W9-CTH-652

Contemporary Literary Criticism

Contemporary Literary Criticism

Excerpts from Criticism
of the Works of Today's
Novelists, Poets, Playwrights,
and Other Creative Writers

Carolyn Riley
Phyllis Carmel Mendelson
Editors

Gale Research Company
Book Tower
Detroit, Michigan 48226

STAFF

Carolyn Riley and Phyllis Carmel Mendelson, *Editors*
Bernadette Meier, *Research Assistant*
Karen M. Hilker, *Editorial Assistant*

Elizabeth Cheslock, *Permissions Manager*
L. Elizabeth Wisniewski, *Permissions Assistant*

Preface

Literary criticism is indispensable to the layman or scholar attempting to evaluate and understand creative writing—whether his subject is one poem, one writer, one idea, one "school," or a general trend in contemporary writing. Literary criticism itself is a collective term for several kinds of critical writing: criticism may be normative, descriptive, interpretive, textual, appreciative, genetic. Conscientious students must consult numerous sources in order to become familiar with "the criticism" pertinent to their subjects.

Until now, there has been nothing resembling an ongoing "encyclopedia" of current literary criticism, bringing together in one series criticism of all the various kinds from widely diverse sources. *Contemporary Literary Criticism* is intended to be such a comprehensive reference work.

The Plan of the Work

Contemporary Literary Criticism presents significant passages from the published criticism of work by well-known creative writers—novelists and short story writers, poets and playwrights. Some creative writers, like James Baldwin and Paul Goodman, are probably better known for their expository work than for their fiction, and so discussion of their nonfiction is included.

Contemporary Literary Criticism is not limited to material concerning long-established authors like Eliot, Faulkner, Hemingway, and Auden, although these and other writers of similar stature are included. Attention is also given to two other groups of writers—writers of considerable public interest—about whose work criticism is hard to locate. These are the newest writers (like Robert M. Pirsig, Erica Jong, and William Kotzwinkle) and the contributors to the well-loved but "unscholarly" genres of mystery and science fiction (like Georges Simenon, Agatha Christie, Robert Heinlein, and Arthur C. Clarke).

The definition of "contemporary" is necessarily arbitrary. For purposes of selection for *CLC*, contemporary writers are those who are either now living or who have died since January 1, 1960. Contemporary criticism is more loosely defined as that written any time during the past twenty-five years or so and currently relevant to the evaluation of the writer under discussion.

References Given to Bio-Bibliographical Material

Notes in many entries directing the user to consult *Contemporary Authors* for detailed biographical and bibliographical information refer to a series of biographical reference books published by the Gale Research Company since 1962, which now includes detailed biographical sketches of about 40,000 authors who have been active during the past decade, many of whose careers began during the post-World War II period, or earlier.

Each volume of *CLC* lists about two hundred authors, with an average of about five excerpts from critical articles or reviews being given for the works of each author. Altogether, there are about 1100 individual excerpts in each volume taken from about 250 books and several hundred issues of some fifty general magazines, literary reviews, and scholarly journals. Each excerpt is fully indentified for the convenience of readers who may wish to consult the entire chapter, article, or review excerpted.

Each volume covers writers not previously included and also provides significant new criticism pertaining to authors included in earlier volumes.

Cumulative indexes of both authors and critics are included in every volume after *CLC-1*.

A Note on Page Citations

Beginning with *CLC-5,* the method for referring to page numbers in the original sources has been standardized. Page numbers appear after each fragment (unless the entire essay was contained on one page). Page numbers appear in citations as well only when the editors wish to indicate, with an essay or chapter title and its *inclusive* page numbers, the scope of the original treatment.

No Single Volume Can be Exhaustive

A final word: Since *Contemporary Literary Criticism* is a multi-volume work of indefinite but considerable size, neither this volume nor any other single volume should be judged apart from the concept that a single volume is but a part of a larger and more comprehensive whole.

If readers wish to suggest authors they are particularly anxious to have covered in coming volumes, or if they have other suggestions or comments, they are cordially invited to write the editors.

A

ACHEBE, Chinua   1930-

Achebe, a Nigerian novelist, short story writer, poet, critic, teacher, and diplomat, writes richly anthropological fiction concerned with conflict caused by change. His successful first novel, *Things Fall Apart*, is still his best known work. (See also *Contemporary Authors*, Vols. 1-4, rev. ed.)

Chinua Achebe's *Things Fall Apart* was published in England in 1958, two years before Nigerian independence. The price of the book was fifteen shillings, which placed it out of reach for the average Nigerian whose annual income in those days did not exceed seventy-five dollars. Achebe's novel, however, had been written not for a Nigerian reading audience nor even for an African reading audience, but, to a large extent, for readers outside of Africa. However, in 1960, when Nigeria became independent, the educational system began to reflect a sense of growing national pride; and in 1964, . . . *Things Fall Apart* became the first novel by an African writer to be included in the required syllabus for African secondary school students throughout the English-speaking portions of the continent. By 1965, Achebe was able to proclaim that his novel in a paperbacked reprint edition priced at a more moderate five shillings had the year before sold some 20,000 copies within Nigeria alone.

In the seven years during which this spectacular change had taken place, Chinua Achebe became recognized as the most original African novelist writing in English. He wrote and published three additional novels (*No Longer at Ease*, 1960; *Arrow of God*, 1964; and *A Man of the People*, 1966), and he became one of the first African writers to build up a reading audience among his fellow Africans. So famous and popular did he become within his own country, that by the time Achebe published his fourth novel it could no longer be said that he was writing for a non-African audience. *Things Fall Apart* during this time became recognized by African and non-African literary critics as the first "classic" in English from tropical Africa. So far did Achebe's influence extend that by the late 1960's his impact on a whole group of younger African novelists could also be demonstrated. (pp. 27-8)

Things Fall Apart has come to be regarded as more than simply a classic; it is now seen as the archetypal African novel. The situation which the novel itself describes—the coming of the white man and the initial disintegration of traditional African society as a consequence of that—is typical of the breakdown all African societies have experienced at one time or another as a result of their exposure to the West. And, moreover, individual Africans all over the continent may identify with the situation Achebe has portrayed. (p. 28)

Although *Arrow of God* is in some ways probably artistically superior to *Things Fall Apart*, it is fated to run a second place in popularity to Achebe's first work. [*Things Fall Apart*] may also be regarded as archetypal because of Achebe's reshaping of a traditional Western literary genre into something distinctly African in form and pattern. (p. 29)

Achebe's dialogue in *Things Fall Apart* is extremely sparse. Okonkwo [the protagonist] says very little at all; not of any one place in the novel may it be said that he has an extended speech or even a very lengthy conversation with another character. And as for authorial presentations of his thoughts, they are limited to two or three very brief passages. Indeed, Achebe relies for the development of his story usually on exposition rather than the dramatic rendering of scene, much as if he were telling an extended oral tale or epic in conventional narrative fashion—almost always making use of the preterit. Again and again the reader is told something about Okonkwo, but he rarely sees these events in action. (pp. 40-1)

I have . . . noted the strong aversion that many Western critics have toward the anthropological overtones present in African fiction, except for the anthropologist, of course, who is looking for this kind of thing. This aversion of the literary critics, however, is no doubt due to their equation of the anthropological with the local colorists at the end of the last century and the beginning of this one. However, in a work such as *Things Fall Apart*, where we are not presented with a novel of character, the anthropological is indeed important. Without it there would be no story. The only way in which Achebe can depict a society's falling apart is first by creating an anthropological overview of that culture, and it should be clear that it is not going to Okonkwo's story that Achebe is chronicling as much as the tragedy of a clan. It is the village of Umuofia, which has been sketched in so carefully, which he will now show as falling apart, crumbling from its exposure to Western civilization. (pp. 43-4)

The piling up of ethnological background, I suggest, is often the equivalent of atmospheric conditioning in Western fiction. Achebe's anthropological passages are what Hardy's descriptive passages are for him—equivalent to Hardy's evocation of atmosphere and mood. Indeed, it is extremely difficult to find a passage of pure description of a natural setting anywhere in Anglophone African writing of the first generation. There is very little that can be related to "landscape painting" in English fiction except for the anthropological passages. (p. 44)

The concluding chapter of *Things Fall Apart* is one of the highlights of contemporary African fiction. In less than three pages, Achebe weaves together the various themes and patterns he has been working with throughout much of his novel. Technically, the most significant aspect of this final chapter is Achebe's sudden shifts in point of view. (p. 57)

The shifting point of view back and forth between an African and a Western viewpoint symbolizes the final breakup of the clan, for *Things Fall Apart*, in spite of the subtitle on the first American edition, *The Story of a Strong Man*, is only in part Okonkwo's story, and, as we have noted, as the book progresses, the story becomes increasingly that of a village, a clan. Achebe clearly indicates this in the final paragraph of his novel where he reduces Okonkwo's story to nothing more than a paragraph in a history book, for history is facts and not individuals, and the history of the coming of the white man to Africa is not the story of the pacification of individuals but of entire tribes of people and even beyond that. . . . Achebe has moved throughout his book away from the individual (Okonkwo) to the communal (Umuofia) and beyond that to the clan. And in the last paragraph, the extension is even further beyond the Ibo of Southeast Nigeria to that of the *Primitive Tribes of the Lower Niger*, ergo, the entire African continent.

The conclusion to *Things Fall Apart* has often been considered over-written, anti-climactic, unnecessarily didactic. . . . Certainly it can be argued that Achebe takes pains to make his message clear, but I feel that the shift to the District Commissioner's point of view strengthens rather than weakens the conclusion. It seems impossibile for any one to read Achebe's last chapter without being noticeably moved, and if it is didactic in the sense of tying things up a little too nicely, then I would have to insist that this was Achebe's intention from the beginning and not merely an accident because of his background of oral tradition. . . . Achebe has written . . . [that] the novelist in an emergent nation cannot afford to pass up a chance to educate his fellow countrymen. . . . [Furthermore], contemporary African literature and other forms of African art have inherited a cultural inclination toward the didactic which in regard to African tradition may be called functionalism.

The ending of *Things Fall Apart* also illustrates the dichotomy of interpretations which cultural backgrounds impose upon a reader. Most Western readers of Achebe's novel seem to interpret the story of Okonkwo's fall as tragic if not close to pure tragedy in classical terms. They cite Okonkwo's pride, his going against the will of the gods (for instance, breaking the Week of Peace, and killing Ikemefuna), and interpret the ending as tragic and inevitable, citing, usually, a parallel to Oedipus. Achebe's own feelings about Okonkwo and the conclusion to the novel, however, would tend to indicate a rather different interpreta-

tion. The most obvious clue is Achebe's title, *Things Fall Apart*, taken from William Butler Yeats's poem, "The Second Coming." Although Yeats's title may be applied ironically to Achebe's story, the indications are that Achebe views the new dispensation as something inevitable, perhaps even desirable. His criticism is clearly of the old way of life which is unsatisfactory now that the West has arrived. This interpretation is supported by several comments Achebe has made about his novel. . . . Lack of adaptability . . . is what Achebe implies led to the collapse of traditional Ibo society. (pp. 59-61)

Of the three major divisions of the book, only the trajectory of Parts II and III resembles the traditional Western well-made novel with conflict—obstacles to be overcome by the protagonist. Part I is especially loose, incorporating as it does section after section of anthropological background. The effect is, of course, to re-create the entire world of day-to-day existence in traditional Ibo society, and Achebe takes pains to make certain that the major stages of life are included: birth, marriage, and death. In the symbiosis which results, Umuofia, rather than Okonkwo, becomes the main character of *Things Fall Apart*, and the transformation it undergoes is archetypal of the entire breakdown of traditional African cultures under exposure to the West.

The novel itself, as I stated at the beginning, must also be regarded as archetypical for the form and patterns Achebe has given it. If we compare the novel very briefly with Joyce Cary's *Mister Johnson* it is readily evident that *Things Fall Apart* is not a story about a character as is Cary's novel and as I feel we tend to regard Western novels as being. For example, Achebe could never have called his novel *Okonkwo*, though it could have been given the name of Okonkwo's village if Achebe had thought that the situation did not extend beyond that one locale within Nigeria. Okonkwo himself does not alter at all throughout the novel. He is the same at the ending as he is at the beginning of the story. Thus, *Things Fall Apart*, because of its emphasis on community rather than individuality, is a novel of situation rather than of character, and this is undoubtedly its major difference from the traditional Western genre, which in the twentieth century, at least, has emphasized the psychological depiction of character. (pp. 62-3)

Let it simply be noted here that the situational plot is indeed the most typical narrative form one encounters in contemporary African fiction. The reason for this is that by and large the major theme of African writing to date has been the conflict of Africa with the West, whether this is shown in its initial stages, as in Achebe's *Things Fall Apart*, or at any one of several different later stages. All four of Achebe's novels are examples of the situational plot, for what happens is ultimately more significant for the group than for the individual whom Achebe uses to focus the situation. The significance, then, is felt by the village, the clan, the tribe, or the nation. (pp. 63-4)

Things Fall Apart does not necessarily give the impression that the story is "plotless" in spite of the fragmentary nature of many of the substories or tales. . . . Achebe's use of the proverb can act as a serious counterpart for the more continuous surface progression of the story. . . . The other unities which he relies on to give form and pattern to the story are the traditional oral tale or tale within a tale—a device no longer in favor with contemporary Western novelists, yet a convention at least as old as the "Man in the

Hill" episode in Fielding's *Tom Jones*. The use of the leit-motif and its associations with stagnancy in Umuofia, masculinity, land, and yam also act as connective links throughout the narrative. It is because of these unities and others, which are vestiges of his own traditional culture, that Achebe's *Things Fall Apart* deserves its position in the forefront of contemporary African writing. Achebe has widened our perspective of the novel and illustrated how a typically Western genre may be given a healthy injection of new blood once it is reshaped and formed by the artist whose vision of life and art is different from our own. (pp. 64-5)

Achebe has increased the importance of dialogue in [*Arrow of God*]—especially dialogue which makes use of materials drawn from traditional oral literature such as the proverb. Hardly a page of his story passes without the presence of a proverb or two; sometimes there will be as many as half-a-dozen, piled one upon another. . . . The use of these oral examples is a primary means of characterization, and it is the adults in Achebe's novel who make the greatest use of these materials—giving the impression of great wisdom. The majority of the proverbs in *Arrow of God* are spoken as dialogue rather than as a part of authorial commentary. The unique aspect of Achebe's characterization, then, is his use of oral literary materials—far more frequently than almost all other African writers. (pp. 150-52)

Achebe's European characters in *Arrow of God* are generally a little less convincing than they could be, for, in truth, they are examined only from the outside, are stereotyped and one-dimensional, efficient little machines meant to do a job in the British Foreign Service, and, necessarily, I suppose, are in too many ways typical of the men who were in the colonial service. (p. 153)

Almost all—if not all—of Achebe's characters in *A Man of the People* are stereotypes, because with this novel Achebe moved into a new area: satire. In many ways the novel is his weakest so far, and I am convinced that its popularity with the African reading audience bears little correlation to its literary merits; however, the novel accomplishes exactly what it set out to do—satirize life in Nigeria in the mid-1960's. Many of the situations satirized can only be appreciated by someone who lived in Nigeria during those years: political corruption, the increasing bureaucracy, the postal strike, the census, the means of communication, the daily news media.

It probably is not fair to criticize Achebe's cardboard characters in *A Man of the People*, since satire rarely is built on believable characters. Even the fact that the story is told in the first person results in no great insight into Achebe's narrator, Odili Samalu, or any of the other characters. The thin story thread is more reminiscent of the novels of Cyprian Ekwensi than of Achebe's earlier works. . . . When the story line gets out of control, Achebe conveniently draws his political morality to an end by having the nation succumb to a military coup. In spite of the de-emphasis on character development, there is certainly more dialogue than Achebe has ever used before, especially in dialects such as Pidgin English, as a means of characterization. The conversation at times is witty, but the whole affair—Odili's entering politics because he has lost his girl —is unconvincing and rather overdrawn. Everybody gets satirized, however, educated and uneducated Africans, the British and the Americans, even the Peace Corps. . . . *A*

Man of the People should be acknowledged for exactly what it is: an entertainment, written for Africans. Achebe no longer tries to explain the way it is, to apologize for the way things are, because this is exactly the point: this is the way things are. The characters are ineffectual, and Achebe's satire itself will be short-lived. The story and the characters have none of the magnitude or the nobility of those in *Things Fall Apart* or *Arrow of God*. (pp. 153-55)

> *Charles R. Larson, in his* The Emergence of African Fiction, *revised edition (copyright © 1972 by Charles R. Larson), Indiana University Press, 1972.*

That Chinua Achebe is essentially a pessimistic writer is apparent both in terms of plot and theme. *Things Fall Apart* and *Arrow of God* portray the disruption caused by imperialism. In the first novel, Okonkwo, the protagonist, commits suicide; in the latter, Ezeulu's mind gives way under strain. *No Longer at Ease*, a study of deterioration under stress and temptation, ends with Okonkwo's grandson, Obiajulu, being found guilty of accepting bribes. *A Man of the People*, a criticism of political corruption, ends with Odili, the narrator through whom we follow the story, rejecting all public involvement and, disillusioned, going into voluntary exile.

Achebe's major awareness is of a heroic past and a debilitated present. (p. 95)

Achebe's sense of history is sophisticated, for he shows not only that the modern character is weak, but why it is weak. To appreciate his analysis fully, one must read all the novels and see them whole. Then, though the direct causes are personal, peculiar to the individual, be he an Odili or an Obiajulu, the indirect causes are more remote, impersonal, and historic. Achebe is more concerned [with presenting] the value of what was destroyed than [with dwelling] on who or what caused that destruction, but when we come to the historic factors, Achebe makes a criticism of colonialism, not so much one of economic exploitation and political suppression—Achebe avoids slogans and easy emotionalism—but of the destruction of social structure and cohesion. As a creative artist, Achebe is more concerned with the individual, so the destruction is shown as it works itself out in individual life and experience. By placing *Things Fall Apart* and *Arrow of God* in the background, we understand better *No Longer at Ease* and *A Man of the People*; by taking the measure of Okonkwo and Ezeulu, we can arrive at a fuller and more sympathetic understanding of Obi and Odili.

Achebe's protagonists are of two types. The heroes are past their prime, courageous, but [end] in defeat that is not only personal but marks the end of much of what they had known and loved. The anti-heroes are the successors, younger and weaker. They are sensitive, initially good intentioned, but being weak, end in failure. Though failing, they survive, disillusioned and damaged: the heroic mold has been shattered, the glory is past.

In *Things Fall Apart* (as in *Arrow of God*) frequent reference is made to the effeminacy of the younger generation. The passing of strength and courage is associated with, if not attributed to, Christianity, since, as preached in the colonies, it stressed meekness and the seeking of justice in a time other than the present and in a place other than this world: "To abandon the gods of one's father and go about with a lot of effeminate men clucking like old hens was the very depth of abomination".... Christianity was also a divisive force, breaking up the unity of the clan, and making military and political conquest easier.... Obiajulu in *No Longer at Ease* sees death as release rather than tragedy. Conrad's Kurtz succumbs to the heart of darkness; ironically, Obi succumbs to "the incipient dawn".... It is post-independence, deep disillusionment: the old home being broken was abandoned, and the new is but a mockery of hopes and expectations. The tragedy seems not only of individuals or of a particular society caught up in historic events, but of universal and permanent significance.... (pp. 107-08)

> *Charles Sarvan Ponnuthurai, "The Pessimism of Chinua Achebe," in* Critique: Studies in Modern Fiction *(copyright © by* Critique, *1974), Vol. XV, No. 3, 1974, pp. 95-109.*

*   *   *

ADAMS, Richard   1920-

Adams, formerly a British civil servant, is the author of the international best seller, *Watership Down*. (See also *Contemporary Authors*, Vols. 49-52.)

Children's literature has a way of becoming adult literature, not when it grows up, but when parents learn how to possess and hence to manipulate the language of their offspring —usually as a substitute for some loss of confidence in their own communicative sets. Lewis Carroll probably realized, better than most, that children's literature seldom pleases children; after all, his tiny Alice has a tendency to fall asleep when being read to out of the big book by her elder sister.... From Aesop to Tolkien, literary history is filled with examples of prolonged adult fascination with children's tales, and there is the faint suggestion that this interest is in part voyeuristic: when the loss of childhood is threatened—by "professional" little leagues, or the vote (and "adult" responsibility) at age eighteen, or the disappearance of special juvenile courts, or wars that make them adults very quickly—we construct an artificial kingdom of perpetual childhood replete with bunnies of one sort or another. Like the fairy palaces of yore, these abodes are always replicas; although they appear as utopias, the realm of childhood is always of the past, never of the future. Maybe it is the closest most of us ever come to confronting what we imagine ourselves to have lost. But, because we lie about its object of address, children's literature is among the most subversive of genres.

Richard Adams' *Watership Down* is one of those adult novels that began, we are told, as a bedtime narrative for his children, only to be awarded the 1973 Guardian and Carnegie Awards for distinguished fiction. The plot is relatively simple: a young rabbit on midnight patrol duty is possessed by a vision of blood in the evening sky, and takes this reasonably natural manifestation of atmospheric refraction as an omen that the warren is being overrun by some mysterious invader. The theme is surely as old as Hamlet's dilemma on the ramparts; namely, how do we reconcile the natural world with the supernatural demands of faith? And perhaps secondarily, *Watership Down*, though not a manual for a Renaissance king-to-be, is a tale about growing up and the necessary exposure to fear and death.

Faced with the dreaded omen, the lapine security council (Owsla) must make a decision that, of course, has antecedents in human history: to abandon their catacomb and to become temporarily nomadic or to attempt to defend what would appear to be an indefensible fortress.... The solution is a sort of compromise exodus: the rabbits leave their ancestral home; cross a river at low tide; encounter and fight their enemies led by the venerable General Woundwort within the urges of the territorial imperative, and eventually intermarry with their enemies following the death of their senior leaders. Only then can the homeland be reclaimed.

This reciprocating motif in *Watership Down*, the cycle of departure and return, is part of the natural synchrony between the creatures of the earth and their seasons. The novel begins in spring and moves us through the terrors of winter and back again to Hazel's death in a heaven "where the first primroses were beginning to bloom." Throughout his novel, Adams makes rich connections between the animal and the human worlds. Of the winter season he writes that man's enjoyment of it is really but a disguised enjoyment of proof against it, whereas for the rabbit, there is always a food problem: "For rabbits, winter remains what it was for men in the middle ages—hard, but bearable by the resourceful and not altogether without compensations."

Far beyond the simple weaving of an entertaining yarn, however, Richard Adams has done something else in *Watership Down*. He has written with the aid of extensive research into the life of rabbits (most of it from R. M. Lockley's *The Private Life of the Rabbit*) a combination of history, mythology, and guidebook. It is both a *genealogy* (and hence a study of beginnings, complete with the rabbit version of Creation: an excessive overflowing of droppings from Frith, the sun god, that made everything fertile) and a *survival* kit (instructions on defending oneself against such untimely endings as that represented by the fox's scent). As such, *Watership Down* is a prophetic book, like the *Bible*, or Blake's *Jerusalem*, or *The Whole Earth Catalogue*—that is, it relates the history of a race of variously "chosen" and "dispossessed" rabbits to the history of their earth itself. In this realm, one's natural history is the same as his human history. Relationships in *Watership Down* tend toward the totemic; that is to say that those events and commandments which under normal circumstances would be regarded as symbolic, have a presence even while absent. Prophetic books present people as being part of their history in a way so very alien to a technocratic civilization with its divisions of labor, generations, time, and space. It offers a genuine "world" complete with its own language and offering the convenience of maps for the lost.

Most myths deal with the themes of loss and renewal or death and rededication and were surely more prevalent when man was closer to the earth which exhibited the same cycle as it rotated about the sun. "Down," after all, is a term equally applicable to a terrain, the geographic equivalent of a fall, and the substance which fills the pillows upon which children dream. Having just about done away with the spontaneous simultaneity of primitive man, our myths now belong to perhaps the only primitives that remain—our children at bedtime. And even that is threatened, because adults make bestselling novels out of them before the kids even learn the rules of the new game, *Watership Down*. (pp. 528-29)

Jan B. Gordon, in Commonweal *(copyright © 1974 Commonweal Publishing Co., Inc.; reprinted by permission of Commonweal Publishing Co., Inc.), September 27, 1974.*

Richard Adams, faced by the daunting task of matching the loud success of *Watership Down*, prefaces his next book [*Shardik*] with quotations from the Odyssey, the Old Testament and Jung—which gives an idea of the scope he has set himself. No world for rabbits, this: it is the world of epic, myth and archetype, bestraddled by the figure of a giant bear that is twice the size of a man, and as full of magic power and significance as a white whale. As in the case of Melville's extraordinary amalgam of prosaic whaling treatise and poetic meditation, *Shardik* is an attempt to create an entire world that is memorably real and, at the same time, incandescent with immemorial meaning. And for a time—at the beginning and again near the ending—it almost works as intended. There can be few books on which more loving, energetic inventiveness has been expended than on *Shardik*. When the great bear lunges out of the forest fire by the Telthearna River on the northern boundary of the Beklan empire, and changes the course of local history, it ushers in a fictional world where everything is made familiar to us, yet startlingly new. . . .

But when the forest magic goes, *Shardik* sinks. . . . The proliferation of exotic detail becomes laborious, the moral drama obvious and over-extended, the bejewelled names and allusions faintly comic. . . .

The book is too long, and too uneven. There is no real grasp of the inward reaches of character, only of the grand simplicities of archetype—and when much of the interest is purportedly centred on Kelderek's individual crisis of betrayal, conscience and moral recovery, this lack is debilitating.

His dark night of the soul is given some strong symbols, but little psychology. And his love-affair with one of the lapsed virgin priestesses is only embarrassing. The epic dimensions of the tale need too many stage-props, create too many moments of bathos, too many eruptions into Marlovian hyperboles, roll-calls, invocations and Victorian-sounding resurrections of the classic epic simile (almost one a page at times, and one of them 17 lines long).

There is enough creative endeavour, careful planning, integrity and sheer multifarious detail in *Shardik* to make a dozen ordinary novels. But, dogged by the ghosts of Rider Haggard and Tolkien and Cecil B. deMille, its intermittent magic, like the great bear itself, dwindles in the cage.

Kenneth Graham, "Bear Garden," in The Listener *(© British Broadcasting Corp., 1975; reprinted by permission of Kenneth Graham), January 2, 1975, p. 30.*

["*Shardik*"] is an exploration of the way an incarnate god works on the human psyche. . . . A picaresque adventure story for sure, but it is much more. Beneath the rich vein of allegory and symbolism, Adams is concerned with how a society worships its gods, chooses its values and raises its children. Adams is a splendid descriptive writer whose only flaw—a minor one—is a fondness for the extended Homeric simile. And he may have created the most evil character ever to appear in fiction, Genshed the slavedealer, who

castrates, mutilates and murders young children for pleasure. This is a marvelous novel of epic dimension, more ambitious, deeper, darker and more richly textured than "Watership." Despite its happy ending, no one under 10 years of age ought to go near it. (p. 77)

Arthur Cooper, "Bear Market," in Newsweek *(copyright 1975 by Newsweek, Inc.; all rights reserved; reprinted by permission), April 28, 1975, pp. 77-8.*

Richard Adams has written a second novel, and may the Great Bear God help him. It seems certain that he is in for a spell of heavyweight reviewing, the kind of borborygmic reappraisal the critical community indulges in when it feels slightly ill and foolish after a gorge of overpraise. What was overpraised, of course, was *Watership Down*, a bunny epic greeted last year as if it were a cross between *Moby-Dick* and *The Wind in the Willows*. The excessive praise was a critical phenomenon that occurs every year or so when reviewers tire of the stinginess that honesty requires, and heap all of their withheld love on some more or less fragile volume.

Seen without regard to its predecessor, *Shardik* resembles good science fiction, unsatisfactorily diluted with Victorian romanticism. . . .

There is no iron to this Iron Age fable. The grimness is fake, the fascination with virginity is a naughty bore, and the monstrous figure of Shardik is cheapened by watery supernaturalism. It is one thing for Kelderek and his primitive fellow tribesmen—a few skeptics to the contrary—to believe the bear is a god, quite another for author and reader to pretend to believe it. This pretense is what Adams insists on, and it smacks of Pan worship, that Victorian silliness in which refined city dwellers pretended that they glimpsed the wicked, goat-footed god as they strolled through an orderly countryside.

Adams begins his tale with an epigraph from Jung: "Superstition and accident manifest the will of God." Perhaps, but not here. The author spins out his romance entertainingly, but without dealing seriously with the questions he raises: of belief and its perversion, of authority and its corruption. Good as he is at nature walks, Adams does not venture far into the forests of the mind.

John Skow, "Ursus Saves?," in Time *(reprinted by permission from* Time, The Weekly Newsmagazine; *copyright Time Inc.), April 28, 1975, p. 93.*

As a sustained act of the imagination, *Shardik* is overawing. Richard Adams has devised for his 526-page story not only characters linked in a complex plot, but an ancient empire as well, complete with new-minted languages and myths, children's games and birdsongs, customs and topographies (maps are provided). The cities of his chimerical realm ring true, as though he had wielded a spade at the digs that excavated them.

Adams's people are not as believable. Like those gallant rabbits in his first book, *Watership Down*, the characters in *Shardik* owe more to literature than to life—stepping out, as it were, in blue blazers from an English boys' adventure tale. The spirit of the prep school pervades both novels, and while this did very little harm to *Watership Down*—it may even have helped that persistent bestseller become one of the few modern novels to be read by both adults and older children—it somewhat undermines the more ambitious *Shardik*, which carries in itself a heavy burden of religious allegory. . . .

Though the end of the journey is disappointing, though Adams's characters have been encountered in other books, still their passage through his invented landscape is worth following. The word "bemused," meaning both "lost in thought" and "stupefied," appears often in *Shardik*. Bemusement seems to be the author's intention. He knows how to tell an adventure that builds hypnotically to a gasp. . . .

There is too much here about castration, torture, sexual abuse, and mutilation. Considering that many of the children who read *Watership Down* will attempt *Shardik*, it is a mistake. Even an adult will be surfeited with its horrors. (p. 53)

> *Ralph Tyler, "The Nature of the Beast," in* Harper's *(copyright 1975 by* Harper's *Magazine; reprinted from the May, 1975 issue by special permission), May, 1975, pp. 53-4.*

Its majestic language, heroic theme and sustained power will make *Shardik* an instant classic; it will still be in print for a long time. Its achievement is awesome: some of its effects move us so deeply that we're surprised to find them made up of words on a printed page. Taking place outside of recorded time, the story begins when Shardik, a gigantic bear, saves the hunter Kelderek from an attacking leopard. . . . Kelderek has been singled out to serve the will of Shardik, the reincarnated power of God. . . .

As in the fiction of Graham Greene, Adams gives an ordinary man the awesome job of serving a God whose mercy sometimes looks like punishment. Kelderek immerses his will in Shardik's, carrying out the Bear-God's message without knowing its nature. . . .

No estimate of *Shardik* can overlook how well Adams' firmly cadenced sentences knit with his epical theme, how his style brings to life his uncanny knowledge of bears—their anatomy, feeding and sleeping habits, and reactions to stress. Shardik is both the power of God and a dangerous, wounded animal, half-crazed by hunger, fire and hunters' arrows. Adams makes the great shambling bear a figure of terror and savage grandeur even in his physical ruin. . . .

Adams filters his acute understanding of human motives through his mighty bear; Shardik embodies the hopes and fears of the people touched by his divinity. The double remove created by the primitive setting and the convention of animist myth lays bare the hidden depths of our basic drives. (p. 29)

> *Peter Wolfe, in* The New Republic *(reprinted by permission of* The New Republic; © 1975 by The New Republic, Inc.), May 3, 1975.*

The world of "Shardik" is wholly imagined, as the enticing map on the inside cover of the book lets us know. It is a cosmos tailored to the order of a story, and the challenge, which Adams meets with his descriptive brilliance, is to make every exotic facet of this world real and convincing: a

world such as we ourselves might live in. Like Tolkien and Mervyn Peake, like Edgar Rice Burroughs, like relatively unsung science fiction novelists such as Ursula LeGuin ("The Left Hand of Darkness") and Frank Herbert ("Dune"), Adams believes that epic events require a world created to their measure. Not the "real world," where only psychological dramas are allowed because the larger frameworks of value have been shattered, but a morally coherent fiction; a world constructed from mythic elements, where mythic events can unfold their energies. It is an old tradition, only recently fallen on bad days, into pulp literature. Its great achievements are "The Epic of Gilgamesh," "The Odyssey," "Beowulf." And in "Shardik," Adams attempts to restore its high seriousness.

The ambition is remarkable; the writer's tools are unique. Yet he does not succeed, and his failure is so resounding that, frankly, it puzzles me. For what fails Adams in "Shardik" is precisely what served him so well in "Watership Down": his genius for storytelling and his affectionate skill in rendering character. (pp. 1-2)

[The] general, kings, courtesans, priestesses and rebels, the entire cast of characters that populate this epic, are rarely more than pulp magazine figures of the crudest sort. They contain little subtlety or surprise. Their motives are schematic, and virtually all their conversation is more wooden than seems possible from a writer whose rabbits spoke in so lively and believable a manner. One concludes that Adams's animals are simply more human than his humans—to the misfortune of his moral and his book. . . .

I would not be surprised if it turned out that "Shardik" was not written after "Watership Down," as the publisher leads us to believe, but before. How else can one explain the amateurish quality which pervades so much of this book by a writer who has previously displayed such masterful gifts? (p. 2)

> *Paul Zweig, in* The New York Times Book Review *(© 1975 by The New York Times Company; reprinted by permission), May 4, 1975.*

There is one good thing to say for *Shardik*. Adams writes about nature—trees, plants, animals, stones, bugs—as though he grew in ground next to wild onions. He talks the natural world into life. But there are few of the usual reasons for reading fiction in *Shardik*. We learn nothing about ourselves here; Adams's people belong with Snow White. He does not create an alternative reality. The novel is a fake antique, a sexless, humorless, dull facsimile of an epic without historical or psychological relevance. Contrary to Adams's wish, *Shardik* transmits no information we need, want, or can use about how we have chosen or employed our deities. *Shardik* is a long-winded Victorian fantasy, a piece of literary furniture properly destined to be unread by tens of thousands of book-club check writers.

> *Webster Schott, "Grin and Bear It," in* Book World—The Washington Post *(© The Washington Post), May 25, 1975, p. 3.*

The rabbit heroes of Richard Adams's celebrated 1974 novel *Watership Down* have swiftly entered the contemporary mythology best articulated by Tolkien and his admiring imitators. As an allegory of survival, that novel escaped simplistic coyness because the closed system of its creatures' ordeal was depicted with a stubborn thoroughness that gave it the unified force of anthropomorphic fable. The inventive consistency of *Watership Down* quieted the snarls of whimsy-haters. Still, the book's imaginative reach was limited; one could resist its blandishments, while recognizing their unpretentious charm.

There is no such defense against *Shardik*—a powerfully compelling prose epic that re-creates the fortunate fall of unaccommodated man, within the history of a splendidly portrayed imaginary kingdom. Adams's cosmos is the remote, long-forgotten "Beklan Empire": for it, he has contrived a wondrously detailed web of topography, flora and fauna, rival languages with their sub-dialects—including a repository of eerie pre-Christian religions, devoutly preserved and faithfully practiced. The people are seekers after an understanding of their place in the creation, through inconsistent communion with the mysterious forces that lead them, past imperfection and error, to wisdom. Onto his heroes' quest Adams has grafted a hymn in praise of the unity of all life. And, before *Shardik* lumbers to its resolute conclusion, it also challenges us with a utopian blueprint for the saving of future generations.

This book *means* to be an epic. The opening scene displays Adams's determination to excite his readers' awe. We are shown the hierarchical confluence of life that fills an enormous forest; next, we hear the throb, along the forest floor, of undercurrent natural forces beating together in complex collusion. But the sound in fact heralds a spreading fire that drives all life before it. (p. 26)

Shardik tacitly acknowledges its obvious models; nonetheless, it seems put together with a shrewdness that is palpably *un*literary—one wants to call it "instinctive."

The imagery is elemental; it always seems unforced—and *natural*. Adams's metaphors are repeatedly drawn from the rituals of nature's processes. Water and fire are the recurring terms. The book opens with a voracious forest fire, concludes at a domestic hearthside scene. In one of its most magnificent set pieces—describing "the passing of Shardik"—the animal's immense corpse drifts downriver on a burning raft, the body of a dead child laid beside it. (Yes, the source is Malory: but I defy any reader to *feel* that it is anything but inevitable, in the context of the world where it occurs.)

Among this book's greatest strengths is its rejection of the modern novel's emphasis on subjective uncertainty. It urges that truth is knowable, and that our intelligences must accept what they recognize for revealed truth—even if it be partial and unsatisfying. Surely, this points to its Christian framework. But isn't there something more, something stretching back still farther?

The language of *Shardik* is primitive and hortatory—as if Adams still held the old pre-civilized belief that words are *things* and can hurt. In the early pages, the sudden appearance of the bear is again and again described with excited rhetorical flourishes (Shardik is " . . . a figure of terror, monstrous beyond the nature even of that dark, savage place"). There are many such passages, in which Adams frankly directs our responses, *tells* us what things mean, how we must feel about them.

It is the way one talks to children—and it gives the impression of words buttressed with gesturing and shaking, as if by a speaker who reminds himself that language is only one of the devices by which we communicate. When the teller tugs thus at our attention, grasps our shoulders, turning us to face him and listen, *listen*. . . .

In reading *Shardik*, we seem to hear again the old stories that were told to us by old people remembering them from past years, knowing we must be made to hear them, that our survival depends upon them. This is a new story, but it has the satisfying wholeness of the great ones it dares to rival; it should be told, and retold, for many generations. (p. 27)

> *Bruce Allen, "Epic in Wonderland," in* Saturday Review *(copyright © 1975 by Saturday Review/World, Inc.; reprinted with permission), May 31, 1975, pp. 26-7.*

I recently spent the best part of a week reading a 600-page novel about some imaginary barbarians who worship an imaginary bear. This is not the sort of thing I would ordinarily do, but I remembered how two years ago I was equally reluctant to start a 400-page book about a tribe of rabbits, and how wrong I was then. By now, over a million people have read *Watership Down*; for many it is a modern classic.

"That rabbit book". . . became an international best seller not just because it was well written and original. It was attractive also because it celebrated qualities many serious novelists are currently afraid or embarrassed to write about. The heroes and heroines of most contemporary novels (including mine) are sad, bumbling failures; hysterical combatants in the sex war; or self-deceptive men and women of ill-will. What a relief to read of characters who have honor and courage and dignity, who will risk their lives for others, whose love for their families and friends and community is enduring and effective—even if they look like Flopsy, Mopsy, and Benjamin Bunny. . . .

Shardik is not about a tribe of bears, but about men, some of whom are just as sympathetic and admirable as the heroes of *Watership Down*. Some critics are skeptical of this, since they know from their own experience, or introspection, that men are basically cowardly, dishonorable, foolish, disloyal, and selfish.

Perhaps Richard Adams was aware of this objection, for instead of setting his tale in any known time and place, he has invented an imaginary primitive world, the ancient Beklan Empire, complete with history, geography, climate, culture, and religion. . . .

Bears, of course, have always been very popular in English literature, though—or perhaps because—they are unknown in English life outside of zoos. From the comic butts of the fables and the enchanted princes of folklore through Kipling's wise, paternal Baloo to Pooh and Paddington, they have always been portrayed as friendly; mischievous or clumsy sometimes, but easily domesticated and affectionate.

Richard Adams's Shardik, the Power of God, is a different sort of animal, more American than English. Like the eponymous hero of Faulkner's "The Bear," he is a figure of terror and mystery, violent and unpredictable. He is Nature, literally red in tooth and claw, both dangerous and beautiful, fearful and desirable. *Shardik*, like *Watership Down*, is among other things an ecological novel, an allegory and history of the relationship of human beings to the physical world. . . .

Irritable reviewers, perhaps thinking of his first appearance in the book [having been badly burned], have compared Shardik to Smokey the Bear; and in a way he is what Smokey would be, taken seriously. Even Smokey has his Faulkner side; he is not small and cuddly, but much larger than the cartoon people he usually confronts. He is generally represented as scowling, even threatening—and what, after all, does he intend to do with that shovel he carries, blade up?

But *Shardik* is not just a possible ecological allegory; it can also be read as a study in the psychology of religion. It cannot be accidental that the central symbol chosen by Richard Adams, the survivor of a Jungian analysis, harks back to what anthropologists have called the oldest surviving evidence of mythological belief, discovered in the mountain caves inhabited by Neanderthal man before 50,000 BC. There, ten thousand years earlier than the wall paintings of prehistoric hunters, the skulls of cave bears were grouped around a fire in the deepest rooms of the caves.

Shardik, like the cave bears, is not really a magical being; he is not anthropomorphized. All that he does is within the range of normal animal behavior; only to those who believe in him does it seem symbolical, an Act of God. Because of this belief, however, lives are changed utterly; hundreds of men, women, and children die; a barbaric empire is destroyed and rebuilt and destroyed again, and finally brought a little nearer to civilized humanism. (p. 34)

[Part] of the book should make some amends to feminists for the condescending treatment of the female rabbits—Flopsys and Mopsys all—in *Watership Down*. Through most of *Shardik*, women are not only important but more admirable generally and closer to nature and the truth than men are. Unfortunately, this does not carry through, and the Good Society established in the happy ending is illogically and disappointingly patriarchal.

In the course of his book, Adams manages to picture most known Western varieties of religious attitude, from the simple totemistic faith of the Ortelgans through the Dionysiac intoxication of the young priestesses of Quiso to the obsessive ritualism or half-superstitious, half-conventional holiday observances of the rich Beklan townspeople. . . . Agnosticism and atheism, both primitive and sophisticated, are not forgotten. . . .

Richard Adams's own position seems to be a variant of that of the Grand Inquisitor. "Superstition and accident manifest the will of God," he quotes (from Jung) in his epigraph. Even if the supernatural does not exist, it is good for men to believe in it—not because it makes them behave better, but because it gives shape and purpose to their existence. In *Shardik*, belief causes men to act cruelly and destructively as well as nobly; the bear is a kind of test which brings out hidden strengths and weaknesses, even in those who do not believe in him. . . .

Gifted writers of fantasy, even when they disclaim belief in magic, often seem to have a supernatural precognition of historical events, so that their books are more relevant

years after they appear than when they were written. H. G. Wells's pretty, silly, commercially exploited Eloi were invented long before the Flower Children; and Huxley's characters blurred the natural depression caused by his Brave New World with Soma well before the discovery of tranquilizers. Authors often disclaim this gift, and even deny that their books might be read symbolically, as Tolkien insisted that Frodo's Ring of absolute destructive power had nothing to do with modern science or the atomic bomb.

Similarly, Richard Adams would probably claim that no thought of the war in Southeast Asia crossed his mind while he was writing *Shardik*. If so, it is merely a lucky coincidence that this brilliant and frightening novel should appear in America just at a time when we, like Kelderek, have finally and fully become aware of how much destruction of the natural world and innocent people, how much mutilation and kidnapping of children, has been done in the name of our gods in the past twenty years. (p.35)

> Alison Lurie, "The Power of Smokey," in The New York Review of Books (*reprinted with permission from* The New York Review of Books; *copyright © 1975 NYREV, Inc.*), *June 12, 1975, pp. 34-5.*

*   *   *

AIKEN, Conrad   1889-1973

Aiken was a distinguished American poet, short story writer, novelist, and critic. His involvement with fantasy and psychology and his concern with sex and morbidity reveal the persistent influence on his work of the theories of Freud and Havelock Ellis. Aiken won the Pulitzer Prize in 1930 for his *Selected Poems*. (See also *Contemporary Authors*, Vols. 5-8, rev. ed.; obituary, Vols. 45-48.)

Aiken's lifelong interest in psychoanalytic theory, especially the work of Freud, is reflected not only in his desire to discover the unconscious elements that are the prelude to all conceptions of and attitudes toward the human role in the universe, but also in his use of myth to depict various levels of human perception and consciousness. . . .

Recognizing that it is fundamentally man's "hunger" for security and grandeur that "shapes itself as gods and rainbows" (*Time in the Rock*, XXVIII), Aiken creates a new mythical concept: God is finally the symbolic expression of man's capacity for full consciousness of the anxieties, conflicts, and longings, the terror of his own limitations, and especially of death, which he has for so long repressed or acknowledged only in distorted and misleading forms; God is at the same time man's consciousness of all that he can achieve and enjoy in the face of the monstrous within himself and nature. The god in man functions in the poet when he employs the chaos of the unconscious mind as the material of creation, imposing order and beauty on its apparent formlessness. In his creation of "Lord Zero" who, he says, is "our dream," Aiken forms a deity out of his consciousness of the lack of purpose and order in the universe; "Lord Zero," in whose honor the poet offers his rites of "devotion" (*Time in the Rock*, LXIX), himself represents the imposition of reason on chaos, and is a creation out of void.

In *Ushant*, Aiken speaks of his realization that "now at last the road was being opened for the only religion that was any longer tenable or viable, a poetic comprehension of man's position in the universe, and of his potentialities as a poietic shaper of his own destiny, through self-knowledge and love. The final phase of evolution of man's mind itself to ever more inclusive consciousness: in that, and that alone, would he find the solvent of all things." In shaping "his own destiny" by rational and aesthetic means, Aiken accepts the loneliness and terror that his own myth of consciousness discloses, and celebrates his "poetic comprehension" that there is none to replace it. (pp. 392-93)

> *Lillian Feder, in her* Ancient Myth in Modern Poetry *(copyright © 1971 by Princeton University Press; reprinted by permission of Princeton University Press), Princeton University Press, 1971.*

For [Aiken] America is not something already completed but a land that is still becoming. It is this vision of America that resolves the paradox of a writer who is at once deeply of a certain place and of everywhere. For the metaphysical poet like Aiken who believes that man is immortal because of his everlasting soul but that man is also tied to nature and therefore mortal and always dying, then paradox is inevitable. But paradox confuses those who will not dig beneath obvious contradictions. (p. 800)

Massachusetts and England represent to Aiken the tidiness and order of the cultivated rational mind, whereas Georgia and Spain represent the disorder and violence but also the rich beauty and deep emotional powers of the unconscious mind. Aiken's two great teachers—Santayana and Freud— also represent these two ways of the conscious and the unconscious. Santayana, part American and part Spaniard, Harvard professor and wandering philosopher, remained loyal to the rational mind; while Freud, the Jew anchored in a dying continental society, plunged deep into the unconscious on one of the greatest voyages of discovery in this or any century. With his love of contraries, Aiken has refused to sacrifice the unconscious to the conscious or the conscious to the unconscious. He has remained loyal to the deepest promptings of his soul, which tell him to accept the particularities of those landscapes that are to him symbols of the basic opposites of man's makeup. (p. 801)

[The] meaning of Aiken's life and work is a resolution of the paradox of the conscious mind with its teaching and preaching functions and the unconscious mind with its dreams and visions and its powerful overflow of emotions. The paradox is resolved in the quest which Aiken has taken into his soul and into the world. And from that quest he has gained increasing knowledge of himself and the world. Possibly more than any other work by Aiken, *Ushant* deals with this theme of the quest and the growth of the power to love and to seek truth. (p. 802)

> *Ted R. Spivey, "Conrad Aiken: Resident of Savannah," in* The Southern Review *(copyright, 1972, by the Louisiana State University), Vol. VIII, No. 4, Autumn, 1972, pp. 792-804.*

One explanation for [Aiken's] absence [from many anthologies of major American verse] may lie in the fact that much of his poetry, including his later verse, remains anchored in the styles of the twenties and thirties, with much in common with the work of Eliot and even of Hardy, and is consequently outdated. But I believe the answer can be found in other directions. The reason for Aiken's neglect, and his consequent crustiness, may be paradoxically the same reason that he is, in my opinion, a poet of stature. The Aiken critic must be attuned to a poetry of philosophical inquiry, rather than to a poetry dependent on the New Critical love of paradox, ambiguity, irony, and other devices of language. Most critics of Aiken's times were not.

Perhaps what Aiken really points to [in claiming academic neglect] is the fact that his corpus has a characteristic that much contemporary poetry and fiction lacks: a real coherence, a staggering thematic and symbolic unity, a philosophical argument, that stretches over forty years across the novels, poems, short stories, and play, *Mr. Arcularis*. Since the late twenties, he has made a single-minded and unwavering attempt to wrestle certain metaphysical themes to a solution and, as a result, all his work is one. Any poet who can play such manifold variations on so vast a subject as the relation of the self to the universe and the acceptance of one's life and death has something to offer us regardless of his precise style of poetry, his "school." At the same time, his single works can be obscure without reference to others, a possibility that has on occasion resulted in harsh judgments.

Because Aiken's writings constitute almost a system, isolated works lose full significance when read alone, and a view of the whole increases the stature of his individual works. Such a case is the play, *Mr. Arcularis*. . . . [One] crucial element in Aiken's unified vision [is] the "great circle" voyage, with its attendant ships, stars, seagulls, and freezing temperatures [which can be traced] through *The Preludes* . . ., the novel *Great Circle* . . ., the short story "Mr. Arcularis," all originally published in the early thirties, and the essay *Ushant*, [as well as] the final version of the play *Mr. Arcularis*, which appeared in 1957, and which remains his final, clearest, and most complete statement of that theme. (pp. 591-92)

In Aiken's work, the voyage itself always takes the form of Thoreau's "great circle." . . . The attainment of the bright pearl of self-knowledge is the goal toward which all life tends in its voyage. Time and again, Aiken enforces this belief that the search for self-knowledge is the ultimate, freeing goal. (pp. 593-94)

This thread passes through all of Aiken's work, and its meaning is plain. The "great circle" is the trip into one's own life, and the Pole Star toward which we all aim on it is the excursion into our own pasts; upon reaching the star, our old selves die and we accept our former lives and death. The final acceptance of oneself, one's death, and the possibility of a rebirth through merging with other selves, "love," brings *Time in the Rock* to a close. . . . (p. 595)

[In the play, *Mr. Arcularis*,] Aiken states powerfully and in public form the point he has been making in his work throughout his career. . . . We must understand where we have been in order to live well in the future; we must embrace all the skeletons in our closets in order to be able to embrace full-bodied life. Far from a Stephen Dedalus-like "nightmare—from which we both will wake" . . ., this moment of self-knowledge remains the goal of all brave men, however painful it must be. We should draw the proper conclusion. We are luckier than Mr. Arcularis because we—like Andrew Cather [protagonist of Aiken's novel, *Great Circle*,]—can still correct past errors, while Arcularis faces an immediate final journey into the "great white light of annihilation."

In this final *Mr. Arcularis* [the play derived from the short story, "Mr. Arcularis,"] a master has put a life of reflection into a powerful symbolic and dramatic form. Here, as in his other work, Aiken has much to tell us—and with an astonishing simplicity, given the complexity of his concerns—once we understand his special artistic code. Perhaps the great circle of Aiken criticism, which began brightly, will end on a note of affirmation. (p. 6)

> *Stephen E. Tabachnick, "The Great Circle Voyage of Conrad Aiken's 'Mr. Arcularis',"* in American Literature *(reprinted by permission of the Publisher; copyright 1974 by Duke University Press, Durham, North Carolina), January, 1974, pp. 590-607.*

[The] verse of Conrad Aiken..., in its time, was decently admired for the virtue of bright finish. About all such writing it is fair to say only that it has a shorter life expectancy than art. To put the matter another way: artifice is the good currency which, for those who will accept it, eliminates any need for the best. (p. 6)

> *David Bromwich, in* The New York Times Book Review *(© 1974 by The New York Times Company; reprinted by permission), April 21, 1974.*

*   *   *

ALBEE, Edward   1928-

Albee, a Pulitzer Prize-winning American dramatist, is widely known for powerful avant-garde works depicting the ills of contemporary society. *The Zoo Story, Who's Afraid of Virginia Woolf*, and *A Delicate Balance* are among his most celebrated plays. (See also *Contemporary Authors*, Vols. 5-8, rev. ed.)

There is nothing "absurd" about [*Who's Afraid of Virginia Woolf*]. Albee has largely abandoned the specific parodic elements and dragooned whimsy of *The Sand Box* and *The American Dream* and the obliquities of *The Zoo Story* and has, if anything, returned to *The Death of Bessie Smith* for savage inspiration and neurotic prototypes. But he has advanced from that problem play. [In *Virginia Woolf*] the action is more inward, and the rhetoric, apart from a few speeches of improbable and high-pitched lamentation, is straightforward, cocky, brutal, knowing and tremendously *au courant* . . . and very funny. (pp. 134-35)

[Albee] is the poet of post-Freudian, post-Riesmanian, post-intellectual, wised-up and not-to-be-had, experiential and disenchanted United States of America 1962 Man. [Note that Gilman's essay was written in 1962.]

But poets, of course, want to sing, discover new lands of the imagination, be healers. That is Albee's self-imposed "task," and it is his downfall. The pressure in him toward the transcendence of naturalism and psychological notation had previously resulted in the painfully coerced denouement of *The Zoo Story* and the descent into incoherence of *The American Dream*. In *Virginia Woolf* the failure is on a larger scale. He has driven into the body of his scrupulously observed *Walpurgisnacht* (the title of Act II; Act I is

called Fun and Games, Act III The Exorcism) a shaft of fantasy designed to point up our sad psychic aridity and fix the relationship between reality and illusion. Its effect is to break the back of the play. (p. 135)

The play ends with the wife sorrowfully accepting the necessity to live without myths while whispering that she remains "afraid of Virginia Woolf," afraid, presumably, of life, art and truth.

There is something doubly wrong with this. Structurally, it leaves the play in division from itself, the psychological realism separated by a gulf from the metaphysical data, just as in *The American Dream* the parody and fantasy lay gasping out of each other's reach. But more than this there is the question of vision, of dramatic truth and rightness, of the proper means to an end, in short, of a "task" and its solution. What Albee has done is to smuggle in an element alien to his physical procedure, asking it to carry the burden of revelation he cannot distill from his mere observation of behavior. He wants to say something profound about the human condition, and he ends, like O'Neill in *The Iceman Cometh*, offering a cliché about illusions.

The sharpest psychological observation will no longer communicate the kind of truth we need and that Albee, with acute but limited sensibility, keeps trying for. As so many developments in art have demonstrated, the psyche is only one element among others and needs to be *located*, tested against other realities, and not simply described. Naturalism gives us nothing but our reflections. However painful, bold and accurate they are, as in *Virginia Woolf*, they are not enough, we are not changed by them, as we are not ultimately changed by this play. The paradox is that human reality can best be apprehended today by indirection, by "inhuman" methods, which means a step beyond the literal, the behavioral, the natural. Our condition is extreme; old measures won't work, but neither will new half-measures, half-dramas such as Albee continues to produce. (pp. 135-36).

> *Richard Gilman, "Here We Go Round the Albee Bush" (1962), in his* Common and Uncommon Masks: Writings on Theatre 1961-1970 *(copyright © 1971 by Richard Gilman; reprinted by permission of Random House, Inc.), Random House, 1971, pp. 133-36.*

Albee, caught between his desire to write a play of ideas and his capacity to write one of melodramatic action, has [in *Tiny Alice*] written neither clearly. The suspense play is full of false starts and red herrings—the mystery impedes the metaphysics instead of establishing a base for it. We cannot accept the demonic trio's change into super-reality because their reality is so murky.

And yet in a peculiar way, *Tiny Alice* is far and away the most significant play on Broadway this year [1965]. . . . More than this, it contains scenes that break down the walls of reticence and safety that mark the commercial theatre.

Most important, it is clearly the work of a playwright who, if his ambitions exceed his capacities, still has ambitions we can respect. Albee characteristically exhibits an eventual failure of mind, an inability to infuse his action with thought, and seeks to cover that up by arbitrary fantasy and metaphysical gymnastics. Nevertheless, a deep stream of dramatic perception and committed passion flows underground in him, and when it occasionally comes to the surface it irrigates our dry theatre the way almost nothing else is doing these days. (pp. 138-39)

> *Richard Gilman, "Chinese Boxes" (1965), in his* Common and Uncommon Masks: Writings on Theatre 1961-1970 *(copyright © 1971 by Richard Gilman; reprinted by permission of Random House, Inc.), Random House, 1971, pp. 137-39.*

When Albee uses *The American Dream* as title of a play (1961), he exemplifies the process of showing disgust with the restricted and conventionalized dream, and he uses the customary satirical method of ignoring the complexities of meaning possible to "dream" and of attributing the inadequate dream to everybody. Thus he has a target instead of a problem, and the shooting can go on forever. (p. 11)

Albee, it seems to me, gives a clue to a good deal of current criticism of American society: it comes out a sense of being let down or treated unfairly by the realm of dreams. People have dreams that cannot be fulfilled because things are the way they are; or dreams are fulfilled, and the dreamers remain unfulfilled; or people rely on dreams that ought not to be fulfilled because they are unfulfilling. Out of disappointment comes the impulse to blame—often broadly and indiscriminately; out of follies comes the impulse to blame those who are foolish. The result is a great cry about the false, the corrupt, the hypocritical; the abuse of American society is acrimonious, savage, unrelenting, and it seems in our day to have reached new heights of virulence. (pp. 11-12)

> *Robert B. Heilman, "The Dream Metaphor: Some Ramifications," in* American Dreams, American Nightmares, *edited by David Madden (copyright © 1970, Southern Illinois University Press; reprinted by permission of the author), Southern Illinois University Press, 1970, pp. 1-18.*

W. H. Auden once remarked that "it is very difficult to conceive of a successful drama without important personal relations, and of such, the most intense is, naturally, the relation between a man and a woman." *Who's Afraid of Virginia Woolf?* is such a drama of personal relations, and no one would ever argue that it lacked intensity. But more important, in this play Edward Albee has backed away from the spirit of nihilism which has dominated most of the contemporary theatre and which was certainly the governing force in his earlier work. Great drama has always shown man at the limits of possibility. In our time we may feel these limits have been drastically reduced, but in *Who's Afraid of Virginia Woolf?* Albee has stretched them some, and in doing so he has given not only the American theatre but the theatre of the whole world, a sense of new possibility.

> *Robert W. Corrigan, "Engagement/ Disengagement in the Contemporary Theatre" (abridged versions originally published in anthologies edited by Robert W. Corrigan, 1962, 1968), in his* The Theatre in Search of a Fix *(copyright © 1973 by Robert*

> *W. Corrigan; used with permission of Delacorte Press), Delacorte Press, 1973, p. 282.*

Albee's *A Delicate Balance*, in which a shriveling playwright tries to disguise that fact with swathings of fake mandarinese and fake metaphysics, is like spending three hours head-down in yards of velour. (p. 26)

> *Stanley Kauffmann, in* The New Republic *(reprinted by permission of* The New Republic; *© 1974 by The New Republic, Inc.), March 2, 1974.*

In his artistic treatment of an intellectually formulated philosophy, Albee, unlike many existential dramatists, succeeds in achieving a unity between the basic assumptions of existentialism and the artistic form in which they are presented. The esthetic structure of *Virginia Woolf* is not so much a subtle blending of realism and existential theory, but is "best approached as a parody of romance: the application of romantic mythical forms to a more realistic content which fits them in unexpected ways," [as Northrop Frye wrote in *Anatomy of Criticism*]. (p. 198)

In *Virginia Woolf* . . . , the romantic mythic modes and roles are parodied. The sterile king becomes Martha's father, the power ruling over the university wasteland, a culture "burdened with a morality too rigid to accommodate itself to the swing of events." The king's beautiful and chaste daughter becomes Martha, the manlike, promiscuous princess who dominates the empty romantic relationship. The dragon-killing hero of romance is George, the ineffectual, dominated simp who reveals a child-like dependence on his bride. Finally, the "monster" in *Virginia Woolf* becomes the western culture's perverted values and unauthenticity. Rather than an idyllic vision of integration and love, the usual conclusion of the heroic quest, Albee's ironic truth is divisive, isolating, and despairing. . . .

Unlike conventional romance, the movement of the romantic quest in *Woolf* is inward and backward, rather than outward and forward. That is, the dramatic action reflects the psychic development of the characters in the exorcism of their illusions, but there is little assurance that the escape into themselves will resolve their problems. By dispelling their illusions, they have only taken the first step. (p. 199)

In *Woolf* the author parodies the ideals of western civilization through an inversion of the romantic form. Thus, romantic love, marriage, sex, the family, status, competition, power—all the "illusions" man has erected to eliminate the differences between self and others and to escape the existential burden of his freedom and loneliness come under attack. . . .

As layer by layer of pretense and artificiality are peeled off, the characters are left with their naked core—which on close examination are destructive illusions. Destroy the illusions of an Albee character and the fear of facing reality is staggering. (p. 200)

In *Woolf* Martha and George take turns playing hero and villain as they engage in a series of combats leading to a final death struggle. Just as the typical villain in romance is associated with moral confusion, darkness, destruction, sterility, Albee's protagonists reveal the same qualities. Even the setting, New Carthage, sets the tone for the drama. Old Carthage was the city founded by the woman ruler Dido who, as the result of a truncated romance with Aeneas, committed suicide. Thus, Albee immediately suggests that he is dealing with an ironic parody of the romantic relationship. (p. 201)

[The] first phase of the romantic cycle involves the mysterious birth of the hero. In *Virginia Woolf* we have the mysterious birth of an "illusory" hero who must be sacrificed to integrate the protagonists into a new state of communion and provide the possibility for a new existential beginning. After George kills the illusory son, he symbolically "eats the telegram" which was supposed to have announced his death. Thus, even the conclusion of *Virginia Woolf* is a parody of the romantic myth. The typical close of the romantic quest is the wedding of hero and heroine suggesting the restoration of fertility and order for the new society. In Albee's play, we have a symbolic death and a parody of the Requiem mass, suggesting the sterility of a barren future. (p. 203)

> *James P. Quinn, "Myth and Romance in Albee's 'Who's Afraid of Virginia Woolf?'," in* Arizona Quarterly *(copyright © 1974 by Arizona Quarterly), Autumn, 1974, pp. 197-204.*

When man's tatterdemalion quest for sodality encounters only poltroonery, he is shorn of all hope and belief. He desponds and is better served by narcotized stupor or inebriation than by meaningful dialogue. Rodomontade passes for discourse and the harlequinade of getting and spending transforms earth into a Principality of Hell.

Albee may not have anything very exceptional or very profound to say, but his way of saying it is disquieting. Although, like Brecht, Albee has been called a dustbin dramatist, and, like Pinter, has been denominated a cataloger of actuality, his forte is baneful banalities and bizarre juxtapositions. (p. 46)

Albee's plays do not remedy society's dissonance. Yet, his stage sets forth what we see without seeing every day. Albee examines emotions and actions most of us would rather not air in public. He flays society's persiflage and the insincere affability of locker room, cocktail party, and annual cotillion. His characters are drones rather than rebels. Few are happy or in good health. Most are ravaged by despair. (pp. 46-7)

Albee does not hesitate to use the scatological or blasphemous. He denounces preconceptions and scores follies. His topsy-turvy world is poised at the edge of an abyss into which we peer at our own risk. Albee's typical man is the jest rather than the glory or riddle of the universe. His plays jolt us with illogic and chortlings. Instead of heart-wrenching melodrama, he presents remorse without regret, grief without resentment. (p. 47)

Who's Afraid of Virginia Woolf? (1962) is Albee's most unqualified success and employs many themes found in his other dramas. The frank treatment of sexual matters is not offensive because it is liberally laced with zany humor. The arrows aimed at man's sadism, mendacity, and sanctimony are not envenomed in *Who's Afraid of Virginia Woolf?* The solecistic humor and obtrusive homosexuality of *Tiny Alice* do not appear here. (pp. 54-5)

The attractive aspect of *Who's Afraid of Virginia Woolf?* is

its view of life—realistic yet not defeatist. Albee rejects Sartre's negativeness and Pinter's depressiveness. Man's inhumanity and unsatisfactory human relations are the warp and woof of this play. A splinter of light is discernible amid the gloaming of nihilism's smog. In depicting the entire gamut of marital emotions, Albee does not omit tenderness. (pp. 55-6)

> *C. N. Stavrou, "Albee in Wonderland," in* Southwest Review *(© 1975 by Southern Methodist University Press), Winter, 1975, pp. 46-61.*

Edward Albee's "Seascape" . . . is a short, wryly witty, and sometimes touching play about discovery. Boldly and simply, it asserts that, at no matter what age and in no matter what time and place, acts of discovery remain to be undertaken. With luck, such acts will be found to have meaning; better still, there is the possibility that they will bear fruit. The plot is a charming toy: a well-to-do middle-aged couple, faced with the bleak certainty of the closing in and shutting down of their lives, have unexpectedly bestowed on them the boon of doubt; through a prodigious accident, they perceive that their lives may yet open out, may yet contain unlooked-for wonders. After many words of despair, the last word we hear spoken, in bright sunlight, under the bluest of blue skies, is a hesitant and yet hopeful "Begin!" And the word is spoken not by a member of the human race but by an enormous speckled lizard, exceptionally distinguished in bearing and utterance, who feels that he has much to learn. So, Mr. Albee hints, do the rest of us. But we must be quick; such willing creatures are not easily come by, even at the edge of our mother the sea.

Of all Mr. Albee's plays, "Seascape" is the most exquisitely written. He has calculated not only every immaculate line of dialogue but every word, every caesura; when the actors fall silent, we hold our breath and wait, as we wait at the reading of some superb long poem. (p.75)

> *Brendan Gill, "Among The Dunes," in* The New Yorker *(© 1975 by The New Yorker Magazine, Inc.), February 3, 1975, pp. 75-7.*

Who's Afraid of Virginia Woolf? is a work of permanence, and the expressions "a Virginia Woolf couple" or a "Virginia Woolf marriage" have drifted into common parlance. In the more than twelve years that have followed, Albee has written seven plays, and all of them put together possess the cumulative magnetic impact of a shelf of dead batteries.

What went wrong? Why are his plays such flaccidly somnolent affairs?

Mainly, Albee has indulged his playwriting defects. Having a very weak gift for plot construction, he took to adapting novels ranging from Carson McCullers' to James Purdy's. . . . After creating the wily priest and the slandering lawyer in *Tiny Alice*, the play that immediately followed *Virginia Woolf*, Albee no longer seemed able to invent any characters that possessed dramatic vigor. They all appeared to be suffering from acute spinal inertia and total mental ennui. Finally, he largely abandoned his strong suit, which was a flair for vituperatively explosive dialogue and bitchy humor. Instead, his characters have spoken for years now with intolerably stilted pomposity, as if they had wandered out of an unpublished work by some minor Victorian novelist.

These treacherous defects are all on parade in *Seascape*. It is not a hateful play; it is bland and innocuous, a two-hour sleeping pill of aimless chatter.

T. E. Kalem, *"Primordial Slime," in* Time *(reprinted by permission from* Time, The Weekly Newsmagazine; *copyright Time Inc.), February 10, 1975, p. 57.*

In . . . "Seascape" Edward Albee seems drained of almost all vitality—theatrical, intellectual, artistic. And vitality was always Albee's bottom line, the one quality that even his detractors admitted he possessed. In the early plays, that vitality was startling, disturbing, explosive, part of a youthful artistic personality that, despite streaks of callowness and derivativeness, expressed the lethal tensions of the American '60s. But after the tremendous impact of "Who's Afraid of Virginia Woolf?" a disastrous thing happened to Albee—he began to think, or rather he assigned his mind to take over on scouting duty, leaving his feeling to clop along in the rear. The prospects for this revamped task force were not good, and sure enough it has wound up lost in the desert. . . .

In "Seascape" his leading idea seems to be that the human species is at the end of its tether, all fagged out in bad faith and decayed energy, and that if sentience and spirit are to persist and prevail in the universe, the lower orders will have to take over.

Albee apparently has been reading recent books about naked apes and saintly dolphins and maybe even right-thinking plants. But he has chosen as inheritors of the earth a brace of lizards. . . . The lizards have scurried out of the deep, driven by a nameless force that Albee's human characters recognize as evolution. The humans . . . are still another squeezing from Albee's eternal married couple. Here, they are middle-aged bipeds whose ostensibly serene life turns out to have really been comfy sterility. . . .

Albee is saying that Nancy and Charlie are about the best humans can do in the way of love and communication, and it's not good enough. So away with them and their rotten world, symbolized by the recurrent roar of planes flying overhead on nasty missions of pollution, useless velocity and potential destruction. . . .

[The] play ends on one of those maddeningly sibyline words Albee has become fond of—"Begin," meaning that the humans will help their amphibious friends up the evolutionary ladder to replace their own tired Judaeo-Christian selves. . . .

Harold Clurman, who has been Albee's most consistently sympathetic critic, saw the playwright's development, at the time of "Virginia Woolf," as moving from "the theater of bewilderment to the threshold of a possible rebirth." My own view is that when Albee grew out of his "bewilderment," that is, his inchoate but authentic vision of contemporary spiritual horror, he tried to replace it with a structure of abstract ideas that would "expand" that vision. But instead of a "rebirth" he only attenuated the force of his work. The process was gradual: "Tiny Alice" retained some hot flashes of Albee's bitter passion, and "Box-Mao-Box" was an audacious attempt to create an abstract theat-

rical form to project his feeling about the drift of human culture toward absurd apocalypse.

But Albee's last two plays, "All Over" and now "Seascape," break down as his shallow but relentless "thinking" undermines his weakening emotional and poetic energy. The tipoff is right at the heart of things—language. The serrated edges of his speech are filed down as Albee experiments with a texture of indirection, notably in "Box-Mao-Box" with the character called, significantly, the Long-Winded Lady. But in "Seascape" that long-windedness has become a constipated language that moves in colonic spasms. Aiming for a Jamesian effect that will achieve great tension by suspending the finality of utterance, Albee achieves only the ultimate in pure nagging.

Jack Kroll, *"Leapin' Lizards," in* Newsweek *(copyright 1975 by Newsweek, Inc.; all rights reserved; reprinted by permission), February 10, 1975, p. 75.*

This simpleminded allegory [*Seascape*] can be interpreted in a dozen convenient, wishy-washy ways, the "lizards" standing for underprivileged minorities, upward mobility, *élan vital*, the instinctual, or whatever; the human beings for the bourgeoisie, the declining West, the Establishment, the victims of the superego, or whatnot. Or any other vague antinomies that must be reconciled so that some great, original philosophic maxim like "Life must go on" or "Life is a continual evolutionary process" might be derived from this splendiferous parable. Banal as all this is, a real artist might have breathed life into it; Albee endows it only with doughy verbiage, feebly quivering inaction, and grandly gesticulating pretentiousness.

There is a canard abroad, originated by Albee himself, that an Albee play has linguistic distinction. It has, to be sure, a style more literary than that of a play by Murray Schisgal or Neil Simon, but so has a sophomore term paper about William Faulkner. Here are some *Seascape* samples: "Continue the temporary and it becomes forever." "We've earned a little life, if you ask me—ASK ME!!!" "They don't look very formidable in the sense of prepossessing." "Nice, isn't it, when the real and the figurative come together?" "Sex goes, it diminishes—well, it becomes a holiday. Not like eating or sleeping; but that's nice, too—that it becomes a holiday." Notice what sorry stratagems are at work in these, for Albee, better-than-average lines. *Figurative* is, inappropriately, dragged in for *imagined* or *wished-for*; *formidable* is, inappositely, hauled out instead of *striking* or *impressive*. And so a platitude or triviality is supposedly ennobled by recourse to solecism. Epigrams like Albee's can be made with a cookie mold: "Continue the singular and it becomes the plural." "Continue not to conform and it becomes conformity." Continue piling up lines and it becomes a play. Ah, but you see, Simon and Schisgal would never use the word *figurative*, even thus incorrectly. This is the *je ne sais quoi* that makes Albee literature. (His *je ne sais*, by the way, extends to French, too; one of his characters is made to say *le petit mort* for *la petite mort*.)

Short as the play is, you feel it being dragged out desperately. . . . Yes, *The Zoo Story* and *Virginia Woolf* were plays; but how long will reviewers and audiences forgive such gaffes as *Tiny Alice, The Ballad of the Sad Café, Malcolm, Everything in the Garden, A Delicate Balance,*

Box Mao Box, All Over, and now *Seascape*, this piece of flotsam washed ashore near Albee's Montauk home? To go on tolerating, however minimally, this proliferation of pratfalls is not to strike a blow for Albee so much as to strike a blow against euthanasia. Such incurable playwriting should have been put out of its misery sooner, while it still preserved a shred of dignity. But, I dare say, Albee is a playwright of ideas for people who have never had an idea.

> *John Simon, "Evolution Made Queasy," in*
> New York Magazine *(© 1975 by NYM Corp.; reprinted by permission of* New York Magazine *and John Simon), February 10, 1975, p. 55.*

[*Seascape*] starts realistically, then becomes a fantasy. It [like *The Sandbox*] is about some sterilities of contemporary life. It, too, is expressed in banalities, but this time there is no reason to think that the diction is satirical. . . .

One welcome change in Albee; as against his recent plays, he has here eschewed fake mandarinese. This dialogue is undistinguished, but at least it is decorated only with artificial broken sentences, not with artificial flowers. However he has clung to his pseudo-Chekhovian mode: a chief ingredient of this early section is reminiscence, in wistful voice, recalling one's silly but charming past self. . . .

In short the play never demonstrates in any degree a real necessity to exist. All it demonstrates is that Albee wants to exist, as a playwright. He cooked up an idea—worth maybe a half hour instead of a bloated hour and a half (including intermission)—and then forced some arbitrary trite points into it in order to justify using it. In character, in texture, in theme, *Seascape* is an echoingly hollow statement of bankruptcy.

I think it's fair to make an inference about Albee's career since *Who's Afraid of Virginia Woolf?* I think that he is caught in a modern trap. He wrote some good plays when he was young; thus by the conventions of our society, he is sentenced to be a playwright for the rest of his life, whether or not he has anything more, really, to write. This wasn't always so: Congreve, Wycherley, Vanbrugh, Sheridan all wrote some fine plays when they were young; then, for differing reasons, quit to do other things. Nowadays this doesn't seem possible if one has been successful early and then begins to run dry. (And it's not just an American phenomenon; see the work of John Osborne since *Inadmissible Evidence*.) I have no gifts of prophecy and wouldn't want them if offered; but Albee's work since *Virginia Woolf* (1962) seems so much more the product of compulsion to be a writer than to write, that there is no reason to hope for improvement. He's still relatively young and could do a lot of other things if he weren't shackled by fear of being thought a burned-out rocket. (For instance, as many of his comments show, he could be a perceptive critic.) (p. 22)

> *Stanley Kauffmann, in* The New Republic *(reprinted by permission of* The New Republic; *© 1975 by The New Republic, Inc.), February 22, 1975.*

It is part of Broadway's unhealthily artificial atmosphere that we receive every new play by a writer of reputation in a state of tension which requires that his work be regarded as either a major event or a disaster. We must *hate* it or

love it. It hardly occurs to anyone that the latest effort of a generally esteemed dramatist may be only a link in a chain of development. That seems to be the case with Edward Albee's *Seascape*. . . .

It is his most relaxed play, a "philosophical" whimsy. You may find it delightful, or, if the nice notion on which it is based does not suit your temperament, you will consider it a drag. In either case it is not something that calls for a hysterical reaction. It is a step in Albee's still green career, a step which, seen in a certain light, augurs well for the future. In an agreeable sense, it is a "little" play. . . .

The play—essentially a one-acter—is, especially in its second half, light and cheerful. It is above all benevolent and, perhaps for the first time with Albee, rather charming. It points to a new direction or disposition on his part and possibly to a spiritual progress away from frustration and venom. If so, I welcome the new vein though, as always, I hope that Albee will eschew his inclination to the purely metaphorical and the abstractly symbolical which has long been a danger to his work. (p. 314)

> *Harold Clurman, in* The Nation *(copyright 1975 by the Nation Associates, Inc.), March 15, 1975.*

* * *

ALDISS, Brian   1925-

Aldiss, a British science-fiction anthologist and critic, writes prize-winning novels and short stories, usually on science-fiction themes. (See also *Contemporary Authors*, Vols. 5-8, rev. ed.)

I find it curious that the overall effect of [the] comic, racy and ingenious novel [*A Soldier Erect*] is in fact rather depressing, monotonous and ingenuous. It is the second instalment of the life and shames of Horatio Stubbs, whose earlier misdemeanours got themselves so compassionately recorded in *The Hand-Reared Boy*. Here, in its successor, this self-abused autobiographist has become a Soldier Boy: he is now larger and older but remains vigorously incapable of feeling anything at all except his erect sexual organ. This disheartening fact is rendered all the sadder by reason of the coincidence that most of the other characters in the book—all of them, like Stubbs, soldiers in India, then Burma—happen to be in exactly the same permanently cocked condition. Nothing, except the faculty of indulging in dialogues of inexhaustible and brilliant filthiness, in any way distinguishes these characters from the masturbatory exhibitionists in the monkey cages of the London Zoo. . . .

What is, I think, more interesting is that on pages 96 and 97 either Horatio Stubbs or Brian Aldiss has constructed what must be one of the finest as it is certainly one of the longest sentences in contemporary pornographic literature. It goes to some 800 words. And Aldiss's real gifts as a novelist appear very clearly in the last chapter, which describes the battle for a little hill in Burma. This chapter is a moving and compassionate piece of writing.

> *George Barker, "Low Feelings," in* The Listener *(© British Broadcasting Corp. 1971), March 25, 1971, p. 389.*

Horatio Stubbs, the hero of ["A Soldier Erect"], first appeared in an earlier book: "The Hand-Reared Boy," and though he is no longer an English student but now an English soldier, he still has primarily one thing on his mind. Whether on embarkation leave in England, on bivouac in India, or in the thick of the Burma campaign of 1944, Stubbs must be the randiest private in the China-Burma-India theater of operation. His zest for whoring declines only during bouts of dysentery.

Along with his priapic location, Stubbs shoulders the burden of being a radio man in some very unpleasant jungle fighting in the mountains of Assam. Mr. Aldiss brings to life this long-dead war, with its vanished mystique and its forgiven and forgotten enemies. He is a military observer who extracts the incongruous humor as well as the horror of the combat soldier's predicament. (pp. 22, 24)

> *Martin Levin, in* The New York Times Book Review *(© 1971 by The New York Times Company; reprinted by permission), August 22, 1971.*

What is important in [science-fiction] is that any situation, however bizarre to present-day conditions, should in fact be logical within its own framework.

It is because of the strangeness of the setting and events in S-F that the author must be doubly careful to ensure that nothing jolts the reader into disbelief. Mr Aldiss tells us that he wished to call this collection of some of his short stories [*Best SF Stories*] 'The Second Best', and one would not quarrel with that. Brian Aldiss is one of the foremost of British S-F writers, one whose talents are not limited to this type, and this collection might serve to interest those readers who have not ventured previously into the pages of S-F, for the quality of English usage is higher than that of most authors today.

The first story is a mocking reflection of man's behaviour. Machines with different grades of brain have taken over various functions of man, working in the fields; mechanical farm labourers. All perform more or less to perfection, the routine being followed as per instructions, when a snag arises. *Warehouse Three* is locked and the field-minder cannot obtain the seed potatoes it requires.

All right, so we accept that machines have taken over from men. What I find baffling is why, with machines in control, the warehouse needed locking in the first place? Are we supposed to deduce that the machines are now so advanced as separate intelligences that they are capable of theft? It is at this point that the logic within the framework breaks down, destroying the illusion of reality.

The second story, *Not For An Age*, is a science-fiction version on a theme written as fantasy in the early years of this century by a woman, May Sinclair. The central character is caught up in one of Blake's eternal circles of damnation in Hell, condemned to ever-lasting torment. May Sinclair's tale, *Where Their Fire Is Not Quenched*, is, in my opinion, a small masterpiece. Mr Aldiss's is run of the mill.

The last story in the collection, *Another Little Boy*, deals with the future, a future in which sex, orgies and orgasm loom large, but take second place to the might of world mass spectaculars, with an agency seeking to put on something vast to celebrate the centenary of August 6th, 1944. First they have to find out why the date is significant—the world has forgotten Hiroshima. But when they find out

what the date means, they celebrate with a repeat performance. Again, all right. But why is the original A-bomb described as weighing 10,000 *tons*? This sort of tiny slip can destroy the illusion out of all proportion.

But between the stories mentioned you can safely assume that there will be something to interest, enlighten, even delight. Brian Aldiss is no mean artist. (pp. vii-viii)

> *John Boland, "In Other Times," in* Books and Bookmen *(© John Boland 1972), August, 1972.*

Science has got out of hand [in *Frankenstein Unbound*] and the solar system is in the throes of an ecological disaster— hence the myth of Frankenstein has particular symbolic significance. Exploring what constitutes myth and what constitutes reality against an unpredictably shifting temporal background can only be taken as an attempt at seriousness. But nothing can alter the fact that having the driver of an atomic car go back two centuries to meet celebrated literary figures ("Shelley was all electricity where Byron was all beef") is nothing if not *extremely silly*. There is a lot of hearty punning between the two poets and Mary Shelley cries "Let your sunlight and my moonlight mingle" to the infatuated Bodenland [the protagonist] who [sounds] less like an American from 2020 and more like the ex-literary editor of a provincial British newspaper from half a century earlier. The writing improves in the desolate landscape at the end, where there's less to be embarrassing about, but not before one of the immortal truths of the last century has reasserted itself: the one about the perils of too much hand-rearing. (p. 1377)

> The Times Literary Supplement *(© Times Newspapers Ltd., 1973; reproduced by permission), November 9, 1973.*

Brian Aldiss disarmingly subtitles [*The Eighty-Minute Hour*] "A Space Opera", which should prepare his readers for the *buffo* element even before they happen on the facetious names of his characters. Glamis Fevertrees, Devlin Carnate and Monty Zoomer take us into a sort of galactic D'Oyly Carte production and, given the author's predilection for referring to literary figures such as Thomas Hardy, we are probably lucky not to have a character named Immanent Will. The plot, like that of most operas, is not easy to follow due to the frequent scene-shifting. Broadly, it concerns a post-holocaust world (of Britain and Ireland nothing has survived save the Koh-i-Noor diamond) whose remaining nations have formed themselves into either the Capitalist-Communist Alliance (no ideological explanation given) or the opposing League of Dissident Nations. There is also a third, more sinister force, the Computer Complex, which is trying to infiltrate and control mankind by means of implanted antennae. Computerized androids and the eighty-minute hour are two more of CC's ambitious projects.

Notwithstanding the intermittent arias for soloists and chorus (in verse), it is a familiar Aldiss libretto . . . [with] the similes more extravagant than meaningful ("He became silent, as silent as greengage jelly"), the mock-Gothic episodes deriving from Peake and Thurber. But just as familiar are those sudden patches where the writing comes alive: the landing of a spaceship on a forest roof two kilometres above the actual surface of a planet whose ecology is based on hydrogen is particularly imaginative. The difficulty is in knowing whether any of it is intended seriously, perhaps as a satirical if apolitical and simplified projection of present trends. Some of the characters are actually computer analogues, but it is never quite clear which, thus ruling out most human interest.

One is left with what Edmund Crispin referred to as the "plot as hero", and this one seems largely concerned with the question of free will. . . . If you find that [his] way of portraying determinism sounds familiar, it is probably because, in common with Mr. Aldiss, you have read *The Sirens of Titan*. But Kurt Vonnegut, for all his sentimentality, did it better; clearer narrative, more serious characters and, above all, *no arias*.

> *"Aldiss and Heaven Too," in* The Times Literary Supplement (© *Times Newspapers Ltd., 1974; reproduced by permission), April 5, 1974, p. 357.*

The Eighty-Minute Hour is Aldiss's Science's Sensations Satirised, a perverse and reversible logomachia. Life, which would mean more under any other name, feeds precariously off the rapidly shifting surfaces of an hallucogenic Earth. Every possible doom has worked its miracle of transformation, and the planet has become a raddled honeycomb of times and tides. Until we grow our sixth and seventh senses, the ultimate pollution must be that of the time continuum—that well-known invention of the realistic novelist. And within Aldiss's "electronic zoomatigina of confusion," time cracks up and displays all the symptoms of *dementia praecox*. . . .

The Eighty-Minute Hour is the *opera bouffe* of the new language, the new Eden from which unhappy silence has been expelled. It is continually surprising with its kollidoscrape of sounds and images, as the movie-go-round goes on for ever and a day. And there are some happy touches: the boardroom of the World Executive Council, the leathery postlude to the Big Bang, "on the walls of which hung among other treasures the only Tiepolo etching to have survived the war. It depicted the flight into Egypt, and was reputed to be more valuable than Egypt itself." Next to it hangs, as the apotheosis of a future hero, an oil painting of Sir Noel Coward. A new design for living. (p. 485)

> *Peter Ackroyd, in* The Spectator *(© 1974 by* The Spectator; *reprinted by permission of* The Spectator*), April 20, 1974.*

*   *   *

ALVAREZ, A(lfred)   1929-

Alvarez is an influential British critic of modern poetry, a poet himself, and a novelist. Throughout his vigorous, idiosyncratic, and firmly subjective criticism, Alvarez examines and endorses the "extremist" artists, those like Plath and Lowell who will pursue their insights to the edge of breakdown—and beyond. His recent highly subjective study of suicide, *The Savage God*, has brought Alvarez' name to the attention of a wide and diverse audience. (See also *Contemporary Authors*, Vols. 1-4, rev. ed.)

Mr. Alvarez is that very welcome character, the subjective critic. . . . [In *The Shaping Spirit*, he] is in reaction against the New Criticism, while paying tribute to the tautening

services it has rendered. For him every poet calls for a different approach, if we are to benefit fully from what he has to impart, even every poem. . . .

What interests him compellingly is the use of language to produce the poetic effect. . . .

Illuminating as Mr. Alvarez's generalizations are, a still greater pleasure is to be got from his sensitive approach to how individual poets use the language to impart their particular apprehension of existence. . . .

[Whatever] disagreements the reader may have with Mr. Alvarez, he will find this an enjoyable book, informed by, to use a phrase of his own, "relish and vitality," an admirable example of that kind of criticism the object of which is "not to find fault, but to discover those beauties that will delight the reasonable reader."

> *"Flexible Criticism," in* The Times Literary Supplement *(© Time Newspapers, Ltd., 1958; reproduced by permission), May 9, 1958, p. 256.*

There are two things that chiefly impress me about this critic. In the first place he accepts the full task of criticism. He not only defines and analyzes [in *Stewards of Excellence*], but he also assesses and evaluates. In the second place he impresses me with the acuteness of his sensibilities.

The result of the first point is that you sometimes violently disagree with him. Personally, I find his dismissal of Dylan Thomas as a man whose poetry is impressively poetic on its creator's tongue and so much "verbal preciosity" on the printed page, a good deal this side of the kingdom of truth. But on the other hand I applaud, from my personal opinions, the partial deflation of Pound and Auden, and the balanced appraisals of Stevens, Crane, and Empson. His championship of the work of D. H. Lawrence caused me to reread the poetry, and this is certainly one of the functions of criticism. I do not find myself completely won over by his arguments, but I am more amenable to the poetry than I was formerly. (pp. 125-26)

There is a thesis in the book: ". . . that 'modernism'—in inverted commas—has been predominantly an American concern, a matter of creating, almost from scratch, their own poetic tradition." This I find interesting, and effectively presented, but the greatest value of the work lies in its individual essays. These are brief, but in each case Mr. Alvarez hits upon a central core of definition that illuminates the entire work of the poet under consideration. Some of these points are well-known, but the critic italicizes them with perceptions and modes of expression that are uniquely his own. . . .

Mr. Alvarez seems to me one of the finest of the younger critics. (p. 126)

> *Paul Petrie, in* Poetry *(© 1959 by the Modern Poetry Association; reprinted by permission of the Editor of Poetry), November, 1959.*

A. Alvarez offers *The New Poetry* [an anthology] as what "really matters" from the last decade and not as a complete guide to the English scene today. Our trouble, he thinks, is that the poetic upheaval which began with the experimental techniques of Eliot and Pound was prevented from coming to anything in this country by a series of "negative feedbacks". First we had the reversion to traditional forms in chic modern guise by Auden in the Thirties, then the high rhetoric and anti-intellectualism of the Forties, and finally the wry flatness of the Fifties Movement. In various ways these all helped to stem the revolution and re-foster our English beliefs in the essential order, politeness and controllability of life. And the result is that "the concept of gentility still reigns supreme" in our poetry. But this genteel stance gets more and more difficult to maintain in an age of mass evil and depth psychology, and the poets who matter now are those who can experience the real underlying disintegration and confront it with the necessary formal skill and intelligence. Those marshalled in this book include two Americans, Berryman and Lowell, and a selection of more recent British names.

We should salute Alvarez for his seriousness, but I don't think his Introduction really comes over as the piece of propaganda he wants it to be. It throws up ideas about verse-forms, emotion, evil, gentility and much else, but in the end does very little to distinguish or relate them all. So that when the "new seriousness" is eventually defined as "the poet's ability and willingness to face the full range of his experience with his full intelligence" we don't feel very much the wiser and have almost no cutting edge for the actual choosing of poems. The anthology itself is in fact far less partisan and more representative than its Introduction pretends: there are no wild inclusions, and if the decade's best poems are mostly here we are still left to our own criteria for picking them out from the rest. Sometimes the chosen poems even seem to conflict with the vague criteria we are given, but there is no attempt to explore this or to ask what it shows. . . . The questions multiply, and it would be silly to think they could all be met in a short introduction (or here). But the danger, if they are not even allowed to arise, is that we shall find ourselves driven back into the personal and irrational attitudes that the "new seriousness" was meant to save us from, while the "new seriousness" itself remains circular and unpersuasive. . . . (pp. 1-2)

> *Colin Falck, in* The Modern Poet: Essays from "the Review," *edited by Ian Hamilton (© Ian Hamilton), MacDonald, 1968; American edition, Horizon, 1969.*

[If] there is any meaning left in a label like "modern intellectual," Alvarez merits it. . . . His issues are vital and engaging, if only because they are ours today.

All this is not to imply that Alvarez is an avid apologist for whatever is new. What is impressive about [*Beyond All This Fiddle*], in fact, is that . . . he is neither an attacker nor defender of current trends. Like Matthew Arnold, whom he obviously admires, his aim is to see things as they are, in the widest possible contexts, and to help create a climate of ideas in which art can flourish. Like T. S. Eliot, he believes that in literary criticism "the only method is to be very intelligent." "What the professor is in theory," he says, "the critic is in practice: an intellectual. He is, I mean, someone to whom ideas are emotionally important, who responds to experience by thinking for himself."

In speaking about Alvarez, one would, were space available, inevitably have to turn to the substance of his ideas, to counter or support them. One wants to quote him, and at length, to communicate how intense his ideology is. A thinker himself, he spurs thought in his reader. And what causes his ragtail collection of subjects to hang together—including essays on three private passions: films, mountaineering, and travel—is not the force of his personality, as with Greene, but the fluidity of his language and ideas, his denseness of texture, his willingness to take chances with great sweeping propositions, his fundamental, clear-headed sanity. His own essay on James ends fittingly: "And he was, after all, one of the most intelligent men who has ever written." The statement typifies Alvarez's consistent dedication to independent thought. (pp. 26, 31)

> *Robert Maurer, in* Saturday Review *(copyright © 1969 by Saturday Review, Inc.; reprinted with permission), August 2, 1969.*

["Beyond All This Fiddle"] is impressive, much more so than are most collections of book reviews, for, despite the diversity of books and topics discussed, it has the unity that comes from the strongly felt, all-pervading presence of a decided and decisive personality. "Beyond All This Fiddle" reminds us of something we tend to forget: that we read good criticism as much for the critic as for the works he deals with. It shows us too just how and why A. Alvarez is so important a figure in contemporary British criticism.

In one of these essays Alvarez takes Dr. Johnson as an example of the writer of what he calls primary criticism, "criticism which, as rationally, deliberately and lucidly as possible, gives a sense of what the poetry is like." He goes on:

"This means it describes not only the mechanics of the verse, the interaction of the various complex elements, meter, imagery and the rest; it also judges the work and sets it down within some scale of values. The values may never be set out formally, but they are everywhere implied in the critic's tone, reasons and choice of words."

This is the critic Alvarez himself aspires to be, and in the last analysis it is his values that give him the peculiar authority he has in British literary journalism at the present time. . . .

[His values] have their being, it seems to me, in his realization of what it has meant to be a Jew in our time, which can be summed up in the words "concentration camp." In his essay "The Literature of the Holocaust," a survey of the imaginative writing that has come out of the camps, he says: "For the rest of us, there was the far obscurer guilt of being Jews who had never been exposed to the camps at all." Elsewhere, in the essay "Beyond the Gentility Principle," which first appeared as the introduction to his anthology of modern verse "The New Poetry," having noted that in our time "mass evil (for lack of a better term) has been magnified to match the scale of mass society," he goes on to suggest that "the forcible recognition of a mass evil outside us has developed precisely parallel with psychoanalysis; that is, with our recognition of the ways in which the same forces are at work within us."

It is within this context that Alvarez conducts his evaluation of contemporary writing. England was scarcely affected by the concentration camps, and the Gentility Principle is, of course, the English principle, the belief that "life, give or take a few social distinctions, is the same as ever, that gentility, decency and all the other social totems will eventually muddle through."

In "Beyond the Gentility Principle" he calls for "a new seriousness" in English poetry. This he defines "simply as the poet's ability and willingness to face the full range of his experiences with his full intelligence; not to take the easy exits of either the conventional response or choking incoherence." It is illuminating that his contemporary heroes in poetry are Robert Lowell, John Berryman and Sylvia Plath, whom he sees as an "imaginary Jew."

Locally, so far as England is concerned, Alvarez is a salutary figure. "The New Poetry," which is essentially a critical anthology, together with its introduction, seems to me a seminal document in the history of recent English poetry, for it sharply rebukes the provincialism and even escapism so strong in English writing today. It is the index of Alvarez's range of reference that he invokes not only American writers as examples of how to cope with the situation of our times but also East European poets and critics, as the essays on Miroslav Holub, Zbigniew Herbert and Jan Kott show. (p. 4)

His favorite adjective of praise, it strikes one as one reads ["Beyond All This Fiddle"] is "intelligent." He gets it, I think from Eliot's formula for criticism: "The only method is to be very intelligent." It is a method Alvarez has made his own. (p. 24)

> Walter Allen, in The New York Times Book Review (© 1969 by The New York Times Company; reprinted by permission), August 17, 1969.

One wishes that Alvarez were more discursive, had more idiosyncrasies, kept a little less strictly to the point [in The Savage God]. He writes briskly and sensibly, with a genuinely sympathetic understanding of the subject [suicide], with a ready control of quotation, and a nicely quizzical way with a good story. But these sturdy virtues don't always prove themselves a match for the gigantic puzzle of self-extinction. Too often the problem of suicide slides elusively from Alvarez's deft, commonsensical scrutiny.

By far the best things in his book are the prologue, a personal memoir of Sylvia Plath, and the epilogue, his account of his own attempted suicide. In these chapters, he lets the details flood in; picks up, like a novelist, the hum and buzz of the ordinary as it converges on its shocking, yet inevitable, climax. . . . The memories are flat, disjointed. They fall into the grammar of the short sentence and the semi-colon —they revive the stale mechanics of seasonal jollity with none of their emotional charge. It's a very precise form, this grammar of anomie, and Alvarez writes it with a moving blend of conviction and control. . . . It's a style of narration in which the impulse to impose oneself on top of the details that press on one has died; a style very close in tone to that of suicide itself.

Most readers will, I imagine, tackle the beginning and end of Alvarez's book first. When they come to the centre of the sandwich they will be disappointed. For it is little more than a summary dossier on suicide through the ages, its literature, sociology and psychoanalysis. Durkheim is glossed, rather too casually. Freud pops in and out of the narrative like a useful if somewhat distant uncle. A number of Professor Xs are exhibited, and made to stand in the corner. In the long 'Suicide and Literature' section, Alvarez is very good, in a non-committal, informative way, on

Cowper, Chatterton and the Young Werther craze. But his quick, analytic, journalist's prose cannot entertain the play of the random that is so important in his accounts of Plath's suicide and his own attempt. Suicide, despite the warnings he puts up in his preface, turns into an act, something that people do, for simple, explorable reasons. (p. 701)

Alvarez's ability to categorise and sort things out leads him to some conclusions that I find merely baffling. In the final chapter of the central section, called 'The Savage God', he extends the argument that he first outlined in his preface to the Penguin New Poetry; the direction of modern literature is into the dimension of death, through an art of risk and violence. And he identifies the two key styles of our time, 'Totalitarian Art' and 'Extremist Art'. On 'Totalitarian Art' I find him wholly plausible. If literature itself suffers a 'psychic numbness' under the pressure of 20th-century history, and enters the closed world of the suicide on his passage to self-extinction, then its symptoms are likely to be silence, exhaustion, and the appearance of ravaged, minimal styles with which to confront head-on the deadly facts of modern experience. . . . In [such] work, we watch literature relinquishing its existence in a deliberate, moral gesture of self-immolation.

But Alvarez confidently couples this style, in an easy otherside-of-the-coin strategy, to the 'extremism' of his famous four, fielded now as bravely as ever before; Lowell, Berryman, Hughes and Plath. It is an axiom of the Alvarez position that these four writers work as a team, dicing with death like crack speedway stuntmen. But do they? Lowell's immersion in his tradition, his quarrying of the past in search of the possible, makes him proudly and profoundly assertive of life. Death exists in his work to be countered, not diced with. And in Sylvia Plath's last poems there is a continuous note of manic triumph, a joy in the achievement of the verse itself, even a kind of jollity, that makes her actual suicide seem more of a terrible contingency than 'a risk she took in handling such volatile material'. Of course she faced her own death in her poems, but it is hard to think of any poet of stature who has not done so, especially if one's criteria are as elastically symbolic as Alvarez makes them in his book. But it seems to me that Tennyson, a writer to whom Alvarez does not refer, comes more dangerously close to the impulse to self-extinction in In Memoriam than many of Alvarez's 20th-century risking heroes. (pp. 701-02)

Our century, in contrast to the Victorian age, has been notoriously bad at facing death at all, and we are both in danger of overvaluing those artists who manage to do so, and, worse, of isolating their treatment of death until it swells out of all proportion to the rest of their work. For Tennyson, the contemplation of suicide was entirely natural; for Sylvia Plath, it meant breaking a taboo. The Savage God shares her excitement and, like her poems, it sometimes achieves art out of questionable arithmetic. (p. 702)

> Jonathan Raban, "Prospect and Horizon Gone," in New Statesman (© 1971 The Statesman & Nation Publishing Co. Ltd.), November 19, 1971, pp. 701-02.

The Savage God's praise of articulate despair is perhaps at times in danger of romanticising suicide, but there is nothing sensational or indulgent about its style, its attitudes, or its conclusions. Alvarez speaks movingly about Burton's rambling mixture of science, pedantry, fable, and personal obsession, and his own book, in some senses also a miscellany, idiosyncratic to breaking-point, has something in common with the *Anatomy of Melancholy*. (pp. 890-91)

Even while he gives full scholarly and critical attention, learned, tolerant, respectful, to suicide, it is the astonishing belief in fortitude that gives the book its dignity and value, that preserves it from melodrama or voyeurism. It helps us to tolerate, too, if not to like, the overconfident simplifications. This treatise on suicide pays very little attention to the economic or the somatic causes. Alvarez works towards (or from) a poetics of suicide. . . .

If the book doesn't always seem in perfect control of its direction, if we are tempted to wonder if Alvarez is "hitching a lift"—his image—from Sylvia Plath, if the psychological and literary judgements are complacent, the human details sometimes reduced or unsympathetic, these apparent flaws are a low price to pay. Perhaps the book's form is a defensive structure, the personal narrative dignified and magnified by history and literary criticism, the Plath memoir providing a particularity which compensates for the sketchiness of his own confession, the confession itself establishing his right to the venture. *The Savage God* is a novel and genuine case of the breakdown of the old stable ego of criticism, more untidy, uncertain, and unstylish than Alvarez's literary criticism, a most moving experiment. This is personalised criticism, blurring the lines between fiction, memoir, autobiography and literary analysis, and revealing its personal concern and motive. We now see, for instance, why the response to 'A Nocturnall upon S. Lucies day' in *The School of Donne* was so impressive. It is a tribute to the book's seriousness to admit that I feel rather ashamed of finding its actual form so interesting. Like so much of the extremist literature it discusses, it is dislocated and fragmented, and while using narrative forms evasively or reticently, it is nakedly exposed as the study of literature seldom dares to be. It is literary criticism become broken and relevantly self-conscious in a way we should praise and emulate. (p. 891)

Barbara Hardy, "Anatomy of Despair," in The Spectator *(© 1971 by* The Spectator; *reprinted by permission of* The Spectator)*, December 18, 1971, pp. 890-91.*

The eternal triangle is at its most bleakly geometric in ["Hers," Alvarez's] novel of sex and self-contempt at an "ancient and famous" British university. In one corner is Sam, a graduate student on the verge of abandoning the academy with a bitter "Goodbye to All That." Opposed to him are his mentor Charles Stone, an eminent literary scholar, and Julie, Stone's cool and wayward German wife. The young man is hungry and sardonic, the older worried about keeping his power and prestige intact. . . .

Sam is hardly a likable character in any of [his several] roles. Since many details of his portrait resemble Alvarez's own background, we are given a choice between two equally uncomfortable interpretations of the book: either Alvarez himself identifies uncritically with Sam's distasteful mixture of opportunism and sentimentality, or else a ritual purgation of the author's self-contempt is being conducted, at which we must be uneasy spectators. In any case, this uncertainty of focus suggests a failure of nerve on

Alvarez's part, an unwillingness to test the limits of his subject.

Through his critical essays and "The Savage God" (a study of literature and suicide) Alvarez has become a leading advocate of what he has termed the "Extremist" poets—Robert Lowell, Anne Sexton, John Berryman, Ted Hughes, Sylvia Plath—who have dared to explore in their art private obsessions with madness, suicide, political terror. "Hers" has some pretensions to being an extremist novel, a making public of private agonies. But the heart of the matter—the truly painful and contradictory nature of sexual freedom—it avoids by sliding away, at the crux, into a very different mode: what Alvarez himself has called "the modern 'cool' style, the art of controlled and detached delinquency."

The apparent sexual extremism of "Hers" comes down to little more than the familiar English obsession with occupying the high ground in the status war—a war that the more spirited prefer to wage in the bedroom, the only place outside the constraints of a pseudo-civility that deadens every other kind of human relation. . . .

Alvarez is further handicapped by his uncertain grasp of the basic skills of a novelist. "Hers" is his first published novel, and it shows. . . .

[But in] spite of its verbal clumsiness, its reliance on tired clichés like dragging in a motorcycle gang as symbols of mindlessly violent youth, this studied, perverse love story still has a sour but definite taste. By its insistence on the eternal contrariness of sexual attraction, it imparts to the relations between its characters a moral strenuousness that is in refreshing contrast to the soggy recitals of sexual victimization now so much in vogue. The combatants in "Hers" are at least evenly matched, the issue between them in suspense; a pity, then, that there is so little reason for the reader to care which fighter can claim to have won. (p. 5)

Paul Delany, in The New York Times Book Review *(© 1975 by The New York Times Company; reprinted by permission), March 30, 1975.*

It is not unlike A. Alvarez to venture out of the ordinary. Best known as a literary critic and a poet, Alvarez often introduces and supports the work of avant-garde, sometimes angry young poets, and, in his famous study of suicide, *The Savage God*, he explores one of the darker sides of literature and of the self. In *Hers*, his first novel, Alvarez quietly plays with inversion and the hidden dimensions of the commonplace. The story is mundane and familiar: a brief, rather dull love affair in one of England's "ancient university" towns (read Oxford). But the relationship is between a professor's wife and one of her husband's students, not the one between the lecherous aging male teacher and the nubile young female pupil that so many "university" novels have trundled out for us. In a damning portrait of the groves of academe, where competitiveness, hypocrisy, and opportunism grow as abundantly as in the outside world, Alvarez shows three people who finally decide to risk a sexual or psychological search for the self rather than just becoming footnotes to the text of existence, thumbing through life as if it were a shelf of books.

That life is not a sunny one. Alvarez heard from his savage

god that an awareness of suicide and self-destructive urges can enrich the meaning of life. In *Hers* people seem already dead, wandering like zombies through set social patterns and professional behavior. It has been said that the passion for destruction is a creative passion; the sad thing here is that it only destroys. The overwhelming sense is one of disgust: distaste for the trappings of the everyday behind which people hide, an unbridgeable gap between the new generation and the old, self-loathing and unsuccessful attempts to shake this feeling through love for others.

A craving for some kind of solution triggers mental journeys into the past. The solution the past offers: resignation, conscious acquiescence instead of despairing passivity. Resignation is probably all we should expect from any character Alvarez cares to create. Like the poets he admires most, these people seem cursed with "open nerve ends." They are excruciatingly aware of what is wrong, but don't have the power to right things—only the strength of a critical sensibility.

Sensitivity of this type is skillfully filtered through Alvarez's intelligence; the story shimmers with the small talk and small thoughts of bright but pedestrian people, and it bears the touch of the poet. An unassuming but interesting novel, *Hers* is also a pessimistic one. It doesn't just spring from a private vision of Alvarez's, however—from his fascination for the "core of darkness" in everyone. The university is the world, and the conditions of the characters universal. How can we wonder at an Englishman telling a darkling tale at this point in time, or balk at the grim grimaces he pulls at what he sees? Alvarez insists that "the real resistance now is to an art which forces its audience to recognize and accept imaginatively . . . not the facts of life but the facts of death and violence." Here is a modest contribution to that form of art. (pp. 26-7)

> *Celia Betsky, in* Saturday Review *(copyright © 1975 by Saturday Review/World, Inc.; reprinted with permission), April 5, 1975.*

The meaning and the value of *Hers* both depend on you. Come to the book fresh from life and be exhilarated; read it with a head full of abstractions, you may be let down. It is not that Alvarez is anti-intellectual in his first novel. Having taught at Princeton, Oxford and the University of New Mexico, he respects the dynamism of ideas and, as shown by his many quotations from authors like Shakespeare, Marvell and Auden, he believes in the interrelatedness of life and literature. . . .

Though Alvarez knows both the jargon and political infighting of academe, he seats *Hers* in the family. The attention he pays to close spontaneous living makes *Hers* a work of domestic realism in the vein of D. H. Lawrence. His insights into personalities under stress also reveal a fresh, conceptless grasp of everyday life that recalls Lawrence. A very first-hand book, *Hers* accepts life without forcing it into a system of philosophical imperatives.

Conveying this acceptance is a style with real lift and bounce. . . .

Alvarez's ability to weld style to his appreciation of the everyday includes dialogue. (p. 25)

A learned novel that, ironically, stresses the limits of learning, *Hers* celebrates both the openendedness and renewability of life. To read it is to join in the celebration. (p. 26)

> *Peter Wolfe, in* The New Republic *(reprinted by permission of* The New Republic; © 1975 by The New Republic, Inc.), April 5, 1975.*

*   *   *

AMIS, Kingsley 1922-

Amis, a British critic, poet, and satirical novelist, has been compared with, among others, Evelyn Waugh, H. G. Wells, Henry Fielding, Samuel Butler, and Ivy Compton-Burnett. His best known work is still *Lucky Jim*, his first novel. (See also *Contemporary Authors*, Vols. 9-12, rev. ed.)

Amis [has expressed] his distaste for an excess of rhetoric or style in fiction. . . [and his] usual reaction to experimental novels is impatience. (p. 39)

Amis feels that it is old-fashioned to praise the experimental novelists; their day is over, and their style has been replaced by a more direct and conventional style—similar to the one which Amis uses himself. (p. 41)

All of this does not mean that Amis throws out everything earlier than contemporary literature. Amis is a great admirer of eighteenth-century literature, and this is his special field as a teacher of literature. The humor and tone of Amis' first novel, *Lucky Jim*, are somewhat reminiscent of the eighteenth-century picaresque novel, and one critic [David Lodge] finds a "Shandean" quality in Amis' fiction.

Amis has said that he feels a close affinity with Henry Fielding. . . . A good deal of the humor and satire in his fiction goes back to Fielding. (pp. 43-4)

Other novels of Amis also have an eighteenth-century flavor. The plot of *That Uncertain Feeling* is reminiscent of Richardson's *Pamela* and of Fielding's parodies of Richardson. (p. 44)

Amis has an even greater affinity with the novelists of the early twentieth century. Quite a few critics see at least a superficial similarity between Amis' Jim Dixon and the heroes of H. G. Wells. Certainly, in terms of attitude towards class they are somewhat alike.

Amis' fictional style resembles that of the writers of this group, like Wells, Bennett, and Butler. Rejecting the verbal innovations and unchronological sequences of the experimentalists, Amis is closer to these pre-experimental writers. His plots, like theirs, are uncomplicated and chronological, and his style is simple and straightforward. A number of critics feel that Jim Dixon's mild rebelliousness and hatred of sham are entirely contemporary phenomena, but to some extent they are similar to Ernest Pontifex's attitudes in Butler's *The Way of all Flesh*. (p. 45)

Amis' criticism is motivated not only by a dislike for experiment and for style in fiction, but by a cultivated Philistinism as well. . . . This is not to say that Amis' criticism is unintelligent or uninformed: the quality of his criticism is high; it is the direction in which the criticism moves which is unusual. Many of his comments seem motivated by iconoclastic impulses, a desire to clear away the rubbish of outworn traditions so that newer forms and values may be considered. Like a good deal of iconoclastic criticism, Amis' comments are at times refreshing and at times hasty and impulsive. His comments about *Beowulf*, for example, fall into the second category. . . . Amis has decided that the price of enjoying *Beowulf* is too high a price to pay; yet to carry this argument to its conclusion would mean that almost every work which is a product of a foreign or older culture is not worth bothering with.

A problem in his criticism is that Amis often does begin to carry this argument to its conclusion. "Filthy Mozart!" says the hero of *Lucky Jim*, and a great chunk of Western Culture falls overboard with a splash. One quickly discovers, however, that Amis is more interested in the splash than anything else. He is too obviously cultured to hate culture that much; one suspects his sincerity. (pp. 51-2)

Amis' humor is mainly satirical. . . . Amis defines modern satire as "fiction that attacks vice and folly as manifested in the individual" [*New York Times Book Review*, July 7, 1957]. His own satire usually follows this definition, though one of his weaknesses as a satirist is an uncertainty in his novels as to what "vice and folly" really are, and who possesses them. In *Take a Girl Like You* Amis satirizes both Patrick's lechery and Jenny's persistence in preserving her virginity. This double satire occurs again in *One Fat Englishman*. Roger Micheldene mocks American customs, many of which are valid targets for satire. But Roger is himself such a snob, bore, and hypocrite that it soon emerges that Amis is satirizing both Americans and anti-American Englishmen. The satire in *Lucky Jim* is much more powerful because it is not divided in this way: Jim Dixon mocks the hypocrisy of his colleagues in the university and refuses to be subverted by it. Here the satire is more powerful because the things being satirized are more boldly defined.

There is a bit of ambiguity even in *Lucky Jim*, however, which two of the other novels, *That Uncertain Feeling* and *Take a Girl Like You*, share. In all three books, very wealthy characters appear who are not satirized, or satirized less than the other characters. (pp. 59-60)

It is difficult to reconcile this trend in Amis' novels with the left-wing views Amis holds and the "class animus" which many critics have attributed to him. To some extent the confusion can be blamed on Amis' own political ambivalence, but it is also true that his political feelings have often been misunderstood and misrepresented.

Part of the confusion came from the "Angry Young Man" appellation: John Osborne was outspokenly left-wing in his political views, and his opinions were attributed to the others in the group, including Amis. (p. 60)

In reality, Amis was only very hesitantly committed to the left. His allegiance to the Labour Party was weak; Labour, to Amis, was only the lesser of two evils. (p. 61)

Amis is seldom partisan, and on particular issues his opinion may vary across the political spectrum. . . . It is this mixture of conservatism and liberalism which helps to account for the seemingly irreconcilable elements in Amis' novels: the anti-Americanism as well as attacks on anti-Americanism in *One Fat Englishman*, or Amis' satirical attacks against class together with his admiration for the wealthy in other novels.

This sort of ambivalence occurs elsewhere in Amis' attitudes and ideas. Since he is a poet, a popular novelist, an anthologist of science fiction, and a literary journalist, he feels more sharply than most writers do the differences between his various audiences. Naturally he will try to

appear more intellectual to his poetic audiences than to the readers of his anthologies of science fiction. If this were all, he would merely be adopting a series of literary poses; but at times his honesty causes him to reverse the roles, and overcompensate. At this point he may write a slangy book review with an anti-intellectual bias or write a very scholarly article on science fiction. Certain things are quite clear: Amis does not care for the experimental writers, a super-abundance of style, or anything that smacks of romanticism. He likes nonallusive, nonsymbolic poetry, straightforward narrative prose, science fiction, jazz, and Henry Fielding. As for terms like "Angry Young Man," or "liberal," in Amis' case they obscure the issue more than anything else. (pp. 62-3)

> *Rubin Rabinovitz, "Kingsley Amis," in his* The Reaction Against Experiment in the English Novel, 1950-1960 *(copyright © 1967 Columbia University Press; reprinted by permission of the publisher), Columbia University Press, 1967, pp. 38-63.*

Amis connoisseurs will find several things [in *Ending Up*] they will expect and several things they will not. The book is compulsively readable and beautifully constructed. There is no writer now alive, other than Anthony Powell, who writes such classically pure English which is at the same time accurately and exactly idiomatic. This is a very rare gift that Mr Amis has cultivated, so that there is nothing he cannot say economically and precisely if he wants to.

He uses this instrument to be wildly and cruelly funny. As each character turns up, he or she is fully realized. (pp. 703-04)

Some of the rather tough jokes in the book arise from familiar Amis situations—the determined non-confrontation between the brigadier and a grandson on blacks, the detailed delineation of the hangovers derived from various drinks, and the frequent (and welcome) references to the need for gratitude that the Red Army has not got here yet. But most of the enjoyment comes from watching people be themselves, after lifetimes [of] being bruised into what they have become.

All that is what we have the right to expect from Mr Amis. He is a craftsman, a true professional. He can get generations right—the old talk of 'wirelesses' and the young of 'radios', as a trivial but correct instance. . . .

What comes as a surprise is the quite extraordinary degree of compassion that Mr Amis shows towards his characters and that they show towards each other. For me, this raises the whole book to very near the top of the Amis canon. You always expect to see the characters clearly delineated in an Amis novel; somehow, I have not really felt that they were meant to be 'understood' in the social work connotation of that phrase. Mr Amis was only nice to characters he liked. In this book, however, each person has a ghastly problem, derived from the fact of being old, and nobody—except the spinster—really feels deeply about anybody else. Nevertheless, they do not only put up, on the whole, with each other; for the most part, they make a go of it, which, of course, most people do. It is a kind of celebration of ordinariness. And the people whom Kingsley Amis is usually pretty cheesed off with—homosexuals, young advertising men, chattering affected ladies—are shown, remorselessly, for what they are, but also with a degree of friendship and liking which is quite remarkably unsentimental. It is as though a jovial, cheerful Mr Amis had decided that as he had got to put up with this lot, he might as well like them for what they are. . . .

The book, has a serious concern with the good and the bad. It ends with a catastrophe, rather like the end of *Macbeth*, which somehow gives point to the brooding sense of disaster, of evil even, that looms over the book. This is reminiscent of *The Green Man*, which deals openly with the supernatural. It is not, I think, just because Mr Amis has recently been writing about Chesterton that there seems to be a Chestertonian flavour to the book. To his extraordinary ability as a writer of colloquial English and his sheer narrative power, there seems to be added a new depth of human feeling.

It is difficult to write about death, and old age. To avoid mawkishness, or sheer horror, and instead to try to be clinically accurate, while writing a novel which is both kind and funny, is a real achievement. Mr Amis has used his strength as a writer on a subject that requires that strength. (p. 704)

> *John Vaizey, "Compliments of the Season,"*
> *in* The Listener *(© British Broadcasting*
> *Corp. 1974; reprinted by permission of John*
> *Vaizey), May 30, 1974, pp. 703-04.*

In some of Kingsley Amis' novels . . . the author's battle with his inner demon is far more dramatic than anything that goes on among the fictional characters. Indeed the true Amis fan—which I count myself—may become more fascinated with this artistic wrestling match than with the actual events of the novel. The suspense is sometimes terrific. Will Amis' blimpishness, as embodied in that gluttonous, overage schoolboy Roger Micheldene, Esq., devour and ruin *One Fat Englishman*? (Almost.) Will his sophomoric snobbishness kill *Girl, 20* stone dead? (It does.) Only in Amis' less "serious" novels—the excellent ghost story *The Green Man* and the sweetly nostalgic *The Riverside Villas Murder*—does he relax his ferocious misanthropy and let fresh air in.

From *Lucky Jim* onward, Amis' heroes, in their preoccupation with food, drink and rather nasty sex, resemble nobody more than England's notorious schoolboy, Billy Bunter. The curse of many English male writers—Amis' idol, Ian Fleming, is an example—is that their attempts to disguise their adolescent fixations merely result in a heavyhanded sophistication that is the indelible mark of the compulsively prankish, fantasy-ridden juvenile. The surprising and heartening thing about Amis' new novel is that somehow, despite himself, a grudging, qualified compassion tempers his basic sourness. *Ending Up* is about old age; it's cruel, upsetting and at times extremely funny. (p. 27)

If *Ending Up* isn't the best Christmas present for your 65-year-old Aunt Cora, it is still a remarkably stoical, even brave little work. . . .

Leaving aside any analogy Amis may intend between the old people's cottage and today's England, he has succeeded in exorcising—at least for one reader—some fears that old age holds for many of us. One can be elderly, semi-senile, crippled with piles and other painful physical indignities, self-deluding and humiliatingly unable to resolve in old age the problems of early life—and still be triumphantly human. It is our good fortune that Kingsley Amis, England's raging, perpetual schoolboy, doesn't go gentle into that good night. (p. 28)

> *Clancy Sigal, in* The New Republic *(reprinted by permission of* The New Republic; *© 1974 by The New Republic, Inc.), October 12, 1974.*

An unabashed admirer of Kingsley Amis since the piping days of "Lucky Jim" (his subversive astringency seemed to me from the first to fall upon and rout the remaining orotundities of Imperial fiction, which may have accounted for Somerset Maugham's calling him what amounted to a cad in a review of the book), I approached his "Ending Up" . . . with anticipatory salivation. Amis, having repeatedly savaged the young and middle-aged, now turns his swift (if not, as the jacket has it, Swiftian) eye upon old age. "Ending Up" concerns itself with a tumbledown household of tumbledown people. . . .

What Amis does with this situation is almost unflaggingly funny; surprisingly, it is also, for him, quite feeling and tender in stretches. . . . But the book is spoiled by its mechanistic structure. It is a short book, a kind of five-finger exercise. That may be why the author considers his people expendable at the end of their palsied romp, but whatever the reason, the ending is forced; it denies the possibilities that all its characters, as the result of hard, thinking work by the author, make manifest in the earlier pages. Too bad. But, naturally, we will hear more—and soon—from Kingsley Amis. (p. 185)

> *L. E. Sissman, in* The New Yorker *(© 1974 by The New Yorker Magazine, Inc.), October 21, 1974.*

I have heard it said that Amis is a real novelist, and I know no one who does not wish that he were, but I hope I'm not giving myself away if I say that for me his best books are *What Became of Jane Austen?* and *On Drink*. Presumably Amis himself has mistaken his talent for a novelist's because he is untiring in his delight in saying nasty funny things about his characters. In *Ending Up* the people are particularly vulnerable because they are over seventy. . . . [A] lot of *Ending Up* is really nasty, and some is really funny. But the characters exist only so Amis can wound them, and when he tires of the fun he just kills them off with casual carelessness. Amis is frightened of life, no question, and much possessed by death, too, but he won't face up to that—which is precisely what Joseph Heller does do—won't make that the stuff of his books. There's hardly need for me to insist on this, since Amis's two most important models, Waugh and Compton-Burnett, could have shown him what's wrong had he wanted to know it. This waste of talent is a great shame. Granted that these are not great days for the English, but others have seen how to be not just funny and nasty when faced with a diminished thing, and Amis has not. (pp. 626-27)

> *Roger Sale, in* The Hudson Review *(copyright © 1974 by The Hudson Review, Inc.; reprinted by permission), Vol. XXVII, No. 4, Winter, 1974-75.*

For a long time now, British fiction has suffered from a

shortage of automobiles. Its characters never go anywhere, and since an author seems limited to the number of people who can fit in a drawing room, they are soon beating tattoos on each other's skin. While this may be fine for the fairly healthy British theater, it limits British novelists to comedies of manners and locked-room detective stories—two highly artificial forms of fiction where the rules are more important than the content—while their vision shrivels like the Empire. A nation of prunes.

A long time ago, Kingsley Amis became famous with *Lucky Jim*, the enduring comedy of a young teacher on the make. But that was during the early days of the "angry young men," those first bright beneficiaries of higher education for the lower classes, who thought they could keep their feet on the streets and their heads above the fog and by sheer toughmindedness break down the pomposities of the British system. They couldn't, and no one else has taken their place. Significantly, Amis' best recent writing has been his most escapist, such as *The Anti-Death League*. Significantly again, *Ending Up*, which starts realistically and degenerates into farce, features life among the very old. (pp. 296-97)

Although all the characters are drawn with a fine, sharp, brittle pencil, there is little shading in their paper-thin personalities. Amis has always had a solid comic sense, and our introduction to his old folks promises a good novel; but after we have seen all their little quirks and quiddities, they have nothing more to do—reading *Ending Up* is like watching a clock run down. When there is nothing more to be exploited from the interactions of his five old people, Amis squeezes out a final drop of humor by killing them all off. While this may be tidy it is hardly convincing; unfortunately it must have seemed permissible in the current denatured state of the British novel. (p. 297)

> *Charles Nicol, "A Brittle Pencil," in* National Review *(© National Review, Inc., 1975; 150 East 35th St., New York, N.Y. 10016), March 14, 1975, pp. 296-97.*

A spare classical work in which nothing is wasted, [*Ending Up*] is presumably well founded on medical reality. Consider the five dreadful seventy-plus inhabitants of Tuppenny-hapenny Cottage: Bernard, retired brigadier (bowel cancer); Shorty, his army but non-officer boy friend of former years (alcoholism with cirrhosis of the liver); George, professor emeritus, Bernard's brother-in-law (stroke with paralysis and nominal aphasia); Adela, Bernard's sister (gastric ulcer and heart disease); and Marigold, her lifelong idol (incipient senility with amnesia). Medically, I suppose that includes all the most probable conditions: if there were room for another human being in the house, he or she would probably have emphysema, and I expect that George's ghastly dog has that.

But true to life, they do not die directly of these diseases: in every case the angel with the darker draught is called Accident, who lives on the stairs, up stepladders, inside medicine cupboards where he mixes up the bottles, or hovering over the dog's ball for pages on end until it gets stepped on. He is a small but effectual angel, often cruel but sometimes kind, as he is to Bernard: a few minutes of shock after a fall is a good exchange for months of terminal cancer. The violent ending, in which all five are carried off almost simultaneously, is however not at all naturalistic, although the de-

tails are carefully worked out. The odds against such an event must be astronomical, as in those detective stories that have five corpses in one country house weekend, including the bishop and the butler. I expect that Amis is alluding to that convention; he must be telling us that, although the characterization, language, and descriptions of the hideous clothes and furniture are as minutely accurate as the medical details, we are to read the book not as a realistic chronicle or a picture of life as lived in Britain today but rather as some kind of fable. But just what kind it is not immediately easy to see.

One clue may lie in what I have read of Amis's journalism. I don't mean only that he himself lives in a sort of middle-class commune, which includes invalids: that is relatively trivial, although it shows he knows what he is talking about. It's more important that he has always been obsessed with music, that great comfort of middle age, preferring late eighteenth-century music (he says his favorite composer is C. P. E. Bach, not J. S.) but also admiring Mozart and others of the Viennese classical composers.

At the risk of incurring Lucky Jim's coarse derision, I will make a guess that he has tried to model the structure of *Ending Up* on a baroque suite or more likely on a classical work with some movements in sonata form. Such a work is likely to be chamber music; and if so, it is presumably a quintet rather than a quartet, so the field is fairly narrow. It could be Schubert's C major quintet, but I think it is more likely to be one of Mozart's: the g minor (K. 516), perhaps, which is believed to be about death and except for the last movement is one of the saddest pieces in all music. In that case the characters not only represent instruments (with Marigold as first fiddle, Bernard as cello, and so on—although their bowels are sometimes used as instruments, too) but also express themes or "first and second subjects." These themes are carefully introduced and reintroduced in musical fashion in the earliest of the forty very short chapters, which can themselves be grouped into "movements" according to the dates of the narrative (October, 1972, to early January, 1973, with distinct gaps).

The first lunch party, in fourteen chapters, suggests to me a first movement in fairly strict sonata form. Can the characters' dreadful habit of repeating themselves be thematic development, their even worse habit of continually interrupting each other counterpoint (like the stretti of a fugato)? The static episodes before Christmas seem like the two slow movements of the g minor; and just as Mozart turns the last movement into a disconcertingly cheerful dance, so Amis moves into a farcical kind of ballet in the penultimate sequence of chapters: during the appalling Christmas dinner people keep falling about in a surprising manner, perhaps more suitable for a Totentanz. I admit I can't make the coda of the story fit the g minor quintet: nevertheless, it does seem to resemble a musical coda. Even if the details of my theory are wrong, I am sure that any careful reader with some musical knowledge will have the sense that chamber music is being played before him, probably Mozart's.

There are no allusions to classical music in the text. The more decayed gentlefolk are uncultivated; the lower-class Shorty is the only musician in the group but he's a Philistine. Nor is the formal structure of the narrative reflected in any formality of language: the quintet and their younger visitors speak and think in varieties of modern British idiom (needless to say, as brilliantly caught as ever): there is nothing of Ivy Compton-Burnett here. But if the essence of classical music (and all classical art) is symmetry, *Ending Up* is richly endowed with this on every plane, narrative and moral. For example, the five are all horrible, but each in different degrees in a different way: Bernard's malevolence, which starts with quiet needling and ends with elaborate and futile practical jokes, is the worst; but Shorty's facetious vulgarity, Adela's stupidity, George's repetitiousness, and Marigold's hideously cute language ("tracklepackle" in her private language means "attractive") are all equally vile.

On the other hand, each is virtuous in his or her peculiar way. Bernard on receiving his death sentence from the specialist keeps silent with military heroism; Shorty tries to cheer up the company with an attempt at verbal wit; Adela is a conscientious housekeeper and a devoted friend; George will not be defeated by his stroke and tries to go on writing for the learned journals; even Marigold deserves credit for trying to be neat and smart. Amis is just to each of them, but nothing excuses their common vices of solipsism and lack of attention, their deep vulgarity of not listening. The book is not a satire, but it contains satire: you cannot satirize people for getting sick and old, but I think Amis means to suggest that you can reasonably expect them to be alert and polite up to the time when the relevant parts of the brain disappear.

There also seems to be some symmetry in the balance of pleasure and pain felt by each of the five. Each suffers, and not only physically; humiliation and irritation are powerfully shown to be the worst scourges of old age. But Amis subtly suggests that each of them is happy too, finding pleasures which the young and restless can hardly know, in routine work, in getting permanently drunk, or, like Bernard, in just passing the time. Almost every sentence spoken is ironical, in that it has at least two meanings, depending on who is listening or, more usually, not listening. Almost every sentence is very sad and very funny. (pp. 32-3)

The book describes the futility and meaninglessness of life as it must sooner or later appear to many old people. Despite his continual joking, and sometimes apparently callous indifference, Amis has written a very moving study of the pain of old age, and he could be thought of as offering a present to Bernard and to others in his plight. If Bernard cannot see his life as meaningful or even see it as whole, then the author can do something like that for him: he won't offer the false comforts of religion or philosophy, but he can give a life some formal pattern, which in the end, as in music, means only itself.

When a writer you have long admired comes up with a book as good as this, it is natural to look up some of his earlier work. When I opened one of them I began to laugh aloud, until I felt the shock of memory. It may be progressive amnesia, but I could not remember laughing aloud at any new book, perhaps at any book, since I first read the library interview in *That Uncertain Feeling*, nearly twenty years ago. (p. 33)

> *Matthew Hodgart, in* The New York Review of Books (*reprinted with permission from* The New York Review of Books; *copyright* © *1975 NYREV, Inc.), March 20, 1975.*

[In *Ending Up,*] Kingsley Amis attempts to make comedy of images of depression, exploring with obsessive attentiveness the horrors of old age. All our worst fears of the future find embodiment here: paralysis, loss of memory, drunkenness, cancer, loneliness, lovelessness, absence of pleasure, impoverishment psychic and economic. The cast of characters comprises the five elderly inhabitants of an ugly, inconvenient rural cottage, bonded by need or convenience, little affection, and occasional younger visitors—relatives or doctor—who feel for them only distaste. . . . At the end—what else?—everyone dies, the novelist disposing of his characters with gay—or desperate?—abandon.

Of course such a novel does not consist only of its raw material, and Amis's wit, his sharp eye for detail, have not left him. If he shows little compassion for the elderly persons he has devised, he displays plausible penetration of the anger and frustration which he imagines as their main emotions. . . . His precision in evoking the factuality of dreariness, his withholding of sympathetic response, give him the commentator's authority. But from what perspective can one properly comment on such phenomena? The young people who visit and detest their aging relatives swear never to resemble them, yet dimly, fearfully, see in these wretched human beings the shapes of their own destinies. The old people may, in fact, allegorize the general condition of humanity. . . . [As in Joseph Heller's *Something Happened*, the] comedy of infuriated acceptance assumes the impossibility of change, the futility of effort. Misery is its subject, misery its true tone; the blinding awareness of misery limits authorial perception. Amis, like Heller, depicts a mini-culture devoid of hope. Like the conversation of the depressed, these novels, turning inward upon themselves, seem distorted by their sense of grievance and their incompletely acknowledged anger. Their obsessive narrowness of vision makes them sound not quite trustworthy. (pp. 585-87)

> *Patricia Meyer Spacks, in* The Yale Review (© *1975 by Yale University; reprinted by permission of the editors), Summer, 1975.*

*   *   *

AMMONS, A(rchie) R(andolph)   1926-

Ammons is an important American pastoral poet in the Emersonian tradition of Robinson and Frost. (See also *Contemporary Authors*, Vols. 9-12, rev. ed.)

All of a sudden, with an unheralded and largely unacknowledged cumulus of books, . . . A. R. Ammons has exploded into the company of American poets which includes Whitman and Emerson and articulates the major impulse of the national expression: the paradox of poetry as process and yet impediment to process. More honestly than Whitman, acknowledging his doubts as the very source of his method ("teach me, father: behold one whose fears are the harnessed mares of his going!"), though without Whitman's dramatic surface, Ammons has traced out the abstractive tendency, the immaterialism that runs through all our *native strain*, in both acceptations of the phrase: to suffer or search out immersion in the stream of reality without surrendering all that is and makes one particularly oneself. The dialectic is rigorous in Ammons' version—the very senses which rehearse the nature of being for the self, the private instances of the sensuous world, must be surrendered to the experience of unity. . . . "Stake off no beginnings or ends, establish no walls,'' the poet urges, addressing that Unity: "I know if I find you I will have to leave the earth and go on out . . . farther than the loss of sight into the unseasonal, undifferentiated stark''—a region, a Death, to speak literally, where there is no poetry, no speech to one's kind, no correspondence perceived and maintained, but only the great soft whoosh of Being that has obsessed our literature from its classical figures, as Lawrence saw so clearly, down to Roethke, Wright Morris, Thornton Wilder. (pp. 1-2)

Yet even in [*Ommateum*, his] first book, especially as we tend to read it with the later work in mind, as a propaedeutic function of that work, it is evident that Ammons has discovered his tremendous theme: putting off the flesh and taking on the universe. Despite a wavering form, an uncertain voice, Ammons means to take on the universe the way Hemingway used to speak of taking on Guy de Maupassant—the odds, it is implied, more than a little in favor of the challenger. (p. 4)

By the time, ten years later, of his second book, *Expressions of Sea Level*, Ammons had extended and enriched this theme to stunning effect—not only in versions of nature and the body, but in terms of poetics as well, enforcing the substitution of the negative All for the single possibility of being. (p. 5)

In *Expressions of Sea Level* we are given a lot more to go on, and consequently go a lot farther, than the persona of Ezra and some rhapsodic landscapes of apocalypse. We are given, with great attention to vegetable detail and meteorological conditioning, the scenes of the poet's childhood in a North Carolina backwoods, the doctrine and rationale of his metaphysical aspirations . . . and the resignation, the accommodation of himself to the tidal marshes of New Jersey as the site of the poet's individual drama. Here is a man obsessed by Pure Being who must put up with a human incarnation when he would prefer to embody only the wind, the *anima* of existence itself:

> So it came time
> 　for me to cede myself
> and I chose
> 　the wind
> 　　to be delivered to.　　　　　(pp. 6-7)

One of Ammons' most interesting sidelines, a lagoon of his main drift, is a concern with archaic cultures whose aspect often reminds us, in its amalgam of the suggestive detail and the long loose line, in its own prose music, of Perse. . . . But not until a more recent book, *Corsons Inlet*, would this mode be brought into accord with the main burden of Ammons' song—the made thing of his impulse. Song may seem an odd word for a verse in which I have descried the music of prose, a verse which is as near as words can get us to our behavior, no more than a fairly cautious means of putting down phrases so that they will keep. Yet though the iambic cadence, and all it implies and demands by way of traditional lilt, has been jettisoned as utterly as Dr. Williams ever decreed, there *is* a song in Ammons' windy lines, a care for the motion of meaning in language which is the whole justice of prosody. (pp. 7-8)

The most luscious of his books so far, *Corsons Inlet* . . ., stands as the farthest and still the most representative reach into, upon, and against Being which the poet has yet made. It opens with a poem that nicely illustrates the perfected diction Ammons has now achieved, a rhythmical certainty which does not depend on syllable-counting or even accentual measure, but on the speed and retard of words as they move together in the mind, on the shape of the stanzas as they follow the intention of the discourse, and on the *rests* which not so much imitate as create the soft action of speech itself. There is a formality in these gentle lines which is new to American poetry, as we say that there is a draughtsmanship in the "drip-drawings" of Pollock which is new to American painting: each must be approached with a modulated set of expectations if we are to realize what the poet, the painter is about. (pp. 11-12)

It is characteristic that so many of [the *Corsons Inlet*] poems—and in the previous book as in the one to come—take up their burden from the shore, the place where it is most clearly seen that "every living thing is in siege: the demand is life, to keep life". . . . (p. 13)

Ammons rehearses a marginal, a transitional experience, he is a littoralist of the imagination because the shore, the beach, or the coastal creek is not a *place* but an *event*, a transaction where land and water create and destroy each other, where life and death are exchanged, where shape and chaos are won and lost. It is here, examining "order tight with shape: blue tiny flowers on a leafless weed: carapace of crab: snail shell" that Ammons finds his rhythms, "fastening into order enlarging grasps of disorder," and as he makes his way down the dunes, rhythms are "reaching through seasons, motions weaving in and out!"

The rebellion against Being and into eternity is put down by the body itself on these expeditions the poet makes, safaris into mortality which convince him that "the eternal will not lie down on any temporal hill," and that he must "face piecemeal the sordid reacceptance of my world." It is not acceptance, but *re*acceptance which must be faced, the world which must be learned *again* as the poet, borrowing Shelley's beautiful image, "kindles his thoughts, blowing the coals of his day's bright conscious" in order "to make green religion in winter bones." In *Corsons Inlet* doctrine has been assimilated into "one song, an overreach from which all possibilities, like filaments, depend: killing, nesting, dying, sun or cloud, figure up and become song—simple, hard: removed." That is Ammons' definition of his aspiration—a long way from the breezy expostulations in *Ommateum*—and, I believe, of his achievement as well: his awareness and his imagination have coincided. (p. 14)

> Richard Howard, "A. R. Ammons" (originally published in Tri-Quarterly), *in his* Alone With America: Essays on the Art of Poetry in the United States Since 1950 (copyright © 1965, 1966, 1967, 1968, 1969 by Richard Howard; reprinted by permission of Atheneum Publishers, New York), Atheneum, 1969, pp. 1-17.

Beyond its experimentation with Poundian cadences, *Ommateum* shows no trace of the verse fashions of the fifties; I cannot detect in it the voice of William Carlos Williams, which indeed I do not hear anywhere in Ammons's work, despite the judgments of several reviewers. The line of descent from Emerson and Whitman to the early poetry of Ammons is direct, and even the Poundian elements in *Ommateum* derive from that part of Pound that is itself Whitmanian.

Ommateum's subject is poetic incarnation, in the mode of Whitman's *Sea-Drift* pieces, Emerson's *Seashore*, and Pound's *Canto II*. The Whitman of *As I Ebb'd with the Ocean of Life* is closest, suggesting that poetic disincarnation is Ammons's true subject, his vitalizing fear. In the "Foreword" to *Ommateum* he begins his list of themes with "the fear of the loss of identity." (p. 257)

Ammons's poetry does for me what Stevens's did earlier, and the High Romantics [Bloom's term, by which he refers to Blake, Wordsworth, Coleridge, Shelley, Keats, and Byron] before that: it helps me to live my life. If Ammons is, as I think, the central poet of my generation, because he alone has made a heterocosm, a second nature in his poetry, I deprecate no other poet by this naming. It is, surprisingly, a rich generation, with ten or a dozen poets who seem at least capable of making a major canon, granting fortune and persistence. Ammons, much more than the others, has made such a canon already. A solitary artist, nurtured by the strength available for him only in extreme isolation, carrying on the Emersonian tradition with a quietness directly contrary to nearly all its other current avatars, he has emerged in his most recent poems as an extraordinary master, comparable to the Stevens of *Ideas of Order* and *The Man With the Blue Guitar*. To track him persistently, from his origins in *Ommateum* through his maturing in *Corsons Inlet* and its companion volumes on to his new phase in *Uplands* and *Briefings* is to be found by not only a complete possibility of imaginative experience, but by a renewed sense of the whole line of Emerson, the vitalizing and much maligned tradition that has accounted for most that matters in American poetry. (p. 261)

The shore, Whitman's emblem for the state in which poets are made and unmade, becomes the theater for the first phase of Ammons's poetic maturity, the lyrics written in the decade after *Ommateum*. These are gathered in three volumes: *Expressions of Sea Level* (1964), *Corsons Inlet* (1965), and *Northfield Poems* (1966), which need to be read as a unit, since the inclusion of a poem in one or another volume seems to be a matter of whim. A reader of Ammons is likeliest to be able to read this phase of him in the *Selected Poems*, whose arrangement in chronological order of composition shows how chronologically scrambled the three volumes are. (p. 263)

Ammons fully claims his Transcendental heritage in his *Hymn*, a work of poetic annunciation in which the "you" is Emerson's "Nature," all that is separate from "the Soul." The *Hymn*'s difficult strength depends on a reader's recognition that the found "you" is: "the *not me*, that is, both nature and art, all other men and my own body." . . .

Emerson's fixed point oscillates dialectically in Ammons's *Hymn*. Where Emerson's mode hovers always around metonymy, parts of a world taken as the whole, Ammons's sense of the universe takes it for a symptom. No American poet, not Whitman or Stevens, shows us so fully something otherwise unknown in the structures of the national consciousness as Ammons does. It cannot be said so far that Ammons has developed as fluent and individual a version of the language of the self as they did, but he has time and persistence enough before he borrows his last authority from death. (p. 264)

The burden of Ammons's poetry is to . . . name that enlargement of life that is also a destruction. When the

naming came most complete, in the late summer of 1962, it gave Ammons his two most ambitious single poems, *Corsons Inlet* and *Saliences*. Though both poems depend upon the context of Ammons's canon, they show the field of his enterprise more fully and freely than could have been expected of any single works. *Corsons Inlet* is likely to be Ammons's most famous poem, his *Sunday Morning*, a successfully universalizing expression of a personal thematic conflict and its apparent (or provisional) resolution. But *Saliences*, a harder, less open, more abstract fury of averted destructions, is the better poem. *Corsons Inlet* comforts itself (and us) with the perpetually renewed hope of a fresh walk over the dunes to the sea. *Saliences* rises past hope to what in the mind is "beyond loss or gain / beyond concern for the separate reach." Both the hope and the ascension beyond hope return us to origins, and can be apprehended with keener aptitude after an excursus taking us deeper into Ammons's tradition. Ammons compels that backward vision of our poetry that only major achievement exacts, and illuminates Emerson and all his progeny as much as he needs them for illumination. Reading Ammons, I brood on all American poetry in the Romantic tradition, which means I yield to Emerson, who is to our modern poetry what Wordsworth has been to all British poetry after him; the starting-point, the defining element, the vexatious father, the shadow and the despair, liberating angel and blocking-agent, perpetual irritant and solacing glory. (pp. 268-69)

The Ammonsian literalness, allied to a similar destructive impulse in Wordsworth and Thoreau, attempts to summon outward continuities to shield the poet from his mind's own force. *A Poem Is A Walk* is the title of a dark, short prose piece by Ammons that tries "to establish a reasonably secure identity between a poem and a walk and to ask how a walk occurs, what it is, and what it is for," but establishes only that a walk by Ammons is a sublime kind of Pythagorean enterprise or Behmenite picnic. Emerson, who spoke as much wisdom as any American, alas spoke darkly also, and Ammons is infuriatingly Emersonian when he tells us a poem "is a motion to no-motion, to the still point of contemplation and deep realization. Its knowledges are all negative and, therefore, more positive than any knowledge." *Corsons Inlet*, *Saliences*, and nearly a hundred other poems by Ammons are nothing of the kind, his imagination be thanked, rather than this spooky, pure-product-of-America mysticism. Unlike Emerson, who crossed triumphantly into prose, Ammons belongs to that company of poets that *thinks* most powerfully and naturally in verse, and sometimes descends to obscure quietudes when verse subsides. (pp. 270-71)

The anguish that goes through *Corsons Inlet*, subdued but ever salient, is more akin to a quality of mind in Thoreau than to anything in Emerson or Whitman. . . . In Thoreau, whatever his final differences with his master, the Emersonian precipitateness and clarity of the privileged moment are sharpened. When I read in his *Journals*, I drown in particulars and cannot find the moments of release, but *The Natural History of Massachusetts*, his first true work, seems all release, and very close to the terrible nostalgias *Corsons Inlet* reluctantly abandons. (p. 272)

[*Saliences*, the] major poem written immediately after *Corsons Inlet*, emerges from stoic acceptance of bafflement into an imaginative reassurance that prompts Ammons's major phase, the lyrics of *Uplands* [and] *Briefings*.... (p. 276)

Saliences thus returns to *Corsons Inlet*'s field of action, driven by that poet's need not to abide in a necessity, however beautiful. Saliences etymologically are out-leapings, "mind feeding out," not taking in perceptions but turning its violent energies out into the field of action. If *Corsons Inlet* is Ammons's version of *The Idea of Order at Key West* (not that he had Stevens's poem in mind, but that the attentive reader learns to compare the two), then *Saliences* is his *The Man With the Blue Guitar*, a discovery of how to begin after a large and noble acknowledgement of dark limitations. *Saliences* is a difficult, abstract poem, but it punches itself along with an overwhelming vigor, showing its exuberance by ramming through every blocking particular, until it can insist that "where not a single single thing endures, / the overall reassures." Overall remains beyond Ammons, but is replaced by "a round / quiet turning, / beyond loss or gain, / beyond concern for the separate reach." *Saliences* emphasizes the transformation of Ammons's obsessive theme, from the longing for unity to the assertion of the mind's power over the particulars of being, the universe of death. The Emersonianism of Ammons is constant; as did Whitman, so his final judgment of his relation to that great precursor will be: "loyal at last." But *Saliences* marks the *clinamen*; the swerve away from Emerson is now clarified, and Ammons will write no poem more crucial to his own unfolding. Before *Saliences*, the common reader must struggle with the temptation of naming Ammons a nature poet; after this, the struggle would be otiose. The quest that was surrendered in *Guide*, and whose loss was accepted in *Corsons Inlet*, is internalized in *Saliences* and afterward.

Saliences approximates (indeliberately) the subtle procedure of a subtradition within Romantic poetry that goes from Shelley's *Mont Blanc* to Stevens's *The Auroras of Autumn*. The poet begins in an austere, even a terrifying scene of natural confrontation, but he does not describe the scene or name the terror until he has presented fully the mind's initial defense against scene and terror, its implicit assertion of its own force.... [*Saliences* includes] seventy magical lines of Ammons upon his heights (starting with: "The reassurance is / that through change / continuities sinuously work"), lines that constitute one of a convincing handful of contemporary assurances that the imagination is capable always of a renovative fresh start. (pp. 276-77)

A poem like [*Upland*] is henceforth Ammons's characteristic work: shorter and more totally self-enclosed than earlier ventures, and less reliant on larger contexts. He has become an absolute master of his art, and a maker of individual tones as only the greater poets can accomplish. (pp. 281-82)

All the poems in *Uplands* have [a] new ease, but the conscious mastery of instrument may obscure for us the prevalence of the old concerns, lightened by the poet's revelation that a search for saliences is a more possible quest than the more primordial romancing after unity. The concerns locate themselves still in Emerson's mental universe; Ammons's *Periphery*, like Dickinson's *Circumference*, goes back to the astonishing *Circles* of 1840 with its insistence that "the only sin is limitation" and its repeated image of concentricity. The appropriate gloss for Ammons's *Periphery* (and for much else in *Uplands*) is: "The natural world may be

conceived of as a system of concentric circles, and we now and then detect in nature slight dislocations which apprise us that this surface on which we now stand is not fixed, but sliding." Ammons calls so being apprised "hesitation," and his slight dislocation is the radiant burst of elk, snow-weed, lichen, white rocks, and verbena that ends *Periphery* so beautifully. (p. 283)

Despite its extraordinary formal control and its continuous sense of a vision attained, *Uplands* is a majestically sad book, for Ammons does not let himself forget that his vision, while uncompromised, is a compromise necessarily, a constant knowing why and how "unity cannot do anything in particular." (pp. 285-86)

From [the] self-imposed pathos [in *Uplands*] Ammons wins no release. Release comes in the ninety delightful lyrics gathered together in *Briefings* (first entitled, gracefully but misleadingly, *Poems Small and Easy*), this poet's finest book. Though the themes of *Briefings* are familiarly Ammonsian, the mode is not. Laconic though transfigured speech has been transformed into "wasteful song." The first poem, *Center*, places us in a freer world than Ammons would give us before. (p. 286)

Briefings marks an end to the oldest conflict in Ammons; the imagination has learned to avoid apocalyptic pitch, but it has learned also its own painful autonomy in regard to the universe it cannot join in unity. With the confidence of this autonomy attained, the mind yet remains wary of what lurks without. (p. 287)

The one particular of dying remains; every unmastered particular is a little death, giving tension to the most triumphant even among these short poems. *Hymn IV*, returning to the great *Hymn* and two related poems of the same title, seals up the quest forever:

> You have enriched us with
> fear and contrariety
> providing the searcher
> confusion for his search
>
> teaching by your snickering
> wisdom an autonomy
> for man
> Bear it all
> and keep me from my enemies'
> wafered concision and zeal
> I give you back to yourself
> whole and undivided

I do not hear bitterness in this, or even defiance, but any late Emersonian worship of the Beautiful Necessity is gone. With the going there comes a deep uncertainty in regard to poetic subject, as *Looking Over the Acreage* and several other poems show so poignantly.... The whole of *Briefings* manifests a surrender of the will-to-knowledge, not only relational knowledge between poetic consciousness and natural objects, but of all knowledge that is too easy, that is not also loss. (pp. 287-88)

Transcendent experience, but with Emerson's kind of Higher Utilitarianism ascetically cut off by a mind made too scrupulous for a new hope, remains the *materia poetica* of Ammons's enterprise. A majestic recent poem like *The City Limits* suggests how much celebration is still possible even when the transcendent moment is cruelly isolated, too harshly purified, totally compelled to be its own value.

Somewhere upon the higher ridges of his Purgatory, Ammons remains stalled, unable . . . to break through to the Condition of Fire promised by *Ommateum*, where instead of invoking Emerson's Uriel or Poe's Israfel he found near identity with "a crippled angel bent in a scythe of grief" yet witnessed a fiery ascent of the angel, fought against it, and only later gained the knowledge that "The eternal will not lie / down on any temporal hill." (p. 289)

> Harold Bloom, "A. R. Ammons: 'When You Consider the Radiance'" (1970), in The Ringers in the Tower: Studies in Romantic Tradition (© 1971 by The University of Chicago), University of Chicago Press, 1971, pp. 257-89.

Imagine . . . Thoreau, his sensibility, his powerful attention to the natural fact, his feet on his rural threshold, his mind contemplative of the newspapers, the *Bhagavad-Gita*, the Harvard Library (with more than 75% of its holdings composed of old sermons and Calvinist treatises), and the behavior of the micro-macro-cosmos, notebook ever in hand. Resurrect him in 1950, and you have, very loosely and maunderingly incarnated, A. R. Ammons as he appears in his *Collected Poems: 1951-1971*. But much diminished though, perhaps by entropic processes. Recall Thoreau as Yankee mystic, poet-manqué devolving into obsessive observer, losing, perhaps necessarily, the grand drift in weltering detail, but having already achieved the metamorphosis of fact into hard, beautiful prose pregnant with wit and probity—and intellectual power. Whereas Ammons, having begun as fervent initiate to the landscapes of the Southwest, and whose voice on the page refracts Pound and W. C. Williams, sometimes also echoing what seems Amerindian poetry as translated by Gibran, ends in this recent decade writing garrulously on the universal quotidian, and (and this is a bad sign) poetics. (pp. 64-5)

Still, what's interesting for 200 pages [that is, the poetry of the first decade] is his religiosity, after all: Ammons talks to the wind and to the mountain, to a "you" that is perhaps Manitou, perhaps our absconded "Thou," and they, He, It, talk back in the seminarian prose of a cuneiform translator. As he gains strength, he leaves that mix of Gibran-McKuen-Sumerian behind . . ., dedicates himself to observations, and begins his long rambles about the Northeastern littoral and riparian scenes, the molecular-galactic, organic-cellular landscapes, chatting about the Creation, as might have Cowper, Goldsmith, Wordsworth, Whitman, were they writing today. Removed from the desert, he has been taken also from the voices of the winds. Instead, he makes his daily American rounds about lawn and meadow, wood, hill, stream, in an easy, articulate, flat, utterly uneventful expository syntax. Altogether unlike Thoreau's sinewy, exacting, apothegmatic prose, and unlike that suavely undulant later Stevens from whom he borrows some of his stanza structures or envelopes, transmogrifying the Master of Imagination into a freshman-text writer who uses the colon for endless, undigestible linkages, never daring Stevens' comma, or venturing Thoreau's period.

As for Ammons' communications? The Scop traditionally conveyed poet-lore until Wordsworth relinquished his *Excursion*. (MacDiarmid and Pound in their long works, Marxist and Fascist bards, both lost bardry, willingly, to the extent they dignified pamphlets of propaganda.) Ammons' world-lore, however, is much better conveyed to us each month by *The Scientific American*. For this poet has by and large done little more than to act as a plain-speaking redactor of such reading matter. That he can summarize our contemporary scientific interests when gazing at the worlds of summer and Ithacan blizzard-winters, or walking the tidal swamp or the maze of geological times, is his chief skill; but it is far, far less interesting, alas, then reading the journals and the science writers themselves, and doing the imaginative work for oneself while strolling and watering one's own lawn. At the end of 20 years and 400 pages, Ammons is lecturing endlessly, mostly on himself writing: he has subsumed flower and storm, flood and glacier to the analysis of himself as provider of the facticities—like the later Thoreau, a failed mystic. For critics and readers who can't meet general science as it comes to us on the newsstand in *Science*, Ammons must seem the very image of a major poet. But there's more *poetry* to be found in a year's subscription to the *Scientific American* than in all of Ammons, more clear evidence of immense imaginative *work* getting done by smart people in the labs, non-writers who write better about the things of this world than this poet does. . . . Five years from now, when they change the communications-engineering jargon again, what will Ammons' efforts at postulating a poetics of the cerebral networks that form the cultural-historical-linguistical-existential anastomosis of conscious-cum-unconscious-consciousness appear to be? Vacuous, as they are to me now. Shoot me quick! but don't talk about major poetry in the central line down from Emerson: this poet is Erasmus Darwin reborn as J. B. Watson! And, by remaining on the exterior of the scientists' descriptions of the exterior side of matter, Ammons has remained exterior to the phenomena of the imagination too. Neither the "Thou" he once cried to in the Southwest, nor we ourselves are likely to be grateful for such a concern and such a printout of toneless, mechanical work. If you like your nature and your nature poetry in hypostasis and at 3rd hand, fine. But if you want the source of such poetry, if you can call it poetry, do read the scientists rather than this stuff. (pp. 65-6)

> Jascha Kessler, "Exteriors," in Kayak (copyright © July 1973, Kayak Books Inc.), Summer, 1973, pp. 64-6.

[Ammons's] work is sometimes interesting, sometimes boring. Men like Harold Bloom, however, are able to find in Ammons' weakest quality—his windy intellectualist rambling—intellectual and aesthetic themes which they can then track back to the work of the Romantics, to Emerson, to late Wallace Stevens . . . a true abstractionist, living in Ulro, is able easily to overlook the fact that the poetry is boring if he can find these themes. Precisely in that lies the evil effect of their laborious prose and Jurassic phrasings. (p. 50)

> Robert Bly, in The American Poetry Review (copyright © 1973 by World Poetry, Inc.; reprinted by permission of Robert Bly), September/October, 1973.

Ammons' strongest thrust is in the nature poem, the contemplative nature walk such as the title poem of the volume *Corsons Inlet* or the poem "Cascadilla Falls." A typical poem—and one of Ammons' best—is "Motion for Motion." After the earliest poems, there is an accrued sense of a precise, contemplative, solitary observer, a whimsical naturist alternating wonder with an abstract and analytical turn of mind. (p. 158)

To isolate these very few poems [from *Collected Poems: 1951-1971*] is to over-simplify the abundance presented, for there is wide variety of tone, subject, voice, form, and persona. There [is] a group of libidinous poems which are typified by the current *hip* parlance; these "Baby" poems, such as the "Guitar Recitivos," are amusing but slight. A more impressive group of poems are the autobiographical pieces about Ammons' Carolina childhood—"Silver," "Nelly Meyers," and "Mule Song"—certainly a vein which the poet has exploited only partially.

Although Ammons has not included the long *Tape for the Turn of the Year*, written in a burst of enthusiasm in 1964 on a single reel of adding machine tape, he nevertheless has included in the latter part of the volume several long and garrulous philosophical compositions, which I will call "project" poems—such as the poem "Art of Poetry" which was written to while away a snow storm, or "Summer Session," likewise written on a self-confessed quota basis during the summer break, or the long piece "Hibernaculum," a chatty, speculative poem in which Ammons gives full rein to his penchant for cataloguing and "philosophizing." In this Christmas vacation project, the startling simile is offered that poetry is like *soup*. More like spaghetti, one is inclined to say, for stringing it out.

Although the impression is distinct that Ammons has allowed himself too much looseness and latitude in some of these recent poems, there are also those poems like "Laser" and "The Arc Inside and Out" that recall the tautness of such earlier, rigorous pieces as "Corsons Inlet." At his best, Ammons leaves the impression of breathless contemplation of interstellar spaces and transcends the merely temporal from the incised image of the felt present; there is a brooding isolative contemplation which is compelling. (pp. 158-59)

With all due recognition of the hyperbole of jacket blurbs, one concludes that this is merely a competent volume by an adept and interesting poet, National Book Award notwithstanding. One hopes that the next collection will be more selective, that his compositions will be more trim, spare, and intellectual. Just this sort of new metaphysical poetry is required to bridge the widening gap between the two cultures. (p. 159)

> *David Jenkins, in* The Georgia Review *(copyright, 1974, by the University of Georgia), Spring, 1974.*

In his collection [*Collected Poems, 1951-1971*] Ammons includes every moment and modulation of his talent: the luminous leafed in with the trivial, the carefully achieved with the self-indulgent, the too long with the too short. One has to wade through a great deal of tentative language before coming upon the fine sparse poems which represent Ammons's best. But the labor is by no means all loss. The very shagginess and roughness of the collection forces the reader to become intimate with Ammons's elusive rhythms. One has the experience not so much of reading a work, as of entering into a process, in the course of which finished poems emerge, like pure crystals, their stony husk refined away. There is power in all of this. The roughness and pro-

fusion of Ammons's work becomes, somehow, a figure for his obsession; the sense of a process rushing brilliantly, though inconclusively forward is, finally, true to the idea of his poetry. As a result of sifting and panning all of this ore —a labor not without tedium—one understands, finally, why Ammons's turn at the banquet table has come.

At a time when the limits of the conversational style have come to be felt more and more strongly, Ammons offers, in great abundance, precisely those qualities neglected during the 1960s: intricate language and conceptual ambition. Reading through many of his longer poems, one is impressed by Ammons's attempt to connect a density of style reminiscent of Gerard Manley Hopkins, with an elaborate reflective framework which recalls Wallace Stevens. The echo of Stevens is inevitable, since Ammons's main concern is to articulate a philosophy of perception which must be simultaneously argued and demonstrated in the poetry. The main point of Ammons's conception seems to be his view that the mind and the world are joined together in a seamless intricacy. It is not simply that the mind and the world mirror each other, for mirrors contain settled forms; they connect but they also interpose limits. Like Alice, the poet has solved the surface of the mirror. He perceives, and renders in language, the interpenetrating gusts of movement by which the mind and the world make each other whole. . . . [The] aim of his poetry is not finishing, but unfinishing; it is to cut the world loose from the illusion of settled forms, and set it flowing in the ever new flood of perception. His words cascade irregularly on the page in a mimetism of released energy. The "idea" is there all right. But the poetry is cold, the experience, for all its intricacy, is thin. And here is Ammons's gravest fault. All too often he fails to connect the conceptual framework of the poem with the local effects of his language. This is especially true in the early work, but it remains true of his longer, more ambitious poems throughout. His images turn moments of experience into sensuous complexities; Hopkins-like compressions of syntax offer the reader "a hundred sensations a second," as Ammons remarks. But a gap yawns between this brilliant seething of impressions and the overarching discourse which Ammons intends as his "idea of order." Between sensuous mimetism and cold philosophy there is a space, which Ammons does not fill often enough. But the space between is where we live. It is where the "idea" thickens into passion, where passions clarify into thought and perception. (pp. 608-09)

Academic critics like Harold Bloom and Geoffrey Hartman have been partly responsible for the enlarged interest in Ammons's work. . . . After years of a poetic style which militated against ideas and repudiated conceptual ambition, they found in Ammons a poet both thoughtful and complex, whose work invites the sort of critical scrutiny which the great works of modernism also invited. Like Stevens, Pound, and Eliot, Ammons in his poetry demands explication. And let us be reminded, explication is not simply a form of detached analysis. It is a mode of reading required by, and appropriate to, complex poems. (p. 610)

But these critics have done Ammons a curious disservice, for they have focused their praise on his weakest quality— his attempt to formulate complicated ideas in poetry—and overlooked what seems to me to be his real achievement: the lyrical articulation of small moments of experience; his ability to organize shapes of language into an epiphany of movement, a frozen flood of perceptions which is visionary not because of any passionate metaphysics, but because of the sheer clarity of the poet's ability to recreate what he "sees." I don't mean to say that Ammons doesn't think well, or that his ideas are not interesting. They are; more important, they provide a framework which releases the intensity of his best short poems. But they do not make good poetry. Unlike Eliot or Stevens, Ammons does not write well about ideas. His conceptual reach does not intensify his language. When he writes "philosophical" poems, or inserts reflective passages into poems, he becomes boring and abstract. Only when his poem plunges into the moment itself does it gain the exhilarating clarity which is Ammons's best quality, as in [the] short poem, "Winter Scene". . . . In poems like these, the scaffolding has been forgotten; the poet is naked in the world, and the world has become naked to him. He is thinking with his "eyes" not his mind, or rather, his mind has let itself loose into the fusing brilliance of perception.

In another mode more special to his vision, Ammons has written poems which are intricate mimetisms of change, expressing his sense of the unceasing movement which is all we can know of experience, and of the world. Such poems succeed when they grasp the form of movement in a kind of visual onomatopoeia, instead of offering conclusions about a metaphysics of change. Given Ammons's obsession with instability and process, it is no surprise that he should have trouble with conclusions, both in the philosophical and in the formal sense. It is only in mid-movement, like a sudden vision of all the drops in a column of falling water, that his poetry attains a sort of cold ecstasy. (pp. 610-11)

Clearly, a poet refuses the dominant language of his time at his peril. Often those poets who succeed create a new language, as Allen Ginsberg did when he wrote *Howl* amid the overpolished tones of the 1950s. At first glance Ammons too seems to be a maverick, working vigorously against the limitations of the plain style, making a case in his work for a new intricacy of conception. Yet his best poems are closer to the plain style than one might think. It is when one hears William Carlos Williams in the background of his voice that the poems work clearly and solidly, not when one hears Hopkins or Stevens. Like so many other poets of the 1960s, Ammons's strengths and limitations derive from his flight into immediacy, his unwillingness to work with or against the limiting framework of culture and tradition. In this sense, of course, Ammons is extraordinarily American. But the impulse to reinvent all language, and all thought, falls short in his work. What survives is Ammons's version of the dream which is at the heart of so much recent poetry: the anticultural, Rousseauean dream of a purer, more articulate nature. (p. 612)

> *Paul Zweig, in* Partisan Review *(copyright © 1974 by Partisan Review, Inc.), Vol. XLI, No. 4, 1974.*

He is neither polemical, esoteric, alienated nor even suicidal. Yet A. R. ("Archie") Ammons has belatedly emerged as a poet of major stature. Given the present state of poetry, that is not an all-out accolade. Yet as his best, Ammons is a poet who finds high images in the familiar. He celebrates earthworms and maggot flies, the trackless ocean and flooding brooks, and sees them all as shapers of a

higher order, an order of diversity and character that makes life infinitely interesting and indomitably self-renewing. If he has a bias, it is praise:

> *for the inexcusable (the worthless abundant) the merely tiresome, the obviously unimprovable. . . .*

Ammons' finest poems meld the hugest images with the most familiar speech to make his points with tight concision. . . .

Of late, Ammons has indulged in several very long poems. They are perhaps verse rather than poetry (verse being what good poets write when they are waiting for a poem to strike). But at least it is verse of a high caliber. . . .

More than any living modern poet, Ammons successfully connects the intricacies of science to the mystery of human nature and what he perceives as the high design of God.

> *A. T. Baker, "Whole Look of Heaven," in* Time *(reprinted by permission from* Time, The Weekly Newsmagazine; *copyright Time Inc.), December 30, 1974, p. 58.*

I am way behind, getting to [Ammons's *Sphere: The Form of a Motion*] only now. And I know why; everything I ever heard about him said that he wasn't my cup of tea. (The Britishness of that idiom is much to the point.) He was, I gathered, a poet who said "Ooh" and "Ah" to the universe, who had oceanic feelings about the multiplicity of things in nature, and the ubiquity of nature's changes; a poet enamoured of *flux*, therefore; and so, necessarily, a practitioner of "open form"—which last comes uncomfortably close for my taste to being a contradiction in terms. In short, he was one whom Harold Bloom had applauded as "a major visionary poet"; and if that doesn't raise my hackles exactly, it certainly gives me goose-pimples.

And everything that I heard is true. Imagine! A poem 1,860 lines long, with only one full stop in it, at the end of the last line; and put before *me*, who likes to think of myself as Doctor Syntax, all for demarcations, a devotee of the sentence! Whatever the opposite of an ideal reader is, I ought to have been that thing so far as this poem is concerned. How could I be anything but exasperated by it, profoundly distrustful, sure I was being bamboozled, sure I was being threatened? And how is it, then, that I was on the contrary *enraptured*? Have I gone soft in the head? Have I suffered a quasi-religious conversion? Shall I drag myself on penitent knees to the feet of the saintly Bloom? No. I am as suspicious as ever I was of Ammons's initial assumptions and governing preoccupations. I still hunger for sentences and full stops, and for a colon that has precise grammatical and rhythmical work to do, instead of being the maid-of-all-work that Ammons makes it into. The cast of his temperament is as alien to me as I thought it would be. And yet I can't refuse the evidence of my senses and my feelings— there wasn't one page of his poem that didn't delight me. . . .

We tend to think that a poetry which celebrates Becoming will find itself in organic or expressive forms; but it is more logical for it to use, as it does here, a form that is inorganic, rigid, mechanical, and arbitrary. Of course this makes for difficulties; the poem is too long, also too dense and exuberant, to be read at a sitting, and yet these open-ended sections provide no resting places, where we can break off and later resume. If, like me, you roughly and provisionally mark places where one stage of the argument is completed and another starts, what is startling and—given the scheme of the whole—very impressive is that these breathing spaces virtually never coincide with the spaces between sections. As for "argument," does it have one? Didn't poems stop having such things, quite some time ago? Apparently not: this poem has an argument; in fact it addresses itself to that hoariest of all arguments, the problem of the Many and the One, no less! (p. 10)

> *Donald Davie, in* The New York Review of Books *(reprinted with permission from* The New York Review of Books; *copyright* © *1975 NYREV, Inc.), March 6, 1975.*

In the coda to his *Collected Poems*, Ammons asked himself for a poem of "plenitude / brought to center and extent," a poem of "periphery enclosing our system with / its bright dot and allowing in nonparlant / quantities at the edge void" —the achievement still denied by his thin *Tape for the Turn of the Year* and tentative "Hibernaculum." *Sphere* is that poem. Inevitably in a work of such length there are patches of tedium, discursive chats and catalogues, as the poet's mind moseys. But then the poem is a deliberate anthology of observations and perceptions that can swerve, with "insweeps of alteration," from a cosmogony to a quince bush, a patchwork that "insists on / differences, on every fragment of difference till the fragments / cease to be fragmentary and wash together in a high flotation / interpenetrating like the possibility of the world." (p. 430)

If the poem has any patron besides the early Ammons, it is Lucretius, the poet of space and solids, of regeneration and reform, of distinctions rather than closure. The lyrical interludes of natural detail in *Sphere* counterpoint its fascination with "the high syrup invisible moving under, through, / and by discretions our true home, not these bodies so much / change makes and ends." The energies of relationships between matter and meaning, and the imposition of the given, are Ammons's "true home". (pp. 430-31)

The deepest motive . . . is finally celebration—the kind of poetic praise that, as Rilke insists, must digest so much of the world's sorrow. *Sphere* celebrates the "heterocosm joyous," the radiance that an earlier poem proclaims all of nature is accepted into. It lies along "the route / from energy to energy," so that "motion is our only place." This "mathematics of stoop and climb" figures the final harmony "in the highest / ambience of diversity." *Sphere* is an unwieldy, absorbing, "abstract" poem; both its ambition and accomplishment are rare, and remind that

> if you do everything with economy and attention, the work itself will take on essentialities of the inevitable, and you will be, if causing,

participating in grace. (p. 432)

> *J. D. McClatchy, in* The Yale Review (© *1975 by Yale University; reprinted by permission of the editors), Spring, 1975.*

*   *   *

ARMAH, Ayi Kwei   1939-

A Ghanaian educated in America and now living in the United States, Armah writes novels, poetry, and short stories. His first novel, *The Beautyful Ones Are Not Yet Born***, was praised for its prose style and compared with work by Joyce.**

Ayi Kwei Armah tends to regard himself as a novelist only incidentally African. On occasion Armah has gone to rather great pains to make it clear that he is writing literature first, and that the Africanness of his writing is something of less great importance. With few exceptions, Armah's two novels [*The Beautyful Ones Are Not Yet Born* and *Fragments*]—and especially the second one—would seem to support this theory, for there are very few "Africanisms" in his work, and his protagonists become alienated men—lonely, isolated individuals confronting a thoroughly dehumanized society in which everyone else seems insane, although it is usually Armah's insular protagonists who, because of their determination to dance to a different drummer, become the accused criminals or madmen. Being thus, Armah's novels fall into the mainstream of current Western tradition, and his protagonists are not very different from a whole line of Western literary anti-heroes: Julian Sorel, Huckleberry Finn, Stephen Dedalus, or Ralph Ellison's Invisible Man.

Like the unnamed protagonist in Ellison's work, Armah's protagonist in *The Beautyful Ones Are Not Yet Born* (1968) is also unnamed, simply referred to as "the man." In addition, like Ellison's Invisible Man, Armah's Man goes on a journey through hell, though unlike Ellison's protagonist, who only slowly comes to the realization that it is his society that is out of joint, Armah's Man knows all along that his society has lost its values and that he is the lone center of value in a society which has long since traded its soul to the devil. It is this awareness from the very beginning that makes the Man's voyage so excruciatingly painful.

The journey itself begins and ends with a bus ride; the Man is riding to work. The emphasis is not, however, on the Man but on the bus itself, the driver, the conductor, and the other passengers, because *The Beautyful Ones Are Not Yet Born* is not so much a novel about a person as it is a novel about a society: post-independent Ghana in the days prior to Nkrumah's fall. (pp. 258-59)

As the Man leaves the bus, Armah begins his graphic description of the Man's hell: a modern wasteland transported to contemporary Africa. Refuse, waste, filth, debris, excrement become the overriding images of his novel. (p. 259)

Everywhere black people are trying to be white. (p. 263)

The Beautyful Ones Are Not Yet Born is a richly evocative work and its publication placed Ayi Kwei Armah in the forefront of the new generation of African writers. In his depiction of a society on the brink of suicide, Armah has created a deeply disturbing picture of the foibles of all decadent political systems—a decadence which has nothing to do with age—of all late bourgeois worlds where morals and values have been lost and even the man of good intentions begins to doubt his sanity, begins to feel that he is the guilty one for not being corrupt. It is a novel which burns with passion and tension, with a fire so strongly kindled that in every word and every sentence one can almost hear and smell the sizzling of the author's own branded flesh. Reading it for the first time, one is almost led to believe that its young author might have burned himself out in the mere process of its creation, but seemingly Armah had not yet sunk to the lowest levels of hell—that near fatal drowning was reserved for his second novel, *Fragments* (1970), which because of its autobiographical nature, its nearness to certain events in Armah's own life, strikes the reader with an even harsher reality than the earlier work as it probes more deeply into the cranium of the artist/ intellectual in contemporary African society, and into the near impossibility of being an artist in Africa today.

The structural complexity of *Fragments* is hinted at in the title and in the dedication: "for AMA ATA & ANA LIVIA." Ama Ata is the Ghanaian writer, Christina Ama Ata Aidoo, an old friend of Armah's. Anna Livia is a character in James Joyce's *Finnegans Wake*. The content or story will be African; the structure (made up of fragments or little pieces like a puzzle) will show an indebtedness to Joyce, though not nearly the amount of obscurity present in Soyinka's *The Interpreters*. Armah does, however, make use of shifting points of view in *Fragments* and of extensive passages of introspection bordering on stream of consciousness. His story here is hardly more plotted than that in his earlier novel though the conflict is much more personalized. Baako, a writer, returns to Ghana after five years overseas and a recent nervous breakdown. Pressured by family and societal conventions, he soon suffers from a second breakdown, more serious than the first because this time it is his own family and country that lead to the collapse. (pp. 268-69)

Armah's picture of contemporary Ghana in *Fragments* is more appalling, more an exposé of corruption than that in *The Beautyful Ones Are Not Yet Born*. (p. 269)

The events in *Fragments* record those which precipitated Ayi Kwei Armah's own mental relapse when he returned to Ghana after studying abroad. As it is suggested in Naana's poignant dialogue with herself, Baako/Armah later exiled himself from his native land, and has since continued his writing in the United States and in Europe.

Ayi Kwei Armah is the most skilled prose stylist in Anglophone Africa today, a painter whose medium happens to be prose. His novel, wrenched from his soul, belongs on the honored shelf with a whole world tradition of autobiographical novels such as André Gide's *Les faux monnayeurs*, James Joyce's *Portrait of the Artist as a Young Man*, Thomas Wolfe's *Look Homeward, Angel*. In his depiction of the stifled artist in contemporary Africa, and specifically of the writer, Armah has turned to a theme almost as old as Western fiction itself but a theme entirely new in African literature. How odd this is, we may think—those of us who are used to reading novels about struggling writers and other artists. We forget, however, that in spite of the fact that the canon of contemporary African literature now includes several hundred volumes of creative work, the printed word is still something relatively new in sub-Saharan Africa, and the theme of the thwarted novelist has been able to surface only now that a second generation of writers have begun their careers and African nations are beginning to close the illiteracy gap. (p. 276)

> *Charles R. Larson, in his* The Emergence of African Fiction, *revised edition (copyright © 1972 by Charles R. Larson), Indiana University Press, 1972.*

Brother Ayi's work, like Fanon's, has very little of the sentimental to it, and is in fact so raw oft-times that one is left dumbfounded as to just how he got into print. He will not make you feel good unless you find pleasure in those stark elements that comprise world-African reality. . . . *Why Are We So Blest?* deals masterfully with perhaps the greatest problem stifling the African Freedom-struggle: the Black man and woman's persistent willingness to send their children off to the oppressor for schooling. . . .

Not only is the content of *Why Are We So Blest?* so very powerful, but the form itself is a locomotive of life's force. The form reminds one at first of diary installments and, indeed, the three main characters of the book are in a sense keeping diaries that we now are reading. Yet, the form goes far far beyond this; it is as a style, a shape, coldly calculated to be life itself, not merely like life. To be specific, we get installments, comments, happenings in the early pages of the book and right on down to the last few moments that we will not understand until the last word is read and reflection on the experience of the book is had. In other words, as in life, we will not understand some occurrences until time has elapsed and brought us the additional insight that comes with more knowledge of the total situation and reflection as such. (p. 86)

Ayi Kwei Armah employs throughout his work what we shall term the *floating symbol*: By this we have reference to how our novelist will utilize/create characters who are symbols of certain real-life factors such as corruption, decadence, waste, and unnerving integrity in the face of these contrapositives; however, each such character is also *actual*, not just a symbol, and thus is not a mere superficial concoction employed as a vehicle toward the perpetuation of some abstract (for better or for worse) literary point. (pp. 87-8)

> *Kiarri T-H Cheatwood, in* Black World *(copyright © March, 1974, by* Black World; *reprinted by permission of* Black World *and Kiarri T-H Cheatwood), March, 1974.*

*   *   *

ARP, Jean   1887-1966

Also known as Hans Arp, this Alsatian-born poet, painter, sculptor, and collagist, was a founder of the dada movement and an important participant in that and the surrealist movement. He wrote poetry in both French and German. (See also obituary, *Contemporary Authors*, Vols. 25-28.)

Over the years, first in his reliefs and then in his whimsical writings, [Arp] developed what he called "concrete art" (as opposed to abstract art)—material and verbal shapes allowed to grow not *after* nature but *like* nature. They arise from spontaneous processes of dream, chance, play, and humor. (pp. 27-8)

Arp had an astonishingly sustained fifty-year career of work. He participated in almost every art movement in Europe without belonging to any. He reached fame slowly without scheming or scandal and avoided personal and political squabbles. . . . The pervasive wholeness of his work tends to obscure the slow evolution it went through. He moved from flat collages and paintings to sculpture in the round, and from tightly constructed poems in German toward more open works, including prose and prose poems in French. . . .

Arp's plastic works and his writings remain childlike, often impish, but fraud does not enter here. Unlike the Surrealists who rarely abandoned a strong sense of decorum (partially in order to be able to violate it), Arp never differentiated between literary genres. Verses, prose poems, fairy tales, reminiscences, declarations of faith—they all fit side by side because of a pervasive whimsy that never detracts from deep communion with nature and life. . . .

Arp is forever looking for, or rather finding, verbal patterns in which sound and sense have approximately equal weight. It often comes off as humor. . . .

After reading a great deal of Arp in both German and French, I have the impression that it is not the unconscious, not any literary tradition, not an assertive talent, but *the language itself that writes the poem.* . . . One does best to relax and enjoy it, and possibly to keep a finger on the French. . . . The nervous exegete, worried about having missed a buried meaning, might fail to hear the sound surfing and syllable sledding. Once or twice the Beatles and Bob Dylan strolled by this way. . . .

His poetry in German is, if not superior to, at least more interesting and varied than his French work. Born and raised in Strasbourg, Arp was genuinely bilingual (plus the local dialect). But he wrote differently in the two languages—more from the inside in German, I should say, less rhythmically and with a little less assurance in French. In both he uses the same techniques of permutating syllables and joining items not by their center (denotative meaning) but by their edges (sound and connotation). And it all contributes to the second point: Arp is a fascinating but almost impossible challenge for the translator. . . .

His literary work stands in a special relation to his art. They form a single reciprocating engine. (p. 28)

> *Roger Shattuck, in* The New York Review of Books *(reprinted with permission from* The New York Review of Books*; copyright © 1972 NYREV, Inc.), May 18, 1972.*

Arp's favourite law [was] the law of chance. . . .

Throughout a long and productive life as a sculptor, reliefmaker, collagist, and maker of torn-paper pictures, Arp remained faithful to this law. In his poetry too he subscribed to its literary equivalent, automatism, and it was this which attracted him towards the Surrealist movement. He always detested 'reason', particularly scientific reason and its fruit, the machine. He revered nature and hoped through his work not to imitate her but to add to her repertoire of forms. To make this clear he invented the term 'concrete art' with the aim of drawing the distinction between what he did and the work of the abstract painters and sculptors. What they were up to, he maintained, was to provide a pictorial equivalent of one or another aspect of the observable world. He hoped to invent artifacts without precedent.

His success was as complete as it is possible to be when surrounded by a universe already overflowing with beings, objects and varied phenomena. Yet his poetry, crammed with imagery (for unlike his friend Schwitters he rarely resorted to sounds and noises), hints, by their collective reappearance, at those few natural shapes which obsessed and inspired him: the egg primarily. There is an egg or eggs in almost every poem, and after that the stone, that infertile cousin of the egg, then the cloud, the navel and the star.

Undeniably he succeeded in impregnating over and over again an apparently simple yet inimitable matrix whose offspring, whether very large sculptures or a few modest lines on paper, were his alone. The 'Arpshape', a term once fashionable in architectural circles, is immediately recognisable and, equally, inimitable. (p. 404)

> *George Melly, "Arpshape," in* New Statesman, *(© 1974 The Statesman & Nation Publishing Co. Ltd.), March 22, 1974, pp. 404, 406.*

Arp's French language poetry has never been given more than a brief introduction or a rapid "appreciation," usually by other artists, in spite of the fact that two major collections of his work appeared during his lifetime. *Le Siège de l'air* (Paris, 1946) contains all his published French poetry from 1915 to 1945, some with important revisions and additions, and a few translations of his German poetry. The second volume, Marcel Jean's careful and thorough edition of the entire volume of Arp's poetry (with a few exceptions), appeared in December 1966 under the title *Jours effeuillés: Poèmes, essais, souvenirs, 1920-1965.* . . . Included in the volume are many previously unpublished poems from 1961 to 1964, as well as many translations from the German. As in German, Arp frequently revised or rewrote his poetry and republished it under the same or different titles. Thus many poems appear twice in *Jours effeuillés*, in slightly different versions. (p. 159)

In general, one can divide the French poetry into two periods, before and after 1957, with a transitional period in the late 1940s and early 1950s. In the French poetry, broadly speaking, there is no marked period of radical experimentation with language, as there is in German during the dada era, and although the later poetry is more conventional, there is a more even and continuous flow of innovative writing and experimentation with form. One might say there is no dada style in the French poetry, that it begins as surrealistic poetry, and that furthermore it remains largely surrealistic in style. This is perhaps partly due to the fact that the earliest French poems (excluding prose pieces and translations) date from the early thirties. The poetry of the 1930s and 1940s is characterized by unexpected images, the strangest possible word combinations, and punning. Basic order—such as time and the size of things—is entirely disrupted. During the transitional period there is slightly less word play and less consciousness of language than in the first period. After 1957 images are less disjointed, or have a greater life span, although they are still constructed with unusual combinations of words, and reference to reality is less disturbed. There is in fact a new style. Lighter, more lyrical, more obscure in the conventional modern manner, childish or foolish sometimes, coquettish and coy, often humorous, this poetry is certainly a degenerative aspect of Arp's style. (p. 160)

Obscure, anomalous, and perplexing at first glance, the French poetry prior to 1957 has an overall characteristic of universal strangeness. The reader must enter a state of poetic receptiveness removed from external reality, abandoning familiar landscapes and feelings. The reality of the poet's life has very little connection with his poetic manifestations, and although there are familiar objects—moustaches, flies, chairs, navels, butterflies, air—they are displaced from their normal contexts and constitute a unity of their own. . . . To the extent that most poems partake of this world of objects, they maintain a coherent structure. That is, they create an internal reality. Some poems refer to the "reality" depicted in another poem—for example, "Notre petit continent" and "Les habitants du continent des chas sans aiguilles." But throughout there is a strong impression of discontinuity, and a space between stanzas (if one may call them that) often represents a break in the structure of internal reality. In fact, by far the greatest number of poems combine such divergent images as to create an impression of irreality, an important characteristic of surrealist poetry in general, to which I shall return.

The poetic techniques described in this paper are more prevalent in the earlier period, although it would be misleading to believe that Arp's style radically changed. There is never an obvious break between "nonsense poetry" and "meaningful poetry." Some of the later poems could easily fit into the earlier period, and some techniques, such as the innovative use of sound association, are maintained throughout. (p. 161)

One can look at *any* poem and find an inactive subject with a verb of action or animation, human or animate qualities applied to inanimate or abstract nouns, personal pronouns referring to things, or encounters of qualities, objects, and actions that simply do not occur in real life, yet all presented in the most direct, matter-of-fact, undisguised manner. It is the regular, correct, and very simple syntax that is responsible for the directness of the images, a regularity that contributes no doubt tremendously to their shock value, and at the same time persuades the reader to accept them as possible. (In his later poetry Arp attempted to free himself from syntax, and some fragmentary sentences or lists of noun phrases occur. But this later poetry is more banal, perhaps precisely because of the slighter degree of contrast between images and syntax.)

While it is certain that the surrealist techniques of automatic writing and the systematic use of chance, dream, and hallucination all contribute to Arp's poetic creation, the surrealist formulation which applies most directly to his imagery is that of the *écart*, or distance between terms. The greater the distance, of course, the better the image, according to the surrealists. Thus the best surrealist images put into syntactical sequence two or more words that do not normally have a logical connection; loss of reality is the result. The pre-surrealist metaphor can bridge the gap between very distant terms, but there is usually a logical (e.g., symbolic, descriptive, causative) relationship that remains undisturbed. In surrealist poetry, as in Arp's, the metonymical relationship replaces the logical one. Unexpected or inappropriate words are juxtaposed to create images that have no apparent meaning, and the usually evident contrast between their semantic anomaly and their syntactic normalcy elevates Arp's images beyond the level of mere automatic or unconscious writing. The animated vision of the world which I see in Arp's imagery owes its existence to systematic use of metonymical substitution. (pp. 172-73)

Arp's series of images create a disjointed, unreal, but vividly animated world which is nevertheless not devoid of emotions. . . . Many feelings are created by these poems, although they are not attached to the traditional subject, the figure of the poet, but rather to other things with which the reader is induced to sympathize. In fact, man appears rarely and is usually not distinguished from animals, plants, objects, and even qualities.

Alfred Liede gives two formulas [in *Dichtung als Spiel*] to describe Arp's relationship to this world: he speaks both of a magic feeling for nature and of a return to the original anarchy of nature. These notions would account for the animation discussed in my study and for the presence of an emotionally charged world of objects, but they do not go far enough to explain Arp's uniqueness. It is the language-consciousness, the consistent exploitation of interrelationships on the linguistic level, that creates the sense of unity and coherence that so strongly opposes any anarchistic quality. Arp's world would be anarchistic were it not for the imposition of his style. . . . A poem of Arp's is as easy to recognize as the clean, curved lines of his sculpture.

Is Arp an innovator? Breton, Eluard, Aragon, Desnos, Soupault, and others employed stylistic devices that Arp used. And Arp was not in advance of them. Nevertheless his use of constellations and configurations, of which he may properly be said to be the inventor, was certainly a necessary prelude to the "discovery" of concrete poetry, the importance of which as a modern poetry movement cannot be denied. An active participant in the surrealist movement, Arp did preserve an individuality and uniqueness of style, which remains intensely personal and is as pleasurable after many readings as on first impression—surely an indication of its quality. (pp. 173-74)

> *Armine Kotin, "Language Techniques in Jean Arp's French Poetry," in* Papers on Language and Literature *(copyright © 1974 by the Board of Trustees, Southern Illinois University at Edwardsville), Spring, 1974, pp. 159-174.*

*   *   *

AYCKBOURN, Alan   1939-

Ayckbourn is a British dramatist, director, and actor. His plays, whether considered biting social commentary or ingenious farces, are always said to display technical virtuosity. (See also *Contemporary Authors*, Vols. 21-22.)

[Ayckbourn] has . . . consistently and uncompromisingly avoided any suggestion of deeper meaning in his plays. Try as we may we cannot find any trace of social or political indoctrination masquerading as harmless diversion, let alone of cosmic anguish. His prime determination is unmistakably to make us laugh and keep us laughing, and all his considerable technical gifts are marshalled to that end alone. It is a tight-rope, and a particularly dangerous, vertiginous tight-rope at that, since if the writer stumbles he has no safety net of deeper significance to fall into: if his plays are not funny they are nothing. And while we are inclined to accept serious intent, however muffed, as a mitigating circumstance for a dramatist, unreasonably enough we see no merit at all in the dramatist who tries to make us laugh and fails.

Fortunately, this has not yet happened to Alan Ayckbourn. Even his less successful plays have always had at least that going for them. (p. 156)

Ayckbourn's particular specialty [is] the comedy of embarrassment, with its characters trying desperately to continue living normal, respectable, suburban lives in . . . very eccentric, public conditions. (p. 157)

> *John Russell Taylor, in his* The Second Wave: British Drama for the Seventies *(reprinted with the permission of Farrar, Straus & Giroux, Inc.; copyright © 1971 by John Russell Taylor), Hill & Wang, 1971.*

Ayckbourn has a sixth sense for the familiar but unrecognised. He sets up a situation or a character so that we can anticipate what will take place. He then plays with our expectations, never letting us down but never losing his capacity to spring surprises. . . .

Maintaining the balance between the predictable and the unexpected is the true skill of the farce dramatist. Ayckbourn, like Neil Simon, is a master of this art, so daring that he's prepared to stretch out the slight material of *Table Manners* over two further episodes. The play is part of a trilogy, *The Norman Conquests*, which takes place over the same weekend in the same house with the same characters, but in different rooms at different times. If we know so much already, what tempts us back to Greenwich? Partly perhaps our admiration at Ayckbourn's skill, the precision of his language and the timing of his wit, but partly too because we've started to feel affectionate towards his characters. He writes in such a way that his . . . cast can take hold of the situations and play around with them.

> *John Elsom, "Home County Table Manners," in* The Listener *(© British Broadcasting Corp. 1974; reprinted by permission of John Elsom), May 23, 1974, p. 677.*

As in *Absurd Person* and the earlier *Time and Time Again*, [Alan Ayckbourn] tends to divide [his characters in *The Norman Conquests*] into two categories, those who exploit and those who are exploited, with scarcely a murmur from the middle ground between. (p. 778)

Mr Ayckbourn has once again succeeded in resuscitating that most comatose of genres, the 'farcical comedy'. Precisely why he's so funny is harder to say. It hasn't anything to do with farcical incident: no bumping into doors, hiding under beds, or mistaking another's identity. It isn't a matter of verbal ingenuity, though Mr Courtenay, in particular, has some neat lines to flourish. Nor is it the embarrassment inherent in the plot, though that adds tension to the evening. Rather, it's Mr Ayckbourn's canny ability to show us, with imperceptible exaggeration, the absurdity of behaviour we'd normally find unfunny and even unremarkable. (pp. 778-79)

> *Benedict Nightingale, "Family Affairs," in* New Statesman *(© 1974 The Statesman & Nation Publishing Co. Ltd.), May 31, 1974, pp. 778-79.*

Death . . . holds no horrors for [Alan Ayckbourn]. Indeed the most audacious thing he's yet written is the second act of *Absurd Person Singular*, in which a rejected wife is wildly misunderstood as she doggedly attempts suicide. Someone helpfully cleans the oven into which she's cramming her head, someone else nearly electrocutes himself mending the light from which she is hanging herself, a third Samaritan begins to replumb the sink where she is swallowing pills. We laugh nervously, perhaps a little guiltily, because the squeamishness and embarrassment we feel about death are being both exploited and undermined; but we laugh all the same. And so we did . . . at *Absent Friends*, three-quarters of whose hilarity depends on our remembering that the main character is in mourning for a beloved fiancée, lately drowned. . . .

[Ayckbourn] has sometimes been called a cold and uncharitable dramatist; but . . . *Absent Friends* should squelch it for good. There is, as usual, much that's unattractive about his characters. . . . Mr Ayckbourn is certainly not an amoral writer: nor is he mocking, gloating, or gratuitously unkind. Compare the play with, say, *Design for Living*, and you'll rapidly see that, unlike Coward, he allows his people to have feelings, that these feelings can be hurt, and that this is cause for regret. . . . There are few sadder things than the slow destruction of youthful optimism, not to mention love, trust and other tender shoots: Mr Ayckbourn makes sure we realise it. . . .

Mr Ayckbourn must at least be congratulated on showing us something we'd quite forgotten, that it is possible to write amusingly and intelligently for social categories A, B, C1, C2 and D. *Absent Friends* comes to us in a popular form, the 'farcical comedy'; its characters, with their subtopian accents, could hail from almost any terrace or housing estate in the country; its main concerns are common human ones, matching and dispatching; and its plot is exquisitely judged to give these two themes freedom and scope. Because Colin is in mourning, and therefore privileged, the others feel obliged to tolerate his intolerable sallies against their peace of mind. Thus, without any offence to credibility, their marriages can be shown in all their pretension and shabbiness, and their constrained, frightened attitudes to death and bereavement simultaneously satirised. The result is a memorable attack on several varieties of falsehood.

> *Benedict Nightingale, "Storms among the Teacups," in* New Statesman *(© 1974 The Statesman & Nation Publishing Co. Ltd.), July 5, 1974, p. 24.*

From the time of *Relatively Speaking* onwards I have been signalling . . . the merits of this alarmingly perceptive dramatist as very much more than those of an expert purveyor of light comedy. Some are still reluctant to accept this fact; others evade the issue by arguing the totally unimportant question whether he is a true writer of comedy or 'merely' an inspired farceur. (I suppose they would have wittered on in much the same way about Molière). But for the most part, with a paradoxical absurdity typical of cultural establishments down the ages, the opinion-formers have finally caught up with Ayckbourn's real quality (and with the general public) in welcoming *The Norman Conquests*, a trilogy which, although the best plays seen in London since his last play, sharply perceptive and almost unbearably funny, is in fact not absolutely on a level with the peaks reached in *Time and Time Again* and *Absurd Person Singular*.

For that matter it is quite possible that *How the Other Half Loves* may turn out to be as impressive as those two. London has not yet seen an adequate production of this one; but even in a mutilated form it drew a sharp picture of the social pressures (too complex to be subsumed under the tired label of 'class') at work on the different levels of middle management's domestic life in provincial English industrial society. Here the situation was seen as immutable, fixed as much by the characters' backgrounds as by their income and status. In *Absurd Person Singular* a similar arrangement of three layers is shown in a process of upheaval. Two professional families—one elderly and exhausted, the other young, half idealist, half destructive—are seen at the mercy of the man both despised, a lower-middle-class financial ferret who finally has them all dancing to his tune. In *Time and Time Again* the core of the play is more personal; against another middle-middle-class background Ayckbourn sets a central figure who is of it, but only in the most literal sense in it—a dreamer, a man of finer sensibilities than the others, but at the same time a corrosive egotist like Dostoievsky's Prince Myshkin, bringing disaster upon himself and everybody else he is involved with. The three plays which make up *The Norman Conquests* pivot upon another such figure. (p. 36)

Out of [the plot materials of *The Norman Conquests*], clearly, one could make a festering O'Neill-style, Freudian drama, a sub-Chekovian wry comedy of hardened attitudes and half-guessed-at disappointments, or the niftiest of television situation farces. It is Mr. Ayckbourn's remarkable achievement to have blended into his trilogy elements of all three genres, and the result—though falling a touch short of the poetry of *Time and Time Again* and the power of *Absurd Person Singular*—is on the simplest assessment a superb trio of entertainments, and beyond that a devastatingly perceptive comment on English middle-class life—on, that is, the lives of most of those who will most delight in it, and who will, in the words of the old song, 'pluck the rose and leave the thorn behind'. . . .

Each play is virtually . . . the off-stage of the others, taking place respectively in the dining-room, the sitting-room and the garden. . . . Mr. Ayckbourn's ingenuity in thus constructing the plays positively makes the head spin if dwelt upon; but of course it should not be dwelt upon, for however valuable the challenge may have been to his inventive powers, it is to us only an incidental pleasure. The value of the work lies elsewhere—in its knife-sharp insights into the long littleness of life and in its unflagging comic exhilaration. (p. 37)

However inhibited or hesitant they may appear, Mr. Ayckbourn's women in these plays—individually called, I had better remember to record, *Table Manners, Living Together* and *Round and Round the Garden*—are pillars of certainty compared to the men. . . . [It is] the pregnant pause which more than anything else [provides] the unnerving element in Mr. Ayckbourn's plays which gives him so much in common with Harold Pinter. (p. 38)

J. W. Lambert, in Drama, *Autumn, 1974.*

Absent Friends . . . is well up to standard. Like most of [Ayckbourn's] work it is based on a simple, rather startling idea: a misunderstanding (as in, say, *Relatively Speaking*) but with a sharper and psychologically rougher edge to it. The theme is death, or rather grief. (p. 61)

Now what does Mr. Ayckbourn mean by all this? Something Sophoclean like no man being able to count himself happy until his wife (at least) is dead? Or Strindbergian?

Mr. Ayckbourn isn't letting on. Like Pinter he just places the character before us and leaves us to draw our own conclusions. But the point is that he manages to make us believe in the sincerity of his hero's unexpected contentment; and, more unexpectedly, he brings it off within the terms of trivial-seeming middle-class comedy: tentative, tactful small talk, long embarrassed silences, evasions of true feeling, clichés which cover up emotional callousness, and a wonderfully timed sense of suburban detail.

We laugh freely at the comedy of English parlour manners: the tinkling of tea-cups and marital tensions, the polite pauses, the affectations, and the display of class characteristics. Then the laughter turns hollow, as if behind it unpalatable home truths had been brewing—and (a point worth remarking in the art of Mr. Ayckbourn) there is no toying with decanters, no need for alcohol to get his people to speak their minds persuasively. (pp. 62-3)

Absent Friends might be compared at certain moments to *Old Times* since its emotional values are so richly retrospective; and yet it seems ambitious to bring Pinter into it. Pinter is a poet, a stylist, and he practises an economy in his theatrical statements which would be out of Ayckbourn's element.

Ayckbourn is more homely, more comforting, more immediately accessible, more easily enjoyed. Witness the crowded audiences of laughing shirt-sleeved holiday-makers. . . . They are never made to frown or allowed to yawn. They are too busy recognizing Uncle Horace or Auntie Flo, young Harry or busybody Betsy—recognizing themselves, or at any rate each other. They are in fact what Mr. Ayckbourn calls his 'source material', and he means to stick close to it, despite his popular success and the wealth it has brought him. (p. 63)

Eric Shorter, in Drama, *Autumn, 1974.*

"Absurd Person Singular" . . . is a brilliant little comedy of domestic misadventure in which, if one troubles to listen closely, a sentence of death is pronounced upon the institution of marriage. Its author, Alan Ayckbourn, has made the play serve as a proof of Murphy's Law—"If anything can go wrong, it will"—and has let us glimpse, behind a shining scrim of jokes, sight gags, and hilarious sudden reversals of fortune, his view of life as nasty, brutish, and short. . . .

From beginning to end, the play is a model of cunning stagecraft; the tiny material of one gag becomes the material for a second, and the second for a third; with each repetition, the material grows richer and more comic. . . . Mr. Ayckbourn, who is said to be able to compose a play of ordinary length in a day or so and a trilogy in a week, attracts our attention by his many hardworking jokes, but he holds it by the profundity of his contempt for how men treat women inside the bonds of marriage. [The] husbands behave viciously toward their wives; the wives suffer and deteriorate. (p. 58)

Brendan Gill, in The New Yorker (© *1974 by The New Yorker Magazine, Inc.), October 21, 1974.*

Alan Ayckbourn has been called the Neil Simon of England. In a series of successful comedies he has converted the social confusion of contemporary England into a fun house of absurdity—as in "Absurd Personal Singular." But

Ayckbourn is much tougher than Simon; he's a behavioral psychologist with a savage streak of satire.

Ayckbourn uses his characters the way a flea-circus professor uses his fleas, making them jump to his bidding in a clockwork farce of sheer inanity. The play's three-part structure—Christmas past, present and future—parodies Dickens, as if to announce the final expiration of jolly old England, in which class tensions can no longer be sloshed over with plum pudding. In this three-Christmas shot the six characters carom off each other, changing their social and personal fortunes in the process.

> *Jack Kroll, "Christmas Cards," in* News-week *(copyright 1974 by Newsweek, Inc.; all rights reserved; reprinted by permission), October 21, 1974, p. 56.*

Alan Ayckbourn has been trumpeted as the Neil Simon of England. Untrue. Neil Simon is a master of middlebrow, smart-cracking social comedy, a manufacturer of character comment that probes just enough to make us laugh indulgently and like ourselves a wee bit more. To judge by *Absurd Person Singular* . . . [Ayckbourn is] much more the Mack Sennett of England—50 percent of Sennett, anyway.

Ayckbourn calls his play a comedy, but it is farce; and essentially it is not theater farce, it is film slapstick. The great farces of Feydeau and Courteline and Piñero are complicated machines of egocentric desire in monochromatic characters, people who desperately want something or other and bump violently into or frantically evade or breathlessly deceive others. Ayckbourn makes no such machine. His characters are monochrome, all right, but few of them *want* anything very much: they just behave in certain ways that are sharply and quickly defined. One wife is a compulsive housecleaner who has an addiction to cleaning, no matter whose house she's in. Another wife is a compulsive, socially pretending drinker. And so on. The result is a series of situations that lead to physical complications that lead to more physical complications. The play is so much like a series of Sennett set-ups that it could very easily be played completely silent with 15 or 20 subtitles.

Ayckbourn understands the secret of this kind of laugh-building. Each of his nests of structures begins with an action that is perfectly credible for its doer and then proceeds perfectly logically: the comedy comes from the fact that this logic has nothing to do with the logic of the other people. For instance, a husband angrily sends his wife out to buy the soda she forgot to get for the party going on inside in the living room. They are both anxious that the guests—business big-shots whom they are eager to impress —should not know of the lapse. The wife goes out the kitchen door, into pouring rain, with raincoat and big hat and boots, her evening dress underneath. When she returns the kitchen door is locked, and she hovers outside the window like a wet ghost, ducking when one of the guests comes in from the living room. Finally she has to go in the front door pretending to be someone else until she can get to the kitchen and change. She has behaved perfectly logically according to her pattern: that pattern simply has nothing to do with what the others, or we, would call sensible. . . .

[Most] of the dialogue itself is quite unfunny. Ayckbourn almost seems to flirt with the idea of an Ionesco-like bar-

rage of banalities, which may be the source of the "absurd" in his title, but the dialogue never quite gets to that level of self-knowledge. If this play were not well *done*, it would be worse than unfunny, it would be embarrassing. (p. 36)

> *Stanley Kauffmann, in* The New Republic *(reprinted by permission of* The New Republic; © *1974 by The New Republic, Inc.), November 9, 1974.*

Mr Ayckbourn is to be congratulated . . . on having done something which, so far as I know, is quite novel in the theatre. His three plays, *Table Manners, Living Together,* and *Round and Round the Garden* [which together compose *The Norman Conquests*] are not a trilogy in the usual sense. They are not three consecutive treatments of the same situation or characters, nor do they present a single problem seen from three different points of view. They are three fragments of the same play, enacted by the same six characters in different parts of one house. When we have seen all three, we know what *A* and *B* were doing in the sitting-room, while *C, D, E* and *F* were in the dining-room or the garden. The three parts fit together to make a space-time continuum, as one might reconstitute a wooden cube that had been carefully sawn into three complex segments.

This is ingenious, and there is some incidental pleasure to be derived from noticing how neatly the parts dovetail together. But what, aesthetically, is the point? I confess I don't see any; the device is a purely mechanical arrangement, which makes the same play three times as long as it might have been, and since the characters cannot develop— being caught at different points of the same week-end—by the third time round we have got to know them rather too well and can anticipate their quirks. One wonders if it would not have been better to take the more telling bits of each play to make a single work, with a change of locale in each act as in *Absurd Person Singular*. The characters themselves are not on a high enough level to bear such lengthy exposure. . . . In other words, a technical gimmick takes precedence over content.

The content itself is farcical comedy . . . [and] Mr Ayckbourn produces some excellent farcical situations. (pp. 64-5)

What, then, is wrong? In the first place, many of the jokes are brought in incidentally, without being properly fitted to the personalities of the characters who utter them or are the subjects of them. . . . In a superior comedy or farce, the jokes are not strung together like daisies in a daisy-chain, but are related to the theme, which they further imperceptibly. In the second place—and this is more important—the farce or comedy is not about anything in particular, except the nondescript muddle in a lower-middle-class household, which lives from minute to minute in a state of petty tension. . . . [The] trilogy is not absolutely different in kind from those dim old Aldwych farces, such as *Rookery Nook* and *Turkey Time*, which read so sadly today. In this respect, *The Norman Conquests* marks a regression since *Absurd Person Singular*, which had the redeeming feature of black humour and an Ionesco-like tingle of awareness. (p. 65)

> *John Weightman, in* Encounter *(© 1974 by Encounter Ltd.), December, 1974.*

[One of the] outstanding critical and box-office hits of the season here [is] Alan Ayckbourn's *The Norman Conquests* . . . [which] is, in fact, three full-length plays—*Table Manners, Living Together* and *Round and Round the Garden*— which are shown on separate evenings. One may see them in any order without a sense of incompleteness. One may see (and enjoy) all three—as I did—without complaining of monotony, though the same six actors appear each night.

The tripartite arrangement is a continuum. When a character leaves the stage in *Table Manners* and goes into the garden, what exactly happens there? We get the answer in *Round and Round the Garden*. When several people leave the garden, they come together again in *Living Together*.

There is no onstage or offstage development: all the action is presented in one or another of the triptych's segments.

This amounts to a dramaturgic tour de force. Alan Ayckbourn's remarkable skill may be explained not only by reference to a natural aptitude for stagecraft but by the fact that he is the staff playwright of a provincial theatre for which he is obliged to furnish one or more scripts every season. It is an old theatre tradition. (p. 286)

Harold Clurman, in The Nation *(copyright 1975 by the Nation Associates, Inc.), March 8, 1975.*

B

BAINBRIDGE, Beryl   1933-

Ms Bainbridge, an English novelist, evokes in her fiction the world of Liverpool's working class with what has been called melancholy realism. (See also *Contemporary Authors*, Vols. 21-22.)

[In *The Dressmaker* (published in America as *The Secret Glass*), Beryl Bainbridge has evoked] with ruthless realism the darkest days of 1944—and, a million miles away from heroics, [adumbrated] in one grim little tale the cataclysm that war created in working-class society. . . .

To have disinterred so many nasty things in the woodshed and yet evoked a workaday image of Liverpudlian optimism and resilience, in so few claustrophobic pages, is a remarkable achievement. Miss Bainbridge's imagination pushes her towards nightmare, and her eye for detail is macabre; but because she writes with taut, matter-of-fact simplicity this seems as authentic as any contemporary image the camera has preserved of that mercifully vanished past. (p. 1101)

> *"Bad Old Days," in* The Times Literary Supplement (© *Times Newspapers Ltd., 1973; reproduced by permission), September 28, 1973, p. 1101.*

Bainbridge's books are melancholy, provincial landscapes in which violence, like a thunderstorm, always threatens, sometimes strikes. Her characters—usually transients between the working and middle classes—wander in and out, grouping and regrouping themselves in an effort to find the most psychologically restful position. For ["The Secret Glass"], she will inevitably be compared with Jean Rhys, Muriel Spark and Iris Murdoch. But her particular sort of understatement, painstaking yet laconic, is very much her own. (pp. 75-6)

Bainbridge is a master of detail and atmosphere, superb at conveying the doggedness of Liverpool life: the oppressive slag heaps, the bomb site that was once Blacker's general store, the dinners of Spam fritters and stewed tomatoes, the young women in public lavatories rubbing sand on their legs to simulate silk stockings. "The Secret Glass" is first-rate as both a psychological and a suspense novel. We often forget how closely woven the two are—how busy life seems before a catastrophe, how mysteriously quiet during it, and how ruthlessly normal afterward. (p. 76)

> *Margo Jefferson, "Violence Under Glass," in* Newsweek (*copyright 1974 by Newsweek, Inc.; all rights reserved; reprinted by permission), August 12, 1974, pp. 75-6.*

Admirers of Beryl Bainbridge's "Harriet Said" . . . will not find that novel's gothic tension in . . . "The Secret Glass." [The latter] has another kind of interest; it will attract readers not for its suspense-entertainment but for its sharp character study and unrelenting Naturalism. . . .

Gone is the eeriness, the gratuitous corruption of "Harriet Said," in which the "innocents" seeking thrills in a lonely landscape brought disaster on a man and his wife. In this book, people are too poor (except for the resented Americans) and too worried about respectability to pursue the eerie or gratuitous thrill. The Lancashire of the earlier novel, with its lonely beach and firelight scenes, . . . is now sobered with Realism: it is 1944, tankers are in the harbor and coal is too dear to be wasted on roaring fires illuminating sexual curiosities to be spied by bored young girls.

In "The Secret Glass" . . . all the deadliness, the wickedness, and even the villain (such as she is) can be tracked to the same dreary source: the narrowness of the working class ethic combined with the hatred felt toward the exotic, affluent Yanks ("pressing young girls up against the wall, mouth to mouth as if eating them") with their jeeps and supplies of cigarettes and nylons and their great dogs on metal chains.

What Miss Bainbridge has written this time is an exposure, both grim and nostalgic, of a type of existence so joyless it turns pathological. . . .

The author is painstaking in her evocation of era and perceptive about the world of manners in working-class Liverpool. She has much to tell us about those pressure cookers of family life and limited means. And she creates memorable portraits of her people. . . .

Against such details of a cramped and deadly existence, the murder at the end of the novel seems like a last-minute frill tacked onto a straitjacket. And when Nellie, sewing a shroud for the victim, excuses the act by saying, "We haven't had much of a life. . . . We haven't done much in the way of proving we're alive," I'm afraid I hear the author trying to justify her sensational denouement by calling sociology to her aid. The "motives" and the events leading up to the murder are too hastily jerry-built into the second half of an otherwise leisurely and careful book. But Beryl Bainbridge, in "The Secret Glass," has the eye and the language of a serious novelist. She can breathe enough life into her people for us to want to read her next time without a murder. (p. 4)

Gail Godwin, in The New York Times Book Review *(© 1974 by The New York Times Company; reprinted by permission), September 15, 1974.*

Beryl Bainbridge's tenure on her world is indisputable. But it's a small, dry place, fenced off like a compound behind barbed wire and vigilantly patrolled by the novelist, who knows rather too well how to keep all her characters within bounds. *The Bottle Factory Outing* is as near to a perfect novel as I've read for a long time. It has both the simplicity and the savagery of one of the nastier folk ballads, along with the ballad's restricted range and the linguistic certainty which comes from working with a foreshortened vocabulary as if it were an eight-note scale. . . .

Miss Bainbridge's prose style is so exactly attuned to the dislocated mental world of her characters that the novelist is able to pass herself off more as an eavesdropper than as an artificer. It is a kind of writing in which world and word are utterly of a piece. (p. 82)

Living in this prose is like suffering from an optical deficiency which causes everything less than six feet away to be magnified, frighteningly sharp, and everything beyond that to congeal into an impenetrable grey fuzz. . . .

It's a style which accepts the extraordinary as normal. A kettle boils. Someone gets strangled. The lavatory cistern breaks down. There are neither causes for events, nor any particular expectations; things just happen. . . .

But to achieve this accuracy, control and perfect pitch, Miss Bainbridge has had to play Procrustes. One might say that her characters are simply the sort of people who are untroubled by thoughts, who lack any sense of their own cultural depth and identity, and who are capable of only the most vestigial feelings, and leave it at that. Or one might accuse Miss Bainbridge of depriving them of the right to think and feel in order to construct a world simple enough to be contained by that pure, lucid but underprivileged prose. A great deal in *The Bottle Factory Outing* can only excite unqualified admiration; but there is, finally and nigglingly, something about it which is as self-enclosed and remote as a monastic cell. (p. 83)

Jonathan Raban, in Encounter *(© 1975 by Encounter Ltd.), February, 1975.*

The Bottle Factory Outing, like [Bainbridge's] earlier books, centers on a pair of women (adolescents in *Harriet Said*) opposite in nature, living in strained, tenuous yet complementary unity. They share life's daily intimacies and larger goals, but their means and styles are grossly dissimilar. Like pairs of magnets endlessly rotated, they attract and repel each other in turn. One is thoughtful, withdrawn, ascetic, the other sensual, blowsy and overweight. One is irritatingly reasonable, the other outlandishly romantic. Freda, like Rita before her in *The Secret Glass*, has the imaginative power to invent an elaborate love affair when in

fact reality has given her precious little to build on. . . . The immense creative will that informs these wild imaginings makes Freda awesome rather than pathetic. But whatever the actual or dreamed erotic entanglements, the essential bond is between the female pair. From this strife-ridden, often destructive yet powerful relationship flows the energy of the story. . . .

This is a wry comic novel of poses and play-acting, the essentials of all comedy. One will remember the characters in extreme gestures of self-parody, like *commedia dell-arte* standbys—the courteous, compliant Latin lover, the red-faced brawling Irish truck driver. And the outing's climax, a bus ride through a safari park (British version of our jungle habitats) is a deftly written travesty: the lions and tigers are oddly dormant, while a dead body waits in the back seat of the parked car. Daily reality seems to be a ludicrous game all agree to play, while far beneath the surface the obscure rumblings of life and death continue, careless and inescapable.

To my mind Bainbridge is not writing thrillers or pseudo-thrillers, as some critics have suggested. Rather she is writing quests. So far, she is asking far more questions than she answers; in our dogmatic age of assertion, this is refreshing. (p. 27)

Lynne Sharon Schwartz, in The New Republic *(reprinted by permission of* The New Republic; *© 1975 by The New Republic, Inc.), May 24, 1975.*

Ms. Bainbridge writes so deftly [in *The Bottle Factory Outing*] about the disasters befalling a pair of witless wenches on a mismanaged company picnic that one can very nearly forgive her black comedy for being no more than a very dirty gray. (p. 95)

Phoebe Adams, in The Atlantic Monthly *(copyright © 1975 by The Atlantic Monthly Company, Boston, Mass.; reprinted with permission), June, 1975.*

* * *

BALDWIN, James   1924-

Baldwin, a distinguished Black American novelist, essayist, playwright, and short story writer, is as celebrated for his prose style as for his powerful evocation of the Black experience in America. (See also *Contemporary Authors*, Vols. 1-4, rev. ed.)

James Baldwin has followed the traditional pattern of the Man of Letters, the Man of Letters with a message, in utilizing almost every means of verbal expression to convey his warnings. But almost anyone so committed to directness of statement is likely to find the odd exigencies of theater more a hindrance than a help. One can tell the truth in novels, especially novels like Baldwin's, more or less directly; one must tell the truth in social essays. But a play is made up fundamentally of the lies of other people's lives. The truth is never in the parts, but in the sum, never stated, but experienced. In *The Amen Corner . . .*, a play derived, to some degree, from the same childhood experience as *Go Tell It on the Mountain*, Baldwin was able to attain something of the stark sincerity of that memoir-novel, despite an excess of rhetoric over plot. But his more ambitious attempt, *Blues for Mister Charlie* (1964), betrays serious imaginative disability.

40

The play was obviously intended as an explosive race-war document . . . , "an attempt," as one reviewer put it, "to give the Caucasians in the audience a white inferiority complex." With some Caucasians the attempt succeeded all too easily, and reviewers paid pious acknowledgments to the justice of Baldwin's anger. But it is an essay in artless bullying, not a play. Its wicked South is faked, its white villains are flat collages of prejudice-clichés—and this despite Baldwin's professed moral experiment (in the wake of the Medgar Evars murder), his generous attempt to imagine a Southern lynch-killer as a human being. There are playable, even moving moments, bits of ritual drama ("Blacktown" talks to "Whitetown"), intriguing shifts back and forth in time. But the dialogue, for the most part, is hopeless: faked banter, faked poetry, doctrinaire racism, dated slang, all conflated with artificial violence and obscenity. The play rarely comes to life, enough life to hurt a serious listener, because Baldwin lacked either the skill or the patience to imagine completely the place, the story, or the people. . . . Baldwin is no playwright—he has difficulty imagining anyone not Baldwin. It provides a perfect example of the relinquishing of judgment by an undiscerning and intimidated white audience. (pp. 72-4)

Each of James Baldwin's three novels [*Go Tell It on the Mountain, Giovanni's Room*, and *Another Country*] has been written out of some personal necessity of the author's, a necessity which it describes, conveys, and, hopefully, enables the author to transcend. Everything he writes—when he writes well—bears this sense of an inner necessity, of the whole of himself told and overcome. From no other contemporary author does one get such a sensation of writing as life; it is all so open and desperate and acute, minute by minute and word by word. The captivation of the reader, the feeling of rightness comes from Baldwin's absolute honesty, from his yielding, however unwillingly, to necessity. A reader *feels* the desperation—if the man had not written this book, and written it so, he could not have survived. Each book is a renewed effort to stay alive and upright through the finding and placing of perfect words. Each book is a staving off of death, a matter of survival.

If this is the case, it can scarcely be considered illegitimate or extra-literary prying to regard the novels as essentially about him, the man, James Baldwin. Autobiographical exactness, after all, is the very source of their sting, their astringent modern taste. It is not anti-literary, therefore, or anti-poetic, to talk of *James Baldwin's* family, or experience, or pain, in these novels, rather than John's or David's. It is no more nasty to write of his inversion than of Proust's. When a writer makes it so clear that he is not lying, one should do him the honor of believing him.

There is more than one kind of honesty in writing, of course. A self-dissolving symbolist may tell truth as well as a self-displaying realist, and Baldwin's honesty is only his, the latest variety: the need to tell "all" the truth, with no pretenses, no fictions, no metaphors—the quality one associates with his best essays. Such a need (cf. Mailer, Genet) may ultimately render unusable all the standard props of fiction. In this new, needful, stripped-bare kind of nervous truth, one tells far more than is customarily told, in order to stay this side of insanity. Baldwin allows himself, for example, none of Ellison's objectivity, very little of his distance from his fictions. Like Richard Wright, ultimately, he is probably more a symbolic Negro than a typical one; but,

again, like Richard Wright, he is no less useful, or even less necessary, for that.

Each novel, for Baldwin, has been a stage; a stage to be lived through, transformed into words, then exorcised and transcended. The next novel begins a new stage, and the process goes on. This does not, of course, mean that he will ever reach the shores of fulfillment and rest. It seems, in fact, highly unlikely, unless he should begin to lie.

Go Tell It on the Mountain (1952) was the first stage, Baldwin's baptism of fire. It is the testament of his coming to terms with, his defining and transcending, the experience of his boyhood—his family, his religion, his Harlem youth. (The story is told again in "Notes of a Native Son"; it is told a third time, far less honestly, in *The Fire Next Time*.) The telling was necessary for Baldwin, in the same way that telling *Look Homeward, Angel* was necessary for Thomas Wolfe. *Go Tell It on the Mountain* has, in fact, much the same kind of effect as Wolfe's great novel, the effect of autobiography-as-exorcism, of a lyrical, painful, ritual exercise whose necessity and intensity the reader feels. The impact on a reader, in books of this sort, appears to be in direct relation to the amount of truth the author is able to tell himself. At the end of *Go Tell It on the Mountain*, the hero, John, has "come through"; one presumes that Baldwin had as well. (pp. 119-21)

Baldwin is as unafraid of glorious prose as he is of honest prose, and the book is woven out of both. But the strength, at last, is that of his own personal necessity, a necessity that the reader can vicariously share. It is the strength of a harrowing prayer, simple and felt, of a small tragic truth that enlarges the heart. The book is carved with love. Because of its peculiar kind of necessary, very personal truth, it remains one of the few, the very few, essential Negro works.

Giovanni's Room (1956) served its purpose too, I suspect. Baldwin's personal uncertainties are not limited to the racial, religious, and familial. (pp. 123-24)

It is certainly one of the most subtle novels of the homosexual world, not as poetic and outspoken as Genet's, not as trashy as John Rechy's; but the emotions are more to be observed than to be shared. It has something of the lyrical allusiveness of *Go Tell It on the Mountain*, of its squeezing, sonnetlike smallness—Giovanni's room is the perfect symbolic setting, as cluttered and oppressively closed as one of Pinter's settings. But the effect, on the whole, is slight. (p. 124)

Another Country, and the sick truths it tells Americans about themselves, had to wait for the emergence of a new style: a style one may designate as New York-1960's. . . . It is used, at its shrillest, most wide-open, by Baldwin, Edward Albee, LeRoi Jones, Norman Mailer, Lenny Bruce, *The Realist*, the new Grove Press novelists, some of the Jewish Establishment journalists and critics (*The New York Review, The New Leader, Partisan Review*), and probably by hundreds of New Yorkers whose names we will never know. It has correspondences with softer manifestations like pop art, Jules Feiffer, Nichols and May, *A Hard Day's Night*. Jane, Vivaldo's "beat chick" in *Another Country*, is a splendid specimen: she is brittle, bitchy, fresh from the shrink, with sex like broken glass; a frenzied neurotic with every nerve bare and bleeding loud, first cousin to Lula in *The Dutchman*.

This style almost entirely carries the book, a style of screaming, no-holds-barred verbal violence. The revolving sequence of events, the inter-ringing figures of the sex dance (everyone mixing with everyone else), even, ultimately, the characters in the dance themselves, white and black, homo-, hetero-, and bi-sexual, exist primarily to provide voices and vehicles for the screamy exchanges, the ear-piercing insults, the excruciating displays of mutual torment. (pp. 125-26)

The race war, as depicted in this novel, is a difficult thing to understand. First of all, Baldwin has almost entirely excluded "average" people, the simple white American bourgeoisie or lower orders, whose prejudice is so obvious and so stupid it bores even more than it disgusts him. The few representatives of *that* world, the upstairs world, who foolishly drop into the plot are usually dissolved into steam with single drops of acid. (A pair of white heterosexual liberals, the Silenskis, so square they are married and have children and make money, degenerate into the crudest samples of sick America before the book is through, despite Baldwin's obvious efforts to be fair. Their racial liberality, it develops, is as fragile as their sexual assurance. So much for "normal" people.)

So all we have left to fight the race war are a few outlaw blacks and highly emancipated whites. In such a context the war loses its social relevance (except perhaps symbolically), and takes on the dimensions of a private duel. But the issues are no less clear. "Somewhere in his heart the black boy hated the white boy because he was white. Somewhere in his heart Vivaldo had hated and feared Rufus because he was black." Baldwin tries, or at least the top of his mind tries, to keep the sides equal, and the fighting fair. The white combatants, Leona, Vivaldo, especially Eric, are created with affection and care: these are no evil, ill-understood Wrighteous puppets. But the Negroes have all the trumps. It is *they*, always, who carry the whip, and no white lover, friend, or reader dares to deny them the right. (pp. 126-27)

At their most intense, these race-war combats always transmute into sex combats—which illustrates Baldwin's theory of the fundamentally sexual character of racism. This aspect of the novel, however, is even more unsettled and unsettling, because of the case Baldwin is trying to make for inversion. (p. 128)

The over-lyrical poeticizing of homosexual love is one of the real flaws of the book. Surely Genet's pictures, or even Baldwin's in *Giovanni's Room*, of the foul *and* fair of inversion, are more just. (pp. 129-30)

Another Country has, in its frantic new writer's world called New York, much of the same necessity, the same quality of desperate exorcism as Baldwin's earlier works. But things here are less under control. Almost all of the thinking, the non-imaginative thinking of Baldwin's essays is sandwiched into the fiction, bearing a suggestion that the man is now writing more from his ideas than his imagination. The piercing one-note tone of repetitiousness of so much of this long book supports this dissatisfying notion. Another dangerous sign is the confusion of narrative authority, very like the confusions of self-identity which mar so many of Baldwin's latest and weakest essays. His own opinions mingle with those of his characters, subjectivity jars with objectivity in such a way as to indicate that the author is unaware of the difference: i.e., that James Baldwin, through the 1950's the sole master of *control* in American prose, in the 1960's has begun to lose control.

What is there to salvage and prize? A number of things. More often than not, between the explosions, *Another Country* reminds the reader that James Baldwin is still one of the genuine stylists of the English language. (p. 130)

He is the most powerful and important American essayist of the postwar period, perhaps of the century. *Notes of a Native Son* and *Nobody Knows My Name* will maintain their place among the small collection of genuine American classics. They have already been adopted as standard texts and models of style in American college courses; and this is not just a "vogue," an offshoot of the Civil Rights movement. Two such books would sustain any reputation, as long as men can tell the true from the false. (pp. 135-36)

Baldwin has shown more concern for the painful exactness of prose style than any other modern American writer. He picks up words with heavy care, then sets them, one by one, with a cool and loving precision that one can feel in the reading. There are no bright words in his best essays, no flashes, allusions, delusions, no Tynanesque "brilliance." His style is like stripped conversation, saying the most that words can *honestly* say. If it hurts, if it ties one down and hammers its words on one's mind, it is simply the effect of his won't-let-go rigor. There is good and bad prose, there is moral and immoral.

This does not of course imply that the style is flat, because it is not like champagne. Baldwin is fully aware of the ambiguities and ironies implicit in his subjects (primary among them the sick paradox that calls itself America), and he weaves these same ambiguities and ironies into his prose. He is also drivingly and constantly self-critical, which is why his writing is so strong and clear, his thinking so often unassailable. His paragraphs work like a witty colloquy of two sharp minds, Baldwin's and his critic's, one within the other: the devastating qualifiers, the cool understatements, the parentheses, the litotes, the suggestions and quiet parallels display the double mind of the self-critic at work.

Writing like this can be more harrowing, more intense than *any* of the works we are considering [elsewhere in the book]. As Baldwin himself admits, Negro literature "is more likely to be a symptom of our tension than an examination of it," and this includes his own three novels, his plays, and his stories. The exhilarating exhaustion of reading his best essays—which in itself may be a proof of their honesty and value—demands that the reader measure up, and forces him to learn. (pp. 136-37)

> *David Littlejohn, in his* Black on White: A Critical Survey of Writing By American Negroes *(copyright © 1966 by David Littlejohn; reprinted by permission of Grossman Publishers), Viking, 1966.*

"If Beale Street Could Talk" is Baldwin's 13th book and it might have been written, if not revised for publication, in the 1950's. Its suffering, bewildered people, trapped in what is referred to as the "garbage dump" of New York City—blacks constantly at the mercy of whites—have not even the psychological benefit of the Black Power and other radical movements to sustain them. Though their story should seem dated, it does not. And the peculiar fact of their being so politically helpless seems to have strengthened, in Baldwin's imagination at least, the deep, powerful bonds of emotion between them. "If Beale Street Could Talk" is a quite moving and very traditional celebration of love. It affirms not only love between a man and a woman, but love of a type that is dealt with only rarely in contemporary fiction—that between members of a family, which may involve extremes of sacrifice. . . .

"If Beale Street Could Talk" manages to be many things at the same time. It is economically, almost poetically constructed, and may certainly be read as a kind of allegory, which refuses conventional outbursts of violence, preferring to stress the provisional, tentative nature of our lives. (p. 1)

The novel progresses swiftly and suspensefully, but its dynamic movement is interior. Baldwin constantly understates the horror of his characters' situation in order to present them as human beings whom disaster has struck, rather than as blacks who have, typically, been victimized by whites and are therefore likely subjects for a novel. The work contains many sympathetic portraits of white people. . . .

"If Beale Street Could Talk" is a moving, painful story. It is so vividly human and so obviously based upon reality, that it strikes us as timeless—an art that has not the slightest need of esthetic tricks, and even less need of fashionable apocalytic excesses. (p. 2)

> *Joyce Carol Oates, in* The New York Times Book Review *(© 1974 by The New York Times Company; reprinted by permission), May 19, 1974.*

The scene [in "If Beale Street Could Talk"] is Harlem today, a long way from Beale Street, but James Baldwin means to tell a story that will move us like one of the great old blues songs—a lyric cry of pain and gritty endurance from the heart of a young black woman whose man is in jail. . . .

[The] music from everywhere in "If Beale Street Could Talk" isn't authentic blues but the stuff that's piped into elevators. Baldwin is never able to find a convincing voice for Tish [the protagonist] who has a dire tendency to utter Words To Live By. "Trouble means you're alone," for instance. . . .

I think I know a bad novel when I see one, though this one fooled me for a while. James Baldwin is a writer one takes seriously; . . . it would be a pleasure to be able to praise his first novel in six years. There are scenes that give one hope: a shouting Sunday service, a family summit meeting to discuss Tish's pregnancy. But "If Beale Street Could Talk" is an almost total disaster.

> *Walter Clemons, "Black and Blue," in* Newsweek *(copyright 1974 by Newsweek, Inc.; all rights reserved; reprinted by permission), May 27, 1974, p. 82.*

Baldwin is a professional fugitive, he is always on the run; from his colour in *Giovanni's Room*, a love story between pure whites; from his class in *Tell Me How Long The Train's Been Gone*; and now the final trick as he escapes from his own sex in *If Beale Street Could Talk*. These so-cial and sexual cells are so vague as to almost defy belief, but Baldwin is clear about his freedom: it consists of the small open space known as romance, that last straw in an ocean of uncertain uncertainties. . . .

Baldwin always stays very close to his material; the structure of the novel is tied to a kind of self-reflectiveness which disobeys the conventional laws of narrative, and the narrative itself breathes with Baldwin's own life as he returns yet again to that primal vision which apparently remains untarnished with the passing of his years. This is the poor, black world of streets and stoops and store-front faith which Baldwin can summon with incantation and which he pours all over himself in an effort to keep his vision clean.

There is that same, impassioned prose—a relic of the evangelical past which leads to sub-headings such as 'Troubled About My Soul' and 'Zion'—and Baldwin constructs the language as if it were the hallowed container of sacred meanings. His novels are attempts to push and pull these truths into some recognisable human shape and perhaps these truths, the gods of that familial hearth which Baldwin has preserved throughout his work, are almost human. They are those of 'life', 'feeling' and 'experience' and Baldwin tills those acres of silent passion which are generally supposed to pass between people at moments of intensity, and which are beyond mere words.

That is why he has never aspired to a casual, Yankee mimeticism, and the model for his black allegories lies somewhere around D. H. Lawrence rather than his ostensible mentor, Richard Wright, whose own writing is nothing more than white journalism plus blood. Baldwin has an impassioned and quasi-Biblical manner which allows him to denounce and lament like a funky Johnny Ray. Its advantages arc fervour (if fervour *is* an advantage) and grace, but what it gains in heat it loses in light, and there is precious little veracity or detail within his sermons. *If Beale Street Could Talk* is composed largely of cardboard, since stereotypes are the only possible vehicles for the single-mineded passions, wordless joys and lengthy silences which Baldwin insists upon discovering in every basement. White policemen and spinsters are always very bad, young blacks and young lovers are thoroughly and undoubtedly good. But even cut-outs can be daubed with a little fresh paint, and Baldwin is adept at that mawkish and slightly camp diction which passes for conversation amongst blacks: "Now the cops who put him in this wagon know that the dude is *sick. I know* they know it. He ain't supposed to be in here—and him not hardly much more than a kid." This is the fantasy of urban America, and in this garish light we may steal away from Baldwin, leaving him to rouge his wounds in public. (p. 22)

> *Peter Ackroyd, in* The Spectator *(© 1974 by The Spectator; reprinted by permission of The Spectator), July 6, 1974.*

Twenty years ago, James Baldwin, the one-time lay preacher, made American Negro gospel-fever the centre of his first book, *Go Tell It on the Mountain*. In [*If Beale Street Could Talk*] the 'holy rollers' are much less sympathetically drawn: he sees them as unresisting inheritors of a vicious, alien religion. . . .

Just as American womanhood is just now beginning the struggle to exist in her own imagination, so the American

Negro has begun to free himself from the prison of a reflected image formed of the stereotypes of the white imagination: he has begun to invent himself.

If Beale Street Could Talk celebrates this new-found capacity for self-creation. It is a sort of fable about the Negro's quest for cultural freedom in the alien environment of present-day New York. . . . [The] black race makes itself finally in its own image.

Disturbingly, however, this image seems to exist simply in opposition to everything white. Though Baldwin has done much to free the American Negro from the 'Uncle Tom' and 'Sambo' clichés of white fiction, he now portrays the white American with equal cartoon crudity. It is as if the black American must now begin to invent the white American, his white American, in order to discover his own identity. Thus, the description of Bell, the cop—one of only two white characters in the book—goes: 'He walked the way John Wayne walks, striding out to clean up the universe, and he believed in all that shit. . . . Like his heroes, he was kind of pin-headed, heavy-gutted, big-assed, and his eyes were as blank as George Washington's eyes.' But between the extremes of black and white, even on Beale Street, there are surely some other shades.

> David Thomas, "Too Black, Too White," in The Listener (© British Broadcasting Corp. 1974; reprinted by permission of David Thomas), July 25, 1974, p. 125.

*   *   *

BARAKA, Imamu Amiri   1934-

Baraka, formerly known as LeRoi Jones, is a prize-winning Black American poet, playwright, director, editor, and community organizer closely associated with Black nationalism. (See also *Contemporary Authors*, Vols. 21-22.)

LeRoi Jones's *Dutchman* earned him a reputation as the Negro scourge of white complacency, an angry, knowing, ultracontemporary playwright. But his . . . short plays, *The Toilet* and *The Slave*, reveal him as an archsentimentalist, a dramatist who uses obscenities and wrath to mask a poverty of ideas and a painfully immature emotional structure. (p. 231)

[*The Toilet*] is entirely unconvincing. There has merely been an undramatized assertion that out of perversion can come love, a sentimental broad jump over all the intervening difficulties. Beyond this, the presence of a [secondary] white character who functions as a voyeur is an infuriatingly juvenile note introduced so that Jones can have it both ways. For the white boy speaks up against the brutality but at the same time is a fairy who clearly doesn't "belong there," where *real* life is going on.

The two plays are united by Jones's adolescent need to have his cake and eat it, to seem to be arguing for peace and reconciliation while flaying whites with every weapon his limited arsenal contains. *The Slave* is a "fable" set at some future time when a Negro insurrection is devastating the country. It is a *pas de trois* among a white liberal couple and the woman's first husband, a Negro who is now the leader of the rebellion. He breaks into their house and holds them at gunpoint, his purpose being to take away the two daughters he had by the woman. Jones's purpose presumably is to have the three engage in denunciation and

counterdenunciation, giving both sides of the racial question. (pp. 231-32)

But on one level Jones writes like nothing so much as a lesser Edna St. Vincent Millay pontificating on the state of world and soul—"I have killed for all times any creative impulses I will ever have by the depravity of my murderous philosophies," the Negro says. On another level Jones employs frequent obscenities exactly the way people in real life do—to preclude the possibility, and danger, of thought. And though Jones allows the white man to call the Negro a maniacal, destructive racist, he stacks the cards ferociously against him. Once more the white is effete, incapable of satisfying the woman as the Negro did, and a liberal whose values pale before the apocalyptic vision of Negro power and healing violence.

In the end the Negro shoots the white man, after which a bomb flattens the house. "The children," moans the fatally injured wife. "They're dead," replies the Negro. Whatever tragic insight resides in these words comes all too late. Jones has simply bypassed a terrain mined with all the explosive truths about human conflict. To traverse this dangerous ground he will need more resources—and more courage. (p. 232)

> Richard Gilman, "Evasive Action" (1964), in his Common and Uncommon Masks: Writings on Theatre 1961-1970 (copyright © 1971 by Richard Gilman; reprinted by permission of Random House, Inc.), Random House, 1971, pp. 231-32.

The Slave . . . is a blatant, unmodulated scream of racial abuse; its primary purpose, one assumes, was authorial self-gratification. . . . It is so devoid of conflict, of dramatic content—the whites are such pappy, wish-fulfilling projections ("Professor No-Dick"), the gunman such a sick, simple noise, that the only reasonable response, white or black, is one of embarrassed and annoyed detachment. Which, perhaps, is what Jones wanted.

The Dutchman . . . is quite another matter. It may be the most important imaginative literary document of the American race war since *Native Son*. And it works. Jones has here channeled his hate equally into *two* antagonists, a young Negro boy and the violent white female (a stunning part for an actress) who accosts him on a New York subway, and has managed to create in their encounter one of the more genuine and irresistible conflicts of the modern stage.

The dialogue between the two is almost perfect. It conveys the shrill, sharp, absolutely open insult-trading of cool modern neurotics, hiding nothing except everything, all very uptight New Yorky 1964. And just beneath it, one can *feel* the peeled-grape hypersensitivity, the heading-for-a-crackup comic tension. (pp. 74-6)

LeRoi Jones has published (in addition to his plays) [his] volumes of poetry, *Preface to a Twenty-Volume Suicide Note* (1961) and *The Dead Lecturer* (1964), and an expressionistic, semi-autobiographical, semi-pornographic prose thing called *The System of Dante's Hell* (1965). He is the most difficult of all the Negro poets, and it is hard to say whether any reader can be guaranteed a just repayment for his efforts. It is hard, in fact, to say anything sensible or useful about a poet who is himself not simply irrational but anti-rational; whose whole approach to poetic language reaches far beyond mere coherence or what we would call sense; who is highly suspicious of the whole nature of verbal communication. This may be one of those many occasions when the wise critic would simply shut up.

> A compromise
> would be silence. To shut up, even such risk
> as the proper placement
> of verbs and nouns. To freeze the spit
> in mid-air, as it aims itself
> at some valiant intellectual's face.

But to give an idea, not to judge, not to interpret: There is, first, a small group of poems that work very nearly in the manner of ordinary sense (at least for a poet). The title poem and "The Turncoat" from the first volume, "Duncan Spoke of a Process," "If Into Love The Image Burdens," "I Substitute For The Dead Lecturer," "Snake Eyes," perhaps "Footnote To A Pretentious Book," and especially "The Liar" from the second volume: these are all quiet, poignantly quiet pieces of introspection, honest and painful, suggestive, intimate, coolly sad: Jones on Jones. They reveal, even in their own moody illogic, a man who wants very much to know who he is, and wants the reader to know and love him too. These are inside poems, straight from the pain. (pp. 96-7)

One familiar with Jones' plays, too, will catch, here and there, the violent racist anger, particularly in the two strong anti-syntactic "speeches," in "Black Dada Nihilismus," a Kill-All-the-Whites manifesto in dada, and in the surrealist abuse of "Rhythm and Blues" and "Green Lantern's Solo," two of his strongest poems. The violence here is a kind of nightmare violence, something one puts together out of frightening fragments. The two latter poems (from *The Dead Lecturer*) may be as close to a testament as Jones will ever offer, if one knew where to find it; the most honest possible expression of a man who simply cannot trust words to stay still.

> I am deaf and blind and lost and will not again
> sing your quiet verse. I have lost
> even the act of poetry, and writhe now for
> cool horizonless dawn...

More frequently, the communication is nowhere so definable. It is a nonverbal communication that uses words and phrases only as little pressures on the reader's consciousness, a communication that has very little to do with normal syntax or denotative structure. One reads, at best, a tone. The *Suicide Note* poems ("early LeRoi Jones"?) like "Hymn for Lanie Poo" have a brash, jazzy, young man's sound—a lot of pop-art black humor, jerky collages à la Rauschenberg of radio serial heroes or comic-strip characters taken seriously. As he admits,

> These words
> are not music. They make no motions
> for a dance.

One is denied even the surface attractions of rhythm, except for a jarring sort of skittery jerkiness, or occasional cool riffs on a theme; the "From an Almanac" poems come nearest to modern jazz. Otherwise, the reader must be content to rest passive, to float along with the unresolved surrealistic progress, as Jones plays about with his parentheses and camp gags and insets of sense in search of a style.

The Dead Lecturer poems are even sparer of sense, less attractive, more steely chill, devoid of even the comic gamey glibness of the earlier Jones. But they are even harder to reject absolutely. We have more odd noodling about with word noises, pages in which no single word group between periods coheres into sense. "Obscure" is too concrete a word: lists, insults, four-letter words, parentheses that don't close, lost commas, cold cuts of sound, allusions, dim suggestions of sex or of characters (there are two hazy "character" sequences, on Crow Jane and Willie Best) blend about in the half light, the murky background of dissonance, not nonsense but not sense. For lines and lines the words may lie positively dead, say nothing at all. Then out of it all leap sudden glints and rills of image or statement or pain, three words, a paragraph, a page. This happens especially in the abstract-expressionist protest poems like "Rhythm and Blues"; the evocative and *crafted* poems full of keen dreams and emergent pain: "A Contract," "The Politics of Rich Painters," all lethal and queerly vivid things. Here, in his non-sense, he attacks with surrealist vigor all the common muck that passes for sense.

It is all, ultimately, anti-rational poetry, an attempt at a new stimulation of consciousness through words made malleable. Jones of course is not the only one practicing it, and his identification with Beat poets like Duncan, Olson, and Snyder is appropriate. Rational criticism is unequipped, in the last analysis, to deal with such an effort, and finally irrelevant. It is poetry for the leisured, the patient, the energetic, for those who do not insist on an immediate show of gain for energies expended. (pp. 98-100)

> *David Littlejohn, in his* Black on White: A Critical Survey of Writing By American Negroes *(copyright © 1966 by David Littlejohn; reprinted by permission of Grossman Publishers), Viking, 1966.*

For whatever reasons, no one has yet examined *Dutchman* simply as a play. Dramatically, *Dutchman* presents a theme developed in a carefully planned structure which itself is the life of this particular drama, and which stands as the turning point in Jones's artistic career.

The theme, as other critics have noted, is one of black identity and its existence in the world. It is presented in the relationship of a black man, Clay, and a white woman, Lula. But because commentators, in a rush to find the tempting "meanings" in their confrontation, have passed over the dynamics of their special interpersonal relationship, much of the play's significance has been lost. (p. 123)

Jones' thematic statement, that the authentic black self cannot survive, is an integral part of his play's dramatic structure. One need not have recourse to biography or sociology to see that Lula's approach, whether as a seductive woman or accusing white person, leaves no room for Clay's existence. It is not surprising that Jones' next play, *The Slave*, should cast his black hero as a revolutionist waging a hopeless war for his existence, for in *Dutchman* his back is squarely against the wall. The notion of an authentic self, and the course of existence it must follow, is central to Jones' works. His sociology bears this out, but it is more instructive to see the theme treated in his fiction, where it remains the key element in his art. Better than his two books of jazz criticism or even his *Home: Social Essays* is the story collection, *Tales*. These sixteen pieces plot the development of a black self, first seeking its reflection in the world of white intellectualism, and finally returning to an opposite set of polarities in authentic black existence. Repeated again and again are the alternatives of "reflection" and "action." (p. 125)

Jones' drama argues the same theme as his most sustained work of prose: that authentic existence is possible only in the vital act of warring against its challenges. His theatre is now self-proclaimed as "Black Arts" and, by necessity, "Revolutionary." White men are taken by the "Experimental Death Unit #1" and shot; "J-E-L-L-O," a play "about Jack Benny and Rochester, and what happens when Rochester diggs hisself," ends with Benny's murder. *Dutchman*, written at the point in Jones' life when he abandoned his white wife and his posture as a Village intellectual in favor of a more racial militancy, is not only substantial drama, but is cathartic within Jones' own career. The black man's self, otherwise repressed in a stifling cultural assimilation, must in fact go underground to preserve its very existence; and Jones' plays become guerilla theatre, treating the theme of a guerilla soul. (pp. 125-26)

> *Jerome Klinkowitz, "LeRoi Jones (Imamu Amiri Baraka): Dutchman as Drama," in* Negro American Literature Forum (© *Indiana State University 1973), Winter, 1973, pp. 123-26.*

Baraka is generally recognized today not only as the first articulater of the requirements for a black literature but also as a kind of spiritual leader of black-poetry writers. Although it seems to me that he has had great difficulty in adhering to his own theory of what black poetry should be, he has nonetheless pointed the way for younger poets. During the late fifties and early sixties, he was a very successful contemporary poet and playwright, whose verse, though unique in its way, was not unlike that of other academic poets: complex, obscure, written primarily for academicians and other poets. After a period of transition, traceable in his poems and essays, he turned his back on the established powers responsible for making him a success, and set about working toward the organization of the black community in his hometown, Newark, New Jersey. His poetry underwent several significant changes (as did his name from Jones to Imamu Amiri Baraka), becoming aggressively militant in its tone and message, and directed, in the manner of Langston Hughes, to the people. Most of the younger black-poetry writers have followed his lead. (p. 16)

> *Donald B. Gibson, "Introduction" to* Modern Black Poets: A Collection of Critical Essays, *edited by Donald B. Gibson (© 1973 by Prentice-Hall, Inc.; reprinted by permission of Prentice-Hall, Inc., Englewood Cliffs, New Jersey), Prentice-Hall, 1973, pp. 1-17.*

LeRoi Jones' poetry describes a quest for a moral order which he feels ultimately impelled to create for himself and on his own terms. It begins as a moral order similar to T. S. Eliot's in *The Waste Land* and similar to the order insisted upon by the comic books and the radio serials of Jones' youth. The moral order Jones searched for is related to Eliot's hanged man, who appears frequently in Jones' work. But it is also related to the hero as something other

than victim: to the existential hero who, like the Shadow, the Lone Ranger, and Green Lantern, can act individually to impose a strong moral order on a disordered world. Yet both of these visions are rejected. . . . All his heroes die; his values are inverted . . .; his only recourse is to become his own hero in the streets, to create his own black gods, and to preach a destruction of the old order as a means of preparing for the new. The pain and anguish he experienced in reaching this point—including the loss of faith in the old heroes and the old moral order—are the subject of the bulk of the poems in . . . three published volumes, *Preface to a Twenty Volume Suicide Note* (1961), *The Dead Lecturer* (1964), and *Black Magic* (1969).

In view of the influences Jones recognizes in his own work, Baudelaire, Duncan, Olson, Ginsberg, to name a few, it may seem strange to isolate Eliot. But Eliot's influence is pervasive: it operates on many levels simultaneously. The fragmented structure of *The Waste Land* figures in many of Jones' more difficult poems, particularly in the poems of the fifties and early sixties. The vision of the world as wasted and infertile; the vision of a world having turned its back on God; the vision of rat's feet through the ruined city all seem as much a part of Jones' poetry as of Eliot's. Rhythms which are decidedly Eliotic crop up in crucial moments in the early—and sometimes the late—poems. And innumerable direct references and allusions to Eliot pepper all the poems, though they are most obvious and most frequent in the middle work. What all this seems to point to is an effort on Jones' part to understand the moral dilemma of his own situation as a black man in a white city, oppressed and displaced in his own land, in the mythic terms which satisfied Eliot and which concerned the ultimate problem of God, moral order, the disregard of man, and the hope of resolution through love and faith. In Eliot we find the thin edge of despair honed to razor sharpness only to be neutralized by faith in a God for whom justice is clear, unambiguous, and thorough—if not sudden and swift. (pp. 112-13)

Jones' almanac is a moral almanac, like Eliot's record of the seasons; both their landscapes are moral landscapes, with the wind and the cold not only affecting, but reflecting the souls of men. The differences in their views lie perhaps in the feeling, on Eliot's part, that though the world has been wasted by man, God could somehow still inspirit it if he wished. Eliot's view is that there is a moral order in the nature of things which man has somehow lost the key to. . . . But for Jones such is not at all so clearly the case. His almanac poems suggest a picture of despair. The winds are cutting, the people infertile, the children impossibly aged. The question of the soul and the question of religion figure strongly in the almanacs as they do in many of the rest of his poems. But Jones has no basic conviction that the basic moral order is there and needs only to be understood anew. Jones in no way renounces his faith in God, but he examines in painful detail his relation to Eliot's God. In these early poems the distinction between Jones' God and Eliot's God seems almost academic. The images Jones uses correspond closely enough to Eliot's to convince us that they are one and the same, the hanged man—Jesus Christ. But the fact seems to be that Jones is examining from the very first the nature of God, that he is trying to see himself in relation to Christ and Eliot's vision, and that he ultimately renounces Eliot's God on the grounds that the moral order is inverted because of the nature of the God himself. If he wishes to set things straight for himself, he must give up the Christian God and find his own. (pp. 115-16)

Critics who have seen nihilism and nothing more . . . in Jones' work are simply wrong. He is looking for something —for a God and a moral code—which will not destroy empires or him. By no means is he fearful of violence or destruction so long as it produces the destruction of the code that destroyed Moctezuma. He sees no irony in the need for such violence: no more than one sees in the destruction of Sodom and Gomorrah, perhaps a reasonable analogy. (p. 119)

It may be said that one of Jones' solutions to the dilemma of what to do about Eliot's God, and what to do about the existential heroes of his comic book youth, is to supplant them both in his own person. (p. 125)

Perhaps it is merely a vatic pose Jones adopts in these poems, and he does not apotheosize himself at all. But there is a curiosity that lingers in the imagination regarding the name he has assumed since the publication of his poems, the Islamic name which appears in the "Explanation" to *Black Magic*. One wonders if God and the comic book heroes are dead forever, or if they have been absorbed into Jones' poetic unconscious waiting to poke out again. His name, Báraka, like Lorca's Duende, means many things. Its root is Hebrew: Brk, and it means a number of things: lightning, the blessed of God, virtue, inspiration, the muse. "Since lightning is a phenomenon everywhere attributed to the gods, *báraka* means the sudden divine rapture that overcomes either a prophet or a group of fervent devotees." It makes one think of the lightning bolt on Captain Marvel's chest, the faith that transformed a Billy Batson at the altar of Shazam, and the consequent faith that out of the scourge of action will come a new order, a new wholeness. (p. 126)

Lee A. Jacobus, "Imamu Amiri Baraka: The Quest for Moral Order" (copyright © 1973 by Lee A. Jacobus), in Modern Black Poets: A Collection of Critical Essays, *edited by Donald B. Gibson, Prentice-Hall, 1973, pp. 112-26.*

The mark of LeRoi Jones' poetry is the mark of his personality on the printed page. He is the most personal so far of the Afro-American poets. For him poetry is the flow of being, the process of human electricity interacting with the weight of time, tapped and possibly trapped on paper. Feelings, impressions, moods, passions move unedited through a structure of shifting images. Quick poems, light on their feet, like a fancy middle-weight. Mostly, his poems carry no argument, no extractable, paraphraseable statement. They operate prior to the pros and cons of rational, persuasive, politic discourse. Even after several readings, one is likely to remember mainly a flavor, a distinct attitude of spirit, an insistent, very personal voice.

His poetry is written out of a heavy anti-rationalist, anti-didactic bias. Its obligation is to the intentions of its own feelings. Its posture is in defiance of criticism. The critic is for him the sycophant and would-be legislator of official (white) reality, an implacable enemy, the best symbol of the spiritually dead pseudo-intellectuality of the West. (Lula in *Dutchman* is a white *critic*, if you watch closely.) Against

the strictures and constipations of this official reality, his poetry is an imposition upon the reader of the actuality, the majesty even (hence, Le*Roi*) of his subjectivity. The personalism of his earlier poetry, particularly, is a challenge to the ready-to-wear definitions of the sociologically defined "Negro writer" lying in wait for him. (p. 127)

All his poems give the notion of being end-of-the-line thoughts, where attempts to reach an understanding dance on the edge of ambiguity. They are the works of an apprentice guru, "stuntin' for disciples," he later decided.

A major source of this creative orientation came from the streets. The hipsterism that nourished his poetry has to be regarded respectfully since whatever its limitations hipsterism was the germ of several cultural and social revolutions still turning in the world today. Hipsterism was a counter-assertion to brand-name, white values and the conformism of middle America, a serio-comic celebration of energies and forms unaccounted for, a mysticism (with some odd resemblances to Zen and other spiritual disciplines) of rhythms and tempos inside of and beyond metronomic, bureaucratic time, reflective of the polyrhythmic time of black music (particularly be-bop) and of the fluid, open time-space sensation of a pot high. Hipsterism was a new, Afro-American ontology, a style of knowing the world and acknowledging in the parody of one's own posture the craziness of a materialistic, hyper-rationalist, racist, self-contradictory square world on the one hand and the absurdity of a universe that mocked human values in its variousness and arbitrariness on the other.

An important aspect of hipsterism that LeRoi absorbed, less familiar than, say, the relationship to black music, was its deep fascination with the ghost-spirits and fantasy-figures of pop culture, the radio, movies, the comic book. (p. 128)

To borrow a figure whose fascination Jones shares with Blake, his poetry passes through a vortex—a point at which physical forces converge—such as the center of a whirlpool. . . . His development has been through one vortex into another (carrying a large segment of creative Afro-America with him). A reading of his works together shows that the crossing was not as sudden as its results were profound. More important, at the convergence-point of these two vortexes the themes, motifs, style, images are common to both, though sometimes inverted.

In brief, what we can see happening in *Black Magic Poetry, 1961-1967* is the despair without reference-point of the earlier volumes discovering its most sufficient cause in the enormity of the fall of man under whiteness. (pp. 129-30)

The vagrant itches of his personal fantasies come home to a new cosmology, much indebted to Elijah Muhammad (see the dramatization of the Yacub myth in *Black Mass*). The natural order of the universe, in which "everything is everything" and man is in harmonious relation to nature and the gods, his imaginative and creative powers equal to his needs, has been interrupted disastrously by the intrusion of a counter-human homunculus (the white man) who maintains its parasitical existence feeding on the blood of living (nonwhite, essentially black) people and their cultures. A crucial image is the vampire. (p. 130)

But to characterize Jones' poetry rather than a particular segment of black nationalist ideology is to recognize the residue of the earlier, personal world-view transformed in the [later] work. For instance, the particular, non-conformist "craziness" of the be-bopper, one indigenous reference point for the adolescent Leroy, becomes the "black madness" of "Black Dada Nihilismus" and then the holier black madness of the intense, fiery, disorienting (to whites) commitment to blackness of the third section of [*Black Magic Poetry*]. (pp. 130-31)

What emerges is a diabolism, incipient from the earliest poems, whose main feature is the blaspheming of the hated religion, in this case the religion of whiteness. It is a commitment implied in the title, *Black Mass*, or in the poem "Black Art" ... or in the whole conception of *Black Magic Poetry*. The black magic motive (*black* meant ironically) is the drive to weave an imaginative spell powerful and compelling enough to counteract in the minds of black people the spell of the white man for "To turn their evil backwards / is to / live". . . . (p. 131)

It is as though his talent were lying around like an empty bag until filled by the spirit-breath of suddenly conscious black people and took stunning shapes from the idioms, rhythms, folklore, the needs and crises, the beauties of a self-defining Afro-America. Some of the *Black Magic* poems adapt the forms of blacktalk: the dozens in "T. T. Jackson sings" and "Word from the Right Wing"; wallwritings like "You cannot hurt / Muhammud Ali, and stay / alive"; hoodoo curses like "Babylon Revisited" and "Sacred Chant for the Return of Black Spirit and Power," raps such as "Poem for Half-White College Students," putdowns like "CIVIL RIGHTS POEM" and neo-African chants such as "Part of the Doctrine". . . . But more of the poems are free-form reflective lyrics, alternately public and private, in which Jones shows remarkable growth as "a long breath singer" in contrast to the telegraphese of the earlier work. In these, where the inspiration is street talk and the long, cascading line of Coltrane and what might be called the Eastern-Astral school of black music, the utterance moves in one unimpedable breath, with its own swoops, cries, distributed vocal parts, sound effects and faultlessly chosen words to its cymbal-crash ending. Poems like "Poem for Black Hearts" and "Black People" are among the few works equal to the intensity and urgency of the black rediscovery years of the sixties.

The incandescent furies of [*Black Magic Poetry*] subside in subsequent poems, some of them collected in *In Our Terribleness* (1970). It is as though Jones sensed that simple, diabolical inversion of white values is another form of flattery and dependency and that the creative motif of despelling the white man had run its course. The later poems, more independently reflective of the spiritual needs of black people, are mellower, less satiric, showing a deeper turn into mysticism. This latest change in a poet who believes in change as a fundamental aspect of reality is signaled by the adoption of a new name, Imamu Amiri Baraka.

There are enough brilliant poems of such variety in *Black Magic* and *In Our Terribleness* to establish the unique identity and claim for respect of several poets. But it is beside the point that Baraka is probably the finest poet, black or white, writing in this country these days. The question still has to be asked whether he has fulfilled the vocation set for him by his own moves and examples. He has called himself a "seer" (one familiar with evil is the way he defined it) and holy man, but hesitates to claim (while vying for it) the fateful name of prophet. (pp. 131-32)

A poet's obligation, by contrast [with the prophet's], is to the integrity of his verbal rendering of his individual sensibility. The problem is whether Baraka's creative impulse, which is essentially underground, hip, urban, and avant-garde, can be made to speak for a nation of black people rather than for a set of black nationalists. Can he transcend the inclination to ad-lib on the changes of black consciousness (the way be-boppers ad-libbed on "Indiana") toward redefining that consciousness in the light of enduring values and in major works of sustained thought and imagination?

"We need a heavy book, like the Bible or the Koran," he writes in *In Our Terribleness*. This is doubtless too much to ask of one man. There are qualities, further, in his creative armament that run counter to that need. He seems to confuse fantasy, which is whimsical and gratuitous (consider "Answers in Progress" in *Tales*, 1967, and "All in the Streets" in *Terribleness*, both beautiful reveries) with myth, which, however non-rational its basis, holds firmly to a certain kind of cause-effect economy. His early avant-garde posture has given way to a mysticism that depends upon other people's orthodoxies, a gnosticism, really, that carries with it the aura of initiates, adepts and degrees of secret lore. The magic of his poetry owes almost as much to his enchantment with figures of pop culture like Mandrake, Lamont Cranston, Plastic Man, and The Green Lantern as it does to African cosmology and Arabic philosophers. Some of his symbols look like paraphernalia left over from a Shriner's convention. In his later work, black nationalism moves toward becoming a subdivision of the occult sciences, whereas something more broadbacked, comprehensive, open, accountable seems demanded by the ethos of black people—the kind of poetry (groping for a reference) Malcolm might have written, had he turned his genius in that direction.

The legacy of hipsterism, then, together with his still rather Baudelairean spiritual elegance, places Baraka's work always underground or aloft in relation to the meat and potatoes' scene where the straight world works out its dull, mediocre gimmicks. His peril is that his work must pass close to that fearful terrain—not conceding to whiteness all of the middle, ordinary world, where humans play out their messy lives—if it is going to take on the amplitude and range of black being.

The limitations I speak of, already dwindling in his latest pieces, really go beyond a consideration of Baraka as poet. *There*, the same qualities are adornments of his invented poetic cosmos, part of the spell-binding conviction of the work, adding tones to one of the distinctive, compelling, haunted modern voices, a voice like the nerve-endings of our terrible times. They are part of the legend, a legend supported by a list of accomplishments impressive in a writer just reaching midcareer. And he *has* become a prophet in the literary sense, establishing modes in which some of the most stirring impulses of black expressiveness have found form. Behind this record, still another title comes to mind for Baraka, one we used to confer only upon ourselves; he is "The Kid of Afro-American Writing." (pp. 133-34)

Clyde Taylor, "Baraka as Poet" (copyright © 1973 by Clyde Taylor), in Modern Black Poets, *edited by Donald B. Gibson, Prentice-Hall, 1973, pp. 127-34.*

BARNES, Peter   1931-

Barnes, a British film critic, editor, director, and playwright, writes gothic comedies, many of which employ historic settings to caricature modern evils.

The Bewitched was the finest modern play I'd read in years: the most extraordinary, the most theatrical and—yes, but without a single nudge or sidelong glance at the audience—the most pertinent to British society in the 1970s. It imposed itself with the feeling of a classic; but this wasn't only because it spoke, as the greatest Elizabethan and Jacobean plays do, to modern concerns in a seventeenth century accent. I knew I was in the presence of something remarkable because, in scene after scene, it led me over ground no playwright had trodden before, to climax after climax of a daring which defied you to imagine how it could ever be staged. Time and again, it produced the effect which A E Housman called the one infallible test of poetry: it made my scalp prickle with cold excitement.

Another sign of a major work of art is that it should bring together, crystallised within a single image or statement, tendencies which have appeared, apparently unconnected, in other works preceding it. In the literature of the 1830s, for example, there is a strain of apparently groundless terror and foreboding which links works as disparate as Tennyson's 'Locksley Hall', Dickens' *Barnaby Rudge* and Bulwer-Lytton's *Last Days of Pompeii*. In Carlyle's *French Revolution* their vague fears and intimations of apocalypse acquire a focus and name: this, you realise, was the great doom hanging over the early Victorian imagination. Similarly, in the British drama of the 1960s, a new tone of comedy and disillusion seems to raise its head. In the black farce of Joe Orton, the metaphysical wit of Tom Stoppard, the Goyescan horror of Edward Bond's *Early Morning* and *Lear*, there is a common note which one could only, at the time, describe loosely as Jacobean—a sense of things falling apart, a bitter delight in their new randomness, an appalled disgust at the superstition and brutality revealed by the collapse of the old order, which brought to mind Ben Jonson, Donne and Webster. By comparison, the playwrights of the 1950s—John Osborne, Arnold Wesker—seemed like survivals from a more confident, neo-Elizabethan age: isolated Raleighs offended by the new era's lack of respect for language, craft, the principle of merit.

Peter Barnes gathers all these threads together in *The Bewitched*. It is a neo-Jacobean play which crystallises, clarifies and pins down what it is that links the Jacobeans and his contemporaries. Partly, it does so by being genuinely Jacobean in thought and texture: only a writer saturated as Barnes is in the language of Jonson, Marston and Middleton (he has taken time out from his own career to edit *The Alchemist, The Devil is an Ass* and *Antonio and Mellida* for contemporary audiences) could have produced the brilliant, thorny, fantastic speech of Carlos' courtiers, the two great verse tirades the stammering king speaks in the lucid aftermath of epilepsy. But more than that, it penetrates to the heart of the Jacobean melancholy which is also our own: the discovery that 'the new philosophy casts all in doubt', that the universe is absurd and all the comforting beliefs in which we were reared are frantic constructs to mask this intolerable truth. (pp. 18-19)

The Bewitched is no more a play about monarchy than *The*

Ruling Class was a play about aristocracy. What makes it bitingly relevant to Britain in the 1970s is the scathing examination of the belief that any category of people, royal or not, is 'special': peculiarly-fitted to govern empires, occupy positions of privilege, command more wealth than others. . . . The most striking difference between the British playwrights of the Sixties and their predecessors of the Osborne generation is that they, the neo-Elizabethans, saw themselves as forerunners of a meritocratic revolution, an opening by universal education of all careers to the talents, which would create a new aristocracy of mind, rather than birth or inherited wealth. Peter Barnes and his contemporaries challenge that definition of equality, satirising with grim Jacobean wit the society meritocracy has built. . . . 'Bewitchment's the cause of our present ills', explains Father Froylan, the royal confessor, to Carlos 'it holds us in dream.' Spain's dream, as Peter Barnes has written it, is our nightmare, pinned down and crystallised. It would be pleasant to think that his mocking, despairing laughter might still wake us. (p. 19)

> *Ronald Bryden, in* Plays and Players (©
> *copyright Ronald Bryden 1974), May, 1974.*

Few plays demonstrate more cogently the shortness of the distance between comedy and tragedy than Peter Barnes's *The Bewitched*. . . . Deeply sensitive to the injustices, cruelties, and absurdity of all hitherto practiced social and political systems, [Barnes] turns his pain into laughter—a laughter that borrows heavily from the most mundane and lowly sources yet grows in dignity and stature as we realize how humane its roots are, and how formidable the sacred cows it has the courage to attack.

The Bewitched deals with Carlos II of Spain, the last of his dynasty, whose death in 1700 plunged Europe into the terrible War of the Spanish Succession. An epileptic, generally sickly, mentally deficient ruler—the product of ghastly inbreeding—whose desperate and vain efforts to beget an heir, preposterously abetted by the entire court, turn the grandiose Spanish empire topsy-turvy, is the proper linchpin for Barnes's anarchist comedy. For Barnes is indeed an anarchist in the best sense: one who execrates all power because he is not afraid to draw the full rather than, as most of us do, the partial consequences of the proposition that all power corrupts. His play is written in rage and despair at royalty, the nobility, the clergy, the army, the police, but also at the most ordinary, simple people, who need only to come into any sort of power to become a public menace. Yet Barnes's sadness and anger are almost always couched in jest—raw and low-down vaudeville or subtly biting irony—and never assume a high moral tone.

The chief device is discrepancy. First, between kinds of humor. . . . A deeper discrepancy lies in the language itself: partly modern, partly archaic, and studded with peculiar apocopes, metatheses, and just plain bad grammar to create a sense of ludicrousness or unease. But the supreme discrepancy is between the pomp and majesty of the trappings of empire and the sardonic or even scatological way in which they are treated; between the horrors of superstition, religious intolerance, mass torture and executions, social exploitation and political assassinations, and the jeeringly absurdist tone Barnes sedulously adheres to. . . .

[This] long play [is] bursting with precise historical documentation that flows easefully into absurdist humor. [The] great lesson of *The Bewitched* is that historical grandeur and terror are ultimately indistinguishable from farce, just as farce has finally to be paid for with high tragedy. What makes the play particularly fine, though, is that its absurdism remains contained and believable, and that the author never loses his sympathy for such basically dreary characters. . . .

Despite venial flaws, *The Bewitched* is the most substantial, skillful, relevant, wise, and necessary play I have seen in years, and fully as funny as it is painful.

> *John Simon, "London Diary VI: The Best,"*
> in New York Magazine (© 1974 by NYM
> Corp.; reprinted by permission of New York
> Magazine *and John Simon), September 2,*
> *1974, p. 56.*

The title [of *The Bewitched*] is puzzling, since though witchcraft, popular hunger for the irrational, and exorcism are introduced as topical elements in the play, they constitute only a bit of trimming. The scene is early eighteenth-century Spain, the story that of assorted efforts to stimulate the deformed, epileptic king Carlos II into producing an heir—the failure of which, in the distorted world of dynastic politics, led to a major European war, to widespread devastation and immense suffering. We may, if we wish, apply its message to our own times, and reflect ruefully or hysterically, according to temperament, on the inadequacies of men in power; but such reflections amount to no more than a wail of dismay at the fact that rulers, whether they are born great, achieve greatness, or have greatness thrust upon them, remain human beings replete with human weaknesses; and whereas Mr. Barnes' other major play, *The Ruling Class*, achieved in a disjointed way a certain sardonic point, *The Bewitched* seems to me no more than a prolonged—very prolonged . . . wallow in disgust for its own sake. (p. 41)

[There is] many a sadomasochistic jape involving, for example, a pet parrot, cripples, Jews and a busy little dwarf (whom we all, cultured fellows that we are, have been happy to recognize as derived from Velasquez) while the assorted rival factions play out their deadly games. The implication is, of course, that meanwhile the people suffer —as god knows they do; but it would require X-ray eyes to detect in the piece much actual interest in or concern for the people. Shakespeare can—as in the night scene before Agincourt—suffuse a whole play with a feeling for the people; Mr. Barnes, whatever his ostensible moral, is here plainly obsessed with the situation he deplores and in his deployment of diverse theatrical techniques, involving a manufactured language of artificial archaisms, deliberate anachronisms, jokey vaudeville interludes ('I'm here to test your faith'—'Testing, testing, one, two, three'. . .), or a bit of song and dance used for what a more sympathetic critic would I suppose describe as devastating irony, and so on. In the interminable mêlée a number of excellent actors swirl round, like bits of clothes in the royal laundromat. . . . [*The Bewitched* is] a tumultuous bore to those unable to accept its author's chosen approach. (pp. 41-3)

> *J. W. Lambert, in Drama, Autumn, 1974.*

Peter Barnes is an enthusiastic antinaturalist with an admiration for Ben Jonson and a delight in baroque verbiage. In . . . *The Bewitched* . . ., he takes a historical subject—the

decay of Spain under its last Hapsburg monarch, the near-idiot Carlos II—which is fascinating in itself and perhaps even in some way relevant to our own predicament, but effectively smothers it under a vast heap of stylistic feathers. The lesson is not that Barnes strays too far from naturalism, for he does not, in spite of his pastiche language, but that like Shaw he cannot allow audiences to approach the play at any point on their own terms, and constantly shouts down their curiosity with his shrill "I'm telling you.". . .

[This] play strives too hard to be significant; it gives out a feeling of strain, which is, as one might expect, a fairly constant presence in the work of these middle generation writers, men as it were liberated but still remembering their shackles. (p. 66)

> *John Spurling, in Encounter (© 1974-1975*
> *by Encounter Ltd.), January, 1975.*

* * *

BARTH, John 1930-

A prize-winning American novelist, Barth writes elegant and highly inventive intellectual satires on the human condition. *Giles Goat-Boy* **and** *The Sot-Weed Factor* **are his best known works. (See also** *Contemporary Authors,* **Vols. 1-4, rev. ed.)**

If we consider one of Barth's most frequent themes . . ., the ambiguity of love, I think that we find not only great consistency in his thinking, but also an increasing tendency to affirm the possibility of love. Barth's tenuous, limited affirmation of love is most clearly defined in the "Menelaiad," but it is an important motif in all the recent short fiction in which he increasingly identifies the dilemmas of lovers with those of artists. Apparently that kind of love which represents a creative attempt to be free from the prison of the self has become for him at least as noble an affirmation as is the artist's comparable attempt to transcend his limitations in his art.

For Barth, however, the possibility of love is never confused with inevitability or necessity. The qualifications with which he has surrounded all discussion of love are almost overwhelming and seem to have provided him with a buttress against the oversimplifications of his own generation. For although Auden has insisted that the distinctive contribution of modern writers has been to explore love in all its complex manifestations and recent publishing history seems determined to prove his truth with a vengeance, one must insist that the special limitation of our age—if not of its most consummate artists—has been its refusal to accept as valid any view of love less laudatory than, say, something like that found in "Dover Beach." Especially during the period when Barth was writing novels, love was popularly supposed to be personally redemptive, if not a universal spiritual panacea. Even in the most absurd of worlds, the argument ran, love could establish something of value, as in Arnold's poem, some refuge against the otherwise universal chaos.

In contrast, Barth has regarded love from the beginning as the very essence of the absurd. Like many comic artists Barth uses man's sexual imbroglios to reveal his essential silliness, but he goes beyond many writers in his insistence that there is not necessarily any sense in any kind of love, not only that which is basely sexual. Barth never denies that love exists, nor does he deny its power; he just consistently denies that it has any necessary meaning and often unfashionably insists on showing its powers to be anything but redemptive. [Characters] are strewn throughout Barth's fiction for whom the experience of love has been both incomprehensible and frightening—at times even disastrous. (pp. 290-91)

What makes Menelaus the proper hero of an "epic" seems to be his commitment, tenuous as it is, to [the] possibility of love. His story ["Menelaiad" in the collection, *Lost in the Funhouse*] represents, therefore, something of a turning point in Barth's fiction. The same affirmation characterizes not only the "Anonymiad," which follows it in *Lost in the Funhouse*, but also the three "epics" which constitute *Chimera*. In the "Bellerophoniad" Barth speaks explicitly of the "ironically qualified fulfillment" of both Menelaus and Perseus in their search for immortality *especially* in the transformation of each into his own voice or life-story. That key word, *especially*, makes it probable that fulfillment might take other forms, too. In each case it is inextricably involved with (if not simply resolved by) the affirmation of the possibility of love.

Barth's emerging position is offered more openly in the closing section of the "Dunyazadiad." Here the narrator approves of Shah Zaman's plea that Dunyazad love him *as if* it might work, implying that pretense, even fiction, is appropriate in a world in which nothing lasts forever, in which not even the conventions of fiction pretend that lovers can live happily ever after. The Arabic tale traditionally concludes that things go well only until the inevitable appearance of "The Destroyer of Delights." Barth's heroes in these recent novellas are those who accept the inevitability of such destruction, who commit themselves to love, not as an absolute value but as a value more precious for its very fragility. To claim the world has "neither joy, nor love, nor light" seems as silly as to trust too completely in the faithfulness of lovers. Instead, as Todd Andrews first insisted [in Barth's early novel, *The End of the Road*], values (like love) less than absolute can be lived by. Barth's recent fiction seems to be expanding on Todd's wisdom, his own position affirming the possibility of love—absurd though that may be. "To be joyous in the full acceptance" of the inevitability of loss, Barth concludes the "Dunyazadiad," "is to possess a treasure." (pp. 305-06)

Harold Farwell, "John Barth's Tenuous Affirmation: 'The Absurd, Unending Possibility of Love'," in The Georgia Review *(copyright, 1974, by the University of Georgia), Summer, 1974, pp. 290-306.*

The mythic Chimera was a divine joke, a trinitarian monster cobbled together out of a lion's head, a goat's body and a serpent's tail. Its three-in-one aspect suffices *Chimera*'s blurb-writer: 'John Barth's new novel bears its name because it, too, is a single whole composed of three very different parts.' A bit pedestrianly viewed, that's so: the task Barth's about is a retelling of the stories of Scheherazade, Perseus and Bellerophon. Like Robert Graves (always), Barth is possessed of the inside story. And in his delightful versions Scheherazade and her sister Dunyazade turn out to be a couple of lesbian women's libbers called Sherry and Doony, and the mythic heroes are well into the male menopause, with phalluses flunking, bellies sagging (too much ouzo and not enough heroic tasks), and the dissertation

writers' questionnaires naggingly bulking their fan mail. Even at this level Barth is a dazzlingly witty putter-back of the mock into mock-heroic.

But that's not all: the Chimera was also a creature of dizzying deceptiveness—now you saw it, now you didn't— so *chimera* equals 'fanciful conception', a bag of tricks. As Barth demonstrates in overgoing Graves's versions of the Bellerophon story (which he quotes), his inside story is usually at least the inside story of the inside story: expectably enough from a narrator who insists the *Thousand and One Nights* isn't the story of Scheherazade but the story of the story of her stories. *Chimera* isn't only a shatteringly clever and scurrilous rewrite of some classic fictions, it's also the trickiest, most shimmeringly elusive of reflections on the art and artificialities of the novel. The least straightforward of the three pieces, *Bellerophoniad* (a title that makes you utter the word 'phoney' while daring you to turn it as a charge against its matter), is smartest of all at challenging any cosy assumptions about writer-novel-reader or fiction-reality relations that errant readers might foolishly bring to this book. To every helix, though, there's always another twist. In *Bellerophoniad*, a revolutionary novelist reapplies for the renewal of his bursary for continuing his revolutionary novel, *Notes*. It will dispense with particularities of character, plot, content and meaning, having 'no content except its own form, no subject but its own processes'. At its navel, there'll be 'a single anecdote, a perfect model of text-within-the-text, a microcosm or paradigm of the work as a whole'. This 'quintessential fiction', advertised thus by *Bellerophoniad*, is to be titled—what else?— *Bellerophoniad*. The financial pleas hit stony ground. And what started by looking like, what *is*, straight Robbe-Grillet, begins to suggest, at least at this turn of its screw, self-parody. But then, you never know quite where you are with Chimeras. (p. 90)

Valentine Cunningham, in New Statesman *(© 1974 The Statesman & Nation Publishing Co. Ltd.), July 19, 1974.*

There is nothing particularly ignoble in a novelist being self-conscious about his craft, but when he imposes these trifling concerns upon the poor reader it becomes a matter of public concern. Mr Barth . . . has chosen to do just that in *Chimera*, a tripartite beast, a novel within a novel within something else on the Chinese principle that a great many boxes are better than a hat. It begins well enough, with a sort of highbrow camp as Barth narrates the narrations of Dunyazade narrating the narrations of Scheherazade (known as Sherry to her handmaidens) to Shahryar. But after that I got them all mixed up, mere pips, as Omar Khayyam might say, squeaking in the bowl of night. These particular Orientals come, in fact, from some pot-pourri known as the *Thousand And One Nights* which Mr Barth thinks of some cross-cultural importance and of which he proceeds to make very heavy weather indeed. . . .

It is all an intolerable mish-mash, and should have remained in the misty land of faery, were it not for people like Mr Barth who have an intolerable urge for systems and meanings. The more unintelligent reviewers will no doubt be taken in by the novel's fanciful contemporaneity, and will talk about its "stark presentment of the boundaries of fiction," "medieval simplicity" and such like, and this may well be Barth's intention: there is no doubt that perspectives appear and disappear as if by magic, and that the prose has its glancings and twinklings as it continually evades the issue (whatever the issue may be). But Barth is trying to spin gold out of the pointless questions which pursue formalists and aestheticians, and he does not realise that the pointlessness becomes all the plainer in a fictional guise.

The offence is compounded by Barth's incursions into classical mythology, in the second and third sections of the novel, which are entitled 'Perseid' and 'Bellerophoniad'. When an American writer touches upon such matters I feel a *frisson* on behalf of centuries of classical scholarship; Americans, being a poorly educated race, take the Greek myths far too seriously and become either pompous or heavily jocular about them. Professor Barth has naturally gone for the jocular 'angle', and has recounted the unutterably boring mythic lives of Perseus and Bellerophon in a suburban demotic that relives the boredom of the original while increasing its capacity to irritate. In the beginning there is darkness, as Perseus recounts his chequered career to Calyx, who knows the stories already and is thus in the same unfortunate position as the reader. . . .

Barth becomes even more self-conscious than the conventional experimental novelist and turns his fables into an elaborate apologia for his own apparently miserable and wasted life. At one point he elevates the novelist (i.e. Barth) into a vatic role, and at the next he belabours himself with a dutiful and tedious modesty. Once you mix this sort of thing with a Bellerophon of a more than baroque complexity—he is preparing a career based upon a reading of the preceding 'Perseid,' setting out a plan for the story he is in fact already telling etcetera—you have a narrative that will not stay still under the reader's gaze. But this complexity is so much a matter of the technical surface of the prose that it takes only a conscious effort of the mind to see through it and, underneath, to find lurking that most fabulous and archaic of mythical beasts, the labyrinth that goes in all directions at once and leads nowhere at all. (p. 86)

> *Peter Ackroyd, in* The Spectator *(© 1974 by* The Spectator*; reprinted by permission of* The Spectator*), July 20, 1974.*

Though the name of John Barth is usually associated with length, he has more recently moved toward works of short-story or novella size, works as noteworthy for their compression as his earlier ones were for their expansiveness. One of the finest of these newer fictions is the last story in *Lost in the Funhouse*, "Anonymiad." This 44-page tale is at once a parodic epic, a pastoral romance, a history of literature, and a treatise on aesthetics. More specifically, it is the autobiography of an anonymous Mycenaen minstrel, anonymous because he has forgotten his name. Marooned alone on an Aegean isle for seven years, the minstrel has chronicled his love for the milkmaid Merope and his love for literature. (p. 361)

Indeed, the invention of writing and literature lies at the heart of the "Anonymiad," as Barth himself has pointed out [in an interview with Joe David Bellamy, *Writer's Yearbook*, 1972]: "I love the idea that he invents fiction and he invents publishing, all on that island. In the obvious way, each one of us *does* invent the art. We find that we're writing poetry and fiction and then we look around to see

who else has done that. But in a way we started it." The minstrel is the archetypal author; he not only invents literature—he exhausts it. (p. 363)

> *D. Allan Jones, "John Barth's 'Anonymiad'," in* Studies in Short Fiction *(copyright 1974 by Newberry College), Fall, 1974, pp. 361-66.*

For John Barth the creative act is both the result and the expression of a radical philosophical freedom. Like his heroes he finds fulfillment in the discovery of new worlds. For him "reality is a drag," a "nice place to visit but you wouldn't want to live there". . . . And his use of "yarns," "elaborate lies" . . . and "flabbergasting plots" . . . is evidence enough that he feels free to take leave of reality. But the freedom one finds in the Barthian world of farcical adventure has two sides, one a blessing, the other a curse, for while it makes possible the search for the new and fantastic, it implies a rejection of the absolute validity of the old. Indeed, the explorative impulse is instigated by an emotional conviction of the absolute untenability of existence: "Who sets me goals to turn my back on" asks Burlingame in *The Sot-Weed Factor*, and then adds, "had I a home I'd likely leave it; a family alive or dead I'd likely scorn it, and wander a stranger in alien towns."

Neither the novelist nor the hero is satisfied with reality. Both, like Don Quixote, sally forth in quest of adventure motivated by the will to alter reality or to imagine alternatives to it. . . . Creating the distance which separates the novelist's dreams from materiality is a desire, the nature of which precludes the possibility of any satisfaction. Barth, of course, accepts with wry amusement the distance between willing-to-be and believing-that-one-already-is and uses it to generate a literature of exhaustion. (pp. 19-20)

> *Edgar A. Dryden, in* Individual and Community: Variations on a Theme in American Fiction, *edited by Kenneth H. Baldwin and David K. Kirby (reprinted by permission of the Publisher; copyright 1975 by Duke University Press, Durham, North Carolina), Duke University Press, 1975.*

*   *   *

BARTHELME, Donald   1931-

Barthelme, a short story writer and novelist, writes witty, imaginative, and brilliant parodies. (See also *Contemporary Authors*, Vols. 21-22.)

[Barthelme's] first national publication . . ., a review of the *39th Annual of Advertising and Editorial Art Design* [appeared in] *Harper's* in October 1961. Looking over the year's best ads, he noted that many "give not so much as a clue to what is being advertised." The award-winning spreads were nothing but form, with content "typically nowhere in sight." But Barthelme knew they were making millions, striking to the core of a new American sensibility, and so it is not surprising that when his own short stories began to appear the same year, their theme and technique followed the same direction.

His basic concern was with the forms of language, even the sounds of words, and he practiced clever disruptions to make people see what was really happening before their eyes and ears. Many stories played with puns, while others were suggestively disconcerting, but in all cases readers were forced to think deeper of the "poppycock" they were accustomed to hear. (p. 435)

With an absolute sense of the shape of sentences and even words, Barthelme found that he could shock readers into a new awareness of the world. For this subject *Snow White* (1967) is his thematic tour de force. The foremost theme of the book is words. "Oh I wish there were some words in the world that were not the words I always hear!" Snow White laments, but she hears only the same old ones, because "I have not been able to imagine anything better." She needs, of course, her prince, but her world is essentially "princeless." It prizes, instead, "equanimity," for anything else would be "bad for business." Its language, we learn, is ninety-nine percent "blanketing," the part of language which "fills in" between the other parts. "'That part,'" we are told, "'the "filling" you might say, of which the expression "you might say" is a good example, is to me the most interesting part'." Of particular importance are "'those aspects of language that may be seen as a model of the trash phenomenon','" aspects which are largely the substance of *Snow White*. Hers is a world of "dreck," of unimaginative life where no one responds to her "hair initiative" because "Americans will not or cannot see themselves as princely."

In a world of one hundred percent trash, its imagination dead and its language simply "blanketing," how does one break through all the blanketing, trash, and *dreck* to a happier reality one hopes would remain beneath? Barthelme's form provides the answer, and in several self-consciously experimental stories written after *Snow White* he plans an epistemological strategy to get at the heart of things. "Robert Kennedy Saved From Drowning," his most famous story, demonstrates the problem. It is an attempt to understand one of the most "blanketed" and obscured events in our recent history, the substance and appeal of the most enigmatic of politicians, and Barthelme's form expresses the near impossibility of the task. . . . "Robert Kennedy Saved From Drowning" stands, intentionally, as a formalistic example of a world of *dreck*. The random juxtaposition of media accounts, documentaries, and personal reports—the raw materials of our own history—add up to nothing conclusive; they are the spatial reality of our age, but a new math is needed to interpret their meaning.

Knowing the world is, for Barthelme, ultimately an achievement of the imagination. His stories are formed on one level by the clever manipulation of words and phrases, and on another by the introduction of startling conceptions, both of which are then worked out in a deft parody of conventional structures. . . . Barthelme's vignettes are not simply arguments in the dialectics of form, but are rather imaginative volcanoes, revitalizing our language, our conceptions, and our experience itself. (pp. 435-38)

Jerome Klinkowitz, in Partisan Review *(copyright © 1973 by Partisan Review, Inc.), Vol. XL, No. 3, 1973.*

Sadness demands not only attention but participation for Barthelme seems to hold Borges's view that literature is a reciprocal process to which the reader contributes by extending and interpreting the suggestions which the writer provides. He might even accept Borges's belief that the reader should not only enter into a dialogue with the writer but that he should identify with him so closely that he almost *becomes* the writer. At any rate it is clear that Barthelme's densely textured stories have more in common with those of Borges than they do with those of Kafka (to whom he has been compared by over-enthusiastic American critics). Admittedly Barthelme shares Kafka's ghoulish 'twilight of humour' (as Max Brod called it) but he lacks that unique ability to express gossamer-subtle imaginative insights in terms at once concrete and limpid. Indeed, some of these stories are so opaque (like some of Borges's) that their significance escapes me altogether. And various pretentious and obtrusive stylistic devices only add to the obscurity.

However, there is enough in *Sadness* to convince the most sceptical that Barthelme has considerable talent. *Subpoena*, for example, is only four pages long yet it manages to encapsulate a complete horrific vision of what the future may hold in store for us. . . . Other stories satirise Hollywood's penchant for including everything but the truth in its epic films, cast a quizzical eye over the updated temptations of St Anthony and take well aimed smacks at psychiatry and the daily grind of family life.

Piers Brendon, "Short Story: Tradition and Experiment," in Books and Bookmen *(© copyright Piers Brendon 1974), February, 1974, p. 59.*

Barthelme is not a dark and obsessed writer. Moreover, he may well be discovering new fictional modes in the very act of presiding over the death of a genre. "The Indian Uprising" carries very far the disintegration of fiction into its raw materials, and may dramatize human consciousness *in extremis*; and dramatize too our capacity to screen ourselves from surrounding violence. The real (?) torturing of real (?) prisoners may seem but the black humor of a film. Or are these glimpses of real lovers "carrying on" in a collapsing world? Is violence fun? Yet I detect in Barthelme less despair over the condition of things (entropy, violence, the increasing per capita production of trash, the mind overwhelmed by phenomena) than bewilderment over the writer's plight—the writer inheriting exhausted language and compelled to shout louder and louder, to escalate literary outrage, in order to gain attention. Or is the escalation demanded by reality? (pp. 27-8)

Barthelme then, unlike Beckett, is on the whole a cheerful historian of collapse. *Snow White*, which is a book about language, is a charming intellectual game: seductive, always comic. "Oh I wish there were some words in the world that were not the words I always hear!" So Snow White, who would like to escape the *trin-trin quotidien*. As in *Alice in Wonderland* there is the fun of people unaware they have been caught off guard, and uttering calm banalities or even wise insights from ludicrous dark places: George typing under Amelia's skirt, and so compelled to automatic writing because he can't see to think. (p. 28)

Barthelme satirizes, with very slight exaggeration, the weird inappropriateness of most speech. "My nourishment is refined from the ongoing circus of the mind in motion. Give me the odd linguistic trip, stutter and fall, and I will be content." Joyce might have added these words to Oxen of the Sun: "It's that we want to be on the leading edge of this trash phenomenon, the everted sphere of the future, and that's why we pay particular attention, too, to those aspects of language that may be seen as a model of the trash phenomenon." Does Barthelme convey . . . new youthful modes of consciousness, rather than merely satirize the old? I am not sure, though one of the narrator's statements would support this: "We like books that have a lot of *dreck* in them, matter which presents itself as not wholly relevant (or indeed, at all relevant) but which, carefully attended to, can supply a 'sense' of what is going on."

The book's rhetorical *trouvaille* is to have given Snow White and her companions French voices, the voices of run-of-the-mill French intellectuals in fact. This is what gives freshness to a book that might, in places, appear very derivative. (There is an entirely conscious recreation of the orator of *The Chairs*. The watching narrator's monotone commentaries as from *Marienbad* or a Godard film, the banalities uttered in the midst of catastrophe, as in Beckett [here, parents living in a parking place since 1936, and rooted to the soil], the parodies of Robbe-Grillet tedium, the enigmatic capitalized headlines as in Godard, with even a Maoist reference—all this is quite openly allusive, pleasures for the intellectual.) The book is drenched in French idiom: a classifying language and recapitulative style down to the smallest components of syntax: "It does not ennoble you, the fever." "Something suggests to me that it is a bad scene, this drink you proffer." "And you others there, lounging about. . . ." "That will be amusing, writing out the charges.". . . Snow White herself has a distinctly French mentality. She effortlessly, glibly measures experience and pours out shapely sentences, the banal or literary formulae that substitute for real thought.

Behind the fun are serious matters: epistemological nightmare and the collapse of language, the widening separation of words and experience, the phenomenological distrust of value: all very French. (pp. 29-30)

Snow White is a remarkably entertaining *performance*. Much of its energy, which almost never flags, derives from rapid changes of context, comic scene, linguistic mode. Yet controlling all these is an authorial voice as distinct as any in contemporary fiction. In diction, in pace and pause and the larger ordonnance of syntax, Barthelme's style really captures movements of thought. It is, even when parodying "sludge" and "stuffing", an exceptionally tight style. Barthelme may have taken the best from the French intellectual while satirizing his glibness. (pp. 30-1)

> *Albert J. Guerard, in* TriQuarterly 30 *(© 1974 by Northwestern University Press), Spring, 1974.*

Donald Barthelme has published . . . dazzling collections of short stories . . . and a remarkably inventive and tightly knit novel, *Snow White* (which is also an excellent woman's liberation tract). Yet a surprising number of readers still speak slightingly of him. They lump him with John Barth (did you ever finish *Giles Goat-Boy*?), Thomas Pynchon (did you ever start *Gravity's Rainbow*?) and others of that ilk, experimental writers with an abundance of technical machinery and almost nothing of interest to express, writers with such a disparity between form and content that their novels resemble devices assembled by Rube Goldberg.

But Barthelme *has* some things to say—and he says them briefly, moreover. Like most sensible people, he has urgent

problems, personal, political, and philosophical. He has thought and read and brooded about them, as we all wish we had time to do. He has approached them from many angles, with the aid of many disciplines, and he has generalized them so that they are recognizably ours. And he treats his readers and fellow brooders as equals, granting us intelligence, sensitivity, knowledge, and a sense of humor. . . .

Most [political] satires have a half-life of perhaps six months; after that they tend to be even less interesting than the men and events they satirize. But Barthelme's approach [in *Guilty Pleasures*] is so imaginative, his sense of outrage is focused so clearly on the essential causes of aggravation, that without being vague or generalized [his] satires can serve as all-purpose and timeless political comment.

> *J. D. O'Hara, "Parodies Regained," in* Book World—The Washington Post *(© The Washington Post), November 3, 1974, p. 3.*

By now Barthelme's fictional landscape is familiar: a plot of undifferentiated clutter, hedged about with manicured non sequiturs. Though [*Guilty Pleasures* is] billed as nonfiction, this collage of pieces reads suspiciously like his past story collections—fragmented, humming with vaguely malevolent absurdities. This book's innocent pleasures stem from seeing how far the author can jump. The *Consumer Bulletin Annual*, for instance, hardly seems a bouncy platform for whimsy. Yet Barthelme somersaults from it into the tale of a hapless soul whose purchases consistently turn out to be substandard. "Consider the case of the bedside clock. 'Check for loudness of tick,' the *Annual* said. I checked. It ticked. Tick seemed decorous. Once installed in home, it boomed like a B-58."

Barthelme turns a parodist's ear to several deserving sources of modern noise. A mock scenario for a film in the manner of Antonioni blurs the line between significant ennui and utter vacuity: "Shot of nail kegs at construction site. Camera peers into keg, counts nails." A news story of four Bunnies, fired from the New York Playboy Club for losing their "Bunny image," provokes a case history: "Bitsy S., an attractive white female of 28, was admitted to Bellevue Hospital complaining that she could not find, physically locate, her own body."

In draping his motley over perishable structures, the satirist risks that they will some day collapse, taking his work down with them. A number of pieces in *Guilty Pleasures* are predicated on Richard Nixon, and their bite has already become gummy. One of the book's funnier stories (*An Hesitation on the Bank of the Delaware*) overcomes this loss through shameless slapstick. George Washington postpones his rowboat crossing until hearing whether Congress will continue to finance his personal extravagances. Speaking in an age when the printed *s* looked like an *f*, an aide informs the general that demands for his horse's accommodations have been rejected: "Both the Houfe Appropriation Committee and the Horfe Appropriation Committee bounced it back." (pp. 111-12)

> Time *(reprinted by permission from* Time, The Weekly Newsmagazine; *copyright Time Inc.), November 11, 1974.*

At a recent dinner party an elderly, much-decorated writer smiled benignly on the bearded man to whom he had just been introduced. "And what do *you* do, Mr. Barthelme?" The instantaneous reply: "I repair typewriters." A mad jest, perhaps rehearsed, yet not inaccurate. Like the Wright brothers, who repaired bicycles, the typewriter repairman has a marvelous invention, the Distant Early Warning Cliché Detector with exclusive Recycling Attachment, which he wheels out into the late afternoon of America. Bring me your tired words, your poor phrases, your huddled sentences yearning to breathe free.

In the late afternoon the light falls sideways on drowsy people and language, heightening colors to fever flush, deepening shadows, pockmarks, fissures; it is an uneasy time of day. "We are adrift in a tense and joyless world that is falling apart at an accelerated rate," says one of Barthelme's narrators. He's right; what to do? The typewriter repairman's machine sends up puffs of colored smoke, warnings against the unreliable blue of the sky. And sometimes a pink party balloon, rising through the smog. "Ennui is the absence of games," says another, ". . . the modern world at its most vulnerable." What Barthelme does in his stories is to pick up the pieces, whatever has fallen apart, polish them and fit them together into a game. Thus armed by the restoration of mystery to what had been debased, we are less vulnerable than before. (pp. 117, 120)

"Guilty Pleasures," a collection of parodies, satires and fables, is the slightest and most accessible of Barthelme's books. It is billed as "nonfiction"—surely a euphemism for inventive pieces that lack the complexity of his more serious work. Some of his targets are broad: Ed Sullivan, the Cosmopolitan Girl, verbs favored by newsmagazines. It's hard to miss such targets, but Barthelme comes on like Robin Hood: his shafts split whatever arrows he finds standing in the bull's-eye. He uses many styles: deadpan, fanciful, poetical, epistolary, metaphysical, reportorial, even surreal collages. It's not surprising that he has come up with the best parody of the White House transcripts:

P: I've never been afraid to be unintelligible . . .
H: Honesty is the best inaudible. Always.

And it doesn't matter that some of the humor is pretty low —George Washington speaks in eighteenth-century typography: "A good bunch of boys, the Fecret Fervice"—because several of these pieces show Barthelme at his best and most joyous, particularly the last one, a demonstration that we cannot through words approach Nothing. The interfering plenitude of life continually nudges us away from an excuse for stopping. The typewriter repairman keeps us in working order still. (p. 120)

Peter S. Prescott, "The Repairman," in Newsweek *(copyright 1974 by Newsweek, Inc.; all rights reserved; reprinted by permission), November 25, 1974, pp. 117, 120.*

Parody is, I suspect, like anchovies: if you like it at all, you love it; if you don't, you detest it. Members of the first category are invited to wallow ecstatically in the first part of *Guilty Pleasures*, a collection of pieces previously published in *The New Yorker* and other magazines. Barthelme has a splendid ear, and at his best he is definitely first rate. "The Angry Young Men," for example, has lines like: "It has been my observation, and I'm not alone in this, other people have made the same observation, a blind man could see it, that the young people today are doing a bloody great

lot of *cooking together before marriage*." And, although it doesn't fulfill the condition of great parody—that it have a worthwhile target—I took an especially wicked pleasure in Barthelme's parody of That Cosmopolitan Girl: "Well, I paid [the cab fare] cheerfully, because I have this magazine I read that teaches me how to be *natural* and *healthy* and *resilient*, but when we got out of the cab he *loaded* this *immense* steamer trunk on my back." The political satire in the middle of the book, I found pretty uncongenial . . .; but the funny parts of *Guilty Pleasures* tip the scales. (p. 357)

Linda Bridges, in National Review *(© National Review, Inc., 1975; 150 East 35th St., New York, N.Y. 10016), March 28, 1975.*

There is no guilt [in "Guilty Pleasures"] for the delighted reader, unless the deliciously pampered guilt of having enjoyed lighthearted pleasures. If anything, Barthelme tickles us with the feeling of our own decent simplicity in these for the most part unprofound pieces of parody, political satire, and fable. This collection is on the whole not Barthelme at his exquisite and concentrated best, but one catches the frail verbal music and not quite melancholy wit of the wise child. (p. liv)

Virginia Quarterly Review *(copyright 1975, by the* Virginia Quarterly Review, *The University of Virginia), Vol. 51, No. 2 (Spring, 1975).*

What does a writer do when he thinks that language no longer communicates effectively, that words have lost their power to move us, that reality is no longer capable of sustaining mythic devices, that telling "stories" of any kind is suspect? Perhaps the most successful recent reply to these questions can be found in Donald Barthelme's *Snow White*, a work which seeks to exploit the decay of language and literature. Like so many other works of art in this century, *Snow White* has as its "subject matter" art itself. It is not the "real world" which it seeks to represent, but the status of art; and as with any significant work of art, we can learn something about ourselves if we respond to it. *Snow White* can, therefore, best be termed a "self-reflexive" work in that even as it is being created, it seeks to examine its own condition. Rooted deeply in a fundamental distrust of most of the conventional principles of fiction, the book also shows an understanding of Wittgenstein's famous distinction between what can be told and what can be shown. Not a description or theory of the conditions and limitations of language and literature, *Snow White* portrays these features in its very fabric. (p. 19)

Although 180 pages in length, *Snow White* is not so much a novel as a sustained collection of fragments, organized loosely around the Snow White fairy tale in what resembles a "collage" method. Barthelme's rendition of the myth is, of course, peculiarly modern. . . . Thus, like Joyce in *Ulysses*, and like a significant number of recent writers, Barthelme has turned to a familiar myth (rather than to "reality") to provide a basic framework for his tale, although the "material" which he places into the framework is drawn from a wide range of literary and cultural sources.

Despite its mythic framework, *Snow White* is likely to leave an initial impression of shapelessness on the reader. . . . Often Barthelme incorporates into his work the sorts of events, names, fads, and data which can be found in the daily newspaper. Even more often, however, these fragments are drawn from cliches of learning—hackneyed opinions dressed up in even more hackneyed styles. . . . Barthelme's use of the heterogeneous mixture of learning and verbal trash does not contribute to any verisimilar design but communicates a sense of what it is like to be alive at a given moment.

If we examine the structure of *Snow White* more closely, we find that, unlike Joyce in *Ulysses*, Barthelme's mythic perspective is prevented from being seriously mythic to any extent. The big problem for Barthelme—as for any writer today who wishes to rely on myth in one way or another—is a self-consciousness about myth that has reached such paralyzing proportions that most contemporary use of myth is overtly self-conscious and is employed primarily for comic purposes. We find exactly this sense of a writer manipulating myth for his own comic or parodic purposes in *Snow White*. Indeed, in many respects the book seems to be deliberately mocking Joyce's painstaking efforts at creating mythic parallels, suggesting perhaps that the condition of both language and reality make such devices unavailable to the modern writer. (pp. 20-1)

Since for Barthelme the changes in modern society make the holding of any mythic center impossible, we find that the mythic parallels in *Snow White* follow only up to certain points, and then find appropriate alterations. The characters openly defy their traditional roles and undercut nearly all our expectations about them.

Like every other literary device in the book, the characters themselves are parodies of their archetypes, uniformly flat and almost comic-bookish in nature. Any sense of their actual identities is minimal and the whole realistic notion of developing a history or background for them is ignored. The book is almost devoid of the sort of details usually provided by novelists to help "realize" the action in their stories. (p. 24)

What does manage to emerge from the blurred personalities of the dwarfs is that they are literally made up out of our society's stock provisions of psychological afflictions, jealousies, introspections, and clichéd opinions. On the other hand, they are obviously grotesquely unsuited for the un-selfconscious, selfless service required of them in the myth. (p. 28)

[Our] expectations, built by previous encounters with literature, are destined to be left unsatisfied. If we are, like Snow White, disappointed with this prospect, we have overestimated language (since it can no longer communicate effectively) and reality (since it no longer produces the kinds of heroes, logical progressions, and predictable feelings which are the stuff of the traditional novel).

If we turn now to the central question of the role of language in Barthelme's book, we find that, more than anything else, the book seems to be "about" the condition of language and the possibilities which exist today for a writer to communicate something meaningful to his readers. (p. 27)

Like Nabokov, for example, Barthelme takes special delight in poking fun at the Freudians. (p. 28)

[The] most pervasive way in which Barthelme demonstrates the bankruptcy of language and literary traditions is the more familiar approach of parodying well-known styles

and methods. Like the "Oxen of the Sun" section of *Ulysses*, *Snow White* is created out of a variety of narrative styles traceable to specific literary sources; in addition, allusions to these works, some direct and others veiled, are everywhere and serve to reinforce the reflexive nature of the work. Often the short sections of the book are created from a hodge-podge of styles, modulating rapidly between specific literary parodies (Stendhal, Rimbaud, Shakespeare, Lorenz Hart, Burroughs), current slang, academic cliché, and advertising jargon. The style, whatever its source, is usually wholly inappropriate to the subject at hand: an eloquent sermon is delivered against "buffalo music," a learned commentary is presented on "The Horsewife in Modern Society.". . .

Snow White is literally created out of the trashy, too-familiar words we have around us every day. . . . Barthelme's book attempts to create new art out of these same words and in the process it exploits the very nature of the debased condition into which language and story-telling have fallen. Steadily it places before us the questions of what resources are left to language, what power to words, images, and stories to move us. (p. 31)

> Larry McCaffery, "Barthelme's 'Snow White': The Aesthetics of Trash," in Critique: Studies in Modern Fiction *(copyright © James Dean Young 1975), Vol. XVI, No. 3, 1975, pp. 19-32.*

The world of Barthelme's *Snow White* supplies only one character who manages to fulfill both a psychological role and a mythical role. Jane, the wicked stepmother-figure, succeeds because her actions are not vitiated by psychological introspection and self-doubt. . . .

As myth fades into realism and realism into absurdity, the identity of the characters is never firmly maintained. One character can be distinguished from another only through a name. When the name changes, the identity changes. (p. 37)

The reader may imagine that he can distinguish one dwarf from another because each has a separate name and each was born in a different national park. However, the dwarfs have the same lover at the same time, experience the same frustrations, imagine collectively—"we had a fantasy" (109)—and even dream collectively. That each was born in a different national park is not, somehow, so striking as that all were born in some national park. Through random narrative switching from "I" to "we," Barthelme emphasizes a common identity among the dwarfs. When the narrative shifts to "I," the reader is never sure which dwarf is "I." When the narrative is third-person dwarf, one is uncertain who is "watching," for at some point in the book, each of the seven dwarfs is "watched" and described by the "third-person dwarf" (as distinguished from the "third-person omniscient narrator" who is also active in *Snow White*).

The reader is thus thwarted in his attempts to identify the author with any one of the characters or even with the voice that speaks for the collective dwarfs. Although a reader usually finds the third-person narrator a point of view from which to judge a novel, in *Snow White*, the omniscient narrator cannot be trusted. (pp. 37-8)

In this way, not only is the reader discouraged from making

any identification with the characters, but he is also prevented from forming any sort of sympathetic alliance with the narrator. In the "classic encounter between patient and psychoanalyst" ("Florence Green") in *Snow White*, the identity of the patient remains a mystery. The reader cannot maintain the role of analyst because the author does not maintain the role of patient. Aware of the critical observer, he builds through the story an elaborate disguise within which he hides his "true" identity. The witty entertainment becomes "a metaphor of the self armoring itself against the gaze of The Other" (59). The characters of *Snow White* offer not clues to the identity of the narrator, but the reflection on a fictional level of the contradictions which exist on the level of the author-reader relationship.

One can be made to believe in a fairy tale set in a fairy-tale world; one can even be led to accept a fairy tale set in a world that pretends to correspond in some respects with the "real" world. However, if the reader cannot ground his point of view in either setting or characters, or in one world or another, he looks to language to direct him. (p. 38)

In *Snow White*, however, language is not a window, but a series of mirrors, each reflecting one another, all equally "real" objects as mirrors, but offering "unreal" reflections, none of which can be depended on by the reader. The basic style takes a deceptively simple and studiedly innocent subject-verb-object form. Yet a style which is studiedly innocent is ultimately mock-innocent and, therefore, basically devious. The reader can accommodate himself to mock-innocence—if it is consistent. However, Barthelme's language continually slides into other styles and thus into other levels of reality. Every shift from mock-innocent to mock-heroic, to mock-poetic, to mock-patriotic, to mock-mythical, to self-mocking is timed to unbalance the reader. . . .

The basic similarity among the different styles lies in the fact that they are all parodies of themselves; yet no single style provides an underlying tone to which the reader can orient himself. The object most consistently parodied is the reader-analyst himself, the victim of Barthelme's ever-changing but always mocking narrative masks. (p. 39)

In addition to setting elaborate verbal traps for the reader, Barthelme has also manipulated the language so that it explodes into meaninglessness in the act of reading. (p. 40)

Barthelme also exploits the less sudden aspects of reader-deception through language by luring the reader into a verbal forest, then leaving him to find some way out: "*The horsewife!* The chiefest ornament on the golden tree of human suffering" (99). Somehow one senses that, whether or not it means anything, it should because it has the *form* of meaning. On the other hand, its form is that of a cliché, language which is so hackneyed that it means nothing. But then, the sentence is not a cliché, because it is not a commonplace phrase, merely in the form of one. Barthelme as patient is presenting the analyst with a puzzle: is the patient disguising significant symptoms in a banal form, or is he creating the semblance of a new form in order to disguise the banality of his symptoms? If every statement the patient makes is either a cliché in form or a cliché in content, then the question is not "are his statements meaningful?" but "are his statements entertaining?" (p. 41)

The reader . . . can find neither the center of Barthelme's world nor even Barthelme himself. Not only is there no central vocabulary, no central point of view, but the fictive entity of the author himself is inconsistent, perhaps even "unreal," a sort of ghost-like virtuoso reflected from the thousand different mirrors of his language, but ultimately hidden from "the gaze of The Other." (p. 43)

> *Betty Flowers, "Barthelme's 'Snow White':
> The Reader-Patient Relationship," in* Cri-
> tique: Studies in Modern Fiction *(copyright
> © James Dean Young 1975), Vol. XVI, No.
> 3, 1975, pp. 33-43.*

*   *   *

BENNETT, Hal   1936-

Bennett is a Black American novelist. (See also *Contemporary Authors*, Vols. 41-44.)

A Wilderness of Vines was a flawed, awkward, at times ineptly written, but insightful and occasionally provocative work engaged in a speculative effort at historical detection that permitted—encouraged, really—large and often uncontrolled displays of compassion and a kind of frenetic energy. It was more an apprentice fiction, a work-in-progress, than a finished novel, and Bennett himself was a writer in search of a style. With this first effort, however, Bennett did succeed in locating his subject: He began to explore the meanings implicit in his vision. He was on his way to elaborating the American racial trauma into a symbol with universal application in his fiction, to creating a very private—yet accessible and historically illuminating—mythology able to penetrate the root strategies and disabling consequences of two other examples of myth-as-history—race and sex. . . . [It] is still somewhat surprising that his performance in *Lord of Dark Places* has not earned him recognition for what he is: one of the most original and gifted Black satirists to come along since Wallace Thurman of *Infants of the Spring*.

Lord of Dark Places is a fine and in many ways an extraordinary satirical novel, a *tour de force* alive with moral intelligence and a knowing, sensuous awareness of the dark, fluid underside of American experience. It offers as protagonist an outrageous Southern youth whom innumerable histories—racial, sexual, religious, national, familial, *etc.*—have conspired to make a phallic hero and records his inevitable victimization and progress over a doomed and all [too] often absurd landscape into eerie recesses of contemporary ambiguity and neurosis, even into the age's sexual yearning for death. At once blackest comedy, savage indictment, and lyric celebration, a strange, disturbing testament to the powers of resilience and moral suasion, the novel illustrates Auden's dictum that in bad times writers turn to satire, for it carries in its depths something of the weight and meaning, the drive and versatility, the despair and defensive optimism of this particular moment in our cultural life. . . . Whatever is finally said about *Lord of Dark Places*, it marks Bennett's emergence as a writer of seriousness and luminous talent wrestling with the demons Myth and History. His achievement, to borrow a figure from his fiction, is that of the magician/priest able to persuade us against all odds, and in the dead of night, of the human possibility. (pp. 37-8)

Like most first novels, *A Wilderness of Vines* stakes out a claim on a fictional territory. It introduces the important thematic concerns of Bennett's novels: his interest in myth and archetype and their recurrence in patterns of social behavior bordering on the surreal, and the controlling imagery and metaphor of his fiction. As it reveals a great deal about his satirical technique and aspirations, it suggests perhaps even more about his highly idiosyncratic vision: its disorienting, yet finally comforting, shifts between jaundiced social comment and sentimentality. Not successful as a novel, *Vines* is important as a prodigiously ambitious first chapter in a history of the post-Civil War Black American to which Bennett's novels and short stories bear witness.... While Bennett's may seem to be a world of excesses ... what one remembers in this fiction is not the extremity of its position, but the achievements of tone and mood, the unnerving reserve and controlled, endlessly provocative understatement: in a word, the disconcerting detachment that informs the fiction at its best moments and that speaks with eloquence, as well as rage, of things mean and dispiriting. (pp. 39-40)

The setting and to a large extent the subject of *A Wilderness of Vines* is Burnside, Va., a farming community of tobacco plantations "owned by Negroes of high complexion, and worked by Negroes who are darker-skinned, or black".... (p. 40)

The central metaphor of *Vines* is that color in Burnside has attained the status of a religion, with clergy and laity, prescriptions and penalties. Burnside's Blacks are impelled, by a certainty of the damnation inescapably attending Blackness, to engage in abysmally degrading and ludicrous efforts at an exorcism made possible by the logic of self-hatred. The satire's content, though, does not always derive its meaning from the satire's form, and emerging from this technical failure is nothing less than a new eschatology, a new mythology, the unexpected drama of myth countering myth. While this eschatology and mythology do not quite amount to a simple matter of color and moral inversion, they do rehearse, albeit for different purposes, certain abused, and abusive, notions of Black sexuality and soul. (pp. 40-1)

Satire, perhaps more than other novel fictions, depends for its success on stylistic and technical facility. As a purely technical accomplishment, *A Wilderness of Vines* is not a good book. Tonal ambiguities, failure to establish and maintain aesthetic distance, expository details excessively, even redundantly, repeated; disorienting shifts in style between surrealistic exaggeration and naturalistic depiction and, hence, problems in authorial voice all combine to limit the success of the fiction as fiction. One effect of these inconsistencies is the satire parodying itself.... At times, the metaphor of the novel is imposed on plot details rather than emerging from them, and the imagery is too frequently obtrusive and self-consciously portentous, which applies as well to the novel's underscoring of theme. Metaphor and imagery comprise the novel's unquestionable area of success and suggest Bennett's concern and very real talent for exploring technical matters. When metaphor and image are integrated into the texture of the novel's experience, they work, and dazzlingly. (pp. 45-6)

What Bennett gives us here is the stuff of racial stereotype at that point where stereotype is transformed into archetype. Bennett is saying what we all know but invariably prefer not to face: that a stereotype could not exist if it did not have something to do with the truth, if it did not reveal with some accuracy what one group of people feels about another. Where Bennett makes his leap is here: stereotype may also reveal with some accuracy what a people feels about itself. It is at this point where common cultural assumption is elaborated "in so accurate and energetic a way" that deepest cultural drive finds expression, where stereotype does indeed become archetype, and fiction myth. Myth in *A Wilderness of Vines* has not been fully elaborated by any means, but the first outlines of such a myth are present. And this, I think, is the real drama of Bennett's fiction, its real subject, and its real meaning both as fiction and as social comment.

The central metaphor of *The Black Wine* is a somewhat shocking Old Testament formulation of the loss of innocence: the world is a whorehouse and all its travelers whores—which suggests something of the tone, the grimness and sense of dismay, and hence of earnestness at work in the novel and at odds with the humor and attempt to achieve perspective-through-exaggeration normally present in Bennett's satire. Bennett, as a matter of fact, is not greatly concerned with the aims of satire in this novel, which is the least satirical of his works and is more consistently effective as historical and sociological study than as fiction. (pp. 46, 89)

Loosely constructed, curiously devoid of dramatic tension, overwritten in spots, poorly written in others, and, as in *Vines*, given to heavy-handed symbolism and underscoring of theme, the novel attempts to impress several of its more obvious meanings upon the reader by endlessly repeating passages.... (p. 94)

Yet ..., *The Black Wine* contains two incredible scenes that far more successful and consistent novels might not equal.... Both scenes are devastating portraits, microscopically observed, of those gestures, self-deceptions and errant stupidities that make for social living and so much of the grief inherent in the human situation. They are also very funny, capturing with seemingly effortless ease not merely the broad outlines of scene and mood, but those richly revealing turns of mind and phrase that define personality and from which all genuine humor obtains. They are very good.

As in *Vines*, the successes of *The Black Wine* do not lie in the areas of plot construction and characterization, so much as they do in its imagery. (pp. 94-5)

[Sex] in this fiction is a mode of inquiry and speculation, a way of plumbing the roots of character and the strategies of culture at the point where sexual obsession originates as much from the logic and ironical perversities of culture as it does from the logic and aberrations of personality. The workings of self and culture comprise a literally fantastic history of sexual misery which, the novels suggest, is the story of race in this country. Implicit in this inquiry is the question of whether a given culture ever fully succeeds in manipulating those mythical structures that surround and in a sense support it; the answer, also implicit but far more tentative and partial, is that at unexpected moments myth may very well exploit culture, astounding its meanings, counteracting its strategies and arresting its rituals in ambiguity. If this is where *A Wilderness of Vines* and *The Black Wine* end, it is only where *Lord of Dark Places* begins. (p. 97) [Walcott's essay continues in the July issue of *Black World*, excerpted below.]

Ronald Walcott, "The Novels of Hal Ben-

nett,'' in Black World *(copyright © June, 1974, by* Black World; *reprinted by permission of* Black World *and Ronald Walcott), June, 1974, pp. 36-48, 89-97.*

Hal Bennett's *Lord of Dark Places* is a satirical and all but scatological attack on the phallic myth, the original American folk drama in which the white female as virgin and bitch goddess and the Black male as defiler and nigger stud are the two central figures. If one accepts America herself as seductive matriarchal player, the phallic myth is also the archetypal drama of incest, and with a vengeance. This is the dominant metaphor of the novel. So it is that that common cultural assumption . . . —the Black man as sexual monster dwelling in the social imagination—finally obtains in *Lord of Dark Places* its essential and, for Bennett, inevitable form.

Lord of Dark Places is where Bennett's fiction has been heading all along, and it arrives in this powerful, aesthetically satisfying, tightly controlled novel possessed of a plot that fairly explodes with incident and invention. It covers territory Bennett has traveled before, but this time, he owns it. For if, as Leslie Fiedler has put it [in ''Archetype and Signature (The Relationship of Poet and Poem)''], literature comes into being at the moment archetype is rendered through a sufficiently complex and singular Persona or Personality, then *Lord of Dark Places* is Hal Bennett's signature. Like Richard Wright before him, Bennett does not deny the logic of the myth so much as he burdens it mercilessly with sardonic affirmations, elaborating his metaphor with muscular energy and dazzling technical facility, consummately and even perversely bringing the myth home to roost. By so doing, he inflicts upon his readers, white and Black, the guilt that attaches to the myth they perpetuate as well as the fear that it might just be true.

At the same time, Bennett attempts to counter the myth of the phallus with the myth of innocence—the controlling myth of his fiction. Eclectic to an extreme—part satire, myth, blues, *bildungsroman*, detective thriller, social commentary, parable, and, as it must be, exorcism—*Lord of Dark Places* explores facets and implications of the Edenic myth as it parallels and can be used to comment on the Black man's American experience from freedom to the trek North: the loss of innocence, the expulsion from the garden (*i.e.*, migration from the South to the North), the attempt to live with the fact and consequences of one's own evil (here, one's complicity in the country's racial madness), and the search for a new Eden—equality, of course, but also a ''reawakening of the ability to love,'' an acceptance of responsibility and morality that ties us not only to ourselves but to each other. It is a search that begins with the individual self and ends, if indeed it ever can end, with the larger self that is society. (pp. 79-80)

[It] is the language that arrests our attention and distances *Lord of Dark Places* from *A Wilderness of Vines* and *The Black Wine*, that aligns it with the verbal resources of Black folk culture, with its metaphorical intensity, earthiness, and facile, if endlessly deceptive, ''naturalness.''

Here for the first time the design of Bennett's fiction is assimilated to a functional idiom that enables the third-person narrative to become, for all purposes and for long stretches, a vernacular narrative. The story is told, it seems, as each of its characters would tell it in his own voice, which means

that it is able to impart a sense of the mystery of personality inherent in language itself. Most of the unique features of the novel follow from the decision to create an individual voice and rhythm for the narrator, a style with roots in an apparently nonliterary and unself-conscious culture. In its flair for the humor and undiminished joy in things physical located at the center of idiomatic expression, the novel demonstrates again and again a sexual vocabulary that takes to startling heights local capacities for improvisation, surprise and lyricism. Not to be confused with the so-often condescending or suffocatingly quaint renderings of folk dialect, this is a technical Black American speech rarely seen in literature, and then in the ''blue blues,'' what Paul Oliver calls [in *Aspects of the Blues Tradition*] the vital thread of vigorous sexual song. (p. 82)

It is [his] affirmation of possibility, rigorously defined and controlled, that distinguishes Bennett's work and pushes it back from the edge of sentimentality. *Lord of Dark Places*, then, as luminous Black fiction and as complex exploration of thesis, is an extravagant satirical comedy in the sense that comedy is tragedy gone mad. And if the novel tells us nothing else, it insists that even in madness there is hope. (p. 96)

> *Ronald Walcott, ''The Novels of Hal Bennett,'' in* Black World *(copyright © July, 1974, by* Black World; *reprinted by permission of* Black World *and Ronald Walcott), July, 1974, pp. 78-96.*

[*Wait Until the Evening*] is, in several important regards, an impressive and provocative piece of work. It is also, in ways not much less important, frustrating and heavy-handed. Bennett writes with grace, humor, feeling and intelligence; he has a vivid, angry imagination that can both shock and delight. But when that imagination runs to excess, as in this novel it does rather frequently, it gets Bennett into trouble.

''Wait Until the Evening'' is narrated by Kevin Brittain, a black man with a sharply developed sense of irony whose story begins in the early years of World War II and reaches its climax in the present. He is a boy when we meet him, living with his parents and grandparents in the Virginia countryside; when the novel ends he is in New Jersey, embittered and ripe for violence. It is the classic American story of the passage from innocence to [worldliness], but much altered by the particular circumstances of being black and by Bennett's extravagant plot. (p. 14)

[When] Bennett is good he is very, very good. . . . His feel for rural Virginia is as strong and accurate as William Styron's. The novel is written very much from a ''black'' viewpoint, but Bennett reveals himself to have a deep understanding of the complexity and difficulty of interracial communication. (p. 16)

> *Jonathan Yardley, in* The New York Times Book Review *(© 1974 by The New York Times Company; reprinted by permission), September 22, 1974.*

*   *   *

BERGER, Thomas   1924-

Berger, an American novelist, short story writer, editor, and playwright, is best known for his novel, *Little Big Man*. (See also *Contemporary Authors*, Vols. 1-4, rev. ed.)

Vital Parts confirms Berger's rank as a major American novelist, one whose stylistic fecundity, psychological insight, and social knowledge are seemingly inexhaustible. Reinhart [Berger's "likeable Midwestern slob"] continues to move, clownlike, through his familiar world of "asymmetrical impulses, like a laughter hopelessly mad, hopelessly free," large in physique, generosity, honesty, gullibility, optimism, and capacity for enduring psychosocial wounds. . . .

As in earlier Reinhart novels, the pace of events in *Vital Parts* is as phenomenally rapid as the tempo of the prose, the outcome is unexpected, explanations emerge late, and one is bombarded with continual novelty. . . .

The laughter threading *Vital Parts* brightens rather than obscures the depth of thought and emotion evoked by Thomas Berger's fiction. In *Crazy in Berlin* Reinhart had expressed in action more than in words the moral distinction between Jew and Nazi. In *Reinhart in Love* he again depicted ideas, in this case the essential humanity of the Negro and the fragility of love. Berger's newest novel dramatizes the tenuous contemporary existence of old-fashioned qualities anathema to Reinhart's son: "Our enemy is liberal, agnostic, rationalistic, moral relativists, 'men of goodwill,' 'common decency,' 'humanitarianism,' and all those frauds."

Will Reinhart, fat, anachronistic fool, survive the 1970s? One hopes so, for he has a basic humanism that should not be lost. . . .

A comic allegorist of the worthwhile Middle American, skillfully wielding a colloquial diction and rhythm of extraordinary expressiveness, Thomas Berger is one of the most successful satiric observers of the ebb and flow of American life after World War II. His prolificacy promises a continued development of the tragicomic mode of vision, something American literature badly needs to compensate for the overextended silence of such formerly active writers as Ralph Ellison, Joseph Heller, and Thomas Pynchon [note that Weber was writing in 1970]. (p. 42)

> *Brom Weber, in* Saturday Review *(copyright © 1970 by Saturday Review, Inc.; reprinted with permission), March 21, 1970.*

At first, it is the ingenuity of Thomas Berger's *Regiment of Women* that fascinates. But, as with his great predecessor, Swift, Berger's storytelling technique is as good as his talent for satire, and it is not long before you are hurrying to unravel the next twist in the plot. . . .

Berger has used rôle reversal and the sex war to raise bigger issues as targets for his satire. Gulliver has travelled through Aldous Huxley's territory to William Golding country.

It is easy to find the appropriate words to describe Thomas Berger: brilliant, provocative, witty, inventive. (p. 61)

> *John Mellors, in* The Listener *(© British Broadcasting Corp. 1974; reprinted by permission of John Mellors), July 11, 1974.*

The main thrust of the comic novel from Chaucer to Vonnegut has been to present stylized exemplars of human behavior—a lineup of types—and then show how completely they represent all of us, despite our pretensions to individuality. Billy Pilgrim and the Wife of Bath may be cut out of cardboard, but are we any deeper? Not much, we suspect; and we laugh out of the shock of such total recognition. Nobody manages this better today than Thomas Berger, whose *Sneaky People* is typecast from beginning to end without invalidating its insight into American life. . . .

This is Berger's seventh novel, following the Reinhart trilogy, *Little Big Man, Killing Time* and *Regiment of Women*. In all of these, he has displayed immense energy and comic invention, a deft hand with plotting, and some of the best dialogue around. *Little Big Man*, unfortunately obscured by the movie, is nothing less than a masterpiece. American history itself provided Berger with his types—a set of buckskin-fringed waxworks bedizened with legend—and in blowing the myths up to ridiculous proportions he paradoxically succeeded in reclaiming history. In *Sneaky People*, Berger is mining less profitable ore. His characters are types pure and simple, not archetypes—not the Custers and Hickoks but ordinary folks [whose] secret lives are no less banal than the ones they live in public. Sensibly, Berger doesn't strain himself, relying on the nostalgic gloss of the '30s and his impeccable sense of timing to keep us turning the pages. A modest but thoroughly enjoyable book.

> *Michael Harris, "A Garden of Devious Delights," in* Book World—The Washington Post *(© The Washington Post), April 20, 1975, p. 3.*

What you do, see, is go out and buy "Sneaky People." Period. No questions asked. Strip off the dust jacket right there, in your local bookstore. Take it from me, you don't want any hint of the splendid, gaudy surprises beforehand. Come at this novel with the same delightful ignorance that Thomas Berger's characters have as their only stock in trade. When did you ever believe a publisher's blurb, anyway? Also, forget the cheap, put-down title. "Sneaky People" is funny, wise and very significant. What more do you need to know?

This is a novel about appearance and reality, person and persona. Berger prefers the padded bra in all of us. (p. 4)

Berger's style has been streamlined for action. In his "Reinhart" series, humor too frequently appeared at the gestural level. Berger would bloodhound metaphors like a Mountie. Now and then they were worn to nervous collapse by the chase. I can recall only one such instance in "Sneaky People." . . . [Comedy] in "Sneaky People" is based on larger misapprehensions, misapprehensions of character and intention. And on colloquial storytelling. This novel narrates in the third person as though that third person were just another middle-class burgher. More and more American novelists have begun to discover what Jewish novelists have known all along: that the omniscient observer is a regular guy, like you and me. He talks, he doesn't write. "Sneaky People," as a result, reads like swift, clear dialogue.

This is a good one. Witty, imaginative, human; solid-state in its masterful construction. Thomas Berger is not an unknown novelist, but he deserves more attention than he has received to date. If word-of-mouth sells books, as every publisher will tell you, let the word start here. Pass it on. (p. 5)

D. Keith Mano, in The New York Times
Book Review (© 1975 by The New York
Times Company; reprinted by permission),
April 20, 1975.

["Sneaky People"] gives us a convincing imitation of the
thirties, and, perhaps because of the nostalgic influence of
the period, a good deal is made of the sticky adolescence
[experience]. Some serious comment on the duplicity of
American society may have been intended, but in essence
this book is simply an exuberant and crudely humorous
entertainment, distinguished from the rest of the drugstore
rack by its professional finish and its zestful language. (p.
126)

The New Yorker (© 1975 by The New
Yorker Magazine, Inc.), June 9, 1975.

*   *   *

BLY, Robert   1926-

**An American poet, editor, translator, and founder of the Fif-
ties Press (which became the Sixties Press and which is now,
of course, the Seventies Press), Bly has been an influential
figure in contemporary poetry. (See also *Contemporary Authors*, Vols. 5-8, rev. ed.)**

Bly does not write verses, with all that the word implies of
a return, a commitment to a constant; he writes *lines*, with
all that the linear implies of a setting out, a movement in
search of a form rather than *within* a form. (pp. 39-40)

[There is, in *The Light Around the Body*, Bly's second
book,] a numbness or torpor, an inertia so new to art,
which by its traditional nature is the celebration of energy,
of mastery, that Robert Bly himself is not always certain of
its accommodation in his utterance; he suffers and thereby
celebrates the inertia of a being who would be saved, redeemed, not because he is he, but because he is here,
merely present with all the lethargy of a life which contains
death—and it is the requisite wonder of Bly's poetry that
the physical qualities of his language rehearse and enhance
the containment, loyal to their artlessness from the start,
unwavering in their oscitance. It is his uncertainty we hear,
I think, when he says—as he sourly said in 1960—"our
poetry, because of its clinging to things and to the surface
of life, has tended to become too barren".... We must
examine what his work betrays but does not parade, what it
reveals but does not translate—a sense of the center sufficiently indicated, perhaps, if we say, merely, that all the
poems, as we pick them up one after the other, are seen to
be *marinating*: they are all at sea. (pp. 42-3)

We start with the first poems in the first book [*Silence in
the Snowy Fields*], the "eleven poems of solitude," where
the Ordeal by Water is of course the Trauma of Birth, and
the longing to return to the womb is the longing for an intro-
jected, incarnate ocean. (p. 45)

The triumph of [the] central group in *Silence in the Snowy
Fields*, however, is not one of Bly's countless committals
of the body to darkness, depth and inertia, to that "silence
on the roads" where "the dark weeds are waiting, as if
under water"; it is, rather, a poem of wakefulness, of inspired consciousness, and the only poem in all his *oeuvre*
not to be devised or derived "Driving through Ohio" or
"Hunting Pheasants in a Cornfield," in that limitless
chthonic expanse which so burdens the vertical self; the

poem is called, exceptionally, "On the Ferry Across Ches-
apeake Bay," and because it is the one piece in the canon
uttered in the actual presence of the real sea, of course it is
that real sea which is put aside ("O deep green sea, it is not
for you / this smoking body ploughs toward death"). The
waking man, Bly discovers, cannot *bring forward* the images which will substantiate another reality; he must listen,
rather, to Nietzsche's advice: "you must be a chaos, to
give birth to a dancing star".... The closing poems of the
book return to the life and to the death-in-life of that Minnesota mariner so amazingly created out of midwestern
elements.... Like Prospero, Bly *drowns* his book with a
final image of renunciation: every hope of distinct and certainly of distinguished life is surrendered for the sake of
"the true gift, beneath the pale lakes of Minnesota," the
treasure beneath the black water.... (pp. 46-7)

Richard Howard, "Robert Bly," in his
Alone with America: Essays on the Art of
Poetry in the United States Since 1950
(copyright © 1965, 1966, 1967, 1968, 1969 by
Richard Howard; reprinted by permission of
Atheneum Publishers, New York), Athe-
neum, 1969, pp. 38-48.

Silence in the Snowy Fields was like a cluster of gnats. No
matter what else I did, I couldn't remain neutral about
Bly's poems. It will be impossible for me to discuss my
change of mind rationally, but I've come to believe that my
reservations about Bly were only nigglings, that measuring
the accomplishment of his work against petty objections is
something like dismissing *Moby Dick* because Melville
loses track of his point of view. Bly is free from the inhibitions of critical dictates many of us have regarded as truths.
He manages, in fact, to write poems that are themselves
suspensions of the critical faculty. The poems had to become what they are. They are quiet, unassuming. They are
uninsistent, unrhetorical; they depend, often, on one another for total effect. They do not lead to the kind of intellectual pleasure (an anti-poetic pleasure) one gets from
having traced down all the allusions in "The Waste Land"
or from having used the unabridged dictionary to come to
terms with "The Comedian as the Letter C"....

Bly's poems do not wear thin. Our inner lives speak in
them, speak out from the silence and solitude of the American midwest. And there is a profound correspondence
between "the man inside the body" ("Silence") and the
oceans of air and water and land through which he moves.
A car is a "solitude covered with iron" ("Driving Toward
the Lac Qui Parle River") and so is the man moving inside
his struts of flesh and bone. For years I felt that Bly's poetry pointed at a mysterious and dissatisfying nothingness
that was a non-subject. But he has one subject that speaks
out from the spaces between lines, stanzas, and poems and
unites them: The Self....

The journeys in Bly's poems are journeys to the interior, as
Theodore Roethke put it. Bly has stopped somewhere and
is waiting for us. He can find no spiritual fathers among
politicians, or the rich, or the self-satisfied (hence his increasing social criticism). But the poet still has friends, a
few people to share the inexplicable inner-life with. When
he is with them he writes quiet, almost melancholy
lines....

Whatever the word means, in *Silence in the Snowy Fields*

Bly is a Romantic. Yeats was not the last. All of our inner men are. But we think we know only what we think. The truth is that the only knowledge worth our while is our knowledge of what we feel. . . .

What we have in Bly is a personal poetry becoming a poetry of social comment. Since the English Romantics first set pen to paper we have been suspicious of the private vision, explaining away our discomfort by saying, weakly, that we are all brothers and that when one speaks personally, subjectively, he speaks for the race. But my inner man, after wars to end all wars, has been driven deeper inside. Bly's poetry assumes, from the beginning, our hurt, and our disbelief that men can do what they have done and are doing. . . .

In *The Light Around the Body* (1967), which won the National Book Award, Bly holds up a mirror to his age. Social criticism becomes intense. In poem after poem we are our politicians' pawns, our generals' statistics, our merchants' suckers.

> *William Heyen, "Inward to the World: The*
> *Poetry of Robert Bly," in* The Far Point,
> *Fall/Winter, 1969, pp. 42-7.*

Bly's political poetry is disorganized, crude in style, with images cranked and shoved together. The untruths are so blatant as to make it impossible to consider them even angry self-deceptions. . . . The government is charged with cruelty and lies; the method of making the charge is to invent wantonly cruel lies. Hate propaganda is always distasteful to hear or to discuss. Bly's political poetry is shameful even for hate propaganda. I hope that such poetry will continue to decline in America. (p. 402)

> *Paul Ramsey, in* Sewanee Review *(reprinted*
> *by permission of the editor;* © *1974 by The*
> *University of the South), Spring, 1974.*

The energy with which the Minnesota poet Robert Bly unreservedly gives himself to his ideas, or in some cases, his prejudices, makes him both one of the most annoying and most exciting poets of his time. Objectivity and judiciousness are not nice words in Bly's vocabulary. . . . Compared with the intense flex and balance of Denise Levertov, Bly sometimes seems like a frenetic farm-boy shying rocks impulsively at anything that moves; but he can often be stingingly on target, and has probably brought home more game politically than any other poet besides Allen Ginsberg. (p. 113)

Most artists are, of necessity, "outsiders" to the larger society and its values, but Bly has been something of an outsider to his fellow poets as well. He has come by this chiefly for two reasons. The first can be called by different names: integrity, independence, stubbornness, egoism. One suspects that many of the critical remarks offered against Bly by his colleagues during the sixties (his theatricality, carelessness of form, lack of music, dilettantism) are only "acceptable" expressions of "unacceptable" irritations and antagonisms they felt toward him. Bly is "no respecter of persons," and often does not play according to the polite rules, whether the game in question belongs to the establishment or the anti-establishment. He is like the pesky student who keeps asking the professor troublesome questions and will not be intimidated. Such traits alone are sufficient

to alienate many, but even beyond this, there is something about Bly in person or print that often makes people uneasy. He is a man with disturbing energy and self-confidence, and an unreserved commitment to the things he does. Earmarks of integrity? or egoism?

Secondly, Bly stands as an "outsider" in that he has been without the support of anything like a Black Mountain, San Francisco, or New York coterie of fellows and followers. (Though a few poets have had affinities with Bly's poetic manner and ideas—Robert Kelly, James Wright, Louis Simpson, Jerome Rothenberg—he stood mostly alone before the *Kayak* poets began to make themselves heard.) Bly's allegiance has been to poets of other languages and of another imagination—the German poets Georg Trakl and Gottfried Benn, the French René Char and Michaux, the Swedish Ekelöf, and especially the Spanish César Vallejo and García Lorca, and the Chilean Pablo Neruda. This inspiration, and the "new imagination" of the poetry that Bly promotes and practices, demands more than casual reading. Bly's poetry is perhaps not so much misread or unread as shallowly read and put easily aside as poetry of the *deep* or *subjective image*. It has been an uncrowded and easy category, a convenient pigeonhole for disposing of poetry that challenges poetry-reading habits. Because the form is strange, it can be focused upon for comment and used as an excuse to avoid a difficult and profoundly unsettling content. Bly has been, then, generally regarded as that poet whom one wishes would take more care "with how things go together," . . . whom one wishes would put a little more trust in the power of "art," and give less energy to polemics. (pp. 114-15)

Bly's interest has always been with content rather than form, and life rather than "art." (Though these pairs are properly not polarities but are related as *ends* and *means*, poets and schools of poetry persist in arranging themselves on one side or another of the dichotomy.) His quarrel with traditional forms and their recent American substitutes is that they cannot carry the content of modern life. That content, he feels, is "the sudden new change in the life of humanity, of which the Nazi Camps, the terror of modern wars, the sanctification of the viciousness of advertising, the turning of everyone into workers, the profundity of associations, is all a part." The "men of 1914" and Eliot in *The Waste Land* made one large raid into this life, but did not persist or widen their foraging; and, in fact, they finally retreated. Bly's view of the modern world is one, then, that focuses on an ugliness that is wider and deeper than that exposed by *The Waste Land*, and which in 1958 had "still not been described." That reality, he suspected, could never be described in the restraints or prettinesses of rhyme, the decorous regularity of iambic meter, the four-letter words of Beat-poetry, the vague suggestiveness of the *symboliste* mode, the impeccable order of poems for *Kenyon Review*, the narrowness of personal or confessional poetry, or the abstract tendencies of contemporary British poetry. What was needed was something at once more vigorous, more powerfully physical, more capable of reaching down into the darknesses and nightmares of the modern sickness. All these are implied in the metaphors with which he describes Spanish poetry, where he finds a power that "grasps modern life as a lion grabs a dog, and wraps it in heavy countless images, and holds it firm in a terrifically dense texture." American poetry was incapable of this because it had sidestepped and never really gone through the experience of surrealism. (p. 116)

Bly's bias [is] against the conscious mind, against the cerebral and the abstract. A poetry that grows from the intellect is like the plant deprived of its soil: true poetry springs from a deeper self, unknowable by the machinery that sorts and labels the produce at the top of the head and makes rational cases for whatever it wishes. The deep imagination swells up from the edges of hallucination and fantasy to produce Picasso's "Guernica," while the superficial imagination finds satisfaction with the usable representational art of Marines planting the flag on Iwo Jima. The images that Bly calls for are not, then, the pictures of Ezra Pound and the Imagists, "petals on a wet black bough," but the images that writhe in the fogs halfway between deep and inarticulate passions and conscious thought. (p. 117)

Bly chooses the poetry of the subjective image because it can carry the content he wants. But is there, perhaps, a closer relationship between the form and the nature of the content it carries? Does the deep image by its very nature, as revealed in the metaphors with which we describe it, lend itself necessarily to a dark, pessimistic, "anti-" or protest poetry?. . . In other words, if we draw images and metaphors from an irrational and chaotic field, will the world they attempt to express be found to be more grotesque and horrible than it perhaps really is? (One thing is at least beyond question—the deep image is by its nature not well suited to saccharine, romantic, or patriotic poetry.) The importance of the question is that, ultimately, one wonders whether Bly's form is a result of his vision, or his vision the result of his form; whether he achieves a more powerful protest because his agonies are deeper, or whether they only seem so because expressed in a more profound form. One is at least confident in claiming that the two influences have reinforced and deepened one another, and that content and form join with a potency that justifies Bly's emergence as one of the most important poets of the sixties. (pp. 117-18)

Bly's first book of poems, *Silence in the Snowy Fields*, is full of rural quietnesses, farmyards, fields, solitudes, and silences. Peaceful and strangely satisfying, the poems attest to a wholeness in the poet who speaks them. The few troubled poems are easily carried by the calm of the rest. But there are touches of discontent here already, and, though far from the spirit of protest animating later work, they do raise themes that become important in *The Light Around the Body*. (p. 118)

Unlike Levertov, in whose poetry death becomes alluring only after the war has undercut a previous vitality, Bly seems always to have sung soft songs to death. "Return to Solitude," "Depression," and "Night" are a few of the poems in *Snowy Fields* where death enters more as friend than intruder. It is as if death were at last the full granting of the solitude and silence that man grabs fleetingly from the night and the fields when he is able momentarily to forget his daylight awareness of man's inhumanities to man. To die is also to be absolved from returning to the agony of moral confrontation and impotence. Death is, moreover, an escape from the self ("My body hung about me like an old grain elevator, / Useless, clogged, full of blackened wheat" . . .), and from the future. . . .

But . . . the dominant vision of *Silence in the Snowy Fields*

is convincingly positive. Much more prevalent than shadow is luminescence; much more prominent than negation is affirmation. (p. 119)

In *Light Around the Body* the specific detail of *Snowy Fields* becomes the generalized subjective image, the inwardness becomes a window on the world, and the "I" becomes "we" or appears only as a point of vision ("I hear," "I see") or means of introducing the image. The "I" of the private vision and of the self apart from the mass of men becomes the "we" of public vision and of the self as part of the community of mankind. . . . In *Light Around the Body* Bly is speaking in the other of his two necessary languages, about the other of his two necessary selves. The private vision of *Silence in the Snowy Fields*, if persisted in, would have atrophied into a wrinkled Wordsworthian natural mysticism evasive of modern realities; the focus of *Light Around the Body*, pursued exclusively, threatens to deteriorate into noisy rhetoric. (p. 121)

[There] are convincing signs that Bly at least *understands* mysticism. That is itself a rare gift. He also seems to have learned, in Eliot's words, "to care and not to care," that difficult passivity that leads to revelation. . . . That kind of "letting go," generally foreign to rational Western man, is usually learned through pain and defeat. Bly, who nowhere shares with his reader the details of his particular personal suffering, has somehow come to the mystical wisdom of passivity:

> There is a joyful night in which we lose
> Everything, and drift
> Like a radish
> Rising and falling, and the ocean
> At last throws us into the ocean. . . .

This understanding, necessarily experiential and not the mere acceptance of the idea by the conscious mind, is for Westerners, if not "mystical," at least a great epiphany. (Denise Levertov's denial of the vain will is a parallel illumination. Allen Ginsberg may not yet have learned to float like a radish, and continues to fling himself against the door that, as Levertov has learned, opens outward.) If the reader bothers to become aware of this spiritual depth in Bly, he is less apt to assume he has read Bly when he has read him only superficially.

Bly's great energy has often earned for him the image of reckless dilettante. In the few public poems of *Snowy Fields* and in nearly all poetry during the war, Bly set for himself the task of jumping up out of the self "like a grasshopper" into the larger soul of the nation to "entangle" in words and bring back some of the strange plants and animals that inhabit it. By seeking to explore the origins and effects of the impulses that make America and Americans physically and psychically what they are, Bly has found himself in the role of "psychologist." Armed necessarily with only a layman's knowledge of Freud and Jung, an imperfect secondhand knowledge of his patient's history, and an inability to hide the simplicity of his thought in arcane official jargon, his analyses have inevitably struck many as foolish and simplistic. . . . Moreover, in exploring the American psyche Bly sometimes comes to conclusions that, contrary to all accepted rules of poetry, he baldly offers in the poems themselves free of charge. These must be acknowledged as disturbing weaknesses: in *Light*, "Men like Rusk are not men" . . ., "We distrust every person on earth with black hair" . . ., "No one in business can be a Christian" . . ., and in *Teeth-Mother*, "The ministers lie, the professors lie, the television lies, the priests lie". . . . Even though perhaps true, these are prose opinions and not poetic insights. Political poetry is always in danger of being taken literally as prose, and the presence of prose passages such as these has helped insure misreadings of Bly's poems. Read as prose, the poems seem more strident and fantastic than they really are. (pp. 122-24)

Like Allen Ginsberg, Bly began his protest against the war long before this country's fighting in Vietnam began. He sensed early that although oppression in all countries was increasingly invisible, it was nevertheless increasingly experienced—"even in America, [oppression] is as common as beauty, for those who have senses which can grasp it." The protest against the war has been for Bly as for Ginsberg (as it was not for a long while for Levertov) part of a larger revolt against the disposition that occasions war and oppresses the human spirit. Bly senses that somewhere hidden in present values and in the American psyche is a dark and terrible cancer, a core of rottenness and disorder. . . . It is this darkness and disorder that Bly seeks to explore, understand, and expose—toward the end that it may heal.

Does this darkness grow out of the black seeds of a national and international malaise, or is it something so pervasive as to hint of a darkness in human or cosmic nature? Is this darkness and this terror, which eventually drives man to "tear off his own arms and throw them into the air," innate in man and the cosmos or in man's political and social structures? The question of Bly's philosophy of man and nature is not immediately easy to answer. He is neither a Hobbesian who believes that man is, except for law, a wolf to man, nor a Rousseauist who sees man as a noble savage diseased with civilization. Nor can he be easily categorized as a Jeffers or a Conrad or a Hardy—he is neither a skeptic nor a pessimist, but senses a darkness in both man and the cosmos that he does not understand. The third stanza of "Johnson's Cabinet Watched by Ants" gives the reader a feeling that evil may be timeless and very much at home in the universe, that it is an old story, ineluctable, contemporal with the primeval ooze. (p. 125)

Generally, of course, Bly's poetry does not seek to uncover the ultimate nature of the universe, but to find the more immediate sources of darkness in man's present society. Some evil may be inevitable, but the poet of *Silence in the Snowy Fields* knows also that man is capable of peace, wholeness, and joy, and that most of the darkness and joylessness of modern man is unnatural. The American psyche Bly finds especially afflicted. (p. 126)

Despite his own personal energy and strength, Bly is the supreme poet of defeat—defeat expressed in deep images of maniacal fury and total inertia. (p. 127)

[His] images are so right and familiar that we are apt to pay too little attention to their richness. Not only in his choice of image, but in his choice of particular words [in "Come with Me"], Bly exactly captures the loneliness, degradation, defenselessness, disorientation, suffocation, defeat, and isolation of modern man. Moreover, we see in these images that man is impelled headlong by forces he does not understand or control, that instead of being in the driver's seat he is driven by a larger impersonal machine and is a

commodity that has no value except that it can be used up. (pp. 127-28)

Though these images are still close to the surface imagination, one can already feel in them an ominous and terrifying note that elsewhere explodes from the deep unconscious with hysterical force:

> One leg walks down the road and leaves
> The other behind, the eyes part
> And fly off in opposite directions. . . .
>
> Wild dogs tear off noses and eyes
> And run off with them down the street—
> The body tears off its own arms and throws them into
>   the air. . . .

Such images haunt *The Light Around the Body* and carry a fantastic horror and degradation. The impossible spectacle of the body tearing off its own arms and throwing them into the air (it has all the mind-crushing-paradox qualities of a Zen *koan*) is the ultimate expression of extreme self-revulsion and longing for mutilation and annihilation.

Because we have been captured by "death," the death-in-life of the outward man cut off from his vital center, Bly believes we long for real death, an annihilation of the alienated self. Undoubtedly influenced by Freud, Bly finds in our hatred and desire to kill others a double proof of our own self-hatred and death wish. According to Freud's theory of projection, we attribute to our enemy the hatred for us that we feel towards ourselves. We thus need to destroy the enemy because we are paranoically sure he is trying to kill us. And by a second law of sublimation and transference, we satisfy our desire for self-destruction by violence against our enemy. (pp. 128-29)

Bly's poems suggest multiple reasons for his and America's obsession with death. Death is variously looked on as the complete solitude and silence, as escape from self and weary realities, as schizophrenic catatonia, as avoidance of the imminent apocalyptic darkness and cataclysm, as annihilation of the alienated outward self, as projected and sublimated self-hatred. Bly further suggests that we desire death as punishment for the guilt of past evils, and as the culmination of our strong anti-life impulses.

We seek death as expiation of the burden of guilt accumulated from the rape of the frontier and the ecology, from Puritanic morality and discipline, from killing Indians, from a history of violence and socioeconomic inequities—Bly's hysterical images of mutilation seem to spiral out of guilt-frenzy. There are anti-life forces at work throughout the modern world, but Bly senses that they have developed most strongly in America because our "progress" has been more rapid. (p. 130)

[Divisions] of the masculine and feminine occur under subtle and sometimes covert forms throughout Bly's protest poetry, and become the most important unifying theme. What for Ginsberg becomes an Apollonian-Dionysiac or order-orgy conflict, becomes for Bly a conflict between masculine and feminine, hard and soft, rigid and flexible, rock and water. The related polarities or subforms are many, and include reason-emotion, active-passive, barren-fertile, cold-warm, angular-curved, stars-moon, frozen-fluid, domination-submission, discipline-love, power-weakness, and light-dark. (p. 136)

Bly's understanding of the history of ideas may not be minutely sophisticated, and his knowledge in many areas may by some criteria be dilettantish. But his pretensions are no greater than those of every other poet: he may venture into fields others avoid, but he makes no claim to professional expertise in any matter except poetry. . . . *Light Around the Body* is a book of many perceptions, and the larger unifying patterns are perhaps largely subconscious rather than calculated. But there is everywhere below the immediate surface of these poems a consistency, integrity, and *coherence* that makes them worthy of the National Book Award. In the award citation the judges, Theodore Weiss, Harvey Shapiro, and Donald Hall, wrote: "If we poets had to choose something that would be for us our Address on the State of the Nation, it would be this book." (p. 152)

Though Bly's poetry [in *The Light Around the Body*] is essentially wasteland poetry—his purposes are to give that landscape fuller expression—he does offer . . . an alternative. It seems at first a private and personal alternative, but it is open to every private person and thus ultimately to the society at large. Indeed, the great revolutionaries have understood that changes in individual consciousness are what is needed, and that changes in the outward political structures are otherwise irrelevant. Those structures are merely the body for which our attitudes are the spirit. (p. 153)

There seem to be two *ways* to promote . . . reunion [between the outward and the inward person] one is to "give up desire," the formula of all spirituality; and the other is to accept the person as sacred. (pp. 153-54)

Bly's is a strange new poetry, more deeply involved, more superficially raucous and polemical. It will not be readily embraced—the rocks on the shore do not easily submit to the sea. It campaigns for a deeper, more spontaneous life, and follows its own advice in its volatile and "uncivilized" subjective images. And yet in the midst of its energy, it understands a tranquil center, a letting go, so that at last, naked as a radish, "the ocean . . . throws us into the ocean." The mountain has not yet altered and become the sea, but partly perhaps because of Bly and other poets against the war, some rocks are falling. (pp. 156-57)

> James F. Mersmann, "Robert Bly: Watering the Rocks," in his Out of the Vietnam Vortex: A Study of Poets and Poetry against the War (© copyright 1974 by the University Press of Kansas), University Press of Kansas, 1974, pp. 113-57.

Robert Bly is the most vocal theorist of his generation, and has helped other writers the most, through his magazine *The Sixties*. But his own poetry—except for the nature poems in *Silence in the Snowy Fields*, which are technically limpid, and full of a not easily expressible peace—seems too much the result of a design for irrational poetry, too little of genuinely unconscious promptings. In his recent surrealistic political poetry, I feel I hear a deep voice choking on its own anger and going shrill; I sympathize, but cannot compare the results with such miraculously heart-whole poems as Snyder's "For the West" or Merwin's "For Now". (p. 65)

> Alan Williamson, "Language against Itself: the Middle Generation of Contemporary

Poets" (copyright © 1974 by Alan Williamson), in American Poetry Since 1960: Some Critical Perspectives, edited by Robert B. Shaw, Dufour, 1974, pp. 55-67.

* * *

BOYLE, Kay   1903-

Ms Boyle is an American novelist, poet, and short story writer, long respected for her intelligent and expertly crafted fiction. (See also *Contemporary Authors*, Vols. 13-16, rev. ed.)

From the time of her first book in 1929, *Wedding Day and Other Stories*, [Kay Boyle's] fate has been occasional high praise and an occasional succès d'estime. Meanwhile, writers far less gifted have been overrated by public and critics alike. At present there are only a few books of Kay Boyle's in print; these fortunately include a hardbound edition of her novel *Monday Night* and paperbacks of *Thirty Stories* and *Three Short Novels* (the last containing one of the masterpieces of this genre in our time, *The Crazy Hunter*). Of her first novel, *Plagued by the Nightingale*, it is safe to say that it is the finest portrait of a French family by a writer from this side of the Atlantic since Henry James fixed his attention upon the Bellegardes in *The American*. Nor is it out of place to mention James here, for Kay Boyle is an important later practitioner in the area in which he worked—"the international theme." Since James, no American except Kay Boyle has concentrated so thoroughly upon that theme.

Despite the excellence of the results, however, Kay Boyle's writing career has had some severe setbacks, partly attributable to timing. She learned to write in the 1920s, when craftsmanship was important, but by the time she began turning out her full-length novels the Depression was on; instead of her subtle penetration of the behavior of Americans in Europe, readers over here wanted what seemed to be the only realities of the moment—rough stories of hunger marchers, factory slaves, or dispossessed tenant farmers. It was a time when entire social classes, rather than individuals, were of dominant interest in fiction, and it was a period when the autobiographical novel was not fashionable; consequently it didn't help Kay Boyle's cause for her to have, in most of her books, a sensitive American girl as the reflector of the action, which usually involved a group of expatriates. Now it may be seen (and I hope it will be seen) that these novels were not indulgently self-centered, not mere personal chronicles, but were rather the reworking of significant experience into fable, intensified by a prose style at once delicate and forcible. (pp. 32-3)

[She is] among the fine women authors of our time who do not write like men (as, say, Willa Cather does), but operate through a distinctly feminine vision (as Dorothy Richardson does), to capture and project experience in a unique and important way. (p. 36)

> Harry T. Moore, "Kay Boyle's Fiction" (originally published in Kenyon Review, Spring, 1960), in his Age of the Modern and Other Literary Essays (copyright © 1971, Southern Illinois University Press), Southern Illinois University Press, 1971, pp. 32-6.

The fates and other bureaucracies have never quite realized

how unprofitable it is to mess with writers. Throw one into jail, prompt the IRS goons to work another over, visit sickness on the family of a third, and the result is ever the same: another book. "The Underground Woman" is one of these. Kay Boyle, I understand, went to jail briefly for attempting to obstruct our recent war in Vietnam; she lost, too, a daughter to one of those horrifying communes, run as religious dictatorships, that sprouted over America in the latter half of the '60s. From these simultaneous ordeals she has wrung a novel. It is a nice, even sweet, book, clearly deeply felt and fairly humming with love and sentiment. Many readers will come away from it convinced they have read a good novel—any reader should instinctly *want* it to be a good novel—but it is not. Probably it shouldn't have been a novel at all. . . .

The novel's problem lies just here. Good fiction feeds upon the particular; imprecision will dent it, a muddled goodwill toward man will corrode it absolutely. Miss Boyle generalizes her characters by identifying them with Greek myths; her generalizations about man's estate should have been left to her readers to infer. We are all one body, she seems to say, and our virtue will move mountains. Probably, if one must emphasize this theme, he had better follow Tolstoy's course and abandon fiction for moral essays. There is good material in ["The Underground Woman"], and some good writing, but I am convinced that Miss Boyle is too close both to her prison experience and her daughter's ordeal in a malevolent commune to turn either into good fiction. This book seems less the product of inspiration than of obligation, and should surely have been told as nonfiction.

Peter S. Prescott, "Life With Daughter," in
Newsweek *(copyright 1975 by Newsweek,
Inc.; all rights reserved; reprinted by permission), January 13, 1975, p. 67A.*

Athena Gregory [protagonist of "The Underground Woman"]—42-years-old, a widowed mother and teacher of a distressingly simple college course in Greco-Roman mythology—finds herself suddenly involved, with many other women, in a protest against the Vietnam war. Facing nine days in the county's Rehabilitation Center, her group prepares for Doom and Tragedy: "What we need is a little optimism around here, if we're going to make it!" one cries. Another says that optimism is not enough: "I think we have to try now to believe that our separate lives are really of no importance."

Such rhetoric is totally disproportionate to the occasion—or it will seem so to the cynical former young who have endured many jails, many cops, many hostile citizens and dangerous inmates, first in the civil rights wars and then in the anti-war wars. But Kay Boyle (author of over 20 works of fiction) is writing, as perhaps she had to, from the viewpoint of older and more sheltered generations. She is writing *for* them, too, trying to draw lessons appropriate to them out of the horrors that Watergate seems to have superseded. . . .

After all it was the sixties that destroyed—perhaps forever—the American family, the authority of public morals, and the credibility of government; no small achievement. That experience has not ended American error, indeed it failed miserably; yet it was in some ways more respectable than the present. Kay Boyle is right to remind us of it (however

imperfect her novel), and to call up again the old circumstances and ideals out of which we might have made so much nicer a country. That jail cells tend to be as alike as Howard Johnsons may seem a small, middle-class perception; but if every patron of HoJo's shared it, things might be better.

Kay Boyle's underground woman is pale and sweet, no relation to Dostoevsky's underground man; and her novel is essentially feminine in its familial concerns, kaleidoscopic feelings, mythical rhetoric and persistent subjectivity; but it speaks to all sensitive and conventional women with bad consciences, and it tries to offer them a way toward self-respect. (p. 4)

J. D. O'Hara, in The New York Times
Book Review *(© 1975 by The New York
Times Company; reprinted by permission),
February 2, 1975.*

Sooner or later it would have happened that a strong voice from the '30s-'40s generation would speak out in fiction about what it is like to be a parent of Vietnam-war-age children. No one's voice is better suited to such witness than Kay Boyle's. *The Underground Woman* . . . comes at the end of a long line of novels (13), short stories, novelettes, four books of poetry, three children's books, and a memorable essay about her experiences during "the bust" at San Francisco State. Her dedication to *belles-lettres* has not made Kay Boyle an intellectual or esthetic elitist. This new book shows what an extraordinary development hers has been. She is, one supposes, much like her heroine, a professor of English in her middle age, an active participant of the Vietnam antiwar movement. She writes powerfully, vividly and with much of her usual irony, of her experiences in demonstrations, of her arrest and brief stay in jail, of her entry into the lives of her fellow-prisoners. The novel ends as she is about to go to jail again.

If this were all, the book might be interesting but not unusually compelling. What gives it an added edge of poignancy is the story of the heroine's daughter, who leaves home to join a commune based upon mindless devotion to a cultic figure, Pete the Redeemer. All the pain of what I suspect might be an event in her own life (Kay Boyle has six children) is contained in this portrait. A woman with a profound personal commitment to human freedom, Kay Boyle shows us the loss of a daughter to a tyrannical movement as one of the tragedies of parenthood.

It might be thought that this issue-centered book would be diminished as fiction. Indeed a recent critic has blamed the book for this, saying that as a result of her concern for current events Kay Boyle's characters lose their believability. My own feeling is that, while this novel is perhaps a lesser Boyle, it is still a valuable fictional document, intensely projected and felt keenly by the reader, of our times, of the pain and trauma of civil disobedience, seen through the eyes of a woman who loves her own family and the rest of the human family with equal passion. . . .

Never lost or isolated in her own identity, Kay Boyle writes of the human condition, in jail, in political action, in the grip of irrational religious fervor. Recently she said: "Nothing can ever make me believe we are helpless as individuals." Her new fiction, and her activity on behalf of amnesty, and for the freedom of political prisoners everywhere in the world are evidence of that conviction. Clearly she has suffered. An earlier novel is called *Nothing Ever Breaks Except the Heart*; for her, heartbreak is the side product of her fight for liberation of people everywhere. (p. 33)

> *Doris Grumbach, in* The New Republic *(reprinted by permission of* The New Republic; © *1975 by The New Republic, Inc.), February 8, 1975.*

There is a kind of telescopic intimacy to Kay Boyle's work that manages to relate the grand concerns of the world to the personal lives of individual people in a way that is both touching and magnanimous. That has always been Boyle's strength, and it shines through again in her latest novel, *The Underground Woman*.

For about five decades now, Kay Boyle has demonstrated her literary abilities in a variety of forms: novels, poems, essays, children's books, and memoirs. Throughout that period she has consistently been able to be topical without being superficial, to be radical without being irrational and to be humane without being hypocritical. Perhaps that is because to her generation—she was a member of that distinguished literary set in Europe in the 1920s and 1930s that included Hemingway, Fitzgerald, Stein, Joyce and Pound —there was no contradiction between social conscience and artistic expression. In any case, *The Underground Woman* is a further extension of her lover's quarrel with the world. As such, it is a plea for the exercise of political conscience on the part of the middle class. . . .

This is a novel about women and about femininity as much as it is about politics; but it is not a feminist novel, in the tendentious sense, any more than any honest novel could be a propaganda tract. Boyle is too good an artist for that. . . .

This is also, in another way, a novel about a group of freaks walking in the shadows of the epic Greeks, a novel about people freaked out of a society that seems unfit for them; about people who, despite their apparent ineffectuality, try nobly to obey the gods of their consciences, their underground men and women, in order to make their lives more meaningful.

The most consistent set of allusions in the book are to Greek mythology, and actually, they form the framework for the novel. To begin with, there is the matter of names. In addition to Athena [the protagonist], there is a famous folk singer named Calisto and a young woman named Calliope. Callisto emerges as Athena's most trusted friend, and Calliope as an admired companion. There are also repeated references to the Greek myths in Athena's thought and speech. And finally, there is the ever-present specter of intrafamilial strife, the central subject of Greek tragedy. . . .

In other words, the characters, the struggles, and the issues in this novel are intended to have a transcendency, to be an "echoing of history." And although the characters are undeniably pedestrian, they are meant to be invested with a certain nobility, a stature grander than their conventional lives suggest. . . .

In *The Underground Woman*, Kay Boyle would have us believe that the grief of the people in her novel sets them apart from those immortal robots who are beyond grief. At

times she succeeds and at times she does not. But whatever the final result her effort is a worthy one, and one thoroughly consistent with those of a writer whose energies have always been expended imaginatively and unselfishly in a constant attempt to enlighten her fellow citizens.

> *Phillip Corwin, "The Telling of the Story," in* The Nation *(copyright 1975 by the Nation Associates, Inc.), March 22, 1975, p. 347.*

*   *   *

BRAUTIGAN, Richard   1933-

Brautigan, an American poet and novelist of the counter-culture, writes witty, fanciful, parabolic fiction. His best known work is *Trout Fishing in America*. (See also *Contemporary Authors*, Vols. 53-56.)

All of Brautigan's techniques [in *In Watermelon Sugar*]— repetition, juxtaposition, fragmentation of time and setting, use of strange lyricism and elements from fantasy and science fiction—come to us through the point of view of the nameless narrator and gradually accumulate toward characterization for negative effect. We obtain the final clue to Brautigan's intention for the novel as a whole when we come to the society's one claim to pure pleasure: communal pride. The narrator repeatedly tells us that he and the others like living in watermelon sugar, that it does suit them; or, in a more defiant vein, "there must be worse lives". . . . Indeed not. The "delicate balance in iDEATH" . . . is the delusion that they can maintain a neutral position disjunct from violence and death without also cutting themselves off from life's fullness. The basic error results in boredom, ritual, and sterility, devoid not only of pleasure but of all feeling and thus all real curiosity, vitality, or a reason for existence. Life in watermelon sugar may be literally the same as dying, since we are told of only one birth . . . to "balance" twenty-two suicides.

Seen in this way, *In Watermelon Sugar* is more than a fad book. It is not a description of "the students' way of life" or a lyric description of a successful counterculture. Brautigan judges his utopian commune and finds it wanting, and the "curious lack of emotion" is the very reason for the negative judgment. Brautigan reminds us that a worse thing than violence and death could be a life without pity or joy. (p. 16)

> *Patricia Hernlund, "Author's Intent: 'In Watermelon Sugar'," in* Critique: Studies in Modern Fiction *(copyright © by* Critique, *1974), Vol. XVI, No. 1, 1974, pp. 5-17.*

On first reading Richard Brautigan's *In Watermelon Sugar*, one senses that something extraordinary has happened to the form of the novel, to the intellectual and aesthetic conventions to which we have become accustomed. Brautigan's work is jigsaw puzzle art that demands more than close reading; it demands an active participation by the reader, a reconstruction of a vision that has been fragmented but warmed by a private poetic sensibility. Three avenues of accessibility, the novel as a utopian instrument, the analogues to the Garden of Eden, and natural determinism converge and create a frame for Brautigan's novel.

Brautigan has created the utopian dream for the post-industrial age of affluence, beyond IBM, and finally beyond curiosity. His longings, unlike other utopian ideals, have no claim on progress, no uplifting of the material condition of man, no holy wars to redistribute the physical wealth, no new metaphors for survival based on the securing of human necessities, and no emotional nirvanas. Other utopian dreamers have responded directly to the events of their age, but Brautigan is responding to the cumulative ages of man, and no response can be significant for him that does not place the entire past on the junk heap (the forgotten works). Nothing will do but a fresh start, with a fresh set of assumptions; *In Watermelon Sugar* takes us back to the beginning for this is Eden, with its syllabic and accented soul mate iDEATH, reconstructed.

The phrase from which the book draws its title is the initial indicator of Brautigan's reconstructed garden, for "In watermelon sugar the deeds were done and done again." We enter the novel during the "again" stage, man's second great attempt to obtain an earthly paradise; the unnamed narrator implies the failure of the past and indicates the social purpose of his creation when he states on the first page, "I hope this works out." Although we shall not attempt here to discover all of the Biblical analogues, we should point out that the narrator of the novel gives us a list of things he will tell us about . . . and that the list encompasses twenty-four items, the same number as books in the Hebraic version of the Old Testament. In addition, the novel is divided into three books, again paralleling the current division of the Old Testament into three sections. In themselves, these similarities are not important, but when coupled with the physical descriptions of the rivers . . ., an analogue to the four rivers traversing Eden, and with the natural setting of piney woods, watermelon fields, and golden sun, the natural beauty and simplicity of an Eden seem apparent. The narrator also describes his simple shack made from natural materials and tells us, "I have a gentle life". . . . (pp. 18-19)

All leads to the obvious, that the narrator is Adam II, that he originated not from the dust, but is rather a creation of rational man-eating tigers who have eaten his parents and left him an orphan. The new Adam emerges, not out of the dust of a universe in chaos, but out of the debris of a systematic and highly developed social order. His navel is intact, but the past is becoming less and less intelligible to him; the forgotten works are a British Museum of discards, the books and wisdom in disarray and intellectually inaccessible, and the physical world a shambles of objects without meaning. The new Adam finds his past as bewildering as the land outside Eden was to the old Adam. Adam II is created, not by the hand of God, but out of a disintegrating social order whose meaning is lost. It is not a world in which God is dead, for God has never existed. Its creative force is scientific, rational, and competitive, in which emotions run high over rights of ownership for materials of survival, and the creation is its antithesis. The tigers incorporate the human qualities of rational discourse and instinctive survival (they eat Adam II's parents not out of malice, but out of hunger). The tigers symbolize the destructive ambiguity of man, his instinct for survival and his rational nature that allows him to explain his acts of violence in terms of survival. As civilization becomes more and more sophisticated, the connections between violent acts and survival become less direct, until finally man loses the ability to connect his deeds with his goals. Such perverted nature is one that needs to be eradicated in Brautigan's cosmos.

If one sees civilization as an elaborate rationalization process, as Brautigan apparently does, then the return to the good life must allow for the destruction of the accoutrements of the rationalistic society. The forgotten works are the destroyed society; as the new society builds it must discover its own realities. The dimensions of iDEATH are circumscribed in new ways from the vanished structure. If man faces up to his biological nature, if he realizes that sophisticated civilized acts grow out of biological instincts and drives, then he must connect his acts directly to his goals in order to return to the essential of existence. Better yet, he must allow himself to become an instrument of nature. From Brautigan's vision, then, grows a natural determinism that is exhibited throughout the novel.

In Watermelon Sugar, like the Old Testament, is a work of teaching and guidance. It sets up the law and creates the myths of the future. In place of a tree of knowledge, we now have the forgotten works, both of which test man's obedience and his curiosity. (pp. 19-20)

Like Eden's, iDEATH's enemy is knowledge and curiosity. Perhaps implied in the assumptions of every utopian work, activity must cease when one succeeds in creating his perfection. The status quo must be maintained for all utopias; only the point at which existence is frozen makes them different. *In Watermelon Sugar* creates a non-authoritarian rule, an intensely self-disciplined society which limits its parameters consciously, while Eden is circumscribed by an outside authority. Brautigan's goals are substantially the same as those of the Old Testament, but he uses a humanistic rather than a deistic device to maintain iDEATH. (p. 23)

In many ways the new Eden is the Bible for the contemporary college generation, a generation that rejects man's mastery over nature, rejects intellectual rationalism, rejects authoritarianism, and emphasizes the natural elements in existence, embraces the environment, and lives collectively rather than individually. The novel finally becomes the new Genesis, the Bible for a new world, with new assumptions, that is carried in the hearts of the young. Such moral stricture according to Brautigan is naturally rather than divinely inspired. Like other utopias, iDEATH creates a sense of boredom, of inaction, and the mundane tasks of existence seem to pale before the activities of an inBOIL who acts out, who literally rebels at the world of pure sensation by his acts of sensory mutilation. Adam II as the passive chronicler is not made of the stuff that we have come to know in traditional prophets, but in a world of new assumptions, he is perhaps the archetype for the future. By any standard, most utopian novels are not exciting reading, and yet an emotional appeal that demands every man to speculate on a future good exerts a pulling force on the reader. Brautigan takes us a step beyond because he bends the language, he shapes a universe of half-inch rivers and grand old trout, statues of grass and a waste land that even the birds avoid. The poet is inseparable from the novelist, so utopia gains a new dimension. (p. 24)

Harvey Leavitt, "The Regained Paradise of Brautigan's 'In Watermelon Sugar'," in Critique: Studies in Modern Fiction *(copyright © by* Critique, *1974), Vol. XVI, No. 1, 1974, pp. 18-24.*

As Richard Brautigan says, his first novel, *Trout Fishing in*

America, is "a vision of America." The work is firmly rooted in the American tradition of Twain and Hemingway, of works whose theme is that man's only salvation lies in escaping from the complexities of city life into the tranquility of the country. While Huck Finn could "light out for the Territory" and Nick Adams could find peace in the Michigan woods, Brautigan's narrator discovers that escape to the wilderness is no longer so simple. Instead of virgin forests, he finds camp grounds so overcrowded that a campsite becomes available only when someone dies. . . . [The] imaginative escape is still possible: such a notion is the heart of *Trout Fishing in America*.

Brautigan presents the idea through a type of metaphor peculiar to him: although metaphor is certainly not his invention, his particular use of it seems unique. . . . In Brautigan's novel, . . . the tenor and the vehicle of the metaphor become fused: the imagined likeness becomes a literal rather than metaphorical identity. For example, Brautigan describes some trout in a stream as being "like fallen leaves." Immediately afterward, however, he says, "I caught a mess of those leaves for dinner." The progression here is important: beginning with the simile "like fallen leaves," an image of how the trout look in the stream, Brautigan converts the simile to a pure metaphor, "I caught a mess of those leaves." The metaphor, then, dynamically moves from a statement of similarity to a statement of identity: the leaves can be caught and eaten for dinner. (pp. 25-6)

[One] interesting implication [of this technique] is that such a use of metaphor—"Brautigan metaphors"—suggests a particular connection between imagination and reality, that the manner in which one thinks of and describes reality can alter reality itself. . . . (p. 27)

[In another incident, merely] thinking about John Dillinger is enough to cause him to appear. The idea that thought alone has the power to conjure up a physical presence is common in the early development both of the individual mind and of human culture in general, for it is basically a magical notion, and "magical" is an excellent description of Brautigan's view of the imaginative faculty, which through language can alter reality by providing a mental escape from its hardships. (pp. 28-9)

[The] theme of the novel is the narrator's development of an imaginative faculty which has the power to change reality. As a boy, the narrator cannot make a flight of stairs become a creek, but as a man he is able to: when he finally encounters the object of his quest, the character named Trout Fishing in America (the essence of the wilderness), the meeting takes place on the Big Wood River . . ., a "wooden" stream where he can catch fish. Brautigan names two of his chapters "Knock on Wood" and mentions the Big Wood River twice, a coincidence of names hardly fortuitous.

The novel's theme, much like that of Wordsworth's *The Prelude*, is the development of the power of the imagination; acquiring such power results in an ability, like that in "Tintern Abbey," to summon imagination to one's aid in times of distress: it provides a way of escaping to nature even in the midst of a city. If Brautigan's novel is "a vision of America," it also reminds us that America is "often only a place in the mind. . . . Through imagination one can still achieve an escape to the wilderness and a salvation from

the anxieties of the city—even a mechanized, urban America from which literal escape and salvation have become increasingly harder to attain. (pp. 30-1)

Thomas Hearron, "Escape through Imagination in 'Trout Fishing in America'," in Critique: Studies in Modern Fiction (*copyright © by* Critique, 1974), *Vol. XVI, No. 1, 1974, pp. 25-31.*

For all its seeming formal disparities and discontinuities, Richard Brautigan's *Trout Fishing in America* explores a very traditional theme, the gap between ideal America and real America, between Trout Fishing in America and Trout Fishing in America Shorty. Continually, Brautigan contrasts temporal and geographic America with a timeless America that is "often only a place in the mind.". . . Despite the disillusionment, the sense of failure and loss pervading the novel, Brautigan attempts to bridge the gap through the artist's power of imagining America otherwise. In so doing, Brautigan becomes a legatee of an uncompromisingly idealistic strain of American writing that wills to redeem America through formal achievement. (p. 32)

The example of *Moby Dick* is instructive in dealing with the structure and style of *Trout Fishing in America*, since Melvillean echoes resound throughout the novel. . . . The sheer quantity of short chapters, their apparently random arrangement, their digressive nature, with a number of chapters seemingly unrelated to the narrative—all reflect the "careful disorderliness" of *Moby Dick*. The characters whom the narrator crosses in his meanderings are the equivalents of *Moby Dick's* various gams, which illuminate central thematic concerns. Stylistically, Brautigan's verbal inventiveness approaches Melville's. *Trout Fishing in America* is loaded with put-ons, parodies, throwaway comments, whimsical irony, pseudo-logic, mock scholarship—for example, the list of fishing books that includes no accounts of "Trout Death by Port Wine" . . ., hyperbole, incongruous juxtapositions, and red herrings too numerous to document. For the careful reader, surprises lurk on every page. Both *Moby Dick* and *Trout Fishing in America* convey a sense of the imagination run wild in their stylistic wit and ingenuity. At times, the tones and rhythms of Brautigan's sentences shrewdly approximate Melville's. . . . Both writers delight in the unlimited freedom of the imagination, and both exhibit boundless pleasure in exploring the resources and possibilities of language. Brautigan's homage to Melville's experimental structure and style is omnipresent in *Trout Fishing in America*. (pp. 33)

In his novel, like Melville, Brautigan seeks an "organic process," a unique form that will revitalize well-worn materials. (p. 34)

Besides the structural and stylistic similarities between the two writers, Brautigan and Melville converge in their use of controlling symbols. Both Moby Dick and Trout Fishing in America are fluid symbols, metamorphic, and chameleon-like. . . . Both entities remain mysterious, unknowable, capable of accruing projected associations and values, yet never revealing their essential meanings. In attempting to arrive at some understanding of such phantoms, Melville and Brautigan circle their subjects again and again, hoping that obliquity will succeed where directness fails. Ultimately, Moby Dick and Trout Fishing in America elude fixed meanings, exist inviolate and indefinable, and retain their freedom in the province of the human imagination. As they should, whale and trout finally resist human grasps and swim free. For both Melville and Brautigan, only the pursuit itself, the continuing quest for the ineffable, holds lasting value. As Brautigan's frustrated, but resigned, Alonso Hagen says: "Somebody else will have to go out there" . . . to search for Trout Fishing in America.

The protean form of the novel allows Brautigan great range in exploring his main theme of ideal America versus real America. Trout fishing as a symbol is metamorphic, surely, but at the same time constant in representing an ideal—the continuing historical appeal that America has for the human imagination as a place where all good things are possible. (pp. 34-5)

As Brautigan traces our downward historical journey through the contrasts and ironies of the various episodes, he reinforces his theme by carefully placing most episodes in specific time contexts: times of day, seasons of the year, ages of the narrator and characters. A consistent cyclical pattern emerges, the parts of which gather very traditional emotional and psychological associations. The framework, in turn, suggests a broader parallel, as times, seasons, and ages are linked to a spiritual record of America. (pp. 36-7)

In choosing to write the kind of fiction that he does—symbolic, parabolic, fantastic—Brautigan clearly aligns himself with the tradition of American romancers, as opposed to that of the realists. The "actual and the imaginary" collide on every page of *Trout Fishing in America*. In his conviction that an imaginative ideal America is the only true America, Brautigan joins the tradition of Thoreau, who says: "Time is but the stream I go a-fishing in. I drink at it; but while I drink I see the sandy bottom and detect how shallow it is. Its thin current slides away, but eternity remains." Hints of the same kind of distant perspective appear in Brautigan's novel with references to time, death, and eternity—particularly in "Trout Fishing on the Street of Eternity". . . . As with Thoreau, all ultimates are absorbed into and transcended by the imagination in an effort to create a universe that "answers to our conceptions." Although Brautigan would happily send that emissary from the actual—Shorty—to realistic writers, he intends to keep Trout Fishing in America for himself. (p. 40)

> *David L. Vanderwerken, "'Trout Fishing in America' and the American Tradition," in* Critique: Studies in Modern Fiction *(copyright © by* Critique, 1974*), Vol. XVI, No. 1, 1974, pp. 32-40.*

"The Hawkline Monster" can be read as one more of Richard Brautigan's surpassingly pleasant divertissements in prose, for it is, like his other four novels, wanly pretty, curious, unexciting, winsome, sprinkled with both sparkling and foolish wit, likable, wispy. Brautigan's writing inspires adjectives, not nouns. The atmosphere is the thing, not events or characters or emotions. Better not dig too deep. No veins of anything solid here.

In "The Hawkline Monster," which is subtitled "A Gothic Western," there is a difference. There are fewer jokes and they are not so amiably odd. Brautigan is more literary. There is sort of a plot, with tension, conflict and relief—if you watch for them carefully and don't blink. Eastern Oregon takes on the look of Yorkshire moors; the mysterious

mansion and the whimsy of the supernatural something below stairs recalls Otranto; and the finale is a grand old device used by many writers but still workable if you can get up a good head of steam. There is an unsung, self-sacrificing hero, and even a moral if you like—Brautigan does not insist on it.

The story is partly satire and partly an excuse. The excuse is for Brautigan's wit, which consists of anecdotes and similes. . . .

Brautigan is, in a word, cute. To be cute is, for the novelist, to enter a dangerous country. It requires a very precise judgment indeed. But Brautigan is the region's Mountain Man—he braves this wilderness fearlessly.

Besides being cute, the action of a Brautigan fiction is as lazy, as airily inconsequential as the behavior of his compatriots in Big Sur. The emphasis is on unflappability. Go with the flow, man. There's a monster downstairs. Gotta kill it. For sure. But the ladies come first. And then dinner. Then the monster.

There is, of course, lots of casual sex, casually described. The sex is less an event that matters than a thing the stick-figure people do to kill time. All the actions here are just as casual. It is as if Brautigan had given up on personalities and their motivations when he began to spend more time on plot. In "In Watermelon Sugar" he presents the reader with a quandary, for the morbid inBOIL and the tragic Margaret do have personalities and do take at least the actions of their suicides seriously, giving the reader a more sympathetic focus for his attention than the pallid, Brautiganian types in the foreground. This could be mastery or clumsiness on the writer's part. The reader is not sure which.

In this latest work it is only the Monster and its shadow that matter to us. The nominal heroes are hired murderers who "could handle any situation that came up with a minimum amount of effort resulting in a maximum amount of effect." A minimum amount of effort is what they take, too, and they have no effect on the reader at all. One would like to care about the Misses Hawkline but, although their creator limns their bodies and their inherited predicament in some detail, they remain chance acquaintances. Perhaps Brautigan is celebrating the obsequies of the persona and I am out of fashion, but it looks more like his characters have all become the shadows into which the Monster at one point hopes to change them.

Richard Brautigan is a popular writer. He is clever and brief; he touches themes and myths close to the current fantasy without being too difficult or too long to complete and understand at a single sitting. He is witty, likable, even literate—a rare virtue nowadays. "The Hawkline Monster" read through once is enjoyable, can even provide a belly laugh. Skimmed through a second time it was, for this reader, unbearable.

It's a merry little book, good for reading by flashlight to friends toasting marshmallows during the next energy crisis, or else to be picked up for 15 minutes in a bookstore. You'll enjoy that quarter hour. (pp. 6-7)

> *John Yohalem, in* The New York Times Book Review *(© 1974 by The New York Times Company; reprinted by permission), September 8, 1974.*

Imagine Zane Grey trying to spruce up Book I of "The Faerie Queen" to make it accessible to readers west of Wichita and you'll have some idea of this fable's disarming appeal. [In *The Hawkline Monster: A Gothic Western* all] the ingredients of A Good Old Myth are present: (1) a remote Gothic house that maintains its own freezing temperature in the summer heat of the Dead Hills of eastern Oregon; (2) a monster said to thrash about in the ice caves beneath the Gothic house; (3a) an unmarried woman threatened by the monster; (3b) her sister, an identical twin; (4) their father, an alchemist consumed by his search for (5) the proper mix of chemicals that will solve the ultimate problem of mankind; (6) two professional killers.

Now for the recipe of the plot. Set aside (4) while (1) freezes in its simmering container. Separate (3a) and (3b), removing (3b) to (6). Bring (3b) and (6) to (1), then blend (3a) and (3b). Let (5) boil over until (2) is overdone. Apply (6) to (2). Allow (3a) and (3b) and (6) to scramble; spice with dirty words. (The sex is inevitable once you have unmarried women troubled by a monster thrashing in their cellar.) And there you have it. The result, I assure you, is as cute as a bucket of oyster stew: you can suck it right down before you remember to put in your teeth. (pp. 82-3)

Richard Brautigan is beloved by college kids [and] is admired for his tenderness toward human vulnerability, for his pose of the *faux naïf*, for his air of sweet inexpressible sadness. . . . Brautigan is a singularly careful writer. . . . Brautigan is a miniaturist who broods about death, who builds his novels from small self-contained blocks. He cannot entirely avoid coyness or dead-end digressions. Yet he conveys a sense of spare economy, of humorous or graceful lines eased in almost imperceptibility. . . .

"The Hawkline Monster is rather more of a pastiche, more of a parody than any of Brautigan's other fictions. It lacks the complexity, the many evanescent refractions of his best book, "Trout Fishing in America," which taps a central metaphor of American literature and deserves to survive the time in which it was written. Never mind. There are enough oppositions here (heat/cold; light/shadow; sex/death) to keep freshman instructors fueled for a decade. And I like the subtitle. Little old ladies waiting in libraries for "Cashelmara" to be returned to the shelves may pick it up, unwittingly. And then won't they be surprised. (p. 83)

> *Peter S. Prescott, "Monster in the Cellar,"*
> *in* Newsweek *(copyright 1974 by Newsweek,*
> *Inc.; all rights reserved; reprinted by per-*
> *mission), September 9, 1974, pp. 82-3.*

Reading Richard Brautigan often gives me the sensation of gazing in a mirror. He and I are nearly the same age, grew up in similar circumstances in small Western towns and cities, and moved to the Bay Area at about the same time. There is, then, a narcissist pleasure in seeing what feels like my own experience given a clarity of expression I have rarely been able to give it. But beyond this shared experience I sense a larger similarity. With a shift in focus I see, "behind" me in the mirror, my society, the social "nature" and its natural setting as they are now, including the social myths that at once unite and divide the society as they mediate its sense (and senses) of reality. Doubtless I assent to the "truth" of this reflection in part because I recognize myself in the foreground, but it is not merely self-love that validates Brautigan's image of society for me. Rather it is

the truth of the self-image, the accurate picture it gives of my ambivalence toward the experience that is "mine" and helped make me "me." We have learned to recognize ambivalence in ourselves; Brautigan's mirror to society shows it at work there as well—and on a scale transcending individual ambivalences, and not merely their sum. *Trout Fishing in America* shows especially well the boundaries and common ground of these two related ambivalences. (p. 29)

Brautigan shows us people balancing, people falling, people long ago fallen. *He* doesn't lose balance, though, even when he temporarily sends his narrator sprawling. Throughout he makes us feel that balance is an aesthetic virtue as well as a key to survival. It can also be celebratory: Brautigan deftly weighs beginnings against conclusions, chapters against chapters, motifs against motifs, not so much to shore fragments against ruins in order to survive as to remind us that, while the play is in earnest, it is still play. If we can follow the line walked among report, reminiscence, and fantasy in "Trout Fishing on the Street of Eternity," say, catching the nuances of feeling that accompany these turns, we can learn to keep our balance elsewhere in the book and perhaps outside it too. The narrator, by putting himself always before us as the narrator, shows himself master of the contradictions as well as their embodiment, yet always behind him is the final fabricator, Brautigan himself, even more the master. He reminds us of this role by the artful juggling of chapters and motifs I mentioned just now, but at the close—like a good juggler—he twice calls attention to his role and person. . . . As the simple and obvious modulation of voice in "Trout Fishing in America Nib" reminds us, the narrator's nib can produce many different effects, express a variety of contradictory myths and facts. He is at home in contradiction, clear-eyed and firm of hand as he creates a fictional world that mirrors oddly but clearly the myth-mediated world of cross purposes that we inhabit waking and sleeping, the world that we inherit and the world that, "growing up," we have shaped in part for ourselves. As Brautigan has shaped him. (pp. 39-40)

[Comprehension], seeing and feeling things and persons as they are along with the myths by which they order and disorder their lives, means most to Brautigan. It permits him and us to recapture the simple while remaining aware of the complex, to fish for trout while aware of all that trout fishing ignores. Most of all, it evades pessimism by offering an escape into other ways of ordering reality into "new" myth. The method requires cunning as well as skill, and so too does trout fishing. (p. 41)

Neil Schmitz's "Richard Brautigan and the Modern Pastoral," in *Modern Fiction Studies*, 19 (Spring 1973), almost decided me against writing this, for besides being excellent it covers *A Confederate General from Big Sur*, *The Abortion*, and *In Watermelon Sugar* as well as *Trout Fishing*. [Excerpts from Schmitz's essay appear in *CLC*-3, page 90.] But while Schmitz calls attention to the power of myth in Brautigan, he seems to me mistaken about how to take it all —or how Brautigan takes it. Schmitz's Brautigan is moved by an "ironic pessimism" to deflate the "posturing rhetoric" of myth. "What exists in history, things as they are" possess for him the greatest power. Like Roland Barthes, whose definition of myth he adopts, Schmitz sees myth as essentially lies to be seen as such and overcome. In this view myth *alienates* signs or words from the reality they name. Since I don't think Brautigan shares this rationalism and know I do not, I have written this essay in qualified praise of myth's inevitable but limited power. (pp. 41-2)

> *Kent Bales, "Fishing the Ambivalence, or, A Reading of Trout Fishing in America," in* Western Humanities Review *(copyright, 1974, University of Utah), Winter, 1975, pp. 29-42.*

[*The Hawkline Monster*] is a 'gothic western' set in Oregon in 1902. . . . Mr Brautigan's arch little chapterettes, laid out with the prissy self-importance of a WI flower arranger, certainly take their toll. The watered style and paper-thin narrative leave so much of the mind free that it zooms hopefully around looking for possible allegory, symbolism or even (cutting its losses) straight-forward hidden depth. One returns to base fatigued and empty-handed. (p. 457)

> *Julian Barnes, in* New Statesman *(© 1975 The Statesman & Nation Publishing Co. Ltd.), April 4, 1975.*

[Brautigan] describes [*The Hawkline Monster*] as a "Gothic Western," and it certainly has that mid-Atlantic and cross-cultural flavour which I associate with extremely bad novels. Cameron and Greer are professional hit-men, who will do anything for the money. Richard Brautigan has obviously learnt something from them. He rattles out his jokes like wax bullets, he almost hits his targets—it is surprising he doesn't get a little closer, since they are the remarkably large ones of conventional horror and conventional adventure—and he uses that ironic and dead-pan manner which is supposed to imply everything but which actually means nothing. (p. 411)

The Hawkline Monster contains a great deal of fancy but no imagination at all—this is presumably what the publishers and Mr Brautigan mean by "gothic"; fortunately, the novel is arranged as a series of brief chapters, and the print is very large, so the tedium of its self-indulgent whimsy is camouflaged for quite long periods. But you can never hide your darkness under a bushel, and Mr Brautigan's prose eventually becomes flat and uninventive, his narrative stale and repetitive. The publishers, of course, tell us that it is "beautifully evocative, funny and observant" but I presume that none of them actually read the book. (p. 412)

> *Peter Ackroyd, in* The Spectator *(© 1975 by* The Spectator; *reprinted by permission of* The Spectator*), April 5, 1975.*

*   *   *

BRENNAN, Maeve   1917-

Maeve Brennan, an Irish-born American, writes meticulously crafted lyrical short stories. She is best known as a regular contributor to *The New Yorker*.

Miss Brennan, who is a specialist at handling the delicate relations of the servant class to the marginal society types they serve, permits her characters to uncoil with all the force that a splenetic imagination can summon. There is a dark lack of sentiment in Miss Brennan's view of these relations, and the fictional life shaped by that view is a cruel, waspish one. There is, further, a terrible sort of satisfaction

to be gotten from the stories, for a punishment invariably befalls those who best deserve it, a punishment that is as spiteful—and sometimes as cheaply ironic—as they themselves are. . . . [There] is contrivance, but it is the best possible sort of fiction: the sort that yields a sense of surprise, and that possibility of continuing surprise, which makes for distinguished fiction. (p. 45)

> *Dorothy Rabinowitz, in* Saturday Review/World *(copyright © 1974 by Saturday Review/World, Inc.; reprinted with permission), March 23, 1974.*

Brennan's moral sympathy for the have-not, her Kiplingesque passion for revenge stop just short of overt moralizing. Interest in [*Christmas Eve*] comes from the witty characters; the balanced, tactile style; the charming, yet irritating, society Brennan criticizes while she describes. But weak plotting undermines much of the interest. . . . This mixture of sophisticated characters and gimcrack plotting is like finding Henry James' people in a script written for the Keystone Cops. (p. 28)

> *Peter Wolfe, in* The New Republic *(reprinted by permission of* The New Republic; *© 1974 by* The New Republic, Inc.*), April 27, 1974.*

Maeve Brennan's characters live in ecological niches of the emotional world. Like birds that nest on the narrowest ledges or the tree that clings to the dust on a rock, they manage to survive within a set of circumscribed, ritualized relations. Because they have so few resources, so little latitude, the tiniest deviation from habit is a great risk, high drama, a roar in the silence of an otherwise tightly controlled universe. One story hinges on the closing of a door, another on a head pulled back from a confidence, a third on who will be warmed by a coveted water bottle.

Two major groups of stories compose "Christmas Eve." The first six take place in a fictional Westchester suburb called Herbert's Retreat, the second six in Ireland, and an entr'acte in a restaurant on West 49th Street. I was initially put off by the Westchester stories which detail the small acts of cruelty and malice of bourgeois households with Irish maids. But what I finally found compelling about them was a mood, like some street scenes of Balthus, of understated, surrealistic malevolence. When Maeve Brennan's maids rebel by a look or a word, it is as if the Papin sisters, the famous murderers who inspired Genet's "The Maids," had run amuck.

The Irish stories are richer, full of the fierce complexities of life. Most describe the cramped, withered, deformed spirits of those who have grown up without love and the accommodations they have been forced to make to survive at all. . . .

The adjective that crops up most often in descriptions of Maeve Brennan's writing is "quiet." What is meant here is the calm, unassuming description of household detail, a literary approach perfectly adapted to Brennan's view of life. In "Christmas Eve" she states the axiom of both her technique and her philosophy, speaking of "the common practices of family life, those practices, habits, and ordinary customs that are the only true realities most of us ever know." In some families these practices serve to establish the existence of love so that "the child grown old and in the dark knows only that what is under his hand is a rock that will never give way."

Through the quiet description of the common practices of family life Brennan reveals the most passionate reality. For the most part, it is the reality of lives devoid of the rock of love, what they cling to and how they subsist. (p. 38)

> *Susan Edmiston, in* The Village Voice *(reprinted by permission of* The Village Voice; *copyright © The Village Voice, Inc., 1974), May 16, 1974.*

Maeve Brennan is the kind of writer who can transform the arrival of a sofa in a lower-middle-class Dublin household or the cleaning of a carpet (one with big pink roses on it) into an extraordinary celebration of family love. She does this by a steady accumulation of detail and alternate flashes of passionate statement and raw insight. The accomplishment is formidable—something few writers attempt without sounding precious, dull, or both.

Her gift is flawlessly demonstrated in the title story from *Christmas Eve*, Maeve Brennan's first book in five years. . . .

Love that is largely unexpressed, and the fear of losing it, dominates the lives of most Brennan characters. All of them, whether they survive in shabby Dublin gentility, bask in fashionable East Hampton, or simply hang on by their fingernails in New York City, live in a world of secret thoughts and elaborate private rituals that they cannot share. Brennan has always specialized in the involuntary victims of such isolation—children and animals. . . .

Her old-fashioned method is the unabashed use of straight description, as in *A Snowy Night on West Forty-Ninth Street*, the one New York story in *Christmas Eve*. It begins, characteristically, in a very low key, as a painstaking portrait of a small French restaurant, and the people who shelter there from the snow. But the author finally produces a freeze-frame of private desperation, the characters savagely revealed in a moment of vulnerability and compromise. (p. 62)

> *Helen Rogan, in* Time *(reprinted by permission from* Time, The Weekly Newsmagazine; *copyright, Time Inc.), July 1, 1974.*

Roughly half of the works in [*Christmas Eve*] are American—upper-middle-class exurban New York; the other half are Irish—lower-middle-class County Wexford. Perhaps some contrast is intended between the styles and values of the two cultures. If so, the point of the contrast is lost in the extreme artistic disparity between the two groups of stories. The American pieces are shallow, obvious, ill-composed and all but devoid of fresh observation, intellectual subtlety and emotional depth. The Irish stories, though unsensational, have a fine, mature, well-knit quality to them. The lyrics may be mournful and repetitious, but the best of them do sing. (p. 5)

If the American themes—money, divorce, and flirtations in the suburbs—seem to have been well-worn by O'Hara, Updike and others, the Irish themes—poverty, sexual repression, anger and domestic sterility—have been unforgettably explored by Synge, O'Casey and Joyce. But

Maeve Brennan demonstrates that familiar, even shopworn subjects and themes, are not necessarily an impediment to fine writing. Nor does it really seem to matter that the author more or less dislikes all of her characters. Oh, it would be nice if now and then a likable character would stick his head in and say "boo" to the tedious, pompous, whining, ill-tempered, selfish, and stupid multitudes. One doesn't expect heroism, but a glimpse of good-natured intelligence would have been refreshing. But Maeve Brennan does not choose to refresh us that way in her Irish stories any more than she did in the American ones. Still—and here, then, is genuine artistry—the Irish characters do earn our sympathy, and their grim, gray, hopeless situations awaken our interest.

I think the reason for this is that Maeve Brennan is a lyrical rather than a dramatic writer. In the American stories, she writes against her own grain. They are full of dialogue and scenes and sets. They are stagey in an unsatisfactory way. Characters are forever making entrances and exits, maids are in and out opening doors, eccentric guests burst out with one-liners and then retreat to a corner, various groups gather for climactic "showdowns." One feels the author laboring beneath the weight of all this theatrical paraphernalia and wishes that she and we could find somewhere to unload it.

In the Irish stories, she finds and keeps her own voice. There is little dialogue, a phrase or a word here and there. The drab row houses and the lovely Irish countryside are not treated as sets. They pervade the thoughts and feelings of the people who inhabit them. There are no clumsily artful build-ups to momentous scenes, largely because nothing momentous ever happens. Life, birth, marriage, death—all seem to become muted, if not stifled, by a vague mixture of fear and nostalgia.

All of the Irish stories deal with family life and the various forms of loneliness which can exist within it. The final piece, "Family Walls," is the triumph of the collection. It is a fictional meditation on a marriage that begins in fragile expectation and ends in vacuity. As in all the Irish stories, it is not a scene or a moment but a mood which is the creative center. (pp. 5-6)

> *Robert Kiely, in* The New York Times Book Review *(© 1974 by The New York Times Company; reprinted by permission), August 4, 1974.*

*   *   *

BROMELL, Henry   1942-

Bromell, an American, is a prize-winning short story writer.

In the vise of inexorable time, all distances prevail, even the slightest which are those between lovers, between husbands and wives, parents and offspring. Love cannot wholly bridge the gap, however briefly the illusion is favored that distances are narrowed. Life is lived balanced "between the temptation to remember and the sympathetic magic" of our still moments of isolated consciousness.

So ponderous a theme this is, albeit a familiar one, that a young writer takes a catastrophic risk in attempting to deal with it. Proust, Borges, and Virginia Woolf remain literary monarchs. But Harry Bromell, at twenty-six, his fiction appearing almost exclusively in the *New Yorker*, has been undaunted. His crystal-clear, tightly spun stories . . . collected [in *The Slightest Distance*] set in chronological order, add up to a surprisingly impressive first novel. (pp. 116-17)

Henry Bromell has proved himself a writer to shout about. (p. 117)

> *Nolan Miller, in* The Antioch Review *(copyright © 1975 by The Antioch Review, Inc.; reprinted by permission of the editors), Vol. 33, No. 1, 1975.*

A delicate nostalgia is the predominant mood of ["The Slightest Distance," a] collection of spare family miniatures, nine stories . . . about the various generations and branches of the Richardson family, all of whom share a common malaise-cum-philosophy: all are slightly out of register with the present moment so that they are almost always either longing or remembering. The "single quivering instant of love" in which one is fully *alive* is brief and rare. All the Richardsons are, in their various ways, aware of this mystifying human predicament, which has to do with the enigmatic nature of time and "the way the heart works." Each . . . voices an explicit variation on this theme. . . . Each of the stories laconically delineates the almost event-less surface of a moment in family life in counterpoint with these moments of numb reflection, or of memory, so seductive and elusive. There seems no real connection between event and event, or event and triggered memory.

This is very restrained, New Yorkerish writing—often a still life, luminous and blank. The whole richness of family life can only be inferred from a gesture as bare as an object or glimpsed in the rear-view mirror of memory. The Richardsons in their puzzled quest for what? can seem maddeningly tepid and tentative; their moments of dazzled realization that they are alive are precious few. Relentless indefiniteness, easing now and then into discreet lyricism, even a slight sentimentality. But the last two stories, "Balcony" and "Old Friends," become more vigorous, candid and explicit and take hold a little more. (p. 16)

> *Annie Gottlieb, in* The New York Times Book Review *(© 1975 by The New York Times Company; reprinted by permission), January 5, 1975.*

Henry Bromell's [*The Slightest Distance*] won the Houghton Mifflin Literary Fellowship Award, no easy one to ignore since past winners include Penn Warren, Elizabeth Bishop, Roth, Clancy Sigal, Robert Stone and Willie Morris. These stories, mostly published in *The New Yorker*, seemed when I read a couple of them there to be too quickly classifiable as made-to-order for the magazine; too quietly knowing about how well-bred stories ought to be written. But collected and read together they changed my mind. Bromell, writing about a family seen through the eyes of its members—particularly one son—doesn't have any fancy stunts or big ideas to get rolling; the stories are no better than they feel in the moment-to-moment development through conversation and narrator-reflection. . . .

Bromell is twenty-six but doesn't have a message from youth to deliver, nor a bee in his bonnet of any sort I have been able to detect. He is willing to hang around his charac-

ters and see if anything will transpire, which means that a reader should have an ear for dead air and less than striking exchanges. It is surely post-post-Hemingway, but done with real modesty and politeness and a tough assurance that suggest Bromell may be no more than a good writer. At any rate these stories are worth looking up. (p. 156)

> *William H. Pritchard, in* The Hudson Review *(copyright © 1975 by The Hudson Review, Inc.; reprinted by permission), Vol. XXVIII, No. 1, Spring, 1975.*

*   *   *

BROOKS, Gwendolyn   1917-

A Black American novelist and Pulitzer Prize-winning poet, Gwendolyn Brooks is one of America's most highly regarded contemporary writers. (See also *Contemporary Authors*, Vols. 1-4, rev. ed.)

Gwendolyn Brooks [is] far more a poet than a Negro [writing solely for the sake of expressing racial experiences]; for she is totally a poet, totally dedicated to her craft. She exercises, customarily, a greater degree of artistic control than any other American Negro writer. Not even Ralph Ellison has attained her level of objective and exquisite detachment. At least one Negro, it is worth noting, in the postwar United States . . . has been able to transcend the assertedly "universal" plight of her race. She is no more professionally black than T. S. Eliot (whose manner and skills she recalls), and should really be read and judged in the colorless company of his followers.

Of all Negro practitioners, only LeRoi Jones demands the same degree of poetic respect as Gwendolyn Brooks. They share a seriousness of poetic purpose, an intensely modern idiom (as opposed to Langston Hughes' "timelessness"), and a coterie audience (as opposed to his popularity). But Jones is a beatific, Blakean disbeliever in words, thrashing out raw problems of self-definition and epistemological truth in hopeless, anti-verbal expressions, all pain and incoherence. For Gwendolyn Brooks, at the other extreme, the issues, the self have all been sublimated into problems of craft, problems which she precisely and coolly solves.

What she seems to have done is to have chosen, as her handle on the "real" (often the horribly real), the other reality of craftsmanship, of technique. With this she has created a highly stylized screen of imagery and diction and sound—fastidiously exact images, crisp Mandarin diction, ice-perfect sound—to stand between the reader and the subject; to stand often so glittering and sure that all he can ever focus on is the screen. The "subjects"—racial discrimination, mother love, suffering—are dehumanized into *manerismo* figurines, dancing her meters. It is *her* intelligence, *her* imagination, *her* brilliant wit and wordplay that entrap the attention. Always, the subjects are held at arm's length away. Whoever the persona—and she is often forced to make the speakers fastidious, alienated creatures like herself—it is always her mind and her style we are dwelling in. (pp. 89-90)

In many of her early poems (especially the *Annie Allen* poems) Mrs. Brooks appears only to pretend to talk of things and of people; her real love is words. The inlay work of words, the *précieux* sonics, the lapidary insets of jeweled images (like those of Gerard Manley Hopkins) can, in excess, squeeze out life and impact altogether, and all but give the lie to the passions professed in the verbs. (p. 90)

She has learned her art superbly. The words, lines, and arrangements have been worked and worked and worked again into poised exactness: the unexpected apt metaphor, the mock-colloquial asides amid jeweled phrases, the half-ironic repetitions—she knows it all. The stylistic critic could only, at his most keen, fault the rare missed stitch of accent, the off-semitone of allusion.

Where, in all of this, is Gwendolyn Brooks? Anywhere? In the proper Donne-to-Eliot manner, she objectifies herself, for the most part, into the figured screen, her "blackness" becomes part of its peacocky color. She is become "all tone," all voice, all fire and air. One can only intuit the inspiring impulses of her works from the intensity of their objective design.

This is not to say she never speaks directly, or communicates ideas—even race-war ideas. There *are* clear direct statements, human portraits, in *A Street in Bronzeville* (1945)—though even in the best ("The Mother," for example) technical overcontrol may prevent the full realization of potential power (a matter of fear?). *Annie Allen* (1950), the Pulitzer Prize volume, is the most Mandarin; but sections VIII and especially XV of "The Womanhood" sequence bring a seething racial intensity of statement that for once gives the controlling art something to control, and produces genuine emotional tension. The latter may be the best statement yet on the latent Jim Crowism of white liberal society. (p. 91)

The same is true, somewhat less deeply, of "Lovers of the Poor" from *The Bean Eaters* (1959), a suave attack on overcultured whites by one who understands overculture, who can treasure herself the riches she mocks. Elsewhere in this . . . book Mrs. Brooks tries to expand her human scale—there are a few poignant husband-wife portraits in the manner of her novella *Maud Martha*, even attempts at jazz. But her fine efforts to take arms (an Emmett Till poem, a Little Rock poem, poems on white snobbery and neighborhood-mixing themes) betray the author through their tissues of arcane allusion, their perfectly chopped metrics. Gwendolyn Brooks has too little of the common touch to be of much use in the war; but she offers, through her painstaking, exquisite art, the example of one woman who has come through. (p. 94)

Maud Martha is a striking human experiment, as exquisitely written and as effective as any of Gwendolyn Brooks' poetry in verse. In thirty-four tiny fragments, vignettes, tiny moments in passage, the reader skims into the life of Maud Martha. First we meet a seven-year-old fat brown girl nobody loves enough; then a dreaming adolescent suffering through dates, living in her books and her satiny visions (the wrong hair, the wrong color, even for a Negro); then the young bride, in a minute kitchenette in a sad gray building in a cold white world, joined to her small-souled, dreamless Paul. He grows numb and unloving from his dreary, daily battle with The Man. He flirts with high-yellows. He hates the demanding pain of her childbearing. Finally, for this black Emma Bovary, there is left only a shrunken life of pretzels and beer, of hard-lipped encounters with the whites, a chapterful of queer neighbors, and glimpses of what might have been. (p. 152)

It is a powerful, beautiful dagger of a book, a womanly book, as generous as it can possibly be. It teaches more, more quickly, more lastingly, than a thousand pages of pro-

test. It is one answer to Langston Hughes' question: "What happens to a dream deferred?" (p. 153)

> *David Littlejohn, in his* Black on White: A Critical Survey of Writing by American Negroes *(copyright © 1966 by David Littlejohn; reprinted by permission of Grossman Publishers), Viking, 1966.*

[Gwendolyn Brooks'] poetry in *Street in Bronzeville* and *Annie Allen* was devoted to small, carefully cerebrated, terse portraits of the Black urban poor. The very existence of the characters she presents is both proof and cause for racial protest, but Miss Brooks handles all with a well-disciplined aesthetic detachment and "apoplectic ice." At this point, there is no rhetorical involvement with causes, racial or otherwise. Indeed, there is no need, for each character, so neatly and precisely presented, is a racial protest in itself and a symbol of some sharply etched human dilemma. This fitted in very well with the literary mood of the late 1940's. (p. 159)

By 1960 the dialogue of the 1940's about protest was as anachronistic as the ancient Platonic *caveat* that too much protest from men of literature might topple the state. . . . Black poets developed a rhetoric of protest and racial confrontation which was relevant for the times. . . . Gwendolyn Brooks' "Riders to the Blood-Red Wrath," for instance, ends with the racially self-confident assertion that the American Black man's long, bloody, and "continuing" Calvary gives him unique insights about man's inhumanity to man. Her Black Everyman . . . concludes that Black America will "Star, and esteem all that which is of woman / Human and hardly human." Indeed, the world will be revolutionized for love by Black America, for out of the Black man's struggle will come the renewal of "Democracy and Christianity." (p. 160)

> *Richard K. Barksdale, "Humanistic Protest in Recent Black Poetry," in* Modern Black Poets: A Collection of Critical Essays, *edited by Donald B. Gibson (copyright © 1973 by Prentice-Hall, Inc.; reprinted by permission of Prentice Hall, Inc., Englewood Cliffs, New Jersey), Prentice-Hall, 1973, pp. 157-64.*

Miss Brooks's first volume of poetry, *A Street in Bronzeville*, . . . translated into vignettes cut like exquisite cameos the experience of life of Negroes domiciled in a large urban Northern ghetto. Her Bronzeville, that is, was obviously Chicago. The immediate occasion for her reception of the Pulitzer Prize was the publication of her *Annie Allen*, a connected sequence of poems tracing the progress to mature womanhood of a Negro girl, the counterpart, in striking ways, except for death in childbirth, of Emily of *Our Town*. Her . . . book of poems, *In the Mecca* (1970), is set in "a great gray hulk of brick, four stories high . . . ancient and enormous, filling half the block north of Thirty-fourth Street between State and Dearborn . . . the Mecca Building." The life of women, particularly Negro women, and the life of Negroes, particularly those who have grown up since World War I in the North, where America's big towns are, figure prominently in Miss Brooks's poetry. Moreover, it does seem true that she is a woman writing, although not in the manner of the damned mob of scribbling women who so distressed Hawthorne—nor because of any mysterious and occult woman's intuition which seems to guide her inner labors. (pp. 81-2)

Miss Brooks, whether she is talking of women or men—sometimes undoubtedly to generate compassion, but, at other times, it well may be, with her tongue in her cheek—constantly speaks as a woman. That she does this in the manner that she is able to sustain only adds a supplemental virtue to the many elemental virtues as an artist which stand her in good stead in her work. For Miss Brooks is one of those artists of whom it can truthfully be said that things like sex and race, important as they are, in the ultimate of ultimates, appear in her work only to be sublimated into insights and revelations of universal application. (p. 82)

Moreover, with Miss Brooks humor is always present or waiting in the wings, perhaps not so genially (and then, perhaps, as genially) as in Langston Hughes, the only other major Negro poet—save, sometimes, Sterling Brown and Tolson in *Harlem Gallery*—for whom humor has been a conspicuous attribute of poetry. But, however she compares as a humorist with other black poets, in Miss Brooks's poetry the humor cannot be missed. It exists, tempering, in Miss Brooks, the irony which abounds in every serious Negro writer's contemplation of the American scene. . . .

Miss Brooks has assimilated, well and easily, her share of avant-garde techniques, and she uses them with no embarrassment or apparent animosity for them. Yet she seems to be a lover of old things, too. Her verse is often free. But often, too, it rhymes, in ways that poets have rhymed immemorially. And one will find that she resorts much to stanzas of the old kind, two lines or three lines or four lines, or more, in regular recurrence or a quickly discernible pattern, as poets once used to do. In *Annie Allen*, even, she has sonnets, at least one of them, "First Fight. Then Fiddle," with a constantly growing circle of admirers for its exceptional qualities as a poem. (p. 83)

Satin-Legs Smith [the protagonist of *The Sundays of Satin-Legs Smith*] superficially is a creature of no consequence; and he is, indeed, the new *Lumpenproletariat par excellence*. His Sundays are the big days of his week. On Sundays he fills (an empty word) his leisure time with diversions which express the best his world, and his conceptions of magnificence, can offer him. And what he does, like what he is, would be comic, were it all not so tragic against the background of the lost promise of the twentieth century. Her *Street in Bronzeville* and her *In the Mecca*, in all seriousness, could be used as reference works in sociology. Her *Annie Allen* quietly demonstrates the wealth of her observation of normal, not abnormal, psychology. . . . Terseness, a judicious understatement combined with pregnant ellipses, often guides the reader into an adventure which permits a revelation of Miss Brooks's capacity for sensitive interpretations of the human comedy. She never writes on "big" subjects. One finds on her agenda no librettos for Liberia, no grand excursus into history like [Robert Hayden's] "Middle Passage." *Annie Allen* typifies her method, the study, as it were, of the flower in the crannied wall. In such a method her genius operates within its area of greatest strength, the close inspection of a limited domain, to reap from that inspection, perhaps paradoxically, but still powerfully, a view of life in which one may see a microscopic portion of the universe intensely and yet,

through that microscopic portion, see all truth for the human condition wherever it exists. (pp. 84-5)

> *Blyden Jackson, in* Black Poetry in America: Two Essays in Historical Interpretation, *by Blyden Jackson and Louis D. Rubin, Jr. (copyright © 1974 by Louisiana State University Press), Louisiana State University Press, 1974.*

*   *   *

BROWN, George Mackay   1921-

A British prize-winning poet, short story writer, novelist, and essayist, Brown still lives in and writes of his native Orkney Islands. His themes, which may be called religious, are derived from Norse sagas and Catholicism. (See also *Contemporary Authors*, Vols. 21-22.)

George Mackay Brown knows where he is. His middle name has the tang-smack of ancient clanship and his poems testify all the time to his fascinated, localised convictions about Orkney-landscape and Orkney-folk past and present. It's like witnessing an absolute at-oneness. Inevitably there's local colour, if not whisky, galore: but not the brand to be mistaken for railway-carriage water-colours or package-deal brochures depicting remote Isles ready-made for recluses craving some ultimate haven-ly cul-de-sac, for neural souls despairing of diseases like noise, for weekend beachcombers seeking bits of bleached history under the shrill mewing Brandenberg-music of Arctic terns. Depict he does, as poets have rightly done ever since vocabulary caught on; and his local colour, in fact his total effect, is of a mature distillation and blend by an excellent and unmistakeable poet patiently subdued by, and to, the demands of his terrain.

For the poem-comber place-names are scattered about like saer-skels: Braga, The Kist and The Sneuk, Skaill, Sulisker, Rockall, Bui, Hoy, and Hamnavoe where

> The kirk, in a gale of psalms, went heaving through
> A tumult of roofs, freighted for heaven. And lovers
>   Unblessed by steeples, lay under
>   The buttered bannock of the moon.

—and except for the kirk we might, just, be under Milk Wood; though in the main Mackay Brown's diction seems as individually home-woofed as his themes and scenes are native. Then, for the wayfarer, curious poetic runes abound: Imagistic, the haikus of Orkney, laconic as milestones or time-stones, like 'Harpoonist':

> He once riveted boat to whale.
> Frail-fingered now
> He weaves crab prisons.

Spare, quiet, visually perceptive, they are idiosyncratic fussless tokens of a way of living and viewing. Aesthetic miniatures, seemingly evocative for their own sakes, appear throughout, like 'Snow' from "Weather Bestiary":

> Autumn, a moulted parrot, eyes with terror
> This weird white cat. It drifts the rose-bush under.

>   (p. 58)

The dead, like the past, are influential, even restorative. History, for both good and ill, is certainly exemplary; and to George Mackay Brown it is also red-haired and blond and cyclic. In . . . *Fishermen with Ploughs*, he has taken on a task indeed: a historical poem cycle in six parts. A 9th Century Norse tribe, refugees from the Dragon of outrageous fortune, sail west, fatalistic but hopeful of an agricultural survival. Settled on Hoy, the generations evolve through religious and political upheavals to compulsory education and the accumulating spurious material lumber of Progress, surely another Dragon, which depopulates the Island till all is desolation and 'Dead Fires'—

> Stars shine through the roofbeams of Scar.
> No flame is needed
> To warm ghosts and nettle and rat.

three lines very reminiscent of his poetic runes.—Ultimately the Dragon is a holocaust that obliterates a city whose few survivors return to the Island, possessed of little more than a primitive hope in agriculture and fishing, but enough to start the wheel turning. This mere summary must not detract anything from Mackay Brown's achievement, from the task itself which is vividly and quietly accomplished with an interesting range of verse-forms and a marvellous prose chorus at the end. All is characteristic: but there's no self-parody, or the sense of being jaded by one's own consistency.

George Mackay Brown knows where he is and writes with a local and natural authority. Most of his work has the Scandinavian quality of the letter K in Orkney, and all his work to date has been a persistent devotion, not because he is running in runic circles but digging, rooting deeper. (pp. 59-60)

> *Harold Massingham, "A Mature Distillation," in* Phoenix *(8 Cavendish Road, Heaton Mersey, Stockport, Cheshire, England), Winter, 1971, pp. 58-60.*

George Mackay Brown is a poet. *Greenvoe* is his first novel. The beauty and precision of his style, where the right word stands in place of three or four near-right words, and the vividness of his imagery all point to the disciplines and perceptions of the poet. That he is also a novelist is demonstrated best in his characters. They are so firmly fleshed and he has endowed them with such vitality that they have that rare quality of seeming to live outside of and beyond the narrative. Novels like this don't come along very often. (pp. 8-9)

> *Ruth Farwell, "There's Life in the Old Novel House," in* Book World—The Washington Post *(© The Washington Post), November 26, 1972, pp. 8-9.*

Magnus is almost a novel, yet more a kind of compilation of narrative and reflective prose, verse, and even one section of drama, round a central theme. . . . Mr Brown is a uniquely observant and skilful chronicler of life in his native Orkneys, past and present; this is the subject he has made his own, which he rarely strays from, and which he treats in writing where everything from a savage terseness to a sustained grandeur of cadence lies at his command. But he has occasionally—here, for example, and in the long poem-sequence, *Fishermen with Ploughs*—sought to arrange it all round one event. The result is a collection of magnificent pieces which do not quite fit together to achieve the desired unity. . . .

Mr Brown begins with the marriage of Magnus's parents and the conception of their son, setting against the dark-age magnificence of the moment the brutal life of the peasantry and the itinerant poor. He passes on through the education of Magnus and his cousin to the outbreak of enmity between them, the afflictions their war brings to the common people, and the final, near-ceremonial quality of Magnus's murder.

The narrative proceeds through these episodes in a series of impressive set-pieces: the weathers of the islands, the sheer colour and smell of land and sea, the earthy, obdurate nature of the people, are fused in these sections in language which is as flexible and precise as it is powerful. Towards the end, much less surely, the story slips into our own time . . . and is intended to suggest the timeless character of Mr Brown's theme: these passages sit uneasily among the rest.

And, despite the story, the Christian moral and the linking symbolism, the book remains an assemblage of brilliant fragments, nothing ever less than superbly observant, and arresting, yet oddly unsatisfactory when put together. In his individual short stories, in his sets of unconnected poems, Mr Brown evokes without strain—and as no one else can—a world of starkness and beauty to which he brings a deep, alert, compassionate understanding. In his more structured books there is a sense of strain about the attempt to draw it all together. The bursting life of the best individual pieces pulls things apart.

> *"Et in Orcadia," in* The Times Literary Supplement *(© Times Newspapers Ltd., 1973; reproduced by permission), September 28, 1973, p. 1101.*

Brown, a fisher of men who but labor in their vocation (Vikings, tinkers, shepherds, poachers, sots at a fair), and a fisher of syntax from every living source of our language appropriate to his poems—although the accents of saga and ballad predominate—is himself an island man, native to Orkney where, having escaped the world's nets, he still lives; his task: "a pure seeking past a swarm of symbols,/ The mill-wheel, sun, and scythe, and ox, and harrow. . . ." The sources of a poet's language are both private and endemic. Scotland and Ireland (possibly Wales) are the *only* places in the English-speaking world where "the people" (not all, but many) are worth overhearing, their daily talk, melodic and inventive, uncontaminated by the international-urban sludge that is fouling the stream of the richest language on earth. . . .

Brown achieved [the] crystallized eloquence [of his "Runes"] with canny sophistication, formed on the way by graduate studies in Gerard Manley Hopkins and the authorship of three volumes of prose fiction. . . . (p. 732)

What he probably learned [from Hopkins] was how to vary his line lengths, and his metres within the line or stanza, how to excite the solemn pace of a devotional verse (cf. respectively, the second stanza of "The Year of the Whale"; "Carol" and "Elegy"). Yet *where*, between Skelton and Keats, would one place the wintry-lyrical next-to-last stanza of "The Funeral of Ally Flett". . .? George Mackay Brown is giving back to poetry much of its ancient courtesy—Greek or Norse: to tell a tale, to commemorate human mischief and to cast spells about our ears. To support my belief that his is the most "wizard shape" to appear in British poetry since Dylan Thomas', I [would] offer "The Condemned Well," a cantata of his skills, a work I have promptly added to my select anthology of great poems about the finite world. (p. 733)

Vernon Young, in The Hudson Review *(copyright © 1973 by The Hudson Review, Inc.; reprinted by permission), Vol. XXVI, No. 4, Winter, 1973-74.*

There are parts of the British Isles so far from London they cannot be called 'provincial'. They . . . are British only by circumstances of history and geography and not identity. (p. 80)

While it would be foolish to claim that George Mackay Brown was an Orkney nationalist, it is still true that the Orkney Islands stand culturally and historically in a comparable relationship to Scotland as Scotland does to England. (pp. 80-1)

George Mackay Brown relies on the exclusiveness of Orkney culture and history in his poems. His poems attempt to make the special case of the Orkneys—and perhaps all remote communities—seem reasonable. He concentrates on a place; and the regret of his poems is that a community, seen to be at one time content with its appropriate ways of earning a living and the kind of society that its cultural inheritance had formed, is on the verge of total alteration, its once necessary unanimity corrupted by individual materialism and collective helplessness. (p. 81)

Loaves and Fishes (1959) was his first commercially published book, and the religious stress is evident enough from the title. 'Holy' was his favourite word: 'the holy earl', 'terrible holy joy', 'their lips/Welded holy and carnal in one flame', 'holy furrow'. Strenuously over-poetic efforts did produce the occasional success. A line like 'the sea grinds his salt behind a riot of masks', while it comes from the stable of over-dramatised visual imagery, that industrious measuring out of incantatory mysteriousness which suffered from the demise of Dylan Thomas's reputation, does however show the quality of Brown's pictorial sense at its most imaginative. It also shows that from the beginning Brown was prepared to associate his writing with outlier Celtic styles, the big bardic puff. (p. 83)

Even if a reader had suspected from *Loaves and Fishes* that what germs of lyrical realism there were in the book would become the most interesting aspect of subsequent poems, the first poem of his next book—*The Year of the Whale*—must have come as something of a surprise. 'The Funeral of Ally Flett' dispenses with naive patter. Imagination perceives what the eye might have seen rather than what the ear can revel in as a substitute for sense. His new idiom is a lucid counterpart of subject, but is at the same time under a formal control that does not neglect musicality. It uses the simplest method of telling a story; episodes and characters follow each other in a sequence of regular verses of eight lines of uneven length. The lyrical finish of the poem is beautifully accommodated to a concrete, visualised narrative. Brown also allows himself words too colloquial for his earlier poems—'tearaway', 'copper'—although to an urban ear, these would already have been replaced.

Brown, as a poet of remote island communities and unindustrial, non-urban landscapes, is at odds with the tradition of modern poetry. He is, in some ways, like Vernon Watkins, who adhered to a post-Modernist climate but maintained interests remote from it, and even antagonistic to the ways of life most contemporary poems arise from. Muir was like this, too, although his commitment to Modernism was critical and thoughtful; it is perhaps the Christianity of these poets that makes them seem apart from the way modern poetry has developed, and at once a criticism of the nature of that development. Local traditions also die hard. (p. 85)

What to an outsider might appear archaic in his poems is held by Brown to be both quintessential and timeless, to be the past alive in the present. His observations of reality are to be seen as corrupt, contemporary life in a time-scale of mundane history, and also in a timelessness of landscape. When excessive alliteration and heavy rhythm (usually to do with the sea) seem to intrude on the contemporary veracity of his observations, it is like an unconscious recall of the past making itself felt. (pp. 85-6)

Brown's best poems are . . . full of names and characters, their typical vulnerabilities, and the virtues of the way of life their personalities prove. He celebrates an ideal of community. At the centre is an imaginary town of Hamnavoe, the microcosm of the Orkneys, and a disguising cipher for the town of Stromness where Brown lives. . . . Scottish poetry is often particularly regional, of a special place—Burns in Ayrshire, Fergusson in Edinburgh. (pp. 86-7)

Unfortunately, Brown has now put forward a quaintly antithetical notion that there is a certain kind of real life for the good men of the Orkneys, and another kind of life in the cities of the mainland which is so vicious that it brings total punishment in the form of 'Black Pentecostal Fire'. In this he is a latter-day Rousseau, to whom the prospect of the brutalisation of pastoral contentment by 'civilisation' is made more real by the fact of civilisation's capacity of self-destruction. This line of feeling exists in Edwin Muir's work, too. . . .

One is entitled to have second thoughts about an imagination whose figments forecast Apocalypse; above all, a mind, like Brown's, that is so defiantly involved in a way of life, that he is prepared to use an imaginative Doom and kill off millions for the sake of a fresh start. Satisfying as an extreme gesture the final blow may be; he imagines it, and in a poetry with such overtly social implications a quick downward thrust of the hand of an atomic God hardly suggests that there is a solution for the problems of remote communities in life. Pessimism too easily takes the form of a hideous mushroom. It is the imagination's answer to the necessity of political engagement—i.e., don't do it; and to some extent it shows a hysterical misunderstanding by Brown of his own passion. . . .

Much of Brown's best writing is to be found in *Fishermen With Ploughs*, which makes his overall meaning doubly unfortunate. Certainly, taken as chronological narrative steps towards future catastrophe, the individual poems don't persuade that holocaust is either inevitable or even likely. (p. 88)

Brown seldom writes about himself. His objectivity is welcome, subordinated to passionate intention as it is. Instead of adopting a representative stance, he shows himself as a poet of community, of shared destiny, whose craft and insights are at the service of his neighbours. He writes from diffused experience, his passion deriving from concerns larger than himself. Even if one looks in his contemporary poems for personal testimony, evidence that what happens to the poet might prove the truth of his generalisations, one is likely to find the absence of subjective attitudes compensated by fidelity to a handful of themes consistently worked. His 'seriousness' is not in question. (p. 89)

[Brown's] is an essentially pastoral complaint; and it is neither an overestimation of Brown's importance nor a misreading of pastoral traditions, to say that he has to an extent successfully re-used methods and feelings of Wordsworth's, as seen in 'Michael'. . . .

But Brown's exhaustive vision, relating as is does to certain patterns of feeling known from the pastoral tradition, has flaws. The first is his rapid dismissal of The City; there is nothing in his writing prepared to admit the possibility of an Ideal Cosmopolis; and he seems unprepared to acknowledge the many writers and thinkers who have imagined such an ideal.

Nostalgia for the better community is, in my view, a valid poetic activity; retrospection is at least one way of visualising an antidote to what in contemporary society has nothing to do with virtue and goodness. Brown may have gone over the score in *Fishermen With Ploughs*, but his complaint is real enough, and magnified by the present activities of those concerned with North Sea Oil. Brown's pastoral mode maintains an awareness of reality; he prefers the socially descriptive and real, and ignores the sophisticated, decorative and sexually delighting—also legitimate elements of 'pastoral'—which are, perhaps, not all that apt in a northern Arcadia. Brown's is a poetry of work and people in an inherited environment, of struggle and compensating pleasures; it is not a poetry of a Golden Age, the unworked abundance. He involves our sympathy for ordinary people, for the idea of a whole community, and not for those for whom they provide—the taxman, the landlord, or the tourist.

When one considers the contrast between the limpidity of much pastoral writing and its motives, and Brown's vision of Orcadia/Arcadia, some sense of his power of literary controlling and merging can be felt. In his best work, he solves all the problems of the poet who wants to be both bucolic, real, hard and northern. (p. 90)

But there are negative aspects to his vision which although admirable to the extent that they are present, are not developed to anything like the lengths Brown's commitment to his ideals might indicate they should be. There is a general rejection of Modernity, for example. It can be noticed in *Loaves and Fishes*, where in 'The Shining Ones' he speaks of 'the great beasts of time' ranging beyond the night, 'a funnel of darkness, roaring with stars'. In the same poem, eternity is described as 'a flower pressed dry/By poets, preachers, all the literate humbugs'. This anxious feeling in Brown's poems for the unknowable scale of time, and the existence of mysterious dimensions, while one basis for the bardic styles he sometimes uses, is also behind his social criticism. His deep hatred of the materialist phase of History arises from mystical conceptions of time, not political ones, and this in spite of a bitter awareness of the root causes of what has altered the Orcadian ways of life. It has more to do with exploitation, capitalist manners, and political neglect, than looking up funnels of darkness at the tantalising galaxies.

But Brown must have it both ways; even a mystical-religious poet cannot evade reality when it washes up the rubbish of the Age on to his beaches. He seems to be saying that the Cosmos as viewed from the Orkneys below is his true subject; the rest is temporal dross, side-issues, a tiresome necessity to face what is only too observable. There is a latent moral strategy in this, a creeping ambivalence. By espousing what is vast and unknowable, Brown is able to think of present time with at least a muted amount of contempt. . . . 'The microcosm', says Beckett, 'cannot forgive the relative immortality of the macrocosm'. Brown's resentment is of that kind. And it is possible to sympathise with a poet in such a dilemma; if only, that is, he would not use his ultimate belief to crucify a world which, whether we like it or not, or whether Brown likes it or not, is the only one we are ever likely to have. For all his fixity and local commitment, Brown is, in poetical terms, unsettled; he is looking at the stars, dreaming of the stars, but round his feet are rusting tin cans, old tyres, beached poisoned fish, while just over the horizon Americans in safety helmets and boilersuits are sinking their oil wells.

Although he dramatises the activities of lairds and landlords, visitations of the taxman, depopulation by the magnet of urban prosperity, there is a wholesale withdrawal in his writing from political decision, or even outright social criticism. Regret, fear, premonitions of a general worsening —moving, and poetic; but the passion that is obviously behind his writing, and the humanity that dictates censorship of self and private emergency in a gesture of communal humility, might also be seen to demand a stridency outwith that represented by the dire trick of Apocalypse. No radical interpretations are offered, only a wiping out. He accepts Time and its consequences, what other men do. He never attempts to answer the question 'What can be done about what is happening to where I live?' In fact, he never asks the question. We are left with an impression of far-off turbulence. He accepts corruption and exploitation with the inert grin of the man happy with what survives, but wanting more because he knows all that there used to be, preferring to outline an ideal by retrospection, creating an image of the past to act as a spell against the present and future.

Having been convinced by the best of what Brown has written, my feeling is that a bit more is called for, a harshness and indignation that Brown might be unsuited by temperament, or poetic beliefs, to provide. (pp. 91-2)

> *Douglas Dunn, "'Finished Fragrance': The Poems of George Mackay Brown," in* Poetry Nation (© *Poetry Nation,* 1974*), No. 2, 1974, pp. 80-92.*

*   *   *

BUKOWSKI, Charles   1920-

Bukowski is a German-born American poet of rough-hewn ferocity. (See also *Contemporary Authors*, Vols. 17-18.)

Charles Bukowski wouldn't even know what you were looking for if you mentioned the philosopher's stone. He is, and has been for more than a dozen books, at the level where all dreck is gold itself, providing it issues from his own self. . . . From his prolific lucubrations, Bukowski is one of those people who must have said to himself sometime, fatally, "Gee, I read Cummings once and Whitman, did I read Whitman? and I listen on the radio to 'symphonic music,' I don't like working, but I do like to be in despair when I'm hung over on dusty Sundays looking out of torn window shade apartment—I *must* be sensitive, if only them bums knew how much, and I have always been on the move, sort of snarling (in poems) at cops and boozing it up with real people in bars—and pretending to like women, taking them on for a feed and fuck,'' which is mere hypocrisy on his part, judging from his talk about women in *Mockingbird Wish Me Luck*. . . .

But the awful thing is that you can have 150 pages of flat stuff without one insight, without one flare-up of language, without an interesting emotion, or even the attempt to devise a poem structured to be conducive to an emotion, without . . . well, one could list more *withouts*, adumbrating thereby an implicit poetics—yours, mine, anyone's.

The question is, however, not those *withouts*, but—*with what* does Bukowski work? With very little, I guess, except the primitive will to scribble self-consciously. I am not sure he wants to project the presence he does: a vain, irritable, miserable, self-indulgent and self-commiserating presence. All those selves, because perhaps he wants it that way. A mean-minded, beery ghost damply haunting the place where he is, in the present, before the person has even been terminated. And, after twelve books of this guff, to seem to some people a plain-speaking poet! There is somewhere here an element of incipient horror, just as there might be an incipient poetry. The horror is what you'd feel sitting an hour among a bunch of winos on a bench on the beach in Venice, California: a flat, dull, stupid, morose horror. Or pick your bums on the Bowery stoops. But the poetry? In the notations Bukowski derives from his memories, which could, for the sake of discussion, be made into poems, if there were a poet present. As it is, there is mostly botched butcher paper. (pp. 230-31)

> *Jascha Kessler, in* Parnassus *(copyright © by* Parnassus: Poetry in Review*), Fall/Winter, 1973.*

[In *Life and Death in the Charity Ward*] Mr Bukowski is obviously following that age-long principle of writing down anything and everything which comes into his head, and he no doubt thinks of himself as the true heir of Shakespeare in never having to blot a line. It becomes increasingly clear in a reading of these stories that he has no critical sense whatsoever, since his talent is a matter of hit-and-mainly-miss. This leads to some vulgar and prosaic passages, since a writer who is not self-aware is condemned to be continually looking over his own shoulder. Bukowski's themes were fads some time ago, and it is now practically impossible to make sex and violence interesting. Of course a man who lives in the past is always the one who has the most to hide from the present, and Bukowski suffers from an inability to perform as much as he promises. Only a bad poet labels himself poet, and only a frustrated man writes about sex with such prurient abandon. A dull character finally emerges, and it is a dullness which spreads through these stories like a stain. (p. 711)

> *Peter Ackroyd, in* The Spectator *(© 1974 by* The Spectator; *reprinted by permission of* The Spectator*), November 30, 1974.*

The last impression I want to give [in this review of *Life and Death in the Charity Ward*] is of an honest and original work mangled, like *Barbary Shore*, by a reviewer's vulgar prudery. As far as originality is concerned, Mr Bukowski is on a very well-travelled path with these picaresque tales of pussy-hunting and boozy male camaraderie in and around Los Angeles. A long way up ahead is Henry Miller (at one point Mr Bukowski wryly acknowledges the distance between them), and throughout there are clear echoes of that huge, under-edited and rather *passé* mob of US chroniclers of dope dreams and groovy pranks, ranging from Kerouac and Tom Wolfe down to the egregious Dr Hunter S. Thompson.

I would imagine that Hubert Selby, Jr figures very prominently in Mr Bukowski's pantheon too; indeed to the extent that if he had any goal it was to make a sort of west-coast *Last Exit to Brooklyn* out of his violent, would-be shocking anecdotes. The reach exceeds the grasp, and it is in contemplating the two so-unequal books that the charge of prudery can best be disposed of. I still find my imagination haunted by some of the images and episodes in Selby's important work. . . . What made Selby's vision so frightening, however, was not the precise details of each sordid event, but the overpowering sense that they were being revealed reluctantly and only because the author was a remorselessly honest man who could not help himself plunging deeper and deeper into the dark recesses of human life.

Unfair or not, Mr Bukowski gives the impression that he is in it only for the shudders. No pioneer probing the edges of experience, but a whipper-up of creepy-crawly *frissons* for jaded appetites. One wouldn't mind even that if only he wasn't such a wretchedly inept whipper-up. But . . . the only possible response to [his] level of blowhard bathos is surely angry laughter. . . . (pp. 838-39)

> *Peter Prince, in* New Statesman *(© 1974 The Statesman & Nation Publishing Co. Ltd.), December 6, 1974.*

Certainly no poet in America as deserving of recognition [as Bukowski] was so long buried, ignored, and even despised by establishment critics, readers in droves, *Rolling Stone, The Whole Earth Catalogue* people, granters of American Poetry Society Annual Awards, etc. I remember how jolted I was when I first read him: I was teaching at the University of California at Riverside and had been given a copy of *Crucifix in a Deathhand*. I carried the book to a string quartet concert one night, began reading it before the concert began, experienced chills, elevations, charismatic flashes, barberpole exaltations, fevers in the groin, etc. I had not read such poems since discovering Dylan Thomas for myself in the fifties. Christ, something awe-thentic at last, I exclaimed, nudging my companion who thought I had gone out of my mind. No poet I was then teaching or reading marched so directly into the poignant grosseries of life, into the depths of soul-body-mind, painted it up quivering and wriggling on the wall, and let in drifts and wafts of compassion to sweeten the dregs. Bukowski was unafraid of life's terror meat-slabs, and he made the angels sing. . . .

To me, he was a super-poet, the best I knew. . . . He made Lowell, Snodgrass, Wilbur, Olson look like dilettantes. (p. 24)

Bukowski has written no better poetry than appears in [*It*

Catches My Heart in Its Hands (1963) and *Crucifix in a Deathhand* (1965)]. . . . In these early poems, the act of writing is for Bukowski "to get . . . feelings down." Now, that's not news, of course; it sounds like warmed-over Shelley and Keats. The crux is the nature of the feelings: are they surface, deep, sentimental, universal? In Bukowski's head, the urge to write, which for him (since he's done so much of it) must be as necessary as defecation, is prompted by his pain. The pain, somehow, is externalized by the writing; or rather, an image allows him to translate pain into a larger testimony of the human spirit. And there is also, he says, "madness and terror" along "agony way." Both are alleviated by the act of the poem. There's something like a time-bomb ticking inside his chest, and if it doesn't go off as a poem it will go off in a fit of drunkenness, dope, sensuality, despair, vomiting, rage. It's as if he's saying that as long as he writes he leashes his terror in its cage. "Beans with garlic" is exactly about this. A terrific idea, beans as loves! And stirring them has to do with writing your poems—words as beans, etc. The idea almost works. (pp. 25-6)

At his best Bukowski produces (invents) his own special rhetoric. Then he is never fatiguing, as he becomes in his later raconteur, gab/barfly manner. Too often his recent voice sounds like one of his army (located primarily in southern California) of inept imitators. His best poems discharge themselves with an Olsonesque energy. One is touched by a vital creative mind loving the creative act, prizing it, despite the booze, etc. This special energy is what earns Bukowski a front rank place among contemporary poets. Call it *originality* if you will; for, to paraphrase T. S. Eliot on Tennyson, Bukowski has (had) originality in abundance.

In *At Terror Street and Agony Way* (1968) a deterioration of Bukowski's talent sets in. His paranoia, traceable in earlier works, is heightened. His temper grows discernibly nasty. . . . It's as if B. wants to spit in your face, dear reader. The situations of the poems become more extreme. It's as if Bukowski is aware that a sycophantic [sic] public expecting outrageous cartwheels and titillating obsenities applauds his showing off. There is a discernible and regrettable drifting from the superb humanity and tenderness of the earlier poems. And there is a troublesome, boring loquaciousness; the finely turned work of the early manner is usurped by rambling, grotty passages of prose masquerading (cut into lengths) as poetry. I continue to read Bukowski nevertheless, because there are still surprises. He remains one of the most readable of poets; and the appearance of any of his books is an event. A core, primitive almost, resides in first-rank poetry—a core of empathy, depth, wisdom-via-suffering feelings. This has shrunk almost away in Bukowski's current work, replaced in part by a regrettable nastiness. (pp. 26-7)

I call [his recent] loquaciousness GAB POETRY. And GAB POETRY seems to be Bukowski's favorite genre these days, particularly if one included the numerous prose pieces, stories and otherwise. The GAB POEM is related to the old fabliaux of Chaucer and the medieval poets, a connection I'm sure Buk will (would) delight in. . . . A travelling narrative (with Chaucer at times presented in skillful verse), garrulous, in which you feel nothing is left out, a sort of gab accompanying spitoon [sic] sounds in some down and out bar. Also, the illusion that the narrator, much

in his cups, is loading your ear as you lean beside him sniffing his loaded breath and working up your own inebriation. (p. 28)

Charles Bukowski is an easy poet to love, fear, and/or hate. He works at developing his own legend as loathsome person, lush, woman-devourer, etc. And he has a winsome, almost childlike, ingratiating side which various people have experienced and enjoyed, frequently to their surprise. He can be the best-behaved poet around, and one of immense charm. Obviously, by discussing his personality I fall into the trap of confusing the personality of the poet with the poetry. . . . And it doesn't matter—none of it—except for the work. My reason for writing this piece is to cut through some of the ordure appearing about Bukowski—much of it sentimental and unabashedly devoted to increasing his celebrity status. He remains a considerable poet who has for the present moved into something of a decline. Yes, say other readers, "but as his poetry worsens his fiction grows better." Perhaps. My own feeling is that poetry remains a more durable and demanding art than fiction, that the depths of the human spirit declare themselves better in poetry than in prose, and that the superior poet is equally the superior man. Buk, climb back up on that fence, grab your beer and your paper and pencil, gaze off over the landscape, and give us a fresh stampede of tremendous poems. (pp. 28, 69)

Robert Peters, "Gab Poetry: The Art of Charles Bukowski," in Margins *(copyright © 1975), January, 1975, pp. 24-8, 69.*

Whether or not Charles Bukowski's "poems" are actually poems is open to legitimate debate, even after the loosening up of our ideas about poetic form that has occurred in the past ten or fifteen years. Certainly they have nothing musical or metrical in their language. But it is also legitimate to evade the question altogether by looking at them simply as chunks of writing, in which case one sees that most of them are really very good. When you compare them with similar chunks—a paragraph from Henry James, say, or one of the portraits from the Prologue to the *Canterbury Tales*—you find the same tension, the same inner unity of image and feeling, the same fully charged language—no gimmicks, no bombast. In terms of language Bukowski is an honest writer.

In terms of substance he is perhaps less than honest, since he idealizes everything dreadfully. His poems are full of stock figures from American romanticism: noble drunks, sensitive whores, downtrodden artists, etc. Everything is seen through a narcotic mist of self-pity and pessimism. Nor has Bukowski added anything new to the mélange, though he has given it a "flavor" of the 1960s and '70s. His strong point is the way he writes clearly about a particular uneventful event—a day, a night, an afternoon at the track, a drive on the freeway—and draws from it a recognizable mood and an understandable meaning. . . . [His poems] are worth reading.

Hayden Carruth, "Images," in Bookletter *(copyright 1975 by* Harper's Magazine; *reprinted from the March 31, 1975 issue by special permission), March 31, 1975, p. 4.*

Charles Bukowski will probably survive as the closest thing to a truly damned poet that our, or any, culture has produced. For some twenty years now he has been a moral spokesman for the American lumpenproletariat, a chronicler of our urban degeneracy, whose dingy furnished rooms, drinking, and fornications are neither bohemianism nor self-indulgence, but a way of life. He writes almost exclusively of violence, dirt, sickness, hopelessness, but with a stoicism and self-honesty, even a sort of good humor, that defeat the implications of such things and make him, or his poetic persona, an improbable hero for our times. A man who has, above all, come through, he demonstrates that human creatures can not only succumb to an ultimate sordidness, but abide there in something resembling dignity. He is like a Henry Miller without epiphanies, or, better still, like a Céline with a moral sense. He is also an excellent poet. (pp. liv, lvi)

> Virginia Quarterly Review (*copyright, 1975, by the* Virginia Quarterly Review, *The University of Virginia), Vol. 51, No. 2 (Spring, 1975).*

*   *   *

BULLINS, Ed   1935-

Bullins, a vital force in the Black Arts movement, is an award-winning Black American playwright, poet, editor, and short story writer. His realistic dramas of the ghetto, immensely relevant for Black audiences, affect profoundly non-Blacks as well. (See also *Contemporary Authors*, Vols. 49-52.)

Bullins has never paid much attention to the niceties of formal structure, choosing instead to concentrate on black life as it very likely really is—a continuing succession of encounters and dialogues, major events and non-events, small joys and ever-present sorrows. . . .

The Duplex is virtually shapeless; it does not really end, merely stops, its central situation unresolved. It is a mixture of styles, from farce to tragedy, a play that works within its own definition of theatre, (and mine), within its own definition of life. It reveals characters and situations that are, for the most part, alien to the white experience. Bullins makes you aware of why blacks have only infrequently attended white theatre. His plays grow out of black life and are written *for blacks*. The white member of the audience is in a sense almost an interloper, looking in on a culture that has a distinctly different texture. (pp. 50-1)

> *Catharine Hughes, in* Plays and Players (© *copyright Catharine Hughes 1972), May, 1972.*

Bullins' plays can generally be divided into two categories: satire and serious. But the line that divides them is sometimes very thin. Plays such as *The Electronic Nigger* and *Pig Pen* are obviously satire. *Electronic Nigger* is a scathing condemnation of the would-be black intellectual, and *Pig Pen* is a laughing look at the world of so-called "revolutionary" integration (about eight black men and one white women). This kind of satire is very explicit and the playwright's position is very clear on these subjects.

The serious plays, however, like *The Duplex, Clara's Ole Man*, and . . . *The Fabulous Miss Marie* . . . do not lend themselves to easy interpretations. *The Duplex* ends, for example, with the older woman, the landlady, going back downstairs in resignation to get her head-whipping from her man because of what she's done. And nobody moves to

help her because supposedly anything her man does is within his right. But, we ask, will that help ease her loneliness? Will that prevent her from seeking out some other young man when things come down on her too hard again? Bullins doesn't say. (p. 52)

> *Lisbeth Gant, in* The Drama Review (© *1972 by* The Drama Review; *reprinted by permission; all rights reserved), December, 1972.*

Ed Bullins' *House Party* is [a] disappointment . . . from a highly talented young writer. It's subtitled 'A Soulful Happening' and on that you'll get no argument from me. What it isn't is much of a play.

We're in 'Black America, in the nostalgic past and now' and nine actors, playing many more than nine roles, have gotten together for some drinks and dancing. One by one, they engage in a series of soliloquies, bridged by musical numbers. The programme labels them 'Woman Poet', 'Loved One', 'Fun Lovin', 'Confused and Lavy', 'Harlem Mother', 'Harlem Politician', 'Black Writer', 'West Indian Revolutionary' and the like. Each has his story to tell, his opinions to voice. But they are abstractions, not people, and only rarely, and then all too briefly, is it suggested that what we're listening to is not 'Black Writer', but Ed Bullins, damn good black writer.

House Party has neither the muscle nor the humour, the pulse nor the pain, of Bullins at his best. It is content with lines like 'No future unless we make it/No hope unless we have it,' which, valid enough in themselves, say nothing that he and others have not said before with more power and passion. A writer as good as Bullins really shouldn't settle for a play as inconsequential as this. (p. 57)

> *Catharine Hughes, in* Plays and Players (© *copyright Catharine Hughes 1974), January, 1974.*

Ed Bullins has often been accused of being negative, of fostering negative images of Black people. His characters are men and women who don't make it, who drift through life using and abusing each other. The unerring honesty of his realistic style makes it impossible for the ugliness of their activities to be obscured or for the viewer to be comfortable. The final act of an Ed Bullins play always takes place after the fact, after the play is over and the audience has separated into individuals who must deal with their collective fate. It is over only when we have dealt with ourselves and the characters and found the distasteful elements in both. Far from being negative, Ed Bullins is concerned with those suicidal practices that render the Black man impotent; that prevent us from reaching the goals so often spoken of in the revolutionary rhetoric of the time. His concentration is on the community as it is, as he sees it now. The dilemma here, however, is that many folks assume that the playwright's stageworld represents a total view of the Black community, when he is, in truth, talking about those who are sick with very specific kinds of illnesses and pretensions. The totality of the viewpoint is relative to the totality of the social phenomena discussed and described.

The Bullins theater is the theater of confrontation. We are forced to look at ourselves and that part of our specific community which troubles us in our quiet moments. [His message is] that we must deal with our own streets, with the choices we continue to make and the dreams we trade for truth. The sounds we hear and the movements we see on the stage disturb us *because* they are rooted in truth. . . . Again, the playwright is caught between the need for new images and the necessity for illuminating the present psychosis.

The duality of Ed Bullins continues even into his craft. To many, he is a pioneer creating new forms for Black expression. Others view his plays as structureless adventures in tasteless dialogue. It is said that "nothing ever happens in a Bullins play." The old bugaboo about plot structure and all of the other characteristics of conventional Western Drama constantly rears its ugly head. Ed, however, continues to turn out pieces which move audiences. His eclecticism defies any definition except his own. Like a jazz musician, he constantly changes and molds his meter. The seemingly straight-down-the-line realism is constantly interrupted with forays into passionate prose and poetry. . . . We may leave the characters in pretty much the same place we found them, but something has definitely been going on. Action has taken place. The work of Ed Bullins is stamped with the feeling of immediacy. It is as if the piece were being created while it is being performed and is subject to the changing moods and urges of its performers. Reading the script, however, tells us the dynamic changes are due to the playwright's stage know-how. They are all plotted moves and nuances. Rather than any rules of dramatic unity and structure, it is the knowledge of his people, his audience, and an unerring understanding of what will and will not work on a stage that directs the Bullins craft. (pp. 16-17)

> *Don Evans, "The Theater of Confrontation: Ed Bullins, Up against the Wall," in* Black World *(copyright © April, 1974, by* Black World; *reprinted by permission of* Black World *and Don Evans), April, 1974, pp. 16-18.*

In his plays, Bullins (a leading playwright of the Drama of Self-celebration) continually portrays [the] Search [for Self-completeness]: Jack and Clara in *Clara's Ole Man* (1959), Cliff and Lou Dawson in *In The Wine Time* (1966), Steve and Grace in *It Has No Choice* (1966), and Steve and Liz in *New England Winter* (1967). In *Duplex*, Bullins elects to make the Search the controlling idea. (p. 22)

Marked by a flowing conversational style, *Duplex* relies on two structural devices to create mood and to transport its unifying idea: (a) unplanned and casual action, and (b) frequently disconnected dialogue. Also, there is very little developed action in the play. (Action "is not here thought of as mere physical activity, but as what the characters do: fight, fall in love, make or evade making decisions, voice their secret thoughts, or harangue either other characters or the audience."). . . The search for structure, then, must focus not on the development of action, but on the development of the theme, the recurrence of hopes for Self-completeness. These hopes are gradually exposed as illusions and are later shattered. Bullins' structural pattern is dissatisfaction with reality, flight into fantasy (or envisioned reality), and a return to an adjusted reality.

An earlier theatrical example of this structural style can be found in the Russian playwright Chekhov, whose simplified plot fabric and apparently unsystematic combination of facts and actions caused his plays to be termed "drama of mood." (pp. 23-4)

Bullins' second structural device [is] desultory conversation. The characters frequently do not listen or respond to each other. Each spins his own yarn to others, who are far more interested in spinning their own. (p. 24)

[The] desultory dialogue highlights the casual action and points to the desperation of the Search for Self-completeness. The remarks are charged not only with the particular meaning for the character who is speaking, but with a special meaning that illumines the Search of the others present. Again, we can turn to Chekhov (to *The Three Sisters* . . .) to see an extensive use of the desultory conversation device. (p. 25)

Bullins selects and arranges his scenes so that they resemble the Search itself: looking, finding, testing, detesting, re-searching. Each character's Search "is examined at length," as [John] Kerr points out. His complaint that the characters are "independent entities," that they "spin off into space without having made vital connection" is the very strength of the play, is in fact the successful meshing of form and content. (pp. 25-6)

> *Samuel A. Hay, "Structural Elements in Ed Bullins' Plays," in* Black World *(copyright © April, 1974, by* Black World; *reprinted by permission of* Black World *and Samuel A. Hay), April, 1974, pp. 20-6.*

"The Taking of Miss Janie," a good new play by Ed Bullins, . . . can be most briefly described as a fugue, whose themes are the feelings and experiences of a number of young people during the nineteen-sixties. . . . As was true of Mr. Bullins' "The Fabulous Miss Marie," each of the leading characters, with a spotlight on him, talks at one time or another directly to the audience about what is on his mind and in his heart and, occasionally, what lies in store for him. . . . Mr. Bullins has rarely been wittier or, for that matter, more understanding and vigorous. "The Taking of Miss Janie" is, according to a program note, a sequel to "The Pig Pen," his most puzzling play. This one may be his most complex, but it is clear. (pp. 61-2)

> *Edith Oliver, "Fugue for Three Roommates," in* The New Yorker *(© 1975 by The New Yorker Magazine, Inc.), March 24, 1975, pp. 61-2.*

The Taking of Miss Janie . . . is a forcefully telling play. It begins with a "flash" of Janie, a white woman who weeps in desperate complaint that she has been raped by Monty, a black man whom we see with her. By the end of the play we have learned that she and Monty met in a poetry class at CCNY where she was struck by his literary talent. Her connection with him is also prompted by the fascination black people arouse in her. She withholds herself from him sexually in an effort to keep their relationship wholly friendly. Monty's feeling for her is perhaps more than desire; there is also rage at her callowness and ignorance of the black world she has entered and her resolve to keep herself chaste with him. The two sentiments mount to physical violence which she, still unenlightened by all she has witnessed and gone through with Monty, terms "rape."

Still, this is not the crux of the play. It is a dramatic portrait of those social elements which gave the 1960s their special stamp. The play focuses on the effect of all those external circumstances—the war, the student demonstrations, the resentments as well as the hopes for radical change—as they play upon the consciousness of articulate black people in particular. . . . But the play's meaning is broader than its specific ethnic background.

What we see is a people—black, white, Jew and gentile—hung up and driven nearly mad by the fearful contradictions between ragged remnants of the American "dream" and the shameful realities of actual existence. There is a strong though fitful will to overcome the resultant disaster but no one is honest, clearheaded, steadfast, informed and disciplined enough to do so. . . . Ploys of escape escape nothing, drugs obliterate reality and lead to nonbeing, diverse brands of racism serve for slogans. Rabid affirmations and hysterical protests eventuate in frustration rather than relief. Nearly everyone is lost in a miserable flow of turbid emotion with no beneficent outlet. All are in the dark and no one is "saved"—not even those who have settled into unquiet compromise or stagnant surrender.

The play, despite its disturbing revelations, is neither mournful in tone nor tendentiously raucous. Vigorously humorous, it does not whine; it growls with a savage grin. Without pleading any special cause, it has sinew and muscle. Bold in its courageous objectivity, it is by no means depressing.

The picture is overcrowded or may only seem so because of the numerous characters and places. . . . At moments it is difficult to distinguish one person from another, but that in part is due to the fact that all are equally, though differently, "in trouble." The audience laughs, shouts and stamps in recognition of the types and situations depicted. It is itself the material of what it beholds and is puzzled on that account. It, too, does not *know*. It finds it impossible "to take sides" and it constantly veers in its sympathies because Bullins does not seek to direct it to any firm conclusion. He is demonstrating, not preaching. His voice here, for all its explosive resonance, is essentially poetic. (p. 414)

> *Harold Clurman, in* The Nation *(copyright 1975 by the Nation Associates, Inc.), April 5, 1975.*

Ed Bullins's *The Taking of Miss Janie* . . . is a modest but steadily engaging play about a black college student's encounter with a liberal white girl who thoughtlessly seeks to have a platonic relationship with him.

The greatest virtue of the play, which is set in the Sixties, is the way it captures the humor that attended campus miscegenation then. . . . As for the final "rape" of Miss Janie, it is also comic, as Bullins makes us see that the idea of rape is essential both to the pride of the black student and to the pleasure of his none-too-chaste concubine. (p. 52)

> *Henry Hewes, in* Saturday Review *(copyright © 1975 by Saturday Review/World, Inc.; reprinted with permission), May 17, 1975.*

[*The Taking of Miss Janie*] begins with a black man raping a white woman. Strangely enough, it is less a brutal phys-ical act than the saddest of requiems. The play ends with the figures of John and Robert Kennedy, Martin Luther King and Malcolm X on a rear stage scrim being spattered with gobs of blood. Thus the rape is, to some degree, an image of the anarchic violence of the '60s.

It is also a double requiem for the defeated hopes of the '60s. As a black girl who has become a lesbian puts it: "We all failed . . . and by failing ourselves we failed in the test of the times. We had so much going for us . . . so much potential. . . . Do you realize it, man? We were the youth of our times. . . . And we blew it. Blew it completely. Look where it all ended. . . . We just turned out lookin' like a bunch of punks and freaks."

Yet it would be quite wrong to think of *The Taking of Miss Janie* as a dirge. . . . Bullins often uses a party as the central structure of his plays, and he does it again here. Even when it is slightly sick, a Bullins party jives. The people talk a vivid street idiom with the fluent opulence of jazz. Their moods dance. They make hot, sly, funny, drunken, sexy scenes together that have the cumulative impact of a seduction. Then they fall apart in revealing stop-motion monologues as if a petal were trying to be a flower. . . .

[The] white heroine Janie is the most pathetic of all. Bullins has drawn a masterly portrait of a befuddled, innocent, college-educated liberal.

> *T. E. Kalem, "Requiem for the '60s," in* Time *(reprinted by permission from* Time, The Weekly Newsmagazine; *copyright Time Inc.), May 19, 1975, p. 80.*

Ed Bullins's [*The Taking of Miss Janie*] is a cartoon allegory, which is a rare genre indeed—at least I hope so. It tries to sum up race relations in our troubled sixties in terms of assorted black and Jewish types, and the allegorical WASP, Miss Janie, who, after ten years of equivocal friendship, is raped by the black hero. Bullins has caught some archetypes quite cleverly, has brought off a few funny routines and pungent lines, and has almost managed not to weight the scales in favor of the black characters. All of this is fine, but what is lacking is a play. The allegory is too simplistic; the attempt to deepen the work by allowing each character a lengthy monologue merely underscores how much has been left undramatized, i.e., undigested fiction rather than theater; and the accumulation of turbulent details in all too many centrifugal destinies only pries an already uncohering play farther apart. . . .

If Bullins thinks that he has written a fairly droll pastiche, good and well; but I have the uneasy feeling he may think of it as serious and searching, too. Alas, if it is not pure pastiche, it is pure pasteboard. (p. 93)

> *John Simon, in* New York Magazine *(© 1975 by NYM Corp.; reprinted by permission of* New York Magazine *and John Simon), May 19, 1975.*

* * *

BURGESS, Anthony 1917-

Burgess, a British novelist, essayist, critic, and composer, is a complex and clever stylist. His best known work is *A Clockwork Orange*. (See also *Contemporary Authors*, Vols. 1-4, rev. ed.)

Like *A Vision of Battlements*, *The Worm and the Ring* is a kind of mock epic. More exactly, it is a mock opera, a burlesque of Wagner's *Der Ring der Nibelungen*. Wagner's allegorical struggle for power between Nibelung dwarfs, giants and gods is translated into a struggle for the control of a grammar school in a little English borough. Wotan, ruler of the gods, becomes Mr. Woolton, Headmaster of the school and an old-fashioned liberal humanist. Fafner, the giant who seizes all and turns himself into a dragon, is "Dr." Gardner (Gard=drag=dragon), a cynical academic Babbitt who has managed to ingratiate himself with members of the business community. With these back-slapping connections, the prestige of a doctorate (earned with stolen treasure, a plagiarized dissertation), personal wealth, and a Machiavellian ruthlessness, he is bound to triumph. . . .

Gardner is wormlike in every respect (AS. *wyrm* = serpent, dragon), but is destined to emerge triumphant, unscathed by the hero, the ruler of the gods or anyone else—a reflection whose bitterness extends well beyond the arena of school politics. (p. 402)

[Burgess's] balanced critical treatment of the extreme of rule based on liberal idealism versus the extreme of cynical autocracy agrees with what we find in [his] other novels. As in his dystopian books, Burgess exposes the inadequacies and dangers of both as governing philosophies. At the same time he suggests that western society is becoming increasingly incapable of accepting a sane, realistic mixture of the two philosophies that would insure the preservation of individual human dignity. That he intends this power struggle in the grammar school to have these much broader political implications is indicated. (p. 404)

Burgess's eschewal of simple answers can also be seen in his treatment of Howarth's rending religious conflicts. Howarth's marriage is nearly wrecked by his wife's fanatical Catholicism, but its salvation does not lie in a total rejection of Catholicism. . . . A careless reading of *The Worm and the Ring* might suggest that its religious themes are either indictments of the Catholic Church or pleas for liberalization. In fact the book contains neither. What keeps Howarth away from the Church in England, in addition to his loss of faith, is the conviction that it is no longer the Church of his Catholic ancestors. . . . He may have no stake in Catholicism, but he cannot bear to see it watered down or modified in the name of progress. His contempt for Catholicism that strives to be with the times shows itself again in a later novel, *Enderby Outside*, where we find a Catholic priest ministering as a spiritual advisor, a kind of Maharishi, to a group of loutish pop-singers. It would be strange then if, in *The Worm and the Ring*, he were beating any sort of drum for updated, liberalized Catholicism. What he is presenting through his characterization of the Howarths is the stresses and anxieties that burden Catholics generally, as well as the sense of alienation they must feel even in a twentieth-century Protestant, though lax and tolerant, culture.

The Worm and the Ring is one of Burgess's better novels. . . . Along with its caustic indictments, it reveals throughout Burgess's extraordinary capacity to make absorbing dramatic entertainment out of the most unlikely material. The hidden comedy and pathos of life in the dreary little grammar school are revealed with sensitivity, sympathy and irresistible wit. (pp. 405-07)

Geoffrey Aggeler, "A Wagnerian Affirmation: Anthony Burgess's 'The Worm and the Ring'," in Western Humanities Review *(copyright, 1972, University of Utah), Autumn, 1973, pp. 401-10.*

Burgess writes with brio, with exuberant sophistication and wit. Because he conceives of [*Napoleon Symphony*] as a comedy of manners, for the most part a novel of conversation, major historical events have a way of happening off stage or just before we join the action. (pp. 85-6)

This setting of fiction in symphonic form works very well for Burgess. It frees him to do what one generally cannot do in novels: that is, pay less attention to the direction of the whole than to the development of the parts. Many of the big scenes that compose this novel are considerable tours de force: walking incognito among the cafés of Paris, for instance, or the retreat across the Berezina River, during which the remnants of the Grand Army construct makeshift bridges that collapse, forcing the survivors to hack through walls of corpses. Occasionally, Burgess is almost too cute—in a Shavian parenthesis that seems to defer to a fashionable theory that in Napoleon lay the seeds of modern corporate dictatorship, Burgess's hero muses on the possibility of inventing gas chambers to eliminate his victims—but then this kind of book accommodates excess. Burgess appears to have had a grand time writing it, cramming into it jokes, puns, rhymes, lugubrious details and some marvelous special effects, yet he has kept it light and bouncy—good fun to read. (p. 86)

Peter S. Prescott, "The 'Eroica' Comedy," in Newsweek *(copyright 1974 by Newsweek, Inc.; all rights reserved; reprinted by permission), May 27, 1974, pp. 85-6.*

A Burgess novel is frequently an embarrassment of riches, a kind of conspicuous consumption of exotic plot thickeners, linguistic games, disturbing tragicomedy. Manichaean trampoline acts and Christian and mythological symbolism. Thematically speaking, anything goes—as Burgess demonstrated . . . in *MF*, a novel of contemporary incest based on an Algonquin Indian myth. In . . . *Napoleon Symphony*, the author, who is also a serious composer, has reached for everything from kazoos to pipe organs. The result is a mock epic about the career of Napoleon Bonaparte that sometimes reads like Dickens, sometimes like Tennyson and Wordsworth, with an occasional gash of Gerard Manley Hopkins' gold-vermilion. "The last section of the book is written in the style of Henry James," Burgess explains without a trace of solemnity, "because Henry James believed he was Napoleon when he was dying."

The novel itself is divided into four movements corresponding to the parts of Beethoven's *Third Symphony*, "*The Eroica*." (Beethoven originally dedicated "*The Eroica*" to Napoleon, but tore up the dedication after the First Consul of France crowned himself Emperor.) At times the Burgess Bonaparte resembles a cross between Charles de Gaulle and Douglas MacArthur. At times he is an 18th century Mafia *capo* trying to manage overextended holdings and control his greedy relatives. Burgess seeks to evoke the heaving spirit of the Napoleonic age by rouging (and *noir*ing) the historical facts with catchy dialogue and fantasy. . . .

On the broader screen of history, Burgess gets his effects by balancing the horrors of war with some of the absurdities of political power and private weaknesses. (p. 92)

As Beethoven is supposed to have said when he retracted the dedication of "*The Eroica*," "*Held, nein* [Hero, no]!" Burgess, the Christian moralist, appears to agree. His reasons are worked out in a fugue of ideas at the book's end where the exiled, cancerous—perhaps even dead—Napoleon encounters a mysterious female apparition. Since she coldly puts Napoleon in his place, she may well be Clio, the Muse of history. In any case, she declares that Beethoven's art is more important than Napoleon's military skill—"an art," she unkindly notes, "highly wasteful of its materials." Napoleon, whose mind or spirit at this point is soaring like the last movement of "*The Eroica*," appears to get the message: musical forms may reveal divine essences, while his own kinetic life has been shaped by a gargantuan but finite will, whose only form was eventually a form of self-delusion. *Napoleon Symphony* is, in some sense, an entertaining and elaborate joke. What the punch line comes down to is the simple fact that even Napoleon thought he was Napoleon. (pp. 92-3)

> *R. Z. Sheppard, "Grand Illusions," in* Time *(reprinted by permission from* Time, The Weekly Newsmagazine; *copyright Time Inc.), May 27, 1974, pp. 92-3.*

Ten years back, Anthony Burgess published a little novel in which he recreated the love life of one "WS," from his first fornicating follies as a lad in Stratford-on-Avon, to his pox-ridden last days in London. Brought out during the Shakespeare quadricentennial, *Nothing Like the Sun* succeeded in offending scholars, biographers and other assorted purists. Now Burgess has gone wholehogger once more and appropriated the score of Beethoven's colossal Third Symphony, the E-flat *Sinfonia Eroica*, to shape a verbal narrative on the last quarter-century of the life of another giant, Napoleon Bonaparte.

No doubt it is the musicologists' and historians' turn to get their hackles up; but no matter. Critics are but bucketfuls compared to the oceans of genius that threaten to swamp this "lump of minor art." For as Burgess himself muses in the heroic-coupleted "Epistle to the Reader" that serves as coda to his new novel, any fictional account of Napoleon must war-and-peace it with Tolstoy, and any musicalization of fiction must swap crescendos with the "Sirens" episode from *Ulysses*. Incredibly enough *Napoleon Symphony* does both. Though writing under the pen-umbrage of Leo and James, and under the longer shadows of Napoleon and Beethoven, Burgess has managed to elude them all and come up with an original, wild, picaresque extravaganza that is pure sunburst and probably his best novel. (pp. 87-8)

[The] fourth part of the novel is probably the most brilliant. In the *Eroica* symphony, Beethoven took a theme from his own Prometheus ballet and worked a number of variations on it. To Beethoven's theme, Burgess sets the phrase INTERFECIMUS NAPOLEONEM REGEM IMPERATOREM (it is singable!), and works the acronym INRI into acrostics in all the rhymed verse passages of the section. It needn't be pointed out—though pedantry demands my doing so—that the four letters also appeared over Jesus on the cross, and since we are concerned here with Napoleon's martyrdom and death on St. Helena, the Latin al-

chemy is a bit mind-boggling. But what of the variations? Burgess gets them in, too, by giving us variations in different styles of the great Victorians—Scott, Wordsworth, Tennyson, Dickens, James, and G. M. Hopkins. And why the Victorians? Because they were, of course, Prometheans!. . .

Napoleon Symphony . . . has as many stops as a full organ, all of them being pulled out by Burgess at an incredible pace. The narrative techniques alone are enough to generate heat for a dozen novels: the shifts back and forth of the narrator—a kind of choric voice given to a unit in Napoleon's army, Napoleon's interior monologues, those writers I mentioned, dozens of verses in heroic (what else!) couplets, footnotes, and naturally Burgess *in propria persona*—as in the general jubilation of all things (animate and inanimate) for Napoleon and Ludwig van Beethoven. . . .

Yet, oddly enough, the structures and techniques of *Napoleon Symphony* are not its greatest assets. A symphony after all unites to create one grand effect, and that effect here is Napoleon. *Pace* Tolstoy, Hugo, Ludwig, Ségur, Caulaincourt, and innumerable other writers of biography and history and apocrypha, Burgess has given us a Napoleon for our time. He is N, *lui*, Napoleon, Bonaparte, Buonaparte, Nabuliune; he is lover, general, doting father, gourmandizer, whoremonger, cuckold, dyspeptic, tyrant, Emperor, genial Mafia cutthroat, martyr, myth. And on all counts he is Prometheus, the fire god; whether fired by passion, by the zeal for war, by his ambition, by the burning certainty of his morality and immortality, or whether chained to the promontories of history, his liver rotted from Courvoisier, his fingers probing the psychosomatic and physical wound. Burgess has given us the elemental Napoleon-Prometheus, caught between fire and Water(loo), and the quintessential Napoleon as well, who "turned the age into himself."

In the long run, I suppose, it is Beethoven who gobbles up Napoleon and Burgess. But I defy anyone to read *Napoleon Symphony*—not while the *Eroica* is playing, but perhaps with the score on one's table—and not evoke new images from Beethoven's music. Burgess should reawaken the fire in all those who have found the symphony growing dull after the hundredth audition, and when the glow is incandescent, should provide them with a literary experience on the scale of the music. *Napoleon Symphony* is alive, lush, lyric, human, witty and wildly comic. (p. 88)

> *Robert K. Morris, "With Flourish of Hautboys," in* The Nation *(copyright 1974 by the Nation Associates, Inc.), August 3, 1974, pp. 87-8.*

Burgess' Napoleon is often very funny [in *Napoleon Symphony*], especially with Josephine. But he is one of history's great mass murderers, even in a comedy. . . . Well, fun's fun. But in Egypt Napoleon found it convenient to execute some 4000 prisoners. It took four days. After the first day they saved bullets by using bayonets. Burgess makes Napoleon dream wistfully of more sophisticated methods, such as gas chambers. . . . Well, Josephine and her kids pounding on Napoleon's bedroom door and screaming, while he sits inside with cotton in his ears, is fine material for comedy; but mass killings, the Master Race, and the terrible crossing of the Berezina are something else; and Burgess must labor to transmute his all too real ogre into a picaresque Punch.

His wand, of course, is words. Burgess . . . loves words, and allusions too. Here Josephine dallies in a gondola under T. S. Eliot's glum eye (Lights lights''), Wordsworth writes of meeting Napoleon as a pudgy gardener on St. Helena, two soldiers plagiarize *The Nigger of the "Narcissus,"* a Jamesian sybil quotes Hopkins, Shem the Penman is everywhere, and of course there's lots of fustian, the literary equivalent of bombardment being bombast.

The idea of a symphony about N was suggested to B [Beethoven] by ex-sergeant Bellejambe, ex-mistress Désirée's husband, future king of Norway, and future traitor. The idea of a novel about N was suggested to B [Burgess] by Stanley Kubrick, who turned *Clockwork Orange* into cinematic trash. The "Eroica" is grand despite its origin, and the *Napoleon Symphony* is high-class entertainment despite its. (p. 32)

> *J. D. O'Hara, in* The New Republic *(reprinted by permission of* The New Republic; © 1974 by The New Republic, Inc.), August 31, 1974.*

Anthony Burgess takes on Napoleon. And not only Napoleon, but Beethoven and Prometheus as well. Does the heart sink? Do the eyes glaze? In prospect, yes. There is often something about his writing that sets up an initial hostility. It is so cocky. Not for him the simple striving to find his own voice to express his own truths. He writes in everyone's voice in turn (stoutly here, denying parody) but louder; indeed his writing is very noisy. Which brings us to the Eroica, which he takes as his starting point. Beethoven began his symphony in honour of Napoleon, and, disillusioned by his hero's venality, ended it as a hymn to Prometheus. Mr Burgess merges the two. His hero is a 'Promethapoleon.''

Mr Burgess avoids obvious intellectuality even though his approach is essentially intellectual. Any possible analysis or commentary has been forestalled by himself; it's all in the text. He stresses in a verse Epistle to the Reader that this 'lump of minor art' is comedy. And there are touches of a truly Groucho humour, as when Napoleon says to guests faced yet again with Chicken Marengo: 'That is already a great historical dish. *Eat it.*' . . .

As much in love with words as ever, Mr Burgess enjoys what he calls 'literal magic', such as his semi-comic dissertation on the significance of the letter W in Napoleon's career. Psychiatrists call 'signs of reference' these apparent associations, experienced in manic states. He is beguiled too by what he calls, knowingly, 'the foolish intimacy of rhyme'. His intimacy with James Joyce may not be foolish but it is all-pervasive, even down to the statutory female soliloquy: Madame Mère surveying her children at a Coronation Anniversary banquet, and planning how she'll sort them out once she gets them back to Ajaccio. Superimposed on this is an explicitly cinematic technique of crosscutting and visual allusion—the novel is dedicated to Stanley J. Kubrick.

So far, so good, and what you'd expect. It is in the final section that something brilliantly special happens. On St Helena the paunchy sick failure talks to girls and ghosts of girls and fights battles. Over his body, doctors argue about

purgatives. And Prometheus is taking over. The glory is never done. 'The hero doesn't have to have existed . . .'. The idea of the hero is what is important. If Napoleon hadn't existed, someone would have invented him. Like all mythical truths, it is deeply corny and deeply moving. Like his Napoleon, Anthony Burgess fingers 'the wafer-thin membrane between the ridiculous and the sublime'. And gets away with it. I surrendered utterly. (p. 435)

> *Victoria Glendinning, in* New Statesman *(© 1974 The Statesman & Nation Publishing Co. Ltd.), September 27, 1974.*

Yes, Mr Burgess is fluent and fanciful and inventive; he is even occasionally fertile. He tells us so himself, in a ''verse epistle'' to the reader [of *Napoleon Symphony*]. And the problem with this book is the temptation to put everything in inverted commas. Its title bears some allusion to the *Eroica* (so the publishers are kind enough to tell me), although the Elizabethan analogy between language and music seems a singularly pointless one at this late date. Certainly the writing has an artificial pace reminiscent of some of the more *troppo* passages of opera bouffe, but Mr Burgess's diction has a generally squelchy quality which one does not associate with anything in particular: ''He hovered voluptuously on the promise of a sneeze but, a strong man, would not yield.'' I like that ''hovered,'' even though it is supposed to be comic.

The secret life of a hero is one of those incurably romantic themes which will remain novelettish despite all attempts to enliven it. And Burgess certainly tries. There is, however, a rule in fiction that there are only a finite number of plots but an infinite number of novelists, and Mr Burgess contrives a rhetorical garishness by shifting the surfaces of his writing around like toy bricks: there are many different voices, letters, deadpan narrative and a number of poetic intervals (although Mr Burgess is by no means a poet). (p. 405)

This is, in fact, a conventionally imagined book which makes use of the iron disunities of our time and which whips up its language to a frenzy for no particular reason. Mr Burgess employs a variety of styles in an excessively self-conscious way, with the result that any dialogue between recognisable human beings seems a trifle cracked. There are some allusions to the *Dynasts* and some odd quotations from Gerard Manley Hopkins, and the literariness of the whole narrative is merely confirmed by a pastiche of *Ulysses* (Burgess seems to have some proprietorial claim to Joyce, although it is difficult to see any similarity) which sets all of the preceding narrative at an aesthetic distance. You could no doubt call the novel a ''sport,'' Mr Burgess being fanciful and inventive and outrageous, but it is only what the closing epistolary verse would call an ''orthodox success.'' We are not particularly amused. (pp. 405-06)

> *Peter Ackroyd, ''Cacophony,'' in* The Spectator *(© 1974 by The Spectator; reprinted by permission of The Spectator), September 28, 1974, pp. 405-06.*

Anthony Burgess . . . [worked] up his Napoleon, got Beethoven in his bones, and ended up with 363 pages of nonsense. You can hear Beethoven in it, but to imitate musical form is to do just that, no more. . . . Not much Beethoven there, more like Pynchon, just as much of the rest is like

Joyce. But Burgess isn't brilliant and sick like Pynchon, or willing to work at it for years like Joyce, or great like Beethoven. I'd love to have a meat breakfast with him on the other side of that bridge, and his Napoleon isn't a bad fellow either, but if Burgess cares about anything here it is probably Jane Austen and Mozart, and he hasn't, or won't, discipline himself to do more than envy them and imitate more modern masters. This is his twenty-first book. It's not bad, but not good either, and so must rank as a disappointment. (pp. 627-28)

> *Roger Sale, in* The Hudson Review *(copyright © 1974 by The Hudson Review, Inc.; reprinted by permission), Vol. XXVII, No. 4, Winter, 1974-75.*

Mr. Burgess's Enderby, visiting professor of English at the University of Manhattan, comes to a tired and not unexpected end in an Upper West Side apartment, his heart given out at last, after the latest encounter with peril, the last round of gluttony. He has not been without his triumphs in a vulgar New York, a milieu full of foreigners, of black and brown hoodlums whose mere appearance in a subway car is enough to send tremors through him, of philistines who have never heard of Gerard Manley Hopkins but are happy to put together a movie called *The Wreck of the Deutschland*, because it is an opportunity to capitalize on a sensational idea. The idea of a film based on *The Wreck of the Deutschland* is in fact Enderby's, the fruit of a careless moment spent in the company of two filmmakers in Tangier. The product is a marvelously updated version of the 1875 *Wreck*, set in Nazi Germany during the Forties. It provides, for the edification of filmgoers in the Seventies, the spectacle of naked, orgasmic nuns, raped or about to be raped by Nazi storm troopers. The result of the film's wide success is that everywhere it has played, there are young savages, apparently inspired by the film, running about attacking nuns. Enderby is of course blamed for letting this contagion loose upon the world, just as Mr. Burgess was blamed for the brutality of *A Clockwork Orange*. But, argues the defiant Enderby, life does not imitate art—it is the other way around.

This novel is Mr. Burgess's answer to critics, and a very good novel it is, too, though not for its retort on such things as the artist's culpability or lack of it (with regard to socially harmful themes), about which Mr. Burgess is apt to get quite tendentious. Far better than any of this is his superb splenetic assault on the destruction of language. It is Burgess's perception—one not unique to him to be sure, but one so richly obsessive as to seem so—that it is the annihilation of the word that has brought us to the abyss in our time. There are flaws in this manysided and vastly entertaining work. Mr. Burgess's choice of satiric objects (New York City, crime, the activist-student lunkheads, the surly black maids) is a bit fashionable, and taking on the host of a late-night television talk show is like shooting fish in a barrel. Yet, it is all immensely well done, properly merciless, and full of sour pleasures, among them Mr. Burgess's unfailing ear for the way in which the enemy talks. (p. 44)

> *Dorothy Rabinowitz, in* Saturday Review *(copyright © 1975 by Saturday Review/ World, Inc.; reprinted with permission), January 25, 1975.*

The much-slighted English poet F. X. Enderby . . . received no public attention until the early sixties, when Joseph Kell published the delightfully funny, grubby and perceptive biography "Inside Mr Enderby." "I'M Enderby" is an Englished "Portrait of the Artist," with its middle-aged Blooming poet struggling against church, state and his dead but unforgotten mother, née Hogg. . . . Some five years later, Kell (now named Anthony Burgess) published "Enderby," restoring Enderby to himself and landing him in Tangier, writing again and visited by a charming irritable muse.

Meanwhile Burgess wrote and wrote—almost 20 novels, including a trilogy he seems to have forgotten—and fame finally came. Not because of his fine writing but because of a slick, coarse, evil movie made from his moral and religious novel "A Clockwork Orange." That experience is now transmogrified [in "The Clockwork Testament, or Enderby's End"] into a chaotic, earnest, satiric, didactic comedy that finishes Enderby off in a mock-heroic explosion of love, warfare and righteousness while Burgess explains what he really and clearly meant in "A Clockwork Orange." Some lighthearted cupidity has led Enderby to sketch a film treatment of Gerard Manley Hopkins's poem "The Wreck of the Deutschland," which has been twisted into an arty, awful sado-porn hit. The resultant fame has landed him a job at Columbia University teaching the definitively nightmarish Creative Writing course.

Meanwhile punks everywhere are mistreating nuns and blaming it all on Hopkins and Enderby, and Enderby— since no one can find Hopkins—must defend art against the age-old charge of perverting men's minds. A staunch Pelagian heretic, Enderby is happy to oblige. Man is not corrupted by original sin, he explains; he is free to choose goodness, and his reason is a sufficient guide. But evil must therefore exist, because choice is the important thing, the sign of our freedom and moral significance. "A Clockwork Orange" had said this, of course, and Enderby can only repeat, variously, the same question: what's it going to be, then? "Die with Beethoven's Ninth howling and crashing away or live in a safe world of silly clockwork music?"

"Testament" begins with a quotation from Seymour Bushe, rushes on to include Joyce, Borges, Nabokov, Shakespeare and Hopkins, and tumbles, slips, splashes and leaps happily in a welter of words until its all too quick end. Some of Burgess's wordy-gurdies are clotted with verbiage; this is not. It is grand, and purists can always ignore the message. Anyone considering a trip to the Big Apple should read it for its street scenes alone. (p. 4)

> *J. D. O'Hara, in* The New York Times Book Review *(© 1975 by The New York Times Company; reprinted by permission), February 2, 1975.*

I would judge that Burgess has a lot invested in Enderby, maybe more than Enderby can quite sustain. The ending of *The Clockwork Testament*, in which the time-traveling schoolchildren from the earlier novels are assured by their teacher that the dead Enderby "is not out of it at all," risks a sentimentality that Enderby alive would have known how to discount. . . . Certainly the book seems thinner, more local, than the splendid *Inside Enderby* or even the less assured *Enderby Outside*, where the pleasure of writing well took precedence over the pleasure of scoring points.

But Anthony Burgess is one of our best, and most serious, fictional comedians, and if the comedy of *The Clockwork Testament* is sometimes too close to a kind of transatlantic farce that others do almost as well, it's also a stirring denunciation of the trivial, the second-rate, the mindless, and a continuously entertaining reminder of how much this marvelously generous—and for all his learning, unacademic —writer has given us in the past two decades. (p. 36)

> *Thomas R. Edwards, in* The New York Review of Books *(reprinted with permission from* The New York Review of Books; *copyright © 1975 NYREV, Inc.), February 20, 1975.*

There are Vonnegut afficionados, Brautigan fans and Pynchon addicts—but can there really be Burgess buffs? There must be, or else the publishers are losing a heap of money. Worldly but world-weary, committed but disengaged, passionate but juiceless: Burgess buffs must be human oxymorons. They must be interesting folks, but aggressive about their supposed superiority. They must be committed to secondary things, to the placing of things, to the construction of attitudes toward things. Don't touch that thing! Make an attitude toward it! Defend that attitude! Burgess has mastered distaste. He loathes things and people involved with things. In the first novel devoted to him, Enderby left his wife when she picked her ears with hairclips, her teeth with a bus ticket and her priest in a dress shop. In this second Enderby novel [*The Clockwork Testament; or Enderby's End*] the distaste is for Enderby's own dentures, the hair in his nose and ears, and his coming end: "the great bloody muckheap of multiplicity . . . from which he wanted to escape but couldn't." Multiplicity confounds schematic attitudes.

The dialogues in *The Clockwork Testament* are straw dialogues, set pieces that Enderby wins outright or wins covertly because the ostensible winners reveal their boorishness by their conquest. These conversations recall that secret desire of smartly verbal people everywhere, at any time: to win with words, to let the wit start winging when the toughs get going. Enderby is better at winging toughs, evidently, than he is at writing poems. But even the dialogues are sour, because they are steeped in Enderby's petty gloating over his petty wins. Having decided that the world is a loathsome place, what joy or seriousness or honor is there in proving the prejudice? Enderby is meant to be a qualified hero, his death a mock tragedy, but it's difficult to take his muddled life as anything more serious than Burgess' recoil from multiplicity while attempting to make a little more money from an old character. Burgess and his editors must think there are more Prufrocks still buying books than I think there are. (p. 29)

> *W. T. Lhamon, Jr., in* The New Republic *(reprinted by permission of* The New Republic; *© 1975 by The New Republic, Inc.), February 22, 1975.*

It is probably not immediately apparent to most readers of *The Long Day Wanes*, Anthony Burgess's huge novel about Malaya, that it was written in three bursts and first appeared as a series of novels. Then it was published as a trilogy; but it has the weight and cohesion of a single novel, and there is little more one needs to know about that penin-sula. Burgess has so many interests (music, linguistics, art history, theology) he can be forgiven for breaking off a long tale to write a symphony or a piece of literary criticism. His gusto and enterprise make most other writers look like rather hoarse prima donnas who apply for fellowships to spray their throats instead of getting on with the job.

Inside Mr. Enderby appeared in the mid-'60s. I think I've read it 12 times: few novels have given me such pleasure, and there is a particular page—a description of Enderby's awful stepmother—that I have committed to memory. The persuasive detail about Enderby is that he is a good poet—a selection of his poems (about 30 poems and fragments exist) could easily be included in a series like the Yale Younger Poets and would get an enthusiastic review in any of the university quarterlies. Space does not permit a long quotation, and it would be unjust to offer anything but a complete poem, but perhaps it suffices to say that Enderby is as great a poet as Nabokov's John Shade. How ironic that two of the best poets of the century are the fictions of great novelists! . . .

In *Enderby Outside* there is an appendix, "Some uncollected early poems . . .", again beautifully written (a sequence of war poems) and well worth studying.

"By God what a genius he had then," Enderby reflects at the end of *The Clockwork Testament*, the last installment of this novel which has been ten years in the works. The echo of Swift is intentional. This is a day in the life of F. X. Enderby—the hectic last day of his life—but it would be wrong to take this book on its own and ignore the previous 500 pages. (p. 1)

[There] is no question that [Burgess] is using his novel to fire a final broadside at the illiterate rabble who have associated him with the egregious movie of recent memory. It is a farewell to America, a good riddance to the cannibal temperament of mass media hacks, and a modest effort to clarify a Christian doctrine. It is also Enderby's end, a disorderly and uncelebrated death for the man who had such high hopes and fine lyrics in Volume One. Burgess's deftness with language is always a delight, but it is underpinned by sustained thought and a great satirical gift. Taken together, the three books that comprise the Enderby saga are a dazzling work, and very likely his best novel. (p. 3)

> *Paul Theroux, "Shades of Enderby," in* Book World—The Washington Post *(© The Washington Post), March 9, 1975, pp. 1, 3.*

"In many ways a dirty book," Anthony Burgess once warned in the columns of the Yorkshire *Post*. "Those of my readers with tender stomachs are advised to leave it alone." Critic Burgess, as it happened, was reviewing a novel called *Inside Mr. Enderby*, ostensibly written by one Joseph Kell but actually the work of a prolific British writer named Anthony Burgess.

Readers who ignored Burgess's cheeky advice may remember that the eponymous poet, F. X. Enderby, was a fairly unprepossessing fellow. . . . Yet Burgess, a man of wit and genius, has been fond enough of this queasy minor poet to devote one, two and now three volumes to him. Why? Because with all his faults, Enderby is a strong booster of original sin, a commodity, Burgess feels, the modern world greatly underrates.

Burgess, in fact, sees the key moral conflict of our age as an extension of the argument that took place between the heretic Pelagius and St. Augustine some 1,600 years ago. Man, preached Pelagius, is untainted by original sin and is thus perfectible through his own efforts. The cynical saint disagreed and ran Pelagius out of Rome. But this humane heretic's views now dominate society, Burgess suggests, through the delusive notion that men are essentially creatures of their environment whose actions must be controlled by benign behaviorists. Disaster, says Burgess. No original sin, no evil. No evil, no moral choice. No moral choice and human freedom becomes meaningless, man becomes a machine.

These views were futuristically dramatized in both Burgess's novel and Stanley Kubrick's version of *The Clockwork Orange*. In *Enderby's End*, Burgess pits the poor poet against the whole city of New York, an area where sin, original or otherwise, is surely not in short supply. Enderby reaches the New World in ways faintly congruent with Burgess's recent career. His name appears among the screenplay credits of a shocking film, and thus notorious, he is offered a teaching post at one of Manhattan's melting-pot universities (in 1972 Burgess lectured at the City College of New York). In Enderby's case, the film is no *Clockwork Orange* but a salacious travesty of Jesuit Gerard Manley Hopkins' poem *The Wreck of the Deutschland*.

The poem is both about Hopkins' spiritual odyssey and an elegy for five Franciscan nuns who drowned when a German liner struck a sand bar off the Kentish Knock in November 1875. Enderby's film producers shift the story to pre-World War II Germany, add a (pre-vow) affair between one of the nuns and "Father Tom" Hopkins, and lavishly document the rape of the nuns by a congregation of SS men.

After the film's release, nuns begin to be raped round the world, and Enderby is blamed for it. . . . In vain he declares that art—even execrable art—is neutral. Loathing the movie more than anyone, he sees it not as a cause but as a symptom of sin. "You ignore art as so much unnecessary garbage," he howls at his tormentors, "or you blame it for your own crimes." Even members of Enderby's creative writing class see him as a "misleading reactionary bastard." He has failed, it appears, to see merit in their "free verse and gutter vocabulary."

Burgess supports his dyspeptic Don Quixote through all sorts of polemical extremities. The reader is lashed with puns and offered poetic tidbits taken from Hopkins. But the book succeeds less as a novel than as intellectual program music. (p. 84)

Enderby's position is too cleverly undermined by irony, too mined with paradox, to prevail. In *The Wreck of the Deutschland* (the poem, not the flick), one of the nuns at the moment of her death "christens her wild worst Best," just as Hopkins himself struggled a lifetime to confirm precisely in private pain and worldly rebuff some clear sign of God's forgiving love. Enderby attempts to perform the same sort of personal miracle. Desperately he tries to see the cruelty, vulgarity and violence not as correctable aberrations but as signs that man is still free, but still in need of God. The attitude makes him something of a sheep in wolf's clothing. Without any assertion that men have souls, it also makes him seem a bit perverse.

Burgess might have risked one more quote from Hopkins. Man, one poem said, "This Jack, joke, poor potsherd/ Patch, matchwood, immortal diamond/ Is immortal diamond." Otherwise, what's so wrong with sun-kissed clockwork oranges? (pp. 84, 86)

> *Timothy Foote, "Wolf of God," in* Time *(reprinted by permission from* Time, The Weekly Newsmagazine; *copyright Time Inc.), March 17, 1975, pp. 84, 86.*

Again [as in *Enderby*, so in *The Clockwork Testament*,] it is Enderby against the world, trying to write and teach poetry in a school, a city, a country that couldn't care less. . . .

Enderby is more than a little like his creator, Anthony Burgess. He even makes the same defense for the violent movie made from his script that Burgess himself made for *A Clockwork Orange*: "if you get rid of evil you get rid of choice." Both are lapsed Catholics with a strong sense of original sin; neither has much hope for America.

Humorously, seriously, even didactically, Burgess examines the state of our culture. Americans are undernourished, physically and intellectually, their schools "a whorehouse of progressive intellectual abdication." Enderby—and Burgess—fight to maintain intellectual standards.

The Clockwork Testament resembles Nabokov's recent novels; like *Transparent Things* it is about death, and like *Look at the Harlequins!* it is about its author (though Burgess, unlike Nabokov, writes in the third person). Nabokov and Burgess are our two leading English-language novelists, and the convergence of their themes is intriguing. (Enderby, afraid that a lady out to kill him has erred, shouts, "'That's Nabokov. . . . not me. *Pale Fire*,' he clarified.") Nabokov and Burgess are both dedicated to words, to language, but Nabokov is detached and ironic, whereas Burgess/Enderby jumps right into the scuffle. Every battle Enderby fights is over words.

He dies as the TV image of a Thirties college musical changes to a poetic film about Augustine and Pelagius. So Burgess uses the popular culture of New York and transforms it into a personal comic vision. The last chapter is a helicopter shot of the city as Enderby lies dead. "Another installment of the human condition is beginning." Very cinematic. (p. 13)

> *Stephen W. Soule, in* Bookletter *(copyright 1975 by* Harper's Magazine; *reprinted from the March 31, 1975 issue by special permission), March 31, 1975.*

Anthony Burgess often seems to be the only living novelist in England. Master of many languages, many dialects of English, and of music (he is also a composer), Burgess is heir to much knowledge and much wit; always totally informed and rarely overburdened, his prose changes directions perpetually because its author knows more possibilities for a sentence than Judge Sirica. He has kept a great tradition alive, and honored his literary father by editing an abridged *Finnegans Wake* and writing two books on Joyce. But unless *Napoleon Symphony* (which I haven't read) is it, Burgess has never written a great novel. Even *A Clockwork Orange* is burdened by his heavy-handed, two-handed symmetry. Yet in language and the faceted shattering of novelistic situations only Nabokov is his master, and only Burgess is in Nabokov's league.

The Clockwork Testament is the third, final novel about his most charming character, Enderby (in the United States, the first two were published together as *Enderby*). Enderby is a poet, a lovably helpless genius with comically obnoxious habits, a willing victim of his own viscera. Just as the first volume was titled *Inside Mr. Enderby* to denote both his mental processes and his indigestion, this third book's subtitle, *Enderby's End*, indicates both the death and the anality of its hero. Other people may "breathe their last," but Enderby seems to excrete rather than expire. . . .

Still, Enderby's innocence makes all this seem comic rather than offensive. Somewhere between a holy fool and an *idiot savant*, Enderby reminds us most of Luzhin, the chess genius of Nabokov's *The Defense*. Like Nabokov, Burgess ridicules the Freudian, determinist view of the artist as a product of neurosis by seeming to make Enderby's anal obsessiveness the central motivation of his character, and then emphasizing it cruelly and absurdly until the reader is forced to admit that is not the point, not the point at all. And Burgess writes by Nabokov's code (the code of any responsible writer): if your character is a genius, you must show samples of his work. Enderby's poems (usually stored in his bathtub) are dense, almost totally obscure configurations of beautiful words. Of course, most people find all decent poetry to be this obscure, and we are at least temporarily convinced that the future might find here something memorable. However, the long poem left uncompleted at Enderby's death is not as convincing as some earlier examples. . . .

As its title indicates, Burgess has used his latest Enderby book as a vehicle to make a statement about *A Clockwork Orange*: he thought the film was good, but lush in its treatment of sexual brutality; while he recognized his book in it, the film was a separate work for which he was not responsible. Leave me alone, I didn't do it.

Putting himself into his novel this way is droll of our author, but in terms of Enderby's character it seems gratuitous. He didn't start out as an autobiographical disguise. Still, there is strong continuity with the earlier books; for instance, we finally get the recipe for "stepmother's tea." And installing Enderby in New York City does allow Burgess to comment on teenage gangs, college students, women's lib, TV talk shows—all the crudities of America. If the urge toward autobiographical justification is at Enderby's expense, that price is still worth paying, for Enderby's hallucinatory experiences in New York between heart attacks are invaluable.

Charles Nicol, "A Poet for Posterity," in National Review (© *National Review, Inc., 1975; 150 East 35th St., New York, N.Y. 10016), May 9, 1975, p. 521.*

*   *   *

BURROUGHS, William S(eward)   1914-

Burroughs, an American, writes inventive, obsessive novels. ***Naked Lunch* is his best known work. (See also *Contemporary Authors*, Vols. 9-12, rev. ed.)**

Naked Lunch belongs to that very large category of books, from Macpherson's *Ossian* to *Peyton Place*, whose interest lies not in their own qualities but in the reception given to them in their own time. In itself, *Naked Lunch* is of very small significance. It consists of a prolonged scream of hatred and disgust, an effort to keep the reader's nose down in the mud for 250 pages. Before reading it I had heard it described as pornography, but this is not the case. The object of pornographic writing is to flood the reader's mind with lust, and lust is at any rate a positive thing to the extent that none of us would exist without it. A pornographic novel is, in however backhanded a way, on the side of something describable as life.

Naked Lunch, by contrast, is unreservedly on the side of death. It seeks to flood the reader's mind not with images of sexual desire but with images of pain, illness, cruelty and corruption. (p. 351)

A book like *Naked Lunch* requires far less talent in the writer, and for that matter less intelligence in the reader than the humblest magazine story or circulating-library novel. From the literary point of view, it is the merest trash, not worth a second glance. (p. 352)

The only writer of any talent of whom Burroughs occasionally manages to remind one is the Marquis de Sade; but if one turns to the pages of Sade after *Naked Lunch* the resemblance soon fades, since Sade, however degenerate he can be at times, has always some saving wit and irony. Burroughs takes himself with a complete, owlish seriousness; indeed, in his opening section he seems, as far as one can make out through the pea-soup fog of his prose, to be offering the book as some kind of tract against drug addiction. (pp. 356-57)

Altogether, *Naked Lunch* offers a very interesting field for speculation, both pathological and sociological. No lover of medical text-books on deformity should miss it. The rest of us, however, can afford to spend our six dollars on something else. (p. 357)

John Wain, "Naked Lunch" (originally titled "The Great Burroughs Affair"; reprinted by permission of The New Republic; © *1962 by The New Republic, Inc.), in* The Critic As Artist: Essays on Books 1920-1970, *edited by Gilbert A. Harrison, Liveright, 1972, pp. 351-57.*

William S. Burroughs is a great autoeroticist—of writing, not sex. He gets astral kicks by composing in blocks, scenes, repetitive and identical memories galvanizing themselves into violent fantasies, the wild mixing of pictures, words, the echoes of popular speech. It is impossible to suspect him of any base erotic motives in his innumerable scenes of one adolescent boy servicing another like a piece of plumbing; nor should one expect a book from him different from his others. . . . [In *The Wild Boys: A Book of the Dead*] he more than ever turns his obsession with cold, callous homosexual coupling into a piece of American science fiction. (p. 4)

Actually, he is a cutup who writes in action-prose, kaleidoscopic shifts, spurts, eruptions and hellzapoppins. But with all the simultaneous and cleverly farcical reversals, noises, revolver shots, sado-masochistic scenes on and off the high wire, the book is inescapably a reverie, the private Burroughs dream state. Whole scenes collide and steal up on each other and break away as if they were stars violently oscillating and exploding in the telescopic eyepiece of an astronomer who just happens to be gloriously soused. . . .

More than anyone else I can think of in contemporary "fiction," he showed himself absolutely reckless in writing for his own satisfaction only. And yet he was so inventive, brilliant, funny in his many wild improvisations (he writes scenes as other people write adjectives, so that he is always inserting one scene into another, *turning* one scene into another), that one recognized a writer interested in nothing but his own mind. . . .

Burroughs is indeed a serious man and a considerable writer. But his books are not really books, they are compositions that astonish, then pall. They are subjective experiences brought into the world for the hell of it and by the excitement of whatever happens to be present to Burroughs's consciousness when he writes. (p. 22)

> *Alfred Kazin, in* The New York Times Book Review *(© 1971 by The New York Times Company; reprinted by permission), December 12, 1971.*

Burroughs has been called a prophet of political doom and a satirist of the American scene, but he has in fact never written about institutions so much as about emotion, never about ideas so much as about the experience of degradation or fear. His political outrage has the meaning of a series of expletives strung together with great intensity. What it communicates is not content but energy—that diffuse, furious revolt that gives his work the edgy power of acid rock. Burroughs' cut-up or fold-in method (take a page or tape, cut it into pieces, and paste or splice together in any order except the original one) is designed not only to destroy any coherent statement, but to dissolve the line between personality and society in a jolting music. This very confusion has served to conceal Burroughs the writer and the hater within his many indistinguishable characters, those anonymous voices choking with nausea at being alive. For Burroughs' final subject is not the particular psyche, nor the social scene, but quaking nerves.

Burroughs' novels are the experience of his orgiastic hate. Passion is the work of demon bacteria, "virus powers" that infect with love, or a craving for heroin, cruelty, or power. Men are no more than the hosts of personality parasites, victims that virus-gods use for food. And the sex parasite is the most voracious. Just as Burroughs politicized heroin addiction in *Naked Lunch* (as the mode of all addictions—of governments to power, of men to cruelty), so in his later novels sex becomes the model for every kind of conflict and degradation. For Burroughs always writes of those lonely, homosexual men who are doomed to be tempted into sex by the likes of Johnny Yen, "the boy-girl god of sexual frustration from the terminal sewers of Venus." His characters tell of lust rolling into degradation and torture, of beautiful boys metamorphosing into slimy green newts. Living is only being wrecked by desire, being violated by men who are not even people. . . .

Yet no matter how far they recede into abstraction, Burroughs' spaced-out men can never escape the sense that every eruption of life is a force for destruction. Burroughs' titles—*Nova Express, The Ticket That Exploded*—tell nearly all: life is a nova express, a fulminating train speeding toward its final, explosive stop. Your ticket to ride is your body, the raging host that makes you ride whether you will or no. (p. 87)

In *Naked Lunch, The Soft Machine*, and *The Ticket That Exploded*, Burroughs wrote of people consumed by their own passions, of lovers spliced together in hate, their intestines locked in a parasitic bond. But in *Nova Express* and *The Wild Boys* he evolved a way of dealing with every agony. In these novels, a man can escape his hate by going out of his mind. Burroughs turns emotion into a psychic event that releases feeling in a brilliant, removed image. . . .

In *The Wild Boys*, Burroughs finally emerges as a fury, the demon artist he calls the Incomparable Yellow Serpent, who "shifts from AC to DC as a thin siren wail breaks from his lips." Pictures "leap from his eyes blasting everyone to smoldering fragments. . . . When comes such another singer?" demands Burroughs.

Burroughs' fantasies are clearly meant to kill off all the straights. What he wants are vindicators, "wild boys," the sudden coming of "a whole generation . . . that felt neither pleasure or pain." (p. 88)

> *Josephine Hendin, "Angries: S-M as a Literary Style," in* Harper's *(copyright 1974 by Harper's Magazine; reprinted from the February, 1974 issue by special permission), February, 1974, pp. 87-93.*

On the eighteenth-century notion that ruins are more sublime than the real thing, [*Exterminator!*] is a novel only by default. It is a continuing series of vignettes, which is an unhip way of saying spliced interfaces. But they all have one thing in common: they are mercifully short.

Heterogeneous people are yoked violently together, and like divers they emerge from Burroughs's shallows more bent than alive. . . . Burroughs's fantasies are from the Eisenhower era, when all good Americans went to Kerouac before they died. And the bad Americans? They stayed in Paris.

Burroughs is at his best when he looks into his mirror and writes. There is a clever satire on a tired old trendy, 'The Coming Purple Better One', who wouldn't say boo to a goose. Especially when it takes the form of a youth-cult, marching en masse and demanding its rights. But this portrait of an innocent at home is the only whiff of clean air among all the cocaine. Much of the novel flirts with 'experimentalism', on the principle that fake diamonds are a writer's best friend. Burroughs's flashes of montage and the occasional rash of block capitals (a variation on plaster of Paris) have the unmistakeable flavour of what the French used to call 'staircase wit', or the lines you should have said before you left the party. Or what Burroughs might call that sinking feeling many times removed. Experimentalism is, nowadays, generally after the fact and most Americans must tiptoe where the French and Irish have already stamped.

There is a desperate conventionality about this 'novel', as if it could explode but only just. (pp. 333-34)

> *Peter Ackroyd, in* The Spectator *(© 1974 by The Spectator; reprinted by permission of The Spectator), March 16, 1974.*

In [Burroughs'] world writers and doctors are the only heroes, while missionaries are sent forth to bring home the genitals of black men. Like Fellini, Burroughs is probably not exaggerating. That's the way he sees things. Characterisation is laughable in the context of the average Burroughs bloodbath. But perversion, the subconscious, the future, whichever terminology you prefer to speak of it in, his world is very much there before your eyes, believed in, relished, detested, lived through. You could say Burroughs was a writer of exotica, too much a creature of his own imagination. [In *Exterminator!*, as in earlier novels, his] world is peopled . . . with all manner of subterranean freaks and failures. On the other hand if there is anyone truly creative in novel-writing today, as distinct from merely interpretative, it must be him. As I said before, it depends on your terminology. Personally I think he's a poet. (p. 455)

Hugo Williams, in New Statesman (© *1974 The Statesman & Nation Publishing Co. Ltd.), March 29, 1974.*

William Burroughs's *Exterminator!* seeks quite deliberately to exploit a mixture of modes. Its styles shift, from a dull, low colloquial, spliced together without punctuation ("You couldn't say exactly when it hit familiar and dreary as a cigarette butt ground out in cold scrambled eggs the tooth paste smears on a washstand glass why you were on the cops day like another just feeling a little worse than usual which is not unusual at all well an ugly thing broke out that day in the precinct . . ."); to an end-of-the-world romantistic ("In the desolate markets the bright fabrics and tinware no longer flap and clatter in the winds of God. There are few purchasers and fingers that touch the merchandise are yellow and listless with fever"); to a brisk documentary ("Sunday August 25: Out to the airport for the arrival of McCarthy. An estimated fifteen thousand supporters there to welcome him mostly young people. Surprisingly few police. Whole scene touching and ineffectual particularly in retrospect of subsequent events"). These styles, and a good many others, occur in discrete and discontinuous sections, united not even by continuous "characters" but only by a common exploitation of the comic-apocalyptic motifs that one easily associates with Burroughs's work.

It is an extremely demanding way to write a book, to begin to do something different every five pages or so, and to bring it off requires not only skill but virtuosity of a very high order. The greatest likelihood is that the book will seem frightfully uneven, demonstrating that its author does some things better than others, which seems to me very much the case with *Exterminator!*. Another likelihood is

that a book so discontinuous will seem, at its end, not to have been structured but only to have grown by accretion, like a scrapbook, and this too seems to me the case with *Exterminator!*. For all of its brutality, there is so much comic-strip stylization to its whores, pimps, junkies, presidential advisers, and scientologists, that the brutality never seems quite persuasive. (pp. 305-06)

Philip Stevick, in Partisan Review (*copyright* © *1974 by Partisan Review, Inc.), Vol. XLI, No. 2, 1974.*

The very name of Burroughs conjures up contorted works of quirky brilliance, a warp of vision through a wild woof of language. [In "The Last Words of Dutch Schultz" we] have instead, astoundingly, the script for a gangster film, pure and simple. Well, not so pure—neither the hero nor the heroin—but very simple, and very good.

"The Last Words of Dutch Schultz" turns out to be a straightforward, skillful piece of work for the movies, a good old-fashioned film biography of a bad old-fashioned racketeer. To suit the genre, the text is in many ways conventional beyond belief. . . .

It's true that there are a few passages that twist and run with the old Burroughs dazzle. . . . But heady passages . . . are very rare; the text remains essentially functional, workmanlike. The genuinely amazing fact is not that the script is a fiction, but that Burroughs has composed a work in the Hollywood vein—relentlessly stereotyped, virtually a parody—that is at the same time congruent with the rest of his unique work. This screenplay makes evident a couple of things about Burroughs that were not nearly so obvious before.

For one thing, it reveals the humorist in Burroughs, the helplessly appalled, obsessed joker. The sequence about the Whisperer, whose voice is a tape recorder, is revoltingly and mirthlessly funny. For another, the screenplay sheds a flickering new light on all those kaleidoscopic hallucinations that go swirling through his books: home-movie loops, of course they are, to be replayed ad nauseam in a tiny theater—the terrified soul. Cinematic extravaganzas, celluloid nightmares. If we are tempted to pin generic labels on anything, it would be a hindsight better to call his novels "Film Scripts in the Form of Fiction." (p. 4)

Alan Friedman, in The New York Times Book Review (© *1975 by The New York Times Company; reprinted by permission), June 22, 1975.*

C

CABRERA INFANTE, G(uillermo) 1929-

Cabrera Infante, a Cuban novelist and short story writer now living in London, writes of both pre- and post-revolutionary Cuba. His fiction is linguistically inventive, brilliant, and humorous. He won the Biblioteca Breve prize in Barcelona in 1964 for *Tres tristes tigres* (*Three Trapped Tigers*)**.**

"Three Trapped Tigers" is a remarkable book. I doubt a funnier book has been written in Spanish since "Don Quixote." Granted, that is not saying much. Literature in Spanish has not been noted for its humor. Yet this, precisely, is one of the book's strongest points: it has savagely refreshed an often portentously solemn heritage. It is also one of the most inventive novels that has come out of Latin America, and that is saying a great deal. The inventiveness of Latin-American fiction since Borges is by now (one would hope) fairly widely recognized.

Finally, its humor is fundamentally linguistic—the pun rate often runs at several per page. First published in Spain in 1964, part of its enterprise is to record the kind of Spanish that is spoken in Cuba—the kind I had imagined to be by definition untranslatable. Not only have Donald Gardner and Suzanne Levine proved otherwise. They have, in collaboration with the author, produced one of the best translations I have ever read. Cabrera Infante's English is known to be excellent—he has written several film scripts in English. What has been done here is to *recreate* the novel—an equivalent version that is never quite the original but that is rarely inferior.

Superficially, this is a story of night-life in Havana shortly before the revolution. It takes us into most of the night-clubs, strip-joints, *barras* and *cantinas* the city could provide—the ones where after-hour *chowcitos* were staged, where people sang songs as if they really cared, and where one might have seen a Negro woman improvising a rumba as though she were inventing dance.

Cabrera Infante (who left Cuba several years ago and now lives in London) has no illusions about what his native island was like under Batista. The book is full of suggestive glimpses of social injustice. "Three Trapped Tigers" is nevertheless an exercise in nostalgia, an attempt, to quote its Carollian epigraph, "to fancy what the flame of a candle looks like after the candle is blown out." The nostalgia is not for the poverty most of the characters were brought up

in. It is rather (I think) a nostalgia for the once-familiar bar, the familiar singer, the familiar friend, for an intensely local yet richly varied world. The novel therefore is a celebration of the small things that oblivion or time demolishes. (p. 5)

A vastly comic novel. A novel where comedy is a strategy against sadness, against mediocrity, against the limitations of an underdeveloped island. "Three Trapped Tigers" is all these things. But, above all, it is a novel about literature, about language. It is an attempt to capture spoken Cuban, an attempt directed against a literary tradition where the act of writing has always been sacredly solemn, remote from the act of speaking.

Cabrera Infante once said he could see no difference between a writer and a bus-driver. His novel is directed against all those writers—until recently, the vast majority in Spain and Latin America—who have believed that to write is above all to distinguish oneself from a bus-driver, to fabricate sonorous, "beautiful" phrases that carry with them the signature "this is literature." Cabrera Infante not only writes a language that has its roots in speech. He also treats us for contrast to magnificent parodies of seven Cuban writers, whom he makes describe the death of Trotsky, "several years after the event—or before." All of them are obsessed, each in a different way, with the flaunting of their impressive "craftsmanship." (pp. 5, 67)

Cabrera Infante's most unsophisticated characters pun, sometimes unwittingly, the pun having often perhaps "revealed" itself at the moment of writing. Language in the page has turned out to be a more complex thing than when it issues from the mouth. The puns, anagrams and palindromes help to illustrate the treacherously elusive nature of diction, its uncontrollable alchemy. The logic of the pun is for instance often the principal motor behind a character's streams of consciousness—as though he were imprisoned by language's own momentum. The author, too, is driven by the logic of the language in his writing as much as by any premeditated aim.

"Three Trapped Tigers" is a novel that meditates on the nature of writing in general and on the nature of its own writing. Its great merit is that it does so in a manner that never obtrudes on the general reader's enjoyment of the book's more superficial but nonetheless joyfully witty qualities. (p. 67)

David Gallagher, in The New York Times Book Review *(© 1971 by The New York Times Company; reprinted by permission), October 17, 1971.*

["Three Trapped Tigers," a] camp epic of night life in Batista's Havana of the 1950's, opens wonderfully, with the emcee of the Tropicana, "the MOST fabulous nightclub in the WORLD," delivering his bilingual spiel while the spotlight swings among the tables singling out the fifteenth-birthday party of Miss Vivian Smith-Corona Alvarez de Real and that perfect emblem of sad celebrity, *"la bella, gloriosa"* Martine Carol. A world is created in five pages, part gritty documentary, part loony fantasy. As a writer, a bongo player, a candid photographer, a small-time actor take turns telling their stories, Cabrera Infante displays ferocious verbal energy, funny expertise in American movies, a sardonic eye for dismal floorshows. . . .

Unfortunately, Cabrera Infante is also a terrible pedant. The second half of "Three Trapped Tigers" dries up into a sandy waste of Joycean punning (what we need least is a Cuban Joyce), heavy literary parodies and assorted monkey tricks of an avant-garde 50 years to the rear (diagrams, numerical puzzlers, a section entitled "Some Revelations" made up of blank pages). The reader impatiently calls for his check before this show is over. (p. 116)

Walter Clemons, in Newsweek *(copyright 1971 by Newsweek, Inc.; all rights reserved; reprinted by permission), October 25, 1971.*

Tres tristes tigres (1967, 'Three sad tigers') . . . is maybe the most original work of fiction to have been written in Latin America, and also the funniest. Yet we must first of all consider an earlier book, *Así en la paz como en la guerra* (1961, 'In peace as in war'), a collection of short stories of considerable distinction, though in an idiom so very different from that of the novel that they scarcely seem to belong to the same man.

Most of the stories in *Así en la paz como en la guerra* were written in the 1950s, during the Batista dictatorship, and with deep commitment to the revolutionary cause. The stories add up to a fairly coherent whole, not only because they present a picture of Cuban life that is always coloured by the author's sense of its injustice and corruption but also because interspersed between the stories there are fifteen linking sketches which describe the repressive violence that was displayed against Batista's opponents. Although the stories were probably written at random they are consequently given a coherent structure, their proposition 'this is Cuba' being counterpointed by the proposition 'this is how it is falling apart' offered by the terrorist sketches.

The Cuba that threatens to fall apart is not an edifying one, although the author never strains to spell the fact out. Neither revolution nor repression is mentioned in the straight stories, yet a subtly suggested sense of menace permeates them. (p. 164)

These sketches have, I think, had a great deal of influence on contemporary Cuban writing, although few people in Cuba would admit it now in view of Cabrera Infante's current disfavour there. There is a school of young Cuban writers like Norberto Fuentes, Jesús Díaz, and Eduardo Heras Leon who have derived from him an unrepentantly aggressive language for the depiction of revolutionary or counter-revolutionary violence. Like Cabrera Infante, they write dead-pan, uncensored stories in which no apology is made for meticulous descriptions of the most gory details of violent death. (p. 165)

[Neither] *Así en la paz como en la guerra*—nor indeed any of the young Cuban writers mentioned—remotely approaches the unprecedented excellence of Cabrera Infante's novel *Tres tristes tigres*. (p. 166)

On one level . . ., *Tres tristes tigres* functions as a documentary of pre-revolutionary night-life, and of Havana in general. . . . The novel will, to paraphrase Robbe-Grillet, be useful to the archaeologist in some centuries time who chooses to reconstruct Havana in 1958. (p. 169)

Tres tristes tigres is mostly about a Havana that the American businessman, over for a weekend overdose of *daiquiris* and professional sex, never got to see, a private, almost secret Havana, dedicated to Afro-Cuban rhythms and to the sound of the *bongos*. Readers who know nothing about Cuban music, and who do not know Havana, will of course miss a great deal in the novel, which in many ways is a local novel—Cabrera Infante has even stated that he wonders how it could be understood in Luyanó, 'a suburb on the outskirts of Havana', so restricted are many of its points of reference to the very centre of the city. . . . Yet even at its most local, *Tres tristes tigres* has the widest possible implications. (p. 170)

Most important, in *Tres tristes tigres* there exists a sense of belonging, of being 'inside', of *sharing* something which all the characters have and which the reader is able to feel despite his possible ignorance of the specific context. For he too may have experienced a similar sense of belonging and of sharing, albeit in a wholly different context. It is one of the trade-marks of *Tres tristes tigres* that it conveys the fundamental sense of what it is like to belong to and to recognize as familiar *any* local situation. And as such it is also very much a novel about friendship, about how friendship is sustained by the existence of a very few, very specific things in common. (p. 171)

Quite unobstrusively, the novel . . . grapples with social realities as eloquently as any socialist realist novel could, more eloquently I think because just as the feel of a local context comes across much more strongly when conveyed from the inside, so does the feel of social injustice when it is an automatic part of what the author is writing *from*, when it is not something he is strenuously attempting to demonstrate for the sake of propaganda. (p. 173)

It is a novel that endeavours to rebel against the manner in which time can abolish a whole epoch that once seemed so significant, a whole local world that was once so rich in associations. No doubt many critics have made or will make any number of sarcastic comments about a man who can feel nostalgic about *Batista's* Cuba. They will of course be crassly missing the point, and not only because *Tres tristes tigres* is a novel about social injustices too. But mainly because Cabrera Infante's nostalgia is directed at the fragile *strategems* people improvise [against] *adversity*, at the rich detail of those perhaps trivial and absurd strategems people have at some point mounted against injustice, but in particular against such fundamental problems as loneliness, mediocrity, and boredom.

Tres tristes tigres is finally, and most importantly perhaps, a novel about language and about literature. For one [thing] the novel is, according to a prefatory note, 'written in Cuban'. This does not mean that Cabrera Infante has emulated the unfortunate linguistic efforts of the regionalist novelists of the twenties and thirties. . . . Like Vargas Llosa, but more so, he seeks to establish a natural, spoken language as the proper language for literature, seeks to rid Latin American literature of its 'literariness', to free the Spanish language from the pomposities of its conventional written forms, from that obligation that writers of a previous generation seem to have felt to *write* a language outlandishly different, so solemnly pompous was it, from the one they spoke. (pp. 178-79)

Throughout the book literary excesses are subjected to merciless ironical contemplation. Gorky cannot be forgiven for writing that 'the sea laughed', Faulkner is mocked for writing that August 'like a languorous replete bird winged slowly toward the moon of decay and death'. There are occasional, unannounced parodies of Hemingway, Proust, and Borges, and other passing parodies of such literary panaceas as the perspectivist novel and the psycho-analytical novel. (pp. 179-80)

A clue to the novel's reflections on the nature of language can be found in its use of the pun. The novel is rife with puns, sometimes at the rate of several per page. Like everything else in the novel, the puns are often just funny, gratuitously, defiantly stupid, part of the book's frequent enterprise to be plain ridiculous for the sake of it, a refreshing one in view of the fact that so much Latin American writing has scarcely been notable for its avoidance of pretentious solemnity. . . . The great inventor Rine invents a space coach worthy of 'H. G. Wells Fargo'. . . . [We see] what happens when Cuban pronunciation is written down, as when Cubans pronounce the names of famous writers such as Shame's Choice or Andre Yi (the distinguished Chinaman). (p. 181)

Yet Cabrera Infante's puns are more than just gratuitous comic effusions. Puns are words that dramatize the extent to which an author can never be in full control of language, because they demonstrate the extent to which a word can be unpredictably complex. Not only does the spoken word unexpectedly acquire a different significance when written down: the written word itself has implications and associations beyond the control of the man *writing* it. . . . [The] streams of consciousness we are offered in this novel usually develop, like those in *Ulysses*, by *phonetic* association rather than by association of ideas. (p. 182)

Cabrera Infante has liberated himself from literary cliché, from vacuous sonority, from self-indulgent embellishment, and from taboos about what can be said'—but [language] is also his master, for no word can be pinned down, no word can be neutralized and made to function innocently in a given context, without it pointing to another context, without it escaping in many other different directions. (p. 183)

> *D. P. Gallagher, "Guillermo Cabrera Infante," in his* Modern Latin-American Literature *(© Oxford University Press, 1973; by permission of Oxford University Press, Oxford),* Oxford University Press, *1973, pp. 164-85.*

CALVINO, Italo   1923-

A member of the left-wing intelligensia in Italy, Calvino writes novels and short stories, blending reality and fantasy with philosophical and moral undertones.

[Calvino's] first significant work of fiction *Il sentiero dei nidi di ragno* (1947; *The Path to the Nest of Spiders*, 1957) revealed that Calvino was capable of more than just the documentary realism and the ideologically inspired adventure narrative of other Resistance fiction, full of blood, violence, and cruelty. Calvino demonstrated his artistic ingenuity by choosing to depict the civil war in Northern Italy from the viewpoint of an adolescent boy, Pin, who is caught up in the Partisan warfare which sweeps over his village and the surrounding mountains. The essential form of the narrative is in the subtle tension between the grave reality of historical events and a courageous boy's insistence on preserving the poetry, if not the innocence of childhood. Calvino has described the book "as a combination of *For Whom the Bell Tolls* and Robert Louis Stevenson." The fable quality of narrative atmosphere maintained by Calvino in this novella is his distinguishing characteristic as a story-teller and has been continued and developed in his short stories, *I Racconti* (1959) and especially in a trilogy of novels; *Il visconte dimezzato* (1952; *The Cloven Viscount*, 1962), *Il barone rampante* (1957; *The Baron in the Trees*, 1959), and *Il cavaliere inesistente* (1959; *The Non-existent Knight*, 1962).

A strong flavor of chivalric epic characterizes all three works of the trilogy which has been republished in one volume under the general title of *I nostri antenati* (1960) and it is hardly surprising to learn that Calvino has an intense admiration for the Ferrarese Renaissance poet-narrator Ludovico Ariosto, author of the *Orlando furioso*. Like his master of the sixteenth century Calvino has sought to utilize a dominant spirit of adventurous fancy to vivify a narrative with a profound moral meaning. Like Ariosto, Calvino does not explicitly insist that his narrative be read within a strict ideological or moral frame of reference; he is content to permit the reader to make whatever interpretation he wishes; and it is indeed possible to read the trilogy without concerning oneself with its philosophical or moral intent. (pp. 161-62)

Calvino has avowed a preference for telling stories about characters who set difficult goals for themselves in life and then work courageously and indefatigably to reach them as part of a search for integrity and wholeness of personality. (pp. 163-64)

The three novels of *I nostri antenati* represent for Calvino three types of experience in self-realization, in the attainment of true spiritual liberty. The moral significance he has skillfully and delicately built into these tales blending fantasy and objective reality is hardly insistent and they offer simple narrative values with a direct, unintellectual fascination, and appeal. Calvino is an unsophisticated, unpretentious stylist with a gift of simplicity stemming from his deep interest in Italian fable literature. *I nostri antenati*, by successfully fusing lyric, epic, and comic elements with a discreet moral view of contemporary man, has provided a fresh viewpoint and technique to recent Italian fiction. (pp. 164-65)

> *Louis Tenenbaum, in* Contemporary European Novelists, *edited by Siegfried Mandel*

(copyright © 1968, Southern Illinois University Press; reprinted by permission of the author), Southern Illinois University Press, 1968.

Calvino is a distinguished Italian novelist, but he is not at his best in these three stories [*The Watchers and Other Stories*]. The first was written nearly twenty years ago and the latest in 1963. Two out of the three have nothing in common except that they have been boiled to savorless pulp over a low flame of symbolism, like overcooked vegetables.

[In the] earliest and shortest story, "The Argentine Ant," . . . the symbolism is extruded from a grim series of events. A young couple with a baby set up house in a village by the sea, only to find that the whole neighborhood is at the mercy of swarms of ants. Nothing helps. One neighbor invents a complicated mechanism for trapping the ants into suicide. Another is obsessed by heading the ants into one labyrinth after another by putting down this poison and that.

The story reaches no climax. In Calvino's world ants are everywhere. Likewise dirt. The hero of the next story, "Smog," is forever washing his hands, since, for him, ants are replaced by dust. And in the third and longest, which gives the volume its name, a left-wing poll watcher is sent into a section of the city run by the Church in aid of cripples and idiots in order to see that their votes are not misused during an election. The ants here become nun-sized and semi-benevolent. Somebody, after all has to look after the rejects of society, and Calvino, if a man of the Left, is a balanced observer, however pessimistic.

He makes things hard for his readers, however, by a portentous manner expressed in cumbrous paragraphs. In less than two pages there are nine bracketed phrases to muffle attention. And at no point in any of these tales do the characters hold any interest in themselves, except as puppets at the mercy of a thesis. Kafka and glue, in fact.

Alan Pryce-Jones, "Kafka and Glue," in Book World—The Washington Post (© The Washington Post), April 25, 1971, p. 12.

Calvino's first novel [*The Path to the Nest of Spiders*] is a plainly told, exuberant sort of book. Although the writing is conventional, there is an odd intensity in the way Calvino sees things, a closeness of scrutiny much like that of William Golding. Like Golding he knows how and when to *inhabit* entirely, with all senses functioning, landscape, state of mind, act. In *The Spire* Golding makes the flawed church so real that one smells the mortar, sees the motes of dust, fears for the ill-placed stones. Calvino does the same in his story of Pin. . . .

"Pin is a boy who does not know how to play games, and cannot take part in the games either of children or grownups." Pin dreams, however, of "a friend, a real friend who understands him and whom he can understand, and then to him, and only to him, will he show the place where the spiders have their lairs." . . . [A] sort of precise, quasi-scientific observation keeps Calvino from the sort of sentimentality that was prevalent in the Forties, when wise children learned compassion from a black mammy as she deep-fried chitlins and Jesus in equal parts south of the Mason-Dixon line.

Pin joins the partisans in the hills above the Ligurian coast. I have a suspicion that Calvino is dreaming all this for he writes like a bookish, nearsighted man who has mislaid his glasses: objects held close . . . are vividly described but the middle and far distances of landscape and war tend to blur. It makes no difference, however, for the dreams of a nearsighted young man at the beginning of a literary career can be more real to the reader than the busy reportage of those journalist-novelists who were there and, seeing it all, saw nothing.

Although Calvino manages to inhabit the skin of the outraged and outrageous child, his men and women are almost always shadowy. Later in his career, Calvino will eliminate men and women altogether as he re-creates the cosmos. Meanwhile, as a beginner, he is a vivid, if occasionally clumsy, writer. . . . Calvino's last paragraphs are almost always jubilant—the sort of cheerful codas that only a deep pessimist about human matters could write. (p. 13)

In 1952 Calvino published *The Cloven Viscount*, one of the three short novels he has since collected under the title *Our Ancestors*. They are engaging works, written in a style somewhat like that of T. H. White's Arthurian novels. The narrator of *The Cloven Viscount* is, again, an orphan boy. During a war between Austria and Turkey (1716) the boy's uncle Viscount Medardo was cloven from top to crotch by a cannon ball. Saved by doctors on the battlefield, the half Viscount was sent home with one leg, one arm, one eye, half a nose, mouth, etc. . . .

The story is cheerfully, briskly told. The Half Viscount is a perfect bastard and takes pleasure in murder, fire, torture. . . .

I note that the publisher's blurb would have us believe that this is "an allegory of modern man—alienated and mutilated—this novel has profound overtones. As a parody of the Christian parables of good and evil, it is both witty and refreshing." Well, at least the book is witty and refreshing. Actually the story is less Christian than a send-up of Plato and his idea of the whole.

In due course the other half of the Viscount hits town; this half is unbearably good and deeply boring. . . . When the two halves are finally united, the resulting whole Viscount is the usual not very interesting human mixture. In a happy ending, he marries Pamela. But the boy narrator is not content. "Amid all this fervor of wholeness, [I] felt myself growing sadder and more lacking. Sometimes one who thinks himself incomplete is merely young."

The Cloven Viscount is filled with many closely observed natural images like "The subsoil was so full of ants that a hand put down anywhere came up all black and swarming with them." I don't know which was written first, *The Cloven Viscount* (1952) or "The Argentine Ant," published in *Botteghe Oscure* (1952), but Calvino's nightmare of an ant-infested world touched on in the novel becomes the subject of "The Argentine Ant" and I fear that I must now trot out that so often misused word "masterpiece." Or, put another way, if "The Argentine Ant" is not a masterpiece of twentieth-century prose writing, I cannot think of anything better. Certainly it is as minatory and strange as anything by Kafka. It is also hideously funny. In some forty pages Calvino gives us "the human condition," as the blurb writers would say, in spades. That is, the human condition *today*. Or the dilemma of modern man. Or the disrupted environment. Or nature's revenge. Or an allegory of grace. Whatever. . . . But a story is, finally, what it tells and no more. (p. 14)

Calvino has now developed two ways of writing. One is literally fabulous. The other makes use of a dry rather didactic style in which the detail is as precisely observed as if the author were writing a manual for the construction of a solar heating unit. Yet the premises of the "dry" stories are often quite as fantastic as those of the fairy tales. (p. 15)

Most realistic and specific of Calvino's works, "The Watcher" has proved (to date) to be the last of the "dry" narratives. In 1965 Calvino published *Cosmicomics*: twelve brief stories dealing in a fantastic way with the creation of the universe, man, society. . . . Calvino has deployed his complex prose in order to compose in words a super strip cartoon narrated by Qfwfq whose progress from life inside the first atom to mollusk on the earth's sea floor to social-climbing amphibian to dinosaur to moon-farmer is told in a dozen episodes that are entirely unlike anything that anyone else has written since, perhaps, Lucian. (p. 17)

In 1967, Calvino published more of Qfwfq's adventures in *Time and the Hunter* [published in America as *t zero*]. For the most part they are engaging cartoons, but one is disconcerted to encounter altogether too many bits of Sarraute, of Robbe-Grillet, of Borges (far too much of Borges) incorporated in the prose of what I have come to regard as a true modern master. . . . On page 6 occurs "viscous"; on page 11 "acid mucus." I started to feel queasy: these are Sarraute words. I decided that their use was simply a matter of coincidence. But when, on page 29, I saw the dread word "magma" I knew that Calvino has been too long in Paris, for only Sarrautistes use "magma," a word the great theoretician of the old New Novel so arbitrarily and uniquely appropriated from the discipline of science. Elsewhere in the stories, Robbe-Grillet's technique of recording the minutiae of a banal situation stops cold some of Calvino's best effects.

"The Chase," in fact, could have been written by Robbe-Grillet. This is not a compliment. . . .

On his own and at his best, Calvino does what very few writers can do: he describes imaginary worlds with the most extraordinary precision and beauty (a word he has single-handedly removed from that sphere of suspicion which the old New Novelists used to maintain surrounds all words and any narrative). (p. 19)

In *Cosmicomics* Calvino makes it possible for the reader to inhabit a meson, a mollusk, a dinosaur—makes him see for the first time light as it ends the dark universe. Since this is a unique gift, I find all the more alarming the "literariness" of *Time and the Hunter*. I was particularly put off by the central story "t zero," which could have been written (and rather better) by Borges. . . .

Calvino ends these tales with his own "The Count of Monte Cristo." The problem he sets himself is how to get out of Château d'If. Faria keeps making plans and tunneling his way through an endless, exitless fortress. Dantès, on the other hand, broods on the nature of the fortress as well as on the various drafts of the novel that Dumas is writing. In some drafts, Dantès will escape and find a treasure and get revenge on his enemies. In other drafts, he suffers a different fate. The narrator contemplates the possibilities of escape by considering the way a fortress (or a work of art) is made. "To plan a book—or an escape—the first thing to know is what to exclude." This particular story is Borges at his very best and, taking into account the essential unity of the multiplicity of all things, one cannot rule out that Calvino's version of *The Count of Monte Cristo* by Alexandre Dumas is indeed the finest achievement of Jorge Luis Borges imagined by Italo Calvino.

Calvino's seventh and latest novel (or work or meditation or poem) *Invisible Cities* is perhaps his most beautiful work. In a garden sit the aged Kublai Khan and the young Marco Polo—Tartar emperor and Venetian traveler. The mood is sunset. Prospero is holding up for the last time his magic wand: Kublai Khan has sensed the end of his empire, of his cities, of himself.

Marco Polo, however, diverts the emperor with tales of cities that he has seen within the empire and Kublai Khan listens, searches for a pattern in Marco Polo's Cities and memory, Cities and desire, Cities and signs, Thin Cities, Trading Cities, Cities and eyes, Cities and names, Cities and the dead, Cities and the sky, Continuous Cities, Hidden Cities. The emperor soon determines that each of these fantastic places is really the same place.

Marco Polo agrees: "'Memory's images, once they are fixed in words, are erased,' Polo said." (So does Borges, repeatedly!) "'Perhaps I am afraid of losing Venice all at once, if I speak of it, or perhaps, speaking of other cities, I have already lost it, little by little.'" Again the theme of multiplicity and wholeness, "when every city," as Calvino wrote at the end of "The Watcher," "is the City."

Of all tasks, describing the contents of a book is the most difficult and in the case of a marvelous invention like *Invisible Cities*, perfectly irrelevant. I shall spare myself the labor; noting, however, that something wise has begun to enter the Calvino canon. The artist seems to have made a peace with the tension between man's idea of the many and of the one. He could now, if he wanted, stop.

Yet Calvino is obliged to go on writing just as his Marco Polo goes on traveling. (p. 20)

During the last quarter century Italo Calvino has advanced far beyond his American and English contemporaries. As they continue to look for the place where the spiders make their nests, Calvino has not only found that special place but learned how himself to make fantastic webs of prose to which all things adhere. In fact, reading Calvino, I had the unnerving sense that I was also writing what he had written; thus does his art prove his case as writer and reader become one, or One. (p. 21)

> *Gore Vidal, "Fabulous Calvino," in* The New York Review of Books (*reprinted with permission from* The New York Review of Books; *copyright © 1974 NYREV, Inc.*), *May 30, 1974, pp. 13-21.*

"Invisible Cities" is a . . . book by Italy's most original storyteller, Italo Calvino. But this time not a book of stories. Something more.

In "Cosmicomics" Calvino found a way to make fables out of evolution. The fables emerged like elemental anecdotes from opening hypotheses, and the biology, the physics, the astronomy, were much more knowledgeable than Calvino the entertainer let them seem. But in "t zero" (which in my opinion was one of the most important works of fiction published during the sixties), Calvino accepted his scientific subject matter less whimsically. He deepened and complicated his vision and voices. He moved into mathematics. He imagined what it might feel like when a one-celled self divides.

In his earlier historical romances that theme of growth had been seen through a kind of uncertain satirical fancy. A young baron takes to the trees in protest against society, and stays there to become an arboreal amphibian, a rebel mutant. A young viscount goes away to war only to be blown apart; his nasty half returns home like some subversion of himself but at long last is rejoined to his long lost good half.

Recently, in "Smog" and in two of the "t zero" stories, Calvino has turned the precise play of his mind upon separations and isolations in urban life. And now, in "Invisible Cities," he has transmuted his themes into something new.

The wonderful phenomena of "Invisible Cities" are seen as through some unfolding nuclear kaleidoscope. Past and future possibility grow out of the prison of an "unlivable present, where all forms of human society have reached an extreme of their cycle and there is no imagining what new forms they may assume."

These words . . . are spoken by an imaginary Kublai Khan, old and pessimistic, for one of the book's two interleaved narratives is his curious, elegiac conversation with his employe, the Venetian traveler Marco Polo. The second narrative—which fills the book's main spaces and makes it not so much a parody of the 13th-century "Travels" as an alternative meditation—is what Marco brings the Khan: an account of fifty-odd cities Marco has visited. . . .

Calvino's twin narratives lean toward and away from each other. The cities, for all their distilled form, represent Mass. The intermittent conversation between the Khan and Marco Polo is Form; it is the will to simplify; it is also a dialogue between the imperial will to impose and possess and the power to rest in the contemplation of multiplicity. (p. 35)

[Though] each city has its special quality, Calvino's gazetteer is elusive, for it embraces perverse paradoxes and sequences within sequences. We are warned not to confuse cities with the words used to describe them; yet we are told that falsehood is not in words but in things. Cities of Signs touch Cities of Memory. The voluptuous Trading City Chloe, where strangers (like figures out of Robbe-Grillet's "La Maison des Rendezvous") consummate strange intimacies in silence, may remind us of that Hidden City of sadness, Raissa, "where runs an invisible thread that binds one living being to another . . . unravels . . . draws new patterns so that at every second the unhappy city contains a happy city unaware of its own existence."

Calvino's elusiveness comes also from the honesty with which he develops his series. "Invisible Cities" is an elegy, autumnal and melancholy. Cities do move more and more toward failure. . . . But the reader finds something more interesting here than decline and fall. Even the cities that exhibit delusion and degeneration remain the possibilities from which, as Marco tells the Khan, any crystal-perfect

community whose molecular form the Khan dreams of must in part be calculated. (pp. 35-6)

I remember those closing stories of "t zero" in which the mind makes new space within patterns of imprisonment, and does so in speculations that accept analysis and technology not simply as the enemy but as models and targets of intense and vital attention. For I believe it is some such space that Calvino has created for his archetypal communities.

If they are forms, they are also like signals condensing in themselves power that awaits its translation into form. And Calvino's book is like no other I know. (p. 36)

> *Joseph McElroy, in* The New York Times Book Review *(© 1974 by The New York Times Company; reprinted by permission), November 17, 1974.*

When we dream of a house, we are dreaming about ourselves. And perhaps, when we dream of cities, it is always Venice we see: magical, unbelievable, its invisible foundations buried in the water, and the painted skies inside the buildings more real than the sky over the lagoon. As with a dream, the fragments are huddled and disconnected, and there is no sense of time or space between them, although at the end of the day, feet are exhausted and eyes are sore. The different components cannot be described in detail. The whole is a great deal more than the sum of the parts. . . .

Invisible Cities is an extraordinary collection, a Baedeker of the imagination. The cities correspond to psychological states and historical states, possibilities and transformations, like the million interchanges in the brain in response to the message from the eye. (p. 253)

> *Emma Tennant, in* The Listener *(© British Broadcasting Corp. 1975; reprinted by permission of Emma Tennant), February 20, 1975.*

Invisible Cities is the poetical notebook of Marco Polo. You might think that there was nothing left to say about Marco Polo, and you would be right. There is a hole right through the middle of this novel, and it lies within the narrator himself who has his circumference everywhere and his centre nowhere. Polo is describing the cities of his travels to the great Khan, and his narrative is arranged as a series of short episodes, with titles like 'Cities and Memory' or 'Cities and Desire' which might mean everything or nothing. They mean nothing. Sr Calvino can employ his conceits as prettily as Borges, to whom he has more than a passing resemblance, but his narrative is written in a relentlessly present tense, with that singleness of mood and emphasis which is the sure sign of an over-developed and under-equipped imagination. There are also some odd anachronisms as "aluminum" (this is known as American *sic*), "radar" and "overpass" clatter through the narrative. But it is no doubt meant to be timeless.

The city of Zaira, for example, consists solely of "relationships between the measurements of its space and the events of its past"; you will recognise here a trace of a 'sixties cult which was known, if I remember rightly, as 'semiology', and *Invisible Cities* is concerned with the signs and the systems of signs which make up what sociologists call the 'modern city'. But academic generalities always have a gaggle of simple and boring moral judgements behind them, and this book is no exception: Sr Calvino tells us, for example, that we can only understand the past by travelling ever onward, that existence "in all of its moments is all of itself", and that you must give form to your desires in order to master them—a somewhat shaky ground on which to build his particular Tower of Babel. But *Invisible Cities* is not completely spurious. Sr Calvino has an unconventional imagination which concentrates upon clusters of objects, upon what is small, hard and visible, and in this way he can substantiate some of the more weightless hopes and anxieties which rarely find a local habitation, let alone a name. His imagination only becomes flaccid when it loses specificity, and retreats into sentimental surrealism. (pp. 214-15)

> *Peter Ackroyd, in* The Spectator *(© 1975 by* The Spectator; *reprinted by permission of* The Spectator), *February 22, 1975.*

Like Jorge Luis Borges and Gabriel García Márquez, Italo Calvino dreams perfect dreams for us; the fantasy of these three Latins ranges beyond the egoism that truncates and anguishingly turns inward the fables of Kafka and that limits the kaleidoscopic visions of Nabokov. Of the three, Calvino is the sunniest, the most variously and benignly curious about the human truth as it comes embedded in its animal, vegetable, historical, and cosmic contexts; all his investigations spiral in upon the central question of *How shall we live?* In "Invisible Cities" . . ., he has produced a consummate book, both crystalline and limpid, adamant and airy, intricate and ingenuous, playful yet "worked" with a monkish care upon materials of great imaginative density and resonance. The book, a sheaf of imaginary cities, combines the slightly brittle and programmatic science fiction of "Cosmicomics" and "t zero" with affectionate mood and elegiac landscapes of his earlier, more naturalistic stories. (p. 137)

Beneath Calvino's tireless shimmer of fancy, his concern over how men live together has carried into our minds. . . . Led to read on by the fascination of the details and the grave beauty of the prose, we find the civic ideal unfolding within us—the same ideal that underlay Calvino's most autobiographical short story, "The Watcher" (1963). . . .

The indirectional, transactional method of "Invisible Cities" is the opposite of that of "Cosmicomics," which announces its idea at the outset—suppose human personalities to be present amid the geological and galactic events modern science describes—and then, more or less amusingly, but a trifle mechanically, executes it. The idea of "Invisible Cities" is not announced; it gradually dawns. (p. 138)

> *John Updike, "Metropolises of the Mind," in* The New Yorker *(© 1975 by The New Yorker Magazine, Inc.), February 24, 1975, pp. 137-40.*

*   *   *

CARTER, Angela 1940-

Ms Carter is an English writer of fantastical short stories and novels. (See also *Contemporary Authors*, Vols. 53-56.)

Fireworks are Gothic tales, not stories, as [Angela Carter] explains in an Afterword. Written 'in a room too small to write a novel in', they are the result of her preoccupation with the imagery of the unconscious. Some of these tales refer to a primitive past, or rework myths. The real world—principally, here, her experience of Japan—is reshaped subjectively so that real cities, real situations, blossom strangely. Her phrasing is superb, and her imagery sometimes unforgettable: 'stagnant eyes' for example. She stalks through many of her own tales, a wanderer 'sad by nature' and attracted to anguish.

The tales are full of puppets, mirrors, forests, sequined eyes, shells, flowers and diffuse lust, like the Dadd pictures at the Tate. It is exciting and provocative; but it is familiar. There have been so many literary variations on the themes of reality, identity, sexual duality. It is the world of Freudian dream and futuristic fiction and pornography; of Edgar Allan Poe, Pirandello, J. G. Ballard and Borges. Familiarity comes perhaps from the fact that the collective unconscious is everyone's stock-pot. But Angela Carter is too aware of its contents. The essence of the Gothic tale—as epitomised by Poe—is its apparent possible innocence. So there may be incest, bestiality, cannibalism; but it is never quite spelled out. Some of her best and most electric encounters are earthed by a pedantic need to explain. Sometimes this is done with a disarming self-irony. 'Do not think I do not realise what I am doing', as she writes at the end of 'The Smile of Winter', proceeding to analyse how it was done. But more often it seems a lack of literary tact. Take a small example from 'Reflections':

> 'Kiss yourself' commanded the androgyne in a swooning voice. 'Kiss yourself in the mirror, the symbolic matrix of this and that, hither and thither, outside and inside.'

The mirror-kiss and its weird consequences had their own force. Talk of symbolic matrices belongs to American Ph.D. theses. We are grounded. Or are we to learn from the author a depth of irony that can make suspect the very symbols that obsess her? Angela Carter is a genius as a word-spinner. She deserves a room big enough to write the new novel in. (p. 229)

> *Victoria Glendinning, in* New Statesman *(© 1974 The Statesman & Nation Publishing Co. Ltd.), August 16, 1974.*

Angela Carter is a talented young English writer of fantasies who means to be taken very seriously. She serves notice to this effect by beginning her . . . novel, "A War of Dreams," with three incisive quotes, one in French, one by Ludwig Wittgenstein and one by that master of the surreal, Alfred Jarry. Her story takes the form of a journey, a device favored by fantasists from Homer and Swift to Carroll and Tolkien. (pp. 6-7)

Angela Carter is at her best with details. Scrupulously, she builds the foundations of her myth out of hundreds of small observations. We soon forget that the terrain she observes with such care is the interior of her own imagination, for the world she describes becomes as real as any naturalist's report. . . .

This is not to say that "The War of Dreams" is without problems. The juxtaposition of the science-fiction elements (the Ministry's computers, Dr. Hoffman's dream transmitters, the Determination Police) with the purer and more potent aspects of fable seems harsh and discordant. And

Angela Carter's ornate and intricately wrought language, although pleasingly mellifluous, often intrudes upon the narrative. At the outset she gives us a world where, thanks to the manipulations of Dr. Hoffman, illusion becomes reality; an old cathedral goes off in a burst of fireworks, an audience of opera goers is turned into peacocks, pigeons quote Hegel from the chimney tops, and in the face of all this abstraction, simile and metaphor become redundant. When the author tells us that "the plaster scrolls and garlands on the pompous exterior of the Town Hall were crumbling like dry sponge cake," we're no longer sure if this is merely description or if she intends us to think that a passer-by could eat the building for dessert.

A tendency toward wordiness, then, and a baroque texture, which at times becomes almost impenetrable, seem the main faults. The devious and complex nature of fantasy demands a simple style. Consider fairy tales and folk stories. A frog turning into a prince is cause enough for wonder without embellishing the event with rhetoric.

But, at her best Angela Carter has created a grotesque and sensual world that calls to mind the texture of Fellini's film "Satyricon" and the violent poetics of Kenneth Patchen's "The Journal of Albion Moonlight." It is a book which deserves to be read and not swept away under that convenient rug labled "speculative fiction." (p. 7)

> *William Hjortsberg, in* The New York Times Book Review *(© 1974 by The New York Times Company; reprinted by permission), September 8, 1974.*

Angela Carter maintains that 'the tale differs from the short story in that it makes a few pretences at the imitation of life. The tale does not log everyday experience, as the short story does . . .; it has relations with subliterary forms of pornography, ballad and dream.' She regards herself as a teller of tales rather than stories. In fact, she seems to me to be most successful when she does 'log everyday experience', but invests it with a dream-like quality. Perhaps the best short stories are half-story, half-tale. . . .

Angela Carter's 'nine profane pieces' in *Fireworks* are set either in Japan, where she has lived, or in dreamscapes, where she considers herself equally at home. Not having the sort of flesh that creeps easily, I remained immune to, although admiring of, most of her Gothic blood-and-thunderstorms; but 'Reflections', a horrifying tale in which the male narrator is forced at gunpoint to seek the mirror-world through the glass, and is raped by a girl whose eyes 'were the eyes that justice would have if she were not blind', came near to destroying my sleep.

On the other hand, the story-tales of Japan enthralled me. 'A Souvenir of Japan' is a delicately-told love story in which the English girl's Japanese lover has 'a passive, cruel sweetness I did not immediately understand, for it was that of the repressed masochism which, in my country, is usually confined to women'. 'The Smile of Winter' makes the lonely December coastline, where the wind comes straight from Alaska and the Japanese equivalent of Hell's Angels can be heard at night weaving their way through the dunes, far more eerie and disturbing than any Walpurgisnacht or Götterdämmerung pastiche. Angela Carter is a highly talented eccentric. I hope she will continue to 'provoke unease'. (p. 416)

> *John Mellors, in* The Listener *(© British Broadcasting Corp. 1974; reprinted by permission of John Mellors), September 26, 1974.*

Angela Carter . . . is our Lady Edgar Allan Poe (and she knows it). So virile is her prose [in *Fireworks*], we may also call her Our Bearded Lady. But she is more still. Like all genuine art, hers breaks through the boundaries of one department of art and extends to others. So she is also a female Nijinsky, possessed by a devil, perhaps by Mephistopheles himself. She is Aubrey Beardsley, but wondrously transformed: divested of two of his essential features, his black-and-white and his consumption, and invested with all the wicked colour and glitter of Gustave Moreau, invested with life. She has also the decadence, the hysteria and the preciosity of Huysmans and Maeterlinck, the doll-like romance of Hoffmann (which she also knows). We can go to the film world, too, for definition: she is also a female Polanski, especially the delightful Polanski of *The Dance of the Vampires*, though, unlike him, never roguish, yet very much a rogue. And like all geniuses, she walks the tightrope on one side of which yawns the chasm of madness, on the other the chasm of bathos. Again like all geniuses, she can topple over and down into both and the next minute be progressing, in full control again, along her tightrope, on tiptoe. In short, she is the anti-thesis of the bourgeois. . . .

[Ms Carter says] of the Gothic tradition in which she writes that it:

> grandly ignores the value systems of our institutions; it deals entirely with the profane. Its great themes are incest and cannibalism. Characters and events are exaggerated beyond reality, to become symbols, ideas, passions. Its style will tend to be ornate, unnatural—and thus operate against the perennial human desire to believe the world of fact. Its only humour is black humour. It retains a singular moral function—that of provoking unease.

A long quote, which I hope both author and publisher will excuse, my excuse being that no one could have said it better than Angela Carter herself. . . .

It is true that fireworks have a brilliance we find in this writing. But theirs is a dead brilliance, while the brilliance of this book is alive. Fireworks, too, can turn out to be damp squibs, so it is a risky term too. Some of Angela Carter's fireworks here come close to turning into damp squibs, but not sufficiently so to justify so precarious a title. Greatest objection of all: fireworks are essentially artificial, and although all art is artifice, all art is not artificial. This writing aspires to be art and nearly everywhere succeeds. . . . The book deserved far subtler labelling. . . .

Of the first three Carter titles [*Shadow Dance, The Magic Toyshop*, and *Several Perceptions*] I liked the first best. Not because the next two weren't better, but because it had an all but unbelievable quality: a *fresh* decadence. But her fourth book, *Heroes and Villains* (1969) was beyond me to enjoy. The post-World War Three world of professors and barbarians she describes in this novel was too obvious an invention, its hairy and bejewelled young savages too symbolic to be interesting. When the girl, Marianne, says to her even symbolically named lover, Jewel: 'You, you're nothing but the invention of my virgin nights' the reader feels too inclined to intrude and interpolate: 'Too true!' When she later throws at him: 'You're not a human being at all, you're a metaphysical proposition!', he feels too inclined to substitute for 'human being' the word 'novel'. And to quote, or rather paraphrase another Carter sentence: 'boredom and exhaustion conspires to erode the novel's complacent idea of itself.' This is not, however, to suggest that a novel should not be a 'metaphysical proposition' for this is precisely what the best novels are. It's just that we don't want them to look like one—we prefer the skeleton covered in flesh. . . .

In *Love* the grubby, stoned young characters in their filthy, lightless flatlet just did not seem to be able to carry the author's metaphysical intention, but after reading the last tale in . . . *Fireworks*, a tale called [''Elegy for a Freelance''], containing not fireworks but bombs and murder, I see that what was really wrong with *Love* was that it ought to have been a short story (or tale) not a novel of 124 pages. (p. 55)

[For] all the highly deliberate, deliberately ornamental embroidery of [her] laden prose, it is the intelligence at work beneath it all which raises almost everything [in *Fireworks*] to the level of art. For intelligence is another attribute of genuine art, and intelligence here is both active and unusual. . . .

There are pieces here, [''The Smile of Winter,'' ''Flesh and the Mirror''], a Woman-Friday piece, called [''Master''] (tribute to Daniel Defoe, 'father of the *bourgeois* novel'— for which, see the author's own farewell note) that don't seem quite to jell—or which didn't seem quite to jell in my mind. This cannot be said of the mirror-world, horror story, [''Reflections''] which begins as science fiction with some splendidly written pages. Here my objection, and I'm sorry to have them, is that the horror becomes a bit bathetic. I wanted to laugh at [many of the metaphors]. . . .

It is true, all the same, it was the sheer, assiduous excellence of this prose that sent me searching for dissonances, waiting to see where the tight-rope walker toppled. . . . Carter can be wickedly satirical and funny too. Not all her humor is black. (p. 56)

James Brockway, "Gothic Pyrotechnics," in Books and Bookmen (© *copyright James Brockway 1975), February, 1975, pp. 55-6.*

*   *   *

CHARYN, Jerome   1937-

Charyn is an American novelist and short story writer. While his early realistic works limn Yiddish New York, his recent writing is increasingly impressionistic and concerned with other aspects of contemporary life. (See also *Contemporary Authors*, Vols. 5-8, rev. ed.)

Rhythm is one important key to the enormous effectiveness of [*The Man Who Grew Younger and Other Stories*,] seven glimpses into the lost world of the Bronx in the early 1940s, rhythm lashed on by fury and graced by all manner of strange delights. Jerome Charyn's New York, which is conveniently sketched in a two-page map at the beginning of the book, is filled with hardened Dead End Kids, bewildered parents, hazardous streets and parks, and a brooding

sense of doom. A good place to grow up absurd, perverse, traumatized, and somehow resilient enough to withstand the blows of adult life—if only one can survive. There is a freshness and yet a face-slapping impact in these stories that one won't find in most slick or academic magazines, and it is also this quality of differentness that makes Charyn's collection unusually forceful and artistically successful. . . .

Charyn's New York is [a] land of horror, brutality, and lurking evil. There is a strange forlorn quality to his stories, which seem like realistic representations of the lower depths of a cruel, teeming metropolis. Redemption comes, if at all, only through a fierce determination to survive, a rhythm of resistance, and a passion to communicate one's fears and wants. Perhaps someone who is not an enemy may be listening after all, and may even be able to do some good.

Samuel I. Bellman, "A Good Place to Grow Up Absurd," in Saturday Review (*copyright* © *1967 by Saturday Review, Inc.; reprinted with permission), January 14, 1967, p. 85.*

Private visions do not always make public benefits. Esthetic distance is all right in its way, but not when it promotes stumbling blocks and credibility gaps. A broad canvas in a novel prevents boredom and yet invites divided attention. All of which points may be quite irrelevant today with the increasing importance of that amazing new literary art form, the subliminal novel.

Jerome Charyn's *Going to Jerusalem*, a wild, zany mélange of sketches, revelations, and epistles, is just such a work. Too disorganized for the narrow, conventional taste, this novel calls up moods and responses below the threshold of consciousness. . . . [Symbols] are not forced on the reader, and the parts of the story have more than surface meaning. We are not dealing here with Hemingway's story-iceberg, or the myths and icons of Freud, Jung, and Fiedler. There is not even a convenient Jamesian ''figure in the carpet.'' Charyn, like the central characters in his book, travels a tortuous road to self-discovery in which purpose, direction, markers, and right-of-way fade into a kaleidoscopic blur. (pp. 34-5)

At the end the reader is left hanging in mid-air.

The high point of the novel is Ivan's encounter with three Negro minstrels, who put on a series of allegorical impromptu acts to express their social protest. Here Charyn is at his best and funniest, and we get the idea that there must be rhyme and reason behind the going-to-Jerusalem traveling game. Perhaps the cruel father (the Admiral), the feckless epileptic Ivan, and the six-year-old chess genius really represent Dostoevskian ideas about good and evil, struggle and strife, that can no longer be meaningfully expressed in conventional terms. This would explain the lack of resolution in the plot and the steady hinting of something big about to happen that never quite does. (p. 35)

Samuel I. Bellman, "Traveling Game," in Saturday Review (*copyright* © *1967 by Saturday Review, Inc.; reprinted with permission), September 9, 1967, pp 34-5.*

The career of Jerome Charyn . . . illuminates the plight, and the opportunities too, of a very gifted young novelist over the decade 1963-73: a writer much aware of contemporary life, fascinated by "real reality", but aware too of what is "going on" in fiction. (Joyce Carol Oates would have provided an example almost as striking). At the beginning of the decade it would have seemed natural, in writing about Charyn's first books, to refer to Philip Roth and Malamud as well as Dickens. By its end one feels affinities with Hawkes (*Eisenhower, My Eisenhower*) and Nabokov (*The Tar Baby*); with, that is, central anti-realist impulsions. Over the decade we see an intensifying effort to make it new, to keep up with changing trends, yet withal a determination to preserve some of the old fictional pleasures, most notably the swarming talkative *vis comica* of subcultures. Charyn is aware too of that other problem that has plagued writers for two generations: how to write about a society and time that dwarf one's wildest imaginings. Can fiction hope to compete, in absurdity and violence, with the newspaper or with the "new journalism"? Finally, not least, Charyn has had to face the economic problem: where has the public gone? How can one write uncompromisingly good fiction, entertaining yet uncommercial, and still win a few readers? (p. 36)

Charyn's talent at the outset was traditional in a fine uninhibited way: Dickensian, but within a New York Jewish world. The impulse to create life and to tell stories was exceptionally strong: "Your loneliness goes down in proportion to the number of characters on a page." "The Man Who Grew Younger" and "Sing, Shaindele, Sing" belong with Malamud's "The Magic Barrel" and Gold's "The Heart of the Artichoke": comic, poignant, rich in personality, wise—great stories all four. Charyn's characters experience various forms of generation gap, and the sadness of a vanishing culture. The Dickensian bent appears in the richly loquacious, irrepressible caricatures of *Once upon a Droshky*, and the climactic mock-heroic scene: a cafeteria become a battlefield. We have a rhetorical embellishment of real reality rather than a magic reinvention of the world. Dickensian too is the tendency to give a child's animistic view of things and to reverse child/parent roles . . . though Charyn's most sympathetic treatment is of adolescents and their attachments to older men: tender father-son relationships, usually disguised. There is not much adult heterosexual love in Charyn's work, nor much that is unequivocally homosexual, and depth psychology has little place. Sexual experience involves a good deal of scatological fun and much language play. Sexuality is *rhetorical*, in the way psychology is for Hawkes and Kosinski. Charyn had discovered, with many others, that this overwrought subject was by the late 1960's chiefly suitable for parody or farce.

Two other traditional drives were evident from the start. The first was the impulse, which few mediocre writers exhibit, to create sympathy for the foolish and the depraved: to discover, in Mauriac's fine phrase, "the secret sources of sanctity in those who seem to have failed." The second was simply the desire to look up, learn, assimilate, relish a great deal of detail, not for detail's sake, but out of an openness to the American scene. Charyn's novels encompass a good deal of knowledge. All this is but to describe a novelistic makeup not unlike that of Saul Bellow a generation earlier, though without Bellow's effort, in the quiet early novels, to reflect a drab quotidian reality. Each talent or thrust is present in Charyn in a more intense, more eccentric form. (Which leads one to ask: Where would Bellow

have gone, how far would he have come, had he first published in 1963 or been born in 1937?)

Charyn's congenial material is evident: the swarming streets, the Yiddish actors and writers, the cafes, the talk: essentially New York Jewish with a background of eastern Europe. But Charyn tried, still in his twenties, to go beyond this given subject-matter. . . . Charyn moved, not too successfully, to upstate New York and a reform school, in *On a Darkening Green*. His narrator is not Jewish, but at one point pretends to be, and a rabbi is surely the novel's most moving personage. . . . There are good moments of comic disorder. But technically the novel is of little interest: conventional in structure, chronologically undisrupted, with a relatively dull narrative consciousness. The method tended to limit rather than encourage Charyn's natural impulse to the fabulous; once again, the world is embellished not reinvented. There is no sign, as yet, that Charyn was fully aware of anti-realist possibilities.

A very uneven book, *Going to Jerusalem*, . . . [reveals] the first definite influence of both Hawkes and Nabokov on [Charyn's] fiction. There is a significant shift, within the novel, from the playful, mildly realistic story of a prodigy's chess tour (with increasing sympathy for his antagonist the aged ex-Nazi Kortz) to more and more surrealist disorder. . . . Rhetorically, there is an interesting pull between the frenetic effort to be more and more lively, more and more *present*, and Charyn's evident talent for impressionist, meditative narration. At the heart of any young writer's situation, of course, is the struggle to discover what will be for him the most congenial form and narrative distance.

Going to Jerusalem is a novel full of fictional ideas, rich in Dickensian geniality and comic life, admirable in its effort to achieve a freer form; finally boring.

American Scrapbook is Charyn's one truly unsuccessful book. . . . [In this novel,] Charyn does use what is, for him, a new technique: multiple voices narrating through interior monologues and recording present action as it unrolls, an exceedingly difficult mode, as Faulkner was to find in *As I Lay Dying*. Charyn had not discerned (and would not entirely in his next book) how uncongenial for him this entrapment in the fictional present could be. (pp. 37-9)

Eisenhower, My Eisenhower is Charyn's first genuinely antirealist, mythologizing extravaganza and first major effort to reflect the absurd aspects of contemporary urban violence: the riots of 1968, I assume, though the novel is laid at the time of an Eisenhower election. (pp. 39-40)

The Tar Baby [is] a novel on the level of all but Nabokov's best . . . and one that must, like Nabokov's, be read intensively rather than casually, with an alert eye for distortion and nuance. (p. 41)

The Tar Baby . . . is a highly involuted novel [which] combines *Pnin*'s comic pathos of the *émigré* and miscast intellectual and *Pale Fire*'s shuttlings between a problematic reality and slippery conjecture; the story unfolds, and a world incrementally builds, but only with the reader's most active collaboration. The resemblances to Nabokov are in fact superficial, though influence is unmistakable: Charyn's voice, even at its most suave, is his own: a compressed, ruggedly accented style, inventive yet precise even in moments of abysmal vulgarity. The exaggerations and comic excursions are those Dickens might have managed had he pushed his way further west and been born one hundred and twenty five years later. Dickens' name suggests itself again because of the need, even in this fairly intellectual book, to create vivid minor characters. The fierce pleasures and unregenerate humanity of *Martin Chuzzlewit* and the American journey! (p. 42)

The Tar Baby is more than any of the earlier books a rhetorical work, manipulating the reader as it shifts tones and modes, and juxtaposes reality with bungling efforts to interpret it. The novel begins as playful satire of academia: the elaborately parodied magazine with its notes on contributors and their absurd careers; the small college in a raw western town, but with its erotic "personal" advertisements and other items of a counter-culture, scarcely underground. In these advertisements, as in Joyce Carol Oates's "Notes on Contributors", real people with real feelings spring to life in a very few lines. (p. 43)

The essential novelistic game is between the parodic and farcical literary stance, the playfulness and brutality of language, *and* a fierce western reality surrendering at last a tragic story. Form and style function, that is, in ironic juxtaposition to the material. Most real for anyone who has visited such colleges, or who has followed the darkest *couloirs* of MLA meetings, is the pathos of the intellectual lost in a raw environment and in a college riddled with jealousies.... Everything, everyone would seem at first glance mere comic stereotype. But the sufferings glimpsed through these screens are real.

The achievement is rhetorical not thematic: an elaborate juggling of a dozen voices, with each new voice leading us to distrust and correct the earlier ones.... The novel's genial tone modulates toward a final monologue of extreme callousness, a vision of total depravity. The impressionist game of shifting sympathy and judgment is beautifully controlled. (pp. 44-5)

The Tar Baby [is] derivative in spots and perhaps in overall inspiration, but by no means the mere pastiche of Nabokov that a *New York Times* reviewer claimed: a book doubtless easy to ridicule through plot summary . . ., its language brilliantly inventive yet sometimes breaking under strain . . . withal a small masterpiece.... There is not one rendered scene of present action on which we can absolutely depend; the reader must turn from mirror to mirror, attendant to shifting profiles, measuring distortion. Yet the whole is rich, comic, sardonic, meaningful. We are entertained; we believe; we care. *The Tar Baby* does contain that fragment of truth for which we have forgotten to ask. (pp. 47-8)

As with Faulkner, so with Charyn one discovers certain constants in book after book: the irrepressible comic impulse and the delight in playful inventive language. All in all *The Tar Baby*, complex as it is, reveals unsubdued the basic energies and impulses with which Charyn began, not least the impulse to tell stories and create life, as much life per page as possible. (p. 49)

Albert J. Guerard, in TriQuarterly 30 *(© 1974 by Northwestern University Press), Spring, 1974.*

About a New York police inspector's attempt to infiltrate a white slavery operation, "Blue Eyes" would have been only a modest study of police deals and dealings—a novel of public information—had not Charyn maintained an in-

tensity of language that characterizes our best novels of private creation. Energized throughout with voice and gesture—the language of character—"Blue Eyes" is a fine work of imagined fact. . . .

Because Charyn attends to . . . details of communication, both as subject and medium, his novel has a page to page fascination and occupies that now underpopulated land between realism and artifice.

Charyn sometimes allows detail to build eccentricity and colloquial vigor to become street jargon, but the results are more entertaining than bothersome. . . . Patrolmen in their "bags" (uniforms), stoolie Arnold "dirtying a car" (planting evidence), "gloms" (dumb cops) chasing "meat-eaters" (whiteslavers)—these do more than prove the author's been on the street. Combined with a conventionally literate diction, good pacing, and comedy of the everyday, phrases like these help return substance to a language puréed by its official users. (p. 6)

Thomas LeClair, in The New York Times Book Review *(© 1975 by the New York Times Company; reprinted by permission), February 9, 1975.*

*   *   *

CLARK, Eleanor   1913-

Miss Clark, an American, writes novels, short stories, and nonfiction. She is married to Robert Penn Warren. (See also *Contemporary Authors*, Vols. 9-12, rev. ed.)

Although [the stories in *Dr. Heart: A Novella and Other Stories*] range over a period of 37 years, they are related thematically and stylistically. Eleanor Clark is an obsessive writer, despite her cool awareness of human frailties, and she returns again and again to "the scene of the crime."

She is interested in the "heartlessness" we all possess. She does not locate the sources for such lack of responsibility—to use one of her favorite words—but she sees it brutally dividing generations, cultures and lovers. . . .

Her natural descriptions—she is, after all, one of our best travel writers—demonstrate her abiding concerns. She gives us so many fighting insects, goats and flies that we accept them as symbols of our inner violence. (pp. 30)

I do not want to reveal the ending of ["The Fish"], or to belabor its juxtapositions of age, consciousness and manners, but I think that it underlines Clark's preoccupations. It is superficially "routine"—what could be more routine than a shopping expedition in the supermarket?—but it is also terrifying as it suggests, along with all the other stories, that life is full of unpredictable, often heartless, violence. It ends appropriately with tears; sympathy triumphs briefly. Knowing the conclusion of other stories, we sense that such reconciliation will soon disappear and the cycle begin again. (pp. 30-1)

Irving Malin, in The New Republic *(reprinted by permission of* The New Republic; *© 1975 by The New Republic, Inc.), January 4 & 11, 1975.*

Eleanor Clark is at her most original when she is being imitative. This is because she is imitative out of love or admiration: the love and admiration originate with her and so, finally, does the result. Thus, in her excellent new novella, "Dr. Heart," her knowledgeable involvement with Stendhal naturally turns her main character into a profoundly Stendhalian hero; in "Rome and a Villa," being reissued . . . after almost 25 years, her immersion in the figurative waters of Rome naturally led her to write in a style effectively approximating the baroque atmosphere of that city of fountains, replete with elaborate ingenious imagery and richly-laden sentences laced with dashes, studded with colons and semi-colons. . . .

Miss Clark's cultivation . . . is an integral element in her art, an art which invites if it does not require a reciprocal cultivation on the part of her reader. . . .

Her sense of past-present as a constantly deliquescing oneness is an obsessive theme with Miss Clark (as water is an obsessive source of imagery), one which makes Rome an eminently suitable subject for her. . . .

Miss Clark on Rome is ultimately autobiographical, as are Izaak Walton on fishing, C. M. Doughty on Arabia, Henry Adams on Mont-St.-Michel and Chartres, Stendhal on Love. But cryptically so. It has to do with the relationship between cruelty and charity, a relationship running through history, creating awesome things while people die. Like the Romans of all these different ages which she describes, she is not outraged by cruelty, she does not find charity where it's been carefully put, and beauty is really important to her. It is an attitude reminiscent of the English poet Crashaw, who fled Puritanism and Right Things to Catholic Baroque Rome. (p. 7)

> Peter Sourian, in The New York Times Book Review (© 1975 by The New York Times Company; reprinted by permission), January 12, 1975.

"It is all one voice, mine—and I don't disown it," Eleanor Clark says about *Dr. Heart,* a collection of her short fiction of four decades. But that's a good question. Is it one voice? Is it any? A writer's voice is more than style, it is subject; the thing that must be said. It is necessity.

These are vague terms. That's a good reason to talk about them. And what better occasion? For along with Clark's story collection comes *Rome and a Villa*, her nonfiction classic, in a new edition in time for Holy Year. *Rome and a Villa* is a travel book in the most glorious sense: your mind travels. So why does the fiction seem so dreary?

Drearier still, the earliest stories are best. They are like forks in the road. . . .

An odd thing about the rest—they are unpleasant. I mean *unpleasant*. Like an exterminator who goes around strangling birds and eventually people; an academic housewife caught robbing another's pocketbook at a party; a bunch of hippies practicing human sacrifice on tombstones. Etc. What is disturbing is that this unpleasantness does not seem to be Eleanor Clark's "voice" either—one could accept that—so much as some notion of what short stories are supposed to be about. In other words, they are "ideas" for short stories; they jab you like hatpins. And when all is said and done, they are still "ideas." It is the difference between pretext and necessity.

You don't need a pretext to write about Rome. Its statues and monuments, its relics of Renaissance and antiquity, its

abundance of impressions, provide their own necessity. There they all are, waiting to be described. And here it all is: *Rome and a Villa* is an idea and an actuality. Clark manages to convey a Rome that is almost catastrophically alive, that threatens to overwhelm the visitor with past and present, and to select, make it her own. There is no question: this is her subject.

> Bette Howland, "Eternal City, Ephemeral Fiction," in Book World—The Washington Post (© The Washington Post), January 26, 1975, p. 3.

Change in Italy and the reader has in no way dulled the flamboyant brilliance of [Miss Clark's] Roman archeology of the mind and eye, and very few works of contemporary fiction can safely withstand comparison with [*Rome and a Villa* (1952),] her remarkable exploration of the Eternal City and the Emperor Hadrian's villa in Tivoli. Neither, unhappily, can her own fiction in *Dr. Heart*.

What exhilarating and youthful audacity there was in the very conception of *Rome and a Villa*! To attempt nothing less than a wholly personal yet flawlessly knowledgeable account of Rome—as a 20th-century metropolis, as a crowded landscape of history, as the gold-and-marble pageant of pagan mortality and Christian triumph. Rarely has the love affair between a modern sensibility and an ancient locale—consummated in every glance, with every step—been more exuberantly recorded. The breadth of Miss Clark's vision is extraordinary—from the grandiloquent splendor of St. Peter's to the humble room where Keats died on the Piazza di Spagna; from Hadrian's calculated hyperbole of stone and yearning in Tivoli to the purring colony of cats in the Piazza Vittorio; from a recapturing of Julius Caesar in the Forum to a recollection of Pope Paul VI on television.

In bringing the volume up to date, Miss Clark has wisely left the main body of her original text unchanged; it was never meant to be a guidebook, it was a response to the *idea* of a city that, through the centuries, has survived everything. (p. 16)

Sadly, neither the novella nor any of the stories in *Dr. Heart* begins to approach this grandeur of mind, reach and spirit. The shorter pieces are either flatly predictable or so insubstantial that they dissolve as you read them like sugar in tea. . . .

The most ambitious and most recent narrative of this collection is the novella, *Dr. Heart,* in which Miss Clark attempts the supremely difficult and self-defeating task of writing a contemporary tale that is also a cunning literary game about Stendhal. Unfortunately, in the course of constructing her elaborate network of allusions and borrowings, whose effect depends on a familiarity with *The Red and the Black* as great as the author's, she somehow loses her fictional point. Even more curious is the idea of writing a Stendhalian story that is totally unconcerned with politics. Stendhal was obsessed with the political and social aftermath of the French Revolution and Napoleon. His despairing contempt for the Bourbon monarchy restored in 1815 is inseparable from his complex, ironic iconography of corruption, romance, heroism, farce, and the precarious survival of the pure in heart.

In place of Stendhal's fiery passion for political intrigue,

Miss Clark lamely substitutes present-day academic and literary infighting. . . .

Moreover, Miss Clark's mockery of the French new novelists is too broad to be witty and too parochial to succeed as farce.

Ultimately, though, the novella fails because it goes perversely against the grain of Miss Clark's talent, which is above all, and gloriously, visual. The power of *Rome and a Villa* derives from the fine art of seeing, of sight as the root of insight. In disappointing contrast, *Dr. Heart* comes to life only in the rare moments when she is describing the mountains that ring Grenoble; it is thus not a sensed experience, but merely a static contrivance. (p. 17)

> *Pearl K. Bell, "The Art of Seeing," in* The New Leader (© *1975 by the American Labor Conference on International Affairs, Inc.), February 17, 1975, pp. 16-17.*

Clark is something of an ironist; that tone governs most of the stories [in *Dr. Heart: A Novella and Other Stories*]. She can be a skillful ironist, but too often her irony seems easy, even lazy-minded. And, incredibly for a writer whose eye seeks the unexpected detail, Clark's characters become stereotypes.

Consider Miss Hinckley, the focal character of the book's first story, "Call Me Comrade." . . . Miss Hinckley is a fussy, spinsterly little woman . . . who hardly knows why she's demonstrating and whose life is so lonely and reduced that she seizes with pathetic desperation on the momentary camaraderie and sense of importance to be had from the demonstrators' adventure.

If what I've just described sounds condescending, it is. Miss Hinckley, who might have been a poignant, even haunting, character, is made out finally to be little more than a pathetic fool. She's a stereotype—the lonely, skimpy-haired spinster—and yet the detail with which Clark observes her . . . is so real that you keep waiting for the stereotype to break, keep waiting for the irony that holds Miss Hinckley at a comfortable distance to give way, so that her pain reaches you. Desperate loneliness is more than pathetic; it's awful, in every sense of the word. It's also universal. When a writer doesn't understand this sort of thing, she seems stupid, or, in the case of a writer of Clark's intelligence, smug.

This tendency to adopt a superior stance toward her characters afflicts Clark, and it badly mars *Dr. Heart*, the newest work in the collection and the most important. The protagonist is Tom Bestwick, a 27-year-old American graduate student, recently divorced and at loose ends. . . . [This] is essentially a novel of the mind (or, as the title implies, the heart), the story of Tom's discovery of some sense of self he can live with.

For a story of this kind to be compelling, the protagonist must be credible, so that one can come to care about him. But Clark is so damn busy mocking Tom that she makes mishmash of him. Half the time, he sounds and acts like a television teen-ager, a dopey refugee from "Leave It to Beaver." The other half, he thinks subtle thoughts, is sensitive to the point of temporary madness, and is imaginatively passionate about Stendhal. The result of this peculiar mixture is that Tom never takes on a fictional life of his own;

he remains a puppet in the author's hands, and a disjointed one at that. (pp. 83-4)

Reading *Dr. Heart*, I kept looking for something to latch onto besides the occasional well-turned phrase or provocative perception that cropped up along the way. I wanted to be drawn into the world of the novel. . . . But Clark's facile irony made that impossible. It made Tom seem trivial, finally, and so his world seemed trivial, and I kept wondering why Clark was wasting her time and mine shooting fish in a barrel when she was obviously capable of doing something altogether more difficult, dangerous, and genuinely engaging. (p. 85)

> *Karen Durbin, "Cheated by the Dozen," in* Ms. (© *1975 Ms. Magazine Corp.), June, 1975, pp. 46, 83-5.*

*   *   *

COLWIN, Laurie   1945?-

Ms Colwin is an American short story writer and novelist.

[Trying] to say why [Laurie Colwin's stories are so] good and so funny (well, they're not all funny; there are a few sad ones) is like trying to analyze the excellence of a good cartoon. Maybe I should say "comic drawing"—I mean the sort of cartoon you see in the New Yorker or Punch, where the way a chair sags or a dog's ears perk up is a delight in itself. Her comedy is the comedy of manners, and it succeeds by its style and observation. The stories aren't anecdotal—I can't give you plot summaries that you can retell at your next party. But when you've read her stories, your next party may seem to you as if Laurie Colwin had written it.

> *Judith Rascoe, "Party Tales," in* Rolling Stone (© *1974 by Straight Arrow Publishers, Inc.; all rights reserved; reprinted by permission), March 28, 1974, p. 56.*

The surprising thing about Laurie Colwin's first book of short stories, *Passion and Affect*, is that it's so good. The stories have a quality of grace and understatement which takes one by surprise. Partly this is the result of Colwin's style, which is often so bare and unadorned as to seem pinched. Yet the style is eminently suited for her subjects. And it can perform wonders.

Passion and Affect is a collection of fourteen stories about people who learn how quietly irrational human beings are. In a sense it is a series of small ballets performed by people who can't, won't, or simply don't communicate. Couples move in slow, graceful circles of bewilderment around one another, and it is men like Harry Markham, in "The Big Plum"—men who try to make a facile equation out of life— who lose their balance. Harry, the world's only supermarket manager who also is working on a dissertation in art history, becomes infatuated with one of his cashiers. Why would a woman who looks like Vermeer's *The Girl with the Pearl Earrings* work at a check-out counter? Harry invents pasts for Binnie that would do credit to Beau Geste, and pursues her with the intention, essentially, of solving her. But there is no "solution" to Binnie. She provides Harry with two different versions of her life and lets him choose for himself. "'What am I supposed to believe, then?'" he asks her. "'Whichever suits you,'" she replies. "'It's your dissertation. Have both. It has nothing to do with me, anyway.' She got up from her chair, did an abrupt dancer's turn, and opened the door for him. 'I'm very serious,' she said."

It is always the dancers who win in Colwin's stories, because they understand movement, and movement is the essence of life. They understand how little they can ever hope to understand about something as shifting and private as a human being—including themselves. Sometimes a character has to make a full circuit around himself before he can begin to grasp even the shape of his life. Max Waltzer—the name ought to be significant—for instance. Max loves his job, loves his house, loves his children, and madly loves his wife. Yet, when he spots water rats in the inlet where his children swim during the summer, he becomes obsessed with the idea of exterminating them. . . . For Max is so happy that he has to invent enemies to protect his family from. And his sudden realization of this, handled skillfully yet almost in whispers, tells the reader what all good art ought to tell him: that "the end of all our exploring/Will be to arrive where we started/And know the place for the first time." (pp. 108-09)

Colwin's great strength is not that she has a theme, but that she has a particularly fertile way of seeing her characters. She obviously believes that life is exciting when people are emotionally alive, and that the quirks and inconsistencies are what the story is all about. She has, in her own words, "the sort of worldliness that spans humor and outrage;" but she has it precisely because she has both humor and outrage and the perception that the very worldliness which incorporates both may, in fact, be either ironic or tragic depending on perspective. In other words: nothing stays; everything is changing into the next thing, and then into the next, before coming back to itself. Colwin's world is alive.

One is hesitant to pin these stories down with a superlative. They are so unassuming that it seems an act of bad taste to trumpet them when they do not trumpet themselves. But *Passion and Affect* is a delightful book. (pp. 109-10)

> *John Agar, in* Carolina Quarterly *(© copyright 1974 Carolina Quarterly), Spring, 1974.*

Laurie Colwin's people in *Passion and Affect* . . . are tired and whipped—but not by poverty or age. . . . Their fatigue is a function of their emotional style; they love intensely, they speak their deepest feelings, and unrequited love can addle their hearts for months. The title of the book's opening story, "Animal Behavior," foreshadows Colwin's treatment of sexual stress. She darts into remote, highly sensitized corners of the human psyche without explaining what goes on there. Like the other animals, man can enjoy sexual love, but he cannot understand or control it; nobody learns from loving. It strengthens and comforts some; others are wiped out by its sharp, aching joys. . . . The main currents of *Passion and Affect* are psychological, not satiric. Personality neither flattens nor falls into patterns. Rather, the reverse applies: the more Colwin says about her groping, decent people, the more she prods our imaginations.

Another imaginative enticement comes from her bright, figured prose. As in Muriel Spark, her short, terse paragraphs transmit sharp-cut images and bright little rips of meaning. . . .

Though saying nothing new about human sexuality, Laurie

Colwin writes with unobtrusive skill, insight, and touching moral passion. (pp. 28-9)

> *Peter Wolfe, in* The New Republic *(reprinted by permission of* The New Republic; *© 1974 by The New Republic, Inc.), April 27, 1974.*

Laurie Colwin's . . . very good in stories of contemporary manners: "The Water Rats," with its upper-middle class family and the husband's almost obsessive need to share, to love, is reminiscent of John Cheever and the best of the Roger Angell-Edward Newhouse-Robert M. Coates *New Yorker* school. "The Smartest Woman in America" is an effective characterization of a female intellectual who would make Norman Mailer tremble; "Mr. Parker" is an expert small piece about small-town provincialism related in terms of a child, her music teacher, and her bigoted mother; "Wet" is a marvelously economical husband-wife story in which swimming becomes a kind of infidelity; and at least half a dozen others [in her collection *Passion and Effect*] are very good indeed. Two of her longer pieces, though, "The Girl with the Harlequin Glasses" and the title story, about a pair of New York intellectuals and their personal problems and their magazine *Runnymede*, are repetitious, long-winded, and soporific. But in the final analysis Laurie Colwin looks and writes like a first-rate writer. (pp. 728-29)

> *William Peden, in* Sewanee Review *(reprinted by permission of the editor; © 1974 by The University of the South), Fall, 1974.*

* * *

CORTÁZAR, Julio   1914-

Cortázar is an Argentine novelist, short story writer, and translator, now living in Paris, whose elaborately experimental fantasies have been compared with work by Borges, Kafka, and Joyce. (See also *Contemporary Authors*, Vols. 21-22.)

Many of the short stories of the Argentine writer Julio Cortázar portray individuals who are afflicted by delusions, hallucinations, and nightmares. These vivid and powerful fantasies are often expressive of the characters' deep alienation, guilt, or fear. In Cortázar's short fiction, the interplay between fantasy and reality is of two different patterns. At times the delusions of the characters act as a positive force, offering consolation and even ironic fulfillment for persons who in reality lead lonely and frustrated lives. Some of the characters nurture their private fantasy worlds through which they reduce their anguish and guilt. In other stories fantasy is afflictive and destructive, serving to intensify the initial anxiety of the character and finally divorcing him entirely from reality, undermining his sanity. (p. 75)

In Cortázar's world, the real or the concrete often turns out to be only a facade that covers the bizarre and the mystifying. Strange forces often well up at night, when the conscious defenses of the characters are relaxed or weakened, either from an extraterrestrial sphere or, more likely, from the subconsciousness of the individuals themselves. For . . . many of Cortázar's characters, the unreal or the absurd asserts itself as the most significant reality. . . . (pp. 78-9)

Fantasy in Cortázar, if positive and ironically fulfilling, can never be sustained and, if negative and destructive, cannot be dispelled. Characters, like the frustrated mother in "The Condemned Door," who retreat into fantasy realms as a means of escape from the pressures or afflictions of reality are caricatured, humiliated, or otherwise defeated. Their illusory worlds collapse and adverse reality triumphs. Delusions of the characters are more often explicitly destructive, as in "Afternoon Nap," when they always triumph over reality. Fantasy in Cortázar is always deceptive or destructive for the characters, because its basis lies in a negative reality of social alienation and emotional turbulence. (p. 90)

> *Lanin A. Gyurko, "Guilt and Delusion: Two Stories by Cortázar," in* Critique: Studies in Modern Fiction *(copyright © by* Critique, *1973), Vol. XIV, No. 3, 1973, pp. 75-90.*

While the literary *cognoscenti* might be disappointed in [*All Fires the Fire,* a] collection of eight stories, the pleasure reader will find them less abstract and more accessible than some other Cortázar fiction. Even though Cortázar fools around with doubles now and then and often indulges in multiple points of view within the same sentence, each story is immensely readable. Dramatically, however, some are more effective than others. . . .

Cortázar seldom wastes a word. His sentences build on each other like spider strands to ultimately form a fragile cobweb spun from one thread. "The Island at Noon" is like that, starting with the moment that the airline steward spots his dream island through the plane window as he looks down on the Aegean Sea. What happens after that builds inexorably and understatedly until the end. But you don't see it coming until you get there. What more can you ask from a story? (p. 69)

> *Deborah Davis, "Webs from a Single Thread," in* Review 73 *(copyright © 1972 by the Center for Inter-American Relations, Inc.), Fall, 1973, pp. 69-70.*

To deal in illusion but not be dismissed as an illusionist is the nearly unsolvable problem of a writer like Julio Cortázar. For him the short story is the perfect form—a fine dazzle, then a quick curtain and nothing left but spots on the retina. But an entire collection of Cortázar's glittering tricky fiction invites the reader's eye to outguess the magician's hand. The mood that results is a profitless mixture of admiration and something not unlike contempt.

The only cure is to wait two months between short stories, and this the reader is urged to do. . . . The special quality of Cortázar's subtle nuttiness deserves much patience.

> *John Skow, "Quicker than the Eye?," in* Time *(reprinted by permission from* Time, The Weekly Newsmagazine; *copyright Time Inc.), October 1, 1973, p. 116.*

It has always been the aim of Julio Cortázar's heroes to find their way to an all-embracing, wholly meaningful experience. They are the heirs of the Surrealist quest for a passage to the "other side", across a magical "bridge" that will lead them away from the irritating mechanics of society to total ecstasy. Such ecstasy is at times glimpsed in his

novels, but it is rarely more than instantaneous, being demolished in the end by the plodding consciousness of its excessively intellectual aspirants. Yet Cortázar's characters often extract a great deal of fun from their search, from their dogged determination not to slip into a social mould. . . .

In recent years Cortázar has become increasingly political in his pronouncements, and through hindsight has tended to interpret his entire oeuvre as a political gesture, as though his questing characters were faltering prototypes for Ché Guevara's New Man. . . .

Libro de Manuel is a liberating, comic book, and presents a heroic notion of revolution difficult to realize. The revolution envisaged will have none of the Puritanical repressiveness of current socialist regimes. . . . It will assert the principle that life is fun, will satisfy man's "erotic and ludic thirst" and liberate him from taboos and social constraints. . . .

Cortázar is aware of the obstacles confronting such a programme, but his novel would be less slight if it came to grips with it more thoroughly. It is symptomatic and interesting that not a single worker appears in *Libro de Manuel,* and if any worker ever got down to reading it, he would no doubt find the book's aspirations somewhat luxurious. *Libro de Manuel* is an unwitting expression of the fact that middle-class intellectual revolutionaries are on a trip all their own, particularly if, like Cortázar, they are Latin Americans living in Paris.

> *"The Fun Revolution," in* The Times Literary Supplement *(© Times Newspapers, Ltd., 1973; reproduced by permission), October 12, 1973, p. 1208.*

Cortázar does not intend to depart from the implications of reason when he employs the fantastic. He believes that reality itself is absurd or irrational. His heresy consists in the fact that he radically metaphorizes the real as he sees it, which is not the way the ordinary reader sees it. . . . He struggles with absurd reality without choosing an alternative to it. In "Carta a una señorita en París" he rebels against the consequences of linear time but stays within it. In using the fantastic for a symbolic purpose, he alludes (inevitably) to the other life-feeling without believing in its power. Unlike Borges, he cannot place his spirit in the world of art and smile or knit his brow, being "in but not of" the real world. Consequently, in Cortázar's work we do not find the momentary relief ["the escape into art," as Wheelock says elsewhere,] that renews us for work on Monday morning; we glimpse the other world but find no real exit from this one. (pp. 6-7)

> *Carter Wheelock, in* The International Fiction Review, *January, 1974.*

[The] eight pieces in "All Fires the Fire" suffer, in the way of collections, from comparison with one another—the story "Meeting" is less stunning than the title piece, and "Instructions for John Howell" ends less satisfyingly than "The Island at Noon." But in sum these eight "mortal games" correct this reviewer's previous impression (gained by that most thrifty of methods, bookstore perusal) that Cortázar was a decadent avant-gardist, a rather desperate innovator snipping autobiography into eye-catching shapes.

True, he cannot get started without a gimmick: there is always a fantastic premise or a startling formalistic deviation, and he does not have Borges's power of persuading us that the strangeness flows from the superior vision of a drastically refined sensibility. But, once the trick is established (and no two devices are alike in this set of eight), Cortázar pushes beyond it with surprising powers of realistic development. (p. 124)

Juxtaposition is Sr. Cortázar's creative habit, and perhaps he is most himself when the juxtaposition is most harsh and least explained; an abyss, narrow as a black knife, gleams in the schizoid split. . . .

[At] his most intense Cortázar floods the gaps and mysteries of his tricky structures with a potent negativity—death, that invisible possibility, made electric and palpable, like the atmosphere before lightning. Whereas a curious immortality, the eternal sprightliness of pure mind, fills the airy spaces of Queneau. Both men convince us that surreality has been elicited from them by the extremity of their ardor for reality. . . . (p. 125)

> John Updike, "Mortal Games," in The New Yorker (© 1974 by The New Yorker Magazine, Inc.), February 25, 1974, pp. 124-25.

Cortázar's tricky fable-stories fragment the World into extra-rational nightmares that question all the Self's "certainties." Point-of-view is hardly sacred (in one story, the interior monologues of separate characters *intersect*; in another, parallel narrative situations are *each* filtered through multiple character-narrators). "Reality" is what you think it is, and confused personae aren't even sure whether they inhabit a Roman gladiatorial arena, or a Paris apartment; the Parisian red-light district in wartime, or an Argentine café. Sometimes Cortázar seems more interested in the sheer fun of the contrivance than in any possible meaning. Example: an airplane steward, fascinated by his vision of a vague island shape floating below, finds himself drawn to the island—where reversed perspective now enthralls him with the image of an airplane overhead. What does it mean? That what we see is only what we *think* we see? Cortázar tells us that "Everything was falsified in the futile and recurrent vision. . . ." But nothing more.

In "The Health of the Sick," a doting family must construct an elaborate hoax to hide family tragedies from their adored, hypersensitive "Mama." With urbane indirection, and perfect pacing, Cortázar allows the hoax to replace the "reality." Best of all is "The Southern Thruway," in which an ominous traffic jam clogs dozens of journeying strangers together in an inexplicable existential impasse. Its victims are in a desert, surrounded by abandoned farmhouses, denied their fixed destination ("a city [that] sparkled in the distance . . ."). Elaborate defenses are adopted, responsibilities delegated, comforting relationships established: a microcosm of society is sedulously constructed. Suddenly, the enigma dissolves—as mysteriously as it had descended. The unity they had accomplished is unceremoniously dispersed, and the unifiers go their separate ways.

One of the things the fictionist can do with "reality" is to play delighted games with it—and make us wonder whether *any* settled assumptions are trustworthy. In Cortázar's inside-out landscape, the staggeringly arranged windows and mirrors are props stolen from the fun-house. (pp. 127-28)

> Bruce Allen, in The Hudson Review (*copyright © 1974 by The Hudson Review, Inc.; reprinted by permission*), Vol. XXVII, No. 1, Spring, 1974.

Julio Cortázar's *Ultimo round*, which first appeared in 1969, is a good example of audience-participation art. In *Rayuela* he had already suggested that the reader choose his own order for approaching the chapters, but *Ultimo round* represents a further step, in that it is now *impossible* for the reader to proceed in a conventional manner. Upon opening the book the reader notes that there are two sets of pages within the binding, and he must immediately decide which of them to read first, and even whether he will go through by reading the top and then the bottom of page one, and so on. In addition, only a few pages—at the beginning and the center particularly—obviously belong together. One example is p. 9, the whole being a picture of Cortázar himself. The top section is already distorted and fragmented by the cutting out and rotation of concentric circles on his face, but if the reader insists on turning the two pages separately he must bear the responsibility for further fragmentation of the author. Any other combinations are purely subjective on the part of the reader: the author wants his reader to feel free to find some personal meaning in a chance combination, whether of two pages whose numbers correspond or in the combination of any other pair of pages. So *Ultimo round* cannot be termed a wholly finished work of art. No work of art is finished until there are "good vibes" between the chaos in the text and the chaos within the reader. (pp. 74-5)

In a sense it is as if Cortázar were reacting to Marshall McLuhan's prediction of the demise of the printed word on the basis of its being a hot medium and hopelessly linear. Meeting the charge that a book is necessarily linear, this work not only refuses to present its divisions in any logical, set order but employs only sentence fragments at many points. . . .

It becomes evident too that in this work the medium is the message. Even if it were possible to arrange the contents of *Ultimo round* logically in a conventional manner, it would lose the major portion of its impact, simply because the greatest effect of the work lies in its very arrangement rather than in its content. (p. 75)

Cortázar appears to conceive of *Ultimo round* as the daily newspaper chronicling the apocalypse, referring to it in the text as a "diario." The format of the cover is that of a newspaper, and this is supported, in some editions, by a light yellow color. The content is like that of a newspaper in that it is miscellaneous and reflects the human condition in transit: there is something for everyone, including ads for a doll repair service, bicycles, and battery recharging.

The book is apocalyptic in its very title, which alludes to a boxing match near its conclusion, and does so in a fragmented language in which one word is properly Spanish and the other an English loan word. (pp. 75-6)

Apocalypse is not simply cataclysm. It is a destruction of all that is in order to rebuild from the most basic beginnings. Therefore if a book is truly apocalyptic it should reflect some attempt at putting the pieces back together in a meaningful order (although not necessarily guided by previously existing canons of "coherence"). The first step should be some sort of return to origins, but in effect Cortázar declares, "De ninguna manera me creo un ejemplo de esa 'vuelta a los orígenes'" ("By no means do I consider myself a participant in that 'return to origins'") . . . . On the basis of the rest of the book, however, I have to conclude that what he has reference to is limited to the search for—as he calls it—the telluric national past, because at another point he states, with apparent approval, "Los personajes de una novela de James Ballard, favorecidos por un mundo en resuelta entropía, tienden a organizar sus sueños en procura de una verdad primordial" ("The characters in a James Ballard novel, favored by a world in determined entropy, tend to organize their dreams in an endeavor to recover a primordial truth"). . . .

So man must pick up the pieces of what has disintegrated in his Self and his environment, just as he picks up the pieces which make up this piece of literature, and build a new world for himself out of them. . . .

The new reality emerging out of the chaos of the apocalypse involves a nonrational way of knowing, a truth which refuses to be captured in the nets carefully passed down from Socrates to the twentieth century. It is a nonlinear truth, not based on the syllogism or symbolic logic, so it is most appropriately contained in a book of random order. It is, as Carlos Castaneda would have it, a separate reality, and all those who may rail against it as illogical are ignored, because not only do they not have currently meaningful answers, they don't even know how to formulate the right questions. (p. 76)

> *William L. Siemens, "Cortázar's 'Ultimo Round': A Bi-Level Literary-Pictorial Experience," in* The International Fiction Review, *January, 1975, pp. 74-7.*

D

DAVIE, Donald 1922-

Davie, an English poet and critic, is best known for his association with "the Movement"—the postwar suspiciousness of the romantic imprecision of some British poetry of the 1940's —and for his contributions to the *New Lines* anthology. Although less coldly intellectual than his early work, his recent poems still exhibit his sense of responsibility to his literary inheritance and his concern for formal elegance. (See also *Contemporary Authors*, Vols. 1-4, rev. ed.)

As poet, Davie is urbane, lucid, and down-to-earth. His best poems are little hymns to rationality. His critical commitments inhibit him somewhat but at the same time they have enabled him to discover and develop the convention that suits him. When imagination and feeling win victories over theory, he achieves what the eighteenth-century critics called "graces beyond the reach of art." (p. 124)

> *William Van O'Connor, in his* The New University Wits and the End of Modernism *(copyright © 1963, Southern Illinois University Press; reprinted by permission of Southern Illinois University Press), Southern Illinois University Press, 1963.*

Generally speaking, . . . the author of *Essex Poems* puts his 'literature' to conspicuously good use. The very last poems in the volume are brutally primitive in a new and admired manner. I would prefer, I think, less 'manner', a more genuine simplicity; or a much longer poem.

Of the many virtues *Essex Poems* displays I would myself single out Davie's handling of metre as the aspect of his formal expertise most worthy of emulation, or envy. Postromantic poetics emphasize sincerity and the 'rhythms of the speaking voice' (generally 'urgent')—as if the poet were actually speaking to us!—whereas the formerly well-advertised satisfactions to be had from a perfect deployment of words within a musically interesting 'tune' are currently undervalued. (p. 81)

> *Michael Alexander, "Donald Davie's 'Essex Poems'," in* Agenda, *Autumn-Winter, 1970, pp. 78-82.*

In Donald Davie's work the relation of the critic to the poet seems deeply ironical. We can enjoy the vitality of the newest experimenters in verse without denying the strength of Mr Davie's warnings against them. . . .

Mr Davie has not been afraid to recommend and use models painfully created by the forebears of our poetry. He has pleaded for aesthetic control and praised moral principles even when they suited the fixed order of society. He has distrusted easy motions and infringed on no legitimate privacies. At the same time, he has utterly rejected provincialism and studied poets who live in regions or speak languages ignored by many of his contemporaries. He has willingly experimented with the styles and structures of three centuries. He has maintained a record of conscious integrity, misrepresenting his character neither to himself nor to others. So he has admitted tergiversations and failures to meet his own requirements.

> *"A Candour under Control," in* The Times Literary Supplement *(© Times Newspapers Ltd., 1972; reproduced by permission), December 22, 1972, p. 1548.*

Mr. Davie is a believer in linearity. Philosophically, he stands in firm but amiable opposition to the submerging of the individual in the cyclical myth. In his craft he finds that traditional discipline is ultimately less restrictive of the poet's intellectual liberty than the traditional eccentricities of free forms and the compulsory convolutions of composition by field. Mr. Davie claims that his natural affinity is to ideas and that for him poetic concreteness and sensuousness are achieved only with the greatest effort. As a result of this self-consciousness, the poet's contact with his own senses is rigorous: never are flamboyant words substituted for honest perceptions of the world. (p. lxi)

> Virginia Quarterly Review *(copyright, 1973, by the* Virginia Quarterly Review, *The University of Virginia), Vol. 49, No. 2 (Spring, 1973).*

Professor Davie's poems tend to make use of a strongly-disciplined, often subdued tone of self-confession or soliloquy, with the intelligence probing or debating upon the situations presented by personal experience, history and landscape—sometimes, perhaps, to a fault. In an early poem, for instance, 'Evangelist', I feel that the interjection of the two listeners at the end of the poem deflects from the dramatic potential of the preacher's personality, well-realised at the start. . . .

Of course, this is to suggest, unfairly, that it has the potential of being a *different* poem. Yet is not the switch from the well-realised *persona* in the first verse, to a comment about attitudes to style and rhetoric in the last, an impoverishing one? Doesn't the reader feel that the rhythms themselves are tamped down, as it were, from the 'dramatic' to the 'literary' by the end? In contrast, the direct voice of regret that ends 'The Garden Party' points its poem up more, and for this reason it pleased as much as any in the early verse. Generally in this early verse, the metre trips along fluently, rather lacking in variation, in a contrast of light and shade. Poems often dwell on 'literary' themes or on matters of personal literary attitude, while some court the dull old maid of obscurity.

In *A Winter Talent*, the fine and well-known 'Time Passing, Beloved' and 'Heigh-ho on a Winter Afternoon' stand out, partly because the rhythms go more naturally and vividly, partly because in them the poet heightens and transcends the reasonable, ironic tone into a confident, direct 'voice'. (p. 77)

After *The Forests of Lithuania*, which are poems on historical incidents that don't rise enough to excite this reviewer, hard though he tried, it is *Events and Wisdoms* where the dramatic heightening and rhythmic heightening combine to give some marvellous, enduring successes—the summit of this poet's achievement, so far. . . . The pastoral and elegiac tone, caught in this collection, especially in these outstanding poems, also catches life . . . at its more vivid and dramatic moments.

In the more recent *Essex Poems*, 'A Winter Landscape near Ely' discreetly but powerfully expresses the theme of waste and death: does not its directness link it to the poems just indicated? But there is surely a levelling-off in this collection. Its 'sparseness' was commented upon at the time when it appeared, but I feel it may really be a thinning of dramatic texture. Some of the poems read like 'notations'—or painter's 'sketches'—rather than fully confident artefacts. The much-noticed 'Or, Solitude' does not fully engage me; Professor Davie sighs for the 'metaphysicality of poetry', but I get the sense of a poem about private poetic attitudes and problems whose public importance has not been firmly enough established by the dramatic force of the poems before. 'A Winter Landscape', for example, is surely moving and metaphysical enough?

I feel the same when Professor Davie talks of 'England'. The England his verse establishes does not convince me as as generally valid as say, the English locality that Norman Nicholson brings to life, or the England of Mr. Larkin. A poem with the title 'England' shows an incursion of a free-wheeling, fragmented, Yankee verse-manner into Professor Davie's poetry that is quite surprising; the poem leaves me standing. (pp. 78-9)

In some of the most recent poems, whose subject touches on the fascinating one of Captain Cook's voyages, and the lives of explorers like Barry and Trevewen, does the verse truly enact the adventurousness, the possibilities, of the theme?

The technique of the 'Six Epistles to Eva Hesse', however, point forward. These poems come through well. . . . (p. 79)

Simon Curtis, "Collected Davie," in *Phoenix* (8 Cavendish Road, Heaton Mersey, Stockport, Cheshire, England), July, 1973, pp. 77-80.

Since the publishing of . . . his *Collected Poems*, Donald Davie's poetry has been moving fast and variously. . . . There seems to be a fresh daring in the creative act. (p. 109)

[A] glance at the *Collected Poems* shows that, from shortly after the beginning of his career, he has been drawn to more sustained works: *The Forests of Lithuania*, *A Sequence for Francis Parkman*, 'England', *Six Epistles to Eva Hesse*. . . . The appeal long poems may have for a writer is clear: they allow him to explore aesthetic structures, and developments and meshings of experience, which would otherwise be unapproachable. And these larger measures are necessary; don't we need to note their rarity more than we do? It's not that long poems are somehow better than short ones, but that we are lacking if almost the only poetry we have is small-scale, however complex, intense, and indeed resonant. Davie's example is important.

The aims of his extended pieces have been varied, as have the means he has found for their articulation. The blurb of *The Forests of Lithuania*, which he seems partly to have inspired, speaks of 'the long poem's privilege of dealing with common human experiences in the way they are commonly perceived, as slowly and gradually evolving amid a wealth of familiar and particular images', and contends that he has 'attempted to win back some of this territory from the novelist'. Certainly, to shift a famous expression of Mallarmé, a decision to 'reprendre *au roman* notre bien' would afford a fertile programme for poetry, and one worth examining further; though it doesn't necessarily involve appropriating the novel's not-quite-modern powers of dense realism. (pp. 109-10)

The later long works abandon the novel as a formal bearing and also come differently at history and geography. The most complex is *Six Epistles to Eva Hesse*, at once satirical, didactic and narrative verse, in cascading octosyllabic couplets. It's a kind of Art of Poetry, which associates certain severe 'English' values: sanity, common sense, a sense of proportion, compassion, with a particular view of history: empirical, linear, individualist, moralising, and with the use of fixed metres and rhyme. This it sets, under the aegis of Comedy, against the Einsteinian and mythic free-wheeling transcendence of history in the open forms of Pound's *Cantos* and Olson's *Maximus Poems*. *Thomas Hardy and British Poetry* has similar concerns.

Six Epistles enacts the discipline it urges. It takes over the documentary method of the *Cantos* and their progeny, in the interests of establishing the poem on a world objectively beyond itself. The procedure is even wittily exaggerated. *The Forests of Lithuania* had adapted a historical poem; *A Sequence for Francis Parkman* had consisted partly of centos of passages from a work of historical scholarship, Parkman's *France and England in North America*; *Six Epistles* has for its immediate pre-text, of all things, a volume of collective literary criticism, Eva Hesse's *New Approaches to Ezra Pound*. (pp. 110-11)

Naturally, *Six Epistles* is a conservative work. It brings to sharp focus Davie's continuing wrestle with Modernism and especially with Pound. His whole career has been an urgent rearguard action, from *Brides of Reason* to *Six Epistles*, from *Purity of Diction in English Verse* to *Thomas Hardy and British Poetry*, against dominant modes of writing and ultimately, indeed, against 'the age'. Could it be that his impingement on poetry in general, through both his poems and his prose, has been essentially, and enlighteningly, critical rather than creative? Here, his showdown with a certain highhanded conjuring with history is wholesome (although one notices that his defence of linearity amounts to no less than a demur about most of modern literature). On the other hand, it's hard to see how his own reading of history, and his prescriptions for 'humanising the globe', generous and self-forgetful though they are, might energise the imagination. (p. 111)

The signs are that Davie is searching. The long works, for instance, bulk large in his output; yet according to Bernard Bergonzi he regards *A Sequence for Francis Parkman* as a poetic luxury not part of his true development, and he claims to have written *Six Epistles to Eva Hesse* lightheartedly. I may be ludicrously mistaken, but I do sense that, having begun with a very clear notion of what he was about, he is now, possibly, undecided, and perhaps at odds with himself. Even *Thomas Hardy and British Poetry*, despite many instructive delights, doesn't, I think, hang together.

This is maybe no bad experience to pass through, for a poet of Davie's gifts. Which I hope I haven't been undervaluing: looking back over what I've written I'm surprised to see so many reservations—no doubt because it's only relevant to discuss his works in terms of major achievement. Let me, then, say the obvious, that the *Collected Poems* already contains any amount of admirable writing, learned, supple, various, and well beyond the attainment of most. And also, that that perpetual severe questioning, from the very beginning of his career, arrests. (pp. 113-14)

> *Michael Edwards, "Donald Davie and British Poetry," in* Poetry Nation *(© copyright* Poetry Nation, *1974), No. 3, 1974, pp. 109-14.*

A handsome production, with many poems that give us passages of that balanced, chaste sort of elegance we expect of him, [*The Shires*] is still an oddly misconceived venture for so fastidious a poet. This collection of 40 poems, one for each county in England—and collectively seeking to explore the writer's 'deep sense of being English'—could have made a fascinating account of the fabric of current English life and landscape. *Could* have, if Professor Davie had stopped, looked, listened, thought and written as assiduously with all of his shires as he has with a few. The book could, alternatively, have been an engaging, perhaps a moving, autobiographical exercise if he had drawn every county (as he does with some) into relationship with his own personal memories. Or, had he concentrated on history and literature, *The Shires* might have come out as the kind of highly individual disquisition so worth listening in to (if not to agree with) when he does it in his criticism. Instead, the book is an uncomfortable mixture of all three. (p. 545)

What is as disappointing . . . as the scantiness of the attention given to most of the shires is the vacuously cryptic quality of many of the reflections to which they give rise. Davie's arcane manner once upon a time, one feels, concealed witty, disturbing, chastening thoughts which it was

worth working quite hard to pick up. Listening closely to his utterances on the English counties, one wonders if there really is much profundity there at all, or if the familiar insouciant precision hasn't somehow slackened here into a mere insouciant ordinariness. . . . The good habit of looking for hidden interest and value in the simplest Davie statements had me wondering over these banalities for quite a time before concluding that the best of poets will sometimes write at a very low pressure indeed. (p. 546)

> *Alan Brownjohn, "Being English," in* New Statesman *(© 1974 The Statesman & Nation Publishing Co. Ltd.), October 18, 1974, pp. 545-46.*

Anyone acquainted with Donald Davie's work will not be surprised at my calling it one of the more considerable ventures in literature in our time. . . . I admire his struggle toward honesty, his intelligence, his defense of the quieter, less impressive, since less assertive, virtues. The struggle he is involved in is nothing other than that of poetry and life itself, not only in a wounded, diminished England, but in the world at large. (p. 113)

After [an] examination of Davie's criticism readers should be prepared to learn from their scrutiny of his poems that they have been, as the flyleaf [of *Collected Poems 1950-1970*] says, "written in the faith that there are still distinctively English—rather than Anglo-American or 'international'—ways of responding imaginatively to the terms of life in the twentieth century." (One might demur, at least a little, for the many poems under the influence of foreign places and poets, especially Pasternak.) And readers should be prepared to hear in the first poem—appropriately, "Homage to William Cowper"—that Davie, even as he is aware with Cowper that "Honor starts, like Charity, at home," regards himself "A pasticheur of the late-Augustan styles." Fortunately he is also rather more than that. The first three formal, witty poems, set apart almost like epigraphs, establish basic themes; all three recognize the troubles and failures, if not horrors, of domesticity, geography, society, and reason—Davie's essential concerns. (p. 130)

It is the human, reflected in ideas and laws, defined by the resolutely other world (though if nature disappears what is that other world but other people and man-made society?), that he is after, and not the identification with that world (usually the "natural") of a Keats or a Rilke. Davie's lyricism is often personal but (as he said of Hardy) in an impersonal, if not "reposeful," way, concerned more than not with lack of feeling and related problems of style. The writing, usually hard and definite, but rather metallic than of carved stone, is rarely possessed of the evocativeness Pound, say, often magically managed. (p. 136)

> *Theodore Weiss, "Between Two Worlds or On The Move," in* Parnassus *(copyright © by* Parnassus: Poetry in Review), *Fall/Winter, 1974, pp. 113-40.*

[*The Shires*] struck me at first as the title of a book in which I would be likely to find an interesting sense of history. No, I was to be disappointed. What I find is a large subject "gone over" in such a way as to reduce it to the scale of the closely personal. Donald Davie has a fine notion of writing. More than anything else, it is "fineness", a deliberately courted delicacy and elegance, that defeats my prior willingness to welcome *The Shires*. Having re-read his *Collected Poems*, I was ready for this new book, and ready to like it.

What irritated me most was its chattiness. . . .

Davie's language is the language of education, of culture. I can see sherries at sundown, comfortable motorcars waiting on the drive. . . .

The Shires carries a weight of reminiscence, autobiography, and private sensation, for which the virtually archaeological title does not prepare us. It is a book by a motorist —"Driving up from Tees-side. . . ." Poet-as-driver is a man I find hard to accept. He's a figure who ought to get out and walk. Or just be in a place, settled. Poets should never learn how to drive. (pp. 85-6)

> *Douglas Dunn, in* Encounter *(© 1975 by Encounter, Ltd.), March, 1975.*

* * *

DILLARD, R(ichard) H(enry) W(ilde) 1937-

A poet, novelist, critic, and short story writer of the American South, Dillard, compared with Borges, Nabokov, and Robbe-Grillet, constructs his own reality. (See also *Contemporary Authors*, Vols. 21-22.)

"The Book of Changes" is a great Chinese box of a novel, strewn with conundrums, masks, misleading clues, disintegrating landscapes, false starts, fake quotations, magicians, werewolves, bumbling detectives, severed hands and heads, and a sinister German dwarf who bumps from scene to scene in various disguises, sexes and shapes. Nothing remains intact for long: Men become women or change into screaming wolves; women appear in men's boxer shorts; suburban folk under the names of Herbert Hoover, Oscar Wilde and the brothers Marx drift in and out of the novel; even that ingenious puppet-maker and puller of strings, Vladimir Nabokov, shows up briefly. The very title of the novel shifts to "The Book of Dillards by R. H. W. Change" on a laundryman's list. Behind these transmogrifications is a world in which the skin "begins to flake away revealing nothing but scaling bone and mold, gray, puffed and swollen, living, dead, decay."

Mr. Dillard leads us gently out of this stale heart of darkness, providing a theory for his elaborate fictioneering. The "post-Einsteinian" novel, he tells us, one demonstrating the intricacies of time and space, "would be concerned with events rather than with characters in the usual sense, would be particulate (composed of small, apparently discrete particles or fragments), would be composed of a number of different but simultaneous time movements, and would finally reveal itself to be formally unified. A modern book of changes." . . .

The problem with all this is that the novel is a more curious beast than the author is willing to allow. The contrivances may fit some rigged time scheme, but they do not shape and gouge the reader's imagination. Mr. Dillard is similar to that Mexican magician in his own book, "complete with brocaded sombrero, up on a low stage squeezing eggs out of his nose with an expression on his face like he had bad sinus trouble." The structure of the novel is transparent, like mad electrical wiring, so that the whole thing becomes a mystery book with only a vague sense of terror: we admire the conundrums but never feel the teeth.

Still, the book does have its pull, mainly because the writer has a marvelous ear for words. It is the small details that keep the book alive: the detective with "his nose veined pale blue with the cold"; the layers of dust that "fur" a room; the octopus in West Berlin's aquarium, eating itself to death at the rate of "half an inch" of tentacle per day.

In "The Book of Changes" Mr. Dillard practices a risky kind of magic: he remains a gifted writer with an obsessive love of conjuring that narrows him and imposes a brittle sense of form upon his book. (p. 4)

> *Jerome Charyn, in* The New York Times Book Review *(© 1974 by The New York Times Company; reprinted by permission), August 25, 1974.*

The Book of Changes is, quite simply, a brain-teaser, labyrinthine and layered. By creation, by imitation, or by grave-raiding, Dillard brings his cast to life and sets them to motion in an involved progression of ciphers and enigmas. They are shadowed by the spirits of Borges, Nabokov, and H. P. Lovecraft (among others), who spring up as passage-markers in the maze.

The characters inhabit four different "time zones," four different fragments of time and experience that seem isolated and unrelated to each other. Longinus, for example, lives perpetually in "winter," the paperboy in constant summer; Pudd's world lasts but three days. What they have in common, aside from being pretty odd, are objects—a coin, a talisman, a scrapbook, a mask, a purloined diamond —objects that retain their integrity and tangibility in the blur of lifetimes that revolve around them, objects that instigate actions and ignite passions in their energetic pursuers. These physical bodies act like magnets in the center of the maze, drawing the characters toward a confluence in time.

The movement is part of Dillard's "post-Einsteinian" novel where "we must concern ourselves with events and not stable bodies," where "time like physical matter is particulate . . . capable of dilation.". . .

This pitch seems a bit too sober and squeaky in the big-top arena of the book. But it enlists Dillard among those writers who view the novel as a separate and more rarefied reality, where the author enacts his own rules, where he plays whatever games he wishes with the reader, and where he ministrates a universe of characters and predicaments and ideas that are alive and moving, but still maintained in a rigorous orbit. The novelist as juggler, tongue firmly placed against cheek.

Dillard does manage to keep things up in the air. Matters begin to spiral toward resolution only in the final chapter. It is a pasticcio of epigrams and explications, the syllabus of Dillard's large and resourceful mythology, and it ties a neat ribbon around the proceedings.

Dillard's prose is a delightful excursion into parody and linguistic pranksterism. The lampoon of the detective genre, from the stodgy Victorianism of Arthur Conan Doyle to the blunt, no-nonsense "diction" of Dashiell Hammett, is teeming with cleverness and humor, and in the character of Fitz-Hyffen, Dillard sires a mutant alter-ego to Holmes who is too funny and too valuable to meet even a fictional death. Add to this the clutter of puns, anagrams, puzzles, and literary allusions, and you have a novel that is teasing and knotty, but happily not Gordian.

Some people prefer to read *about* detectives. Others relish the opportunity to be literary Sherlocks themselves, to enter the landscape of fiction, carrying greatcoat and glass, and stalk the demons of imagination. *The Book of Changes* accommodates both types of reader. R. H. W. Dillard writes like a criminal who subconsciously wants to be caught, and the clues are plentifully strewn throughout his novel. It is well worth the chase. (pp. 2-3)

> Stephen Hall, "In Juggler Vein," in Book World—The Washington Post (© The Washington Post), *November 3, 1974, pp. 2-3.*

*   *   *

DRABBLE, Margaret   1939-

An English novelist, playwright, short story writer, and author of critical biographies, Ms Drabble writes intelligent and insightful traditional novels. (See also *Contemporary Authors,* **Vols. 13-16, rev. ed.)**

Ours is certainly an age of great, even heroic, biographies and autobiographies, and Margaret Drabble's richly detailed and wonderfully sensitive critical biography of Arnold Bennett is very much of our time. Though Bennett's reputation is not that of certain of his famous contemporaries, the intensity of Drabble's appreciation of him, and her ability to communicate that appreciation in both emotional and intellectual terms, will lead many of us to a new assessment of Bennett's major works. (p. 34)

That so highly acclaimed a young novelist as Margaret Drabble should spend many, many months researching Bennett, talking with innumerable people about him, always on the lookout for stray items of his ephemera—as well as fighting London traffic on a bicycle, back and forth between the British Museum and her home some distance away—seemed to me simply baffling; until I realized that this book is no ordinary biography. Of course, it satisfies every academic demand for factual accuracy, and then some; but it is also Margaret Drabble's analysis of her own origins and her own tradition, both as a person from Bennett's part of England—possibly related to him by way of a maternal great-grandmother—and a writer in his tradition, brought up to admire realism and social concern in literature.

Drabble understands her subject from the inside, in a way that no American critic could hope to approximate. To know what London and England are like, one can do no better than to read Margaret Drabble; it's doubtful that there is any single American writer who represents the diversity and near-chaos of our culture, as Drabble represents the tone of contemporary English culture. Her imagination is both refined and robust, slyly satirical and profoundly moral: there is no one quite like her writing today, and her work is especially valuable because it shows with what grace the uniquely contemporary personality can deal with traditional and timeless subjects. . . .

Margaret Drabble analyzes her own background, then, and provides her readers with the means by which better to understand her own novels, especially *Jerusalem the Golden* and *The Needle's Eye,* which deal with moral issues of a kind not translatable into contemporary American terms. Art transcends regional and parochial particularities, of course, but the artist generally writes out of a fierce love-hate relationship with those particularities, in an attempt to discover just what they are and how one has been shaped by them. In *The Old Wives' Tale* and the "Clayhanger" series, as well as in other of his novels, Bennett dealt with a world and with people who stand behind, in a manner of speaking, the Londoners of Margaret Drabble's fiction. They are of the same stock, shaped by the same religion and the same class-consciousness. (p. 35)

Like Drabble's earlier studies of Wordsworth and Virginia Woolf, *Arnold Bennett* contrasts sharply with the kind of grudgingly appreciative—and occasionally cruel—academic criticism that is standard fare from university presses, written by scholar-critics with no sympathy for their subjects. This book is generated by Drabble's feelings for Bennett, written "in a partisan spirit, as an act of appreciation". . . .

[Margaret Drabble] struck me (and perhaps I struck her the same way: there is a great deal of similarity between us) as a young woman intensely interested in nearly all aspects of experience, but not one who would care to experiment, personally, in anything very much out of the ordinary. Warm, humorous, gently intelligent, she possesses the Jamesian talent for discerning possibilities of adventure, as well as the Jamesian caution (or wisdom) that values most highly the position of observer. After all, it is those who survive, those who observe carefully and sympathetically, who have something valuable to communicate to the rest of the world. Robert Frost speculated on what one might make "of a diminished thing"—assuming that the drama of an extraordinary life was no longer possible—but Margaret Drabble, like Bennett and like her own fictional characters, would declare the daily experience of life itself something extraordinary. (p. 36)

> Joyce Carol Oates, "Bricks and Mortar," in Ms. *(reprinted by permission of the author and her agent, Blanche C. Gregory, Inc.; copyright © 1974 by Joyce Carol Oates), August, 1974, pp. 34-6.*

Although the primary theme in Drabble's fiction is her intense preoccupation with questions of fatalism and will, her work also involves—both explicitly and implicitly—feminist concerns. Because the central protagonist (even in *The Needle's Eye*) is always a woman and the society in which she lives is always depicted, accurately, as deeply patriarchal and class-bound, the problem of the individual's capacity for self-determination is inevitably tied to the feminist perspective. (p. 176)

After *The Garrick Year,* Drabble's novels become more complicated psychologically and philosophically, partly because the heroine's family and social origins become an additional aspect of fate to be consciously reckoned with in her comprehension of the present and her vision of the future. And of all Drabble heroines, Clara Maughm of *Jerusalem the Golden* is most heavily burdened by the circumstances of her childhood. (p. 178)

Drabble's portrayal of Clara is not particularly interesting and not completely convincing; it is difficult, at the end of the novel, to reconcile Clara's intelligence with her reaffirmed pledge to force a modern fairy-tale fate out of human materials whose realness and vulnerability have been so palpably revealed. Through Clara, Drabble makes a sort of straw man of the efficacious will; the will that serves misguided desire substitutes for the will that serves the intelligence and inevitably gets knocked down by the dictates of justice and the free rein of authorial manipulation. Consequently, the most pressing question implicit in Clara's situation—how far she could conscientiously and realistically rise above the confines of her past—is virtually bypassed. In contrast to her handling of Clara, Drabble's gently controlled and affectionate portrayal of Rosamund Stacey in *The Millstone* raises more serious and subtle questions about the relationship between will and character, character and fate. Moreover, in the mild atmosphere of Rosamund's basic acceptance of past influences and present occurrences, the occasional exertions of her will in the service of a selfhood deeper than any fate offer a particularly effective challenge to the deterministic assumptions of the book. *The Millstone* incorporates the beginning of a subtle complexity in Drabble's notions of fatalism and related feminist issues, a complexity that thickens with the heroine's destructive submission to fate in *The Waterfall* and finally, in *The Needle's Eye*, breaks through into a new vision of possible freedom. (pp. 179-80)

Drabble has come a long way, in *The Needle's Eye*, from the artful construction of fatalistic circumstances to which Emma and Rosamund must yield and from the creation of the fatally destructive monolithic natures of Clara and [Jane Gray, in *The Waterfall*]. *The Needle's Eye* is a complex and passionate evocation of a fatalism deriving from the human condition and the nature of the world; Drabble's vision no longer imposes an idiosyncratic pattern on the materials of life. Perhaps the most authentic aspect of fatalism in her last novel is its political basis; Rose and Simon are both motivated in everything they do by a humanitarian consciousness. (pp. 187-88)

The Needle's Eye is a portrayal of political and personal existential struggle shadowed by a belief in the "double-bind" of man's psychic make-up: man is possessed of "just enough illumination . . . to suffer for failure, and too little spirit to live in the light, too little strength to reach the light" (*NE*, p. 172), and, although he strives for individual identity, as "the property of two parents with equal claim," "he is condemned for survival to partition" (*NE*, pp. 260-61). (p. 188)

The Needle's Eye is unusually complex among Drabble's works largely because it contains two central protagonists; it is the story of Simon Camish, as well as of Rose Vassiliou, and in a sense Simon's reaction to Rose constitutes the primary growth of consciousness in the novel. (p. 189)

In so far as it is convincing, fatalism in *The Needle's Eye* rests on the author's careful construction of interlocking double-binds relating both to the general psychological and political nature of man. But without betraying the delicate balance of her ironic vision of reality, Drabble might—as she says—have enabled Rose to remain alone with her children, "might have allowed her her freedom.". . . Feminism, as an issue, does not figure strongly in *The Needle's Eye* mainly because Rose, more than any other Drabble heroine, transcends conventional femaleness in her person and because her primary struggle is with questions of will and fate that affect women and men alike. (p. 190)

One of the qualities which makes Margaret Drabble unique as a writer—with the exception of Doris Lessing in some of her work—is her acute sense of the value and beauty of children, and her almost uncanny perception, usually without abandoning the adult point of view, of the child's inner life. She understands, better than most novelists, the power of an individual child's nature to affect the adult experience, as well as the force of a child's needs in shaping his parents' decisions and, if they are sensitive, their psychic development. (p. 191)

> *Marion Vlastos Libby, "Fate and Feminism in the Novels of Margaret Drabble," in* Contemporary Literature (© *1975 by the Board of Regents of the University of Wisconsin System), Vol. 16, No. 2, Spring, 1975, pp. 175-92.*

Margaret Drabble is an English girl who writes novels. Not just novels but bestsellers. Not just bestsellers but books which are critics' darlings. She is called the George Eliot of her generation, which pleases her very much, and the Charlotte Bronte, which doesn't please her at all. C. P. Snow tells me she is one of England's best novelists. (p. 255)

Is she a woman's novelist? Critics (of all sexes) say she is.

"Proust is a woman's novelist; Angus Wilson is a woman's writer; Joyce Carol Oates writes 'men's books'; a lot of men write best about women, with a woman's sensibility." The argument is tenable. Drabble has created some memorable men. Simon Camish, the introspective, self-analyzing lawyer of "Needle's Eye," is a man to remember. One would like to know the absent husband, the guitarist, so suggestively dismissed in "The Waterfall." (p. 262)

In style and form she is traditional. But what she is saying is not traditional. She is writing about revolutions in values. She is concerned with privilege; she does not believe in it. She is writing about the effect women are having on society; she is quite sure that the "woman's role, the rift between the sexes," is going to change society completely, and in probing these changes and anticipating further changes. "I and most women are writing about things that have never been written about, really."

She is writing about the universals in private experience, themes and subtleties which sustain the novel as an art form, make it more than a good story, and inspire good readers. The questions she is asking are recording the social history of an era. (p. 263)

She never thinks about keeping her audience. She has an absolutely heroic disregard of them. Hers, as Faulkner said of his work, is the standard which has to be met. . . . She is not arrogant but realistic. Reality for Margaret Drabble is the fiction she's creating, far more than the constant variable of popularity.

Then why is she so popular?

"There must be a lot of people like me. A lot of people have got exactly the same worries and problems . . .". (p. 264)

Drabble is answer and example to women who think the role into which society stereotypes them *necessarily* limits them, or makes them losers in life. She is a sweet reminder to stereotypers of women that women no longer swing in the ancient orbits. (p. 265)

Nancy Poland, "Margaret Drabble: 'There Must Be a Lot of People Like Me'," in The Midwest Quarterly *(copyright, 1975, by* The Midwest Quarterly, *Kansas State College of Pittsburg), Spring, 1975, pp. 255-67.*

If the family as a social institution disappears over the next 50 years, Margaret Drabble's novels will become a documentation of its painful survival into the second half of the 20th century. The long and silent lifetime relation of brothers and sisters, the strain of grownup children's relations with aging parents, the fatigue-heightened experience of mothers with infants, the breathing, rib-close love and hatred of husband and wife, they are all there in what has come to be a rather sizable body of work.

But Drabble is not interested in documenting anything. One of the most obvious aspects of her work as a novelist has been her lack of passivity, her reluctance to be shaped by rather than shape the culture in which she lives. With her last novel it has become impossible to ignore what has always been a part of her attraction as a writer: her quest for the good life. Such an old-fashioned undertaking involves her not in turning the clock back but in moving more responsibly into the future. Fortunately she has none of the complacent purposefulness of one who knows where the world should be heading; her novels are full of our contemporary failures and confusions. Her characters drift on the swirling waters of our daily experience, but they do so with a kind of moral evaluation of their own drift. (p. 21)

Drabble is one of those writers who believe we do not make life, and yet human beings have a responsibility for what they do. . . .

Taking responsibility for the life one has drifted into does not always mean doing the right thing. Indeed *The Needle's Eye* is unlike any of Drabble's other novels just because Rose does. She decides it is not enough to know the right thing to do. One must do it. No matter how irrational, how mad it may seem—for example, giving away one's millions to an African country—one must do it. At the end of the *The Millstone*, Rosamund can not perform such an act; she lets George go rather than behave in an uncivilized way by throwing herself at his feet. . . .

But Rose is a kind of saint, a saint who yells at her children and fights with her husband, but who from childhood has asked with Bunyan's pilgrim: "What is it I must do to be saved?" She has given away her inherited wealth and fought her way back from a privileged position to that of the ordinary mortal. And what is most important about her is her support of the normally vulgar world. At the end, Rose pats the ugly broken lion outside the sports arena and thinks of the beautiful handmade lion in front of her father's estate. She lays her hand approvingly on the ugly lion. "It was gritty and cold, a beast of the people. Mass-produced it had been, but it had weathered into identity. And this she hoped, for every living soul."

That concluding prayer-like line has a generosity that is to be found in almost every line of Drabble's recent biography of Arnold Bennett. Although much of the detailed recounting of his literary life is uninspired, she praises his love of and respect for the ordinary. In an earlier book on Wordsworth she had also drawn the reader's attention to the moral as well as psychological implications of a writer's response to vulgar reality. (p. 22)

Her novels celebrate moral awareness; her characters attempt to make out of the rhythm of experience a meaningful life. (p. 23)

J. O'Brien Schaefer, "The Novels of Margaret Drabble," in The New Republic *(reprinted by permission of* The New Republic; © *1975 by The New Republic, Inc.), April 26, 1975, pp. 21-3.*

E

EVERSON, William 1912-
(formerly Brother Antoninus)

An American poet formerly associated with the San Francisco Renaissance, Everson was until recently a Dominican monk. (See also *Contemporary Authors*, Vols. 9-12, rev. ed.)

The work of Brother Antoninus begins, first of all, with a very emphatic content, characterized by him as follows: "A poem, like a dream, is a 'whole' to the extent that it registers the mystery of the psychic complex which produced it." *The Hazards of Holiness* is a collection of specific tests, of "scalps torn dripping from the skulls of interior adversaries," which last way of speaking will not outrage those who are willing to admit that a "Dark Night of the Soul" may exist for a man who attempts to find himself in relation to God. Again as Brother Antoninus says, "These are the terrible wrestlings his verse begins to register; and this is the harrowing ambiguity, so fraught with terror and mystery and meaning, that cross-riddles this demon-haunted realm."

Such a way of speaking will have, of course, an immediate impact, and it will either be one of respect and sympathy for the man who has so endured, to speak, or it will be perhaps a questioning of such an invention of agony in a world so substantially tormented. Either response will here depend on the reader's own relation to the literal facts dealt with, the faith in God which is the issue. But, in either case, there can be without such question a simple response to the ways the words are working. (pp. 42-3)

I cannot avoid nor deny the force of [his] language, despite my own characterization of it as often melodramatic, that is, an enlargement of occasion purely willed. What the poems effect is a language, itself a formality, a distinct way of engaging feeling, a testing of tones of response and recognition. They speak in one voice because their occasion—despite the variation of subject—is always the same, the search for substantial faith. (pp. 43-4)

> *Robert Creeley, "'Think what's got away . . .'," in* Poetry (© *1963 by The Modern Poetry Association; reprinted by permission of the Editor of* Poetry), *April, 1963, pp. 42-4.*

The Rose of Solitude concerns itself with the reverbera-

tions of a single event: the speaker of the poem, a religious, goes to bed with a pleasant woman who, thinking it over afterwards, declines to repeat the experience. Out of this germ, which might have been quieted by the confessional, come 125 pages of overheated verse, and a lengthy prose preface which may represent the fullest statement of a narcissist theology yet made in our time.

The book's faults lie in its disproportion and in its irresponsibility. Antoninus assumes an identity of microcosm and macrocosm: the human sufferer is not only a type of Christ, he *is* Christ. Moreover, the human sin is excused by suffering, since only when he is confronted by sin and suffering is God in a position to grant forgiveness. The concept of the *felix culpa* has seldom been more strained than here, or more psychologized; eventually the doctrine is perverted into a general congratulation to Antoninus for having been good enough to suffer so much.

The language of the book is, like its substance, overblown. Antoninus makes a simple equation between suffering and unintelligibility: the greater the pain, the more tortured the syntax. In pursuit of this relationship he arrives at distortions which can best be called grotesque. (p. 693)

> *William Dickey, in* The Hudson Review (*copyright* © *1968 by The Hudson Review, Inc.; reprinted by permission), Vol. XXX, No. 4, Winter, 1967-68.*

It isn't only the insistence on the urgency of the poet's self that sets Antoninus's work apart from other poetry of the last twenty years. There have been other poets who have tried to scrape away as many layers of the skin. Antoninus, in a period when the poetic idiom has become dry and understated, has an almost seventeenth century richness of language and expression. He has a closer affinity to Vaughn, Crashaw, Alabaster—the Christopher Smart of *A Song to David*—than he does to the insistent objectivity of Robert Creeley or Denise Levertov, or to the complex allusiveness of Charles Olson or Robert Duncan. I don't think he was influenced by the metaphysical poets—he was from the beginning a Jeffers' disciple—but the feeling in the poetry is of a man, like the earlier poets, who has been driven by the torment of his life to the most intense poetry he can find language to express.

Antoninus's language is so intense, so vivid, that the poems can almost be read in clusters of words and phrases—"Far trumpets of succinctness," "a treading of feet on the stairs of redness," "I think moons of kept measure," "I felt the new wind, south/Grope her tonguing mouth on the wall," "The wind breaking its knees on this hurdle, the house," "Birds beak for her!" "In the high peal of rivering lips," "The low freighters at sea/Take in their sides the nuzzling dolphins that are their death." He has a brilliant sense of alliteration. From *In The Fictive Wish*,

> Wader
> Watcher by water,
> Walker alone by the wave-worn shore
> In water woven.

And he doesn't hesitate to extend the flash of phrase into a poem's inner tensions. He uses a long, wavering line at points that near the stillness of a moment of contemplation.... But at moments of deepening intensity the line tightens to an abrupt, insistent rhythmic unit.... None of this has the flat speech rhythm that sets the dominant tone of most contemporary poetry. Duncan has his own kind of rhetorical verbosity, and Ginsberg has some of the rhythm of the synagogue chant, but the modern poet has usually been less emotional—his own responses kept at an objective distance from the poem. Antoninus has none of this restraint—the phrase, the phrase rhythm, function as a direct expression of his emotions. Part of the felt affinity with the earlier group of metaphysical poets is this emotional extravagance, this sense of poetic hyperbole.... [In] "The Song The Body Dreamed In The Spirit's Mad Behest," ... [the] image and the language could almost have come from [Donne.] (pp. 97-9)

It's true that of all the contemporary poets Antoninus is the only one with some kind of persona—his identification with his holy order—that he can put between himself and his work, and it could be that this has given him the situation he needed to open his emotional stance. When he took his vows in 1951, after more than a dozen years of publication as William Everson, he had, as Brother Antoninus, a reach of expression opened to him that had been inhibited while he was still writing as William Everson. Nothing in his secular poetry has the grinding fervor of his religious writing. But is the poet William Everson? Is the poet Brother Antoninus? The two persons of Antoninus have never fully merged—even now that he has left the order and married, and the complex currents of his poetry express this continuing duality. Not confusion—I don't think there is any confusion of his separate identities in Antoninus, only a deep consciousness of their differences. But the emphasis of the poetry has moved—since 1951, when he was thirty-nine—from the preoccupations with the self to the more specific emotions of his religious self. Everson is still present in Antoninus, as the man who is Antoninus was a presence in the poems of Everson. (p. 100)

It is possible to be unmoved by the religiosity of the later work, and to pass over the Jeffers'-like cadences of the first poems, but this period of his life was one of deep personal unhappiness, and the humanness of his loss is directly, and strongly, moving. So much seems to be slipping through his hands, and one moment of loss slides uncertain and confused into only another moment of loss. Artistically they become some of his most fully formed poems. The images of his earlier work—earth, the sea, the smells of weeds, the distances of hills and fields—have spread and extended through the lengthened lyric impulse of his dominating unhappiness. Since the poems come near his moment of crisis their resolutions are temporary—their sense of imminent despair tangled and heavy through their loping lines. *In The Fictive Wish*, from Oregon, 1946, has perhaps the most fully realized flowering of beauty, since it centers on one of his points of almost complete resolution. *The Blowing Of The Seed*, from Sebastopol, California, in 1946, is agonizing in its pained cutting of his body in its sudden despair. "There Will Be Harvest," from Berkeley the next year, in the collection *The Springing Of The Blade*, is dominated with the weight of his life's details, and its involvement with the crisis of his physical love.

In The Fictive Wish is a sustained lyric outburst, its syntax and form left ambiguous, but its emotional clarities brilliantly sustained. From its opening lines the difficulties of understanding are obvious, but the poem's great beauty also begins to unfold with its first hesitant breath. (pp. 100-01)

The poetry that emerged from his years in the Dominican Order increasingly shared the violent physicality of the metaphysical poets—the acerbation of celibacy on a body that is unable to deny its desire for fulfillment. In his book *The Rose Of Solitude* the violence of desire and its turmoil becomes the central problem of the poem—and the desire expressed in the poem is open and explicit, forced in on him by the real embrace of a woman. (p. 103)

The guarded tone of most modern poetry does give the impression of a cautious withdrawal from a social environment so hostile that anything except a kind of guarded mistrust seems too naive as an emotional response. Whatever anyone has believed in as a kind of center for himself or the society has turned out to be mostly useless. This doesn't mean that other poets haven't been involved with the implications of sexuality, haven't brooded over the failure of what Antoninus would call Man and Woman to resolve their differences—it only means that they've decided to let less of themselves be measured against the force of this confrontation. Antoninus refuses to step out of the way, just as he has refused to deny any of the physical implications of his mature work. (pp. 104-05)

Even when the imagery is most strained, the language most driven, these moments in the later work only more deeply etch the complex portrait of himself that the poetry gives us. (p. 106)

Samuel Charters, "Brother Antoninus," in his Some Poems/Poets: Studies in American Underground Poetry Since 1945 *(copyright © 1971 by Samuel Charters), Oyez, 1971, pp. 97-106.*

[After] a long silence, William Everson offers his readers a collection of poems: *Man-Fate, The Swan Song of Brother Antoninus*. These poems are, as he tells us, "a love poem sequence." They explore the implications of his break with monastic life and his new union with Susanna and her infant son. This volume is comprised, he says, "of troubled verse." Indeed. But the trouble does not lie with the subject matter, as Everson fears. Most contemporary readers are sophisticated enough to accept with equanimity the transition of a monk to the lay marital status. My quarrel with Everson arises from his squandering of an enormous talent in gusts of undisciplined verse. The long introductory poem, "Tendril in the Mesh" with its heavy thump of alliteration, affected diction, and baroque metaphors reads like a bad translation of some fourteenth century Northumbrian verse. . . .

After such a buffeting of bathos I probably over-reacted in joy to the quietly lovely "Ebb at Evening." However, this poem and "Man-Fate" seem to me to be eminently successful works of art. Here Everson is master of his craft.

The agony that pulses just beneath the surface of his work establishes a rhythm that is dangerous, threatening, but controlled. Poems such as these and "The Black Hills" demonstrate that Everson remains an artist with reserves of power he has yet to tap. (pp. 124-25)

Claire Hahn, in Commonweal *(copyright © 1975 Commonweal Publishing Co., Inc.; reprinted by permission of Commonweal Publishing Co., Inc.), May 9, 1975.*

F

FORSYTH, Frederick   1938-

Forsyth, a novelist and journalist, is best known for *The Odessa File* and *The Day of the Jackal*.

"The Day of the Jackal" was a taut if occasionally long-winded thriller in which the assassin's beat-the-clock planning meshed excitingly with the book's action. "The Dogs of War" force-marches the reader through more than 300 pages of mercenary "Cat" Shannon's preparations to take over a platinum-rich African country, Zangaro, for a rapacious English mining magnate—only to reach a climax that lies there like lead.

It may be that Frederick Forsyth has got himself stoned on the "Mission Impossible" formula, in which technical know-how substitutes for substance. So much of "Dogs" is concerned with the washing of illicit funds in Brussels and Zurich, the setting up of dummy companies and funny-money dodges, the bribing of gunrunners and government officials with cash and contracts, that the novel gets lost in the intricate shuffle of paper work. (pp. 68-9)

> *S. K. Oberbeck, "Straw Dogs," in* Newsweek *(copyright 1974 by Newsweek, Inc.; all rights reserved; reprinted by permission), July 22, 1974, pp. 68-9.*

The Dogs of War, like *The Day of the Jackal*, is ingeniously plotted, an impressive blend of fact and fiction, written in tight, lucid, masculine prose. In *The Day of the Jackal* we learned, step by step, how to go about knocking off a chief of state. In this one, we learn in equally fine detail how to acquire the personnel, the arms, and the logistical support necessary to invade an African nation. It's a complicated process, and it gets just a bit heavy two-thirds of the way through, but few novelists writing today have Forsyth's flair for building suspense by piling up relatively mundane details.

The Dogs of War is a first-rate thriller, with a beautifully handled opening set in Biafra and a satisfying, though slightly stagy, conclusion. The only real problem is one of characterization. Many of Forsyth's mercenaries are relatively trite figures, their motivation insufficiently explained. And this is a shame, for there is no more interesting and enigmatic group of men. (p. 880)

> *John R. Coyne, Jr., in* National Review (©

National Review, Inc., 1974; 150 East 35th St., New York, N.Y. 10016), August 2, 1974.

Like *Robinson Crusoe*, . . . *The Dogs of War* pays tribute to the skilful management of complex affairs: both novels interest you in process, and Forsyth's novel, like Defoe's, is besotted on the detailed processes of capitalist enterprise. And reading either is corrupting, because you're encouraged to believe that with money all things are possible, and that this is enviably acceptable and proper. The large sums of money freely flashed all over Forsyth's fiction effect a kind of hypnosis. But, in the end, he fails to be as thoroughgoing as Defoe, and bids finally for redemption with a surprising bet-hedging dodge. Shannon [the protagonist], the epilogue reveals, knew all along that he had lung-cancer and only a few months to live—and so is turned into that tomorrow-we-die desperado-cum-epicurean figure of less interesting and more usual fictions. . . . This . . . does nothing, though, to minimise the novel's consistent and protracted celebration of the power of money—not to mention Shannon's own persistence in earning fat wages precisely at the hands of the profiteers. (p. 389)

> *Valentine Cunningham, in* New Statesman (© *1974 The Statesman & Nation Publishing Co. Ltd.), September 20, 1974.*

*   *   *

FRIEDMAN, Bruce Jay   1930-

Friedman is an American short story writer, playwright, and novelist with a talent for evoking the black-comic aspects of contemporary Jewish life. (See also *Contemporary Authors*, Vols. 9-12, rev. ed.)

Bruce Jay Friedman's [play] *Scuba Duba* is a nearly perfect product of the new pseudo-sophistication, being a compendium of varieties of dishonesty, an icon of simulated seriousness and fake wit, a gross indulgence masquerading as a work. And it has been taken up overnight by an audience which constitutes the complement of the exploiters, their target and body politic, an audience wised up to Broadway and avid for what it considers—or has been told to consider—"real," au courant, hit-'em-where-they-live drama, absurd, cocky and daring as hell. (p. 188)

Thematically [Friedman] seems to be dealing with some exceedingly pertinent contemporary social and psychological material, and dramaturgically he appears to be in the full recent tradition of what we might call the scatalogical-absurd. In the stage's new climate, where anything goes and everything is bound to come, it is nevertheless an impressive feat of exploitive playwriting to fuse two such disparate elements of audience appeal—hip sociology and advanced bawdry—into the simulacrum of a dramatic experience. Negroes and tits, together with a dash of Jewish mother-fixation, all of it served up with what has come to be known as "irreverence" or "if cultural rape is inevitable, lie back and enjoy it": such is *Scuba Duba*, whose very title conveys that distinctive lilt of the current imagination as it sets off to appropriate the games other people play. (pp. 188-89)

[Nothing] is going to bring conviction, comic or otherwise, to a play that [exists] as a fraud, an exercise in self-indulgence, and one whose chief interest in social phenomena lies in literally getting back at their seriousness through japes, fashionable wit and the most vulgar kind of mockery. For Friedman's comic impulse, whenever it isn't simply drilling down into that exhausted mine of neurotic Jewishness (mothers, psychiatrists, hypochondria, self-pity) is capitalizing on the tensions and terrors of the interracial situation by letting us hear, in that liberating communal atmosphere the theatre is supposed to provide, the "things we haven't yet dared say" about it. (pp. 189-90)

[A] vocabulary of insult and invective runs through the play as its verbal leitmotif and functions as that kind of sterile catharsis which is obtained whenever something previously forbidden is allowed a temporary and revocable release. It is hermetic, cut off from true feeling and thought, not part of any dramatic action or purpose, sent up into the air in the interests of coarse therapy, of "acting-out." And yet in the play's most cowardly procedure it is all made safe, legitimized by the playwright's having seen to it that we are made aware of our inferiority, that the Negroes come off better, that they get the girl while we, poor schnooks who have been suffering with the hero all along, get the bird. That masochism has long been a mainstay of American commercial theatre, Broadway audiences having reveled in the exposure of their middle-class deficiencies and delusions, is a commonplace observation; the bright new fact is that masochism has spread to the outlying precincts where an audience purportedly hungry for truth and art has really been waiting for its chance at homeotherapy. (p. 190)

[If] Friedman had written a true play, if he had a dramatic imagination (as *Stern* clearly showed he has a novelistic one), his substance would have altered under its pressure, even while his "subject" remained the same. But lacking a dramatic imagination, not knowing how to set people or faculties in confrontation or how to force a histrionic reality out of raw experience, he is left with that experience at its level of deprivation of meaning and form. What he seems to have done to compensate for this is to have picked up information on how other writers have gotten by with their non-plays in this era of formlessness and the cash value of gratuitous outrage. (pp. 190-91)

The damage is to the pretense that we are witnessing something more than a situation comedy. A black comedy if you will, but one whose darkness seemed to me to lie in its revelations of what is likely to be esteemed for some time to come in certain quarters as wit, imagination, theatrical zest and social sophistication. (p. 192)

Richard Gilman, "Anatomy of a Hit" (1967), in his Common and Uncommon Masks: Writings on Theatre 1961-1970 *(copyright © 1971 by Richard Gilman; reprinted by permission of Random House, Inc.), Random House, 1971, pp. 188-92.*

I remember buying a hard-cover copy of Bruce Jay Friedman's first novel, *Stern*—an impulse purchase, made on the strength of the book's first paragraph. Although its brittle style might seem in retrospect a bit facile, too easily imitable (Friedman went on to imitate it badly himself) something was *there*: a sense of the swallowed terror in an ordinary man's ordinary life. Friedman's new novel, *About Harry Towns* . . . comes with the publisher's promise that Friedman has returned to the "moving and serious" work with which he began his career. . . .

The narrative voice of this book sticks close to the consciousness of Harry Towns, who, though melancholy and self-judging, is not what you would call articulate, and the book depends on the irony of inadequate statement. . . . There are episodes in which this spare method works, particularly Towns's pathetic effort to entertain his son while entertaining himself in Las Vegas; and his failure to do what he intends for his parents ("He was Captain Almost"), who die within a few weeks of each other, or, as Towns puts it, "back to back." But in the end you're asked to invest more in Towns's agonies than he seems to do himself. (p. 128)

Richard Todd, in The Atlantic Monthly *(copyright © 1974 by The Atlantic Monthly Company, Boston, Mass.; reprinted with permission), May, 1974.*

The attitudes and assumptions about success, marriage, family, and the Bourgeois American Dream bodied forth in *About Harry Towns* are by this time so shopworn and hackneyed as to require no recapitulation. As the book moves along, the narrator seems to develop a kind of condescending affection for Harry Towns. Nevertheless, as he is portrayed here, Harry is throughout this book a study in enervation and failure; devoid of any moral or imaginative energy; riddled with warranted guilt and self-doubt, but for all the wrong reasons; disaffected to the point of autism; lacking, despite the enviable opulence in which he manages to maintain himself, any visible involvement in work—a man who in middle age suddenly seems to find himself, for reasons beyond his ken, and for reasons never made clear to the reader, living a life that depresses and depletes him. He is, in short, a singularly distasteful and unengrossing individual, and one can only wonder what exactly it is about him that Bruce Jay Friedman expects us to find of moment. (p. 26)

Jane Larkin Crain, in Saturday Review/ World *(copyright © 1974 by Saturday Review/World, Inc.; reprinted with permission), June 1, 1974.*

"The thing I like about Harry Towns," a character comments, "is that everything astonishes him." The thing about Bruce Jay Friedman is that he's a seasoned pro who continues to astonish—leveling off a career which has included three novels, two books of short fiction, a shot at

Hollywood and two very successful plays—with *About Harry Towns*, a collection of recent stories which tickle, depress, gouge below the belt and at second or third reading hold up as nothing less than a joy. . . .

Harry Towns is something of an ordinary language philosopher; his crutch and salvation, his argot, the wide-eyed cynicism of New York street talk, has not been done better since Joseph Mitchell's 1930s New Yorker profiles of odd Manhattan characters. . . .

What Bruce Jay Friedman has accomplished in *About Harry Towns* is to have created a character straight out of a fiction writer's dreams: unique, haunting and completely memorable. Short fiction is possibly the most demanding prose medium, in that one has so little space to sketch so much. Each of Friedman's Harry Towns stories stands on its own (and has) and each complements the other brilliantly. The book is novel, it is short fiction, it is essay. It is a goddamn heartbreaking delight and you are a fool if you miss it.

> *Toby Thompson, "Oh Dad, Poor Dad," in Book World—The Washington Post (© The Washington Post), June 16, 1974, p. 2.*

A number of our toughest novelists have gone so far in the direction of comprehensive in-joking, cosmic cynicism, urbane oversoul that they've out-toughed themselves, out-orbited modernity, and checked themselves back in with the basics—parents, children, marriage, friendship, gutted tradition. Their over-experienced, flailing heroes have reeled through all the circles of our hip Inferno and are now ready to retest their reactions to certain establishment values even if the retesting process hurts. And it does hurt.

Case in point: Bruce Jay Friedman's unheroic but swinging compendium of vulnerabilities named Harry Towns. . . .

[*About Harry Towns* is a] book . . . of brilliant chapters, a series of episodes with little development, change that is no real change, irresolute resolution. . . . Friedman solves nothing for his well-meaning protagonist. . . . (p. 32)

> *James R. Frakes, in The New York Times Book Review (© 1974 by The New York Times Company; reprinted by permission), June 23, 1974.*

Bruce Jay Friedman's "stand-up comic" routines . . . have become an essential trademark of a very impressive body of drama and fiction. In Friedman's comedy, however, there is a disquieting quality. His play *Scuba Duba* was accurately subtitled "a tense comedy," alerting us to the fact that in his work laughs come always at the expense of overbearing psychic pain. His heroes are worriers, with an uncomfortable inheritance of guilt from their Jewish past.

About Harry Towns, Friedman's fourth novel, has much in common with the manner and narrative method of *Stern* and *The Dick*. Harry Towns is more successful and self-assured than the heroes of these earlier novels but he too has to work very hard to keep his guilt at bay. . . .

Friedman's art thrives on the incongruous, the unexpected. Readers familiar with his play in which a steambath turns out to be the afterworld run by a Puerto Rican attendant, with *Stern*, in which a rest home proves to be a place of fierce excitement and activity, or with *A Mother's Kisses*,

in which a Kansas land grant college is virtually taken over by an aggressive Jewish mother, will not be surprised at some of the curious juxtapositions in *About Harry Towns*. . . .

Friedman is a gifted chronicler of the fantasy life of the urban and suburban Jew. The emphasis in *About Harry Towns*, however, is less conspicuously Jewish than in the earlier three novels, the Jewish ingredients largely restricted to the death of Towns' parents. Harry's mother has virtually none of those traits that we associate with the Jewish mother, so dominant and vocal a presence in his other work.

Despite the toning down of Jewish elements, there is much in this novel that echoes his earlier work. Towns' Bryn Mawr girlfriend has appeared before in *Steambath*. Harry's relationship with his son, which is never quite satisfactory, resembles Stern's bumbling filial gestures. Marriages do not work out very well in any of his plays or fiction and promiscuity, real or imagined, is always much in evidence.

The occasional sense of *déjà lu* that one gets from reading *About Harry Towns* reinforces our feeling that Friedman's admirable work is all of a piece. With remarkable consistency, he continues to catch the verbal rhythms that we associate with Philip Roth, Wallace Markfield, Irvin Faust, Jay Neugeboren and other American-Jewish writers who came to maturity in the 1960s. (p. 28)

> *Melvin J. Friedman, in The New Republic (reprinted by permission of The New Republic; © 1974 by The New Republic, Inc.), July 27 & August 3, 1974.*

About Harry Towns specialises in that sour and dead-pan American prose which has been untouched by human hand. But any writer who can create sentences like Ascot hats—"I am Mary Jo Smith, your waitress for tonight, and here is your special chilled fork for the Brazilia Festival Salad"—can't be all cardboard. (p. 183)

[Harry's story] . . . would be the usual blues of urbanised and industrialised Man, but Friedman's flat and sour prose comes into its own very quickly and becomes a very effective description of the toneless way in which Americans conduct their affairs and the bland way in which they conduct each other. I enjoyed this book. (p. 184)

> *Peter Ackroyd, in The Spectator (© 1975 by The Spectator; reprinted by permission of The Spectator), February 15, 1975.*

Bruce Jay Friedman is . . . refreshingly unpretentious, though it will inevitably be added that he has plenty to be unpretentious about. *About Harry Towns* is a . . . walkabout novel: a discursive, anecdotal evocation of the urban male menopause. . . . It is a book that needn't have been written which is probably one of the reasons why it's so easy to read—fluent, droll and moderately likeable. (p. 250)

> *Martin Amis, in New Statesman (© 1975 The Statesman & Nation Publishing Co. Ltd.), February 21, 1975.*

*   *   *

FRIEL, Brian   1929-

Friel is an Irish dramatist and short story writer. (See also *Contemporary Authors*, Vols. 21-22.)

The "real" world of Brian Friel's short stories reaches from Kincasslagh in the west of Donegal through Strabane, Derry City, and Coleraine to Omagh and County Tyrone. Alongside, at times superimposed on, these actual places are the imagined towns, villages, and country districts—Beannafreaghan, Glennafuiseog, Corradinna, Mullaghduff. These are composites and extensions of reality, given substance by an intense receptiveness to the atmosphere of a day or season, to the run of landscape, the play of light and shade, all the tangibles that localize a time and place. The vibrant solidity of the settings is perhaps the strongest single impression left by the world of these stories, memorable because never merely a background décor. (p. 31)

[The] protagonists of [Friel's] stories often have very strongly the feeling that they are of a piece with a place. They are, however, anything but creatures of circumstance. The kinship between man and place may satisfy because it has the assurance of familiarity. But the familiarity may be harsh, demanding; and it is inexhaustible, liable always to disclose unsuspected outlines. There is a process of learning and readjustment. The individual remains his own man. (p. 33)

Friel's regional background and his period give him a quite different point of departure from that of O'Faolain's squireens and peasants. Yet [he] produces similar perceptions of past working into present, of waning life, and the prospect of new growth. For all its melancholy, "Foundry House," like "Among the Ruins," leaves as its final impression, "continuance, life repeating itself and surviving."

It is an arduous survival. Adversity, self-deception, illusion, are the constant challenges in the homogeneous world that knits together . . . from the stories. We are not in the stereotyped Ireland of holy peasants and farcical roisterers. Defeated, or clinging to reality, the characters have the perplexed humanity that earns them Friel's compassion. Though they will not confess, they may recognize, their own illusions, which do not supplant reality but make it tolerable. (p. 42)

The realities of . . . life are subsistence farming and parish horizons, romantic to the tourist, but for the locals meaning drudgery and, often, little-minded parochialism. This parochialism figures in the Ireland of these stories, along with its aging bachelors and outnumbered women. It has its share of stifling respectability, ever ready to be outraged or titillated. (pp. 43-4)

The environment of his stories is a Catholic one. He is not an artist of the whole community, Protestant and Catholic. It is likely impossible that he could be. So widely are the two groups set apart by different school systems, by divergent historical loyalties, by sectarian government, that neither has any real and natural intimacy with the other. . . . [None] of the Northern Writers, of either persuasion, has been able to "transcend the divisions of the region," where sectarian politics thrive on the archaic enmities it is their business to foster. Yet it is also true that Friel's stories betray no least hint of rancor in their author, and, though not "political," irradiate political correspondences, in their recurring motifs of flight and exile, and the whole complex medley of the shifting alliances between man and place.

Friel's settings are mostly rural and the people he writes about poor. . . . [Although] the characters are often hardy, spirited, and their presentation lighthearted, the tone of the stories seems to me predominantly elegiac: for loves, friendships, observances, past or fated to pass. They establish a transient but crucial mood, generated by the traffic between past and present, place and person. The moments to cherish are those that isolate the quality of a life, of a relationship with one's fellows or one's region. The participants sense rather than define their significance; and the stories' purpose is not only to state the moment but to preserve that indeterminateness. As Bernard feels at the end of "Aunt Maggie, the Strong One" . . . , knowledge "of all he had witnessed could no longer be contained in the intellect alone but was dissolving already and overflowing into the emotions." The stories too retain within themselves a core of meaning that resists paraphrase. (pp. 46-7)

Philadelphia [Here I Come!, Friel's first major play, was] of a totally different order of achievement from its predecessors. . . . The logic of the play is not in plot contrivance or "what-happens-next," but in its delicate montage of past and present experience and feeling.

Technically, the most striking device is the representation of Gar by two actors, one the Public, the other the Private, self. Through them, we see him, within the present of this life with father, relive his crucial memories. (pp. 62-3)

The situation and its people exist in depth, through Friel's discerning management of the kinds of statement made accessible by Joyce and O'Neill; and to an extent, though Friel would disagree, by Beckett, if one can conceive of Beckett without the grotesque.

It is a statement first of all, and necessarily, about particular people in a particular grouping. More generally, it is a statement about Ireland, the Ireland of religious and sexual frigidity, of overbearing old age, of joyless, close-mouthed rural puritanism; and of their opposites. The play's humor reflects them and is often, understandably, savage enough. . . . Beyond these peculiarly regional truths, its ironies and an underlayer of certain images carry the play to a wider statement still. Gar's—especially Private's—eloquence, and the inarticulateness it operates on and variously responds to, set up a pattern of speech and silence that enlarges the personal failures of communication. Ample scenes, notably in Gar's symbolic recollection, accentuate the restrictions of closed-up doors and streets, material images of their spiritual counterparts. Ultimately, the play is talking in the broadest terms about estrangement, loneliness, and human hopes of understanding and intimacy. Unequivocally "Irish," *Philadelphia* traverses its regional boundaries.

The language of *The Loves of Cass McGuire*, like that of *Philadelphia*, is naturalistic. Raised and tensed above its actual speech models, it is perfectly authentic in all its registers, remarkably so in Cass's own Americanized idiom. Again, too, it is the language that carries the transitions of mood and, especially here, of perception. For *Cass*, like some of the short stories, is about escape, and the accelerating process of escape, from reality to dreams, an impairment of vision willed or accepted. (pp. 69-71)

In *Philadelphia*, in *Cass*, in *Lovers*, high spirits, laughter, whatever opposites they may have to contend with, are genuinely a release. *Crystal and Fox* has no uncompromised gaiety. At his most lighthearted, there are reservations in Fox, undeclared but evident in how he goes about what he says and does. There are cracks in Fox's behaviour—his bitterness, his enthusiasms and sudden bland indifferences—which are tokens of the faults beneath. A stage-direction suggests their nature: *"his exultation . . . has also a cold brittle quality, [an] edge of menace."*

In *Crystal and Fox* the menace is always at hand. Its most obvious manifestation is in physical brutality, on and off stage. . . . This violence echoes the destructive impulses in him that he half willingly lets take command. (pp. 93-4)

The setting, and the characters that go with it, are different [from his preceding plays]. The only—distant—relative of devices like the Private Gar, direct address to the audience, the "rhapsodies," is the play-within-the-play and the audience at Fox's show. There is no Gar to voice hidden thoughts, no Cass to soliloquize. The method of *Crystal* is more fully naturalistic. Linguistically, too, it is in comparison stripped and severe, working to other purposes the manner of scenes like Master Boyle's leave-taking in *Philadelphia*, where words touch obliquely on feelings. These purposes, most important of all, darken the humor, and in *The Gentle Island*, Friel's next play, trace in human illusions and suspicion the roots of violence. (pp. 94-5)

This is in a way Friel's most Irish play. Its point of departure is the peculiarly regional one of the depopulated off-shore islands. The point of departure, however, is exactly that, a certain state of affairs in a particular locality, circumstance, family. Its purpose is not to elegize the past, to interpret social causes, to attribute any superior "reality" to the simple life. Though all these notions glance through the action, they are not its subject, nor does the play tidy them into answers. The action itself generates its own questions. (p. 97)

The Gentle Island is not only about Inishkeen. Ireland has been historically, and is, a violent land. The play makes an image of this which, in one aspect, has the significance of Seamus Heaney's "The Last Mummer." It expresses also a sense—or the loss of a sense—of possessing, and of belonging (to farm, region, culture), the ownership of land: closely woven, in Irish life and writing, with the violence and bitterness that Yeats, if he did not commend, acknowledged. More broadly, it is a parable of human groping after communion and permanence, and the elisions of contact that frustrate it. *The Gentle Island* marks a new direction in Friel. It very firmly develops new themes and, in the ways indicated, new methods.

The Gentle Island is as different from its predecessors as *Philadelphia* was, promising a continuing evolution in Friel's approach to his medium and what he has to say in it. The two years after *The Gentle Island* precipitated for him a dramatic fable that insisted upon yet different forms to image the continued Northern violence. *The Freedom of the City* . . . took shape over those years, though its origins shelve further back. As a play about the present North, set in Derry in 1970, it engages the problem of maintaining the prismatic individuality of character in a situation—that is, the real-life situation—readier to assume the simplicities of political dogma. (pp. 99-100)

Friel observes an urban face—and catches the urban as accurately as the rural voice—of the society familiar in his work. He has observed in it its "peculiar spiritual, and indeed material, flux." The imprint of that we may identify, for example, in Gar or in Fox; as we may, differently manifested, in *The Freedom of the City*, the same individual

search for some covenant with dissolving, once familiar, prospects. Its methods too—the recurrent dissolves of scene, the forceful management of shifting viewpoints, the commentaries—are revisions of technique that appropriate the new location. The play is recording tremors of a social mutation. (pp. 105-06)

Of . . . Irish dramatists, Friel has unquestionably the body of work most distinguished by its substance, integrity, and development, well able to stand with that of his English contemporaries. Their writing has a variety and intensity which, even where he does not particularly take to it, Friel much admires. There is no question, however, of an "influence" from any of these sources other than in [an] indirect way. . . . Nor is it easy to enter Friel into any of the Irish "schools." His plays are obviously not isolated from the Irish traditions; but he is a Northern Catholic, the first important dramatist from that background, which inflects his distinctive, personal voice.

"I would like," he has said, "to write a play that would capture the peculiar spiritual, and indeed material, flux, that this country is in at the moment. This has got to be done, for me anyway, at a local, parochial level, and hopefully this will have meaning for other people in other countries." This is a fair description of the plays Friel has already written, regarded as a composite, a single, continuing testimony. Their content has its own interest, but the content does not explain its force. . . . In each of his plays Friel achieves the process of dramatic organization, the conjunction of its parts, that discovers order in observed facts, and conveys their meaning. In each of them too, . . . he has varied his method and changed the point of attack.

This inventive command of design gives Friel's plays their excellence. (pp. 109-10)

Both his short stories and his plays supply the creative premises where writer and audience collaborate. In the plays his development has been toward a greater simplicity, but no less subtlety, of method. (p. 110)

> *D. E. S. Maxwell, in his* Brian Friel (© *1973 by Associated University Presses*), *Bucknell University Press, 1973.*

Brian Friel's *The Freedom of the City* is about the troubles in Londonderry, Northern Ireland, during 1970. It is marred by several narrative knotholes. . . . But the author is not aiming at suspense nor does he desire his play to be "thrilling." He is setting forth a simple stream of events which have a meaning he wishes us to contemplate in a quasi-Brechtian mode.

It may also be objected that, given the play's subject matter, its tone is much too mild. On the other hand, it is possible that the low key Friel employs may be intended to undercut the accusations of mere "propaganda" that often are leveled at such plays. He avoids the specific political issues involved. What he shows is the innocence of most of the people hurt—in this case, killed—in such social struggles, and, more important, what moves them to take part in them when they are ignorant of what is basically at stake. . . .

The play's importance for me is that it deals with an immediate situation typical (or symbolic) of much more than itself. Its very lack of sensational dramatics or clamorous partisanship lends it a peculiar pathos. Such plays are perhaps more telling and useful at present than fashionable declarations of cosmic "absurdity." *The Freedom of the City* is decently written with quiet touches of humor which make it the more affecting. (pp. 315-16)

> *Harold Clurman, in* The Nation *(copyright 1974 by the Nation Associates, Inc.), March 9, 1974.*

*   *   *

FUGARD, Athol   1932-

Fugard, a South African award-winning playwright, essayist, and short story writer concerned with the tragedies of his native land, is South Africa's best known dramatist.

Boesman and Lena is the third work by the South African dramatist Athol Fugard to be produced in this country: the previous ones were *Blood Knot . . .* and *Hello and Goodbye. . . .* Fugard is white and, as writer and director, has devoted himself to theater with "non-Europeans" in his country. . . .

[*Boesman and Lena*] is not a protest play, though the pain of race hatred flames through it; it becomes, quickly and surely, a drama of all human beings in their differing captivities, suffering from and inflicting hate. Boesman and Lena are brown, the old Kaffir man is black, and the specifics of their wretched lives are caused by the history and policies of their country; but Fugard makes very clear that, within the circumference of their lives, they represent the larger world. He is not saying—not by the wildest stretch of self-coddling imagination—that racial injustices do not signify; he is saying that those injustices are an extremity of the cruelty in all men. The reason that his play achieves towering height—as in the main it does—is because it *includes* the agony of *apartheid* and shows that *apartheid* is not devil-inflicted but manmade, and that Boesman is a man, too.

Fugard works with small means: his previous plays had two characters each, this one has three. The influence of Eugene O'Neill has always seemed strong in him, particularly in *Hello and Goodbye*, which dealt with some rather egregious symbols of a (white) family's doom. O'Neill's influence seems strong again here—but here it is the later, greater O'Neill, not the patent symbolist. What is this play but another long day's journey into a very dark night? And the quintessential dynamics is like that in late O'Neill: drama not by the encounter of obstacle but by the stripping naked of lives. This "moment" of two hours is an ontogeny

that recounts our phylogeny: because Fugard has seen that, by telling crystalline truth about these wretches, with no clutter of theatrical device, he could not possibly leave us out. He has embraced these people so fiercely and lovingly that in their rags and drunkenness and cunning and persistence, they move through a small epic of contemporary man. I can think of no naturalistic play since [Gorki's] *The Lower Depths* that—far from using its subject for clinical study—so completely converts almost protozoan characters into vicars for us all. . . . (p. 16)

This play comes before us sublimely innocent of the news that this kind of theater is supposed to be dying, as many (including me) have said, with reason enough. *Boesman and Lena* is the kind of play that "nobody" writes any more, representational, sequential, mimetic; but it is rooted in such a felt need, its symbolism is so thoroughly assimilated, its tragic view so wholesouled, that it again proves a sometimes forgotten truth: no art-form is dead so long as it fits the purpose of a committed and talented artist. (p. 25)

> *Stanley Kauffmann, in* The New Republic *(reprinted by permission of* The New Republic; © *1970 by The New Republic, Inc.), July 25, 1970.*

Athol Fugard . . . is South Africa's most prominent playwright. By virtue of this reputation, Mr Fugard is also therefore one of the South African government's most prominent critics. His criticism is not polemically levelled, however, at pigmy politicians, but is expressed in a canon of dramatic writing which registers, in anguished and poetic terms, the suffering endured at the hands of those who rule and legislate. (p. 34)

> *Michael Coveney, "Challenging the Silence," in* Plays and Players *(© copyright Michael Coveney 1973), November, 1973, pp. 34-7.*

[Plays] dealing with burning questions of the day are surely to be welcomed, provided that they are not mere agitprop exercises; and those of Athol Fugard most certainly are not. Indeed, Mr. Fugard's pictures of life in the dustbins of South African society have been widely hailed for the wrong reasons; readers of many reviews of them might easily suppose that these too were mere propaganda exercises. Though they have their faults, notably a sort of sentimental *nostalgie de la boue*, they are nothing of the sort, but at the least deeply sympathetic studies of ill-equipped people in miserable circumstances. (p. 22)

> *J. W. Lambert, in* Drama, *Spring, 1974.*

G

GARDNER, John   1933-

Gardner, a medieval scholar and a prolific novelist, is often cited as one of America's most brilliant and exciting writers of fiction.

The previous Gardner novels I've read [that is, before *Nickel Mountain*]—*The Wreckage of Agathon, Grendel* and *The Sunlight Dialogues*—were interesting (particularly from a technical standpoint) and, in some instances, engrossing; but they all had a disturbing bloated quality. For one thing, Gardner's language never seemed to let up. Sheriff Clumly of *The Sunlight Dialogues* couldn't simply wince; he had to wince "as if he bit into a lemon.". . . In addition to the inflated, often awkward, prose, the reader had to contend with the author's incessant preaching. Gardner has been called a "philosophical novelist," and to some extent he is, if by the term one simply means a novelist who explores various ideas and concepts. All well and good. We appreciate such exploration. But too often in these three novels Gardner's ideas were merely recorded, not dramatized, with the result that the "characters" became mouthpieces for the author, and the ideas, presented with little or no subtlety, seemed pedestrian and obvious. No wonder the reader grew weary of Grendel's terribly stylized ranting and raving, Agathon's contrived meditations on freedom, and the Sunlight Man's all-too-perfectly calculated, at-the-drop-of-a-hat speeches on freedom, irrationality, order, and assorted subjects. Gardner seemed to be an incurable preacher. Only in a John Gardner novel would you find a dragon saying: "The essence of life is to be found in the frustrations of established order." Even in his epic poem, *Jason and Medea*, an eminently forgettable volume, he was determined to deliver ideas, even if they appeared ludicrous ("How, that is, does an astral apogee come to know more about upright action than a vertical line or the loudest possible physical thump?").

The reader of *Nickel Mountain*, then, is relieved to discover that in this "pastoral novel" (Gardner's term) the author has dispensed with blatant philosophizing and has toned down his language. . . . Theoretically, *Nickel Mountain* should be a fine book, the kind of straight, unpretentious novel of character and environment we hoped Gardner might write for a change of pace. Sadly enough, it reveals that although the author does have a gift for describing rural life—in this case, a small Catskill community

of the nineteen-fifties—he doesn't have much talent for creating characters or for sustaining sufficient interest in them. . . .

Gardner may have been attempting to "modernize" the pastoral form. But what he has created is simply a traditional novel that doesn't succeed in traditional terms. The dust-jacket notes claim that *Nickel Mountain* is warm and moving, but these are exactly the traditional virtues that the book so badly lacks. The characters fail to touch us and involve us because they haven't been fully realized and because what often happens to them recalls events in second-rate fiction and drama. . . .

John Gardner has indeed come down to earth in this novel, but, unfortunately, he seemed more comfortable in his own special realm, the one populated, in part, by intensely philosophical prisoners and dragons. (pp. 536-37)

> *Ronald De Feo, in* Commonweal *(copyright © 1974 Commonweal Publishing Co., Inc.; reprinted by permission of Commonweal Publishing Co., Inc.), March 1, 1974.*

Where Gardner's *The Sunlight Dialogues* was a mock nineteenth-century novel about a real twentieth-century dilemma, [*Nickel Mountain*] is (or is trying to be) a real nineteenth-century novel about the timeless ordinariness of most of our lives, measured out as they are in universal events and rituals like marriage, childbirth, illness, mistaken kindnesses, and accidental death. The language, compared with Gardner's earlier, flashier excursions, is much chastened, and only occasionally falls into swooning simile. . . .

Several things go wrong, though. First, people crack up in the country (and in this novel) too, and since Gardner, like most writers, is more at home with people cracking up than he is with people just going about their humdrum business, the contrast between city and country begins to pale a bit. Second, the traffic between sophisticated writers and simple lives can go only one way. You can show, that is, how complex simple lives are when you look at them closely, and here as in *The Sunlight Dialogues* Gardner does this well. What you can't show, if you're a complicated writer, is how simple simplicity is. All you can offer is a set of mirror images of your own complication. Then again, you can show how simple people delve into meta-

131

physics in their own language, and Gardner, again, does this rather well. I don't think you can presume, with any success, to render their obscure states of mind in your own grand, speculative manner. . . .

Here as in his other fiction, Gardner shows a marvelous gift for making *stories* ask balanced, intricate questions, for getting his complex questions into tight stories. . . . (p. 22)

> *Michael Wood, in* The New York Review of Books *(reprinted with permission from* The New York Review of Books; *copyright* © *1974 NYREV, Inc.), March 21, 1974.*

I happen to like *The Sunlight Dialogues*, perhaps because I am fond of magicians, and the novel's moving force is a lunatic illusionist. But although the characters are thoughtfully drawn and the scenes work well, the book does provoke the same doubt raised by such mighty works as, for instance, Barth's *Giles Goat-Boy*: namely, whether the author has assembled fictional engines unnecessarily huge and powerful for the ideas that are to be moved about the stage.

Nickel Mountain is quite another matter. It is gentle and pastoral—meaning, I suppose, that all the beasts in its country landscape are tame and that the reader can afford to dream a bit without worrying that he will be savaged. The author knows exactly, of course, the restful calm he has created, and the very strong attraction of the novel lies in the art with which Gardner guides the dreaming. (p. 1)

The effect of the novel is astonishingly strong. The characters have been criticized for being vague and unrealized, but this, I think, misses the point. Gardner's intention, it seems clear, is to portray time, the strange slow drift in which we are all carried along. It is not that events do not have meaning, or that we do not sometimes see ourselves and others with sharp understanding. But time's huge flow is so utterly mysterious, the author seems to be saying, that smaller mysteries and perceptions blur and become reverie. There is nothing in the least arcane or literary in this haunting sense of time's movement; a boy can feel it as he lies on his back in meadow grass listening to crickets and an old man can feel it thinking of the boy. Gardner has caught the mystery in this simple and mysterious novel.

Gardner himself, on the contrary, is not yet caught. His remarkable progression of novels does not seem to have defined his limits. There is no evidence that he is merely a talented dabbler in different modes, or less than a wholehearted artist. (p. 4)

> *Jack Skow, "Time's Slow Reverie," in* Book World—The Washington Post *(*© *The Washington Post), March 31, 1974, pp. 1, 4.*

[The] beautiful hues of Gardner's New York State landscape and the auras emanating from his leading characters [in *Nickel Mountain*] . . . appear to be more the function of the viewer's lenses than of the things and people themselves.

Forty years ago, William Empson dismissed such writing as a form of pastoral. . . . In a book that he calls "a pastoral novel," John Gardner has attempted once again the paradoxical task of speaking for the speechless and feeling for the numbed. But he does so by meeting Empson's objec-

tions directly, dispensing with the traditional methods of realism and returning to the root form of such narratives. Thus he does not attempt to test the values of the class he writes about but, rather, of the class to which he belongs and for whom he writes. (p. 759)

No page of *Nickel Mountain* lacks the imprint of [his] fulsome prose in which highly colored natural description takes precedence over questions of human psychology and narrative action. The effect is, moreover, closer to lyric than epic, scene after painted scene linked in the reader's mind by virtue of the feelings engendered by Gardner's moving descriptions rather than any logical connections between one notation about a character and the next. Despite carefully planted assurances that by the end of the novel Soames has "discovered . . . the idea of magical change," no transformations of character or action have occurred. Thus, while the setting of *Nickel Mountain* resembles that of Gardner's *The Sunlight Dialogues* . . . , no scene could be further removed from the fields where order struggled with chaos and time with decay. Here thought vaporizes and metaphysics shrivels into the plodding sententiousness of Henry Soames pulling off his socks at the end of a day and "wondering what it all meant."

Each of Gardner's previous novels does in fact present itself, as well as any novel can, as a dramatization of "what it all means," and each concludes with the death of the main character as if to suggest that death—and the endings of novels—stand as the final response to all conjecture about meaning. In the last chapter of *Nickel Mountain*, Gardner leads Henry Soames to the edge of a grave. But he cannot make him die. Although Soames has a "heart condition" and feels "as old as the mountains," the range to which he compares himself is the fairy-tale chain in a region where death has no dominion. In his world without end, only the prose lives, flares up, flickers, fumes, and finally gutters out. Gardner has presented us with the final version of pastoral. (p. 760)

> *Alan Cheuse, in* The Nation *(copyright 1974 by the Nation Associates, Inc.), June 15, 1974.*

With seven books published in the past five years, Novelist John Gardner, has confounded the theory that quality can only come slowly, and in small doses. Gardner . . . has managed to lob serious, stylistically adventuresome fiction over the barricades of academic coteries and onto the middle levels of America's bestseller lists. He is also a fabulist with a heart, capable of making the arcane both accessible and emotionally stirring. Near the end of *The King's Indian*, Gardner briefly introduces himself as a man who, "with the help of Poe and Melville and many another man, wrote this book." The attributions are graceful but hardly necessary, for Poe and Melville rattle around in this book like a couple of dybbuks. Gardner seems possessed by their eagerness to stare into the black holes of transcendental optimism, and two of his nine tales flatter the 19th century authors with unabashed imitation.

In *The Ravages of Spring* a middle-aged country doctor on a round of house calls finds himself threatened by a string of tornadoes. He seeks shelter in a clapboard-gothic house and lands in the middle of a Vincent Price movie. It includes a mad scientist, a demented, beautiful woman and a terrible secret: through genetic tinkering, the scientist claims to have discovered how to populate the world with exact duplicates of himself and his companion. Solipsism teeters toward the edge of reality. The storm explodes the house like an inflated hypothesis, but the doctor survives— and so, in a way, does the scientist.

The King's Indian, the title story, is a much longer and more complex pastiche. Shanghaied aboard a whaling ship, young Jonathan Upchurch is forced to play Ishmael to a crazed Ahab of a captain. The ship's quest is not for a white whale but, as Upchurch slowly learns, for the mysterious duplicate of itself, reported sunk on its last voyage. Is he surrounded, then, by ghosts? Or is the captain out to smash determinism by carrying his ship safely past a meeting with its foreshadowed self? As adventures and mysteries multiply, a third possibility begins to appear: a hoax, launched by a vaudeville magician, swelling out of control, may be engulfing both perpetrators and dupes alike. . . .

Gardner does not restrict himself to century-old American settings. He is also at home in classical antiquity (*Jason and Medea*) and the late Dark Ages (*Grendel*). He fills pages with royalty and serfs, knights, monks, prisoners and jailers. Magic is taken for granted; humble facts are made to seem miraculous. A lesser writer might stretch the profligate inventiveness of this single book into a long career.

Gardner uses exuberant creations in the service of a stern task: to sneak up on truth without startling it into sham abstractions. As one of his characters says: "The part [of life] we understand is irrelevant." So Gardner sets conflicting metaphysics whirling, then records the patterns thrown out by their lines of force. One situation constantly recurs, as it did in Gardner's ambitious *The Sunlight Dialogues*: traditionalist meets anarchist; an inherited past must defend itself against a plotless future. In *Pastoral Care*, a young minister tries to remind his complacent congregation of Christianity's revolutionary roots. A bomb-tossing student takes him at his word, graphically reminding his appalled mentor of the etymology of the word radical.

Gardner knows that such bedrock dualities never change and are never resolved. He also shows that they can crop up anywhere, in the most mundane or marvelous of forms, and that stories can preserve more of their truths than battle reports from competing ideologies. His stories—fanciful, allusive, studded with archaisms ("erumpent," "zacotic," "flambuginous")—are diverting jaunts around central mysteries. With Gardner as tour guide, getting there is all the fun.

> *Paul Gray, "American Gothic," in* Time *(reprinted by permission from* Time, The Weekly Magazine; *copyright Time Inc.), December 30, 1974, p. 56.*

[Five] stories, all somber in tone, make up "The Midnight Reader," which is followed [in *The King's Indian*] by three "Tales of Queen Louisa," spoofs of love and war in a medieval setting. "The King's Indian" itself is an amazing novella which incorporates elements from *The Rime of the Ancient Mariner, Moby Dick, The Narrative of Arthur Gordon Pym*, and much else—in line with Gardner's evident belief that the problems that plague us have persisted throughout history. (p. 1)

These are excellent stories. Nobody writing today is better than Gardner at clothing the idea in flesh. Nonetheless, there is something about *The King's Indian*—the amount of sleight-of-hand, perhaps, or the fact that the characters' concerns are so exclusively philosophical—that keeps it from having the impact of its literary antecedents. [But] Gardner himself [is] aware of the dangers of playfulness. . . . (pp. 1-2)

Gardner's chief value, one suspects, is less that of the individual artist—the Poe or Melville or Kafka or Dostoevsky sunk in his own life and theorizing with desperate, often naive, seriousness—than that of the intellectual, in touch with a tradition, who is skilled enough to connect us with the past. And in an age of lost traditions and broken connections, this is indeed a considerable value. (p. 2)

> *Michael Harris, "A Limitless Shadow," in* Book World—The Washington Post (© The Washington Post), *January 12, 1975, pp. 1-2.*

The stories in *The King's Indian* allow John Gardner to put on a variety of narrative masks, from that of teller of hip fairy tales about anxiety, madness, and marital strain to jaunty impersonations of Poe, Kafka, Melville, and John Gardner. And of course the beauty of masks is that they can come off whenever an effect is required. For example, "John Napper Sailing Through the Universe," a tale of *la vie bohème* centered on an artist with the same name as the illustrator of Gardner's *Sunlight Dialogues*, is told by a narrator named—like a good many other people in the book —John, a college teacher who like Professor John Gardner lives on a farm in southern Illinois and is writing an epic poem about Jason and Medea. . . .

I wish Gardner weren't so eager to join the game of self-conscious fiction. Insisting on the arbitrariness of illusions puts all the cards in the novelist's hand, and I feel a little surly about Gardner's assumption that I, the reader, am safely "real" (how can he be so sure?) while letting me see that "John Gardner the man that . . . wrote this book" is just another disguise of a trickster who, like any teacher, has reserved the real power for himself.

It's not inevitably a bad thing for a novelist to teach in a college and know a lot about literature and modern thought. One of the best stories here, "Pastoral Care," takes place in a college town in southern Illinois beset by revolutionary student unrest. To be sure, the troubled protagonist is a clergyman, not a teacher, but the professions have their resemblances. Elsewhere the voices are those of a literate country doctor, a medieval monk, a prison administrator, a smart parent amusing his kids with more than they're likely to grasp; and in all these clerkish voices one hears an academic man trying out hypothetical other selves in situations in which a literary education can exercise itself to greater effect than it usually does on campus.

Gardner's Grendel and Sunlight Man were deracinated professors, too, speculative minds placed in situations whose hostility or indifference provided a splendid tragi-comic stage for eloquent failure. And *Nickel Mountain*, his most restrained and best novel, has fine moments in which "ordinary" people are granted the emotional equivalent of intellectual subtlety, moments that work because self-consciousness and self-irony are not attached to them.

Nothing in *The King's Indian* matches these successes. The recurrent motif is craziness, not the depressing madness of the real world but in the more amusing sense of "crazy" that in bookish conversation (like "marvelous," "incredible," and "unbelievable") simply means exciting and imaginative. . . .

Much of this is made tolerable by Gardner's great gifts for language and moral atmosphere. But only in the title story, "The King's Indian" (referring, appropriately, to a chess gambit), is there anything like the amplitude of form and conception needed to keep Gardner's eloquence from swamping the fable. . . .

Academic vaudeville can be good fun, and Gardner in these stories does play with classic American uneasiness, the mixture of fascination and mistrust toward portentous appearances, the yearning to strike through the mask even as you fear that there will, after all, be nothing much behind it. But *The King's Indian* is irksome in its reaching for the outrageous, the crazy, the (I'm afraid it must be said) cute, and I can only hope that it has done this immensely gifted writer some good to get these things out of his system. (p. 34)

> *Thomas R. Edwards, in* The New York Review of Books *(reprinted with permission from* The New York Review of Books; *copyright © 1975 NYREV, Inc.), February 20, 1975.*

Though I admire John Gardner's talent, ambition, and inventiveness, I've never been able to warm up to his work. The author has what might be called a sweet tooth for philosophy. He is often so determined to inject philosophical dialogues, concepts, and references into his work that he will introduce them even if they break the mood of the tale he is telling, interrupt the action, appear totally absurd, pretentious, and contrived in context. For example, in *Grendel*, Gardner's clever, though at times stifling takeoff on the Beowulf story, the title character visits a dragon who speaks in the following manner: "Importance is primarily monistic in its reference to the universe. Limited to a finite individual occasion, importance ceases to be important." The reader is, of course, willing to accept the fantasy of the book and go along with the talking monster business, but must he contend with a dragon who sounds as if he's conducting a seminar in philosophy? Such a passage not only destroys the mood of the fiction (for we can only believe that the philosophic author is spouting these very carefully chosen words), but it also gives the piece a bloated quality.

Almost all of Gardner's books have suffered from this peculiar brand of inflation and heavy-handedness. Although the reader appreciated the meticulous rendering of small-town life in *The Sunlight Dialogues*, he couldn't accept the contrived philosophical tug of war between Sheriff Clumly and the Sunlight Man (whose at-the-drop-of-a-hat monologues were too artfully structured to be believed). Once again, in the poem *Jason and Medeia*, a long, misguided venture, Gardner's characters often became mere mouthpieces for their obsessively philosophic creator. *Nickel Mountain*, Gardner's next work, was almost a welcomed change of pace. In this somber rural tale focusing on an inarticulate outsider, the irritating philosophical passages were noticeably, mercifully absent. The novel really didn't work—it was too cold and studied and the characters never truly sprang to life—but at least it did promise a less pretentious Gardner to come.

Unfortunately, *The King's Indian* . . . is filled with the same type of self-indulgence that marred so many of his earlier efforts. And to make matters worse, there is in this collection of tales a good amount of still fashionable, though by now tedious, literary game-playing—in-jokes on narrative technique and the art of fiction, allusions to other writers and their work, the use of contemporary jargon in historical pieces. . . . The three stories dealing with mad Queen Louisa are supposed to be sparkling and witty, but come across as silly sketches tossed off by a professor between classes. . . . Of the two stories with a contemporary setting, "Pastoral Care" is the more accomplished and substantial. In fact, this refreshingly quiet piece, focusing on a Presbyterian minister's encounter with a student, shows that Gardner can do without his bag of tricks—the story is direct and effective.

Sadly, that bag of tricks is fully employed in the title story (a novella, actually) and the results are maddening. "The King's Indian" is a huge crazy comic invention in which a host of authors are evoked and parodied—Melville, Hawthorne, Poe, Coleridge, Charles Brockden Brown, to name only a few. Jonathan Upchurch's narrative, describing his voyage on a whaling ship populated by an insane cast of characters, is totally outrageous, containing enough twists and turns of plot, hoaxes, conspiracies, coincidences, to support dozens of tales. Gardner obviously had fun writing it, and I wish I could report that I had fun reading it. But one gets the idea soon enough, and the tale, for all its mad energy, rapidly becomes a bore. (pp. 234-35)

The King's Indian surprises me on two counts. One, that a writer of Gardner's sophistication could settle for such philosophical and literary doodling. And two, that so many critics could be charmed by the performance. This kind of encouragement Gardner surely does not need. (p. 235)

> *Ronald De Feo, "A Sweet Tooth for Philosophy," in* National Review *(© National Review, Inc., 1975; 150 East 35th St., New York, N.Y. 10016), February 28, 1975, pp. 234-35.*

All but two of the stories in [*The King's Indian*] . . . are cast in specialized literary forms—fairy tales, allegory, sea yarns, gothic horror stories. . . . The first thing that strikes one in a reading of this and others of his derivative writings is Gardner's sly and exuberant affection for his literary models, coupled with his own meticulous craftsmanship and inventiveness. After a while, though, one begins to suspect that underneath all the razzle-dazzle and the fancy footwork rather less may be going on than meets the eye. Whether Gardner is in fact "celebrating" (as he puts it) the writers he imitates or merely playing around with them, his achievement suffers by the comparison; his piecemeal allegorical and symbolic schemes, lacking intelligible structure, come more and more to resemble, rather than to illuminate, the metaphysical mystery land through which he journeys. (pp. 25-6)

> *Jane Larkin Crain, in* Saturday Review *(copyright © 1975 by Saturday Review/World, Inc.; reprinted with permission), March 8, 1975.*

Ever since 1971, when *Grendel* burst upon the scene, all "heaped-up howls of rage" and "monstrous energy of grief,'' John Gardner's books have erupted at frequent intervals with a mighty thump and glitter. Dazzled by the display, reviewers have stood at a safe distance, marveling at the chunks of pure poetry interspersed with interminable metaphysical ramblings, and murmuring, ''O my! O my!'' like Mole.

Stupefaction has been guaranteed, for not only does Gardner put on a good show, but he's a virtuoso, too. *Grendel* was a reworking of the Anglo-Saxon *Beowulf*; *The Wreckage of Agathon* a satire set in ancient Sparta; *Jason and Medea* an epic poem 354 pages long; *The Sunlight Dialogues* a vast, clotted meditation on the laws of the universe as demonstrated in upper New York State; *Nickel Mountain* a romantic pastorale that moved at a snail's pace.

Gardner's work consistently wins such extravagant praise that it looks as if people are responding to something more than the books themselves, which, for all their grand design, have moments of monumental unreadability. . . . The likeliest explanation for such unguarded optimism seems to be that, when so many current novels are just slick and sexy products or slapdash journalese, weary reviewers, homesick for literature, are seduced by Gardner's rampant *writerishness*: his obsession with form, his literary in-jokes and elaborate imitations.

In *The King's Indian*, a collection of eight short stories and a tale, this writerishness is more marked than before, which is terrific for those who want to feel reassured about the continuity of literary tradition, et cetera, and for devotees of genre writing (in particular ghost stories, horror stories, and sea yarns), but disappointing for everybody else. Four of the best stories are to be found under the heading ''The Midnight Reader'' and have, as central characters, a priest, a doctor, a monk, and the warden of a prison. By tradition, all of them are the guardians either of authority or of an established system of belief, which makes them powerfully symbolic figures. Each man is exposed to some uncanny threat, a sinister undermining of the foundations of his life, and by extension, society itself. It's Gardner's old preoccupation, seen most clearly in *The Sunlight Dialogues*— man's imposition of his own intellectual order on an indifferent, chaotic universe and his reluctance to face ''reality.'' Here he borrows from Poe and Kafka to make ''reality'' especially terrifying. (pp. 3-4)

These stories have a certain eerie fascination but lose their effect because they're so self-consciously clever. Gardner does love to show off. . . .

Short stories seem to bring out the worst in Gardner, for when he's not being arch, he's plunging headlong into romantic agony, and fretting tirelessly over the fact that life has no meaning. . . . Whoops and gasps and reels and shrieks worked in *Grendel*. They were thrillingly new, but used too often they're nothing more than good sound effects. . . . His whole stance, of one who has dared to peer into the void, begins to look like a spectacular but ham performance. . . .

[An] essential part of Gardner's success [is] his relentless belief in the writer as hero or holy man, and the devastating *hubris* with which he demonstrates it. Such single-mindedness has its attractive aspects, and the pomposity that tends to accompany it has in the past been diluted in the comfortable narrative sprawl of his longer writing, or outshone by his poetry. But this time he has shown himself standing squarely center-stage, performing, haranguing, and lecturing, and never quite holding the crowd. (p. 4)

> *Helen Rogan, ''Whoops and Gasps,'' in* Bookletter *(copyright 1975 by Harper's Magazine; reprinted from the April 14, 1975 issue by special permission), April 14, 1975, pp. 3-4.*

* * *

GENET, Jean   1910-

Genet is a French playwright, novelist, and poet; but, Sartre has written, his eternal essence consists in his being a thief. After the early prison poems, Genet wrote the autobiographical novels, deliberately antisocial accounts of homosexual love and criminal violence which led some to call him a ''black magician,'' before turning to drama, for him the perfect literary form for the incantatory expression of dream and ritual. (See also *Contemporary Authors,* Vols. 13-16, rev. ed.)

The concept of sovereignty has always obsessed the imagination of Genet. Sartre believes that Genet chose evil because that was precisely the realm in which he could hope to reach a status of sovereignty. In *Miracle de la Rose*, in those passages where the character Harcamone is meditating in his cell, the ideal of sovereignty is ascribed to the assassin who is about to be executed. The state of evil is the reverse of the state of holiness. Genet plays on the two worlds because he finds them similar in the sense that the extremes of both are forbidden to an ordinary man, and that both are characterized by violence and danger.

The theory of alienation is prevalent in contemporary literature, and it has never been orchestrated so richly, with such tragic and sensual poignancy, as in Genet's books. The existences evoked in his novels and plays, which are obviously his own existence, cannot find their realization. These characters fully understand how estranged, how alienated they are, and they are both obsessed and fascinated by this state.

Genet began writing in prison with the avowed purpose of composing a new moral order which would be his. His intention was to discover and construct a moral order that would explain and justify his mode of life. (pp. 51-2)

The central drama is always the struggle between the man in authority and the young man to whom he is attracted. The psychological variations of this struggle are many. Each of the novels is a different world in which the same drama unfolds. (pp. 52-3)

The hallucinatory beauty with which Jean Genet has expressed his system of morality and his philosophy of evil increases the difficulty of defining his tradition and assessing his worth. He is the arch-romantic, far more the artist than the philosopher. His nature is essentially religious. His is also a nature of extreme passivity. In this sense, he is more comparable to Baudelaire than to Rimbaud or Lautréamont. He is the opposite of the revolutionist and the reformer. He is the man living just outside of the normally-constituted society. He has no desire to play a part in society, especially no desire to mount in society, to triumph over it. He is therefore the opposite of Balzac's Rastignac and Stendhal's Julien Sorel. (p. 53)

> *Wallace Fowlie, in* Contemporary European Novelists, *edited by Siegfried Mandel (copy-*

The Maids, The Balcony, and *The Blacks* are three fine examples of metatheater. Genet's characters act out, as in a play within a play, the parts which their fantasy craves. Each one is in a sense the author of his own play. Genet brilliantly develops the theme that illusion is inescapable. Like O'Neill in *The Iceman Cometh*, he is seeking to demonstrate that illusions are indispensable to life, but there is a basic difference between his work and that of O'Neill. Whereas Genet's protagonists know that they are embracing illusion, O'Neill makes it clear that his alcoholic derelicts, who are unable to cope with reality, are better off nursing their pipe dreams.

What distinguishes Genet as a playwright is that he breaks down the barriers traditionally interposed between imagination and reality. A homosexual and thief who discovered art as his means of deliverance, he is a perspectivist who beholds reality not as a fixed, empirical datum, but as something to be shaped. Reality, as he portrays it, remains enigmatic and paradoxical. Struggling to transcend the limitations imposed by the life of reason, he strives to go beyond the artificially devised dualism of fact and fantasy, matter and mind, reality and dream. Genet is the savage iconoclast for whom truth is but false appearance. The vision he projects on the stage is no more to be relied on; it may be false too, but at least it serves a good purpose in exposing the collective conspiracy of falsehood. . . . (p. 67)

From the beginning of his literary career, Genet, like Ionesco, was concerned with the problem of determining what is reality, what is truth. Reality is full of disparate, deceptive, and conflicting elements. Even the imagination is impotent to recapture the truth of the past, for this past is reconstructed by the medium of memory and the flow of dream imagery. Like Gide and Rivière, Genet is unsparing in his efforts to achieve full sincerity; he is concerned, above all, to know himself. What fascinates him is the rich potentiality of the drama as ritual; it ceases to be an aesthetic spectacle and becomes a communion that involves both actors and audience. That is how Genet seeks to batter down the obstacles that prevent communication. He tears aside the veils of dissimulation society uses to cover up its festering vices.

The Maids ingeniously exploits the resources of the theater in order to challenge and subvert the conventional notions of what reality is. Genet builds up a facade that seems eminently plausible and then proceeds to tear it down and reveal what lies concealed behind it. The play deliberately employs a technique of mystification. It is extremely difficult, in following this dialectic of dissimulation, to disentangle the imaginary aspect from the real. If Genet is attracted to the theater by the element "of fake, of sham, of artificiality," he offers no version of what we can confidently accept as the truth. . . . *The Maids* brings out the extraordinary degree to which all men, in their shifting roles of subordination, play the staged game of duplicity. . . . (pp. 67-8)

The Balcony offers a striking example of a play that endeavors to shatter theatrical illusion by showing that *all* is illusion. From her balcony, by means of her peep-hole sys-

tem, Madame Irma sees that her customers betray no inclination to gain their ends in reality; their gratification comes from the knowledge that all this takes place in a realm of fantasy. They know they are not what they seem; it is only the illusion they crave. Genet focuses on the brothel as a microcosmic reflection of society. Only in Madame Irma's establishment does the true character of reality emerge. At the end of the play, Irma addresses the audience directly; she will prepare her costumes and studios for the following day, when business will go on as usual, regardless of which political regime is installed in power. . . . (p. 70)

The Blacks presents the fantasies of revenge by a whole group, all of whom are Negroes. The actors arrange themselves in two bodies: those who by gesture, speech, and action will reveal the fantasies cherished by the Negro race, and the masked Negroes (representing the whites) who will portray what the Negroes imagine is the white man's conception of the Negro people. The Negroes act out the murder of a white woman, since this is what the whites imagine Negroes are capable of. The fantasy of "projection" is powerfully built up: the alleged sexual potency of the Negro, the rape, the murder of the white woman. The clownish element is exploited as a way of making this display of homicidal hatred bearable to the whites in the audience. Genet stresses the ceremonial aspects, reminding the spectators that this is only a ritual performance, a play within a play that shuttles back and forth between reality and illusion. Mirrors, mask, ritual, dream, fantasy: these are the devices Genet uses to bring out the grotesque contradictions of reality. The Negroes in this "clown show" see themselves as the whites see them, but since the whites are Negroes masked as whites, even this image is a reflection of their own tormented consciousness of color. (p. 71)

[If Genet] had not existed, Sartre would have had to invent him; fortunately "God" invented him to provide Sartre with a perfect Existentialist subject for his *Saint Genet*. His system of values is as symmetrical as a French formal garden, and his sense of hierarchy and ceremonial detail is almost as acute as if he had been brought up under the *Ancien Régime* at Versailles. But what he presents us with is an inverted mirror-image of the "average" world. His is literally an underworld or counterworld, a realm of night or hell which stands in black opposition to the moderately tragic operations of daylight existence. (p. 289)

[Genet's] heroes are criminal riff-raff, often with exotic names indicating international origins. But they all speak French argot, and over them all Genet spreads the rich decoration of his own sumptuous literary French.

Not the least surprising thing about him is that a child brought up in what one imagines to be a desert of illiteracy should have acquired this unerring distinction of language. His underworld speaks its own peculiar tongue, which is also, of course, his own native idiom, but he himself constantly describes it in the most refined style of the upper world. . . . Aristocrats, after all, are only people who are confident that they are the best. Genet decides to have this confidence, at least linguistically, and so he turns prison yards into courts of love, condemned murderers into holy martyrs, and tattooed thugs into Lancelots and Guineveres. This extraordinary imaginative effort succeeds to a surprising extent, and it is none the worse for also containing its own ironic negation. Genet's books are typically modern works of art in that they build up a deliberate illusion as if it were the truth, while at the same time suggesting that, in matters of this kind, there is no truth other than varieties of willed illusion. (p. 290)

[His novels] might . . . be considered as different volumes of the same work. They take the form of rambling, fantastic memoirs, which dodge about between the first person and the third, and show no respect for clarity of narrative. They are not ordinary books written with an eye to the reader, but rather private ruminations or celebrations in which Genet goes over the past and works it up to the poetic pitch at which he can, in a sense, become reconciled to it. (p. 291)

Genet's writing expresses strong emotion only in the direction of sublimity. He is so steeped in pornography and dirt that he deals with it quite unselfconsciously. It is there and, whenever the need arises, he refers to it directly by means of . . . obscene terms. . . . But his real interest is in psychological detail and the poetic superstructure. He both wants to see the situation as it is and to transmute it into noble terms. . . . To read Genet is to be whirled through a succession of appearances: male changes into female and vice versa, darkness into light, horror into ecstasy. And the doomed sump of humanity appears more moving and obscene through being lit by this fitful glow than if it were described with straight and conscientious sordidness. (pp. 291-92)

His most memorable scenes have a sad, detached poetry about them, and sex and excretions are present only because these are what his imagination has found to work on. . . . Genet has a marvellous way of suggesting the strange and ludicrous aspects of sex as well as its lyricism and mystery. This comes out most clearly not in *Miracle of the Rose* but in the astonishing copulation scene in *Querelle de Brest*, which is like an amplification, in poetic prose, of Rimbaud's powerful homosexual sonnet.

Since I have a high opinion of Genet's writing and, indeed, think he is quite unique within his given range, I would like to indicate his limitations. Being a rapturous monologuist like Céline or Henry Miller, he has little sense of over-all literary structure. You just have to accept each "novel" as a flux in which he moves from incident to incident without warning or explanation. Sometimes an episode is completely elaborated, but often the scenes are merely hinted at or not developed enough to become fully intelligible. Some readers may feel that this adds to the literary effect of sinister chiaroscuro; but I often find it disappointing and think it arises from the fact that Genet is writing primarily for himself and not completely objectifying his experience. Also like Céline or Miller, he is an egoist with little or no gift of characterisation. In *Miracle of the Rose*, he keeps referring to different boys by name . . ., but it is impossible to get an individualised picture of any of them. They are all in a sense the same boy, and no doubt versions of the author, wavering between masculinity and femininity, fidelity and betrayal, courage and cowardice, defiance and abjection. They have hardly more substance to them than figures in a courtly romance, such as *L'Astrée* or *The Faerie Queene*. (pp. 292-93)

Genet is only concerned with their sexuality and the emotions of power and humility connected with sex. They have no personal quirks, no ideas, hobbies, or ambitions. . . . [For] Genet, respectable society is a compact, foreign bloc, like capitalist America for a naïve Russian Communist or Soviet Russia for a naïve American right-winger. In *Miracle of the Rose*, he can thus build up Harcamone, the condemned criminal, into an august sacrificial figure, around whom the prison community moves, like the faithful around the figure of Christ during the Passion. This is the ultimate point of inverted Romanticism, and I don't believe in it for one moment. But I think I see why he needs it to complete his topsy-turvy psychological structure and maintain his imaginative stance. (p. 293)

[Even if Genet's] account is valid only for a small minority or for himself, it gives one of the most convincing and moving visions of psychological distress to be found in contemporary literature. (p. 294)

> *John Weightman, "Genet's Black Chivalry," in his* The Concept of the Avant-Garde: Explorations in Modernism (© *1973 by John Weightman*), *Alcove, 1973, pp. 289-94.*

In Genet's work, the essential alienation is conveyed by and through the ritual, symbolic and allegorical resources of the theatre. The world, the writer, his beliefs, dreams and art, the play itself, are all wrapped round each other; and yet Genet's plays are authentically political, obsessed as they are with a fundamental theme, the relationship of the rulers to the ruled. The two maids, the clients of the brothel in *The Balcony*, the blacks in *The Blacks*, all *perform*, acting out their lives in a conscious acknowledgment of the circumstance of their own incarnation, which is theatre. Thus they are both the subject and the object of art; art comes back at them, helping them (not always conclusively) to bridge the gap between their predicament and their aspirations. . . .

Genet . . . provides us not only with multiple reinsurance against illusion and empathy, but also with a delicate commentary on the interplay of art and reality, on how content emerges from the dialogue between subject and form. He uses myth, symbol, ritual and allegory to delineate the levels of consciousness and political aspiration operating in the world outside the theatre. (p. 66)

> *David Caute, in* TriQuarterly 30 (© *1974 by Northwestern University Press), Spring, 1974.*

Genet creates—and destroys—his characters solely to serve the turn of his pleasure. When he hears the voice of God on the Day of Judgement, it will be his own. . . .

[One] of the triumphs of [*Our Lady of the Flowers*] is the metamorphosis of reality. Trivial and sordid things become elevated and beautiful: but they remain trivial and sordid as well. It's almost impossible to achieve this effect without language. The soldier Gabriel, for example, is described by Genet as the Archangel: but he also wears boots and a sagging belt. . . .

Genet offers us emblems to play with—he wants us to create for ourselves.

Stewart Trotter, "Flowers," in Plays and Players *(© copyright Stewart Trotter 1974), May, 1974, p. 43.*

Jean Genet's five novels have secured him international recognition as one of the masters of modern French fiction. He wrote "Querelle" in the late 1940's after he had finished "Our Lady of the Flowers," "Miracle of the Rose," "The Thief's Journal" and "Funeral Rites." In many ways "Querelle" is the purest and the most austere enactment of those romantic situations that Genet's envy of handsome young men caused him to return to again and again. The charming little queens who graced "Our Lady of the Flowers" have disappeared, but they have been replaced by the more complex Lieutenant Seblon, a naval officer who maintains a severely masculine exterior in order to disguise the fits of ecstasy he rehearses in daydreams about his steward, Querelle. Whereas Querelle and all but one of the other adult men in the book are heterosexual and stupid, Lieutenant Seblon is clandestinely homosexual and as brilliant, devious and eloquent as Genet himself. We are treated to many excerpts from the Lieutenant's diary, and Genet mentions parenthetically: "While the other characters are incapable of lyricism, which we are using in order to re-create them more vividly within you, Lieutenant Seblon himself is solely responsible for what flows from his pen." What flows are poetic effusions celebrating desire and masochism—and Querelle.

Genet is in an awkward, dishonest—no, an ambiguous relationship with his reader and his characters. At the beginning of his novel, he announces that he is writing for homosexuals. But Genet cannot resist scandalizing his reader who, if homosexual, must also be a prude and a hypocrite—indeed, Baudelaire's "hypocritical reader, brother, counterpart." Thus Genet can write, after a violent scene, that he trusts the reader "to complete, with his very own malaise, the contradictory and twisted windings of our own vision of the murder." Not only is the reader made an unwilling accomplice to Genet's fiction, he is also bullied and confused by the narrator. The climactic scene is placed too early in the book, and Genet insolently acknowledges that he is breaking "the habitual rules of narrative logic." The conclusion is speeded up because, as Genet admits, he has become impatient with his tale. Worst of all, the book is left incomplete, unfinished. . . .

Strangely enough, Genet is also on an odd footing with himself. Throughout much of the book, he is the solitary dreamer conjuring up his elegant brutes and placing them in tableaux that excite his lust and cruel imagination. He sides with his characters and defies his readers. This is the posture he assumed in his earlier novels as well. But by the end of "Querelle" "the character escapes from its author, becoming its own, singular being." Indeed, one senses that Genet is frightened by Querelle, the monster he has created. The murderers in earlier books had flaws. They were cowards, they were caught, they were executed. Querelle seems to be getting away with it. Uneasily, Genet shifts his sympathies to the bourgeois reader. He begins to speak of "that sense of true justice that lives in everyone." Perhaps Genet laid his book aside in horror, not in disdain. . . .

In "Querelle" the mythological and the analytical powers seem to be perfectly in balance. By mythologizing his hero, Genet makes him as bright as not just a star but an entire constellation; through analysis, Genet delineates the subtle dynamics that relate one character to another. As his ability to dissect action became more and more powerful, Genet abandoned fiction and turned to plays (in his plays we encounter nothing but analysis of social machinery). Then, his work finished, the master embraced silence. (p. 4)

Edmund White, in The New York Times Book Review *(© 1974 by The New York Times Company; reprinted by permission), September 8, 1974.*

This disquieting novel, ["Querelle,"] first published in France in 1953, demonstrates once again Genet's unique gift as an artist and conjurer. Querelle is a sailor, thief, murderer, and waterfront prowler whose ship is temporarily docked in Brest. He has murdered more than one man and, for reasons he cannot articulate, has come to depend on thievery and acts of brutality for the liberating effect they have on his spirit. Two murders take place: one committed by Querelle, the other by a young mason. The mason acts out of confusion and passion, but Querelle murders his victim (a friendly messmate) calmly, and with no apparent motive. Genet's celebration of violence, his descriptions of homosexual lechery, and his opulent nihilism are sometimes extraordinarily interesting, sometimes repellent, and sometimes simply dull—but his uniqueness lies elsewhere. It is in his ability to create a wholly private, totally idiosyncratic world that is as poetically "pure" as its components are blunt and coarse. His quayside haunts, vaporous docks, and handsome young toughs have an almost mythic power to disturb one. (pp. 188-89)

The New Yorker *(© 1974 by The New Yorker Magazine, Inc.), October 21, 1974.*

The more I read Genet, the more I feel that his is a case where the biography of the writer is fallacious (in the sense the New Critics once argued all literary biography to be), that his life has no bearing on his work. . . .

Doubtless Genet's experience as a prisoner, and between imprisonments as a petty criminal, has provided him with a wealth of material, a plethora of the factual detail documentary novelists love. Yet Genet is not a documentary novelist. You can probably learn more about the actual life of French criminals from the memoirs of surviving Devil's Island convicts or from perusing Simenon with care than you can from reading *Our Lady of the Flowers* or *The Miracle of the Rose*.

This does not mean, however, that Genet is an inferior author. On the contrary, he is better than most novelists writing in France today. What I am suggesting is that, far from becoming a writer because he was a criminal whose life provided him with something to say, Genet is a natural artist who happened to become a criminal, and whose experiences in that role have merely assisted him in presenting his romantically metaphysical visions.

Indeed, the source of Genet's visions is to be found not in the underworld he has inhabited and described, but in the long vistas of French literature. Genet is hardly a literary freak. He stands firmly and centrally in the French "anti-tradition," the line of great amoral moralists beginning with Sade and Laclos and continuing through Balzac and Stendhal, Baudelaire and Verlaine, to Gide and Céline, Camus and Malraux.

While English and German romanticism foundered in Gothic nightmares and amorous idylls, French romanticism made the criminal its hero, and linked the artist with the outlaw in an alliance that, in the cases of Verlaine and Genet, has amounted to identification. This explains French romanticism's extraordinary vitality, for no conflict is more enduring than the one between the individual and society; and no situation in life or fiction represents that conflict more intensely than the relationship between the criminal and the policeman, the convict and the jailer, the condemned and the executioner. (p. 19)

[No] one can read Genet without being reminded of Vautrin, the Satanic malefactor of *Pére Goriot* or, for that matter, of Stendhal's Julian Sorel. But of course there are differences. The crimes of Vautrin and Sorel are seen by their perpetrators as direct challenges to the corruption and tyranny by which society sustains itself. Rebellion is explicit, whereas in Genet it is only implied. In this way, his people are really closer to later, more nihilistic figures of French literature, Gide's Lafcadio and Camus' Meursault, antiheroes who commit *crimes gratuits*, motiveless acts of emotionless violence. Criminality for Genet is autonomous, and is described with a curious artifice that lifts it completely out of a naturalistic realm.

This sense of crime as artifice—and the novel as well—is enhanced in *Querelle* by Genet's stylized description of Brest and its fogs (giving the book a tone of haunting remoteness reminiscent of Marcel Carné's film *Quai des Brumes*) and by the remarkably elaborate passages of psychological analysis. These take on the nature of an arabesque decoration unrelated in any immediate way to the characters or their actions. The verbal surface of the novel is extraordinarily well-worked in the original: Much that we take at first for profundity is in fact a skillful arrangement of ideas and images into evocative but ambiguous fictional patterns. Unfortunately, this aspect of Genet's writing is largely lost in . . . translation. (pp. 19-20)

Genet is not the deep or subtle thinker some critics have taken him for. Although he, like Sartre and Camus, deals with extreme situations, he does so in terms of evading them rather than facing them; in the final analysis he is nearer to grand symbolists like Proust than to the novelist-philosophers. His criminals are significant not for what they tell us about the relationship between society and its enemies, but for what they suggest to every man about himself and about those pure impulses—diabolical yet innocent because they are beyond good and evil—that demand liberation from within each of us. (p. 20)

> *George Woodcock, "The Satanic Tradition," in* The New Leader *(© 1974 by the American Labor Conference on International Affairs, Inc.), October 28, 1974, pp. 19-20.*

[*Querelle*] is the last of Genet's "novels" and the nearest to being an example of the genre, since it clarifies out into a group of interlinked stories, whereas the earlier works, such as *Pompes funebres* or *Miracle de la rose*, are more in the nature of rhapsodic meditations with anecdotal passages embedded in them. The central character, Georges or Jo, who bears the unexplained but apparently aggressive nickname of "Querelle de Brest," is not merely a beautiful hoodlum; he is also a sailor in the French navy, and this

allows Genet to make great play with the *matelot* type of homosexual lyricism, which seems to be common to various nations. Querelle's consciousness of the way the uniform moulds his limbs, his characteristic sailor's walk, the fact that he comes from the sea and will go back to the sea after committing certain deeds in the fog-laden and sailor-haunted air of the port of Brest—all this adds up to a thick, steamy, *"Quai des brumes"* poetry, such as Genet bestows, in other contexts, on reformatories and prisons. If, at times, it appears to verge on sentimentality, Genet very soon corrects the impression by showing, as usual, that his sense of the human, all-too-human, is accompanied by the bleakest cult of evil. He is a much better writer than the Marquis de Sade as regards subtlety of style and precise detail of notation, but he is every bit as relentless. . . .

Genet creates his habitual subject/object patterns of power and sexuality, which read like deliberate illustrations of existentialist psychology, although there can be no doubt that Genet had evolved them long before he had even heard of Jean-Paul Sartre.

> *John Weightman, "Kind of a Drag," in* Book World—The Washington Post *(© The Washington Post), November 3, 1974, p. 3.*

*   *   *

GERHARDIE, William   1895-

Gerhardie, born and raised in St. Petersburg, is an English novelist and autobiographer. At the age of seventy-five he published the four-volume novel *This Present Breath*, upon which he had worked for twenty-five years. (See also *Contemporary Authors*, Vols. 25-28.)

To date [1971], *My Wife's the Least of It* is the last, the most extensive and not the least of William Gerhardie's novels. It also represents his first and only foray into the hilarious Pickwickian tradition of novel writing. Its structure is episodic, for it's an offshoot of the picaresque novel and relies on a high proportion of dialogue. Since people do not behave logically in life, neither should they do so in fiction. But in Gerhardie's books they *attempt* to do so. What he shows us is the lunacy of logic, and the illogical quagmires into which the straight and narrow path of logic unerringly leads us. His dialogue catches this illogical paradox, or paradox of logic, marvellously well, and his meticulously odd speech rhythms, repetitive yet with intricate variations, are like a musical refrain serving to orchestrate the idiosyncratic behaviour of his characters.

Like much of Gerhardie's fiction, the literary value of *My Wife's the Least of It* does not depend upon suspense or dense plot construction. It is a sane study of general insanity, and the technique which Gerhardie employs to heighten this insanity is one that he had first put to use 16 years earlier in *Futility*: perpetual deferment. Ostensibly this novel is the expanded version of an original manuscript written by Mr Baldridge, a one-time novelist who, following his marriage to a mad millionairess, rises to a position of unprecedented public esteem in the administration of charities. This device enables Gerhardie to portray Mr Baldridge's inside history . . . without identifying himself with his central character. . . .

[This] is a sad book—not depressing, for it is wonderfully fertilised by humour, but remorseless, like a Chinese torture. The unfortunate Baldridge is never the pessimist: it is

his continual optimism that exhausts him. As the lost opportunities multiply and the absurdity rises almost to a
screaming pitch, we may protest, 'Surely this is enough.'
But we are not to be spared. The pointless unavailing activity spins us round faster and faster; the switchback of
anticipation and disappointment jolts us ever more mercilessly up and down until we cry out in desperation—and
still we are not heeded, but ingeniously carried, without
regard to our feelings, on and on.

Gerhardie does not tell us that all hope is vain. He shows
us that hope, if harnessed exclusively to the external world,
must take us nowhere in the end. The intimations in *My
Wife's the Least of It* are of money, not immortality; and
the paradise that is so tantalisingly deferred is of this world
alone. He has not written a social satire. . .; he has given us
an illustration, detail by dire detail, minute by minute, of
our life in time. . . . Through *My Wife's the Least of It*,
hidden to closed hearts, there runs the whole gamut of the
Word from the Garden of Eden to the Garden of
Gethsemane—the malaise, only recently apparent, about an
undue anthropocentrism of pervading human theology.

My Wife's the Least of It is remarkable for the number of
characters from Gerhardie's other novels who, as in some
final curtain call, reappear. . . . This trick of reintroducing
his own characters in slightly altered connotations was one
subsequently employed by Evelyn Waugh. But Waugh's
tone is less gentle than Gerhardie's and in its component
parts (as opposed to its cumulative effect) more exaggerated. During the Coronation of George VI, Gerhardie's
Aunt Minnie, who originally appeared in *Of Mortal Love*
and whose enthusiasm for the ceremony is second to no
one's, drops off to sleep on the balcony where, hours later,
having dreamt of the procession but not actually seen it
passing below her, she is found in the drizzling rain, happily
waving a miniature Union Jack. The way Evelyn Waugh
would have treated this scene . . . is to send her toppling
over the rails, and possibly not content with this, he would
have had a parrot overbalance her to her death. . . .

Among his novels of the 1930s *My Wife's the Least of It*
occupies a place similar to that of *Doom* in the previous
decade. Both are prophetic, concerned with the future, but
the limited future. Of the possibilities beyond time, which
Gerhardie revealed in *Resurrection*, there is no hint—unless it is in Gerhardie's clairvoyant humour which implies
another dimension and provides a detached, but not unfeeling, appraisal of Baldridge's predicament. For Baldridge
himself, such clairvoyance is more difficult to achieve, for
indignation threatens him with loss of humour.

After the desolation in *Of Mortal Love*, . . . the hilarity of
My Wife's the Least of It was welcome, and the book was
generously received by almost the entire London press
when it was first published in 1938. It was, as John Davenport commented, 'a tardy tribute'. But at last nothing (bar-
ring a war) seemed able to prevent Gerhardie's novels receiving the general acclaim they had for so long been on the
very point of receiving.

> *Michael Holroyd, "Lost Opportunities," in*
> New Statesman (© *1971 The Statesman &*
> *Nation Publishing Co. Ltd.), July 23, 1971,*
> *p. 120.*

I don't consider myself at all well read. . . . However, I do
make a point of knowing which authors I should have read.
That much at least I owe to literature. When these three
novels [*Futility, The Polyglots*, and *Of Mortal Love*] by
William Gerhardie arrived, I was taken aback. Review
excerpts didn't come from the Placebo, Arkansas *Bee-
Examiner*. They came from C. P. Snow, H. G. Wells, G.
B. Shaw, Edith Wharton, that sort. . . . I had never read
William Gerhardie. I had never even heard of him before.

I should have. And so should you. Gerhardie is one of the
most important and most rewarding novelists to have
written in this English century. . . .

His first two novels, *Futility* (1922) and *The Polyglots*
(1925), are quite similar: eyewitness accounts of the hugger-
mugger intervention [of the Allies, during the Russian Re-
volution] exalted to marvelous comic fiction by a sensitive
absurdist eye. A British eye. Red areas on the globe circa
1910 indicated nations where detached observation was
going on. Asides to the audience: understated, elegant of
style, somewhat separate, always somewhat privileged.
You know, Waugh, Greene, and the others; they are Gerhardie's heirs. It was part of British colonialism and commerce that the foreign was exploited in fiction. There are
other rapes than the one Lord Elgin pulled off.

But a gentle human tension pervades *Futility* and *The Polyglots* that, say, the author of *Black Mischief* would not
even deign to RSVP. Gerhardie's subject is double: the nation and the family. The nation is huge, quite mad, divided
against itself, disintegrating. The family is huge, quite mad,
divided against itself, and yet obdurately cohesive—perhaps because of inertia and selfishness, perhaps because of
love (which is often, in aspect, selfish and inertial).

British fiction has invented better, more engaging eccentrics than any other literature. Gerhardie's two families—
Russian in *Futility*, English-Belgian in *The Polyglots*—endure chaos extra- and intramural. Their insane quirks are
comic but also defensive, even therapeutic. Monomania
confronting the polymania of generals and bureaucrats and
terrorists. It is these family groups, set against an ancient
world's catastrophic end, that give Gerhardie's first two
novels the high strain of resilient social tissue and loyalty,
which, no matter how absurd at its surface, stands for
human magnificence. He may be pardoned for using such
an extraordinary theme twice. Novelists are seldom so fortunate in their biographies. *Futility* is a fine novel. *The Polyglots*, which refines it, must rank with Waugh's very best,
with Ford Madox Ford's *The Good Soldier*, amongst the
three or four most superb examples of that peculiar and
significant British fictional vision.

Futility announces a proviso. "The 'I' of this book is not
me." But, as far as any first person can be the author in fiction, Gerhardie's first person is Gerhardie. *The Polyglots*
has no proviso. It/they are a young first person, both
charming and honest. Though perceptive, they do not
judge. Their detachment, moreover, has been pleasantly
flawed. They are in love. As Britain discovered excuses to
intervene in Russia, these young British officers intervene
in families for love. Each family has one beautiful, perverse, silly, self-interested young lady. Love fascinates
Gerhardie. In its insane vagaries and destructiveness it
parallels war. But young ladies are Gerhardie's problem
both as first person and as novelist.

In *Of Mortal Love* (1936) Gerhardie faced the ultimate fictional challenge at ten paces: to create a loveworthy woman. Perfect eyes or that special uptilted profile have no legal tender on the page. Men can be loved for their professions: artist, hero, citizen of the world. Women, 1930s women anyway, can be loved only for what they are. It comes down to dialogue and the odd action. Dinah has been given a boost over her capricious predecessors, but not enough of one. Gerhardie put governors on his comic sense, so that she should not be tainted by it. Yet Dinah is vain, fickle, overpassionate, full of childish inconsequence. At her tragic death, face powder is delivered from the chemist just too late. Dinah doesn't seem worth Gerhardie's time. Not so much of it at least.

And Gerhardie seems uncomfortable at home. *Of Mortal Love* is first rate, but the novel has only England in peacetime as a counterpoint. Perhaps he sensed this. Many chapter headings designate their subject matter by a place name; ordinary British folk make abortive cameo appearances in trams, in streets. It's as though these devices were intended to give the novel greater geographical and social breadth. Dinah has a St. Petersburg history and a large staff of relatives, but they are peripheral, they serve rather as live flashbacks. Gerhardie's other young women, less well conceived than Dinah, comic figures, were justified by both family and nation. Which all means: *The Polyglots* does tend to spoil one. (pp. 403, 405)

A novelist of this stature deserves more than twenty years' determined silence. (p. 405)

> *D. Keith Mano, "Before Waugh and Greene, Gerhardie," in* National Review *(© National Review, Inc., 1975; 150 East 35th St., New York, N.Y. 10016), April 11, 1975, pp. 403, 405.*

* * *

GINZBURG, Natalia   1916-

Ms Ginzburg, an Italian novelist, short story writer, and autobiographer, employs a straightforward prose language characterized by deceptive simplicity.

Natalia Ginzburg's entrancing characters [in *No Way*] are a group of Romans who could be right out of Chekhov.... All of [their] relationships are assembled by Natalia Ginzburg through a brilliantly defined series of epistolary connections that have the intricacy and the fragility of an ant city. The wit is mordant and comes directly out of paradox. The keynote is struck by [one character] when he comments on [another's] life style. "One can't understand it," he says. "And yet one can understand it very well." (p. 14)

> *Martin Levin, in* The New York Times Book Review *(© 1974 by The New York Times Company; reprinted by permission), September 1, 1974.*

Natalia Ginzburg, in Italy accepted as one of the foremost writers to emerge after the war—one whose work, in fact, is partly engendered by the trauma of war—is hardly a household word here in America. And that is our loss, because Ginzburg's is a unique voice, pure and unmistakable. The contours of her sentences linger in the ear like phrases from great music, familiar, basic truths. Her characters, sad, thwarted, often drab types, are memorable in the manner of people one knew very long ago....

[Her] two books of remarkable essays [are] like nothing I know being written in English today: in incredibly simple language, they combine an adolescent ingenuousness with the ripe sagacity of a woman who has endured the isolation of growing up Jewish in Turin, the war, the loss of a loved husband to German persecution, and the aftermath. (p. 26)

No Way . . . deserves to be read and relished. It should become a part of our permanent memory because it is about the things we cannot afford to ignore.... (p. 27)

> *Lynne Sharon Schwartz, in* The New Republic *(reprinted by permission of* The New Republic; *© 1974 by The New Republic, Inc.), September 14, 1974.*

In "No Way" . . . [Natalia Ginzburg] creates a marvellous and saddening world in the scope of a hundred and sixty pages. This is, in a sense, the world of the Finzi-Continis: though her family and its circle are not Jewish, they are a group of bourgeois confronted by events beyond their control and floundering in despond and apathy. The time is the early seventies, when in Italy money still buys privilege and mobility but no insulation from the unease of the times....

Signora Ginzburg has been compared to Chekhov, and, indeed, her characters are failed and sweet, like his. But their situation is worse: Chekhov's rural petty gentry were at least rooted—chained, if you will—to the land and to the whole codex of Russianness; Ginzburg's rootless Romans can find nothing to believe in. (pp. 185-86)

[Their] maddening vagueness, [an] unwillingness to commit oneself to any relationship, to any ideal, is the true theme of the book. Even the most admirable character, Oswald, a bookseller, is a walking ambiguity, a presumed bisexual who cannot bring himself to maintain a relationship with either man or woman but abases himself—to gather credit in the Heaven he cannot possibly believe in—by running the most menial errands for the acquaintances who take constant advantages of him. He is Ford Madox Ford's good soldier without a cause. (p. 186)

What makes this book so wonderful—magical, even—is that we are never bored by the imprisoned pacings and abortive flights of its people. They all become real and individual and fascinating through the technical gifts of the author. In a short compass, with the most rudimentary of tools (the epistolary form, an utter minimum of stage-setting and description, and language as spare and declarative as Hemingway's), she creates a whole society of irretrievably lost dreams....

"No Way" is a novel of the curdling of aspirations and the enfeebling of powers among those who heretofore held sway. Its quality lies in its reportorial accuracy, in its fine, warm, rueful equanimity, in its balance in the face of toppling worlds. It is a most remarkable book. (p. 188)

> *L. E. Sissman, in* The New Yorker *(© 1974 by The New Yorker Magazine, Inc.), October 21, 1974.*

No Way is a very short novel, bare and bleak as bones. Its ominous English title is appropriate enough for its mood, except for the easy current slanginess of that phrase, mouthed by so many of us now on trivial occasions. In Natalia Ginzburg's Italian it was simply *Caro Michele*

["Dear Michael"] (1973), the form of salutation in the letters that tell much of the story.

This story is quite ordinary, the author seems to want us to take the people as ordinary, and yet to me they appear entirely out of the ordinary, different from any society I have ever known. Not that it is news to any of us that life can be depressing, but to live in a state of such daily depression as we have in *No Way* seems not to be living at all. These people are in one way like people in a stupid novel, where it is depressing to think the author supposed such creatures could exist or that they would be interesting if they did. But Natalia Ginzburg is far from stupid and the novel is far from depressing to read. Perhaps it is as she has one of her characters say, "One of the rare pleasures in life is to compare the descriptions of others with our fantasies and then with the reality." . . .

What seems so very odd and appalling—not beyond the reach of our fantasies, to be sure, but of an extremity certainly beyond our everyday experience—is the way these people talk to one another and the way they write their letters. Of course we have been familiar in literature for a generation with the emptiness and despair of a good many *outré* characters, but here we must suppose that if we were Romans, reasonably good bourgeois folk, these would be our friends and neighbors, all of them. . . .

Their lengthy and expository correspondence seems no more unlikely than that of other epistolary novels, and perhaps Italians are given to writing such deadpan missives to one another, just as they used to talk loudly all the time in Italian, wave their arms, wear pointy shoes, and roll their eyes in that hysterical, futile, and charming manner. It is the bleak, flat recognition of the emptiness of themselves and of the others that goes beyond the stoic wastes into some other region I do not know. I feel sure it is not supposed to be funny. (p. 39)

Perhaps we are to imagine for [the characters], out of her clarity and out of our mercy, feelings deeper than those they claim for themselves—or perhaps we are simply not to condemn them for living in this frozen despair. For the knowing despair, neither witty, defiant, bitter, nor surprised, seems not to be caused by . . . death . . . or by their own deadly loneliness. It is a kind of weather they live in as though there were no other and no getting out of it. There are no evil people here, no really bad deeds done that might require mercy. So I suppose this is simply Natalia Ginzburg's Italy.

It was not always like this. An earlier novel by Natalia Ginzburg, *A Light for Fools* (. . . 1957), dealing with an earlier period, makes the time of Mussolini and of the Second World War a brave era. Here there were villains and heroes aplenty, fiery characters, peasants and gentry, and real adventures. The essential elements, though, are similar, all but that fatal atmosphere. (pp. 39-40)

A Light for Fools is a marvelous tale, full of the most distinct characters and manners, shaped with the knowledge of how children are born and grow up and then die or get old. (In *No Way*, the mother says, "They have never been young, so how can they grow old.") There is absolutely no moral dithering at all. The Germans are quite simply the Germans, and nobody has to wonder if he should blame himself for what the Germans did. The Germans did what Germans do. The peasants want to kill Germans, "any

dirty blackguard of a German." That view of good and evil is old-fashioned, healthy, intelligent, and perhaps quite behind us now. It was a great pleasure to come upon this novel, and upon *No Way*, and I intend to find the other books of Natalia Ginzburg too. (p. 40)

John Thompson, in The New York Review of Books *(reprinted with permission from* The New York Review of Books; *copyright © 1975 NYREV, Inc.), January 23, 1975.*

* * *

GODWIN, Gail   1937-

Ms Godwin is an American novelist and short story writer. (See also *Contemporary Authors*, Vols. 29-32.)

Coming after the first wave attacks of women's liberation writing, with the virtues and faults of propaganda literature, the more subtle examinations of the categories of power in terms of male/female struggle deal with "power" in a far deeper, far more abstract way—hence, Gail Godwin's two novels [*The Perfectionist* and *Glass People*] may be read, instructively, as about the precarious battle for identity of two young "new" women. But this is simply one level and perhaps not the most important one. Miss Godwin is preoccupied with the relationship between private, individual selves and larger, more mythic selves. (p. 8)

[*The Glass People*] is a formally executed, precise, and altogether professional short novel which deepened my long-cherished belief about certain forms of art: that in exploring extremities of human behavior, in forcing us to wade through real or metaphorical blood, such art saves us from these experiences and is cathartic in the best sense of the term. (p. 10)

Joyce Carol Oates, "Transparent Creatures Caught in Myths," in Book World—The Washington Post *(© The Washington Post), October 1, 1972, pp. 8, 10.*

The Odd Woman [is a] generous, sensitive, intelligent, humane, and literate book that, despite its generosity, sensitivity, humanity, and literacy, manages to be a deadly bore. . . . One of the book's chief weaknesses is that so much of the dialogue is couched in flat, dull universityese. ("This is the price we pay for evolving: the deadly drain on our energies . . . when we dare to open our mind and let another examine its contents.") But an even greater weakness is that almost every scene has the same tone and emotional texture, so that after a while one begins to feel as if one were reading an endless . . . letter from a nice but hopelessly gabby friend. (p. 234)

The New Yorker *(© 1974 by The New Yorker Magazine, Inc.), November 18, 1974.*

Like several recent novels, *The Odd Woman* owes much of its dialectic structure to Doris Lessing's *Children of Violence* pentalogy, in which Martha Quest explores herself and the world around her over many years and two continents. Martha was often as exasperating a character as Jane [Godwin's protagonist] but we stayed with the slow parts of her story because Lessing's emotional and intellectual sweep invited confidence. The confidence was justified by the imaginative completion of *The Four-Gated City*.

Godwin merely confirms our fears that Jane's tentativeness won't lead to a confrontation with anything outside itself. *The Odd Woman*'s schematic organization is unpleasantly rigid, and Godwin has little to say.

Jane responds to students too frequently with a quote that doesn't answer anything, and she evades her own basic questions by thinking of characters with whom she wants to identify. *The Odd Woman* is full of literary allusions that backfire. When Jane compares herself to Isabel Archer or Gwendolen Harleth, we see the foolishness of the comparison; and we may wish that we were back reading *The Portrait of a Lady* or *Daniel Deronda*.

Dwelling on literature as a way of stalemating one's self is a potentially interesting subject for a novel, but I was never convinced that Godwin was aware of the problem. Jane approaches life as though it were a doctoral thesis that could be completed with mental note cards, and Godwin presents all of Jane's literary references so solemnly that the novel is footnoted like a thesis. The title is a footnote: Gissing's *The Odd Women*, which Jane is preparing to teach, is evoked so frequently that it becomes Godwin's novel-within-a-novel. Jane, trying to work out her life, makes a chart of Gissing's characters and the solutions they found. Gissing's 19th-century feminists and unhappy spinsters have problems that offer Jane no help with hers; but before Jane reaches that conclusion, Godwin has spent an inordinate number of words on a novel that is like her own only in the use of "odd" to mean "unmarried."

The flaws of *The Odd Woman* are crippling, but I may have made the book seem less promising than it is. One is always aware of Godwin's struggle with the demands she has made on herself, and there are places where her novelist's intelligence breaks through.... In the successful scenes Godwin is returning to the tone of her earlier work, and I'm not suggesting that she should simply go back to what she is good at. She was right to know that she couldn't grow as a writer by continuing with those little fables about sexual apocalypses and exquisite neuroses. But now she has to find a subject. (pp. 26-7)

> *John Alfred Avant, in* The New Republic *(reprinted by permission of* The New Republic; © 1975 by The New Republic, Inc.), *January 25, 1975.*

* * *

GOLDBARTH, Albert 1948-

Goldbarth, a prolific poet, has been called "one of the substantial voices of contemporary American poetry." (See also ***Contemporary Authors,* Vols. 53-56.)**

Albert Goldbarth has achieved success with the long form and has employed for the purpose both imagist and surrealist techniques, as well as some which sound a Shakespearean note in America. *Opticks: a poem in seven sections* releases lines with the jollity of the Henry IV plays and with language as beautiful as that of *Lear*.

On one level Goldbarth's *Opticks* is simply delicious as a linguistic offering. The first section not only establishes the theme of "how glass came into my life", it sets the driving rhythmical and tonal power of the whole poem. Using asterisks as breaks between run-on stanzas, Goldbarth weaves a "latticework of crosses", telephone poles, and barbed wire which is at once imagistically intriguing and shot through with internal off-rhymes. The poet's ability to spin an endless array of interrelated images is quite amazing. This could, of course, become cloying if it were not for the accompanying sound, and for the awareness on the reader's part that all of this cross imagery has something to do with glass, though *what* remains for the moment unclear. (p. 37)

In *Opticks* Goldbarth has seen, as Blake says, a world in a grain of sand, but, to the Chicago poet's credit, he has not gone to this or other such well-worn quotes for his sources. Instead, he has ranged far and wide—Egypt, the Illinois tollway, Germany of World War II, a Middle Ages glass makers guild—to demonstrate that "everything's in the window." Other than the specific inspirations mentioned in the poem, I wonder what poets Goldbarth was reading at the time of composition. This fine poem makes me think of Lear after he is blinded, of Louis Zukofsky's *A*, with its variations on the I's (pronounced *eyes*) and its blend of colloquial and scientific languages, without there being any suggestion of direct influence. Despite a surrealistic playfulness and an often derivative type of recent inclination for exhausting the possibilities of single images, Goldbarth's sources are finally and essentially very personal ones.

The result is a long poem with a singular impact. Many voices speak, some with excitement and some with concern, but the ultimate force of the poem comes from the poet's sureness of touch in working his almost epic loom. Or, to change the metaphor, for a treatise of sand, *Opticks* is a banquet so heaped with juicy treats that it proves Goldbarth's truly one of the most fertile imaginations going. (p. 58)

> *Dave Oliphant, "Goldbarth's Vocabulary Banquet & Treatise of Sand," in* Margins *(copyright © 1974), December, 1974, pp. 37, 58.*

Goldbarth's innovative dramatic monologues demand comparison with Richard Howard's original dramatic poems. Howard is superior in creating autonomous characters and intense dramatic situations, though the Pulitzer winner might envy this twenty-six-year-old's gift of vivid language. Browning provides a more instructive comparison, not only because Goldbarth adapts his monologue form but also because the modern poet's dense texture, his chiaroscuro of grotesque images alternating with flaring insights, and the long, energetic, alliterative lines, all suggest that Victorian model.

However, Goldbarth updates the Romanticist epistemology, according to which the poet extends his own experience and authority by projecting himself into dramatic personas. (pp. 96-7)

> *Dillon Johnston, in* Shenandoah *(copyright by* Shenandoah; *reprinted from* Shenandoah: The Washington and Lee University Review *with the permission of the Editor), Winter, 1975.*

Coprolites [the title of one of Goldbarth's recent books] are fossil feces which, when the archeologist cracks them open, reveal "a clock/stopped once and saying its message/forever." . . . Everything that T. S. Eliot advised about "the historical sense, which we may call nearly indispensable to anyone who would continue to be a poet beyond his twenty-fifth year," is at work in Goldbarth, except that for him, of course, it is a prehistorical sense. At the end of his title poem . . . Goldbarth passes himself "to a new generation," like a wry, metaphysical Whitman addressing his body, and the leavings thereof, as "good manure". . . . What may seem a preoccupation with the basic bodily functions serves . . . throughout the book an almost sacramental purpose. What is man, after all, but a complex of bodily functions—his curious body grown, in the late Pleistocene, out of older curious bodies that left themselves, and their coprolites, dead and buried in limestone better than half a billion years—and what did they leave us but marks in the stones?—and what do the poets leave us, here in the sixth millenium of written history, but marks in the (printer's) stones? (pp. 221-22)

The brilliant nonsense of Goldbarth's "Singing the Tree" . . . reveals Goldbarth's uncanny gifts at their most playful. . . . "Play's the thing," Frost said in his great praise of Robinson, and Goldbarth has made a poem . . . full of play, the free play of an exhilarated and exhilarating imagination—child's play of the most truly serious kind. . . . It is probably evident even in "Singing the Tree," but Goldbarth's one large fault is his enviable impulse to make a *tour de force* of every poem. Among his most impressive are the three "dialogues" in Section II of *Coprolites*. They each consist of two monologues broken into pieces and knit into one another like the spread fingers of two hands meshed together: the first is interrupted always in mid-sentence while each segment of the second forms a complete paragraph. Goldbarth's technique exploits the complementary effects of fragmentation and interrelation, further augmented by the fact that, in each case, the speakers are isolated in time by a minimum of nearly two centuries. (pp. 224-25)

Albert Goldbarth has extended his range perhaps broader than any other poet of the mid-seventies and, in so doing, has taught himself more tricks than most mature poets could use by the end of the century. I couldn't suggest a course of development, but it seems to me that, tricks aside, anyone who can write lines like [those] from the end of "The Fisher's Wish" will secure himself somewhere, among those who bank the fires in the next dark age. . . . (p. 226)

> Michael Heffernan, "Good Manure," in The Midwest Quarterly (copyright, 1975, by The Midwest Quarterly, Kansas State College of Pittsburg), Winter, 1975, pp. 221-26.

[Goldbarth's] poetic blitz overwhelms us with fresh images, thought, imaginative scope, but also—as wherever mass is the product—buries us with the unfinished detritus of a mind (and an ego) whose accelerator is frozen. *Opticks* is a great vine of a poem sadly etiolated by haste and demonstrative of Goldbarth's racy faults.

Opticks is one poem in seven parts, an afflatus of "through a glass darkly." Its metaphor is all glass. (p. 227)

Goldbarth's subtlety is noticing his lack of subtlety, but he only underlines its absence. He wants to be patted on the back and told "Yes, you are witty, little buddy." It is, of course, immaturity and it ribs the entire poem. He is every-

where stepping forward as poet, sometimes apologetically, to sneer at his reader. He poses and prances. . . .

Immaturity translates to self-ishness in *Opticks*. It flecks style, tone, subject, and shaping. False modesty is always transparent; effort's integer is obvious. Luxuriating in adjectives, in fragile variations, is too often self-deluding, especially when self is the sole subject. Shortcuts don't replace nouns and verbs, but make a mirror for the self to wallow in. (p. 228)

Beyond the self-conscious sickness of this poem, beyond the tinny irony and windiness of march, a greater sickness seduces the best of Goldbarth. François Mauriac wrote that "the despair of modern man is born of his belief in the absurdity of the world." Our poets and poet-trainers hold such absurdity sacred. It leads them to write of boredom. We ask, do they really live so inconsequentially? If true, the flesh they celebrate must be atrophied, the life excessively dull and indulgent. But too much paint merely blurs the canvas. Goldbarth's recurrent image for this boredom, this dissolution of the vital, is surgent in each section of *Opticks*, as in so many of his poems: shit, turds, dung, feces, crap, coprolites, drit. He is more excremental than Swift, and I, for one, am bored with the stink. Let those who will, freud-like, handle the ramifications of what Goldbarth calls "ass-comfy." For those who cannot be satisfied with Goldbarth's predominant foci of interest, he adds another: the vagina, and it, too, as Cummings might have said, exudes. Perhaps if Goldbarth explores additional landscapes, he will find the world not so absurd, not so boring. At any rate, he works at a dead end. (p. 228-29)

I haven't praised, as I might have, some of the fine things in this poem. I must, however, applaud Goldbarth's energy, his willingness to challenge big tasks, his refusal to accomplish the easy. Even the worst of his poems demonstrate his marvelous equipment, his intelligence, his straining for vision. This book is an ego-sop, but it will die so that he may write other, better books. (p. 229)

> Dave Smith, "Drit under Glass," in The Midwest Quarterly (copyright, 1975, by The Midwest Quarterly, Kansas State College of Pittsburg), Winter, 1975, pp. 227-29.

The collection of fifty poems in *Jan. 31* is broad enough to show why Albert Goldbarth is more than minimally surviving and has become, in the words of Nelson Rockefeller, "a hot commodity." . . . [His] work is distinguished by its imagery, its language, its structure, its erudition and its mood. (p. 230)

He stakes the success of his title poem, and ultimately the success of the book, on his ability to establish the idea that the natural order of things is cyclical and if, like space curving back on itself, history repeats its processes of human bondage and suffering, then it likewise regenerates knowledge and strength. During our various metaphorical winters, this understanding, along with our basic physical pleasures, will provide us both hope and comfort. Goldbarth often casts himself in the role of mythmaker, and stanzas relating in detail the customs of an ancient civilization as an archetype for some general aspect of contemporary life are not uncommon. (p. 231)

Another strategy Goldbarth uses to stress the interconnectedness of things is the metaphor in which an image the reader expects to be merely a detail in the narrative framework suddenly hatches its own vehicle which grows enormous and elaborate, taking wing to live its own life among the archetypes of the poem. . . . Goldbarth is ingenious at this. (p. 232)

What, then, are the limitations of [*Jan. 31*], and of this poet with his knowledge of sciences and humanities, his intellect and his command of language? One criticism that I have read of his earlier work proposed that his images occasionally become so elaborate that the direction of the poem is difficult to follow. This, the reviewer suggested, results from Goldbarth's too-conscious employment of the situation of the writer writing about the use of language. I do not find either of these problems among the poems in *Jan. 31*. The images, even when elaborate, do not seem inappropriate and Goldbarth's poems—so many of which deal with language—are saved individually by the portrayal of sex, love, speech, writing, and bodily functions as so many different languages through which one touches, or attempts to touch, different sources of strength.

My own inclination, considering Goldbarth's youth and obvious gifts, is to ask questions not only about this book but about the function of poetry today and the more immediate problem of where Goldbarth goes from here. The poems in *Jan. 31* are largely repetitive in mood. We come to understand very well that the loneliness we feel, the submission to external forces, and the lack of faith are all parts of a cyclical process—perhaps something in our human nature—but there is almost nothing in this book that refers to any contemporary event outside the poems themselves. Granted that Goldbarth's winter is metaphorical—are we struggling against anything that is peculiar to our time? Is history really more a circle than a spiral? Are not even metaphorical winters caused by events political, social, economic, ethnic, demographic and scientific—and by the events themselves, not the theories they engender or support, or their historical archetypes or analogues? In an everyday world of particularized experience, what are some of the promised "ways of surviving"?

I know we have all been taught to let poems justify themselves, and perhaps I am sounding increasingly Matthew Arnoldish. In any case, the title poem of *Jan. 31* is one of the best poems I have read in years, and the reason it alone must save or almost save this collection, despite the dazzling language throughout the book, is that it happens to be the one poem that connects with a political reality underlying the metaphorical winter. . . . (pp. 232-33)

> *Jonathan Katz, "Sing Goddamm," in* The Midwest Quarterly *(copyright, 1975, by The Midwest Quarterly, Kansas State College of Pittsburg), Winter, 1975, pp. 230-34.*

*　　*　　*

GORDIMER, Nadine 1923-

Ms Gordimer, a South African novelist and short story writer, works at the center of the emerging South African literary tradition. She has said that, in South Africa, "society *is* the political situation"; hence, her fiction continues to explore the immorality of *apartheid* and other, often political, aspects of contemporary life in an uneasy multi-racial society. (See also *Contemporary Authors*, Vols. 5-8, rev. ed.)

Far and away the best thing in *A Guest of Honour* is the description of Africa. It is a wonderfully rich description, drawing on a fine feeling both for nature and history, and an exceptional knowledge of individual African character. . . . [The] note of authentic observation runs everywhere through the book.

Yet this is not a novel like, say, Conrad's *Nostromo*, passing on to us the personal experiences of a representative group of inhabitants of an unstable country, and allowing us to draw our own conclusions about them, and their nation's plight. It is not even the account of one man's private experience of Africa. Bray, without actually telling the story in the first person, is a kind of attendant mind throughout the book until he dies. But Bray's train of thought is frequently commandeered by a sort of pirate voice. As a responsive person in a specific setting, at those times he fades away, and we get pages of informative and argumentative summary of the historical and political situation. They are supposed to be Bray's reflections, but they carry little fictive conviction. What it amounts to is that deeply enmeshed in the book is a long, straight article by Miss Gordimer herself about African affairs. It has a case to make—the case, in brief, for African socialism—but it has little in common with the oblique and uninsistent processes of fiction. And it needs to be tested by reference to the facts about real African countries, and exposed to debate in terms of political principle and economic theory, in a way it is sheltered from in this guise.

The novel, as a novel, is gravely limited by this fact. And Bray, as a character, suffers particularly badly from his liability to disappear from the scene like this. But it is not his only difficulty. In so far as he does in fact draw conclusions and make decisions he is accorded a respect, even a kind of reverence, by Miss Gordimer that makes it equally hard to see him clearly as a person. (pp. 66-7)

> *Derwent May, in* Encounter *(© 1971 by Encounter Ltd.), August, 1971.*

The Conservationist is a tremendous imaginative stocktaking of Mehring [the protagonist] and his estate; and to write the book Miss Gordimer has had to reconstruct, piece by piece, a sensibility, even a historical consciousness, quite alien from her own. She has taken on Mehring's contemptuous, powerful sexuality and has felt the world through the stirrings of his genitals as well as simply watched it through his eyes. On this level alone, there has been no novel with which to compare it since Angus Wilson's *The Middle Age of Mrs Eliot*. She writes about being a man with more curiosity, passion and intelligence than any man could bring to the subject. But this sexual transposition is only the springboard for an amazing and dangerous dive into the mirrorlike otherness of Africa. As a liberal herself (it wasn't by accident that the title of that brilliant short novel, *The Late Bourgeois World*, came from Ernst Fischer's *The Necessity of Art*) she has entered imaginatively into the state of mind which takes *apartheid* for granted as a moral good. As a white, she has adopted the resigned, bovine perspectives of Mehring's "boys," their wives and children—people who are as much part of Mehring himself as his other goods and chattels. As a writer, she has created a rich prose—not a satiric idiom—for a mind accustomed to thinking of any kind of art or extended introspection as being a poor substitute for the material blessings of life.

This prose is her triumph; but it comes close to being her undoing too. The main drive of the writing through the book is its acquisitiveness; it sucks in details like a Hoover. A field, a farmyard, a room, a desert, a continent . . . everything is appropriated as soon as looked at. Nor is it the style of an inventory. It is a luscious, crowded prose, rhythmical and rich in metaphor. (p. 81)

The extraordinary thing is that Mehring is so complete and powerful a fictional character that he survives all of Miss Gordimer's efforts to trip him up. He only stops his prose when his brains are blown out. And he, not Miss Gordimer, finally dominates the novel. We are supposed to respond to the tragicomedy of his arrogant attempt to own Africa; as it is, we just watch him owning it as confidently as any 18th-century squire. His affairs turn into tolerable peccadillos; his racial attitudes are easily ascribable to customs of the country. When I came to the end of the book, at once puzzled and wholly persuaded, I wondered if Miss Gordimer felt like Frankenstein. (p. 82)

> *Jonathan Raban, in* Encounter *(© 1975 by Encounter Ltd.), February, 1975.*

More than Doris Lessing, a fellow South African who is a bit too much of an English *yenta* for my taste, and even more than Alan Paton, who has been rather quiescent of late, Nadine Gordimer has become, in the whole solid body of her work, the literary voice and conscience of her society—and how I wish I could say this about any contemporary American novelist. In the sense of being a completely South African writer and insisting on remaining there, Ms. Gordimer is a "regionalist." But her region is really the whole Third World, to which she has increasingly dedicated her literary work. . . .

As in all of Ms. Gordimer's works, the farm's blacks [in *The Conservationist*] are described beautifully. She has a fine grasp of the language they speak—both among themselves and to their masters. She knows their customs, habits, superstitions, holiday ceremonials, and tribal rituals. And she sees right through the deceptive masks they wear for their dealings with the whites and even with the Indian settlers in South Africa: All this is no mean achievement for the sheltered South African English girl of good family that Nadine Gordimer was at the outset of her career. . . . Beside the blacks' tribal and communal richness, which is never sentimentalized or patronized in Gordimer's work, the whites of the chronicle emerge as very pale and alienated individuals indeed. (p. 24)

I am not suggesting that *any* white South African writer can really penetrate the black African consciousness. For that we may have to await the native black artists of that continent, who are historically about to emerge and tell their story. But what Nadine Gordimer brilliantly here describes once again is a terrified white consciousness in the midst of a mysterious and ominous sea of black humanity. . . .

As things stand, Nadine Gordimer is one of the very few links between white and black in South Africa. She is a bearer of culture in a barbaric society. And she is a luminous symbol of at least one white person's understanding of the black man's burden. (p. 25)

> *Maxwell Geismar, "Black Man's Burden," in* Saturday Review *(copyright © 1975 by Saturday Review/World, Inc.; reprinted with permission), March 8, 1975, pp. 24-5.*

It seems a naïve kind of compliment: to say of a novel that nothing in it is wasted, that its episodes, images and phrases reverberate throughout the length of its narrative and by repetition gain significance. Is this not the condition to which all novels should aspire? And yet most of them, even the best, are ragged things. Many novelists distrust perfection of craftsmanship, as if it in some way inhibits vitality and inspiration. "The Conservationist" is above all taut and careful; complex and thickly textured, it is the kind of novel that delights critics and English professors (failed white hunters, all), who will chase with excited yelps its spoor of themes and symbols. (p. 74)

With economy and skill, Nadine Gordimer develops her story's physical and moral landscapes simultaneously. Her narrative advances by means of interior monologues interrupted by dialogue, by remembered conversations poking through present perceptions, by imagined scenes and confrontations. Symbols germinate and multiply. . . .

This is an excellent novel that forces its own slow pace upon the reader; it rewards—indeed, to appreciate all that it offers, it requires—a second reading. (p. 75)

> *Peter S. Prescott, "Down in the Dirt," in* Newsweek *(copyright 1975 by Newsweek, Inc.; all rights reserved; reprinted by permission), March 10, 1975, pp. 74-5.*

Nothing in Nadine Gordimer's earlier work—five admirable novels and five volumes of short stories dealing mainly with her native South Africa—prepared me for the incredible power, the intellectual and poetic authority of *The Conservationist.* . . . To be sure, she has always written with genuinely unhortatory intelligence about the harsh dislocations and indignities of apartheid, which taints every South African with its moral squalor. Yet *The Conservationist* is not simply Miss Gordimer's finest novel by far, it is a book intricately different in kind from what she has done before; the realities of power and oppression emerge in a new way, no longer dependent on the reassuring simplicities of condemnation.

Rarely is a writer in mid-career . . . invaded by a character who asserts so audacious a force of discovery it is as if a key has been turned in a door the novelist didn't know was there. All the prudent habits of imagination, judgment and language are swept away before this indomitable wave of energy, and the novelist, willing or not, is obliged to accept the challenge of transcendence.

Such a character is Mehring, the conservationist of Miss Gordimer's ambiguously ironic title, and he is so absolute and commanding a presence—is there any other woman who can write with this shrewdly intuitive sympathy about the inner life of a man?—that he threatens to take up all the space there is. It is no small part of the novel's achievement that we can see Mehring in proper perspective, though much of the time we are trapped inside his head, eavesdropping on a clamor of memory, fantasy and sexual greed. (p. 17)

The conservationist wants South African society to remain unchanged, and he protectively assures that the birds and reeds and grassland on his farm—initially bought on impulse, as a tax-loss deduction—are tended, nurtured, made to yield fodder, natural beauty and order, "the simple things of life that poorer men can no longer afford." To conserve is to possess; ownership is power. Striding confidently around his land Mehring declares, "My possessions are enough for me."

But he is forced to learn, finally paying for the lesson with his life, that he cannot attain absolute dominion over the South African veld, expropriated by white men yet cared for by the blacks who belong to it, just as he cannot control his coldly reckless sexuality. (pp. 17-18)

These bare bones . . . only dimly convey the stunning richness and teeming density of Miss Gordimer's prose, which one can scarcely credit to the same hand that wrought the cautiously subdued style of her earlier books. The predatory Mehring has liberated his creator from the inhibiting reticence of the well-formed story, and given her the courage of a driving extravagance that, remarkably, is never excessive. With unerring control, she builds a deceptively erratic structure of minutely observed natural detail, hypnotic rumination, and deftly interpolated glimpses into the black compound on the farm. The threads of heightened metaphor and carefully manipulated symbol, shuttling back and forth between the veld and the irascible introspective landscape of Mehring's solitude, pull him, urgently, resonantly, toward his doom. With *The Conservationist*, Nadine Gordimer has triumphantly left the timid league of minor novelists behind. (p. 18)

> *Pearl K. Bell, "Confronting Hateful Legacies," in* The New Leader *(© 1975 by the American Labor Conference on International Affairs, Inc.), March 31, 1975, pp. 17-18.*

[*The Conservationist*] is a magnificent novel about an African farm and about its owner, Mehring, a rich industrialist who is its conserver and its victim, enacting a timeless rivalry between man and land wherein land inevitably triumphs. . . .

Though *The Conservationist* has been greatly praised in England, I would expect it to be even more widely admired here, where stories about man and the land—the one transient, the other abiding—recur and eternally fascinate; it is a theme which has preoccupied American writers from Cooper to Hemingway (but seems not to occur much in the English novel, except perhaps in Hardy). The "conservationist" must impose himself on a landscape that is peculiarly African, but is universal and timeless, too, a rare mixture of particularity and generality that characterizes this distinguished book. . . .

Gordimer has the range and concerns of a mature and brilliant artist. Her writing has the tough precision of poetry and the closely observed naturalness of everyday life. It has all the power of romantic writing about nature but none of the defects, of overwriting and metaphysical pretentiousness, that sometimes mar this mode. *The Conservationist* is intensely impressive.

> *Diane Johnson, "Out of Africa," in* Book World—The Washington Post *(© The Washington Post), April 6, 1975, p. 3.*

Miss Gordimer's vision of Africa is the most complete one we have, and in time to come, when we want to know everything there is to know about a newly independent black African country, it is to this white South African woman and "Guest of Honor" (1970) that we will turn.

If we want an overview of bewildered whites, well-intentioned liberals, foundation men, lost Africans and burnt-out firebrands, her collection of stories, "Livingstone's Companions" (1971) is an invaluable guide. Now that the black South African writers have chosen silence, exile or cunning, only Miss Gordimer remains to record the complex fate of a continent that had a mere decade of notoriety before lapsing into tropical senescence. (p. 4)

> *Paul Theroux, in* The New York Times Book Review *(© 1975 by The New York Times Company; reprinted by permission), April 13, 1975.*

The power of *The Conservationist* is in its rendering of South African life—farm, city, veld, shanty town—and in the questions it poses about the nature of civilization: how much of it is worth conserving? . . . This bare, beautiful novel resists sentimentality. Troubling, spare, and often lyrical, it takes shape from Gordimer's sense of the eternal verities. (p. 12)

> *Frances Taliaferro, in* Bookletter *(copyright 1975 by* Harper's Magazine; *reprinted from the April 28, 1975 issue by special permission), April 28, 1975.*

Blacks outnumber whites in South Africa: how many of THEM are there? It used to be thirteen million. These days the figure has climbed, in one ambitious instance, to twenty-two million . . . of THEM. But then WE have grown in numbers too. . . . We English-speaking whites, together with the Afrikaners (we counted them with us in this one instance only) were a small white island in a vast black sea which would sweep us all to oblivion sooner or later. (p. 49)

Nadine Gordimer is one of the few South African writers (themselves few in number) who set out early on to chart our diminution. She has examined the nature of the predicament of the whites in Southern Africa, alternately cosseting and sublimating our sense of guilt which, however we may try to bury it, springs to life again from the grey ashes of our lives, a terrible phoenix. Much of her best work is written in the knowledge, both exhilarating and finally saddening, that there is no other theme for the artist in South Africa. Miss Gordimer can write about other things, and has often done so in her short stories. But these, for all their craft, cannot rank except in exceptional instances beside the novels in which her attention is focused with all the limitations inherent in the situation on the dangerous and dull banalities that constitute life in Southern Africa. (pp. 49-50)

It is a strange thing that those creations of Miss Gordimer's which most expand in the mind are not those of the living, made by the most painstaking attention to psychological detail, but rather, her dead. In that thin and disappointing novel, *The Late Bourgeois World*, the image of Max, the one-time political revolutionary who drowns himself by driving his car into Cape Town harbour and has betrayed his cause and his friends, swims most powerfully in the consciousness. It is difficult to say why this should be so, why the dead should have more substance than the living.

South Africa is palpably there in all Miss Gordimer's novels: the Greek corner cafés, the bleak little mining towns of the Transvaal, the great mining camp itself, Johannesburg, with its black townships squatting at its feet like unwanted children, and the extravagant idiocies of the well-heeled white madams and masters in their green and sanitized suburbs. . . . One might say that she perceives how deadly dull so much of it is, and she can sometimes be boring with it. At best there is her admirable fidelity to the landscapes she describes, at worst she drives home her points, tediously and sententiously, leaving nothing to the imagination.

Perhaps this is why one grasped so eagerly the new perspective on Africa which she offered in *A Guest Of Honour*. Here was Africa again, but it was an Africa with which few of her white South African readers would have been familiar. How could they be? The Africa to which James Bray returns from England as an honoured guest and then to a post in the department of education at the invitation of the President, Mweta, is very different to their home ground. It is *out there*, beyond the Zambesi. Yet, as one read through *A Guest Of Honour*, one realized with growing amazement that the black state and its people about which she wrote, though they were most certainly black, seemed for all the world like US. Now nothing could be more shocking to the white sensibility than that. It undermines the central pivot on which our entire existence in Africa is based: that we are, well, different, and though of course we are all equal, we are, you know, separate, and we'd rather like to keep it that way—not through choice, you understand, but because we realize that there are those essential, God-given differences. Such a radical challenge to our cherished beliefs in our uniqueness, separateness, whiteness, is the astonishing achievement of *A Guest Of Honour*. It offers no parallels, draws no comparisons, makes no concessions to our pet phobias. We are put in our places not out of mind, perhaps, but out of the picture. (pp. 52-3)

[The] brooding presence of the dead who will not lie down, this powerful influence in so much of Miss Gordimer's writing, has become in *The Conservationist* the major theme. (p. 54)

In this, at once the most dour and desolate of her novels, Nadine Gordimer has come closest to revealing the manner in which we will lose what we have set out most fiercely to conserve. (p. 55)

> *Christopher Hope, "Out of the Picture: The Novels of Nadine Gordimer," in* London Magazine *(© London Magazine, 1975), April/May, 1975, pp. 49-55.*

With a swirling intensity that often leaves names and identities implicit or incomplete, Miss Gordimer summons up [in "The Conservationist"] the well-to-do, deceptively secure world of a South African industrialist referred to simply as Mehring. . . . The title is ironic: while Mehring is aware of every threat to the natural harmony of his farm, he is blind to the consequences of his smug, instinctive aggressions. Through Miss Gordimer's eyes, he sees his land with the lucidity of a true lover, yet his whole life is based on use and exploitation. His character, like those of the other people in this novel, suggests something of the factitious quality of South African society, yet the book is not a tract. Mehring matters to us as if he were someone we knew, and his habits of thoughtlessness can be found anywhere. (pp. 141-42)

The New Yorker (© 1975 by The New Yorker Magazine, Inc.), May 12, 1975.

The way Nadine Gordimer's fiction connects to her political views and activities makes a complex picture that our own writers tend to begrudge us. It is a picture of what the literary critic Leslie Fiedler has called "the relationship between the truth of art, the truth of conscience, and the truth of facts."

Gordimer's books are very far from the purposeful political "novel" that dresses a cross section of a society in ideological sandwich boards. In [*The Conservationist*] for instance, characters think about and bait each other with politics the way people do in ordinary life. (p. 39)

[The] land is the dominant "character" in *The Conservationist*. Its presence courses through the book like the river in *Huckleberry Finn*: destructive and the source of life, receiving and uncovering everything, in time. (p. 40)

> *Veronica Geng, "Disputed Territory," in* Ms. *(© 1975 Ms. Magazine Corp.), July, 1975, pp. 39-41.*

*   *   *

GOYEN, (Charles) William   1915-

Goyen is a Southwestern American novelist and short story writer in whose work physical and emotional detail merge to form a unique, and perhaps undervalued, fiction. (See also *Contemporary Authors*, Vols. 5-8, rev. ed.)

Goyen's prophetic second novel, *In a Farther Country* (1955), . . . is not only [his] most significant novel, but also a highly relevant document, published years ahead of its time, examining in those pre-Rachel Carson years such environmental and ecological problems as air and water pollution and the extinction of numerous species. . . .

At the time of publication the book was received with indifference and incomprehension. Part of the reason Goyen's message fell on deaf ears was, perhaps, a matter of technique. He treated these problems, his themes, not in a naturalistic or realistic manner at all. Goyen did not aspire to become the Upton Sinclair of the ecological or the urban crisis. Instead, he attacked the problems within the elusive framework of a romance. . . . (His first book, *The House of Breath*, was also very much a romance rather than a novel, but was less quixotic in its integration of imagination, memory, and perception. . . .) (p. 213)

The romantic genre was a propitious choice for Goyen, allowing the poetic writer a freedom of time and place and movement unknown in the realistic novel. His central characters, all people who are displaced in locale and in spirit, can freely shuttle back and forth in place and time, imagining themselves to be where they are not. Once the heroine, one Marietta McGee-Chavéz, acquires the totem "road runner" for herself (in reality a faded-out macaw), she dreams herself out of her city apartment and into an adobe house on the plains. Most of the book's action occurs within the field of her dream. The book bears no more resemblance to the usual novel than, say, Virginia Woolf's *Orlando*. (p. 214)

Its last two paragraphs, which form a Coda to the book, reveal that all the characters and actions which preceded were dream-products of the heroine, mere imaginative projections from an embroidered curtain upon which the lifeless prototypes had been stitched. (pp. 214-15)

The frailty of the flesh, of the thread, and of the ancient art of the Colcha stitch from which the curtain was created, are all recurring motifs in the Romance. The tapestry which contains them and into which Marietta enters is like the looking-glass through which Lewis Carroll's Alice passes. It is significant that Goyen, in the very last sentence, raises the additional possibility that, instead of the company having been dreamed by the heroine, the curtain itself was dreamed by the company. This is quite like Carroll's Alice asking, in the last chapter of *Through the Looking-glass*, who it was who dreamed it all.... Carroll's Alice and Goyen's Marietta share this and other uncertainties revolving about the unreality of the real. (p. 215)

Marietta's Southwest in the romance is but a Southwest of the mind. Displaced and unhappy, a victim of what Saul Bellow has called "deep city vexation," she nevertheless must remain in the city and therefore begins in her unhappiness to move in a field which is almost exclusively mental. (pp. 215-16)

The book's title, then, comes into focus when we acknowledge "the farther country" to be not Spain or New Mexico, and certainly not New York, but rather the farther reaches of the imagination which can salvage the spirit in a bad time. One of the book's essential themes is the survival of the imagination in a world where imagination is dying, an insensitive world established in the very first paragraph, where the constant stream of trucks on West Twenty-third Street emblemizes the omnipresent threat of mechanization. . . .

This romance, then, is about exiles—animals exiled from their natural habitat, but more especially human victims of the unnatural environment man has created. (p. 217)

Man has killed off species before taking the time to study their value or to perceive the consequences. He has not taken things in their season, which is the great lesson of *In a Farther Country*. Toward the conclusion, in one of the most beautiful passages William Goyen has given us anywhere, the author makes a plea, in purest poetry, that we not force the world into an unnatural state. . . . (p. 220)

> Robert Phillips, "The Romance of Prophecy: Goyen's 'In a Farther Country'," in Southwest Review (© 1971 by Southern Methodist University Press), Summer, 1971, pp. 213-21.

[*Come, The Restorer*] seems a splendid synthesis of some of Goyen's original themes—the struggle between the spirit and the flesh; the loss of integrity in a time of ecological travesty—with his later comic manner, first evidenced in *The Fair Sister* (1963).

While critics can debate the place of *Come, the Restorer* in the Goyen canon, it also seems of value to reassess the novel which launched Goyen's literary trajectory, which has twice been a play, which has been translated into several languages, . . . and which many feel he may never surpass: *The House of Breath* (1950). It is a book so rich, so original, that even a quarter of a century later there is little agreement on its "meaning" and implications. (p. 248)

Certain critics have found its ultimate meaning totally elu-

sive. . . . Nonsense. Rather than being incomprehensible, *The House of Breath* is a novel shimmering with so many implications and resonances that it requires many readings before comprehension.

I suggest two entrances to this novel, two ways of seeing the materials Goyen has ordered, ways of sharing his intentions. The first is a matter of secrets kept by each main character. In a somewhat plotless novel, one in which chapters are mere refractions of the teller's memory, the revelation of a secret (or secrets) by each protagonist is an important dramatic element uniting the book, and one which no critic has before touched upon. Indeed, "Everything in this world is not black and white," as Goyen instructs at one point. And it is . . . the gray areas—the unclear, the undifferentiated—which he explores most extensively. (p. 249)

While the secrets are clandestine, certain symbols and symbolic acts within the novel are very open. They need only be pondered to be understood, and once understood, to contribute to understanding. For the most part, Goyen's symbols are highly elemental—invoking air, earth, and water for association. (In . . . *Come, the Restorer*, he adds the fourth element, fire, while maintaining the other three.) (p. 251)

> Robert Phillips, "Secret and Symbol: Entrances to Goyen's House of Breath," in Southwest Review (© 1974 by Southern Methodist University Press), Summer, 1974, pp. 248-53.

William Goyen's first novel in a decade [*Come, the Restorer*] is a welcome event. Panning in on his native Texas, Goyen has given us the history of the "rich and conservative city" of Rose during its "days of wonder and joy before the world went bad." . . .

Evoking this vanished world with brilliance and verve, Goyen the fabulist awakens in us "the expectation that everybody has, at one time or another . . . [of] something going to return; or something going to arrive, bright and fresh and changing everything." This done, he reminds us gently that there is no return, that in all probability nothing wondrous will happen—leaving us enriched but with a deep sense of loss. (p. 111)

> Peter G. Kramer, in Newsweek (copyright 1974 by Newsweek, Inc.; all rights reserved; reprinted by permission), November 11, 1974.

* * *

GOYTISOLO, Juan 1931-

Goytisolo, a prolific and talented Spanish novelist, was born in Catalonia and has lived in exile in France since 1957.

Although he has lived in exile for most of the past two decades, Juan Goytisolo, at the age of 43, is generally considered to be the foremost novelist of contemporary Spain. Within his own country all of Goytisolo's work—six novels, two books of essays—is on the swollen blacklist of "outlawed writers," mainly, of course, because the author is an intransigently outspoken enemy of the Franco regime. (p. 15)

[Like] that Irish exile James Joyce, with whom he is often,

perhaps extravagantly, compared by European critics, Goytisolo has become more and more passionately obsessed with his despised and beloved country the longer he lives beyond its suffocating reach. His new novel, *Count Julian . . .*, is a violent, irresolvable quarrel between the severed halves of a Spanish exile's nature, one part exultantly free of a world that "compels us, against our wills, to be spokesmen for something," the other inescapably bewitched by a man's unbreakable ties to his homeland.

The word "novel," it should be pointed out, is simply a label of convenience for *Count Julian*. The book is really an anti-epic, a brutally untraditional meditation—now apoplectically enraged, now cruelly and deceptively playful—on the barren wastes of Spanish history and the putrescent stench of 20th-century Spanish "progress." That Goytisolo faces the defiling realities with totally agonized despair, disbelieving in the possibility of change, he makes appallingly clear by casting the entire work in the form of a single sentence, which uses many types of punctuation but never the period. *Count Julian* is literally a drama of vicious continuity that has no end. (pp. 15-16)

The standard device of modernism is the wrenching of conventional forms out of their placid, familiar alignments, in order to explode the desiccated habits of inherited response; to offend and mock and jeer as a majestically subversive means of eliciting new ways of seeing, hearing, thinking, feeling. But because Goytisolo limits the scope of his assault so narrowly to abuses of the word, he finally defeats himself. When his own language becomes a vehicle of incomprehensibility, Goytisolo seems as much the victim of the word as he is the enemy of its abuse. (p. 16)

> *Pearl K. Bell, "Exile's Revenge," in* The New Leader (© *1974 by the American Labor Conference on International Affairs, Inc.), June 10, 1974, pp. 15-16.*

Juan Goytisolo, . . . an exile from Franco Spain since 1957, has written a tortured, labyrinthine novel [*Count Julian*] that leaves a ragged scar across the land from Port Bou to Algeciras, from La Corunna to Almeria. He rapes the language and castrates the culture. In a sado-masochistic rage he seeks to purge and purify—to shake Spanish stoicism to its very foundations with a massive dose of corruption.

To this end Goytisolo has constructed an elaborate psychosexual metaphor in which Count Julian urges that the Moorish conquest be repeated.

Nothing escapes the fury of Count Julian. History, tradition, ritual and that which goes by the name of progress are all lacerated. Seneca, the great Stoical philosopher who opened his veins in the most futile of all gestures, symbolizes what Goytisolo obviously regards as the absurdity of Spanish nobility, the poverty of Spanish philosophy.

But the very end of the book provides an insight into the true relationship between Count Julian and Spain across the straits. "tomorrow," he says, "will be another day, the invasion will begin all over again"

There is no period at the end of that sentence—the last in the book. What could possibly be more stoical than that? . . .

Count Julian is an effort to revise the Spanish language and bring the Spanish novel into the 20th century. It is the spir-

itual heir of *Ulysses*, most of Beckett, *Naked Lunch* and *Last Exit to Brooklyn*. It has minor flaws such as the obviousness of much of its symbolism and the obscurity of some of its historical allusions, but its overall success in mapping the hell of Julian's mind is an impressive literary achievement.

> *Stephen Klaidman, "Heart of Darkness," in* Book World—The Washington Post (© *The Washington Post), June 16, 1974, p. 2.*

[*Count Julian* is] a very *literary* achievement, an elegant and accomplished novel about impotent rage rather than a cry of rage and impotence itself, and a little too civilized for all the violence it keeps threatening to conjure up. . . .

I say this because the book occasionally behaves as if it were a genuine political act all on its own—it is no more political than any good novel is, and it is less political than some. What it is, is a Spanish work of fiction which has learned the language of phantasmagoria and feigned free association from Latin American writers of the Sixties (*Count Julian* was first published in Mexico in 1970). . . . I don't mean that Goytisolo is imitating or plagiarizing Cortázar, or Lezama Lima, or García Márquez, I mean that the occupied language of Spain is here set free by the emancipated example of other novelists writing in Spanish; once free, having once found what he calls in another context the absolute kingdom of the improbable, Goytisolo creates his own remarkably fluent and funny and intelligent idiom. . . .

Nothing is sacred, nothing is spared. Everything Spanish, from Fray Luis de León to Federico García Lorca by way of Unamuno and Menéndez Pelayo, comes under the hatchet of this exile's scorn. The attack is too undiscriminating in the end to be anything other than an implicit portrait of the attacker, and this is the force of the allusion in the book's title. (p. 40)

> *Michael Wood, in* The New York Review of Books (*reprinted with permission from* The New York Review of Books; *copyright © 1974 NYREV, Inc.), August 8, 1974.*

"Count Julian" is the vengeful and surrealistic daydream of a kif-smoking Tangiers dweller who is obsessed by dreams of revenge-through-decadence over the Spain which has exiled him. It combines the flavor of de Sade with the contemporary continental traditions of novelists like Robbe-Grillet and Cortázar: there is also, like a footnote, a young boy guide in the Gide tradition.

The narrator is launching a revolution which he says will consist of sex and intelligence, with support in passing from the international pop culture. At first the attack is limited to squashing flies and spiders between the pages of various Spanish classics, but the author also clashes with a doomed and corrupted Seneca and the fantasy culminates, finally, in the invasion of the mainland by Count Julian, a famous and ferociously perverse Spanish traitor.

It is an extremely sensitively written narrative and comes across with surprising gentleness considering that it amounts to a poison pen letter to Spanish society, comparable perhaps to Picasso's very personal hate-filled comic strip showing the defeat of a pestilent France. Yet even such a vivid scene as the death of an American tourist lady who is fatally bitten by a snake she has been enticed into holding for photographers remains, in the quietly seething flow of phrases, hallucinatory, with not much more weight than conjecture. At such moments, Goytisolo seems to satisfy himself by playing with shock.

The movement of his narrative, a flow of phrases half severed and half connected by colons (a protest against colonialism?), has the effect of a gently delirious reverie; I felt like I was living through an illness with beneficial side effects. I admired "Count Julian" but must say that generally the vagueness of delineated idea combined with the high quality of its style made it come across as a fine patina without the statue. (pp. 25-6)

> *Martin Washburn, in* The Village Voice *(reprinted by permission of* The Village Voice; *copyright © The Village Voice, Inc., 1974), August 15, 1974.*

Goytisolo is a most ingenious traveller and writer, and far from monotonous. He has . . . been an exile since 1957. He was born in Catalonia and educated at the Universities of Barcelona and Madrid; his name is Basque. The only point in mentioning this is that Basque and Catalan cultures are by tradition violently hostile to the classic role of Castile in Spanish history and literature. The Catalans see themselves as dramatic personal volcanoes, as "modern" eruptions in a country vowed to the cults of death and custom. It is natural that Goytisolo should immediately bring Joyce, Malcolm Lowry, Beckett, and even Nabokov to mind, for he looks beyond his country. Exile unites such writers in one important aspect. The exile loses his country, and his only luggage is his language—a smuggled capital or hoard. He locks himself up in it and it becomes a speculative magic, and he himself becomes—as Joyce and Nabokov became—a grammarian of his hatreds and defeated love. (p. 173)

The pain in ["Count Julian"] is not only the pain of exile. The recurrent symbols of the snake, poison, infection, the fighting weapons of insects introduce elements of excess and cruelty that go back to some personal horror which threads the moral indignation of the book. The cripples and beggars are like mutilated insects; on a higher plane, the Spaniards (or, as he would say, the Hispanos) are ridiculed for a sexual puritanism induced by their fierce religion or by the cults of virginity, the mother, and the traditional feeling for racial or ideological purity; the narrator is haunted by a dreadful fantasy of homosexual assault in childhood and of obsessive guilt. This is one of the recurring themes in the elaborate mosaic into which his outcry falls. It, of course, enlarges the sense of rebellion against disgrace and complicity in it. As a diatribe, "Count Julian" is black comedy. It suffers from journalistic punning and a touch or two of the kind of café fantasy more likely to erupt in Barcelona (the home of the fantastic cathedral of the Sagrada Familia) than in the cliché-ridden tertulias of Madrid. The interesting thing is that the love-hate, like Joyce's in "Ulysses," should take the form of a revolt against language forms and syntax; in this century, literature and the arts have been prompt to record the seismic tremors that have dislodged our certainties. Yet "black" though it is, "Count Julian" has a note of jubilation and a devastating, satirical wit. (p. 175)

> *V. S. Pritchett, "Man Without a Country," in* The New Yorker *(copyright 1974 by V. S. Pritchett; reprinted by permission of Harold*

Matson Co., Inc.), October 7, 1974, pp. 173-75.

Properly speaking, *Count Julian* should be read as part of a trilogy. The first volume is *Marks of Identity*, the second is *Count Julian* and the third, the about to be published *Juan Without a Country*. (p. 250)

Marks of Identity is a departure from the previous Goytisolo novels which were done in the super-realistic mode which had a grip on Spanish literature, and stemmed directly from the political miseries of the calamitous Spain of the late 1940s and 1950s. In *Marks of Identity*, Goytisolo begins to do a variety of things. Obvious political statement, he feels, is not enough for a novel; he starts to break with form—using a variety of first, second and third persons, he is looking and listening to the breaks in language and, at the same time, he begins to break with form—in the attempt to describe what he is really seeing and feeling, his work becomes less abstract. The autobiography, in broken form, or new form, is begun. Like Joyce, Goytisolo's exiled hero starts at a long voyage, and finally begins with himself, his own childhood, his own town—Barcelona. We see, filtered through the photos and dialogues inside the hero's head—that hero who, walled in by bitter loneliness and rage, is "installed in Paris"—the world of Alvaro. [Alvaro, who dreams up Count Julian, is Goytisolo's Stephen Dedalus.] . . .

When one reads *Count Julian* in proper sequence, with its bold, raging, poetic, incantatory rhythms, marvelously translated by Helen R. Lane, it is a book far more accessible to the reader. (p. 251)

Count Julian has been reviewed in this country as the masterpiece of Spain's greatest living writer. Albeit true, the statement is of little use to the reader unless the novel is put into its proper context. Carlos Fuentes, in his *New York Times* review, did a magnificent job of explaining the relation of Spanish history to the use of the legendary Count Julian. Michael Wood, however, in *The New York Review of Books* confused matters by assuming that Goytisolo learned his techniques from the modern Latin American novelists. The life force in Goytisolo's work is Spain—and has nothing to do with Latin American genius. Goya, Buñuel, Madrid, Barcelona, outrageous wit—all these play in the formation of Goytisolo's style and his very Spanish way of being obsessed by Spain. Like many Spanish geniuses before him, including Picasso, Goytisolo appears to have benefited by subjecting Spanish passion to French thought. Clearly, in addition to Joyce, he has been influenced by Céline, Jean Genet and the techniques of the *nouveau roman*. While some of those techniques have produced novels that appear to be somewhat listless—the French novelists in the last decade often seem to lack a subject on which to hang their techniques—in the hands of this Spanish novelist, raging against Spain, the results are explosive. (pp. 251-52)

> *Barbara Probst Solomon, in* The Nation *(copyright 1975 by the Nation Associates, Inc.), March 1, 1975.*

*   *   *

GUNN, Bill   1934-

Gunn is an American novelist and playwright. (See also *Contemporary Authors*, Vols. 13-16, rev. ed.)

The first thing to be said about Bill Gunn's play "Black Picture Show" . . . is that its author is obviously gifted. The second thing to be said about the play is that it is not a success. And the third thing to be said about it is that, ironically, the nature of its failure heightens one's certainty of Mr. Gunn's talent, for that *any* dramatic action capable of interesting us for an entire evening could be wrested out of the ill-chosen, long-since-shopworn subject matter of "Black Picture Show" approaches the miraculous. We are again, and how reluctantly, in the presence of a hero who writes. Writes and suffers, and his suffering, like that of a thousand other writers in plays, novels, and movies, is induced largely by the fact that he has sold out. For nothing more important than money, he has committed his divine spark into the hands of hucksters; he who should have been an O'Neill has become a hack. Moreover, his lacerating self-reproach is made all the more painful by the fact that the hucksters who have seduced him are white and he is black. He has done a grave injury not only to himself but also to his people.

Where to begin in the dismissal of such conventional claptrap? Almost the first rule that one learns on taking up a career in letters is that a writer mustn't write about a writer writing. (Prodigious exceptions, like Joyce and Proust, are imitated at one's peril.) A second rule, which need never be mastered, provided that one obeys the first rule, is that a writer's occupational sufferings are apt to be much less interesting than those of a truck driver or a lacquerer of tea trays; his flushed flutterings on the brink of literary prostitution quickly prove tiresome. In any event, the first-rate artist who sells out and therefore becomes second-rate is mostly a figment of the imagination of the second-rate artist who has sold out and who would never have been first-rate; or perhaps, more amusingly, it is a figment of the imagination of the third-rate writer who has sold out and has unexpectedly advanced to second-rate, with the hope of someday being first-rate dimly glimmering before him. "Black Picture Show" prompts other musings. Why is it worse for a black to sell out to a white than for a white to sell out to a white, or, for that matter, for a black to sell out to a black? Except on grounds of racial snobbery, with its implication that all blacks ought to be able to be counted on to behave more honorably than all whites, why should the question of color arise?

Mr. Gunn may well have been troubled by some of these questions and may have sought to divert our attention from them by the overingenious intricacies of his cat's cradle of a plot. He constantly scrambles time and place: the hero is now a middle-aged man going mad and dying in the presence of a young son, now himself a young son uneasy in the presence of his father; the bleak dayroom of the psychiatric ward of a hospital in the Bronx is at the same time the vulgarly overfurnished living room of a large country house. These pranks of dramaturgy, though they serve to keep us on our toes, fail to illuminate the characters; the story is essentially a simple one and gains nothing by having an apparent complexity imposed on it. . . . The murderous conversations between the hero-writer and his wife and between the producer and his wife compare favorably with the classic oral assassinations of "Who's Afraid of Virginia Woolf?" Mr. Gunn is at his best in these scenes. (p. 61)

> *Brendan Gill, in* The New Yorker (© *1975 by* The New Yorker *Magazine, Inc.), January 20, 1975.*

Until recent years, no one could have imagined that rage would be peddled as theatrical entertainment. In its osmotic effect, this viciousness of attitude poisons whatever theme the playwright may have thought he had. The playgoer leaves the theater in a state of psychological dishevelment as he might a hospital room after visiting a patient who is running a dangerous fever.

In *Black Picture Show*, Playwright Bill Gunn's hero is already hospitalized, or rather, confined to a Bronx, New York City, mental home. Alexander . . . has gone mad, but he has been a black poet, playwright and screenwriter of merit. Fragmented episodes indicate how he has bobbed for the white man's Golden Delicious apple and drowned in economic and psychic abasement. He is dying; perhaps he is already dead. Obfuscation ranks high among Playwright Gunn's defects.

What is Gunn driving at? He is saying that Alexander, an artist of seemingly impeccable integrity, has sold out and been destroyed by his yen for lucre. This is twaddle. No artist has ever been corrupted or humiliated by the quest for cash unless he was a willing accomplice. . . .

Need one add that Playwright Gunn is not at all satisfied to make this a human fallibility? He persists in what has become for some an article of faith and fallacy—that some whitey somewhere is prostituting the black brothers for gain. Just to spell it out in the corniest imaginable terms, Playwright Gunn has Alexander's wife sue for a contract with a white homosexual film producer . . ., and she has to kneel on the floor to pick up the largesse he languidly strews in the form of $1,000 bills. Meanwhile, the producer's wife . . . sashays round the room in a cocaine-sniffing trance. Racism is abhorrent; let the same be said for reverse racism.

> *T. E. Kalem, "The Blame Game," in* Time *(reprinted by permission from* Time, The Weekly Newsmagazine; *copyright* Time Inc.), *January 20, 1975, p. 76.*

Bill Gunn comes late to the ranks of anti-white black writers. In his 1964 novel "All the Rest Have Died" his leading character, Barney, also a black writer [as is Alexander, the protagonist of "Black Picture Show"] says: "I am not concerned with what I am racially. . . . I am the rapist and the raped. I am victimized and I am responsible." Now in "Black Picture Show" there are lines like "White heaven is colored hell," which have an unconvincing, bandwagon ring. Maybe Gunn's consciousness has been raised, but I think Barney's words represent Gunn's real feeling as a writer, and I think the real theme of his play is the agony of the artist in a world where art is a dirty word. . . .

This is almost the first black play to deal with this theme, and it's too bad Gunn has gotten it out of focus. Even the key, violent quarrels between Alexander and [his son] J. D. are thrown out of whack by a racial overlay. J. D. has become a successful director of chic films (very murky, this), and he represents, he tells Alexander, the black counter-revolution—"from freedom to indifference." The real pathos of this father-son relationship is that it stands for two sides of one split spirit—J. D.'s "indifference" is really Alexander's own temptation to abandon the imperatives of art for self-pity.

Put simply, I believe Gunn's mistake was his attempt to

write a "black" play. Black writing at this point—Toni Morrison, Ishmael Reed, Ed Bullins—has out-distanced the simplicities of Gunn's belated racial polemics.

> *Jack Kroll, "Black-and-White Picture," in* Newsweek *(copyright 1975 by Newsweek, Inc.; all rights reserved; reprinted by permission), January 20, 1975, p. 83.*

Judging by his *Black Picture Show* . . ., Bill Gunn as dramatist and director is a man of notable but as yet undisciplined talent. There is strong feeling in the play; there are passages of excellent writing and, in dialogue and staging, one brilliantly conceived scene. But the play lacks steady focus. . . .

Further, the writing veers from a crudely effective vernacular to prose-poetry and perhaps verse. The latter fails to register, not merely because it is indistinctly spoken but because it serves no dramatic function. It seems even more a "decoration" than the music which accompanies much of the action. Gunn tries to do too many things at once; the play becomes disordered. Yet one recognizes a genuine heartbeat; it is a living experience. (p. 94)

> *Harold Clurman, in* The Nation *(copyright 1975 by the Nation Associates, Inc.), January 25, 1975.*

[*Black Picture Show*] is, basically, a simplistic work about an idealistic black playwright and his opportunistic film-maker son struggling in the white man's show-biz, both characters apparently modeled on Gunn himself, a screenwriter-director with a history of troubles with Hollywood. Dying in an asylum, the father hallucinates the key moments of his life, involving a drunken mother, a loyal but castrating wife, a loving but difficult son, and a mysterious friend who doubles as a butler. It is all about family infighting and flamboyant guilt feelings, plus, of course, the obligatory white-hating scene, the play's cornerstone, in which a bestial Hollywood producer and his whacked-out wife come to dinner and humiliate their black hosts while making white pigs of themselves.

This could have been your standard undistinguished play except for some patches of keen Albeesque bitchery to make it a bit better, and a great deal of pretension to make it a lot worse: Strindbergian expressionism, scramblings of time and place, an onstage band playing irrelevant music . . . with occasional supererogatory lyrics by the author, and periodic lapses into spoken verse, of which Gunn seems enormously proud though they sound like a cross between a college poetry magazine and a Hallmark card. (p. 51)

> *John Simon, in* New York Magazine *(© 1975 by NYM Corp.; reprinted by permission of* New York Magazine *and John Simon), January 27, 1975.*

H

HACKER, Marilyn   1942-

Ms Hacker, an American poet now living in England, won both the Lamont Poetry Prize and the National Book Award for *Presentation Piece*, her first collection.

The titles of the poems [in *Presentation Piece*] are fashionable ("Pornographic Poem," "Landscape for Insurrection," "She Bitches about Boys"), but a close look reveals a collection of technical exercises: villanelles, sestinas, perfect iambic pentameters and far from perfect free verse. The poems seem created, not with urgency or commitment, but to display craftsmanship. Yet, it is the craftsmanship which distorts. Hacker's world of sexual liberation sounds somewhat ludicrous propped by 17th-century verse forms.... Hacker also has a predilection for the recondite. How can the reader respond to [her] grab bag of images, set in what passes as free verse? (p. 3)

> Norma Procopiow, in Book World—The Washington Post (© The Washington Post), May 26, 1974.

Presentation Piece . . . [is] a very good book. . . .

The American poetry scene is so large and diffuse that it's hard, perhaps impossible, to generalize about it. But there does seem to be a resurgence of interest in tight, formal poetry and Marilyn Hacker's poems show the rich possibilities inherent in structure; her book is filled with sonnets, sestinas (61), villanelles, blank verse, even heroic couplets (but with distinctly modern tone)....

The poems are personal, intense, often oblique and sliding toward the surreal; these last, though sometimes interesting, are the least successful, hardest to get at. . . . But the book is filled with poems not only strongly realized but which say something about and to the human condition. "The Navigators" is a fine long poem about the complicated, sexual relationship of three people. "The Dark Twin," "Exiles," "She Bitches about Boys," "Imaginary Translations" and "Elegy for Janis Joplin" are poems with deep feelings controlled and directed by technical skill and wit reminiscent of Howard Nemerov's poems. I suppose it is still fashionable to think that intellect and wit are somehow incompatible with deeply felt poetry—one can't be romantic and ironic at the same time—but *Presentation Piece* encourages me to think that the fashion may be changing. (p. 24)

> Peter Meinke, in The New Republic (reprinted by permission of The New Republic; © 1974 by The New Republic, Inc.), September 7, 1974.

Marilyn Hacker stands squarely, and very elegantly, in the indirect T. S. Eliot line. She is sharp-eyed and -edged, cool, very acute about sophistication and its falsities, and very witty. Her wit is at its best when it is at one with her humor and her good humor. "Presentation Piece" shows a great many skills, and doesn't just show them off. At times, it does wax philosophical about what poetry deeply is—but then elsewhere it furnishes the best sort of self-criticism: poems which are likewise about poetry but are rich with comedy and insinuation. The exquisitely sinister sestina, "Untoward Occurrence at Embassy Poetry Reading," for instance, which pays back its tacit debt to W. H. Auden tenfold; or the sardonic sonnet "Apologia pro opere suo".....

She is a most deft rhymestress—the feminine form of "rhymester," which Marilyn Hacker may dislike (when she lists her interests and causes, she juxtaposes houseplants and radical feminism), compresses rhythm and prosody ("stress") with rhyme. There is a weird amplitude of spirit in her steely erotic poetry, as in the cheerful city grubbiness of "Elektra on Third Avenue"; or the mock-prim suggestive silence (total, just where you least expect it) of "Pornographic Poem"; or the laconic crackle of "Imaginary Translation II"; or the seductive accents of "Nimue to Merlin"; or (best of all) the rhythmic disintegration into a hurrying longing, which gives itself away, of "She Bitches About Boys".... (p. 2)

> Christopher Ricks, in The New York Times Book Review (© 1975 by The New York Times Company; reprinted by permission), January 12, 1975.

Marilyn Hacker . . . is a poet of emerging womanhood and the decaying American city. Her lines have a nervous intensity and a taut, glutted texture expressive of their subject. (p. 46)

Miss Hacker's dense line makes for interest and sometimes high adventure; but it also makes for strain and for an opacity which at times seems willful. More than most first volumes, *Presentation Piece* demands to be read in its entirety, since the poems reflect on one another, and with repeated readings a vocabulary of images begins to emerge. Over and again one encounters images of the body, especially the tongue; of salt upon the tongue; of the sea, cliffs, a beach; of lovers awakening. And it becomes apparent that the poet is attempting to formulate, in these and related images, a language of instinct and feeling—of a woman's bodily awareness—and to express the body's longings, including its "inadmissible longings", as they are shaped and repressed in personal relationships. That such a language has yet to be created, or yet to be discovered, is both exhilarating and a cause for anguish. (pp. 46-7)

These poems grope not only through languages but also through forms, as though nothing quite sufficed to express the pain of isolation. About half of the poems employ traditional forms: sonnets, villanelles, sestinas. When these pieces succeed, as does a poem entitled *Forage Sestina*, they express powerful emotions powerfully restrained; and they seem to confirm the traditional forms. Often, however, the sonnets and sestinas fall victim to artifice and do not confirm much of anything. Whatever their origin might have been, they read like formal exercises. On the whole, the poems in freer forms are more convincing. If, like the shrill, unreadable *Elegy* for Janis Joplin, they sometimes fail, it is not for lack of insight or feeling but for lack of the restraint so evident in the more traditional pieces. (p. 47)

> *Ben Howard, in* Poetry (© *1975 by The Modern Poetry Association; reprinted by permission of the Editor of* Poetry), *April, 1975.*

[Marilyn Hacker's] anger forms [her] work, and in each case is set against a delicate lyricism; this tension is what makes [her] poetry extraordinary. Marilyn Hacker, with her complex imagery and mastery of rhyme and conventional poetic forms, seems to be creating word puzzles against chaos. (p. 48)

[The poems in *Presentation Piece*] seem . . . to be autobiographical, but as I read more deeply, they seemed as much about language as life. There is something very disturbing about her images, the kind of disturbance you feel jostling through an unfamiliar street: everything is too vivid. And there is her uncontemporary love of tight forms. Hacker ends *Presentation Piece* with a sonnet sequence called "A Christmas Crown," but her favorite form seems to be the sestina; the book has seven.

In a sestina the last words of the six lines of the first stanza are repeated in a different order to end the lines of the other five stanzas. The limitation this places on the poet adds to the excitement of writing a poem. (p. 113)

> *Honor Moore, in* Ms. (© *1975 Ms. Magazine Corp.), April, 1975.*

*   *   *

HAILEY, Arthur   1920-

Hailey, an English-born Canadian novelist and playwright, has won enormous popularity with his slick and engrossing formula fiction. *The Final Diagnosis, Hotel, Airport,* **and** *Wheels* **are among the most widely read of all contemporary novels. (See also** *Contemporary Authors,* **Vols. 1-4, rev. ed.)**

"Wheels" is at once an exposé of and a salute to the auto industry. The exposures are directed largely at the work force, who may well deserve them; at car dealers, who are certainly not without sin; and at the M---a, which controls the crime rampant in all auto plants. On the other hand, Mr. Hailey plays a diligent Boswell to management's Doctor Johnson. He describes the pox-marks on his subject's cheeks, but finds him to be an admirable fellow.

The book (a Hailey hallmark) is crammed with information about the design, manufacture and marketing of automobiles. It has a Tolstoy-sized cast. Its plot has more windings than a Byzantine intrigue. That is not to say it is hard to follow: Mr. Hailey is nothing if not a competent craftsman; his directions are as easy to understand as an A.A.A. road map. What is more, his novel is interesting, since he has the natural storyteller's gift of keeping a reader avidly turning the pages. One's attention does wane, briefly, when he writes lines like: "Later they made love to find the old magic had returned." But these are momentary irritants—and one races past them. (p. 48)

Mr. Hailey produces not a single scene with explicit sex, and few terms likely to offend anybody's moral sensibilities. The strongest word in the book is "s-o-b," usually directed at Emerson Vale, a critic of the industry and author of a book "The American Car: Unsure in Any Need." . . .

Mr. Hailey goes on and on, until he decides he has given the reader his money's worth. And he has. In my judgment, his chances of escaping blockbusterdom are nil. (p. 49)

> *John Reed, in* The New York Times Book Review (© *1971 by The New York Times Company; reprinted by permission), September 19, 1971.*

Arthur Hailey lives in a world of diminishing opportunities, perhaps a victim of his own success. Since he perfected the formula for his kind of novel, with *Airport*, a lot of other writers have moved onto his turf—not necessarily imitators, but certainly competitors, gobbling up ideas in a field where basic themes are not all that plentiful. Frederick Forsyth, for example, wrote the novel that Hailey might have called *Coup* or *The Mercenaries*, calling it instead *The Dogs of War* and hitting best-seller lists for a good long stay. John Godey's *The Taking of Pelham One Two Three* might just as easily have been a Hailey book called *Subway*. And there are two books either of which Hailey might have written under the title of *Skyscraper: The Tower* and *The Glass Inferno*. It's getting crowded out there in the world of what we might call the "information novel."

But if he ever runs out of industries and enterprises suited to his particular style, Hailey does have one last resource; he can always do a novel with autobiographical overtones called *Potboiler*. It would chronicle in minute detail the daily routines of a man who lives well by writing 500-page books which are almost fact and almost fiction: the travels to interview people for background information, the carefully arranged boxes full of little index cards with key details, the slow elaboration of a multilayered plot and the writer's search for places in the bulk of his novel where he can slip in a fact or an opinion like nuts and raisins in a muffin. Above all, it should explore the unique formula for this kind of book. Start with something large and complicated, a business or institution that touches the lives of large numbers of people and is not fully understood by the public. Ideally, the subject should have a touch of glamour and some element of risk in its routine activities. The writer takes the reader inside this subject, letting him see it from various points of view and tossing in an occasional little sermon on public responsibilities. Numerous characters are formed out of available material (cardboard will do nicely) and they are set in motion by a series of crises, small, medium and large, which illustrate the nature and particularly the weaknesses of the activity that is the real subject (in a sense the real hero) of the book.

The Moneychangers fits this pattern beautifully. Its hero is First Mercantile American, a large bank in Cleveland (the locale is carefully disguised throughout, but on page 200 an editor let slip the information that one of the bank's officers lives in Shaker Heights) that sometimes resembles the Bank of America. FMA faces a number of problems and/or decisions: the mysterious disappearance of $6,000 from a teller's cashbox; a rash of counterfeit credit cards; the question of whether to continue funding a low-cost housing development or to float a massive loan for a multinational conglomerate; policy decisions on whether to open new branches, how to advertise its services and which to encourage (credit cards which are a trap for many weak-willed clients, or savings accounts which build the nation's moral fiber), whether to put money into slow-but-sure home mortgage investments or to go after various fast-buck opportunities. Above all, the bank faces the choice of a new president, whose personality will naturally affect many key decisions: Roscoe, an unimaginative man but good with money whose eye is fixed firmly on the bottom line; or Alex, dynamic, innovative, socially aware but solidly committed to traditional fiscal virtues—you can tell from these summaries which one Hailey is rooting for.

The plot involves (besides a modest quota of sex) a large and cleverly contrived demonstration by poor people, undercover operations in a counterfeit ring, a bit of embezzling, a little blackmail, some high-level corporate hanky-panky, a major financial disaster, a localized panic and run on the bank, some kidnapping and torture, several visits to an insane asylum, a chase scene, a suicide. And in little niches strategically located throughout the plot, we get what I suspect most people read Hailey for: a panoramic view of the banking industry, its security arrangements and profit margins, the philosophy of the credit card, the attractions of foreign currency, the inside of the stock market, the EFT (electronic fund transfer) system which may eventually replace money, the principles of trust fund management, the question of interlocking directorates, the relation of banks to savings and loan institutions, the plans for a new American currency which will baffle counterfeiters, the dynamics of short-term money trading among big banks, tax dodges and shelters, the techniques of a surprise audit in a branch bank and much more. We might say of Hailey what one of his characters says of a call girl who is employed by a large conglomerate, that he gives full value for the money.

What he gives, actually, is the feeling that you are learning something—that, by the time you finish page 472, you really know what's in banking. This is largely illusion, of course; even with this size and such a restricted subject,

the book has to sacrifice depth to achieve breadth. But it is ideal reading for those who feel guilty about wasting their time on mere fiction. And if you wonder whether there are many such people, just watch the best-seller lists. (pp. 1-2)

Joseph McLellan, "Cash on the Line," in Book World—The Washington Post (© The Washington Post), *March 23, 1975, pp. 1-2.*

Arthur Hailey's novels are such genuine publishing events that to criticize them is like putting the slug on the Rockettes. It's not going to change anything. No sooner is his contract inked than mighty lumberjacks start to make their axes ring. Paperback houses and book clubs fairly whimper to give him money while the work is still in progress, and Ross Hunter calls up the old actors' home to begin casting his next blockbuster. At the publication party itself the last deviled egg is still to be consumed when his book busts through on the best-seller lists. In view of all this hoopla, the fact that Mr. Hailey's books aren't any good seems to be almost beside the point. They are already winners.

Still, there is such a thing as degree, and it must be reported that "The Moneychangers" represents a step backward for Mr. Hailey. It is neither as interesting as "Hotel" nor as arresting as "Airport."

The side of the street Mr. Hailey is working runs through an old and respected neighborhood. The novel that brings the reader news of places and people far removed from his own experience has been a staple of the craft of fiction since Defoe started the whole thing. For better or worse, and I'm not so sure it has always been for worse, the novel has been as good an illuminator of our time as nonfiction. Good novelists, even clumsy ones with a story to tell, have always been able to take us behind the scenes. Dreiser rubbed our noses in the stench of the machine shop, and Auchincloss can still give us a dazzling, muted tour of the board room. They had stories that went somewhere peopled with characters you wanted to know more about. And while they were at it, they told how things worked.

Mr. Hailey doesn't have a story to tell that hasn't been done better before. His characters swarm through his books like bores at a cocktail party you forget the second they depart and have to be reintroduced when they reappear. And his detail work gives less information than a well-constructed Sunday piece in a newspaper. Mr. Hailey is one of the new purveyors of plasticized fiction who promises to take us to distant places and then stashes us in a nearby Hilton hotel.

In his latest ["The Moneychangers"], Mr. Hailey draws a bead on the banking business and somehow manages to miss that inviting target almost entirely. Ben Rosselli, president of the First Mercantile American Bank, announces that he is at death's door—which at least gets him out of the book early. This sets off an unseemly struggle for power reminiscent of the plot of "Executive Suite" which is resolved in largely the same way. If you think the vice president who is in favor of the little people of this world doesn't win, you haven't been reading many Arthur Hailey novels. It's enough to make you search out Tolstoy's clean old peasant and strangle him.

There are a few subplots included not so much to illuminate the main story I suspect, as to take our minds off it. There is a whiff of Robert Vesco in the character of a crooked financier, a credit-card counterfeiting scheme of surpassing crudity and the mandatory love story.

This represents fairly sparse plotting for a Hailey novel, and I think it was a mistake. Books such as "Hotel" kept driving the reader forward by switching among seven or eight relatively boring story lines, until he had invested so much time he hung on just to see what happened. You can bail out of "The Moneychangers" at any time. You've been there before. (p. 40)

> *Peter Andrews, in* The New York Times Book Review *(© 1975 by The New York Times Company; reprinted by permission), May 18, 1975.*

*   *   *

HAMBURGER, Michael   1924-

Hamburger is a German-born English poet, translator, and critic. Hamburger has achieved a sturdy reputation as a poet; in addition, he is the outstanding translator and interpreter of German poetry for English readers. His collected translations of Hölderlin and Hugo von Hofmannsthal are considered definitive. (See also *Contemporary Authors*, Vols. 5-8, rev. ed.)

Mr. Hamburger's book [*The Truth of Poetry*] gave me most furiously to think, not only because of its high level of thoughtfulness and sensibility, but because it is so disturbingly informative. To be told about poet after poet, from country after country, to be shown examples of their work, to be introduced to their theories about poetry, and their views of the universe, and their personal circumstances, and the titles of their books, and the kind of thing they said in their letters, is to be (as another contemporary poet has put it) "bombed with information." Because Mr. Hamburger knows so much about poetry, in so many languages, and has thought about it so deeply, and is such a good poet himself, and explains it so clearly without minimising the difficulties—because of these things, his book is truly frightening: I mean it makes me want to get up from my chair and run away. For what his book really demonstrates, as he knows perfectly well, is the sheer *chaos* of modern poetry, the lack of agreement about anything at all. . . . [The] great strength of this book, and also what makes it unsettling, is that it demonstrates how little the poets of the modern world, with all the force of their art and the logic of their persuasion, have been able to convince one another. (p. 53)

> *John Wain, in* Encounter *(© 1970 by Encounter Ltd.), November, 1970.*

Ownerless Earth is an important book. It reveals the full range of Michael Hamburger's poetry, selecting from work published in six previous collections (from *Flowering Cactus* of 1950 to *Travelling* of 1969), and including a good deal of very recent poetry. Furthermore, it contains his best and longest poem to date, the superb sequence called 'Travelling', previously available only in a limited edition booklet. This book makes one more than ever aware of Hamburger's true stature as a poet—for he is, or so I believe, one of the few really first-rate poets writing in England today. Hamburger's fine intelligence, his sensitivity, his feeling for the craft of poetry, his seriousness, and his pleasantly grumpy humour and satiric ingenuity, are all

qualities which should have won him a far greater audience than that which he actually has.

Hamburger's concern is with the existence—and of ever-growing threat and damage to that existence—of natural and human orders which speak, in whatever various ways, of beauty and individual quality, of decency and love. It is a concern very much like Hopkins' in the last century, except that the damage (and the threat of continuing damage) to these orders is far greater than in Hopkins' time; and that Hopkins's concern was partly motivated by religious belief, whereas Hamburger is a humanist—though one whose world is not without "aura". It is, in fact, this quality of "aura"—or rather, of indefinable senses of life which arise *between* the hard physical things by the way in which these are presented in the poem—which constitutes much of what Hamburger is about, and which is present as much in many of the poems Hamburger labels "of time and place", and the ones of human interaction, as those which are called in the present book "dream poems." (pp. 139-40)

> *David Miller, "Michael Hamburger: Some Remarks on His Poetry," in* Agenda, *Autumn-Winter, 1973/4, pp. 139-48.*

If Hamburger's poems can be taken as manifestations of the moral consciousness of the modern European Jew, which they can and must be, it is necessary to add immediately that the poet's ancient, glittering eyes are gay. His work is not very often flawed by the puritanical and solemn earnestness characteristic, for example, of some of Jon Silkin's poetry. . . . If Michael Hamburger writes with an outraged moral consciousness, and he often does, he is also a connoisseur of the chaos that outrages him and threatens to destroy his world. (p. 46)

Hamburger writes . . . straight political poems, sometimes satirical or ironic, sometimes more or less didactic; there are poems that manage to transmute even the most recalcitrant (including political) materials into more or less purely formal structures; and there are poems in which the magician and moralist in Hamburger meet and fight it out. Throughout, there is a preoccupation with the possibility of falling into silence, and there are many poems about language, about words: "I can't do without them. / But I hate them as lovers hate them / When it's time for bodies to speak." (p. 47)

[He] continues to investigate the relationship between language and possession of all kinds, and he travels. [*Ownerless Earth*] may seem at first to be a journey toward that point at which the Efficacious Word is finally found and uttered, a point (in space, in time, in mind) which becomes, by naming it, real and one's own. But it is in fact a journey well beyond that point (or delusion) through an ownerless earth indeed, an earth not to be possessed by language (or any other human instrument), though it may be encountered in terms of language, travelled or experienced in terms of its strange agency. (p. 48)

> *John Matthias, in* Poetry *(© 1974 by The Modern Poetry Association; reprinted by permission of the Editor of* Poetry), *April, 1974.*

[Michael Hamburger] learned British English. And it is possible to think that he learned it too well. National characteristics are mostly mythical: through most of his history the English man has been flamboyant and histrionic, as he is today; but for perhaps 200 years influential classes chose to cultivate a different image, of the Englishman as tight-lipped, reticent and laconic, a specialist in understatement. Michael Hamburger perhaps acquired this code of speech and behavior with the peculiar fervor of the exotic seeking assimilation. To me, who was brought up to embrace the same now superannuated code, this is very attractive and touching. But it will come as a shock to readers who know Hamburger chiefly as exemplary translator, particularly of the schizophrenic visionary Friedrich Hölderlin.

Nevertheless the translator and the poet do not live in separate apartments. It is true that an early poem called "Hölderlin," is one of Hamburger's worst; and 20 years ago, when he tried to emulate Hölderlin's Hellenism directly, it came out as sub-Tennyson. But his translator's devotion to German poetry has been essential to his sense of his own identity—. . . . And if the other half or greater half of that identity was English (and very precisely located too, in London suburbs south of the Thames), that English suburban scene is registered in mysteriously spare and dancing lyrics like "Grey Heat," "The House Martins," "The Jackdaws," by a sensibility that has manifestly acquired the sensuous but uncloying opulence of German poets like Trakl or Rilke. As for the Jewish allegiance, it is acknowledged at moments all the more hair-raising for being few and far between, as when it surfaces suddenly in a poem of typically British domesticity and wry deprecation:

> I hear my children at play
> And recall that one branch of
>   the elm-tree looks dead;
> Also that twenty years ago I
>   could have been parchment
> Cured and stretched for a
> lampshade,
> Who now have children, a
>   lampshade
> And the fear of those winds. . . . (pp. 30-1)

Michael Hamburger is a contemporary whom I respect without reservations and an English poet who will be read and remembered long after more flashy and quarrelsome talents have burned themselves out. (p. 31)

> *Donald Davie, in* The New York Times Book Review (© *1974 by The New York Times Company; reprinted by permission), April 28, 1974.*

In one respect, [*A Mug's Game,* Hamburger's autobiography,] is not a *poet's* tale of a poet's life. Hamburger has always been acutely aware—sometimes restrictively so—of roles, masks, personae, of disparate selves for separate functions. Here he plays the chronicler, not the poet. Here he is expressly dealing with remembered superficialities, knowing full well that 'the most intense, most formative experiences may have eluded the chronicler because they have no context, no frame of reference in time and place'. Those experiences he leaves to the poet, who compiles a different book. (pp. 102-03)

Doubts that he could write good poems in English because it was not his first language, because word and thing did not lie naively close, left their mark on his poetry in a certain austerity of diction. This may account for his relative lateness in finding an individual voice; it does account for his most distinctive achievement: the body of translations from the German he has given to the English tradition. All the self-effacement and adaptability to other men's voices that bedevilled his own beginnings as an independent poet stood him in triumphant good stead here: one thinks of his life-long service to Hölderlin, which began when he was still a schoolboy, devoting his talents to another poet's work at an age when that other marvellous boy, Hofmannsthal, whom he has served equally devotedly, was pouring out his own first flood of lyrics. The scrupulousness he practised in rendering other men's rhyme and rhythm has brought its reward in his own performance. Translating functioned as five-finger-exercises for him, sustained him through dead periods, enabled him to explore the nuances and exactitudes of his all-but-own, of his own language. . . . He is a poet of fine precision, not of broad effect, and I suspect that much of [his] finesse has been learnt from his craft of translating. (p. 104)

> *Joyce Crick, "The Chronicler and the Poet: Michael Hamburger at 50," in* Poetry Nation (© *copyright* Poetry Nation, *1974), No. 3, 1974, pp. 102-08.*

If ever poems were autotelic, these [in *Ownerless Earth*] are. The voice is a poet's in the agony of poiesis. . . . From the beginning, thirty years ago, Hamburger's has been a tyrannical muse, demanding feeling and knowledge, the solemn and the facetious. The poet is called to see what is there, but also what is not there and what is beyond. (p. 73)

Life is a pilgrimage into deprivation, into death. Death is the polarity of satiety, but it is also the completion of need, and thus a synthesis of the entire dialectic. Again and again, Hamburger offers death as coterminous with life. Beginning and end coalesce. (p. 74)

His relief from the agony of poiesis is the taking up of his heritage, in some sense at least a heavenly heritage. By putting birth and death together he can

> . . . look up and see
> A strip of sky . . .
>
> Begin again, saying:
> Mountain, Lake. Light.
> Earth. Water. Air.
> You. Nothing more. No one's.
>   ("Traveling IV")

It is in these very poems of noetic synthesis that Hamburger recaptures the felicities of form he lost in his prosaic 1950's . . . and his crab free verse of his 1960's. . . . Those were arid years, without the oases of couplets from "Palinode," skillful off- and slant-rimes from "The Sacrifice," and the flawlessly metaphysical "Mathematics of Love," a poem worthy of Jack Donne. The voice of the poet seems reborn as he approaches rebirth. . . . (pp. 75-6)

> *Tony Herbold, in* Parnassus (copyright © *by* Parnassus: Poetry in Review), *Fall/Winter, 1974.*

*   *   *

HAMMETT, (Samuel) Dashiell   1894-1961

Hammett, an outstanding American crime novelist, was best

known for *The Maltese Falcon, The Glass Key,* **and** *The Thin Man.*

Hammett, who created the most powerful of [the] new heroes in Sam Spade, had been a private detective and knew the corrupt inner workings of American cities. But Sam Spade was a less obvious projection of Hammett than detective heroes usually are of their authors. Hammett had got his early romanticism under strict ironic control. He could see Spade from outside, without affection, perhaps with some bleak compassion. In this as in other respects Spade marks a sharp break with the Holmes tradition. He possesses the virtues and follows the code of a frontier male. Thrust for his sins into the urban inferno, he pits his courage and cunning against its denizens, plays for the highest stakes available, love and money, and loses nearly everything in the end. His lover is guilty of murder; his narrow, bitter code forces Spade to turn her over to the police. The Maltese falcon has been stripped of jewels. . . .

The ferocious intensity of the work, the rigorous spelling-out of Sam Spade's deprivation of his full human heritage, seem to me to make his story tragedy, if there is such a thing as dead-pan tragedy. Hammett was the first American writer to use the detective-story for the purposes of a major novelist, to present a vision, blazing if disenchanted, of our lives. Sam Spade was the product and reflection of a mind which was not at home in Zion, or in Zenith.

> *Ross Macdonald, "The Writer as Detective Hero" (copyright © 1964 by* Show Magazine, Hartford Publications, Inc.; reprinted by permission of Harold Ober Associates Incorporated), in *Essays: Classic and Contemporary, edited by Richard W. Lid, Lippincott, 1967, pp. 307-15.*

Seven detective stories by Dashiell Hammett, written between 1923 and 1930, are collected in "The Continental Op." . . .

[The stories] tend to be fast and neat, flickering with static, rudimentary scenes—like the panels of a comic book—in timeless drama. For example, the narrator says, "That day was Thursday. Nothing else happened that day." His week is made of days as a list is made of items in required sequence, with no ordinary human feeling of passing time. Sentences move this way too—at a brisk, consistent pace, with no wasted moves in syntax or sense. . . . Facts and sharp pictures accumulate, not impressionistic complexities.

The characters in these stories tend to be types or caricatures, wittily constructed of psychological and physical peculiarities. They are stuck rigidly in themselves—exactly as the narrator insists they are. . . .

[For example, when] Porky Grout [previously termed a coward] shows the virtue of courage—because he falls in love with an evil woman and tries to stop the narrator from capturing her—he is smashed to death by the narrator's speeding car. Thus the narrator determines, if nothing else, that his original description of Porky Grout can never be refuted.

Like days of the week, events of the plot are automatically sequential, but they are no mere progression of cause and effect; they can seem to be expressions of colossal hatred.

The narrator says when he realizes fully that he has just run over and obliterated (or murdered) a courageous Porky Grout: "'That was Porky. That was Porky.' It was an amazing fact." The important thing, then, is not whether or not that was Porky, but that a fact is a fact, more or less amazing.

Characters usually exchange information with the narrator, rather than conversation, and everyone tends to be as logical as Aristotle even when they lie, which is often. Mainly they live in a theoretical city called San Francisco. It has specifically named streets and specific addresses, but in these detectival places (analogous perhaps to mysterious, potentially exciting places of the human body) there is no authentic ambience, sensuous reality or anything that threatens to confuse the lucid presentation of plot. But it might be more accurate to say these stories present problems, not plots, and they are developed or organized like essays intended for intricate understanding, not made like stories for intuitive apprehension. (Sooner or later someone will compare them to the fiction of Kafka, Beckett, Handke, et al., if somebody hasn't already made that mistake.)

Despite strenuous organization, these stories are usually absurd—unintentionally absurd, I think. Nevertheless, they create a feeling of strict, antiseptically determinate form, and they show remarkable variations within it. They are then remarkable and interesting, but if these adjectives appear in an advertisement for the book, tell your friends the stories are not worth reading unless they please you: They are a special, literate experience. It takes place in a mental region where subterranean impulses are cultivated and a species of imaginative vegetation seethes into shape, feeding on its own sick juice.

I was hypnotized by the energy of these stories and pleased by their deft, technical achievements. For example, rapid description of character: ". . . he was the kind of man who combs his hair before he shaves, so his mirror will show an orderly picture." Or: ". . . a little man whose meek face had the devil-may-care expression of a model husband on a tear." (p. 1)

[However, a description of a beautiful and aristocratic-appearing woman] suggests the conjunction of physical presence and class ideal, which, in the same story, through a verbal tumble, becomes racist and vicious: "loafing Mexicans" and a "greasy orchestra." This is . . . from Hammett's detective (not Hammett). . . .

The woman described is really a lady. She is . . . British and rich. Unfortunately, she loves somebody and, like Porky Grout, she is hideously murdered. Again, Hammett's detective, the narrator in these stories, seems too much an author of these stories. Perhaps—despite his racial slurs, his respect for superior classes, his slimy eroticism based on a woman's dark or white or yellow type, his contempt for artiness in men—he is, ironically, just as democratic and decent as Hammett himself, in his fundamental conception of human beings. Classy or greasy, if they feel, they die.

The stories, then, are not only the achievements of form, but are overcontrolled by Hammett's detective. Virtually everyone he describes in graphic psychological, physical or stereotypical detail seems fated to suffer just for having been seen by him. The stories are, for this reason, only ambiguously controlled by Hammett. He might not know everything he might be saying, through his detective, about himself. So much of the pleasure, meaning and value of these stories is surrendered to such a creep. However, whatever it is Hammett says through his detective, it is exciting and ugly; and the important point remains—that the way he says it, through his detective, is interesting insofar as it tends to be strangely and ambiguously inevitable. (p. 10)

[The] stories might be compared, in their formal character, to games in which a detective must invent horrible applications of the rules. While those who need him are dropping all around, he goes about intimidating, dominating, manipulating, analyzing, and at last arranging events so that they have the result he requires—the solution, or the dissolution of the story and its problem. It is hardly noticeable, but the solution can matter little to the people who were, in the first place, most concerned; they are usually dead.

It may be slightly too much to say that, insofar as this detective sees people precisely he tends to see them as morally disgusting; but it does seem to be his personal problem to make events prove that people are what he sees. The revelation of courage in Porky Grout was an embarrassment—amazing, but trivial really because, as the detective says, "he wasn't even human." At least the events he makes do prove that people get theirs whenever he thinks he gets their number. Hammett's achievement, in these stories, is to have fixed the aura of paranoia in literate forms. (p. 14)

> *Leonard Michaels, in* The New York Times Book Review *(© 1974 by The New York Times Company; reprinted by permission), December 8, 1974.*

Written over forty years ago, these stories [collected in *The Continental Op*] of the tough, nameless, dryly witty warhorse of the Continental Detective Agency still make Hammett's imitators and competitors look like fugitives from a kindergarten. (pp. 122-23)

> *Phoebe Adams, in* The Atlantic Monthly *(copyright © 1975 by The Atlantic Monthly Company, Boston, Mass.; reprinted with permission), February, 1975.*

In the early Fifties, when I first read Dashiell Hammett, he seemed to fit perfectly an image my friends and I had then of a writer who had made being a writer into a romantic occupation. He had lived in "the real world," he had suffered years of obscurity and poverty as he learned to write a clean, honest prose, he had written books that were out of print and hard to find, he had gone to Hollywood and drunk too much and stopped writing, he had chosen to go to jail rather than talk at a communist conspiracy trial, he had some undetailed beautiful relation with Lillian Hellman. Compared to that, Fitzgerald and Hemingway were too gaudy, available for anyone's romancing.

About Hammett's writing, I now see, we held an ambivalent attitude that bespoke an uneasiness we could not recognize. On the one hand we pointed to the battered paperbacks we had struggled to find and said: "There, with Op and Spade and Nick Charles, is the real thing, serious writing about crime and detection." On the other hand we

implicitly diminished that achievement by dreaming that in the intervening years Hammett had been struggling to write a great, a "mature" novel that would show the world he was as good as we wanted to claim he was. When pressed, I would admit to preferring Raymond Chandler, even to hankering after new young toughs like John D. MacDonald and John Ross Macdonald. But Hammett was the first, and the years of writing stories for *Black Mask* had to be honored somehow. . . .

[Lillian Hellman's] 1965 memoir, which may well be the best thing either of them ever wrote, did much to make Hammett into the heroic figure we had all vaguely created years earlier; it was then published as the introduction to ten Continental Op pieces called *The Big Knockover*, and that volume, plus *The Novels of Dashiell Hammett*, which had been published a year earlier, gave his best work the permanence it deserved. . . .

The Continental Op [is] a new book of seven stories selected and introduced by Steven Marcus. . . . The stories are inferior work—Marcus might well have done better by rescuing the few minor tales that have never been reprinted from *Black Mask*—and those who come to Hammett for the first time via this volume will get only snatches that show why anyone should read him. With a writer who is very limited at his best, this kind of exposure is especially unwelcome.

Yet one can see what Marcus has in mind, perverse though it seems to be. He wants to take those stories which have almost no interest either as conventional fiction or as conventional detective fiction and to claim that this is where you find Hammett pure. . . . Then:

> It should be quite evident that . . . the end of the story is no more plausible—nor is it meant to be—than the stories that have been told to him by all parties, guilty or innocent, in the course of his work. The Op may catch the real thief or collar the actual crook—that is not entirely to the point. What is to the point is that the story, account, or chain of events that the Op winds up with as "reality" is no more plausible and no less ambiguous than the stories that he meets with at the outset and later.

Thus Hammett becomes a candidate for existential sainthood. What makes Marcus's point useless is that in so far as it is true it is mostly a sign of the mediocrity of the stories. We assume, and the Op assumes, that in each case his job is like that of the classic detective: winnow true from false, fact from fiction. We do not assume that a nameless and faceless figure, operating out of a named but equally faceless San Francisco, will act like Philo Vance or Ellery Queen. Nor does Hammett offer his characters in such a way that anyone can care who did what to whom. But if the Op's account of events isn't plausible, it's meant to be, even if it isn't tidy or illuminating. If it isn't to the point that he catch the real thief, then his whole demeanor as an operative—who seeks no reward for himself, who is never violent wantonly—is a fraud. When it doesn't matter what the Op or anyone else does, and that is certainly true in many pages here if not true of whole stories, it makes for very dull reading. (p. 20)

The Op is like the queen in chess, able to move both

straight and diagonally, as it were, in a world of pawns, bishops, and rooks. But he is a piece, more truly within his world than are most detectives.

This is precisely what's wrong. When the cast is cardboard, when the relations among the characters are devoid of interest, when the Op succeeds by allowing for no human motive except the most simply conceived greed and lust, when the plot moves these figures around like wind-up dolls, there is nothing to make any of it matter. No theory, furthermore, true or false, that Marcus can supply can create an interest by saying "But that's the point" and by going on about contingencies and fiction-making detectives. Hammett was not a hero to himself, but he took himself seriously, and Marcus's way of making him pretentious only has the effect of making him trivial. (pp. 20-1)

[Hammett] was pretty thoroughly committed, from habit or design, to the idea that human beings were not very interesting, so no character he could invent could hold his interest. Now and again he came up with a good plot which could give his writing some purpose, but since he had to keep writing, good plot or no, there was little for him to attend to most of the time but the prose itself. When that happens, the prose becomes stylized almost immediately, words are pieces in a jigsaw. (p. 21)

To do [his best work] he needed someone besides the Op, whose anonymous integrity had worn pretty thin, and he assayed three different characters with three different styles in his last three novels: Sam Spade in *The Maltese Falcon*, Ned Beaumont in *The Glass Key*, and Nick Charles in *The Thin Man*. It is at this point that we can turn to the otherwise deflecting question of which is the best book.

Hammett himself preferred *The Glass Key*, and so, to judge by what he later did with the private eye form, did Chandler; there is much to be said for the preference. *The Maltese Falcon* isn't all that much different from the Op novels, and if Spade is a clearer figure it is mostly because he is more openly selfish and nasty, and there isn't much Hammett can do except let him bark away. *The Thin Man* is silly fun, warmed by the relation of Nick to Nora, warmed as Hammett himself was by his new relation with Lillian Hellman, but otherwise an inconsequential effort to make a casual virtue out of casual plotting. Yet *The Glass Key* is the best because Hammett here tries to make the style of his hero matter; Ned Beaumont's poses are poses, capable of costing something. It is a fumbling book because Hammett wouldn't commit himself enough to what he was doing, wouldn't try to assess how much Beaumont dummies up because of his feeling for a friend, or how much it matters to him that he seem more a gentleman than a thug.

The code always said that one doesn't talk about such things, and the success or failure of *The Glass Key*—and all Hammett, all Chandler, all Ross Macdonald, too—depends on how well the hero's relation to this code is handled. Hold to it completely, act as if there were no prices for so doing, and you have the boring Op; begin to act as if there were prices to be paid and inevitably self-pity begins to creep in: I kept my word, and I took my beating, etc. can lead to some dreary and immoral posing. What Hellman has shown us, however, is that Hammett himself believed in the code, and suffered because he did; the dignity with which he was willing to do so tinged his life with greatness. Better, then, to let the self-pity come in if it

must, better to deal with it openly as best one can. Better to say life matters, especially if you really think it does.

Hammett cannot handle all this in *The Glass Key*, but he tries. . . . The writing in this book is on the edge of all Hammett himself could not write about, but that is not a bad place for his writing to be. . . .

No need to complain that [the early] stories are crude, primitive, effortful; no need, either, to elevate these very qualities into high art. He did quite a bit in his ten years of writing, and he was a real pioneer. If the best of Chandler and MacDonald and Macdonald is better than his best, if the middling stuff of quite a few writers is better than his middling stuff, there isn't one who doesn't know how much he made them possible. (p. 22)

> *Roger Sale, "The Hammett Case," in* The New York Review of Books *(reprinted with permission from* The New York Review of Books; *copyright © 1975 NYREV, Inc.),* February 6, 1975, pp. 20-2.

Dashiell Hammett created the American Private Eye in 1923 when he sent his first Continental Op story to *Black Mask*. Probably the best introduction to Hammett, *The Big Knockover*, contains a number of these stories as well as Lillian Hellman's beautiful description of their author; their love affair was legendary, and continued until Hammett's death in 1961. But his writing life had lasted only ten years. Tuberculosis, drinking, some Communism, some months in prison during the McCarthy era, and finally cancer—these just begin to explain the long silence. Perhaps the clue lies in the way Hammett abandoned the Op for three new detectives in his last books: Sam Spade in *The Maltese Falcon*, Ned Beaumont in *The Glass Key*, Nick Charles in *The Thin Man*. Perhaps what he had to say began to change too fast for any character to keep up with it. Perhaps he had too much to write about.

The Continental Op contains, along with an introduction by Steven Marcus, seven more stories about the Op. Unfortunately, Marcus makes Hammett sound like Borges or Pirandello, juggling the evanescent planes of subjective reality; supposedly the Op, who starts out to unravel a reality not of lies, ends up by constructing another, "no more plausible and no less ambiguous," that is equally fictional. Surely, this over-cerebral interpretation demeans the Op, who does actually succeed in finding the truth behind the phony setup. If Marcus means only that the Op deliberately ignores some crimes, and will send up a crook for the wrong crime if he can't get him for the one he did commit, then Marcus is confusing the Op's "fiction-making" actions with the Op's certain knowledge of the truth. Hammett's hero sees a dirty world; he doesn't need to invent it all over again. (p. 2)

The stories in *The Continental Op* are almost all among Hammett's first, long on ballet and short on music. But it would be a mistake to view this collection as history; every story is, if not memorable, at least highly readable. The Op —even early Op—hasn't dated.

When Hammett was finished with the Op, he created Sam Spade, who lives beyond the code. He swims in corruption like an eel in a rockpile, or rather, wears it like a used suit that he discards only when he finds it doesn't fit. Without it he seems naked and anxious for another dirty wardrobe. . . .

Hammett was, like Mark Twain, a natural; he created his own style and his own characters out of dirt and junk, and had to work hard to keep them from slipping back into the slime. (p. 3)

Charles Nicol, in Bookletter *(copyright 1975 by* Harper's Magazine; *reprinted from the March 31, 1975 issue by special permission), March 31, 1975.*

*   *   *

HANDKE, Peter   1942?-

Handke, an Austrian novelist, playwright, poet, and essayist, is considered an exciting writer earning international stature.

Wunschloses Unglück [published in English as *A Sorrow Beyond Dreams*] is a sensitive account of the life of Peter Handke's mother, a life which ended in suicide. It is an attempt both at writing about her and recording the difficulties of doing so. . . .

The work is dominated by a single aesthetic imperative: not to sell reality short, not to become "reified into some machine for manufacturing memories or stereotypes". The resultant novel operates on two levels (rather in the self-analytical manner of *Der Hausierer*): the unadorned account of this woman's life and a commentary on the shortcomings of the biography as it develops. Certain misgivings are voiced at length before the account begins, and the narrative is interrupted every so often when the author feels that his material is shifting from fact to fiction.

Handke has always been less concerned with problems of narrative perspective than with the narrator's linguistic precision when describing what he is permitted to observe. Here, the narrator assumes an attitude of virtual omniscience towards his mother (although the tone rarely jars)— and his main interest is not in whether he *can* know so much about her, but rather whether he has done justice to what he *does* know. . . .

In this delicately balanced novel, the reader witnesses Handke pitting his desire for an authentic account against the elusiveness of reality. But *Wunschloses Unglück* does not just note (and even at times take evasive action to resist) the danger of slipping into the rituals and rhetoric of confessional biography. There are times where Handke is not beyond exaggerating the fictiveness of his approach. For his mother functions here as both individual and "instance": a paradigm against which not only the resilience of language but also the pressure of literary clichés can be tested. And fact and paradigm inevitably clash on occasions. Hence the novella-like beginning of the work, the occasional arch mannerisms of *Sprachskepsis*, or the discussion of the problem of writing about poverty in literature and avoiding the pathos and emotional commonplaces of "nineteenth-century" writing.

Certain pitfalls seem to appear in the novel simply in order that the narrator may theorize about them; the old Handke-gestures have not been eradicated any more fully than the literary clichés have. (The narrative confesses as much, as the sobre, unilinear biography is abandoned in favour of a series of final, disjointed anecdotes.) Yet on the whole, Handke shows a newly-acquired respect for tangible reality in *Wunschloses Unglück*, and a compassion for his subject. The result is a salutary ability to contain his linguistic diffidence within bounds appropriate to its material.

"Fictively Filial," in The Times Literary Supplement *(© Times Newspapers, Ltd., 1972; reproduced by permission), December 1, 1972, p. 1449.*

The Ride Across Lake Constance . . . confirms [Handke's] seriousness, his accomplishment and his utter 'foreignness'. English language drama does not breed writers with such preoccupations as are evinced here.

For Handke is a writer who does away with surface altogether. He writes, as it were, from the nine-tenths of speech and behaviour that go unsaid and undone, rather than the one tenth that passes right through the system and actually communicates itself to others. In *Lake Constance* we see not so much an edgy encounter between several persons, in what is presumably the neutral ground of an hotel, as a subterranean account of unexpressed desires, fears, fantasies, nightmares and manoeuvres in a game of dominance and submission. . . .

The inherent difficulty in the play, for Handke as well as for us, is that the focus constantly changes, indeed it's a multiple focus, so that productive ambiguity sometimes gives way to impenetrable confusion. Having set himself such an ambitious and complex schema, Handke has not resolved all the considerable problems that it throws up. . . .

In *Lake Constance*, if someone holds out a hand, nobody shakes it. Rather it will be examined, stared at, kissed or have something placed on it. But that notion, that verbal and behavioural transactions are like business transactions, bobs up again throughout. It seems that one of Handke's central preoccupations is with the (somewhat jaded) thought that we're all on the make even in social situations, that the undercurrent of our behaviour towards each other is a jockeying for position, profit and territory. (p. 48)

It's almost a case for aleatoric playwriting, of which many might feel this piece to be an example. But I don't think Handke is that sort of a cynic. His plays are immensely serious, even grave. My only carp about *Kaspar*—which I look upon as an otherwise perfect play—is a feeling of portentousness, as though Handke were slightly burdened with an awareness of writing an important, a seminal play. *Lake Constance* is not such a superb structure but neither does it feel portentous. At moments, I'm reminded of Spike Milligan. . . . But Handke never permits himself to touch the sublime heights of Milligan's agility with concepts and their destruction. Milligan, a Celtic anarchist, fires off random shots . . . all the time. And, when he's pissed off, he turns to something else. Handke, being a Teuton, works systematically through, imposing an order on chaos. If not portentous, *Lake Constance* is pretty daunting. It makes you work at it. And indeed I can't put my hand on my heart . . . and swear that Handke has made me ponder on the implications of these matters for my own existence. Milligan wouldn't try to, but he can provoke you into making connections. Handke, burdened with a whole play to write and a schematised intent, is always too bogged down to take glorious Milliganesque flight. But then Milligan is a genius. . . . Handke may yet prove to be a genius but he is certainly well worth grappling with meanwhile. (p. 49)

W. Stephen Gilbert, in Plays and Players *(© copyright W. Stephen Gilbert 1974), January, 1974.*

Handke is a securely established star of the German-speaking literary world, [called by various writers] "the darling of the West German critics" . . ., "long since the key figure of his generation". . . .

He first attracted attention in 1966, with an acidulous attack upon the "descriptive literature" that he considered predominant in West German fiction. Since then he has himself produced industriously and managed to appeal to both the middlebrow press as an enfant terrible and to various highbrow camps. A "literary technocrat," in the words of one critic, he can draw readers from those who approach art politically (by his matter-of-fact, vaguely Brechtian rejection of conventional fiction's comfortable fat) and from those more concerned with "pure art" (by his persistent concern with a blend of ostensible avant-gardism and self-conscious literary historicism).

Above all, Handke is an original, both in his work and in his person. His industriousness has been matched by the central-European critical establishment; . . . when he was only 30, there had already appeared a 393-page anthology of essays on him, complete with a 35-page bibliography of books and additional articles deemed too insignificant to include in the book. . . .

[*Short Letter, Long Farewell*, a novel,] is hardly a very endearing piece of prose. The title suggests the bones of the plot: on a visit to America the Austrian protagonist receives a short, flat farewell note from his wife ("I am in New York. Please don't look for me. It would not be nice for you to find me"), then spends the rest of the book traveling across the country, sensing his wife's presence in a series of threatening, melodramatic incidents, and finally encountering her again on the West Coast where the "long farewell" is consummated. (Actually, the "Langen Abschied" of the title is a direct and characteristic reference to Raymond Chandler's "The Long Goodbye," which the translator, Ralph Manheim, has missed; on the whole, Manheim does a decent job, although the very self-consciousness of Handke's style and his near-fetishism about language makes translation problematic from the start.)

Needless to say, the first-person account of the hero's wanderings is hardly meant to be the whole story, nor is it recounted naturalistically: every time Handke ventures into dialogue he becomes a candidate for a bottom-of-the-page New Yorker item. But of course descriptive realism isn't the point here. Handke has a view of the world that he is trying to recreate through language and through art, and this novel is part of that attempt. Its hero perceives the world out of existential insecurity, his ego constantly shattered by outer reality (nature), inner reality (dreams) and time (chilling, cinematic flashbacks). . . .

The two central points of reference in a book full of references are Gottfried Keller's novel "Der grüne Heinrich" and the films of John Ford. In his continual, even obsessive citations of Keller and Ford, Handke identifies his book with the tradition of the German *Bildungsroman* (a novel in which the hero learns through his experiences) and with Ford's larger-than-life, heroic Americana, and yet also distances himself from them ironically. Handke values Keller's Heinrich because "he didn't want to interpret things; all he wanted was to be as detached as possible." Ford, who himself enters the book as a character at the end, assumes the role of patriarchal deus ex machina, wearily re-

solving tensions between history and nature and husband and wife, and making possible the peculiarly inconclusive "happy end," as Handke called it in an interview.

How all of this will strike the non-German reader will be a matter of taste. Sometimes the artificiality and the (deliberate) downright silliness of his assertions ("'We Americans always say "we" even when we're talking about our private affairs,' said John Ford") will strike one as dated, unpleasant, foreign or simply inept. The most immediately striking parts of this book are the moments in which Handke opens up Kafkaesque vistas—dreaming instants of remembered horror—and an occasional set piece, as in the description of the desperately doting lovers the hero encounters in St. Louis.

But for those who respond to complex and clever artifice, Handke has much to offer. The writing may be careful and calculating, but it is enormously intricate. . . .

The sheer density of the in-jokes and cross references and philosophical curve balls throughout this book will keep a generation of German scholars busy and happy, and will no doubt attract something of an American discipleship as well. And there is an undeniable, intriguing fascination to it, one that makes one curious indeed about how Handke will evolve in coming years. It's just all very, very cold. (p. 5)

> *John Rockwell, in* The New York Times Book Review *(© 1974 by The New York Times Company; reprinted by permission), September 15, 1974.*

The Austrian writer Peter Handke is . . . a dramatist of deservedly high international reputation. He has also written volumes of poems and essays and . . . novels. His third novel, the first to be published in English, was *The Goalie's Anxiety at the Penalty Kick* (1972), a subtle and fine use of mental disintegration as an analogue of the questions explored by Wittgenstein: connections between one's inner self and the world's knowledge of it.

Handke's fourth novel [*Short Letter, Long Farewell*] is about mental integration. This short, superbly wrought, understated yet powerful novel can be described, in one aspect, as a scale model of America made with absolute verism but then bathed in a slantwise light that shows the fantasy hidden in the fact. Handke also uses this process with his first-person narrator. At times we feel that the man is imagining some of the things around him, but then there are scale corroborations that confirm that he is only seeing the "imaginary" in the real. . . .

From the beginning of the book, two cultural elements dominate: the Germanic culture of the narrator and American culture—but the latter is encountered in nothing like the Dickens-Trollope-Nabokov visitor's vein. Here the young European brings a good deal of the American culture *with* him from Europe, chiefly through the media of American pop music and films. He "recognizes" the US, not just because he has been here before but because, since childhood, it has been affecting him. (p. 29)

The book's dual process of reality and . . . parareality, its duality of European and American cultures are structurally aligned to the dual theme at the center: fear—of existence itself—that the narrator brings from Europe, along with a perspective on that fear that he gains in America. . . . The second paragraph . . . begins: "As far as I can remember, I seem to have been born for horror and fear". . . . The "comparisons" in America give him a means of dealing with the fact (and terror) of being alive, as if—something like Handke's wonderful play *Kaspar*—a grown person, previously devoid of language, was here acquiring a means of identifying and ordering environment and experience. . . .

Handke's novel is thus—to use a weary word validly, I hope—existential: the narrator (and in the background his wife) finds modes of living through an extreme situation that summons up everything in him, from his childhood memories of hiding under blankets to his reliance on the "safety" of American rock and film. . . .

Its being is in the way it is written—a book of secrets to which we are made privy, full of sharp visions and of disquieting proportions, disquieting because true. Handke makes his narrator's minor moments empty their contents just as fully as the major ones. . . .

Short Letter, Long Farewell, like *The Goalie*, can be read too quickly. Like *The Goalie* it is so intensely distilled that it seems easy to negotiate. Handke doesn't raise his voice or perorate; but every word he speaks has consequences. (p. 30)

> *Stanley Kauffmann, "It All Happened," in* The New Republic *(reprinted by permission of* The New Republic; © *1974 by The New Republic, Inc.), September 28, 1974, pp. 29-30.*

The Austrian narrator of *Short Letter, Long Farewell* ends an odyssey across America by paying a visit to director John Ford in Southern California: "He took us to his study and showed us a pile of movie scripts; writers were still sending them to him. 'There are some good stories in there,' he said. 'Simple and clear. The kind of stories we need.'" Few readers are likely to find Peter Handke's novel either simple or clear, but it seems to me precisely the kind we need. (p. 17)

It is important for two reasons: its narrative technique and the landscape of America against which the narrative unfolds. The latter shows us a country we have not seen so clearly since, perhaps, Nathanael West.

In this America—the imitation of a Hollywood fantasy instead of the other way around—a tense drama is given shape. Central to it is the narrator himself, whose reflections suggest the influence of Ludwig Wittgenstein. "Philosophy," Wittgenstein wrote in *The Blue Book*, ". . . is a fight against the fascination which forms of expression exert upon us." Handke's protagonist battles against language's tyranny over experience. . . .

Two things are going on in *Short Letter, Long Farewell*: The hero, desiring pure experience, fights his own intellectual formulations, while Handke, as a writer, combats the novel-as-literary-formulation. At the least, the latter contest is won, and the victory is complete and powerful.

Handke's method—to question the nature of experience, including literary experience—is most economically seen in the poems in *Innerworld*. But, again, these are no more like what many readers have come to think of as poems than

Handke's novel is like an Oates melodrama. Handke cares less about entertaining than changing the reader.

Many of the poems present a series of language-descriptions of "the same thing." "The Three Readings of the Law," for example, begins: "Every citizen has the right—/applause/to develop his personality freely—/applause. . . ." In the poem's second section this idea is rephrased: "Every citizen has the right—/applause/to develop his personality freely within the framework of the law—/exclamations: Hear! Hear! . . ." And in the final section: "Every citizen has the right/to develop his personality freely within the framework of the law and standards of common decency/. . . *General, stormy, nearly unending applause*." Language enslaves us, and the bitter irony is that we can enjoy being enslaved. . . .

What interests Handke, as always, is the relationship between the language and the experience. (p. 18)

> *Charles Deemer, "Combating the Tyranny of Language," in* The New Leader (© *1974 by the American Labor Conference on International Affairs, Inc.), November 11, 1974, pp. 17-18.*

This too-slender novel [*A Sorrow Beyond Dreams*] is the story of a mother's life seen through the eyes of her son. A suicide in her early 50s, she had grown to womanhood in Germany in the years just before World War II. She had felt the excitement of the new order under the Nazis, the pleasure of feeling at one with everyone in the nation, of having a purpose. But her nature and the nature of her society were such that she was not long destined to enjoy purpose or happiness of any kind. She was different from those around her, her son thinks: a careful but rebellious woman in ways that showed themselves only rarely. Mr. Handke's portrait is weighty and moving, slender though it is; he has a gift for the concise phrase, for the exact proof that shows, in a line or two, the nature of the character under his scrutiny. This is an astonishingly sad and possibly deceptive work; one has been persuaded that one has seen a life pass by, a life wholly crushed and joyless, when in fact one has seen a summation. But it is persuasion of precisely this sort that is the novelist's business, and Mr. Handke brings it off, desolate though it is. (pp. 27-8)

> *Dorothy Rabinowitz, in* Saturday Review *(copyright © 1975 by Saturday Review/World, Inc.; reprinted with permission), March 22, 1975.*

[Handke's] plays and other works have made him perhaps the most interesting young writer in German today. (p. 20)

[Richard Gilman, in *The Making of Modern Drama*,] rightly [observes] that Handke is in some way a philosophical dramatist [and] finds him to be very like Wittgenstein. It is true that Wittgenstein called philosophy "a battle against the bewitchment of our intelligence by means of language," and that Handke shows himself to be very suspicious of language as the means by which we are induced to accept "reality"; indeed he sometimes hates it and speaks of its "idiocy." But these similarities, even if not misleading, are not sufficient to justify the conclusion that "nothing could be closer in spirit" to Wittgenstein than Handke, and I am not surprised to learn that the dramatist has himself rejected the comparison.

Wittgenstein was concerned to avoid errors arising from a failure to understand the workings of language. This is not the same as to wish to "learn to be nauseated by language," as Handke says he does, and as he says we should if we are to achieve consciousness. But Handke's theory is not fully articulated, and there is excuse for confusion. He believes language to be an agent of social oppression and mystification, so there is a political aspect to his theory; but Handke seems to me less interested in this for its own sake than as the symptom of a more radical distress. Language makes us sick, perhaps makes us wicked (his theory is really quite Rousseauistic), and if we can find a single dominant motive in Handke's work it is that as a writer he is always having to love what he abhors. The consequence is that he is a poet above all else, and almost always in a state of fright or horror. (pp. 20-1)

The nausea which he says he feels, and which he compares to the nausea of Sartre's Roquentin about *things*, arises less from the brutalization of people by (the abuse of) language than from disgust at having to deal with the corrupt and systematic independence of language itself.

Hence for Handke language is what prevents us from being in the world as it is, a set of debilitating fictions. He is faithful to the puritanism of the avant-garde in general when he says that "the progress of literature consists of the gradual removal of unnecessary fictions," and his earliest effort was to destroy the fictions that are habitual in the theater. He sought to strip it of all its familiar trappings, going beyond the point where Beckett leaves off, trying to make audiences understand the "produced" quality of what they were seeing, to abuse the theater and the audience too, in so far as it contributed to the theatrical fiction. In his early plays, there is no action, no character, no fourth wall; there are people in a room, and all that is happening is language. Of course the theater can be seen as a model of other forms of social lying, all dependent on language. Attack language, Handke seems to be saying, and you attack the root of evil.

Using language to attack language sets problems Handke is always aware of. His anti-theater is very theatrical, his anti-language has great linguistic and rhetorical resource. The words of his *Sprechstücke* ("speak-ins") are not, he explains, "pictures"; they point not to a world beyond them "but to the world in the words themselves." This words can do only by insisting on themselves as interesting, as opaque rather than transparent, exactly as the atheatrical quality of his plays requires constant reminders that we are in a theater and nowhere else. The expectations of the audience are constantly maintained by assertions that no conceivable curiosity or expectation of theirs may hope to be satisfied. . . .

By constantly and aggressively challenging expectations Handke makes his anti-play playable, the anti-language speakable, intelligible to a language-corrupted audience. *Self-Accusation*, a less *épatant* piece [than *Offending the Audience*], explains the process of corruption: one is born, one acquires with language desire and anxiety, one commits crimes indiscriminately social and linguistic. *Offending the Audience* is said to be based on rock style and rhythms; *My Foot, My Tutor* is all mime. But these are evasions; language, as game or disease, dominates the entire enterprise.

Kaspar consummates Handke's theatrical treatment of this topic. According to the author it is "anarchic, and negates everything it comes across. I don't care whether this yields a positive utopia . . .". (p. 21)

Handke's poems . . . are series of sentences bound together by linguistic and rhetorical devices of the kind that are currently interesting practitioners of "text-linguistics" or "discourse-analysis." Above all they are encounters between the poet, a self-confessed traitor to silence, and his enemy the language. . . .

Of the novels *The Goalie's Anxiety at the Penalty Kick* is most immediately impressive. It is of course obsessed with language and the anxieties it induces; but despite this attention to its own medium of communication it is a highly wrought story. (p. 22)

There is a trick ending, well prepared; and yet we can no more take it as its narrative face value than we can suppose the repetitions of words and motifs have the kind of sense one would expect in a more normal novel. They are indices or symptoms of the language-disease. The book has frontiers with Kafka and with the *nouveau roman*, but its peculiar pathology makes it decisively different from either. . . .

New readers of Handke might do well to start with [*A Sorrow Beyond Dreams*], for here his deviations are less puzzling and better marked than in the early plays. Certainly he is not to be thought of only as a playwright; his place is wherever language needs to be examined or purged. He has the fertility and the resource to maintain himself alive in this extraordinary combat. Perhaps Handke is a little preoccupied with his own originality, and with the specificity of his own terrors. He nevertheless offers, with prodigality, evidence that the obsessions of modernism still afford the possibility of greatness. (p. 23)

> *Frank Kermode, "The Model of a Modern Modernist," in* The New York Review of Books *(reprinted with permission from* The New York Review of Books; *copyright © 1975 NYREV, Inc.), May 1, 1975, pp. 20-3.*

Among contemporary writers, Samuel Beckett has made an honorable specialty of composing a text and then cutting it, or shrinking it, beyond bare bone to the marrow, in the end producing something that feels like an irreducible minimum but still evokes its ampler versions. Beckett's *The Lost Ones* was one such text; Peter Handke's new book [*A Sorrow Beyond Dreams*] is another, though Handke offers the reader considerably more than Beckett in the way of colorful phenomena to hold on to and linger over. Easier to read, it has something of the same self-generalizing force as *The Lost Ones*, however; and the dreadful poignancy of the theme—the suicide of the narrator's mother—suffuses a maze of particulars which both scald and sustain him. A gentle, candid searching-out of her life develops into a tough inquiry as to what a writer, and a compulsive one at that, can make of grief, shock, and indignation.

One answer is: as short and as loaded a book as possible; no fat, no *longueurs*, no self-indulgent melodrama. Another is to recognize in the act of writing, as Handke's narrator (Handke himself?) does, that objectification or getting something off one's chest is impossible. Objectified, the hurt becomes a groomed presence that is the more upsetting for being out in the open. One never gets the text off one's chest. As the narrator says toward the end, "It is not true that writing has helped me . . . the story has not ceased to preoccupy me.'' Earlier, he explains that he ''experienced moments of extreme speechlessness and needed to formulate them,'' only to discover at the halfway point the twin evils of over- and understating. These ''two dangers'' slow down his writing ''because in every sentence I am afraid of losing my balance.'' In fact, as he says, this story is ''really about the nameless, about speechless moments of terror,'' and it's impossible to read it without sensing in every sentence an ontological vertigo that makes him write only a bit more than it doesn't. From that faint but sovereign impetus comes a text that feels wrenched-out, choked on itself, self-rebuked. . . .

It is a profoundly affecting story, counterpointed throughout by the narrator's offended hesitancy and his weird but utterly comprehensible pride in what she's done. A giggle here, a self-conscious image there (''In these tempests of dread, I become magnetic like a decaying animal''), only sharpen the impact. Some day, the narrator promises himself, he'll write about the whole thing in greater detail. One hopes not. Subtitled as it is—''A Life Story''—*A Sorrow Beyond Dreams* not only implies an alternative genre, the death story, but also crams two lives into one death. Brief as it is, the text seems radioactive, professionally unprofessional in its abrupt, blurted pain. The writer is almost as much at a disadvantage as, say, a lion-tamer or a TV repairman who has to express grief entirely in the idiom of his calling. A better developed, less panicky, book wouldn't be half so disturbing.

As it is, we have here some mordant death-chamber music from an Austrian writer who gets better all the time. . . . The titles of two previous Handke novels, *The Goalie's Anxiety at the Penalty Kick* and *Short Letter, Long Farewell*, strangely prefigure this new book: it's not often you find the elegist's anxiety at the elegy so naked and concise.

> Paul West, ''Mother's Days,'' in Book World—The Washington Post (© The Washington Post), *May 11, 1975, p. 2.*

*   *   *

HANLEY, James   1901-

Hanley is a British novelist, playwright, short story writer, and essayist. His most distinguished works are his novels of the sea and of war in which he exhibits a tragic vision of solitary man sometimes compared to Hardy's.

A Woman in the Sky is a variation on what seems to have become [Hanley's] favourite theme: the importance attached by the lonely to the lives they have made for themselves. Every invasion, however well-meaning, is an erosion of their liberty. Usually they defend their little worlds of obsession or fantasy against all comers. In [this] book these worlds have already collapsed. . . .

Like *Another World*, [this] novel carries all the confidence and conviction that Mr Hanley has brought with him from his ten-year stint as a playwright. The density of narrative which distinguished the major novels has been replaced by a kind of skeletal framework, the barest points of reference to time and place and situation.

The genius here (is it too strong a word?) lies in the way in which a characteristic density of effect builds up from such a tremendous economy of means; and in the way the simplicity, even the poverty, of common speech, the abrasive sounds of the near-inarticulate, acquire through stubbornly persistent rhythms and repetitions a richness and a depth that reveal the endless subtleties and inconsistencies of the characters, and the magic of the private worlds they create.

> ''*Up and Out*,'' in The Times Literary Supplement (© *Times Newspapers, Ltd., 1973; reproduced by permission*), October 5, 1973, p. 1157.

A Woman in the Sky is not so much about the bleakness of the cold, impersonal urban landscape—which is not to underestimate the outrage with which Hanley depicts it—as it is about the resources people find to contend with it. The most valuable of those, Hanley suggests, is human intimacy, and that is the real subject of his novel. . . .

Hanley unfolds [his] tales of intimacy slowly, lovingly, until at the end the reader is totally engaged with the human fabric he has woven. There is true desperation in all these lives—the scene in which Mrs. Kavanaugh, alone in her room, cries out in terror against the night is profoundly frightening—but there is also compassion. Its embodiment is Lena Biddulph. She is a strange, harsh woman, who greets strangers with drunken sarcasm and shouts angrily at chilly bureaucrats. Yet the tenderness with which she cares for Brigid Kavanaugh—writing letters for her to her imaginary son, steering her through battles with the bottle, shielding her against loneliness—elevates her to a sainthood that is quite unexpected and wholly affecting.

A Woman in the Sky is a small book—terse and, when to be so is most important, reticent. But it is large with compassion, concern, understanding. It is a beautiful piece of work, with a dignity to match that of the two women who march in such odd triumph through its pages. (p. 28)

> Jonathan Yardley, in The New Republic (*reprinted by permission of* The New Republic; © *1974 by The New Republic, Inc.*), *March 30, 1974.*

James Hanley . . . became immediately notorious for his *Boy* (1931), an angry novel about the humiliations and indecencies suffered by an adolescent on a merchant steamer. Finally suppressed under British obscenity laws, the book became a *cause célèbre* and Hanley's reputation seemed secure. His popularity reached its flood in the late 1930s and early 1940s with several first-rate novels about the war at sea and at home in England, and with the opening volumes of his Furys saga which traced the generations and fortunes of a lower class, Liverpool-Irish family. And then it ebbed. Though praised for his ''importance'' by such writers as Auden, Forster, Herbert Read and Henry Green, save for a fierce and respected coterie, Hanley was hardly read in Britain by the 1950s and practically unknown in the States. In 1962, with some twenty-two novels and fifteen books of short stories behind him, and studied neglect before, Hanley published a novel, *Say Nothing*, and abandoned the writing of fiction. . . .

[In 1972] Hanley broke a decade of silence with *Another World*. Set in Wales, where he has lived for the past forty years, it is a novel of pursuit and salvation, telling how a minister tries to save a lady recluse from a hell as private and claustrophobic as the room in which she lives. The book proved that Hanley had lost none of his force as a novelist, nor any of his compassion for those marginal people who, whether adrift at sea, terrified in a London blitz, or alone in a small Welsh rooming house, retreat to their own painful fantasies within rather than face the nightmare realities without. Like *Another World, A Woman in the Sky* is also a novel about loneliness and age, about that apathy bordering on the total loss of will power, and about the need to foster obsessions, if not, in fact, about the compulsion to pursue them. But it is a much bleaker and more terrifying book, and one which makes us feel the sting of death even as we witness the desperate uncoiling of life. (p. 601)

Hanley's spare style . . . and his long passages of staccato dialogue . . . strip all melodrama from the interplay of feelings, yet leave all emotions naked and still vastly human. . . .

A Woman in the Sky is a reaching out: not to push down barriers, or to collar the reader with message and moral but to tear away the fabric society weaves about old people, more often concealing their vulnerability than protecting their individuality. (p. 602)

> *Robert K. Morris, "Saved and Damned by Imagination," in* The Nation *(copyright 1974 by the Nation Associates, Inc.), May 11, 1974, pp. 601-02.*

On the evidence of *A Woman in the Sky* Hanley is a writer to be taken very seriously. His prose is spare, clipped, almost palpably *careful*, yet it is charged with a deep undercurrent of emotion. Hanley is writing about people who "don't matter," and with great tenderness he shows us how very much indeed they do matter. (p. 538)

A Woman in the Sky is one of those books that we reviewers persist in calling "minor," as if we were reluctant to go on record with the vigorous praise we actually feel. So let me say that this novel is not minor at all. In compassion, feeling, sheer human understanding, it is enormous. Hanley's people are as real as any you will meet anywhere, and their unexpected, quirky triumphs will move you profoundly. (p. 540)

> *Jonathan Yardley, in* Sewanee Review *(reprinted by permission of the editor; © 1974 by The University of the South), Summer, 1974.*

*   *   *

HAYDEN, Robert   1913-

Hayden is a prize-winning Black American poet and anthologist.

Robert Hayden's "Middle Passage," [which this critic believes to be one of the "finest poems by Negroes," has a position] in the literature of the race war . . . analogous to *Invisible Man* among the novels and *The Dutchman* among the plays. The effect . . . is irresistible and entire, the hurt . . . is lasting. It inheres in part, this pain, in the very hell of their subjects, in each case so completely evoked. The effect is certified, though, by the satisfying, spherical fullness of the design, the exactness of the craft. (pp. 83-4)

[It is a long poem] in which one could scarcely change a word with any hope of increasing the rightness or the

power. [It is] bloody, graphic, even documentary in [its] detailing of the horror; but so certain and controlled one can *use* the torment. . . . [Nothing] less than extensive quotation . . . could acknowledge the brim-full rightness, the necessary alteration of mode and effect. . . . Hayden, a "major" Negro poet, has written many other poems, professional and stylish: Communist and African-memory poems, war poems, Negro hero poems, poems overfilled with a sort of decadent delirious excess of hallucinatory imagery. But it all now seems, in unfair retrospect, apprentice work for "Middle Passage." (pp. 84, 86)

> *David Littlejohn, in his* Black on White: A Critical Survey of Writing By American Negroes *(copyright © 1966 by David Littlejohn; reprinted by permission of Grossman Publishers), Viking, 1966.*

Hayden's . . . surrealistic *A Ballad of Remembrance* is chilling with its whirling, glittering images and rhythms and its feeling of nightmare and irrationality. It captures the black experience, but filtered through the poet's sensitive subjectivity. . . .

In *Middle Passage* and *Runagate Runagate*, Hayden incorporates all the innovations of the experimental poets of the 1920s: varied and expressive rhythms; anti-poetic materials such as quotations from handbills, legal documents, ships' logs; scraps of poetry, hymns, spirituals; fusing all these together to make two exciting narratives of the beginning and of the escape from slavery. (p. 228)

> *Dudley Randall, "The Black Aesthetic in the Thirties, Forties and Fifties" (copyright © 1971 by Dudley Randall; reprinted by permission of Doubleday & Co., Inc.), in* The Black Aesthetic, *edited by Addison Gayle, Jr., Doubleday, 1971, pp. 224-34.*

History has haunted Robert Hayden from the beginning of his career as a poet. In 1941, . . . he worked on a series of poems dealing with slavery and the Civil War called *The Black Spear*. . . . This effort was no juvenile excursion, to be forgotten in the years of maturity. Though some of the poems have not been reprinted in *Selected Poems* (1966), *The Black Spear* survives in a severely altered form in Section Five of that volume. What remains is not simply "O Daedalus, Fly Away Home" and "Frederick Douglass," but a preoccupation with a continuing historical ambition. This was the desire to record accurately the yearnings, the frustrations, and the achievement of an enslaved but undestroyed people. "Middle Passage," "The Ballad of Nat Turner," and "Runagate, Runagate," all written later, share this concern. In these poems noble Blacks, Cinquez, Nat Turner, and Harriet Tubman, rise from oppression and obscurity. (p. 96)

A generation later Hayden displays an attachment somewhat less strong to historical themes. . . . Though the commitment to interpreting history is still present, the emphasis has changed. The poems of *The Black Spear* emerge from the suffering of Black people before Emancipation and record their assertion of manhood, more than the simple ability to survive, but those in "Words in the Mourning Time" describe the agony undergone by Malcolm and others to achieve spiritual liberation in our own day and the search for meaning in history upon which that liberation depends. What has endured through the years is the central importance of history in Hayden's poetry—not history as the poet would like it to be, but history as he has discovered it. (p. 97)

[A dominant influence] was Stephen Vincent Benét, whose long historical narrative *John Brown's Body* (1927) moved Hayden to think of approaching slavery and the Civil War "from the black man's point of view." Indeed, Hayden has acknowledged the fact that the title of his sequence of historical poems, *The Black Spear*, comes from Benét. (p. 98)

[One] of the differences separating Benét's poem from his own [is] the richness of his documentation. The accurate touches that come from Hayden's wide reading are impressive . . . [and] display evidences of extensive research in the slave trade. (p. 100)

History, formal and folk, serves Hayden's purpose, and that purpose in the early historical poems is to describe the mystical emergence of freedom from circumstances that appall and degrade, and the making of a man, a Black man in America. (p. 106)

> *Charles T. Davis, "Robert Hayden's Use of History" (copyright © 1973 by Charles T. Davis), in* Modern Black Poets: A Collection of Critical Essays, *Prentice-Hall, 1973, pp. 96-111.*

Although many of his poems deal directly with the experience of being black in America . . ., Hayden has stressed in his public statements, that he does not want race to enter into judgments of his poetry. . . . He obviously does not feel he inherited a black aesthetic with the color of his skin. Today when many of the young black writers in their understandable wrath against the criminal treatment of their people seem to be saying that suffering is an exclusive property of their race and that black writing is for blacks—honky, hands off—Robert Hayden's attitude must sound suspiciously like the poetic version of integration. (p. 277)

At the core of Hayden's work is suffering, but the suffering is not limited to that caused by racial prejudice. One finds it in personal sounding poems, in poems of Negro History and contemporary violence, in those about the Mexican poor, and even in his religious poems that center on Baha'u'llah, the cult figure of the Baha'i religion that Hayden professes. But also at the core of his work is hope —tough, unsentimental hope that challenges the pain. . . . (pp. 278-79)

Hayden's most characteristic style is [an] explosive one . . ., filled with alliteration and complicated sound effects supported by a rather expansive vocabulary. At times his music and diction are reminiscent of Wallace Stevens, more often of Hart Crane, and in a few places, where the rhythms are most pronounced, of Vachel Lindsay. (p. 280)

> *Michael Paul Novak, "Meditative, Ironic, Richly Human: The Poetry of Robert Hayden," in* The Midwest Quarterly (*copyright, 1974, by* The Midwest Quarterly, *Kansas State College of Pittsburg), Spring, 1974, pp. 276-85.*

Hayden aims at finding his own best self, using . . . models and traditions irrespective of race. Hayden and his critics both agree also that Hayden wanted to be not "just" a Negro poet. Although he identified strongly with Negro life, he wanted to be free—to feel that he was free—to be any kind of poet he cared to try to be. It was important to him, in other words, that he should be as integrated as he wished. In practice, incidentally—or, really, most significantly—Hayden largely realized his own professions. Beauty of form he often achieved in his work. This beauty he compounded with a wealth of substance usually racial in its derivation, yet frequently enough not too racial to keep him from incorporating into his work practices from poets who were well thought of in the circle of the Establishment.

One can see him very well at work in such a poem as his "Middle Passage," as fine a moment, it well may be, as one could want in the treatment of a Negro theme. (pp. 76-7)

"Middle Passage" is a title which, like ["The Waste Land"], speaks both through literal allusion and a rich metaphor of millions of people and more than one historic epoch. In literal allusion "Middle Passage" refers to the idiom of the slave trade. Slave ships typically sailed a triangle, the so-called triangle of trade. . . . The middle leg, the voyage over water from Africa to America, in which the ship was crammed with blacks to be disposed of as if they were not human, was called the "middle passage." Literally, then, "middle passage" speaks of a horrible transition. Figuratively it obviously refers to the unfinished odyssey of a people. It is the whole "blackamerican" experience since Africa. To say the words "Middle Passage" within the context of Hayden's poem is to speak of something real and big. One need not even read the poem to begin to explore an epic theme. One can stop, as it were, with the title and still possess a poem.

Out of a richly freighted title, then, grows a richly freighted poem. (pp. 77-8)

The selection of "narrators," as Hayden uses it in "Middle Passage," not only adds to the immediacy and the special credibility of a dramatic method to the poem. It also invests the voices of the poem with a quality of objectivity. It is not as if the poem writes, or rewrites, history. It is, rather, as if it repeats history, as if it actually performs the impossible miracle of "playing back" the past. . . . [The] poem maintains a constant flow of suggestion and allusion: here, a turn of language, "black gold, black ivory, black seed"; there, an echo from Shakespeare, from a song in *The Tempest*; at one point, mere wisps of Methodist hymnody; and, near the poem's end, a resentful reference by the Spaniard of the *Amistad* to John Quincy Adams. Myriad voices speak, indeed, in "Middle Passage." Hayden, a careful, painstaking, deliberate workman, sensitive to the infinite possibilities for the management of form in poetry, close student of the poetic mode approved by the New Critics, and, like Tolson, an esteemed teacher as well as a dedicated poet, may be adjudged in his performance in "Middle Passage" virtually the artist whom he hopes to be in his conception of the ideal poet.

He did not always write, as in "Middle Passage," of the Negro problem. His experiment in verse that seems almost physically to dive, "The Divers," for example, has absolutely no connection with Negroes as Negroes. But he did not deliberately avoid writing about Negroes. Quite to the contrary, his fundamental impulse has always seemed, not to be not black, but . . . to write as the spirit moves him. If it moves him racially, well and good. If not, well and good also. (pp. 79-80)

Blyden Jackson, in Black Poetry in America: Two Essays in Historical Interpretation, *by Blyden Jackson and Louis D. Rubin, Jr. (copyright © by Louisiana State University Press), Louisiana State University Press, 1974.*

* * *

HEANEY, Seamus 1939-

Heaney is an award-winning Irish poet, best known for his collection *Death of a Naturalist.*

There have always been three intertwined stands in Seamus Heaney's poetry: exploration of the hidden self, the Hidden Ireland, and the hidden artist, working underground or undercover as he moves along or spins the web of these worlds. The web has increased in intricacy and fineness with each successive book, and 'The Last Mummer' offers a more complete account of Heaney's poetic personality than his previous incarnations as 'big-eyed Narcissus', eel ('A Lough Neagh Sequence') or blacksmith. . . . [In] *Door into the Dark*, I noticed a particular fascination with terrain where land and water meet—and its connection with a sense of boundaries within the self blurring and dissolving, or of horizons being extended. This kind of focus is even more conspicuous in *Wintering Out* with its 'softening ruts', bog (of course), 'melted snow', 'alluvial mud' mound-dwellers who 'break the light ice at wells and dunghills', rushy fields, riverbank, while the poet

> . . . fords his life
> By sounding.
> Soundings.

or on firmer ground 'senses the pads / unfurling under grass and clover'. The images of breaking ice, or 'panes of flood' and a favourite word 'membrane' [suggest] the penetration of skins, of protective covering to the truth, or horror, that lies beneath: 'a flower of mud- / water blooms up to his reflection'. Like Wodwo Heaney 'sounds, with his senses, as agents or spies: he literally keeps his ear to the ground, 'small mouth and ear / in a woody cleft, / lobe and larynx / of the mossy places', 'senses', 'fingers', 'cocks his ear', 'eavesdrops', as he quests for 'antediluvian lore', origins, essences, bearings. . . . There is a striking new preoccupation with language itself: not a self-conscious aesthetic awareness—though it casts light on his physical relishing of words and phrase—but directed towards and capturing that point of articulation at which landscape becomes vocal, language tangible (another boundary crossed). . . . His loquacious waters, 'soft gradient / of consonant, vowel meadow' not only dramatise the interpenetration of word and thing as they reproduce the making of words in the mouth and their reverberation in the ear, but also suggest that language is the final medium to be sensually inhabited: 'a mating call of sound / rises to pleasure me'. (pp. 87-8)

'The Wool Trade' enacts the difference between English on the tongue of an Englishman and an Irishman . . . [and] indicates both how completely Heaney himself has absorbed the whole linguistic tradition available to him, and how intimately his language is involved with and presents the physical contours of Ulster. (p. 88)

The meeting of land and water primarily expresses the personal 'soundings' of *Wintering Out*. Its more social and historical soundings are accompanied by an imagery of dark yards and outhouses (as well as by 'flecks of blood' and 'carrion'.) This imagery seems to reflect both the twilight existence of the Hidden Ireland during the slave-centuries and the shadowed life, shadow-life of Ulster during the past four years. Sometimes, hopefully the yard is lit by a circle of lamplight which makes explicit the whole poetic process of illumination. Heaney has occasionally been attacked locally for not writing directly about the Troubles, but for him head-on confrontation has never been a congenial or rewarding strategy. 'A Northern Hoard', which contains the least oblique images of violence, in part explains the real agony and involvement, as well as preternatural understanding of complexities and inevitabilities, which imposes numbness:

> What do I say if they wheel out their dead?
> I'm cauterized, a black stump of bone.

Images of magic, superstition, spirits of the countryside, primitive cultures (we picked flints, / Pale and dirt-veined') define the tribal origins and nature of the conflict.

This is not only a very powerful but also a very beautiful volume, comprising a greater range of tone than its predecessors. Two of the more separated pieces in the second half of *Wintering Out* attain a real tragic dimension, 'Bye-Child' and 'Limbo'—while the compassion of 'The Tollund Man' ('his peat-brown head, / The mild pods of his eyes') as well as a proliferation of flower imagery ('my arms full / of wild cherry and rhododendron') also point to an enrichment of spiritual resources. (Who was the reviewer who said Heaney couldn't deal with *human* nature?) Technically, he will have to take care that the flexible quatrain does not become a cliché, but altogether on every level *Wintering Out* touches new springs. (pp. 88-9)

Edna Longley, "Heaney's Hidden Ireland," in Phoenix *(8 Cavendish Road, Heaton Mersey, Stockport, Cheshire, England), July, 1973.*

Seamus Heaney has already assembled a body of work of extraordinary distinctiveness and distinction. . . . [He] has been proclaimed an exciting talent by many and a possibly major poet by several. Single-mindedness of purpose, a fertile continuity of theme, high competence in execution, a growing unmistakability of voice: these are Heaney's strengths and they place him in seriousness and maturity beyond hailing distance of most younger British poets.

These make him sound dull, whereas Heaney writes a verse that achieves, but does not depend upon, immediate impact. The most eye-catching feature is a use of rawly physical metaphors for things in and out of the physical world: frogs are 'mud grenades, their blunt heads farting'; granary sacks are 'great blind rats'; a quiet river wears 'a transfer of gables and sky'; a pregnant cow looks as though 'she has swallowed a barrel.' Heaney's metaphors are so right, so conclusive that they generate within the poem and across the canon an axiomatic quality that is perilously close to being self-defeating; they can even in cumulation constitute their own kind of preciosity. In consequence, the poet occasionally gives the impression of a man hastening to patent a style. Craft, with which unlike most poets today

Heaney is preoccupied, is not merely honest skill but also Daedalean cunning. He will seemingly not be deflected from working his enviably rich vein as he strikes deeper and deeper towards some unseen mother lode. The metaphor is apt, for Heaney's theme thus far has been 'working the earth,' and his exploitation of this coincides with the 'whole earth' movement in Britain and the United States. Just as important, it coincides with the attempts of several writers in Northern Ireland to delve beneath the violent surface of life in the province into lore, history and myth, on the principle that the poisonous plant can best be understood by its roots. Heaney may have been engaged upon this before terror struck in 1969, but the 'Troubles' have surely lent his poetry urgency and authenticity.

Troubles or no, digging deep has always been a hazardous business in Ulster, for it is to resume the dark, in Heaney's phrase, and the dark is fearful. It is arguable whether or not the fear with which Heaney's poetry is soaked is justified by the trove he has brought back from the Ulster heart of darkness. The impersonal insights are undeniable and remarkable, but the poet's degree of emotional involvement is more problematic. And has the poet up to now worked deep, in conceit and extended metaphor, at the expense of modal variety? These are questions not to be answered until the tangy and peculiarly seasoned quality of Heaney's poetry has been savoured. Should he reach perfection in his present mode, he will have become a notable minor poet. Should he instead widen his themes, break into new modes, and learn to trust his feeling, Seamus Heaney might well become the best Irish poet since Yeats. (pp. 35-6)

Early Heaney poetry startled with its physicality. What a pleasure it was to come upon for the first time imagery so bluff, masculine and dead-on. . . . Heaney's first volume, *Death of a Naturalist* . . . is as heavily laden with assonance, alliteration, imagery of touch, taste and smell, and with synesthesia (the buzz of bluebottles visualised as gauze) as the flax is with sods. Extensive description of a static scene can, as we shall see later, lead Heaney into confusion, despite a Ted Hughes-like vividness. Heaney is on firmer ground when recreating the *processes* of the earth and how man interacts with nature through ritual, custom and work. Not only are Heaney's poems about manual work on the farm—ploughing, planting, harvesting, horseshoeing etc.—but they are themselves manuals on how the work is actually done. . . . Of course, by dint of education, travel and rural changes, Heaney is no longer at one with his rural origins and so his rehearsal of the customs he witnessed or participated in as a child assumes the quality of incantation and commemoration. The poems, he would have us believe, are substitutes for the farmwork he was once close to. (p. 36)

It might be said that in *Death of a Naturalist*, with its prolific use of elementary poetic devices and overplus of image-making, Heaney was merely learning how to handle the turf-spade. It is likely, however, that the spade, wielded with whatever expertise, is too restricted a tool for Heaney's intellect and sensibility. At any rate, his second and third volumes evidence the pen metamorphosing from spade back again to pen.

Yet digging in one form or another remains the archetypal act in Heaney's poetry. What is found when the earth is overturned is sometimes good, such as the cream-white healthy tubers in 'At a Potato Digging,' though in the same poem we are reminded that this was not always so and that 'wild higgledy skeletons/scoured the land in 'forty-five,/wolfed the blighted root and died.' Deeper down, finds are liable to be more interesting. Because of the strange power in bog water which prevents decay, much of Ireland's past has been preserved within the three million acres of bog—utensils, jewellery and most characteristically the wood from Ireland's vanished oak forests: 'A carter's trophy/split for rafters,/a cobwebbed, black,/long-seasoned rib/ / under the first thatch' ('Bog Oak'). The laid open turf-bank is also a memory-bank, permitting us to read 'an approximate chronological sequence of landscapes and human cultures in Ireland going back several thousand years. Digging turf can often be interrupted—or continued—to become excavation. (p. 38)

Death of a Naturalist was Heaney's preliminary and noisy spade-work, the clearing of brush and scrub. Gradually there is a movement towards the spare and vertical shapes of *Wintering Out*, serious attempts to sink shafts narrowly and deep. Between the surface clatter of *Death of a Naturalist* and the striking downwards in *Wintering Out* comes the intermediate task in *Door into the Dark* of striking inwards, recognising the inner fears to be overcome before the real digging is begun. . . . Excessive respect for the dark is shared not only by children and religious adults, but by primitives. The dark blurs the distinction between pagan and Christian. Raised a Catholic, an upbringing that has shaped 'In Gallarus Oratory,' Heaney has nonetheless kept intimate traffic with the elder faiths of the Irish countryside which lie, bog-like, beneath the visible Roman Catholicism that has often coopted them. (pp. 39-40)

Door into the Dark is not a sustained assault upon the dark but a series of forays. . . . Heaney has a marked reluctance to strike inwards, to cross the threshold, to explore the emotional and psychological sources of his fear; and fear therefore outweighs understanding in his work, as darkness outweighs illumination. We might choose to see his Roman Catholic upbringing coming into play here. Heaney's feeling in Gallarus oratory is indistinguishable from the penitent's desire to confess inside the dark confessional or pray inside the monastic sanctum. (The suggestion of defiance in 'No worshipper/Would leap up to his God off this floor' surely stems from Heaney's being native to a fundamentalist corner of Ireland whose majority abhors kneeling and the monastic tradition.) But Heaney is no readier to confess his personal feelings to his readers than the penitent is to discuss his confession with anyone other than his priest. The privacy of religious belief becomes the privacy of poetic feeling. (pp. 40-1)

In the meantime, the poet remains masterly at composing the signals and symptoms of fear into verse as compactly layered as good turf. At the poetic centre of *Door into the Dark* is a fine group of poems called 'A Lough Neagh Sequence.' Accounts of how the lough fishermen catch eels, interwoven with accounts of the life-cycle of the fish, are brilliant public metaphors for that psychic disturbance in Heaney's poetry whose precise meaning remains as intractable as bog oak. The sequence also interweaves the key Heaney motifs of descent, homing and darkness in the fashion of a metaphysical conceit. The eels travelling overland at night form a 'horrid cable' that encircles the poet's world of experience, threatening it with mysterious and malign power yet defining its shape and continuity. The completed circle of eels is also an 'orbit' of fears, and this implies a gravitational tendency to descend as well as to circumscribe.

The conceit lies at the heart of *Door into the Dark*. The volume is a marked improvement over *Death of a Naturalist* in terms of surer control and more effective conservation of energy. But the tautness of the conceit and the dramatic distancing it involves can obscure psychic and emotional issues as readily as immature and uncontrolled fertility. Moreover, the particular conceit of Heaney's choice—that of the circle or orbit—threatens to make his poetic philosophy a closed system, a state of affairs which is not helped by what I earlier called the axiomatic rightness of his images. (p. 41)

[For] most of *Wintering Out* he is still content to impersonalise his feelings. If, for instance, natural and preternatural fears are more honestly evoked and allayed than in either of the two previous books, it is by dint not of greater emotional investment but of sounder analogies.... Heaney's fear of the dark becomes in *Wintering Out* a fear of the violence in ... 'the immemorial peasant tradition which dominates the heart of Ireland' and of the way this violent and sacrificial past fingers out through analogy and recurrence to the present. A group of ... poems in *Wintering Out* is concerned not with depth-readings of the Irish earth but with topography. Above as well as below the ground are the signatures of the past inscribed for us to see. In these 'topographical poems' which are also 'language poems,' parts of speech and parts of landscape are identified as a Catholic Ulsterman looks and listens around and considers what he has gained and lost by living in the planted North. (p. 43)

For Heaney, obsolescence can be a primal state and, insofar as the obsolete is preserved in custom, speech or bog, can exert an influence on the present. It is this obsolescence-primality-nativeness of the Irish that will resurge.

When we have figured this out, we have yet to decide if Heaney is referring to a linguistic or cultural resurgence (or both) and what form it is to take.... Unfortunately these resourceful poems are so cerebral that when they fail as arguments (not necessarily by being false but by being unclear), they fail ultimately as poems. (pp. 45-6)

The ambiguity of the language-poems does, however, reflect Heaney's dilemma as a poet, suspended between the English and (Anglo-) Irish traditions and cultures. Correlatives of ambivalence proliferate in his verse: the archetypal sound in his work (and to be savoured in the reading) is the guttural spirant, half-consonant, half-vowel; the archetypal locale is the bog, half-water, half-land; the archetypal animal is the eel which can fancifully be regarded (in its overland forays) as half-mammal, half-fish. (p. 46)

If Heaney becomes the best Irish poet of his generation, it will be because he has remained true to as great an Irishness in diction, setting and theme as he has already achieved, while taking the emotional risks of his great antecedent Yeats and his contemporary Thomas Kinsella. His sure sense of miniaturist form, learned from the English poets of the 'fifties and 'sixties, is a solid foundation from which he needs to launch into a variety of modes. Time, shall we say, to lay aside the spade and bring out the heavy machinery. In the meantime, there is little contemporary poetry that has bettered the quality and fruitfulness of Heaney's solitary digging; few poets have enlivened their work with a more remarkable gift for seeing afresh the physical world around us and beneath us. (p. 47)

> *John Wilson Foster, "The Poetry of Seamus Heaney," in* Critical Quarterly, *Spring, 1974, pp. 35-48.*

Seamus Heaney himself must be not far short of attributive status. Certainly his name will signify to most readers of poetry today the mysterious power of words to recreate in the mind the reality of the physical world; to provide the verb to every created thing in a way that confounds Auden's linguistic pessimism, and justifies Heidegger's definition of language as 'speaking being'. This power is exercised with the confidence we have come to expect in Heaney's ... volume *Wintering Out*. In 'Gifts of Rain', for example, ... in images that serve as sudden earths: 'stepping stones like black molars/ Sunk in the ford', a cow's afterbirth 'strung on the hedge/ As if the wind smarted/ And streamed bloodshot tears', 'The cobbles of the yard/ Lit pale as eggs'. But to those critics underprovided with negative capability who have all along asked the irritable questions 'what next, what else?' Heaney's third book also suggests some intriguing answers. Generally, one can say that Heaney has become more self-conscious; both about his material, language, and also about his volatile and even dangerous subject-matter, Ireland. It's remarkable how many of these poems turn in on themselves, taking the words of which they are composed as part of their subject. It is as if Heaney has suddenly decided to explore the implications of his own poetic faculty. Thus one can read the first poem 'Fodder' ('Or, as we said,/fother, I open/my arms for it/again'), with its new attention to words themselves, as an image of the poet's provident storing of his materials, 'multiple as loaves/ and fishes', for his future sustenance. (pp. 85-6)

The other self-consciousness is political. Heaney is no protest poet, but nor can he remain indifferent to the bombs, snipers, and internment camps that maim the body of his land. The image of Ireland as the tortured body of a woman is implied in 'Land' here, and becomes explicit in poems which he has since published in *The Listener*, 'Bog Queen' and 'A New Life'. It is a traditional image used with new urgency, and containing new menace; a menace which is also communicated here in 'The Last Mummer', when the mummer 'catches the stick in his fist/ and, shrouded, starts beating/ the bars of the gate'. There are no dates or names here, no indictment; the guilt like the terror must be shared among too many. But there is some risk of the contagion of despair. The sense of this is best communicated by a question Heaney quotes in his prologue poem, a question chalked on a Belfast wall: 'Is there a life before death?'. The idea of death, of course, is not quantifiable; but we may wonder whether Heaney and his chalker of slogans have not the most need of the word at the present time, as a verbal event that is very much rooted in their reality. (p. 86)

> *Damian Grant, in* Critical Quarterly, *Spring, 1974.*

Although twenty-six years younger than [R. S.] Thomas, Seamus Heaney shares Thomas' intimacy with the soil, and resembles him in having moved from dread of nature to reconciliation with it. Heaney has concentrated upon graphic, imagistic descriptions of the northern Irish countryside of his youth, has set out to commemorate in undistorted fashion "things founded clean on their own shapes." The various and abundant sensuous phenomena crowded into his verse testify to his pleasure in physical experience. . . . (p. 328)

[He] is intensely conscious of the awesomeness of living energy . . . [and] has come to recognize living energy as a positive force countering the ruthlessness of existence and the inevitability of death. . . . Heaney intensifies the sense of throbbing energy through the frequent use of what are perhaps most appropriately described as "explosive images." Frogs sit "poised like mud grenades," and in "Trout" the fish holding itself steady in the current resembles a "fat gun barrel." (pp. 328-29)

> *Julian Gitzen, in* The Midwest Quarterly *(copyright, 1974, by* The Midwest Quarterly, *Kansas State College of Pittsburg), Summer, 1974.*

*   *   *

HELLER, Joseph   1923-

Heller, an American novelist and playwright, won immediate recognition with his first novel, *Catch-22*, a "lethal blend of farce and fantasy, sick humour and icy casualness." Heller's long-awaited second novel, *Something Happened*, is a depressing and profoundly affecting statement about the condition of modern mankind. With the publication of this second work, Heller is recognized as a major contemporary novelist. (See also *Contemporary Authors*, Vols. 5-8, rev. ed.)

[The] alternating play of humor and horror [in *Catch-22*] creates a dramatic tension throughout that allows the book to be labeled as a classic both of humor and of war. It is not "a comic war novel" despite the fact that comedy and war are held more or less in solution, for the war is *not* comic but horrible—this we are not allowed to forget. The laughter repeatedly breaks through the tight net of frustration in which the characters struggle only to sink back as the net repairs itself and holds the reader prisoned in its outrageous bonds. (p. 190)

[The] artistic strategy relating to the thesis of the novel, . . ., put simply, is this: War is irrational; and the representative things that happen in war are likewise irrational, including man's behavior in war. This thesis is an underlying assumption, a donnée, illustrated not documentarily but imaginatively throughout the book. It is, in terms of the book, unarguable—you take it or leave it—for the author has seen to it that all the evidence favors his thesis. What he asks, and it is everything, is that his readers accept the credibility of his characters and their actions, if not at face value, then as wild, ingratiating exaggeration that nevertheless carries the indestructible truth that war is irrational. (p. 191)

The responsive reader of *Catch-22* is . . . made to walk a tight-rope as he leans first to riotous humor and then tips to the side of black tragedy. There is much in the book that illustrates Charlie Chaplin's dictum that humor is "playful pain." . . .

The humor in *Catch-22*, we are forced to conclude, is only secondary. Where Heller comes through in unalleviated

horror is where the message lies. The book's humor does not alleviate the horror; it heightens it by contrast.

It is not therefore the disinterestedness of pure humor that we find in *Catch-22*. It does not accept the pain of life with wry resignation. Instead it flaunts in bitterness the desperate flag of resistance to the wrongs of this life—wrongs suffered, not by the wholly innocent, but by the insufficiently guilty. And the wrongs are perpetrated not only by unscrupulous, ignorant, and power-hungry men, but also by the inscrutable Deity. (p. 197)

> *Louis Hasley, "Dramatic Tension in 'Catch-22'," in* The Midwest Quarterly *(copyright, 1974, by* The Midwest Quarterly, *Kansas State College of Pittsburg), Winter, 1974, pp. 190-97.*

[In] Joseph Heller's very fine, wrenchingly depressing new novel (his second), *Something Happened* . . . Bob Slocum is the narrator. The book is his story—his ruminations, memories, gags, guilts, self-analysis, fears-at-the-abyss ("I've got anxiety; I suppress hysteria")—a parable for our times (Heller's clear intention), a contemporary *Job* (here robbed even of Jewishness), a sort of *Pilgrim's Stagnation*. . . . (Personally, *Catch-22* and I never really got on. It seemed to me a succession of terrific and then not-so-terrific punch lines, and when it meandered, so did my attention.) But *Something Happened* is very different. It gnaws at one, slowly and almost nuzzlingly at first, mercilessly toward the end. It hurts. It gives the willies. (p. 78)

Something Happened is composed with complete deliberation, of a series of conditions of survival (some call it living) that are being constantly recapitulated and subject to all the various tones and moods at Slocum's articulate command (anger, self-mockery, stoic frankness, confession), and that loop back on each other in ever-tightening coils. The central theme is fear—fear in every aspect of his life, at work, at home, out on the town. Fear is seen as the necessary webbing of the social order. Sometimes fear is almost a thrill to Slocum. At work, he wants and expects small but appropriate displays of fear from those who work under him (as he provides same to those above); absent such displays, he feels threatened and confused. The safety valve is mockery: for example, Slocum doodles company organization charts showing lines, not of responsibility, but of "envy, hope, fear, ambition, frustration, rivalry, hatred, or disappointment."

What's wrong with Slocum is that he has become sharply aware of fear as a set condition of his every movement, of his every human relationship. It provides him with some very sharp insights. . . . It also leads to many jokes, on which he hones his guilt. Slocum is in extreme pain. He mocks it in order not to succumb to it entirely; otherwise, he might simply scream, like one of Bacon's popes.

The story—there are plots and subplots—is an accounting and a self-analysis, and it is truthful. But as a process of therapy, it does not and cannot work for Slocum—nor can it work in Heller's view, for any of us. Slocum's agony is not from "something" that "happened" to him that can be exposed and thereby defused, but instead seeps up through the accretion of everything that happened to him, everything that he is, all the circumscribing circumstances of his life—including his articulation of self-consciousness, all the yearnings, guilts, and clever japes. Slocum's agony is thus not a sickness that can be healed, but an appropriate response to his reality, to the way life now is. *Something Happened* is like a dirge, a chant. It is Heller's diagnosis of the modern human spirit, which, he says, is living in hell, has got the willies, is near to death. (pp. 78-9)

Eliot Fremont-Smith, "Heller's Hell," in New York Magazine *(© 1974 by NYM Corp.; reprinted by permission of* New York Magazine *and Eliot Fremont-Smith), September 30, 1974, pp. 78-9.*

Like Ralph Ellison in these if in no other respects, Joseph Heller is notable for being a slow worker as well as for being one of the few American novelists able to sustain a reputation on the basis of a single book. With hindsight, it is possible to see that *Catch-22* (1961), Heller's first and only other novel, was a well-aimed bomb. To cite works only in its own direct line, the novel has clearly been the intellectual sire of the film "Dr. Strangelove" and, more recently, of the movie and now television series, "M.A.S.H." It brought comedy to the essentially grim subject of war, and thereby demonstrated its utter absurdity. Before the appearance of *Catch-22*, anti-heroism in American fiction was well on its way to being established; it took things a step further, however, and can be read as a mass over the death of heroism itself. It held that, in the mad, impersonal killing of modern warfare, heroism was a joke, and only seeing after one's own survival made sense: in an insane world, only the man who pretended to insanity can be judged sane. Beginning as a cult novel, *Catch-22* spread in popularity to the point where, along with Paul Goodman's *Growing Up Absurd* and the novels of Kurt Vonnegut, it has to be accounted one of the key books to understanding the fashionable nihilism of the past decade.

There was a catch in *Catch-22*, as the novel's more perceptive critics pointed out. The catch is that Heller, till nearly the end of his novel, does not mention the Nazis, and thus nowhere suggests that, absurd though modern warfare most truly is, there really was no alternative, except the unthinkable one of knuckling under to Hitler's Third Reich. Evil is the missing component in *Catch-22*, and if one is to go all the way with one's nihilism, as Heller was not in this novel, then one must proclaim World War II to have been an outright fraud, which Heller was not prepared to do. Still, it took a certain courage for Heller to use World War II as the background for *Catch-22*—Korea was then available, and of course today Vietnam would be an absolute patsy for demonstrating his argument. On the other hand, it may come down to no more than the fact that Heller's own experience was of World War II, and he is not a writer who works well outside the boundaries of his own experience.

Despite the flaw running up the center of *Catch-22*, the novel had a winning exuberance and a wealth of comic invention. Between its energy and its comedy, Heller was able for the better part of 400 pages to sustain interest in the grotesquely mad world he set before his readers. More than with most novelists, the universe of Heller's novels is a self-enclosed one. Accept his assumptions and his conclusions inevitably, sometimes hilariously, follow. The assumptions of *Catch-22* are that courage, bravery, liberty, love of country, and other human virtues are all a joke, a hideous cover-up for the urge toward self-advancement, the

will to power, and simple craziness. Interestingly, in its assumption *Catch-22* is a precursor to much of the fiction that arose out of the past decade, but with an even deeper skepticism about conventional explanations of human character and how the world works. In the fiction of Donald Barthelme, Leonard Michaels, Thomas Pynchon, and Robert Coover, among others, this skepticism slices to the bone: character counts for nothing; plot is a laugh, since cause can no longer be held to explain effect; and language itself is no more than the stick of a blind man, a thing which we use to grope our way around in the dark but which really lights up nothing. A curious symbiosis is at work here; as Heller's first novel, directly or indirectly, fed the fiction of these younger writers of the generation following his own, so Heller's second novel [*Something Happened*] seems to feed off their work. . . .

Something has happened, all right, but it is in the nature of the kind of novel Heller has written that we never learn what, specifically, it is. The quality of life is less good than it once seemed, relationships between husbands and wives and parents and children are impossible, the country is going to hell in a handwagon. "The world just doesn't work. It's an idea whose time has gone." All these points are duly, even repetitiously and dully, noted, but what exactly has happened to bring about the malaise that constitutes the only emotional climate of *Something Happened* is never pinpointed beyond this.

As a novelist, in *Catch-22* as in *Something Happened*, Joseph Heller's method is never to explain but to let description suffice. "Description," wrote Wallace Stevens, "is revelation." Instead of an analysis of the malaise, then, we get a description of it. In the nearly 600-page monologue provided by Bob Slocum, there is no attempt to understand what is going on, but only to describe what it feels like to live under the malaise. Much as if he were talking to a tireless and well-paid psychoanalyst, Slocum rambles on confessionally, formlessly, repetitiously. Anxieties elide into fantasies, fantasies into terrors, terrors into nostalgia. It is almost as if we, the novel's readers, are in the psychoanalyst's chair, notebook on lap, a decanter of hot coffee on the desk, patiently awaiting the completion of the analysand's tale, so that we might then return to the quiet of our study, reassemble the data, and offer an answer to what exactly has happened. (p. 1)

Something Happened has none of the joyous energy of *Catch-22*, nor much of its comic invention. It is a novel of bleak landscapes and shadowy characters. It begins in anxiety and ends in despair. Nothing happens in *Something Happened*.

This is by deliberation. The nature of Slocum's work remains unknown. Most characters are not described, except for their deformities: a limp on one, a bit of spittle on the corner of the mouth on another, the overweight of a third. Like so much fiction of its kind, physical description is kept arid and abstract; concretion, interestingly enough, is lavished only on sex. Slocum's wife's buttocks, breasts, and other parts are described in detail; nothing is said about her face. Perhaps this is not surprising; perhaps it comes down to no more than a technical problem. If a novelist has no interest in plot, if he has no interest as well in character, if he cannot believe in the first and is bored by the second, then drama, the twists of plot out of which character is formed or revealed in fiction, is denied him also. This, if one wishes to write at novel length, leaves sex. . . .

Pornography is a dead end in literature; it is better portrayed, if we must have it, in the movies. But given the loss of credence in character and in plot that is part of Heller's novelistic equipment, pornography is all that is left him, or any other writer who works under what is called the post-Modernist sensibility. Under this sensibility, despair is assumed, defeat is assumed, hopelessness is assumed. (Oddly, an ample audience for all this bad news is also assumed.) What results is, in effect, Kafka with screwing—which, as anyone who has looked into Kafka knows, isn't Kafka at all. It is merely writing about screwing under the guise of higher purposes.

If *Something Happened* turns out to be of slight interest in itself, it is of wider interest in demonstrating that fiction written under the assumptions of the post-Modernist sensibility cannot sustain itself over the length of a large novel. A Donald Barthelme can float a story or sketch under these same assumptions for eight or ten pages on sheer brilliance. But at greater length, things tend to flatten out—the literature of exhaustion itself in the end proves exhausting to read. In Joseph Heller's case there is an irony here that an ironist such as himself might perhaps appreciate. Thirteen years in transit, when the milk train of his second novel finally arrived at its destination the cargo had gone sour. (p. 2)

Joseph Epstein, "Joseph Heller's Milk Train: Nothing More to Express," in Book World—The Washington Post (© The Washington Post), *October 6, 1974, pp. 1-2.*

Mr. Heller might have . . ., at least somewhere in ["Something Happened"], used conventional, Chekhovian techniques for making us love a sometimes wicked man. He might have said that Slocum was drunk or tired after a bad day at the office when he spoke so heartlessly or that he whispered his heartlessness only to himself or to a stranger he would never see again. But Slocum is invariably sober and deliberate during his monologue, does not seem to give a damn who hears what he says. Judging from his selection of unromantic episodes and attitudes, it is his wish that we dislike him.

And we gratify that wish.

Is this book any good? Yes. It is splendidly put together and hypnotic to read. It is as clear and hard-edged as a cut diamond. Mr. Heller's concentration and patience are so evident on every page that one can only say that "Something Happened" is at all points precisely what he hoped it would be. (pp. 1-2)

"Something Happened" is so astonishingly pessimistic . . . that it can be called a daring experiment. Depictions of utter hopelessness in literature have been acceptable up to now only in small doses, in short-story form, as in Franz Kafka's "The Metamorphosis," Shirley Jackson's "The Lottery," or John D. MacDonald's "The Hangover," to name a treasured few. As far as I know, though, Joseph Heller is the first major American writer to deal with unrelieved misery at novel length. Even more rashly, he leaves his major character, Slocum, essentially unchanged at the end. . . .

The uneasiness which many people will feel about liking "Something Happened" has roots which are deep. It is no casual thing to swallow a book by Joseph Heller, for he is,

whether he intends to be or not, a maker of myths. (One way to do this, surely, is to be the final and most brilliant teller of an oft-told tale.) "Catch-22" is now the dominant myth about Americans in the war against fascism. "Something Happened," if swallowed, could become the dominant myth about the middle-class veterans who came home from that war to become heads of nuclear families. The proposed myth has it that those families were pathetically vulnerable and suffocating. It says that the heads of them commonly took jobs which were vaguely dishonorable or at least stultifying, in order to make as much money as they could for their little families, and they used that money in futile attempts to buy safety and happiness. The proposed myth says that they lost their dignity and their will to live in the process.

It says they are hideously tired now.

To accept a new myth about ourselves is to simplify our memories—and to place our stamp of approval on what might become an epitaph for our era in the shorthand of history. This, in my opinion, is why critics often condemn our most significant books and poems and plays when they first appear, while praising feebler creations. The birth of a new myth fills them with primitive dread, for myths are so effective.

Well—I have now suppressed my own dread. I have thought dispassionately about "Something Happened," and I am now content to have it shown to future generations as a spooky sort of summary of what my generation of nebulously clever white people experienced, and what we, within the cage of those experiences, then did with our lives.

And I am counting on a backlash. I expect younger readers to love Robert Slocum—on the grounds that he couldn't possibly be as morally repellent and socially useless as he claims to be.

People a lot younger than I am may even be able to laugh at Slocum in an affectionate way, something I am unable to do. They may even see comedy in his tragic and foolish belief that he is totally responsible for the happiness or unhappiness of the members of his tiny family.

They may even see some nobility in him, as an old soldier who has been brought to emotional ruin at last by the aging process and civilian life. . . .

We keep reading this overly long book, even though there is no rise and fall in passion and language, because it is structured as a suspense novel. The puzzle which seduces us is this one: Which of several possible tragedies will result from so much unhappiness? The author picks a good one.

I say that this is the most memorable, and therefore the most permanent variation on a familiar theme, in that it says baldly what the other variations only implied, what the other variations tried with desperate sentimentality not to imply: That many lives, judged by the standards of the people who live them, are simply not worth living. (p. 2)

Kurt Vonnegut, Jr., in The New York Times Book Review (© *1974 by The New York Times Company; reprinted by permission), October 6, 1974.*

Joseph Heller's "Catch-22" was only ostensibly a novel about combat during World War II. Yossarian's war was a dodging, twisting exercise in survival within a surreal bureaucracy, and he might well have flown the banner of Walt Kelly's Pogo: "We have met the enemy and he is us." "Catch-22," reread, is as wonderful as I thought a dozen years ago, Dickensian in energy, inventiveness and exuberance. I went back to it because I was having a hard time with Heller's second novel, in which he has come home to a Manhattan office and a Connecticut suburb. . . . The new book is as morose, slow and thoughtless as the first was morose, fast and buoyant. Heller has not written "Son of Catch-22"; if he had, we would all jump on him. But "Something Happened" will take time to digest. I don't like it as much as I'd hoped to. (p. 116)

Heller has staged a kind of Dance of Death of the Quotidian. Those who are aggrieved that the best American novelists have often seemed to work outside ordinary life will find that Heller, confining himself to the family and the job, has written an epic of the everyday. "Something Happened" has a Tolstoyan normality, an open-hearted appetite for the ordinary, a willingness to explore inadmissible feelings—early-morning aversion to one's wife, hatred of one's children, fears of homosexuality, the sudden desire to strike out at those who arouse uncomfortable feelings of pity, the craven indifference to worthy causes ("Soon there'll be no more whales. My wife and I will just have to make do without them").

There is so much to admire in this long, funny, very affecting—and sometimes monotonous—book that I wish I could wholeheartedly believe in its final pages. . . . The event is as horrible as Snowden's death in "Catch-22" and as lengthily foreshadowed. I don't think it can be read without tears. But it leaves an aftertaste of contrivance.

I hardly have to tell you to read Joseph Heller's novel. He is a writer who arouses affection, and "Something Happened" has been awaited with the eagerness with which we once looked forward to a new work from J. D. Salinger. My own bemusement may be a result of exaggerated hopes. (p. 118)

Walter Clemons, "Comedy of Fear," in Newsweek *(copyright 1974 by Newsweek, Inc.; all rights reserved; reprinted by permission), October 14, 1974, pp. 116, 118.*

What can a writer do for an encore who has already been compared—by a critic as restrained as Robert Brustein—to the Marx Brothers, Kingsley Amis, S. J. Perelman and Al Capp? For 13 years, ever since *Catch-22* became an unparalleled publishing phenomenon and a cult book all over the world, that has been Joseph Heller's problem. . . .

To announce that *Something Happened* is a terrific letdown is only to make the obvious comment on publicized great expectations. But how exactly does it fail? To try to answer that question is to get into certain kinds of bankruptcy that have to do not only with American lives but also with the novels that struggle to record them.

Something Happened, for instance, cannot really be read apart from *Catch-22*. It represents the second installment, so to speak, of Heller's *War and Peace*. Over ten years ago Heller explained: "The hero is the antithesis of Yossarian —20 years later." Of his Syrian-American bombardier in

Catch-22 he had written: "It was a vile and muddy war, and Yossarian could have lived without it—lived forever, perhaps." Of his WASP business executive, Bob Slocum, in *Something Happened*, Heller might have written: It was a vile and muddy peace, and Slocum was dying of it—dying in slow motion.

With 100 little winks, grimaces and ha-has, Slocum describes (and mercilessly redescribes) himself and his life in a flat pattern of total recall. . . .

"Something did happen to me somewhere that robbed me of confidence and courage," Slocum concludes from the depths of his boredom and anxiety. Endlessly he rummages through his childhood sexual initiations for clues. But it is not what has happened, but what has not happened to Slocum that constitutes his main problem—and Heller's. Can anything be more difficult than constructing a novel about a weightless figure with no pull of gravity morally or emotionally—a cipher whose brief sensation is of "standing still"? For brief, affecting moments Slocum feels love for his bright, affectionate nine-year-old son. But Heller clumsily resolves the relationship by making Slocum responsible for the boy's death. Improbably, he smothers him with a hug. Rather than being shocked, or moved, the reader is embarrassed by this climax, so abrupt, so calculated, in its symbolism. The son's death simply seems scripted in desperation to wrench the novel out of its passive mood, to interrupt at any cost the compulsive drone of self-pity—to break at last Slocum's death grip not only on his son, but also on the reader and on Heller himself.

"There are really so few things that *can* happen to people in this lifetime of ours, so few alternatives, so little any of us *can* become." Does Slocum's confession of impotence speak, too, for Heller's predicament as a writer with a dead-end novel on his hands?

A little naively, perhaps, readers still look to novels to provide models, or at least styles, for their own lives. From *Catch-22* they received the antic message: In a mad world, the sane man runs for his life. What does *Something Happened* have to say? A tired retread of the anti-hero—a dated update of *The Organization Man* as crossed with Kafka—Slocum kicks his doubtless hand-cut English shoes against his casket and pronounces the epitaph on himself and his novel: "I wish I knew what to wish." (p. 87)

Melvin Maddocks, "Boring from Within," in Time *(reprinted by permission from* Time, The Weekly Newsmagazine; *copyright Time Inc.), October 14, 1974, pp. 87-8.*

The way [*Something Happened*] is told really is the plot and the circumstance, is itself recognition and reversal, as our doctrine these days says it ought to be. The manner of revelation is itself what is revealed. And therein may have lurked, for Heller, a key miscalculation—but I will come back to that.

It would be easy to dismiss *Something Happened*, and probably wrong. For as he did so unforgettably in *Catch-22*, Joseph Heller pushes at us here a deadly moral and we may well find ourselves impaled on it. This is not just another punishment of the same old organization man. No, Slocum's scummy, slimy nature is calculated to trap us in his horror as surely as Yossarian's adorable boyish farce did in *his* horror. *Something Happened* does not have anything like the marvelous clowning, the poignant camaraderie, the wild caricature, the pure acetylene contempt of *Catch-22.* (p. 24)

Surely nobody expected Heller even to try things like that again. Nor can we expect that *Something Happened* is likely to enjoy the fate of *Catch-22*, progressing from random cheers and groans to cult observances and then, through the years of a hideous American history it seemed to predict, to its place as a "contemporary classic" by mass acclaim and academic instauration. . . .

But the ruminations of Slocum do become as insidious as muck. The voice is so familiar. . . .

Joseph Heller has to an unusual degree the power to disturb. I recall thinking about *Catch-22* back in 1961 that I didn't want women I knew to read it, a squeamishness perhaps strangely enough projected—not sufficiently unlike, perhaps, Slocum's own deadly tenderness. Some of us at least are going to be reminded by this book of too many things we put away in unmarked places, the bad luck of too many deaths too close to home, too many bad habits of the way some of us live, too much bad faith, bad dreams, and how we are still frightened by things long after we should have gotten over them. These accuse personally. Yossarian's innocent revelation only accused the world. "They're trying to kill me." "No one's trying to kill you." "Then why are they shooting at me?" "They're shooting at everyone. They're trying to kill everyone." "And what difference does that make?" "You're crazy." Ah, to be crazy again in that harmless fashion.

I can deny Slocum is now or ever has been any *semblable* of mine or any *frère*. Maybe I will deny that his life is in any way the life of myself, of my generation, my USA, my era, or even, to spill Slocum's secret that Slocum never quite spills, that his nasty life is human life—is the life of the hearth, of the tribe, of civilization itself. But no less a rough great stake than that does Heller try to leave us stuck on.

It is too much. Heller's man may induce in some of us qualms of recognition but he will not bear the burden of being Everyman. I believe it is not overinterpretation to say that Heller expects him to do this. . . .

At least since Salinger, there has been a strong movement in American fiction to persuade us that it would be better for all of us if we could remain little boys—and Slocum does the brave favor for his little boy of granting him this absolution. By this view, we are not to ask whether or not in our gray flannel suits (our denims, our double knits) we are better or worse than the other monsters of history, the men of Caesar or Attila, of Hitler. In those terms, on that level, of course it is foolish. It cannot be one of the great human evils to sound exactly like *Esquire* magazine, crazed by a glimpse of hide between trouser and sock. There is some radical loss of perspective here. *Catch-22* may well be, for a generation, its book of War, but *Something Happened* cannot team up with it to make a *War and Peace.*

And then there is that slight miscalculation I mentioned, about the way the story so artfully stays all in the hero's mind. . . . Slocum's essence comes from what he is, from sounding like *Esquire*, from not letting his kid become a man by not being one himself—not from actual physical murder. When he is made to do this, his story becomes a case history rather than a sad predicament. Nor will its great nameless "Company" serve to make it an allegory. (p. 25)

Good stories make conflicting morals. Heller probably tries too hard to make his stories cover all the moral points, and readers, or critics anyway, tend to forget the value of the narrative as they ponder the moral of Yossarian's desertion, and as they may ponder the moral of Slocum's murder. Heller's imagination is serious, really serious. I don't know how many today urge us to the depths where things, rather than being merely and easily absurd, truly resist our categories of what ought to be. But Bob Slocum, I am afraid, does not quite take us along. We have all heard those tour guides who think to charm us by showing how they seduce themselves with their own voices. Slocum is exactly such a one, and far too long-winded ever to talk us all the way down with him. (pp. 25-6)

John Thompson, "Caught Again," in The New York Review of Books *(reprinted with permission from* The New York Review of Books; *copyright © 1974 NYREV, Inc.), October 17, 1974, pp. 24-6.*

[There] is evidence everywhere in [*Something Happened*] that Heller's originality is of the order that depends on the constant reexamination of imaginative premises and the deepening exploration of more and more complex areas of consciousness. Its driving impulse is self-renewal rather than self-imitation, and the terms of its expression are those wholly appropriate to the new work, hence derivative of nothing antecedent to that work. There can be no doubt that the author of *Catch-22* wrote *Something Happened.* Tonal and stylistic continuities between the two books are numerous and unmistakable. But Heller has objectified his now greatly darkened vision of life through very different and much more complicated materials. He has discovered and possessed new territories of his imagination, and he has produced a major work of fiction, one that is as distinctive of its kind as *Catch-22* but more ambitious and profound, an abrasively brilliant commentary on American life that must surely be recognized as the most important novel to appear in this country in at least a decade.

The size of Heller's achievement is perhaps best demonstrated by his success in coming to terms with what is unquestionably the most difficult problem facing the American novelist today: how to give dramatic life and, above all, dramatic concreteness to individual experience at a time in our cultural history when the most urgent awareness is of the *un*dramatic nature of individual experience, and when the typifying obsession stemming from that awareness is with abstract states of consciousness—shifting and largely morbid psychological moods, anxieties arising out of a pervasive sense of the running out and running down of vital energies, entropic processes in society and within the self, the collapse of moral and social structures that once helped to give purpose and continuity to the individual life and provided the novelist with readily dramatizable materials. (p. 18)

[The] characteristic personal dilemma of our time is one in which the individual suffers, not from a conflict with oppressive social forces, but from the apparent absence of social forces that may effectively be engaged in conflict. This afflicts him with a helpless sense that society at large has no relation to him personally. . . . His mental state is shaped by chronic feelings of loss divorced from an understanding of what precisely has been lost. Hence, his response to the world is not heroic combativeness—since he cannot identify the enemy—but aggressive paranoia—since in a society seemingly governed by no principle of sanity or coherence literally anything can happen and probably will, and literally anyone may suddenly and for no reason *become* the enemy. The only reality is the constant likelihood of disaster, for nothing can reliably be known or relied upon, and the behavior of people, when they share no common moral assumptions and have no reason to be kind to one another, is altogether unpredictable. "A man was shot today in the park," says Heller. "Nobody knows why." "No one's in charge." The separation of action from motive, event from cause, creates anarchy in the public world and anomie in the individual. (p. 19)

To humanize a dehumanized condition in a novel would seem to be achievement enough. But to humanize a condition in which dehumanization is not merely the primary fact of life but the primary subject of consciousness is a nearly miraculous artistic feat.

Heller accomplishes this by making brilliant use of the technique of psychological realism. His theme is social and psychological entropy, and his material is the flow of impressions and memories through the mind of his protagonist, a middle-aged corporation executive named Bob Slocum, whose obsession is with the gathering evidence of the entropic processes at work within himself and his society. Slocum's consciousness is the very center of the drama and, in fact, constitutes the drama. The objective reality of the life he experiences is of small importance when compared with his subjective view of it. Hence, it is perfectly proper that the social context in which and upon which the action of his consciousness is played out should be rendered only marginally. His family, friends, business associates, and mistresses are finally realized in his perception of them, and it is his perception of them that creates their most significant reality. Like Dostoevski's Underground Man—and the whole of the novel is Dostoevskian in its compulsiveness and pathological morbidity—Slocum is a man raging in a vacuum, and the character of his raging identifies him as belonging squarely in the anti-heroic tradition.

In presenting such a portrait of Slocum's consciousness, Heller was faced with yet another technical difficulty: how to dramatize a condition of acute psychic disturbance, which may well be the most common and *normal* condition of our time, without making it seem actual mental derangement and thus untrustworthy as the locus of the novel's point of view. He also had to cope with the problem that it is of the essence of Slocum's exacerbated vision of reality that there should be so little objective justification for it. (pp. 19-20)

Heller has confronted, with an authenticity few writers possess, some of the most unpleasant truths about our situation at this time, and he has dramatized a crisis that is manifest in far more ominous ways than in shortages of fuel and natural resources, a failing economy, and the spoliation of our physical environment. In so doing, he has created a darkened, demonic, perhaps partly hallucinated fictive portrait of contemporary America, but one that has at the same time a disquieting verisimilitude. We hear from everywhere

that we have fallen away from some large conception we once had of ourselves, a conception that gave meaning to the past and promise to the future and made the present endurable. Something happened. Heller does not attempt to tell us what. Like most major artists, he is an adversary force, offering no comfort whatever and recognizing no obligation except to honor his subversive vision of the truth. (p. 21)

> *John W. Aldridge, "Vision of Man Raging in a Vacuum," in* Saturday Review/World, *(copyright © 1974 by Saturday Review/ World, Inc.; reprinted with permission), October 19, 1974, pp. 18-21.*

Something Happened is a monstrous effort to make literature out of pettiness. Relentlessly analytical about mean and mixed human motives, riveted to cynicism, essentially standstill, it unmercifully grinds out the paltriness to which one "successful" man's life, willy-nilly, can amount. Though no one could mistake its assiduity, the novel is a rout of creative drive and imagination, omitting as it does the low sun of Possibility against which its apparently huge, snarled ball of gnats could be measured. The book acquiesces in its own meanness with a clever shrug. It abdicates—and why if not out of punishing unbelief?—the high critical function of art.

Heller's popular *Catch-22* was, by contrast, brilliantly empowered with rage. To be sure, it failed to suggest what was worth living for, but at least it showed, with fair and breath-stealing exaggeration, what was not worth dying for —the greed and ambition of other men. It was the work of a common sensibility with uncommon independence, a balking Falstaffian *sense*. (p. 377)

In *Catch-22*, the war, as Yossarian kept pointing out to slower minds, was trying to kill him, but Slocum [protagonist of *Something Happened*]—a tamed-down Yossarian with a wife, three children, and an acre in Connecticut— has nothing to fear from the company in which he is a minor executive except that it could "fire" him. Whatever its drawbacks—and with his ruthless instinct for honesty Slocum underscores these—at least it provides him with self-esteem, pays well, offers refuge from the piranha pool of his family, and even condones philandering, though not on company time. What else could a man want?

Slocum's smallness consists in this, that he doesn't know. (pp. 377-78)

Slocum seems to have suffered no more than the usual fears consequent upon being born an infant and mortal, and except for his anxieties about his older son—a pint-sized version of the sweet chaplain of *Catch-22*—his passes at panic, depression and *Angst* are the only perfunctory moves in a hard-working book. His "demons" might have been ordered from Sears, and neither metaphysical Dread nor the dark Unconscious proves a living power in the book. . . .

But though Slocum cries "Wolf" for nearly 600 pages, the only wolf in sight is lubricious Slocum himself. In truth, he is not so much helpless as complacent. Just enlightened enough to be ashamed of his life, he doesn't try to change it because its sensual and egoistic gratifications are adequate, even considerable (for instance, he boasts, in reference to his wife: "No Women's Liberation for her. Lots of male chauvinist pig"). His emotional adolescence has proved so die-hard that he has taken the easy course and let it live.

Behind the sociological scrim of the book, its illustrations of William H. White's *The Organization Man* and Paul Goodman's *Growing Up Absurd*, beyond its depiction of what Goodman called the "apparently closed room" of modern America, in which "a large rat race [is] the dominant center of attention," beyond the examples of children "early resigned" to growing up with neither an "open margin" nor Faith, that sense that the world "will continue to support the next step": beyond all this squats the real villain of the piece: slothful, selfish human nature—equipped though it happens to be with a tirelessly rummaging mind that turns up every innate contradiction. The cultural allusions could all fall away and the substance of the book would remain undiminished, unaltered, unrepentant: quarrelsome, clever, horny, deceitful humankind. . . .

[A] poorly reasoned capitulation to the worst in human nature justifies a self-interest that in Yossarian, given the horrendous circumstances, proves sympathetic: it is an interest, after all, in keeping alive. But Yossarian is no less self-centered than those who want to exploit and kill him. For Heller, there was simply nothing outside biology but lies. Now, investing self-serving behavior with neither mitigating circumstance nor inventive zaniness, he has built a repellent, granitic monument to it—in effect accepting it as all there is.

Heller's skepticism about culture, as opposed to involuntary vitality, is of course in the mainstream of modernism—that strong acid stream that wells as from the mouth of Nietzsche, passing now, in part, through the work of several American novelists (examples: John Hawkes, Joyce Carol Oates). If it were a service merely to look selfishness, in Slocum's phrase, "squarely in the eye," however dulled that eye, then *Something Happened* would rank as a serious contribution to modernism. But in fact it looks at selfishness askew, indulgently, and conceals beneath its clever surface a diagnostic ineptitude. . . .

[The] novel is almost totally without dramatic impulse and significance—a "closed room." . . .

Although *Something Happened* fails to justify its frequent repetitiveness or its interior ordering, still, to give it its due, it proves readable, largely because of its gritty perceptions. The middle class—in its offices, its homes—has seldom been so remorselessly observed. All the same, how chafing that the book should rest content with what could not, after all, have taken much effort to discern. (p. 378)

> *Calvin Bedient, "Demons Ordered from Sears," in* The Nation *(copyright 1974 by the Nation Associates, Inc.), October 19, 1974, pp. 377-78.*

Joseph Heller's [*Something Happened*] is exhaustive and exhausting, a major contemporary novel. . . . I was often bored and exasperated by it, the way we are bored by so many of our unpleasant friends. But I would have kept reading for as long as he kept talking, the way we keep listening to those same awful people spill out their trouble and bile. The fascination of the abominator.

Bob Slocum is no true friend of anybody's. He is a woefully lost figure with a profound emptiness, a sad, absurd, vicious, grasping, climbing, womanizing, cowardly, sadistic, groveling, loving, yearning, anxious, fearful victim of the indecipherable, indescribable malady of being born

human. Heller goes the Beckett route (the novels) in creating Slocum. The book is a monologue with remembered dialogue, almost static in terms of time, but with some progressions eventually. It reads like a self-analysis and memoir dictated nonstop over a few weeks, but it covers a longer, not-quite definable span in which Slocum has a family disaster at about the same time he is promoted in his job and gets to do what he wants most to do in life: make a three-minute speech at the company's convention in Puerto Rico. . . .

The speech is the metaphor for everybody's immediate, pressing but meaningless goal, the way the company is the framework for the society we live in, the way the combat group in *Catch-22* was the framework of the war society. Heller is a big metaphor man. (p. 17)

The book is a baring of what Heller thinks is everybody's soul, at least everybody who shares the values of the corporate state, the company scramble, the family debacle. It will be a rare man anywhere, but especially in America, who doesn't see something of his own soul in Slocum's disastrously honest confession. (p. 18)

There is no way to sum up all Heller has put into this book. It is as rich in wit, social and psychological insight, American irony and memorable conversations as it is devoid of any story, plot structure, tidy continuity and other accoutrements of the conventional novel. His chief stylistic tool is repetition. . . . It is peculiarly Heller's and it echoes the repetition that gave *Catch-22* such an original tone.

The new book will doubtlessly be compared to *Catch-22* . . .; but this work is so unlike the first that similarities are important only because of their irrelevance.

Heller has learned from Beckett, Camus, Kafka, but he is clearly himself, a novelist who will be looked upon as one of the world's most interesting writers. (pp. 18-19)

> *William Kennedy, "Endlessly Honest Confession," in* The New Republic *(reprinted by permission of* The New Republic; © *1974 by The New Republic, Inc.), October 19, 1974, pp. 17-19.*

[All] good social anthropology has an intricate mythology carefully concealed within it, giving credence and structure to our urban lies; but when Heller spells it out [in *Something Happened*] and when its ligaments are revealed in all their breathtaking banality, the whole business lies down like a corpse and refuses to provide plot or character.

Somewhere there is life—endless, muggy life—outside these large corporate structures and Joseph Heller is not about to be undone. Bob Slocum has learned to live happily and wisely by copying everyone else—he even has an unhappy wife and unhappy children to complete the illusion. All of this is conveyed in an even and dispassionate prose, in which a falling cadence is a necessary part of the 'meaning': "There is no one else I would rather be than me, even though I don't really like me and am not even sure who it is I am." And no one else does, either. There is just this writing, sardonic and pathetic in turn, which leaves out no subordinate clauses and which spreads like a stain, only resorting to brackets, "(Ha Ha)", to relieve the more profound, more childish and less syntactically correct of gripes. The section headings are like cut-out cards, 'My daughter's unhappy', 'My little boy is having difficulties', but the shades of the prose-house darken this simple and direct little world.

A deadpan prose is not readily at the service of cheap sentiment; it is one which can make suburban dialogue sound as unreal and as funny as it really is, and one which can also conceal the most complex intentions. . . . Time seems to be coming to an end very slowly and very elaborately, and nothing actually happens to shake these musings among the ruins. (pp. 541-42)

It is true that the last section of the novel contains the remotest hint of action when Bob does something nasty to his son and is, at the same time, promoted in his company—like a transverse Oedipus. But any analogy with classical myth is spurious since with *Something Happened* we are in a world of flatulence and self-doubt with which no god or prophet will interfere. It may be something of a backhanded compliment to note that the novel conveys this monumental inactivity with some panache, but someone must make chaos out of our order and Mr. Heller has done it. (p. 542)

> *Peter Ackroyd, "Long Longings," in* The Spectator; (© *1974 by* The Spectator; *reprinted by permission of* The Spectator), *October 26, 1974, pp. 541-42.*

Catch-22 was more than a wildly successful work. It was also heralded as the classic fictional statement of [its] passionately antiwar decade and its nay-saying, antinomian, black-comic Zeitgeist. Though Heller was writing about World War II, his contemptuous denunciation of all war perfectly suited the American mood of mockery and disgust in the time of Vietnam.

Yossarian, Heller's exuberantly self-devoted hero, unequivocally rejecting the idiotic and lethal notion that any country, any cause, any ideal is worth risking one's life for, became a heady symbol. By asking a simple question—"Why are they shooting at me?"—Yossarian gave the lie to every bureaucratic claim to a soldier's patriotism, and an Army psychiatrist declared him crazy because "he has no respect for excessive authority or obsolete traditions." In Heller's brilliant inversion of the military ethic, Yossarian's fears became a heightened, a manic form of sanity: If he acted crazy because he didn't want to be killed, that proved he must be sane, since "a concern for one's own safety in the face of dangers that are real and immediate is the process of a rational mind."

Heller's was a vast and immovable paranoid vision of existence. He was an early laborer in the vineyards that nourished as well such quintessential novelists of the '60s as Pynchon, Vonnegut, Kesey, and Burroughs, although his gusto and openness made him far more engaging and humanly accessible than the others. Yet, if the most spontaneous and delightful quality of *Catch-22* was its powerful mocking vitality—untamed, extravagant, boisterously hyperbolical, coarse, raucous, bursting with irrepressible energy—the final impact of the book was seriously weakened not only by the author's surprising blunders into bathos but, worse, by his intellectual confusion. Until the end, Yossarian's enemy was the stupid and corrupt American military hierarchy; in the last episode, though, Heller remembered the actual enemy, Hitler, and suddenly Yossarian, the outrageous antipatriot deserting to Sweden, was

replaced by Yossarian the moral idealist. This strange turnabout threatened the very foundations of the novel's irreverent comic scheme, and we were left with a point of view that was blurred and confused. (p. 17)

With *Something Happened* our confusion is twice compounded. For I can think of no other novel that reads like such a willful, disastrous exercise in futility. Throughout its almost 600 pages we are forced to listen to the turgid, self-pitying, unintelligent, scandalously repetitive, childishly narcissistic, suffocatingly tedious monologue of a faceless organization-man named Bob Slocum. In especially desperate moments during my Sisyphean struggle to finish *Something Happened*, I felt, paranoid as Yossarian, that Heller was trying to murder me—with boredom, not bullets. Enslaved by the tyrant of conscience, I persevered, discovering in the process that not until this trial by tedium had I really understood the term "bored to tears."

Ironically, the novel's opening pages promise a rare feast—a minute, unrelenting and unflinching confession of the representative Man of Anxiety in the waning decades of this mad century. . . . The premonitory rhythm of doom and decay is superbly sustained, for a few pages.

But soon we realize that the rest of the book is an endlessly repetitious movement within the same mood, circling the same unvaried ground over and over like a disoriented bird. In the first chapter, the dog-eat-dog pecking order of Slocum's company is described in exhausting detail; in keeping with the menacing abstractness of his working life, we never learn what product or service the company exists to sell, only the malevolence of its hierarchical and bureaucratized relationships.

Slocum's pointillist self-portrait becomes a dank web of distrust and dishonesty, lust and infantile rage, envy and hatred, punctuated with hollow cries of despair: "Is this the most I can get from the few years left in this one life of mine?" Everywhere he turns, burrowing into the past and enduring the present, Slocum is confronted with breakdown, madness, suicide, betrayal, and sloth. Within and without, his world is an unregenerate swamp of rack and ruin. Pathologically dissociated from himself, Slocum is a chameleon, taking on the gestures and vocabularies of whichever colleague he is with; even his handwriting is a forgery, borrowed from a boyhood friend. . . .

When something finally does happen, it is so motiveless, so arbitrary, so perversely vague as to seem only another of Slocum's furtive dreams of murder, and it may well be only that. Even Heller seems to have dozed over his text at times—we are frequently informed that Mrs. Slocum is a churchgoing Congregationalist, but on page 472 she suddenly becomes Jewish! By then, however, I was beyond caring. If Slocum is meant to be a distillation of present-day America's pervasive sickness, Heller does not render this contaminating despair with sufficient urgency, and Slocum never extends beyond the bog of his sordid, dull particularity. He is not Everyman but no-man, and he can move us neither to pity nor to rage.

There is scarcely a link, an echo, a family resemblance of style or tone to be found in Joseph Heller's two novels. What happened to the manic wit, the running gags, the loony inventiveness and corrosive horror of *Catch-22*? Where did Heller mislay his descriptive agility, the violently grotesque gift for caricatures like Milo Minderbinder and General Dreedle? In *Something Happened* everything is merely told, in a spiraling proliferation of remarks that begin nowhere and fall in upon themselves.

Quite clearly, Heller has attempted here to write a particularly contemporary major novel. During the 19th century, authors aimed at showing reality objectively, by means of an omnipresent and unobtrusive narrator in absolute command of everything that occurred. But today's most innovative writers have abandoned this method. As though reality in our time has become increasingly incomprehensible, ungraspable, a mad world that cannot be contained within old-fashioned frames of reference assented to by novelist and reader both, books like *Herzog, Portnoy's Complaint* and now *Something Happened* do not present life, they describe it; and they do this in one voice, from a single point of view, apparently because life no longer lends itself to a wider, more dramatic manipulation of experience. But unlike Bellow and Roth, Heller has confined himself in *Something Happened* to a sensibility that is narrow and humorless, static and toneless, without the reverberations of variety. In the end Slocum—or Heller—is talking only to himself. For that reason we do not care. (p. 18)

> Pearl K. Bell, "Heller's Trial By Tedium," in The New Leader (© 1974 by the American Labor Conference on International Affairs, Inc.), October 28, 1974, pp. 17-18.

Something Happened is a lump compared with *Catch-22*.

Both novels resemble great stonelike objects, slabs of uniform consistency that may be cut up without disturbing the essence. One reason for this is that both come out of a terrible, indeed a heroic, simplifying urge, a monomania that can only elaborate more variations, illustrations of itself. Both in *Catch-22* and *Something Happened*, the terms of the hero's plight are circular, solipsistic, and the novelist is prepared to demonstrate the logic of it until Doomsday (which will never dawn). Both Yossarian and Slocum are stuck in an eternal present time that never changes or holds out prospects of ending, except in death: everything except death repeats itself; the fear of death especially repeats itself. Yet *Catch-22* was buoyant, *Something Happened* sinks. *Catch-22*, a perfectly serious comic novel with a point to drive home, was loaded with belly laughs; *Something Happened*, also serious and with a lesson to teach that is not all that different, provides at most five natural laughs in more than five hundred pages. It is an unrelievedly dreary book—perhaps only a comedian when he isn't cracking jokes could be as dreary. Slocum is given to making mirthless puns and comments on his own complaints, following these up immediately with an indicative, crippling, parenthetical "(ha-ha)." . . . Yossarian was scared stiff and dead serious all the time, and never spoke directly to the reader (he was Heller's creature); Slocum buttonholes the reader and doesn't let go (there may be questions where the dividing line is between him and the novelist). Better say that the sense of humor that vitalized *Catch-22* has been reduced, pinched down, into a small solitary nerve of dreary irony. (pp. 78, 80)

The essential dreariness of *Something Happened* can best be compared to the feel of another novel of the early 60's, Philip Roth's *Letting Go*, that catalogue of contemporary misery every entry of which the writer rubbed his reader's face into. If anything, *Something Happened* is more thoroughly dismal than *Letting Go*, for Heller is hopeless where Roth is mean. . . .

The seed planted in *Catch-22* has come to bloom in *Something Happened*. Although it is doubtful that eight million readers really took this to heart, Heller's easily-interpreted real message in 1961, not unconnected to his experiences in World War II, was that everything eventually stinks, albeit with hysterical and sensual consolations. His clear message now . . . is that life is absolutely rotten and apparent consolations are tricks. As it turns out, not the war or the army was at fault, but modern life is the villain—in short, life—and people are its agents. . . . *Catch-22* was a nightmare that it was theoretically possible to wake up from (on V-E Day?); *Something Happened* chronicles wide-awake reality through Slocum. *Here is life—smell it*, the book is saying. *Here are people—aren't they vile?* Insanity is institutionalized as if hell were mundane, and nothing extraordinary or allegorical about it. Things are what they seem, neither heightened for effect nor symbolized. Now there is no hope even, for this ordinary state of war will never end—"I hate my neighbor," Slocum says, "and he hates me." (p. 80)

The terrible thing about this potentially is that Slocum is a fellow with compassionate, loving urges—particularly toward his normal son. Because these are not developed much, the book seldom generates the quality of everyday terror that Slocum is supposed to be feeling ("the willies"). The quality conveyed is of dreary whining grievance against life's built-in corruption factor. . . .

Slocum sounds more like Heller's mouthpiece, like a troubled, interesting middle-aged male creature of our times from whom Heller must maintain a certain artistic detachment but doesn't. (p. 82)

Throughout, the style Heller gives Slocum is ideally suited to the purpose of low-grade complaint, unsuited to the more difficult purpose of evoking terror or accusing God. *My soul is weary of my life.* . . . Slocum isn't Job by a long shot, he isn't even marked by that residue of Congregationalism that Cheever's or Updike's authentic WASP suburban sufferers wear like a whimsical nimbus while they learn to be satisfied with crabgrass and good whiskey. Slocum's suffering, real enough no doubt, is an overgrown boy's, not a man's. The long ingrown parentheses on every page are the perfect scheme for handling his adolescent irony. (pp. 82-3)

Something Happened was meant to be simple, and it is, so Heller ought to be credited with another achievement, which is roughly artistic. By having Slocum sell out 100 per cent, Heller was faithful right to the end to the main idea of *Something Happened*, and thanks to this the book is finally more coherent and even more of a simple piece than *Catch-22* was. It is a novel fashioned in cold blood—a cold stone of a book, braver than most, braver than *Catch-22*, not brave enough. . . . By comparison, although there may well be something jejune, even sinful, in the simplicity of Heller's vision in this second book, there is little doubt that his success in cleaving to it for all these years and pages gives *Something Happened* a sort of heroic, massive integrity so dense the book sinks under its weight. (p. 84)

> Edward Grossman, "Yossarian Lives" (reprinted from Commentary by permission; copyright © 1974 by the American Jewish Committee), in Commentary, November, 1974, pp. 78, 80, 82-4.

[In *Something Happened*,] Heller writes what I'd call the first person compulsive. His first person, Bob Slocum, is the sort of lapel-eating talker you come across in Holiday Inn bars at 2 A.M. Slocum's style, his whole schtick, is repetition. Sentences come in syntactically matched sets, like dinnerware: five will begin, say, with the same word; half a dozen will be draped on the same noun-adverb-verb armature. Slocum poses himself rhetorical questions, "What would happen if. . . ." Then supplies rhetorical answers, "I know what would happen: nothing." He uses tautology as an ironic undertone. "The figures are photocopied on the latest photo-copying machines." Bad jokes are labeled "ha-ha," for your convenience. He backspaces himself with interjections, digressions, contradictions. Indeed, half the text is prophylactically sealed in parentheses. *Something Happened* could be an Evelyn Wood primer. It taught me to skim. If you miss a paragraph, a page, a chapter, it hardly signifies, you'll catch Slocum's drift next time around. . . .

Reading, I remembered three old girlfriends—who are they now?—and my dead father's favorite gesture caught itself in my hands again. This is an effect of fine writing; there's no other way to account for it.

And yet the book irked me. It's a prejudice I have against spendthrift effort. The fact holds: you can start *Something Happened* on page 359, read through to the end, and still pass a multiple choice test in plot, character, style. It isn't cricket, I understand that, to criticize a marathon for being 26 miles long. Great length is the thing's nature. Recapitulation, compulsiveness, flashbacks to the same spot, the treadmilling define Slocum's character and his milieu. But you and I, we catch on fast enough, 300 pages would give us the gist. Who needs that much gist anyway? *Something Happened* is overlong, a bit of an imposition. Maybe it's Heller's trademark. A friend once told me that *Catch-22*, in first draft, was *Catch-17*. I believe him.

D. Keith Mano, "Fine Writing That Irks," in National Review (© National Review, Inc., 1974; 150 East 35th St., New York, N.Y. 10016), November 22, 1974, p. 1364.

Slocum [the narrator of *Something Happened*] is not an ordinary neurotic. (Who is?) He tends to be a symbolist. He makes doors metaphysical entities. He is confined to his decaying body; he does not know what lies outside it, what awaits him in some *outer* world.

Slocum is so obsessed by doors that he tends to regard others as shadows behind frosted glass. He cannot really allow them to be fully seen. He has to keep them hidden. Thus when his wife and children try to appear as *persons*—with ambivalent motives and needs—he retreats into his mental office. He shuts doors on them. (pp. 272-73)

Slocum is an *outline himself*. He stands at times outside of his activities; he perceives his perceptions. He is no longer himself: "I miss my mother again when I remember how poignantly I missed her when I woke this morning. I miss the forsaken child. He's me. But I'm not he. I think he may be hiding inside my head with all the others I know are there and cannot find, playing evil tricks on my moods and heartbeat also. I have a universe in my head." Slocum is "suspended"; he does not understand where he begins or ends. *He fears measuring his universe's limits*; he refuses to go through doors by suicide.

"Suicide." The word haunts him. Is it because his father killed himself? Would he like to become his father? Does he dare to defend himself? Such questions trouble Slocum. He does not have the will to answer them once and for all. He prefers instead to say one thing—choose one role—and then another. He multiplies questions and metamorphoses; he won't stay put. He lacks the will to commit himself. Although we admire his crafty transformations, we also note, as he secretly does, his mad passivity. He kills himself every day. . . .

Obviously, Slocum is a "maladjusted" man, but he perfectly adapts himself to other disturbed men. He is the organization man. He recognizes other workers as his reflections. He knows what to say, what to wear, what doors to open and close. And it is the final irony that Slocum, who seems so uncontrolled, finally "gains command."

I find that I have been so seduced by Slocum's personality that I have not bothered with his voice. His style perfectly reflects his concerns. He speaks in a flat, repetitive, charted way. . . . He chooses his words with care. . . . He is, however, so controlled in his speech that he forgets—or, better yet, neglects—the content. "Person," for example, is just another word. . . .

Slocum . . . is, finally, *something* that happened. I will not easily forget Slocum and his doors. (p. 273)

Irving Malin, in Commonweal (copyright © 1974 Commonweal Publishing Co., Inc.; reprinted by permission of Commonweal Publishing Co., Inc.), December 20, 1974.

Joseph Heller's long-awaited second novel, *Something Happened* . . . was the best book I read this year. Not because it's perfect ("A novel is a prose narrative of some length that has something wrong with it" in Randall Jarrell's handy definition) but because it interested and bothered me most; it sticks in my mind and won't be settled. The craven Bob Slocum, circling and recircling the question of what went wrong with his life, is a comical and disturbing success. "I wish," he says, "I knew what to wish." I sometimes wished I were elsewhere—rereading "Catch-22" for instance—but this is a prodigious book. (p. 63)

Walter Clemons, in Newsweek (copyright 1974 by Newsweek, Inc.; all rights reserved; reprinted by permission), December 30, 1974.

"Something Happened" is . . . a dead novel of manners. Its characters maneuver for status like ghouls in a mausoleum. One poor wretch signals his failure, as with a leper's bell, by invariably wearing the wrong clothes. The hero, Bob Slocum, claws his way through the web of power and fear known as "manners" in order to give a three-minute speech at the company convention.

The bit-players are called things like Mr. Brown and Mr. Green, indicating pieces in a game, and this is perhaps a little *too* dead. People who work in such organizations are actually named after long and interesting numbers. But anyway we bookfolk will not settle for last year's satire, however pertinent. We've already done dehumanization (like pollution) and we can't do it again. We want a satire for the future, however aimless and untrue.

Heller, a book person himself, seems to have felt the same thing. (His career maps cultural history like the traces of a glacier.) Back in the Pleistocene Age, when the book began, office satire was very much the thing. But since we all moved to Stamford, the Family took over, and so Heller changed his crawl to that direction, producing to my mind an extraordinary piece of work.

The subject is still manners, the tearing down and building up of protocols, and the application of management techniques to living people. Slocum tries the same silky manipulations and power-grabs, but his son is too good for them, and his wife too slyly vague, while his daughter resorts to anti-manners, the paralyzing weapon of the young. Slocum is rendered helpless by her lethal blasts of rudeness. Love, the alternative to manners, is unfortunately beyond him, buried under layers of performance. Or else lost in the mail room.

Reactions to "Something Happened" have been so disproportionate that one senses some nonliterary nerve being tapped. Heller's droning repetitions obviously have something to do with it—yet these match the set phrases people actually use and the set thoughts behind the phrases: those obsessions lined up like toothaches which one's tongue returns to maddeningly. In Heller, Manners is what you do while playing with your toothaches, to keep you from boring and maiming other people, and some readers may feel that a whole book about this is just too damn cute and nerve-wracking.

Well, so is life, according to Heller and I daresay to many people. Amy Vanderbilt's . . . etiquette book . . . is as airless and obsessive as any Heller, and I was mildly astonished to hear that some 2,750,000 are in print and moving. . . .

> *Wilfrid Sheed, "The Good Word: The Novel of Manners Lives," in* The New York Times Book Review *(© 1975 by The New York Times Company; reprinted by permission), February 2, 1975, p. 2.*

The monotone of depression controls and shapes *Something Happened*, a novel of rigorous neurotic logic in which all significant causality is internal and nothing that can conceivably happen in the external world will make any real difference to the tortured sensibility of the protagonist-narrator. (p. 583)

Bob Slocum's life is a cliché: the fact defines his hopelessness. The book that contains him is not. Its manipulation of the commonplaces of late twentieth-century experience comprises an assault on the reader's sensibility as sadistic as the narrator's manipulations of other people. No one could *like* such a novel: its demand for attention to the minutiae of a distasteful man's distress torments us. Not a criticism of life but an imitation of the action of enraged misery, its expressive authenticity—however dismal the substance of what is expressed—compels the imagination, persuading the reader to participate, persuading him that he *already* participates, in the anger and despair that shape the novel and its protagonist. The familiarity of Slocum's life makes us almost as miserable as it makes him. One is tempted to attribute to the author a contempt for his society, his audience, and the creatures of his fantasy. The novelist, expertly evoking our masochism, implies that his punishing

vision of upper-middle-class anguish reflects the truth of our condition. Acknowledging the partial validity of his claim, we may yet wonder about the implications of such reflecting—which lacks the energy or focus of satire, sounds too despairing to generate serious social criticism, seems totally implicated in the misery it depicts. Such profound depression as Slocum's amounts to pathology; can art consist in pathology's imitation? (pp. 584-85)

> *Patricia Meyer Spacks, in* The Yale Review *(© 1975 by Yale University; reprinted by permission of the editors), Summer, 1975.*

*   *   *

HILL, Geoffrey   1932-

Hill is a British poet.

Hill's use of language, and choice of words, has been noticed, often, one feels, to the detriment of his themes. One sympathises with the reviewers. The compressed language is intimately bound up with what it is conveying. This is true of many poets, but true to an unusual degree with Hill. It is true in another sense. The language itself is unlike most other writing current, and coupled with this is an unusually self-conscious pointing on the part of the poet to the language. This is not because he wishes to draw attention to it for its own sake, but because the language both posits his concerns, and is itself, in the way it is used, an instance of them. Moreover, his use of language is both itself an instance of his (moral) concerns, and the sensuous gesture that defines them. It is therefore difficult to speak of his themes without coming first into necessary contact with the language.

Hill's use of irony is ubiquitous, but is not, usually, of the non-participatory and mandarin sort. It articulates the collision of events, or brings them together out of concern, and for this a more or less regular and simple use of syntax is needed, and used. (p. 145)

In pointing to the importance of the Imagist movement as it has affected English and American poetry, one is of course considering how central the image has become both in the writing, and for the considering, of twentieth-century poetry. . . . The image becomes that point at which an ignition of all the elements of meaning and response takes place; that is, not only do the meanings and their impulses get expressed, but at that point are given their principal impetus. Even with the hard clear image calmly delivered this occurs. Hill has been both the innocent partaker and victim in this. He has used and been used. This is partly because of course the age as it were reeks of such practice. But with Hill one also feels that the choice has been made because he has come to recognise that the use of the image can properly communicate the intensity he wishes to express. Through it he can express the intensity, but fix it in such a way that it will evaluate the concerns of the poem it is embedded in without its intensity overruling the other parts. The intensity finds in its own kind of formality its own controlling expression. At the same time, the image as artefact has a perhaps satisfactory and not unmodest existence. It can be regarded, but it is also useful. Curiously enough, although the impression of imagery in Hill is, in my mind at least, strong, checking through the poetry, one is surprised at how controlled is the frequency of the kind of imagery I am thinking of. There are many instances of images used to represent objects, creatures, events. But it is as though the image whereby one object is enriched by the verbal presence of another, combined with it, and a third thing made—as though such a creation were recognised as so potentially powerful, and so open to abuse, that he was especially careful to use it sparingly. And he is, rightly, suspicious of offering confection to readers who enjoy the local richness without taking to them the full meaning of the poem, which is only susceptible to patience and a care for what it is as a whole thing. (pp. 147-48)

Hill has more recently been concerned to accumulate meaning and response in a more gradual way. But, in the earlier work especially, the intense evaluation, response, judgement—all are released at that sudden moment of expansion which is the moment of visualisation. Hill's poetry has more often consisted of, not continuous narrative, but a conjunction of imagistic impulses. A conjunction of intensities, sometimes sensuously rich, and nearly always scrupulously evaluative. (p. 150)

[In his] longer poems, sequences and extended work that demand some correspondingly developed structure . . . , [Hill is fearful] of sacrificing the imagistic purity of his work, of sullying that compression, of impairing a dramatic enactment, or mimesis of psychological impulses, [and so] prefers to accumulate intensities than involve them in accumulating and continuous action. This may partly be due to the preference Hill shows for writing that, by dramatic mimesis, introduces to the reader internal impulses rather than dramatic action. (p. 152)

> *Jon Silkin, "The Poetry of Geoffrey Hill" (copyright © by Jon Silkin), in* British Poetry Since 1960: A Critical Survey, *edited by Michael Schmidt and Grevel Lindop, Carcanet, 1972, pp. 143-64.*

Geoffery Hill, though not broken down, writes from a Christian sensibility bruised to blackness; he seems to harbor a relish for cruelty that violently repels him. In *Mercian Hymns* we catch a glimpse of a boy loving "the battle-anthems and the gregarious news" on the wartime wireless and "huddled with stories of dragon-tailed airships and warriors." Hill seems to be that boy grown up, still fascinated by terrible killers but with an equally terrible burden of guilt. Why else write thirty prose poems about the little-known eighth-century king Offa, envisaging him as charismatically callous? (p. 84)

Fragmentary, furiously reticent, these poems were not written to instruct: their life is as lustrously dark as your own face when you see it, no longer your own, looking back from a well. I distrust Hill's need, frigid as it is, to live imaginatively among murderous men.

Yet these poems, which give the eerie impression that contemporary West Midlands is twelve centuries deep, not only focus mesmerically the arbitrary violence and capricious human authority of the world today; for all their questionable fascination with self-possessed authority, they are themselves exquisitely self-possessed. They are new without the slightest uncertainty, masterfully chiseled. . . . The writing is at once austere and passionately sensuous, the two qualities coming together in a kind of menace. Hill's manner, if elegant, has the impersonal driving force of those frightening machines used to tighten nuts to bolts; his concision is formidably reticent. (pp. 84-5)

In Hill's two earlier volumes his reticence was as much a weakness as a strength. His poems often read like notes jotted down at some remarkable poetry reading, like the sweepings of the fine things. They were all in pieces, as if too fastidious for the vulgarity of connections. Tautly held back, Hill was like a panther crouched for a spring he was too cautious to take. Now he has sprung, and the surprise is that he stays air-borne for the entire volume: the poems lie in a suspenseful shadow, under a tameless intention that is forever impending. Not that Hill's method has much changed: the *Hymns* are like an antiquary's collection of exquisite shards. But the shards are convincing pieces of lost wholes and slightly larger than Hill used to offer. Then, too, he has applied his method more repeatedly to the same subject. One has time, as it were, to learn to see in his dark.

Oblique yet penetrating, *Mercian Hymns* is a severely wrought achievement of language and a successful experiment in a stark, disjunctive rendering of life. In the sustained spell of its fusion of Mercia with the modern Midlands, and of the legendary with reeking life, as in its excavatory method and curious reticent conviction, it is something new in English poetry and, I think, a substantial addition to it. (pp. 85-6)

> *Calvin Bedient, in* Parnassus *(copyright © by* Parnassus: Poetry in Review), *Spring/Summer, 1973.*

*   *   *

HOFFMAN, Stanley   1944-

Hoffman is an American novelist.

[Stanley Hoffman's first novel, *Solomon's Temple*,] is a vulgar book, populated by grotesque people doing unpleasant things, and if I were to think hard I could probably come up with any number of nits to pick. It is also an extraordinarily audacious piece of writing, boldly conceived and beautifully executed, hilarious and tragic at the same time, the sort of book Philip Roth attempted (and failed) to write in *The Breast*. (I was about to add that it is a fresh breath of air, too, but then I remembered that much of it concerns certain indelicate functions of the intestines.) Its subject is fat. . . .

Laughter and terror are Stanley Hoffman's tools and he wields them with masterful and telling effect, often on the most unlikely subjects: a ghoulishly seductive potato salad (it sings in the night, calling and beckoning from the refrigerator), the boys' room of a yeshiva, the candy aisle of a supermarket, an unspeakable Thanksgiving dinner, and the sight of a pretty girl walking across a lawn in shorts. (There is also a lot of sex, most of it grotty. Brilliantly grotty.)

He even gives fresh life—if that is quite the word for it—to that most shopworn of contemporary stock companies, the Brooklyn Jewish *lumpenproletariat*. In Hoffman's hands, Jay Solomon is no mere character in a novel, no mere figure in a tapestry of words. He is a living, breathing, painfully human metaphor of all of us in this strange, inchoate country: he believes in the perfectability of man and the efficacy of simple remedies. While assiduously tending the temple of his flesh (first feeding it, then starving it and finally exercising it into a boulder of muscle), he has totally ignored the garden of his spirit, and it is rank with weeds. His failure is the failure of us all, a very American tragedy.

If a finer, more bitter and truer work of fiction has appeared within the last 12 months—with the lonely exception of Judith Rascoe's superb *Yours, and Mine*—I have not seen it, and I doubt that it is there. (p. 2)

> *L. J. Davis, in* Book World—The Washington Post (© *The Washington Post), February 10, 1974.*

[The hero of "Solomon's Temple"] puts his pudgy finger on what goes wrong with this book: "The inevitability of progress, after all, tends to lose its excitement after a while." With his shamelessly stereotyped Jewish parents, Jay Solomon is a smeared carbon of Portnoy, without Roth's terrifying comedy. His prose is too often unbelievably phony.... You keep hoping it's all a stylistic joke, a sly technique of characterizing a pathetic, self-pitying schlepp, but lamentably, you soon see that it's not, that Mr. Hoffman is no more certain of his attitude, his tone, toward Jay than is the reader. A spontaneous laugh, even if cruel, can justify the most tasteless of jokes. A twinge of empathetic agony, even in response to a freakshow, can excuse what smells like exploitation of authentic misery. "Solomon's Temple" has neither joy, nor love, nor light, nor help for pain. (pp. 37-8)

> *James R. Frakes, in* The New York Times Book Review (© *1974 by The New York Times Company; reprinted by permission), March 24, 1974.*

* * *

HOLLANDER, John   1929-

Hollander is an American poet, critic, and anthologist, best known for *Visions from the Ramble*, a sequence of poems about his childhood. (See also *Contemporary Authors*, Vols. 1-4, rev. ed.)

The soul lies buried in the ink that writes, John Clare said in a famous fragment . . ., and we are all, since then, turned grave robbers and vandals, eager to disclose the smelly cave under the Doric pediment, to disinter, still smoking, the pythoness' lair beneath the neat pillars, even if we have to push them down to get to it.

Hieratically disposed, but with a characteristic invitation for that very reason to pillage, to *profanation*, the works of John Hollander, monuments indeed, shapely at times to the point of a glassy impenetrability, stand before us in an alluring perspective worthy of Poussin for its rhythmic passage of saliences and recessions, its fair *attitudes*; and though I intend to violate these marbles as relentlessly as Lord Elgin looted his, for it seems to me that Hollander is precisely the poet of an obsessive, overpoweringly confessional necessity, I think it is only justice to pause first and marvel a little at their presence among us as *completions*. In effect, it is because his exigencies are so painfully inward that this poet has been obliged to take a stand against his own hurt, lest he go flying off in all directions, fragmented indeed, the slivers as jagged as any connoisseur of chaos could require. Such surface complacencies—one of Hollander's critics once referred to him rather angrily as an armored tank, betraying what I think is our mistrust of a poet's express preparation to enter the engagement ironclad; we seem to want the wounds on the outside, where everyone can see them—bewilder us only if we fail to re-

alize that surfaces are not only intimate, but are insolent with depths. (p. 201)

Believing, then, in the poem, relying in an almost unparalleled way on the art of poetry as a redeeming possibility, Hollander sacrifices nearly everything to that art, and it requires a considerable excursion into his work, on the reader's part, before the rewards of such an oblation are clearly discernible. From the poem, the thing made, Hollander seeks an escape from remembering, or an end to it, a cure for forgetting, or a tranquilizer, and though the poem —certainly from his second book onward—abides his question, permitting him to stand like an Oedipus before an endless avenue of sphinxes, only twice in his entire career, I think, is his obsession abreacted, his desperation answered by the very instruments to which he has entrusted his questions. The powers of memory and oblivion are too strong— though they are not so easily lined up with life and death as their ordinary positive or negative charge would suggest. In fact, let us consider the uses of forgetting before we decide with Proust that remembering is where salvation lies. Salvation, after all, *lies*, and that is Hollander's torment, his theme and, in its secular acknowledgment of a sacred severance, his release. (pp. 202-03)

Memory . . . is not only murderous when it is inordinate, as we see in Borges, in Beckett—it is mendacious in its normal form; and this is where Hollander suffers most from its abuses, discovering and dramatizing in his own biography the post-Freudian truth that what is remembered is not at all the same thing as what occurred. The mind creates its past, not recalls it, and the only escape, the only issue from these endless, crowding productions of memory is a kind of death—the death administered by language, the infliction of meaning upon being. (Thus it is memory that insists upon a death, forgetting that offers the gift of life.) No doubt, a poet's language kills no one. Yet when Hollander speaks, in his climactic vision of himself, of "that tall fat man," death, a real death is announced and already present in his language; his language means that this person, who is here, now, can be detached from himself, withdrawn from his existence and presence and suddenly plunged into a nothingness of existence and presence; his language signifies, essentially, the possibility of such destruction; it is, at every moment, a determined allusion to such an event. Of course Hollander's language kills no one. But if that tall fat man were not actually capable of dying, if he were not at each moment of his remembered life threatened with death, a death linked and united to himself by a bond of essence, Hollander could not achieve that ideal negation which is his poem, that postponed murder which is his language. It is therefore quite exact to say of this poet's speech: death speaks in and through him. Death, the death dealt by an adequate language, is for Hollander, in the poem, a rescue from the hypertrophy of memory, an escape from the fallacious past, from what Tolkien calls the burden of deathlessness, that kind of immortality or rather endless serial living which is (in fairy tales like Hollander's *The Quest of the Gole*) the deepest desire, the Great Escape.

Hollander's accommodation of this thanatomachia, his way of *embodying* the war to the death with oblivion and recall, is a dialectics of the seasons. It is the most conventional, yet the most radical of the available tropes, the widest yet the most familiar of poetical themes: the response to the cyclical, and the transcendence of the cyclical. His own emphasis on winter cannot surprise us, once we have realized that what is death to nature is life to the poet who would engage it *on his own terms*. The terms are hiemal ones—though we cannot speak of any season without implying them all and without implying something which leaves "all time, all seasons, and their change" behind. (pp. 203-04)

No other poet of his generation, I think, has found out the secret so perfectly of fitting words together in the music that created the English lyric from Campion to Marvell; from the beginning, Hollander's practice is more than practicing, more than the recreation of an epigone—it is the freedom of a man who by submitting in all good faith to the responsibilities of an achieved form (experience entrusted to an expressive convention: his true Daedalus was Dryden, etc.) relies on the poem's moment to bear him beyond its teeming surface to some high place. (pp. 207-08)

Visions from the Ramble is a major effort in American poetry to recover for the art some of the energy and inclusiveness we now tend to associate with fiction. As it seems to me, all of Hollander's previous work prepared him for this enterprise, and he has here, by a rare willingness—call it *need*—to risk *himself* in the undertaking, succeeded in fusing all that he knows with all that he knows he has forgotten, until we can merely say of him (but if we fail to say it, our reading of his *oeuvre* is no more than the vain coincidence of a shadow and a transparence: commentary is survival) what *he* has said, and we have already quoted, about his choice of poems for children: "so this book's end explores the world that is beyond Winter, and yet does so by speaking of nothing more than what we are." (p. 229)

> Richard Howard, "John Hollander," in his Alone With America: Essays on the Art of Poetry in the United States Since 1950 *(copyright © 1965, 1966, 1967, 1968, 1969 by Richard Howard; reprinted by permission of Atheneum Publishers, New York), Atheneum, 1969, pp. 200-231.*

John Hollander's . . . "The Night Mirror," belongs with a vengeance to the poetry of the new nostalgia. In a sense, it is a brave book, ignoring just about all of the changes that poetic language has undergone in America since Ezra Pound first convinced everybody that they should "make it new." Hollander's motto instead is, make it old. The book is so full of selected echoes that the effect must be intentional. Hollander's use of "turbulence" for example ("Away we turn, awakening/A long memorial turbulence") to describe the experience of mystical insight, recalls Yeats's use of the word in "The Magi" ("Being by Calvary's turbulence unsatisfied"). In another poem, the lines "We took to the clear water/Writing our names in the book," recall Keats's famous epitaph: "Here lies a man whose name is writ in water." These are only some of the ghosts which haunt "The Night Mirror."

Hollander is at his best among the generalities of the high style, which he manages with a sort of brilliance. At times a genuine rhapsodic sweep lifts his language, as in . . . "In Fog, Tacit, Outside Cherbourg". . . . The language is antiquated, but the extended swell of the lines is managed with skill and suppleness. The best poems in "The Night Mirror" have a similar quality of old-fashioned brilliance. A few of them are frankly imitations, like the elegy for An-

drew Chiappe, entitled "Damoetas," which echoes Milton's "Lycidas." Reading "Damoetas" is like entering a museum. All the paraphernalia of the pastoral elegy are present: the swans, the stone bridges over brooks in green meadows, the mourning of the seasons, the pastoral pseudonym. To resuscitate these old forms verges on eccentricity, but the poem has genuinely moving moments. . . .

I found myself admiring the performance, while I wondered why it was being given. In many of his poems, Hollander is like a virtuoso without a subject matter. The language soars in complicated trills, but in the end it becomes clear that no secrets are being told. (p. 4)

By guiding his language into . . . glittering generalities Hollander sets himself an insoluble problem, for the life of the emotions will not enter here. That is a shame, because there are moments of real strength in "The Night Mirror"; [in], for example, . . . the opening poem in the book . . . [the] images are crisp and strong, creating a felt connection between the inward and outward worlds. If "The Night Mirror" had answered the promise of lines like these, it would have been a different, and a far more moving book. (p. 20)

> *Paul Zweig, in* The New York Times Book Review *(© 1971 by The New York Times Company; reprinted by permission), October 17, 1971.*

In 1969, when John Hollander published *Types of Shape*, a collection of twenty-five emblems whose texts supply their own pictures (shapes of type, then, or as the poet polemically puts it in one of them, "no ideas but in forms"), he probably distracted his readers and viewers as much by providing (next slide, please) a respectable lineage for *Swan and Shadow*, say, or *The Figure in the Carpet* in the Alexandrian Greeks or George Herbert or Apollinaire, as by displaying the imperturbable *sprezzatura* of his typing. And what he distracted us *from*, I think, by the apparent gadgetry on the one side and the archaic governance on the other, is the entire congruence and continuity of these figured—even calculated—creations with the noble work which had preceded them, *Visions from the Ramble* (1965) and especially with his new book *The Night Mirror*, published in the fall of 1971. The very premonitory titles of so many of the iconographs—*A possible fake, Playing an obsolete instrument, Crise de coeur, Vanished mansard, Work problem, Blots, Broken column, Last quarter*—declare the mortality, the evanescence and the wreckage of even these splendid things, their fallings from us, then vanishings, "the eclipse of old moonlights by the darkness of origin." The emblem book constitutes a handsome muscle —hinge, holding action, decorous hurdle—between the two valves, the secreting ovals which have perfected pain into pearl: the major poetry of John Hollander.

Such poetry is the way language behaves—not only acts but acts out—when subjected or even objected to certain extreme circumstances, chief among which, "where mean and mode unite", will be the negative. Hollander's grand celebration will be of failure, obscuration, nightfall, the world darkened by his own shadow, "a long memorial turbulence." . . . As I have elsewhere remarked of the glorious *Visions*, it is by fusing all that he knows with all that he knows he has forgotten; and as I would say of the glamorous *Types,* it is by letting his language "pour into forms it molds itself'', that this poet articulates the conflict and concert of naming and making . . .; so I can see that this latest book [*The Night Mirror*], with all its mastery of natural objects (the music volute, the Alaskan brown bear, the slice of sequoia) and its mystery of mechanical or made ones (the spinning phonograph record, the golem, the night mirror itself), reflects, as its divided title insists, a phenomenology of dark/light, repetition/accident, memory/loss, affirmation/ dissolution. Thus the form of Hollander's poetry (and ''forms stand for their maker,'' as he told us in *Types of Shape*), the behavior of his language, will be *not this but THIS*, a negative assertion clearing the ground (or digging a grave) for what may yet stand, a decreating mode which will permit reality *to have transpired*. . . . (pp. 300-01)

The Night Mirror is not merely a book, it is a glyph of self-disclosure, glosses on a text of identity-as-debilitation. . . . It is why sentences here are so *hard*—they are death sentences. Hollander will not let his lines go until they have turned and, grammatically, blessed him. The sentence must be saturated, filling all its primary sites (the subject, the verb, the object) with expansions, interpolations, subordinate clauses, determinants; of course this saturation is utopian, for structurally speaking, there is no reason to end a sentence—*something more* can always be added, never the truly conclusive addition. Only to the Muse will Hollander say ''I gave. I recall.'' And those four words with their terrible pun, those two absolute sentences are the program; but the realization, but *the performance*, in long circumstantial accounts of a city childhood, a travelled maturity, . . . must be elaborated, worked out indeed, so that all the resources of making may fulfill the negative (''crackling of no flame, crunching / of no particular paper'') by reflection of return, by the mirror of verse, of revision, recuperation, *getting back*, as may be said of all this intelligent, beautiful work. . . . (p. 302)

Richard Howard, in Poetry (© *1972 by the Modern Poetry Association; reprinted by permission of the Editor of* Poetry), *August, 1972.*

The Night Mirror loses much of its music when Hollander speaks from his ''own'' self, when he takes himself as his theme. In his personal poems—the meditations on his childhood, the addresses to colleagues and friends, the meditations on places and things—he foregoes his natural grace and humor for a fiendishly knotted pattern of syntax, meter, and metaphor. Poems of this sort are puzzles, but in Hollander's case they often lack the leavening touch of playfulness that makes the puzzle a pleasure to solve. Reading *The Night Mirror* can be a strain, a ferocious struggle with opacity and hermetic effect. (pp. 168-69)

Hollander *needs* to compose poems in the first person singular: he is most at home with epigrams, invectives, apostrophes, and declarations, whatever their mood or message. But whether the speaker is called John Hollander or Adam, is, or ought to be, beside the point, because what is really at stake is an act of faith, a kind of self-effacement, a leap into language that gains a voice while leaving the everyday self behind. (p. 170)

Richard A. Rand, in Parnassus (copyright © *by* Parnassus: Poetry in Review), *Fall/ Winter, 1972.*

I don't know an American poet better at turning out sophisticated, hard-nosed (but good-hearted too) social verse than John Hollander, and it ends up not feeling ''light,'' like light whiskey, at all. [*Town and Country Matters*] is made up of Erotica and Satirica, ''translations and fresh creation'' of ''a world of classical urbanity''. . . . John Hollander's dirty mind is excellently displayed throughout. . . . The idea of setting out to be dirty and daring is a depressing one, but in fact these poems don't let themselves get locked into lubricious points. For me the best things in a never less than interesting collection are eighteen ''Sonnets for Roseblush''. . . . But the gem of the volume, and I would claim the best poem Hollander has ever written, is a long one called ''New York,'' spun off from Juvenal, the friend ''Rus'' leaving town for good because living in the city has grown impossible, the poet staying behind to reflect on the meaning of living there. Written in strong couplets the verse twists and moves rapidly through the junk and glories of urban life. . . . Hoving as seen through Dr. Johnson seeing through Juvenal (''In full-blown dignity see Wolsey stand'') or Pope (''In office here fair Cloacina stands,/And ministers to Jove with purest hands'')—the poem is filled with eighteenth-century lines. Other institutions are similarly seen through and dispensed with by the exile. But after he leaves, the poet has his own fling at seeing through life in the country (''Dilapidated walls in cold Vermont'') and eventually comes to a moving account of why he (Hollander in no disguise) will stay put to ''see the ending out from where we should''. . . . I have not come across any better lines than [his] recently. (pp. 590-92)

William H. Pritchard, in The Hudson Review (copyright © *1973 by The Hudson Review, Inc.; reprinted by permission), Vol. XXVI, No. 3, Autumn, 1973.*

[In *The Head of the Bed*,] Hollander has composed an enthralling, though essentially plotless, meditation on the alien majesty of sexuality. The poem is a male dream of female otherness. It is necessarily in some degree a nightmare. Yet, in its final stanzas, one hears the note of triumph as well as resignation, and the ''lids slammed down over darkened glass'' of its opening line have begun to see truly at the end. ''The Head of the Bed'' takes over the slow, circling manner of Auden's ''At the Grave of Henry James,'' and, quite apart from the triadic arrangement of stanzas, it owes much to the style of the later Stevens. Like the imagination of its hero, however, the poem at last wins through to an individuality that is more than the sum of its parts. (p. 6)

Taken with its commentary [in David R. Godine's chapbook edition,] ''The Head of the Bed'' emerges as a learned, slightly mad and absolutely delightful book. It will probably become a collector's item and it certainly has a place among the true small wonders of modern literature. (p. 7)

David Bromwich, in The New York Times Book Review (© *1974 by The New York Times Company; reprinted by permission), June 16, 1974.*

John Hollander writes poems that are all mostly panoplied, at their best not at their most hermetic (''The Head of the Bed'' . . . breathes too much the exhalations of Stevens) but rather at their most graceful, in the poetry of compliment, like the poem given with a gold chain. . . . Something apparently momentous but too often unintelligible is presumed in these poems—portents, allegories, hints. . . . There is an elegy for Auden (written in fact for his 65th birthday) in which, in a courtly bow to convention, Hollander turns the dead into a constellation. . . . It is an elegy stylized and stylish, fulfilling Milton's command to poets, that they should "with lucky words favor [each other's] destined Urn,/And bid fair peace be to [the] sable shroud." In this elegy and the one for Mark Van Doren, Hollander shows how his gifts, too easily veering by themselves into complication for complication's sake, can be saved by a given occasion. (pp. 29-30)

Helen Vendler, in The New York Times Book Review *(© 1975 by The New York Times Company; reprinted by permission), April 6, 1975.*

*   *   *

HOWARD, Maureen   1930-

Ms Howard is an American novelist. (See also *Contemporary Authors*, Vols. 53-56.)

Maureen Howard's *Before My Time* . . . seems to me a very good novel indeed, one of the best I've read in quite a while. . . . The tone is breezy, pushy enough to give us a sense that Laura's story will be a story, but so scrappily involved with itself, with the implications of the previous sentence, that it may need no plot to get that story told. Anyone who has read Howard's first two novels, *Not a Word About Nightingales* and *Bridgeport Bus,* will recognize this as her distinct voice, but it also bears an easy unselfconscious relation to the great monologuists of the last decade: Bellow, Mailer.

The great difference between Maureen Howard and anyone else I can think of who is remotely like her is that *her* assurance, her breezy way of letting one sentence twist off from the one before, carries with it no heavy burden of self. Here is Laura Quinn, and Jimmy Cogan, and Laura's husband, and Jimmy's mother, father, brother and sister, girl friend—here they are all, the book is like a series of short stories—but Howard not only doesn't work to give them distinct voices, she doesn't work very hard, in the normal sense, to make them characters. What they have, more precious almost than voice or self, is lives they are leading. (pp. 221-22)

In a book that just keeps moving off its own energies, that spins off stories with abundance, there are problems, no matter how wonderful the writing is page by page. The obvious one is focus, and if Howard rightly knows she must abjure big scenes that will smell of the lamp and inkhorn plots, she also wants it to come together. . . . There's not a page in this book that I could point to and wish it were different, yet I did not feel it all working out quite right at the end. Perhaps all I really hope is that she has or will soon have a novel called *My Time* to follow this one, because my dissatisfaction here was certainly no greater than what I felt finishing the separate books of other sequences I've liked very much, like Frederic Buechner's and Robertson Davies's. Howard has taken fifteen years to write her three novels, so that we know the apparent ease of her prose is not something she finds easy, and her books are so good, so

capable of lingering in the memory, that perhaps one must not press the point. But I do hope she hasn't finished with Laura Quinn. (pp. 223-24)

Roger Sale, in Sewanee Review *(reprinted by permission of the editor; © 1975 by The University of the South), Winter, 1975.*

"Before My Time" is both a direct descendant of [Maureen Howard's] first two books ["Not a Word About Nightingales" and "Brideport Bus"] and a departure, a sport, an evidence of how many unrepetitive subjects and persons Maureen Howard's head is capable of imagining and then fixing in perfect language for our understanding. As in the others, there is no message, only an urgent, desperate meaning; the medium in which it grows is a further display of her sane, evocative, simple and exact prose. The story's overall coloration is once again Irish-Catholic, because that world seems to be the American world Howard knows best, but it is in no sense limited to that milieu.

"Nightingales" was a paradox of a novel. It convinced through the originality of its parts, at the same time that, throughout, it seems to echo familiar fictional themes. . . . What is not reminiscent . . . is the writing, the creation of memorable characters. . . .

"Bridgeport Bus" is another matter. For the richness and complexity of its extraordinary central character, Mary Agnes Keely, 35-year-old virgin, novelist-in-the-making and figure of fun, who escapes her mother and life in Connecticut aboard a bus to New York, I can think of only one parallel: Gulley Jimson in "The Horse's Mouth." Both characters are word-mass creations whose creative spirits are not so much talked about as displayed by the force of the novel itself. Mary Agnes is one of the few characters in recent fiction (she tells the novel herself) to persuade me that she *is* the gifted, original, talented person she is depicted to be. . . .

There is no story to "Bridgeport Bus"—unless it is the picaresque tracing of a tragic parabola, the journey of the gaunt, self-educated, superbly aware and talented woman in search of life and art. . . . The women in this novel are as good as any I can think of: consider the thin and often anemic, thinly disguised self-portraits that novelists often give us. . . .

After Maureen Howard's latest novel has been properly noticed, its admirers will want to go back to savor Mary Agnes's cruel wit, her mixture of "cool intelligence and fire."

In "Before My Time" we meet two interrelated Irish-American families. . . .

What happens in these lives (the thematic pattern is so much the same in the three books that one comes to see that Maureen Howard is using all her ingenuity to the same inexorable end) is precisely nothing. . . .

Again the theme of an uneventful, deeply felt, nonprogress, of captivity in the sacrament and ritual of marriage, of life as a series of inconsequential events, poignant and terrible, signifying little. And again it is an unremitting catalogue of the snares and delusions of family life: it "is like the classics played in modern dress by an amateur troop. Vulgarized versions of the old tales.". . .

Maureen Howard has the gift of being unobtrusively present in her fictions, like the good children who are neither seen nor heard. But her hand is felt, controlling events, keeping them in their assigned comic or poignant rings, preventing excess and promoting restrained yet agonized, circular movement. Reading her, one is made to return to the inevitable, to the conclusions that things do not end satisfactorily so much as they happen; they seem to mean something for the moment and then disappear into memory, which is what fiction is to this extraordinary talented writer. . . . (p. 5)

Doris Grumbach, in The New York Times Book Review (© 1975 by The New York Times Company; reprinted by permission), January 19, 1975.

Certainly Miss Howard's stylistic virtuosity cannot be disputed; every inch of her prose [in Before My Time] is trimmed and polished with meticulous skill. Yet from the first, the principal thread of her narrative is yawningly familiar: still another invasion of middle-aged suburban order by rude youth. . . .

Miss Howard tries hard to freshen her tired scene with an abundance of eccentric characters, whose outlines are cleverly suggested but whose substance is perilously vague, and whose place in the scheme of the novel is irritatingly fuzzy. Only one of the portraits acquires incisive clarity—Jimmy's mother, a disappointed and blowzy Irish beauty tied to a chronic gambler for drab life, tippling herself away in a squalid Bronx tenement with secret nips of gin and yearning. Everyone else, including [the protagonists], remains hazy and dim, though Miss Howard's prose is never less than elegant.

Before My Time, alas, is impaled on its very perfection; in the end there is almost nothing to grasp and hold and savor. One feels consistently cheated by the "fine" writing, the artfulness of all those tentative ambiguities, the ornate fretwork of dissonance and dependence that registers so little thought and feeling about the ongoing war of American generations. At no point does Miss Howard take any chances, make the kind of reckless flying leap that Diane Johnson carries off with splendid bravura on practically every page. . . . Before My Time is merely an exquisite bore. (p. 18)

Pearl K. Bell, in The New Leader (© 1975 by the American Labor Conference on International Affairs, Inc.), January 20, 1975.

The tricky construction of [Before My Time] partly damages it: the relationship between woman and boy never gets fully dramatized. It remains a muffled, theoretical "given" —the peg on which family stories are hung. But the family stories are a glinting lantern show of American success and failures—primarily Irish (contrasting Boston and New York subspecies, '40s and '70s generations), with supporting Italian and Jewish examples.

Two stories, out of many, are particularly moving. Jim Cogan's younger brother and sister, secretive, inseparable twins, enjoy a friendship with a neighboring Italian baker whose in-laws went back to Calabria to buy a husband for their unmarriageable Angelina; the twins, quizzing the immigrant about his life, "learned . . . about their own world

though they never suspected it. The kids thought they were listening to tales of another land." Equally absorbing is the tale of the Cogans' luckless father making his salesman's calls on a patriarchal Jewish tycoon, retained as a decorative artifact in his sons' new office building: "They should put me out in the lobby with the Lipchitz," says Hoshie Feinmark. "I'm part of the museum. A work of art. This old man in the cashmere jacket and silk shirt is Poppa, a success. They never called me Poppa when they were little but it's quaint now, Jewish. Sometimes I want to laugh." Maureen Howard is subtle, oblique and precise. I like her novel a lot.

Walter Clemons, "Lantern Show," in Newsweek (copyright 1975 by Newsweek, Inc.; all rights reserved; reprinted by permission), January 20, 1975, p. 76.

Traditional novelists toss pebbles into domestic pools and then take notes. The postwar fashion has been to track these projectiles directly into the muck below, but there is another, older way. As masters like Henry James and Virginia Woolf knew, the ripples on the surface can bedevil the eye and engage the mind. Before My Time brushes up this earlier technique. It transforms a brief disturbance of hearth and home into an age of anxiety. . . .

Before My Time conveys a range of details and events that would be impressive in a novel twice as long. Although the design appears casual, the book's power is in its language. Time and again, a part is successfully substituted for a whole. One swallow can a summer make, if described with enough care, just as one scene can conjure up a lifetime. So a costumed hippie wandering the streets is pinned with words: "A child who has lost its role in the Christmas play." Quietly dropped epigrams cause wide ripples: "Family life is like the classics played in modern dress by an amateur troop. Vulgarized version of the old tales.". . . "I would like to write faster," [Maureen Howard] says, "but life intervenes." That, triumphantly, is exactly what happens in her novel.

Paul Gray, "Lost Generation," in Time (reprinted by permission from Time, The Weekly Newsmagazine; copyright Time Inc.), January 27, 1975, p. 78.

In . . . Before My Time, Maureen Howard deftly and movingly captures the feel of family life most of us have experienced, its contradictions now so deep within us that we forget how they shaped our growing up and growing old. Howard's art helps us to remember. (p. 25)

Before My Time begins and ends with Laura Quinn; her history, and her encounter with Jim Cogan, frame and focus the novel. They do not make up the whole of it. Before My Time is also the story of all the Murrays [Laura's family]. (pp. 25-6)

The Murray saga, Boston and the Bronx, is virtually a novel itself. It unfolds in fragments, set pieces, short story-like chapters . . . that fascinate in their own right, interlock, overlap and create a very special resonance for the Laura-Jim plot. Howard is not using technique simply to play a Rashamon game with her readers, though we can surely delight in her craft as mysteries are explained and episodes intersect. The structure and detail of Before My Time establish a world of family relationships—between siblings, between generations, with those important adults who are not one's parents. Even minor characters in this novel (neighbors, housekeeper, secretary, clients and boss) are shown in some family role, as Howard dramatizes from multiple perspectives that mix of intimacy and isolation, safety and competition, present and past the family provides in our time.

Howard's last novel, *Bridgeport Bus*, was a funny, sad work some readers were fortunate to discover and then eager to pass on to friends. *Before My Time* is a richer, more complex, perhaps more difficult novel, but also funny/sad. . . .

Howard knows that all her characters are ordinary, and very precious: women and men, old and young, post-Kennedy liberal intellectuals and barefoot seekers of revelation. She knows that the personal truth of each is to be found in the meeting of private experience and historical moment, lets us see those truths, and then reminds us that we see them because she has trained our vision. (p. 26)

> *Elaine Ruben, in* The New Republic *(reprinted by permission of* The New Republic; © 1975 by The New Republic, Inc.*), February 8, 1975.*

* * *

HUGHES, (James) Langston   1902-1967

Hughes, a Black American poet, also wrote a novel, short stories, and the humorous "Simple" sketches for which he is best known. (See also *Contemporary Authors,* **Vols. 1-4, rev. ed.; obituary, Vols. 25-28.)**

Not Without Laughter deserves notice . . . as an antidote to the many shrill and artificial Harlem Renaissance novels.

It is not easy to define Hughes' achievement without making him sound corny or soft. Formulations of his work come out like Faulkner's stodgy explanations of his own novels, even to the motifs of "affirmation" and "endurance." *Not Without Laughter* belongs with the fiction of its simpler time. It is a gentle sequence of well-sketched social views, like so many Negro novels of the period—the family gatherings, the colored ball, the pool hall. It even includes the standard caricature of the Episcopalian, anti-watermelon dicty.

Its special value, like that of DuBois' social essays, lies in its completeness and truth, its control and wide humanity. It is probably the most genuine inside view of Negro life available in the fiction of the period, comparable to later works like Ann Petry's. Like almost all of Hughes' work it is sad, to a degree, but never violent or bitter; it is touching, but never falsely sentimental. It is very small, really, in outline—a collection of the more or less connected stories of a family of very average, very attractive small-town Negroes in Kansas; but the stories flow with the warmth of genuine life. (p. 52)

Langston Hughes . . . remains the most impressive, durable, and prolific Negro writer in America. His voice is as sure, his manner as original, his position as secure as, say, Edwin Arlington Robinson's or Robinson Jeffers'. He is the one sure Negro classic, more certain of permanence than even Baldwin or Ellison or Wright. By molding his verse always on the sounds of Negro talk, the rhythms of

Negro music, by retaining his own keen honesty and directness, his poetic sense and ironic intelligence, he has maintained through four decades a readable newness distinctly his own. . . . Hughes is a true professional, like the hero of his fictions only deceptively "Simple." . . . He has . . . produced, for the white reader, a convincing, singing source book on the emotional life-style of the lower-class urban Negro in America, as valid as the blues. (pp. 54-5)

Langston Hughes is as skillful and durable a storyteller as he is a poet, a master at the ironic little social comedies of Negro life—a type he seems almost to have invented, so sure now is his hold and possession. His work lives as a potent reminder to the critic of the enduring primacy of "the story." He is an ingenious and happy craftsman in the best tradition of Somerset Maugham or O. Henry; his stories can be read, enjoyed, and understood by the man of simple common sense who dwells, presumably, in everyone. It would be folly to condescend; to suggest, effetely, that one is past such things: one never is. There is much to be admired in a small perfect circle. If Langston Hughes' stories are not deeply, endlessly resonant, or are not richly laden with awesome suggestion, they are still honest, deft, amusing, and provocative, reading after reading. They endure. He is lesser than Ellison or Baldwin only because his scope is so much smaller, not because his work is cheaper or less complete. But comparisons are foolish for a writer so attractive and secure. . . . He really "tells stories" rather than writes fiction, and he rarely makes mistakes. Although he has written of many things, his most comfortable subject is the urban Northern American Negro, his jobs, his play, his churches, his women. He can deal with various classes, but seems most at home with the poor. His text for Roy de Carava's rich photo essay, *The Sweet Flypaper of Life* (1955), is as total an example of Langston Hughes, of his bittersweet participation in the lives of his people, as anything else he has written. There seems to be no distance, really, between author and subject, no artist's detachment—which is doubtless the effect of very careful art.

His tone has that intimate, elusive, near-tragic, near-comic sound of the Negro blues, and is equally defiant of analysis. His theme is not so much white oppression, as the Negro's quiet resistance to it. His writings typify (and probably support) the famous and useful myth of Negro endurance—the knowing grin, half-smile half-smirk, of the bowing but unbeaten. They may thus not find favor with more militant Negroes, who regard the very myth of endurance as treacherously pacifist, supported if not invented by whites.

The "Simple" stories, one or two pages long, offer little barbed home truths about Harlem life, the cost of living, domestic unbliss, and especially the various ludicrous paradoxes of America's racial double standard. Jesse B. Simple is a sort of comic no-good (a stereotype turned to use, written by a Negro for Negroes) with perpetual lady troubles, cadging beers off the straight man who tells the stories in exchange for another of his twisty bits of folk wisdom about "the ways of white folks."

On the whole, Hughes' creative life has been as full, as varied, and as original as Picasso's, a joyful, honest monument of a career. There is no noticeable sham in it, no pretension, no self-deceit; but a great, great deal of delight and smiling irresistible wit. If he seems for the moment upstaged by angrier men, by more complex artists, if "different views engage'' us, necessarily, at this trying stage of the race war, he may well outlive them all, and still be there when it's over. Much of the greatness of the three major Negro novelists derives from their singularity, their essential aloneness; Hughes' at least seems to derive from his anonymous unity with his people. He *seems* to speak for millions, which is a tricky thing to do. (pp. 144-47)

> *David Littlejohn, in his* Black on White: A Critical Survey of Writing By American Negroes *(copyright © 1966 by David Littlejohn; reprinted by permission of Grossman Publishers), Viking, 1966.*

Langston Hughes . . . has perhaps the greatest reputation (worldwide) that any black writer has ever had. Hughes differed from most of his predecessors among black poets, and (until recently) from those who followed him as well, in that he addressed his poetry to the people, specifically to black people. During the twenties when most American poets were turning inward, writing obscure and esoteric poetry to an ever decreasing audience of readers, Hughes was turning outward, using language and themes, attitudes and ideas familiar to anyone who had the ability simply to read. He has been, unlike most nonblack poets other than Walt Whitman, Vachel Lindsay, and Carl Sandburg, a poet of the people. He often employs dialect distinctive of the black urban dweller or the rural black peasant. Throughout his career he was aware of injustice and oppression, and used his poetry as a means of opposing or mitigating them. Two early poems, "The Negro Speaks of Rivers" and "I, Too, Sing America," testify to his abiding hope for the fulfillment of the American ideal—not only for black people, but for all the dispossessed of the land. Until the time of his death, he spread his message humorously—though always seriously—to audiences throughout the country, having read his poetry to more people (possibly) than any other American poet. (pp. 7-8)

> *Donald B. Gibson, "Introduction" to* Modern Black Poets: A Collection of Critical Essays, *edited by Donald B. Gibson (© 1973 by Prentice-Hall, Inc.; reprinted by permission of Prentice-Hall, Inc., Englewood Cliffs, New Jersey), Prentice-Hall, 1973, pp. 1-17.*

Good Morning Revolution [compiled by Faith Berry] is a collection of selected articles, stories and poems by Langston Hughes. Most have not appeared in book form prior to Faith Berry's creative effort. The wealth of materials brings into sharp focus Hughes the poet, possessed of a powerful social, revolutionary vision, revolution in his work characterizing a creative concern for change in the social process that will guarantee maximum well-being for all men. Here the reader will see how he dared to dream of a sane society, how he focused his hope on creative change, how he yearned for humane treatment for blacks and other oppressed people. . . .

No poet has evidenced deeper concern for the dignity of the masses, freedom, justice and the equality of the sons of man than he did. (p. 29)

> *James D. Tyms, in* The New Republic *(reprinted by permission of* The New Republic; *© 1974 by The New Republic, Inc.), January 5 & 12, 1974.*

Negro jazz, itself an obvious convention of the Negro folk —especially during and after their transplantation from the South to the North—almost seems to haunt all of the early verse of Hughes. It appears sometimes in the rhythm and the arrangement of the line. It appears sometimes in the language—which may be, upon occasion, veritably a jazz *patois*—and sometimes in the mood. And then in both Hughes's blues and his jazz there is almost always something else, a something else that links Hughes and his poetry, and the people presented in his poetry, to a convention seemingly universal in its hold upon ordinary people, all ordinary people. That something else is the technique of the ballad. [Read] Hughes's "When love is gone." Therein a voice speaks; a story is told to us by the character with this voice who informs us as we would be informed in a play. The method, the resort to dialogue or dramatic monologue, is the ballad technique, the same technique which may be found, for example, in a ballad like "Sir Patrick Spens." It is a favorite technique with Hughes. He does write lyric poems. But in his "lyric" *persona* he is often able to copy this social convention of the Negro folk, their use of the method of the ballad, to tell others how they feel. In this same "lyric" *persona*, also, he is able to reflect in subject matter the kind of happenings which ordinary Negroes tended to notice during the Renaissance and in theme the issues which those same Negroes tended to discuss in their familiar intercourse with each other.

In Hughes, indeed, the conventional life of the Negro folk is made to come alive, and that, of course, is the life of the Negro folk as they are. It is the life that, in America, has set the Negro masses apart from whites. Why do *they* act like that? signifies only that a middle-class white has observed a custom which he does not share. It signified for Hughes, who understood much of the *why* and managed often to incorporate insights into its nature in his verse, that he was, of all the Renaissance poets, the true New Negro of the Renaissance poet's definition. He made his poetry act like that. . . . [His was the] common touch, the touch that really mattered.

Perhaps, however, Hughes's touch may have been (for he was, of course, not perfect) in his art too much of precisely that, a touch. As he can be related to the ballad, he can also be related to Impressionism. Indeed, it is hardly too much to say that all his poetry ever does is collect impressions. It is highly probable that, in all of Negro literature, he must be accorded the title of the Great Impressionist. Thereto, of course, attaches a limitation. Impressions tend to lack depth, if not also concentrated power. Hughes's impressions do come from the right places. They are taken by an artist who does not stand in his own light. And they do witness to the reality of a group experience of American life. Yet they are still impressions. Hughes was not a genius at synthesizing big things. He could, and yet he could not, quite see the whole forest as some writers do. It may have been his greatest lack and probably the reason he has never seemed as "serious" as writers like Ellison and Wright, or Tolson at his best. Even so he saw enough . . . to be a leading interpreter of the Negro in twentieth-century America and twentieth-century literature. (pp. 56-8)

> *Blyden Jackson, in* Black Poetry in America: Two Essays in Historical Interpretation, *by Blyden Jackson and Louis D. Rubin, Jr. (copyright © 1974 by Louisiana*

State University Press), Louisiana State University Press, 1974.

*   *   *

HUXLEY, Aldous   1894-1963

Huxley was a British-American novelist, short story writer, and essayist whose work is distinguished by tremendous variety and brilliance. One critic has written that Huxley was "able to articulate the intellectual and moral conflicts being fought in the collective soul of the twentieth century" and, indeed, all of Huxley's work may be read as a search for values in the absence of traditional sources of value—love, religion, and family life.

Fictionally, Huxley reveals himself many times as an experimenter in technique; and there is nothing tentative or uncertain in the achieved form of his prose-poems [Stanford is reviewing Huxley's *Collected Poetry*]. Quite apart from the virtuosity and wit which they so scintillatingly reveal, they are of importance in showing how much Huxley was influenced in his poetry by French models. Reading them, one thinks of Baudelaire and his experiments in 'the other harmony of prose', of Rimbaud, Mallarmé, and—more obviously still—Laforgue. . . .

[Especially to be noted is] Huxley's one individual masterpiece in verse—his long eighteen-page picaresque elegy *Soles Occidere et Redire Possunt* ('Suns set and rise again; but we, when we die, go down to the eternal night'). . . .

[Huxley was a] subtle, intellectual and acrobatic poet. (p. 57)

> *Derek Stanford, in* Books and Bookmen (©
> *Derek Stanford 1971), March, 1971.*

Huxley's verse, collected [in *The Collected Poetry of Aldous Huxley*] for the first time, has mainly a historical and biographical interest. No one of my generation could fail to be touched rereading these yearnings after ideal love, this disgust at lust; the attempts, mainly with an outworn style, to bring modern properties and the intellectual life into verse. [Richard] Church is right in his introduction to point out Huxley's quality of innocence as a young man, an innocence all the more quaint in its alliance with the encyclopedic cleverness and the wish to shock. But he was rarely a poet who looked like staying the course, though one shouldn't underestimate the labour put into a number of extended pieces, and a good many idiosyncratic and original turns. However, I think it's true to say that what is really novel and striking here belongs properly to prose. . . .

Nevertheless, Huxley's interest in the potential scope of poetry stayed with him right until the end of his life, and one must pay proper tribute to it. There are two early essays on the subject—'Subject-Matter of Poetry' in *On the Margin* (1923) and 'And wanton optics roll the melting eye' in *Music at Night* (1931). The ideas here are gathered and amplified in the little book *Literature and Science* that he published in the year of his death. His main plea is for poets to feel science as they feel the traditional subjects of poetry, so that poetry may deal with it; and he points out that the commonly held notion that poets in this century have put back into poetry great tracts of life and thought . . . long considered inappropriate must be subject to severe qualification. The latter was a timely observation in 1923

and even in 1931, but it is extraordinary that *Literature and Science* fails to refer to Auden's remarkable work in the intervening years, to say nothing of other poets and critics of scientific temper, like Empson. Still, this book is well worth attention and, of course, it makes explicit what Huxley was trying to do in the side of his verse that we must find most interesting today. . . .

The end of the poetry more or less coincides with the end of Huxley's first fictional period—that is to say, with the publication of *Point Counter Point* (1928). What a dazzling, if over-forced, decade of creativity! Our reservations about the verse must be tempered with admiration for its prolixity, and in a time of enormous fictional and other output. I think the work of this decade will inevitably separate itself off from the later and, on the whole, disappointing books; and in that event the verse will play a minor but essential part in the reading of Huxley by future generations.

> *Roy Fuller, "Gilding by the Ruolz process—Roy Fuller Considers the Poetry of Aldous Huxley," in* The Listener (© *British Broadcasting Corp. 1971; reprinted by permission of Roy Fuller), March 18, 1971, p. 343.*

Aldous [Huxley's] non-meshing with surrounding life leads to his failure in his novels either to invent characters who are convincing human beings or to write (as he sometimes thought he was doing) artificial comedy in the manner of Peacock. His characters seem to fall halfway between some real-life model (Lypiatt, the artist in *Antic Hay*, Rampion in *Point Counter Point*) and puppets invented to demonstrate attitudes and behavior. One reads them for passages which affect one as essays. *Brave New World* is far and away the most successful of his fictions because it is scarcely a novel at all and most an essay. (p. 21)

He was a gifted writer who distrusted his own gift and distrusted still more the kind of prestige that today attaches to art and to being a writer. He was a very clever man who not only sought humility but really attained it. One of his clearest insights, which he states frequently in his letters, is that human beings are conditioned by their circumstance into types which have very little comprehension of one another's psychological premises. This being agreed, it is implicit in his writing and his letters that he represents a point of view which is largely the result of his conditioning: his family, his physiology, his near-blindness.

Because his limitations are implicit he can be convinced and convincing without being dogmatic, wrong-headed without being wrong. One is always brought back to what is personal in him, his being, his essence, the intelligence, the good will, together with limitations of which he is so conscious that they do not exclude—indeed they indicate—the possibility of other points of view. As well as being a humanist, he is divinely human. (p. 24)

> *Stephen Spender, "The Conscience of the Huxleys," in* The New York Review of Books (*reprinted with permission from* The New York Review of Books; *copyright* © *1971 NYREV, Inc.), March 25, 1971, pp. 21-4.*

If there is not, in [Huxley's] long shelf of books, a single masterpiece, there are a number that live in the mind. *Brave New World*, which might have been his *Gulliver's Travels*, is unconvincing today because its picture of a future dominated by ease and plenty, by technology in the service of a fat-bellied hedonism, is so remote from the dark, hate-ridden barbarism that has actually resulted from twentieth-century scientific premises. But it is, in the terms of the 1920s, an interesting failure. *The Perennial Philosophy*, Huxley's attempt at a *Summa Philosophica* based on the entire range of his reading, shares the fate of most systems—after the lapse of a few years, it seems merely a monument to work for work's sake—but it speaks for the forties as the early satire speaks for the twenties. And the voluminous essays, though nothing they have to say seems important now, remain impressive in their willingness to find something to say about such a huge range of subjects— so much of history, of art, of literature, of manners and customs, of hagiography and mythology and psychology, fell under his restless eye. (p. 27)

I am simply going to avoid saying anything about Huxley's poetry, apart from the initial admission that it is not very interesting. In fact, it had a certain interest: the diagnostic. Huxley began to publish poetry in 1916 and stopped in 1931. His verse-writing life thus spanned the Great Divide, the years when the idiom of poetry, throughout the English-speaking world and very largely elsewhere, changed out of recognition. His first volume was published a year before Eliot's *Prufrock and Other Observations* and his last a year after Auden's first *Poems*. He thus illustrates the case of the gifted minor poet who is forced, by the accident of his birthdate, to adapt to a colossal change. Having formed his expectations and habits on the verse of the late nineteenth and early twentieth centuries, having already invested a certain effort and achieved some reputation, he is faced with a sudden complete shift in sensibility. What does he do? Call it a passing fad and wait for it to disappear? Run after the new fashion with his head if not with his heart? Or genuinely strip away existing attitudes, switch on his radar, and devoutly wait to see if the signals that are coming to other people will come to him too? (pp. 27-8)

Huxley's verse—literary, cultivated, sensitive, but never getting anywhere near the grain of experience and always following linguistic convention, never leading it—shows the helplessness even of his clever and adaptable mind in the face of this situation. He writes like the Georgian poets; he writes like Keats; he writes like Verlaine; he tries his hand, once or twice, at free verse in the plangent and rhetorical manner of his friend D. H. Lawrence; but none of it will do; he simply cannot find a way of making major statements in verse. His poems remain, obstinately, a series of minor footnotes on his prose works. The fact that he gave up at the age of 37 seems to indicate that, fine literary critic as he was, he saw the situation clearly and accepted it. (p. 28)

John Wain, "Poems of a Prosaist," in The New Republic *(reprinted by permission of* The New Republic; © *1971 by The New Republic, Inc.), September 11, 1971, pp. 27-8.*

Huxley could never have entered the front rank of novelists, for a reason that can be found in a comment he made on the style of T. E. Lawrence: "He wanted to write well, and he wrote about as well as a conscious will can make one write. But the consciously willed style always stops short of the best. . . ." In the same way Huxley's ability as a novelist was a consciously willed one; he lacked the natural gift (as he himself would have acknowledged) of a D. H. Lawrence or E. M. Forster. Yet those early novels are at least as good as the early novels of Anthony Powell or Angus Wilson—two novelists who, whether consciously or subconsciously, must obviously have been influenced by him. (p. 405)

Francis King, "An Older Aldous," in The Spectator *(© 1974 by The Spectator; reprinted by permission of* The Spectator*), September 28, 1974, pp. 404-05.*

Huxley's development as a writer is generally regarded as a decline from the *romans à clef* of the Twenties about ego-eccentrics of the British intelligentsia to the homilies of the Forties and Fifties on the evils of overpopulation and assorted disasters of the modern world. And it is widely agreed that after the early period his fiction includes nothing to equal *Antic Hay* and a few of the stories— "Young Archimedes," for one, in which he manages to construct an absorbing tale around a demonstration that the square of the hypotenuse of a right triangle is equal to the sum of the squares of the other two sides. Yet of all his books, *Brave New World* (1932) is the most assured of a place in history, if not literature, and, arguably, his narrative skills increased in some of the later nonfiction, in *Gray Eminence*, for instance, and in the essay on Maine de Biran.

At the same time, Huxley's development as a person can be looked upon as an ascent from mere brilliance into wisdom, from superiority into humility, from the satirist of individuals to the philosophical activist for the human condition. The question, then, is whether literary criteria are applicable to the later works. After all, the best of them are admittedly didactic, and while some, including *Ape and Essence* and *Island*, employ fictional forms, these neglect even the minimal requirements of the novel. Huxley himself rejected literary criticism as "pharisaical" and useless as a paradigm for the criticism of life. (p. 9)

Robert Craft, "Huxley at Home," in The New York Review of Books *(reprinted with permission from* The New York Review of Books; *copyright © 1975 NYREV, Inc.), January 23, 1975, pp. 9-12.*

Readers of my generation used to think of Aldous Huxley as a leader of the revolt against "Victorianism"; the word was then still entirely synonymous with "repressiveness." It wasn't only that the characters in *Antic Hay* or *Point Counter Point* led freer sexual lives than those in Victorian novels: they also felt less obligation to society as a whole, claiming the freedom to develop as individuals along private guidelines that might lead to asceticism and mysticism as often as to hedonism. Those characters who seemed to have the approval of their creator—there weren't many— did not seek to preserve the *status quo* or set the world to rights by revolutionary means: a separate peace would satisfy them, although they never managed to attain it, somehow. *Brave New World* (1932) did much to destroy the faith in scientific and technological "progress" that had survived almost intact from Victorian days. In the later 1930s, when intellectuals all over Europe were rejecting individualism in favor of collective movements, whether of the Left or Right, Huxley showed his freedom from trendiness by publishing *Eyeless in Gaza* (1936). Anthony Beavis, its protagonist, finally decides that his ideal is "Unity with all being.". . .

[It was] the didactic element that makes his nonfiction so valuable but causes a steady decline in the artistic quality of his novels. . . . [But] Aldous never attempted the thrilling rhetoric of a prophet; it was the firmly reasonable tone of the pedagogue that weakened the spell cast by the storyteller. (p. 118)

What I can't forgive him is his artistic treatment of sex—what Miss Bedford rightly calls his "Swiftian and Baudelairean horror." In spite of his own experience on the one hand and of his admiration for D. H. Lawrence on the other, Huxley always presents sex in his novels as nasty and/or destructive. If his hypocrisy in this matter was largely unconscious, so is that of the stereotyped Victorian male. . . .

I fully intended to do my homework on Huxley, rereading some of the earlier work and tackling for the first time *Eyeless in Gaza* and some of its successors, the books that my generation (now aged 55 to 65) either disliked or ignored. I began with *Antic Hay* (1923), which I couldn't remember having read before, and soon detected a familiar tone in the narrator's voice: the Beckett of *More Pricks Than Kicks* (1934) and *Murphy* (1938) must have been an admirer of Huxley and his polymath's allusiveness. I next planned to reread *Point Counter Point* (1928), but 50 pages of its knowingness and snobbery were enough; I felt I'd have been better occupied rereading Huxley's model for this novel, Gide's *The Counterfeiters*. *Eyeless* was more satisfying, perhaps Huxley's best novel: a long Victorian lay sermon on sin and repentance, spiced by some of the sexual frankness of the 1920s.

After trying *Island* and being put off by its simplistic didacticism, I have given up Huxley for the present. When I take him up again, I'm going to read his nonfiction—apparently I'm too old to accept a treatise disguised as a novel. Significantly, it was my younger son who urged me to read *Island*. From 1930 on, although I'm sure he never dared believe it, Huxley was writing for a generation still unborn. Now that that generation has grown up, they have taken him to their hearts. They recognize his anti-utopia, *Brave New World*, and they believe in his Utopia, *Island*. He had a far clearer vision of the immediate future than H. G. Wells, for instance, and lived long enough to say, "I told you so" in *Brave New World Revisited*. It was unfortunate that his serious experiments with LSD and mescaline gave a specious legitimacy to a hedonistic use of drugs that his Victorian self deplored.

Without question, Huxley's writings have influenced the course of history—how much, it is still impossible to tell—but I believe they have done more good than harm so far. He created no great work of literary art, but then the works that he most admired belonged to arts he could not master, music and painting. (p. 119)

> Vivian Mercier, "A Victorian Anti-Victorian," in *The Nation (copyright 1975 by the Nation Associates, Inc.), February 1, 1975, pp. 118-20.*

[The] greater part of Aldous Huxley's work is already stone-dead. He had a veritable genius for titles. "Crome Yellow," "Antic Hay," "Point Counter Point," "Brave New World," "Eyeless in Gaza" lead a brilliant, disembodied life in their own right, almost eclipsing the Shakespearean or Miltonic context from which they are taken. But what of the novels themselves? Why have they faded so quickly from imaginative authority? Why does "Point Counter Point" rely for what vitality it has on the presence among its characters of a distorted but suggestive portrayal of D. H. Lawrence? What has made of "Brave New World" and, even more emphatically, of Huxley's later utopian fantasy, "Island," merely historical occasions in contrast to the urgent power of George Orwell's "1984" or, indeed, of the speculative fictions of H. G. Wells? (p. 103)

Though committed to the sharpest possible sense of the future—scientific, political, psychological—Huxley was perhaps the last of the Victorian sages. This may give a clue to our real problem: the mustiness, the datedness that hang like gentle dust over novels once so dashing, so up-to-the-minute.

Victorian sagacity will often have within it a streak of silliness. Probe the solid front of rational energy and you will turn up the faddist, the occultist, the practitioner of animal magnetism and cold ablutions. The genius of the Victorian middle class seems to contain an ineradicable retardment, a deliberately cultivated prolongation of childhood. We find it in Jowett, in Gladstone, even in Darwin. Nursery and school reach into adult existence with an unchallenged authority—part nightmare, part heart's longing. (Lewis Carroll precisely captures the ambiguous note.). . .

Aldous Huxley's flash of intellect, his mental reach, his articulacy were legend. But the confident obtuseness, the immaturities are no less striking. ("The idea of using his knowledge in order to make himself better never seems to have occurred to him," says Huxley of Proust.). . . Aldous Huxley's investments in [extraterrestrial theories and similar] matters are not accidental. On one level they reproduce, almost uncannily, the table-rapping, ectoplasmic, mesmeric trials of his Victorian forebears. The arrogant innocence that marks the relations of the Victorian agnostic to the charlatan carries over into the modern man. On another level, they are the touchstone of Huxley's radicalism, of his search for a "breakthrough" into new dimensions of understanding. The fineness and the silliness are inseparable. It was a recipe that drove D. H. Lawrence, toward whom Huxley was persistently generous, to black rage. (p. 104)

As modern research has revealed, narcotics and attempts to enlarge consciousness through hallucination played a large part in the Romantic movement and Victorian art and literature. Huxley was in this respect an heir to Coleridge, De Quincey, Baudelaire, and the *fin de siècle*. The utopian, socially directed aims of his explorations in "self-transcendence" were, on the other hand, entirely modern and prophetic. . . . The liturgical cadence, the paternalistic fervor [of his drug avocation] are unmistakable; they descend directly from Victorian evangelism or the robust confidence of the Victorian secularist in a sunrise future for mankind. We know now that Huxley's pharmacology was irresponsible and that "The Doors of Perception" is, at the very most, a profoundly ambiguous contribution. (p. 105)

It is, most likely, [his] cultivation of rootlessness, so contrastive with D. H. Lawrence's or James Joyce's anguish of exile, that makes much of Huxley's work brittle. He was, to use yet another late-Victorian idiom, marvellously clever rather than intelligent (the remark on Proust being a grim illustration of the difference). A giggly smartness turns up even in his most solid writings, such as "The Devils of Loudun." It reduces a fair proportion—think of "The Gioconda Smile" and "The Genius and the Goddess"—to a novelettish, Hollywood level. He wrote too much, and under almost constant financial pressure.... Huxley's ability to make himself glossy, to deliver the scripts and the magazine articles, ... points to an essential weakness. He may not have wished to end as a mass-media guru, but he filled the part all too well. (p. 106)

George Steiner, "The Last Victorian," in The New Yorker *(© 1975 by The New Yorker Magazine, Inc.), February 17, 1975, pp. 103-06.*

J

JENNINGS, Elizabeth   1926-

Elizabeth Jennings is an English Catholic poet and scholar who established her literary reputation as a member of "the Movement," a group of writers which included Kingsley Amis, Thom Gunn, and Philip Larkin. The dignity and composure that characterized the early work of the "Movement" writers is evident in all of Miss Jennings' poetry.

In declining to use rhetorical gestures, startling images and metaphors, or to render the physical world with any vividness, Miss Jennings severely limits her range. She asks to be read as a poet of the mind, to be read for her insights and the play of ideas. And she selects topics about which one might write a prose essay. She likes such subjects as the nature of symbols, myth, kingship—all of which call for intellectual reach and subtlety. (p. 125)

> *William Van O'Connor, in his* The New University Wits and the End of Modernism *(copyright © 1963, Southern Illinois University Press; reprinted by permission of Southern Illinois University Press), Southern Illinois University Press, 1963.*

[Elizabeth] Jennings's poetry inhabits a moral world, and that is a rare thing these days when the pat phrases of ideological indignation are as far as many of our poets get in exploring the universe ethically considered. Didactic poetry, like didactic judgment, can appear harsh and off-putting; but her poems are saved from this by her vulnerability to the fact of pain and her fund of sympathy. She is also a wise, as well as compassionate poet and knows that self-pity is 'death to the human heart'; which is one reason why she tells us 'Never blame/Anyone but yourself.'

Her most frequent themes are hurt, sorrow and aloneness (whether of herself or others), but she does not seek to hug these states, rather to understand and transcend them. So she sees the roots of so many of our moral and spiritual dilemmas in an egoism turning inward. . . . (pp. 100-01)

> *Derek Stanford, in* Books and Bookmen *(© copyright Derek Stanford 1972), December, 1972.*

In 1967, Elizabeth Jennings' *Collected Poems* appeared. Edmund Blunden described her poetry as uniting "the deepest sensibility with a poetry of restraint and yet of great candour". [Hers is] . . . a formal restraint rather than a tentativeness of statement. Her prose poems are her most successful deviations from strict form, while the free-verse or aformal poems at the end of the *Collected* are the least successful. Miss Jennings requires traditional form, and she uses it with authority. Her temperament is not innovative in this sense. With her, form helps to discover order or disorder, rather than . . . order or disorder discovering form. Form is a primary poetic necessity rather than a device in Miss Jennings' poetry. Early on, she saw it, rather as Donne did, controlling the otherwise inarticulable. (p. 82)

Her central preoccupation is not, then, with technique—something she takes for granted and uses skilfully. Nor does she worry much about "what poetry is"—she recognises that it is essential to her, and it would be solipsistic in her to tease out the reasons for this urgent necessity. If anything, poetry is a mode—perhaps the only mode—she has of reaching beyond her individual isolation and discovering relationship. When her poems are aesthetic in preoccupation, she is usually exploring the applicability of art to experience, or its vital relationship with experience. Most often her preoccupation is with suffering of various sorts, with loss, and occasionally fine celebrations of love. She is . . . a poet who is still developing, within her chosen formal confines, towards a new clarity. She began as a love poet and has developed into the poet of complex relationships. Her best poems are not descriptive but exploratory of relationships. She seems at present to be putting aside rather than losing her earlier, more complex language, her aesthetic frame of reference, and her for a time obsessive mental hospital themes for direct confrontation with relationships. Some of the recent poems strike one as sentimental: simplifications rather than lucidities. But the best of them are her finest work to date, rediscovering meaning in apparently overused words, finding a linguistic spareness and clarity which render the poems direct and to the heart. The stylistic transition is almost complete.

Love, shadows, the mind, silence—all these are basic themes in her work. Time, too, obsesses her, and time rather than space is the poet's plane, through which she moves. Her images from nature are usually explicated, allegorised. The poems with plots (especially the early poems) become archetypal in her treatment, and effectively so. (pp. 82-3)

From this tendency to archetypes, Miss Jennings has proceeded on her course. The imagined and generalised has become realised. Intellectual preoccupation, where the mind implied thought, has become preoccupation where the mind implies perception in the widest sense—moral and human perception. There is no more hypothesis. The experiences of loss, the uncertainty of continuous identity, unfulfilled or frustrated longing, the ephemerality of landmarks and timemarks, a failure to find roots and security, to establish permanent relationships with nature or with human beings, have become the burning concerns of Miss Jennings' poetry. "It is acceptance she arranges", one of the recent poems says—perhaps this is the almost sacramental function of her art, expressed earlier in "Visit to an Artist". There the host and wine, the offering—which the experience underlies, validates, sanctifies—are most real and impart an ultimate validity to the poetic act.

"It was by negatives I learned my place. . . ." Without ever having been a genuinely confessional poet, Elizabeth Jennings has explored more territory in more depth than most poets writing today. Her recent work continues with the preoccupations of the earlier, but moves always closer and closer to bedrock. It is strange for a poet, at the outset of a career, to foresee intellectually most of the problems which will become realities for her later on. To have kept course and cut always deeper as she went and goes is a remarkable achievement. (pp. 83-4)

> *Margaret Byers, "Cautious Vision: Recent British Poetry by Women" (copyright © by Margaret Byers), in* British Poetry Since 1960: A Critical Survey, *edited by Michael Schmidt and Grevel Lindop, Carcanet, 1972, pp. 82-4.*

* * *

JOHNSON, Diane 1934-

Ms Johnson is a highly regarded American novelist. (See also *Contemporary Authors*, Vols. 41-44.)

[*Burning*] may well be the song the sirens sang, so fresh it is, so beguiling that you'll never be able to resist it, even with wax in your deadened ears. A Southern California novel without a single lousy movie starlet, a tale of fire in the hills and drugs in the system, of a Bel Air heroine who, "except for being plain and a terrible housekeeper," was a perfect wife, of children who thrive on neglect and pizza and Chicken Delight, of firemen who have more sex appeal than Francis X. Bushman but nourish tidy consciences, of a guru psychiatrist who uses drug-and-sex therapy, eats only cream and orange juice, and agonizes over neglected fleshy succulents more than over his patients . . . oh, I tell you this is a swinging novel!

So much is going on here that it's like trying to describe a twelve-ring circus in standard prose. . . .

The literal holocaust threatens from page one, and when it finally roars through the pathetic sprinkler systems, swimming pools, and protective rings of ice plant, it comes almost as a relief, a confirmation of the absurd disaster inherent in this social landscape. Neither the characters nor the reader knows whether to scream or laugh. . . . Mrs. Johnson superintends this asylum with cool disdain and a remarkable neo-classic elegance of phrase, sentence, and chapter. It's comforting to know that someone competent is in charge.

> *J. R. Frakes, "Siren Song," in* Book World —Chicago Tribune *(© 1971 Postrib Corp.), September 5, 1971, p. 2.*

Diane Johnson apparently has hit upon the solution to all those kooks, cultists, junkies, bogus professionals, displaced Midwesterners whose innocence is awash, police, firemen, Chicanos, Negroes and social workers who inhabit the easy cliché of Los Angeles: Simply burn the damn place down. At least this is what happens to an appreciable part of that sprawling metropolis toward the end of "Burning," and once the Biblical wrath and apocalyptic quality of this great fire is certain, the reader will probably issue a sigh of relief. Not because our continued and restless suckling on various moral tenets is finally vindicated by the flaming purification of Diane Johnson's Los Angeles à la Sodom and Gomorrah, but simply because the author has found the means to bring her book to a close. Phew. (p. 6)

> *Tom McHale, in* The New York Times Book Review *(© 1971 by The New York Times Company; reprinted by permission), September 5, 1971.*

Firemen, policemen, government investigators and welfare workers are important to Miss Johnson's Los Angeles setting [for "Burning"], increasing the surrealism that attends all California fiction. . . . Even Miss Johnson's sex scenes are unexpectedly cheery. She is witty and serious, I think, but tries to be both at once and doesn't make it. Her book should have been either much funnier or much grimmer or, failing that, she should have been much better. (p. 118)

> *Peter S. Prescott, in* Newsweek *(copyright 1971 by Newsweek, Inc.; all rights reserved; reprinted by permission), October 25, 1971.*

It is news to nobody that the leisured end of American society tends to produce bored and baffled Freud-ridden ciphers who are willing to accept any seemingly authoritative estimate of themselves and their needs, so the comedy [in *Burning*] is pretty thin. Group-therapy and the drug-induced self-analysis of depressed citizens have been done to death as satirical material. The most depressing thing about the book is that Miss Johnson is plainly too intelligent to be unaware of this. Living as she does at the current spiritual battlefront of civilisation, she must simply snipe away at the dismal targets that offer themselves, knowing that the small-arms fire of *Burning* is unlikely to bring them down. (p. 706)

> *R. R. Davies, in* New Statesman *(© 1971 The Statesman & Nation Publishing Co. Ltd.), November 19, 1971.*

Diane Johnson is one of our most interesting contemporary writers, and one is surprised at the lack of attention her three novels, *Fair Game* (1965), *Loving Hands at Home* (1968), and *Burning* (1971), have received. She is the kind of writer Virginia Woolf says in *A Room of One's Own* it is very difficult for a woman to be: she is in control of her material, communicating not personal anger nor frustration but her own vision through novels about Los Angeles in the last third of the twentieth century—of the conditions of life itself; and she has followed her own artistic impulses rather than the fads of the moment.

What seem to be Johnson's virtues may account for her relative lack of popular appeal. She is not sensational, sentimental, nor simple-minded. Although her central characters are women about whom she writes perceptively, she is increasingly aware of the complexities of their dilemmas and the impossibility of separating women's lives from men's. Her characters' situations are increasingly tangled, and her resolutions increasingly tentative. She writes in the satiric-comic-realistic tradition, in a mode that may not appeal to readers nurtured on the personal, subjective, and doctrinaire.

The lack of serious critical attention is another matter. Her novels both require and reward careful attention, particularly when seen as ever more successful variations on a few central themes: the conflict between individuals' desires and society's institutions and conventions, institutions which cannot either channel individuals into constructive and integrated lives or even control the destructive, disintegrating forces which are equally inherent in life; the dangers of venturing outside established boundaries, but the futility of looking for security within them; the need to become aware of the exciting yet frightening possibilities of life.

In each of Johnson's novels a woman who *has* ventured outside the boundaries has a shocking experience which sends her back inside, but only temporarily until another experience within the only apparently safe boundaries either sends her outside again or changes her whole perspective. In each novel characters and scenes symbolize the allurement, mystery, promise and terror of the life outside, and in each the overtones are satiric-comic-grotesque. These elements are progressively more closely integrated with the realistic elements, so that the third novel, *Burning*, is at once the grimmest and the funniest. (pp. 53-4)

Burning is her most satisfying novel. At one level it is a satire of our regulatory agencies: child welfare, police, firemen. At another, it is a satire of both our contemporary culture and our counterculture. At its deepest level, it is a compassionate yet unsentimental examination of our difficulties in coping with ourselves, with one another, and with our natural environment. (p.60)

Diane Johnson is not . . . a "feminist writer" in the contemporary sense. She is a contemporary writer with an interest in dehumanization, loss of personal identity, rents in the social fabric; and she sees these conditions as affecting women perhaps even more acutely than men. Her novels are not merely topical, though their surfaces may be; they deal with the essential fragility of life and the defenses we build against both its freest and most dangerous expression, a situation whose realistic, comic, and grotesque elements she explores. She has a sense of form that enables her to integrate symbolism, narrative, and characterization into a coherent whole. Johnson is at her best in episodes combining social commentary with revelation of an individual's development. . . . Though some of the situations are depressing, the novels are not; Johnson's comic sense provides a perspective. All in all, she is already a good novelist and, as she is also a young novelist, she may become a very good one. (p.63)

> *Marjorie Ryan, "The Novels of Diane Johnson," in* Critique: Studies in Modern Fiction *(copyright © by* Critique, *1974), Vol. XVI, No. 1, 1974, pp. 53-63.*

The Shadow Knows is no mystery novel. Rather, it is an extraordinarily vivid, intricate and affecting account of one week in the life of a young woman caught in the grip of terror. On the most immediate level, it is a novel about what it is like to be a woman—and it is so vastly superior to the run-of-the-mill "new woman's novel" that to place it within the genre would be an insult to its author. On a larger level, it is a novel about what it is like simply to be a human being trying "to find your way in the dark" of inexplicable evil. . . .

[N.'s] obsession becomes the identification of [her] real or fancied would-be murderer. . . . As she is drawn ever more deeply into her obsession, N. falls into a realm where fact and fantasy are confused. The incidents are real enough . . . —but are they anything more than a chain of unrelated circumstances? All we know is that N. is desperate, and that she is seeking ways to cope with that desperation. Torn between "life and death thoughts," she looks around for—and finds—ways to see in the dark.

The breadth and depth of Diane Johnson's accomplishment cannot be overstated. Taking her title from a once-popular radio melodrama ("Who knows what evil lurks in the hearts of men? The Shadow knows!"), she has elevated pop to art. The novel is a consideration of "what's lurking in people's hearts," in particular the heart of N. herself. Her voyage through terror becomes that classic American story, the voyage to self-discovery, told with astonishing complexity and subtlety. A self-centered and somewhat frivolous girl becomes a whole woman, capable of dealing with life on its harsh and mysterious terms.

Read *The Shadow Knows*, if you wish, for its suspense; there is plenty of it, brilliantly sustained. Read it for its insights into a woman undergoing the shock of liberation. Read it for its wit, its compassion, its flawless prose, its wells of feeling. But by all means read it. It is as fine a novel as we have seen this year—and this is a year in which we have seen some very fine novels.

> *Jonathan Yardley, "What Evil Lurks . . .," in* Book World–The Washington Post *(© The Washington Post), December 22, 1974, p. 1.*

In Diane Johnson's remarkable . . . novel, *The Shadow Knows . . .*, we are told nothing whatever about the heroine's childhood and early youth, about her parents or their social and economic class, about her brothers and sisters or her favorite traumas. Nor are we given a dutiful sketch of that tiresome ancestral symbol in current fiction, the all-powerfully influential grandparent. In fact, we do not even learn the narrator's first name—she is only N. Hexam throughout.

Yet I can think of few characters in recent fiction whose being is more lucidly concrete and intricately alive, more compelling and distinct. . . .

Miss Johnson . . . insists that her heroine simply stand up and *be*—in the discontinuous, remorseless present and the immediate mess of her life, never looking back nostalgically to vanished years for excuses and explanations. . . . It is all we need to know, for Miss Johnson has an uncanny gift for infusing an evocative intensity into the here and now. (p. 17)

Miss Johnson, astonishingly for a woman writer in 1974, has not been seduced by fashionably bitter feminist ideology. Despite circumstances that are appallingly bleak and unlikely to improve in the near future, N. is too self-mocking to seriously indulge in the tiresome litanies of grievance and complaint that militancy inspires. She is too quirky and sardonic for slogans, yet also more recklessly self-committed than most feminists. . . . Where treacherous reality ends and N.'s terrified fantasies take over is the unresolvable conundrum at the heart of this memorable book, and in the end the only tangible certainty is N.'s unique talent for surviving on her own terms, for defending the best of herself even when the enemy is only her own darkest imaginings. With [this] novel . . . Diane Johnson becomes one of the genuinely arresting voices in American writing today. (p. 18)

> *Pearl K. Bell, in* The New Leader *(© 1975 by the American Labor Conference on International Affairs, Inc.), January 20, 1975.*

"*Sola, perduta, abbandonata!*" exclaims Puccini's Manon Lescaut—alone, lost, abandoned—the ultimate female cry of woe. And the three words are still drifting into our lives from the pages of the past, like unconquerable dust. Or so Diane Johnson's . . . novel, *The Shadow Knows,* seems to tell us. (p. 728)

Revolving like a grim carrousel around the torment—the paranoia—of the victim, . . . *The Shadow Knows,* is first of all a sort of bitter parody of a genre invented by 19th-century men: the detective novel. Its heroine-narrator, who guardedly names herself "N.," quite early in the book decides that she is being stalked by a murderer, perhaps along with her four children and her black maid, Ev. Her increasingly frantic attempts to discover the criminal's identity . . . and her imaginary dialogues with a tweedily contemptuous famous inspector make up the substance of the novel.

As the story unfolds out of the hectic spinnings of N.'s mind, it resonates like Charlotte Brontë filtered through Kafka, or like a strange dream in which Agatha Christie is transformed into a feverish metaphysician. The victim become detective, trying to solve the crime without even knowing what it is. How many novels by women . . . must develop that plot less explicitly but just as passionately? (p. 730)

[N.'s] terrified broodings echo those of Jane Eyre, for whose is the "low, slow ha! ha!" Jane hears in the attic at Thornfield, what is the shadow that haunts Jane and Rochester if not the same murderous darkness that moves too often between men and women, victor and victim, seducer and betrayer?

For this reason, because it is ultimately metaphorical, Johnson's plot is hard to unravel. There is a flash of uncertainty at the end of the book, as if the novelist herself, even while trying to finish the story on a hopeful note, recognized that there is no simple solution to the mystery, no easy way out of the mad tangle. "*Sola, perduta, abbandonata!*" N. quotes the phrase herself—each woman must struggle with her femaleness in her own way, survive betrayals through unique strategies. The literary implications of all this are what critics . . . should begin to examine with more care. (pp. 730-31)

> *Sandra M. Gilbert, in* The Nation *(copy-*

right 1975 by the Nation Associates, Inc.), June 14, 1975.

*   *   *

JOHNSON, Uwe   1934-

Johnson, a novelist, was born in East Germany and moved to West Berlin immediately after his first novel was rejected by an East German publisher. All of Johnson's work portrays his concern with divided Germany and the confrontation of two cultures, a sociopolitical situation which represents, for him, the partition of the world. He has been both praised and criticized for his fiercely realistic depiction of modern Germany. (See also *Contemporary Authors*, Vols. 1-4, rev. ed.)

Wallace Stevens noted: "In the presence of extraordinary actuality, consciousness takes the place of imagination." This helps me express my dissatisfaction with *Two Views*, effective as it is on its own terms. Johnson reports a grim situation excellently, without flinching or exaggerating. But the overall effect of the book, despite some insight into behavior under stress, is not imaginative. The situation remains itself in the reader's mind; it does not expand in significance. But as an American far from the battle (and one not particularly interested in politics), I feel uncomfortable about saying this. Another kind of reader may find the book more suggestive. (p. 110)

> *David J. Gordon, in* The Yale Review *(© 1967 by Yale University; reprinted by permission of the editors), Autumn, 1967.*

Almost exclusively, Johnson dedicates himself to the phenomenon of the divided Germanies: "the border: the difference: the distance." Although the nature of freedom has been dealt with by philosophers and historians, it gains deeper dimensions in the fiction—or literary journalism—of Johnson. (p. 100)

Johnson's methods have been compared with those of Joyce and Faulkner, but methods, although they bear similarities, do not make art. Joyce and Faulkner's people live through their full and sensual apprehension of experience; Johnson's people live through their fragmented and lugubrious cerebrations. One is art while the other is artifice. (p. 105)

To the extent that the author disclaims omniscience, [*The Third Book About Achim*] becomes reportage and an ingenious game. Yet the novelty of portraying an honest "attempt at an attempt" to corral truth forces the reader into involvement and participation in the search—a rare accomplishment in the modern novel. With *The Third Book about Achim*, Johnson went beyond the sterotypes so numerous in *Speculations about Jakob*; with *Two Views* he demonstrated a sureness of touch with less unconventional methods. (p. 108)

In no other novel is the dividedness of the two Berlins and the two Germanies—culturally and politically—rendered with such precision of language and feeling [as in *Two Views*]. Jakob, Karsch, Karen, Achim, and Beate are personifications of the anguished internal dialogue and conflicts taking place. . . . In the East German language, Johnson is "Ein Objektivist," a person politically unreliable because he sees both sides of an issue and questions both. Although Johnson knows that "freedom" in the East is obsolete, he has refused to become a propagandist for the

West either as a novelist or as a public figure. Possibly to avoid the very tangible pressures that have been placed upon him, he takes frequent trips abroad. Yet, his writings speak honestly and clearly of impartial compassion and they report his experiences, without naïve optimism for the future. (p. 109)

> *Siegfried Mandel, in* Contemporary European Novelists, *edited by Siegfried Mandel (copyright © 1968, Southern Illinois University Press; reprinted by permission of the author), Southern Illinois University Press, 1968.*

Johnson's first novel, *Speculations about Jacob* (1959), focuses on speculations about the mysterious death of Jacob Abs. . . . Is his death an accident, suicide, or liquidation? The novel seems to reveal the truth of the matter through fragments of conversation, reports, monologues, and reminiscences, none of which, however, manages to go beyond superficial evidence. All the remarks about the hero remain pure conjecture, and the reader finally realizes that he has been exposed to the hideous atmosphere of everyday life in a totalitarian state, one in which everyone is suspected and no one knows what really happened. . . .

The differences between the two Germanies are even more evident [in *The Third Book About Achim*] than in Johnson's first novel. Various linguistic means make their alienation particularly visible: for instance, when two speakers using the same word have two different conceptions of its meaning. Once again everything remains shrouded in vagueness and speculation. For this reason, Johnson clings intensively to detailed descriptions of tangible objects, thereby pointing to that realm alone in which clear assertions are possible.

Two Viewpoints (1965) indicates even in the title the author's intention to present East and West from varied perspectives. The building of the Berlin wall separates the West German photographer-journalist, B., and the East German nurse, D., who had been brought together by a superficial love affair. In this clearly structured book B. and D. are presented in alternate chapters. Their separation does not particularly affect either of them. In spite of their physical intimacy B. and D., abbreviations for *Bundesrepublik* (West Germany) and *Deutsche Demokratische Republik* (East Germany), can find no meaningful mutual relationship. It is remarkable that Johnson handles a highly political subject quite unpolitically. Political realities are implied in the fortunes of the characters without polemics or propaganda. In no way does Johnson intend to present the West German nation in more favorable light than the East German. The author's own position on the dividing line where the two Germanies touch as well as diverge is appropriate to the subject of his works. (pp. 392-93)

> *Diether H. Haenicke, in* The Challenge of German Literature, *edited by Horst S. Daemmrich and Diether H. Haenicke (reprinted by permission of the Wayne State University Press; copyright © 1971 by Wayne State University Press), Wayne State University Press, 1971.*

Among the literatures of postwar Europe, German writing occupies a special and difficult position. It has had to be created virtually from nothing, because the twelve year period of Nazi rule between 1933 and 1945 constituted a hiatus; writers at home were silenced or brought into line with state policy in artistic matters, and those in exile, like Brecht and Thomas Mann, were cut off from their linguistic and cultural roots. . . . None of the writers who have achieved eminence since 1945 has been either able or willing to elude the necessary confrontation with the facts either of his country's crimes and of its total and crushing defeat, or of the terrible poetic justice meted out by the devastating, pillaging, and raping soldiery of the allied armies repaying eye for eye and tooth for tooth. Nor has it been possible to ignore the obscenity of the continued division of the country. . . . And in the international sphere, finally, the German writer has spent much of the post-war period overcoming his cultural isolation: for, after the long years of Nazi censorship, Joyce, Hemingway, Faulkner, and above all Kafka, had to be rediscovered. If novelists like Uwe Johnson occasionally appear to have been excessively influenced by these forebears, it is quite understandable, and certainly pardonable.

All these factors—the trauma of the defeat and subsequent political division of his country, the need to recreate the literary tradition, and the problem of relating to a self-satisfied and philistine society—are present in Johnson's work, which I find aesthetically the most accomplished to have come out of Germany in recent years. He constitutes, for me, the genuine avant-garde: beside him, Böll appears ponderous, Grass flashy, and Walser arch. And yet his work to date centers on one obsessive theme (the mutual incomprehension of the two Germanies), and certainly lacks the richness and complexity of the world we associate with his rivals: . . . he has produced a masterpiece by concentrating rather than by diffusing his focus. The masterpiece—dominating head and shoulders his other work—is *The Third Book About Achim*, which is concerned with the foredoomed effort to "fix" the real, to determine its true importance and accuracy, and to solidify the past moment in all its sharp vividness. Reality is not grasped by language, but created by it: language not only delimits the world as Wittgenstein rightly perceived, it also structures it. Johnson—like Nabokov, Simon, and Borges among the other great neo-modernists—has seized upon this essential truth, and explores it with dazzling virtuosity and invention. (pp. 81-2)

[All] Johnson's works ask the same question: what is the truth, what is the reality behind the appearance? The answer invariably given is that there are many possibilities for interpretation, that there are no absolute truth-values, that enquiry must remain open-ended and ambiguous, and any report cannot help but be elliptical, cryptic, and allusive. (pp. 83-4)

> *John Fletcher, "The Themes of Alienation and Mutual Incomprehension in the Novels of Uwe Johnson," in* International Fiction Review, *July, 1974, pp. 81-7.*

It is a suspect occasion when I find a book so large in its aspirations, so fresh in its attitudes, so militant in its inventions, and so unmistakable in their realization that I must call it a masterpiece, even though it is not (yet) the entire work. Here is the first half of Uwe Johnson's fourth novel [*Anniversaries: From the Life of Gesine Cresspahl*]; the second will appear next year. Yet I do not hesitate to speak maximally about the book under review, any more than I would have hesitated to call the first installments of *Little Dorrit* or *Middlemarch* masterpieces when they appeared serially, as novels always used to do. For there is a unified, if not a uniform, impulse of composition here that justifies the division into parts, into successive volumes, and I believe I can speak above suspicion for the integrity of the book even though the author's ultimate intention has further designs upon me. (p. 38)

Uwe Johnson has never before been so explicit, never so committed to the toll that the actual takes upon what *we* take for our real lives. He is the author of three previous novels, and characters from all of them appear in *Anniversaries*: Apparently he believes in the cumulative evidence of his imagination. The fragmentation of narrative in all of his books, the displacement of compositional interest from what is told to the telling itself, suggest that from the start Uwe Johnson has been so possessed by his own place and his familiar people that he can give himself up to a sort of stupefaction of storytelling, an invoked ecstasy of utterance without explanation or stage direction.

None of the earlier books, despite or perhaps because of the enormities of the immediate, the perishable, the "journalistic" that Johnson wants to accommodate in them, is much fun to read: None of them focuses on an eroticized central character, which is what we mean by a "sympathetic" one. Instead, the hypertrophied devices, the obstructed "tellings" are the focus, and the novels take the shape of exacting spirals wreathed around an empty center, a cold heart. These books have been praised and given prizes—through gritted teeth, as it were: The moral poverties of East and West are not heightened by grotesque comedy, as in Günter Grass, or relieved by divertissements of suspense, as in Heinrich Böll; endurable hunger and unsatisfactory pleasure are the poles, the extremes of these fictions. . . .

Anniversaries is the first of Johnson's books to be written with—though not about—love, to dramatize characters with whom we identify because they have an identity themselves, because they love themselves. And, of course, because they hate themselves. In an America destroying Vietnam and disabling her own cities—the year is 1967; the place is New York City, chiefly the upper West Side—the characters *misgive* themselves, to warp a phrase, for enjoying their own freedom.

From the Life of Gesine Cresspahl is the second part of the novel's title. We have met this appealing, "eroticized" young woman before. She is the toughminded young translator in *Speculations About Jakob*. . . .

Uwe Johnson has come into possession of—has been possessed by—a world, the mythology of a town (Jerichow), and a family (the Cresspahls), which he is enabled to criticize and distance by the very circumstances of their presentation in exile, their gentile diaspora. . . .

[Nothing] is endorsed in *Anniversaries*, though a great deal is identified—insight, not advocacy, is the undertaking here. . . . *Anniversaries* substantiates a claim that it is not, or not only, some universal historical process, some ideology, or some other large abstraction that embodies and enacts morality, but rather certain realizations of our own conscious lives within the rehearsed limitations of a given society—national socialism, Marxist communism, capitalist democracy. (p. 39)

One thinks of the portraits of New York by foreign writers, from Dickens to Robbe-Grillet, and nowhere in that catalog of despisals does there occur so loving and so accurate a delineation of the city as that in *Anniversaries*. One might expect the descriptions of German landscape, German weather, German gesture, but the surprise is the affectionate, funny, and searching scrutiny of New York. One would not look for the proper sociology of West End Avenue from such a visitor, but Johnson has a Balzac's passion for the telling detail, the revealing exactitude. He can afford to tamper with narrative, to interrupt, and even to impede our interest with random notations, because he is so sure of his facts, so convinced of his *realia*. . . .

It would be comforting, as a New Yorker, to assume that my city and America herself had bestowed, somehow, upon this gifted and intricate novelist the saving graces of affection and humor that had appeared to be in default in his more strictly German books. But I cannot think that local color is rose color. Rather, I think that Uwe Johnson, at 40 and at ease with his own arsenal of means, has collected together what he had all the time wanted to say, and that he has been "released," by what Proust would call the accidental and inevitable occasion of New York, into his first mastery.

Is it a mastery of the novel, one might ask, or of journalism, as I have suggested? I think the risks Johnson takes, as he has always taken them, with the day-by-day are great risks indeed, for we sense . . . all the dross of a life merely lived out, which is to say eluded. Yet so momentous is the judgment passed upon that life—upon all our lives—by the form it takes, and refuses to take, that I think the journalistic mode is no more than the means by which this fiction obtains access to reality, to the expressed values of existence. So intensely are the figures imagined . . . that the ballast of Manhattan fact is needed to keep the book on the page, to keep the life in focus, to keep the agony from getting *out of drawing*. (p. 40)

> *Richard Howard, "City Spirals," in* Saturday Review *(copyright © 1975 by Saturday Review/World, Inc.; reprinted with permission), February 22, 1975, pp. 38-40.*

Clearly, Johnson is his own man, even to the extent of not worrying overmuch about national membership and he joins those other expatriate writers—Beckett, Nabokov, Borges, Jakov Lind, Cortázar—who have focused their material the better by leaving it behind or have discovered new material of more ecumenical clout. If Johnson has an abiding theme, it is deracination; and if he has a typical mental movement it is that of emigrating in the mind—as he did in West Berlin when, after reading Faulkner (banned in the East), he Yoknapatawpha-ed *Speculations*, entirely recasting it. Overland, or in the mind, he is a novelist of transits, borders, hinterlands, spatial simultaneities, and, above all, history lodged in the head like contraband.

Yet he is far from being a novelist of fragments, a rootless experimentalist, as *Anniversaries* proves at some length. He does permit himself a certain scrambling of narrative procedure—unexplained tilts from voice to voice, or from one time to another, or from *I* to *we*, even from a plural-feeling *I* to a singular-feeling *we*—but these are far from innovational, and he emerges increasingly as an orthodox novelist occasionally given to mystification and quaint chronic overlap, as if Mann's *Buddenbrooks* were being ghost-written by the Faulkner of, say, *Requiem for a Nun*. . . .

[In] reading his dense, allusive, mighty intelligent book [*Anniversaries*], I felt my head much exercised but my pulses moved only by the pulsations of history. Johnson's grave plethora is that of a pensive, moral, intact man who prefers speculation to the known and is given to longwinded trance. Nothing wrong with any of that; but, as several speculative novelists have shown (among them Claude Simon and Cortázar), the multiple choices in the enigma-novel need to be at least twice as vivid, as garish even, as the established facts in the novel that gives what's-known-for-sure. It's odd that Johnson, in the mold of the chronicle-novel, has created a long work in which what happened next seems almost irrelevant to the heroine's life. She's a fine mirror, even as a distorting one, but for insistent, integrated presence she doesn't compare with the woman in Heinrich Böll's equally complex *Group Portrait with Lady*, which Leila Vennewitz translated with the same ingenuity and scruple.

> *Paul West, "Uwe Can't Go Home Again,"*
> *in* Book World—The Washington Post *(©*
> *The Washington Post), April 6, 1975, p. 2.*

* * *

JORDAN, June   1936-

Ms Jordan, a Black American poet, has also written poems, fiction, and nonfiction for children. (See also *Contemporary Authors*, Vols. 33-36.)

June Jordan assembles *Some Changes* out of the black experience, and she does so coherently. Her expression is developed out of, or through, a fine irony that manages to control her bitterness, even to dominate her rage against the intolerable, so that she can laugh and cry, be melancholic and scornful and so on, presenting always the familiar faces of human personality, integral personality. She adapts her poems to the occasions that they are properly, using different voices, and levels of thought and diction that are humanly germane and not disembodied rages or vengeful shadows; thus she can create her world, that is, people it for us, for she has the singer's sense of the dramatic and projects herself into a poem to express its special subject, its individuality. Of course it's always her voice, because she has the skill to use it so variously: but the imagination it needs to run through all her changes is her talent. Moreover she seems not to have rejected on principle what has been available to poets in the way of models; in other words, you can see all the white poets she has read, too. She has been assimilating their usages of phrase and stanza; she sees with her own eyes through them, speaks them with her own voice, which is another way of remarking that she is interested in poetry itself. No matter how she will use her poems, and most of them are political in thrust, she has the great good sense, or taste, not to politicize her poetry. There is a difference, even in love poetry, nature poetry, and she has some of that sort, between speaking as yourself and editorializing for others. She is both simple and strong; she is clear in the head, besides. . . . When June Jordan goes through her changes, she does it; she doesn't talk about doing it. For us there is pleasure in that, because we can go through them with her. And that means she has poetry near her. (pp. 301-03)

> *Jascha Kessler, in* Poetry *(© 1973 by The Modern Poetry Association; reprinted by permission of the Editor of* Poetry*), February, 1973.*

June Jordan writes ragalike pieces of word-music that serve her politics, both personal and public. (p. 48)

[Her] political poems are the most powerful and beautiful in [*New Days: Poems of Exile and Return*] . . . and among the greatest of their kind. In the *American Poetry Review* . . . she wrote: "I expect a distinctively Black poem to speak *for me*-as-part-of-an-*us*." But she never sacrifices poetry for politics. In fact, her craft, the patterning of sound, rhythm, and image, make her art inseparable from political statement, form inseparable from content. [She] uses images contrapuntally to interweave disparate emotions. (pp. 49, 113)

Her *New Days* is a substantial book of five sections: "Conditions for Leaving," "Poems of Exile," and three sections written after her return from Rome. "Poems of Exile" culminates with the long "Roman Poem Number Five," about visiting the ruins of Pompeii. In it Jordan describes her contradictory feelings on seeing mummified citizens in the lava-frozen horror of unexpected death: *living visitors admire the poise/of agony the poise of agony is/absolute.*" And there are love poems, breathtaking in their simplicity. . . . (p. 113)

> *Honor Moore, in* Ms. *(© 1975 Ms. Magazine Corp.), April, 1975.*

K

KAVAN, Anna (pseudonym of Helen Ferguson Woods) 1904-1968

Born in France, Anna Kavan lived in the United States, Burma, Norway, New Zealand, and England. She was a novelist and short story writer. (See also *Contemporary Authors*, Vols. 5-8, rev. ed.; obituary, Vols. 25-28.)

Anna Kavan's novel, *A Scarcity of Love*, is written with alarming intensity. Its fairy-tale touches and allegorical hints, combined with a structure which seems dictated by the progress of obsession rather than the conventions of a plot, suggest extraordinary violence and disorganization of feeling.

The story starts in a castle and ends with a dreamlike suicide in a jungle river, and the characters are seen clearly outlined, like a child's drawings, against frozen mountains, lush tropical gardens, vast mirrored hotels. At the centre of the story is a snow queen woman, who rejects her baby, forces her husband to suicide, and devotes the rest of her life to the worship and preservation of her beauty and the incidental destruction of men, who serve her as acolytes rather than lovers. The baby she abandoned is returned to her as a girl already mutilated by a loveless childhood, and the second half of the novel watches the girl grappling feebly for some possible life, disliked by her mother, spurned by a young husband, until she offers herself gratefully to that river in the jungle.

The landscapes of the book are projections of the girl's fogged, distorted perceptions, and the novel's considerable interest lies in what is a kind of territorial ambiguity, a constantly shifting uncertainty about the reality of the experiences which are so lucidly described and even explained. There is mindless cruelty on the one side, passive suffering on the other; or is this the way the world looks through tormenting paranoia? People, landscape, objects acquire monstrous and menacing properties. The more wraithlike and drained the girl becomes the more solid and bold become her visions of corruption and the characters who embody evil for her.

> *"Death by Drowning," in* The Times Literary Supplement *(© Times Newspapers, Ltd., 1971; reproduced by permission), February 5, 1971, p. 144.*

Anna Kavan's *Ice* is labeled science fiction on its jacket, but its major quality is that surrealist murkiness so fashionable among the more abstruse literati of the past decade or so. What is so disconcerting to me is the unspecified nature of every character, location, and even event (proper nouns seem to be an unknown quantity to the author). An unnamed narrator returns to his unnamed homeland from somewhere else in search of a girl (thereafter referred to as "the girl," no emphasis on *the*). Over this country hangs some unspecified disaster (a nice ice age, *perhaps*; much is made of the constant cold and snow); there already seems to be a state of near anarchy prevailing. The girl, for reasons best known to herself, flees, followed by the narrator who pursues her to another unspecified place which seems to have no political or social ties to any locale. . . . Nothing much ever happens, and one is never told just why the world is in the state it's in. I can but admire the author for maintaining any kind of narrative with characters lacking names. It's a sort of *tour de force*, and Kavan does not lack other skills. The constant sense of gloom and cold is consistently conveyed. It's the only book my mind's eye has ever conjured up entirely in black and white. But the vague problems and conflicts of these nebulous characters in these mysterious locales simply did not engage me at all. (pp. 25-6)

> *Baird Searles, in* The Magazine of Fantasy and Science Fiction *(copyright © 1971 by Mercury Press, Inc.), October, 1971.*

'And he ravished her. He simply took her body and ravished it.' It has been a long time since a fictional heroine had such a complaint to make and in such language, but Anna Kavan's novel [*Let Me Alone*] is 44 years old, a pioneering effort for Women's Liberation first published in 1930. . . . *Let Me Alone* will have a special significance for her fans because it is here that Anna Kavan first appears, not as an author but as the fictional heroine of the novel. Miss Kavan was born Helen Ferguson and wrote several books under that name, including this one. After *Let Me Alone* this unusual woman took the extraordinary step of renaming herself after her own fictional heroine, Anna Kavan, rather as if Dickens had changed his name by deed poll to David Copperfield. It is even more interesting when you consider that Kavan is not the heroine's original surname but the name of the hated and despised husband of the novel. Rhys Davies, in an introductory note, also points out that after the change of name Miss Kavan's actual appearance changed in a remarkable fashion. . . .

Miss Kavan's style with its repetition of words resembles that of D. H. Lawrence. There are certain passages which also could be mistaken for Lawrence. . . . The spirit is Lawrence's too. Anna, the heroine, is disenchanted like Lady Chatterley. . . . She is a sort of reverse Constance Chatterley because she cannot stand to have her husband touch her. But the husband's brutish insensitivity is very Lawrence and the jungle which surrounds her house haunts her in a Lawrentian way and the natives are sensitive, delicate, natural men and women. This echo of the great English novelist is not a bad thing. Even the repetition of words works fine and makes you wonder, as with Lawrence, why we have acquired the odd notion that to use the same word twice in a sentence is a sign of bad writing.

> *Stanley Reynolds, "Jungle Dust," in* New Statesman (© *1974 The Statesman & Nation Publishing Co. Ltd.), January 11, 1974, p. 55.*

It's certainly not unusual to find yourself reading a novel by D. H. Lawrence when you thought that it was written by someone else, but it is unusual to find yourself responding with almost the same assent that you give to Lawrence, because the assimilation of his style is so completely successful. This confident assumption of a master's style, common enough in music and painting but rare in literature, would give *Let Me Alone* a secure claim to interest, if it did not already have a biographical claim. . . .

Clearly, stress generated an intense animus, and Lawrence's impassioned iconography, his development of a highly selective, obsessive mode of characterisation, gave her just the technique she needed to express it. (p. 248)

> *Roger Garfitt, in* The Listener (© *British Broadcasting Corp. 1974), February 21, 1974.*

Anna Kavan's fictions were all done inside the wail: and they rarely went in for laughter. *My Soul In China*, consisting of manuscripts left unpublished at her death in 1968, does include a couple of stories that might be essaying the lighter touch, 'Gosh, I never expected the happy ending', exclaims the narrator at the end of yet another of Ms Kavan's bleak forays among ghastly freakers-out and assorted libbers: nor did the reader. Unconsolation is what's more usually settled for in this enclosingly anguished world of mirrors and fish-bowls. (p. 424)

> *Valentine Cunningham, in* New Statesman (© *1975 The Statesman & Nation Publishing Co. Ltd.), March 28, 1975.*

["Julia and the Bazooka" is a collection of fifteen] powerful, pure, anguished short stories by an extraordinary English writer who died in 1968 at the age of sixty-seven. Anna Kavan's life, which is plainly mirrored in these stories, was one of almost unmitigated loneliness and despair. There were lengthy sojourns in mental institutions, several suicide attempts, and, for the last thirty years, an addiction to heroin, which she believed (and her doctors seem to have agreed with her) she required to keep going at all. None of

these stories searches for any redemptive truths about the human spirit. All are bleak, angry records of a vision of life as a dangerous trap and the world as a menacing place filled with grotesque, cruel, remote creatures. Miss Kavan was a writer of such imagination and such chillingly matter-of-fact, unself-pitying vigor, however, that her vision transcends itself. Whether she is writing about a woman recently released from a mental institution who finds the outside world as much of a prison as the one she's just left, or a humid, erotic fantasy about a leopard, or a premonition of her own death, these stories have a wildness and beauty that are completely original and deeply moving. (p. 139)

> *The* New Yorker (© *1975 by The New Yorker Magazine, Inc.), April 28, 1975.*

The facts of one's difficult existence do not guarantee literature. Anna Kavan is not interesting because she was a woman, an addict or had silver blonde hair. She is interesting because her work comes through with a powerful androgynous individuality and because the stories are luminous and rich with a fresh kind of peril. She knows how to pull us into her world, her dreams and nightmares—how to have all of it become ours.

She will remind you of John Fowles; other times, notably in the story "Fog" in "Julia and the Bazooka," she reminds one of Kafka. Her novel "Ice," a gorgeous amphetamine dream book with the games and elusiveness of "The Magus," also brings Baudelaire to mind. But Anna Kavan is as coolly contemporary as Joy Williams.

She holds her experience up to the light of her imagination like a sheet of plate glass and smashes it. The images stay there on the fragments like jigsaw bits of mirror, and the pieces will fit together. (p. 47)

> *Jill Robinson, in* The New York Times Book Review (© *1975 by The New York Times Company; reprinted by permission), May 11, 1975.*

*   *   *

KAWABATA Yasunari   1899-1972

Kawabata was a Japanese novelist and short story writer, the winner of most of Japan's literary awards and, in 1968, the Nobel Prize for Literature. He is widely read in the West, where his novels *Snow Country* and *The Master of Go* are particularly popular and his elegant and simple prose style is much admired. (See also obituary, *Contemporary Authors*, Vols. 33-36.)

Thousand Cranes would certainly be a hot contender for the No-tell Prize, since the most attentive reader, and the most prurient, will be hard put to know what exactly is going on at times. The 'story' concerns the relations of a young man with two of his late father's mistresses— but these crude European terms are probably quite inapt here, 'relations' and 'mistresses' in especial!— and with the legitimate daughter of one of those old mistresses. Where the book comes alive is when the characters are talking about tea-ceremony bowls and other ritual accessories. Symbols are they? But why bring in symbols to express what elsewhere you are carefully suppressing?

Does one's recognition of the sensitiveness of the writing prohibit one from complaining that the characters are so faintly drawn as to seem hardly two-dimensional even? I suspect that the occasional awkwardness of the translation here, as compared with the overt skill of the same translator in *Snow Country*, is less an indication that the translator has taken on more than he can manage than that there is simply less to manage. (p. 191)

[When] the characters don't know why they do what they do or feel how they feel, it is hardly up to us to pronounce on what they do or how they do it. The ending is quietly cryptic, and that is all. A Chinese reader whose opinion I solicited declared that the story left us with grave suspicions—a highly unsatisfactory state of affairs! And if I might venture a racial generalisation—bad taste though it be to do so—I would suggest that on the whole the Chinese prefer to know what is being done and who is doing it to whom, whereas by comparison the Japanese are willing to be unsure. Such ignorance, or rather non-knowing, is not exactly to be described as bliss, but seems to be regarded as a spiritual or aesthetic condition distinctly superior to ordinary wisdom.

Snow Country is distinctly superior to *Thousand Cranes*, I should think. If Kawabata is to be prized as a psychologist and more particularly for his female psychology, then there is more interesting psychology and more particularly female psychology to be found here. If he is to be prized as a stylist, as a prose writer in the tradition of *haiku* (those open-ended poemlets), then there are more *haiku* and more interesting ones to be found here. The plot is thin, even emaciated, and concerns a love affair (though 'love' is not quite the word, nor is 'affair') between a dilettante from Tokyo and a hot-spring geisha. (p. 192)

[Perhaps] the most vivid presence in this novel is that of the snow country itself. Sensitively and adroitly as Kawabata conveys sensuality in inter-human relationships, the relationship between humans and nature is more strongly and more interestingly sensual here—as in *Thousand Cranes*, it may seem, is the relationship between humans and art objects. Human effort goes to waste, men and women are like the dew which soon dries up and vanishes, but the snow country endures. This novel ends—or open-ends—as cryptically as *Thousand Cranes*, but on a firmer note. Though Shimamura is nothing, Komako, usefully or not, is something, is alive. She is probably one of the best, most engaging, most touching, female portraits in Japanese fiction—outside that written by Japanese women. (pp. 193-94)

> *D. J. Enright, "The Japanese Novel: Yasunari Kawabata" (1969), in his* Man is an Onion: Reviews and Essays *(reprinted by permission of The Open Court Publishing Company, LaSalle, Illinois; © 1972 by D. J. Enright), Open Court, 1972, pp. 190-94.*

The Sound of the Mountain is particularly successful in evoking the atmosphere of the home in Kamakura and the moods which affect Shingo. In line with Japanese tradition, Kawabata uses natural phenomena to suggest not only the changing seasons but also the feelings and fears of the characters. Rain, wind, flowers and trees, even the food various members of the family buy and eat are made to play their parts in reflecting what is going on in the minds of the participants. Similar use is made also of minor incidents, as when a mongrel bitch who has attached herself to the household has a litter of puppies beneath the house.

This is very much a Japanese novel, and some of the nuances may well be lost on people who do not know the Japanese scene and do not fully understand the nature of Japanese social and family relationships. Kamakura, for instance, means so much more to those who know its geography and history. Some help can be, and, indeed, is given by footnotes dealing with items of life peculiar to Japan—e.g. the kotatsu is explained as "a quilt covered frame over a sunken brazier for warming the extremities"—yet the difficulty with explanations like this is that they may sound strange or even meaningless.

> *"Head of the Family," in* The Times Literary Supplement (© *Times Newspapers Ltd., 1971; reproduced by permission), August 20, 1971, p. 987.*

Japanese tea gardens are seldom large, but many elements in them conspire to give you a sense of spaciousness and to keep you from racing through them. The stepping stones, for instance, are often of irregular sizes and shapes, and they are placed so as to impede your progress. You are forced to pause for an instant, look up and enjoy a particular view.

The narration of "The Lake," a short novel which the Nobel Prize-winning Kawabata wrote in 1955, is full of similarly artful hesitations. Moments that any other writer would have dropped or speedily summarized are dilated and returned to again and again. This curious method of composition is not just a trick but rather the book's way of getting back to the specific moment, the exact play of light, the precise details of a dream or the inexplicable flash of violence that shivers through a lover's romantic daydreams—the original sensation, not the falsifying, simplifying recollection of that sensation. . . .

Language . . . and our traditional modes of writing, force us to lie about what we have felt at any given moment. A tale, any tale, gathers random atoms of experience into coherent, structured molecules of narration. Kawabata doesn't lie, and that is why his books are hypnotic and shocking.

He is is especially shocking in his treatment of those contradictory impulses which are usually abstracted and harmonized into an unreal sentiment called love. In "The Lake" Kawabata plunges "love" into an acid bath in which it disintegrates into its constitutents of vanity, lust, an itch for adventure and an old, inconsolable ache to be whole, to be fulfilled by someone else. . . .

Circles upon circles of memory, coincidence after coincidence, innocent themes followed by their sinister, scarcely audible overtones and echoes—all the effects Kawabata has achieved function like filters slipped over a light until it acquires the precise psychological hue and density of the present, which, after all, is inevitably colored by the past, by repetition, by accidentals. So present is this book in its hallucinatory descriptions and relaxed but terrifying dialogue that the reader is surprised, in looking back through its pages, to realize it is not literally written in the present tense.

[With its] juxtaposed qualities of beauty and terror . . . "The Lake" is as compact and immense, as natural and contrived, as the ideal tea garden. (p. 7)

> *Edmund White, in* The New York Times

Book Review (© 1974 by The New York Times Company; reprinted by permission), June 23, 1974.

Beneath the shining surface of *The Lake* there is an underlay of erotic intimations and dimly perceived happenings, which are designed themselves to coax the reader into voyeuristic participation. Delicately, Kawabata explores the feelings of an old misogynist who is seeking the eternal woman, the compassionate mother; he lays bare the greed and deceit of a woman servant conspiring to win for her daughter their mistress's lover; he describes the revenge plotted by a spiteful young woman determined to get back at the man who stole her youth. This dredging of the sexual depths is at once so intriguing and sordid, poetic and allusive, that one senses here the presence of an intensely Japanese, yet universal, master of the erotic. (p. 25)

Susan Heath, in Saturday Review/World *(copyright © 1974 by Saturday Review/World, Inc.; reprinted with permission), July 27, 1974.*

[Kawabata's] fiction seems to be most valued in Japanese for those qualities that are most difficult to render in translation: precision and delicacy of image, the shimmer of haiku, an allusive sadness and minute sense of the impermanence of things. . . .

Kawabata possessed a delicate sense of the tie between victim and criminal, the kinship of guilt. And of the kinship of sex and death, which the artist, in whatever deformed guises, labors to transcend through art itself.

Lance Morrow, "Kinship of Guilt," in Time *(reprinted by permission from* Time, The Weekly Newsmagazine; *copyright* Time Inc.*), July 29, 1974, (p. 66).*

Yasunari Kawabata's last novel [*Beauty and Sadness*] is a consummately skillful arrangement of space and stillness, a brush drawing of love and vengeance not ultimately convincing, but perhaps ultimately not meant to convince. Yet the novel's measure is that its most fascinating feature may be the face of the writer bleakly regarding the reader from the dust jacket. . . .

Kawabata's face is that of a man who has indeed reached an ending, and speculation, though idle, is unavoidable. In what seems to be the only unguarded paragraph in the book, Kawabata's hero, a middle-aged writer, wryly asks his wife the proper retirement age for a novelist. The novel itself is an answer: it is time to stop writing when there is nothing left but professionalism. . . .

What is unsatisfactory about [this novel] is not that it rings false, but that it does not ring at all. The final appalling scene is meant to strike a gong, but there is no resonance, no reverberation. The characters and their pain disappear from the mind with the turn of the last page.

John Skow, "Sound of No Bell Ringing," in Time *(reprinted by permission from* Time, The Weekly Newsmagazine; *copyright* Time Inc.*), February 24, 1975, p. 65.*

Why [Kawabata] committed suicide . . . is unknown, but it is in character that [his] admiration of French Impressionism as it took root in Japan, his delight in young love, and his brooding death are the distinguishing elements in his posthumous novel [*Beauty and Sadness*].

The story embraces five characters, and it begins when Oki, a successful middle-aged novelist of Tokyo, is on his way to Kyoto with the sentimental hope of hearing the New Year's bells with Otoko, the girl he seduced twenty-four years ago and never forgot. She was fifteen at the time of their passionate affair, and when their baby died at birth she attempted to kill herself. After a slow recovery she began to paint, and is now an established artist in the Japanese Impressionist tradition.

Otoko shares her guesthouse on the grounds of an old temple with Keiko, a girl of astonishing beauty with a talent for swift, abstract canvases. Keiko is fiercely devoted to the older woman; she knows of the early tragic love affair and out of jealousy will exact revenge by seducing either the novelist or his immature son.

The beauty of the novel comes from its lovely descriptions of the flower paintings and of Otoko's portraits, which are in contrast with Keiko's impulsive abstracts such as the undulating green impression of the tea plantation. The suspense arises from the relighting of the old love and from young Keiko's relentless tantalizing: she is daring, and her murderous impulse flares up repeatedly.

Much of the story is told in dialogue, translated by Howard Hibbett in a manner that is quite true to life. But these people talk around and about; they repeat themselves to the point where the reader yearns for them to decide. It is a mark of Kawabata's genius that what one remembers is Keiko's painting of the plum blossom, the soothing summer evening on the balcony of Ofusa's tea house, the famous old stone gardens of Kyoto, the classical beauty of Japan as it is embodied in the dignity of the heroine, Otoko. (p. 144)

Edward Weeks, in The Atlantic Monthly *(copyright © 1975 by The Atlantic Monthly Company, Boston, Mass.; reprinted with permission), March, 1975.*

["Beauty and Sadness," Kawabata's last novel,] is the most consciously plotted of Kawabata's works and explores the relationship of art to life; it is a tale of fearful asymmetries and a terrifying nemesis, an inexorable linking of beauty and sadness. (p. 3)

Kawabata was nearly always a painter, most memorable perhaps for the interplay of red and white, rich and shimmering, that marked "Snow Country" and the "House of the Sleeping Beauties" and for the opposing black and red that moved through "Thousand Cranes" like a dialectic. "Beauty and Sadness" is explicitly concerned with painting, yet its colors are muted, and its predominant image is that of a stone garden.

This last novel is distinguished by purity, supreme clarity of line and sustained elegiac tone. It is cold, in many ways, colder than "The Master of Go," and all the more disquieting for that, since it is a tale of passionate love. This is not Kawabata's sensuous best, certainly not his richest work, but it is endlessly provocative to the mind and, as is everything else he wrote, original, indisputably his own. In such a case, why quibble? Kawabata was a writer of rare intensity. Reckoned by word count, his output was small.

His self-imposed silence is final, which means that the little we have is all that we shall have, and very precious. (p. 4)

A. G. Mojtabai, in the New York Times Book Review *(© 1975 by The New York Times Company; reprinted by permission), March 2, 1975.*

["Beauty and Sadness" is a] dark flower from the delicate hand of the 1968 Nobel Prize winner—his last work before he committed suicide, in 1972. Gloomy, stiff, and suffused with an occasionally intolerably lush eroticism, this somewhat inaccessible (to Western readers, at least) novel perches like a butterfly on the undulations of emotion emanating from a famous middle-aged writer; his former mistress; a beautiful, amoral girl who is now the ex-mistress's protégée and lover; and, to a lesser extent, the writer's wife and daughter. There are many exquisitely visual passages, showing the continuing strong influence that Kawabata's early interest in painting had on his writing; sometimes it seems that a splendid pageant is taking place when all that is happening is that someone is lifting a teacup. More often, however, the endless spate of rich kimonos, serene mountains, elegant sunsets, and sombre stone gardens and temples tends to overwhelm the few tortured, lost souls that inhabit this strange, frozen book. (pp. 125-26)

The New Yorker *(© 1975 by The New Yorker Magazine, Inc.), March 17, 1975.*

*   *   *

KENEALLY, Thomas   1935-

Keneally, an Australian Catholic novelist of Irish ancestry, has written eight novels. His most recent novel, *Blood Red, Sister Rose*, will undoubtedly establish his international reputation.

A Dutiful Daughter is a disquieting novel and in many instances a moving one—qualities which testify, above all, to Thomas Keneally's skill in using to his advantage a subject which in less capable hands might have looked merely grotesque, or even ridiculous. Not that the grotesque is in short supply—for two of the four principal characters have been afflicted by a horrific physical metamorphosis which has left them half animal, half human.

Barbara and Damian Glover have kept secret their parents' sudden, inexplicable change into what might best be described as bovine centaurs. Damian, now at university and beginning to find a life outside the terrible emotional claustrophobia in which his sister remains trapped, is becoming increasingly divided between a concern for his parents' plight and a need to break away from them, and from an obsessive relationship with his sister. Barbara, meanwhile, tends to her parents much as she might tend ailing cattle, although her commitment to them is more than filial. . . .

The parents are, as it were, kept from us in the opening stages of the book, though we know something of their suffering, and this cleverly organized suspense leaves us almost fearing their appearance. They remain for some time offstage: heard but not seen; and we are given shocking (because almost specific) details by way of frightening props—the medication Barbara is preparing for her mother, for example, has instructions which read: *"Dispose of infected bedding . . . aborted foetuses . . . and afterbirth by deep burial in quicklime."* But more than anything, it is the

sense of the quotidian, of the impossible accepted as fact that lend the book its own bizarre credibility. The story seen as fable or metaphor—though that is obviously part of Mr. Keneally's design—seems not to overwhelm the characters, nor leave us hunting symbolic meanings in every turn of events. The second-person narrative gives the impression that Damian is being addressed by the narrator—or more probably addressing himself—and the accusatory (or self-accusatory) tone mellows, at times, into a sort of bemused recollection which fits precisely the painful, hopeless approximations to normality of the whole family. The success of the book lies in that tone—in the way tragedy, black comedy and emotional chaos are made to reside in acts of simple concern.

"Horses for Courses," in The Times Literary Supplement *(© Times Newspapers, Ltd., 1971; reproduced by permission), April 23, 1971, p. 465.*

One of the soundest laws of modern literature goes like this: novelists with the most damned consciences tend to write the most blessed prose. On the lengthy roster headed, of course, by James Joyce, Thomas Keneally supplies another case in point.

Like Joyce, Keneally once studied with a view to the priesthood. Joyce could not decide whether to define hell as Dublin or the nuclear family. Keneally agrees with Joyce about the family. His alternate hell seems to be his native Australia, and like Joyce again, he takes his hell both ways.

In *A Dutiful Daughter*, Keneally creates a presumably commonplace family—the Glovers—plunks them down on an isolated outback farm, and pronounces the scene his ninth circle. . . . Observing that "absolutely millions of people" are mad with "family pride," he concludes that "the only way for them to get humility is through learning they're—you know—beasts." Accordingly, like a Greek mythologist with the heart of a gloomy seminary student, Keneally makes original sin literal by turning Father and Mother Glover into bull and cow from the waist down.

This violent act of surrealism accomplished, Keneally continues as if nothing had happened. He has the special power of a poker-face comedian telling a gallows joke. Father and Mother Glover, for instance, spend their perfectly average evenings kneeling on all fours before the telly or pawing over a *Reader's Digest*.

Beside this terrible banality, Keneally's suggestion that family is another name for incest seems positively matter-of-fact. Further Keneally theories: an exceptional child is doomed to play Joan of Arc—martyr—to parents, who compulsively burn as witch that truthful spirit in the child that sees the beast in its elders and, worse, announces it. "Parents, for all their preaching and threats, turn out to be the children," the remarkable Barbara observes. This freedom to speculate, Keneally may be saying, is the only freedom.

How does a martyr escape from family, from original sin, even from Australia? Like Joyce & Co., Keneally is better at seeing the trap than seeing a way out. "We're cemented, you, me, them," Barbara cries. In the end, Keneally looses a Jehovah-like flood on the outback and the Glovers, washing himself clean of his creation. But in the meantime, writing like an angel, he has forcefully raised an ancient question: What is the demon in man that so often makes him a monster to those condemned to love him—including himself? (pp. 95-6)

Melvin Maddocks, "Family Circle," in Time *(reprinted by permission from* Time, The Weekly Newsmagazine; *copyright Time Inc.), June 7, 1971, pp. 95-6.*

Strictly speaking, heresy is dead, but its contentious spirit lingers in Thomas Keneally's work. *A Dutiful Daughter* is the boldest expression yet of his war against moribund doctrine and its crippling of living religious faith. He has stopped writing within the system, so to speak, as he did in his previous novel, *Three Cheers for the Paraclete*—where his spokesman was a sardonic young priest—to take an imaginative leap well over the parish wall. Where earlier Keneally's quarrel with the Church was revealed in civilized, scholarly rumination, now he exalts it to an almost apocalyptic vision, a modern Book of Revelation. His indictment of the Church's sclerosis takes on a grander sweep, a sharper urgency, through the symbolic acts and images available to him in the parable mode.

The narrative is modeled loosely on the Christian legend of redemption, the course of the savior who assumes the suffering and fate of man, including, in the author's view, his carnality. If we are to be restored to human wholeness, our animality must be accepted without a sense of sin and admitted to the province of divine grace. More radical still, he bestows the attributes of the Christ figure on a woman. "A woman . . . is a state of crucifixion." . . .

[Keneally tells us] that, in the face of our evolving knowledge (as, for example, Freudian sexual concepts), the old rules are less than human, with their legacy of guilt, fear, shame, and a bigoted spiritual pride. . . .

To call this book a "Catholic novel" is limiting. For one thing, such a description could scare off whole ranks of readers, which its intricate artistry deserves. Keneally has written a sophisticated, robustly high-spirited version of the modern crisis of faith. The fierce, original geography reminds us that these dilemmas have too long been confined to the gloomy tunnels of city streets. Like another Catholic existentialist, the philosopher Gabriel Marcel, Keneally's theme is not naïve optimism but hope as an affirmation of a state that is yet to be. Even to nonbelievers, this stimulates irresistible directions for speculation. (p. 52)

Muriel Haynes, in Saturday Review *(copyright © 1971 by Saturday Review, Inc.; reprinted with permission), July 24, 1971.*

In the kitchen of a small farm in an Australian approximation of Yoknapatawpha County, astigmatic, intense Barbara Glover prepares a syringe of antibiotic. Students of analogy will note the echo of "barbarous" in her first name and, perhaps, excavate from the family name as muffled "lover." Thomas Keneally is constructing a complex fable, and the reader must keep his wits about him in case he muffs a level of meaning. And Barbara does throb with thwarted sexual energy. But, then, Mr. Keneally might have named her at perfect random; one of the characteristics of his sustained exercise in the baroque is a diabolical ingenuity, and it is sometimes difficult to ascertain, amongst the flux of startling words and events, what is significant and what is not. . . .

This spirited expressionist performance has stylistic affinities with American high Gothic (e.g., Djuna Barnes and Jane Bowles) and thematic ones with James Purdy's parent-child fable, "Malcolm," though Mr. Keneally's tale lacks the stark outlines that characterize the fable as a mode. He offers an embarrassment of symbolic riches, and his prevailing Firbankian archness sometimes effects a tinkling queasiness of tone. One doesn't know whether one is cued in for a belly laugh, a nervous giggle or a shudder of horror.

The book's immense undertow of tormented sexuality is often expressed in a rhetoric that puts a strain on the predominant narcissistically decorative prose. The style is in subtle conflict with the Buñuelian woes of puritanical Catholicism, pubertal disorientation, unnaturally prolonged virginity, exacerbated frustration and sexual guilt, that are the monsters typified by the half-beasts Barbara hides in the byre with their television, knitting and tobacco.

But the novel sticks in the mind . . . because [of] the remarkable surreal vision of the father, the bull-man, . . . running through the little town, "a fable, a figure of speech, an accident, groping beneath genuinely municipal lamp posts." The metamorphosis itself is self-sufficient. It is authentically marvelous; one may provide the symbolic underpinning as one pleases from the wealth of material provided. (p. 53)

Angela Carter, in The New York Times Book Review *(© 1971 by The New York Times Company; reprinted by permission), September 12, 1971.*

For solid performance every time out, [one of] the best of [the] Catholic novelists is also the youngest, Thomas Keneally. He has built up his vision of a world "between-gods," with patience and growing economy, through six novels: "The Place at Whitton," "The Fear," "Bring Larks and Heroes," "Three Cheers for the Paraclete," "The Survivor," and "A Dutiful Daughter." The last is best; it puts the Cheiron myth to better use than Updike had, takes Joan of Arc's witchcraft more seriously than either Shakespeare or Shaw did, and details nightmare in daylight realistic style without any reliance on Kafka. ["A Dutiful Daughter"] is an extraordinary book in every way. (p. 20)

Garry Wills, "Catholic Faith and Fiction," in The New York Times Book Review *(© 1972 by The New York Times Company; reprinted by permission), January 16, 1972, pp. 1-2, 14-20.*

Perhaps a mild disappointment . . . awaits admirers of Thomas Keneally, Australian author of the much-praised *Chant of Jimmy Blacksmith*. With *Blood Red, Sister Rose* he has chosen to explore the Joan of Arc legend, producing a novel that, while always accomplished, seems in the end several degress less than memorable. To put it crudely, the problems with using a very familiar story as a basis for a novel is that, knowing to one's bones how it's all going to end, one expects so much from the getting there: some extraordinary insight, perhaps, or a marvellously exciting retelling of the familiar tale . . . anyway something pretty special. Mr Keneally has had the nice idea of making his warring knights converse in the idiom of Mafia mobsters, and he is sharp on the class-distinctions operating in 15th-century warfare (for the knights a courtly game, for the peasantry a brutal slaughter). But still, finally, that something special isn't quite there. (p. 513)

> *Peter Prince, in* New Statesman *(© 1974 The Statesman & Nation Publishing Co. Ltd.), October 11, 1974.*

[The] novels of the Australian writer Thomas Keneally seem to grow rougher in style and more eccentric in substance as he gains in experience. The awkwardness of his earlist work was the kind you expect from any first novelist. Through those that followed—*Bring Larks and Heroes, Three Cheers for the Paraclete,* and *The Survivor* (good books, all)—there was an orderly development of narrative skill, and his work gradually assumed a certain professional polish. With *A Dutiful Daughter,* Keneally's work took a strange and very original turn . . ., the book featured animal metamorphoses and sudden irrationality, and was surely one of the oddest books in a decade of odd books. And while there was nothing so very bizarre in the story of Keneally's superb next, *The Chant of Jimmie Blacksmith,* the author seemed to do all he could to subvert the strong narrative of his novel—and to do so quite consciously. It seems he doesn't wish a narrative to come between himself and his reader: Thomas Keneally has an absolute horror of being understood too quickly. . . .

Although Keneally takes Joan [of Arc] seriously enough—she is [in *Blood Red, Sister Rose*] neither the witch that Margaret Murray made her out to be, nor quite the firebrand that Bernard Shaw portrayed—this does not mean that he takes her solemnly. His intent, in fact, seems to be to reduce her and her legend to recognizably human dimensions. Jehanne, as he refers to her (in the interest, I take it, of historical accuracy), is very much the peasant girl as the account begins—though never quite what you would call a simple peasant girl. Cow-herding, milking, working in the fields—none of this is much to her liking: she has yearnings for a grander life. When she is only 13 and her "voices" begin, she is delighted for she knows they will set her apart and suspects they will grant her entry into the great world to which she has always aspired. . . .

She is somewhat intimidated, if not finally appalled, by her prolonged exposure to warfare. As practiced in the 15th century, it is a game—but a deadly one whose carnage gives *Blood Red, Sister Rose* its most real moments.

There is some irony in this, for Thomas Keneally seemed determined to write a sort of antihistorical novel, one that would expose the pettiness of war's political basis—at least that of the Hundred Years War. He would expose the royalty and the nobility as no more than silly. He would present war in its bookkeeping details. In this way, the book dithers along for the first 200 pages, through a lot of chatty nonsense. . . . It comes almost as a surprise then, that two-thirds of the way through the novel, Keneally's narrative suddenly roars into life as he describes the separate battles fought to lift the siege of Orleans. It is as though Keneally could suppress his story-telling instincts no longer. His high intentions are brought low by his successful story-telling.

What were those high intentions? To expose war as the most vain of human vanities because the most destructive. Just as strong, though less explicit, seems to be his wish to attack the sainthood of Joan, the religious commissar of all French forces. Keneally, an ex-seminarian, is no doubt disturbed—just as you or I or any thinking person should be—that history (sacred history, at that) accepts it that the Divinity should actually have mucked about in French politics through the agency of some deluded adolescent. The longer you think about it the more absurd it becomes. Which accounts, I suppose, for the willful absurdities of *Blood Red, Sister Rose.*

> *Bruce Cook, "Suspicions of Sainthood," in* Book World—The Washington Post *(© The Washington Post), January 26, 1975, p. 3.*

Thomas Keneally's new novel [*Blood Red, Sister Rose*] is a version of the Joan of Arc story, and interesting enough for the amount of information—whether fact or lore—that has gone into it, and for the imaginative reconstruction of the horrors of 15th-century warfare. The characterisation of Joan—Jehanne—is unusual. A sexually abnormal peasant girl, her life in *Blood Red, Sister Rose* is as blood orientated as even so bloody an age could provide for. . . .

That the book has pretensions to being more than an 'historical novel' is evident from the sanguinariness and the preoccupation with political management: we are meant to learn something about the price of power and its unchanging nature. But it does not get beyond being an excellent historical novel—not quite in the Mary Renault class, perhaps, but a match for Helen Waddell or T. H. White. What imprisons the book is the Keneally trade mark—the use of modern, and transatlantic modern, colloquialism for dialogue. But you cannot help enjoying it, for all that. For one thing, the narration is not a first person monologue—believe me, a rare pleasure these days. (p. 190)

> *Neil Hepburn, in* The Listener *(© British Broadcasting Corp. 1975; reprinted by permission of Neil Hepburn), February 6, 1975.*

We all know the story, the big scenes: the Voices, the Dauphin's court, Orleans, Rheims, Rouen, the pyre. . . . It would seem foolhardy to attempt to revive these worn tales again. Yet Australian novelist Thomas Keneally has done it and carried it off with aplomb. [In "Blood Red, Sister Rose,"] Saint Joan lives again, robustly, in a way we have not known her before. . . .

Portrayed here is the brilliant, doomed, gala day of the mock king, who must pay the price when the sun goes down. The institution of mock kings and temporary kings is familiar in many cultures and has been well documented by Frazer in "The Golden Bough." "Blood Red, Sister Rose" recasts the Saint Joan legend within the framework of this broader tradition. The result is startling and, at the same time, amazingly plausible. . . .

Keneally's Jehanne, alone, is supple and fully dimensional. She is, at times, sharply nostalgic for the world of ordinary loves and lives she must leave behind. . . .

The story is a tragedy, yet "Blood Red, Sister Rose" is a romp. Queen Yolande, giving the go-ahead for presentation of the girl at court, is reported to have said: " 'Although such people always abound in times of emergency it could be useful to have a prophetess on the staff . . .'." Accordingly, a subcommittee is set up for validation of the girl's virginity. When Jehanne fends off a common soldier who is making a pass at her, she reminds him of her Voices and says: "God help any man who has me." He is properly unimpressed and replies "You only want to sleep with knights."

Irreverent? Not in the final analysis. For none of this diminishes Joan. It ennobles her sacrifice by making it real. (p. 7)

A. G. Mojtabai, in The New York Times Book Review *(© 1975 by The New York Times Company; reprinted by permission), February 9, 1975.*

The original legend of Joan of Arc was all ethereal voices and uprolled eyes. George Bernard Shaw's *Saint Joan* suffered from an opposite flaw: a 15th century French farm girl with 19th century English socialist leanings, she seemed all pragmatism and muddy boots.

Between this Joan-too-spiritual and that Joan-too-earthy, a third Joan has been waiting to be born. In his eighth novel, Australian Thomas Keneally, who once studied for the priesthood, slowly and thoughtfully reconstructs a whole Joan, less spectacular than the first two but decidedly more convincing and perhaps, at last, more moving. . . .

At her simplest level, the Keneally Joan can be very simple indeed—obstinate but rather dull with the protuberant brown eyes of a cow: "Looking at her, you nearly went to sleep." She is an object of manipulation. The knights wave her like a banner to win battles. The "fat clergy" cash in those victories as new ecclesiastical revenue. The Dauphin, of course, uses her to gain his crown. Keneally graphically savors the irony of this visionary innocent ("our little he-nun") ending up in the midst of disemboweled and headless corpses, moving from battlefield to bloody battlefield in the company of assassins, whores and lice.

But this clownish dupe, Keneally also knows, finally outmanipulated all her manipulators. To Keneally she is the incarnation of an idea whose time had come—the peasant striding into the council of kings and lords of the church. As rude as common fare, she serves notice on the feudal system that knighthood is no longer in flower. As she lifts the siege at Orléans and pushes her balky Dauphin with the "fat, unhappy lips" toward his coronation at Rheims, she is hurrying onstage not a monarchy but the modern nation-state. The descendants of this Joan are the bourgeoisie.

But the Joan that ultimately fascinates Keneally is Saint Joan. To him, her voices are as real as she is. Why not? Keneally's world of 1420 is full of voices—from all sorts of prophets, astrologers, witches. Every oak grove is "enchanted timber." *The Golden Bough* seems to coexist with the Gospels on these pages, finding common ground in the ritual of sacrifice. From the first, Keneally's virgin, who never even menstruated, is predestined to shed blood as scapegoat for her unworthy King. "All she wanted to do." he sums up, "was achieve her own victimhood."

Were the voices then holy or demonic? It depends on who is listening, Keneally seems to say. But if he has no new answer, he has a new question. His Joan—part battle flag, part rebel and part saint—adds up to a heroic surrogate for the absurd and contradictory in Everyman, "the feel of the frayed edges of all the world's foolishness coalescing in her guts." Is her mystery, he asks, harder to explain than the mystery of any reader's life?

Melvin Maddocks, "Joans of Arc," in Time *(reprinted by permission from* Time, The Weekly Newsmagazine; *copyright Time Inc.), February 10, 1975, p. 76.*

Australian novelist Thomas Keneally's revisionist portrait of Joan of Arc [*Blood Red, Sister Rose*] retells the conventional story from an ironic viewpoint that dares surprising omissions and emphasizes the profane dimensions of a doomed adventure into spirituality. The novel attends dramatically to "Jehanne's" sieges of Orleans and Rheims, but ends with the coronation of the ridiculous Dauphin, thus made Charles VII of France. Only in an epilogue is there mention of "the witch's" capture, inquisition, and martyrdom.

Keneally concentrates on the formation of his heroine's bewildered sensibility. . . .

The novel's organization reflects an unsuccessful search for a parallel structure that will convey the reduction of otherworldly aspirations to a muddle of banality. . . .

How purity burns itself up in the lower air of mundane intrigues: that is the point. But the point should never have been allowed to dominate, much less replace, a story whose pristine internal logic demands that it be told to its conclusion, or not at all. (p. 12)

Bruce Allen, in Bookletter *(copyright 1975 by* Harper's Magazine; *reprinted from the March 31, 1975 issue by special permission), March 31, 1975.*

*   *   *

KEROUAC, Jack   1922-1969

Kerouac was an American novelist and poet. Along with Ginsberg, Burroughs, and others, he was also an original member of the group which, in the middle 1940s, became the Beat movement. Kerouac's own work was an effort to "invent a new prose," specifically American, which was to reflect in its spontaneity and formlessness the vastness and beauty of this country. (See also *Contemporary Authors*, Vols. 5-8, rev. ed.; obituary, Vols. 25-28.)

Jack Kerouac's *Visions of Cody* is at once an epitaph and a rhapsodic celebration of the American beat world of the late 1940s and early 1950s. A long, voracious and uneven novel, it is an important addition to his published work, though for any but the initiate or aspiring novice it is a book to be left well alone, or blasted through at a single sitting. Never previously published in its entirety, it has been known only as an underground legend. Kerouac wrote the novel between 1951 and 1952, immediately before *On the Road*, which itself waited five years before its publication in 1957.

Both books deal with the same hero and the same period. Cody Pomeray is Neal Cassady of *On the Road*, but whereas the later book is a fairly straightforward example of the American picaresque, *Visions of Cody* is a much more ambitious, much more revealing, and probably a much more honest book. Certainly it makes the symbiotic relationship between the narrator, Jack Duluoz, and the beat hipster, Cody, a good deal clearer. Kerouac's admiration for the restless energy and raw egocentricity of Cody is at root that of the American college dropout's respect for the real thing. . . .

Cody, son of a Denver drunk, brought up homeless and motherless during the Depression years, . . . and living as a youth among society's misfits and outcasts, was dispossessed from birth. . . .

That Cody, born into this world, should be able to act at all is what Kerouac celebrates. The will to fulfill the self through sex, pot, peyote, jazz, and a total acceptance of the moment, are not for Cody, as they are for Duluoz, part of a gesture, a rejection the American dream turned sour. . . .

Kerouac, the compulsive recorder of his chosen world, calls the book his "record of joy", but time is the enemy of the arch-Romantic. "Whenever I realize I'm going to die, I no longer can understand the meaning of life." Movement, however frenetic, leads only to death. "All you do is head straight for the grave, a face just covers a skull awhile. Stretch that skull-cover and smile." The split between Kerouac's twin roles as celebrant and elegist is never resolved. Ever contradictory, he is at one moment full of love and tenderness, and the next adopting the stance of the quintessential American male chauvinist. . . . Yet the novel is repeatedly shot through with the pathos of Kerouac's desperation, and marked by moments of self-recognition. . . .

Self-indulgent? Yes. But not pompous or self-regarding. Kerouac's naivety, his unawareness of his own charisma, are virtues. . . . Kerouac was no prophet; he was a suffering, self-destroying talent, desperately attempting to encompass his experience, his America, by recording its losses and its ecstasies, an heir of Whitman without his genius.

> *"Hobo Concerto," in* The Times Literary Supplement (© *Times Newspapers, Ltd., 1973; reproduced by permission), November 2, 1973, p. 1333.*

The best that can be said of Jack Kerouac's posthumous *Visions of Cody* . . . is that it contains some very fine writing and gives as convincing and detailed a portrait of a complete love-friendship between two men as we have in American literature. Unfortunately, the perhaps seventy-five pages of fine writing makes up less than a fifth of the book; a painful amount of the rest is taken up by tape transcriptions of drunken conversations between Kerouac and Cody. . . . Moreover, Kerouac and his admirers thought that Kerouac was Huck Finn—boyish, compassionate, fleeing big bad society armed only with his charm and his zest for life, sweetly sad that others could not be as naturally good as he. And it is true that the best passages of *Visions of Cody* could have been written by a Huck Finn jaded into the twentieth century. There are tenderly passionate character sketches of persons seen only fleetingly, prose denunciations of the worst aspects of American Life, the insights that became the clichés of the protest movements of the sixties. But mostly, what emerges is a portrait of a couple of latter-day Tom Sawyers—con artists oblivious to the hurt they inflict on others, inflating their own egos and deflating others, chortling over their own cuteness, crying over self-inflicted wounds, constantly reopening the wounds that were not self-inflicted. Despite the impression Kerouac tries to give—that the beats were beaten by modern American middle-class establishment philistine bourgeois materialism—we see Kerouac and Cody beaten by their arrogance, by their pretensions to

wisdom when they lack even elementary common sense. (pp. 88-9)

> *Lee T. Lemon, in* Prairie Schooner (© *1974 by University of Nebraska Press; reprinted by permission from* Prairie Schooner), *Spring, 1974.*

[Although] many readers of *On The Road* have thought it a modern version of the picaresque, its structure is formidably complex. Here is no loose scribbling of notes whose only organization is geographical and chronological, but a delicately constructed account of the relation between the narrator, Sal Paradise, and his friend, Dean Moriarty—an account built according to a classic dramatic design. *On The Road* is a love story, not a travelog (and certainly not a call to Revolution). It is told with all the "art"—the conscious and unconscious shaping of verbal materials—one expects from the best writing. Kerouac may legitimately be, even on the basis of *On The Road* alone, a great American author—an author the equal of Mailer himself. (pp. 200-01)

The book begins with the narrator's construction of distinctions and boundaries; it ends with his discarding them—a discarding which indicates his desire to suspend opposites in a perhaps continuous state of flux. The book moves from hierarchy to openness, from the limitation of possibilities to their expansion. (p. 201)

One of Kerouac's accomplishments in *On The Road* is in fact to unify the open ending (in which all points of view in the novel are combined without being resolved) with a time-honored novelistic and dramaturgic structure. (p. 202)

> *George Dardess, "The Delicate Dynamics of Friendship: A Reconsideration of Kerouac's 'On The Road',"* in American Literature *(reprinted by permission of the Publisher; copyright 1974 by Duke University Press, Durham, North Carolina), May, 1974, pp. 200-06.*

Though [Kerouac's] writing seems loose and colloquial, careless, written on the run, its influence—and the influence of his personality imprinted in it—entered the stream of American life and literature and rushed it to unexplored possibilities. The Kerouac "charisma," as Seymour Krim called it, affected individual writers like Norman Mailer and helped mobilize literary movements like the San Francisco Renaissance. More pervasively, his charisma reached out to a wide and dispersed group of adorers who pursued him years after his immediate fame had dimmed. To them he was the legend he imagined himself: their fantasies and his coalesced. . . . The constant confusion inherent in his wild cross-country circuits—futile except for their ultimate conversion into fiction—his depression, dependence, and self-destruction reached pathological intensity. That he became a legend in this time tells us that his pathologies were not private. They had, and continue to have, cultural relevance: they are part of a shared vision; and what must disturb us in that vision are the political implications of an exemplary life that seemed rebellious and exhilarating, and ended in inanition. (pp. 415-16)

What about him inspired a generation of followers to idealize him as a rebel of social and political meaning? Was it because he told how he did not like the "mean old cops" he encountered on the road? Or that he did not like sub-urban houses and TV sets—though proud of having bought both for his mother? Was it because he liked Krazy Kat, hiding in an alley with a brick for the cop? But that, pat-ently, is childish social criticism. When infrequently he faced political problems straight on, he resolved them by simple and sudden intuitions that "everything would be all right." It just would. (p. 416)

Political commitment assumes the possibility of power, and through power, of change. Kerouac lived with a profoundly defeated sense of helplessness, reflected in his prolonged, or rather his unending, adolescence. He had an appalled vision of life as empty, meaningless, and futile. His readers saw him as a modern Whitman affirming life and beckoning them to its open roads. But his obverse side was nihilistic, and his refrain that of Beckett—born to die. In a late book, *Vanity of Duluoz*, he gave his testament to the young, a message from Ecclesiastes: "No 'generation' is 'new.' There's 'nothing new under the sun.' 'All is vanity.'" From his very first book, *The Town and the City*, with its image of a dying fish hooked and suffering, he sought meta-physical support for his personal sense of helplessness. He believed we were all victims, born victimized by "meta-physical causes," as he called them in *Vanity of Duluoz*—yet simple and obvious causes: that we were born to die. Believing this, he was relieved of social responsibility and could justify his "apoliticalness"; since the causes of suf-fering were beyond help, there was nothing anyone could or need do.... He valued energy, went after "the wild ones," as he said in a famous passage in *On the Road*; he gambled on his energy and won for a while—and then lost. He died at the age of forty-six. His life raises troublesome questions about the fate of energy in America and of art committed to energy. Like Jackson Pollock, with whom I find many affinities, he tried by sheer energy to vitalize his art, to force life and art into union.... Kerouac attempted an impossible coalescence of life and writings, and he did as well as anyone. That, I think, is his appeal, that his books, even the weary ones like *Tristessa*, reach us immediately, sometimes confuse and even alienate us, but always imme-diately, as if the person in his complexities and his childish-ness were there. This effect of immediacy comes in part, I believe, very strangely from the sense of helplessness the books convey. They start usually at the end of his story, when he stands depleted by the experience he is about to recount. Life and fiction merge, and he is trapped, moving in a circle from the experience he pursued in order to have something to write about, which having been captured, leaves him with nothing except something to write about. And there he is before us, writing. (pp. 417-18)

Kerouac believed in a mimetic art. He sought a language and a form to give shape to "shapeless experience," exper-ience as he found, made, and conceived it. But I believe that shapelessness is an *illusion* he created through a dis-cernible and definable form he gave his novels. (p. 419)

Regressive, narcissistic, dependent, and neurotically hostile towards those upon whom he depended, Kerouac has, nev-ertheless, the power to possess us still as once he possessed his generation. We share with him a sense of loss; and day by day nowadays, that loss becomes sharper and more poignant as the dream of America recedes like his dream of innocence. When energized, he vitalized us by his romantic vision of movement, experience, ecstasy, and transcend-

ence. When tired and worn out, as often he was, he tells us the romantic dream is delusive, and the open road, "a nightmare place." Like Beckett, a much greater writer, with whom he shares a vision of nihilistic despair, he found himself gripped by the compulsion to write; and through his books, as through Beckett's, the human voice persists and reaches us: that is [one] secret of the immediacy of his art. In her biography [*Kerouac: A Biography*], Ann Charters reminds us to listen to this voice, for it spoke of American dreams hopes, and defeats. Through his voice, going on incessantly from one autobiographical novel after another, Kerouac established his style. That style has both ener-gized and depleted us—and disturbed a generation. We, too, suffer its disturbance. That is why we must look at it ... deeply ...—to see how in the past it possessed us as an adolescent dream, and how in the future we can move beyond it to responsible maturity while possessing still its vision of freedom. (pp. 421-22)

Blanche H. Gelfant, "Jack Kerouac," in Contemporary Literature (© *1974 by the Board of Regents of the University of Wis-consin System), Vol. 15, No. 3, Summer, 1974, pp. 415-22.*

[Although] the continuing communal stream ... did largely spring from the fountainhead of [Kerouac's] "spontaneous bop prosody" sagas, his real-life sentences were penned in solitary, born of suffering, alienation, and an idealism as genuine as that of his beloved Thomas Wolfe. He rejoiced in the writing, like anyone who sweats to join others to-gether, but he harked back constantly to the theme of modern man in search of a soul—articulating the common loneliness hitherto more often celebrated in American folk-song and spirituals, and in the cry of jazz and blues.

Coleridge distinguishes between Mechanic, and Organic "Form as Proceeding"; Kerouac's forms are of the latter kind, emanating directly from his personal experience with a strong oral bias and phenomenal recall....

[In her biography, *Kerouac*, Ann Charters] confirms that *The Subterraneans*, which I've always taken to be his most honest and revealing testament, writ in three nights, to chronicle his tempestuous affair with a black girl for whom he eventually proved too soft, "was closest in its desperate-ness and vulnerability to the way Kerouac actually lived." For all his anti-intellectualism he was pretty badly stuck in the impotent grooves of the 'white negro'; and yet his real love of the dark sun of America comes across, paradoxi-cally, as effective literature—which has since catalysed diverse upheavals for the better, in observation that was typical and accurate for all that it was vastly sentimen-tal....

It's not as a mystic or prophet or spokesman that I value him ..., but as a compulsive writer who insisted on laying down his vision of reality, bleak as well as exultant; beatific in squalor, he uniquely held his mirror to the nature he saw and knew. With Dylan Thomas before him, Bob Dylan unsuspected ahead, Kerouac was essentially a word-magi-cian and a bard: but ... being constitutionally incapable of either running with the radical commitments of his imme-diate poetic peers, or staying within the limits of even the newest open verse forms, he kissed the leper of prose—and cured it! His purity is what was unique. Insofar as he pro-jects himself, it's hardly the spectacle of a man attaining wisdom, but rather all the awkward complexity of a weak and puritanical/average-sensual seeker after truth, declaring his quest with a kind concern and compassion for the people he encounters on it—not forgetting the reader; hence presaging the renaissance of authentic human communion looked for by that other late-lamented jazz-poet, Kenneth Patchen: "Men were made to talk to one another. . . . The writing of the future will be just this kind of writing—one man trying to tell another man of the events in *his own heart*." And hung-up though he was on his 'legend,' Kerouac was saved by a fine excess of inspirational energy from wasting his words to polish a monument, carve an acceptable image or jostle with literati for reputation. His heroism was not in the 'holy goof' who sadly, in the closing chapter of his life, seemed to degenerate into almost a caricature of rednecked lush-hood: it lay, even then, in sticking to his last: whatever happened (and a helluva lot did, in his forty-six short years) "bringing it all back home," from travels and travails to notebook and type-writer, 'artificial aids' notwithstanding.

> *Michael Horowitz, "Those Were the Daze," in* The Spectator *(© 1974 by The Spectator; reprinted by permission of The Spectator), August 10, 1974, p. 181.*

Jack Kerouac is . . . mawkish enough for a whole literature and *Maggie Cassidy* . . . is a book fatally flawed by Kerouac's single-minded devotion to his own passions. He employs that familiarly incantatory prose which has won the hearts of Eng. Lit. students everywhere, and in this story of awakening adolescence it summons up squads of emotion with code-words like "tragic," "brooding," "sad," "alone," "incredibly" to much the same purpose and with much the same effect as Pepsi glamourise their Cola.

It was a prose which worked magnificently in *The Town and The City*, a first novel which showed the depths to which Kerouac could aspire as a romantic novelist, but in *Maggie Cassidy* it is a weaker and looser thing, becoming so loose, in fact, that it connects with no 'reality' other than the wayward burst of Kerouac's sentiment. It is quite in character that the novel should be dominated by Kerouac's ulterior ego, a snivelling French Canadian known somewhat archly as Jacky Duluoz, and the narrative is much concerned with his secret passions, his sporting prowess, his first love and his delayed maturity. The titular heroine hardly gets mentioned, and becomes yet another sacrificial victim to Kerouac's pathetic and abandoned sense of chronology.

Maggie Cassidy is indeed a pallid book, casting post-impressions like dried petals and capitalising hugely on the universal and sympathetic attractiveness of 'first love'. Every event and every character is mediated through Kerouac's reverent but gaseous memory and the narrative is interesting only if you happen to find Kerouac interesting. When he forgets about his own emotions, the prose reverts to that low and monotonous hum which is characteristic of generators waiting to be utilised. His occasional genius lies only in expressing the most conventional emotions and the most conventional impressions with an exuberance that makes them apparently his own, but they remain stubbornly unoriginal for all that. The depths of this book's [particular] solipsism can be measured in the fact that large areas of dialogue are altogether pointless and unreal. The book falls apart into a number of fine and memorable phrases which I have, unfortunately, already forgotten. (pp. 246-47)

> *Peter Ackroyd, in* The Spectator *(© 1974 by The Spectator; reprinted by permission of The Spectator), August 24, 1974.*

When Jack Kerouac died was it that we felt it was the end of an era or we felt we ought to feel it was the end of an era the day that Jack Kerouac died? . . . It's like the end of an era, we said and we had to mark it, like lighting bonfires on the year's shortest day to warm the world back to life, to stop it going any further into cold and darkness. What's kerouac? the uni students said when I talked about getting a room for free to hold the wake. We'd had readings against the war and readings against censorship, now we would have readings for seasons of the year, a reading for kerouac, or the winter solstice. (p. 65)

What's kerouac? Kerouac is a registered code name, like Kodak® or Coca-cola®. It is a magic incantation. It represents the out, the other, the away. . . . I'm reading *On the Road* . . . and lying in bed . . . holding my kerouac, that's what it is, a talisman. (pp. 65-6)

> *Michael Wilding, "Bye Bye Jack. See You Soon," in* Stand *(copyright © by Stand), Vol. 16, No. 2, 1975, pp. 65-6.*

*   *   *

KINNELL, Galway   1927-

Kinnell, an American poet, novelist, and translator, delighted critics with a long Whitmanesque poem, "The Avenue Bearing the Initial of Christ into the New World," in his first book and his reputation as a superior lyric poet, "the only one who has taken up the passionate symbolic search of the Great American tradition," has continued to grow. (See also *Contemporary Authors*, Vols. 9-12, rev. ed.)

The poetry of Galway Kinnell . . . is an Ordeal by Fire. It is fire which he invokes to set forth his plight, to enact his ordeal, and to restore himself to reality. It is fire—in its constant transformations, its endless resurrection—which *is* reality, for Kinnell as for Heraclitus: "The world is an ever-living fire, with measures of it kindling and measures of it going out.". . . The agony of that knowledge—the knowledge or at least the conviction that all must be consumed in order to be reborn, must be reduced to ash in order to be redeemed—gives Galway Kinnell's poetry its astonishing resonance, the accents of a conflict beyond wisdom as it is beyond piety: "I don't know what you died of," one of the characters in his novel says, "whatever it was, that is what will bring you alive again." (pp. 259-60)

The fire opens Kinnell's first book, where it is seen benevolently enough as the vital energy of earthly things:

> *Cold wind stirs, and the last green*
> *Climbs to all the tips of the season, like*
> *The last flame brightening on a wick.*
> *Embers drop and break in sparks . . .*

The sense of the self-consuming candle as the characteristic avatar of flame is one that will remain with Kinnell to the end—as in *Black Light*, where he speaks, about to blow out the candle, of "the point of the flame, that shifting instant where the flame was turning into pure spirit." (p. 261)

The ecstasy of knowing oneself a part of the world's *physis*, of knowing that within oneself there is the same pulse on which "the world burns," the radiant interchange between mind and love, between body and earth, between water and fire, is [in "Alewives Pool"] registered in Kinnell's happiest key, when Being is so wrought up in its oneness of possibilities—"the air flames forth"—that a man's "days to come flood on his heart as if they were his past." (p. 263)

By his ransacked, purified, literally inflamed imagination, Kinnell is able to ransom his world, having reached in his most sustained effort ["The Avenue Bearing the Initial of Christ into the New World"] that place where everything which is is blessed.

It is no easy thing to write a sequel to the apocalypse, and one feels, often, about Kinnell's second book, *Flower Herding on Mount Monadnock*, something of the strain, the broken impulse that commands the versification as well as the patchy moments of pyrophany. . . . By the time he gets to the title poem at the end of this short book, Kinnell has earned for himself what he says of Villon in the introduction to his "factual, harsh, and active" version: "He writes in a passion for reality and a deep anguish at its going . . . it is a cry not only over the brevity of existence and the coming of dark, but also over this dying life, this life so horrified by death and so deeply in need of it." In the final section of "Flower Herding," a ten-part journal of natural devotions, Galway Kinnell makes his penultimate accommodation of the life that is being consumed in the fire —it is an accommodation so transfigured that it can be expressed, finally, in a few simple declarative sentences, the ecstatic constatation of the death that is in being, the being that is in death. (pp. 266-68)

Humbled, reduced, but reduced in the sense of *intensified*, concentrated rather than diminished, life, having passed through what Arnold called "the gradual furnace of the world," life for Galway Kinnell becomes a matter of sacred vestiges, remnants, husks—as he says in his third book of poems published in 1968, *Body Rags*. (p. 268)

In these poems of astonishing metamorphosis, Kinnell has been concerned to enact, by his "dance of solitude" as he calls the shaman's performance in "The Bear," to articulate the truth of Goethe's great dictum: One learns nothing, but one becomes something. Ever larger in these late poems bulks or—for bulk is not what we get, but rather a flickering ballet around the circumference of what is guessed at in the darkness—breaks in upon us the awareness that in order to achieve transformation the ritual imagination of burning must in our time be abjured for a natural process, with all its attendant waste and weariness: "our faces smudged with light from the fingertips of the ages." (p. 269)

Richard Howard, "Galway Kinnell," in his Alone With America: Essays on the Art of Poetry in the United States Since 1950 *(copyright © 1965, 1966, 1967, 1968, 1969 by Richard Howard; reprinted by permission of Atheneum Publishers, New York), Atheneum, 1969, pp. 258-71.*

In the decade and a half since his first book appeared, Galway Kinnell has emerged as one of the most powerful and moving poets of his generation. His is an elementary poetry—a poetry of dark woods and snow; of wind and fire and stars; of bone and blood. His subjects are perennial: love illumined and made more precious by the omnipresence of death. . . . Kinnell has posed the most anguished of all our questions: "Is it true/the earth is all there is, and the earth does not last?" If it does not, it can still be irradiated and somehow made sacred, if not by God then by the poet. (p. 24)

Patrick Keane, in The New Republic *(reprinted by permission of* The New Republic; © 1974 by The New Republic, Inc.*), July 27 & August 3, 1974.*

Galway Kinnell attained early fame with his very ambitious poem "The Avenue Bearing the Initial of Christ into the New World", which is still arguably as good as anything he has written. It reminds one of Crane and early Lowell in its sonority, but more of "The Waste Land"—if, indeed, of anything in literature—in its ability to include a seething cauldron of urban sensations, of randomness and ugliness, yet hold its own poetic shape. What it lacks is an underlying vision or concern, beyond mere awe at the weight of humanity, the "instants of transcendence" and the "oceans of loathing and fear." At the rare points where it tries to conceal this lack through rhetoric, the poem becomes abruptly stagey. Both the strengths and the weaknesses here are prophetic for Kinnell's later work. He continues to have the most over-vaulting and Marlovian style of his contemporaries, but it is a double-edged advantage, since his share of the generational directness, and his personal fondness for metaphysical clichés, make any hamming more obvious, and less likely to be mitigated by surrounding beauties, than it would be in a poet like Crane. On the other hand, his later poems succeed in uncovering the real feeling behind the Avenue C poem and making it, itself, the subject. It is the sense of a violent, impersonal, unseemly energy behind life, stunning the ego and bringing both "transcendence"—because it makes a continuum of the personal self and the cosmos—and "loathing and fear," because it is inseparable from the threat of change and death, "the pre-trembling of a house that falls." In poem after poem, Kinnell resuffers one identical ordeal, accepting death in order to be able to accept life, and concomitantly— like his Thoreau in "The Last River"—accepting cruel appetites in order to accept his full animal being, and avoid a crueller sado-masochistic spirituality. At times the acceptance seems as negative as that, at least; but at other times it has its own special serenity, as at the end of "La Bagarede", where "the seventh / of the Sisters, she who hid herself / for shame / at having loved one who dies, is shining." Kinnell's form has not altered substantially since his second book, just as his central experience has not. It is a sequence of generally very short, always numbered free verse units; the isolations somewhat take the place of rhetoric in conferring a brooding intensity on details; and the poet is free to move quickly from himself to nature to vignettes of human life, while keeping our primary attention on the pattern that moves us into terror and out again into some form of resolution. Kinnell's poetry has a very narrow range of purely personal experiences. He can really handle only those that directly touch on his cosmic vision— passionate love, being with the dying and the newly born, political imprisonment in the South—but of these he writes extraordinarily well (offhand, at least, "Under the Maud

Moon" seems as good a poem about the first year of life as I have read). But one looks in vain, in Kinnell's poetry, for the personal roots of his own vision and his repeated self-trial; though I am struck by the recurring theme of self-hatred, the special self-hatred of the large man presumed to be brutal by others, to be imprecise and blundering by himself—as it appears, for instance, in his feelings about his size at birth ("It was eight days before the doctor / Would scare my mother with me"). But I have dwelt too much on limitations, not enough on what makes the poetry convincing or overwhelming—the moments of stunned sensation in which human beings turn into force and object, and nature into embodied metaphysics, before our eyes.... (pp. 63-4)

> Alan Williamson, "Language Against Itself: The Middle Generation of Contemporary Poets" (copyright © 1974 by Alan Williamson), in American Poetry Since 1960: Some Critical Perspectives, edited by Robert B. Shaw, Dufour, 1974, pp. 55-67.

Galway Kinnell is a man who hungers for the spiritual, who has no special capacity for spiritual apprehensions, who has been culturally conditioned moreover to resist the very disciplines that might have opened him up to the spiritual apprehensions he hungers for. By writing poems which thrash in and out of the impasse thus created, Kinnell has made a great reputation—which suggests that there are many readers who are walled up in the same bind, and ask nothing better than to churn and agonize within it. (p. 9)

It is very hard to see what "Jesus" or "Christ" signifies for Kinnell. So far as I can make out, it means in his mouth roughly what it means in the mouth of a Unitarian. But it really would be nice to know. And until we do know, his making so free with it cannot but seem—and not just in the eyes of Christians—an unpardonable vulgarity. (p. 17)

No poet can be blamed for his inability to make the act of Christian faith. But what one can ask of any such poet is, first, that the impediments to faith be real, substantial, and such as to command respect; second, that having declared his incapacity for the sacramental and incarnational act of the imagination in the forms inherited from his own culture, he should be wary of pretending to make those acts in the terms presented by cultures that are not his at all; and, third, that he should not, having turned his back on the Christian dispensation, continue to trade surreptitiously in scraps torn arbitrarily from the body of doctrine he has renounced. On all three counts, whereas an honest atheist like Hardy is in the clear, Kinnell stands convicted. For in the first place, in both of the poems which most explicitly deny the validity of the Christian Incarnation (in "Easter" its invalidity is already taken for granted), the case is argued through the experience of a child; and in at least one of those cases, "First Communion," the objections are appropriately puerile, a misplaced matter-of-factness, materialistic and indeed mercenary. The claims of Christianity are nowhere in Kinnell brought to the bar of an adult intelligence. On the third count, ... Kinnell continues to import a religiose fervor by tossing the name of Jesus around. But it's on the second count that the case against him is most flagrant and most far-reaching, since it's something that he shares with many other poets of his generation. (pp. 17-18)

[It's] obvious that poetry composed for or at "the podium"

must be, as compared with poetry for the solitary reader, loose in weave and coarse in texture [Kinnell has said that most of his revisions were made, impromptu, while reading to audiences.] So it is in "The Avenue Bearing the Initial of Christ into the New World." Certainly the poem is powerful, certainly it is inventive, yes it is keenly observed; but inevitably for the solitary reader it telegraphs its punches, as when, needing to allude to the Nazi extermination camps, it can do so only by printing in full a blank form announcing death over the signature of a Camp Commandant.

Kinnell may mistake this point, and his admirers certainly will. We are not asking for more beauty and less power, or for feelings that are tenuous and fugitive rather than those that are vehement; we are asking for feelings that shall be tracked with scrupulous and sinuous fidelity, rather than a general area of feeling expansively gestured at. (p. 20)

> Donald Davie, "Slogging for the Absolute," in Parnassus (copyright © by Parnassus: Poetry in Review), Fall/Winter, 1974, pp. 9-22.

Galway Kinnell [is] truly rural (and therefore good on cities).... [He] began with a keen gratitude to William Carlos Williams, about whom he wrote a bad poem (its humor curdles to sarcasm), and likewise with a gratitude to Frost (ditto), and so to the most enduring of his gratitudes, to "the mystical all-lovingness of Walt Whitman."... Whenever Kinnell is doing the hushed bated-breath thing, all portentous self-attentive first-personry ("I wake in the night," or "I sit listening/To the surf"), the importance comes on as winsome self-importance, or "Song of My Self-Importance." The cosmic browbeats the comic. Yet ... there were fine poems in which self-importance, the intelligent exclusion of humor, was dramatically right because the poems were about rapt young lovers and how they manage temporarily to exclude so much and are fearful of humor....

The best of Kinnell, which is very good, comes when he resists the expected humorlessness of rural-piety poetry (which often disguises its humorlessness behind wisps of whimsy), and when he is not claiming to be either a sensitive plant or a sarcastic cactus. There are such penetratingly humorous poems as the parable, half-town and half-country, "Indian Bread"; or the gruff aggrievedness of "Duck-Chasing"; or the teeming townscape, humane, fascinated and therefore fascinating, of "The Avenue Bearing the Initial. ..."; or the miniature country vignette, "Spring Oak" ..., a tiny industrious earthquake, committing itself to the spring and revealing itself, all with affectionate banter and without any of the pomposity which the American Mother Earth sometimes gets from her poetic children....

Galway Kinnell is in the direct Whitman line. (p. 2)

> Christopher Ricks, in The New York Times Book Review (© 1975 by The New York Times Company; reprinted by permission), January 12, 1975.

The Avenue Bearing the Initial of Christ into the New World is one of the most vivid legacies of [The Waste Land] in English, building its immense rhetorical power from the materials of several dialects, litanies of place, and a profound sense of the spiritual disintegration that Eliot divined in modern urban life. And like Eliot's, Kinnell's is a religious poem, in which the chaotic forces of survival (in this instance, the turbulent, jumbled life of New York's lower East Side, along Avenue C) ultimately preside over the terror latent in our late stage of civilization. Since it is impossible to isolate any single passage from the magnificent sprawl of this poem, I can only suggest its importance by stressing that my comparison of it to [*The Waste Land*] was intended to be less an arbitrary reference than an effort to estimate the poem's durable achievement.

The very early poems of his apprenticeship distinguish themselves from most such offerings in the quality of their feeling, their naturalness and depth of insight. Kinnell is in possession of a gift that so few poets have now, with their emphasis on subdued, laconic diction. Almost any stanza from his first two books yields the fierce vision refined later on. . . . (pp. 301-02)

There is a wonderful variety in [*The Avenue Bearing the Initial of Christ into the New World: Poems 1946-1964*]; reading through them all at once, one becomes aware of how much he has struggled to exercise his imagination, writing out of the deepest sources of contemplation, sketching in the temper of an afternoon with a few fine strokes, recording his immense love of the texture of experience, awaking in a forest "half alive in the world", and knowing "half my life belongs to the wild darkness". As a companion to the diffuse and dream-like experiments of *The Book of Nightmares* and *Body Rags*, the publication of a Selected Poems is well-deserved; what is so remarkable is that these earlier poems should constitute in themselves such a major work. (p. 302)

> *James Atlas, in* Poetry (© *1975 by The Modern Poetry Association; reprinted by permission of the Editor of* Poetry), *February, 1975.*

* * *

KOCH, Kenneth 1925-

Koch is an American poet and playwright almost as well known for his advocacy of teaching poetry writing to elementary school children as for his own fine work. Koch, together with John Ashbery and Frank O'Hara, was a principal of the "New York School," a group of poets working in the middle 1950s to transcribe the essence of "abstract expressionism" in painting for poetry. (See also *Contemporary Authors*, Vols. 1-4, rev. ed.)

George Washington Crossing the Delaware . . . [is] the funniest play I have seen this year. (p. 236)

I have a feeling it's the funniest play by an American in a lot longer than that. Oh, and a very indigenous play, one about which Birchers and beats can agree, or at least break bread at. For while it is a parody, or set of interlocking parodies, the purest kind of fantastic innocence—such as probably prevailed at the birth of our nation and such as still prevails on the level of presentation at high-school patriotic pageants—continually warms the scene, that décor of cut-out boats, horses and guns and those costumes of splendid sashiness, tri-corned *élan* and big-buttoned spirit-of-'76 which Alex Katz has designed so brilliantly.

You see, Koch really loves George Washington, the way we are supposed to but can't until all the parodiable elements are worked through and burned away. The play is the recovery of a childlike vision of American origins and one strain of our persisting reality, the child having been helped to see freshly through the sharp wits and memory for eras of language of the adult looking over his shoulder, the one who prompts the actors to mock Shakespeare, the diction of masques, melodrama, Barbara Frietchie, cigarette ads, Max Lerner and Fulton Lewis, Jr. And the distortion that emerges, the verbal and visual minor miracle, is of the order of Picasso's women, truer than the mirror, or of Kafka or Beckett when their language moves into the most uncomplicated yet primally mysterious play.

So then, if you want to hear Cornwallis say wonderingly of the father of our country that "he walks as he rides!" or of the British cause that "love makes it right," if you want to hear the Redcoats pray "If only we could win him over to our side!" and hear George himself declare that "We have nothing to fear but death" and then settle back for a nap with a murmured "Goodnight America"; if you want to see "democracy in action . . . actuality exemplified in a military situation"—I strongly urge you to cross the Delaware, or whatever river separates you from the play. . . . No better investment around at any price. (pp. 236-37)

> *Richard Gilman, "'George Washington Crossing the Delaware'" (1962), in his* Common and Uncommon Masks: Writings on Theatre 1961-1970 *(copyright © 1971 by Richard Gilman; reprinted by permission of Random House, Inc.),* Random House, *1971, pp. 236-37.*

Koch's position in modern poetry is not easy to determine. It may help to begin by pairing him with a long-established older poet to whom his relations are obviously close enough in some respects, and absurdly distant enough in others, to be instructive. In part he is one of those "literalists of the imagination" who are commended by Marianne Moore in a well-known poem and whose principles are exemplified in her own work. Like Miss Moore, Koch is fond of making poetry out of poetry-resistant stuff. Locks, lipsticks, business letterheads, walnuts, lunch and fudge attract him; so do examples of inept slang, silly sentiment, brutal behavior and stereotyped exotica and erotica. . . . But Koch never submits [any] kind of phenomenon to any Moore-like process of minute and patient scrutiny. He is eminently an activist, eagerly participating in, rather than merely observing, the realm of locks and fudge. And if, like Marianne Moore, he is always springing surprises, he does not spring them as if he were handing you a cup of tea. Her finely conscious demureness is not for him. For him, the element of surprise, and the excitement created by it, are primary and absolute. In short, "life" does not present itself to Kenneth Koch as a picture or symbol or collector's item. "Life" talks, sighs, grunts and sometimes sings; it is a drama, largely comic, in which there are parts for everyone and everything, and all the parts are speaking parts. . . .

Apparently Koch is determined to put the reality back into Joyce's "reality of experience," to restore the newness to Pound's "Make it New," while holding ideas of poetry and of poetic composition that are essentially different from those of the classic modern writers. In his attempt to supersede—or transform—those writers, Koch has drawn upon far-flung sources. They range from Kafka to certain recent French poets (including Surrealists), to Whitman, Gertrude Stein, William Carlos Williams and others in the native book. . . .

[He] will flee the sunlight of approved poetic practice, staking his poetic chances on whatever wonders may turn up in the wet weather ("rainways") of *unapproved* poetic practice. He will talk to himself, improvise, consult his dreams, cherish the *trouvaille*, and misprize the well-wrought poem.

Such, as I make it out, is Kenneth Koch's unprogrammatic program (or a part of it), and the calamitous possibilities in it are obvious. Like the similar program of certain of the Beats, it could turn the writing of poetry into a form of hygiene. It could and does: some of Koch's efforts, like many of theirs, suggest the breathing exercises of a particularly deep-breasted individual. . . . Consulting the sybil of the unconscious, he occasionally gets stuck with large mouthfuls of predigested images and with lines of verse that make no known kind of music. . . . And if his verse is sometimes lacking in the delights of a reliable style, it also offers few of the conveniences of a consistent lucidity. To me his idiom is often a Linear B that remains to be cracked. (pp. 10, 12)

> *F. W. Dupee, "You're Welcome," in* The New York Review of Books *(reprinted with permission from* The New York Review of Books; *copyright © 1963 NYREV, Inc.), May, 1963, p. 10, 12.*

Kenneth Koch's first book, published in 1959, is a comic epic (though in fact all epics are comic for they are recounted *at length*, they rest or come to rest in *duration*) called *Ko, or A Season on Earth*. By truncating his own name (one shimmering self indeed), the poet gets his Hero's, conveniently that of a Japanese baseball player. . . . The success of this enormous poem of vignettes —and it will be the success of all Koch's projects, a prowess which marks, which *is* the borderline between accident and will, between hysteria and method—amounts to the tension between the moment of ecstasy and the movement elsewhere; to the pressure built up in the reader's mind—"in nervous patience till the glory starts"—as the result of a promise to remain at the center yet a *practice* of eccentricity. (pp. 282-83)

Having ransacked every genre, every convention, every possibility of outrage and confiscation—"never stop revealing yourself"—Koch has in "The Artist" and in several other uproarious instances ("You Were Wearing," "Locks," "Lunch," "Down at the Docks") produced poems which are entirely *his own*. That is their limitation of course, but it is their great resource too, their great and problematic *interest*, flickering between the intolerable moment and the intolerable movement, the unendurable *now* and the unendurable *next*, an oscillation which, as the poet himself remarks, can conclude only "when Kenneth is dead". . . . (pp. 290-91)

> *Richard Howard, "Kenneth Koch," in his* Alone With America: Essays on the Art of Poetry in the United States Since 1950 *(copyright © 1965, 1966, 1967, 1968, 1969 by*

> *Richard Howard; reprinted by permission of Atheneum Publishers, New York),* Atheneum, 1969, pp. 281-91.

Written over the decade 1953-1962, the brief plays of Kenneth Koch burlesque the occasional pageants of academic or patriotic tradition. The blurb on the cover of his *Bertha and Other Plays* claims that the plays "use and parody a wide variety of theatrical models and traditions." Rather than parody, however, which is mockery of a specific work or author, Koch's plays are burlesque, containing a wider mockery of a genre or style. (p. 310)

Koch is an able mocker, but his targets are limited—history, legend, patriotic and contemporary clichés. His wit is of cabaret quality, depending on brevity and expert timing. So far, none of his plays has the sustained drive of a *Knight of the Burning Pestle* [a Restoration drama ascribed to Beaumont and Fletcher] or *Critic* [a satire by Sheridan]. As in his equally witty and more imaginative volumes of poetry, Koch runs the danger of repeating his own facility. (p. 312)

> *Ruby Cohn, "Kenneth Koch," in her* Dialogue in American Drama *(copyright © 1971 by Indiana University Press), Indiana University Press, 1971, pp. 310-12.*

In Kenneth Koch's "The Postcard Collection," there is little pretense at surface "realism"; but a convincing personality is evoked, by sheer powerful concentration on exposed nerves and agitated emotions. The "collector" tries to decipher literal "truths" from unintelligible messages scribbled on postcards. He's naggingly conscious that he's a poet, and may be "reading too much in." Do people try to give a formal order to their lives, he wonders, by preserving in "messages" certainties that fail to apply in their lives? Or is this only the delusion of the literary man, who cannot see straight "reality" in its unruly simpleness? It is quite a trick, to render this confusion between the Self and the World so affectingly—while relying so nakedly on the viewpoint of "the artist." Koch is a marvelous, fluidly graceful writer. (p. 121)

> *Bruce Allen, in* The Hudson Review *(copyright © 1974 by The Hudson Review, Inc.; reprinted by permission), Vol. XXVII, No. 1, Spring, 1974.*

*   *   *

KOTZWINKLE, William   1938-

Kotzwinkle is an American novelist and writer for children. (See also *Contemporary Authors*, Vols. 45-48.)

Here it is only March, man, and we already have the funniest book of 1974. [*The Fan Man* is] the story of Horse Badorties, man, a fellow who says man a lot and who has a lot to say to any man. . . .

Horse Badorties is obviously an unusual person. So also must be William Kotzwinkle who has invented Horse in this short, artfully structured, supremely insane novel about a freaky quasi-Hindu-shmindu brahman who is one with the ridiculously filthy, worn-out world. It is Buddha's story turned inside out, glopped up and set in Manhattan, notably the East Village where Horse's ever-shifting shit pile is situated.

Kotzwinkle's artistry is such that you take the allusions to Buddhism and Hinduism for granted as merely arcane tidbits from the weird, eclectic Horse Badorties speech pattern. But the fan obsession, man, begins to form a religious pattern of its own. . . .

And so as Horse gallops along through his densely packed realm we perceive him not as another Ginger Man, which at times he seems to be, but as a lowest-level saint of dreck and yecch, a holy man climbing up from the oily, filthy bottom muck of Central Park lake, following Buddha's path, lugging a red, white and blue hot dog umbrella to protect himself, moving toward a cosmic consciousness of all things. (p. 32)

Wearing one Japanese, one Chinese shoe, uncoding the Tibetan Book Of The Dead and dealing Acapulco produce via Colorado, Horse walks into American literature a full-blown achievement, a heroic godheaded head, a splendid creep, a sublime prince of the holy trash pile. Send congratulations to William Kotzwinkle, also a hero, man.

This must be Kotzwinkle month. Since the above was written, two more Kotzwinkles have surfaced, one new, one three years old. The new one is highclass porn, *Nightbook*, a paperback original, and the old one is new in paper, a collection of stories: *Elephant Bangs Train*, published first in 1971. Neither book has anything like the impact of *The Fan Man*, which though short and episodic is nevertheless ambitious and cohesive. But both new ones are erratically funny and *Nightbook* is nifty dirt. (p. 33)

> *William Kennedy, "Horse Badorties," in* The New Republic *(reprinted by permission of* The New Republic; © *1974 by The New Republic, Inc.), March 2, 1974, pp. 32-3.*

William Kotzwinkle holds the minority opinion that sex can be funny. Amid the sex education mania that has already slowed United States population growth to zero, this novelist is a prophet of the ludicrously lubricious. Small wonder that ["Nightbook"] contains recurrent references to Demeter, goddess of fertility. Kotzwinkle characters are plugged directly into the life force, albeit subject to frequent short circuits.

"Nightbook" is something of a parody consisting of alternating ancient and modern episodes—all dirty. The author throws around references to Herodotus, Plutarch and Homer, although his real antecedent is visibly Henry Miller. Semiramis and Artemis rub elbows, etc., with 42nd Street peepshow girls and contemporary freaks. In his mingling of the scatological and the mythological, Kotzwinkle is into legends that might have surprised Bullfinch. He doesn't seem to know Ishtar from Aphrodite, or, for that matter, Sophocles from Aristophanes. No matter. There are plenty of classical scholars, but there's a scarcity of earthy, Demetrian humor. (p. 38)

> *Martin Levin, in* The New York Times Book Review *(© 1974 by The New York Times Company; reprinted by permission), March 17, 1974.*

The only thing interesting about William Kotzwinkle's lame "Exultate! Jubilate!" from what seems like the pre-dawn age of lower-East Side hippiedom is how he manages to get so many "man"'s ("And here, man, beneath a pile of wet

newspapers is a shirt, man, with one sleeve") onto every page [of "The Fan Man"]. On page 69, there are fifteen, but the jackpot is probably page 126, with twenty-three. (p. 142)

> *The New Yorker (© 1974 by The New Yorker Magazine, Inc.), March 25, 1974.*

William Kotzwinkle has other celebrants, and is felt by many to be on a leading edge of American fiction. For my part, I think [*The Fan Man*] is so cute it could hug itself. (p. 129)

> *Richard Todd, in* The Atlantic Monthly *(copyright © 1974 by The Atlantic Monthly Company, Boston, Mass.; reprinted with permission), May, 1974.*

William Kotzwinkle's *The Fan Man* is a modishly bizarre offering that comes both admired by Kurt Vonnegut, Jr. and professing admiration for Kurt Vonnegut, Jr., but nevertheless does contrive its own engaging brand of egocentrically crazy talk. Talking is Horse Badorties, man (every sentence, man, has 'man' in it somewhere, man), a special kind of junkie, zestfully piling his pads with garbage and sheet music. . . . [The] novel scrapes into redemption, just, through its hero's loving-hating involvement with New York City. . . . *The Fan Man's* energetically disposed reflections on urbanity will at least earn it a footnote in someone's thesis on city fiction. (p. 871)

> *Valentine Cunningham, in* New Statesman *(© 1974 The Statesman & Nation Publishing Co. Ltd.), December 13, 1974.*

*   *   *

KROETSCH, Robert   1927-

Kroetsch is a Canadian novelist, short story writer, and poet. (See also *Contemporary Authors*, Vols. 19-20.)

Robert Kroetsch's three novels, *But We Are Exiles* (1965), *The Words of My Roaring* (1966), and *The Studhorse Man* (1970) reveal an increasingly confident literary personality. . . . [His] assertive view shows itself in the novels as a species of vitalism: Kroetsch's heroes are compulsive actors, doers, drawn into the paradoxes of apocalyptical romanticism, especially in sexual terms. . . . Kroetsch has been aware from his first novel of the duality in his romance of the extreme situation. The drive to freedom is also a quest for death. Whatever the egotistical assertion achieves, it is an ambiguous triumph. This is extended, furthermore, into the artist's relations with his created world. In his Introduction to *Creation* [an anthology he edited] Kroetsch quotes Heinrich Zimmer in *The King and the Corpse:*

> The involvement of the gods in the web of their own creation, so that they become . . . the harried victims of their creatures, entangled in nets of not quite voluntary self-manifestation, and then mocked by the knowing laughter of their own externally reflected inner judge: this is the miracle of the universe. This is the tragicomic romance of the world.

The "harried victim" of his own "creatures", the artist is

mocked by what he makes. The act of creation is a tragic-comic revelation. The "externally reflected inner judge" refers directly to what Kroetsch [has called] . . . "this *doppelgänger thing*"; the romance of assertion, and the grandeur of defiance, are always mocked by the "inner judge". What is surprising . . . is that Kroetsch has evolved so rapidly from the manner of *But We Are Exiles,* where "this *doppelgänger* thing" was a grim wrestling match indeed. Kroetsch's priapic hero has been transformed from the principal in a claustrophobic, inward-turning personal catastrophe, to the fool in a cosmic comedy.

The theme of *But We Are Exiles* is drawn, as the epigraph suggests, from the myth of Narcissus. . . . Even in outline, Conradian analogues suggest themselves, particularly *The Secret Sharer.* The quest for the Other, the river journey motif, and, in the pilot role, the typical Conradian theme of freedom-through-mastery may be noted. (pp. 54-6)

It is not Kroetsch's indebtedness here which concerns me. It is possible that *But We Are Exiles* was his personal Battle of the Books, but, more generally speaking, it is the *moral* opposition the analogues suggest which throws most light on his development to *The Studhorse Man.* For [another] analogue is with Kerouac's *On The Road* or even, perhaps, the frenzied car-drives of [Robert Penn Warren's] *All The King's Men.* The Conrad/Kerouac opposition is between disciplined self-mastery and the ultra-romantic dream of total Experience—that other myth of "freedom" which consists of the repudiation of all law save the egotistical assertion. (p. 56)

The Words of My Roaring offers few easy literary analogues. The questing hero undergoes a significant revision, however, as the scene is shifted from the Mackenzie to rural Alberta. While the mythic structure of *But We Are Exiles* and the large natural symbols of river, sea, and annihilating snow can hardly be ignored, the texture of the prose, even the frequent thought-stream passages, is essentially realistic. But the prose is itself a product of Guy's consciousness: being repressed, cryptic, and unable to respond adequately to the power of the Mackenzie setting. Almost as if he sensed the lost opportunity of his first novel, Kroetsch expressed the expansive, potentially poetic Hornyak-consciousness in *The Words of My Roaring,* abandoning Guy's taut limitations. [Guy is the pilot of the Mackenzie River working boat whose mission in *But We Are Exiles* is the search for the drowned body of Hornyak.] In Johnnie Backstrom, undertaker of Coulee Hill, the priapic hero is now comic. (pp. 57-8)

Self-conscious use of myth is one thing; self-conscious self-parody in the use of myth is another. In [*The Studhorse Man*] Kroetsch has moved from the dramatic fable to the complex and essentially comic "fabulation".

The Studhorse Man is narrated by Demeter Proudfoot, a madman who chooses to spend his time in the asylum seated in his bath-tub. His name, and the device of the "tale told by an idiot", proclaim the assault on realism which persists throughout. . . . While the Narcissus myth provides the central thematic thread of *But We Are Exiles,* the myths of Demeter and Poseidon . . . are fragmented and distorted schemes of reference in *The Studhorse Man.* Their order is mocked as it is utilized. What *is* consistent is a wholesale pattern of recurrence, an unabashed use of coincidence and analogy so that a *sense* of order is implied despite the lack of a binding metaphor. The texture of *The Studhorse Man* is rich and various; what may be suggested here . . . is the manner in which Kroetsch gathers up the threads of his past fiction in this . . . work. (p. 61)

In tracing Kroetsch's progress from fable to fabulation certain conflicts appear. They are embodied—and there is some self-mockery here—in the person of Demeter Proudfoot. The observer sitting in his bath is surely derived from the famous example of Diogenes the Cynic, who took up residence in a Tub best to display his contempt for luxury and the sensual world. For Kroetsch's priapic heroes are seen . . . as essentially absurd questers compelled by the sensual itch yet denied the consummation they so passionately wish. For all the energy and joy of Kroetsch's fictional world, it is realized by a mind which distrusts its own compulsions. As the name Demeter suggests, furthermore, the goddess of fertility and growth becomes, in *The Studhorse Man,* the cause of . . . death and, by extension, the reducer of Poseidon's myth to prophylactic technology. It is a "cynical" conclusion. (p. 64)

> *Peter Thomas, "Priapus in the Danse Macabre,"* in Canadian Literature, *Summer, 1974, pp. 54-64.*

Although Robert Kroetsch is primarily a western writer, he is intrigued by the North. It was the setting for his first novel, *But We Are Exiles,* and . . . in his fourth book [*Gone Indian*], he attempts to encounter fully the significance of this half-real, half-hallucinated northern landscape, this unknowable region where the world is reduced to its basic elements and beyond that to a final void. (p. 103)

Gone Indian is the concluding work in Kroetsch's Out West trilogy, which has now moved from the depression thirties (*The Words of My Roaring*) through the forties (*The Studhorse Man*) into the seventies. Each of the novels in the trilogy deals with the passing of an era, a moment of crisis which forms one more chapter in the history of the Apocalypse: each examines the particular myths by which its society defines itself, wittily interweaving other mythic structures drawn from the larger western tradition, and—in *Gone Indian*—blending in Indian myth as well to form a complexly layered whole beneath a deceptively simple surface.

The title changes that this final book of the trilogy went through suggests the several ways the novel works. The original title, *Funeral Games* (Kroetsch says he abandoned it as "too Graeco-Roman"), invokes Book V of the *Aeneid,* where the funeral games for Anchises celebrated by Aeneas and his men serve as a kind of societal passage rite marking the death of the old Trojan order and the turning toward the yet to be created Roman world. Within the novel the Notikeewin winter games serve a similar function. . . . Kroetsch's second working title, *Falling,* emphasizes the personal aspect of the novel: Jeremy's perception of his life as perpetual falling/failing, and his final realization that falling toward death is an inevitable part of life and that falling is the payment for flying. Finally the title *Gone Indian* (with the intentional ambiguity of "Gone") catches a number of the dominant themes in the book: the North American fascination with and search for the Edenic, pastoral world; the novel's ironic play with urban man's romanticization of the Indian and the lost culture he represents; and finally its very serious play with the Indian trickster myth. (pp. 103-04)

These various levels of the novel work together to say something about the society that Kroetsch visualizes as coming to an end in the seventies: the competitive, technological, highly rationalistic order. . . .

Gone Indian is a fine book, providing a fascinating conclusion to Kroetsch's vision of the development of the Canadian West as emblematic of twentieth century social change. It is a book which should be read at least twice to penetrate beneath its surface, but that is a compliment to Kroetsch as story teller. (p. 104)

> *Russell M. Brown, "Freedom to Depart,"* in Canadian Literature, *Summer, 1974, pp. 103-04.*

*   *   *

KUMIN, Maxine   1925-

Ms Kumin, a Pulitzer Prize-winner, is an American poet, novelist, and writer for children. Her poetry is distinguished by sharp images of closely observed natural phenomena. (See also Contemporary Authors, Vols. 1-4, rev. ed.)

Maxine Kumin's book ["Up Country"] acknowledges its debt to Thoreau, though in my opinion Kumin's poetry gives us a sharp-edged, unflinching and occasionally nightmarish subjectivity exasperatingly absent in Thoreau. The most valuable, because most powerful, statements of the transcendental experience are those rooted firmly in existence, however private or eccentric. . . . The experience of "Up Country's" 42 poems is dramatic and visionary, but above all convincing. (p. 7)

> *Joyce Carol Oates, in* The New York Times Book Review *(© 1972 by The New York Times Company; reprinted by permission), November 19, 1972.*

Mrs. Kumin is no imitator but very clearly her own writer (and a distinctive novelist too). In these poems [*Up Country*] she steeps herself—sometimes adopting the figure of "the Hermit" to intensify the feeling of solitary humanity in the midst of nature—in the actualities of soil, pond, trees, beans, local topography, animal tracks in the snow, an ancient bathtub used for a watering trough, the gravestones of an old cemetery, the variety of insects frequenting a pond, the hundred-and-sixty-year-old markings in an attic, a handbook of simples, and so forth. As John Ciardi says of her accuracy with respect to the reality her poems render: "She teaches me, by example, to use my own eyes. When she looks at something I have seen, she makes me see it better. When she looks at something I do not know, I therefore trust her." That is high praise, and also traditional praise. Many a younger poet at the present time should perhaps be compelled to earn it. (pp. 222-23)

> *Ralph J. Mills, Jr., in* Parnassus *(copyright © by Parnassus: Poetry in Review), Spring/Summer, 1973.*

Wonderment, in these numb and wary times, is a rare response to fiction or to anything else, and Mrs. Kumin's fourth novel, "The Designated Heir," evokes it over and over. So did "Up Country: Poems of New England," which last year won her a Pulitzer Prize. In both verse and prose she brings tastes, sounds, textures, smells and the look of things to vivid life. . . .

"The Designated Heir" abounds with such perceptive distinctions. It is not a novel of much action or wide scope, but its texture is a marvel and its people are so vivid they take up permanent residence in our minds. (p. 10)

> *Jane Howard, in* The New York Times Book Review *(© 1974 by The New York Times Company; reprinted by permission), June 23, 1974.*

Maxine Kumin is a woman who writes like some male writers, specifically like Erich Segal, author of the novel *Love Story*, which was an earlier and highly successful variation on Kumin's theme of love, domesticity and money [in *The Designated Heir*]. Her plot is simple: Can Robin Parks, a highborn Bostonian and the "designated heir" of the title, find happiness with Jeffrey Rabinowitz, a nice Jewish boy from East 62nd Street? The answer is not absolutely certain, although a probable "yes" seems safe. (p. 25)

Maxine Kumin uses a lot of literary devices—sections from Jeffrey's Peace Corps journal; symbol and metaphor applied like band-aids or perhaps tourniquets—to mask the essential banality of her plot. They are not enough. She is fond of words like "argufy" and "horripilate" ("she read still omnivorously, horripilated by modern fiction, yet determined to keep abreast"). She has an unerring eye for the inept simile: "from the rafters vegetables hung down as simply as shoelaces" and "the porcelain cup and saucer rode in his left hand as easily as a sailboat at its moorings," to cite two. She also likes to pass on aphoristic wisdom, better when it comes by way of Thoreau, whom she quotes frequently, than from the author. Here are three examples of hers: "the art of capitulation is grace"; "the real primal scene is the first time you have to be a parent to your parent. The first time you have to be the forgiver"; and, "love means different things to different people." (Lest we forget, love also means never having to say you're sorry, and *pace*, Erich.) When Robin is told, "your head is a bank vault stuffed full of useless aphorisms," the reader cheers.

Such infelicities might not be so surprising in a creative writing student, but Kumin is an experienced, indeed an honored, writer. . . . Clearly she is not an amateur, which is why I read this book twice, thinking, hoping that I'd missed something the first time. But no. I didn't believe it the second time either. *The Designated Heir* is a marshmallow of a book—sticky, sweet and soft in the center, and suitable for roasting. (p. 26)

> *William McPherson, in* The New Republic *(reprinted by permission of* The New Republic; *© 1974 by The New Republic, Inc.), August 10 & 17, 1974.*

L

LARKIN, Philip   1922-

Larkin, an English poet, novelist, critic, and essayist, has been called the finest British poet of his generation. Although he has little in common with Kingsley Amis, Thom Gunn, Donald Davie, Elizabeth Jennings, and the other "Movement" writers, Larkin contributed his well known Wordsworthian poem "Church Going" to Robert Conquest's *New Lines* **anthology and so is often associated with "the Movement." Larkin's brooding meditations, sometimes likened to work by Hardy, are loosely constructed around his personal everyday experiences in his provincial home in Yorkshire. Anthony Thwaite has said that there is an "agnostic stoicism in his work which confronts change, diminution, death with sardonic resignation." (See also** *Contemporary Authors,* **Vols. 5-8, rev. ed.)**

If Larkin is minor, then it must only be because of the small size of his body of work: he has published [few] collections of verse. The first, *The North Ship* (1945), though it contains some good poems, and is certainly worth detailed consideration, is perhaps more interesting as the early work of someone who became a very good poet indeed than for its intrinsic merits. . . .

Larkin is not only a poet: he has written two fine novels, *Jill* (1946) and *A Girl in Winter* (1947). His penetrating and witty literary criticism makes one wish he wrote more—unless it took up time he would otherwise write poems in. . . . (p. 1)

Larkin has been considered by many to be the best of the Movement poets. . . . I cannot agree . . . partly because I think Larkin does not share the faults of the Movement, and partly because Larkin's poetry does not seem to me to be so typical of that produced by the Movement that it may be picked out to epitomise its virtues. (pp. 9-10)

Technically, Larkin is an extraordinarily various and accomplished poet, a poet who uses the devices of metre and rhyme for specific effects, not just because, in Robert Frost's phrase, he likes to play his tennis with a net. His language is never flat, unless he intends it to be so for a particular reason, and his diction is never stereotyped. He is always ready, like Thomas Hardy, to reach across accepted literary boundaries for a word that will precisely express what he intends: into archaism, as in the 'accoutred' of 'Church Going'; into Americanism, as in the 'store-bought clothes' of the recent 'How Distant'; into coarse colloquial, in such phrases as 'books are a load of crap' from 'A Study of Reading Habits'; and even into the extremely uncommon usages of another poet, as in the 'prinked' brasswork of the ships in 'Next Please', a word surely used in the sense in which Hardy uses it in 'Beeny Cliff', where the tops of waves are 'prinked' by the sun.

Larkin has a sympathy with the different that is lacking in the work of many of his Movement contemporaries. (pp. 19-20)

Most important, perhaps, Larkin's attention is not turned inwards upon himself and his art—at least, this is true of his poetry after *The North Ship*. Though . . . twenty-five per cent of the poems in *New Lines* use the words 'poem', 'poet' or 'poetry', Larkin's mature poems do not include any of those words. And this is true of all the poems of *The Less Deceived* and *The Whitsun Weddings*, not just the selection printed in *New Lines*: poetry is his medium, not his subject. The Movement was a valuable force, and from it emerged a body of excellent writing. But Larkin's poetry seems to me better and more important than what was generally produced. (p. 20)

He has said that poetry is 'born of the tension between what [the poet] non-verbally feels and what can be got over in common word-usage to someone who hasn't had his experience or education or travel-grant'. In common with Dr. Johnson, Larkin sees in life 'much . . . to be endured and little to be enjoyed'; and like the blues singer's art, Larkin's poetry mediates between this experience and his audience. His forms are 'traditional' rather than 'modern', though they are various, and unmistakably a full response to contemporary life. (p. 21)

Larkin has written only two novels, *Jill* and *A Girl in Winter*. . . . [It] seems to me that the more worthwhile thing for Larkin to do is to write poems. He is certainly a better poet than novelist, on the evidence we have before us. (p. 36)

Jill is not so much about conflicting social situations, and the stresses attendant on crossing class boundaries, as about our reactions to life and our expectations of it. John [the protagonist] is unable to cope with life when he has no fixed context within which to live. He demands continuity, and fixed objects by which to determine his position. The question, 'How shall I behave?' is always answered for John by reference to his place in a scheme. The lesson he learns is that life's landscape really has no such fixed points, no constant pattern. We cannot expect anything from life because in the end we have no control over it, no more than the trees have control over the way they bend. (p. 43)

Larkin has commented that both his novels are really extended poems: he was careful, he said, if he used a word on page 15, not to use it again on page 115. Certainly, we may criticise *Jill* for being too 'poetical'. Sometimes detail is so fine as to be pedantic, and not at all illuminating. It may flesh out John's background for us to know that his mother tied his sandwiches 'firmly, but not tightly'; but we are no better off for knowing that the apple eaten by the clergyman who shares John's railway carriage as he travels to Oxford is russet, nor that it is peeled with a *silver* pen-knife. In this first novel Larkin was too often lured into description for the sake of showing how well he can do it. Similarly, the young novelist is often carried away into drawing comparisons through similes that in no way advance the story or illuminate the theme. . . . Such similes are striking, but, not being organic, stand out unnaturally from the narrative. (p. 44)

But if Larkin's description of particular objects is sometimes over-precise, it seems that his general presentation of war-time Oxford is less precise than it should be. . . . Though there are many of the real trappings of war-time—black-outs, rations, and so on—many of the events of the novel . . . belong to an earlier, gayer decade. (pp. 44-5)

It is unfortunate, too, that John's character is not consistent. Larkin wanted to present us with a naïve young man, quite out of things in the company of a group of young sophisticates. . . . And yet when he becomes involved with the fantasy Jill, he has a perfect command of the idiom appropriate to a girls' boarding school.

These points are niggling, perhaps in view of the novel's many good qualities. (p. 45)

Like *Jill*, *A Girl in Winter* is a novel about maturing, coming to terms with the facts of our lives, accepting what is real, rather than depending on false expectations to make living worthwhile. (p. 46)

A Girl in Winter is a better novel than *Jill*, largely because of the stylistic improvements on the earlier work. As a story, it is slighter—much more an 'over-sized poem', which Larkin now considers both novels to be. But the prose, in the main, is much sparer. There is still the occasional redundant simile, as when Katherine's vacillating emotions are compared at length to a flock of birds swooping first to one corner of a field and then to another. Really, for a state already fully described, we do not need to be given an explanatory image that adds nothing new. There is much less self-conscious 'fine writing' than in *Jill* [and] Larkin has a firmer grasp of the complexities of character in *A Girl in Winter*. (pp. 51-2)

Larkin's critical writings, mainly in the form of reviews of poets he likes, have outlined the concept of poetry Hardy gave him—a set of beliefs that have remained remarkably constant over the years. The most important of those beliefs is that a poem should directly depend on actual experience. (p. 59)

Moreover, these experiences should be 'unsorted'. One of the chief defects of modern and contemporary poetry, Larkin believes, is that poetry is losing touch with life because the experiences that inform it are too often of a rarefied kind. . . . This explains one of Larkin's most widely quoted, and most widely misunderstood remarks. . . . 'I . . . have no belief in "tradition",' Larkin wrote, 'or a common myth-kitty or casual allusions in poems to other poems or poets, which last I find unpleasantly like the talk of literary understrappers letting you see they know the right people.' The statement has been taken again and again by those who dislike Larkin's poetry as evidence of a 'provincial', even philistine frame of mind. The charge has no substance if we appreciate fully what Larkin is saying: he is objecting to '"tradition"' (the quotation marks are important), the 'myth-kitty' and those 'casual allusions' in so far as they are considered separate from other experience. Of course, reading a poem or knowing a poet is as much a part of experience as what happens at work, or watching two horses grazing; but that is the point: poems and poets are not things apart. He objects to '"tradition"' considered as something above and beyond life; to a 'myth-kitty', a stock of special 'poetic' myths which are to poetry as stage properties are to drama; to 'casual allusions', which are not organic to the poem, and are not really casual at all, but a way of showing off. Poetry should have a direct relationship with life, then, in that it should be regarded as being a part of life, not separate from it, and it should look to life for its subject matter.

More than this, Larkin has consistently maintained that a poet should write about those things in life that move him most deeply: if he does not feel deeply about anything, he should not write. This explains his small poetic production, and his conviction that a poet should not make his living by writing. He believes that poetry will only be written well when it has to be written. . . . (pp. 60-1)

It is surprising, perhaps, to consider that Larkin's suggestions are in the same spirit as Wordsworth's, that 'poetry is the spontaneous overflow of powerful feelings'. Surprising, in view of the fact that Larkin has been singled out as a poet who has little emotional intensity in his verse. . . . Larkin himself is puzzled by critics' finding his work unemotional. . . .

The feeling of responsibility to the experience justifies Larkin's conviction that content in poetry is more important than form. (p. 62)

Larkin has [no] . . . contempt [for] form. . . . It is just that originality, for Larkin, consists not in modifying the medium of communication, but in communicating something different. (pp. 62-3)

But though Larkin considers his prime responsibility to be to the experience he is trying to preserve, he has a keen sense of the audience for his poems. (p. 63)

Larkin seeks the general audience. He has commended Kipling, Housman and Betjeman for their 'direct relation with a reading public', obtained by being 'moving and memorable'. . . . [He] deplores the obscurity of the moderns, taking as their representatives Pound in poetry, Picasso in painting, and in jazz Charlie Parker, the saxophonist who did most to engineer the divergence of jazz into 'modern' and 'traditional'. Larkin considers ours 'an age so determined to make hard work out of reading poetry', and complains that this is to a large extent the fault of critics. . . . Larkin . . . considers it nonsense for a critic to claim to know a poem's meaning more accurately than its author. (pp. 64-5)

Larkin is certainly anti-intellectual pretension, anti- that kind of cleverness designed not to enlighten but to confuse and exclude; but not anti- the intellectual in itself. (p. 65)

Larkin has never condemned Yeats for his difficulty, though Yeats is at times a difficult poet. So is Larkin himself, one might add. (p. 66)

Larkin's concern is not that poetry be read merely for pleasure, but lest study by the 'dutiful mob' replace poetry's enjoyment by the wider audience. Such study is 'no substitute' for that enjoyment; but it is not wrong in itself. The critics are damaging only when they abstract poetry from life. . . . Larkin objects to 'culture in the abstract', not to culture; indeed, he wishes to see 'culture' in its narrower sense restored to its place in our 'culture' as a whole. (pp. 67-8)

When Larkin's poems do strive after a universal statement, they work best when they grow out of the kind of experience Larkin evokes in 'Myxomatosis'. His themes are almost always personal or perennial ones, and he is sometimes criticised for not writing about the impact of such specifically contemporary phenomena as Hiroshima and Auschwitz. . . . He is a contemporary man, and his observation of life is deeply influenced by the phenomena of contemporary life; but these things are part of the texture of his vision. He does not need to write about them directly to show that he is aware of them. (pp. 72-3)

Larkin showed in *The Less Deceived* that he did not write poetry that blows off the top of one's head, to use Emily Dickinson's metaphor; but the collection did show that he wrote movingly and memorably about aspects of life that were of great importance to his readers as well as to himself. He showed that he was a witty poet with immense verbal facility, capable of the most subtle modulations of tone, speaking a language vitalised by its relationship with the idiom we speak. He showed above all, to use his own phrases, that he was a poet 'capable of strong feeling' and 'of conveying strong feeling in poetry'. (pp. 90-1)

> *David Timms, in his* Philip Larkin *(copyright © Text David Timms 1973; by permission of Harper & Row, Publishers, Inc., Barnes & Noble Import Division), Barnes & Noble, 1973.*

Larkin collections come out at the rate of one per decade: *The North Ship*, 1945; *The Less Deceived*, 1955; *The Whitsun Weddings*, 1964; *High Windows*, 1974. Not exactly a torrent of creativity: just the best. (p. 65)

Now that the latest Larkin [*High Windows*] is finally available, . . . [one finds] that it all adds up even better than one had expected: the poems which one thought of as characteristic turn out to be more than that—or rather the *character* turns out to be more than that. Larkin has never liked the idea of an artist Developing. Nor has he himself done so. But he has managed to go on clarifying what he was sent to say. The total impression of *High Windows* is of despair made beautiful. Real despair and real beauty, with not a trace of posturing in either. The book is the peer of

the previous two mature collections, and if they did not exist would be just as astonishing. But they do exist (most of us could recognise any line from either one) and can't help rendering many of the themes in this third book deceptively familiar.

I think that in most of the poems here collected Larkin's ideas are being reinforced or deepened rather than repeated. But from time to time a certain predictability of form indicates that a previous discovery is being unearthed all over again. Such instances aren't difficult to spot, and it would be intemperate to betray delight at doing so. Larkin's "forgeries" (Auden's term for self-plagiarisms) are very few. He is more original from poem to poem than almost any modern poet one can think of. His limitations, such as they are, lie deeper than that. Here again, it is not wise to be happy about spotting them. Without the limitations there would be no Larkin—the beam cuts *because* it's narrow.

It has always seemed to me a great pity that Larkin's more intelligent critics should content themselves with finding his view of life circumscribed. It is, but it is also bodied forth as art to a remarkable degree. There is a connection between the circumscription and the poetic intensity, and it's no surprise that the critics who can't see the connection can't see the separation either. They seem to think that just because the poet is (self-admittedly) emotionally wounded, the poetry is wounded too. (pp. 65-6)

It ought to be obvious that Larkin is not a universal poet in the thematic sense—in fact, he is a self-proclaimed stranger to a good half, *the* good half of life. . . . What's missing in Larkin doesn't just tend to be missing, it's glaringly, achingly, unarguably *missing*. (p. 66)

["The Building,"] I think, is the volume's masterpiece—an absolute chiller, which I find myself getting by heart despite a pronounced temperamental aversion. The Building is the house of death, a Dantesque hell-hole—one thinks particularly of *Inferno V*—where people "at that vague age that claims/The end of choice, the last of hope" are sent to "their appointed levels." The ambience is standard modernist humdrum: paperbacks, tea, rows of steel chairs like an airport lounge. You can look down into the yard and see red brick, lagged pipes, traffic. But the smell is frightening. In time everyone will find a nurse beckoning to him. The dead lie in white rows somewhere above. This, says Larkin with an undeflected power unique even for him, is what it all really adds up to. Life is a dream and we awake to this reality. (p. 69)

There is no point in disagreeing with the man if that's the way he feels, and he wouldn't write a poem like "The Building" if he didn't feel that way to the point of daemonic possession. He himself is well aware that there are happier ways of viewing life. It's just that he is incapable of sharing them, except for fleeting moments—and the fleeting moments do not accumulate, whereas the times in between them do. The narrator says that "nothing contravenes/The coming dark." It's an inherently less interesting proposition than its opposite, and a poet forced to devote his creative effort to embodying it has only a small amount of space to work in. Nor, within the space, is he free from the paradox that his poems will become part of life, not death. From that paradox, we gain. The desperation of "The Building" is like the desperation of Leopardi, disconsolate yet doomed to being beautiful. The advantage which accrues is one of purity—a hopeless affirmation is the only kind we really want to hear when we feel, as sooner or later everybody must, that life is a trap.

There is no certain way of separating Larkin's attitude to society from his conception of himself, but to the extent that you can, he seems to be in two minds about what the world has come to. He thinks, on the one hand, that it's probably all up; and on the other hand that youth still has a chance. On the theme of modern life being an unmitigated and steadily intensifying catastrophe he reads like his admired Betjeman in a murderous mood—no banana blush or cherry telly teeth, just a tight-browed disdain and a toxic line of invective. "Going, Going" is particularly instructive here. (pp. 69-70)

Larkin loves and inhabits tradition as much as Betjeman does, but artistically he had already let go of it when others were only just realising it was time to cling on. Larkin is the poet of the void. The one affirmation his work offers is the possibility that when we have lost everything the problem of beauty will still remain. It's enough. (p. 71)

> *Clive James, "Wolves of Memory," in* Encounter (© 1974 by Encounter Ltd.), June, 1974, pp. 65-71.

Debate about what Philip Larkin's high windows actually are, and why they qualify as the title of this profoundly beautiful and remarkable book, could go on endlessly; missing the fact that they have had a special significance in his poetry from the beginning. In this title-poem, as is already well-known, the equivalent found for the speaker's ambiguous envy of the new sexual liberty of the young (their long *downward* slide to happiness) is the envy his elders possibly felt about his own new freedom, when young, from religious fears and constraints. But then comes the sudden switch away: no more of sex or religion, no more analogies, no rueful last twist—simply the one lucid, scaringly serene image:

> the thought of high windows:
> The sun-comprehending glass,
> And beyond it, the deep blue air, that shows
> Nothing, and is nowhere, and is endless.

That 'deep blue air', standing powerfully beyond, is one of those inscrutable spaces, pure because they are so empty and still, which arrive somewhere in every Larkin volume. Whether showing up as an 'unearthly dawn', or a 'padlocked cube of light', as 'attics cleared of him', as moments by the 'unfenced existence' of the sea or when simply staring into clear water, as solitary hours under clear, unhindered moonlight, or in *High Windows*, as blank pages in a diary or 'flawless weather', Larkin is repeatedly turning aside to them from the soiled territory of living: living among others, or private living with its fears and shames, or the insoluble anguishes of any living. Such areas of chaste emptiness open up as eerily important mental experiences.

Despite his disavowal of a poet's obligation to develop, *High Windows* does show an indisputable development in Larkin. The early *North Ship*, and *The Less Deceived*, were building up steadily to that overwhelmingly sad sense in *The Whitsun Weddings* (it was the predominant statement of that volume) that nearly all human expectations were pathetic delusion and folly, betrayed by the hidden forces pushing death inexorably closer. The most positive

feeling was that some kinds of ritual observance (work in 'Toads Revisited', nuptial customs in the weddings poem) made sense for staving off death, or as excuses for very limited hope. Also that love, commemorated on the Arundel tomb (under light, incidentally, which 'thronged the glass' each summer) did justify our existence, perhaps.

The difference and development in *High Windows* is partly in Larkin's breaking away from that one dominant theme. Here, *all* the different Larkin motifs have come together in precisely adjusted balance, in a collection in which all his well-known virtues and skills are enhanced, validated and drawn together by the ethereal and compelling image providing the title. Once again there is consummate control of the various verse forms. Accurate details are summoned and ordered with astonishing ease: nostalgic in 'To the Sea', or made harrowingly cumulative in his hospital poem, 'The Building'. And there is that same unalterable exactness—other words would *not* have fitted—about a diction which everyone must surely now realise as authoritative because of its reticence, not somehow in spite of it; response to its finest effects is an index of awareness of the undiminished resourcefulness of modern English (and response to its magnetic quality and sheer serviceability is seen in critics' constant use of phrases from Larkin to help them when writing *about* Larkin.)

But it is the new emphases which are interesting and which might provide clues as to whether, for Larkin, the pull of the deep blue air is towards life or death: ultimately the most important question to resolve. Clearly new here is the greatly strengthened fascination with the value of habits and rituals: he has never given these things a more arresting dimension. And it is all intimately linked with the ways, the places, the times in which Larkin sees life as having meaning and fulness. (p. 854)

Larkin's lack of personal hope and expectations for any of us finally leaves him resting faith in the continuance of some good, habitual things just as they are (though sometimes they can only be remembered, since the catastrophes of 1914 and 1929 destroyed so much innocence). It is about the seaside always being there, the Show always going on—though the hotel furnishings now exist only in wistful recall. These things represent the concealed values in the poems. When Larkin states this underlying conservatism openly, the whole thing gets oddly weakened ('Going, Going') or blimpishly absurd ('Homage to a Government'). We might be thankful that Larkin is so rarely explicit about what he believes; on the other hand, very thankful that he isn't fitting stained glass into the high windows to complete the syndrome.

It's doubtful whether a better book than *High Windows* will come out of the 1970s. . . . [Almost] every Larkin poem grows larger and clearer as the years go by. (pp. 854, 856)

> *Alan Brownjohn, "The Deep Blue Air," in* New Statesman (© 1974 The Statesman & Nation Publishing Co. Ltd.), June 14, 1974, pp. 854, 856.

Taken as a whole, Philip Larkin's poetry has the effect of a sustained attack upon the philosophical idealism of romantic literature, and more specifically upon its "decadent" stepchild, modernism. For virtually his entire career he has been writing at least implicitly on this subject, sometimes openly attacking modernism in poetry and jazz music, presenting himself as a skeptical, "less deceived" observer of contemporary life. (p. 331)

The traditional view of his development has him casting aside romanticism in favor of an empirical, Movement poetic; thus the British critic Colin Falck [in *The Modern Poet*, edited by Ian Hamilton,] has described the progress of his poetry since *The North Ship* as a repudiation of an "impossible idealism" and an "ever-deepening acceptance of the ordinariness of things as they are." This view needs qualification to the extent that Larkin was probably never a romantic in the technical, philosophical sense.... From the beginning, Larkin's work has manifested a certain coolness and lack of self-esteem, a need to withdraw from experience; but at the same time it has continued to show his desire for a purely secular type of romance, a romance he must have felt in Vernon Watkins' "impassioned and imperative" readings [of Yeats, at the Oxford English Club in 1943] even if he could enjoy it only at second hand. (p. 333)

Larkin's problem is that in his apparent rejection of philosophical idealism he has become wary of all romance, including the passion and the sense of active rebellion which gives modernist literature much of its humanity. If the right-wing, visionary poetry of Yeats represents a flawed thesis, then Larkin's poetry, which has its own conservative instincts, represents a flawed antithesis. Colin Falck seems to be addressing this problem in his essay on Larkin, which concludes with a call for a poetry of "lucid barbarism"; my chief disagreement with Falck is that I resist having to choose such an unhappy alternative as he presents. Surely we can have the "passionate intensity" which is often missing in Larkin, but without the antihuman barbarism, obscurity, or escapism which is the repellent side of modernist literature.

In any case, poems such as "The Whitsun Weddings" show that Larkin is trying to assert his humanity, not deny it.... They also suggest that the greatest virtue in Larkin's poetry is not so much his suppression of large poetic gestures as his ability to recover an honest sense of joy and beauty. There are times when Larkin's skeptical, disillusioned self takes over entirely; he seldom presents himself as anything but an onlooker, and his collections are full of bitter poems about failure. He can make us feel the pain of an empty life, as in a poem like "Home is so Sad" ..., but such verses would not hurt so much if Larkin did not retain the desire for a "lost world," a yearning for the way things ought to be. Beneath his irony and his potential lack of feeling, there is a sympathy which now and then breaks through to create a powerful effect. Thus some of his best poems are purely secular epiphanies, "tender visitings"; his Movement style is thrown into relief by his occasional discoveries of strong feeling, and the moments of light, always highly qualified by the grey that surrounds them, become extremely valuable. Perhaps that is why, in the last lines of the last poem in *The Whitsun Weddings*, Larkin cautiously offers an "almost-instinct" which he has found "almost true": "What will survive of us is love." (p. 344)

James Naremore, "Philip Larkin's 'Lost World'," in Contemporary Literature *(© 1974 by the Board of Regents of the University of Wisconsin System), Vol. 15, No. 3, Summer, 1974, pp. 331-44.*

Philip Larkin's book of poems, *High Windows*, ... has sold out its first edition of 6,000 copies. My guess is that, for a living English poet, only a collection by the Poet Laureate will have topped that figure. Larkin's runaway success confounds those who assert that the general reader will not buy good poetry and yet it will dishearten the many lesser poets or publishers of little magazines who are struggling to approach anything like a sale of 60, let alone 600. Larkin is a withdrawn, inaccessible poet; unlike Betjeman he needs to be read with concentration, and repeatedly, to find the meaning behind the surface words. To get some idea of his method of working, it is illuminating to look at his worksheets of 'At Grass' (now part of the British Museum Collection of Modern Literary Manuscripts), ... over 40 verse variations, some of them abandoned altogether, some worked over again and again, for the final five verses of the poem. (p. 125)

Elizabeth Brownjohn, in New Statesman *(© 1974 The Statesman & Nation Publishing Co. Ltd.), July 26, 1974.*

All is not well with Larkin. The poems have revealed a personality both wry and self-deprecating; after a dull childhood ('I Remember, I Remember'), he seems to have arrived at his current situation and attitudes through no very conscious choice ('Dockery and Son', 'Send No Money', etc.), and can only expect now 'age, and then the only end of age'. But if life is slow dying and love solves nothing, at least in the past he has always viewed the human condition with some compassion. What seems to have happened now [in *High Windows*] is that he, or his poetic persona, has come to feel so out of touch with the world around him that his capacity for looking at it sympathetically has largely disappeared.

Perhaps one might have guessed at something of the kind. *The Less Deceived*, published in 1955, contained two poems—'Coming' and 'Wedding Wind'—which were in their different ways direct celebrations of joy. Ten years later *The Whitsun Weddings* marked something of a retreat. 'First Sight', true, is about the surprise of pleasure to come—for lambs; but one or two low-keyed poems have crept in, and one rather coarse one. Dramatic monologues of the 'Wedding Wind' type have disappeared. Emotionally, Larkin has played progressively safer. But there is a difference between emotional caution and lack of any emotional life at all; and whereas, poem for poem, *The Whitsun Weddings* was the equal of *The Less Deceived*, [*High Windows*] is much less good than either. The manner and strategy are recognisable; but for the most part the longer poems are lifeless, the lyrical ones don't work, and both language and subject-matter have become coarser and more banal. The only development is along the lines of 'A Study of Reading Habits'. (p. 13)

I re-read Larkin constantly. From this volume I shall want to turn to 'Vers de Societé'—the theme of 'Wants', rather in the manner of 'I Remember, I Remember', witty and exact and 'Dublinesque', an Irish street-scene almost in the old delicate, lyrical manner. Perhaps while the book is out I shall read the title-poem. And then—a sigh, and back with relief to the two earlier volumes. It is intensely sad. (p. 17)

Humphrey Clucas, "Unsatisfactory Age," in Agenda, *Autumn, 1974, pp. 13-17.*

Philip Larkin is the *other* English Poet Laureate, even more loved and needed than the official one, John Betjeman. To the literary English now, with their thinned, overwatched sensibility, Larkin is grateful proof that at least one plangent "English" string can still be sounded, thrill through them. Ted Hughes is like an ephebe of Shakespeare run wild in the woods; Charles Tomlinson like a staid valley tree, with philosophical murmurings. Where in these is that grand sweetened pathos most readily recognizable as English poetry? But Larkin's small infrequent volumes—once a decade—read like prudent petitions to a National Anthology Committee. With well-behaved order—here are the stanzas, there the rhyme—he speaks to the heart and says of the world: Is this all there is? Is *this* what we deserve? He takes one back to Edward Thomas and Thomas Hardy. Indeed, despite his hangdog air, his wised-up verse, he takes one back to Keats.

Like Robert Lowell, Larkin endears himself, in a deflected age, by feeling inward with life as "tragedy." His all but "passive apprehension of suffering"—his phrase for Hardy—gives him an unignorable intimacy with pain. He locates the sore spots and presses them tenderly. *How* he presses them—his liability is sentimentality. If he is not so formidable as Hardy, if for all his exquisiteness he approximates mass entertainers like Rod McKuen and Leonard Cohen, it is because his feeling swells protectingly before the situations he describes. He escapes them through compassion—tames them into pathos.

Indeed, Larkin force-feeds his pity, as if regret were all he could feel, and feel he must. His poems are not discoveries but bashes of sympathy. Reading him is like being stroked during a bereavement. . . .

In its black-draped guise as the might-have-been, Larkin's Romanticism, which is like Hemingway's gone softer still, gives us the stature of a scarcely utterable, voided capacity for happiness. Reading him, we mourn ourselves. No matter that, again like Hemingway, he throws to the Cerberus of total self-consciousness, of our aggressive moral skepticism against the feelings, the sop of an unaspiring idiom. ("I just think it will happen, soon," "However we mess it about," "And this is all right," "in a pig's arse, friend.") His language is not the denigration of high expectations that it seems: it is the paring of Romantic overreaching, a paring redolent of the pulp it has lost. (p. 3)

There is not and (since his second volume, "The Less Deceived") never has been any question of Larkin's skill, and more: he has, often enough to confound, that superlative felicity, that hard-to-explain strong effect, that makes the best poets finally useless as models—wonders apart. Though "High Windows" suffers from repeating the tones and tricks of "The Less Deceived" and "The Whitsun Weddings," it is nonetheless a trove of pleasures. Even if you want to cash in the sad, generous feeling, what undoubted poetry remains.

To begin with, there is, with occasional lapses, that piercing, "bleakened" quality to the word, the line, that makes one think: "Why, of course it took Larkin 10 years to write these twenty-four poems." Again one thinks of Hemingway—of the bullfighter's "purity of line." Impressions are cleanly made, firm, immediate. . . . Only what Larkin wants us to see is there, utterly distinct, everything else fallen away. . . .

[How] he can write! His hard, laconic, evocative style pulls against his obvious desire to drown everything euthanasically, in tears of defeat. His descriptions are not "loving," but just for that reason, like Hemingway's, they will last. They are, as it were, what the world *will* say for its own beauty and interest—even through a poet disenchanted with it.

Larkin's management of poems is no less superb. A Larkin poem does not just happen; it is as concentrated as heart surgery. Everything, from the voice that takes you in through its matey casualness only to lead you unawares into naked solemnity, from the modulation of wryness into awful personal need, to the fresh notations, the subtle metrical pulls, and the unforced consummations—everything, as a rule, is precisely judged. And how Larkin's characteristic rhythm, with its unhurried emphases, as if to assert, "There is not much to note, but note it, we owe it that"—how this assured movement works with the rhyme and plain diction to give a compelling presence to what he says.

There is slightly more variety in "High Windows" than in the earlier volumes, considerably more attachment to public union and ongoingness: summer beaches, country shows, "The secret, bestial peace" of the "lamplit cave" in "The Card-Players." But who will predict for Larkin a new beginning? Indeed, his poetic identity is so sharply flavored that—for all his emotional limitations and excesses—a change could scarcely help seeming a dilution. His sad tenderness is the condition of his strength. Let him appeal, then, as he is—rather unadventurous, a disciple of tradition—to that committee on anthologies. Few could be admitted more deservedly. (p. 14)

Calvin Bedient, in The New York Times Book Review (© *1975 by The New York Times Company; reprinted by permission), January 12, 1975.*

Larkin first came to critical attention when *New Lines* was published in 1956. This was an anthology of young poets (quickly labeled "The Movement" by the media) whose bond of union was their hatred of Eliot's obscurity and the lush romanticism of Dylan Thomas's besotted followers. They aimed at clarity, directness of language, communication from one civilized and literate being to another. Larkin seemed to fulfill the credo of the Movement better than anyone else, and he was often singled out, as much for damnation as for praise, by those looking for the ultimate Movement poet.

Now comes *High Windows*, a niggardly 42 pages of well-leaded print. Is there a new Larkin? No. The one conspicuous change is that today he is not shy about using an occasional four-letter word, but even this bow to more permissive standards is severely controlled by a taste that is impeccable. He turns to the people's Anglo-Saxon only when some poetic purpose is served.

In the new book, Larkin continues his quiet exploration of the daily human scene, but simply does it better than ever before. The poet's sense of the exactly right combination of words is uncannily accurate, as when in one poem he refers to "A white steamer stuck in the afternoon" and in another to "Lit shelved liners" that "Grope like mad worlds westward." . . .

If the book has one central subject it is the advance of age, viewed without joy but also without sentimental self-deception. . . . He is as somber as Thomas Hardy, but more nimble with language.

Larkin, like Eliot, Yeats, and a number of others, is emotionally something of a conservative. He sees an England in which meadows, lanes, and carved choirs will disappear into museums while concrete and pollution cover the land. . . .

Larkin's conservatism shows up also in his unashamed fondness for the traditional poetic workhorses, iambic pentameter and rhymed stanza forms. Any young poet, cutting his poetic teeth on verse of the "open form" type, would do well to take a prayerful look at *High Windows* before dismissing the ancestral tools of the trade. In the hands of Larkin, they are as fresh as though just invented.

Having showered this poet and his newest book with praise, what is there to say against it? Certainly, for the most part it consummately does what it attempts. At times, though not often, the wit and verbal cleverness become just a little cute. And some subjects are more suitable for Larkin than others. Though he can put together a nature poem exceedingly well, the Wordsworthian territory is not his best base of operations. One senses less of his distinctive voice even in such a good poem as "The Trees." . . .

All in all, *High Windows* is cause for rejoicing; the sheer success of poem after poem lifts the spirit. And it is also heartening to find this major achievement scored by a poet who quietly goes his own way, at his own pace, paying little attention to changing poetic fads and trends. By being himself he has written one of the few books of verse certain to survive and gleam from a lackluster period of British poetry.

> *Chad Walsh, "Long Slide to Happiness," in* Book World—The Washington Post (© The Washington Post), January 12, 1975, p. 3.

It is only now, by hindsight, that [Larkin's two novels, *Jill* (1946) and *A Girl in Winter* (1947)] seem to point forward to the poetry. Taken in their chronology, they are impressively mature and self-sufficient. If Larkin had never written a line of verse, his place as a writer would still have been secure. (pp. 383-84)

[The] novels are at ease with a range of sympathies that the later poems, even the most magnificant ones, deal with only piecemeal, although with incomparably more telling effect.

Considering that Evelyn Waugh began a comic tradition in the modern novel which only lately seems in danger of dying out, and considering Larkin's gift for sardonic comedy—a gift which by all accounts decisively influenced his contemporaries at Oxford—it is remarkable how non-comic his novels are, how completely they do not fit into the family of talents which includes Waugh and Powell and Amis. *Jill* employs many of the same properties as an Oxford novel by the young Waugh—the obscure young hero is casually destroyed by his socially superior contemporaries —but the treatment is unrelievedly sad. Larkin's hero has not an ounce of the inner strength which Amis gave Jim Dixon. . . . All the materials of farce are present and begging to be used, but tragedy is what Larkin aims for and what he largely achieves. . . .

[*A Girl in Winter*] is as disconsolate as its predecessor,

leaving the protagonist once again facing an unsatisfactory prime.

A contributory grace in both novels, but outstanding in *A Girl in Winter*, is the sheer quality of the writing. Larkin told [Philip Oakes in a *Sunday Times* profile] that he wrote the books like poems, carefully eliminating repeated words. Fastidiousness is everywhere and flamboyance non-existent: the touch is unfaltering. . . .

Why, if Larkin could write novels like these, did he stop? To hindsight the answer is easy: because he was about to become the finest poet of his generation, instead of just one of its best novelists. A more inquiring appraisal suggests that although his aesthetic effect was rich, his stock of events was thin. In a fictional texture featuring a sore tooth and a fleeting kiss as important threads, Zen diaphanousness always threatened. (What is the sound of *one* flower being arranged?) The master lyric poet, given time, will eventually reject the idea of writing any line not meant to be remembered. Larkin, while being to no extent a dandy, is nevertheless an exquisite. It is often the way with exquisites that they graduate from full-scale prentice constructions to small-scale works of entirely original intensity, having found a large expanse limiting. Chopin is not too far-fetched a parallel. Larkin's two novels are like Chopin's two concertos: good enough to promise not merely more of the same, but a hitherto unheard-of distillation of their own lyrical essence. (p. 384)

> *Clive James, "Sad Steps," in* New Statesman (© 1975 The Statesman & Nation Publishing Co. Ltd.), March 21, 1975, pp. 383-84.

Centrality—other than in a parodied middle-class myth— [Larkin] has not; in volume his work remains slight; in range it narrows as it deepens; in metrics, diction and form it develops with shrewd tactics and without strategy. *High Windows* offers the refinement and toughening of a talent which thrives on being peripheral, even eccentric, but in the process its true unevenness is revealed. Here Larkin's readiness to speak without the protection of wit can expose his banality and integrity in equal measure. His honest and moving awareness of wider perspectives of spirit and desolation can leave him at the mercy of plangency. . . .

His bluff-realist anti-self can be toughened to the point where it moves from crass modishness . . . to crass moralising. . . .

But in thus pushing against the boundaries of his talent and submitting to far more open tones in this volume Larkin draws more than sympathy from the reader. In several of the shorter pieces his subtlety is made to gravitate around the poet's own attitudes without the defence of a puppet persona. His new stridency, "Groping back to bed after a piss" ("Sad Steps"), clears the air for a debate on pretentions and nervous unease, for which he takes full responsibility. . . . Making the joke at his own expense "Posterity" colours clichéd satire with warmth and leads to real discovery; and even more valuable, Larkin has found his way towards celebrations which are not conditioned by archaic diction. The young survive his own losses in "Sad Steps"; in "Solar" fastidiousness of phrase accumulates a true praise of giving; and in "Cut Grass" Larkin's profound restraint allows sensitivity quietly to overwhelm the sense of defeat. . . .

If *High Windows* leaves no doubt of the dangers to which Larkin's art is exposed it also proves how valuable are its hard-won achievements. (p. 76)

Desmond Graham, in Stand *(copyright* © *by* Stand*), Vol. 16, No. 2, 1975.*

High Windows is the most exciting literary event since Larkin's last collection, *The Whitsun Weddings* 1964, and we should make the most of celebrating Larkin now, for if his pattern of publication continues, his next collection will appear in 1984. That is, if anyone is still reading poetry then.

For the moment Larkin's few detractors, critics who applaud his technical mastery while deploring his negative pessimism are silent, and if Larkin ever chucks himself off the new Humber bridge even Al Alvarez might rush forward to canonise him. Does Larkin's gloom exceed that of Houseman, Hardy, Eliot or Edward Thomas? I'm sure it doesn't and anyway it is so often set off by a quality they, on the whole, lack, a very healthy sense of humour. "Vers de Société" (in this collection) for instance is a poem that makes one laugh out loud despite its gloomy conclusion.

High Windows is as excellent in total as the two previous collections but in its balance between the plain unadorned style he developed in *The Whitsun Weddings* and the more poetical side of his talent it is like *The Less Deceived*. Some poems, like "Solar" and the middle section of "Livings" recall the richer imagery he was using from *The North Ship* 1945 to his pamphlet *XX Poems* 1951. Change and development in Larkin's work is not willed change, as it often seems to be in Auden or Lowell, but a slow evolution, a gradual deepening of themes and variations already stated. Technically Larkin is still a traditionalist but his forms, metres, rhythms and syntax are as effortless and varied as ever. There are some new departures, "The Explosion" retrieves for serious purposes a meter that had seemed unusable since Longfellow; the form and metre of the last poem in the sequence "Livings" recalls his love of Praed; in "Cut Grass" the beautiful but melancholy cadences are as moving as anything in Christina Rossetti. But all have the stamp of Larkin's unique voice. In one of the longest poems in the book "Show Saturday" massive stanzas easily carry the sprawl of apparently random details in a way that is new but pure Larkin. Although it is true that parts of the poem bring to mind earlier successes, it doesn't seem like self-imitation. (p. 87)

In Larkin's last book, age, decay and death, though prominent were inclined to be abstract. Now, ten years on, they have become horrifyingly concrete in one of the finest poems in the book "The Old Fools". A model for any poet [is] its mastery of tone, long line and long stanza. . . . [One] of his strongest qualities is his skill in *re-enacting* rather than re-creating emotion. As he said himself 'poetry is emotional in nature, *theatrical* in operation'.

Throughout *High Windows* the pessimistic side of Larkin is more compelling than the affirmative side, perhaps because his emotional responses are now much stronger, because he is that much nearer to old age and death. Very fine as the affirmative poems, "To the Sea" and "Show Saturday" are, they lack the poetic resonance of poems like "Church Going" and "The Whitsun Weddings". (pp. 90-1)

George Hartley, "The Lost Displays," in

Phoenix *(8 Cavendish Road, Heaton Mersey, Stockport, Cheshire, England), Spring, 1975, pp. 87-92.*

[In 'High Windows,' the title poem of Larkin's new collection,] two speculations are juxtaposed, the first on the younger generation, whose sexual freedom Larkin envies, the second on Larkin's generation, whose emancipation from religious constraints may have been envied by *his* elders. . . . The poem's point is not whether freedom is real, or one more real than the other, since both are matters of the observer's guesswork; rather that imagined freedom is always located as if in an unreachable elsewhere seen through 'high windows'. . . . Given the nature of Larkin's world, one may think of a university tower, a high-rise block of flats, a hospital. But wherever the windows are, they define the limits of human life; real freedom is on the other side and, man not being a bird, his 'long slide / To happiness' would mean a quick drop to extinction. In the face of that total freedom whose other name is death, human 'freedom'—choice and responsibility—extends no further than 'the right', in Kenneth Allott's phrase, 'to decide in no question'.

More sharply and sombrely than before, what this volume confronts is 'last things'. Death has always haunted Larkin's poetry, but now it looms inescapably distinct; no longer 'a black-sailed unfamiliar' or 'the only end of age' (chilling as those euphemisms were), it stares in "The Old Fools", through the lineaments of senility. (p. 96)

Some poems make me suspect that Larkin gains release, even a sense of exhilaration, by expressing so openly his blacker moods. (p. 97)

In terms of shape and definition, each poem in this fine collection is a distinct entity; there is an impressive technical range (no form is used twice) and an equally impressive range of tones and voices, the most striking that of the defiantly lonely lighthouse-keeper of "Livings (II)". . . . But what is perhaps more impressive is the sense that develops of the volume as a thematic totality. The effect of reading and re-reading is stereophonic, as cross-references of word and feeling clarify and deepen one's initial response. Larkin's picture of life and death is not all-inclusive —the loneliness that sharpens his vision leaves some things outside the frame; but what he does see is both real and important, and he speaks of it with an authority based on skill and the determination to be completely honest.

He also speaks with compassion. Central to the unity of this volume, as it is central in position, is "The Building". . . . The 'building', it becomes clear, is a hospital; but nowhere is that word used, perhaps because Larkin wishes to leave the reader's mind unbiassed by 'scientific' preconceptions (which might suggest false hope) and open to his investigation of its essential hopeless purpose, which is 'a struggle to transcend / The thought of dying'. The building is in fact a secular cathedral, where medicine replaces religion and individuals, their 'homes and names / Suddenly in abeyance', are reduced to their fundamental frightened humanity. . . . The 'intensely sad' vision which Larkin attains to here is his most moving achievement in this volume, and the fusion he can bring about between the ordinariness of his subject-matter and its inherent pathos has rarely been so poignantly exemplified. . . . The view we see is drab and local; the regret we feel, universal. (pp. 99-100)

Philip Gardner, "Bearing the Unbearable," in Phoenix *(8 Cavendish Road, Heaton Mersey, Stockport, Cheshire, England), Spring, 1975, pp. 94-100.*

A glass case in a room called "The English Tradition" is where some people, Americans especially, think that Philip Larkin's poetry belongs: they imagine he is a kind of old-fashioned taxidermist who fluffs up the wings of dead ducks, like the iambic pentameter and the rhymed quatrain, for a public devoted to almost extinct birds. His admirers, mostly British, feel that he writes with more precision than any other living poet about real people in real places; they can quote him, because his mastery of rhyme and meter enables him to write memorably; and they count among their favorite books of the century *The Less Deceived* and *The Whitsun Weddings*. . . .

What he does in *High Windows* is the most difficult thing of all, and it only looks easy because he does it so well: he makes poetry out of common situations in ordinary lives. . . . [These are] poems about living and dying in a farcical, sad, and constricted world, in which he finds less to celebrate now than ten or twenty years ago. Metaphysical despair consoled by an earthy sense of humor pervades his poetry. Time, fertility, and death remain his underlying themes, and oblivion is nearer than ever. But he still enters each poem empirically through actual experience, "letting the door thud shut," keeping all his wits alert for what's going on inside.

He avoids speaking as a "poet," preferring to sound like a man of common sense, or some familiar recognizable type. He seems to be saying with unaffected modesty, "These thoughts go in verse because that's the way they feel right to me"; and he leaves it to us to decide if we wish to treat what he's written as poetry. His language is plain conversational English, not mandarin, not literary. . . . Attached to things as they are, he enjoys debunking with mockery, and even self-mockery, any notions he thinks are unintelligible, untenable, or absurd. Religion, magic, and mythology are not his concern, but there *is* a kind of magic one can believe in, which he often employs: free of hocus-pocus, it concerns the tangible world of jobs and food and clothes and journeys we're disagreeably lumped with by fate, and it consists of naming them so accurately that they seem to be changed into objects or gestures or motions we can love. (p. 30)

The renewal of a style so translucent and so richly complex as that of the "Lines on a Young Lady's Photograph Album" or later "The Whitsun Weddings" is probably no less difficult than the invention of a different style; especially since the world Larkin writes about, in which "life is slow dying," has enjoyed no radical change, rebirth or revolution in this period. England, without her empire, is still his paradise, more regrettably lost than ever, under "bleak high-risers" and motorways with no foreseeable chance of being regained. . . .

He seems in [*High Windows*] to have reached that dangerous period in a writer's life where Bergotte was stranded by the time we meet him in Proust's novel, trapped in the limitations he needed to perfect his early style. Larkin's real achievement first came from a deeply resolved acceptance of life's limits, and from always being "the less deceived." . . . [His] writing was deeply distrustful of all gods, heroes, myths, ideologies, and foreigners (which, among poets, included Yeats as an Irish Celt and Pound as an American "culture-monger"). The annulling and the distrust have continued without letup or development. (p. 31)

The title poem, "High Windows," is worth examining closely; since youth, sex, time, and oblivion all come together in the space of a few lines. In true Larkin style, it contains a couple of interior dramatic arguments, which tend to cancel each other out, "each one double-yolked with meaning and meaning's rebuttal," themselves put down by an astounding conclusion. It begins with human farce, and ends with a note about the universe. It starts in free verse and evolves quite naturally (gathering more and more life as it grows) into a lyrical rhymed quatrain. The opening lines are brutally coarse; and the last four as pure as anything in modern poetry. This itself is a puritan dichotomy: the poem is truly in the tradition of the regicides against the martyrologists. . . .

It's a poem in which Larkin gives us a look down one of those "long perspectives" of time. He uses idiom to convey a sense of utter remoteness between the post-Chatterley Anglo-American classless voice of the present and the old-fashioned lower-class puritanical English voice of the past, both of which are suddenly transcended by the true voice of the imagination (modulating from a minor into a major key) giving us the crystal image of the last quatrain, a celebration of the void. One could scarcely predict the poem's surprising destination from its beginning: from murky roots it grows with genuine mystery up into the "deep blue air." . . .

I think Larkin is [close] to E. M. Forster in what he thinks poetry ought to do: what matters for him is to make separate lives, or fragments of life, connect in a work of art. The best of these poems are "connectors" in this sense: "To the Sea," which brings families together at an annual ritual; "Solar," which assembles most fertile and generous images in a celebration of the sun, almost in free verse, a fine achievement; and a bewildering triptych called "Livings." (p. 32)

Larkin's finest lines—and how easy they are to remember! —earn their freedom by submission to that ancient tyranny ["of rhyme," as Proust wrote]; and they do it so well that I believe he is one modern poet who has really confuted by practical demonstration a famous dictum of William Carlos Williams: "I say we are *through* with the iambic pentameter as presently conceived, at least for dramatic verse; through with the measured quatrain, the staid concatenations of sounds in the usual stanza, the sonnet": advice which has misled a whole generation in America into thinking that freedom in poetry may be attained directly by writing in free verse. *High Windows* shows in a living way that meter and rhyme, when skillfully handled by an artist who knows how to conceal his art, can still have useful and noble functions to perform in poetry. (p. 33)

Richard Murphy, "The Art of Debunkery," in The New York Review of Books *(reprinted with permission from* The New York Review of Books; *copyright © 1975 NYREV, Inc.), May 15, 1975, pp. 30-3.*

Le CARRÉ, John (pseudonym of David Cornwell) 1931-

Le Carré, an English novelist, is one of the few thriller writers—Eric Ambler and Graham Greene are two others—able to create serious fiction, distinguished by insight into motivation and personality, without sacrificing the best qualities of the thriller novel. After his tremendously successful novel *The Spy Who Came In From the Cold* and several other thrillers, le Carré apparently abandoned that genre for "serious" fiction; but critics and audience alike were delighted to receive his most recent thriller, *Tinker, Tailor, Soldier, Spy*, regarded by many as his best book to date. (See also *Contemporary Authors*, Vols. 5-8, rev. ed.)

In case you were wondering, John le Carré is still the master of the spy story. Thirty pages into [*Tinker, Tailor, Soldier, Spy*] should find you breathing heavily and mumbling penances for hours wasted with Ian Fleming and Frederick Forsyth. Le Carré's work is above all plausible, rooted not in extravagant fantasies of the cold war but in the realities of bureaucratic rivalry summoned up through vapors of nostalgia and bitterness, in understated pessimism, in images of attenuation and grinding down, in "a sense of great things dwindling to a small, mean end," as le Carré's hero puts it. Recently, le Carré has seemed anxious to abandon the bleak authority of his spy fiction (his last novel [*The Naïve and Sentimental Lover*] was a windy, conventional romance), but this story marks a return to the straight and elaborately constructed entertainment. . . .

Whether le Carré has adopted the shadow world of spies as a metaphor for much of our contemporary style of life I do not know, but it has served him well in several books as a frame in which to put many brief but striking portraits of destroyed and hunted men.

> *Peter S. Prescott, "Smiley vs. the Mole," in* Newsweek *(copyright 1974 by Newsweek, Inc.; all rights reserved; reprinted by permission), June 17, 1974, p. 104.*

During a cold war, when battles are fought by spies instead of soldiers, spy novels, particularly those written in response to the exigencies of everyday political life, seem to flourish. . . . In a world politically split, with neat *Schrecklichkeit*, into Us and Them, the spy novel boomed with hectic inventiveness. However far-fetched and implausible, it nonetheless touched a raw nerve.

But as history moved beyond confrontation between the two superpowers to a more diffuse, amorphous, constantly shifting arena of multiple antagonisms and unpredictable alliances, the spy novel itself changed from a hyperbolic reflection of a comprehended world to a rather poignantly anachronistic echo of a world that is gone. As a result, the novels of John Le Carré, who is unarguably the most brilliantly imaginative practitioner of the genre today, are "historical" novels even when they are ostensibly set in the present. And because of their historical perspective, they can register a skepticism and moral ambivalence, even outrage, about many aspects of espionage that would have been unthinkable to Ian Fleming and Helen MacInnes, the straight-and-true descendants of St. George. In contrast to the razzle-dazzle adventure tales of those authors, neither of whom harbored the faintest doubts about good and evil or which is which, Le Carré's books appear to be enriched

with the insight and subtlety of a complex literary sensibility—or, at the least, a muckraking insider's view of Intelligence work as a very dirty game, a brutal contest that leaves no one on either side clean or unbloodied.

As Kingsley Amis has acidly pointed out, this seeming philosophic detachment renders Le Carré acceptable and "true" and "realistic" to highbrows who would ordinarily disclaim any interest in a writer of mere thrillers. . . . Yet Le Carré's genuine strength is precisely and strictly that of a first-rate spy novelist. To distort his admittedly unconventional view of British Intelligence, seeing in it a symbolic representation of Larger Issues; to draw high-toned moral profundity from the exhausted seediness of Alec Leamas, the spy who came in from the cold, is to misrepresent and distort Le Carré's extraordinary achievements as an original and mesmerising writer working within the strict boundaries of a difficult genre.

It is myopic and unjust to link Le Carré with high art: The criteria for judging literary fiction are simply irrelevant to his superb entertainments and can only muddle a reader's pleasure. One takes up Le Carré's books not for his style, though he writes with exceptional grace and wit; not for his delineation of personality, though many of his characters are drawn with a lively eye for their singular eccentricities and foibles; and certainly not for his pseudoprofound comments on the moral implications and underlying rot of Intelligence work, which he offers with extreme reticence and veiled, slyly mocking solemnity. Rather, Le Carré is a master craftsman of ingeniously plotted suspense, weaving astoundingly intricate fantasies of discovery, stealth, surprise, duplicity, and final exposure. And the good news is that after *The Naïve and Sentimental Lover*, a recent limp venture into "straight" fiction, [with *Tinker, Tailor, Soldier, Spy*] he is back at the very top of his form. (pp. 15-16)

> *Pearl K. Bell, "Coming in from the Cold War," in* The New Leader *(© 1974 by the American Labor Conference on International Affairs, Inc.), June 24, 1974, pp. 15-16.*

[*Tinker, Tailor, Soldier, Spy*] is le Carré's first Circus act since a mildly lamentable foray into straight fiction (*The Naïve and Sentimental Lover*—1972). If it is not exactly a three-ring literary homecoming, it is a splendid assemblage of the virtues displayed in previous le Carré thrillers. Fine public-school scenes (*see A Murder of Quality*). Gently savage reminders that lingering old-boyism from the heroic days of World War II can lead to lethal folly in the crocodile world of modern espionage. Brisk demonstrations that hell hath no fury like that of feuding bureaucrats (*The Looking Glass War, A Small Town in Germany*). . . .

Le Carré can still raise Circus shoptalk to the level of art. The intricate procedures of his baby sitters (bodyguards), lamplighters (watchers, safe-house men), and pavement artists (shadowers) rarely palls. . . .

[The] book remains something of a paper chase. Why? In part, one suspects, because the struggle occurs mostly in Little England, a political shire now shorn of power and purpose, where there may simply be too much central heating for the spy who comes in from the cold. . . . The remorseless world of international espionage is thus transformed into something very like a traditional English detective story with the suspects figuratively locked in the English country house as the sleuth (Smiley) pokes around and the tantalized spectators wonder if he will dare pin it on the butler. (p. 91)

> Timothy Foote, "Playing Tigers," in Time (reprinted by permission from Time, The Weekly Newsmagazine; copyright Time Inc.), June 24, 1974, pp. 88, 91.

John Le Carré's new book ["Tinker, Tailor, Soldier, Spy"] . . . reconfirms the impression that Le Carré belongs to the select company of such spy and detective story writers as Arthur Conan Doyle and Graham Greene in England and Dashiell Hammett, James M. Cain, Raymond Chandler and Ross Macdonald in America. There are those who read crime and espionage books for the plot and those who read them for the atmosphere; the former talk of "ingenious puzzles" and take pride in "pure ratiocination"; the latter think themselves more literary, worry about style and characterization, and tend to praise their favorite writers as "real novelists." Le Carré's books—like those of the six authors just mentioned—offer plenty for both kinds of readers.

"Tinker, Tailor, Soldier, Spy" is fluently written; it is full of vivid character sketches of secret agents and bureaucrats from all levels of British society, and the dialogue catches their voices well. The social and physical details of English life and the day to day activities of the intelligence service at home and abroad are convincing. Unlike many writers Le Carré is at his best showing men hard at work; he is fascinated by the office politics of the agency since the war. He even has a go at such "novelistic" effects as interlocking themes of sexual and political betrayal. Yet the plot is as tangled and suspenseful as any action fan could require, and the inductive skill of the diffident, intellectual hero should bring joy to the hearts of the purists. The scale and complexity of this novel are much greater than in any of Le Carré's previous books. . . .

Le Carré's career has been erratic from the start. Unlike most genre writers, he has never simply cranked out books according to a formula. His first two novels—a modest spy story, "Call for the Dead," in 1961 and a rather poor detective story, "A Murder of Quality," in 1962—gave little sense that Le Carré would ever amount to very much. But his third book—"The Spy Who Came in From the Cold" in 1963—was manifestly the work of a strong and original popular novelist and was greeted with enthusiasm by such British worthies as C. P. Snow, J. B. Priestley and Graham Greene (who called it "the best spy story I have ever read"). . . . His next book, "The Looking Glass War" in 1965, also sold well but it was distinctly less exciting, more of an atmospheric short story than a novel, for all its length. "A Small Town in Germany" in 1968 sold less well but is a most impressive popular novel; yet after it Le Carré abandoned the genre to write "The Naïve and Sentimental Lover," a book that failed with both critics and public.

"Tinker, Tailor, Soldier, Spy" is a full recovery, which in many ways consolidates Le Carré's career. (p. 1)

Le Carré's originality and distinction as a popular novelist lie in his use of the conventions of the spy novel for purposes of social criticism. . . .

However, are not Le Carré's novels, even at their best, falsely comforting? For all their angry social criticism, they always offer us the pleasures of imagining the world as it was portrayed in the good old-fashioned English novel of class and character, manners and morals: the surface details of the physical and social world are clearly seen; people's looks and voices are immediately categorized and brightly reproduced; the plots are complex, suspenseful, full of historical details, but they are always triumphantly concluded, all mysteries and ambiguities neatly resolved. The psychology is straightforward; motives tend to be unmixed; the tangles of sex and family life are simplified. . . .

Quite inadvertently Le Carré's novels reinforce the sodden liberalism they claim to condemn. They are nostalgic and given to self-pity; they offer two-dimensional models of human experience, melodramatic or sentimental answers to political dilemmas, and the simplistic and self-comforting suggestion that good men (and readers) should give up politics for lost and—like the victimized boy Candide—go cultivate their gardens. Le Carré's books repeatedly express a horrified, morally outraged but essentially naïve retreat from the full imagination of politics and society. . . . When Le Carré tried for depth in his last novel, he failed; modernism and the ironies of the literary novels of the 1960's are beyond him; but when, as in this new book, he shows the surface of experience in that good old-fashioned way, he is thoroughly entertaining. (p. 2)

> Richard Locke, in The New York Times Book Review (© 1974 by The New York Times Company; reprinted by permission), June 30, 1974.

[In le Carré's spy novels, not] only human motives, but the mechanics of history itself, are lost in an infinite regression of wheels within wheels. The machinery, set in motion in the past by some unknown hand, is everything. Why, you may wonder, do these unhappy men continue with their ridiculous power game? The answer, it seems, has to do with conditioning.

Bred on illusions, they have neither the equipment nor the desire to overcome the loss of these, and must find new forms of illusion. Patriotism mutates to sentimental homosexuality, to an irritable departmental esprit de corps, to a bureaucratic rationale which demands the appearance of action even if it is all about nothing. Besides, to shut up shop would be to concede victory in the power game to the United States, or the Soviet Union, or both—a fait accompli which these bloody-minded civil servants admit only to themselves, and in defiance of which they fight tooth and nail. Hence the aura of superannuated gentility, the feeling one gets from le Carré that time stopped in about 1950. Le Carré creates a very plausible, but finally unreal world. Is there really a British Secret Service, one finds oneself asking, and if so is it anything like this? Has the sophisticated, seedy version any more documentary value than the vulgar, glamorous one of Ian Fleming?

> Derek Mahon, "Dolls Within Dolls," in The Listener (© British Broadcasting Corp. 1974; reprinted by permission of Derek Mahon), July 4, 1974, p. 30.

Tinker, Tailor, Soldier, Spy . . . marks [Le Carré's] return to the spy thriller after a brief and disastrous excursion into the pseudo world of the modern so-called 'straight' novel with the appalling [The] Naïve and Sentimental Lover. . . .

The first-mentioned novel marks the return to the centre of the stage of Le Carré's finest creation, George Smiley, brilliant spy and totally inadequate man. Smiley becomes involved in a plot of unbelievably complex proportions. . . . This story—which is brilliantly complex, and makes *The Spy* [*Who Came in from the Cold*] look like a gentle Henty romp—is, moreover, apparently only the first in a series of rounds between Smiley and [a] new Russian mastermind in which, it seems, Smiley is himself to become Control. . . .

Le Carré claims that the popularity of his work depends on a human fascination with deceit, and with treason as a capital form of deceit. Everybody in his books is a deceiver, almost everybody a potential traitor. James Cameron, in a recent brilliant critique of the books, stresses their fascination as novels of *manners*, in which the style and world of the characters—the obscure code-names, the apparently impenetrable but easily explained obscurity of the professional spying jargon—come to have a sufficiency of their own.

I am not sure that Le Carré altogether sees the implication of his own generalisation about his own work; nor that the critics . . . see the real and simple quality of the affirmations of the Le Carré characters. One speech of one such character that will ring for a long time in my ears is a passage from *A Small Town in Germany* in which a Foreign Office official makes a deep and bitter pronouncement, markedly nostalgic in character, on the decline of British power, the horror of that event, and the righteous anger to which human complicity in its occurence should give rise. It is this feeling, lying behind all the taradiddle of complexity, psychologising and shabbiness which gives the Le Carré spy novels their power.

And I want to develop the argument a little further. In the new book there is a whole series of characters—Jim, the battered, physically crooked, morally integral, ex-spy schoolteacher is the principal one, and a fulcrum of the action—who are modernised and more complex versions of the larger than life heroes of Buchan and his followers. Beneath the hatred of his country's decline, and the hatred of those responsible by their lack of vitality for it, and beneath his dark and seething regret for the past, John Le Carré is an adventure story writer in the grand British tradition. By his skill, and his extension of the range of his models, as much as through his own confused understanding of his heritage, he surpasses the general run of the modern novelists, and achieves, with this book, which is the best he has written, a great thriller.

> *"Crime Compendium," in* The Spectator *(© 1974 by* The Spectator; *reprinted by permission of* The Spectator), *July 6, 1974, p. 21.*

Enthusiasm is not the best tactical posture. For a reviewer alive to the sophisticated attractions of jaundice it's also an abdication. All the same I find it difficult to be temperate about saying how much I enjoyed John Le Carré's new novel. *Tinker Tailor Soldier Spy* marks his return to the spy format after an exploratory peep into the straight world. Straight but parallel also: the contours of Le Carré's densely imagined, filthy landscape of deceit and murder are complementary to the features of normality, one reason why his descriptions of the underworld are so cogent. With no journalistic accumulation of technicalities in the manner of Forsyth, none of Len Deighton's obsession with gadgetry, Le Carré concentrates on inflections, submerged mannerisms, the elliptical shorthand of an obscure professionalism.

Here he plays the values of ordinary life off against 'trade' values, not to shock or to differentiate but to point out how close the spy is to the citizen. George Smiley, the shambling, paunchy hero of this novel and also of *Call for the Dead* is a top-class intelligence man, yet his responses remain profoundly conventional. So far from behaving like a spy in private life he tries to behave decently in the professional life, with disastrous consequences. It is precisely this vulnerability which makes him such an engaging figure. The same goes for his colleagues, despite their heavily meaningful names (autocratic Control, aloof Alleline). One is shocked not by their capacity for deceit but by their inclination to trust. . . .

A perceptive reader [is] entranced not so much by the ramifications of the plot, beautifully engineered though it is, as by concern for the characters, a rare thing in thrillers. (p. 52)

> *Timothy Mo, in* New Statesman *(© 1974* The Statesman & Nation Publishing Co. Ltd.), *July 12, 1974.*

Tinker, Tailor, Soldier, Spy . . . [is an] outstanding novel, based on England's Kim Philby affair, by the man who gave depth and dimension to the agents lurking behind the headline stories of the Cold War. It would be a mistake to describe this as merely a thriller; there is a fullness of characterization here that is found in few novels of any sort today, and the felicity of expression alone would justify reading it. Not to mention, of course, that Le Carré tells an absorbing story. (p. 1)

> Book World—The Washington Post *(© The* Washington Post), *December 8, 1974.*

John le Carré's *Tinker, Tailor, Soldier, Spy* . . . is a detective story about spies (a Russian agent has burrowed deep into England's intelligence service), rooted not in extravagant fantasies but in the realities of bureaucratic rivalry. Through its vapors of nostalgia, bitterness and understated pessimism, we learn a lot about mendacity, greed and complacency, the self-delusion that governs the lives of able and intelligent men. (p. 62)

> *Peter S. Prescott, in* Newsweek *(copyright 1974 by Newsweek, Inc.; all rights reserved; reprinted by permission), December 30, 1974.*

[Le Carré] . . . is really dull and really pretentious in *Tinker, Tailor, Soldier, Spy*, plodding and gloomy. Eric Ambler gave the spy story good plots and well-observed exotic atmospheres; Le Carré offers only boring shoptalk, in the name of telling it like it is, presumably, the spy business is just a business, see, so who is to complain if he sounds like Sloan Wilson in *The Man in the Gray Flannel Suit*. Where Joseph Heller tries, and tries and tries, to find edges and sadnesses to the clichés about big company bureaucracies, Le Carré accepts them, literally, gloomily. I kept wondering if he were trying to find some way to fool all the people all the time. (p. 626)

Roger Sale, in The Hudson Review *(copyright © 1974 by The Hudson Review, Inc.; reprinted by permission), Vol. XXVII, No. 4, Winter, 1974-75.*

*   *   *

LEHMANN, Rosamond   1905-

Rosamond Lehmann is an English novelist and short story writer. Although Ms Lehmann has published little since the early 1950s, critics urge rediscovery of her skillful and convincing studies of young women growing up and mature women in love.

Rosamond Lehmann has limitations which are severe enough to exclude her from the first rank of novelists of her period. More importantly, they have affected her productivity, so that after *The Ballad and the Source*, the Everest of her career, she had nowhere to go but down, and back, to *The Echoing Grove*. She is a demanding and scrupulous writer—her slight critical writing attests to that—and, when the source was running dry, as it obviously was in *The Echoing Grove*, she stopped, perhaps permanently.

But there is a reverse side to the coin. Some of the qualities [critics have termed] limitations—"reminiscence, whimsy, delicacy, unfulfillment," "memories of childhood and youth"—are the very qualities that distinguished *Invitation to the Waltz* and *Dusty Answer* and that contributed to *The Ballad and the Source*. They became limitations only when Miss Lehmann could not reach beyond them to the more vigorous qualities necessary for a mature and wide vision of life. One expects a Bildungsroman of a young writer, but not of a mature writer, and certainly not a continuous one. Her world may be a "half-world," . . . it may be limited in theme and vision; but within its bounds it is real. Within her range, narrow as it admittedly is, Rosamond Lehmann has done superb work; and at least two of the novels, the third in time, *Invitation to the Waltz*, and the fifth, *The Ballad and the Source*, are genuine works of the imagination.

To attempt to place Miss Lehmann in relation to other novelists of the between-the-wars period poses a difficulty, for she is not easily categorized. Unlike the majority, she has no discernible moral or intellectual, social or political philosophies. She is not a satirist of the contemporary scene, as are Huxley and Waugh. She does not rail against the destructiveness of the industrialized world to the individual, as did Lawrence. She is not preoccupied with the problem of good and evil, as is Greene. If she has a religion, it does not reveal itself in her novels, nor does her political attitude. Although she has experimented with technique, she is not an innovator in the sense that Joyce and Virginia Woolf were. And, although she greatly admires the work of Forster, she can hardly be said to share his interest in intellectualizing the novel.

There is in one sense, however, a link between Miss Lehmann and E. M. Forster: their shared belief that it is personal relationships that matter most in life and in art. Forster's "only connect" philosophy permeates Miss Lehmann's work, not in an explicit philosophy, but in a concentration on personal relationships to the exclusion of practically everything else. (pp. 22-4)

There is nothing narrow in this concept of the principal concern of the novelist. On the contrary, it places Miss Lehmann in the mainstream of the English novel. (p. 24)

Rosamond Lehmann has, generally, three themes. The first, though not in importance, centers around the romantic relationships between men and women, or, more specifically, *women in love*. This theme dominates *The Weather in the Streets* and *The Echoing Grove*. Her second theme, *adolescence* or the *celebration of youth and beauty*, is the basis of *Dusty Answer* and *Invitation to the Waltz*. Her third theme, growing out of the second, can best be termed *loss of youth* or *nostalgia for lost youth*. This is the principal theme of *A Note in Music*, but it also informs *Dusty Answer* and *The Echoing Grove*.

In fact, one can almost conclude that the disillusionment implied in *nostalgia for lost youth* is her principal theme, and the other two merely variations on it. . . . Even in *The Ballad and the Source*, the one novel in which Miss Lehmann breaks the bonds of her normal visionary world, the innocence of the child-observer Rebecca is shattered by the glimpses she has of adult corruption.

This pervasive theme of disillusionment with the adult world is indicative of one of Miss Lehmann's limitations. Disillusionment is, of course, a legitimate theme—perhaps it is *the* theme of the Age of Anxiety—but to use it time and again, without comment and without *thought*, is to reveal a narrow view of human life. Her major characters are almost without exception feeling, not thinking people; and, since Miss Lehmann does not act as commentator on their points of view, one is left with the conclusion that the vision of life represented by the characters is that of the author too.

A second limitation is in the range of her characterization. She seems unable to create a fully realized, three-dimensional male character. All of her protagonists are women. (pp. 25-6)

Rosamond Lehmann's world is a world of young girls and women—growing up, falling in love, regretting, growing older. The men who are there exist in the shadows; one knows them, with the exception of Rickie, only through the eyes of the women. The social background of these women is the upper-middle class: indeed, the impression is overwhelming that Judith, Olivia, Rebecca, Dinah, and Madeleine come from the same family. The fathers, at least, of all of them, although fleeting in appearance, seem to be the same man and bear a strong resemblance to Miss Lehmann's own father. . . . (pp. 26-7)

1927, the year of *Dusty Answer* and of Elizabeth Bowen's *The Hotel*, both first novels, was also the year of Virginia Woolf's *To the Lighthouse*. The significance of this otherwise unimportant coincidence is that, if Miss Lehmann can be said to resemble any other novelists of her era, she resembles not only the woman who began her novelist career at the same time, but also the older writer whose most perfect work appeared in 1927. The similarity lies mostly in the poetic sensibility which all three possess, a sensibility which is peculiarly feminine. There is something of the lyric poet in all three, as well as a deep knowledge of the feminine psyche.

The Woolfian influence, if it can be called that, is in the style—the gossamer poetic quality of the prose. With Elizabeth Bowen, Miss Lehmann also shares a similarity of character and situation. The former's portrayals of young girls approaching the adult world and of young women in romantic situations resemble Miss Lehmann's. Such a novel as *A World of Love*, though not good Bowen, could almost have been written by Miss Lehmann. (p. 27)

Rosamond Lehmann's move from the enchanted adolescent world of *Dusty Answer* to the defeated adult one of *A Note in Music* effects an enlargement of technique but a diminution of emotional power. The fault lies in the nature of the theme; for—without the ennobling touch of tragedy, or at least some vital response in the narrator—such material is bound to appear arid and meaningless: a denial of the value of human life. If life's value is denied, then surely the art that represents the denial becomes irrelevant. Because most of the vitality of *A Note in Music* belongs to the prose and not to the characters, the result hovers close to an intellectual exercise in despair displayed against a background of beautiful prose.

In her third novel, *Invitation to the Waltz* (1932), Miss Lehmann makes an abrupt turnabout and, eschewing despair, returns to the enchanted adolescent world she began with—with a difference. (p. 57)

[A] variety of age groups, social classes, and points of view gives *Invitation to the Waltz* a broader base than *Dusty Answer* and, in spite of the restricted time scheme, offers opportunities for contrasts lacking in the earlier work. At the same time, unlike *Dusty Answer*, in which Judith is pictured almost completely apart from family and assumes thereby a kind of floating isolation, Olivia is firmly rooted in family life with a definable background in time. The novel gains in solidity from these differences. (p. 59)

Invitation to the Waltz is not merely a delicious trifle. It is a microcosm in which an adolescent's experiences during a single week reflect the adult world she will soon know. Hints of tragedy, of illness, of despair, of cruelty, and of lust abound in the book; and, if one comes away from it remembering only the charming James and the humorous awkwardness of Olivia, the fault lies with the reader, not the book. The dark side of life is there, always balancing the lighter, though never, because Olivia is young and still undisillusioned, overwhelming it. Perhaps [George] Dangerfield is saying more about himself than about *Invitation to the Waltz* when he remarks that the older characters "answer to something in us that is mature and disillusioned." (pp. 74-5)

Like *Invitation to the Waltz*, *The Ballad and the Source* is a near perfect union of technique and substance; but the world described is [quite different]. One needs no "willing suspension of disbelief" for *Invitation to the Waltz*; one needs it in abundance for *The Ballad and the Source*. Not that there is anything supernatural in the book, but the highly colored, highly romantic story it tells treads close to that thin line between drama and melodrama; and the method by which it is told in some ways taxes the credulity of the reader. The enormous success of the book is indicated by the fact that few of its articulate readers have been unable to grant it the necessary "suspension of disbelief."

The technique of *The Ballad and the Source* is unlike anything Miss Lehmann attempted previously. (pp. 89-90)

The point of view . . . is not just the double one of the narrator as character and observer (both adult and child), but rather a many faceted point of view in which five people, including the narrator, look at a three-generation tale of intricate human passions and psychological motivations, and emerge with often contradictory impressions.

The technique is in part that used by Henry James in *What*

Maisie Knew, but with obvious variations. James employs the third-person point of view; Miss Lehmann, the first. Maisie is the focal point of the events, her life wholly dependent on their outcome. Rebecca Landon in *The Ballad and the Source* is only indirectly involved in the events. Maisie learns through observation; she is not told what is going on. Rebecca is the recipient of confidences, but she also uses her powers of observation to form her own conclusions. The narration of *What Maisie Knew* is straight forward; that of *The Ballad and the Source* moves forward and backward in time. Where the two books are most alike is in their use of the consciousness of a child-observer to illumine the effect of adult experience on childhood innocence. More than one critic has suggested that not only the technique but the spirit of *The Ballad and the Source* is Jamesian. . . . [There] are Jamesian qualities; but not all of them are peculiarly Jamesian. Conrad, for one, also wrote [psychological mysteries emphasizing psychological motives], and one could make out quite a good case for a Conradian influence on Miss Lehmann's book. The Jamesian influence can easily be overemphasized to the point of absurdity, for a comparison of *What Maisie Knew* and *The Ballad and the Source* reveals very striking general differences between the two writers. James is a moralist; Miss Lehmann is not. James's work is sharply intellectual; Miss Lehmann's is highly emotional. The prose styles of the two writers are as far apart as one can imagine; the delicate lyricism of Miss Lehmann would have been anathema to James.

In theme, however, *The Ballad and the Source* does bear a resemblance to the work of James, among countless others; for it is concerned with the difficulty of ascertaining the truth about human character. (pp. 90-1)

Sibyl Anstey Herbert Jardine [is] the central character of *The Ballad and the Source*, and one of the most fascinatingly complex characters imaginable. The search for truth which is the central theme of the book, is the search by Rebecca for the truth about Mrs. Jardine. . . . (p. 92)

Without doubt this portrait is Miss Lehmann's masterpiece. Mrs. Jardine's very ambiguity insures her hold on the reader's imagination; for, when the book is finished and laid aside, she refuses to loosen her grip on the reader. Part of her power stems not merely from the complexity but from the elusiveness of her character—from her refusal to be pinned down to any simple interpretation. . . .

She is of course vicious, egotistical, disagreeable; but she also possesses those qualities that make Gil and Rebecca love her—her concern for truth, her kindness to children, her respect for individuality. In other words, it is possible both to admire her and to be horrified by her, even to pity her. Mrs. Jardine victimizes others but she is also the victim of her own delusions. There can be no doubt that her later life consists of an unremitting search for self-justification; she must always have a listener against whose reactions she can test the validity of her behavior. The seemingly self-possessed woman is never completely certain. . . . (p. 106)

Diana Trilling concludes that "the reader is left with the heavy burden of Mrs. Jardine's ambivalent morality; even in Mrs. Jardine's lies we have been taught to see a certain truth." This is the answer to the fascination of the book: the fact that, even at the end, one cannot be sure what Mrs.

Jardine is. It is also the characteristic that links *The Ballad and the Source* with the earlier *A Note in Music*, in which Miss Lehmann attempts with less success a similar exploration of the nature of reality. . . .

Mrs. Trilling admires the "moral and technical imagination" of the book but deplores the lack of what she terms "moral passion." One has the impression, she writes, that Miss Lehmann cares "more about the outcome of a story than about the outcome of life itself." This seems an unfair judgment, for, after all, what Mrs. Trilling really objects to is the fact that the narrator does not take a moral stand on the character of Mrs. Jardine. But if Rebecca did, the whole point of the book would be lost since Miss Lehmann's aim is to show the difficulty of making correct moral judgments. . . . Miss Lehmann leaves moral judgments to her readers, who, at the last, know more than any of the characters. If the narrator intruded herself anymore than she does, the novel would lose one of its most potent qualities—the fascination of a many-sided truth. (p. 107)

From the enchanted adolescent world of her first novel, *Dusty Answer*, to the disillusioned adult world of her last, *The Echoing Grove*, the pendulum of Rosamond Lehmann's vision of life swings back and forth between enchantment and disillusionment, childhood and adulthood, in a strikingly regular pattern which is broken only once, by *The Ballad and the Source*. In this novel alone does Miss Lehmann break the mold of her vision to emerge into a larger world in which vitality, even though it be destructive, is at least possible to adults. Mrs. Jardine may not be an admirable human being, she may even be criminally destructive, but she is always alive. She would never—as do Norah and Grace, Madeleine and Dinah—resign herself to a monotonous existence in which everything worthwhile belongs to the past. She has too vivid a conception of the source of life to entertain such negation: "'The source, Rebecca! The fount of life—the source, the quick spring that rises in illimitable depths of darkness and flows through every living thing from generation to generation. It is what we feel mounting in us when we say: "I know! I love! I *am*!" Do you understand me now?'" (p. 139)

In view of Mrs. Jardine's character and past, one can consider this speech ironic; but the basic validity of the idea offers an insight into Miss Lehmann's failure to find much in adult experience which does not end in disillusionment. Elsewhere in *The Ballad and the Source*, the adult Rebecca, remembering the qualities of her grandmother, speaks of her "energy with a core like the crack and sting of a whip. It was this, this last that had left our house, and perhaps most similar houses at that period. . . . Looking back now, one might express it by saying there seemed disillusionments lurking, unformulated doubts about overcoming difficulties; a defeat somewhere, a failure of the vital impulse". . . . Surely Miss Lehmann is speaking here, not only *as* the character of Rebecca, but *through* the character, in order to express her own dissatisfaction with the contemporary world. (pp. 139-40)

One must assume . . . that, since she offers no reasons for the prevailing disillusionment of her adult characters, she is saying that disillusionment is an inevitable result of growing up and that adulthood for her is equated with disillusionment.

Where Miss Lehmann fails in her adult novels—*A Note in Music, The Weather in the Streets*, and *The Echoing Grove*—is not in her choice of theme but in her creation of characters to embody it. With the exception of Olivia, her major characters in these novels are, it must be confessed, close to "the impoverished, so frequently non-adult, dull and neurotic novel-figure of today" that she herself deplores [in "The Future of the Novel?"]. It is not life that defeats Norah and Rickie and the others, but themselves. One has the feeling that they are condemned to futile lives, not because they have grown up but because they have refused to grow up. Masquerading as adults, they are really children pouting because they have been denied some pleasure they have set their hearts on. They are representatives of the "failure of the vital impulse." (pp. 140-41)

It is for this reason that Miss Lehmann's major novels are *Dusty Answer* and *Invitation to the Waltz*, the two primarily concerned with childhood and adolescence, and *The Ballad and the Source*, in which adolescence is the mirror of the adult world. In these three Miss Lehmann reveals not only the "vital impulse," but the source of her own creative center, which is her extraordinary ability to recreate the visionary world of childhood and youth. The major characters of these novels are alive, vital, unforgettable—in every way superior creations. *Dusty Answer* . . . must be labeled a qualified success because of its failure in the last portion; but the other two are first-rate works of the imagination in which technique and substance blend into a superb unity. (p. 141)

Perhaps the conflict between generations ["imaginatively treated," according to this reviewer] would be better termed a conflict between generations of women. In none of the novels does the father of the family make more than a brief appearance, and in every case he is older than the mother, scholarly in tastes, and tolerant toward human frailties. In *Invitation to the Waltz* and in *The Weather in the Streets*, he is ill; in *The Echoing Grove*, he dies after a long illness; in *The Ballad and the Source*, he "set[s] out without complaint upon his slow heart-rending journey into the shadows". . . . The conclusion is inescapable that the same man posed for all the fathers and that he is probably Rudolph Lehmann. Autobiographical implications aside, the similarity of the fathers and their shadowy presences in the family groups illustrate the most salient of Miss Lehmann's limitations as a novelist—her inability to create a fully realized male character.

In four of the novels—*Dusty Answer, A Note in Music, Invitation to the Waltz* and *The Ballad and the Source*—her inability to penetrate the male mind is not a serious disadvantage because the nature of her material does not demand a major male character. But in the two novels which center on the relationships between men and women in "the love game," the limitation is fatal. Miss Lehmann attempts to evade the problem in *The Weather in the Streets* by confining her characterization of Rollo to an outside view; he is seen through Olivia's memory of him, and with Olivia in scenes described in the third person. But never for a moment does one have any idea of what he is thinking. If Miss Lehmann's point of view in the novel were always that of Olivia, this would not be so important; but occasionally she utilizes the points of view of two minor characters, Kate and Mrs. Curtis. The result is a novel in which some of the minor characters, including Lady Spencer, are more vivid than one of the two major characters.

In *The Echoing Grove*, on the other hand, Miss Lehmann, bravely facing her problem, utilizes an internal approach to the male of her triangle and gives him as much attention, if not more, than she does the two women involved. The end of the love affair, in the "Morning" section, is told mostly from Rickie's point of view; but unfortunately Rickie is little more than the stereotyped weak, vacillating, inadequate man. When, in the "Midnight" section, Miss Lehmann unexpectedly attempts to give Rickie stature, thereby destroying his validity even as a type, Rickie as a character is dead. And so is the novel. (pp. 143-44)

Rosamond Lehmann's world is a feminine world, whether the "she" be a child of ten listening intently to stories of a life she has yet to know, or an aristocratic dowager defending her rigid standards of conduct against the assault of her son's mistress. She is usually of the upper middle class, but she may be of the aristocracy, or she may be a prostitute. Whoever she is, Rosamond Lehmann knows the secrets of her heart as few novelists can.

Much has been said about the limitations of Miss Lehmann's art; but, in the final analysis, it is fairer to judge her not by what she fails to do, but by what she succeeds in doing. Equipped with an understanding of family life and of social classes, and gifted with a beautiful prose style and an extraordinary insight into the thought processes of children and women, she has created out of her vision six novels, every one of which attests to the mark of the superior craftsman, and two of which lie close to that faint line which separates the near-great from the great novel. If she is not a Bach of the novel, she most assuredly is a Chopin. (p. 144)

> *Diana E. LeStourgeon, in her* Rosamond Lehmann *(copyright 1965 by Twayne Publishers, Inc.; reprinted with the permission of Twayne Publishers, A Division of G. K. Hall & Co., Boston), Twayne, 1965.*

The recent interest in women's fiction, studies, and points of view has revived many literary reputations from Mrs. Gaskell to Anaïs Nin, but has, so far, apparently neglected Rosamond Lehmann. Twenty-five or thirty years ago, however, Miss Lehmann was frequently discussed as fully the equal of Elizabeth Bowen and almost the equal of Virginia Woolf, all three drawn together under the heading of "feminine," a term that did not seem so condescending then as it does now, that connoted the delicate, the perceptive, the working of insight in a smaller area often missed by the blunter, clumsier, "masculine" sensibility. The 1945 American publishers of *The Ballad and the Source*, Miss Lehmann's best-known novel, trumpeted this "feminine" fiction with a lemon-pistachio cover and raspberry letters. Part of the reason for the current neglect of Miss Lehmann's work is clearly her silence. After publishing four novels in the first decade of her career (1927 through 1936), she has published only two novels, five short stories, one play, and a slim volume of "fragments of an inner life" since 1936—and no fiction at all in the last twenty years. But I have assumed there must be other reasons as well, attitudes expressed within the fiction, perhaps not unlike those attitudes contained in Doris Lessing's recent *The Summer Before the Dark* that caused so many of the reviewers to complain because Lessing had not provided some blazingly affirmative new role for her forty-five-year-

old heroine. Another reason, more valid critically, might be flaws in Miss Lehmann's work not so easily visible a generation ago. (p. 203)

From her third novel on, from *Invitation to the Waltz* (1932)—a brilliantly compressed novel that presents only two days, her seventeenth birthday and her first dance, in the heroine's vibrant search for experience, much like a less thematically underlined version of some of Katherine Mansfield's stories—Miss Lehmann's central character is always placed within a family, has relationships to react against as well as those to establish. The point of view is invariably that of the second daughter, attracted to and in rebellion from her fair, devoted, more conventional, and complacent older sister. They have a kind, intelligent, remote father, an old upper-middle class professional who gradually weakens and dies over a period of about ten years; a competent and managing mother, secure socially, who attempts to hold the family in place; and one or two (depending on the novel) younger siblings, the youngest the only boy whom everyone worships. The family structure is a locus of settled time, place, relationships, and emotion from which the heroine must break in order to find herself. The search for identity and love is not, however, confined to the adolescent, for, in the later novels, like *The Echoing Grove* (1953), the second daughter becomes the mistress and the older daughter the wife in a novel about the strains of a man in love with each of two sisters. Miss Lehmann's second novel, *A Note in Music* (1930), avoids the centrality of the family unit, but the point of view is still that of the woman committed to something that restricts her. (p. 204)

Miss Lehmann's heroines are all initially protected members of the upper-middle class and invariably confront representatives from other classes as they break away.... [At] each moment, the sense of possible vitality in a relationship is undercut by an awareness of class distinctions. Each person, underneath, is lonely and defeated; each longs for a connection and is sensitive to just those exterior elements of speech, behavior, and attitude that make connection most difficult. (p. 205)

All Miss Lehmann's heroines have a sense of history that is both personal and general and are part of a past they are struggling to repudiate or recapture, sometimes both simultaneously as in *The Weather in the Streets*. *A Note in Music* takes its title from a quotation by Walter Savage Landor: "But the present, like a note in music, is nothing but as it appertains to what is past and what is to come." Throughout that novel, the characters try to seize the "moment," to crystallize an identity out of the flux of experience, a process like that sometimes achieved by characters in Virginia Woolf's novels, but, in Miss Lehmann's fiction, the "moment," the unique present, never appears or is illusory or immediately dissolves. Historical flux dominates.... *The Ballad and the Source* links the personal history of one family to the more general decline of the English upper classes in the first twenty years of this century, providing the adolescents of 1920 with "reminiscent conversations" so that "their identity, to themselves so dubious, so cloudy, becomes clarified."

The extensions of the sensitive self into society and history give density and meaning to the fiction, but they give no permanence or consolation to the characters. A hard sense of the inconsolability of human experience dominates the fiction: all emotions change, no love is fully matched or requited, all human beings die. . . . All the novels bring the characters to the recognition that death is the "dusty answer"—an answer that is both unsatisfactory and inescapable—to the human search that is "hot for certainties," to refer to the quotation from Meredith that reverberates throughout Miss Lehmann's work. Invariably, human sexuality is the principal means for an attempt to impose the self upon experience, to create an intense connection that can assuage the inevitable forces of time, history, death. And the sexual impulses described are sometimes, in a muted and secondary way, homosexual, particularly in *Dusty Answer, The Weather in the Streets*, and *The Echoing Grove*, for the sense of sexual connection, of expressing the self in close relationship, is more important than the nature of the relationship's object. Sex is primarily a release of self, not a search for an appropriate or particular kind of other. In all the novels, the sexual connections are transitory, defeated, the heroines left alone at the end with the recognition that they have nothing beyond themselves. In *The Echoing Grove*, in which two sisters have loved the same man, now dead, and in which the ending suggests that, for the mistress, her sister has always been more central, more loved, and more the adversary than has the man, the collapse of the affair is summarized with a line from Blake: "Go love without the help of anything on earth." Reviewers and critics have sometimes mentioned the disillusionment as a principal limitation of Miss Lehmann's fiction. Yet it is only a limitation from a perspective that asserts a human capacity to triumph over or in spite of time and death. And the simultaneously sharp and sympathetic refusal to console is also the "limitation" implicit in Housman's poems, in Chekhov's plays and stories, and in Arnold Bennett's serious fiction.

Reviewers of Miss Lehmann's fiction when it came out pasted the judgment of "feminine" as another "limitation," described her work as "sensitive," as seeing things always from a woman's point of view and unable to depict men convincingly. As a fact, although not as a charge, the designation of a "feminine" perspective is accurate. In *Dusty Answer*, at the end, the heroine deplores the Cambridge atmosphere that "disliked and distrusted her and all other females." The heroines, too, are always conscious of their femininity, aware of how they look, how their clothes both enhance and characterize them (the use of clothes is particularly well done in *Invitation to the Waltz*), how others respond to them. And, at times, for example in *The Weather in the Streets*, heroines instruct themselves on how to be the appropriate mistress to a married man, somewhat in the manner of Helen Gurley Brown's *Cosmopolitan*, although Miss Lehmann's characters are always far more sensitive to the emotional strains and ambivalences involved in acting out such a code. But this kind of "feminine" perspective is only a "limitation" from a point of view that regards world currency exchange or international religious movements as vastly more significant than personal relations or love, that adheres to a hierarchy of occupational values. In addition, I find the characterizations of Miss Lehmann's men most convincing and effective. Particularly in *The Weather in the Streets* and *The Echoing Grove*, the men at the apex of adulterous triangles, each caught between two women (both of whom he loves), are presented with an insight that can shatter the male ego. In Miss Lehmann's world, the men, only apparently "passive" and invariably reacting to difficult situations with superficial

calm, can love more spontaneously or with more equanimity than the women can, but they also love more irresponsibly and are less sensitive to the emotional obligations love entails. They sacrifice both a sense of history and of consistency to keeping their cool. Miss Lehmann makes no moral judgments on the sexual roles. Rather, with considerable density of detail, with intelligence and a refusal to settle for easy slogans, she develops the implications of some of the differences between men and women in love.

Critics have always praised Miss Lehmann's prose, its clarity, its finish, its sensitivity, its "beauty," sometimes as a kind of minor compensation for the major limitations of her femininity and her disillusionment. . . . And the prose is invariably sharp and sensitive, an instrument that formulates as much of human impulse, chaos, and effort as, in Miss Lehmann's terms, one can. Like the love affair that, in one novel, is the temporary refuge from the "rain, wind, fog" of London winters, protection from the "weather" in the streets, the prose, never merely decorative, is the protection of the human perspective, the impermanent hedge against death. But there is also sometimes another note in the prose that I find less easy to accommodate as the instrument of a sensitive, lucid, and unconsoling human formulation. This is a kind of rhapsodic prose, an occasional flight into the mysteries of organic nature. . . . These interludes seem almost animistic, sensitive to spirits permeating the natural world, closer in ways to the prose of John Cowper Powys than to that of Katherine Mansfield. This rhapsodic prose is most apparent and given most room in *The Ballad and the Source*, the novel in which the attempt to discover the "source," the beginning of the mysteries that influence three generations, "the fount of life," is most conscious and articulate. The central figure of the novel, Mrs. Jardine, is seen as "savage," "unearthly," an "enchantress" of considerable charm or an "Enchantress Queen in an antique ballad of revenge.". . . [It] lacks, for me, the immediacy of the other novels, dissipates its force in long confessionals and melodramatic revelations. Animistic prose has its drawbacks and it does not, at least for Miss Lehmann, seem integrated well into the form of the novel. In fact, as apparent in *The Swan in the Evening* (1967), more recent experience has caused Miss Lehmann to focus more and more on the animistic and the mystical, and she has not written fiction at all. One kind of personal experience, most often that which refuses consolation, is transmuted into fiction; another kind of personal experience, less publicly communicable, more mysterious and more recondite, is transmuted into "fragments of an inner life." Yet hints of the mystical, bits of the animistic, are occasionally visible in all her prose.

The fact that implications that can be derived from her different kinds of prose are not fully integrated into a single kind of fiction might be one reason that Miss Lehmann's work has been so unjustly neglected. More probably, however, the reasons are less valid critically. Rosamond Lehmann is neither strident nor teachable; her work cannot easily be either extrapolated into a simplified and positive perspective, a message, or analyzed meaningfully in terms of an imagistic pattern or structure that yields what was not visible before. Unlike the novelists with whom she was most frequently compared, Virginia Woolf and Elizabeth Bowen, Rosamond Lehmann does not expand or reveal under the stress of rigorous analysis. Virginia Woolf, in her fiction, attempted to define identity, to say "there she was," in terms that dealt simultaneously with both individuals and a generalized essence of humanity. Although Miss Lehmann enthusiastically admired Woolf's fiction . . ., she never strives for that kind of metaphysical coherence, never organizes a novel around reaching a lighthouse. Elizabeth Bowen's fiction, particularly her best-known work of the thirties and forties, carefully shapes and structures the moral dimensions of the characters she creates, has heroines, monsters, and various stages in between. Miss Lehmann's fiction relentlessly refuses to judge. Metaphysically and morally, although not stylistically, her novels are closer to those of Arnold Bennett than to those of either Virginia Woolf or Elizabeth Bowen. (pp. 205-10)

I [have] found myself drawn to the more sprawling "adult" novels, to *A Note in Music, The Weather in the Streets,* and *The Echoing Grove,* novels of greater subtlety, complexity, and density of experience. . . . The country pubs and hotels in England in the thirties show every physical and social timber in *The Weather in the Streets;* what it was like for a woman to live with two growing children in the country during World War II is conveyed with thorough brilliance in long short stories such as "A Dream of Winter" and "Wonderful Holidays"; an older English family, in its reticences, its follies, and its braveries, is seen, without sentimentality or nostalgia, in "The Red-Haired Miss Daintreys." Miss Lehmann's images are often strikingly suggestive descriptions. In one story set during the cold winter of 1939-40, the winter of the "phony" war, "The war sprawled everywhere inert: like a child too big to get born it would die in the womb and be shovelled underground, disgracefully, as monsters are, and after a while, with returning health and a change of scene, we would forget that we conceived it." Less definably historical or geographical experience is also presented: the sense of begrudged time all around in the man divided between a wife and a mistress, the defenses that preserve a marriage, and the sisters who can reconcile by betraying the dead man they both wanted in *The Echoing Grove.* All of these, admittedly, are simply atoms of experience, not a pattern to explain, judge, or transform that experience. Yet the atoms are interesting and alive, and they radiate, with a sense of total honesty, an intelligent woman's version of her time and place. (pp. 210-11)

> *James Gindin, "Rosamond Lehmann: A Revaluation," in* Contemporary Literature *(© 1974 by the Board of Regents of the University of Wisconsin System), Vol. 15, No. 2, Spring, 1974, pp. 203-11.*

* * *

LELCHUK, Alan   1938-

Lelchuk is an American novelist. (See also *Contemporary Authors*, Vols. 45-48.)

[In *American Mischief,* a] Dean at Cardozo College, right outside Boston, keeps a harem and tries to talk like Moses Herzog about the pleasures and pains of being a contemporary man who goes about and visits women. A student at Cardozo admires the Dean for the "honesty" of having a harem, and hates him for his old-fashioned politics and morality. So, after warming up his campaign of guerrilla politics by raping a fourteen-year-old virgin, murdering Norman Mailer, and sacking the Fogg Museum, the student kidnaps the Dean and a group of other literate liberals

and carts them off to a hideout in New Hampshire where the older folks are to be educated in the task of reshaping America.

Now there is no Cardozo College, but there is a Brandeis, a Norman Mailer, a Fogg Museum, and a New Hampshire. Presumably there is a dean somewhere who keeps a harem, and there certainly are guerrilla students who would like to kidnap old-line liberals. But still, *American Mischief* is not a novel. It is as real as [a] State Farm ad, and one hopes that quick identification of its phoniness will give us better things to argue about in 1973. . . .

Lelchuk is hard pressed to get anyone to believe he wrote all that . . . pornography [in the opening section] just to draw an "accurate picture" of decadent America. . . .

[In] the next section a student leader, Lenny Pincus, describes his transformation from a thoughtful radical loner to a gorilla trying to get more in touch with raw current reality. . . . [This takes] up half the book, and we are supposed to revalue our earlier position and realize the Dean may have had something when he insisted that the trouble with the kids is that they didn't know guerrillas turned into gorillas. Having done that, we are supposed to think back to the Dean and his filthy harem and feel caught deep in some moral ambivalence about modern America.

We all know that the point about pornography is that it is meant to happen to readers, not to characters, so we know, reading the first 150 pages, that we—those of us who are male—are supposed to admit our envy of the Dean's antics or else be condemned as liars. But the rest of the book is like that, too; nothing happens to anyone inside, it's all meant for us alone. If, guiltily but willingly, we repudiate the Dean and his harem, we do so realizing America has brought its leaders to this pass, and therefore side or sympathize with the guerrillas who want to change all that. But by the time a black girl shits on one of the Dean's mistresses in the New Hampshire snow, we are meant to see what a bind the country is in, caught between the decadence of the Dean and the barbarism of the kids. But because none of the characters realizes any of this, the novel seems like pornography.

Lelchuk seems to be trying to confront us with a moral dilemma when in fact he is giving us only a crude political choice. The effect of the fictional method is not even to insist upon the choice but to let us have it both ways. Ostensibly we will feel that if we aren't damned as liberals or revolutionaries we will be damned as libertines or prudes. In fact we are free to be excited by the black girl's defecation *and* to be repulsed by her animality, to accept the pyrotechnic use of Mailer's own language to imagine his murder, *and* to go along with Lenny when he says later that rhetorical murders are false and a sign of incomplete political thinking. The book seeks to have no life of its own, only to repulse or excite or frighten its readers.

American Mischief reads right along, dirty and brutal and effortless, but it takes four full working days to finish, and at the end I could only hope that by some miracle no one would ever feel obliged to argue with me, or with anyone, about it. (p. 21)

> *Roger Sale, in* The New York Review of Books *(reprinted with permission from* The New York Review of Books; *copyright © 1973 NYREV, Inc.), February 8, 1973.*

When a large novel is badly organized but one is nonetheless determined to praise it, one calls it "ambitious." When the same novel lacks anything resembling a moral center, giving its readers no sense of where the author stands in regard to the issues his book has raised, then one who still wishes to praise it refers to its author's "appetite for the contradictory and the bewildering." At any rate, that is how Philip Roth dealt with the most egregious flaws in Alan Lelchuk's *American Mischief.* . . . As for Alan Lelchuk, he is the man who has conducted elaborate interviews with Roth about his last two books. These interviews are notable above all for taking each book at its highest possible valuation. . . . When two people agree to overestimate each other, it is sometimes called love. When two writers do the same thing in print, it is called literary politics. . . .

What of the novel itself: its content, its quality, its power as a statement about American life in our day? Set for the most part in Cambridge, Massachusetts, in the late 1960s, *American Mischief* is a work of the greatest possible contemporaneity—a book, in fact about yesterday. Its subject is the wild scrambling of values—sexual, political, ethical, social—that began to take place in American life during the middle 1960s, and that found its most active centers in university communities. The Dissolution, the Greening of America, the Shaking of the Foundation, call them what you will, these years have been crucial for America—except for the Depression, perhaps the most crucial years of the century. It is as if a cultural tidal wave had rolled in, touching everything, and even after it began to roll back, as it appears to be doing now, had left in its wake a film over every aspect of American life. It is a big subject, a throbbingly significant one, and Alan Lelchuk proposes to take on the whole of it in *American Mischief.* (p. 3)

"Family Talk" is the title Lelchuk gives to the dean's memoir of life with his six women, and it is written in a style intended to be wittily pornographic. Such a style demands the most sensational sexual details combined with the most humdrum commentary. Henry Miller is the father of this style in English, and it is exemplified in one of his *Tropics* novels when, in the midst of some extremely fancy fornication, his partner's purse drops and some coins spill out on the floor. "I made a mental note to pick them up later," Miller writes. It was funny when Miller did it; it was even amusing when Roth did it (if you didn't bother to reread it, that is); but it is funny no longer. It has all been done—and to death.

How exhausted this vein of literary pornography has become is clear when one recognizes that the mechanics of sex, never all that multifarious to begin with, now always take backseat to sundry psychological twists. The kicks, in other words, are nowadays in the kinks. (p. 8)

Toward the end of *American Mischief* . . ., Dean Kovell suggests the underlying cause of Pincus's troublemaking: "Too much Dostoevsky, I'd say." A similar, lower-level diagnosis of Alan Lelchuk's fiction comes to mind: Too much Philip Roth, I'd say. . . . How shriveled the novelistic vision has become over the past decades! For a novelist such as Malraux a man was the sum of his actions in the world; for such novelists as Roth and Lelchuk, a man seems to be the sum of his actions in bed.

Tolstoy once said that "anyone writing a novel must have a clear and firm idea as to what is good and bad in life." Philip Roth has said of Lelchuk that nothing so rouses him "to robust delight" as "the contemplation of confusion." Which qualifies Lelchuk as an ideal reader for his own novel, for it is a highly confused affair—as botched a piece of literature as has come along in some while. It is botched, first, in the most fundamental ways. Dialogue, plot and character are rudimentary. Everyone speaks exactly alike. . . . Although careful attention has been lavished on details, the plot itself, and especially the way the book ends, is slipshod and disappointing—not because Lelchuk is contemptuous of plot but because he lacked either the patience or artistry to bring it off.

It might be argued that *American Mischief* is not a well-made novel in the conventional sense because it is not a conventional novel—it is instead that supposedly higher and grander creation, a novel of ideas. Lelchuk gives fair warning that this is what he intends by quoting Goethe in an epigraph: "General ideas and great conceit tend always to create horrible mischief." General ideas and great conceit are the qualities Lelchuk himself appears to have in greatest abundance, and the combination, as his novel demonstrates, creates not merely horrible mischief but literary havoc.

American Mischief is long on general ideas—though the word "notions" describes them better—and short on the novelistic craft required to make them the property of fiction. It seems a book designed as a vehicle to carry the cultural clutter its author has acquired over the years. . . . Some of this clutter is quaintly out of fashion—as, for example, his attack on Herman Kahn, whom no one has bothered to defame since the early 1960s—and some of it is up to the moment. But in the end it is just clutter, the kind of junk a young, with-it professor of literature would, predictably, attempt to stuff into a novel. (pp. 8, 9)

[If] the novel really does die, it will be the novelists themselves who have killed it off. They will kill it, as Alan Lelchuk here kills a potentially great subject, by choosing the flashy over the serious, by inept craft, and by a narrow vision both of the novel's possibilities and of life itself. (p. 9)

> *Joseph Epstein, "General Ideas and Great Conceit," in* Book World—The Washington Post *(© The Washington Post), February 11, 1973, pp. 3, 8-9.*

The first 164 pages of ["American Mischief"] . . . [take] the form of a sexual memoir . . . [which] is spicier than anything Timothy Leary could have brought back from the spiritworld, [but which] becomes pure boredom. . . .

This first part is really a cultural sociology of the Cambridge scene in the late 1960's, though the book is unconvincingly set in the spring of 1972. It is an essay studded with case histories rather than people and could have come out in *Ramparts* as "Sex: A Liberal's Betrayal in His Own Words." Frankly, I had no idea what Alan Lelchuk was capable of until I came to the body of the novel. This is a fast, wily, melodramatic comedy about the Bomber Left written from a point of view that is unsure of its sympathies but finally shows itself thoroughly commercial-minded in its opportunism. With unresting provocativeness it reports a student uprising at Cardozo, the orgiastic destruction of the college museum's Pollocks, Matisses, etc., the spreading of the "revolutionary" flames to Harvard's museums, the burning of the Widener Library. Then, after a lecture by Norman Mailer at Harvard, Lenny Pincus murders Mailer in a Cambridge hotel room, just to show what the crisis of our time demands of a Mailer admirer who must exceed him—and succeed him. Lenny shoots him through the rectum.

This episode was interestingly rewritten in proof after the real Norman Mailer protested to Lelchuk. . . .

The book ends with Lenny violently suffering in jail, all too visibly the victim of an idealism that struggled in vain against the system—of an education in Dostoevsky and Nietzsche that ill-prepared Lenny for the realities of power in America. Or for the realists on the Bomber Left.

Once he gets to Lenny himself, Mr. Lelchuk turns out to be a lively enough writer of narrative, entertaining above all in his provocativeness. For unlike [Dean] Kovell, that caricature of a dishonest father-figure, Lenny is real to Mr. Lelchuk, who loves him but doesn't know what to think of the outrages he brashly has him commit. But the reason Mr. Lelchuk loves Lenny is that this is a novel not about "revolution" but about fiction and fame. It is a book less about the contest between fiction and reality—Lenny's stated problem—than it is about well-known American writers as characters. I don't know another current novel that is so much about the love-hate toward "established" writers. Naturally, this calls for a lot of sycophancy, too. (p. 2)

Mr. Lelchuk is too intellectual for my taste and much too conscious of the latest intelligence in the academy, where the far-out is always in style, too late. Mr. Lelchuk is a novelist with no voice of his own, no point of view that gets to the reader after so many ritual sacrifices of libraries, museums—and other writers. The "treatment" of the out-of-date campus uprising is tentatively satiric but finally settles on the tragedy of poor Lenny. From his preoccupation with intellectuals, critics, literary sons and fathers, I would guess that Mr. Lelchuk, though openly opportunistic to the point of doing himself in, does have a real theme. Lenny is offered as a tragedy because he is young, brought up on fiction and, with these two inadequate weapons, has taken on "America" itself.

Of course Lenny hasn't taken on anything but his own consciousness raising. So to give the book drama, it becomes a try-out of profanation. The "Jewish novel" must go. Jewish intellectuals must go. That devil Isaac must now drag poor old Father Abraham to the place of execution— and will not let *him* off. All the old (Jewish) culture authorities must go. Among the intellectuals kidnapped to the New Left camp in New Hampshire for re-education are the authors of "Communitas" and "The Liberal Imagination"; the latter especially is made to look superfluous to the "revolutionary" generation, just as Mailer must be shot in the most demeaning way possible.

And yet the profanation is never serious, coming as it does, not from Nazis who did burn libraries and murder authors, but from Lenny Pincus. The profanation is unserious, too, because while Mr. Lelchuk clearly suggests that Lenny did his best, that Lenny is quite noble, that Lenny was done in at the end by an America unworthy of him, Mr. Lelchuk himself seems as audience-conscious, as up-to-the-minute as Johnny Carson, Abbie Hoffman, Germaine Greer and the latest professor scornfully announcing the death of literature to a cheering group at the Modern Language Association. What terrors to the status quo! Or as Lenny Pincus's mother could have said about him, "Such a radical!" (p. 3)

Alfred Kazin, in The New York Times Book Review *(© 1973 by The New York Times Company; reprinted by permission), February 11, 1973.*

American Mischief is one of those rare first novels that achieves prior to publication the kind of scandalous notoriety that assures for a work and its author such few good things as the literary life has to offer. . . .

The center of the scandal is the appearance, in a small but pivotal role, of Norman Mailer. . . . [From] the book's style, from its incompetent attempts to demonstrate the relationships between the ideas of its major figures and their sexual behavior, one has a sense that Lelchuk crawled out from under Mailer's overcoat—or at least the one he wore while writing *Barbary Shore, The Deer Park, An American Dream*—that Lelchuk is taking him on, much as Hemingway once claimed to have engaged in combat with *his* masters, Turgenev and Flaubert among them. The difference here being that Hemingway never put words in their mouths, placed them as historical figures in extreme fictional situations, and attempted to imagine how they might respond.

This, too, represents a kind of perverse homage to Mailer. For if he was one of the leaders of the movement to apply the techniques of the novel to the writing of journalism, why is it not equally cricket to use him—or, more precisely, his journalistic persona (which, paradoxically, is a partially fictional creation in the making of which he has enthusiastically conspired)—in a fiction? And having done that, why can't you bring Paul Goodman on to make a speech to Harvard students, or show Leonard Bernstein having a hysterical breakdown while conducting a concert, or imagine that Red Auerbach, general manager of the Boston Celtics, has written a dumb-jock letter to one of your characters?

Legally, of course, it's possible, given the doctrine that the price of celebrity is surrender of most of one's rights to privacy. And since Mailer and Bernstein, at least, have worked hard to achieve that status, one doesn't feel too sorry for them. (Auerbach, a quiet man not much known outside his field, is a different matter; and I'd be willing to contribute instantly to a legal fund for him to bring a test case against Lelchuk for making him look stupid. . . .) (p. 49)

Lelchuk has the bad ear that betrays his breeding. He cannot accurately reproduce, let alone parody, something as simple to handle as a *New York Times* news story or one of its editorials. No more can he capture, let alone satirize, the rich, full absurdity of intellectuals engaged in the tribal ceremony of a panel discussion. And despite a breezy, knowing manner about social details, he mixes them up. . . .

But the failure in matters of this kind, though telling, is insignificant compared to his structural failures. . . .

[There] is too much . . . inner [debating], and [the debates] are too crudely stated, too repetitive to hold our interest. . . . [The protagonists] never engage in the kind of conflict that might (a) meld the two major sections of the book together; (b) explicitly state the novelist's position in regard to the issues he raises (implicitly, I think, he favors "the kids," but he also knows who reviews books in this country); or (c) break through the thick crust of his own rhetoric and show us his people acting, *living* waywardly, impulsively, contradictorily as people—even liberal professors and student activists—really do in life. Only in the passages dealing with sexual congress does he write with any excitement or real feeling, and that seems to me largely voyeuristic in character. For the rest, he attains at best a prosody and a level of insight no higher than that of journalism. And not Mailerian journalism, either; it's more the sort you get on Sundays when the boys are writing from the clips. . . .

[This] is certainly fit country for a novelist to traverse, no question about that; that a sensitive psychological probing of both the liberal academic mind and the student radical one is currently in order, and that the failure . . . is perhaps the most lamentable of the many failures of *American Mischief*. (p. 50)

> *Richard Schickel, "Tailing Mailer and Other Literary Mischief," in* World *(copyright © 1973 by Saturday Review, Inc.; reprinted with permission), February 13, 1973, pp. 49-50.*

American Mischief . . . is one of those success-story books —the kind (and they are much rarer than one is apt to think) that through concentrated planning and a good deal of luck enjoy a lot of newsy publicity and fashionable chatter and invested money well before their public launchings (usually called "literary *events*") as physical, purchasable objects with printed pages that you and I might actually *read*.

American Mischief was known about in the book trade last summer; the paperback rights had been bought for a rumored fortune, the book clubs were talking about almost nothing else . . . , and Philip Roth, who doesn't spread his praise lightly, had decided to go all out for it. "A brilliant and original comedy," he wrote. . . . No novelist has written with such knowlege and eloquence of the consequences of carnal passion in Massachusetts since *The Scarlet Letter*."

As if all that weren't enough, others clambered aboard the bandwagon with enthusiastic references to *The Possessed, Look Homeward, Angel*, and *The Naked and the Dead*. Philip Roth, Saul Bellow, Germaine Greer, Bernard Malamud, Nathaniel Hawthorne, Fyodor Dostoevsky, Thomas Wolfe, Norman Mailer—Wow! That's practically everybody except Shakespeare and Dick Tracy. And Lady Luck. But she was not far behind; in fact, she arrived in the form of Norman Mailer, who, with lawyers assembled, protested. (p. 75)

Well, ancient history; but worth outlining here for several reasons. . . . *American Mischief* . . . has genuine literary and intellectual quality. But it also has had, because of all the chatter and money and scandal involved in it, a great handicap. And that is simple bloodlust: after all the noise, if the book didn't measure up to the highest standards (a Dostoevsky, no less), it would be attacked. And attacked it has been, with all the proper genuflections to disappointment

and, behind that, with a certain amount of (only human) satisfaction. (pp. 75-6)

Now . . . suppose such a work of literature comes along and one finds it simply, literally, unreadable. That is, one finds that little chunks of it are aptly phrased, acutely insightful, delightfully intelligent and clever and funny (this guy is no hack), and even fashionably "relevant" (a dopey word, by the way)—but one simply cannot, no matter how hard one tries, sit down and read the whole thing through, from beginning to end. . . . Is one simply *refusing* to read? . . . *American Mischief* comes as a new, ready-made classic; it turns out to be, among other things, good and bad, immensely repetitive and boring. We have all stumbled through books that are boring and thought the better of ourselves for doing so, but this is a book that, above all else, was supposed to be *anything* but boring. In sum, the expectations that have been instilled for *American Mischief* by calculation and happenstance—all quite outside the book itself—that have made the book a success in the first place and brought it to everybody's attention, have also had the greatest part in doing it in. The other part, I am afraid, does —and at last—belong to the author.

American Mischief is clever, funny, and fashionable. It is set in the environs of Cambridge, Massachusetts, and everything is named, from the very real Harvard Square restaurant, Chez Dreyfus, to the murdered writer, Norman Mailer. Or almost everything: much of the action takes place at Cardozo College, an apparent misspelling of Brandeis University; and there are various luminaries (Lionel Trilling, Paul Goodman) who are not named but who are easily identifiable by those "in the know." There are references to Marx, Hegel, Freud, and the Charles River, so everybody should be quickly clued in that this is no dumbbunny story. (pp. 76-7)

[In] a variety of ways the book can stand as a definitive monograph on feces—the meanings of, the metaphors about, enticements to, their political and literary transcendental possibilities, etc. . . .

[The story] is, of course, fleshed out with a lot of sex and cruelty and violence and names. . . . Plus the irony. Now the irony is very rich indeed: the viewpoint is Pincus's, through which we see, ironically, Kovell's, and then, way back, through the mists, Alan Lelchuk's. *His* viewpoint turns out to be—oh, say, akin to Katherine Anne Porter's in *Ship of Fools*, or to Shakespeare's "What fools these mortals be"; you get the idea. Actually, it's not so much a viewpoint as 501 pages of raised eyebrow. . . .

Had [the book] been condensed to 150 less self-indulgent pages, it might have been far better; it also might never have been a book club selection or enjoyed Roth's praise or Mailer's disgruntlement, or been heard about every again. Life is unfair. (p. 77)

> *Eliot Fremont-Smith, in* Saturday Review *(copyright © 1973 by Saturday Review, Inc.; reprinted with permission), February 17, 1973.*

American Mischief is 500 pages of unremitting explicitness and tendentious detail, but for all the recipes of realism, it reads like pure fantasy. (p. 94)

The point about realistic novels, of course, is that they

have to be realistic. *American Mischief* is realistic only in method, not in substance. If the novel had been written by the Nabokov of *Pale Fire*, we could have read it as though Lenny Pincus and Bernie Kovell had invented each other. If it had been written by the Vonnegut of *Breakfast of Champions*, the author and his fantasies would have been transformed by the fiction. If it had been written by the Kosinski of *The Painted Bird*, we could have read it as a representation of how our fantasies about the lust and cruelty of student radicals have contaminated what goes for reality. But the realistic method will not allow us to read the novel in any of these ways. The method will not allow for the uncanny. And it is precisely the uncanny world of multiple unrealities as represented in the work of modernist writers that protects us from being conned or bullied by the fantasies of reality-instructors such as Alan Lelchuk. (p. 95)

> *George Stade, in* Harper's *(copyright 1973 by* Harper's Magazine; *reprinted from the May, 1973 issue by special permission), May, 1973.*

At some point in *Miriam at Thirty-Four*, one of the novel's supporting characters—a painter and front-runner in Miriam's stable of lovers—delivers himself of a diatribe about the egregiousness of critics. His outburst has been provoked by the hostile reception with which his own work has been greeted by those (as he himself would have it) who are too pietistic to understand his treatment of the erotic and who lack the artistic imagination necessary to appreciate a brilliant talent like his own.

Mr. Lelchuk's fantasies notwithstanding, it is unlikely that *Miriam at Thirty-Four* will provoke much outrage; a lot of it is, in fact, "dirty," but it is rather ridiculous for him to intimate that sex scenes could raise eyebrows—let alone inspire puritanical fury—in 1974. If this very silly novel does, like Mr. Lelchuk's first novel, go largely unappreciated, it may solace him to believe that he is being victimized by deficiencies ingrained in the American spirit. Anyone who reads his book, however, will know better. (p. 26)

> *Jane Larkin Crain, in* Saturday Review/ World *(copyright © 1974 by Saturday Review/World, Inc.; reprinted with permission), November 16, 1974.*

At a time when feminism is flourishing and Freud is enjoying a new respectability in its ranks, this novel [*Miriam at Thirty-Four*] about a 34-year-old intellectual whose just-discovered sexuality turns her life around might seem to offer intriguing possibilities. Instead, reading it made me feel as though I'd walked up to a handsomely-decorated building and, a couple of hours later, found myself dumped smartly into the back alley, glaring back in wonder that the facade had turned out to be hollow and most of the inhabitants glib hired hands. Let us at once avoid confusion: female sexuality is hardly the private property of female writers . . ., but Alan Lelchuk's exploitation of its concept in this novel leaves readers holding a bag of demonstration sex scenes and pretentious modern moralizing while the author has slipped out to the latest Sam Peckinpah/Clint Eastwood double feature. . . .

The serious writer who wants his audience to witness detailed sex and then the punishment and humiliation of a central character has a delicate task indeed. He must at all cost avoid the easy voyeurism that he risks, the idea that this kind of pleasure and punishment is simply titillating and thus deserving of detail. More important, novels and movies that specialize in lengthily-depicted violence as retribution against their central characters—often blameless innocents—justifiably irritate audiences because they implicate us in the rage of their creators, rage that seems to miss its real targets and splatter off the page or the screen onto us.

This novel depends on our recognition of up-to-the-minute cultural and political trappings instead of developing character or plot; being subjected to the detailed, self-sought rape of the central character while the author insists that he is really exploring the ironies and tragedies of female masochism and his heroine's conflict between new pleasure and old self-hatred, goes considerably beyond irritation. The narrative emerges as the same old innocent-town-tramp-gets-gang-raped plot to me, and since bad-girl mythology has it that punishment must follow innocent pleasure, it's punishment that Miriam gets, in spite of her author's assurance that she has a right to her own sexuality. And it's in the intensity of this punishment that we can see clearly that the novel's supporting characters—Cambridge intellectuals, artists, rather smugly-typed women's movement figures, Miriam's lovers—have all been used to debase the character whose sexuality they've either denied or encouraged.

Pleasure and punishment aside, if possible, the truth is that people just don't exist as simply sexual beings, and Lelchuk's attempt to depict them that way ends up in tired stereotyping—the groovily free 19-year-old flower child who has attracted and liberated a bright and awesomely, to the author, well-credentialed middle-aged professor, the aggressive, hard-line "heavy" at the women's meeting who must, therefore, turn out to be a lesbian, the handsome Middle American who makes love so well that he's got to be dumb. The author never succeeds in granting any of the characters, with the exception of the repressive ex-husband, more than fleeting dimension.

A final but not niggling trouble is that this novel is remarkably, almost amusingly, class-bound; it assumes with a straight face that its readers are as impressed with such phenomena as Harvard degrees, profitable academic prestige at 33, and even fashionable furniture, as are its approved, non-authoritarian characters (the authoritarian ones fare far less fashionably). It is thus especially hard to attribute more substance to the extravagantly described sex scenes than to the Design Research decor or the marinated fresh fish and asparagus in hollandaise sauce. This kind of detail should be absorbing at least from the perspective of upper middle-class social history—we can listen entranced to a cataloguing of what people wore to a wedding or the contents of the menu at a dinner party, for what they tell us about the lives of the people who were there—but here it's strictly a prestigious stage set, to be struck as soon as Miriam moves off toward the violence Lelchuk has in store for her.

For all its smart patter (there's a lot) about liberated sexuality, the clenched quality with which this novel demonstrates its concerns is weirdly out of synch with its apparent surface, as though an elaborately casual hipster were telling a German fairy tale. And in presenting Miriam and everyone else in only one dimension—the sexual—Lelchuk has at once sensationalized and trivialized the culture and the character whose life he means to illuminate. (p. 50)

Sara Blackburn, in The New York Times Book Review (© 1974 by The New York Times Company; reprinted by permission), November 17, 1974.

Lelchuk's novel [*Miriam at Thirty-Four*] hasn't made a splash on the book-front, but certainly could be the perfect object for ideological squabble: the Liberated Woman is likely to see this as one male's cheapshot revenge on her sex—reducing "liberation" to sexual freedom, then doing in the freewheeling practitioner. On the other hand, the book fits perfectly into the hands of anyone sick to death of the cant of Finding Oneself, even at the Radcliffe Institute for Women; or one muses that anybody who runs around Cambridge taking that many pictures (Miriam is a serious photographer) deserves what happens to her.

Yet the real problem is not ideology but style, and here perhaps opposed temperaments could find common meeting-place. Even if Lelchuk is eventually out to punish his heroine, he early on establishes full complicity with her through his style. . . . (pp. 149-50)

As with Lelchuk's previous *American Mischief*, the present novel is superb in its presentation of Greater Boston, particularly the "accepted insanities" of Cambridge. But onto this realistic, scenic base is grafted Tall Story Superstructure; Kovell in the earlier book had six lovers, and Miriam here has three, alternating—a sort of Ginger Rogers *Tom, Dick and Harry* movie brought up to date thirty-five years later. . . . Lots of fun, but you can't move from this atmosphere to parables of self-destruction [or] self-fulfillment. At least I couldn't. (pp. 150-51)

William H. Pritchard, in The Hudson Review (copyright © 1975 by The Hudson Review, Inc.; reprinted by permission), Vol. XXVIII, No. 1, Spring, 1975.

Like John Dos Passos, Alan Lelchuk may become the chronicler of our cultural fancies. *American Mischief*, his first novel, fictionalized the vagaries of student revolution in the sixties, and *Miriam at Thirty-Four* is meant to do the same for women caught in the throes of feminism. His heroine, Miriam Scheinman (M.S.) has some interesting edges. (p. 118)

[At the end of the novel], she is raped and left naked except for a sweater, a long shirt, and [her] cap. Afterward she walks into an ice cream parlor with the shirt tied round her waist and sits down, obviously naked but still wearing the cap. This last scene is the final dare in a series of dares out of which Lelchuk makes his novel.

To begin with, he appropriates the plot of the standard feminist narrative: woman wakes up in empty trough of marriage and leaves husband to find identity. With your attention on this convention, his next dare is to shift the content of the plot so that Miriam maximizes her liberation not as much by her professional competence—she is a photographer—as by her sexual liaisons with her three male lovers. This does make men rather more central than orthodox feminism (a shadowy antagonist in the novel) might wish. . . . Lastly, when the novel of a woman who has discovered how to use her power in bed ends by her being

gang-raped, it invites the suggestion that someone is seeing to it that she is punished.

But these dares are only drawing cards for the main show in which the novelist replaces certain simplistic feminist notions with his own formulations. Which is fine except for the last scene in the ice cream parlor. One would like to believe that this novel of a woman's many successes over her repressive training ends with yet another triumph: by her public appearance over ice cream, the heroine tacitly acknowledges what feminists have been slow to see—that rape is not the worst thing that can happen to a woman and that to see it as catastrophic is to acquiesce in the identification of a woman with her body.

And if Miriam's liberation comes through her body at first, her final scene read in this way would put the body in perspective. . . . But Lelchuk has actually only rewritten the oldest of stories: the one which identifies the worst that can happen to a woman with the violation of her body. The half-naked Miriam is having ice cream because she is half-crazy. It's the standard refrain: a woman's spirit is punished in the body.

This is the tired conclusion to what began as a frisky essay on women. As a novel it bears the same relation to the art of fiction as textbook sex does to the art of love. There is an absence of felt life, which is all right in an essay or a sex manual but is definitely not all right in either art or love. And although one might accept the novelist's thesis that some women (but by no means all, as he implies) needs to be liberated from sexual shyness more than from anything else, his fiction does nothing to engage and convince the imagination.

Lelchuk's style is so lumpy that background information about the characters is frequently delivered in parentheses near their names—as if the writer ordered out for it, and it arrived late. The sexual language appears soiled, like the cue lines in someone's jerk-off book. . . . It is hard to see how sex written of in this way can appear liberating; it is more in the line of hard work—a subject better suited to Lelchuk's talents, judging from the good passages about Miriam's photography.

The pity of all this is that the novelist has expended a great deal of sympathy and energy in this portrait of a woman without ever establishing fictional roots which will allow his ideas to take hold. (p. 120)

Elizabeth Turner Pochoda, "The Oldest Story Ever Told," in Ms. (© 1975 Ms. Magazine Corp.), April, 1975, pp. 118, 120.

* * *

LEVERTOV, Denise 1923-

Ms Levertov is a prize-winning British-American poet of Welsh and Jewish parentage, sometimes associated with the Black Mountain or "projectivist" poets. Her principal poetic concern has always been the relationship of form and content; her search for an "organic" poetry, a "manifestation of form sense" discovered by the poet in all things, has led her to endorse Hopkins' "inscape concept." Her graceful, powerful, and irreducible poems, "obstinately precise," are among the finest in contemporary American literature. (See also *Contemporary Authors*, Vols. 1-4, rev. ed.)

[It] is not by heaving her up onto the double standard of

penis envy that we can see this poet plain. Beyond her monostrophic discipleship to the Boys, and the relic imagism that labels her still one of the Girls, Denise Levertov has a further—and happily, decisive—range of experience which she has committed to the language, that makes her poetry important and makes it in fact *her poetry*: for her, the poem is a sacramental transaction, permitting, even enforcing access to a released state of being, an ecstatic awareness that is not so much concomitant to a religion, with its stern implications of community and service, as to a gnosis. The contradictions of her mode and her mood, the pressure of events and the price of evangelism have all worked to her harm, somewhat, upon what I take to be her authentic and native impulse, and if I am often confused by her poems—as I was in writing about her work several years ago, when I had reported her "a moralist whose manner forbids her to develop what she *knows*; yet whenever she manages to defeat the assumptions of her mindless mode, her authority convinces me utterly"—I am also convinced by them and prompted, in the course of six books, to . . . admiration. (pp. 293-94)

Gently, . . . Miss Levertov undertakes the approach to life as a continuum and to poetry as a rite by which its rhythms may be recorded. . . . The longing for rituals, the need to "transform into our flesh our deaths" is the subject, then, of all her later poems, though their object is generally elsewhere, out *in the world* which, as much for Miss Levertov as for a poet like Gautier, absolutely exists as it is. Her undertaking will be to convert: to connect as by a kind of magic that can be neither criticized nor institutionalized nor brought to a full expression of its own intentions, the eternal consciousness of disparities into a momentary unity of association. The literary conventions available—by conquest—to her for this transaction are not always adequate to the ultimate ambition of her task, but in two of her latest books, published in 1963 and 1965, and called *The Jacob's Ladder* and *O Taste and See*, "something sundered begins to knit. / By scene, by sentence, something is rendered / back into life, back to the gods." The titles of these two books suggest the poles from which the poet must swing—on the one side the Jacob's Ladder which is the "path between reality and the soul, a language excelling itself to be itself," and on the other the delectation in the world as *data*, as given: "The world is / not with us enough." Between transcendence and immanence. Riven often into chaos by discrepant and indeed divided allegiances, Denise Levertov has so far devised three principal tactics for reconciling herself with her own spirit, her own flesh. One is the return to an esoteric wisdom—Hasidism, Zen, and that impulse of energy-worship which runs through English and American poetry from Blake and Whitman to Lawrence and Olson—a doctrine that must stand for her as a danger as well as a lure. . . . Another is the intensificaiton of momentary consciousness to ecstasy, a kind of *via corporis naturaliter* of which she speaks in "The Depths". . . . And the third is the exploration of her own history, "something forgotten for twenty years," [demonstrated in] one of her finest poems so far, "A Map of the Western Part of the County of Essex in England" (pp. 300-01)

There is another world, Paul Eluard once exclaimed, and it is in this one! So Denise Levertov has discovered, though the other way round: in her longing for "miracles," and "otherness that was blessed," she has come upon the

world, *this world*, and in it, out of it, has created the forms, the rites that grant her access to that first, divined reality which is the object of her faith: they are her poems. (p. 305)

> *Richard Howard, "Denise Levertov" (originally published in* Tri-Quarterly), *in his* Alone With America: Essays on the Art of Poetry in the United States Since 1950 *(copyright © 1965, 1966, 1967, 1968, 1969 by Richard Howard; reprinted by permission of Atheneum Publishers, New York), Atheneum, 1969, pp. 292-305.*

Denise Levertov has remained the romantic she was in her early poems: She retains the attitude toward creativity that in her English period was most amply discussed and exemplified by the British poet and critic Herbert Read, whom she had known in her schooldays and with whom she shared so much in terms of sensibility. When I read the excellent passages in *The Poet in the World* on the difference between organic poetry and free verse (organic poetry never loses sight of the poem as a whole), when I encountered observations like "Form is never more than a *revelation* of content," and "There is a poetry that in thought and in feeling and in perception seeks the forms peculiar to these experiences," I heard the voice of a true romantic. I noted rather sadly, too, that the name of Read never appears in her book.

But Levertov's views are derived only in part from Read and from her other neo-Romantic associates. They represent in addition the wisdom of half a lifetime of writing poetry, and what impresses one constantly is her interest in the practicalities of creation, not to mention her sensible avoidance of faddish cults. For example, she cuts through the cant about poetry being dependent on the physical voice to point out that some poets simply have terrible voices, and that in any case a poem is controlled by "the rhythm of the inner voice."

What Denise Levertov herself identifies as one of the great differences between her English and her American poetry is that through emigration she learned "to engage my capacities as a poet in the crude substance of dailiness." This was not merely a question of relating poetry more closely to colloquial speech or to the minutiae of an ordinary woman's life. (The latter would certainly not have been anything new; I remember publishing in 1947 a fine Levertov poem on "Folding a Shirt.") It was likewise a matter of getting involved through teaching in the lives of the young. Teaching, she says, "has opened my life . . . towards people, towards a political and social understanding." Indeed, there are essays in *The Poet in the World* on the teaching experience that anyone who has combined teaching with writing will find familiar and sensible. But there are also essays on political activism about which, I confess, my feelings are more ambivalent. In the '40s, when I was an anarchist activist, Denise Levertov was perhaps loyal in sentiment to the cause, although not herself in any way active. During the '60s she became an activist, and her actions certainly proved her sincerity. What disappoints one in her writing on this subject, however, is that it rarely goes beyond emotional generalities. (pp. 19-20)

In the world of politics the wings that are the poet's strength become as clumsy and inept as those of Baudelaire's albatross. This lesson the poets of the '30s learned, painfully; doubtless it must be learned again.

Far Eastern connoisseurs avoid the pot that has no flaw; it has achieved the perfection that is death. Imperfection is a sign of vitality, and if I have sought and found a flaw in *The Poet in the World*, let me present it as the reassuring blemish in an otherwise excellent and fascinating book, one of the best books a poet has written about the poet's craft. (p. 20)

> *George Woodcock, "Pilgrimage of a Poet," in* New Leader *(© 1974 by the American Labor Conference on International Affairs, Inc.), March 4, 1974, pp. 19-20.*

Levertov . . . objects to the notion that the poet attempts only a limited re-creation of simple experience, or thera-peutic self-expression. A poet must do more than label or confess. He must find a way to bring his understanding of the world to his reader in such a way that the reader too feels a part of the "translation." (p. 795)

Levertov has provided contemporary writing with a direc-tion, a tone, even an organ bass. It is true that her poems have shown great variety of form—although the pervasive Levertov voice is serene, moderate, marked by verbal music and metaphor. Yet, varied as their shape may be, the poems speak consistently for Levertov's solemn view of life. She sees life as renewing, joyful, majestic; a promise to be held tenderly; a duty to be performed earnestly; and her poetry, as an art originating in, and expressive of, that mys-teriously compelling vision. (p. 796)

> *Linda Wagner, "Matters of the Here and Now," in* The Nation *(copyright 1974 by the Nation Associates, Inc.), June 22, 1974, pp. 795-96.*

Denise Levertov's new prose work, *The Poet in the World*, is a valuable, almost necessary, book for the writer and reader of poetry, and indeed for anyone sensitive to the motivating and celebratory quality of words. . . . [In it, she] responds to the most insistent issues for the contemporary poet: the function and technique of poetry, the artist's role in the classroom and political arena. Yet despite her em-phasis on the poet's work in and with the world, her recur-rent image of birth brings to the surface one of her most se-rious underlying themes, the genesis of poetry, of life, and of a humane society. (p. 435)

As a poet Levertov feels that she must act in the world. As a maker and instrument of poems she also struggles to bring forth her unique celebration of life.

The Poet in the World fills the gap that too many writers leave open, the chinks between their poetic, personal, and political ideas. In her new book Denise Levertov presents a wholistic vision of the poet in her surroundings. At the very least Levertov answers the persistent question about how she can reconcile her poetry with her political activism. At the most the book awakens us sleepers and communicates some of that energy which enables us, too, to live crea-tively in the world. (p. 437)

> *Susan Hoerchner, "Denise Levertov," in* Contemporary Literature *(© 1974 by the Board of Regents of the University of Wis-consin System), Vol. 15, No. 3, Summer, 1974, pp. 435-37.*

Balanced and *whole* are words that have perhaps best char-acterized the work and the person of Denise Levertov—at least until the late sixties. The second line of her first volume of poetry speaks of the "systole and diastole marking miraculous hours," and it is inside just such a pulse of balanced polarities that her poetry finds its stable center. She knows that "Strength of feeling, reverence for mystery, and clarity of intellect must be kept in balance with one another. Neither the passive nor the active must dominate, they must work in conjunction as in a marriage." Her poems seek the middle way not because they are dull or timid, but because the eye that finds the poetry inside the flux is sane and confident. There are no excesses of ecstasy or despair, celebration or denigration, naïvete or cynicism; there is instead an acute ability to find simple beauties in the heart of squalor and something to relish even in negative experiences. While her poetry experiences the world with a finely honed and precise sensibility, it ac-cepts necessary human suffering and the world's imperfec-tion with a deep strength. . . . But it is more than just that— it is incomparable and unique poetry that tastes in the hard and difficult world a satisfying savor and at times a deep, if limited, joy.

Levertov's sanity and balance are not of the kind that ex-cludes mystery—indeed, in addition to her interest in dreams, all her poetry seeks to discover the mystery that lies beyond the surfaces of things. Allen Ginsberg shares a reverence for mystery, but one realizes immediately that it means for him something different: Levertov is concerned with an internal and natural mystery rather than a tran-scendent or metaphysical one (though at their deepest core or supreme circumference they are the same).

If any of the three elements—feeling, mystery, and intellect —has outweighed the others in Levertov's poetics, it has surely been intellect, but intellect in its highest manifesta-tion as *claritas*. *Claritas* is more than oiled reason (though Levertov only partly shares Ginsberg's Blakean anti-intel-lectualism); it is the clean, precise perception that arises from attending closely while the will is quieted and the in-tellect is warmed by the emotions. *Claritas* arises from the unforced union of all the senses and faculties—but if one has to single out a primary synecdoche, the *eye* immedi-ately recommends itself. Levertov's poetry is a poetry of the eye in that it is concerned with *seeing into* experience and discovering the order and significance that her poet's faith tells her is really there behind the surface chaos. Her poetry is of the mental and spiritual eye, however, and not primarily a poetry of phanopoeia or visual image. . . . Her own work reminds us of Joseph Conrad's dictum that art is "to make you see," except that Levertov's intention hints less of indirect didacticism: her poetry is not so much to make someone else see as it is a *process of seeing* for the poet. Perhaps, "art is to make the artist see" or "art is the way an artist sees." Through poetry she reaches to the heart of things, finds out what their centers are. If the reader can follow, he is welcomed along, but although the poetry is mindful of communication and expression, its primary concern is discovery. Her poetry seeks *instress* or the *apperception of inscape* not only of natural objects but of emotional and intellectual experience as well. It seeks analogies, resemblances, natural allegories: "such a poetry is," as she has noted, "exploratory."

Levertov's attitude towards art and experience is of primary importance in understanding her first reactions to the Vietnam War. Whereas Ginsberg sees war as the ultimate reification of artificial control and imposed order, the natural activity of a judgmental Moloch, she sees it as ultimate unreason and disorder, as the clouding of *claritas* and the violation of the innate order at the heart of things. In Ginsberg's heirarchy of values, *touching and experiencing* is preeminent; in Levertov's, *seeing into and understanding* is most important. Ginsberg does not seek *in-sight* as much as sensation, motion, and flexibility. His war is against pattern, restriction, limitation; her struggle is to discover the true patterns, to find the limits and definitions of things. He is concerned about pressures that impinge upon his flesh and space; she is concerned about forces that block and limit her vision. Thus in Ginsberg's poetry combat and orgy are juxtaposed; in Levertov's poetry carnage is juxtaposed against "my clear caressive sight, my poet's sight," and mutilated bodies are contrasted with the beauty of man's eyes, "flowers that perceive the stars."

It is the loss and contradiction of vision that makes the war horrible to Levertov, and this may be said without any denigration of her compassion or humanity. Her concern is not a coldly aesthetic one: she cares not so much about the loss of the possibilities of art as an end in itself, but about the loss of the clarity that strikes to depths where the highest art and fullest life are inseparable. (pp. 77-9)

Levertov tries to give her poems the shape and pattern she discovers outside the poem; the poems embody and concretize experience at the level of its orderliness, at the point where it touches the natural mystery in the heart of things. Though she might agree to some extent with Ginsberg that poetry can and should be "a transcript of consciousness," it must be of a consciousness composed and quieted to a deeper seeing, and not a random and undiscriminating "free-mind." Poetry should not be *prima materia* or liquid protoplasm: poems should "become definite bodies, as protoplasm becomes a living and solid creature, and moves as such a creature will move in its living." Levertov dislikes the ossifications of Moloch or of poetic conventions as much as Ginsberg does, and yet realizes some kind of skeleton or integument is essential to all living things. She dislikes poems that are "mere quivering pieces of autobiographical raw material." Giving the poem a structure or skin and keeping it "together" is a way of keeping the mind or consciousness together, and vice versa. Though it should not shape itself to external demands, every life and every poem must discover a form and attain a precise and substantial shape: it may grow its own organic hide but it cannot do without one. Levertov does not share Ginsberg's desire to "go naked" physically, psychologically, or aesthetically....

> It's not a question of
> false constraints—but
>   to move well and get somewhere
> wear shoes that fit.
>
> To hell with easy rhythms—
> sloppy mules that anyone can
>   kick off or
> step into.
>
>   (pp. 81-2)

The hard, clear form of Levertov's poetry ... between 1955 and 1965 ... offers no doubt that she is in control, moving attentively and perceptively through experience with a confidence more common to poets before the First World War. Not a naïve or romantic poetry, but a poetry of a healthy psyche, it is unlike much poetry written in the fifties and sixties. Either because severe self-doubt did not exist or was kept outside of the poetry, the work before 1965 is able to devote its attention to the balanced seeing and savoring of life.... Because of the Vietnam War the same cannot be said of *The Sorrow Dance* (1967), *Relearning the Alphabet* (1970), and *To Stay Alive* (1971).

Alongside her obvious relish for life, Levertov's poetry has always carried a measured note of austerity and sadness. She finds beauty everywhere, yet it is seldom an effervescent or exaggerated outflowing; it is a beauty harbored deep within the heart of a paradoxical sadness and limitation. Such limitation is accepted as inevitable and good, not to be destroyed or rebelled against, but to be looked into to discover how beauty keeps its mysterious habitation there. (pp. 82-3)

While Levertov was never oblivious to pain and sorrow, she was always able through poetry to find in all experience an order and significance that explained and elevated it. At the least, poetry by speaking of sorrow was able to clarify and distance it so that it could be handled.... The shadow of the Vietnam War comes to alter all this: vision is clouded, form is broken, balance is impossible, and the psyche is unable to throw off its illness and sorrow. (pp. 85-6)

[The] first of the "war poems" ... sets out the primary theme of her poetry on the war—the loss of vision and poetic power.

Those critics who have over the years complained that Levertov's poetry is too limited in subject matter have usually not been clear about what that limited matter was; but one can easily argue that too much of her poetry centers on the role and method of the poet, the experience of being a poet, and the act of creating poems. The propensity for *ars poetica* carries over into the war poems. (pp. 87-8)

The war casts a disabling shadow for Levertov because hers is a poetics of order and of the presumption of order: "my notion of organic form is really based on the idea that there is form in all things—that the artist doesn't impose form upon chaos, but discovers hidden form by means of the poet's attentive listening, not only his listening but also his feeling, his meditating upon his experience, and by means of his accurate transcription of that experience into words."... Her tendency to see war as "black confusion" and ultimate disorder suggests war is all shell and without the kernel that poetry seeks. (pp. 89-90)

[Desperation] does not really describe the feeling flowing out of Levertov's poems on the war. A few notes of *The Sorrow Dance* sound something like hysteria, and later poems move beyond desperation, through mild catatonia toward intransigent rebellion. One fact is apparent in the changing moods: evil has been encountered by Levertov in a way it had not been encountered before, and the effect has been profound. (pp. 92-3)

After the violent images of "Life at War," "Two Variations," and "Advent 1966," Denise Levertov comes to avoid specific description of the war's horrors, "the crimes of war, / the unspeakable—of which, then, / I won't speak" ("Interim," in *Relearning* ...). But knowledge of them is ever present and forms, as Bly warned, "Particles / The grass cannot dissolve." (p. 95)

Because poetic vision and poetic form are so closely allied for Levertov, it is natural that her verse about and during the Vietnam conflict should be troubled with a loss of form as well as a loss of vision. Thus, just as "The Pulse" and "Life at War," dealing with loss of vision, introduce the war poems in *The Sorrow Dance*, so "The Broken Sandal," concerned with the loss of form, introduces the long section of war-related poems in *Relearning the Alphabet*.

> Dreamed the thong of my sandal broke.
> Nothing to hold it to my foot.
> How shall I walk?
>   Barefoot?
> The sharp stones, the dirt. I would
> hobble . . .

[This] poem . . . asks to be read as *ars poetica*. It is of course also more than that, except that for Levertov the art of poetry includes the whole art of living. (p. 96)

Different poems begin to look like an attempt to go barefoot or put on a different sandal in quest of greater sufficiency of content and form. Two long political poems in *Relearning the Alphabet*, "An Interim" and "From a Notebook: October '68—May '69," mix stanzas of various lines and rhythms, handbills, news stories, prose letters, much in the manner of Williams's *Paterson* or Pound's *The Cantos*. They are marked too with a new spirit, a new polemical subjectivity. Though she is not completely comfortable within the "revolution," she knows that it is "revolution or death" and that

> It's in the air: no air
>   to breathe without
> scent of it.   (p. 101)

The revolution is at least an activity in a time when activity seems impossible, a way out of darkness and lassitude. If a poetry of the swing of the birch catkins seems trivial in the shadow of Vietnam and People's Park, then poetry must find a revolutionary voice. The poetry of "discovery" no longer satisfies the hunger for meaning when what it discovers are objects without meaning. The earth does not satisfy the needs of man, and life must become more than the intently haphazard tourism of the senses. (pp. 101-02)

Levertov is not, however, fully at ease within the movement, and her hunger is somewhat different or larger than that of most of those within it. She is not comfortable in verse that is not "exploratory" and is uneasy with the "few flippant rhymes" she is able to "bring forth out of . . . [her] anger". . . . Subsequent poems reveal her awareness that the idiom and traditionless iconoclasm of the revolution are not hers. The new shift in poetic manner further complicates an already alien predicament: she has changed continents and cultures and is "without a terrain in which, to which, I belong" . . .; and because her roots are in the nineteenth century she is not only without a country but without an era. That this predicament (the pressing needs of the revolution weighted against the strong need for poetic integrity) is the cause of great anguish can be seen, despite the carefully modulated rhythms. . . . There is, then, in *Relearning the Alphabet*, a "politicized poet" and a "pure poet," which are at times distinct, at times indistinguishable. The one has not replaced the other, but they exist side by side. (pp. 102-03)

But though the old poetry is still for a while a possible po-

etry for Levertov, the war and the revolution have opened new fields and new spiritual understandings. Certain poems of *Relearning the Alphabet* at last show the spiritual depth that one might always have looked for from a poet of such extraordinary fortitude and strong *Hasidic* background. One cannot be sure whether the understandings here evident are new to the poet or are only now allowed to manifest themselves because of a changing aesthetic. But the title of the 1970 volume, the tentative manner in which some ideas are set forth, and the long tradition of exploratory poetry lead one to believe that the shape of the book is not a matter of art alone, but of spiritual autobiography, a true relearning. The book is not an aggregation of separate poems but an admirably unified work: its shape is that of a *Bildungsroman* or, better, a mystical hagiography. The voice moves through defeat and death of the will to a new peace and hope, a new sense of human possibility. Though every life changes under a multitude of influences (the mere passage of time alone having profound effects), it seems clear that the war and the social malaise have occasioned the darkness, and that "the movement" and Levertov's spiritual heritage have brought on the new light. Such at least is the configuration of the poetry in *Relearning the Alphabet*.

It should not be surprising that a volume of poems written in years when death seems ubiquitous should be heavily colored by its influence. Death invades these poems in a variety of meaningful ways. It is there from the beginning in the burning babes, the broken sandal, the spreading circles of red, the graveside poems, the starvation in Biafra, and indeed in the chapter heading "Elegies." (pp. 103-04)

"Relearning the Alphabet" is rightly neither protest poem, war poem, nor political poem, and yet there can be no doubt that its experience is shaped in the matrices of war, politics, and protest. It is in many ways an "Ash Wednesday" poem in which the poet "relearns" the joy of simplicity; accepts the cycle of

> Endless
> returning, endless
> revolution of dream to ember, ember to anguish,
> anguish to flame, flame to delight,
> delight to dark and dream, dream to ember . . .

and realizes that transcendence is not a matter that may be forced by the will or "sharp desire." (p. 109)

Denise Levertov's poems on war . . . are for the most part not poems of the same viability or aesthetic autonomy as the earlier precise poems of immediate experience. Those were "made objects" with a life of their own, true to experience, true to a moment and to a context, and once made were able to walk off on their own power, no longer dependent. In place of the earlier sonnet-sized *closed* and ordered poems, her later work moves to long *open* and unbuttoned poems, which are very much, in Robert Duncan's sense, "Passages" of a continuing larger Poem in which the order is the constant shifting of orders. In some sense the early poems are undoubtedly more perfect and enduring works of art, more timeless and less datable, but they are, for all their fineness, only teacups, and of sorely limited capacities. The war-shadowed poems are less clean and symmetrical but are moral and philosophical schooners of some size. . . . *O Taste and See* is incomparable poetry, but one would be dissatisfied if it were the only kind of poetry: and one would ultimately be dissatisfied with Levertov if it were the only kind of poetry she could write. The war, by offering much that was distasteful and unsightly, prompted a poetry that asks the poet to add the light and weight of her moral and spiritual powers to the fine sensibility of her palate and eye. (pp. 109-10)

[*To Stay Alive* reveals] Levertov's growing bitterness about the war and the state of the American soul. . ., [a] note of alienation, [and] an increasing sense of unbridgeable distance between Levertov and her opposition. . . . But her own humanity is still very much warm and alive. Both revolution and anger are still essentially foreign to her nature, and she would almost prefer death rather than immersion in the intransigent and aggressive acts of revolution. . . . (p. 111)

> *James F. Mersmann, "Denise Levertov: Piercing In," in his* Out of the Vietnam Vortex: A Study of Poets and Poetry Against the War *(© copyright 1974 by the University Press of Kansas), University Press of Kansas, 1974, pp. 77-112.*

[Levertov's] poetic theory . . . is essentially psychological . . . [in that] she emphasizes the mental condition of the poet rather than the qualities of the finished poem. The state of mind which she regards as most conducive to successful writing resembles Negative Capability as described by Keats. (p. 328)

Singling out for approval a related Keatsian pronouncement that "The Genius of Poetry must work out its own salvation in a man: It cannot be matured by law and precept, but by sensation & watchfulness in itself," she asserts that a poet who would write well must bring to his subject the "ecstatic *attention,* the *intensity,* that would penetrate to its reality" ([*The Poet in the World*], p. 97). . . .

While Levertov's conception of the poet as an intense Keatsian observer shapes the core of her theory of "organic form," she also makes use of Hopkins's term "inscape" in extended form. Beginning with Hopkins's definition of "inscape" as an object's "intrinsic form," she argues that "intellectual and emotional experience" as well as objects or living beings may possess "inscape," and that the poet conscious of such form may seek to reproduce it by analogy in a shaped poem. The author seeking to recreate a given inscape must "contemplate" it with Keatsian watchfulness. If his attention remains steady, the first words of the poem eventually will come to him. (p. 329)

Like Stevens, . . . she conceives of imagination as being more closely akin to understanding than to fancy or fantasy, and she probably would agree with Stevens's conclusion that imagination seldom fruitfully transcends reality, but performs a vital service in illuminating or modifying the real. For example, she assumes that imagination is responsible for Keatsian empathy. . . . The imagination, then, as Levertov conceives of it, is the power of mentally recreating reality. (p. 330)

Her attention to physical details permits Levertov to develop a considerable range of poetic subject, for, like Williams, she is often inspired by the humble, the commonplace, or the small, and she composes remarkably perceptive poems about a single flower, a man walking two dogs in the rain, and even sunlight glittering on rubbish in a

street. In fact the majority of her poems concern the happenings of everyday life. Their attractiveness stems in part from Levertov's gift for discovering the uncommon features of commonplace (and frequently overlooked) objects or events. (p. 333)

She bears an additional resemblance to Williams in her admiration for vitality, energy, movement, for "life that wants to live." It is noteworthy that her verse, like that of Williams, makes comparatively few references to death. (p. 334)

Her efforts at political and social reform are entirely consistent with her personality and outlook, for her practice of counting the misfortunes and wrongs of others as her own intensifies her social consciousness, while her belief that vitality is synonymous with change encourages her to assume that social or political change is likely to be beneficial. (p. 340)

> *Julian Gitzen, "From Reverence to Attention: The Poetry of Denise Levertov," in* The Midwest Quarterly *(copyright, 1975, by The Midwest Quarterly,* Kansas State College of Pittsburg*), Spring, 1975, pp. 328-41.*

* * *

LEVINE, Philip   1928-

Levine, an American poet, writes tough but compassionate poems about "pigs, thistles, thorny people who refuse to die." He studied under John Berryman and admires Ginsberg, Snyder, Kinnell, and Ted Hughes, but claims that no other writer has particularly influenced his work. (See also *Contemporary Authors,* Vols. 9-12, rev. ed.)

Philip Levine's sixth book, *1933,* is filled with persons and images from his past: his grandparents, parents, uncles; black Packards, knickers, Roosevelt, World War II, his childhood, first loves. Because he looks "in the corners of things" his poems are grounded simply on simple observations that somehow expand into tantalizing ambiguities. . . . Levine is not a flashy poet . . . and these poems are even "quieter" than those in *They Feed They Lion,* his previous book (1972). But his dark vision, which picks out mostly unpretty, visceral images, has remained constant: "the scattered intestines of purses," "great tubs of fat," "thumb prints/on an oily knife," "the cold meats of the deep," "the rich harvest/of the alleys," "the rats/frozen under the conveyors," etc.

One new element is a certain nostalgia, natural in poems looking backward. (p. 24)

Although Levine tends to look on nature as an antagonist, and his memories tend to be memories of loss, and the "air crackles" with the anger of the dead, these poems have a stoical strength based on the existence of love. His short two- and three-beat lines heavy with nouns and verbs support a nonsentimental view of life that gives value to the smallest, least elegant, action. . . . (pp. 24-5)

> *Peter Meinke, in* The New Republic *(reprinted by permission of* The New Republic; *© 1974 by The New Republic, Inc.), September 7, 1974.*

The landscapes of Philip Levine's latest book, *1933,* resemble those of his earlier poetry; the poet experiencing them is not so familiar a figure. Levine once identified as major obsessions: "Detroit. The dying of America. Search for communion. Admiration for cactus, pigs, thistles, thorny people who refuse to die." In the harsh light of the Depression and midwestern waste, these scenes and people are revisited. But Levine imagines them this time without the flashes of anger which in the past have made his poetry vivid as a scar. *1933* may well be Levine's *Life Studies*—like Robert Lowell's book, a ghostly reunion of family and friends, an autobiography, a tribute, an exorcism. (p. 41)

On the Edge was an astonishing debut. Where most first books pay poetic debts and shed other poets' skins, *On the Edge* was a clear announcement by a prickly poetic personality. As prologue, it prepares us for the more anecdotal and narrative character of his next few books. (p. 43)

[The] felt hostility between poet and reader, [the] disregard for the reader's comfort, is the strength of some of the best poems in *On the Edge*. Among these, "Gangrene" is a real shocker.... "Gangrene" works by making a reader anxious as to just how close to life, to truth, the poem may take him. (pp. 44-5)

They Feed They Lion ... is to my mind Levine's finest book precisely because it forces us to enter ... virtually indescribable states of mind and to recognize them as our own. Levine not only takes on, once more, his resistant roles, but also strains at grammar and snytax to draw us into unfamiliar worlds. The title poem is an apocalyptic chant where revulsion is gathered into awe, where appetite becomes a lion rather than a universal wolf, and where man preying upon man is not only part of the order of things but also something for fearful celebration.... The fierce conjunctions ... and the jammed grammar of this poem forestall all discrimination, all efforts to tell detritis from nourishing earth. (p. 47)

[*1933*] is a book of beautiful passages, but not of whole poems. There are moving moments.... But read through, one poem after another, there is too much incantation. That Levine gets a great deal of this ritualizing effect from the Spanish poetry which stimulates many poets these days is neither here nor there. The mode doesn't accommodate the anger and hostility which, in earlier books, were clearly part of his impetus for writing.

It is not that contradictions, the twinning of violence and beauty have disappeared from his work. What's gone is the tension, the way he stretched the language and forced us to acknowledge contradictions.... [Contraries] are swallowed by litany, each line given coordinate value and somehow lulling us with the way of the world. (p. 49)

> *David Kalstone, "The Entranced Procession of the Dead," in* Parnassus *(copyright © by Parnassus: Poetry in Review), Fall/Winter, 1974, pp. 41-50.*

[Compared] with *They Feed They Lion*, Levine's new book [*1933*] is less splendid, though quite as sordid. What was wonderful about that last book—and what is missing, or missed, in this latest one—is just the conviction of splendor, the just conviction which balances and ransoms the conviction of sordor, the unjust conviction. Poets often suffer from, even exult over, the trough-of-the-wave syndrome in those organized articulations of their *oeuvre* they call their books, their volumes; the crest for Levine was

certainly a poem like *Breath*, which ended *They Feed They Lion* with these axiological pulsations:

> I give
> the world my worn-out breath
> on an old tune, I give
> it all I have
> and take it back again.

And the trough is here, when Levine apostrophizes "the world" with that same shuddering fall, that urgency of deprivation, that starved energy of shared lives brutalized by displacement, by promiscuous sociability rather than society, by labor rather than work, by agglomeration rather than cities. Addresses to flesh and bone, these poems work by breath, though they do not always "work", as I say—they break down, they break off, they break up.... And yet ... It is so difficult a thing Levine has undertaken, this balancing act of his, where at a certain pitch of revering identification "one comes," as he said as long ago as in *Not This Pig*, "to be a stranger to nothing." And the more difficult because he does it by breathing, by that systole and diastole of air taken in and given out, the impulse caught up and released, which makes any equilibrium a danger, a suffocation even. He wants, preposterously, to bless; he would transform blasphemy into blessing by no more than making the poem, by no less than uttering it—in all Indo-European languages, *to do* is initially *to revere*.... He would have us know that if we are dismembered, we may—in a total apprehension of magnificence, of terrestrial power—be remembered. For if it is the *conviction* of splendor which fails in *1933*, it is never the assumption. Levine has in fact enlarged his premises, or brooded upon them till they are the more unmistakably his, and therefore ours, in these indeterminate litanies. He has breathed the world in and out, he has made the earth itself the contents of a single infinite and eternal human body, his own.... (pp. 354-55)

Levine *names*, and in his fragmentary devotions here he achieves a kind of splenetic salvation, he assumes the world, which is to say he takes it on as a filthy garment, and takes it on, too, as a challenger, "naming / the grains of the sea / and blessing ...". (p. 356)

> *Richard Howard, in* Poetry *(© 1975 by The Modern Poetry Association; reprinted by permission of the Editor of* Poetry*), March, 1975.*

Over the last few years Philip Levine has become so striking a poet that I'm surprised he's not more highly valued than he is. Of course he always wrote forceful poems, but were they always so original? An early admired one, "That Distant Winter," seems now, in retrospect, not to be Levine at all, has varying echoes of Lowell, Jarrell, Trakl, and some of the dramatic properties of Lawrence's "The Prussian Officer," which probably inspired it. Another, equally admired, "On the Edge," sits with the ghost of Weldon Kees, who has haunted the poet elsewhere. But it's when we come to his latest collections, *They Feed They Lion*, ... and the recent *1933*, that the particular Levine style and strategy continue almost uninterruptedly from page to page. The fine savagery of the earlier volume is manlier, more immediate in its appeal; the later volume is smoother, craftier, a bit muted, but is an advance, I think, deeper, certainly, and more humane.

Levine's is a daunting, brooding art, often without solace. Scorn and sympathy seem to be there in equal measure, "so much sorrow in hatred," as he says. The bonds of family, work, class, Levine as householder in America, knockabout wanderer in Spain, the wars of man and nature, wilderness and town—these are the different features of a difficult face, "human and ripe with terror"—and with knowledge. Recognition through confrontation, behavior under pressure—obviously these do not come easily to him.

An antagonistic strain, what he calls the "sour afterthought," rubs off on practically everything he touches. Essentially he's a poet of solitude, presents not "the bliss of solitide," Whitman's theme, but solitude as recoil from attachment or obligation, solitude that has him as a poet in middle age ruminating on remnants of a boy's dream "of a single self / formed of all the warring selves split / off at my birth / and set spinning." And it is just these selves or their later incarnations—Levine as husband, father, friend—which he keeps discovering or despoiling again and again.

He manages, I suppose, two things probably better than any of his contemporaries, at least those born in the middle or late Twenties. The old *mon semblable, mon frère* business of Baudelaire is given renewed American vigor in a number of his poems—for instance, "The Midget," "Baby Villon," "Angel Butcher," parts of "Silent in America." More important, he can create the sense of a milieu, the sound, feel, geography of a place, a time, a people, the flavor of what's been happening among us and what continues to happen, which seem to me almost totally lacking in most other serious poetry today. His portraits, in particular—those in *They Feed They Lion* and *1933*—are troubling, mysterious, delicate, wrathful, constitute a sort of litany of the industrial (Detroit) and immigrant (Jewish) backgrounds which formed him and follow him. They define the poet to himself and his world to us. . . .

The tenor and power of the language are often colloquial, yet subtly, sparsely musical too. Musical, I suppose, in the traditional sense that the words on the page always await their proper pitch, can only be arranged in a certain way, deviate from the necessary sequence and the mood is not sustained, the melody lost. And that's important since Levine's metaphors are not always the strongest, his subject matter can seem repetitive or astringent. One really has to *believe* what he says, the way the breath shapes its particular truth. And I do (which doesn't always happen when I read poets). . . .

Levine, though, has one particular fault. Naturally he's a master of *la belle indifférence*, but that sort of stoical orneriness can become, I think, a bit of a trick. A few of the poems, especially those in *They Feed They Lion*, affect an odd air of concealment and exposure, reminiscent of the American thriller, the taut abrupt tone of Bogart with his buried vein of idealism, the Bogart who says, "Don't be too sure I'm as crooked as I'm supposed to be." It's that sort of cockiness, and the threatening calm behind it, that makes him laugh at, for instance, what he calls those "twitch-nosed academic pants-pisser poets" of the Fifties, or that has him count a bit monotonously the cost and grit of experience, insisting upon its value even while chafing against it, or has him write declamatory phrases that sound great but don't always make much sense: "I shit handfuls of earth." Still he's obviously a rugged burdened animal. The best of his obsessions seem to me always muscular,

always authentic, his characteristic posture being, in fact, that of a horse in harness, moving restively backward or sidewise, who balks but endures. (p. 20)

Yet though his poems are not inclusive, though they are built on a continual narrowing down of sentiment or comment, the incompatibilities in them—the opposition between grievance and balm, fierceness and tenderness, between himself "made otherwise" by another's pain—do ultimately merge, as they do in Whitman, although not in joyous surrender, but simply of necessity. (p. 21)

Robert Mazzocco, in The New York Review of Books *(reprinted with permission from* The New York Review of Books; *copyright © 1975 NYREV, Inc.), April 3, 1975.*

*   *   *

LOGAN, John   1923-

Logan, an American Catholic of Irish ancestry, is a poet and critic. His characteristic poems are intense and often extremely personal.

Though it is true (at least in my opinion) that his poems about saints and martyrs are not his best, the surprising thing about this part of Logan's work is that the churchly bookishness is not dry and dead; it is oddly alive and *felt*, for in addition to being a Catholic, Logan is a man for whom intellectual excitement exists. Even so, to a religious outsider like myself, his formidable and detailed knowledge of church history and ritual is rather forbidding, and there are a good many times when I get lost in it. If one is patient, however, one comes to see that Mr. Logan's sense of what is sacred in his own experience is by no means limited to what is officially supposed to be sacred; it does not in the least depend on his having read Saint Augustine or on any of the rest of his orthodox or unorthodox learning. His poems at their best—and Mr. Logan's work is remarkably "level," with few peaks and declines—convey to a remarkable degree that degreeless and immeasurable and unanalyzable quality which Albert Schweitzer has called, in our century's greatest phrase, "reverence for life." In the face of this feeling, which is constant throughout Mr. Logan's writing, one does not really care much about talking of his literary means. His technical abilities are relatively slight, and really begin and end with an uncommon capacity for coming up with a strangely necessary and urgent observation and setting it among others by means of ordinary, unemphatic but rather breathless language which makes his lines read something like a nervous, onrushing prose. The heavy machinery of his religious symbology looks at times a little incongruous in this setting, but Logan himself never does. (p. 166)

James Dickey, "John Logan" (1962), in his Babel to Byzantium *(reprinted with the permission of Farrar, Straus & Giroux, Inc.; copyright © 1956, 1957, 1958, 1959, 1960, 1961, 1962, 1963, 1964, 1965, 1966, 1967, 1968 by James Dickey), Farrar, Straus, 1968, pp. 164-67.*

[When] we read, in the dedication of Logan's third volume: "The Redemption has happened. The Holy Ghost is in Men. The art is to help men become what they really are," it is apparent, even before we expose ourselves to the poem's action upon us, that we are not in the hands of a mere pietist, that Logan is possessed by no theory but a thirst.

Tautologically enough, in the understanding of Christianity, for a man to become *what he really is* means that he does not become something else, does not undergo or initiate upon himself a metamorphosis, which is the central symbol of divine love as the understanding of Paganism conceived it. For Logan, a man initiates or undergoes a *transfiguration*, is made over only by becoming more intensely and ecstatically himself—becomes what he really is to the exclusion of accident and change. That is the lesson, for him, to be learned from the lives of the saints and the deaths of the martyrs, and to be rehearsed, dreadfully enough, in the very *realia* of his own existence, no less profound for being the more profane: "if some people find my subjects less religious now than they used to be, the reason is that I now think poetry itself more religious than I used to do.... It's not really the skeleton in our closets that we fear, it's the god."

John Logan's most remarkable and happily most characteristic poems, then, will not be versified accounts of the torture and death of the British poet-martyr Southwell, or even Freudian *aperçus* into the overmothered life of a Heinrich Heine, individual and even indicative as the latter are.... Logan's highest achievement, I think, the basis and perhaps the residue of all the other poems, are those—they are to be found in all of his books, more densely in the later ones—of confession, the kind of writing in which experience has not been mediated by knowledge, or at least by learning, and in which the risk, consequently, attendant on transfiguration is greatest precisely where it is run most egregiously—fastest. The autobiographical mode allows this poet to exploit to intense profit the confusion, if not the identity, of his beliefs in God and in the Oedipus Complex. Sometimes indeed I am not so sure about God, but the Western tradition of parricide and piety is certainly furthered here, whether acknowledged baldly ("Man's central difficulty is his old hell with his prick") or in the terms of violent metaphor. (pp. 307-08)

[As] James Dickey has pointed out in one of the few critical notices of Logan's work that signifies beyond the jacket blurb, this poet's technical abilities are relatively slight, and really begin and end with an uncommon capacity for coming up with a strangely necessary and urgent observation and setting it among others by means of ordinary, unemphatic but rather breathless language "which makes his lines read something like a nervous onrushing prose." (p. 313)

[Logan writes]: "A poet is a priest or a necromancer of the baroque who dissolves by the incantations of his cadenced human breath the surface of earth to show under it the covered terror, the warmth, the formal excitement ...". Cadenced human breath, call it, as an instrument to get at transfiguration. The energy of spiritual substance driving through endless labyrinths, the very corridors of the lungs, which occasionally coil into form. There is a strange innocence about this voice, for all its ecclesiastical knowingness and all its bookish insistence, the innocence of a man who does not say, like Jarrell's despairing Woman at the Washington Zoo, "Change me! change me!" but rather, "Make me Myself!" Besides the centripetal mode of confession he

has come upon, the one I think most effective and convincing in his repertory ...—besides this guilt-ridden litany which manages never to sound like Robert Lowell even if it does so at times merely by not being very accomplished, Logan has two other means of approaching transfiguration: one is the historical commentary ..., which in *Spring of the Thief* he brings to a characteristic pitch of laceration, as in "The Experiment That Failed".... The other mode of access to transfiguration is the ecstatic identification of the poet's consciousness with objects, with landscape, with a weather intromitted into the self [exhibited] in his "Eight Poems on Portraits of the Foot".... (pp. 315-16)

The wish for some geniune change other than our death, the transfiguration of life not in immortality but in the living of it—that is Logan's manfully shouldered burden and his quest: the body of this man's work *cries out* to be poems, and in that exploration, which is his own form of prayer, who can doubt he has already succeeded and will—over his towering argument as over his tottering art—prevail. (p. 317)

> Richard Howard, "John Logan" (originally published in Chelsea), in his Alone With America: Essays on the Art of Poetry in the United States Since 1950 (copyright © 1965, 1966, 1967, 1968, 1969 by Richard Howard; reprinted by permission of Atheneum Publishers, New York), Atheneum, 1969, pp. 306-317.

If the usual academic distinctions between major and minor have any validity, then it must be said that John Logan is a poet of major importance. Without question, Logan violates—and quite blithely—many of the currently accepted canons of poetic taste. In a generation which treasures the concrete and the visual, Logan does not hesitate to invoke a richly sensuous experience supported by all the linguistic devices he can muster. While the spontaneous, the immediate, even the "found" is being elevated to poetic dignity, Logan continues to make poems about the extraordinary, the fantastic, even the surrealistic and totally imagined experience. (pp. 69-70)

> Harold Isbell, in Commonweal (copyright © 1970 Commonweal Publishing Co., Inc.; reprinted by permission of Commonweal Publishing Co., Inc.), March 27, 1970.

Yeats knows that our existence would be unrelievedly tragic if from our dying we could not create, so that dread can become hope, even in the face of biological decay. Much of John Logan's recent poetry faces directly this kind of awareness. He places his sense of man's tragic bondage against two equally powerful resolutions: the momentary obliteration of both dread and hope that comes through identifying himself with the dying *animal*, and the momentary release of the soul through identification with a creating spirit that transforms human hope and dread into grace. So much of his recent poetry seems generated from anxiety attending the uncertain fate of hope and dread because in life one resolution is likely to exclude the other. But only the two together would allow the dying animal to become the man who generates and creates *through* death. The soul of the man then must be embodied in what he can create beyond his body, as his words name and so release him (in the act of writing) from the animal obliterations of "dying" in all its meanings. . . .

What keeps his recent poems from being in any narrowly conceived sense confessional is his stark drive to clarify ways in which all private losses are understood as dyings that can generate new insight. Many of the poems deal with the failure to achieve this. Once belief in the religious meaning of a personal quest is shaken, the problem of discovering new meaning from repeated losses is a problem of discovering new piety *in* the losses, not simply as a result of them—the solution that failed Wordsworth and many other converts. But John Logan is converting *out* of orthodox belief at the moment when religious myth is being tested against actual experience, and so his search for transcendent meaning in particular experiences is part of a further refusal to invest religious energy in religious objects (on the model of childhood's "faith" in parents, and adult man's "faith" in his institutions and beliefs). The search for meaning in new relationships is as well a search for new access to divinity, through which precariously freed identity might be extended and confirmed. But this is putting it backwards: the odyssey of losing old identity and confronting new selfhood opens up a quiet and patient freeing of awe and even worship. It is a search for reverence through turbulence, reverence sometimes mocked by institutionalized faith. (p. 19)

There is . . . an exploration for grace in Logan's recent poetry and a testing of its loss. Grace is found anew as the process of making and unmaking meaning is enacted; grace comes with the solemn urgency of a momentary deliverance, but it can be frozen too in the deliverance. Its picture, like the poem itself, needs constantly to be remade. Those things in personal relationships most fugitive and powerful thus become centers of its definition. (p. 22)

What John Logan's poetry gives back to life, out of the huge awkward torn cry, comes with an extraordinary economy and a desire to give release to the reader by shaping and controlling emotional response. It comes through the exercise of a craft that builds on all the resources commanded through echoing associations by turning one emotion into its opposite, so that the slow and deliberate paces, interrupted with more abrupt verbal gestures, are both guiding and assuring in the way they make inclusive meaning out of polarized feelings. His own assurance against leaving the reader with the work of inventing speed and contour is what he joyfully praises in Cummings' experiments with controlling how words are received. (p. 23)

[We] long for the "spirit of health." No poet, since Freud's discoveries have become the common property of the mind, has written with fuller mastery of the circumstances in which this longing finds itself baffled and fulfilled than John Logan. He has gone far to answer Freud's misbegotten charge that poetry is another form of fantasy; for he has dramatized the meaning of fantasy at work in his hope, then dramatized the way the need for transcendence goes beyond fantasy to become actual. He writes of our instincts for transcendence and discovers their lineaments without then turning upon them as if they were merely part of the child's primary illusion. This gives the Romantic concern with the self the added gravity of analyzed emotion, freed from the disguises and displacements of personae, but freed too of the reductive truths of psychoanalysis—where the

meaning of the poet's particular and immediate situation is often analyzed in terms of its "original" significance. What is unique in his recent poetry is the drive to return to those origins and make them conscious, so that their meaning for the "spirit of health" can be included in his re-understanding of them. He goes down to the private sources of feeling through time and recovers them for the inclusive present. When he emerges changed, like us through him, it is with the sudden wakefulness of a newly created presence, vulnerable again, and "unpredictable as grace." (p. 24)

William H. Chaplin, "Identity and Spirit in the Recent Poetry of John Logan," in The American Poetry Review *(copyright © 1973 by World Poetry, Inc.), May/June, 1973, pp. 19-24.*

Logan has found, invented, has convulsed his way to that listening body which in viridescent America is generally identified not so much with a readership as with witnesses, people who prefer performances to books, the young:

> *I want to open (willingly) the mouth*
> *of my youth*
>   *and breathe musical breath*
>   *into it.*

And so he does; he does want to, and he does breathe it— into his youth, their youth, whatever youth is around, "for our conscience views itself / in the mirror of the flesh." With a choking intensity altogether characteristic of a man so deep-throated, so large-hearted, Logan has labored to divest his poetry . . . of all that is arduous, exacting, exclusive, professional, to make it efficient outside the clique of the learned. By efficient I mean *operative*, working, irresistible even, upon that kind of cursive exposure, which is not at all sure it will have—or require—a second occasion. This is poetry for the first time around, when the first time is at once acknowledged to be the last as well. . . . [The] designs upon us which Logan's language will have cannot afford that larger-scale ceremonial of hovering expectations —expectations met, violated, restored—which depend upon a unit, a model constituted by at least the line, at best the paragraph or, decorously, the stanza (the *room* in which to turn back, to walk up and down). A hand-to-mouth music is to be heard here, there is no time for setting the table, for courses; the rhymes are discovered in passing, and like anything which passes, they vary in quality, but they are there, usable, functional—they serve to mark the end of something which language itself accommodates, the end of effort.

But before I lounge a little among the dissipated ardors of *The Anonymous Lover*, with its idiosyncratic landscapes, photographs, paintings, inventories and addresses, I want to look back first to its predecessor, *The Zig Zag Walk*, which gathered up Logan's poems from 1963 to 1968. I want to look back, because I want to show, in brief, what it is that this poet has labored to divest himself *of*; what the baggage is, or was, that Logan is now the lighter for having jettisoned. In an earlier account of Logan's work . . . I remarked upon his versions of transfiguration, achieved by fervors of dedication to dead poets and mages, to landscapes and objects, and to his own insulted and injured experience, his confessed biography. In the case of past masters, Logan's apostrophes are always to *them*, not to their achievement. That is wonderfully so in the Keats elegy from *The Zig Zag Walk*, a representative (and gorgeous) achievement. . . . Logan's enterprise here is indicative of all that he has decided no longer to bother about.

If not despairing, then desperate in their fluttering apostrophe, Logan's "Lines for the Twice-drowned" (once in death, again in the realization of death: "You, Keats . . . and I . . . drown again / away from home . . . as you once drowned in your own phlegm, / and I in my poem. I am afraid.") [offers] that typical terror of process which is this poet's signal—his signal to write poems, one might say, at any rate, at any cost, to break silence by that fond utterance of the situation, that Recognition Scene he sets over and over again. Logan's zeal of identification is of course to the *man* Keats—the Keats of the letters quoted in the epigraph and of the terrible deathbed so hallucinatorily figured in the body of the poem itself—rather than to the poet Keats, the Keats of the Odes, say. The slow, unpersuadable triumph registered by a poem like "To Autumn" is not to be collected from an exile in the sopping Roman graveyard. Logan cannot, in his own poem, keep from casting experience in its charnal terms, for so the occasion appears to demand of him ("Since my birth / I've waited for the terror of this place"), but his capacities and his task as an artist come to his rescue here, save him from being no more than the Beddoes of the affair. For the care he takes with notation, indeed the almost musical play against each other of things heard and felt and seen . . . is warped by the end into a kind of patience: reluctantly, painfully, the revelation is given; the living poet can read the gravestone of the dead one. He can learn, by fraternal concession, that there *is* a process in that final fierce violet, as in the "furious August rain" which, if only acknowledged, if only *imagined* intensely enough, can permit the kind of ultimate acceptance which so loads "To Autumn". For all Logan's pangs, he achieves or is granted a patience, for that is what patience originally means: a *suffering*, here a sufferance of the worst in order to gain not the best but no more than being—that ongoing life which is writ in water indeed, "streams that shape and change", for we must alter in order to exist.

There are not many poems in *The Zig Zag Walk* so good as the Keats elegy, nor need there be; there is throughout the book a passionate striving between language and experience to represent each other—an energy *toward* that transfiguration of experience which will relieve Logan of the process, the patience. . . .

In [*The Anonymous Lover*], there is no patience to be relieved; the transfiguration has always and already occurred —*elsewhere*, outside the poems, which are merely the marginalia of metamorphosis, a prolegomenon to any future ecstasy. It is foolish to speak any longer of Logan's "task" as an artist, for these poems are the discovery of a method which will obviate tasks, their mastery, and in a sense their mystery. The poems of *The Anonymous Lover* are perhaps the first in the history of the art which are set down, by an authentic artist, to take care of themselves; hence the buckshot lines, the broken words, the determination of movement by the "revealed" rhyme of language off the transfigured tongue-tip. In the representative achievement here, the final poem "Tears, Spray and Steam," Keats is indeed mentioned (there is someone around who "knows / all the Odes / by heart / as well as many / bawdy songs"), but he is merely a prop, not a passion now. Logan is past passion in

these exploded notations—he is ready and willing to let the language wash over him, noticing its casual arrests, and declaring, there! that will be the poem. The risk of his decision is ours, and of ours, his. (p. 7)

> *Richard Howard, in* The American Poetry Review *(copyright © 1973 by World Poetry, Inc.; reprinted by permission of Richard Howard), September/October, 1973.*

This book of love poems [*The Anonymous Lover*] makes me feel the way all good poems do—both humble at the incredible gift one writer is displaying and also strangely peaceful—that sense that perhaps he has shown us all the way to write a poem we thought we never could even try. (p. 46)

> *Diane Wakoski, in* The American Poetry Review *(copyright © 1974 by World Poetry, Inc.; reprinted by permission of Diane Wakoski), January/February, 1974.*

John Logan is keyed to immediacy and his senses are extremely sharp; he is essentially a poet of sensibility. Line breaks are extremely important for him, and no one else breaks the poetic line quite as he does. Often the break occurs in the middle of a word, creating surprise but never surprise alone. Logan distinguishes between the different syllables in a word and often wants to emphasize one which is not the last; as a result we find a sequence like "All the heavy / wet- / ness" and are forced to rethink our concept of the line break. Logan's breaks are never arbitrary; they provide emphasis and make an interesting point about language—that ultimate syllables are often flat and ponderous, and have little place at the end of a poetic line.

The poems have an admirable honesty and directness; Logan looks at the world and his life intently, and there are almost no "effects". He is honestly sentimental. The carefully pitched voice of the poet can go on at considerable length, and many poems are not at all concise. But something quite remarkable often happens. At a certain point in the poem the entire world seems to come into existence by virtue of his way of looking at it—not just selected details, what is pretty, or what he has managed to transform. The poems do not consist of high points and "successes"; instead, each is a much larger package based on a way of looking at the world that can accept any detail with which it is presented. The poems have few pinnacles or startling cliffs one can admire; they proceed by very small increments and build up into large, deliberate structures with a high point at the end which we realize is high only after the rather flat voice has stopped, the poem ends, and we are falling from it. This happens in "The Dead Man's Room," "Three Poems on Aaron Siskind's Photographs," and "Only the Dreamer Can Change the Dream". It is the entire poem which has created a highly metaphorical structure out of ordinary, everyday details. These metaphorical structures are the world as we know it. (pp. 171-72)

> *John R. Carpenter, in* Poetry *(© 1974 by The Modern Poetry Association; reprinted by permission of the Editor of* Poetry*), December, 1974.*

*   *   *

LOWELL, Robert   1917-

Poet, playwright, translator, critic, and man of letters,

Lowell is one of America's most outstanding writers. All of his work reflects the complex tension between his Puritan New England background and his mature conversion to Catholicism. Donald Hall, himself a distinguished poet and scholar, has written that Lowell "has the potential to become the major poet in English of the last half of this century, as Yeats ... was the major poet of the first half." (See also *Contemporary Authors*, Vols. 9-12, rev. ed.)

Viewed as a whole, Lowell's treatment of American history [in *The Old Glory*, three plays] presents a tangle of tonalities, his varying attitudes sometimes jarring against each other in a single poem or in different versions of the same poem. His feelings about the past have been in a state of flux throughout his career, history intersecting with self in a shifting drama. That self has been immersed in an anxious, violent present which is our common property, and that immersion has helped give Lowell's handling of our past its intense and protean nature as well as its public scope. (p. 40)

Lowell's handling of American wars appears to have tapped very different currents of feeling in him at different times: he combines a pacifist's hatred of violence with an armchair general's fascinated regard for combat. (p. 47)

In [some] of Lowell's poems, ... the past repels; in [others] it attracts, putting the present to shame. But this description is misleading, for on occasion the two attitudes come together in a single work, and such poems are the most interesting of Lowell's treatments of the past, exhibiting the conflicts of a mind in which the events of history will not stay pigeonholed. (p. 49)

[An] attraction to their power keeps Lowell's sensibility tied to the very fathers he is trying to reject, producing a warring of elements in his poems about the past. Ancestors, familial or spiritual, are renounced, but duplicitous assent to them somehow enters, and the ancestral tradition is continued in the self or the spirit of the poems, rather than being terminated by it.

There is at least one poem of Lowell in which this process seems to be recognized. In its original version, "Rebellion" ... marked the rejection of a violent past enshrined in family heirlooms, notably a flintlock. But the poem contains a paradox, apparently undiscerned in the first version: the son, in rejecting the violent past, was committing a violent act in the present, sending his father crashing into the heirlooms, the flintlock breaking on his head. In its revised version, the poem's original focus on ancestral guilt (through reference to Bunker Hill) is replaced by a recognition of the son's guilt. (pp. 56-7)

The view that prevails throughout the trilogy might be fairly summed up in this way: some of the men depicted won, some lost, all were in the wrong. There is a troubling glibness in this view, a sense that a scheme has been imposed too easily on the materials by an observer who is too emotionally removed from them. The exacerbation, admiration, or confused conjunction of both, evident in the earlier Lowell's images of the past, have given way to an Olympian repugnance before the spectacle of history, a tone which is something other and lesser than the controlled presentation, discussed above, of mixed emotions and mixed materials. The relatively objective form of the drama has, in Lowell's hands, resulted in more auctorial objectivity than one wants, and a more trivial past than one

believes in. Curiously enough, Lowell has said that *The Old Glory* "is partly a tribute to the past. . . ." Would that it were. The plays might have been richer, more persuasive, and more moving than they are. (pp. 63-4)

> Alan Holder, "The Flintlocks of the Fathers: Robert Lowell's Treatment of The American Past," in The New England Quarterly (*copyright 1971 by* The New England Quarterly), *March, 1971, pp. 40-65.*

Robert Lowell is [a] confessional poet who has done an odd thing. He's revised the lovely *Notebook 1967-68* without improving it. As a set of discrete throwaways it had charm, which he otherwise doesn't. Revising the book forces us to see it as a Work which needed revision. He belongs to the rewrite school; everyone who grew up around Kenyon does. Young poets I talk to can't afford to work that way—if it isn't right the first time they chuck it, and if their work is less dense there are more surprises. The New Critics think in terms of individual poems, which must announce themselves as such. The younger crowd tend to think of individual poems as incidents in a larger event called writing poems. Why revise when you can write another? If my proofreader eye can still be trusted, page-for-page comparison of the old and new versions comes to this: in general the old versions are metrically rougher (usually more interesting), and verbal changes destroy as often as they improve. The additions are genuinely unnoticeable, except for the ones on Mary Stuart, Robespierre, and Mozart. I *think* the "Rembrandt" alterations are for the better, but miss the old version of "For Norman Mailer." . . . At the end of *Love & Fame* Berryman prays; Lowell addresses Berryman. They aren't much like each other. Each is trying to get out of the horrible equation of poem and lyric, by writing little things which make a big thing. MacDiarmid did it in 1926, in *A Drunk Man Looks at the Thistle*. He went on to write excellent nonlyric verse. Berryman and Lowell are still trying for that and so, creaky as they are, still count as Younger Poets. The solution, when it comes, will not be a matter of revision. (pp. 207-08)

> Gerald Burns, in Southwest Review (© 1971 by Southern Methodist University Press), *Spring, 1971.*

A good many critics have paid their routine respects to the *scale* of what Robert Lowell has done in *Notebook* and in *History*, its latest revised version. He aims at world stature —the argument seems to be—both in themes and in personal achievement as a poet, and although he may not wholly succeed we should respect him—in this age of hole-and-corner over-privatised poetry etc., etc.—for at least trying. But should we really? (p. 124)

Unlike the jumble or jungle of *Notebook* [Lowell's own terms, in his preface to *History*], *History* is arranged chronologically by its ostensible subject-matter. Beginning in mythic and Biblical times we are taken on a long journey through recorded history with the names of several score of famous historical personages as our main stopping-places. When we eventually reach our own times and the poet himself comes on the scene, the scope widens to include contemporary politics, people (frequently artists) the poet has known and a variety of things and events he has experienced or reacted to. *History* has its sources not only in

Notebook but also in Lowell's other early poetry, a good deal of which is cannibalised or else simply re-written into the new fourteen-line form; it also contains a lot of translations, some of them re-written from *Imitations* and other early books. If *Notebook* ('my last published poem') is a poem, then *History*, with all its further re-orderings and revisions, must presumably be even more of one. The indications are, in fact, that Lowell's whole poetic output may from now on be eligible for this process of self-digestion, the resulting enormous work-in-progress being offered to us as a continuously mutating single poem. But one might also wonder if the revisions are heading in a very sensible direction: the jumble or jungle of *Notebook* seems in many ways a more fertile arrangement (if there is fertility here at all) than the would-be objective chronologising of *History* with its rather arbitrary hiving-off of more intimate matters into another volume.

The more so since *History* is thoroughly personal anyway. The real *raison d'être* of nearly all the famous names who crowd these pages, from Sappho and Alexander through Napoleon and Goethe to Robert Kennedy and Sylvia Plath, seems to be as pegs to hang Robert Lowell poems on. (p. 125)

Obviously it is not history that Lowell is writing. There are times when the historical vehicle takes over—moments of empathy, briefly and capriciously sustained—but for the most part the history in these poems is present only as exploratory metaphor: at the centre of them we find the poet himself and his already well-documented concerns and anxieties. Lowell—no chameleon poet—is ransacking the universe for emotional support. If there were doubt about this it would be resolved by the poems' diction alone: as with the translations, the idiom is unmistakable Lowell—febrile, spiked with anachronisms, harshly ultra-American. Orestes wonders whether he can call the police against his own family, Cicero is garrulous on a sofa of magazines, Trojan chivalry is shit, and so on. Lowell's diction is a unique poetic argot, powerful enough on occasions but also guaranteed to deracinate an experience from anywhere except the corpus of this one poet's work. It would be possible to suppose that Lowell's imperious colonising of history expressed some kind of half-buried philosophy—about the unchangingness of human nature perhaps, or some version of the eternal return. One is reminded sometimes of Auden's almost geological readings of our cultural past. But Auden's interest was always quizzical and detached; here it is inescapably the poet's own world which is the real subject and to which everything is appropriated, and within that world it is the poet himself. *History* eventually homes in on the present, and when it does so the poetry—though almost always rather boring in its assumption that the poet's self-preoccupation and most casual experiences must *eo ipso* be interesting to a reader—is not particularly problematical. Lowell can be momentarily engaging . . . but otherwise . . . the second half of *History* is mostly self-centred biographical material without any of the power or poetic urge behind it of *Life Studies* or *For the Union Dead*, with which it is in some ways continuous; the metaphorical tension is collapsed almost entirely and we are made to follow the poet in his unrelieved self-involvement. Such interest as the poems have is mainly borrowed from their subjects, as when they touch on publicly known events or persons. It is the earlier, more historical-looking poems of *History* which are the most rewarding; they have an air of would-be *tour*

de force about them, even of vulgarity—rather as Pound's *Propertius* did—but they also contain most of the book's poetry. They are poems about Lowell in the guise of poems about something else; proof perhaps—if we needed it—that egocentricity works better as a subject for poetry than as a *faute de mieux* substitute for it.

The privacies of *For Lizzie and Harriet* and *The Dolphin* are really very much a part of *History*. . . . The essential subject is still Lowell himself, since the relationships dealt with only really establish themselves in their capacity as sources of concern for the poet. There are some impressive lines, but they nearly always arise out of the poet's meditations on his own destiny, on the possibility of happiness, or on his ultimate solitude. . . . No one but the poet himself is convincingly realised in these poems. (pp. 127-28)

How much does Lowell's egocentricity matter? Not at all, perhaps, in the sense that any strong feeling can be a source of poetry. It does on the other hand seem to undermine the rather obvious drive to greatness which all these poems exhibit. Lowell, like John Berryman, has allowed his life—if one can judge by the poetry—to be consumed in the effort to produce art, and the result is a moral impoverishment at the heart of the poetry itself. If poetic greatness can be driven towards at all it would seem to require a more subtle and flexible approach than Lowell has so far shown himself capable of. Lowell's way with words in these latest books is as gladiatorial and unsubmissive as ever; his ability to remain in doubts and mysteries seems as untried as it was when he took the universe by the throat in *Land of Unlikeness* and *Lord Weary's Castle*. What is miraculous is that in the interstices of all this personal turmoil he has been able to give us poetry at all. Like an anxious swimmer who flounders more and more desperately instead of trusting himself to the water, Lowell seems unable to relax and simply allow things to happen. . . . And yet in the teeth of all the probabilities he has produced his poetry.

In *Lord Weary's Castle* Lowell dealt with his personal problems in religious guise, but what was most striking was not so much the vehicle chosen as the savage manhandling of language and rhythm with which the poems were put together. On the face of it nothing could be less religious—and in the end perhaps, by the same token, nothing could be less genuinely poetic. The emotional material of these poems is never for one moment allowed to discover and declare the verbal rhythms which will properly express it; it is treated instead as an antecedently and separately known thing which needs to be forcibly manipulated—and which is in fact buckled into antecedently and separately chosen poetic metres. The violence with which this is done is really the true subject of the poetry, or rather its subject *manqué*; but it remains almost entirely uncomprehended and has no proper embodiment in what the poems say. . . . Lowell's spectacular abandonment of this kind of formal fanaticism in his *Life Studies* sequence was surely his liberation as a poet. Behind the low-keyed diction and the understated, bitten-off emotion of the *Life Studies* poems we can sense the poet facing up to the possible chaos and emptiness of life and doing so without any religious mitigation or bombast; and against this possible chaos or emptiness we see Lowell measuring himself and his own life. By taking himself as subject, and by seeing himself as exemplary for all of us, Lowell achieved an authentic impersonality in his verse despite the extreme subjectivity of its surface manner. The authenticity was also underwritten by charm and humour, qualities which these poems share with the autobiographical piece *91 Revere Street* but which were not very conspicuous in the earlier verse. (Lowell's decision to write *Life Studies* as verse rather than prose is surely one of the happiest near-accidents of modern poetry.) The process begun in *Life Studies* is carried further in *For the Union Dead*, where Lowell's concern with survival is projected outwards into a concern for the survival of anything of enduring human value and into a controlled anger on behalf of all humanity against what is being done to us. This is Lowell's first move towards historical and political material, and together with some of the poems of *Life Studies* it begins to seem now like the high point, both poetically and morally, of his work. In a poem like 'The Mouth of the Hudson' the real world is there, just as the real other people of *Life Studies* are there, and the buried rhymes, the blurring of transitives and intransitives and the many other Lowellian hallmarks of the diction (which even so remains low-profile and near-to-naturalistic) combine to convey the frustration which is the poem's subject. . . . The more elaborate title poem of *For the Union Dead* has many of the same qualities. These poems find their own rhythms—and they are allowed to do so. Despite the central place which most of them give to Lowell's personal anxieties, the anxieties are redeemed as poetry by being located in a recognisable and shareable world; the comparatively low-keyed diction ensures that this world is created in the poem rather than appropriated into it; the poet speaks for himself and for us all.

It looks as though Lowell's humanitarian phase could now be over. His concern with the common fate seems to have dwindled and hardened into a concern with personal survival and fame; the poetry has curved back into an egocentricity of content which matches the egocentricity of form with which it started out. Lowell's publication of *Notebook* was an act of arrogance which a less famous poet would never have been allowed to get away with. . . . [These poems] are almost wholly kinetic in nature—untransmuted (if personally hallmarked) passages from life and history—with only rare moments that approach any kind of artistic stasis. Almost any quotation from the later part of *History* —whatever its interest as subject-matter—would serve to illustrate the extent of this artistic impoverishment. (pp. 129-31)

What we look for in poetry, directly or indirectly, is images of hope or beauty or fulfilment. The poet's task is to find these. Not to find them in the modern world is one thing, and the failure to find them is a source of one kind of modern poetry. But not to find them anywhere in life at all is to verge on a bankruptcy both poetic and personal. At times Lowell has come near to this. We are left by his latest three volumes with only the slenderest sense of a world out there to be trusted or believed in. There are glimmerings of hope, particularly in *The Dolphin*, but they amount to very little in terms of realised poetry—and they are not helped in any case by the structural enfeeblement of all this recent work. The verse in these books is almost without exception rhythmically dead, and the fourteen-line form with its sloppy pentameters amounts virtually to a formal abdication. In too many of these poems one feels the poet trying simply for something which will click as poetry; mostly it doesn't, but the fourteen-line form enables him to stop after fourteen lines without a feeling of awful inconsequentiality. Without the fourteen-line receptacle the majority of these

poems would never know when to stop—or perhaps would never have had the courage to start. Once they are given this undemanding space to expand into the poems spend most of their time courting luck for a good image or ending. Lowell has improved individual lines from the *Notebook* stage of many of these poems, and particularly many of his endings, but somehow it doesn't seem to make much difference. One knows that the real obligation towards the creation of a finished poem has been allowed to lapse. *History* seems less of a disordered flux than *Notebook* because it is objectively arranged, but in the end it comes no nearer to an imaginative coherence—and may even be further away. Lowell has evaded his real task here, which was to quarry a few real poems—or even conceivably a properly organised super-poem—out of the subjective matrix of *Notebook*. The worst condemnation of this recent work perhaps—and it is surely a crucial test—is that almost none of it is memorable. Can Lowell even now retrench and start again, recovering perhaps the sense of rhythm and of what actually makes a poem which gave us *Life Studies* and *For the Union Dead*? (pp. 133-34)

> *Colin Falck, "Overtrained for Poetry," in* Poetry Nation *(© Poetry Nation, 1974), No. 2, 1974, pp. 124-34.*

[The] fundamental and crucial truth [is] that poetry is a special kind of *act of language* which in the vital connections it makes necessarily implies such things as attitudes, joy, indignation, compassion, pity, rage, commiseration, empathy, and other thoughts and emotions none of which necessarily implies an act of language.

Such an act of language is Robert Lowell's "Skunk Hour," which does not expressly attempt to define the function of the poet, but among other things does just that. The speaker perceives and describes the moral landscape of his time. He looks out and describes corruption and perversion: ecclesiastical, political, economic, social, sexual, and artistic, in the hermit heiress, the mystery of the "summer millionaire," and the homosexual interior decorator. In twenty-four lines of remarkable linguistic density and symbolic condensation, Lowell gives us a masterful survey of what is wrong with society. In the remaining twenty-four lines the speaker turns the moral spotlight first (in twelve lines) on himself, on the corruption within the speaker himself, and then (in the final twelve lines) on the ironically healthy, purposeful skunks of the title. The speaker's moral condemnation is complete: all are corrupt, including the speaker, who is without self-righteousness. Only the amoral skunks are (ironically) innocent, and in their ignorance seem to tacitly point a way for our redemption. The mood is indeed dispirited, and yet not without a suggestion of hope. The poet does not tell us that which he would no doubt like to hear nor that which we would like to hear except insofar as that might happen to be part of what he in fact finds in his questioning vision. (pp. 738-39)

> *R. P. Dickey, in* Sewanee Review *(reprinted by permission of the editor; © 1974 by The University of the South), Fall, 1974.*

At first a poet of denunciation and doom, in the spirit of Milton's Lucifer or Savonarola, intoning the discordant but frequently resounding measures of Melville by way of Hart Crane, Robert Lowell has recently loosened *(to a degree)* the knots in his uptight diction and re-emerged as, by influential consent, the dean of confessional poets. This role has followed the period of political activism during which Lowell was celebrated for his civil insurgence and his imprisonment as a Conscientious Objector. . . .

If Lowell is not the greatest poet of post-war America, who is? I prefer not to answer the question after proposing it—or rather, after deriving it empirically from current critical opinion. In these times, when such-and-such a poet (novelist, painter, whomever) is nominated as the greatest, the distinction, probable or not, tends to disqualify for serious attention all others who are not nominees, or who might be if it were agreed that *their* kind of genius is as valuable as the kind being elevated by the preferences of the hour. That Lowell is formidable no critic would be foolish enough to dispute; that the poems he wrote between 1946 and 1959 are surpassed by few written in America during the same period is equally beyond debate. Their gritty resonance and inquisitorial power are proven; they have unshakeably entered the language (i.e. the language inherited by those whose consciousness is formed by unique configurations of the written word). Few poets could be expected to sustain the pitch of those years without dire consequences. (Lowell's were dire enough. Dylan Thomas exploded.) There is no such exaltation of language in the three volumes confronting me [*History, For Lizzie and Harriet,* and *The Dolphin*], no such polemic and no such confinement to wrathful theology or to the reflexive self-disinheritance that agitated the bulk of Lowell's earlier poems.

The fever remains, and the lightning flashes of masochism, the abrupt modification of introductory subject, the veering detour from topic sentence to distant kindred. Principally, he can still be defined as a poet of free association, an expressionist undeniably vivid yet consistently uneven, since he is under incessant pressure to reveal *all* of himself in his poems: the private life, the public notoriety, the objective excursions to outposts of history and nature, the recoils of personal chagrin or expiation. A bewildering magnitude of squandered energy is the result: splendors of observation consort with embarassing intimacies and gratuitous generalities which should be unacceptable to anyone of mature judgement. . . .

Lowell is indeed a prodigious and arresting poet with astounding avenues of survival—yet I would personally sacrifice all his output for a half-dozen poems of Anthony Hecht, published in *The Dark Hours* (1967). Having said that, I have still to cope with the contents of the three Lowell volumes I have sketchily introduced.

Singularity of form is the first notable feature of these verses. Curiously, all but a very few are pseudo-sonnets: i.e. they are unrhymed and offbeat stanzas of 14 lines, a system that controls their limits without serving the intentions of the original structure—neither that of the Italian octave-and-sestet division, nor of the mounting tension and epigrammatic release of the triple quatrain and couplet in the Shakespearean sonnet. There's no earthly reason Lowell shouldn't employ the model in his own way but there are multiple occasions for which his employment doesn't work. A resolution is prepared which never takes place or, with an appearance of lyric integrity, the unit's measures are destroyed as soon as you try reading them aloud. (p. 22)

Obscure meaning is not clarified by disjunctive shape and forced alliteration; the multi-stress pentameter combined with two, three, four or five-syllable lines, amusing in its own way, could have been disposed in several other arrangements, to the advantage of sight and sound. I dwell on these incongruities not to be pedantic but to support inquiry. Lowell knows what he is doing; am *I* sure I know *why*? (pp. 22-3)

Nearly all Lowell's greeting-card poems—to ex-wives or for old friends, or those that supply banal quotations from eminent contemporaries—make me feel uncomfortable; they name-flash, they assume a pandemic curiosity I don't happen to share. I like Lowell least when his subject is himself and there are, I hasten to amend, impressive scores of such subjects among these hundreds. . . . Within the covers of *History,* the scope of his response to historical personalities is astounding. If you discount the interloping, solipsistic verses, you could declare his subject in these pages to be an idiosyncratic rediscovery of the past. His sense of history is tinged with delirium and weighted by caricature, with none of the obsessional longeurs of Ezra Pound: an anthology of intuitions. And the illuminations with which he reveals Clytemnestra, Hannibal, Caligula, Dante, Rembrandt, Goethe—many more—are sulphuric, as if we had seen the character in question by the sputtering flare of a match before darkness again resumed its eternal reign. Which is perhaps why his contemporary closeups are far less striking; he must look askance to see clearly—to see, that is, in the only way a poet of his order can see, with a degree of untruth that no longer matters. The truth of documents is often no more substantial than the moment seen by matchlight. (p. 23)

> *Vernon Young, in* Lugano Review, *No. 1, 1975.*

*   *   *

LURIE, Alison   1926-

Ms Lurie is an American novelist whose "outstandingly intelligent" fiction has earned for her an international reputation. (See also *Contemporary Authors,* Vols. 1-4, rev. ed.)

Miss Lurie's central female characters, Emmy in *Love and Friendship*, Katherine in *The Nowhere City,* Janet in *Real People* and Erica in *The War Between the Tates* share some preoccupations. They have a powerful call to pleasure which is countered by an equally strong cry for decency, candour and moral fastidiousness. They want to have a good time, they want the people round them to have a good time, but why do they—why does everyone else—have to be such hypocritical, censorious, devious, vain, cruel bastards? What had been a low, enlightened murmur of discontent in *Love and Friendship* is transformed into a fierce, controlled song of rage and frustration in *The War Between the Tates*. It is as if a powerful classical soprano were giving a recital which she interspersed with very funny stories; the skill of the performer is so exceptional that the audience feels at the end that it has witnessed such a great act that to analyse how the effects are achieved would be an impertinence. (pp. 126-27)

Miss Lurie's treatment of Wendy [in *The War Between the Tates*] . . . constitutes, in my view, a damaging element to the subtle moral and comic balance of the book. To all the other characters Miss Lurie extends what might be described as a concealed warmth—a belief that for all their moral failings she likes them. The appalling children; her hypocrite husband; her sluttish friend Danielle; Sandy, the local guru-shop owner, each possess—or have possessed—radiant saving graces. Though she tries, Miss Lurie fails to be just to Wendy. She hates her mindless devotion to Brian Tate, her degradation of language, her careless, futile half-bakedness. She seems even to hate her youth. The result is that the funny scenes and incidents involving Wendy have a malice about them which isn't to be found in any of Miss Lurie's other books, though she has frequently and foolishly been accused of bitchiness in the past.

The novel is beautifully constructed. Moving between the present and past historic tense we watch the declaration of war, the recruitment of allies and the marshalling of commanders and troops; we see the intricacies of espionage and the complex development of tactics sometimes from the front line and, sometimes from a further, higher vantage point. Vitally important skirmishes between some of the contenders are left unrecorded, as in the chaos of war itself, when smoke, shouts and fear distort and destroy communication. This large simile is never stressed, and only by the very end of the novel is the reader aware of its richness. He feels the elation and fatigue which follows battle.

What distinguishes *The War Between the Tates* from so much other good American fiction is its fearlessness. Vonnegut, Updike, Mailer, Philip Roth may lay claim to greater literary inventiveness—but none of them [tells his] truth with the sophisticated directness of Alison Lurie. An obsessive hatred of deceit and a minutely exact response to the surface and inner substance of ordinary life go to produce her art. (pp. 127-28)

> *Julian Jebb, "Ordinary Life," in* London Magazine, *(© London Magazine, 1974), December 1974/January 1975, pp. 125-28.*

There is some firm evidence in the five novels she has so far published that Alison Lurie should be a better novelist than she is. Her reputation up to now does not indicate that she has been widely appreciated for the qualities she does possess, although she has acquired over the years a certain small cult following, and . . . *The War Between the Tates* appears to be winning her the kind of popular attention which may prove only that her limitations have at last begun to be recognized as seeming more attractive than her virtues. That novel, at any rate, represents a descent from some relatively serious level of intention into a flossiness which was only occasionally detectable in her before and which may well be attracting her natural public.

Yet from time to time even here and in the best of her earlier work Miss Lurie reveals qualities that merit—and have seldom been given—close critical consideration. She has a satirical edge which, when it is not employed in hacking away at the obvious, is often eviscerating. She writes a prose of great clarity and concision, an expository language that efficiently serves her subject but that does not stylize upon it. She has many true things to say about the various modes of self-deception and distraction by which we endure the passage of life in these peculiarly trivializing times, and she often says them in a manner she has earned entirely by herself and that represents an authentic fictional voice. Yet there is also something hobbled and hamstrung about her engagement of experience, something that causes her again

and again to fall short of what one feels to be her full capacity to extract the truth of her materials. She seems regularly to be aware of more than she can imaginatively comprehend, to be able to describe more than she can make thematically significant. Above all, there is a lack in her of the kind of adventurousness usually associated with important talent, a conventionality or timidity that frequently causes her to make formulations of reality which in a part of her mind she must know to be clichés, and to pass over without examining certain possibilities for satire which a more radical talent would recognize as the most fertile possibilities to be found in her chosen subject.

These deficiencies manifest themselves perhaps most clearly in Miss Lurie's heavy dependence on sexual intrigue for the dramatic complication of her fiction. In all her novels except *Imaginary Friends*, which seems to have no recognizable place in her canon, there is a monotonous sameness of situation which might appear to represent a ringing of changes on, and a progressively deepening exploration of, an obsessive subject until one sees that really there is no changing or deepening. *Love and Friendship, The Nowhere City, Real People,* and *The War Between the Tates* all have to do with the experience of adultery . . . [in] the university community or artist colony . . . and as a rule the sexual drama is given such force as it possesses through being played out against the background of the dreariest middle-class respectability, boredom, child-breeding, and generalized spiritual and material shabbiness. What usually happens is that as a result of having good sex with somebody not one's legal spouse, the errant husband or wife achieves some temporary sense of rejuvenated identity which may or may not be to the ultimate advantage of marriage and community.

It is one of the older saws of criticism that extramarital sex in literature is not of terribly much interest in itself, however graphically it may be described. Its value lies in the illumination it gives to character and in the extent to which it poses some fresh challenge to the always fragile balance of tensions existing between the erotic imperatives of the self and the official hypocrisies of the public world. The penetration of the illusion that snobbery generates is, in Lionel Trilling's excellent phrase, the proper aim of the social novel, and adultery is one of the traditional, if hackneyed, modes through which this aim is accomplished. But Miss Lurie seems never to grasp the implications of the melodrama around which four of her five novels are constructed, and there are insufficient moral prohibitions in the society she describes to give it the depth of implication she is unable to perceive within it. She appears to feel that it is enough if her characters dare to commit the heresy of climbing into bed with one another. That is enough to insure their meaning as characters and to justify their presence in her novels. Her treatment of adultery suffers, in short, from arbitrariness and inconsequence. The insight it affords us into the natures of the people who commit it is finally reducible to some idea of the beneficial or destructive effects of orgasmic liberation, which is repeatedly seen as in and for itself an apocalyptic experience. . . . [The] lives of these people either do or do not undergo some important change—a sufficiency of meaning perhaps in the one-dimensional world of the soap-opera serial, where what happens next may finally be all that matters, but a gross insufficiency in novels that seem to promise some genuine revelation of character on a plane subtler and more complicated than that simply of the variety of sexual things one does to others or others do to one. (pp. 79-80)

Miss Lurie can be seen to share the dilemma of any satirical novelist of manners whose work must depend for its vitality in some direct way upon the vitality of the life he is attempting to satirize. The dilemma is deepened, furthermore, when the novelist's subject is contemporary academic manners, for nothing is more obvious to anyone familiar with the university scene of the last twenty years than that the dramatic possibilities for a fiction dealing with academic life are not what they once were—nor has the gradual growth of an encrustation of cliché around some of its most typifying characters and situations made the problem any less difficult. It seems scarcely conceivable that a novelist of whatever degree of talent would be able to write academic fiction today without being obliged to write *through* the precedent established by such classic practitioners of the genre as Helen Howe, Mary McCarthy, Randall Jarrell, Robie Macauley, and Bernard Malamud, at the same time that he would necessarily be writing without most of the advantages which these writers possessed. (p. 80)

In Miss Lurie's fiction of academic life a situation that may once have been crucial may seem to be of uncertain significance or to have a merely hoked-up significance just because the actualities of academic life have depleted it of drama. . . . [In *The War Between the Tates*, the] problems would seem to be swollen with dramatic, not to say melo-

dramatic, possibility. But they actually are not because we recognize that behind them there is absolutely nothing at stake—no risk, no threat, no anguish. The society in which they and the characters exist is much too limited, drab, and morally diffuse to give them consequence. . . . It is a society made for and by the burgeoning new population of academic Babbitts, and it is the ideal medium for their relentlessly bourgeois pursuits.

There is evidence in Miss Lurie's novels that she has some awareness of this aspect of academic life, but she treats it as little more than stage-setting for her favorite drama of sexual intrigue. Perhaps it would require a talent the size of Mailer's or Bellow's to recognize that just here, in the contrast between the professional function of academics and their way of life, is to be found what little remains of interesting literary material in the university scene . . ., and it could form the basis of a great subject. But Miss Lurie's novels do not engage it because her imagination remains trapped amid the clichés of academic life, in situations which history has rendered obsolete and crises which have lost their power, in both actuality and art, to matter very much. (p. 81)

John W. Aldridge, "How Good is Alison Lurie?" (reprinted from Commentary *by permission; copyright © 1975 by the American Jewish Committee), in* Commentary, *January, 1975, pp. 79-81.*

M

MacBETH, George   1932-

George MacBeth is an "arrogant" and inventive Scottish poet. (See also *Contemporary Authors*, Vols. 25-28.)

Macbeth has exuberance. He loves to write. But what he writes is so often, at least in [*Collected Poems, 1958-1970*], premeditated whimsy. A sense of imagination that, as in the case of many British poets today, cannot express itself with honest freedom, as Kerouac, but one that is fettered by structure. His poems, no matter what the subject—and the range is broad—fall into a traditional order of spacing, rhythm, and length (a six martini discussion of "life"). Attempting amusement and intense subjectivity, he creates contrived sets of words—statements after the fact of feeling. Perhaps in this paradox lies Macbeth's appeal. And, to the credit of his paradoxical nature, he is best in the section on the child in man, where there are fewer jarring shifts in tone: for example, these lines from "When I Am Dead": "And I desire to be laid on my side/ face down: since I have bad dreams/ if I lie on my back." (p. 1019)

> *Jon M. Warner, in* Library Journal *(reprinted from the March 15, 1972, issue of* Library Journal, *published by R. R. Bowker Company, a Xerox company; copyright © 1972 by Xerox Corporation), March 15, 1972.*

Early in his career, George Macbeth acquired a reputation as the *enfant terrible* of English poetry, which his subsequent lively publicity has done its best to play up. . . . Sadly, if we ignore the sinister packaging, we find that Macbeth is not quite the diabolical revolutionary he is made out to be. A look at the poems themselves, rather than the notes on them at the back of the book, brings the expectant eye to focus on a rather traditional product: accomplished, but not in any important sense original. The poems strike a violent posture, to utter a mild truth: publicity by Mr. Hyde, poems by Dr. Jekyll. "The Son", for instance, has the following note: "A mortuary attendant rapes the body of a dead woman. He associates her with his mother, who died of a liver disease". Yet the poem itself is robustly healthy at its core, and familiar in its impulse. . . .

The technique of these poems is not to match complexity with a complex texture, but to provide a powerful simplifi-

cation. They refer complicated contemporary situations back to primal myth. (p. 29)

It is perhaps significant that there are a number of Science Fiction poems, for much SF writing is precisely what I have tried to indicate in Macbeth, the use of a complicated theory to establish a very simple human situation. (p. 30)

Christianity seems to be an irritant to Macbeth. He tries to debunk it, but it's a frame of reference that he can't resist. . . . [It] is the invariable symbolism in which new beliefs must clothe themselves, as if it has become an obsessive force in the collective unconscious. The roots of this in Macbeth's own experience are perhaps explored in "St. Andrew's", a dispassionate poem which, by describing exactly the barrenness of the mystery, expresses the hopelessness of established religion more vividly than the irony wrung from religion elsewhere. That Macbeth does have a certain animus against Christianity is clear. What is left obscure is the reason for this, and the relevance of it, beyond a convenient source of emotive references, to his poetry. . . . The animus remains inarticulate, barren in its own spite. Macbeth has not harnessed his anger as a creative force. (p. 33)

[Macbeth] is not a revolutionary wit but a hack satirist, dependent on the continuance of the Establishment. The pity is, there are signs he could have been something more. He has an unusual sympathy, but not the passion to drive him far beyond the obvious. He has an acute mind, but not a clear head, for it is buzzing with effects.

The tendency to elaborate the surface, rather than strike to the substance, is one that recurs throughout Macbeth. It is mirrored in his style, which tends more to an accretion of detail and an accumulation of verbal effect, than to one incisive choice or a single stroke of language. Despite, or because of, all the surface clutter, there is a distance from the object. . . . This distance in the writing is probably a habit now, which Macbeth shows recent signs of trying to break, but initially the distance was deliberately sought, and not, I think, as an aid to perspective, but as a protective measure. Macbeth has been widely praised for his powers of invention. It is equally possible to see his work as a series of attractive diversions, skirting immense areas of silence. . . .

[The] discovery of a distancing device acted as a release,

made it possible to write about difficult personal material. The pity is that this is not a release but an evasion. A divorce grows between the impetus and the expression. Interest shifts from the real to the apparent subject, from the clarification of a complex experience to the forging of a simplified one. And so there is this division of energy in Macbeth, between the lurid façade of the note and the wholesome commonplaces of the poem. Presumably the real subject, the material that was of difficulty and might have been of value, lies lost somewhere in the cabbala of the note: and what we have in the poem is *kitsch*. (p. 34)

He has often been praised for his versatility. I'm not sure it isn't his worst enemy, for it seems to extend the fundamental dissipation of energy. There are several subjects on which he has written a cluster of poems, treating the same material in a variety of styles, from a straightforward selection from the facts through several degrees of decoration to extreme artifice. The neatest example is the sequence on the death of his cat: in quite a brief space of time he seems to have run the whole gamut. Here the critical conclusion is not simple: the precise account is moving, but the formal lament is even finer—only, beyond the lament, lie two more variations, a surrealist dream-poem of only moderate quality, and an intricately woven sequence of twelve sonnets that is quite preposterous. There are other clusters where one can simply say that the quality is consistently mixed. In the White Goddess poems he seems all the time to be circling his material, feinting as often as he attacks: intricate footwork, but only rarely does he draw blood. The ironic reflections on Christianity are similarly inconclusive. (p. 35)

Had his creative impulse been intensive rather than extensive, Macbeth might have given us at least one moment of utter reality, wrought into imperishable form. As it is, he has given us a body of verse, most of which is already disposable. (p. 36)

Macbeth's style was impressive from early on. In recent years it has not acquired significant new strengths: rather it has become muscle-bound. The bold use of the associative force of words, which was particularly Macbeth's achievement, has been developed into a violent element of style; odd instances are effective, but the constant use of it turns surprise into a mannerism. (p. 47)

[The] publication of *Collected Poems* comes at a very odd time, when the author is clearly at a transitional stage. (p. 48)

[In] recent uncollected poems there are signs of a more direct, personal voice, and a gentler mood, though the voice is often blurred by stylistic ambitions, with a particular tendency to rhetoric. "In Winter" escapes these vices: a delicate development of a small, unextraordinary moment.

One of the current epitaphs that Macbeth likes to sport is "extraordinary gifts arrogantly wasted". On the evidence so far, I rather think that we have seen a distinct but limited gift, artfully deployed. He has worn the guises of Surrealist and Expressionist, but he is by natural sympathy a neo-Romantic, with inclinations to the sentimental. Thus his best work has, in fact, been in a domestic setting, with tinges of humour: for in this vein the postures aren't possible, or else they're material to be debunked, but the sentiment can be real. Macbeth is clearly concerned to be "the important poet", but he has perhaps not realised where his own strengths lie. Until recently, the use of masks and de-

vices has dissipated most of his "important" material. On present form, he may well find himself with classic status, but not on the same podium as Byron: he is more likely to be cherished as a twentieth-century descendant of Edward Lear, with a certain infusion from A. A. Milne—but that is no mean compliment. (pp. 48-9)

> *Roger Garfitt, "George Macbeth" (copyright © by Roger Garfitt), in* British Poetry Since 1960: A Critical Survey, *edited by Michael Schmidt and Grevel Lindop, Carcanet, 1972, pp. 29-49.*

In the better poems in George MacBeth's new collection [*Shrapnel*] one senses that the real life of the poems moves on a level quite separate from the aspirations of the language. The personal poems that conclude the book are sustained by moments when Mr. MacBeth edges towards a conversational tone. . . . This is a new tone in his work, and almost stifled at birth by habits of style: a fallen calf lies "on stones of unconcern", a friend's phone call comes "through troubled iron of my own concerns", a thank-you poem celebrates "ceremonies of beneficence". How much better these poems could have been if their candour was not at the mercy of grandiloquence. Even so, they represent an advance.

> *"Aspirations," in* The Times Literary Supplement *(© Times Newspapers Ltd., 1973; reproduced by permission), March 9, 1973, p. 270.*

George MacBeth has frequently been called one of the half-dozen best British poets now writing, but to me he is still down the bank, reaching about, uncertain where he is going. Often he is reduced to the conscious effort of entertaining, for which he lacks a happy touch; nor is he any happier when searching, for he seems to speak from outside his lines, leaving them stranded. He describes more than he evokes, and his mind is seldom on what he depicts; it lacks imaginative tact and precision. (pp. 69-70)

> *Calvin Bedient, in* Parnassus *(copyright © by Parnassus: Poetry in Review), Spring/Summer, 1973.*

Prayers occurs at a point of confluence between two familiar George MacBeth tendencies: the poem as self-referential comic sport, and the poem as gravely liturgical ritual. On the whole the latter element predominates: these are exotic, priestly offerings, more aptly chanted than read, addressed to an array of real or mythical life-forms (Lord Squirrel, Fire Bird, Last Rose) whose powers are solemnly petitioned. . . . It is all good fun, but smells strongly of the poetic sacristy. . . . Mr. MacBeth, as this pamphlet shows well enough, has considerable technical competence; all he needs now is something to say. (p. 997)

> The Times Literary Supplement *(© Times Newspapers Ltd., 1973; reproduced by permission), August 31, 1973.*

George MacBeth's *Poet's Year* is not a bouquet of seasonal garlands but simply an accumulation of what he wrote between the months of September 1971 and September 1972. The book's blurb directs one to "death and sexual energy" as the mainsprings of Mr. MacBeth's work, but also comments that there is a greater concern "with time and the effects of time" than has been evident in his earlier collections—hardly true if one compares, say, "A Death in the North" (in *The Broken Places*, Mr. MacBeth's first mature collection, published in 1963) with "On the Death of May Street" in the present book: both speak with the same slow-paced elegiac gravity of "time and the effects of time". As for "sexual energy", there is a poem called "Porn" which is written in a characteristic MacBeth fashion of fragmentary lewdness, and a couple of resolutely unpleasant excursions into the erotic ("Lovers" and "Lovers Again"), written in stark quatrains. The term "energy" does not come readily to mind. An elegy for Andrew Young, a congested, formally dense but impressive poem called "Birth", and an exuberantly Kiplingesque performance on "The World of J. Edgar Hoover" must be counted among the successes of a typically uneven and entertaining collection. (p. 1276)

> The Times Literary Supplement (© *Times Newspapers Ltd.*, 1973; reproduced by permission), October 19, 1973.

[*The Transformation*] is short and lush, more an intricate game than a novel. Guy Sebring changes into a woman called Alcestis and embarks on a series of splendidly bisexual encounters as time wheels dizzily between the *Belle Epoque* to the late Thirties, and space shifts similarly from central Europe to an Edwardian country house. Mr MacBeth sets up an atmosphere of erotic expectation which only the *Story of O* could fulfil; and it is his pleasure gently to disappoint his reader, which he does with a sanguine aplomb worthy of the depraved figures in his fantasy. (p. 216)

> Elaine Feinstein, in New Statesman (© *1975 The Statesman & Nation Publishing Co. Ltd.*), February 14, 1975.

[The questions] which George MacBeth asks are unsettling, enigmatic, subversive—questioning not the senses but the motives, the bases of perception. . . . [His] new collection, *Shrapnel and A Poet's Year* (which was originally published, in England, as two separate volumes), is ruthlessly bizarre, with a vicious nervousness about many of the poems. They are compelled by a gothic ritualism, which educates the sensibility to that predicament which has so many names—evil, ego, imago, and which inevitably accomplishes the collision or collusion of energy and design. The categories of personal, social, and aesthetic experience are fused by MacBeth until we are left uncertainly caught in a web of imaginative intrigue, bound fast by a metrical concision that is as deft as a magician, as tight as the knots he ties. Some of the pieces are slight, but "Even the most ordinary detail/Can be a surprising wonder . . ." as poets and their readers have always known. And the best of these poems are small, nerve-wracked masterpieces, especially the "War Poems," and most especially "The Broken Ones." . . . (p. 127)

MacBeth is uncannily adept, moving from an intricate aloofness to a relaxed conspiracy. . . . And the juxtapositions which he effects are rather like capriciously and hugely arrogant metaphors. . . . It is a very good volume of poems. (p. 128)

> J. E. Chamberlin, in The Hudson Review (copyright © *1975 by The Hudson Review, Inc.; reprinted by permission*), Vol. XXVIII, No. 1, Spring, 1975.

*   *   *

MADDEN, David   1933-

An American poet, novelist, playwright, and essayist, Madden is also the editor of *American Dreams, American Nightmares*, and *Rediscoveries*, two excellent critical collections. (See also *Contemporary Authors*, Vols. 1-4, rev. ed.)

David Madden wrote of Joyce Carol Oates: "She is one of the few writers today who has the vision to disturb my sleep, to frighten me when, in banal moments, I involuntarily recall a mood from one of her stories. After reading Miss Oates, one's casual moments are not one's own." Up to now Madden's own curious, lively writing has never threatened me in this way. His criticism has been sharp and far-ranging, his fiction uneven. At times he seemed to be experimenting for ways to retell the same adventures, searching as it were for the exact form to come to terms with whatever haunted him, whatever forced him to write. Finally, in *Bijou*, he has managed to put it all together. Two weeks after having read this deceptively quiet work I still think about it, about how, in his story of a year (1946) in the life of Lucius Hutchfield of Cherokee, Tennessee, Madden has finally managed to catch a vital part of our American experience. *Bijou* is an important novel.

In *The Poetic Image in 6 Genres* Madden discussed the two imaginative extremes of his own Tennessee childhood. One was listening to his grandmother's tales. "I sense that my grandmother was aware of the effects her storytelling had on me, and, even as a child, I was aware of another part of myself that stood at a distance, observing the dynamic interplay between teller and listener." More important in terms of *Bijou* was Madden's passion for the movies. "From age four until fifteen, I saw three 'shows' a week, usually twice each. . . . I wanted to be able to affect people the way the movies affected the spectators around me; but the only way I could deal with the magic powers of the movies was to write down my own versions . . .". (p. 29)

In the introduction to one of the many volumes he has edited (*American Dreams, American Nightmares*) Madden states that today, in our collective field of vision "in which we perceive mainly the nightmare, the idea of the 'American Dream' has become a cliché." But Madden then cites Wright Morris: "Every cliché once had its moment of truth." This truth, of course, is both factual and imaginative. Wright Morris is one of Madden's literary heroes, and in fact he wrote a full-length study of Morris' fiction. But even more interesting in light of *Bijou* is Madden's book on, of all people, James M. Cain. Discussing Cain and other tough guy writers Madden notes that this unusual genre has become part of our patrimony. "Their manner of dealing with the universals of sex, money, and violence presents a somewhat expressionistic picture of American society and culture in the 1930's and 1940's and provides insights into the American Dream-turned-nightmare and into the all-American boy turned tough guy." Whether or not Lucius turns sour is not the point of *Bijou*. Madden's novel, after all, captures only one crucial year. More Tom Sawyer than Huck Finn, Lucius is obviously doomed to a life of telling stories and reshaping his past. Whether or not anyone listens will decide his fate. (p. 30)

"Bijou," set in 1946 in small-town Tennessee, stars Lucius, a 13-year-old who is not only a movie freak but also an usher in one of the local theaters, where he gets to watch, over and over, the scenes he reconstructs and fantasizes about during the rest of his life. And so the real details of his days . . . are disguised, surrounded, submerged into Alan Ladd and Veronica Lake plots and Hedy Lamarr dreams.

The movie plots, actual and imagined, take up an embarrassingly large portion of the novel's considerable length. It's not that they're either pretentious or artificially constructed, but they are immediately and unceasingly boring, and Lucius as a character is finally overwhelmed by them. . . .

No one would deny that Lucius, like millions of kids, used the movies to keep sane while getting through adolescence; the point is that fiction can't support a dogged, literal description of the details. (p. 35)

> Sara Blackburn, in The New York Times Book Review (© 1974 by The New York Times Company; reprinted by permission), April 21, 1974.

The time [of *Bijou*], one quickly sees, is 1946, and at one time or other we are bombarded with names of movies, songs, and best sellers, with newspaper and newsreel headlines. Lucius writes stories, dreams of being a writer, and gradually moves from stories based on movies to stories based on popular fiction to stories based on his own life, which in turn is based on that of Thomas Wolfe.

Now I am only a year older than Lucius Hutchfield, and was raised in a small city not unlike Cherokee. (p. 24)

In a sense, then, I am close to Madden's ideal reader. Yet long before I felt *Bijou* was terribly long, I felt first nervous and then repulsed by it, in the same way one can feel about a *roman à clef* when one knows who the people are behind all the characters. The nervousness arises the moment one realizes how much work one is doing for the author, how much supplying from one's own memory is going on, how blank it must all seem to an innocent reader, of a different place or time, who cannot do this work. The repulsion begins when one sees that what makes the book so static, so long, so unresponsive and even irresponsible about itself, is the use of nostalgia, pure, unruffled nostalgia, as the impulse behind the entire creation. Long before one wants to call the book bad in any sense it becomes intolerable.

Nostalgia is one of the impulses behind a great many very good works of literature. . . . But nostalgia, by itself, traps moments into images that are beyond intelligence and reproach, beyond the interference of the older person doing the remembering. All the movies Lucius Hutchfield saw in 1946, all the books he fondled, all the songs he heard, all the letters and stories he wrote, all the days and weeks, all are important, and equally important. . . . [The] naming is right and the naming is all Madden can or need do.

But the importance that nostalgia gives to names and places is precisely what deprives nostalgic creations of humanity, since all feelings are equally important and equally pleasureable. No understanding is needed, no shaping or judging can take place, in *Bijou*. . . . Madden . . . doesn't care who Lucius Hutchfield is, for all the attention he has apparently lavished on him. When moments are trapped in this way, they can be lovingly and precisely written and still be beyond the power of the writer to save them. (p. 25)

> Roger Sale, in The New York Review of Books (reprinted with permission from The New York Review of Books; copyright © 1974 NYREV, Inc.), June 27, 1974.

* * *

MAILER, Norman   1923-

One of the most vociferous and declamatory American social critics of our time, Mailer, a novelist, essayist, and film-maker, is as eclectic a writer as the controversy his writing incites. (See also *Contemporary Authors*, Vols. 9-12, rev. ed.)

In a *New Yorker* interview published after *The Naked and the Dead* had scored its sensational success, Norman Mailer said of his novel: "It has been called a novel without hope. I think actually it is a novel with a great deal of hope. It finds . . . that even in man's corruption and sickness there are yearnings and inarticulate strivings for a better world, a life with more dignity." This statement is a remarkable example of how erroneous an artist can be about his creation.

The yearnings and inarticulate strivings of men for a better world of which Mailer speaks are shown in *The Naked and the Dead* with a sense of hopelessness about their achieving it. This is conveyed in a passage of startling beauty. As the platoon approaches the island of Anopopei in its landing craft, the men look upon it in the sunset with a strange rapture. ". . . The island hovered before them like an Oriental monarch's conception of heaven, and they responded to it with an acute and terrible longing. It was a vision of all the beauty for which they had ever yearned, all the ecstasy they had ever sought." But this vision cannot last, and, as the sunset fades, the men are left with the reality of the terror and blackness of life. . . .

The island of Anopopei, which presented itself as a bright vision, proves to be a nightmare. It is the mysterious world in which men live, working in unfathomable ways to confuse, terrify, and destroy them. (p. 291)

The only ones to whom Anopopei is not terrifying are the reactionary General Cummings, a coldly calculating machine, and Sergeant Croft, his enlisted-man counterpart, who finds in killing the satisfaction of his powers. Each believes that life contains a pattern that he can either control or identify with, not a vaguely perceived sinister cosmic conspiracy. (p. 292)

The action and dialogue as well as the setting and atmosphere suggest . . . that there is a pattern, [and that] it means . . . the presence of a malign supernatural power. . . . God, it seems, is like General Cummings, unconcerned with the personalities and fates of individual men and reducing them to the point where they cease to be individuals. As the cynical petty racketeer Polack responds to the question, "Listen, Polack, you think there's a God?". . ., "If there is, he sure is a sonofabitch." (pp. 293-94)

Charles Shapiro, in The New Republic *(reprinted by permission of* The New Republic; © 1974 by The New Republic, Inc.), March 30, 1974.*

The climb up the mountain and the long haul of carrying Wilson bring to the men an epiphany in which they attain a fleeting vision of a cruelly indifferent God. It is this experience which gives the title to the novel. Mailer had used the word "naked" several times earlier to mean open, vulnerable. (p. 294)

> *Paul N. Siegel, "The Malign Deity of 'The Naked and the Dead',"* in Twentieth Century Literature *(copyright 1974, Hofstra University Press), October, 1974, pp. 291-97.*

Why Are We in Vietnam? . . . at first appears to be little more than an egotistical, obscenity-peppered tirade; its story of a rite of passage seems remarkable only for its derivative themes.

The plot concerns two boys who are taken on a hunting trip in the Alaskan wilderness; disappointed by failures of courage on the part of the adults in the party, the two go off into the wilderness on their own. To prove themselves, they leave behind most of their equipment; by the time they return to the camp, after a series of encounters with wild animals, they have a newly acquired sense of maturity.

Even this brief outline conjures up a bevy of allusions. The journey of the young men resembles the one Huck and Jim take on their raft; and like Salinger's heroes, they possess a precocious ability to sniff out moral flaws in their elders. If the bear in the novel is not precisely like Faulkner's, it is because it is distantly related to a much-hunted great white whale. The noble savagery of Mailer's Ollie the Indian is part Rousseau, part Fenimore Cooper. And the rite-of-passage theme is a bit bedraggled after long years in the service of maturing heroes like Prince Hal, Raskolnikov, and Stephen Dedalus.

But Mailer does not deny his literary antecedents. His protagonist acknowledges the influence of Shakespeare, Mark Twain, Melville, Joyce, Dostoevski, Rousseau, and Salinger. After tipping his hat to his predecessors, Mailer sets out on his own: the novel may be allusive, but it is not derivative.

It is in handling mythic themes that Mailer proves himself most original. The familiar initiation story is supported by an animistic substructure, so that the novel's use of myth resembles that of primitive literature. Because our culture considers animistic beliefs irrational and superstitious, Mailer is to some extent forced to conceal his purpose. This he accomplishes by using obscene language as a distracting element, and by describing animistic phenomena in scientific language. Cleverly, Mailer uses the most mysterious phenomena in science to introduce the animistic themes.

Animism implies that entities usually considered inanimate or subhuman have the ability to think and communicate; moreover, it often posits the existence of a world spirit which perceives all thought and acts as an intermediary in telepathic communication. In *Why Are We in Vietnam?* one finds this sort of animism, and electromagnetic radiation is used as a metaphor to describe how such animistic thought processes work. (p. 298-99)

During the daytime one's consciousness is dominated by rational thought, and so, especially for civilized man, there is little sensitivity to psychic phenomena. But by following procedures to clear the mind it is possible not only to receive M.E.F. [Magnetic-Electro Fief, Mailer's invention, supernatural counterpart of the electro-magnetic field] signals during the daytime, but also to receive them from animals. The purification ceremony for D.J. and his friend Tex Hyde begins when they enter the Alaskan wilderness after having divested themselves of all but their most rudimentary equipment: in doing this they throw off artifacts of civilization and technology which inhibit psychic sensitivity. (pp. 299-300)

Not only do D.J. and Tex experience initiation in a conventional sense, but their initiation also occurs on a supernatural plane. This sort of dichotomy, in which supernatural events underscore the physical action, again brings the novel close to the techniques of mythic and primitive literature.

The struggle of the hero in primitive stories is often simultaneously an ordeal in the natural world and a battle on a supernatural plane. Homer, for example, does not draw a sharp distinction between Odysseus' battle to preserve his life in a raging sea and his effort to escape the wrath of Poseidon. Not only is the sea controlled by Poseidon; in a sense it is Poseidon. Primitive mythology at times extends this idea and gives life to inanimate entities by introducing a pantheistic system which encompasses the entire natural world. The result is a network of intercommunication which connects all disparate entities and finally gives universal significance to every apparently discrete event which occurs.

Modern works which attempt to use myths are often limited by the omission of this sort of animistic underscoring; in a rational, skeptical culture one can hardly expect myths to be as significant as in a culture where a belief in animism is universal. But since we all retain remnants of animistic belief from childhood (as Jean Piaget has shown) it is possible to use some animistic themes even in a culture which outwardly retains its skepticism.

Mythology can be seen as an example of pre-scientific thinking, that is to say, an attempt to satisfy human curiosity about events which cannot be explained rationally. This in fact is what Mailer does in *Why Are We in Vietnam?* He uses inexplicable scientific phenomena as metaphors for mysterious human events, hinting that when they violate ordinary experience such phenomena (like superconductivity or imaginary numbers) involve psychic forces. Rationally we may be certain that such forces cannot exist; but there is a powerful underlying residuum of childhood thought which insists that they do. This childhood belief in magic and the supernatural provides the unconscious rumblings which make the mythic themes of a work like this one persuasive.

For his technological metaphors Mailer chooses mainly phenomena in which antithetical entities, on the model of anode and cathode, are juxtaposed. The nodes of the antithesis are at opposing extremes, but eventually their differing potentials unite them in sparklike discharges of psychic current. In intercourse the polar extremes are male and female; their union produces a current in the psychic world which is analogous to superconductivity in the physical world. (pp. 300-01)

In this fashion Mailer compares scientific antitheses (like the poles of a magnet, positive and negative charges, rational and imaginary numbers) with human antitheses (like black and white, good and evil, rational and irrational thought, courage and dread, male and female). Most of the novel's mythic structure follows this pattern: its supernatural aspects are given technological explanations; for the familiar, rational processes in the world, Mailer posits corresponding irrational processes. (p. 301)

Dread finally turns D.J. and Tex into obscene creatures: young soldiers who look forward to the brutal scenes they will encounter in Vietnam. Since their friendship is now corroded by the fear of an ultimate confrontation, they will kill strangers to demonstrate their prowess, to discourage one another from seeking a confrontation. Yet the Cain-Abel rivalry can never be eliminated, because peaceful gestures in this vicious cycle are always misconstrued as signs of weakness.

The last words of the book express D.J.'s eagerness to be off to the battleground: "Vietnam, hot dam." In a book filled with explicit sexual descriptions and scatalogical language, this mild phrase—an indication of D.J.'s lost ethical sensitivity—is perhaps the most obscene.

The novel's mixture of violent and obscene passages is used to emphasize the moral differences between violent words and violent actions. A reader who rejects the novel because of its obscenity will miss many of the underlying ethical issues. Ironically, those readers who cannot see beyond the novel's obscenity illustrate one of Mailer's favorite satiric situations, when rigid ethical fastidiousness turns out to be a mask for ignorance, cowardice, or corruption.

But more than this, Mailer is saying that an inability to hear certain words, the very process of calling a portion of the vocabulary obscene, indicates a personality which refuses to acknowledge an obscene, irrational part of itself. Such a refusal, founded on the belief that everything in life must be orderly and rational, makes one vulnerable to destructive forces in the psyche. America's campaign to suppress obscenity, in other words, is understood as a symptom of its irrational brutality in Asia. The country is being ravaged by the effects of repressed irrationality; it is time Americans made an attempt to confront and understand their irrationality. In a sense, Mailer is urging an immature nation to undergo an act of psychic initiation.

Mailer's story, like some of Conrad's tales, deals with an initiation which measures the hero's ability to become aware of and confront irrational elements in the psyche. Both writers present conventional initiation stories on the surface of their fiction; and both use the supernatural to provide metaphors on a psychological level. In "The Shadow-Line," for example, the ghost of the dead captain is a metaphor for a destructive force within the hero which undermines his strength in the crisis which proves to be his initiation test.

This is very similar to Mailer's technique. The animism in his novel serves both to bring his story closer to primitive myth and to provide a metaphor for psychological forces. Mailer uses obscenity as Conrad used symbolism: to conceal the deeper level of his story in an effort to duplicate the subtlety of psychological forces at play in daily life. One undesirable side effect of this method has been that many of the early readers of Conrad and Mailer saw only the surface story, and were virtually unaware of the duality of this naturalistic-psychological form.

This dual form ties in with the dualities Mailer sees in human life. He refers in the novel to Mani, the founder of Manicheism . . . and Manichean dualism to some extent operates in portions of the book. Many of the key themes in the novel are presented as antithetical halves of Manichean dichotomies. The most important technical metaphors fit in well with the Manichean dualities: anode and cathode, the charged antithetical nodes of a single entity, resemble the Manichean belief that matter is a mixture of good and evil elements. And Mailer's juxtaposition of rational and imaginary numbers, to indicate that natural objects have their counterparts in the supernatural world, echoes the Manichean belief in the interplay and struggle of the forces of light and darkness.

This dualistic approach is utilized in many other areas of the novel. When obscenity and brutality are understood as expressions of the same violent force in different modes, their connections can be explored. In similar fashion, Mailer considers problems of race relations, moral cowardice, sexuality, and ecology using this dualistic method. Perhaps most subtle and ingenious is his decision to use scientific language to describe supernatural events, linking the opposed nodes of magic and technology.

One aspect of Mailer's skill in this novel is the ease with which he combines these disparate and antithetical elements. His eclectic interest in modern social and psychological problems is never inconsistent with his use of animism and mythic techniques. Mailer blends these levels so that the primitive elements add emotional impact to the novel without robbing it of intellectual sophistication. In this sense his novel is—despite first impressions—both original and profound. (pp. 303-05)

> Rubin Rabinovitz, "Myth and Animism in 'Why Are We in Vietnam?'," in Twentieth Century Literature (copyright 1974, Hofstra University Press), October, 1974, pp. 298-305.

Jewish cultural audiences, which are generally pleased to hear Saul Bellow and Bernard Malamud identified by critics as Jewish writers, are perfectly content that by and large Norman Mailer, with all his considerable influence and stature, should go forth onto the lecture platform and the television talk shows as a writer *period*. This is obviously okay too with the author of *The Deer Park* and *An American Dream*, to name just two of his books with heroes he chooses not to call Cohen. It is pointless to wonder what Jews (or Gentiles) would have made of those two books if the author had had other than an O'Shaugnessy as the libidinous voyager or a Rojack as the wife-murderer and spade-whipper in his American Gomorrah, for that an identifiably Jewish hero could perpetrate such spectacular transgressions with so much gusto and so little self-doubt or ethical disorientation turns out to be as inconceivable to Norman Mailer as it is to Bernard Malamud. And maybe for the same reason: it is just the Jew in one that says "No, no, *restrain* yourself" to such grandiose lusts and drives. To which prohibition Malamud adds, "Amen," but to which Mailer replies, "Then I'll see ya' around." (pp. 25-6)

Philip Roth, "Imagining Jews," in The New York Review of Books *(reprinted with permission from* The New York Review of Books; *copyright © 1974 NYREV, Inc.), October 3, 1974, pp. 22-8.*

* * *

MALAMUD, Bernard 1914-

A Jewish American novelist and short story writer, Malamud is the Pulitzer Prize-winning author of *The Assistant, The Tenants*, and *Rembrandt's Hat*. (See also *Contemporary Authors*, Vols. 5-8, rev. ed.)

Bernard Malamud is a bit of a puzzle to many readers, though they often find it difficult to articulate their mystification. Anybody, however, who is not charmed by Malamud or not convinced of his talent, need only turn to "The Tenants" after a surfeit of contemporary fiction and he will discover that here is something distinctive, here is the elastic strength of a genuine prose style in the hands of a genuine writer. Malamud may not have solved his basic problems with plot, and he has, seemingly, tried to evade them here with a mirror trick, reproducing his own image on the career of his hero, thereby justifying his own failure; but whatever his difficulties along this line he has created and spoken through some very real people. And, hiding behind the protagonist's person, Malamud is able to unburden himself of a great many thoughts about writing. . . .

Much of what Malamud says about writing is nothing more than the old ideal of artistic integrity done up in new words. The blunt but crudely eloquent pleas for a new literature as voiced by Spear, however, give a new dimension to the whole debate; Malamud has crystallized the question that is bothering many a critical mind as everybody turns again to the problem of art. The book is inconclusive, in part a tract on the critical dilemma, but beautifully written, solid, substantial.

William B. Hill, S. J., "'The Tenants'," in Best Sellers *(copyright 1971, by the University of Scranton), October 15, 1971, p. 316.*

Compared with his earlier collections of stories, *The Magic Barrel* and *Idiots First*, [*Rembrandt's Hat*] seems rather bare at first sight, evoking less of the rank smell of rooming-houses, and the heat of people living close together. But if the surrounding atmosphere has thinned, the human encounters have become sharper and more extraordinary.

It was always, anyway, personal rather than material poverty that was Mr. Malamud's theme—poverty of spirit, the tight emotional economy that sets the price of friendship or trust or love. . . .

Whether the subjects are grotesque or drab, Mr. Malamud's style retains its lucidity, strength and truthfulness. It never looks imaginatively strenuous—there are few eye-catching flourishes—but it succeeds uniquely in conveying the many-sidedness and wholeness of a situation. . . .

Mr. Malamud's stories are as important as his novels; the present volume confirms that. And indeed, his sense that the writer's responsibility never lets up is one of his most distinctive qualities.

"Poor in Spirit," in The Times Literary Supplement *(© Times Newspapers Ltd., 1973; reproduced by permission), October 5, 1973, p. 1158.*

[Malamud] is a seeker and practitioner of an imaginative language which will go beyond the usual humanistic terminologies, or of a music of fiction which will immediately and absolutely *mean*. At the same time, I have to add that I can't make an observation like that about a fellow writer without feeling a twinge of doubt concerning the whole business. In what sense, for instance, could *Pictures of Fidelman: An Exhibition* (1969) be said to aspire to any music at all? Isn't it just a bad book, pathetic in its attempts to relate art to life, full of feeble jokes and forgettable characters? Well, yes, but then remember the Malamud of *The Assistant* (1957) and *The Fixer* (1966). These are not masterpieces, but they are amongst the more decent bits of fiction we have had in English since the Second World War. They engage with life's textures, they make their comment on the bleakness of existence, they come back to speak of an experience of chaos which still finds joy in the selecting of appropriate metaphors and the making of memorable rhythms. (pp. 71-2)

[In *Rembrandt's Hat*] Malamud is playing the one tune in different keys, and no doubt with variations, but precisely what the original might be never becomes clear. . . . Brilliance, Mr. Malamud, yes, but brilliance is not enough. Who ever felt satisfied after a meal of it? (p. 72)

Robert Nye, in Books and Bookmen *(© copyright Robert Nye 1974), January, 1974.*

[Malamud] has had what, I suppose, we must all now recognize as the extraordinary fortune to inherit, more or less direct, that Yiddish tradition of story-telling which reached its height in the work of Isaac Bashevis Singer. (p. 137)

John Mellors, in London Magazine *(© London Magazine 1974), February/March, 1974.*

[There are] in the work of Bernard Malamud . . . tendencies . . . so sharply and schematically present as to give Malamud's novels the lineaments of moral allegory. For Malamud, generally speaking, the Jew is innocent, passive, virtuous, and this to the degree that he defines himself or is defined by others as a Jew; the Gentile, on the other hand, is characteristically corrupt, violent, and lustful, particularly when he enters a room or a store or a cell with a Jew in it.

Now on the face of it, it would seem that a writer could not get very far with such evangelistic simplifications. And yet that is not at all the case with Malamud (as it isn't with Jerzy Kosinski in *The Painted Bird*), for so instinctively do the figures of a good Jew and a bad goy emerge from an imagination essentially folkloric and didactic that his fiction is actually most convincing the more strictly he adheres to these simplifications, and diminishes in moral conviction and narrative drive to the extent that he surrenders them, or tries, however slyly, to undo their hold on him.

The best book—containing as it does the classic Malamudian moral arrangement—is still *The Assistant*, which proposes that an entombed and impoverished grocer named Morris Bober shall by the example of his passive suffering and his goodness of heart transform a young thieving Italian drifter named Frank Alpine into another entombed, impoverished, suffering Jewish grocer, and that this shall constitute an act of *assistance*, and set Alpine on the road to redemption—or so the stern morality of the book suggests.

Redemption from what? Crimes of violence and deceit against a good Jewish father, crimes of lust against the father's virginal daughter, whom the goy has spied upon naked and then raped. But oh how punitive is this redemption! We might almost take what happens to the bad goy when he falls into the hands of the good Jew as an act of enraged Old Testament retribution visited upon him by the wrathful Jewish author—if it weren't for the moral pathos and the gentle religious coloration with which Malamud invests the tale of conversion; and also the emphasis that is clear to the author throughout—that it is the good Jews who have fallen into the hands of the bad goy. It has occurred to me that a less hopeful Jewish writer than Malamud—Kosinski, say, whose novels don't put much stock in the capacity for redemption, but concentrate rather determinedly on the persistence of brutality and malice—might not have understood Alpine's transformation into Jewish grocer and Jewish father (with all those roles entail in this book) as a sign of moral improvement, but as the cruel realization of Bober's revenge. "Now suffer, you goy bastard, the way I did." (p. 25)

I know of no serious authors who have chronicled physical brutality and fleshly mortification in such detail and at such length, and who likewise have taken a single defenseless innocent and constructed almost an entire book [*The Fixer*] out of the relentless violations suffered by that character at the hands of cruel and perverse captors, other than Malamud, the Marquis de Sade, and the pseudonymous author of *The Story of O*. . . .

The careful social and historical documentation of *The Fixer*—which Malamud's instinctive feel for folk material is generally able to transform from fiction researched into fiction imagined—envelops what is at its center a relentless work of violent pornography, in which the pure and innocent Jew, whose queasiness at the sight of blood is at the outset almost maidenly, is ravished by the sadistic goyim, "men," a knowledgeable ghost informs him, "who [are] without morality." . . .

In *Pictures of Fidelman* Malamud sets out to turn the tables on himself and, gamely, to take a holiday from his own obsessive mythology: here he imagines as the hero a Jewish man living without shame and even with a kind of virile, if shlemielish, forcefulness in a world of Italian gangsters, thieves, pimps, whores, and bohemians. . . . [In] *Fidelman*, unfortunately, natural repugnance and constraints, and a genuine sense of what conversions cost, are by and large dissolved in rhetorical flourishes rather than through the sort of human struggle that Malamud's own deeply held sense of things calls forth in *The Assistant* and *The Fixer*. It's no accident that this of all the longer works generates virtually no internal narrative tension (a means whereby it might seek to test its own assumptions) and is without the continuous sequential development that comes to this kind of storyteller so naturally and acts in him as a necessary counterforce against runaway fantasy. This playful daydream of waywardness, criminality, transgression, lust, and sexual perversion could not have stood up against that kind of opposition. . . .

[The] book has an air of unchecked and unfocused indulgence, which is freewheeling about a libidinous and disordered life more or less to the extent that nothing much is at stake or seriously challenged. (p. 26)

[Whereas] in *The Assistant* the lusting goy's passionate and aggressive act of *genuinely* loving desire for the Jewish girl takes the form of rape, and requires penance (or retribution) of the harshest kind, in *Pictures of Fidelman*, the Jew's most wayward (albeit comfortingly passive) sexual act is, without anything faintly resembling Alpine's enormous personal struggle, converted on the spot into love. And if this is still insufficiently reassuring about a Jew and sexual appetite, the book manages by the end to have severed the bisexual Fidelman as thoroughly from things Jewish as *The Assistant*, by its conclusion, has marked the sexually constrained, if not desexed, Alpine as a Jew forevermore. Of all of Malamud's Jewish heroes is there any who is by comparison so strikingly *un*-Jewish (after chapter one is out of the way, that is), who insists upon it so little and is so little reminded of it by the Gentile world? And is there any who, at the conclusion, is happier? . . .

[It is] the disjunction between act and self-knowledge that accounts for the lightheaded dreaminess of *Fidelman*, and that differentiates it so sharply from those wholly convincing novels, *The Assistant* and *The Fixer*, where no beclouding ambivalence stands between the author's imagination and the objects of his fury. (p. 27)

> *Philip Roth, "Imagining Jews," in* The New York Review of Books *(reprinted with permission from* The New York Review of Books; *copyright © 1974 NYREV, Inc.), October 3, 1974, pp. 22-8.*

*   *   *

MALOFF, Saul   1922-

Maloff is an American editor, literary critic, and novelist. (See also *Contemporary Authors*, Vols. 33-36.)

There has been some speculation in psychological jargon that one must first find one's father before being able to reject him. With a new twist, to this insight—such as it is—Saul Maloff has written a novel ironically called "Happy Families." With the closest possible eye for detail and with perceptions that are sharpened to razor-edge, we are introduced to the American Family as a moribund institution. The emphasis, however, is on the father-daughter syndrome in our great society.

With a devastating irony, we are treated to a kind of epiphany—and a palimpsest too. Filled with unconscious reflections of a literary nature, we unmask layer upon layer of narration to produce an idea—and the idea is a simple one, though rather unpleasant. Truth, as Mr. Maloff indicates, is often unpleasant. And as we read on we learn—over and over again—that fathers with seventeen-year-old daughters have problems, to say nothing about the problems the seventeen-year-old daughters have with fathers. . . . It would seem that these young creatures are careless, insolent, flaunting, instinctual, mammary and fleshy, smoldering—and, in some cases, much more. . . .

There is superb craftsmanship here as ideas come and go, that are fragmentary and elusive. Mr. Maloff has the ability to bring us into direct contact with the minutiae of life, its feel, and color, and smell, its nuance and humor. The characterization—especially of Mr. Kalb's boss—is superb. (p. 208)

Clara M. Siggins, in Best Sellers *(copyright 1968, by the University of Scranton), August 15, 1968.*

Happy Families . . . is actually less a novel than a long psychiatric nightmare conceived in despondency and executed in a kind of manic misery. The wish-fulfilling, therapy-begging ending is of a piece with the rest of the fantasies, oblique interior monologues, and shadowy comic encounters in the book: stuff that dreams are made of when the spirit is being torn apart on a torture rack of intolerable circumstance. But there is a not unwholesome fascination in staying with the author through his dark night of garrulous catharsis. We soon realize that Saul Maloff is not going to tell us much of a story, yet something very exciting emerges.

Kalb is the standard loser of much Midwestern or New York-based fiction since World War II. Herzog without the academic extras. Jonathan Baumbach's "man to conjure with," only in terms of a daughter instead of a son. Herbert Gold's Herbert Gold, but with one girl instead of two, and minus the acquired sophistication. To be sure, Kalb's head is full of literary references and camp (the book wouldn't be a bad cram text for an advanced degree in English or Popular Culture).

Samuel I. Bellman, "Incestuously Lusting Fathers," in Saturday Review *(copyright © 1968 by Saturday Review, Inc.; reprinted with permission), September 7, 1968, p. 46.*

The principal difficulty with Saul Maloff's intelligent and entertaining new novel [*Heartland*] is that the ground it explores has already been rather thoroughly plowed. Its central theme—that of the vaguely intellectual New York Jew set uncomfortably down on a corn-fed provincial campus—has been examined by, among others, Bernard Malamud in *A New Life* and John Updike in *Bech*. The bizarre ritual its protagonist encounters is out of *The Golden Bough* and bears striking if entirely coincidental similarity to the tale spun by the whilom movie actor, Thomas Tryon, in his current best-seller, *Harvest Home*.

Still Maloff is a novelist of skill and wit, and there is much to recommend in *Heartland*. . . .

Maloff has described *Heartland* as "a comic fable," and at its best the comedy is indeed good. (p. 30)

Heartland is nothing if not a "New York novel" in point of view, conscious and deliberate; for Maloff seems to recognize that New York provincialism is as ripe a subject for satire as heartland provincialism. At times, however, [his] satire is heavy-handed . . . [and] may not make Saul Maloff many friends in the heart of the heart of the country, but it is, on the whole, provocative and perceptive. (p. 31)

Jonathan Yardley, "Jew among the Alien Corn," in The New Republic *(reprinted by permission of* The New Republic; *© 1973 by Harrison-Blaine of New Jersey, Inc.), September 29, 1973, pp. 30-1.*

Starved for good humor, I was ready for what *Heartland*'s advertisers promised—a story that would tickle and absorb. I needed a whole loaf of the stuff lost somewhere between Camelot and Operation Candor. But I wound up eating cake.

Some cake! More like crumbs, tiny bits of stuff that had to be pressed hard between thumb and forefinger and rolled together before they could be made to resemble an edible mass. Now, if Saul Maloff were a new bride who couldn't boil water, his latest novel's faults might have been easier to swallow. But he is a writer of considerable skill and experience. And *Heartland* is a concoction so blatantly tasteless in parts that it might've been cooked up by the folks who brought us C-rations. . . .

Oh, there were good moments in *Heartland*, chiefly when Maloff prepared a smörgasbord of colorful demonstration scenes, familiar entrées from the 1960s which he molded to suit the current taste for Zionist theatre. But if the setting was colorful, the hero was all wrong. Superstars who give mass movements bounce have the talent to concoct a heady brew, but Maloff's hero, Isaiah Greene, produces a watered-down *vin ordinaire*. (p. 282)

Greene (and therefore *Heartland*) struck me as a literary gimmick that happened to coincide with the Mideast crisis and the decline of the vocal, militant segment of the women's movement: a slick, plastic robot in a Dynel wig, properly tousled to create the right effect, all done up in baggy corduroys with suede patches at the elbows just the way somebody imagined an aging New York Jewish academic ought to be. . . .

Some day, I hope, male anxieties and prejudices won't be presented in fictional form projected as women's faults, a defensive and dishonest approach to humor which makes true satire impossible. If the book has any redeeming value, it lies with the women Maloff introduces. Such women! They supply all the action, for good or ill. But unfortunately they are only pseudo-women, cardboard mock-ups of the army of flesh and blood serfs already on their feet and marching, breaking out of the cookie-cutter stereotypes that generations of male and male-oriented writers have produced. This novel is a contribution to that movement. And that is something. (p. 283)

Bonnie Stowers, "Low Pressure at High Altitude," in The Nation *(copyright 1974 by the Nation Associates, Inc.), March 2, 1974.*

*   *   *

MANNING, Olivia   1911-

Olivia Manning is an English novelist and short story writer whose most important and ambitious work is her "Balkan Trilogy," composed of *The Great Fortune, The Spoilt City*, and *Friends and Heroes*. (See also *Contemporary Authors*, Vols. 5-8, rev. ed.)

A solid, monolithic theme projects from Olivia Manning's *Balkan Trilogy* and that is "uncertainty." The series concerns itself neither with abstract or metaphysical theories of time, refashioned or shifting ideologies, nor various plays for power or status; but with the often bare, ironically conditioned facts of living in uncertainty—uncertainty not as an accident, but as a constant of life—in a world over which hangs the certainty of ruin. . . .

Miss Manning's [sequence] is [neither] self-conscious [nor] arty; [it is] one of the [more] knowledgeable about common experience. It strives not for effects but for a single effect: to show a society teetering on, about to plunge into, an abyss, and to show people caught up in the making of history at a time when the mere debacle of the First World War was about to yield to the holocaust of the Second. Yet to show all this with something rivaling an antiepic, antiromantic sweep, to show how in this extraordinary decade the everyday world, through uncertainty, runs down.

For most of the trilogy Miss Manning's extraordinary world is Bucharest during the early years of the war, a city crammed with its complement of adventurers, expatriates, emigrés, opportunists, money barons, civil servants, and princes who suddenly find themselves on the threshold of history. Part comic-opera Ruritania in its feudality, its gilt and gaudiness; part political nightmare in its ferment of royalist, liberal, and fascist factions, Bucharest reflects the pretensions and tensions of a Rumania as heterogeneous as Durrell's Alexandria or Burgess's Malaya. It is a presence, a force of some magnificence before it squanders "the great fortune" (the title of the first volume in the sequence) to become "the spoilt city" (the title of the second). Pressured from within and without, part of a country neutered by its fence-sitting neutrality, ransacked of its dignity, culture, wealth, and civilization, Bucharest becomes the battleground for a kind of primal survival, and, as Miss Manning makes symbolically apparent, a Troy fallen anew.

Also, the mood of the capital, alternating between euphoria and hysteria, acts as a barometer for the fluctuations of history that counterpoint the less frenzied, but more closely woven lives of the ambassadors of the everyday world, Guy and Harriet Pringle, people ordinary without being mediocre, relevant and meaningful without being vitally important. . . . It is precisely Harriet's growth in the series (her progress from an intransigent realism in her view of the world and of Guy, to an understanding that "to have one thing permanent in life as they knew it was as much as they could expect"), and the chastening of Guy's selfish idealism, that make the novels so personal a statement on the laboring for continuity in the face of change. (pp. 29-31)

Miss Manning questions persistently the need for questing after permanence at times of drastic flux. Indeed, the idea that survival is to be valued in and for itself submits to its own self-irony. Undoubtedly for this reason the author (at points in the series) overshadows hero and heroine with her one true original, Prince Yakimov, part pander, part cad, part Pagliaccio, whose . . . rise and fall are interwoven with the fate of the Pringles. As they move toward their own feeling of what is permanent in life and endure, seeking permanence as a ballast in the sea of change, he founders and goes under. Yaki becomes the victim of uncertainty; the Pringles (in however limited a sense) become victors over it. (p. 31)

Like Powell, Miss Manning focuses on the trivial because in living, we do also. Like him, too, she juxtaposes the trifling and the momentous to comment on the absurdity of the human condition. Yet trivia is never expanded—as in the prolonged farces of Evelyn Waugh, say—but contracted into two faces of the human condition: the personal and the historic. (p. 40)

Harriet, of all the characters in the trilogy, comes out on top because she has done more than survive the uncertainty of life and the tragedy that ensues from that uncertainty. She has not been trapped by her ego or good intentions or the solipsism of self alone, but has risen to heights of sensitivity and responsibility, has gained (in Iris Murdoch's words) a "sense of the other."

The novel is at its best in showing Harriet's unfolding and maturing, and actually "works" through radical shifts or displacement of earlier relationships. Harriet, though early alerted to the potentialities of people, continued to think of them as relating to herself or Guy. Now she sees them as they are, not how they might or should be. (p. 45)

In a most conclusive way the repeated breakdown of things for the Pringles—the breakdown of the Balkans, the breakdown of the Pringles's old values, of their dependency on others, of "illusion and disillusion"—is actually the dismantling of any notion that "romance," in the sense of happy means and happy endings, might control life. What does control life is the antiromantic, the unexpected and uncertain, which, in Miss Manning's trilogy, are forced to a higher exponent. Living in *any* way during wartime can only be a postponement of life as we might know it. Perhaps in no other situation of comparable intensity and involvement are appearances so identical with reality. Life *is* what it is!

As is death. Yaki's fatal shooting is less gratuitous in the weird scheme of a world operating under war than the *actes gratuits* of other modern novelists who kill off their protagonists without so much as a by-your-leave. Miss Manning seems indeed faithful to the historic moment—as Durrell, say, has little or no respect for it at all—and is not interested in pulling rabbits out of hats. Reversals or the "suddenness of things" are not intended to beef up the limited action. (If one is not in sympathy with Miss Manning's characters to begin with, even action will never satisfy.) Rather, the tissue of change connecting life and death is built leisurely, faithfully, organically. Ideally, change overrides chance and seeks to stabilize the impermanent through the permanent; but in the *Balkan Trilogy* we see impermanence become a way of life and death in itself. . . . In simplest terms war is life, just as Harriet says.

The implications here are perhaps the most unique to be found among the contemporary novel sequences. Change becomes the unexpected, chance the expected; and any romantic vision that would see otherwise is accountable to the darker truths of reality. . . . But, as Mary McCarthy has written, "the quest for certainty is itself a hero's goal," a paradoxical, testy, incontestable notion that is supported again and again by Miss Manning's trilogy. . . . To be sure, as the sequence closes, one scarcely gives a second thought to the Pringles. No longer fictional, they are no longer historic. But while in the foreground Guy and Harriet, nonheroic heroes consigned to the world of "friends"—a world capricious, absurd, often meaningless, forever changing, forever uncertain—loom as large and important as history itself. (pp. 48-9)

Robert K. Morris, "Olivia Manning: The 'Balkan Trilogy,' The Quest for Permanence," in his Continuance and Change: The Contemporary British Novel Sequence *(copyright © 1972, Southern Illinois University Press; reprinted by permission of*

Southern Illinois University Press),
Southern Illinois University Press, 1972, pp.
29-49.

Olivia Manning's *The Rain Forest* is one of those novels often described as 'old-fashioned': it gives all the satisfactions of a thoroughly planned and developing structure, a generally unobtrusive (but all too conscious) symbolism, an extensive roll of sharply outlined characters, subplots which refract and distortedly echo the principal story, and —most 'old-fashioned' of all, I suppose—a wholly professional and detached authorial voice, serenely encompassing the upsets and explosions it describes, arranging effects and set-pieces and settling accounts with impersonal calm. It's the novelist's grand, disposing narrative manner, and when it works as well as it does in *The Rain Forest*, it exists above fashion, old or new, as a particularly lucid way of getting a novel written and a story told. (pp. 486-87)

[The setting is] Al-Bustan, an island in the Indian Ocean where the Empire is slowly and pompously winding down. Half of the island is the steamy mixture of British colonial snobbery and incompetence, rich Western decadence (at the exclusive Praslin hotel), Levantine plotting, seedy nightclubs and the Residency garden, which this sort of setting invariably suggests in fiction; the other half of Al-Bustan is the primeval rain forest of the title, territory forbidden to the island's inhabitants. This said, any longtime reader of novels will know that a revolution is in the offing, that the Fosters [the protagonists] will suffer estrangement but rescue their marriage, and that some of the cast will penetrate the forest and—because it's primeval—in some way be renewed by it. Yet this summary, close enough to the events of the novel, does not suggest the delicacy of Olivia Manning's evocation of Al-Bustan, nor the effective eccentricity of her imagination: the world of plum-faced British residents, mummified by the conventions of a century before, takes on an oddly surreal and vivid awfulness, as in a film by Buñuel. (p. 487)

Peter Straub, in New Statesman *(© 1974*
The Statesman & Nation Publishing Co.
Ltd.), April 5, 1974.

*   *   *

MATTHIESSEN, Peter   1927-

An American novelist, short story writer, and nature writer, Matthiessen successfully incorporates his knowledge and experience as a travel and nature writer into his fiction. (See also *Contemporary Authors*, Vols. 9-12, rev. ed.)

["Blue Meridian: The Search for the Great White Shark"] is a trove of shark lore, a suspenseful adventure yarn, and a decent man's account of the way other decent men behave toward one another when they are under great pressure. . . .

Matthiessen is especially good at tracking down images fit to represent the sensation of diving. . . .

Memorable too is Matthiessen's account of how the prey that hunted its hunters looked beneath the ocean's surface. (p. 92)

For Matthiessen, . . . the search was a fine adventure come to a fine conclusion. . . . And the place to look for the important things, as Matthiessen shows, is at the far edge of things, just beyond the reach of light, where the white shark comes from. (pp. 92-4)

Geoffrey Wolff, "Man-Eater in the Deep,"
in Newsweek *(copyright 1971 by Newsweek,*
Inc.; all rights reserved; reprinted by permission), April 26, 1971, pp. 92-4.

Peter Matthiessen, who began as a fiction writer, has become through his travels and study of anthropology a walking book of knowledge. But his speculation about human prehistory [in *The Tree Where Man Was Born*] tends to clot his prose, leaving the reader behind. However, if one does not fuss over his technical terms and reads with a skipping eye, the firm truths are there: about the generalized *Homo* who used hand axes half a million years ago, about the early worship of cattle by the migrating people who subsisted on their milk and blood drawn from a vein, and of how when men of Asia brought wheat, barley, sheep, and goats to the Lower Nile, the desert expanded and the drought was advanced "by the goats which ate the thorns that had sewn tight the land that soon unraveled into sand." Much fateful history is packed into those few words.

Entwined with this curiosity about the dim past is Mr. Matthiessen's second and to me more engrossing theme: his observations of the natives, the landscape, the wildlife he encountered on his two expeditions to East Africa. . . . Matthiessen is a professional and his thumbnail sketches of those who helped him on his way . . . are a pleasing human thread. From them he gets the prescience of the natural forces, the hatreds, and the hunger which threaten to change what is. (pp. 125-26)

Edward Weeks, in The Atlantic Monthly
(copyright © 1972 by The Atlantic Monthly
Company, Boston, Mass.; reprinted with
permission), November, 1972.

["The Tree Where Man Was Born"] is the first nonfiction book on Africa with a surprise ending. Of course [Matthiessen] is not your ordinary long-haired itinerant. His first chapters are the quality journalism he, like Rebecca West or Norman Mailer, can do. He never sees just birds, but mousebirds and bee-eaters, never just antelope, but kongoni or gerenuks. His people are members of any of 50 tribes, painted authentically in place and time, always in a landscape.

It is a plethora of information in The New Yorker fashion —damn near more than we can stand. With him we feel like privileged, intelligent tourists. But he drives us and is driven, and the beautiful chit-chat goes on and on. We are almost lulled by this quietly frantic monologue and Eliot Porter's monumental color photographs into a coffee-table slump, fascinated and slightly irritated.

Throughout, the narration of his trip affirms the singleness of man and nature. . . .

In spite of the delicate sensibility and tough willingness to risk and push on, there are no personalities and no real satisfaction. . . .

His mind races along with his Land Rover, cutting swaths of information overkill in the great Serengeti plain. It is there, in Tanzania, where things begin to change, and it is hard to know how much of this change in Matthiessen's story is conscious and deliberate. In the Serengeti the theme of the vast spectacle of herds and carnivores is death —the "Rites of Passage," which seems to open a door.

Now officials, zoologists and guides begin to become people . . . [and] a barrier is clearly crossed.

South of the Serengeti are the remnants of a hunting-gathering people, the Hadza. Destined inevitably to be destroyed by distant politicians, they are . . . a happy, intelligent, dignified people in the moment before oblivion. Meeting them, Matthiessen smiles his first truly glad smile in 218 pages. . . .

[They] represent what we have lost: not an innocence so much as a profound sophistication—nonwant, repose, communal society, attention to what is alive and good. Rushing down on them is the raging ideology of want and technomania, the spurious and degrading intoxication of nationalism. Much earlier it swept across Europe and North America. The hunters will at last come to the end of their million years of peace of the heart and ecological harmony, which began, perhaps, in the same country of the sacred baobab tree where Matthiessen ends his narration. (p. 31)

> *Paul Shepard, in* The New York Times Book Review *(© 1972 by The New York Times Company; reprinted by permission), November 26, 1972.*

With gusto, Mr. Matthiessen draws us [in "Far Tortuga"] into the comical rude dialect of the turtlers, and, in the exquisite prose one has come to expect from his nature writing, sketches the ravaged but still awesome Caribbean. Portents appear: disrupting winds, unlucky currents, a trailing sharklike shape, a disappointing haul. The book skillfully grows in resonance, and we begin to relish the familiar echoes: the storm at sea, the captain's rages, the dumbstruck sailor lashed to the mast. We enjoy the clever way—with words grouped in blocks and squiggles of unconnected type—in which Mr. Matthiessen brings his tale to stark, insistent life. In the end, the exact significance of the book has to be surmised. Is it a parable of nature's vengeance? A postscript to pirates' crimes? A lesson on searching and illusion? In any case, it is a superb feat of storytelling. (pp. 118-19)

> The New Yorker *(© 1975 by The New Yorker Magazine, Inc.), May 19, 1975.*

[Most] reviewers owe Peter Matthiessen reparation for the shabby, yawning condescension with which, ten years ago, they greeted his marvelous novel, "At Play in the Fields of the Lord." I hope ["Far Tortuga"] will be more carefully read, for it seems to me a beautiful and original piece of work, a resonant, symbolical story of nine doomed men who dream of an earthly paradise as the world winds down around them. (p. 85)

To convey [his] haunting story Matthiessen has invented a structure made from the sparest descriptions of time, weather and place—"Midafternoon. The tide still falling. A mosquito whines"—and blocks of dialogue unencumbered by attribution to specific characters; we come to learn from the dialogue itself who is speaking. The rhythms of these sailors' speech are both colloquial and formal: Matthiessen

reproduces the West Indian dialect exactly but often allows the words to fall into lines of about fifteen unstressed syllables—the result is not poetry, but not far from it, either. Then, as if to slow our progress through his narrative, or emphasize its reverberations, Matthiessen introduces unequal amounts of white space between paragraphs and sections of his story.

The effect is rather like that of a film script, or of a surreal painting: a sharply realistic story that is precise, even informative about details, and yet one in which the figures we observe point symbolically and metaphorically beyond themselves. In sum, this is a moving, impressive book, a difficult yet successful undertaking. I haven't read anything of similar stature for a long time. (p. 86)

> *Peter S. Prescott, "The Last Turtles," in* Newsweek *(copyright 1975 by Newsweek, Inc.; all rights reserved; reprinted by permission), May 19, 1975, pp. 85-6.*

From its opening moment, with daybreak over the Windward Passage, the reader [of "Far Tortuga"] senses that the narrative itself is the recapitulation of a cosmic process, as though the author has sought to link his storytelling with the eye of creation.

Sea stories are usually existentialist fables; "Far Tortuga" is not—and the fact that it is not creates a certain imbalance in its structure. The insights here are sublime, but they are not within the humanistic scale. In a way there is only a single insight, the unity of things beneath an ever-changing multiplicity of forms. Matthiessen's characters are very much the carefully individuated, positivistic creatures of traditional good fiction, outfitted with speeches, histories, destinies. Their alienation from and ignorance of the essential unity of which they are a part is common to most people and "true to life," but now and then—as in the case of the psychic, Wodie—they are a little too obviously exotic constructs, a touch too predictable, a shade too close to registering as literary "originals" to serve the book's informing vision.

Yet they are effective characters, the reader becomes thoroughly involved in their fate, and the book works well even on what I take to be its secondary levels. "Far Tortuga" is an important book, its pleasures are many and good for the soul. Peter Matthiessen is a unique and masterful visionary artist. (p. 2)

> *Robert Stone, in* The New York Times Book Review *(© 1975 by The New York Times Company; reprinted by permission), May 25, 1975.*

Literary sea voyages often carry a heavy ballast of allegory. The potential, after all, is readymade; it requires no great leap of imagination to see a ship as a tiny world adrift in eternity. *Far Tortuga* shuns such metaphysics in favor of hard surfaces. Avers is no Captain Ahab, nor is the *Eden* a ship of fools. The captain and his crew simply make up an exotic collection of drifters, drunks, petty criminals and indefatigable optimists, worth knowing, this novel implies, for their own sakes. . . .

To prove this point, Matthiessen writes the novel (his fifth) as if he were on board the *Eden* and living on short rations. Every fictional resource is jettisoned except snippets of descriptive prose and huge chunks of West Indian pidgin dialect. . . . He does not even allow himself access to his characters' thoughts. As far as this novel is concerned, they are what they say.

Far Tortuga therefore sets sail with a babel of unattributed dialogue swimming in blinding expanses of white space. Pages go by bearing single words: "Polaris," "horizon." Taken singly, these pages seem too easy, too close to the work of lazy poets who write a word like "loneliness" in the middle of a blank piece of paper and call it an insight.

But soon a wind starts to whistle somewhere behind those empty spaces. The rhythmic monotony on board ship ("Will relieves Buddy, Byrum relieves Will, Wodie relieves Byrum") is broken by staccato quarrels and spurts of activity when the turtles are hauled in. The crew members emerge from anonymity as their speech patterns and private obsessions are repeated. The dialects begin to tease the ear with unheard melodies. Descriptive passages, when they occur, achieve a haunting beauty: "Where the bonita chop the surface, the minnows spray into the air in silver showers, all across the sunlit coral."

Matthiessen is a noted explorer and naturalist as well as a novelist. Back in 1967, he sailed on a turtle boat out of Grand Cayman. As thoroughly as possible with words on paper, he has duplicated that experience, creating along the way an uncommonly successful mixture of fact and fiction. *Far Tortuga* is a treatise on turtling, an account of the dying days of sailing ships on unspoiled waters, and a history of a locale that winter tourists tripping through the Caribbean rarely see. Most memorably, it is a spare adventure tale about simple men driven to the extremities of pain and death by ignorance, greed, weakness and inexplicable fate.

> *Paul Gray, "Sea Changes," in* Time *(reprinted by permission of* Time, The Weekly Newsmagazine; *copyright Time Inc.), May 26, 1975, p. 80.*

In his undergraduate short stories, . . . through his expeditions to the Amazon, the Sudan, New Guinea, and more essentially, in his seafaring as a commercial fisherman and his adventures searching for the great white shark, Peter Matthiessen has lived with the potential that at some time he would write an exceptional novel. This is it. In its impressionistic form, with its humor, its melody, and its drama, *Far Tortuga* is a sea story the like of which I have not read since *Lord Jim.* (p. 92)

> *Edward Weeks, in* The Atlantic Monthly *(copyright © 1975 by* The Atlantic Monthly Company, *Boston, Mass.; reprinted with permission), June, 1975.*

In his new novel, *Far Tortuga* . . ., Peter Matthiessen recounts the catastrophic last voyage of a decayed Grand Cayman schooner, the *Eden,* fishing for green turtle off the Nicaraguan coast. . . .

Far Tortuga is . . . full of unfortunate typographical experiments. Many of the pages are literally agape with blank white space that I suppose is meant to symbolize the blind infinity of the sea. On one page some unevocative phrases ("trade wind, rain glitter, wind, sun, wind," etc.) are arranged in the shape of a ship's mast; another contains a

single word, "horizon," with a wavering line below. When, at the disastrous climax, the ship strikes an unexpected rock off Far Tortuga, a cay not found on any chart and most likely "a mere dream and legend of the turtle men," the page reads in its entirety "THE SHIP STRIKES."

Where did the rock come from? It was put there, of course, for the symbolizing convenience of Peter Matthiessen, whose prose has been holding its breath until terrible mortality could take its mythical toll. But so accidental is the rock's appearance that the destruction of the *Eden* and its crew seems wholly factitious rather than tragic. Though *Far Tortuga* has been deliriously praised by such early readers as James Dickey and Eleanor Clark, in my mind it has already turned into 408 pages bereft of any words or deeds or moral I want to remember. . . . (p. 18)

> *Pearl K. Bell, in* The New Leader *(© 1975 by the American Labor Conference on International Affairs, Inc.), June 9, 1975.*

*   *   *

McCARTHY, Mary   1912-

An American novelist, essayist, short story writer, and critic, Ms McCarthy is known for her social and political criticism as well as for her popular novels *The Group* and *Birds of America*. (See also *Contemporary Authors*, Vols. 5-8, rev. ed.)

Though hardly an allegorist, Mary McCarthy is one example of what I mean by the academic novelist. An abrasive critical intelligence and a formidably incisive prose writer, Miss McCarthy has not written a first-rate novel. Mainly she has not because she is unable (or unwilling) to create characters capable of defying their maker. They are not quite like some of Robert Penn Warren's, embodied abstractions; but for all their simulation of a kind of life, they are not quite human beings either; they are artifacts of real people. Miss McCarthy holds them up to the fluoroscope of her critical intelligence and finds them sterile and absurd, mean and pretentious, deceitful and corrupt, and worse. How comic and unpleasant we all are! And the secret is, she knew it all the time. She has schemed her characters as moral deformities in the first place. The best of her novels, *The Groves of Academe*, treats with nice comic distance the machinations of an academic failure who makes himself seem a victim of persecution in order to retain his small position in a college that seems as hypocritical, mediocre and unpleasant as the man himself. Written with a cold Augustan eye, a scrupulous aversion for mortal weakness, *Groves of Academe* is a vicious and amusing satire, unbloodied by any real traces of human behavior. For all the wit and intelligence that informs her fictional world, it is devoid of compassion, an unlovely wasteland. And what comfort to feel superior to her people! What small, hateful comfort! It is not so much a vision of the world that Miss McCarthy gives us but an attitude, a series of rigidly preconceived attitudes, which denies her characters the limited freedom of self-motion, and in the process the possibility of discovery which is the miracle of the novel's art. (pp. 8-9)

> *Jonathan Baumbach, "Introduction" to his* The Landscape of Nightmare: Studies in the Contemporary American Novel *(reprinted by permission of New York University Press; copyright © 1965 by New York Uni-*

versity), New York University Press, 1965, pp. 8-9.

Whole sections of *Birds of America* read like a valentine to Fanny Farmer.

Picking one's way through the author's loving, Whitman-esque lists of foods, flowers, and other impedimenta of a lost domestic paradise, one wonders at times if this is a novel or a course in home economics. One wonders, too, if we—both Mary McCarthy and her readers—have not seriously misjudged her real ambitions as a writer. Is it possible that our leading bitch-intellectual, so renowned for her cold-blooded hatchetwork on the pieties of the liberal mind, has all along been harboring a desire to assume the mantle of Mrs. Beeton? Unserious questions, you may say. But alas, this is the kind of mental tick-tack-toe the reader of *Birds of America* is reduced to for pages—for chapters—at a time.

There are, to be sure, some characters in this novel, though they are distinctly less important—less real—to the author than are *things.* . . .

There is also, in a manner of speaking, a plot—a small, poor, badly undernourished, somewhat dehydrated little cliché of a plot, but a plot all the same. . . . Despite the hailstorm of "ideas" that can be heard hitting the roof—all those long, long thoughts about nature, taste, progress, democracy, and America—all we are really offered in *Birds of America* is a few pathetic scraps from the Jamesian banquet.

Still, better novels have been written on flimsier and no less hackneyed materials. The dispiriting quality of *Birds of America* owes as much to its style as to its theme. For the truth is—dare one say it?—that Mary McCarthy cannot write a novel. She lacks the essential fictional gift: She cannot imagine *others.* Missing from the powerful arsenal of her literary talents is some fundamental mimetic sympathy. We can no more imagine her being haunted by one of her characters than we can imagine Proust, say, *not* being haunted by one of his. There is, indeed, a more vivid sense of character in almost any one of her literary or political essays than in her fiction, and for a very good reason. In her essays, Miss McCarthy is not obliged to do the impossible: invent the people she is writing about.

To understand the method and the texture of a Mary McCarthy novel, one must go back to the beginnings of her literary career—to the bright, brittle, wickedly snobbish reviews of Broadway shows she once wrote for *Partisan Review.* For the fact is, she has never stopped writing these reviews, even in her novels. But whereas even third-rate Broadway comedies once provided the theater critic with substantial enough characters to write about, the novelist must create her own, and this Miss McCarthy cannot do. In *Birds of America*, neither Peter Levi nor his silly mother is ever really *there;* the author simply "reviews" their ideas and their actions at stupefying length. They do not even enjoy the kind of reality that, in most of Mary McCarthy's writing, is given to the butts of her satire, for the author is more than a little in love with these characters. The satirical thrust is reserved for their adversaries in taste.

Really, it is all too tedious to be endured. Although—as always in Miss McCarthy's writing—there is a good deal of free-floating snobbery in the book, the issue of snobbery as a social or spiritual value is never joined. We shall have to look elsewhere for the novel we need on this theme.

Nor can *Birds of America* be said to have a value as social reportage, for its account of the sociology of taste is totally out of date. While the entire country is half-mad with dreams of culinary glory, with herb gardens flourishing, and the smallest hardware stores in the tiniest villages of Maine boasting ample supplies of preserving jars by the dozens, Mary McCarthy imagines that all these things belong to some prehistoric past. This is really the only good joke to be found in this novel—that its author is so preposterously out of date about the objects of her concern. (p. 2)

> *Hilton Kramer, in* Book World *(© The Washington Post), May 23, 1971.*

Birds of America strikes me as another book that has gone wrong. . . . [My] complaint is that [Mary McCarthy] tries to fit a running political, social, and ecological commentary-cum-satire into the form of a novel that cannot or will not sustain it. At best, it strives to become a contemporary *Candide*, but hardly succeeds, mainly because Peter's innocence is more irksome than it is refreshing: he seems badly in need of a father as well as a mother. (pp. 463-64)

> *Jay L. Halio, in* The Southern Review *(copyright, 1973, by the Louisiana State University), Vol. IX, No. 1, Spring, 1973.*

I find MMcC too full of herself when she writes of wars and military trials and great events [in *The Seventeenth Degree*], so that one sees her figure looming large in the foreground of her fine prose, hears her too-certain, too-loud voice sounding out over the roar of guns and planes and testimony of soldiers in the background, and this grows irritating after a while. One paragraph of the first essay will illustrate this. Even if your ear is poor you will not be able to miss the dominance of the first-person pronoun, her ego over the matter. . . . As always, MMcC is her own favorite story. (p. 33)

> *Doris Grumbach, in* The New Republic *(reprinted by permission of* The New Republic; *© 1974 by The New Republic, Inc.), May 25, 1974.*

Mary McCarthy is an American novelist who was known, chiefly, to a small band of other novelists, whose novels she respectfully reviewed in small literary magazines and who respectfully reviewed hers, until she broke out of that rarified circle and, momentarily, into the real world of Hemingway and Steinbeck (the latter whom she refers to in *The Seventeenth Degree* as a "fool"), when she came up with one called *The Group*. Buried in it was a passing account of a lesbian, which attracted a film company, because in those pre-Jacqueline Susann days, lesbians were few and far between in novels by respectable lady authors. With that episode highly emphasised, the film was a hit and the titillated rushed out to buy the book, only to find those passages too vague to get much of a kick from, and so Miss McCarthy went back to writing novels which were read by reviewers in the little literary magazines and hardly anyone else. She was reputed to have a private income.

She was, of course, devoted to John F. Kennedy and was prepared, one assumes, for there is no evidence to the contrary, to be as devoted to Lyndon Johnson, until she noticed Vietnam. It had been there all along, of course, under Kennedy, but it was not an important war, not important enough, at any rate, to arouse the tigress in Miss McCarthy. No important numbers of Vietnamese were being slaughtered, and not much American money was being spent. But when Johnson followed, to the letter, Kennedy's battle plans (perfected by his previous military adventure, the Bay of Pigs), and the loss of lives and money became noticeable, Miss McCarthy, suddenly aflame, demanded that he stop. Johnson didn't stop, if indeed he ever heard of her demand, any more than Kennedy or any other Commander-in-Chief would have. Even when Robert Lowell, a poet whose blank verse sways 8,765 Americans, refused to attend a White House Festival of the Arts unless his host stopped that war forthwith, the Festival simply chugged along without him.

Miss McCarthy, Mr. Lowell, and many other of our most prestigious military planners, took out full-pages in the *New York Times*, denouncing the President as a blood-drinking colossus, obsessed with destroying the little brown people of the world when it was perfectly clear that Vietnam was a nagging circumstance he had inherited from the Kennedys that he didn't know what in hell to do with, except somehow to win, and that his towering achievement, the achievement closest to his damaged heart, was the civil rights legislation, which the Kennedys and the McCarthys and the Lowells had long whined about and done nothing about, but which he wheedled and bullied through Congress to give dignity, at long last, to the black and brown people of America.

There were lots of Mary McCarthys around in the 'sixties and early 'seventies; Jane Fonda and Joan Baez were the best known. They said and wrote much which they are, understandably, embarrassed by today, but not our Mary. She wrote pamphlet after pamphlet in those days. She should be grateful today that they were ignored even by her friends on the little literary magazines, and that nobody bought them, but like a surly fighter who fought a wild and foolish fight, and lost, she insists on running the videotapes of her performance again in this collection [*The Seventeenth Degree*] and to the same empty rooms. The running theme of this new collection is that the North Vietnamese (and their allies, the Russians, the Chinese and the Viet Cong) were saints and the Americans and the South Vietnamese were bums. The disorder of Saigon disgusted her. The perfect order of Hanoi charmed her. . . .

It was in Hanoi "we heard Johnson's abdication speech. All of us . . . dancing . . . kissing, hugging each other, took a bit of credit for ourselves. We had helped to bring the war to an end. It could not last much longer."

What the Mary McCarthys helped to do was bring Nixon into the White House and prolong the war four bloody years longer.

Al Capp, "American Farce," in The Spectator *(© 1975 by* The Spectator; *reprinted by permission of* The Spectator*), February 15, 1975, p. 182.*

The Vietnam war and its subsequent wrangles turned Mary McCarthy into a pamphleteer. Until 1964, when she became interested and eventually obsessed by America's part in the war, her writing was characterised by a patrician wit and a humane political sense. She did not cease to be humane with her concern in the war—far from it—but her forthrightness became blunter still and her writing almost wilfully inelegant. And something else, a mingling of new tones, the first a zealous and enterprising Mother Superior's ('This belief of mine was what was prompting me, like an apostolic "call", to put aside my normal work and go'), the second reminiscent of the chatty radicalism of the Princess Casamassima ('At my desk I had rather pleasant reveries of going to jail. It could be peaceful: no telephone'). In this collection of long, related pieces [*The Seventeenth Degree*] two are new and three have already appeared in book form. They are all linked in some way to Vietnam and though none is news they constitute a thoughtful appraisal of what is by no means an ended war. How right she was. (p. 311)

For anyone who doubts the value of Mary McCarthy's survey, charging her with republishing something that has outworn its usefulness, it is well to remember that President Ford is urging Congress to increase military aid. No supply of arms can possibly be handed over without men to act as advisers, and we could well be back to the days of 1963, before—as Orwell put it—we were jerked out of our deep sleep by the roar of bombs. If that happens, Ms McCarthy's book will not be history but prophecy, and there is no question that this is part of her pamphleteering intention. (p. 312)

Paul Theroux, "Mother Superior," in New Statesman *(© 1975 The Statesman & Nation Publishing Co. Ltd.), March 7, 1975, pp. 311-12.*

*   *   *

McCOURT, James   1941-

James McCourt is an American novelist. (See also *Contemporary Authors*, Vols. 57-60.)

James McCourt re-orders priorities [in "Mawrdew Czgowchwz"]. Like La Tosca, his creatures live for art and live for love. They are operaphiles, and opera is the most important thing in the world—at last someone has had the courage to say that.

This excuses them and McCourt from the charge of frivolity, which might otherwise have been leveled at the likes of Halcyon Q. Paranoy, Dame Sybil Farewell-Tarnysh, Merovig Creplaczx and Tangent Percase, people who casually utter gems like "What is laughter but somehow the cabaletta to grief?" and "Not for the squeamish?—Who are they, a sect?" and "Reality does not occur, it is enforced."

Amidst follies thick as post-performance traffic, McCourt tells the tale of Mawrdew Czgowchwz (pronounced "gorgeous"), "the diva of the moment," the ultimate opera singer of the fifties. Ever since her solo flight from newly Russified Czechoslovakia ended in a crash landing on the Champs Elysées, she has held the imagination of the world in thrall. The lady combines the onstage temperament of Callas with the offstage amiability of Tebaldi and a soupçon of De Los Angeles melancholy and Nilsson wit. She is the first "oltrano," possessing a range of three and a half octaves to F-sharp in alt and a repertory that includes Mélisande, Orfeo, the Queen of the Night, Norma, Brünnhilde, Katisha, both Dido and Cassandra in "Les

Troyens,'' both the Marschallin and Octavian in ''Rosenkavalier,'' and both Leonora and Azucena in ''Il Trovatore.''. . .

''Mawrdew Czgowchwz'' is not a parody of anything in particular, but a mélange of fantasies, the author's daydream of what the world could be if a few discrepancies in the perfection of reality were set to rights, something like Nabokov's ''Ada'' or Vian's ''Mood Indigo.'' This is a world where hunger strikes occur to protest the Met's firing of a singer, where blizzards vanish in a day, permitting audiences to attend the opera, where crowds gather and respond on cue, as do clouds. Everyone is wise and good save for a few wicked on whom divine retribution swiftly falls. Central Park is free of muggers and available for masquerades.

McCourt declaims his love for opera as it should be and for old New York as it never really was and brings to the task extraordinary talents for epigram, for style, for juxtaposition, for sheer nonsense. He shines a light on the arabesques of the English language at an unusual angle, so that weird and wonderful configurations pop out of it.

The result is delectable but may be too cluttered for some tastes. The style keenly recalls Ronald Firbank, whose appeal is a specialized one, despite recent claims for his universality. The prose is luminous enough to be lurid. Events are almost too busy being described to happen. McCourt has Firbank's vast supply of improbably stylish phrases, his knack for sketching a character lightly but complexly, his eye and love for nonsense in the name of social amenities. But he is less far out. He has not Firbank's taste in perversity—the most scandalous event in ''Mawrdew Czgowchwz'' is the rape of the diva by her conductor minutes before her first Isolde. Firbank's novels are perceived through a hazy scrim of non sequiturs, compared with which McCourt's prose is straightforward. McCourt is as florid as the Bel Canto composers but, as someone once said of Puccini, ''he gets on with it.''

''Once upon a time (time out of mind)'' begins this remembrance of things past that never were; McCourt escapes time not only by recapturing the Old Met that no longer exists outside memory, but also by gilding his memories in so literally fantastic a manner that only mind could contain them. But for the delectation of what other minds is this one displayed? ''Mawrdew Czgowchwz'' is not written for any isolatable cult—knowledge of opera would give added pleasure but the novel exists independent of that. The reader must be prepared, however, to follow the silver-tongued writer throughout an outlandish landscape, unquestioning. Reason would be out of place here. She would upset the ecological balance of a rich and delicate world. From which, into ''time out of mind,'' McCourt ultimately sends his gorgeous heroine, and the Czgowchwz moment goes on and on. (p. 6)

> *John Yohalem, in* The New York Times
> Book Review *(© 1975 by The New York
> Times Company; reprinted by permission),
> January 26, 1975.*

The tale of Mawrdew Czgowchwz, a Zuleika Dobson of the opera world, the ultimate diva with a working range of three and a half octaves, is a work of *altissimo* camp. This could be suffocating. But James McCourt is an ecstatic

fabulist, robustly funny and inventive, and touchingly in love with his subject. His work gives him pleasure, and so it's a pleasure to watch him work. (p. 61)

McCourt is unfailingly exact about every detail of operaphilia and about such '40s esoterica as the murder of composer-conductor Alexander Hollenius by Christine Radcliffe. I noted only one infinitesimal misquotation of a Cole Porter song title. He writes a joyous cadenza on the Old Met waiting line: ''Like the more heroic, if not necessarily more valiant, bread lines, soup lines, and picket lines of the venerable prewar urban populist network, the postwar opera line *stood* for something . . . which since the demolition of the Old Met has forever and for ill been lost, forgotten, even forsworn.'' (pp. 61-2)

McCourt's novel is both special and precious, in the most honorable senses of those words. (p. 62)

> *Walter Clemons, ''Opera Madness,'' in*
> Newsweek *(copyright 1975 by Newsweek,
> Inc.; all rights reserved; reprinted by permission), January 27, 1975, pp. 61-2.*

It's hard to imagine what we would have made of [*Mawrdew Czgowchwz*] a dozen years ago, before the appearance of Susan Sontag's ''Notes on 'Camp'.'' That essay provoked considerable excitement because it mapped out a sensibility we hadn't known how to deal with before. Not in America, anyway: Wilde and Firbank we had accommodated, but they were English (or Anglo-Irish) after all, and everybody knows how odd foreigners can be. Now *camp* is one of the reviewer's favorite words, shorthand for all kinds of excess and silliness. Paul Morrisey's *Frankenstein*, Bette Midler and the Pointer Sisters, wedgies and flamingo-emblazoned rayon shirts, Burt Reynolds in the buff—too much our tacky popular culture takes to its bosom is described as camp, and we have to start from scratch with our definitions. We need Susan Sontag back, and she *is* back, in a way: the publicity handouts list her (along with Lewis Mumford and Joyce Carol Oates) as one of the early supporters of this remarkable book.

It's the real article, *le vrai* camp. . . .

A funny, loving, uneven fantasy. It's true camp because despite all the glitter it's fundamentally serious. The novel playfully suggests the completeness, the absolute value of the esthetic vision. McCourt acknowledges storm troopers, breadlines, the Cold War. But he knows, with Yeats, that ''poets . . . are always gay,'' that Ophelia and Cordelia ''do not break up their lines to weep.'' When MC jumps her cue and sings the *Liebestod* in Erse, she does so gloriously, but it is a shocking intrusion of life, MC's life, into art, the interrupted performance a symbol of universal chaos. Civilization's great task is to bring MC back, in the words of her therapist, to ''her libidinal life's task,'' ''performative utterance.'' In celebrating the supreme importance of performance, with its divinities, its bloody Olympian battles, its fiendishly demanding but adoring believers, McCourt says some weighty truths—indirectly, comically—about civilized life and the heroic worth of these shining secular rites.

And he says them, much of the time, with great verve and inventiveness. The accounts of MC's appearances—in opera, in concert, at parties by the baby grand—are an undiluted joy, and at the same time a knowing send-up of the language of music criticism, hilarious and thoroughly convincing. I have to admit the book is less winning in carrying out some of its more workaday novelistic tasks. McCourt has taken Firbank as his mentor, I think, and while the names of the characters would not shame the creator of Miss Miami Mouth—Halcyon Paranoy, the Countess Madge O'Meaghre Gautier, Achille Plonque—the characters themselves often turn out to be a lot less interesting than they sound. The prose is mannered to a fare-thee-well, yet it doesn't often have the Master's other-worldly wit or his lunatic genius for skewered syntax. And, sad to say, there's something warmed-over about the ecclesiastical and witchcraft foolery. But *Mawrdew Czgowchwz* is all style and assurance when it cleaves to its subject. It's also nice to see someone paying such tender homage to Gotham, the City, without which there would be no temple and no rites, no gods, no worshippers. The poor old girl hasn't had a song like this sung about her for a long time. (pp. 26-8)

> *James Boatwright, in* The New Republic *(reprinted by permission of* The New Republic; © *1975 by The New Republic, Inc.),* February 8, 1975.

*   *   *

McELROY, Joseph 1930-

McElroy is an American novelist whose work has reminded critics of Heller and Pynchon. (See also *Contemporary Authors*, Vols. 19-20.)

["Lookout Cartridge"] is not an easy novel to describe. It is something like the movie "Blow-Up," let us say, in that its hero thinks he spies with a camera what his naked eyes have refused to see. And it is something like the novels of Robbe-Grillet in that its prose is deadpan, toneless, under a spell, looped in its own obsessions, words whispering inside the head of a madman. It is like Pynchon's "Gravity's Rainbow" in that its symbolic and allusive formulae come from science and technology rather than from literature and other art, and in that one reads through it as one might move through sets designed by a secretive and paranoid demiurge. It is like many novels written by authors from Dostoevsky to Michel Butor in that its unexpected harmonies and novel dissonances sound against the conventions of the mystery novel. It is like the recent work of Norman Mailer in its hero's attempt to sniff out and soak up the power, energy, magic or mana released by violence and fear. "We are in the grip of forces," says Cartwright, the hero whose mind is the "lookout cartridge" of the title, "and also of their absence.". . .

For Cartwright, who is brawny and wears a trenchcoat, as for Sam Spade, Philip Marlowe and Lew Archer, the way to uncover a mystery is to make waves. But "waves aren't simple; they hit each other; they interfere, take each other's force, but also reinforce." Cartwright makes things happen that make things happen to him. He becomes the killer behind the killers who do the actual killings, none of which would have occurred without the waves he has made or the powers he has poached. His quest leads him over "fork upon fork, fibres sprouting deltas, alternatives routed into huge parallel families ignorant of each other." Each mystery solved discloses others and provides the motives for new mystifications. The more Cartwright learns, the greater his power, but the less he understands it. He is moved to formulate a law: "You will not have both power and the understanding of it."

The clues to the knowledge and power he seeks are always broken, or buried, or on the periphery of his attention—Mayan calendars, Stonehenge computers, the properties of liquid crystals, the forgotten art of wheelwrighting, Gerardus Mercador, a character in "The Woman in White," his son's interrupted talk about elevation grids, his daughter's resemblance to a number of other women, the relations between his wife and his ex-mistress, a surpressed name, an uncompleted phrase, a bit of history, a section of landscape, a piece of equipment, a face flashing by, something colored orange, the word PROBE on a newspaper headline the rest of which is covered by an iron weight marked LIFE: collages in time and space of memory, perception and illusion. Cartwright comes to understand that he is immersed in "some oceanic conspiracy of refractions.". . .

The systems of power—financial, criminal, political, domestic, erotic and psychotic—that extend through and around him wheel at all angles to each other and at different speeds. And yet they have the look of subsystems waiting for a supersystem to subsume them.

They have that look because so many bits in one system reflect or echo bits in the others. "No such thing as randomness," says Cartwright, whether hopefully or fearfully, but there is no certainty, this side of godhood and paranoia. The novel ends (with a bang) this side of godhood or paranoia, the issue unresolved, except by violence. "I was not sure what I had seen, but I knew what we had done" are Cartwright's last words to us. And neither are we sure what to see in the flickers of analogy and homology among parts of the systems that wheel through and around Cartwright, but we know that they signal the main sources of anxious fascination and eerie power generated by this novel.

And we leave this novel—the author's fourth long work of fiction in only nine years (his two most recent books were "Hind's Kidnap" and "Ancient History")—with a renewed sense of the systematic disconnection and sinister relatedness among the power systems we detect from our own lookout cartridges, or consciousnesses slotted between what is within us and "the times we live in." As I said, this is not an easy novel to describe. Nor is it easy to read—or to put down. The rewards, for once, are adequate to the effort required. What is easy is to predict that 1975 will not produce many novels as good. For its technical brilliance, its unremitting intelligence, for the rich complexity of the homologies and analogies between its systems and the fearful times we live in, "Lookout Cartridge" is the rarest kind of achievement. (p. 3)

> *George Stade, in* The New York Times Book Review (© *1975 by The New York Times Company; reprinted by permission),* February 2, 1975.

Lookout Cartridge is not a novel to be savored in a comfortable armchair by the fire. It should be read at a metal desk in a pale green office under fluorescent lights—or perhaps over a cup of coffee at some long-forgotten Automat. It is a mean and lonely piece of work. . . .

The plot . . . seems unimportant next to the problems presented by McElroy's prose. He puts words together in a manner so unrelenting that reading the book for long stretches of time induced in me actual physical discomfort

—a kind of vertigo with an accompanying tightness in the cords of the neck. McElroy has created a style with all the syntactical complexity of Joyce, but without the lush Celtic melody to carry you along over the bumps.

Whether McElroy is a superb writer or merely a difficult one is too fine a point to answer after one reading of one novel. But he's certainly in earnest and is to be taken seriously if one is tough enough to take him at all. (p. 55)

> *Carol Holmes, in* Harper's *(copyright 1975 by* Harper's Magazine; *reprinted from the May, 1975 issue by special permission), May, 1975.*

Barthelme and Barth sometimes; Handke, Hawkes and Baraka frequently; Mailer lately; Heller and Pynchon always; and now, with his fourth book [*Lookout Cartridge*], Joseph McElroy: these are our writers of stoned fictions. They've altered our rhythms, stuttered our speech, toyed with our timing and besieged us with noise. They've poised their fictions between order and disorder, meaning and nonmeaning, something and nothing, the mainstream and being at sea, the main man and the outlaw. Posing choices, they've pushed us to edges. And from the edge, they've veered not back into certainty, resolution or coherence, but out into seeming chaos, instability and easy-to-mock vulnerabilities. Their fictions are spacy yet jammed with information. But their greatest information lurks in their rhythms, noise-to-signal ratios, and links of bits to other bits. Their greatest information lurks between their items of news. . . .

Unlike McElroy's earlier fictions, *Lookout Cartridge* makes it impossible for readers to fall back on "connectedness," "coherence" or any other rainy day staple of complacent experience. Nothing in this book *makes sense.* Rather, *Lookout Cartridge* and other stoned books show a sort of "nothing" where people *sense without making.* For his 531 dense pages, McElroy builds no visible structure, edifies not at all, resolves only in flashes. As its main character says, the book is finally "like some instance of Hindu Maya that lets us believe in the rest that may not really be there."

The book takes place in the mind of an American named Cartwright. . . .

Cartwright thinks of his consciousness as a cartridge whose meaning will be revealed by its surrounding past and projected future, by the making and viewing of the film, but both the past and its future are so specifically uncertain that even his own content is in doubt. And if he is a cartridge to be inserted in some prefigured scheme, who's the inserter? These are some of the questions McElroy poses but to which he refuses clear answers. Is anything left?. . .

From homebody to being at "home with the unexpected" is the distance Cartwright travels in his tale. And that is also, if crudely, the tale of the shift from straight to stoned fiction. *Lookout Cartridge* does create spaces "not previously there." It's a book that repays rereading and yes, it only grows stronger in hindsight. Still, one wishes in frustration for more of what Cartwright calls "concussion." And that's one of McElroy's nicest touches, for while he seems to defuse his perils he actually compounds them. The deaths in his story are as accidental as its full plenty of details and its ultimate destruction of concrete mean-

ing. . . . The concussions in *Lookout Cartridge* are muffled, the tracks erased, and hieroglyphic shimmerings are all that remain. It's not a cheap thrill, not a gas, not a hit, toke or rush. After all, it's a stone. (p. 28)

> *W. T. Lhamon, Jr., in* The New Republic *(reprinted by permission of* The New Republic; © 1975 by The New Republic, Inc.), May 3, 1975.*

*   *   *

McGAHERN, John   1935-

McGahern is an Irish novelist in the Celtic literary tradition. (See also *Contemporary Authors*, Vols. 19-20.)

"What a coffin this schoolroom would be without the long withdrawing tide of memory becoming imagination," reflects Patrick [in "The Leavetaking"], an Irish schoolmaster on the day he is fired for having married a divorced woman. This insistence on death in the face of love is a constant of Patrick's personality. Perhaps it is traceable to the deathbed of his young mother, from which he was torn by an insensitive father. Or perhaps this perception of mortality is a Celtic literary tradition going back to Joyce's "Dubliners," which includes a memorable celebration of the funeral. In any event, Patrick thinks of life as a collection of "small deaths," and he is obsessed with the big sleep even in the act of love. His somber memories are a lowering backdrop for his attempts to free himself from an unhappy past.

John McGahern paints an almost Victorian family portrait of heavy father, submissive mother, and the cruelties they inflict on each other. The author has a lyrical touch that translates his hero's hard times into some dark imagery that lingers long after you have closed the book. (p. 10)

> *Martin Levin, in* The New York Times Book Review *(© 1975 by The New York Times Company; reprinted by permission), February 2, 1975.*

I doubt there is another practicing writer of fiction in English as good as John McGahern who is so little noticed in this country. You would have to poke around, even among those who read books for a living, to find the few who have read him. I infer this in part because the jacket of his fourth book ["The Leavetaking"] carries four excerpts from American reviews, one of them revised to make it exquisitely ungrammatical, but all once written by me. An embarrassment for all of us, surely, yet the Irish know him: they awarded his first novel, "The Barracks," their highest prize and then banned the publication of his second, "The Dark." Censors, more than most of us, believe in the efficacy of literature and take steps accordingly. The English know him, too: the Times Literary Supplement has put McGahern "among the half dozen practicing writers of English prose most worthy of our attention."

Perhaps this new story, lighter and more optimistic than its predecessors, will fare better here. It is romantic, a love story, unfashionable in its concern for dignity and courage. An Irish schoolteacher and an American divorcee—his background is poor and mean, hers rich and mean—find, after many wrong loves, a right love, an ecstatic pleasure in living. After a period of concealing their delight in each other and their marriage from those who have an economic hold on them (her father is possessive, his school will dismiss him for marrying a "married" woman), they elect to cut free their moorings and embark on their own course. (pp. 90-1)

In summary it is the stuff of soap opera. McGahern was never an innovator. What makes the story significant, even compelling, is the design that he has imposed upon it, the precision of his observation, and his care for the language of Joyce and Yeats. McGahern means us to read slowly, to hear the sounds, feel the weight of his words. The story begins with the teacher brooding on his imminent dismissal. Moving through the school day's routine he remembers the loss of his mother, whom he greatly loved, and that involuntary, life-denying loss is set against a voluntary, life-affirming decision to lose his job. For the loss of love (I suspect this is the story's undeclared message) cannot often be repeated before it becomes the loss of life. McGahern's novel, then, is about the conscious decision to recover life, and it is done very elegantly indeed. (pp. 91-2)

> *Peter S. Prescott, "Super-Soap," in* Newsweek *(copyright 1975 by Newsweek, Inc.; all rights reserved; reprinted by permission), February 17, 1975, pp. 90-2.*

McGahern's exquisitely written book [*The Leavetaking*] reminds us that the brutality and despair of much modern fiction is not the whole or the only story. Sex is not necessarily an existential booby-trap, and some of the promises life holds out may even, once in a while, be realized. . . .

A writer must convince his readers that he has truly earned the right to speak, as McGahern does at the end, in the accents of exaltation; that he has reason for proclaiming, in D. H. Lawrence's words: "Look, we have come through!" *The Leavetaking* compels our assent—as brilliant literary art alone can do, and as soap opera cannot. McGahern's imagery, for all its haunting melancholy, is flawlessly precise. Like Nadine Gordimer, he can fuse past and present in a dazzling stillness of thickly layered time.

But this burnished eloquence derives its weight from the bitter fidelity that stamps McGahern's rendering of Ireland. It is a country as holy and narrow, as intransigent and seductive, as the Ireland that drove Stephen Dedalus to arm himself with silence, exile and cunning. . . . The choice made by McGahern's lovers seems insignificantly private set beside Joyce's Promethean defiance in the cause of art. Still, the taproots, deep in Ireland's incorrigibly tragic experience, are the same, and so is the luminous purity of the novelists' courage. (p. 18)

> *Pearl K. Bell, in* The New Leader (© 1975 *by the American Labor Conference on International Affairs, Inc.), March 31, 1975.*

*   *   *

McHALE, Tom   1941-

McHale is an American novelist, best known for *Farragan's Retreat*.

Three years ago, McHale published two exhilarating novels in quick succession: *Principato* and *Farragan's Retreat*. In both he revealed wild comic gusto, a youthful, vengeful rage at certain vagaries of the Roman Catholic Church, and a visceral knowledge of middle-class Irish and Italians

around Philadelphia and the Jersey shore. McHale was never a stylist; he made up in energy what he lacked in elegance.

In *Alinsky's Diamond* he quits his familiar landscape and sets out on a literary crusade nearly as unfortunate as the one he describes in this novel. . . . *Alinsky's Diamond* is not so much a case of an overcomplicated plot, in fact, as a whole flea market full of story lines.

Though at first McHale's worst problem seems to be the exhausting narrative, the real dilemma is that for the first time he is writing about people he does not know. The crusaders, the thugs, the conmen in these pages are strangers to the author. McHale has clearly shown that he can be a dazzling extemporizer, but he badly needs familiar roots. The very restlessness demonstrated in *Alinsky's Diamond* may contribute to something enduring in the future. For now, though, McHale's imagination can do without this kind of exotic melodrama.

> *Martha Duffy, "Pilgrim's Regress," in* Time *(reprinted by permission from* Time, The Weekly Newsmagazine; *copyright Time Inc.), September 30, 1974, p. E3.*

In his third novel [*Alinsky's Diamond*] Tom McHale has drastically altered the geography of his world but left intact his fascination with the curious and the grotesque, especially in their religious manifestations. *Principato* and *Farragan's Retreat* bore the marks of their Philadelphia origins where the strong ethnic ties and bitter conflicts of Irish and Italians share a common root in the soil of cultural Catholicism. No matter how faint their actual belief, neither Principato nor Farragan can escape their inherited religion, complete with kooky or conniving clerics, ironbound conventions and occasional comforts. . . .

[In this novel a] wildly picaresque element lends an exotic flavor to McHale's already highly spiced religious imagination, but he pays for the gain with a less convincing cast of characters.

The comic extravagances in the earlier novels grew out of a recognizable sense of place. The outrageous things McHale's creations said and did were merely blown-up versions of what we read about in the daily papers. By shifting the locale to France and assorted points between there and Jerusalem, and by introducing the almost mythic title character, Meyer Alinsky, the author has moved further down the road from realism to abstraction and allegory. Ideas have always been present in McHale's fiction—questions about revenge, belief, patriotism—but in *Alinsky's Diamond* the overriding issue of retribution and vicarious sacrifice is central.

McHale's facility at comic invention and his talent for creating a believable and lovable "hero" [Frank Murphy] outweigh the novel's defects. . . .

In creating Frank Murphy, McHale has remained true to previous form; along with Principato and Farragan, Murphy is quintessentially *l'homme moyen sensuel* forced to deal with true believers ("As always, when he was in the company of men who had an intense personal discipline of one sort or another, Murphy felt a consummate shame"). . . . Murphy's innate skepticism makes him the perfect foil for McHale's darkly comic vision. No one need tell him that the world is absurd. From the moment he unaccountably escaped from the Midwestern tornado that took the rest of his family, Murphy has lived with the blessings and the curses of an irrational Providence. Moving deeper into the monomaniacal world of Meyer Alinsky, Murphy refuses to surrender either his basic common sense or his appreciation of just how awry the universe really is.

Aside from the comedy generated by Murphy and his perceptions, McHale, as we have come to expect, also provides us with a number of very funny set pieces. But as the novel progresses both slapstick and satire give way before an unrelenting and often savage irony. Even more than McHale's earlier novels, *Alinsky's Diamond* is intended as a "serious" comic novel, and in large part it succeeds. My only objection is that the theological issues of guilt and atonement sometimes threaten to swamp the narrative. (p. 24)

> *John B. Breslin, in* The New Republic *(reprinted by permission of* The New Republic; © *1974 by The New Republic, Inc.), October 19, 1974.*

I read both of [McHale's] earlier books with hope for his talent, though disappointment in his technique, and I approached ["Alinsky's Diamond"] with expectations. Alas, I found it almost literally unreadable, for it piles a farfetched and fake-picaresque plot teeming with unlikely, dimensionless characters upon a prolix corpus of strained and awkward prose. I couldn't finish it; I was wholly put off by clotted sentences like . . . "'Violence! Violence!' Gervais suddenly shrieked, with an elaborate Mediterranean gesture that told, despite his careful professional accent, that he was probably Marseillaise [*sic*] or at least came from somewhere in Provence." I have not abandoned hope, but I wish that McHale would, in the reputed words of Ettore Bugatti, "simplicate and add lightness". . . . (p. 185)

> *L. E. Sissman, in* The New Yorker *(© 1974 by The New Yorker Magazine, Inc.), October 21, 1974.*

Tom McHale is as *relaxed* a novelist as any we have, and that is a refreshing, though limited, virtue. It certainly makes for readability; *Alinsky's Diamond* flows along free from any narrative tics or stylistic self-consciousness, all surface casualness and poise. . . .

The point of tension . . . becomes the relation of Murphy [the protagonist] to Alinsky—the one passive, disillusioned, ineffectual; the other manipulative, amoral, obsessive. Alinsky is full of a passionate intensity (he murders, imprisons, corrupts); Murphy lacks all conviction. The process of the book is Murphy's moral rehabilitation accomplished through the negative example of Alinsky.

McHale's Murphy is of the same stuff as [Herbert] Gold's Curtis [in *Swiftie the Magician*]. They are victims/observers, playthings of the fates and fashions, witnesses to their own and the world's disintegration. Caught in a world of passionate excess, they are beset by the same dilemmas: how to be reasonable in the face of hysteria, how to feel compassion in the face of pervasive brutality, how to maintain coherence in the face of cultural chaos. Their philosophy, such as it is, is this: in a tidal wave, it is better to be a cork than a dam.

This is the new passivity. It is successor to the embattled innocence of the Fifties and early Sixties, Salinger's rants and Ginsberg's raves. It is part of a post-New Frontier, post-Vietnam, post-New Left exhaustion. There is a sense in these characters of having seen all things, felt all emotions, tested all beliefs, taken all drugs, loved all women. What remains is a tasteful self-deprecation and a distaste for extremists. . . .

The adversary is no longer those who feel too little but those who feel too much—the Swifties and Alinskys of the world. Not insensitivity but hypersensitivity is the enemy, not complacency but fanaticism. Bellow gave early expression to this mood in the person of Sammler; Gold and McHale, in their more modest achievements, bring the attitude further up to date. . . .

McHale [aligns himself] with the sober majority, and after all the trafficking in exotica, [his book ends] in celebration of simple domestic virtues. The ambivalence is striking: the fascination with things contemporary that ends by rejecting them in the name of a sober decency. . . .

[McHale is] well immersed in the mainstream. . . . What [his new book points] up is a general drift toward cosmopolitanism, facetiousness, and casualness, toward the topical and the urban, the novel as sustained flirtation with the world. (p. 112)

> *Michael Levenson, in* Harper's *(copyright 1974 by* Harper's *Magazine; reprinted from the November, 1974 issue by special permission), November, 1974.*

In *Alinsky's Diamond* Tom McHale spatially extends the world of his earlier fiction, the two novels *Principato* and *Farragan's Retreat*, but he does not really alter it or its laws. The several reviewers who faulted the new book for sketchy or unbelievable European and Middle Eastern locales, instead of the familiar Philadelphia (where on the whole they would rather have McHale be) surely cannot remember . . . the earlier books very well, and they make McHale out to be much more a local colorist than he is or tries to be. His strengths, like his weaknesses, are elsewhere. If a dilapidated bar in Philadelphia could be equally in New York or Boston, then why not make it a café in Italy? If an American Irish Catholic can assume the identity of the Italian Principato, then why not let him be an American expatriate drinking himself to death in the French provinces?

In fact, the dimensions of McHale's world, which depend hardly at all on physical environment, are remarkably constant. At its center is a single man—Angelo Principato, Arthur Farragan, and now Francis Xavier Murphy—who can be young or middle-aged, failed or successful, impoverished or comfortable, but who *will* be pleasant, passive, and reasonably humble, manipulated by, uncomprehending of, and finally, subtly, rebellious against the events and people about him. The events strike the reader as very funny when they happen . . ., but they turn out to be either slightly sinister or malignant in the extreme. Most of the people, the supporting cast, turn out to be the way they seem initially, also malignant in the extreme, and their incapacity for change reflects the shallowness of their conception. . . . [One] of the best things about the protagonist, who, unlike his adversaries, does have some depth and ability to work toward self-knowledge, is simply that he is gentler than the nasty people in his family. That means that he cusses less than they, though all McHale's characters spend a lot of time cussing, and that unlike them he doesn't say, or says only when coerced and then with uncommon embarrassment, words like jap, yid, and nigger, a sure index of nastiness in McHale's world. (pp. 459-60)

[There] will be in every book not only celibate priests and gluttonous gigolos, as well as occasional homosexuals and practitioners of deliciously odd perversions, but the man who is or seems to be totally impotent. . . .

The most important fact in McHale's consistent fictional world is the practical joke that God played on the protagonist when He made him a Catholic and mated him for life, maybe longer, with guilt. You don't have to be a Catholic, of course, to feel guilty about all things, perhaps especially the absence of anything rationally requiring feelings of guilt (witness poor Portnoy, trapped in a Jewish joke as Principato *et al*, are trapped in Catholic jokes—leading legions of dust-jacket-cited critics to call McHale, preposterously, a Roman Roth), but McHale seems to think it helps. . . . Guilt is the real antagonist in these books, the enemy within the pleasant hero's sullied skin. (p. 460)

Farragan must die because . . . he did not find it enough to live, in himself or in his son. He is guilty of not holding onto life. Long before his time is due, as his friend Fitzpatrick charges, Farragan starts "going back: acceding to the inner dyings and crumblings, embracing the lush grayness of senility. . . ." This is wintry indeed, with a touch of the epiphanic chill of Joyce's *The Dead*.

This terror at the heart of *Farragan's Retreat* is McHale's one signal fictional achievement. Beside it, *Principato* appears unresolved and *Alinsky's Diamond* anarchic and flatly anti-climactic. It's too bad, because even in *Farragan's Retreat* McHale's success is attained in spite of his prose, a very remarkable feat, and when success is partial, as in *Principato*, or dubious, as in *Alinsky's Diamond*, his prose becomes more than one can reasonably ignore. How does one describe it? At best, perhaps serviceable, capable of conveying information, though with none of the richness, inventiveness, and complexity that McHale can give to incidents (part of the trouble may be that the incidents come too easily, that McHale's imagination is so prodigal that he finds no need to temper its products). At worst, which it is much of the time, hackneyed, flaccid, and dreary. When someone says something in earnest, he says it in dead earnest; when someone is awakened, he is rudely awakened. I wish that McHale wouldn't allow Murphy to become "suddenly enthused" at something. (pp. 461-62)

Still, McHale is a serious, purposeful writer, and he clearly had big ideas for *Alinsky's Diamond*. Maybe, like John Steinbeck in *East of Eden*, he is trying too hard. In their humility, which is not always quite so authentic as it seems, McHale's heroes are all Christ figures, of a sort; their Christ-likeness, however, never presumes to be pure but is interestingly mixed with something else: Farragan's with the obedience of Abraham, Murphy's with the ambiguous luck of, oddly, Barabbas. (p. 462)

McHale can get away with caricatures because they do serve, somehow, to define the problems and environment of the protagonist, but he does not allow them equal time. [But in *Alinsky's Diamond*] we are to believe in Alinsky for himself, as something more than a phase of Murphy's dysfunction, and yet he too is a caricature. . . .

Objectively horrible things happen in *Alinsky's Diamond*, plenty of them, but they are arbitrary and gratuitous. They are not, as they absolutely are in *Farragan's Retreat*, a cruelly definitive interpretation of everything that has gone before. . . . In *Alinsky's Diamond* one can never really understand why the characters should get what they get, and the dozens of often comic episodes do not, finally, revolve about a single moral hub. What McHale can do at the top of his form, as he has shown once, is make you shudder, though I don't think many readers will shudder at *Alinsky's Diamond*. I don't want this novelist to go back to Philadelphia, but I hope he will follow his third novel with a book worthy of his second. (p. 463)

> *Mark Taylor, "McHale's Retreat," in* Commonweal *(copyright © 1975 Commonweal Publishing Co., Inc.; reprinted by permission of Commonweal Publishing Co., Inc.), March 14, 1975, pp. 459-63.*

Alinsky's Diamond is not funny, not savage, and not brilliant. It is a terrible novel. Its humor is supposed to be worldly and mordant. It is, however, based on whatever comedy resides in the situation of a whore, a pimp, a drunk, and an abortionist making a religious crusade from France to Jerusalem. Not very funny per se, and not much funnier for the addition of Meyer Alinsky, an ex-Iowa halfback who conceived the whole sordid business for reasons of his own. Murphy, the drunk, is pointedly presented as a Christ figure; Alinsky turns out to be a megalomaniac with a secret sorrow; Alinsky's mother is a salty, improbable combination of Molly Goldberg and the Mater Dolorosa. The plot is correspondingly gimmicky; it leaves a vacuum unfilled by virtuoso writing, Redeeming Social Value, or even pornography.

I feel victimized not by McHale but by the whole apparatus of book merchandising, by the marketing of trendy writers as commodities. I am repelled by the glibness of jacket copy that assumes the existence of a "McHale tradition"— after two novels. I am also ashamed of the feeble willingness with which I periodically succumb to this sort of cant, and there must be thousands like me. Of course it's our own fault if we choose to read *Alinsky's Diamond* instead of *Middlemarch*, and no Reign of Virtue is going to legislate the permanent availability of the good, the true, and the beautiful. I just wish we weren't so regularly offered the overpraised, the tacky, and the meretricious.

> *Frances Taliaferro, "Victim of the Zeitgeist," in* Harper's *(copyright 1975 by Harper's Magazine; reprinted from the May, 1975 issue by special permission), May, 1975, p. 46.*

* * *

MERCER, David   1928-

A British writer for stage, screen, and television, Mercer is best known for his screenplay, *Morgan*. (See also *Contemporary Authors*, Vols. 9-12, rev. ed.)

[Looking] back now, it is possible to see the whole body of Mercer's work as depicting in various ways the birthpangs of a private man. His characters are all involved, one way or another, in the battle to assert their individual, unique natures within, or if necessary outside, the framework of normal everyday life, of social, political or psychological categories. To say that all are involved in this struggle does not necessarily mean that all of them consciously engage in it, and it certainly does not mean that they all win out in the end. Some seek comfort in anonymity, uniformity, some contrive to contract out of the struggle, some are shattered by it and destroyed. But behind the action of all Mercer's plays is a consciousness of individuality as something which is constantly under attack, and which has to be fought for with all one's strength if it is to be preserved.

This continuing theme in Mercer's work gives unity and direction to the expression of his various personal preoccupations. The principal preoccupations are political and psychological—or are usually categorized as such. But it seems to me that the attempts of various commentators to define Mercer's work in terms of a 'polarity' between politics and psychology, Marx and Freud, are finally quite beside the point, in that there is no appreciable tension between the two concepts, or two ways of looking at things, in the plays themselves. Instead, both are seen as essentially the same thing, or rather, one might say, both are interchangeable metaphors for the real subject: the relationship between the individual and the institution. (pp. 41-2)

> *John Russell Taylor, "David Mercer," in his* The Second Wave: British Drama for the Seventies *(reprinted with the permission of Farrar, Straus & Giroux, Inc.; copyright © 1971 by John Russell Taylor), Hill & Wang, 1971, pp. 36-58.*

David Mercer has always had a tendency to fix us wedding guests in the eye and force us to look at the collection of albatrosses he carries tied round his neck and drooping down his shoulders; but he's rarely been so bald about it, so artless and interminable, as in *Duck Song*. In a recent interview he announced that the play was 'about confusion', which I believe. He added that 'the confusion is sort of lucid', which, without some enormous emphasis on that 'sort of', I find less easy to swallow. And he then declared that it concerned 'the terrible, awful, unforgivable, inexcusable ineptitude of our society and its values', which it simply isn't. It doesn't invite you to look objectively at society, and judge it, but subjectively to share Mercer's general bewilderment and ennui. It's an internal weather report, told by a meteorologist who prefers to free-associate behind his desk than to study the data in detail and depth: squalls, sleet, showers of blood, plagues of frogs, frost at night, fog for most of the day. But often, alas, only the fog is discernible. . . .

In defiance of the laws of argument and of drama, the play inexorably dwindles into a melancholy monologue for several voices, all of which seem to be Mercer's own. Imagine if, instead of writing all those tragedies, Shakespeare had herded together Macbeth, Hamlet, Troilus and Timon to tell us, in plaintive half-sequiturs, that life's but a poor player, that outrageous fortune has a lot of slings and arrows, and so on; and you'll see how clogged and unmanageable are his musings on sex, love, colonialism, capitalism, cruelty, ignorance and death. And this from a writer whose precise wit we've so often admired in the past! (p. 232)

> *Benedict Nightingale, in* New Statesman (©

> *1974 The Statesman & Nation Publishing Co. Ltd.), February 15, 1974.*

David Mercer . . . has scarcely strayed from the well-known paths of naturalism. His latest play *Duck Song* (1974) suggests desperation: its first act is pure domestic comedy of the most banal kind, while its second act, refusing to meet any of the cheques drawn in the first, takes refuge in a series of unexplained and inexplicable (except in theatrical terms) events such as the disappearance of the scenery and the death of a character who later gets to her feet again. Perhaps Mercer is trying at last to turn and rend his dead language, or perhaps he is rather belatedly satirising absurdism, but the result certainly looks like a swan-song in the feathers of a dead duck. (p. 65)

> *John Spurling, in* Encounter (© *1975 by Encounter Ltd.), January, 1975.*

* * *

MERWIN, W(illiam) S(tanley)   1927-

Merwin, an American who has lived most of his life abroad, is a major poet, a translator from French, Spanish, Portuguese, Latin, Yiddish, and other languages, and the author of the short prose pieces collected in *The Miner's Pale Children* and one play, *Favor Island*. At the heart of Merwin's poetic sensibility is what Karl Malkoff has called "the sense of an allegorical universe [and] the appeal to central symbols and mythic patterns" to shore up against the "nothingness that at all times threatens." Merwin was awarded the Pulitzer Prize for Poetry for his 1970 collection, *The Carrier of Ladders*. (See also *Contemporary Authors*, Vols. 13-16, rev. ed.)

"Among all dictions," Merwin seeks "that ceremony whereby you ['love,' or the imagination, or poetry] may be named / perpetual out of the anonymity / of death." It is in the rhetoric of completion that Merwin utters his longing for the partial, since

> *Mention, though*
> *It be the scholiast of memory,*
> *Makes yet its presences from emptiness . . . .*

The paradox is a true one, and explains why *The Dancing Bears* of 1954 takes its title from Flaubert's bitter remark that "human speech is like a cracked kettle on which we pound out tunes fit to make bears dance, when what we want is to win over the stars." The figure of art as a cosmic failure, a grotesque second-best instead of a sympathetic magic—that is the ironical sign, affording a tremendous field to his talents for assimilation and apprenticeship, under which Merwin inscribes his elegance and his eloquence (did not even his first book [*A Mask for Janus*] borrow for its epigraph an assertion from John Wheelwright "habit is evil, all habit, even speech . . ."?). The aspiration to commanding utterance ("the dicta for the only poem") is from the start renounced, decried, and the dandy's posture of supreme defiance, cast up to the indifferent stars, justifies the *made* music (as opposed to the miraculous natural harmonies) of these further poems; furthermore, there is a gaudy acknowledgment that in the decrepitude of "the only poem," that Orphic spell which might hold the world in thrall, plurality with all its chances and changes must make do, and "in defeat find such re-creation" as the world's disguises afford:

> *I walk multifarious among*
> *My baubles and horses; unless I go in a mask*

How shall I know myself among my faces?

In the poet's repertory, then, there are to be found again among the titles "songs," "runes," a "colloquy" and three of the long, ode-like Provençal love-poems called "canso" —all thus labelled to reinforce the *wrought* (rather than the *given*) aspect of Merwin's enterprise:

> . . . *As though a man could make*
> *A mirror out of his own divinity,*
> *Wherein he might believe himself, and be.* (p. 361)

Perhaps the single decisive poem in this book . . ., the one that best accounts, in terms of the poet's identification of his own role, for the discipline which keeps these bears dancing, the suffered discrepancy between the music of the spheres and of the side-show, is the address to Columbus, "You, Genoese Mariner." Here, in a single sentence, characteristically tormented into an ironic salute that is 31 lines long, the poet apostrophizes the resolute explorer . . ., hails him as himself (the identification is made abruptly by no more than an anacoluthon, the dash which separates "you . . . who fancied / earth too circumscribed / to imagine . . . the unfingered world" from "I whose face has become / suddenly a frame / for astonishment"), thereby associating the Columbus who voyaged West for "gilt and spice" with his own disaster as a lover, as a poet, and closing on both "mistaken sailors" staring in sad wonderment at the world's "unknown dimension." The shared delusion was to believe that a Westerly direction, a held course

> *Must by its own token*
> *Continuing, contain*
> A grammar of return . . .

The line I have set in roman defines Merwin's entire project so far, for all the devices and designs of this courtly despot tend toward a cyclical theory of existence, the notion—so comforting to a poet who has the imagination of recurrence—that one can move onward only by preparing to move back: yet the vision fails, the changeless and diagrammatic universe ("an utter prey to mirrors") of the Genoese mariner as of the American jongleur dissolves in the forfeits of a lifetime, in fact of time itself. Ruefully, Merwin takes leave of his fantasy of perfection:

> *I, after so long,*
> *Who have been wrong as you.*

The navigational error discredits, for Merwin if not for us, his grammar of return (that magnificent phrase for a poetics of immutability); but . . . the mistake, like Christopher Columbus', was a creative one: the result in both cases was the discovery of America. (pp. 363-64)

[When] two years later in 1956, Merwin's *Green with Beasts* was published, that quarrel with the methods and measures of immutability (which had hitherto found expression . . . only in an exasperation of surface, a hypertrophy of the verse paragraph often eschewing rhyme for, instead, an archaizing involution of syntax) had utterly transmuted the poetry. His discontent with an orbific music which might charm into an imaginative unity all the disparates of experience now led Merwin into an expression so sharply disjunct from his initial achievements that we must look hard to see what bearing those earlier charged counsels of perfection could have on these long looping lines, these distended paragraphs of slackened expatiation unstarred by an incandescence of vocabulary or syntax, any rich and strange transformation of the very bones of speech.

It is another harmony these poems assert (one which fastens to the Eliot of the *Quartets* and later verse plays), just as it seems a different poet altogether from the celebrant of the Final Festival who now addresses himself to the world as a suffered presence, an endured pressure rather than an encompassed plaything; *how* different is evident not only in the gravamen but in the very grammar of the lines, no longer a "grammar of return" but of realization:

> *And I moved away because you must live*
> *Forward, which is away from whatever*
> *It was that you had, though you think when you have it*
> *That it will stay with you forever . . .*

The titles, as before, indicate the nature of the material, and that the material has altered: of the 39 new poems (set up on the page in long blocks of language, without the shapely stanzas and refrains which had given the work in the past its demurely marshalled aspect) only one, the "Mariner's Carol," makes the old generic commitment; the rest come to grips with their action without the mediation of a regular form: "Burning the Cat" or "The Eyes of the Drowned Watch Keels Going Over." The poems tend, then, to be ruminations or arguments, affording what Miss Moore calls "a gallantry of observation" rather than the exuberance of design—they are not prose, but they have some of the virtues of prose, for they are able to accommodate the ordinary sights and sounds of life without transforming them into myth, without impairing their specific quality as events. (pp. 364-65)

The notion of somehow becoming a vehicle for vision, rather than a manipulator of it, is what informs or even commands these poems, imparting an air of submission to the lines ungirt on the page, a certain droning resonance which, for the poet of so many rimes and sestinas, is a tremendous risk, but one knowingly taken. The critical poem in this third series, I think—critical in the sense that it defines the *crisis* of the poet's project, and also in the sense that it offers a conscious reflection on what Merwin has undertaken—is "Learning a Dead Language"; the "dead language" is of course unspecified, for it is not Latin or Greek but poetry itself, with its "grammar of return" and its "governing order," that is at issue. (p. 366)

In 1963, Merwin published his fifth book, *The Moving Target*, whose very title suggests, and whose contents enforce . . . a paroxysmal shift in the order of discourse lest the poet "not contain but be his own process of reversion." (pp. 371-72)

Merwin now invites the participation of silence as he once warded it off with all the words in his armory. There are six or seven generating nouns here, around which experience gathers in figures of force like filings in a magnetic field; once we perceive the web constituted by *lock* and *key*, *knife* and *mirror*, *clock* and *stone*, as well as the basic movements of *opening* and *closing*, we can track Merwin like a *moving target*, indeed—like the dangerous quarry he has become in his flight from the menagerie of mannerliness; if we read this book through not as a set of discrete poems but rather as a sequence of *sentences* in the full meaning of the word—not only a judgment and a "musical idea," but a discernment by the *senses*—as a notation of the central man who has cut away almost all the connective tissue of rationalization that made, once, his circulatory system so easy to trace, then there is no obscurity here, though the outrage, the brilliant abruptness is certainly stunning. . . . The whole burden of Merwin's discovery that "I'm not the fire" is the shift from a posture of mastery to one of submission or of resistance to submission ("to just sit down and let the horizon ride over me"); the corollary is that if I am not the fire, I am what the fire feeds on, and consequently there is a certain grandeur about the victimization:

> This must be what I wanted to be doing
> Walking at night between the two deserts,
> Singing.

It is a grammar of departure, now, that Merwin employs, without any of the comforting associations that had kept the world familiar; here *things*, natural objects, are seen or somehow acknowledged with such clarity that for the moment nothing else exists except the space around them. (p. 374)

In 1967, four years after *The Moving Target*, Merwin brought out his sixth book, *The Lice*. . . . [These] are all poems of a visionary reality, hallucinatory in their clarity of outline, their distinctness of detail. . . . The poems are entirely unpunctuated, and the virtuosity of their accessibility is great, for the continuities are extended beyond those of the last book, the voice sustained for longer units of expression; but (in keeping with Merwin's habit of articulating each of his modes in pairs of books) the work, whether wisps of a couple of lines and a single image, or deliberations of several pages and almost novelistic detail, are of the same inner coherence, the same outer necessity as those in *The Moving Target* ("May I bow to Necessity," he prays in "Wish," in the new book, "not / to her hirelings"). All the poems appear to be written from one and the same place where the poet has holed up, observant but withdrawn, compassionate but hopeless, isolated yet the more concerned, at least in quantity of reference, by the events of a public world. . . . It is as though the poet had decided, or determined, his own fate, which is one of dispossession and the *aigre* wisdom to be derived from it: "Now all my teachers are dead except silence / I am trying to read what the five poplars are writing / on the void." . . . Merwin is free ("I know I'm free / this is how I live / up here") to attend to his visionary task, his responsibility to others. . . . [There is] a detachment from the glamor of language as the canonical order had wielded it, from the glare of reality as the discursive impulse had submitted to it, and even from the gleam of vision as the latest web of fragmentary correspondences had invoked it. . . . [There] is a chill, almost a silence that lines his speech, and a difference about his notation of the world which I take as the final achievement of his vast mutations; it is the welcoming of his destitution among men in this book (as in the last it was the encompassing of his death in a private history) that sounds the special note of *The Lice*. . . . [Perhaps] what I have called coolness and detachment is merely the effect of a poetry which has altogether committed itself to that encounter with identity we call, at our best, reality; for no poetry, where it is good, transcends anything or is about anything: it is itself, discovering its own purpose and naming its own meaning. . . . (pp. 378-80)

> *Richard Howard, "W. S. Merwin," in his* Alone With America: Essays on the Art of Poetry in the United States Since 1950 *(copyright © 1965, 1966, 1967, 1968, 1969 by Richard Howard; reprinted by permission of*

Atheneum Publishers, New York), Atheneum, 1969, pp. 349-81.

W. S. Merwin's *Writings to an Unfinished Accompaniment* has a symptomatic title. Mostly his poems are the stuff poems are made of, but the makings stir: regrets, glimmers, nostalgias, religious adumbrations, in a bleak, somber, emptied yet resonant world, the pieces somnambulistically (druggedly?) adrift. He has a fine ear, and his verse includes and goes beyond short-line free verse; accents focus perceivings, yet his lines move long, away from heavy beats into syntactical repeatings and shifts. "A Door" ("What is dying") is a good example of the different motions unified. Excitement, fear, and a wide blankness of dissolvings. The poem concerns the lack of entry into one's secret self, death, eternity, silence, armies and lightings failing, yet opening into "the endless home." Is it of fear, gazing on the wastes of time and potentiality? Is it in favor of death as escape from the burden of consciousness? Does it offer hope of drifting into some blessed state? All three or none—how can one tell? If its themes are taken seriously, it raises religious questions the poetry does not face. How relate drifting emotion and insight to mysticism, salvation, good and evil? As poetry it is beautiful, but defective compared to Henry King or Henry Vaughan, who can be as strange and dark as Merwin and show a greater grasp of human experience and more comprehensible formings. Merwin is highly intelligent when he wishes to be, but it is not intelligence he cultivates. (pp. 397-98)

> *Paul Ramsey, in* Sewanee Review *(reprinted by permission of the editor; © 1974 by The University of the South), Spring, 1974.*

A running theme through all of W. S. Merwin's books is sight: vision: knowing: re-learning: discovering. Sometimes poems on these topics are too vaporous, they talk too much smoke, their lips are lost in fog, their words rise into clouds and disappear from the lens of consciousness. . . . If we retain anything it is retained under some tarpaulin in the basement, some storage spot that hasn't been touched since youth, a place upon which we do not focus yet which our minds nudge while turning over in their sleep.

Seemingly we have changed, we have become less, we have compromised and slowed, we have found in our acquisition of information and knowledge that life was more mysterious while we were innocent of all this mentalizing. Eyes are key symbols for Merwin—they are instrumental in keeping secret all that spoils life: either eyes betray us by seeing how burdened with varnish we have become, how common and removed from the electricity of spirited life, how remote we are from what we used to be, or else eyes are the talismans that bring us the crystal freshness of stepping into life almost for the first time amazed, in awe, loving with the full sting of love.

What returns us to that pristine state? What comes closest to levitating our consciousness to where it battles nothing but only flows with constant purity and affirmity—security and soundness—and unquestioned joy? What offers a wholesomeness inaccessible to adults? Perhaps the elements as only a child can know them; plus a mystification of reason. Not irrationality, but a left-handed throw of the dice, a despecifying that removes the packaging from around our Understanding. This is why, I believe, there is such a heavy reliance upon words such as "light", "stone", "sun", "tongue", "sleep", "wings", "silence", "shadow", "summer", "wind", "trees", "clouds", "mountains", "water", "fire", "animals", and "dark".

He shys away from making things definite. Premium is placed upon indistinctness, presumably to permit more possibilities, vagueness being a virtue almost in itself, something that suspends the unpleasant evidence of the ego's intervention in social commerce. Contingency, after all, is property of no one thing. Monolithic thoughts become sand moving across a desert. What was self-evident becomes conditional, relative—we come closer to dream, closer to literally extracting sunbeams from cucumbers.

On the other hand, [the poems in *Writings to an Unfinished Accompaniment*] are an ontological argument for the spirit living in all substance. They virtually convince us that they are the first scratchings upon our tabula rasa. So, escapism or not, they quietly work upon our being, teasing lost parts of our mind out of hiding.

Certainly there is an artlessness at play. Merwin is such an advanced stylist that he can make his poems appear, or so it seems, at the snap of his fingers, iron filings converging into words at the whisk of a magnet, a touch of fire under a sheet of paper slowly drawing words from the white grain. They come with such ease, they have certainty, there is little question that they belong, that they are the correct and only words possible. They seem no more deliberated upon and labored over than leaves floating down a creek. This pleases me, but I can't help wondering why Merwin has this concern to have his poems exist, as it were, so distinctly separate from the self. Can it be that he feels they carry more authority being "untainted by human ego"? That in sounding more from the "mind of God" they will be more readily accepted as truth? Pound insisted that "the purpose of writing is to reveal the subject". This Merwin does often with a single stroke, but in stepping out of his poems he makes it more difficult to "square with reality", something else that Pound insisted on. Then, too, Pound, in his later years, repudiated everything he said or wrote, which brings us back to Merwin's poems. What Merwin frequently does is seize upon a situation or a state *in* being that is regulated by the mind, then go directly to it, illustrating its dilemma by use of imagistic analogies—little stories with stones and silence and light playing the component parts of our mind's functioning. This is indeed advanced poetry. But because of its abstract pursuit, when Merwin does reveal his subject with a single stroke it characteristically takes on the guise of mystification and will appear recondite. In other words, Merwin doesn't so much square with tangible journalistic reality as he does with subjective reality as interpreted by the mind. It is his psychology that is translated into imagination—but more. Life and death are in the same hammock, for Merwin, with joy and sadness. Individual situations are ever being seen in complete context, all tenses applied, destiny working its way simultaneously through all channels of the mind, beginning begetting end, cause begetting effect, reason embodied in result.

Merwin starts with the result, then gives us the process, or at least something of the blueprint from which the result is derived. His poems activate the leit motif *behind* formal sight and comprehension. We know what they are saying, they confirm our suspicions. Through Merwin's effort we amend our own version of reality. The knowledge is there, all it takes is the guidance of his poems to make such knowledge salient. (pp. 176-78)

> *Douglas Blazek, in* Poetry (© *1974 by The Modern Poetry Association; reprinted by permission of the Editor of* Poetry), *June, 1974.*

W. S. Merwin writes about nameless, unseeable, untouchable, bodiless feelings that have no thrill of flesh, about spent echoes, lost light, the most rarefied, highflown absences. He is a spider at the spinet, playing sonatas for the deaf. Not human, a wall, a wind, a wolf, a water current reading the braille of the riverbottom. Hawksighted, he sees empty spaces birds have left in the blue. . . .

"Writings to an Unfinished Accompaniment" [is a collection of] poems caught out of the side of the eye, heard past the edge of hearing, just brushing the spirit's fingertips. Most are beyond meaning, but not meaningless. . . .

When I began reading Merwin his poems were butterflies that vanished from the net. Now I follow even his thinnest hints to their point of disappearance, and read them happily. Despite the often missing wingbolts, no aids are needed. (p. 20)

> *Donald Newlove, in* The Village Voice *(reprinted by permission of* The Village Voice; *copyright* © *The Village Voice, Inc., 1974), July 4, 1974.*

W. S. Merwin's . . . book (*Asian Figures*) is a serially-structured compendium of proverbs, aphorisms, and riddles from Japan, China, Korea, and other oriental countries, all "translated" by the poet from English translations into clean, hard, and often vulgar American-type language. Merwin's *Figures* are at once epigrammatic and lyric; the providential truth behind each aphorism is nicely undercut, and, at times, short-circuited by the use of odd juxtapositions and uncertain rhythms, so that the ultimate meaning of each, though familiar, is also elusive. . . . (p. 296)

As with any good aphorism, a little of this goes a long way. . . . [This] densely monotonous, white-on-white bible of thousands of proverbial figurations is the product of an intriguing concept, one that fascinates the reader even as it reduces him to a kind of IBM computer of home truths. (p. 297)

> *Gerrit Henry, in* Poetry (© *1974 by The Modern Poetry Association; reprinted by permission of the Editor of* Poetry), *August, 1974.*

From the beginning, Merwin has demonstrated a concern with reticence, with not speaking; *A Mask For Janus*, published in the Yale Series of Younger Poets (1952), consisted of ballads in archaic diction, songs, and mythic parables. Auden, who was then editor of the Series, noted in his introduction "The historical experience which is latent" in Merwin's poems: "By translating these feelings into mythical terms, the poet is able to avoid what a direct treatment could scarcely have avoided, the use of names and events which will probably turn out not to have been the really significant ones." What Auden meant was that these poems had been composed in a language devoid of immediate social content, abstract and imprecise. Their ornate, peculiar diction, an absence of all qualities distinguishing the modern, a derivative, self-conscious voice: this was the result of Merwin's decision to "avoid what a direct treatment could scarcely have avoided," and it has plagued his writing ever since.

Even so, an intelligence comparable to that of Wallace Stevens, though lacking Stevens' enviable grace, was at work. . . . Rhetorical and stylized, Merwin's earliest poems conformed to the procedures of the English poetic tradition, even borrowing inversions ("The frame that was my devotion/ And my blessing was"), words ("in priestly winter bide"), and characters (huntsmen, lords, and kings); while almost no traces of this lyrical, delicate style remain in Merwin's later collections, there are undeniable resemblances between what he was writing then and a mode that owes less to some identifiable period than to the language of English literature. (pp. 72-3)

Idiosyncratic in his themes, concerned less with a private self than with ill-defined motifs that wavered between the pastoral and metaphysics, Merwin [in his middle period] had mastered the techniques of writing and then amplified their truths. It was not until the publication of *The Drunk in the Furnace*, though, that his own temperament became visible, his Being-in-the-world; voyages at sea, motifs of loss, and the phenomenon of surviving death, witnessing that moment of collective disaster when "our cries were swallowed up and all hands lost," had become obsessive concerns. In several poems, such as "Bell Buoy", "Sea Monster", "Cape Dread", and "Sailor Ashore", the sea mirrors and exemplifies our own alien condition; its meanings are interpreted as allegorical; a ship leaving port "has put/ All of disaster between us: a gulf/ Beyond reckoning. It begins where we are." And the closing lines of "The Bones" recall Kafka's parable of "Infinite Hope, but not for us". . . . Merwin's tacit longing is to live among whatever he names, entering the world again in some other, elemental form. His is the chore of "giving/ Shapes" to things, altering their appearance, transmuting them, just as our presence in the natural world enacts a sea-change on what surrounds us.

In opposition to this eternal, devastating sea, imposing in its immense and silent depths, is urban life; this other solitude, arriving in pool halls, wretched hotels, and old men's homes, evades "the real dark" of existence, concealed in a vast, incomprehensible universe. (p. 75)

The Moving Target . . . announced Merwin's departure from the disciplined versification and controlled narrative style of his earlier collections. Sprawling, unrhymed lines, idiomatic speech and the notation of trivial thoughts, irrational similes ("I bring myself back from the streets that open like long/ Silent laughs"): there was in these unusual poems an oratorical "I" whose abrasive complaints echoed Eliot's dramatic monologues. . . . Or the speaker's was a disembodied voice, addressing some unknown Other, or talking out loud; irrational comparisons, partial syllepses ("Night, I am/ As old as pain and I have/ No other story."), and puns proliferated, while the repeated use of animism ("the horizon/ Climbs down from its tree") imbued the poems with a Surrealist confusion. . . . [An] absence of distinction between words and things . . . lies behind *The Moving Target*, where Merwin's belief is in the similitude, even synonymity, of image and object.

His departure from the discursive revelation of objects becomes more noticeable in the closing poems; interruptions of thought, intrusions of unconscious mind are more pronounced, until in "The Crossroads of the World etc." all punctuation has been omitted, except a question mark that ends the poem. After that, there is none in this volume, or in the two that have succeeded it. Line breaks appear to be random, the words themselves are arbitrary, verging on hysteria. . . . (pp. 76-7)

Merwin in his later poetry . . . still resists the real significance of what he practises; the disruption of language is no more than a device in *The Lice* (1967) and *The Carrier of Ladders* (1970). Monotonous, interminable, self-imitative, each poem exudes unbearable exhaustion; none supports a close analysis. (p. 78)

The Miner's Pale Children exploited a genre that extends from Baudelaire through Rimbaud and Mallarmé to Francis Ponge in France, that shares affinities with Lichtenberg and imitates Kafka: the prose poem. These pieces, less fiction than parable, explore an odd region where events are unexplained, where animals talk among themselves, where hope has been "a calm lake in early spring, white because the sky above it was the color of milk." Like the fables of Donald Barthelme, or Beckett's *stories and texts for nothing*, Merwin's episodic, elusive stories exist in a dimension of the mysterious, spoken through some unidentified voice. The language is dense and detailed, but about nothing, or, to be more specific, about the problem of nothingness. . . . [In] these prose pieces, the lessons . . . could be: to write is to determine the world's actual properties. (p. 80)

> James Atlas, "Diminishing Returns: The Writings of W. S. Merwin" (copyright © 1974 by James Atlas), in American Poetry Since 1960: Some Critical Perspectives, edited by Robert B. Shaw, Dufour, 1974, pp. 69-81.

*   *   *

MICHENER, James A(lbert)   1907-

Michener is an American writer of epic-like works of documentary fiction and fictional documentary. He is still best known for *Hawaii*. (See also *Contemporary Authors*, Vols. 5-8, rev. ed.)

Within this amazing super-novel [*The Source*], which contains a prodigious variety of narratives comprising an integrated whole, there are stories worthy of the talents of Sholem Asch, I. B. Singer, Bernard Malamud, and other "classic" interpreters of the Jewish experience. There are innumerable philosophical discussions worthy of our most talented moralists. And there is also, of course, a certain amount of trite and contrived storytelling, but this does not by any means obscure the high merits of the book. . . .

True, *The Source* does not "define the sensibility of an age," as the greatest novels are supposed to do. But it does provide an invaluable examination of the circumstances surrounding the origin and development of Judaism, and it enhances this with an extended consideration of the parallel developments of Christianity and Islam and relations between adherents of the three faiths. . . .

The social and religious (and therefore political) problems of present-day Israel are cunningly dealt with . . ., but interesting as are some of the dialogues on the what, why, and where of Jews in Israel and the U.S., the portion as a whole does not represent Michener at his best. . . . Far superior are many of the tales relating to different levels of the dig, each having its own appropriate archeological symbol. . . . In the later-level sections Michener rises to lyric heights and seems utterly possessed by his story, and as this is transmitted directly to the reader the impact of *The Source* is enormous. . . .

Throughout *The Source* Michener, true to form, has been unusually responsive to possibilities for detailing violence and large-scale bloodshed, and the Crusades (in which innumerable Christians were *also* massacred by the Germanic barbarians) offer him a first-rate opportunity. No summary can do justice to this ghastly but compelling section, nor to what is probably the finest section of all, "The Saintly Men of Safed". . . . Here, in his picture of the Spanish Inquisition and the remarkable refugees who came to Safed, a few miles from the site of Makor, Michener has produced a document that might have been written by a Jewish writer of the first rank bent on awakening his people to their glorious heritage.

The crux of Michener's book? Despite all of the age-old persecutions and exterminations of the Jews, in the Galilee and in other parts of the world, Jews hang on somehow and remain attached to their ancient land. "Something was going on here that the history books did not tell us." Related to this is Michener's idea, advanced through Cullinane and debated by Eliav and Tabari, that the Jews' moral right to Israel is based on custodianship. However controversial that might be, it is hard to dispute Eliav's reflective summation, at the conclusion of the book, of the Jewish concept of God:

> We seek God so earnestly, Eliav reflected,
> not to find Him but to discover ourselves.

> *Samuel Irving Bellman, "Tales of Ancient Israel," in* Congress Bi-Weekly, *June 14, 1965, p. 18.*

Colorado was admitted to the Union in 1876 and therefore is known as the Centennial State. You all know what is going to happen in 1976. Can Mr. Michener's subject and his title [*Centennial*] be a happenstance? Shall we give him the benefit of the doubt? Or do we sense a certain cunning, does a mote of dust from the fields of Philistia irritate our inner eye?

If you think that Mr. Michener is going to begin with Christopher Columbus or Eric the Red, or with those arrivistes from Europe and the British Isles; even if you think he's going to begin with the buffalo and the Asian hunters who followed them, you have another think coming, and another one, and many more thereafter. No. He begins billions of years before there is hide or hair of *homo sapiens*. Indeed, he begins at the *beginning* when the North American continent is still under water. . . .

Many a long year and many a long page later we get down to brass tacks and start winning the West. (p. 1)

We make treaties with Indians and break them; we are scalped by Indians and we scalp them back; we give the Indians Taos lightning and we drink good whiskey ourselves; we go to pow-wows. We bring Texas longhorns to Colorado and Wyoming and we are forever and a day on the trail; we slaughter the buffalo; we trap beaver; we go to Pike's Peak and placer-pan for gold; we mine silver; we learn to irrigate and become truck farmers. We come down with and die of cholera. We die of rattler's bites, of gunshot wounds, of rattler's bites, of amputation of limbs by tomahawk, of rattler's bites. We eat a lot of jerky and sourdough biscuits [for which Michener supplies recipes]. The buffalo stampede; the cattle stampede. There are awful blizzards and awful invasions of locusts.

The sheepmen come in; they and the cattlemen start a-feuding and a-killing. The Iron Horse comes in. Dudes from Europe shoot the buffalo from train windows. Paleontologists arrive to look at fossils and prehistoric bones. The bones of the now nearly extinct buffalo are collected for fertilizer. Mexicans lounge around in saloons in Denver during the winter and eat hot tamales. Cowboys driving the cattle up from Texas sit around the campfire at night and sing cowboy songs and tell tall tales. Colorado is admitted to the Union. . . . We scrounge our way through the Depression and through the devastating dust storms of the early 1930s. We enter World War II.

Now in the 1970s, we have ski resorts; we have a western movie festival in Cheyenne, Wyoming, showing John Wayne in his finest roles. We are concerned about endangered species. . . .

Mr. Michener has written another book [a pamphlet, actually,] which, however, is not for sale [but is available free to libraries and schools]. It is called *About Centennial: Some Notes on the Novel.* In it, he tells us about his writing devices. Sometimes he is asked whether he ever uses himself as the model for a character. "Not really. But in this novel the grizzled old bison Rufous comes rather close to representing the author." Now when Rufous was in his prime during one rutting season, "for no apparent reason, (he) began suddenly charging at cottonwood trees along the riverbank. . . . The next day as he was walking idly toward the herd he felt an uncontrollable compulsion to throw himself on the ground, twisting and turning in the dust a dozen times until he was laden with sand. Then he rose, urinated heavily in the wallow and threw himself into it again, smearing the muddy urine over his head and body as if to announce to the world, 'When you smell that smell, remember. It belongs to Rufous.'" What an extraordinary self-portrait!

Ars longa, vita brevis est. In the case of *Centennial*, the opposite obtains. (p. 2)

> *Jean Stafford, "How the West Was Lost," in* Book World—The Washington Post (© The Washington Post), *September 1, 1974, pp. 1-2.*

Michener and monumentalism are no strangers; in size, scope, and chutzpah, *Centennial* is every bit the equal of his previous blockbusters, *Hawaii* and *The Source*, not to mention Mt. Rushmore. (How long ago and far away that fresh and lively first novel out of World War II, *Tales of the South Pacific*, now seems.) . . .

Counting animals (a dinosaur, a prehistoric horse, bison, sheep, locusts), vegetables (grass, corn, wheat) and minerals (the Rockies, gold and silver, and, if one employs the term loosely to include elemental forces, the river, glaciers, blizzard, drought, even mass migration urgings to Siberia and back), the book's characters number in the hundreds. Among the many things Michener is not hesitant about is anthropomorphism. My own favorite character is an aging but sweet-natured female diplodocus, who, lacking proper molars and strong digestive juices, swallows large round stones to help churn and grind the food in her stomach. Her exact location in time, however, is uncertain even to Michener; she lived 136 million years ago on one page, 140 million on another, and 160 million according to the flap copy. Humans, each with a story—there are about 120 identifiable plots in *Centennial*—appear very late in time but fairly early in the book. (There is a limit, after all, to how much a best seller can focus on other species.) So, following Lame Beaver, come, in fairly quick succession, white trappers, mountain men, Oregon trail homesteaders like the Zendts, cattle-ranchers and cowboys, fortune hunters, actors, politicians, industrialists, real-estate operators, ecologists, and our professor. It is all quite neatly done: one sinks into this book in the same way that it sinks into the history of a small patch of ground. One can also pop back out of it at any time; the prose is stolid and solid, and not what you'd call entrapping or bewitching.

Three important things are going for this book, and make peripheral and impertinent both serious fault-finding and incipient giggles. One is the momentum of the vast conception; it does carry one along. (The movement of the book is both vertical, into and up from the past, and horizontal—the endless changes on the face of the land, the travels and migrations of people and animals, passing through, staying awhile, settling, moving on.) Another is the sheer bulk of information that the book imparts—once upon a time a central purpose of the novel. The third is the sense of sharing that Michener constantly evokes. The subject of *Centennial* is our country, our history. If nobody else will throw it a party, Michener will, and everybody's invited in for a piece of the cake. You don't throw stones at this kind of book—though some grinding of same might have helped the old digestion.

> *Eliot Fremont-Smith, "A Piece of Cake," in* New York Magazine *(© 1974 by NYM Corp.; reprinted by permission of* New York Magazine *and Eliot Fremont-Smith), September 2, 1974, p. 62.*

James A. Michener is the literary world's Cecil B. De-Mille, a popular novelist with an awesome audience for his epic narratives, an unpretentious, solid craftsman. . . .

As with his previous best-sellers "Hawaii" and "The Source," Michener burrows back into prehistory to build a story that unfolds with the inevitability of geologic strata. [In *Centennial*] his theme is the settlement of the American West as focused in the fictional town of Centennial, Colo., whose growth is researched by a college history professor, for a special issue of US magazine.

Like DeMille, Michener stocks his horse-cum-soap-opera with scores of characters, some of them believable . . ., others as thin as the air at the summit of the Rockies. (p. 82)

Michener is one of the most didactic of novelists, cramming his books full of lessons in geology, anthropology, history and sociology. The novel's stated theme may be the settling

of the West, but its underlying concerns are the relationships of men to the land—and to each other. (pp. 82-3)

The book has its flaws and is swollen like a river in spring. Yet Michener manages to make his new novel readable and, yes, likable even while he dispenses a sugar-coated historical pill. . . . (p. 83)

> *Arthur Cooper, "Eohippus Opera," in* Newsweek *(copyright 1974 by Newsweek, Inc.; all rights reserved; reprinted by permission), September 16, 1974, pp. 82-6.*

As a writer Michener has many attributes. He tells a good story. The massiveness of his research is impressive. His reportage of history is lively and often persuasive. He holds dear, as he made explicit in his *Kent State*, all the more generous, the more commendable liberal attitudes. We find him sharply opposed to the prejudicial rigidities so prevalent in what he calls, in *Kent State*, Middle America, of which, as he suggests, the West has its full share. The hospitality of his mind, his genuine sympathy for history's victims of prejudice and bigotry emerge clearly in *Centennial*.

But somehow Michener falls short. His weakness, as I see it, and sadly enough, is his art. He is history's journalist; he is not an artist. For all his recording of the Western scene he fails to *evoke* in his reader any sense, any genuine feel for this most dramatic of countrysides. His style is bereft of nuance, his diction shorn of any fringes of suggestiveness. He has no verbal equivalents for states of mind and feeling. He favors his character Elly Zendt who keeps a journal on her way west and who is admittedly one of Michener's better creations, yet he sees her coming close to the ideal of unimaginative Germanic historians, "reporting things as they actually happened." A general lack of subtlety of imagination is manifest, too, in his characterization that often sheers toward types and the melodramatic. There are no truly memorable characters in Michener because he makes no plunges into the recesses of the mind; he never explores nor brings to light the myriad paradoxes of human personality. Perhaps his scope is too vast; his effort is horizontal and hence clings to the flat. Or perhaps his self-admitted tendency toward didacticism forces him to say it out straight rather than depend on the obliqueness of dramatization. The last chapter in *Centennial* is a tract, a polemic, undoubtedly deserved, against small-mindedness and vulgarity but a polemic nevertheless, and Paul Garrett a poorly disguised spokesman for the author. (pp. 21-2)

> *Stuart James, "Stately American Novel," in* The New Republic *(reprinted by permission of* The New Republic; *© 1974 by The New Republic, Inc.), September 21, 1974, pp. 21-2.*

Michener's manifest love of the land he writes about can be moving. The almost hubristic sweep of his conception is impressive. He has a busy curiosity about family dynasties and bloodlines. He writes especially well about the technique of things: how Indians chipped their arrowheads, what breeds of grass and cattle best survived in the inhospitable prairie. He is also one of the few modern novelists who order their works with a sense of civic conscience, here notably in his discussion of Indians and of the depradations of commerce. . . . *Centennial* is indeed a monumental birthday present and in its way, a generously entertaining one. As an epic vision of America, however, it may suffer from a familiar Michener mistake—erring on the side of the grandiose.

> *Lance Morrow, "Happy Birthday, America," in* Time *(reprinted by permission from* Time, The Weekly Newsmagazine; *copyright Time Inc.), September 23, 1974, p. 96.*

Like a modern Noah, James Michener has not so much written as constructed *Centennial*, a vast and overcrowded Ark of a book designed to preserve for posterity representative forms of life from the American past that Mr. Michener believes are worth saving. A commendable motive and especially welcome in an age devoted to perfecting disposability. The results are another matter, since Mr. Michener has felt compelled to supply not merely the Ark but the Deluge as well. Whatever strengths *Centennial* may have as a novel are washed away in a surging torrent of information and instruction which ultimately drowns the interest of even the most determined and sympathetic of readers.

Good storytelling commands the narrator to begin at the beginning. Mr. Michener, in a burst of literal-mindedness, takes this to mean somewhere just this side of Genesis as he lectures lengthily and learnedly on the geochronology of the mythical town of Centennial. . . . So lavishly is Centennial's geohistory detailed that it is page 112 before the year 9268 B.C. is reached and the first human character, prehistoric man in the form of a flint-knapper, makes his appearance. Meanwhile, however, the knapper has been preceded by prototypical specimens, in their correct evolutionary order, of the diplodocus, the eohippus, the bison, the beaver, the rattlesnake, and the eagle, all anthropomorphized to a degree that would make Uncle Remus wince. . . .

Michener tries to systematize history by projecting prototypes. Unfortunately for his purposes, while the technique may work for geologic time and zoologic evolution, it is not applicable to human beings in all their rich contrariety and never-duplicating complexity. In short, Michener's characters are victims of his urge to instruct. They are cartoon-strip figures whose effect is to illustrate rather than illuminate, and it is on this fundamental weakness that *Centennial* founders. When it is impossible to tell one good guy from the next; when the bad guys are equally indistinguishable one from another; and when both could be beavers or bison for that matter, it is plain that as fine fiction, *Centennial* offers bulk but not much nourishment. . . .

If *Centennial* was intended to convey anything beyond [a] stupefying mass of incidental information, it is that the forces which shaped the contours and the character of the land it celebrates, and the values and skills developed by the men who first knew it, merit our respectful attention. True and unarguable. But half a million words seems an ironically excessive number for what is essentially a conservationist's message.

> *Rene Kuhn Bryant, "Michener's Deluge," in* National Review *(© National Review, Inc., 1974; 150 East 35th St., New York, N.Y. 10016), November 22, 1974, p. 1365.*

James Michener's whole interest is in straightforward narrative, and *Centennial* takes up so much shelf space be-

cause it is nearly an anthology of a dozen separate but related novels. Each of them has convincing characters, well visualised action scenes, thematic concerns. A third of the way into it, the idea of reading a novel about activities from four billion BC to 1974 on a portion of the earth's surface now housing a small Colorado town actually seems plausible. The early chapters—mini-novels, really—about dinosaurs and bison tend to be overcute in that almost unavoidable way which emerges from conflating animal 'personalities' with strong story lines. But after these chapters, Lame Beaver strolls onstage, and the whole long story of Indians and settlers and hunters and cattlemen unreels.

To make this preposterous venture work (and much more, to make it actually engrossing) requires narrative skills of the highest order. Michener is an easy target, and his huge popularity makes him an almost embarrassing author to like —he's always been the epitome of the serious-minded, rather plodding middlebrow novelist. But I would argue that he has a deep, nearly infallible instinct for the mechanics of fiction, and something like a genius for skating near enough to sentimentality to tap wide areas of emotion, without ever falling in. (pp. 794-95)

Michener [has] kept his integrity by virtue of his great curiosity about human beings, his moral liveliness and his felt responsibility to his own fantasies. If those virtues seem elephantine, well, *Centennial* is a very friendly elephant of a book. (p. 795)

> *Peter Straub, in* New Statesman *(© 1974 The Statesman & Nation Publishing Co. Ltd.), November 29, 1974.*

* * *

MILOSZ, Czeslaw 1911-

A Lithuanian-born poet now living in the United States, Milosz wrote for the Polish underground in Warsaw during World War II then fled to Paris. There he wrote *The Captive Mind*, a prose work, in which he explained the effects of Communism on creativity. He is considered a major poet in Poland and writes primarily in Polish. (See also *Contemporary Authors*, Vols. 1-4, rev. ed.)

Unless they are ideologists, and unless they are low on essential intelligence, poets perhaps inevitably write of the great public events of the world, of matters of state, in a tone which if it isn't ironic sounds rather like it. Milosz keeps the balance well and honorably between the evil and the good of the world, if at times he seems to be dipping a thumb lightly into the tenderer scale. When people are ready to assume that versified professions of universal compassion and protests against generalized tyranny are in themselves signs of nobility of mind, then they are likely to believe that irony in poetry is a sign of meanness of spirit. Fear of this may account for Milosz's slightly comic warnings and for the occasional deliberate-sounding paean in his later work. . . .

[It] is rare for Milosz to be portentous or solemn. Neither is he wittingly or unwittingly "confessional": a mode of mixing the public and the private whereby, though the result may be distasteful, no one cares to express a dislike for it in public. Frequently—something I have forgotten to mention—Milosz is extremely amusing: an epithet not to be used dismissively, or even lightly. He has one great advantage, at least poetically speaking, and one great quality: his wounds are not self-inflicted ones, and he does not wear them on his sleeve.

D. J. Enright, "Child of Europe," in The New York Review of Books (reprinted with permission from The New York Review of Books; copyright © 1974 NYREV, Inc.), April 4, 1974, p. 29.

Milosz's poems are compact of judgment, and in two senses of the word: discernment and condemnation. . . .

Milosz is clearly one of James's "people on whom nothing is lost." Reading these poems one has the impression that all his life experience is constantly available to him. This has the result that much of the book is what one suite of poems is called, an "album of dreams." The dream-work fuses the last waking thought with shards of distant or buried experience, foreshortens and warps the space-time of the poem, resulting in a sort of meta-tense, the everlasting Now that came into being with Milosz (and thanks to these poems will outlast him). . . .

Milosz's poetic voice is defined by two extremes: stark parataxis, each line a sentence, with no subordination, on the one hand, and on the other a skillfully controlled long surging period that gathers force from line to line. (p. 37)

Clarence Brown, in The Village Voice (reprinted by permission of The Village Voice; copyright © The Village Voice, Inc., 1974), May 2, 1974.

Although [Czeslaw Milosz] is considered by many to be the greatest living Polish poet, his writing is scarcely known here, aside from one prose work, "The Captive Mind," which appeared at the height of the McCarthy era, when it was received as simply another anti-Communist testimonial. But "The Captive Mind" is far more than a work of political invective; it is an elegy for destroyed values and, indirectly, an autobiography. In it, Milosz argues that Marxism had not been a belief for Polish intellectuals so much as a form of escape from the anguish of personal identity. Twenty years later, the book remains one of the finest ever written about the lure and the inner cost of totalitarian ideology. It is also a key to Milosz's conviction that poetry must be a moral as well as an esthetic discipline, that poetry must translate the anguish of personal experience into a framework of values which defend against "skepticism" and "sterile anger" and thereby defend against the lure of ideology. . . .

[On] the evidence of ["Selected Poems"] Czeslaw Milosz seems one of the few genuinely important poets writing today. His "Selected Poems" is a carefully constructed book, spanning the work of 40 years. Its central portion is devoted to poems written during and shortly after World War II, when Milosz was a freedom-fighter in occupied Warsaw. Its first and last sections contain the poems of exile, among them many of the finest he has written. (p. 6)

Although Milosz is a poet of many subjects, the experience of loss casts shadows across all his work and amounts to an interpretation of life itself. . . .

To be born, for Milosz, is to join the diaspora of the living, expelled into the world of strangers, taught to speak a stranger's tongue. It is also to learn the utterly gratuitous power of the world to crush the life it nurtures. One hears, in the background, the experience of the adult whose world has collapsed without meaning. The diaspora of steel and brutality; the hand which strangles absurdly or, equally absurdly, caresses.

Milosz differs from modernist poets like Yeats or Stevens who erected private systems of belief because they no longer trusted the solidity of traditional values. Milosz's language asserts the continuity of his culture simply and unself-consciously. Although he uses the elliptical techniques of modern poetry, there are frequent references in his work to the Bible, Polish history and Christian morality. Perhaps this is a special form of militancy on the part of Milosz, resembling the discreet militancy of Russian poets like Pasternak, Mandelstam or Brodsky. Against the strident claims of an ideology that pretends to wipe clean the slate of history in order to create new values and a "new man," against the discontinuity of war and exile, the poet offers a modest voice, speaking an old language.

But this language contains the resources of centuries. Speaking it, one speaks with a voice more than personal. In its idiom, exile is not simply an autobiographical but a Christian experience. Milosz's power lies in his ability to speak with this larger voice without diminishing the urgency that drives his words. . . .

[Since] Milosz settled in the United States, an important new element has entered his poetry. The images of Poland that provide nostalgic substance in his later work are answered by a counterpoint of speedways and white California cities, by images of Point Lobos and San Francisco, above all by the interrogating presence of the American wilderness. These more recent poems are among the finest Milosz has written. In them, he carries on the same crucial argument about the limits of human nature that towers starkly and simply in the poems written during the war. But his adversary is different now. It is not the faceless abyss of Nazism, or the leaden routines of totalitarian existence; it is American innocence. It is the American belief that a life without limits is possible, and necessary. . . .

Milosz reminds us that animals undoubtedly killed their prey in Eden, too, that our "purest" pleasures may be a form of self-deception, "an artifice of cunning self-love." Without the acknowledgment of human limits—what Christianity calls original sin—man is all too easily captivated by the devils within who "play catch with hunks of bloody meat." (p. 7)

Paul Zweig, in The New York Times Book Review (© 1974 by The New York Times Company; reprinted by permission), July 7, 1974.

Even though he has a great many other interests, Czeslaw Milosz regards himself primarily as a poet. He has also written prose, some of which, like The Captive Mind, has been translated into many languages. . . .

Although Selected Poems focuses primarily on the last ten years, it goes back several decades and includes poems written in Nazi-occupied Poland. . . .

In intellectual scope this collection is breathtaking. In displaying the poet's originality and freshness of imagination, the poems glitter in all colors of the rainbow. There is an underlying unity of style, but there are hardly two poems alike. Milosz never strikes exactly the same chord. In 1944 in Warsaw, the poet felt that his poetry was "like an insult to suffering humanity." A short poem, "Gift," sings high notes of almost angelic bliss. Perhaps the most representative of the poet's irony are the opening lines of his "Counsels": "If I were in the place of young poets / (quite a place, whatever the generation might think) / I would prefer not to say that the earth is a madman's dream." (p. 156)

> *George J. Maciuszko, in* Books Abroad *(copyright 1975 by the University of Oklahoma Press), Vol. 49, No. 1, Winter, 1975.*

A political refugee who sought asylum in America, Milosz is considered one of the best contemporary Polish poets. More lyrical than an Auden, he combines a somewhat didactic though just analysis of modern ideological hell with a moist, earthy Slavic tenderness. His scrupulous insights into recent history with which he is all too familiar shape themselves into accurate and acrid epigrams. One may imagine him cultivating his California garden, almost in bliss, and yet aware of how untrue and dull our moral landscape has become. (pp. lx-lxi)

> Virginia Quarterly Review *(copyright, 1975, by the* Virginia Quarterly Review, The University of Virginia), *Vol. 51, No. 2 (Spring, 1975).*

* * *

MOJTABAI, A(nn) G(race)   1938-

Ms Mojtabai is an American novelist.

"Mundome"—the title is a grammatically impossible juxtaposition of the Latin words for "world" and "self"—is an extraordinarily pure novel, pure as the contained landscapes inside glass paperweights in which the snow falls endlessly on minute figures, preserved from dust and decay by the absence of air. It is a novel singularly free from designs upon the reader; it tells its story, but unlike the similarly hypnotic Ancient Mariner it appends no sermon. Like its central characters, it asks only that it be allowed to express itself without being meddled with. . . .

"Mundome" is a gem of a book: small, brilliant, cut with lapidary precision, and static. It is a novel in which little happens but much is said, and it is said remarkably well. . . . The writing is flawless, by which I mean that moments of clumsiness and disbelief are not allowed to intrude. A. G. Mojtabai writes like an angel, but as a knowledge of angels may suggest, her book is somewhat bloodless; it is a little like a sampler, an illustration of mastered techniques. Flourishes of language embellish the central characters, but neither engages our sympathy, and each would scorn to try: to do so, in this vacuum of a world, would be to risk contamination. (p. 6)

> *Margaret Atwood, in* The New York Times Book Review *(© 1974 by The New York Times Company; reprinted by permission), May 12, 1974.*

[*Mundome* is a] first novel of extraordinary originality and purity which beautifully, if often obscurely, portrays a world of tenuous human connections and lost meanings. On the surface, it is about a man, Richard Henken, a nine-to-five archivist at a large New York library (his specialty is "ephemera and fugitive material"), who spends all his free time caring for his mentally disturbed sister. . . . In the course of the book, most of what Richard thinks is exposed as illusion; his distinctions between healthy and unhealthy, good and bad, and even sane and insane are constantly mocked or deflated by his sister's childlike responses to the world. As the book progresses, we see that, in fact, he shares many of her perceptions. More than that, he admires them, and longs to leave the "real" world and enter hers. In the hopeless, damaged relationship of the sister and brother, the author creates not only a kind of schizophrenic cosmology but a brilliant, challenging fictional form. (pp. 108-09)

Mrs. Mojtabai's language is stark, playful. The terrain is something like Nabokov's, something like Beckett's, but without Nabokov's sensuality and without Beckett's lyricism. One misses both qualities. The book's single failing is that it mirrors dysfunction and disaffection somewhat too exactly. One feels pressed into a black, glittering cave that offers almost no air or light—nothing but darkness. (p. 109)

> The New Yorker *(© 1974 by The New Yorker Magazine, Inc.), June 3, 1974.*

A reviewer for whom I have the highest respect has described A. G. Mojtabai's *Mundome* as "Nabokovian." That did not occur to me while first reading the novel, but in large measure it is accurate. Mrs. Mojtabai . . . does write with a touch of the Nabokovian manner, and her novel is very much a psychological puzzle of the sort he likes to play. But I have little affection for the work of the Master, finding much of it to be cold-hearted and self-indulgent—and neither of those weaknesses bothers *Mundome*. (p. 540)

It is a real pleasure to encounter fiction that is written with the intelligence and command of language that A. G. Mojtabai has brought to *Mundome*. Madness, need it be said, has been widely used as a metaphor in postwar fiction, and by no means only by American writers, but rarely has it been as effectively—indeed devastatingly—employed as in this novel. *Mundome* is brief, enigmatic, and fascinating. It is not easy fiction to read because it constantly challenges the reader's own imagination, but meeting the challenge is immensely rewarding. (pp. 541-42)

> *Jonathan Yardley, in* Sewanee Review *(reprinted by permission of the editor; © 1974 by The University of the South), Summer, 1974.*

* * *

MOORCOCK, Michael   1939-

Moorcock is an award-winning British writer and editor of fantasy and science fiction. (See also *Contemporary Authors*, Vols. 45-48.)

He only does it to annoy. Or desires to make your flesh creep. Or tilts at windmills. Michael Moorcock does all those, and more. Reading him is rather like trying to drink tea from a sieve; one gains very little from the experiment. . . .

[His] works are filled with merry pranks, japes and wheezes that appear to be aimed at entertaining nine-year-old mentalities, rather than saying anything of significance or that has not already been written.

Moorcock's writings should perhaps be taken in small doses, if at all. Certainly after a few pages this particular reviewer suffered mental indigestion. Presumably the fault is in me, for other reviewers have praised Mr Moorcock highly. This I can understand in part, for underneath all the baroque ornamentation in these books there is clear evidence of a considerable talent, struggling to express itself. (p. 80)

One must admire Mr Moorcock for his industry, although the sum of it all is, for me, a nothingness. Let us hope that soon he will avoid self-indulgence as a writer and produce a work that says something, for he clearly could do so, accepting the necessary discipline. (p. 81)

> *John Boland, in* Books and Bookmen *(© copyright John Boland 1972), October, 1972.*

The Oak and the Ram has no claim whatever to be considered SF. [It is] "Volume the Second of the Chronicle of Prince Corum and the Silver Hand" ["Volume the First" was *The Bull and the Spear*] and hovers in a pastiche-like world of *Beowulf*, Arthurian romance and Celtic legend. All the characters seem to be kings or archdruids, and finding one's way through their names is like being lost with a Hebridean road map. The story itself is opaque, but seems to be about endless sword-fights in a damp climate. Oddly enough, . . . it is quite well written. But after a page or two the whole thing becomes a welter of dirks and stallions, baying hounds and the clash of byrnies. The lovely Medhbh wears a smock of blue samite and the grim stones of Craig Dôn resound to harps and war-axes. After 168 pages the great sword Retaliator is hung up to await the third volume. Frankly, the whole folksy, heroey, legendy, whimsy sub-Tolkien world should be loaded into a coracle and pushed off the Western Isles; it would not be long before the wailing died away. (p. 1377)

> The Times Literary Supplement *(© Times Newspapers Ltd., 1973; reproduced by permission), November 9, 1973.*

["Breakfast in the Ruins," a] shrill, ambitious novel, will remind readers of "Candide" and "Mother Courage." Its pages are laden with caustics and ironies and parodies and bloody scenes of destruction. British writer Michael Moorcock, the author of some 40 books, is generally associated with science fiction. The present work is a dazzling historical fantasy with one glimpse into the future. . . .

The rigid structuring of the chapters allows the reader to prepare for shocks, so the earlier chapters are the most effective. . . . But it is the author's poisonous imagination, sense of humor, and professional attack that propel the book forward. If you are looking to replenish your supply of hope for man, look elsewhere. This is meant to be scathing and it is. (p. 38)

> *John Deck, in* The New York Times Book Review *(© 1974 by The New York Times Company; reprinted by permission), May 19, 1974.*

I have never understood the cult of Michael Moorcock. I know he is very big in Notting Hill Gate among drugsters

and students from Essex University, but I have remained untouched. This may well have been callow ignorance, since I was impressed by at least two thirds of *The Sword and the Stallion*. It opens emptily enough as Moorcock proceeds to embroider a banal little story about wars and rumours of wars with a diction which is unpronounceable but which must exist somewhere between Welsh, Icelandic and demotic Greek. . . .

But, as soon as Moorcock forgets about his humanoids and their blank solial detail, the narrative takes off on a flight of consciousness which left me breathless if not bowed. . . . And when Moorcock goes in pursuit of his vision, his prose has a cadence and a simplicity which remind me of some of the more notorious passages of Malory. . . .

I do not understand why Moorcock wants to bother himself and his readers with tales of battles and human passions when he can construct a prose of such imaginative strength. Malory was able to sustain it for some twenty books, and there is no reason why Moorcock should not devote himself to the rediscovery of those forbidding depths. (p. 182)

> *Peter Ackroyd, in* The Spectator *(© 1974 by The Spectator; reprinted by permission of The Spectator), August 10, 1974.*

The second in a projected three-volume series called "The Dancers at the End of Time," "The Hollow Lands" is buoyed up by the same agile imagination which made "An Alien Heat" such a splendid, sturdy bubble of science fiction. One such novel may appear from time to time, two are difficult, but three, when the third is issued, will be almost impossible. Yet one's confidence in Mr. Moorcock is strengthened with every page, for he is secure in his abilities and his "end of time" is a glittering, seductive environment. (p. lii)

> Virginia Quarterly Review *(copyright, 1975, by the* Virginia Quarterly Review, *The University of Virginia), Vol. 51, No. 2 (Spring, 1975).*

*　　*　　*

MOORE, Brian 1921-

Moore, an Irish-born Canadian novelist living in New York, is widely acclaimed for his sensitive delineation of the inner struggles of his frail and luckless characters. (See also *Contemporary Authors*, Vols. 1-4, rev. ed.)

At the end of Brian Moore's . . . novel, *Catholics* . . ., an abbot kneels in front of the tabernacle in the abbey church to lead his monks in prayer. He believes the tabernacle to be empty; he knows that the effect of his prayer will be his own experience of horror at the emptiness of the universe. In Moore's first book published in 1955 [*The Lonely Passion of Judith Hearne*], a neurotic spinster appalled by her growing conviction that the tabernacle is empty, blasphemously assaults it in an effort to discover if God is inside. The question of the vacancy of the tabernacle or its overwhelming fullness lies at the center of Moore's work, for to that question are tied two others with which he has struggled in his novels, out of which he has created his novels. With the fullness of the tabernacle, Moore associates an objective world which is created and ordered by a father whose absolute power is synonymous with a terrible sadistic energy. With its emptiness he associates a void in which a person floats, trapped forever in his own solipsistic dream. On the great presence or the great absence depend the reality of the world outside the mind and the legitimacy of the novelist's commitment to his own imagination.

The creating of fictions is the central subject of the seven novels Moore published between 1955 and 1970. In each of them, he presents a single character whose every vital energy is given to a private life in fantasy. That character, no matter the facts of biography or of sexual designation, is very strongly identified with Moore the novelist, although it is not until his fourth book that the fantasizer emerges as a novelist. In each of the first four books [*Judith Hearne, The Feast of Lupercal, The Luck of Ginger Coffey,* and *An Answer From Limbo*], the dream life of the central character is a guilty one, for he has treacherously withdrawn from the morally valid world of the father; in each book he is rightly punished for that betrayal. Yet the world which the fantasizer has denied is one in which he has been brutally humiliated by the very power which has created it—and created him. As Moore develops as a writer, the rebellion of the fantasizer against the father as God becomes personalized, explicitly attached to Moore himself and to his complex relation to his own father. In his first two books, however, the fantasizer's struggle against reality and defeat by it are presented through a study of the lives of two aging and powerless celibates in the Belfast Catholic community. Both characters are carefully dissociated from Moore personally. . . . The rebellious artist is disguised in these first two books as a spinster alcoholic and an impotent schoolmaster; the overwhelming father is hidden in the powerful social institutions of Catholic Belfast—family, church, school. The concealment gives the apparently dispassionate realistic studies of two wasted lives in a restricted provincial town an extraordinary intensity. (pp. 13-15)

Moore suggests [in *Judith Hearne*] that withdrawal from the community into the isolated imagination is a contemptible regression to childhood. At the same time, however, he shows that the community insists that its adult members remain forever in a sanctioned childhood. (p. 22)

The community breaks its members, but it also guards them. It both destroys and protects the individual person.

The book does not resolve this contradiction, and the reader is in effect trapped within it. In spite of a clear indictment of family and religion as the parts of a ruthlessly repressive mechanism, the presentation of the sheer human decency and happiness of the O'Neill family justifies the system, and the values on which it is based. The reader must accept at one and the same time the irreconcilable notions that Judith Hearne's problems would have been solved if only she had been pretty enough and lucky enough to have attracted a good Catholic husband, and that she cannot marry because she is the victim of repressive cultural forces. . . . The reader is left at the end of the book in a state of painful confusion, a confusion I would suggest, which is the counterpart of Moore's ambivalence toward the ordered world over which his father presided. In his second book, *The Feast of Lupercal* . . ., Moore solves the technical problems raised by this ambivalence. He creates as his victimized central character a person who, unlike Judith Hearne, does have a reasonable chance for happiness and whose inability to actualize that chance is rooted solely in the conditions which have formed his experience. (pp. 23-4)

At the opening of the book, Devine is what everyone in his world expects him to be. He is steady, solid, unfailingly reliable. He appears to be an adult acting responsibly in society; however like Judith Hearne, he is trapped in a prolonged childhood, a fact which the external circumstances of his life reveal. (p. 25)

Dev's childlikeness, like that of Judith Hearne, is shown to be contemptible, and contemptible for the same reason. He too has withdrawn from the community into the isolated world of fantasy. (p. 33)

In the withdrawal inward to fantasy, Dev has done what the community does by religion—he has escaped the generational realities of sex and death; he has denied his humanity and the significance of the daily actualities of his life. The imagination in this book, as in Moore's first, merely isolates; it does not liberate from the life-denying abstractions of the community ideal. In Moore's Belfast, there is no Stephen Dedalus. The spinster alcoholic and the impotent bachelor who once thought of himself as the Irish Baudelaire lack the intelligence of Stephen Dedalus, but more crucially his power and his sense of the overriding validity of the life of the imagination. (p. 34)

The realistic surface of *The Luck of Ginger Coffey* remains opaque unless we view the book in relation to the recurring concerns of Moore's fiction and in relation to the essential biographical fact that Moore made a reputation for himself as a serious novelist with two books that were written in Canada about life in Belfast. The relation of the failure Coffey to the successful writer Moore is the source of the novel's complexity and interest. (pp. 35-6)

Coffey represents what should have happened to Moore. Coffey is a character in a coherent and embodied fantasy who gets the fate which his creator at a deep and irrational level believes that the fantasizer deserves.

In *An Answer From Limbo* . . ., Moore explores all the aspects of the struggle between his condemnation of the fantasizer and his own career as a successful novelist. Beneath the realistic surface of this novel, as in *The Luck of Ginger Coffey*, lies a demonstrably coherent symbolic pattern which is concerned with the activity of the novelist himself. The underpattern in the Canadian book conveys its author's guilt at his successful exploitation of his Irish past. The underpattern in *An Answer From Limbo* ties authorial guilt to complicated aggressive forces which are felt to impel the creation of fiction. The figure of the fantasizer appears here at last in the shape in which its relation to Moore in unmistakable, that is as the Ulster-born novelist Brendan Tierney. The facts of Tierney's life are not precisely the facts of Moore's, but Tierney represents Moore as he conceives himself in the role of novelist. (pp. 49-50)

The idea that writing a novel is an act of destruction is implicit in the way in which Moore varies the narrative perspective within the structure of the book, and it is an explicit element in Brendan's thinking about his art. (p. 50)

This linking of punitive aggression and literary creation should be related to the linking in *The Feast of Lupercal* of sadistic punishment and sexual intercourse. . . . In both these books, Moore uses man's sexual punishment of woman as the paradigm for all expressions of power. All creation—physical, cosmic, aesthetic—involves the punitive exercise of masculine energy. In *An Answer From*

Limbo, spirit is persistently associated with the male. Aesthetic and actual fathers fade into God, as does the hierarchy of fathers at St. Michan's in *The Feast of Lupercal*. Mrs. Tierney in her judgment dreams sees her own father in the role of God the father; Brendan in writing his book becomes an omnipotent creator. Women, on the other hand, are shown to be rawly corporeal, inviting and obscurely deserving the punishment they receive. The omniscient perspective gives the suffering and death of Mrs. Tierney and the sexual degradation of Jane the weight of inevitability. When Brendan withdraws from them, they are abandoned to a fearful punishment which the linking of events in the narrative suggests comes to them from an all-knowing, unforgiving, brutally sadistic God. (pp. 51-2)

[Moore] implies that women can be protected from divine sadistic energy only by the love of the men who have proper authority over them within the family system. . . .

Yet the generational world is a horrifying one. Though human love within marriage and the family mitigates its brutality, its essential processes are inseparable from masculine cruelty and feminine degradation. (p. 55)

The change [in his life] which Moore acknowledges [in interviews] . . . is clearly reflected in his fiction, not only in *The Emperor of Ice-Cream* . . ., but also in the two novels which followed it [*I Am Mary Dunne* and *Fergus*]. *The Emperor of Ice-Cream* shows significant changes in the recurring patterns of Moore's fiction. Once again he gives us the conflict between the fantasizer-son and the rigidly authoritarian father, but this time the conflict lacks the deep, driven pain characteristic of its earlier appearances, and the issue of the conflict at last is the reconciliation of father and son, the father's acceptance of the son's triumph. It is interesting that at this point in his career, the Christ-as-victim pattern disappears entirely from Moore's work. (p. 64)

The transformation of the omnipotent sadistic father into comic components and the frank authorial affection for the fantasizer hero are significant changes in this book [*The Emperor of Ice-Cream*] which should be related, I think, to its weakness. The book is flawed by Moore's use of the techniques of narrative realism when he no longer has a view of the world which can be expressed by such a convention. The view behind the first group of Moore's fictions is that there exists outside the mind a world fixed and defined in eternal validity, created and ruled by paternal power. Against this rigid order, as we have repeatedly seen, the fantasizer builds an inner world, subversive of the true one, and therefore evil. The use of the Wallace Stevens poem to name this book suggests Moore's new perspective on the world, one in which the imagination is at last accepted as legitimate. The poem's view of mind, however, remains unarticulated in the form of the novel. The poem itself seems awkwardly used in the book. It is quoted in fragments . . . at wide intervals in the book, but Gavin's understanding of it seems subservient to his delight in discovering that other people know the poem too. (pp. 69-70)

Moore is clearly interested in writing a timeless fable of testing and reconciliation which has particular significance for himself as an artist. But Moore's fable gets tangled with the trappings of a realistic novel: a very large cast of characters, careful description of the physical terrain of Belfast, and location in a specific and limited historical period. In the earlier books, realistic elements are charged with their own being and with hidden meaning in relation to the fantasizer. In *The Emperor of Ice-Cream*, they exist only as background for the testing of the hero and they lose validity. . . .

In *I Am Mary Dunne* . . ., the reader is at every point made aware that the closely woven realistic density of the novel is a triumph of the creative imagination. Moore's title echoes Flaubert's "*Madame Bovary, c'est moi*," and in so doing establishes the fact that the character Mary Dunne is the creation of the novelist Brian Moore, and that in the character as artifact, he will reveal himself. The epigraph of the book reinforces the point: "O body swayed to music, O brightening glance,/How can we know the dancer from the dance?" In this book, the novelist will reveal himself in the practice of his art. (p. 71)

A new attitude toward experience which Moore reveals in this novel permits him to view the creation of fiction, both in private fantasy and in the work of the artist, as a morally acceptable action. Since every person's perception and experience of the objective are seen to be shaped subjectively, the life in the mind is no longer a solitary aberration of the impotent and rebellious, but a universal fact of human experience. In *An Answer From Limbo*, Moore's sense of the fictional world as subversive of the real and the true caused him to present the novelist character as the destroyer of Mrs. Tierney. In *I Am Mary Dunne*, his more complex view of the interaction of the subjective and the objective in human experience permits him to present himself as novelist in the act of creating Mary Dunne. (p. 74)

Moore's presentation of Mary Dunne shows that a humane tolerance has replaced the rigid moralism of the first four books. This new tolerance frees Moore to reveal in the book itself his own skill in the act of imaginative creation. (p. 79)

Fergus . . . explores the objective and subjective experience of a single day in the life of Fergus Fadden. Fadden is Gavin Burke grown up and Brendan Tierney grown older. (p. 81)

Moore brings *An Answer From Limbo* and *The Feast of Lupercal* into this novel. Like his predecessors, Fergus made his peace with the powerful ghost by withdrawing from Ireland into the imagination. His own name expresses a retreat, for Fergus is the deposed king in the sagas of the Ulster cycle whom Yeats presented in a poem admired by Stephen Dedalus as a man who left the real world for the world of dream. What Fergus realizes on the day of his revelations is that he is the source of his own guilt and fear, that the tragically tormented Sweeney element of his being, is like his life and his work, his own creation. (p. 83)

Fergus can at last demythologize his father, accept him as a man, release him from the role of tyrant and god he has held for so long in the depths of his son's being. (pp. 87-8)

Seen in the light of Moore's previous work, *The Revolution Script* is clearly an exercise in projection: Moore's historically existent revolutionary youths and middle-aged men, disembodied by the media, distanced from him by nationality, are given in the book a shape of particular significance to Moore. There is something unethical in this projection of the deeply personal onto public events involving real persons. The subject matter of Moore's book demands the scrupulous impersonality of the journalist, not the private emotional energies of the novelist. This naive and self-indulgent book sentimentalizes and degrades Moore's constant and honest preoccupations. We are given precisely what the title promises: the script for a media melodrama in which there are heroes and villains, and in which human suffering is reduced to a cheap cliché. "The hearse moved off on Pierre Laporte's last automobile ride, the journey to the grave." . . . Such casual brutality is only possible in a context from which all of the weight of common humanity has disappeared.

In *Catholics* . . . Moore restores the hierarchically ordered objective world which he attacked in the first phase of his career and disintegrated in the second. In this . . . [book], he approaches a structured and divinely sanctioned world from the viewpoint of the order-giving father, rather than that of the rebellious child. It is true that he presents that world at the moment of its disappearance, but the fiction is ordered to show that the disappearance is the ultimate proof of that world's validity. *Catholics* is quite literally an apocalyptic book, and apocalypse as Moore conceives it depends on the existence of God and of the Roman Catholic Church. The book is set in the 1990s; the ominous year 2,000 hovers just beyond its range. The Roman Catholic Church, committed to ecumenism and social change, is about to absorb yet one more world religion—Buddhism. (As every Catholic school child used to know, just before the last day, there will be one fold and one shepherd.) Images and lines from Yeats's "The Second Coming" flash through the book, and a helicopter out of Bergman's apocalyptic *Through a Glass Darkly* violates Muck Island with its inhuman menace. (pp. 92-3)

In this book, Moore returns to the old view of the world as objective and ruled by God through a human network of fathers, and to Ireland for setting. The media paradigms for experience, as used in *Fergus* and *The Revolution Script*, have vanished, their only trace the Bergman helicopter. This book is intensely literary; in it Moore seems at pains to join himself to the great Irish writers who opened the century which his book implies is the last one. Moore's Abbot is a hawklike man, . . . a man like the old artificer whom Stephen Dedalus recognized as his father. Yeats's "Second Coming" is closely woven into the language of the book, and Synge's journal of life on the Aran Islands is woven into both its content and its language. Moore . . . seems at peace, for the moment, with all fathers. Like the Abbot, he seems to be now in the world of the father, which is a complex and mysterious new one, waiting to be explored. (pp. 95-6)

Jeanne Flood, in her Brian Moore *(© 1974 by Associated University Presses, Inc.), Bucknell University Press, 1974.*

Catholics, [Brian Moore's] last, much-acclaimed novel, was a tight, controlled, intensely projected story about an isolated community of monks who courted modern heresy by their sturdy adherence to the Old Church. In *The Great Victorian Collection*, his 10th novel, he is again concerned, less interestingly, with the real world as it impinges upon the ideal—or in this case—the dream world. And he has added a new concern: the artist, responsible for his own beautiful creation, is taken over and profited from by commercial interests. His life is, ultimately, lost, destroyed by the "collection" he creates.

Or is it possible that the novel is about something else entirely: the nature and power and destructive force of dreams?

The story is so simple that it may be hard to believe in it in the bare telling, a difficulty which also arises in the reading. Maloney, an obscure young historian of the Victorian age, an assistant professor at McGill University, sleeps one night in a motel in Carmel, California, dreams of a magnificent collection of Victorian antiques, artifacts, erotic books, tools and general memorabilia. He wakes. Outside his window in the motel parking lot *is* his dream collection, every detail of it perfect, more real than the actual objects in existence, certainly real because some of the objects no longer exist except in the written accounts which Maloney, in his research, has read.

"I am a historian who was witness to that first moment in history when a man's dream literally came true." Maloney at first exults at his responsibility for the secular and scholarly miracle. Like any true artist he gloats over its completeness, hovers over it, refuses to leave it because he suspects his presence is necessary for its integrity (indeed the one time he leaves Carmel a sudden, local rainstorm showers down upon the collection). The outside world questions its authenticity, his account of its conception, ridicules his person and, finally, takes it from him. . . .

The idea of the book is intriguing and the Victorian descriptions are wonderfully, accurately, detailed and interesting (in the same way that Evan Connell's *The Connoisseur* held the reader fascinated because it communicated so well the lonely passion of the collector). The whole, however, lacks the kind of convincing force, the propulsive persuasion that *Catholics* carried. Parable or science-fiction, psychodrama or fine flight of fancy, whichever, the novel's hinges and structural wires, its blueprint, show too clearly. The characters are actors in the parable rather than people, playing out the ingenious but indecisive events and leaving us, like people in a dream, unconvinced.

Doris Grumbach, "An Antic Dream," in Book World—The Washington Post *(© The Washington Post), June 1, 1975, p. 2.*

Brian Moore's *The Great Victorian Collection* is a bit of a dangler—a fast moving and gripping novel, mixing science fiction fantasy with hard California fact, but it's unresolved, quirky, occasional. When I'd finished it I had to go back to *Judith Hearne, The Luck of Ginger Coffey*, and *I Am Mary Dunne* to recall what it was that made me think Moore great. What can be said so far about the Moore oeuvre is that it exhibits a keen sense of the observable mannerisms of various psychologies and that the novels are as important or unimportant as the characters Moore chooses to portray. The situations of Mary Dunne and the others reverberate in universal experience. The hero of *The Great Victorian Collection* is curious but not important. (pp. 64-5)

[Two] things point to a seriousness in Moore's purpose: the death of this hero . . .; and a compelling documentary style. . . .

What, exactly, does Moore have against Tony? His youth? His academic position? His failed marriage? Surely it can't be just dreaming a dream. There's not the slightest suggestion anywhere that Tony has isolated himself in an ivory tower. He transgresses no value in the story for which he must be punished.

At one point I thought that Moore was having a go at the Anglo-Irish philosopher Bishop Berkeley ..., who said that the world exists because God continues to think it. A character even says that Tony, an atheist, has brought about "the first wholly secular miracle in the history of mankind." A madman picketing the collection with a placard saying Only God Can Create seems to add support. Something was perhaps being said about the doom of proud materialistic man, but Moore never connected these ideas.

Again I wondered if Moore was attacking the kitsch cult, and John Fowles' manipulative spin-offs. . . .

The failure of *The Great Victorian Collection* is that although Tony is as real as Judith Hearne, Ginger Coffey, or Mary Dunne, he's trapped in a butterfly net and he's too much of a gentleman to break out. Tragedy becomes farce when the hero's plight is strange, wonderful, and particular. Fantasy doesn't mix with Moore's psychological insights. Poor Tony is too real to be even a clown. He's neither Lear nor Loman; attention need not be paid. (p. 65)

> Anne Montagnes, "Dreaming a Victorian Fantasy," in Saturday Night (copyright 1975), July/August, 1975, pp. 64-5.

* * *

MORTIMER, Penelope 1918-

Ms Mortimer, an English novelist, short story writer, screenwriter, and critic, is best known for her novel *The Pumpkin Eater*. (See also *Contemporary Authors*, Vols. 57-60.)

A distinctive image which recurs in Mrs. Mortimer's novels is the mirror into which you look, fearfully, to find some confirmation of your own identity—and there is none. *The Pumpkin Eater* might be described as a novel about a woman who has clung so long to her illusion of identity (by endless childbearing and by sheltering in strong, protective male arms) that the glimpse of herself, alone, afraid, and free, causes a breakdown. It remains Mrs. Mortimer's best book.

Some men—since many of them will no doubt find [*My Friend Says It's Bullet-Proof*] very much "a woman's book" too—might dismiss as characteristic feminine masochism, or even vanity, the way in which, once again, her heroine has this desperate need to be "corroborated" by the men in her life, to face the painful and frightening knowledge that she is alone, and to have the courage and generosity to accept reality, however much it hurts. . . .

My Friend Says It's Bullet-Proof is, as we now expect from Mrs. Mortimer, brilliantly planned, taut, intelligent, unobtrusively skilful in tangling and disentangling the past and present crises in her characters' lives. Muriel's confrontation, first with the illusory horrors of her blind father's existence, and then with the fact that her own damaged life has similarly distorted the outside world, is beautifully patterned. There are some waspish little comic scenes—though perhaps American PR and energetic matrons are too crude a target for Mrs. Mortimer's talent—and the despair behind some of the snatches of dialogue (non-communication, barriers impossible to bridge) sketches in some of the minor characters with fine melancholy wit.

> "She Alone," in The Times Literary Supplement (© Times Newspapers Ltd., 1967; reproduced by permission), October 12, 1967, p. 953.

There is still a fashion among lady writers for being paranoia strip tease babies, blackmailing the sensitive reader with titillating ennui and fashionable anxiety. . . . *Long Distance*, as a connoisseur of novel titles might suspect, is set in a place and in a mood which will be familiar to those accustomed to the nouveau Italian cinema: a well-appointed mansion which is both grandiose and eerie, a heroine who does not know whether she is coming or going but remains solemn on all occasions, and absolutely no plot at all.

A sensitive and mysterious "I" inhabits this book with a proprietorial air which events do not actually justify, and it, or she, or what I will call from now on Miss X, is escaping from an equally mysterious and oppressive "you." Without the benefit of first-name terms, it becomes all too easy to get the characters completely confused and to leave the novel feeling that you have been banging on closed doors in vain. This, of course, may well be the point. *Long Distance* is couched relentlessly in the present tense, and becomes an intelligent woman's guide to phenomenological method, and it is written in what in more enlightened times was known as a 'feminine style.' Miss X is tremulous with self-conscious reactions, and Miss Mortimer allows her heroine to spread her sensations somewhat thinly in all directions at once. It is not as if she were the only nut on the beach; somewhere a play is being performed which Miss X finds melancholy, Miss X now has children and plays the part of a disturbed and vulnerable little goose so dear to the hearts of modern novelists, Miss X has an affair with someone or something, and Miss X ends up by transcribing some dubious tapes. The whole business is so resolutely mysterious that there must be an allegory somewhere.

But I cannot believe in mystery which is so easily created: a positive fog of meaning and intention is imposed upon the narrative from the beginning. . . . Is the mansion a mental hospital? Are the characters real? Are they figments of a past life? Is Miss X here or there? Am I still reading this book or have I fallen asleep? None of these questions is satisfactorily answered. (pp. 710-11)

[In] *Long Distance* . . . there is something precious about the endless self-reflection and self-analysis which make up the soft belly of the book. This is not to say that the book is altogether too conventional to be rewarding: Miss Mortimer's prose has a plangency and a sonority which occasionally hit the high note of an authentic Anglo-Saxon misery: "The tea, the biscuits, the joint, the pudding, the sleep." This list is an appropriate litany for the little world of the selfhood, but programme music is not enough. I found the manner of the book too easily achieved to be valuable. (p. 711)

> Peter Ackroyd, in The Spectator (© 1974 by The Spectator; reprinted by permission of The Spectator), June 8, 1974.

There is no anchor of reality [in *Long Distance*]. The landscapes are created by the self, and are liable to sudden, treacherous change. The reader, swung from memory to mirage to urgent reporting, must make up his or her mind how the pieces are meant to be put together, and what they ultimately mean.

The trouble . . . lies in the mishandling of fantasy. . . . A fantastic landscape needs to be as convincing as a recognisable, realistic one. (pp. 808-09)

[What] does stand out is the difference in the writing between the 'real' scenes (when magically transported, for instance, to a dirty house with plates to be washed up and a horde of demanding children to be cared for) and the fantastic ones. In the former, all Ms Mortimer's talent for detail and desperation is in evidence. In the latter . . . she lacks conviction: she is not sufficiently interested in fairy tales herself to make a fairy tale interesting. (p. 809)

> *Emma Tennant, in* The Listener *(© British Broadcasting Corp. 1974; reprinted by permission of Emma Tennant), June 20, 1974.*

["Long Distance"] is an ambitious modern novel in that there is not much going on in it, and such action as there is has been nicely obscured beneath a very slick surface. Roughly: a woman in her middle years enters some sort of institution. . . . The woman narrates and she is anonymous too. In the dim mood of the story one picks out Kafka, then something more stagy and clinical, perhaps Pinter, until at last one reaches the happy lulled state known as indifference.

Penelope Mortimer has really not done a great deal to make it matter. . . .

"Long Distance" [is] . . . not only bizarre but also impossible. . . . But a mode of allegory that is at once facile and opaque seems to be a great temptation in our time, and Miss Mortimer, a realistic writer of modest gifts, has yielded to its thrall. . . .

At her best, Miss Mortimer recalls another New Yorker, Penelope (Gilliatt), and her small truthful observations are worth a thousand planted allegorical ones. Her commonplace assets are a decorous style, a good ear for talk and an approach to every crisis—consciously brave, tender, and blessed with a native toughness—which it would be hard to find unsympathetic. Correspondingly, she has the drawbacks of a lyrically fluent "femininity." The quotation marks are necessary: this is indeed the hothouse [of feminine] sensibility. . . .

But in any event it is not the author who needs scolding; she was simply too weak to ignore trendy bad habits; no, "Kafkaesque" itself is to blame, a poor, arch and silly thing, most unworthy of its master. Vague allegory of this order should be given a decent burial. One would dub it a two-legged monster, undecided between realism and fantasy, except that it has a third limb to confound reality and fantasy, and so it stands neatly as any tripod, ready for action and firmly supporting nothing in particular. (p. 3)

> *David Bromwich, in* The New York Times Book Review *(© 1974 by The New York Times Company; reprinted by permission), September 22, 1974.*

Long Distance is an original, distinguished, often puzzling novel. Unwittingly I was absorbed into it as surely as I remember being into Franz Kafka's *The Trial* and *The Castle*, and for the same reasons. My whole attention was captured by its first paragraph, and I was engrossed by its complex ambiguities, wandering without will through the endless fictional maze, watching every signpost for clues. Ultimately the novel goes nowhere, but instead settles its heroine into her endless future: "I live at a long distance from everything I knew, seeing it clearly." And throughout the long-distance journey to nowhere I was impressed by Mortimer's subtle, inventive mind and her lucid prose; impressed, captivated, *entertained* in the classic sense of being "held," bound, yes enthralled.

If you know *The Pumpkin Eater* (1963) or some of her later fiction like *My Friend Says it's Bulletproof* (1967) you will remember Penelope Mortimer's interest in time and timelessness, in the heights (and depths) of ordinary household maternal and sexual experience. . . . Both novels are short and pointed; both achieve extraordinary density for their length because the prose is terse, direct and because of her use of auxiliary devices to give the narrative depth—journals, dreams, psychiatric interviews. They have a rich, split-level texture; in Mortimer's fictional houses there are many rooms, vertically arranged and furnished with the precisely placed, elegant furniture of her style.

To me *Long Distance* is the culmination of her eight books or at least as many of them as I have read. I have rarely read a more intriguing novel. It is a great puzzle, a Chinese box of a story inhabited by an unnamed woman. Where is she? Far from us, from anyone she has ever known (in one sense), unvisited, in a great white mansion. In a mental institution . . . ? Perhaps. . . .

In the White House itself? Perhaps. . . .

The level I incline to is eschatological. The theological word itself parallels the title of the novel, deriving from the Greek *eschatos, ex*, furthest out. The mansion is the house of death, after death, located in heaven or hell, it makes no difference, clearly there is no distinction made here. (p. 23)

Much . . . happens, or seems to happen, too full, too significant in detail and symbol to spoil by exploring completely. But the addition of it all, in mood and tone and meaning, persuades me that we are in a House of the Dead in which she yearns for direct physical contact but is allowed only sterile, interminable reruns. At the end of the novel, the first stage of her stay being over, her immortality begins. She is resigned to her room ("where I hope to live forever") and to the mindless continuity of eternity: "I have accepted the fact that I'm simple and live through old songs . . . I now believe the purpose of this place is to repeat experience until it is remembered." Life after death, in dreams, in memory, is destined to be relived, at a long distance from itself, in a house with a reflecting pool by a woman who has lived a woman's life, and in eternity still does. What a marvelous book! Am I entirely right in this reading of its locus? Perhaps. (p. 24)

> *Doris Grumbach, "Hail to a Distinguished Novel," in* The New Republic *(reprinted by permission of* The New Republic; *© 1974 by The New Republic, Inc.), September 28, 1974, pp. 23-4.*

Of England's practicing long-distance novelists—those of middle years who have written ten books or so—few are as intelligent as Penelope Mortimer. . . . For Mortimer the construction of an intricate metaphor may become so absorbing that such joy as her fable affords is reduced to symbol hunting, the identification of an allegory. (pp. 101-02)

Peter S. Prescott, "Mates and Inmates," in Newsweek *(copyright 1974 by Newsweek, Inc.; all rights reserved; reprinted by permission), September 30, 1974, pp. 101-02.*

A woman, who is never named [in *Long Distance*] arrives at a kind of rest home or therapeutic community—never defined—isolated on a large estate, somewhere, some time not in the past, separated from someone she has either known or longed for. She meets the other inmates, notably a man with the odd name of Gondzik, who becomes her lover, as he may have been in another time; he also becomes a tyrant, a bully, an advisor, a lover of other women. All along, it is at length revealed, he has been a spy for the ever-looming Administration. If he is all men, then the anonymous narrator is all women, the Administration is society, and Basil Gondzik's surname may be taken as a way of saying that life, love, and what-all have Gone Sick.

One might also suggest, more reluctantly, that the novel itself, in this most polished and serious manifestation, has lost something of its rude vigor, confined not to an oppressive country estate that mirrors the unsatisfactory world, but to the author's comments on reality. A novel must be reality. . . .

In *Long Distance*, . . . Miss Mortimer has made a valiant attempt to find a new way of commenting in a general sense on the very specific evolution of a woman. The narration seems to be very subjective; the source of the incidents matters only and perhaps not at all to the author (depending on the length of her distance from them). . . .

Long Distance is an honest book, one that shows an intent familiarity not only with psychoanalysis and Watergate but with the private struggle for self. One cannot help but wonder if the book is an unusual form of autobiography, a journal of a mind's struggle to keep itself together through all the problems of womanhood. It is knotty with insights: we must, for one, repeat experience until it is remembered. If we are honest, we trap ourselves; but if we accept our prison it proves to have more doors and more possibilities of decor than we had thought. A woman who has raised six children and written nine books may feel the most important things about herself must be said indirectly; but discretion stifles the demons of art. Ironically, more people would be drawn to this book if it were not so diligently written.

Mary Richie, "Dial 'N' for Novel," in Book World—The Washington Post *(© The Washington Post), October 6, 1974, p. 3.*

N

NERUDA, Pablo   1904-1973

A Nobel Prize-winning Chilean poet, Neruda is best known for his early masterpiece *Residencia en la tierra* and *Twenty Love Poems and One Song of Despair*. Neruda has been called the "Latin Walt Whitman" for his epic poem *Canto General*, and he is considered one of the finest surrealist writers of all time. (See also *Contemporary Authors*, Vols. 19-20; obituary, Vols. 45-48.)

The Nobel Prize in literature is perhaps best known for the writers who never won it. . . . It was, therefore, to the company of non-winners, the most distinguished writers truly associated in our minds with the prize, that Sartre aspired when he recently rejected the honor, saying it should have gone to Pablo Neruda. Each time Neruda doesn't win, it becomes more obvious that he is too big for the prize and that the only way for the Swedish Academy to achieve literary dignity is for it to accept the largesse Neruda's name could bestow on its award. [Neruda *was* awarded the prize in 1971.] . . .

In our country, Neruda is still largely unknown for two reasons that are the main weaknesses of this present volume [*A New Decade: (Poems 1958-1967)*]: one, a problem in the poet's art; the other, a difficulty in the translator's practice. Neruda is an openly Communist, often eloquent, sometimes flatulent, revolutionary writer whose politics disturb some Americans, offend others. For this reason he has never been properly taught in the schools where foreign poets may gain a base for their reputation here. (p. 383)

The best things in this selection . . . are the implicit lyric autobiography and esthetic credo of an aging poet. It is not a volume to win a Nobel Prize, nor is it half so good as *The Heights of Macchu Picchu* . . . ; but it may, after all, introduce Americans to one of the biggest and most powerful of poetic voices, a voice so vast, even in its later days, that it encompasses its own failures as part of a personal authenticity and derives highest praise, perhaps, from accolades withheld. (p. 384)

> *Ronald Christ, in* Commonweal *(copyright © 1969 Commonweal Publishing Co., Inc.; reprinted by permission of Commonweal Publishing Co., Inc.), December 26, 1969.*

Neruda's poems are spoken by a generic "I" who is not quite the living man Neruda, they describe a generic landscape and are addressed to a generic "people." There is a great deal of idealization in his work, and of attitudinizing. He makes a penetrating statement about this in his own prefatory note to *Splendor and Death of Joaquin Murieta:* "This is a tragic work, but it is also, in part, a *jeu d'esprit.*" (p. 197)

Neruda writes fluently, easily, abundantly, a poetry of enthusiasms and attitudes that are ready at hand in the world, not a poetry of facts, perceptions, and difficult knowledge. Vallejo's poetry was an event in the Spanish language; and like MacDiarmid, Vallejo has written for the life and spirit of his people. Neruda works in the middle style, with a middle consciousness, and what he writes belongs to literature. . . . (p. 198)

> *Richard Pevear, in* The Hudson Review *(copyright © 1973 by The Hudson Review, Inc.; reprinted by permission), Vol. XXVI, No. 1, Spring, 1973.*

After reading the ample selections from the *Residencia* [in *Selected Poems*] there can be little doubt that, as Robert Bly has said, Neruda has given us "the greatest surrealist poems yet written in a Western language." The surprising thing is that one could even speak of Breton and Aragon as Neruda's peers. Nor can one come away with anything but great admiration for the *Odas*. The things ensnared there—chestnuts, books, tomatoes, and so forth—are given fresh, original poetic life.

Unfortunately, the weakest part of the book happens to be its translations of Neruda's greatest poem, the *Canto General*. It is not that Anthony Kerrigan's efforts are poor; the failure, rather, arises from exclusiveness. Something essential is lost in this section of the book and underplayed through the entire book: the ideological, political Neruda. The *Canto* arose out of the poet's experience in the late forties in Chile; after the government outlawed the Communist Party, the poet, who continued to speak out, was pursued by the Secret Police, went into exile, traveled clandestinely through the continent, and finally flew from Mexico to France. The *Canto*, like the never translated *Las Uvas y El Viento (The Grapes and the Wind)*, contains some embarrassing political pieces which fail to go beyond propaganda. But it also contains some of the greatest political poetry of the century, pieces which while written to appeal to and arouse the masses are still very great poems. None are included here. In fact, nothing from Books V to X of the *Canto* is represented. It is a most extraordinary gap, for gone are some of the poems in which Neruda is most humanistic, most ideological, most humane, most socially conscious. One comes to the conclusion that behind the *Selected Poems* is an orthodox sense of the relation of poetry and politics. Such a sense does not serve contemporary South American literature at all. Writers such as Neruda are deeply politicized, for good reasons. To depoliticize them is to destroy one of their great qualities. While South American leftist criticism has overemphasized the political elements in Neruda, the *Selected Poems* does the reverse. (pp. 446-47)

> *Philip R. Yannella, "The Poems of Pablo Neruda," in* The Southern Review *(copyright, 1973, by the Louisiana State University), Vol. IX, No. 1, Spring, 1973, pp. 445-48.*

[It] may be said that Neruda's tumultuous life as a poet was dedicated in great part to a political end in Chile which looked for a time as though it had a healthy chance of coming to attainment. Neruda had more acclaim and attention than almost any other poet has been lucky enough to come by in a lifetime: but I felt that Allende's victory in 1970, and Neruda's subsequent appointment as Chilean Ambassador to France, gave Neruda a kind of joyful satisfaction on a wholly different plane. Nor was that appointment a gratuitous gift on Allende's part: Neruda was a seasoned diplomat, if not always an acquiescent one, and he took his ambassadorial function with the utmost seriousness. When, in 1971, Neruda was awarded his Nobel Prize, Allende declared a national holiday. The reports which seep out of Chile now, of the sacking of his house at Isla Negra, of book burnings, of vicious acts of retribution on the part of the military junta, can only have the effect of giving his poetry a heroic stature. Much of his poetry *is* heroic in its vision, and that he should die in the ashes of that vision hurts more deeply than the simple fact of his death.

Neruda must without question be the most widely circulated poet in history, mainly because of the huge spate of translation, particularly in the Soviet Union and in China. Yet his work is not at all well-known in the English language, although in the last few years selected editions and odd single volumes have appeared. Even that is curiously misleading, for it gives little or no sense of the huge bulk of his work, his persistent changes of manner and matter, his torrential poetic appetite, the almost planetary range of his poetry. (pp. 437-38)

It is unlikely, however industriously translators keep mining away, that Neruda will come across into English. For one thing, he was in many ways a careless poet, one who preferred to leave his poems behind him for the sake of new preoccupations. For another, some of his writing smacked unabashedly of political tract-writing, and is forgettable as such. For a third, he was fundamentally a Chilean and a Latin American, and Latin America, even although it seems to me to be generating the most exciting literature in our present world, never quite loses for this country the aura of a never-never land, a vague continent of

names rather than realities. Moreover, the context of English poetry is a comparatively eccentric and private one, given over to private language and personal reference, a poetry of closely perceived subtleties. For that reason, the grand scale of Neruda's most elevated manner, the great hymns of his *Canto General*, his invocations of the Latin American continent in all its vegetal and historical vastness, come to rest somewhat uneasily in English, or at least lose the hugely inspiring tone and scale which emanate from Neruda's Spanish. I find I can never read his poems without hearing that slow, carefully-paced voice behind them, that peculiarly languid cadence which gave the words a kind of stone permanence. . . .

His great poetic virtue was that he never repeated himself. (p. 438)

The number of Chileans who know Neruda's strongest poems by heart, the number of Latin Americans who feel him to have summed them up and given them heart, will clearly outlast any temporary horrors. The intervention of the military junta in Chile, always the most human and worldly of the Latin American countries, has been a crude shock: but I feel very firmly that it has small chance against the durable humanity of Neruda, and the sheer human abundance of his poetry. (p. 439)

> *Alastair Reid, "The Chilean Poet Pablo Neruda, 1904-1973, by His Translator, Alastair Reid," in* The Listener *(© British Broadcasting Corp. 1973; reprinted by permission of Alastair Reid), October 4, 1973, pp. 437-39.*

Neruda's greatest poetic resource lay in his historical imagination. . . .

Neruda's historical imagination shaped some of his finest political poems such as "They Reach the Gulf of Mexico (1493)". . . . These poems have a depth of reference and a recreative energy unequalled in American poetry. . . .

For Neruda the turbulent revolutions of the natural world meant change, change man could grow with. His essential image, especially in the last years of his life, was replenishment. He lived facing the ocean where the surf and swell that threaten human life in Eliot's poetry were what Neruda learned from as he wrote.

> *John Felstiner, "Pablo Neruda, 1904-1973," in* The New Republic *(reprinted by permission of* The New Republic; *© 1973 by The New Republic, Inc.), October 13, 1973, p. 27.*

After 1953, Neruda called for a poetry that would reach ordinary people, announcing the new programme in "Obscurity and Clarity in Poetry." Determined to become more simple, he uttered phrases that were stripped of the Baroque strain of the earlier work. And yet if his commitment to human suffering led him to compose in a more severe style, it did not change his insistence on "pure" poetry: "And I sing because I sing because I sing," he declares in a later poem.

Nor did his knowledge of destruction alter his poetic concern with the things of this world. Until the end of his life, he wrote powerfully of the air, the wind, fire and bread—and, in effect, of the earth on which he lived.

Unhappily, [*Five Decades: A Selection (Poems 1925-1970)*] does no more to convey Neruda's extraordinary achievement than many other English versions have done. In fact, by now it is hardly surprising to American readers that the poetry of Neruda is not what his translators would have us think it is. . . .

Although I cannot recommend the present volume, I must say that it might make some readers angry enough to get out the dictionary and read only the Spanish across the page. While a faithful translation encourages dependence on the translator, and even a good prose paraphrase serves as a substitute for the original, a weak translation can, paradoxically, force attention on the poet's own words.

> *Grace Schulman, "A Translator's Transgressions," in* Review 74 *(copyright © 1974 by the Center for Inter-American Relations, Inc.), Winter, 1974, p. 73.*

There are rare human beings whose mere presence has a quality of meditation, and Pablo Neruda was such a man.

It is a quality which flows with compassionate energy in his poetry, as if the poems were sustained throughout by a deep inner hum. The words emerging with romantic eloquence, translate the hum into language. It is not the poet who is speaking, but the world rendering itself darkly, angrily, sensuously, laughingly, into a spiritual medium. In this sense, Neruda's great poems are hymns. They are not about anything, or rather their subject matter is merely a sort of incarnation which the hymn has chosen. So many of the poems in *Residence on Earth* give the appearance of being incomplete. That they actually do have a beginning, middle and end is a concealed and secondary fact: the reader experiences a moment of dark song which is exposed to him, momentarily, from the ongoing hum of experience. The poems do not so much end, as they wind down and hush temporarily. . . . In each poem, the poet names the animals, the passions, the miseries. And the naming goes on, delighting in its incompleteness which is simply evidence of the world's abundance.

Pablo Neruda wrote abundantly too, as if he needed to match the outer world with his inner wealth. . . .

Extravagaria . . . is not one of his important books. The *Residences, The Heights of Macchu Picchu, The Elementary Odes* are, by far, greater achievements. In comparison, *Extravagaria* resembles a sort of finger exercise. The poet has taken time out to rehearse his instrument, trying out all the friendly turns of language which have served him so well. (p. 75)

The themes of *Extravagaria* are the familiar themes of Neruda's great poetry: love and nostalgia, the appetite for experience, the celebration of interior life. As always the poems intone a massive elegy in which grief becomes succulent and lovely, and turns into its opposite. . . . [It] is a while before we notice that the tones [of the chants in *Extravagaria*] are a little faded; that the inner hum has fallen silent, leaving the verses to perform out of habit, lapsing all too frequently into melodrama instead of surprise, sentimentality instead of compressed passions, formulas instead of incantations.

The mystery of poetic achievement is exquisite. in *Extravagaria* the magnificent elegiac space is there, but the life-breath is fitful, and the generous frame of the poem sags. *Extravagaria* is one of those books which remind us that even a great poet has clay feet, that he stands on the same earth we do; that the difference between us, therefore, is puzzling and troubling. It would be easier simply to venerate his "genius," and sit back, happy that there is nothing we need to do. But Neruda won't let us off. His greatness and his failures are merely human. (pp. 75-6)

> *Paul Zweig, "The Poet Rehearses His Instrument," in* Review 74 *(copyright © 1974 by the Center for Inter-American Relations, Inc.), Winter, 1974, pp. 74-6.*

"We are many" is the title of a rather unconvincing poem by Pablo Neruda about his own multiple selves. The phrase could be applied with greater force perhaps to the translators of Neruda into English. They really are many. . . .

They are many and they are not, on the whole, very good. Only Robert Bly and Anthony Kerrigan make Neruda sound in English as if he might be a good poet in Spanish. . . .

The author of *Extravagaria* may well be a great writer (and is, in my view), but in this book he is merely flexing his muscles, playing his scales and paying a few debts. The work is casual, whimsical, silly, sometimes charming, occasionally clear and strong . . . , and almost willfully minor when set beside *Residence on Earth*, or any section of the *Canto General*, or beside the later *Memorial de Isla Negra*. . . .

[The] besetting sin of Neruda's translators is a refusal to leave him alone, a reluctance to say what he says, a perverse, elaborate flight from the tone of the original. Silent mothers become mute matriarchs, true love becomes unfalsified ardor, forgetting is almost invariably oblivion. Gloves become gauntlets, coins currency, flowers blossoms, and hard cavities become adamantine hollows. The comic climax to all these attempts to bundle Neruda off into some sort of Pre-Raphaelite old folks home comes in *The Heights of Macchu-Picchu*, where Tarn translates the ordinary Spanish word for glass (*vaso*) as chalice, and Robert Pring-Mill, in an introduction to the volume, comments on the "religious overtones of such an image." There are religious overtones in the work, as it happens, but none of them accompanies that modest glass.

In one sense, of course, Neruda is an old-fashioned poet, but that is because he prolongs traditions, not because he tries to sound archaic and lofty. Many of his favorite poetic strategies belong to the nineteenth century (or even earlier) rather than to the twentieth. He prefers similes to metaphors; he likes to personify moods, conditions, landscapes; he is fond of operatic exclamations and of directly addressing countries, provinces, shades of the dead, features of the natural world like stars, rivers, and the sea; he is fond of decorous, elegant inversions, of formal antithesis (summer-winter, life-death) and of asymmetrical pairs (silence and slime, suits and pride, drunkards and jasmines, yesterday and Valparaiso). He likes dying falls and melting conclusions.

He is a poet who has not so much rejected or retreated from modernism (in the English meaning of the term) as he has managed to get along without it, to preserve older forms without seeming nostalgic or reactionary. He will not break with the poetic past so long as it will nourish the poetic present; and if he often, in spite of all this, seems more modern than he is, it is because he skillfully *alludes* to modernity quite a lot—borrows from the languages of mathematics and science, for example. He is a thoroughly *rhetorical* poet. Rather than wringing eloquence's neck, as Verlaine advised, he gives eloquence a new lease of life by making it discreet and direct. But this is the point. Neruda's vocabulary, apart from an occasional excess of fragrance, twilight, and autumn, is entirely comtemporary and prosaic—even in the early *Residence on Earth*, where he achieves surrealist effects by means of the most commonplace objects and animals: beds, brooms, shoes, dogs, coffins. Neruda's best poetry is born in the interplay between this everyday language and those courtly, often intricate poetic manners. (p. 8)

[Even] Neruda's greatest poetry is merely part of a larger picture, just an element in a pattern of life and writing which embodies and pleads for a whole set of Latin American possibilities: the poet in politics, the politician who is a great poet; the public man with the incomparable common touch; the popular poet, even the oral poet, since people who can't read still know and love and recite and sing poems by Neruda, who receives international critical acclaim. It is a vision of a vast but integrated personal life, and beyond that a vision of a multifarious but coherent community, summarized in one exemplary individual. . . .

The Heights of Macchu-Picchu, written in 1945, is a sequence of twelve poems, a section of the *Canto General* and a major work in its own right. It is perhaps the best of all introductions to Neruda, since his gifts receive their full expression there and since it is also a form of spiritual autobiography, a description of a moral and aesthetic journey out of baffled solitude into a sense of poetic mission. It points backward toward *Residence on Earth*, Neruda's early masterpiece, most of which was written before 1935, and forward to the *Canto General* (1950), into which it was incorporated. It parodies earlier manners and scouts for later ones. Above all it balances perfectly two insistent, enduring strains in Neruda's work: the desire to clear up confusions and the desire to hang on to them.

"I am sure / of the unmoving stone," Neruda writes in a later poem, "but I know the wind." He loves the stillness and ideal geometry of Macchu-Picchu, the spectacular Andean ruin of an ancient Inca city, but he finds a battery of questions and uncertainties there, change and extinction among that rocky permanence: "Stone upon stone, but where was man?" Was Macchu-Picchu a city erected, like so many others, on misery and hunger and death, and who will speak now for the vanished laborers who built it and supplied it with meat and grain? They themselves can't return from subterranean time, as Neruda puts it, but perhaps the poet's concern for them will lend their voices to his poem. In effect Neruda is asking for their blessing on the whole of the *Canto General*, a colossal, unequal monument, a long celebration of the American continent, an angry, at times sentimental, at times very compelling plea for the wretched of the American earth.

It is hard to see where a poet could go after such a book— Whitman, in similar circumstances, just kept adding poems to his. Neruda's life's work was done by the time he was forty-five, and there is a sense in which he simply managed to outlive himself elegantly for twenty years, remaining as

prolific as ever without really finding a subject that mattered enough. Many people admire the four books of elementary (or elemental, or both) odes . . . but for me they have, along with *Extravagaria* (1958), too much the tone of the great man showing us how humble and playful he can be. . . .

On the other hand, there is the remarkable verse autobiography, *Memorial de Isla Negra* (1964), which is really casual and relaxed in the way that *Extravagaria* merely tries to be. Without pretensions of either humility or grandeur, the poet remembers patches of his life: his father, his family's friends, his loves; places, thoughts, moods, moments. I should say also that early and late in his career (and in between) Neruda wrote incomparable love poems, and that he seems never to have written a bad poem about the sea.

But *Residence on Earth* remains, in my view, the greatest of all Neruda's books. Neruda himself came to regard it very harshly. It helped people to die rather than to live, he said, and if he had the proper authority to do so he would ban it, and make sure it was never reprinted. No doubt there was an element of pose in that pronouncement since, as Rodríguez Monegal remarks, Neruda never took any steps to keep the baleful book out of his collected works, and continued to regard it as one of his best volumes. . . .

It is a painful, brilliant, despairing work, full of surprising turns of phrase and marvelously simple, inventive imagery. "I understand the harmony of the world," Paul Claudel once wrote, "when shall I come across the melody?" *Residence on Earth* in its earlier parts—the last section is devoted to the Spain of the Civil War—presents a man who understands neither the harmony nor the melody, who sees only chaos and multiplicity, a busy or bored, frantic or lethargic alien world in which he has no place or purpose. Neruda wrote much of the book in India, when he was intensely lonely, and the whole of the exotic East parades across the text like a broken-down circus, an array of odd, cruel customs which add up only to nightmare. As late as in *Memorial de Isla Negra* we hear Neruda saying, "And if I saw anything in my life it was one evening / in India, on the edge of a river: a woman of flesh and bones being burned."

Yet there is a curious quality to all this unmistakable anguish, and I quoted Claudel . . . because both appear to have had exceptional propensities for despair, which they simply smothered in orthodoxy—Neruda's communism seems to have served much the same purpose as Claudel's Catholicism—and conjured away in expansive displays of ingenuousness and optimism. More important—and this is the point of the comparison here—the despair which speaks in the early works of both men is not the spleen and self-doubt of Vallejo or Kafka or Proust or any other of those heirs of Baudelaire whom we think of as paradigmatically modern men, but a sense of separation, a sense of uselessness, of a life of pure contingency in a profuse, pointless universe, which is accompanied by a seemingly entire and undiminished self-confidence. . . .

Neruda's very impermeability to the attractions of the East is a form of strength, the sign of a substantial, unshaken identity. Like Claudel, Neruda rarely doubts himself but constantly frets about his lack of connection with others; and it is this connection with others that Neruda finally encounters in Spain—in poets and companions first of all, in Lorca and Rafael Alberti, and then in a whole attacked nation. From Spain, Neruda can return to Chile by way of Macchu-Picchu, and feel at one with the dead and the living of his continent. (p. 10)

The loneliness of *Residence on Earth* takes on a special, metaphysical edge because it is *not* the loneliness of a generally tormented, unhappy man. ''Perhaps I was condemned to happiness,'' Neruda says in a later poem; but then the sentence was in many ways severe, for until his Spanish experience Neruda seems to have failed to find in the world any answer to his own energy and generosity and abundance. Perhaps health has its neuroses, Nietzsche wrote. *Residence on Earth* reflects the hovering dementia of the insufficiently demented, the echoing solitude of an undivided self. (pp. 10, 12)

> Michael Wood, ''The Poetry of Neruda,'' in The New York Review of Books (*reprinted with permission from* The New York Review of Books; *copyright* © *1974 NYREV, Inc.*), October 3, 1974, pp. 8-12.

Does cataloguing plants, animals, the parts of the human body, and the events of injustice make a great poet? Chopped up Whitman in a surrealistic, inorganic soup often seems to be Neruda's substitute for imaginative lyricism. A squirt of Marx is sometimes added, and floats irrelevantly on top like oil on seawater. When he denounces oppression selectively, when he lists poetic things without being poetic, he is a propagandist rather than a poet. And yet there is something fine in him, as if a strong man's body were buried under the fat of a glutton. (p. lxi)

> Virginia Quarterly Review (*copyright, 1975, by the* Virginia Quarterly Review, *The University of Virginia*), *Vol. 51, No. 2 (Spring, 1975).*

Pablo Neruda, recipient of the 1971 Nobel Prize for Literature, has been translated more than any other Latin American poet of the last decade. All too often I have wondered why the translators bothered. Ben Belitt's reckless translation of *Joaquin Murieta* was plainly awful and Robert Bly's many translations sounded exactly like Robert Bly. Donald Walsh's rendering of *The Captain's Verses* was accurate and sympathetic but the collection was too limited. But *Estravagaria* was one of Neruda's personal favorites, and its translation by Alastair Reid is the first real proof *in English* that Neruda deserves an international reputation. Though one might quibble over Mr. Reid's Latinizing of the title in *Extravagaria* . . ., little fault can be found with the poems. Further, the collection has a higher, more consistent quality than previous publications. I have always been uncomfortable with Neruda's random mix of images and abstract nouns which frequently seemed hurried and unreined. There is some of this . . . [yet] in some lovely sections, images are developed and sustained. . . . If one wishes to read Neruda, *Extravagaria* would be well chosen; Mr. Reid's translations are certainly well done. (p. 89)

> W. G. Regier, in Prairie Schooner (© *1975 by University of Nebraska Press; reprinted by permission from* Prairie Schooner), *Spring, 1975.*

NICHOLS, Peter   1927-

A British writer for stage, screen, and television, Nichols is best known for his black comedy, *A Day in the Death of Joe Egg*.

From almost every point of view *Forget-Me-Not Lane* looks like a summary of Nichols's work to date, gathering together its various threads and presenting them to us in a satisfactorily rounded whole with even more dazzling skill than *A Day in the Death of Joe Egg* or *The National Health*. And yet it is a real play; it gives completely the illusion (if it is an illusion) of organic growth; it resolutely shows us everything, tells us nothing. That is why we understand so much from it. And indeed the success of Nichols's campaign to broaden our dramatic responses probably derives first and foremost from the fact that he never set out to mount such a campaign, never had any intention except to write single plays mirroring an aspect of the world as he sees it. (p. 35)

> John Russell Taylor, ''Peter Nichols,'' in his The Second Wave: British Drama for the Seventies (*reprinted with the permission of Farrar, Straus & Giroux, Inc.; copyright* © *1971 by John Russell Taylor*), Hill & Wang, *1971, pp. 16-35.*

It would be hard to review *Saved* without mentioning the stoning of the baby in Act Two, or, for that matter, to expatiate on *Macbeth* without revealing that the main character kills a King of Scotland. Both events seem to explain so much that occurs afterwards. But the promoters of Peter Nichols's *Chez Nous* ask us critics to remain mum about certain revelations made early in the evening, and I'm not the man to shirk a challenge. Let me tell you, then, that the play involves two English couples [Dick and Liz, Diana and Phil], one somewhat smugly in possession of a converted barn in the Dordogne, the other on a visit. . . .

Believing with E. M. Forster (as I do) that character and theme are rather more important than 'that low atavistic form', the story, I must spill the beans. First, Dick and Liz announce that their 13-year-old, Jane, is the mother of the baby Liz is jubilantly passing off as her own. Then it emerges that Phil is the father. . . . [It] is, of course, the characters' longer-term response to their shock that really matters. 'What have I done wrong?' wails [Liz], and that 'I' is typical. All think first of themselves, second of their teetering marriages, and not at all of the teenage tot most intimately involved. We never meet Jane, and so little concern is expressed for her by the adults that Nichols is moved to indicate his disapproval of their egos in an unconventional way. Thunder intermittently cracks and booms, making the lights flicker and suggesting (so it seemed to me) that the authorial gods are not pleased; and a jet screams alarmingly low over the roof, as if practising for kamikaze. Mr. Nichols is clearly in the cockpit, a furious grin on his face, buzzing his characters and itching to strafe them.

Some may think this a fanciful interpretation of mere casual additions to the general atmosphere. But since Nichols ends his play by treating a hen's egg not just as a symbol, but as one with two or three meanings, I chose to believe he has more artistry and purpose than that. This is a very intelligent, careful play, which regards its protagonists with humour, horror, exasperation and compassion, though not always in equal proportions. Dick emerges pretty poorly, not least because he's written some pop sociology which advocates pubescent liberation: this public audacity sorts oddly with his private cowardice, his fear that Jane's baby will somehow damage his career. Liz is self-satisfied and insensitive: an emotional clod-hopper who likes to compare herself to Tolstoy's wife. Diana and Phil prove rather more sympathetic—she for all her fastidiousness and melodramatics, he, with his ostentatious crudity, his pathetic yen for youth and craving for paternity. Their reconciliation, in which she unfurls the hysterectomy-scarred body she's always kept hidden, is unexpectedly moving, a declaration that affection can survive a mangling. As Nichols sees it, men are in thrall to their sexual drives, women doomed to humour them, but both sexes more tenaciously committed to marriage than they sometimes realise. (p. 232)

> *Benedict Nightingale, in* New Statesman *(© 1974 The Statesman & Nation Publishing Co. Ltd.), February 15, 1974.*

Chez Nous is another evening of the familiar marital tug-of-war *chez* Nichols. . . . [One who] expected to meet old friends [would be] right. Dick is a slightly older brother to Bri in *Joe Egg* and Frank in *Forget-Me-Not Lane*: another impossibilist for whom daily married life is a Colditz from which he endlessly plots fantastic escapes. Liz is a greyer, cheerier version of Bri's Sheila and Frank's Ursula: the loving, patiently matter-of-fact gaoler who forever punctures her mate's fantasies with her walking reminder that you can have real emotions only about reality.

Unfortunately, it becomes clear in *Chez Nous* that this recurring opposition expresses an equivalent tug-of-war within Nichols' talent. Part of him is Bri-Frank-Dick, using his plays as play: as fantasies exploring the alternatives to real life. The other half is Sheila-Ursula-Liz: the realist who drags her yoke-fellow back to fact, reminding him that his play-acting emotions are only theatre. I'd be sad to see either excluded from the process of his creations, but I've no doubt that his best plays are the ones in which Sheila and Ursula, respectively, kept the upper hand. In *The National Health*, the spirit of Bri-Frank-Dick ran away with the evening and I felt, weakened it. The serious argument that each of us is entitled to his own death, with the real emotions proper to it, was overlaid by Nichols' farcical elaboration of the alternatives by which we evade these—euphemism, the cult of the Surgeon, the nursery-ritual of hospital life.

For too much of *Chez Nous*, as well, a sense of the play-as-play predominates. (pp. 27-8)

Its central incident is an improbability, a deliberate alternative to real life, engineered as a play-experiment to see what emotions one should have about it. Because it's unreal, as the Sheila-Ursula-Liz side of his talent should have told Mr Nichols, most of the emotions it generates are unreal too. (p. 28)

All right: the situation *Chez Nous* is built on is improbable but not impossible. It could be real. What real emotions could people have about it? Phil has two: shame . . . [and] sheer joy. . . . Liz has two more: fury . . . [and] delight. . . . Mr Nichols recognises their reality and approves of them,

giving them place of honour at the end—I haven't said anything, I hope, which suggests that he's capable of writing a really bad play. But he spends far too much of his evening exploring all the unreal emotions. (pp. 28-9)

[The] ending . . ., rightly, has been hailed as one of the finest things he's done. But in the meantime, his indulgence of fantasy has made things too artificial for . . . much conviction. (p. 29)

> *Ronald Bryden, in* Plays and Players *(© copyright Ronald Bryden 1974), March, 1974.*

[Peter Nichols] is a dramatist who has hitherto seemed possessed of as vivaciously original a comic talent as anyone presently operating in the theatre, and it is as surprising as it is dismaying to find that talent—which has risen buoyantly to the formidable challenges of being joyously and inoffensively entertaining even about spastic children and death in a geriatric ward—foundering bleakly in contemplation of the menace of the motor car, which is what *The Freeway* is about.

At least, that is what it is about on one level. Perhaps fuming frustratedly in his Peugeot in some bank-holiday traffic-jam and cursing the affluence of the age which permits so many other people to have cars to impede the progress of one's own, he has biliously imagined a future in which all but the abysmally underprivileged and handicapped are motorists and the pride of the nation is a vast motorway—the F1—running the entire length of Britain. Warming to his testy invention, Nichols has further envisaged an eighty-mile jam on this motorway in which the vehicles have been kept stationary for three days with rapidly dwindling food supplies, water meagerly rationed, no civilised sanitation and the general atmosphere of a city under siege. It would plainly be possible to develop the situation pretty humorously, but Nichols on this occasion seems to be altogether too embittered (he must have had some really terrible times in the Peugeot), and it is a measure, I suppose, of his desperation—and of the extraordinary fall in his standards of comedy—that he is reduced to the desolate business of trying to get a laugh or two out of people going to the lavatory in rather primitive circumstances.

In the little section of the jam presented on the stage, he offers us some stereotypical caricatures of the working-class and of the aristocracy, and it is hard to say whether his patronising view of the former or the quaint naïveté that informs his disdain for the latter is the more painful. Neither, though, is quite so distressing as the fact that his F1 and the trouble that develops on it are a tortured metaphor for British democracy, class-ridden and acquisitive, careering along a freeway to disaster. He is, of course, entitled to his point of view, but I strongly suspect that this is a case in which one might agree with what he says but oppose to the death his tedious way of saying it. (p. 472)

> *Kenneth Hurren, in* The Spectator *(© 1974 by* The Spectator; *reprinted by permission of* The Spectator), *October 12, 1974.*

Nothing dates faster than the future; and [*The Freeway*,] Peter Nichols's vision of a Britain transformed into countless car-parks linked by gigantic freeways already seems less apt than it would have in 1971 or 1972. . . . [He should] show an industry in slump, hit by the cost of oil and raw materials, by the relative poverty of the home market and the exasperating tendency of foreign buyers to want engines that start and doors that don't fall off. The England of 1984 would become a land of old bangers fuelled by hope and paraffin, threading round the clumps of grass that would by then be sprouting from the motorway tarmac. I have seen the future, and it walks. . . .

[Mr Nichols] sometimes seems more interested in feeding us a series of extracts from *Whitaker's,* Anthony Sampson's *Anatomy of Britain* and the RAC *Book of the Road,* 1984 editions, than in constructing a living, growing plot to demonstrate his hopes and fears.

But if plot is defined as characters changing in response to events, and events occurring because of the interaction of characters, then Mr Nichols's *National Health* was a pretty static affair, too. There's nothing wrong with a play that's mainly concerned to anatomise a given situation and discuss the issues raised—provided, of course, it is all done with depth as well as breadth. But here *The Freeway* seems suspect. . . .

We learn that individual self-indulgence can produce social misery; that labour tends to equate happiness with possessions, and that capital is only too glad to keep its power with the odd handout; that freedom, in short, may be slavery. But anyone who has read a little 19th-century history, or even heard a few economic discussions on *Panorama,* will want to see more slippery questions tackled. How, without real economic growth, can everybody in this country expect a reasonably secure life? How, with growth, can we avoid desecrating the environment, with houses and factories and perhaps even freeways? And do working people want cars from a vague acquisitiveness, or a wish to compensate for childhood deprivation, as the play suggests? . . . It's as if a physician were diagnosing a complex disease without taking all the necessary X-rays.

I found *The Freeway* not unenjoyable, a deliberately negative recommendation. As a play of ideas, it could be more provocative; as a comedy about people in a jam, more trenchant and amusing. . . . Mr Nichols's tendency [is] to substitute reportage for show. We hear tales of theft and violence; but all we see, apart from the principals and their cars, are lounging soldiers, a desultory queue of disgruntled motorists at the end of Act One, and the occasional figure skulking anonymously in the background. Given the size of the theme and the human resources [involved], it seems a dreadful swindle.

> *Benedict Nightingale, "Scrubbers," in* New Statesman *(© 1974 The Statesman & Nation Publishing Co. Ltd.), October 11, 1974, p. 515.*

"The National Health" . . . is a play about the physical and spiritual indignities of sickness, old age, and approaching death. It takes place in the men's ward of a hospital somewhere in England; the dreadfulness of suffering and the still greater dreadfulness of the certain end to suffering hang in the antiseptic air. . . .

Hard as it may be to believe, Mr. Nichols' play is an unbroken series of successful jokes: gallows humor of a kind that makes us simultaneously gasp and laugh. It is a play in which the disgustingness of our failed mortality—the bedpans equally with the senile loss of reason—is transformed and rendered acceptable. Mr. Nichols implies that the price we pay for living is almost intolerably high, but "almost" is the word he emphasizes and celebrates. . . . Mr. Nichols' close, compassionate scrutiny of life and death heightened my sense of well-being instead of diminishing it; we forget at our peril that the artist is the best of physicians. (p. 60)

> *Brendan Gill, in* The New Yorker *(© 1974 by The New Yorker Magazine, Inc.), October 21, 1974.*

In a brief two decades, the young British dramatists who railed angrily at the Establishment have been succeeded by caustic young playwrights who acidly mock the welfare state. Underlying that mockery is a sour nagging resentment of the present sorry state of England. Thus it is no unintended irony that *The National Health* is set in a hospital ward for the dying. . . .

Silence ought to be the motif of such a room, or so one might think. Instead, it is raucous with gallows humor. There is probably not an outright comedy on Broadway at which one could clock more smiles, snorts, giggles and guffaws. Quite apart from the patients' sometimes grisly jests, the response of the audience obviously has complex, uneasy, psychological roots. Laughter is a wonder drug by which man anesthetizes his consciousness of mortality. (p. 90)

No one in contemporary theater orchestrates mordant laughter with a surer hand than Playwright Peter Nichols. His forked tongue darts at everything, but his compassion is deep and pure. Those who saw *A Day in the Death of Joe Egg* know that he confected humor out of a situation in which parents were coping with a mongoloid child. One miracle deserves another, and Nichols has performed it again in *The National Health.* (pp. 90, 93)

> *T. E. Kalem, "Ballet of Death," in* Time *(reprinted by permission from* Time, The Weekly Newsmagazine; *copyright Time Inc.), October 21, 1974, pp. 90, 93.*

Peter Nichols is . . . intelligent, witty, mordant and lazy-minded. *A Day in the Death of Joe Egg* . . . had a strong central premise: two young parents with a mute immobile child and the comedy-fantasy life they build around her. Having got the premise, Nichols thought he had the play and, after he had gone on for an act, he had to patch together a story out of rags and tatters. *Forget-Me-Not Lane* was the narrator's memoirs of his youth and didn't do much more than exploit the (British) audience's recollections of period minutiae and the trite poignancy of characters who, we know as we watch them, have since died.

Now comes *The National Health,* set in a North London hospital (the Sir Stafford Cripps Ward!). Again Nichols' assets are plain, including his ability to write good parts. (He was an actor for five years and he knows how to write for actors.) But again the laziness. Here he leans—with some talent but nonetheless just leans—on the inevitable horrors and comedies and ironies in a hospital ward. In an assorted cast of characters, some die, some leave, some come back, and they don't all behave predictably in relation to those facts. But *that's* predictable: and Nichols doesn't go much further. Maybe he thought the title itself would help, with its connotations of, well, of national health. No luck. It doesn't fill the hole at the center of the concept.

He does filigree his play with two devices. The first is show-biz fantasy. He interweaves a series of episodes called "television time": romance between a young Scots doctor and a Puerto Rican nurse, as well as one between the doctor's doctor-father and a Scots nurse, done as a cartoon of TV soap opera but really as a cartoon of pop adulation of the people in whose hands the lives of the patients rest. An orderly steps out of the play frequently to act as caustic interlocutor. Vaudeville of the serious is not exactly new and Nichols doesn't use it as well as, say, Charles Wood did in his script for Lester's *How I Won the War*, but the montage of deathrattle and raillery has its effect.

His second device is mode-mixing in the straight scenes. He ruthlessly combines barrack-room gags (inopportune farts), realistic horror (a cancer patient's chilling screams), glib religious satire (a missionary and a chaplain lampooned), insightful humor (a woman doctor so overworked that she falls asleep on a patient's chest while listening to his heart), and moving moments (an ulcer patient trying not to worry about his young son). He also revives a few antique jokes ("If my old friends were alive to see me now, they'd drop dead"); still the constant changes of key give the play a tart, unfooled air.

But neither they nor the fantasy sequences redeem it. In all his work so far Nichols has shown irreverence for sentimentality and theatrical taboos but, fundamentally, not much more. He *seems* to bite bullets—in *Joe Egg* the anguish of having a brain-damaged child, in this play the implacability of the hospital beds waiting for every one of us —but he just mouths them for a while before he spits them out, he never really crunches. We keep waiting for the author's gravity as distinct from the subject's. And waiting and waiting. Nichols' talent so far is for choosing subjects and modes, not in what he does with them. (p. 32)

> *Stanley Kauffmann, in* The New Republic *(reprinted by permission of* The New Republic; © *1974 by The New Republic, Inc.), November 2, 1974.*

The Freeway is set at some unspecified time in the near future, possibly 1984.... [It] is clearly meant to convey the Plight of the Nation by means of a major symbol. (p. 64)

[Apparently] we are meant to believe that the country is partly in the grip of a neo-Fascist organisation, with its private force of armed rangers, which owns The Freeway, a toll-highway that has superseded the motor-roads. How this organisation operates in conjunction with the elected government, or whether it is an authoritarian organ of the government, is not shown, or I did not understand. I suspect that Mr Nichols has taken the vague hints of authoritarianism in the air and linked them to the hated motor-car to produce the simple contrast: freeway=road to slavery.

True in one sense; the paradox of the motor-car is that it makes each individual free in the first instance, and then produces total nonfreedom, if all individuals want to avail themselves of their freedom at the same time. In other words, it is a perfect illustration of Existentialist liberty leading to the freeze-up of the practico-inert.

This is a problem which politics will have to solve, but it is not in itself a political problem; it is a pure consequence of technological proliferation. I find it difficult to imagine a neo-Fascist organisation centring on roads or motor-cars. I fancy it would be more likely, in an advanced society, to facilitate traffic movement and to clamp down elsewhere. Why not keep people buzzing from *A* to *B* and from *B* to *A* in the illusory conviction that they are doing something real, are accomplishing a *projet*? Movement could be the opium of the people (as indeed it already is to a large extent). I don't think Mr Nichols has thought out the whole psycho-phenomenological question of the motor-car in an interesting way. I have never owned a car, have never learned to drive, and would vote for any government that proposed a return to the bicycle; but it is a waste of time to be metaphysically naive or flatly negative about the motor-car, which is a poetic object for most people, whether they know this or not. . . .

Equally weak is his treatment of the opposition between nature and culture. The Canadianised ex-Cockney has known the independence of the wilds and, when hunger threatens, he gathers mushrooms and blackberries, and shoots a pigeon. At the end, he walks off on his own with a confident smile, as if only he were at home in the "natural" situation created by a suddenly demotorised world. But this is an unjustified and sentimental implication. No "natural" man could survive for long in Britain without recourse to civilisation, although he might manage better for a time in the remoter parts of Canada. But even in Canada, he would not really be "natural", because Man is, by definition, the species which has, even in the most primitive situation, added culture to nature. Robinson Crusoe and Tarzan of the Apes are both highly civilised types, who convey an illusion of naturalness because of the very selective brand of culture they present us with. Man cannot return to nature; he can only choose between varieties of culture. All this has been debated *ad infinitum* since the 18th century, but Mr Nichols seems to go no further than the popular, non-philosophical clichés to achieve his theatrical effects, and therefore they cannot form a compelling pattern. Perhaps we can put it this way: *Joe Egg* and *The National Health* were good, because Nichols has a direct personal perception of physical or medical evil; *The Freeway* fails, because he does not sense with equal clarity the nub of political evil. (p. 66)

> *John Weightman, in* Encounter (© *1974 by Encounter Ltd.), December, 1974.*

Peter Nichols's *A Day in the Death of Joe Egg* (1967) had the characters directly addressing the audience so as to streamline the presentation and give a hearty music-hall humour to a gloomy subject, but the basis of its considerable appeal for audiences was that it dealt in straightforward naturalistic terms with a topical problem—what is it like to have a spastic child? His second play, *The National Health* (1969), counterpointed the fantasy naturalism of television soap-operas about hospitals with the "straight" naturalism of a "real" hospital. In *Chez Nous* (1974) he seems to have fallen back completely on the old domestic comedy routine, using language ostensibly directed from one character to another, but actually turned outwards to amuse the audience. In his latest play, *The Freeway*, he models himself unprepossessingly on Shaw. [One] might well feel depressed about the outcome of the Reformation if he had only Nichols's development before his eyes. (pp. 64-5)

John Spurling, in Encounter (© *1974-75 by Encounter Ltd.), January, 1975.*

O

O'BRIEN, Edna   1932-

The male-female relationship and the condition of women, especially their sexual repression, in her native Ireland are principal themes in Ms O'Brien's novels and short stories. Because of her outspoken but sensitive treatments of controversial subjects, her books, such as *The Lonely Girl* and *A Pagan Place*, have been banned in Ireland. (See also *Contemporary Authors*, Vols. 1-4, rev. ed.)

Inside every short story is a bigger story—which ought not to be trying to get out. Inside each of Edna O'Brien's stories is a full-length novel: quiescent, let it be said. The converse is also true; each story could be part of one and the same novel. They integrate: [*A Scandalous Woman*] is a collection, not a gallimaufry. Scandalous Eily, of the title, is the victim of the God-like rage for respectability. More than an eye for an eye: for a tumble in the lime-kiln—marriage for life. There are glimpses of her after her shotgun wedding, growing odd, her lovely hair falling out, and then growing wild, a figure of fun and terror in the street; finally, her hair permed, her spark gone, serving in her husband's grocery store. In a 'land of shame, a land of murder' and sacrificial women, she has paid the price.

'Over' is the lament of a left-off woman. The absurd shifts and fantasies of misery define her as the betrayed, the unliberated, hanging on grimmer than death. She knows what she has lost and she exposes her lover more mercilessly than she does herself. 'King Lear says women must be kind, or something to that effect.' The effect will have to do.

'The Favourite' dead-pan but piercingly tells of the decline and fall of a little empire. Tess, a third child, was born on the Sabbath day. She is not strong on imagination and lives by virtue of the facts. With *her* luck, facts are a virtue. They are also means and an end. She swans through life. But even she, when her turn comes, does not know if she has been happy, and asks: 'Is this how it is when one begins to be unhappy?'

'Honeymoon' is a classic case of disappointment. Not that the honeymoon itself is classic—these two have been living together for months. Nor are they a classic couple: he is twice her age and has had 'two other wives of different nationalities'. Nevertheless, she 'obeyed him in everything, even in the type of shoes she was to wear—completely flat

shoes which as it happened gave her a pain in her instep'. They meet a hunchback who curses them when they decline to rent her steaming wet cottage. They disappoint the hunchback, and a lonely couple longing for company, and he disappoints her. "Marry in haste, repent in leisure,' she thinks. But how much and how often will she disappoint him? And thus be the third wife not to come up to his quite reasonable expectations?

In 'A Journey' there is an attempt to sound the man's emotions, but only as surmise. Suppositions are all the woman can have. In 'Love-Child', Hickey, the workman, desperately tries to cope, but he is unequipped: brings too many cabbages, shoots the uneatable wild goose and wastes himself. He dies, leaving a ridiculous memory and his dreadful 'love-child'. This man had love but did not know what to do with it.

The Creature's deformity is her soft heart. It is not human to be kind, nor even womanly—whatever King Lear said—and only the beasts of the field have cause for humility. So she is always referred to as 'The Creature'. However, she is not without hope. For twenty years she has lived on a 'last high tightrope', which is twitched from under her, to release a 'gigantic and useless sorrow'. Appropiately, it is all done by kindness.

The last story, 'The House of My Dreams', describes a mental breakdown. With this subject, it is so easy to pile the agony on the joy, splendours on miseries. With a writer like Edna O'Brien the result is still worth reading for the juxtapositions. (On the other hand, a writer whose technique is based on surprise might do well to remember that the trouble with punchlines is that eventually the mind tends to duck.) When the last crumbling woman is taken away to the place where 'she and others would be under supervision' these Kathleens have learned their bitter lesson. There can be no liberation from love—it was, after all, Adam's rib. (p. 316-17)

A. L. Barker, "Bondmaidens," in The Listener (© *British Broadcasting Corp. 1974; reprinted by permission of A. L. Barker), September 5, 1974, pp. 316-17.*

[*A Scandalous Woman And Other Stories*] offer the pleasures [Edna O'Brien's] readers have come to expect: the brisk and deadly pleasures of fairy tale. She is adept at evoking gardens of Eden: a rural Irish childhood-Eden and the Eden of sexual delight. Snakes abound. Penalties threaten. The dangling apple is too bright to be wholesome, but the girl approaching cannot gain this grim knowledge without risk. As though exhausted by this primal dilemma, Miss O'Brien's heroines seem, once fallen, unable to rise. Their Fall is always sexual. If they do totter to their feet, it is to fall again. . . .

Despite feminist efforts on behalf of their kind, Miss O'-Brien's sex-dazzled heroines continue to race like lemmings toward unhappiness. Biology, for them, is still inflexible destiny and, with the possible exception of a quick, free abortion on the National Health, no social advantage is going to change things for creatures whose passivity rivals that of Sade's Justine. . . .

A highly successful writer, she nurtures her fiction on the compost of defeat. Doom, as in a *Totentanz*, is visibly present at the happiest moments. . . . [The] legitimate woman, a constant though faceless figure in the O'Brien triangle, is the foil and antithesis of the scandalous heroine. The legitimate woman has the social virtues. She keeps her man in the end because she calculates, choosing happiness —a long-term affair—over ecstasy, a much dicier value. Miss O'Brien does not care for the social virtues. . . .

Although a feminist republic of free, responsible women might be tempted to ban Miss O'Brien's defeatist writings, they should rather, I think, be grateful to her. Her stories are bulletins from a front on which they will not care to engage, field reports on the feminine condition at its most acute. Only a woman fiction writer can safely and authentically explore feminine passivity to the full. She can experience it totally in her characters while protected from its virus by the fact that she is, qua writer, simultaneously active. Miss O'Brien explores with persuasive thoroughness. (pp. 3-4)

Miss O'Brien's range is narrow and obsessional. The larger world does not interest her. Her social settings are perfunctory. Like Racine's queens, her sex and self-absorbed women are undisturbed by the day-to-day. Nothing intervenes to prevent their passion reaching boiling point. Unlike Racinian passion, however, theirs never boils over. There is no explosion. No climax. The slice of life is chopped off more or less neatly and a few sentences of melancholy Stoicism tie it up.

Hers is the archetypal Romantic attitude: a yearning to cage the minute, arrest time at the childhood phase or the moment of sexual ecstasy or, all else failing, to recapture it through art. Her talents are for sensuous evocation, shimmering surface seduction. She can make us share her dreams, taste those cakes, feel, see and touch as she has done. What she does not seem to be able to do is to get experience into perspective. She cannot judge or structure it and so she seems forced—a variant of Santayana's sentence on those who forget history—to rework it. The story is forever the same.

As Miss O'Brien's fictional world is cyclic, it would be unreasonable to expect of her the explosive condensation sometimes aimed for in the short story. There is no moment of insight or understanding either, since the world is not to be understood. A quietistic and elegant shrug is her usual way of ending a story. . . . (p. 4)

Julia O'Faolian, in The New York Times Book Review *(© 1974 by The New York Times Company; reprinted by permission), September 22, 1974.*

The premise that the happiest of lives will one day be deprived and that, for the most promising and the most beautiful, there is destined a time of madness and emptiness, is not a new one in literature. What is notable about Edna O'Brien is the gaiety, the genuine spirits, that lighten the life of [the] stories [in *A Scandalous Woman and Other Stories*] before the darkness sets in. Miss O'Brien's talent, as evident in the long title story, is to create characters in the full belief and the immediacy of the moment, characters whose lives may go this way or that, who exist innocent of their fate, and who somehow keep the reader innocent with them. The collection is not at its best in cluttered stories like "The House of My Dreams," a rambling work told from the point of view of a mind unhinged. But madness is Miss O'Brien's strong suit, particularly the sort of madness that is the product of loneliness and age, of the unexpected, unprepared-for vacancies that lie in wait for one. It is evident in "The Favorite," a stark, chilling story and one that is steadfastly ordinary, ordinary in its details and its assumptions in the way that most human life is ordinary. It is a steadfastness that distinguishes most of the stories here and that makes Edna O'Brien so enormously readable a writer. (p. 28)

Dorothy Rabinowitz, in Saturday Review/ World *(copyright © 1974 by Saturday Review/World, Inc.; reprinted with permission), October 5, 1974.*

Miss O'Brien's women unhesitantly acknowledge sexual necessity while living independently of public concerns; her feminists rarely recognize that their cause is public. Instead their object is love, and their sorrow is its loss. . . . The fear of loss is an ever-present burden of living; moreover, it is a dominant attribute of love. (p. 10)

Still a second factor exposed by Miss O'Brien's literary stethoscope should cause more discomfort than this exclusive submergence in the love theme, and that is the thoroughness with which one's choice of someone to love defines the entire range of one's personality; it exposes a streak of masochism, describes one's pathetic ideals, or reflects conditions of loneliness. (pp. 10-11)

In the final analysis, loneliness and independence must be acknowledged as dominant themes in Edna O'Brien's fiction. Stresses, especially those of loneliness, most dramatically take the form of a quest for someone to love, and that person not only has a body but also reflects the protagonist's state of mind. (pp. 12-13)

[Sexual] failure, where it occurs in Edna O'Brien's works, is often the result of choice and of religious background and is countered by a staunch independence that all Miss O'-Brien's heroines, though some are unaware of it, exhibit (Mary Hooligan of *Night* turns an array of sexual, and other, reminiscences into triumphant humor and rebounds from her last disappointment with admirable courage to face the future). Of the reader's retention of sexual stresses as the dominant impression of her books, Edna O'Brien remarked [that] in a story of 70,000 words 3000 at most might deal directly with sex [and] 'if these 3000 are pored over to the virtual exclusion of the other 67,000 whose fault is that?" (p. 14)

That Miss O'Brien has been called a feminist develops not so much from an ideal or from a philosophical cause but from a realistic appraisal of the female condition and of the male-female relationship. Asked what the Cinderella motif means to her, as it appears in *August*, where Ellen wants a certain kind of man who would "control and bewitch" her, Edna O'Brien said, "I mean the metamorphosis from being outcast to being queen, to being accepted." Of the Prince Charming in this role, seven years after *August* was published, Miss O'Brien said, "As for the man who would bewitch her, I think I would use a stronger word now, the man who would possess her. I have a very strong pull and obviously conflicting pull towards god and the devil." (p. 39)

In Miss O'Brien's hands the god who should mate with Cinderella and establish her in a new kingdom of happiness merges with the evil principle, so that, for example Dr. Flaggler [of *Night*], a veritable Mephistopheles, chortles "You are not going to escape me, not now, not ever, you are not going out of my sight, you poor zealous wretch".....

This archaic instinct in Miss O'Brien's work becomes a trenchant elucidation of the physical processes of maturation and age. As a result of self-development her characters realize that they must free themselves from the evil force, and generally they gather courage and walk away, as in the short story "How to Grow a Wisteria." (p. 40)

In a sense Miss O'Brien's work may be viewed as a process of change from romance to realism—from the innocent view that an alignment with a male means happiness ever after to the stark realization that such is not possible. Actually, the popular Cinderella story is fraught with marital suicide in that Cinderella has lost the connection with abstract Wisdom or cultural benefits. In Edna O'Brien's work, Prince Charming is Eugene Gaillard, attracted to Caithleen Brady for her naïveté, but later finding her repulsive for the same quality.

Rather than representing Wisdom, which was originally a combination of Love and Knowledge, today's Cinderella must acquire Wisdom. (p. 41)

August marks a transition between the heroine's earlier quest for self-development through marriage with a hero and the later knowledge that such is impossible. That dream was almost relinquished in *Girls* and was retained only in the ideal of a lover in *August*. Thereafter the Edna O'Brien heroine keeps the dream as a shadow of reality but alliance with a rare desirable male always, for some reason, proves impossible. The woman builds her future in direct strife with a male, as does Zee [of *Zee & Co.*], or independently with an added burden of revenge for the damage caused by a man in the past. (pp. 47-8)

The style during these years has developed from the simple and barren naïveté of the young Caithleen with her revealing touches of ingenuousness ("I felt badly about being the cause of sending them solicitors' letters but Eugene said that it had to be") to the discursive ruminations of Mary Hooligan who reels off exhaustive lists like those of Samuel Beckett's *Watt* and converses with herself in a stream-of-consciousness-with-plot technique somewhat like that of

Molly Bloom. Most of the fiction is written in the first person, which enhances both its verisimilitude and, one suspects, the critical tendency to treat it as autobiography. The best passages of the early novels are those scenes which reveal contrasting personalitities—in *The Lonely Girl*, when Gaillard comes to tea with Joanna, when the deputation of virtuous god-fearing farmers calls upon the agnostic Gaillard to retrieve Caithleen's honor, when the locals in the pub insult Gaillard and Caithleen—and these point to a successful career in drama. *Girls in Their Married Bliss*, the most discomforting of the novels, is blunt and direct in diction. The same attitudes on love, or the female condition, or religious friction may be phrased more subtly in the later works. The progression in style has permitted experimentation in technique, notably in *A Pagan Place*, which is written in the second person with the child-heroine identified only as "you," the father as "he," and the mother as "she." The two kinds of ficiton—the Irish and the urbane —are produced from two life styles in Ireland and in England. Caithleen from County Clare is . . . a "right looking eejit" (a Clare expression), and a heroine may appear "streelish" in Ireland and "wanton" in England. The last novel, *Night*, marks a maturity not only in style and content but also in perception about the home land. Using real Irish names, Miss O'Brien has now created a territory as Faulkner did with Yoknapatawpha. (pp. 77-8)

This mergence of Irish geography with artistic vision develops naturally from Miss O'Brien's concern with memory. The technique of *A Pagan Place* and of *Night* is the use of memory through contrasting personalities; but the similarity between the "you," who makes a "mind and soul trip" into childhood, and the mature Mary Hooligan is the Irish background. (p. 79)

In the short story collection, three stories—"The Rug," "An Outing," and "Irish Revel"—evoke the atmosphere of Joyce's *Dubliners*. (p. 80)

"Irish Revel," the best story in the collection, offers a West of Ireland version of Joyce's classic, "The Dead," although, as the title indicates, the living here are mostly concerned with living. (p. 81)

The influence of Joyce, and especially of "The Dead" [can be noted] in *The Country Girls*. Also the style of *A Pagan Place* echoes the early pages of Joyce's *Portrait*. . . . *Night* features a rural stripling, "a fellow with unmatching eyes," who recalls the blind stripling of *Ulysses*; and Mary's "winding effluvias" evokes a flickering gleam of Anna Livia Plurabelle. *Night*'s greatest resemblance of Joyce is in its indebtedness to the soliloquy of Molly Bloom with the particular Edna O'Brien touch of attachment to the Irish past. (pp. 82-3)

The evolution of Edna O'Brien as a writer, however, bears as its closest resemblance to James Joyce her regard for authenticity. (p. 83)

Yet, if Edna O'Brien has learned from Joyce, in particular in the rich prose of Mary Hooligan, she remains her own woman. (pp. 83-4)

Grace Eckley, in her Edna O'Brien (© *1974 by Associated University Presses, Inc.*), *Bucknell University Press, 1974.*

O'BRIEN, Flann (pseudonym of Brian O Nuallain)   1911-1966

O'Brien was an Irish novelist and humorist whose comic masterpiece was *At Swim-Two-Birds*. He was best known in Ireland as Myles na gCopaleen, his *nom de plume* for his Irish Times column. (See also *Contemporary Authors*, Vols. 21-22; obituary, Vols. 25-28.)

When I looked at *The Poor Mouth* by Myles na Gopaleen —alias Flann O'Brien—I had a sinking feeling that this translation from the Gaelic was going to prove an Important Irish Novel. So I consulted an Irish friend and he confirmed my worst fears: it is an important satire on modern Gaelic literature. 'But,' my friend added, 'it's very funny.' Reassured, I read—and he was right, it is very funny. It is a ludicrous exaggeration of one's worst prejudices about bog-Irish, living with the family pigs, in non-stop rain.

The Poor Mouth tells the story of the life and times of Bonaparte O'Coonassa, Gaelic peasant growing up in the village of Corkadoragha 'in that part of Ireland where only Irish is spoken'; oppressed by the elements and his own Gaelic-ness, drunkenness, idleness, superstition and ignorance; patronised by learned pro-Gael gentlefolk from Dublin; and victimised by English-speaking domination— which begins during his first and only day of schooling, when the master beats him soundly for giving his Gaelic name, and renames him, identically with every other child in the school, James O'Donnell, and ends with his sentence to 29 years in prison, like his father before him, for a crime he did not commit after a trial he could not understand. Occasionally, the inhabitants of Corkadoragha get their own back: O'Coonassa's grandfather, 'the Old-Grey-Fellow', dresses all his piglets up in clothes to qualify for a Government award for all English-speaking children; and when one of the disguised pigs escapes, it wins the family half-a-crown and a flask of whiskey by being mistaken for a real Gaelic speaker by a German linguistics professor with a tape-recorder. But, on the whole, the Gaels suffer continually from the attacks of a malign universe. (pp. 93-4)

> *Sara Maitland, in* The Listener (© *British Broadcasting Corp. 1974; reprinted by permission of Sara Maitland), July 18, 1974.*

Always a satirist (often an indignant one), O'Brien could be scathingly funny about causes in which he believed—the value of the Gaelic language to Irish culture, for instance. He was also the most thoroughly *literary* comic writer since Joyce, lampooning not only the Irish but the clichés of attitude and language with which ten centuries of Irish writers have belabored their compatriots. . . .

If "The Poor Mouth" is not quite a comic masterpiece, it nevertheless shows a comic genius working close to his best capability. Humor of this quality, this intensity, is very rare; as witty in its language as in its invention, it cries to be read aloud.

> *Peter S. Prescott, "Galloping Gael," in* Newsweek (*copyright 1974 by Newsweek, Inc.; all rights reserved; reprinted by permission), October 21, 1974, p. 112.*

'Tis the odd joke of modern Irish literature—of the three novelists in its holy trinity, James Joyce, Samuel Beckett and Flann O'Brien, the easiest and most accessible of the

lot, O'Brien, is the one ignored by the American public. Flann was the boy who stayed in Ireland and masked his corrosive humor under the decencies. He practiced eerie magic within the homespun bounds of Irish myth and folktale, detective story, even out and out comic parody and engaging nonsense in a regular newspaper column. Though in his two great books, *At Swim-Two-Birds* and *The Third Policeman*, he would veer respectively toward the experimental play of Joyce and the bleak dead-end dementia of Beckett, Flann was too much his own man, Ireland's man, to speak in any but his own tongue and cheek. And O it's marvelous stuff. A book by this rogue (who will drive you and the branch librarian crazy with his pseudonyms . . . is tasty as the fairy tales gobbled up in childhood. (p. 1)

What is *The Poor Mouth* about? The stone, bone-breaking poverty of the Gaelic-speaking farmers of the Irish West, and a hero, Bonaparte O'Coonassa, who spurns these older brethren, takes refuge in fairy tales and through a lark of fate finds himself rewarded with a haven of sorts for his middle age.

Nothing is in the mouths of these potato diggers but sweet Gaelic. And that is the nourishment of "the poor mouth": language. Though translated out of the original into harsher English, the heroic mockery of the tale rings out, rocking even Noah's Ark in its wild waves. I will not spoil a stone sober jest by relating what awaits O'Coonassa in the Irish paradise on top of the mountain, Hunger Stack. I can affirm his words, it *is* better for a man to die on the heights from celestial waters. . . .

Strains of the Bible and the old Icelandic saga make themselves felt in lines of *The Poor Mouth*. . . .

At first glance one might imagine that the chapters of *The Poor Mouth* . . . are simply Irish tall tales. Only deceptively and stealthily Flann O'Brien has been dropping the seeds of a fabulous vine in his wake and it suddenly appears in full flower, the spine of a grim plot waving in your face as you put the book down. Its crown may be high in the cirrus and cumulus of fable, but its roots grip the rocky bottom of Corkadoragha. . . . It is a parable of doom for the Irish-speaking folk of the West spun out of the stuff of anecdote, joke, side-of-the-mouth sarcasm, in which the old heroic literature, *The Tain*, can be heard, twisted to modern usage. Half child's tale, half political cartoon, there is a far off reverberation of Dean Swift's gifts in it all. (p. 3)

> *Mark Jay Mirsky, "Gael Force," in* Book World—The Washington Post (© *The Washington Post), January 19, 1975, pp. 1, 3.*

The recurring case of Flann O'Brien alias Brian Nolan, a civil servant, alias Myles na Gopaleen, a newspaper columnist, seems to end up with the same verdict—quite possibly a major comic writer. But a forgettable one, apparently, who has to be rediscovered every time a book of his swims into our ken. . . . This present hilarious book ["The Poor Mouth"] was written in Gaelic in 1941 for an Irish audience about a local situation. You read with a hypothetical American kibitzing over your shoulder and he seems to laugh at the wrong places. The reasons are cultural and amplify a chronic minor ache of Irish lit.—how American (and English) readers misinterpret the writing of a small rural country in ways that suppress its truest voice, its rootedness in a culture as alien as Aztec or Senufo, to which the Irish language gives immediate access. . . .

O'Brien [uses] the language itself with a hard-edged almost Swiftian precision. He knew Irish (and French) literature backwards (his puns in Gaelic are Joycean), had a pub's-eye view of the world, and a savage streak of misanthrophy. He brought irony along with him into the closed Gaelic Revival universe much as the Captain Cook brought measles to the Easter Islanders. (p. 25)

In the original, [the story] is conveyed in a Gaelic distinguished by its purity of locution, its supple phrasing, its precision of meaning and double-meaning. The language itself is both subject and vehicle of the story and so suffers a double compression that constantly tests its toughness and delicacy. The references raise a whole Atlantis of Gaelic literature . . . only to destroy tracts of it, but in the process adding the best modern book ever written in Gaelic. The man who blessed the language by so using it was of course designated an enemy of the people or rather of the revivalists who never forgave him for producing at their expense what they all wanted to see—a masterpiece in Gaelic. . . .

In English the purity of the folk-style comes up a little too wide-eyed. The finest uses of that style are the parodies of the Irish sagas in O'Brien's best book, "At Swim-Two-Birds" (1939), and in James Stephen's "The Crock of Gold" where the simplicity is successfully estheticized.

The original was written in a moribund language about a moribund language for a vanishing audience. Yet for almost any Irishman, the language calls up a primary culture, a lucid and devious state of mind to which only the language gives access, and which is compromised by most of the Irish literature fitted so handily into English lit. courses in this country. O'Brien's very modern ironies give as much access to that world as anyone who doesn't have Gaelic can get. And for the generations that suffered the excesses of the language revival, the book is a mythic construct, a sort of companion to the "Portrait of the Artist," in which the hero—the Irish language—suffers bitter repressions before it is exalted. (p. 26)

> Brian O'Doherty, in The New York Times Book Review (© 1975 by The New York Times Company; reprinted by permission), January 19, 1975.

The Poor Mouth is a very unlikely piece of fiction. To begin with, it was originally written in Modern Irish—Gaelic, if you prefer—a language used by only a few thousand people. Second, it is actually a parody of a literary genre known only to fanatics on Irish literature, namely Autobiographies Dictated by Illiterate Gaelic Peasants. And, most unlikely of all, even if you know none of these facts, it's a fine book, hilarious, moving, gorgeously written.

Brian O'Nolan . . . probably would have become much more widely known had he chosen to write in English. He did write a very popular newspaper column in English for The Irish Times under the name of Myles na Gopaleen. But his fiction, published in Irish under the name Flann O'Brien, "went down the bung-hole," as the Celticist Frank Kinnehan recently put it. Irish was O'Nolan's adopted language; he used it because he loved it. His small audience of Irish readers did not love his fiction, however, because he vigorously satirized all forms of Irish vanities, including venerated literary traditions. His books did somewhat better in English translation, and greatly appealed to other writers, such as Dylan Thomas, S. J. Perelman, and James Joyce.

Joyce probably admired O'Nolan's fiction because in certain ways it resembled his own. Like Joyce, O'Nolan used his abundant imagination to spin together complex mythological themes and archaic literary styles. He especially enjoyed producing parodies of ancient sagas, which he wrote in Old Irish—impressive labor, especially when one considers that the language which Old Irish most closely resembles is Sanskrit. (Both tongues have the same ancestor, Proto-Indo-European, their major differences being that Sanskrit has its own form of written script and is easier to learn. In fact, the only language that surpasses Old Irish for sheer complexity is Navajo.) You might think that a writer using so many problematic devices would produce rather pedantic books. Actually, most of O'Nolan's Old Irish parodies show up in a work called At Swim-Two-Birds, which Brendan Behan called "just the kind of book to give to your sister—if she's a loud, dirty, boozy girl." Not pedantic.

In The Poor Mouth, O'Nolan mostly stuck to Modern Irish, but not the variety now taught in all Irish schools by government decree. (This official Gaelic only came into existence after the Revolution of 1916, and is a thoroughly artificial language seldom used in real life.) O'Nolan wrote in genuine Modern Irish, a direct descendant of Old Irish which has survived only in a few small areas in the western part of Ireland known as the Gaeltacht. The people who live in this remote section preserved their ancient speech and customs throughout centuries of British oppression mainly because the British found them totally useless. They had nothing, they did nothing: they just lived in abject poverty and spoke pure Irish. In the days of the Irish literary revival, Anglo-Irish authors like Yeats and Synge took a great interest in these living relics of Ireland's past. Synge even went to live with some of them in the Aran Islands, where he found much inspiration for his plays.

O'Nolan did something quite different. In The Poor Mouth he adopted the language and persona of a Gaeltacht native and wrote a memoir from that point of view. Through his own words we follow the life of Bonaparte O'Coonassa from his birth to his incarceration in a British jail for a crime which, naturally, he never committed. Until that sad day, O'Coonassa lives with his grandfather, the Old-Grey-Fellow, in a fictional place known as Corkadoragha and characterized chiefly by potatoes, poverty, and torrential rain. Pigs die from their own stench; people drink, dance, and starve themselves to death; and the Sea-Cat, a horrible beast, goes on periodic rampages. This may not sound funny, but Corkadoragha turns out to be the world headquarters for gallows humor. (pp. 116-17)

The Poor Mouth jigs along a narrow path that winds between outright horror and downright blather but whose foundation is historical reality. O'Nolan based his narrative on the actual memoirs of Gaeltacht residents, published in the 1930s. His book not only satirizes Irish life in general, but he specifically parodies the style of these memoirs. . . .

O'Nolan did not save the Irish language itself with books

like *The Poor Mouth*, a fact he laments. . . . But by writing in Irish, O'Nolan did preserve the spirit of its great tradition, in much the same way Isaac Bashevis Singer has rescued the spirit of the old Yiddish traditions from oblivion. These are generous acts for writers to perform. (p. 118)

> *David McClelland, "Spuds and Rainwater," in* Harper's *(copyright 1975 by Harper's Magazine; reprinted from the February, 1975 issue by special permission), February, 1975, pp. 116-18.*

An Béal Bocht [published in English as *The Poor Mouth*] is a satire; the object of the satire is the Gaelic language, or more properly the Gaelic language revival; but since the book was written in Gaelic and is itself a product of that revival, the satire inevitably turns in upon itself in ways that defy unerring passage through nuances and shades of meaning (and double meaning) from one language to another. We are told, for example, in a brief preface, that O'Brien is at times parodying the style of certain modern Gaelic writers—Máire (Séamus O Grianna and Tomás O Criomhthainn)—but to readers ignorant of Gaelic and unfamiliar with the originals, the parody, if recognizable at all, is not likely to mean much. . . .

Poverty, famine, flood, drunkenness, squalor and thievery are the principal coordinates of existence in [Corkadoragha, the fictional setting of *The Poor Mouth,* and the] worst of all possible worlds. Bonaparte, a Gaelic Candide, accepts his existence as if he were, as indeed he is, one with the rocks and the rain and the bogs and the sea, one for whom calamity is a natural condition of being, one of those creatures whom Yeats, describing the inhabitants of William Carleton's *Traits and Stories of the Irish Peasantry*, spoke of as "only half-emerged from the earth."

This is not what our English cousins would call a jolly book, and some of our Irish cousins—those with minds more literal than literary—would hardly think it a funny book. But to those who know the folly of which even a good man in a good cause is capable, *The Poor Mouth* is a small Gaelic classic in the classical tradition of satire that ranges from Juvenal to Swift, to Voltaire, to Joyce, to—God help us—even to Evelyn Waugh. The deadliest weapon, the sharpest blade in the armory of satire is irony, the talent for turning the world upside down or, failing that, standing men on their heads so that true, or at least fresh, perspective is possible and there is once again a chance of knowing what the world is actually like to look at. The satirist in this is like those prophets of the Old Testament who lashed men from their idolatries—whatever image man's pride takes in whatever age—back into human shape again. Flann O'Brien is here deflating the heroic myth of the Gael (which was anyhow largely the contrivance of non-Gaelic Anglo-Irishmen) and at the same time instructing the Irish establishment of his day that a language, even the sweet, melodious tongue of the Gael, is less important than the men and women who speak it; that the Gaeltacht—those areas in which only Irish is spoken—cannot continue to exist as linguistic ghettos; that Gaelic made compulsory (as it was in Irish schools until a few years ago) is pointed in the direction of eternity where, like Latin and Greek, it may embalm a culture but can no longer express the life of a people.

The final irony in *The Poor Mouth* is of course that while it

pokes fine (and unrefined) fun at the Gaelic revival, it is at the same time proof of the success and continuing vitality of that revival—*on se moque de ce qu'on aime*—a success and vitality sufficient to have stimulated and sustained a satiric work of the first rank. (p. 312)

> *Kevin Sullivan, "'A Bad Story about the Hard Life'," in* The Nation *(copyright 1975 by the Nation Associates, Inc.), March 15, 1975, pp. 311-12.*

O'Nolan (hereinafter to be called O'Brien) was something of a *seannachie*—a Gaelic word for that singular Gaelic person, the storyteller. But he was not the sort of *seannachie* who writes novels. His novels are no more novels than Carroll's Alice books are, being vehicles for a play of wit and fantasy, lyrical, satirical, and surreal. Flights and gags and conundrums are preferred to plot, character, and conclusion, and set up a system of internal relations which resembles the structure of a symbolist poem. It is of Carroll that his novels (hereinafter to be called novels) vividly remind one—as much as of Joyce, by whose works, and legend, and devoted tribe of simpleton American thesis-writers O'Brien seems to have been obsessed. For Myles na Gopaleen, O'Brien's journalistic self, James Joyce was "a complete prig, a snob, and a person possessed of endowment unique in the archives of conceit": this might be the voice of a wounded love. Thirteen years earlier, in 1944, the same journalist had asserted that, apart from Joyce and Yeats, Irish writers were "literary vermin, an eruption of literary scabies."

Irish writers were faced, in the Thirties, with a choice between contributing to a nationalist concern with the protection of Gaelic culture and the folk tradition, and siding with those who wanted to be Modern and to follow Joyce into a literal or figurative exile. This *seannachie*, who was also a Gaelic scholar, stayed at home: but he did not side with the nationalists, and what he wrote, in Gaelic and out of it, was distinctively Modern. Irish literature since Yeats and Joyce has known a striking austerity—evident in the novels and plays of Beckett, the verse of Patrick Kavanagh, and the stories of O'Brien: three grim men, who appear to bring news, among other things, of a society in which sex is wrong and in which violence and drunkenness are more widely honored than they are in most places. (pp. 31-2)

Pleonasm is a use of language which displays elaboration or excess, and at different levels his was a pleonastic art. His novels contain duplication and repetition, and incorporate parodies of other people's writings; one subplot is mirrored in another; doors open into the room you are about to quit. (p. 32)

O'Brien's cresslike cresses, pointed points, an imaginary title like *The Closed Cloister*, his elaborations and embellishments, his seemingly unending cycles and recurrences—these can look like a fulfillment of the hereditary patterns and predilections of Celtic art. His excesses recall, and occasionally imitate, the rhetoric of classical Gaelic poetry, the grace notes of bagpipe music, the convolutions and circularities of the illuminated manuscript, of the brooch, of the Celtic cross. The snakelike snakes of his stories have a way of swallowing their own tails: his interest in such shapes, and in bicycles, being that of a man who is interested in eternity (he is also interested in hell).

These interests may be interpreted as belonging to an art which is practiced for its own sake, which is austere, self-sufficing, pure. But there may be those who interpret them with reference to the circumstances of O'Brien's own late-Gaelic society, and who insist that this is an art of tautology, a gratuitous art, a celibate's art, in the sense that it appears to belong to a country in which climaxes are considered disgraceful, and who are reminded, by a purple patch of O'Brien's about an arsenal of bombs and guns, of the pure and austere mutilators who compose the IRA. Here, it might be thought, is an art which repeats itself, goes in circles and does not end, and which gives a picture of the neverendingness of Ireland, of its over and over again, its forever after and its waiting for Godot. It is both an old and a new art: each of his works, in the self-sufficing Modern way, lies enclosed in the cloister of its peculiar language, but that language, to the extent of its capacity for piety and for parody, opens onto the works of the ethnic past, each with its own enclosures and excesses.

The truth is that O'Brien's excesses, and those which have preceded them, are a complex business, and are difficult for a foreigner to interpret. There are occasions when this abundance can seem like a figure of speech for its opposite —for scarcity or dearth. We seem then to be in a world— any one of a succession of Gaelic worlds—where watercress is as good as a feast because there is not much else to eat, and where one thing can hardly be compared to another because there is only the one thing. (pp. 32-3)

The Poor Mouth is a copious treatment of the subject of scarcity, and it reaches its climax, such as it is, in an imagined abundance, a magic windfall feast complete with fairy gold. History does not exist for the people of the tale. The present has swallowed the past, there has always been dearth, and the folk mind thinks hard about potatoes.

This wonderful book was published in 1941 . . . [and] is a better book, in my view, than either *At Swim* or *The Third Policeman*. All three books represent collections of episodes, but *The Poor Mouth*, copious but short, has more of a point, a pointed point. It has none of the desultoriness which the unending can produce, and which is produced in the other two works. It even has an ending. *At Swim* appears, significantly enough, to have been cut down to publishable size by another hand (so, of course, was *The Waste Land*). O'Brien prided himself on the "plot" of *The Third Policeman*, but this may have been codology. He also talked, in the same breath, of the narrator's being in hell, and of his being a heel and a killer. But the narrator is experienced by the reader as courteous, forlorn, and delightful, and he does not appear to experience the pains of the damned. (p. 33)

No one who is curious about the three Gaelic literatures should fail to read *The Poor Mouth*. (p. 34)

Karl Miller, "Gael in Wonderland," in The New York Review of Books (reprinted with permission from The New York Review of Books; copyright © 1975 NYREV, Inc.), May 1, 1975, pp. 31-4.

You would eagerly buy and read . . . [*The Poor Mouth*] if you had read *At Swim-Two-Birds* (O'Brien's best) or *The Third Policeman*. If you have not previously read O'-Brien's English novels, you might still be interested in The

Poor Mouth's subject, the Gaelic language movement and its effects on the Irish. But even if you aren't, the treatment of this subject deserves the attention of all punsters, tall-tale lovers, fanciers of farce, enemies of cliché, and just plain people who like a good laugh. O'Brien's comic style, here as in his other works, is incredibly elastic. It stretches characters and events to their utmost—and then goes further. Gaelic is as intelligible as pig Latin? Well then, who should speak "Gaelic which was so good, so poetic and so obscure" but a drunken piglet in breeches? Of course the poor true swindling Gaels in O'Brien's always-raining Cork-adoragha all live like swine and eat potatoes. As Flann O'Brien in his novels and as Myles na gCopaleen in his *Irish Times* columns, Brian O'Nolan was a satirist who saw that the Irish habit of mythmaking is destructive when it aggrandizes and glorifies the unworthy. But he could also see that these myths, taken as works of language art, are glorious testaments to the continual supremacy of the Irish way with words. James Joyce forged an Irish myth to capture the conscience of his race and in so doing he captured many other men's consciences as well. O'Brien's works strongly affirm such achievements and they further them too. "A real writer, with the true comic spirit," Joyce says in a rare dustjacket puff. It's too bad that for 25 years very few have paid attention. *Do* read O'Brien. He's a really funny writer. Believe *me* if you don't believe James Joyce. (p. 681)

Rosa Cumare, in National Review (© National Review, Inc., 1975; 150 East 35th St., New York, N.Y. 10016), June 20, 1975.

* * *

O'CASEY, Sean 1880-1964

O'Casey was an Irish dramatist who dealt in all his work with political and social change in Ireland and with the suffering of Irish townspeople during periods of strife—the Easter 1916 Uprising, the revolt against England in 1920-21, and the Irish Civil War of 1922-23. Although most critics believe O'Casey's dramatic talent and range were limited, his influence on his contemporaries is never questioned. To Americans, O'Casey is probably best known for his six-volume autobiography, *Mirror in My House*.

[O'Casey] changed the nature of Irish drama from peasant comedies to a presumably realistic urban drama of Dublin slum life, tragicomedies which O'Casey himself labeled "tragedies." (p. 12)

The reputation based on the first three full-length plays [*The Shadow of a Gunman, Juno and the Paycock*, and *The Plough and the Stars*] has remained as an ultimate verdict on Sean O'Casey, even when critics have failed to agree on the bases for their judgment. O'Casey himself cautioned against viewing the plays as photographic realism. (The dramatist's detractors have often dismissed them as only that, while several of his defenders have admired the plays for just that quality.) He went on . . . to quadruple the body of his dramatic output, experimenting often in expressionistic and other nonrealistic techniques, and maintaining throughout that the spirit of such experimentation was already operative in the Dublin plays [just mentioned]. Many commentators have also assumed that these early plays were essentially formless, an almost accidental throwing together of a variety of characters who play out their individual slices of life on O'Casey's stage: O'Casey has therefore been credited with utilizing a fortuitously free-form drama, and has also been criticized for careless formlessness. Eventually a handful of critics appeared who praised the dramatist for the intuitive sense of stagecraft which made these same plays so eminently successful. . . . [His] subject matter remained almost exclusively Irish, with only one or two exceptions, and for over thirty years he kept in touch with political and social changes in Ireland, mirroring them in his new plays and remaining a persistent critic of essential elements of Irish life under the Republic. (pp. 14-15)

It is a 1940 comedy, *Purple Dust*, that serves as an introduction to the later O'Casey style, the plays of comic fantasy. This remained the essential vein of his dramatic work until his death almost 25 years later, interrupted occasionally by such propaganda pieces as *Oak Leaves* and by his most autobiographic statement in drama, *Red Roses for Me* (1942). The latter exists for many as a unique piece of O'Caseyana, a personal, poetic, and tender statement from the dramatist, recalling the power of his naturalistic efforts of the 20s, but blending these with touches of fantasy and expressionistic poetry in the third act, and incorporating some of O'Casey's finest comic elements. (p. 18)

The O'Casey of the *Purple Dust* vein cast a cold eye on the paralysis of rural Ireland (abandoning the Dublin urban scene in which he had lived for 46 years for the small town, the village, and the farm community in which social change was even slower in making itself felt than in the capital city). Here he uncovered the dead hand of the parish priest, the self-aggrandizing grasp of the new Irish landowners, and the occasional defiant fist of a socially aware rebel. The landlords are still British in the 1940 "wayward comedy," but thereafter in *Cock-a-Doodle Dandy* (1949), *The Bishop's Bonfire* (1955), and *The Drums of Father Ned* (1958) they are Irish parvenus, graduated to councillors and mayors and elected as papal counts. Hand in glove with the bigoted clergy, they keep a tight grip on the politics, economy, mores, and morality of their petty fiefdoms, attempting to stem the natural tide of freedom, love, rebellion, and life itself. O'Casey's young people often demand the right to shape their own futures, for romantic love and passion, for song and dance and an open investigation of all closed issues, and when denied these rights by parent and priest they opt for emigration to England rather than atrophy in Ireland. In the rare event of victory over the forces of the dead past, they jauntily take command of their world, leaving the rulers of the old society to atrophy. O'Casey's technique in these late comedies parallels that of the Dublin plays in their blend of the tragic and the pathetic with the wildly comic, but with strong elements of fantasy for leavening. Supernatural birds, superhuman heroes, mysterious priests who stir the youth to rebellion—all embodiments of the Life Force—take command in the more optimistic of the plays (*Purple Dust, The Drums of Father Ned*, and the shorter "Figuro in the Night") and usher in the O'Caseyan future. But in the more somber dramas, despite the many flashes of hilarity and song, the mood of bitterness predominates, and the fallen angels retreat, refusing to serve the fierce god and tyrannical master, often leaving behind those of their fellows who cannot muster the courage to take a stand: *Cock-a-Doodle Dandy, The Bishop's Bonfire*, and O'Casey's last full-length play, *Behind the Green Curtains* (1961). (pp. 19-20)

[Many] of O'Casey's dramas concern some of the most important political events in Irish and European history during O'Casey's lifetime. His individual attitudes dominate the action of these theatrical recreations, but every important facet of twentieth-century history is mirrored here, as well as in the six autobiographies collected in 1956 under the cumulative title of *Mirror in My House*. (pp. 20-1)

Between Synge on one end of the chronological spectrum and a yawning void on the other, Sean O'Casey stands as Irish drama almost by himself—and one of the best dramatists writing in the English language in his time in any country. His imperfections were enormous. He insisted upon utilizing melodrama, and he dangerously juggled genres; he was heavyhanded in his diction, propagandistic with a vengeance, and even derivative. He had faults enough to demolish any other writer—yet he mastered his art, polished his techniques, took his chances, and survived his mistakes, rarely concentrating them to any great extent. He emerged with a voice of his own, a style of his own, and a body of artistic work that reflected his personality and thinking with flair and color. (pp. 24-5)

By the time he began to write plays O'Casey was already a dedicated socialist, but the early tenement plays are devoid of propagandistic evidence. He concentrated on real events, their complexities and their multiple effects on the people he knew, rarely showing his hand to his audience. (The same Dubliners who were being dissected and lampooned in these comic tragedies sat in the theatre and roared at themselves, until the full brunt of O'Casey's satire struck home in *The Plough and the Stars*.) Laughing at himself was as important to the dramatist as mocking others, and in both *Juno* and *The Plough* he was capable of a satiric caricature of rather unlovely socialists. (pp. 37-8)

O'Casey's characters are destined to be remembered—particularly his unique comic creations—and no one more than his Paycock. The development of "Captain" Jack Boyle and his butty Joxer Daly in *Juno* is probably O'Casey's finest achievement. He continued thereafter to vary the possibilities of the character type, the indolent, self-indulgent braggart whom he saw at the crux of the paralytic condition in Irish life, but whose boisterous wit and élan always brought him at least halfway back to redemption. In dozens of varying situations O'Casey proved that variations on the type could be endless, and few of his plays were without them. (pp. 53-4)

O'Casey throughout his career allowed himself a broad range of play in handling the paycock as a type, often stressing the individuality of the character at the expense of known characteristics, and finding some more redeemable than others. That they strut with a measure of self-importance, that they fabricate outrageously to preserve their self-esteem, and that they often see others around them as reflections of themselves serve to establish the type. How they react when the chips are down often distinguished the individual. (pp. 54-5)

O'Casey's young heroines share with the mother-figures of his plays a unique position: they far out-number the male heroes, most of his men being too weak and too conventional to rival the strong-minded and vibrant women. (p. 85)

A pretty face, an ample bosom, and tantalizing legs may seem more appropriate for Hollywood than for serious drama, but O'Casey sees them as hopeful signs of life worth living. (p. 118)

Sean O'Casey could capsulize into character description that handful of personality elements which encompass a person . . . , and in concise dramatic form he etched those few strokes to delineate a character as he saw it in his mind's eye, and then allowed that character to prove himself by acting out his own personality in response to the events that confronted him. Whenever he assumed the novelist's prerogative in editorializations about his fictional people, he was careful to justify that usurpation by embodying the underlined characteristics in speech and in action. . . . [He] was skilled in making political statements and revealing the strongest of his personal ideals through the simple expedients of setting a scene and introducing a human being onto his stage. Few committed artists in the theatre have been as successful in having reality and poetry carry the major responsibility for the writer's convictions as has Sean O'Casey. (pp. 118-19)

> *Bernard Benstock, in his* Sean O'Casey (© *1970 by Associated University Presses, Inc.), Bucknell University Press, 1970.*

Distinguished drama historians praising [*The Plough and the Stars*] speak of it as a naturalistic, mass drama having little structural design. . . . [If] *The Plough and the Stars* truly has little structural design, the acknowledged greatness of this play would make unassailable the position of those critics who maintain that greatness can, no, *should* be achieved in rebellion against the "tyranny of the plot." But although the design of the play does not readily reveal itself, it is an intricate and firm design with at least three interdependent plot-structures. (pp. 203-04)

[At the end of the first act], we do not yet know who the character central to the plot is, but we already have a sense of firm structural design and we have aligned ourselves with Nora. (p. 205)

[The events and characters of the second act] are all essentially thematic and tonal elements. However important they are to the play's dimension and its comic and satiric power, however successfully O'Casey controls their textural harmony in the whole formal design of the play, they are not shaped into a plot-structure. The various actions of these characters have no logical unity and do not move the play forward. (pp. 205-06)

Nora absorbs our interest and sympathy more than any other character in the play, but she is not central to the plot; she does not advance the action of the play, she is not a doer of acts that cohere into a complete plot-structure. Clitheroe, on the other hand, does have a plot-structure, although not the main one. The logical unity of his action is worked out in relationship to Nora. . . . Because he has no part in the final action of the play, which takes place in the significant fourth act, he cannot be central to the plot.

Who, then, is central? There is no question that Nora and Clitheroe are our main focus of interest—but the advance of the play's action and its culmination belong mainly to Bessie. She, indeed, has two plot-structures, the main one in relationship to Nora, another in relationship to Mrs. Gogan. The first of these is the main plot-structure of the play. . . . (p. 206)

We may note in O'Casey's structural design, as fundamental to the play's sense of wholeness, that Bessie's plot-structure has Clitheroe's involved in it. . . . It is [the] interdependence of plot-structures . . . that makes each integral to the whole. (p. 207)

The contemporary welcome accorded the so-called "plotless" play may well issue from a misunderstanding of the modern structural mode. . . . [Being] the primary formal principle the plot-structure must be perceived if there is to be accurate and full artistic apprehension.

There are critics who also fail to see syllogistic plot-structures in the theater of the absurd. . . . As in such expressionistic plays as Strindberg's and as in plays written in the mode that Chekhov invented, the plot-structure of absurd plays is submerged—but it is there and is formally essential. Without it the plays would collapse like a body without a skeleton. . . . Common to the new modes of theater in the twentieth century is the submerged plot-structure, which is not the main focus of interest. (pp. 208-09)

> *Seymour Reiter, in his* World Theatre: The Structure and Meaning of Drama (© *1973; reprinted by permission of the publisher, Horizon Press, New York), Horizon, 1973.*

Grief is the wood-note wild of the Irish soul. Rarely has a people's sorrow been sounded with such resonant purity as it is in Sean O'Casey's *Juno and the Paycock*. Despite moments of bathos and some soap operatics in the construction of the plot, this play is one of the granitic masterworks of modern dramatic art. . . .

Tragedy or not, what is O'Casey celebrating? A trinity of profound, if currently unfashionable values—God, country and family. Not for a single moment during *Juno and the Paycock* is one unaware that Roman Catholicism, Ireland and the Boyles' intense awareness of themselves as an embattled entity have shaped the people that we see before us. Not for the good, necessarily. O'Casey had as sharp an eye as James Joyce for the foibles of his race, though it sometimes brimmed with an un-Joycean compassion. He knew the perils of being priest-ridden, the curse of drink, the terrible gift of hurting one another that has remained constant from the 1916 "Troubles" to the present sad day. Yet he set it all down to the ineffable music of English that rarely sounds sweeter than it does on the Irish tongue. And he relished the Irish fondness for gossipmongering, playacting, and scene-making that has made them, after the greeks and the Elizabethans, the greatest dramatists of the Western world.

> *T. E. Kalem, "Irish Trinity," in* Time *(reprinted by permission from* Time, The Weekly Newsmagazine; *copyright Time Inc.), November 18, 1974, p. 95.*

O'Casey pretended to—and sometimes possessed—the homely uncorrupted sagacity of the crow of our animal tales, and regarded himself as called on to administer stinging wasp-like rebukes to social and artistic complacency. Yet . . . he was often simple-minded rather than innocently wise, and querulous, even mean-spirited, instead of intellectually valorous. . . .

Anomalies and contradictions abound in his writings and in the zone of estimation that surrounds it. What is his place, this troublesome, erratic, autodidactic Irishman? Was he really one of the great modern playwrights, as so many textbooks and so much popular consideration would have it? I remember the litany from my student days: Ibsen, Strindberg, Chekhov, Shaw, O'Casey, O'Neill—the recent masters. . . .

But it's not true. O'Casey can't bear the weight of such an apotheosis, which threatens by reaction to diminish his limited achievement. There are too many bad and even deeply embarrassing plays in his *oeuvre* ("Within the Gates," "The Star Turns Red," "The Bishop's Bonfire," et al.) and too many esthetic sins of naiveté, rhetorical excess, sentimentality and tendentiousness in all but his very best work: "Juno and the Paycock," "The Plough and the Stars," the late and only half-successful "Cock-a-doodle Dandy." I suspect that O'Casey's inflated reputation in the textbooks and in certain theatrical circles is largely a set of extra-artistic circumstances: the sterility of the English-speaking theater in the twenties when he came to prominence with his "Dublin" plays at the Abbey Theater; his ferocious battle with censorship; his own "dramatic" story —slum childhood, self-education, lifelong nearblindness, self-exile. . . .

The peculiar violence of O'Casey's circumstances, his beleaguered physical and economic condition, his struggle with Irish prudery and provincialism, make him something other than a fully representative literary figure, but he *is* representative in having been frequently unconscious of the true nature of his work, in having felt simultaneously misunderstood and touched with glory, and in having doggedly insisted on his inspiration even when it was leading him to imaginative disaster. (p. 1)

He wanted to experiment, to mix structures and styles, to be more "poetic." Yet his sensibility and theory of drama, grounded in what he acknowledges in a letter to be a strange equality of admiration for Shakespeare and Dion Boucicault, were scarcely up to the job. With "The Silver Tassie" in 1928 he fell into some of the most flagrant delinquences—bathos, ideological cant, pseudo-poetic rhetoric—of the then dying Expressionist movement, and most of his plays from then on exhibit the same malfeasances.

The controversy over the Abbey's rejection of "The Silver Tassie" is fascinating and instructive. . . . Speaking for the Abbey's directors, W. B. Yeats told O'Casey that the play suffered from both inadequate technical prowess and imaginative unconvincingness. . . . Yeats was right . . .; there was no failure to discern his genius.

Convinced, though, that the play had been rejected because of its disturbing originality, O'Casey seized on and built up a role as prophet unhonored. He was given ample material: the bannings of his plays in Ireland and Boston, the abuse of outraged jingoists and bluenoses. But political irreverence, anti-clericalism and sexual honesty aren't enough to constitute literary genius. Good as his best work is, emotionally accurate as it occasionally can be, O'Casey's theater mostly lacks that mysterious agency by which experience is shaped by form into new consciousness. (pp. 16, 18)

He was not ahead of his time: to see this one has only to compare his "experiments" with those of Brecht and Pirandello, who wrote during much of the same period. (p. 18)

Richard Gilman, in The New York Times Book Review (© *1975 by The New York Times Company; reprinted by permission),* March 16, 1975.

[Sean O'Casey's] reputation for genius begins, and I think ends, with the early plays, the Dublin cycle which comprises *The Shadow of a Gunman, Juno and the Paycock* and *The Plough and the Stars.* That in any event is the commonly accepted critical judgment on O'Casey which only his most fervent admirers, on the one hand, or a handful of disenchanted begrudgers, on the other, would care to dispute. The reputation is sustained, but not powerfully supported, by *Purple Dust* and *Cock-a-Doodle-Dandy,* barnyard farces which are probably to be ranked next after the earlier tragicomedies. The experimental plays such as the controversial *Silver Tassie,* an experiment in expressionism, or *The Star Turns Red,* an experiment in ideological symbolism, are interesting as experiments but hardly memorable as works of art. Even the dramatic readings given to the early installments of O'Casey's six-volume autobiography—*I Knock at the Door* and *Pictures in the Hallway*—are more effective as drama than are his formal experiments with drama itself. So effective indeed that Brooks Atkinson saw in these readings—a bare stage, a handful of actors with scripts open before them, all plot, props, personae totally subordinate to the power and grace of language—that drama, stripped to its essentials, is and can be no more and no less than "a plank and a passion."

Sean O'Casey was above all a passionate man and his genius, if granted, is concentrated in this quality of his life which only occasionally carried over into the work. It was, and when we encounter it in the theatre can still be, a disarming passion; it disarms criticism by its directness and simplicity, by the purity of its intent and intensity, by the unashamed fact of itself. "Sean had no learning," O'Casey wrote in the last book of his autobiography, "no knowledge —what he set down were but his feelings moulded with words; there they were and there they'd stay." O'Casey's personal staying power was impressive—he lived on into his 80s—and the staying power of his language, despite the moldy edges of much of it, is in direct proportion to the passionate quality that informed the whole of his life. (p. 55)

[Perhaps] more than any other writer of his stature O'Casey is innocent of ideas; his mind, unencumbered by education and uninhibited by discipline, was that of a poet, albeit a poet *manqué,* and he had, though he did not know it, an instinctive abhorrence of the abstract in any form. But forms of the abstract, though naturally abhorrent, were also insidiously attractive, and he was drawn to them like some old desert saint tempted beyond endurance to the embrace of an illusion he cannot dispel. O'Casey's embrace of communism was of this order—he thought and spoke and wrote of himself as a Communist, and like any old saint not knowing what he's about he made a bit of a fool of himself in the clinches. . . . The old saint's instincts, however pure, are corrupted by ideas, the spirit rigidifies in the embrace of ideology, the humanity of the man—his most endearing characteristic—all but disappears in a fog of abstractions. (pp. 55-6)

O'Casey is not after all a writer of the first rank if that rank is determined by the presence of fellow Irishmen like

Yeats, Joyce, Shaw, Synge and Beckett. O'Casey himself, I think, would be the first to admit this. But if he is not profound he is important and plays a significant role in the history of 20th-century drama and the story of modern Irish literature. (p. 56)

> *Kevin Sullivan, "O'Casey's Plank and Passion," in* The Nation *(copyright 1975 by the Nation Associates, Inc.), July 19, 1975, pp. 55-6.*

*   *   *

O'FLAHERTY, Liam   1896-

O'Flaherty is an Irish realistic novelist and short story writer.

For many years O'Flaherty was classified with Joyce and O'Casey as a realist, although this label indicates chiefly a reaction to the writing of Yeats, Synge, and A.E. Yet O'Flaherty's novels still possess a depth and range that deserve reexamination. From the standpoint of literary history, O'Flaherty examines in his novels major shifts in the Irish psyche in the first half of the twentieth century; he describes in detail the effect of social and economic change on the peasant or country man; futhermore, his protagonists fit into significant psychological and existential patterns.

In general, O'Flaherty writes a realistic novel with readily recognized settings and characters, but the theme and plot revolve around a neoromantic protagonist. Although O'Flaherty has naturalistic leanings, he never makes the meticulous examination of environment of a Zola or Dreiser, in part because in his work environment does not control the protagonist. Instead, O'Flaherty's chief characters, often driven by obsessions, plunge into disaster. At times these protagonists have a Nietzschean will, but they are generally limited in intellect and judgment. As a group, O'Flaherty's novels deal with the dominant images affecting modern Ireland.... Historically, O'Flaherty's novels study the Irish psyche from the famine of 1846-47, through the land war of the 1870s, through the revolution of 1916-23, and into the new Irish Free State that was struggling to establish its own social and political forms. But generally O'Flaherty does not attempt to depict historical attitudes with precision; with some exceptions, his peasants, rebels, landlords, priests, and shopkeepers speak for similar values, whether in the 1840s or the 1920s. (pp. 36-7)

In his . . . novels O'Flaherty does not experiment with the role of the narrator. . . . O'Flaherty seems untouched by the work of Henry James and Conrad. Almost always O'Flaherty's narrator is the classic third person omniscient narrator, a *persona* excited by strong protagonists and unusual events. As an observer of modern man, he attends closely to the instinctive and passionate reactions; he is sensitive to man's crippling obsessions and alert to man's tendency to blunder into nets from which he cannot extricate himself. But his narrator seldom shirks his duties as storyteller; he advances the narration rapidly; he idles only briefly, if at all, for comment; he avoids with a clean narrative outline the bypaths of reminiscence or speculation. While the narrator generally explores sympathetically only the protagonist, he rests with a common-sense view of the conflicts within secondary figures. Despite his well-established views on Communism and the Church, he seldom promotes

Marxism or anticlericalism in his novels. On occasion he develops a scene at two levels, mainly to show the confused mind of a protagonist. In *The Neighbour's Wife*, for example, Father McMahon listens to the simple confessions of the peasants as he torments himself with doubts about the teachings of the Church; in *The Puritan* Francis Ferriter similarly tries to explain a murder he has committed to a priest as he relives in memory a host of associations with his suppressed love for the whore whom he killed.

O'Flaherty avoids poetic devices in his prose, although an occasional epic simile recalls his training in the classics. So intent is O'Flaherty on raw experience that he emphasizes man's suffering and turmoil at the expense of precision of expression. At times the narrator rushes along, dropping clichés, awkward phrases, and sentences that ring hollow. Frequently he fails to exploit ironies inherent in the situation of the protagonist. Whether the narrator's directness derives from de Maupassant, the Gaelic storytellers, or other influences, he respects the visible, physical world. His narrator is consumed with the necessity for sketching the immediate situation and laying bare at once the feelings of the characters. The reader is never in doubt about external circumstances. (pp. 54-5)

A serious flaw in O'Flaherty's novels is his frequent failure to distinguish between scene and summary, between drama and exposition—that is, he lacks the gift of the skilled novelist to select and treat background expeditiously and to concentrate on the development of simple or complex scenes. In *Skerrett*, for instance, the author leaves many scenes half-developed or only touched upon. . . . O'Flaherty's consummate skill in the stories of sketching in people and places often fails him in the novels where the context requires extended dramatization.

As a novelist, O'Flaherty has weaknesses in vision and technique that prevent his work from attracting widespread attention, but in works like *The Black Soul* and *Skerrett* he treats problems of the modern temper with a raw vitality appropriate to the experience of his protagonists. O'Flaherty must be accounted a perceptive observer of the dominant images of his countrymen and of western man. He probes the void, the emptiness of men whose faith has been broken, whose imaginations have been twisted by the social, political, or economic demands of the age. Often brusque in presentation, O'Flaherty nevertheless pursues the unassimilated experience of modern life, projecting it in novels that have been too readily neglected by critics and ordinary readers. (pp. 56-7)

Despite O'Flaherty's reputation as the novelist of the Irish Revolution, only two of his fourteen novels have settings during the period of 1916-23: *The Martyr* (1923) and *Insurrection* (1950). Two other novels, however, may be included in a group of war novels, *The Informer* (1925) and *The Assassin* (1928), for *The Informer* deals with gunmen and a revolutionary cell, and *The Assassin* studies the split mentality of a gunman, though in a postwar period. In dramatizing man's recourse to violence O'Flaherty preferred the small intense world of Ireland to the larger world he knew from military service and travel. Somehow his love-hate relation to Ireland fired his imagination. But despite his Irish settings O'Flaherty is a close student of the modern temper. . . .

Even a brief discussion of O'Flaherty's war novels, however, should include comment on *The Return of the Brute* (1929). This crudely and evidently hastily written novel hardly rises above a conventional protest against the horror of trench warfare. In *The Return of the Brute*, O'Flaherty reinforces his theme with repeated references to the bestiality of man. (pp. 58-9)

In the short stories . . . O'Flaherty builds in deceptively simple stories vivid images of the basic instincts of man. Somehow by stripping away the covering of civilization and the superstructures of reason, he penetrated to a bedrock of experience. It is indeed a complex critical problem to account for the simplicity and directness of his best short stories. To O'Flaherty these stories were secondary to the larger themes and characters of his novels; in fact, the stories sometimes resemble vignettes that could be extracted from his novels on the Aran Islands and the west of Ireland. (p. 93)

Through contemplating simple people and animals and the relatively uncomplicated forces of nature O'Flaherty may have hoped to present an instinctive response to a life that had been mangled or smothered by industrialization, cities, and wars.

This search for an accurate rendering of man's instinctive life marks both his short stories and his novels. In the novels, oversized Dostoevskian figures dominate the work; their dreams of perfection, twisted and fanatic as they generally are, represent man's upward movement to a perfection implicit in the evolutionary process. In the short stories O'Flaherty falls back on peasants, animals, and children; the setting is that of farm, sea, or village. . . . In both novels and short stories, a Gaelic influence is manifest in the directness of narrative, the simplicity of language, and an elemental concern with primary emotions. One of the most noticeable differences between novels and short stories, however, lies in the use of melodrama, which is employed in the novels mainly in the interest of psychological realism. Melodrama seems to be his technique for showing the explosive emotions of his protagonists; for O'Flaherty it is a means to express a heightened level of intensity. The short stories, however, seem to be born in a different literary climate. Sean O'Faolain . . . questions the melodrama in the novels but praises the composure of the short stories. Among novelists, he says, O'Flaherty is a Don Quixote, an inverted romantic in search for an ideal beauty, hard to define because of the fury with which he rushes against his enemies. But the short stories have a different ambience: "In those lovely short stories, however, he is at rest. There he has found something that bears resemblance to his ideal, not in men, but in birds and animals; and often men are seen as cruel creatures who hunt and torment these dumb things." (pp. 94-5)

O'Flaherty's prevailing concern, [in fact], is not with war, but with peasants and animals, or as one critic states, with the land. His purpose is not to present a realistic or naturalistic view of the Irish peasant; his stories lack the harsh objectivity and ironies of Chekhov's story "Peasants," a severe indictment of the ignorance, drunkenness and brutality of the peasant, and a more severe indictment of the masters permitting this suffering. Instead, O'Flaherty generally uses the simplicity of peasant life to depict elemental reactions and instincts. Although he does not ignore cruelty, ignorance, or the sporadic eruptions of rage or mad-

ness among the peasants, he uses character and event to dramatize the uncluttered working out of creative and destructive forces in man and nature. He prizes feats of strength, unexpected moments of joy and grief, those dramatic interstices in man's struggle against social and natural forces that may injure or annihilate him. (pp. 96-7)

By freeing himself from the necessity of making an intellectual gloss on objects and people, O'Flaherty concentrates on people, things, and events with his full energies devoted to expressing their intrinsic being. He takes peasantlike delight in an unfettered examination of a wave, the birth of a cow, a daughter going into exile; the object, person, or event so captivates his imagination that nothing seems to intrude between the author and the unfolding of the destiny of his subject. In this state of mind he writes with a clear-eyed intensity and immediacy that seems almost a total surrender of the author's personality to the nature of things outside of himself. (p. 97)

Collectively O'Flaherty's short stories describe two or three generations of life in the Aran Islands and the west of Ireland; perhaps they reach back even further, so little did life change in those areas until the end of the nineteenth century. In the short stories, O'Flaherty makes little effort to assign a time to the events; peasants have always fished from the cliffs, fought the sea, and tilled their fields. . . .

Among peasants O'Flaherty has a fondness for crotchety and slovenly old people, eccentric individuals who see themselves as bearers of a tradition. Perhaps his most impressive creation of this type is Brian Kilmartin in *Famine*, a man who clings to his land despite the famine, knowing that bad years will be followed by good years. Often these peasants are upset by new leaders, new money, and new goods. (p. 98)

In O'Flaherty's stories there are few love scenes, and those few are not well developed, but he senses the unstated affection that unifies a family or holds individuals together in a world in which untimely death is frequent. Like Synge, O'Flaherty finds some of his most poignant stories in separation and loss. (pp. 100-01)

O'Flaherty does not escape some of the pitfalls of stories about peasants. Some yarns, possibly adapted from the oral tradition, seem to have only a surface; the author delights in too facile an exaggeration or in a comic hoax. (p. 101)

In method, O'Flaherty's stories have a simplicity that suggests Hemingway's studied effort to select specific details that create scene or character and provide at the same time the means to elicit the right emotional reaction. But O'Flaherty selects his details on a much simpler level. He is not interested in symbolism as such; he relies on an inherent rather than on an analogical symbolism. He uses the natural order as a Gaelic storyteller, because of his interest in the person or event itself; he depends on the narrative movement of the story. . . . O'Flaherty is most effective when he remains close to the oral tradition, when the storyteller presents events and people simply and directly. When O'Flaherty indulges in philosophy or manipulates symbolism or overstates themes, his stories tend to collapse. But . . . the oral tradition may also beguile O'Flaherty through ingenious situations. O'Flaherty's achievement in the short story may best be grasped, I believe, by considering two types of stories in which he excelled: the lyric sketch and the comprehensive fable. Both types, as used by

O'Flaherty, have close ties with the oral tradition and O'Flaherty's search to discover or rediscover an elemental life in man.

By far the greatest number of O'Flaherty's stories are lyric sketches, with a simple narrative, a limited plot, and with scene and characterization governed by what is immediate and readily observable. O'Flaherty does not neglect the narrative, but the effect of the narrative in his shortest works is similar to that of a lyric poem; in fact . . . in these sketches the entire story is an epiphany. The uncomplicated plot discloses the inevitable working out of an emotion or a rhythm of nature. There is little attention to any causal arrangements of events; O'Flaherty holds tightly to the present tense; people speak and act; storms arise and fall without analysis. In the short stories, as in the novels, he does not experiment with point of view; he utilizes a reliable narrator who is clear-eyed, sane, and shrewdly alert to the forces in man, society, and nature, that maim or crush the individual. Neither does he psychoanalyze his characters; he has little use for flashbacks or the probings of memory. Similarly, O'Flaherty limits his language to ordinary words; at times he lapses into pedestrian phrases or clichés; he disdains style. In his theory the raw urgency of action and reaction should not be impeded by fastidious diction. Yet in the best of his lyric sketches, O'Flaherty places his men and women close to the earth or sea in narrative that is stark, unsophisticated, and accurate for evoking a sense of the relentless working out of man's instincts.

O'Flaherty's stories lack the breadth and complexity of those of Joyce, O'Faolain, or O'Connor, and he deals with an external world foreign to men in an industrial, urban society. Yet his simple world is perfectly attuned to the passions and instincts that he wishes to stress. Like Yeats and Lawrence, he selects his material to rediscover the wellsprings of man's emotional life. Although he does not explore as widely as these writers, he acquires, as Yeats would say, an intensity through simplification. His setting, characters, and language cling to the physical order in which all men must live. (pp. 103-04)

As an artist, O'Flaherty is engaged, then, in the creation of cultural images, temporary though they may be, to supply what the civilization does not furnish—cultural images that lead to an integration of personality or, in Yeats's terms' to a unity of being. Beneath O'Flaherty's absorption in the physical, external world lies a belief in the evolutionary process, of men, especially artists, finding fulfillment in the struggle for perfection. This perfection may be elusive, even nonexistent, but nevertheless it is still the highest goal for man. (p. 117)

> *James H. O'Brien, in his* Liam O'Flaherty *(© 1970 by Associated University Presses, Inc.), Bucknell University Press, 1970.*

*   *   *

O'HARA, Frank   1926-1966

O'Hara was an American poet, playwright, and art critic. (See also *Contemporary Authors Permanent Series*, Vol. 1; obituary, *Contemporary Authors*, Vols. 25-28.)

Frank O'Hara, who died at [forty] in an accident, run down on the beach at night in the summer of 1966, had a constant apprehension of what death must reveal in the life of his personality—or rather, a constant conviction that it was death itself which would reveal that life. . . . Without death, the opacities of a selfhood would mean nothing to him, would deprive him of eternity. . . . Mere life, more and more living, would strip the poet of that senseless creature inhabiting him, that self to whom he owed the best of his illusions and his conflicts. Only his flaws, properly nursed, could "save" him, allow him to *keep* for the rest of us. . . . O'Hara urged himself—with a loyalty astonishing in a poet who prayed for "grace to be born and live as variously as possible—the conception of the mask barely suggests the sordid identifications," even *obliged* himself to see life as an ensemble of impulses not for resisting but for bearing us toward death: "I don't think I want to win anything I think I want to die unadorned." (p. 397)

It is obvious that for the artist obsessed with his expressive vocation—and I take an obsession with personality to *be* an expressive vocation, the need to *manifest* that personality, to invite for our amusement and even instruction its distinctive postures—anything and everything is doomed to become occasion, including the pursuit of occasion. . . .

Yet no occasion is ever adequate to the impulse that wants to make it an occasion—all poetry is in this sense the acknowledgment of failure, the aporia of poetry's impossibility ("if you don't eat me I'll have to eat myself"), and what is required of the poet is to make this submission, this admission, this fidelity to failure as Beckett calls it, into a new occasion, a new term of relation between the poet and his poem, a new expressive act. This requirement O'Hara fulfilled from the first. (p. 399)

Passing into myth, Pasternak had said, and surely O'Hara would have recognized his death on that beach, the onslaught of a monster sent against him by the very powers of meaninglessness he opposed—would have recognized his death as the death of Hippolytus (his true Phaedra was New York), and that death does deny accident, leaving behind the hero's name and his poetry which is the nomination of what he was:

> *the momentary smile and underneath, a small irresponsible glory that fits.*   (p. 412)

> *Richard Howard, "Frank O'Hara," in his* Alone With America: Essays on the Art of Poetry in the United States Since 1950 *(copyright © 1965, 1966, 1967, 1968, 1969 by Richard Howard; reprinted by permission of Atheneum Publishers, New York), Atheneum, 1969, pp. 396-412.*

Now that Knopf has given us O'Hara's *Collected Poems* they had better rapidly produce a *Selected Poems*, a book that wouldn't drown O'Hara in his own fluency. For the record, we need this new collection; for the sake of fame and poetry, we need a massively reduced version, showing O'Hara at his best. His charms are inseparable from his overproduction—the offhand remark, the fleeting notation of a landscape, the Christmas or birthday verse, the impromptu souvenir of a party—these are his common forms, as though he roamed through life snapping Polaroid pictures, pulling them out of his camera and throwing them in a desk drawer sixty seconds later. And here they are— some overexposed, some underdeveloped, some blurred, some unfocused, and yet any number of them succeeding in fixing the brilliance of some long-forgotten lunch, or the curve of a body in a single gesture, or a snowstorm, or a childhood movie. If these poems are photographic in their immediacy, they remind us too of the rapid unfinished sketches done by an artist to keep his hand in, or to remind him of some perishable composition of the earth. If there were a movie equivalent to a sketch, some of these poems would be better called verbal movies—the "I-do-this, I-do-that" poems, as O'Hara himself called them. (p. 5)

[Two] aspects of his work tended to do O'Hara in: his radical incapacity for abstraction (like Byron, when he thinks he is a child) and his lack of a comfortable form (he veered wildly from long [poems] to short, with no particular reason in many cases for either choice). The longest poems end up simply messy, endless secretions, with a nugget of poetry here and there, slices of life arbitrarily beginning, and ending for no particular reason. . . . The theoretical question O'Hara forces on us is a radical one: Why should poetry be confined in a limited or closed form? Our minds ramble on; why not our poems? Ramblings are not, to say the least, the native form of poets with metaphysical minds, but O'Hara, in his fundamental prescinding from the metaphysical, believes neither in problems nor in solutions, nor even in the path from one to the other. He believes in colloquies, observations, memories, impressions, and variations —all things with no beginnings and no endings, things we tune in on and then tune out of. . . . The inherent limitation seems not to be a formal one within the poem, but rather an external one—the limited attention span of the poet or his reader. (pp. 5-6)

The wish *not* to impute significance has rarely been stronger in lyric poetry. It happened, it went like this, it's over. Why is it worth recording? Because it happened. Why is what happened worth recording? Because what else is there to record? And why should we want to read it? Because what else is there to know except what has happened to people? Such a radical and dismissive logic flouts the whole male world and its relentless demand for ideologies, causes, and systems of significance. The anarchic elasticity of O'Hara's poetry depends entirely on his athletic effort to make the personal the poetic—the personal divested of religion, of politics, of mysticism, of patriotism, of metaphysics, even of idealism. . . . O'Hara's designedly light explanation of his theory of poetry (which he winsomely named "Personism") rests on intimacy and immediacy. (p. 9)

The reason O'Hara can be truly aerial is that he genuinely has no metaphysical baggage. No religion, no politics, no ideology, no nothing. . . . Dismay followed by elation, comfort succeeded by loneliness, getting mad giving way to a shrug, apathy followed by quickening—these are O'Hara's dimensions and out of them he creates his poetic space. There are ominous sighs in the later poems, sighs especially about America, that make us wonder whether O'Hara could have kept up the verve and bounce and amplitude of his best poems, but even a sad poem wafts up, often enough, a comic energy. (pp. 18-19)

Guessing, observing, looking, reading, comparing, reflecting, loving, writing, and talking, he takes us through life as though he were the host at a spectacular party. We may regret the equableness and charm of our guide, and wish him occasionally more Apollonian or more Dionysian (the sex poems aren't very good, though they try hard and are brave in their homosexual details), but there's no point

wishing O'Hara other than he was. The scale he works in is deliberately, at least by past ideological standards, very small. Klee might be the painter who seems comparable, in his jokes, his whimsical collocations, his tenderness, his childlike naïveté, his sprightliness, his muted levels of significance, his sentiment. In O'Hara, modern life is instantly recognizable, and a modern ethos of the anarchically personal receives its best incarnation yet. If it satisfies some portion of us less than a more panoramic ambition, we are self-betrayed in recognizing the frailty of our own supports. We cannot logically repudiate ideology and then lament its absence (though Stevens made a whole poetry out of just that illogic). O'Hara puts our dilemma inescapably before us, for the first time, and is therefore, in his fine multiplicity and his utter absence of what might be called an intellectual syntax, a poet to be reckoned with, a new species. (p. 20)

> *Helen Vendler, "The Virtues of the Alterable," in* Parnassus *(copyright © by Parnassus: Poetry in Review), Fall/Winter, 1972, pp. 5-20.*

Frank O'Hara is one of the nicest bores around. The less of him you read the better he is. [Where] O'Hara really shines is a poem or two anthologized with strangers. Why is this? An O'Hara poem is fresh, cheerful, and impudent. The line is alive, and he can be funny and affectionate without pose. It's not that he is never serious; when he gets serious he giggles. But a pound of O'Hara makes you wonder how frightful the solemnity is he's always chasing away. It's the reverse of waiting for those presidents carved in rock to grin. Vive la bagatelle. There's nothing worse than Bly or Piercy (or Lowell) being serious, unless it's these magnificently printed happy poems in bulk. Think if Picasso had painted nothing but plates and funny sculptures. Such unrelieved gaiety calls up the sort of *Paradise Loft* he never wrote, full of broken bones and real pain, not these sailings after lunch. They are social and bright, like what technicolor does to New York apartments in clever films. They are nostalgic for the present. He is a gifted writer determined to be trivial, and while his fribble is better than other people's mush or woof, there is that lack in the poems of what one imagines in the man and, lacking, resents.

> *Gerald Burns, "Portrait of the Artist as Charming," in* Southwest Review *(© 1974 by Southern Methodist University Press), Spring, 1974, p. 201.*

"One need never leave the confines of New York to get all the greenery one wishes—I can't even enjoy a blade of grass unless I know there's a subway handy, or a record store or some other sign that people do not totally *regret* life." This speaker in "Meditations in an Emergency" is, of course, Frank O'Hara's creation and not O'Hara himself, but he speaks (with some irony) for a poet who moved to New York as Marvell did in his garden, who made from details of the landscape an oddly significant vision.

O'Hara does not write about the city; he lives in it. In friendly reciprocity, a New York has come to live in the poems that no longer exists in fact. More likely it never existed. Knowing that once there was a Golden Griffin bookstore or a Ziegfeld Theatre, knowing that there is indeed a Seagram building not to mention an Allen Ginsberg, a literary tourist would be deceived into imagining that the whole of O'Hara's New York once had a geographical reality. His ceremonious naming makes the reader forget that the persons, places, things thereby gain meaning in a poetic universe rather than mass in a physical one.

Illusion suggests, even in many of his best-known poems, that the poetic narrative retails experience "as it happened." Behind this, however, stands a structure of personal encounters—their potentialities, their actualities, their aftermaths—working on all the senses to characterize his special world.... It is a necessary quality of this poetry that it speaks above or through the noise of cars and buses —in New York it's not volume but style that earns a hearing in a big cocktail party. (pp. 109-10)

The appearance of coincidence works for O'Hara in the city as does a suggestion of surrealism, a dramatic style of conversation, and a musical notion of prosody. The city worked for him in providing not just the events and encounters but a special pace, a sense of gathering—images, tones, ideas. O'Hara placed himself at a center by working, throughout his poetic career, at the Museum of Modern Art. He had started out as a music student; by 1950, apparently, he was dividing his time between his poetry and others' painting. In addition to work (as curator by the time of his death in 1966) at the Museum, he wrote [art] criticism for *Art News* and *Art & Literature*.... His close friendships with artists working in and near New York contributed to [his] book on [Jackson] Pollock, produced poems like his "Ode to Willem de Kooning", "Ode to Michael Goldberg ('s Birth and Other Births)", and the lithographs made with Larry Rivers. (p. 112)

O'Hara on Pollock seems truly to be talking to himself: "Surrealism," he notes, "enjoined the duty, along with the liberation, of saying what you mean and meaning what you say, above and beyond any fondness for saying and meaning." Saying and meaning like this demand activity on an appropriate scale and, toward the end of the essay, O'Hara describes Pollock's discovery of what came to be called Action Painting, when "the scale of the painting became that of the painter's body." As O'Hara extends this notion of "scale, and no-scale," he touches a reader's sense of the poet walking the city in "The Day Lady Died": what impresses itself as the shape and substance of the poem is, again in O'Hara's words for Pollock, "the physical reality of the artist and his activity of expressing it, united to the spiritual reality of the artist in a oneness which has no need for the mediation of metaphor or symbol." (pp. 112-13)

O'Hara directed formidable technical resources toward his poetic goals. In his brilliant memoir, "Frank O'Hara and His Poems" [see excerpts in *CLC*-2], Bill Berkson says, "An early notebook shows studies of Ronsard, Heine, Petrarch, Anglo-Saxon charms, Rilke, Jammes. There were imitations of Coleridge, translations of Hölderlin," and, one could add, references to Eliot as well as Olson, Stevens as well as Stein. O'Hara experimented with rhyme and off-rhyme in early poems like "After Wyatt" and "The distinguished / and freshly dusted Apollodorus-type." He developed a prosody that permitted the unobtrusively electric effects of even his most prosy works, but his intense artistic concern with syntax reached farthest and deepest.

O'Hara's remarkable way of making a sentence, or not-making a sentence, shapes his poems from 1951 on. Syntax covers anything from minute dependencies in a three-word sequence to massive interrelationships in the longest poem; it gives the poet a handle on time. O'Hara's sentences held firm around any range, any reference he reached for. (pp. 114-15)

O'Hara's poems after 1960 or so insist instead on separate moments. Syntax becomes a means of separating one moment's perception from another's, and the infrequent pattern that works like sentences signals a special occasion, a moment worth extending over time and space. (p. 115)

Inevitably syntax involves time, and time held prizes for O'Hara throughout his career. It *acts* in his poetry dramatically. Some private sense of menace may have endowed him with enormous respect for time's paradoxical uses. (p. 116)

> *Susan Holahan, "Frank O'Hara's Poetry"* *(copyright © 1974 by Susan Holahan), in* American Poetry Since 1960: Some Critical Perspectives, *edited by Robert B. Shaw, Dufour, 1974, pp. 109-22.*

Read in conjunction with the *Collected Poems* (1971), [the] set of essays [*Art Chronicles 1954-1966*] suggests to me that O'Hara will eventually emerge as the Ezra Pound of the postwar period. His poetry—brilliant, droll, exciting, iconoclastic—may not measure up to the *Cantos*, but like Pound, O'Hara helped to bring about a revolution in artistic sensibility....

Despite—or perhaps because of—this great range of interests, the academic establishment, ready to enshrine an Adrienne Rich in a Norton Critical Edition, still refuses to take O'Hara seriously. His poems, written at odd moments of the day or night, are accused of frivolity, formlessness and excessive in-jokes. No doubt, his art criticism will be similarly dismissed by certain academics as being too impressionistic. True, O'Hara is likely to refer to paintings as "tragic," "demonic," "sullen," "somber," "tender," "luminous" or "joyful," without backing up these adjectives with any overt theory of art. Yet his impressionistic criticism takes on a different cast when one notes that, like Pound, he had an unerring eye for genius, an amazing sense of the difference between the first-rate and the second-best. (p. 23)

O'Hara was ... always testing critical commonplaces; like Pound's, his approach to art was insistently individual, independent. By the mid-'60s, when the human figure began to reassert itself, O'Hara was one of the first to discern its new potential. (p. 24)

> *Marjorie Perloff, "They Were There," in* The New Republic *(reprinted by permission of The New Republic; © 1975 by The New Republic, Inc.), March 1, 1975, pp. 23-4.*

*   *   *

OLSON, Charles   1910-1970

Olson, a major American poet and scholar, was the mentor of the Black Mountain poets and a proponent of objective verse. He is best known for the Maximus poems and for his study of Melville, *Call me Ishmael.* **(See also** *Contemporary Authors Permanent Series***, Vol. 1; obituary,** *Contemporary Authors***, Vols. 25-28.)**

For Olson the line becomes a way to a movement beyond the single impact of the words which go to make it up, and brings to their logic a force of its own. Instead of the simple wagon which carries the load, he makes it that which drives too, to the common logic, the sense of the poem. . . .

Olson is a good deal more than a competent technician. . . . [He exhibits] a range of subject and a depth of perception that mark him exceptional. His language is exact, hangs tight to the move of his thought.

> *Robert Creeley, "Charles Olson: Y&X," in* Montevallo Review, *Summer, 1951.*

[Olson's] *The Maximus Poems* are, or seem first to me, the modulation of a man's attentions, by which I mean the whole wonder of perception. They are truth because their form is that issue of what is out there, and what part of it can come into a man's own body. That much is not sentimental, nor can anything be sentimental if we make it that engagement. The local is not a place but a place in a given man—what part of it he has been compelled or else brought by love to give witness to in his own mind. And that is *the* form, that is, the whole thing, as whole as it can get. (p. 157)

> *Robert Creeley, "Charles Olson: 'The Maximus Poems, 1-10'" (1953), in his* A Quick Graph: Collected Notes and Essays, *edited by Donald Allen (copyright © 1970 by Robert Creeley), Four Seasons, 1970, pp. 157-58.*

As a "post-modern" philosopher, Olson has little patience with the nineteenth century transcendental idealism of Emerson and Thoreau, but his methodology is often similar to theirs. Like them, he writes as a dogmatist, lecturing in the manner of a Yankee original, theorizing independent of the academy. He is a bookish man, with a wildly diverse taste for books (his writing often seems an immediate, direct response to something he has just read), but he remains at heart an enthusiast, a poet-preacher rather than a professor. In scientific matters, Olson is a self-educated man, as much an amateur mathematician and physicist as Thoreau was a gentleman botanist and zoologist. Olson's friend Robert Duncan once recalled affectionately, "Charles is just like I am. He sits around and reads all day." Like Melville, Olson reads to write.

Like Emerson and Thoreau, Olson is fiercely involved in the uniqueness of the American experience. He has stated in *Proprioception* that America is the inheritor of "a secularization which not only loses nothing of the divine but by seeing process in reality redeems all idealism from theocracy or mobocracy, whether it is rational or superstitious, whether it is democratic or socialism." But while he can be rhapsodic over the promise of the democratic experiment, he is also disillusioned over the exploitation of natural resources and the prevalence of human greed. (pp. 17-18)

Olson theorizes about the universe without quite the total comprehensiveness necessary to account for the complexity of life with God in the street, the result of the secularization of His part in the world of things. (p. 20)

Olson's philosophy of projective space, that quantity is the basic principle of the universe and that process is its most interesting fact, brings him directly to his method in *Call*

me *Ishmael*. As Robert Creeley has pointed out in his introduction to Olson's *Selected Writings*, the theory of projective space eschews criticism as a descriptive process. Attacking Plato and Aristotle's systems of logical notation and categorization, Olson insists instead on criticism as an "active and definitive engagement with what a text proposes." This engagement strikes cautious readers as a mishmash if they expect a book like *Ishmael* (subtitled "A Study of Melville") to be organized according to some perceivable system of developing logical relationships. The organization of *Ishmael* is perceivable, but only to the inquiring, intuitive eye. (pp. 20-1)

If man chooses to treat external reality any differently than as part of his own process, his own inner life, then he is mistreating external reality for his own arbitrary willful purposes. To Olson, academic criticism destroys "the energy implicit in any high work of the past" because such criticism uses the methods of description, generalization, and logic—all inimical to the creative process since they blur or destroy the outlines of external reality. . . . [*Ishmael*] is constructed like the acts of experience themselves, "on several more planes than the arbitrary and discursive which we inherit can declare."

To comprehend fully how Olson conceived *Ishmael*, the reader must keep in mind that what really matters for him is not generalization or logic or a coherent intellectual framework, but the Thing Itself. (pp. 21-2)

Call me Ishmael is Olson's study of Melville as prophet—the first American writer to realize the principle of projective space. But *Ishmael* is also Olson's own emergence as prophet. If his first birth was his entrance into life, his second was his appearance as philosopher and poet in his first book: "Art is the only twin life has." (p. 22)

From Melville, Olson first realized what he later came to understand was known by Lawrence and Pound, that the past was usable. . . . The philosopher in Olson was ready long before the poet took courage, but with Melville as spiritual mentor, Olson found his voice.

This voice was Ishmael's, the philosopher, the witness. (p. 23)

Olson's Ishmael *is* Olson. With his philosophy he places himself in an unpopular camp; for insisting upon God's place in the street, he is as much an infidel as Mohammed, who claimed descent from Ishmael the son of Abraham and thus brought the name into disrepute.

Through the mask of Ishmael and while in the guise of a Melville biographer and scholar, Olson speaks as a philosopher of projective space and an interpreter of the American experience. The drama of Olson's book, its becoming in its own way as extended a prose-poem as *Moby-Dick*, lies in its structure. *Ishmael* may be felt as a re-creation of *Moby-Dick* according to the theory of projective space, with Olson as Ishmael and Melville as Ahab. The re-creation is intuitive, not rigorously schematic. It is the record of Olson's response to Melville offered in the terms of quantity as intensive. . . . Olson's Ishmael is witness to the triumph and tragedy of Herman Melville, like Ahab finally defeated—according to Olson—in his effort to master space. (pp. 24-5)

Although Olson's concerns are those of a philosopher, his prose is that of a poet. . . . Typography, the image of the word, the thing-ness of physical perception are in Olson's concept the basic materials of poetry. His underlying philosophic concern with continuous space leads him to history, geography, economics—*facts* rather than imagination. Unlikely materials for a poet, but as Ishmael, Olson animates them for his interpretation of Melville. (p. 30)

Melville is fascinated by the philosophic state of mind and leaves Ishmael's perceptions soon after the *Pequod*'s voyage gets under way. The essential difference is that Olson has committed himself to a particular philosophy, whereas Melville holds no single belief. For Melville, dogma of any kind is impossible. . . .

Establishing a close parallel between *Ishmael* and *Moby-Dick* was less important to Olson than animating his thoughts about Melville. (p. 31)

The three forces acting on Melville "to bring about the dimensions of *Moby-Dick*" were tragedy (Shakespeare), myth (Noah and Moses), and space (lordship over nature). *Ishmael*'s Part I is the force of space on Melville. Part II is source, Shakespeare. Part III is Moses, Part V is Noah—myth. . . . This is what *Call me Ishmael* is explicitly about. . . . Olson organizes his book like a poet. The process of simply getting through the text is a major part of the reader's experience, and probably for most readers the act of reading the book generates in itself a more vivid impression than what the book is specifically about. (pp. 32-3)

With its structure a brilliant dramatization of Olson's philosophical theories, the contents of the book—Olson's demonstration that Melville was the first American "poet of space"—next requires careful scrutiny. In everything Olson writes, his meanings are complex, never mere description or logical argument. Over a hundred years ago, Emerson said, "Let us answer a book on ink with a book of flesh and blood" [Perry, *The Heart of Emerson's Journals*, p. 162]. As a literary and biographical study of Melville, *Call me Ishmael* is no academic book of ink. It is Olson's personal vision of what Melville *is*: Melville's experience interpreted by an eyewitness. (p. 38)

If Olson's idea about Melville's involvement in space is meant to be taken on faith alone, as a religious belief, then *Call me Ishmael* has the power of myth. Melville's experience becomes archetypal, prophetic of the experience of "Pacific man"—including Charles Olson himself. The reader who decides to continue the experience of *Ishmael* beyond the first fifteen pages must take on faith (or be willing to suspend unbelief) Olson's view of Melville as the first American poet of space. (p. 50)

It suited Olson's purpose to stress the inspiration he sensed Melville getting from Shakespeare, since what Olson himself had found in Melville paralleled the relationship he saw working nearly a century before between the two writers. When Olson refers to what Melville saw as an "American advantage" over Shakespeare [*Ishmael*, p. 41], for example, it is to find a similar "advantage" for himself over Melville. . . . The advantage is, as Olson wrote in his *Bibliography for Ed Dorn*, that "You is an American (no patriotism intended: sign reads, 'Leave All Flags Outside—Park Yr Karkassone')." There is no flag waving in *Ishmael*, but there is a strong cry of political idealism. The chapter titled "Shakespeare, concluded" is Olson's most extended discussion of the American advantage, the golden promise and the bitter reality of the "strongest social force," democ-

racy. . . . Ahab is "the American Timon," assailing through his extra-human hate "all the hidden forces that terrorize man," and dragging his crew and himself to violent death through his solipsism. (pp. 54-5)

Olson is writing as a social philosopher, not as a literary critic, using *Moby-Dick* to project a description of what he sees as the myth of America. He interprets Melville's experience of being witness to the failure—the tragedy—of the American experiment through greed, "solipsism," the lust to possess space. This is as explicit as Olson gets on the subject of what exactly Melville was as a "poete d'espace." (p. 55)

[Olson's] book may be read as either philosophy or poetry, for it is both. What it is not is conventional literary criticism —Olson turned back to this only after the "original, aboriginal" creative expression of *Call me Ishmael*. (p. 64)

> *Ann Charters, in her* Olson/Melville: A Study in Affinity *(© copyright 1968 Ann Charters), Oyez, 1968.*

Writing under the shadow of Pound's Cantos and Williams' *Paterson*, Olson has tried [in *Maximus Poems IV, V, VI*] to delve back further than Pound into pre-history and to create a more sharply defined image than Williams of a modern city.

There are passages where Olson succeeds very well in evoking and satirising the realities of urban living. . . . Gobbets of local history are lovingly dredged up and patiently reassembled. Modern wit sometimes flashes brightly through the historical material but the poem as a whole is maddeningly uneven. His method prevents him from providing linkages. The material must be allowed to speak for itself without any explanation of its relevance, and he incorporates long stretches of (apparently) verbatim quotation from documents which have a bearing on local history, assuming that his placing of them inside his structure will suffice to make them meaningful. It doesn't. At its best, though, his writing has a vitality in common with [Robert] Duncan's. He is often very successful in making the movement of the verse imitate the movement he is describing. (pp. 85-6)

What should not have been inevitable is the variation in the amount of pressure behind the lines. There are passages where historical, geographical, geological, and archeological elements are all fused and illuminated in the same flash of awareness and where the versification contributes its full share to the statement Olson is making. But there are also long passages where he bogs himself down in obscure incidents from the past which have no apparent relevance to the present and where the poetic line is loose and sprawling. Sometimes he seems to think that each genuine piece of local history possesses its own alembic to distil itself into poetry. (p. 86)

> *Ronald Hayman, in* Encounter *(© 1970 by Encounter Ltd.), February, 1970.*

Charles Olson died in January, 1970, after 24 years of publishing poems. One of the driving forces behind the Black Mountain educational experiment, Olson influenced the college's poets in ways as large as the man himself. Robert Creeley and Robert Duncan in particular claim loving debts to the poet Duncan calls a "Big Fire Source. One of the ones we have to study." But if these poets and many others know Olson's importance in American poetry, critics too often ignore him, finding his poems difficult, obscure, and sometimes cranky (when they find them at all). The major work, the *Maximus Poems* sequence, which takes Gloucester, Massachusetts for America as W. C. Williams claims Paterson, is published separately. [*Archaeologist of Morning*] contains all other poems Olson authorized for publication in his lifetime, including previously uncollected works from journals and magazines. Now, with such magical pieces as "The Kingfishers" and "The Librarian," among others, readily available, surely attention will be paid where it must, to a poet who searched valiantly for the breath of verse beyond and before the received forms of the schoolmen he despised and loved. (p. 284)

The Antioch Review *(copyright © 1971 by* The Antioch Review, Inc.; *reprinted by permission of the editors), Vol. XXXI, No. 2, 1971.*

I have never been happy with the waffly tone of *In Cold Hell*, elliptically allusive and aggressively folksy, a teaching machine with its sleeves rolled up. (p. 296)

[A] cheap way to tell a lot about a reader would be whether he'd rather read good Olson or good Stevens. Olson is more immediately social, at least in the drinking-bout sense, and there are more people in his poems. If he hasn't solved the artist/public split, he tries, a great many ways. He wants to write poems a sailor could read, rather than fodder for scholars. What kills him is a taste for 30's experiment and a gluey wish for certainties of the *sort* he thinks he finds in traditional European culture. Unlike Joyce he seems a bit embarrassed by being a writer, and will put in a strange word because he is ashamed of it. Which is why the sailors I know go around quoting Masefield. For a writer so clever at seeing why so much professional literature is deadly, he is oddly crippled by the self-conscious man's love of the awkward, which is his obverse fear of the formal. It gives him one advantage over Fifties Slick—not even Creeley is better at struggling to be graceful (compare Creeley's "Dancing" to Olson's "how to dance/sitting down"), and they both love the tristely minimal assertion, the content for which that figure was invented. Creeley hasn't Olson's need to play with Big Ideas, like Henry Miller's abortive book on Lawrence; by being born later (and a genius), it is enough if he can sort out his feelings. Olson's generation were covert Shelleyans, their writing something magical if not mythical, that might (if you looked the other way) even make things happen. He really does want an audience of human people, even when he writes as if the final judge were Maxwell Bodenheim. . . . [The] Olson his students discovered and loved (as he discovered them) is . . . in *Archaeologist [of Morning]*. The *O'Ryan* series is nothing much, Chandleresque tough, but the last little ones on color are something he should have done more with. (pp. 296-97)

Gerald Burns, in Southwest Review *(© 1971 by Southern Methodist University Press), Summer, 1971.*

"Archaeologist of Morning" [contains] all the poems Olson published in his lifetime, apart from the "Maximus" sequence. . . . Undoubtedly many poems exist in manuscript that have yet to appear, so this collection is incomplete against the larger effort of his lifetime; nonetheless, we are grateful for it. It is a beautiful and impressive tribute to Olson. . . .

Olson is unique, and probably the most difficult of recent American poets. No other poet requires such an effort, equivalent to learning a new language, or rather to adjusting the sense we have of the old one, so that we hear the precision of his, and learn to experience a world through it. There are Olson poems I doubt anyone will ever understand except in their general aspect. Others are line and sunlight clear. The best of them hover between formal clarity and the larger obscurity of the man's mind, a mind so rich that hosts of poets not of his school have paid him the tribute of a Socrates.

His shifts are subtle though major. It is as though in his hands the American language is once again in touch with its roots. He is not quite archaic though he is full of archaisms. His syntax is too alive to be archaic. His focus stops in the noticing of something where you least expect it, and the sudden concentration that is felt brings about a rearrangement of all that has gone before. . . .

To view the collected poems as this volume forces us to do is to get a confused sense of subject. There are poems that weave classical images through contemporary instances; that create Piero di Cosimo effects, luxurious yet deft. Poems that burst upon the tide of an established myth and seem to vivify it, as the beautiful ode to Aphrodite, "The Ring Of." Poems written in the heat of Olson's dig among the Maya, unfolding his theories of body (and eye), against his enmity for modern civilization, and its usury of spirit. Poems that try to place everything in a happy parataxis of Sumerian drift, that root out beginnings to beginnings, pre-logic, pre-liminary. Broadsides directed to The Gloucester Times against the dismantling of old houses to make way for the plastic and the new. Poems on what America was, meant, like his "West" series.

Olson on the subject of America (in the glory of its possibilities) is beautiful. Confronting America, as it radiates out of Gloucester and environs, his poetry often breaks step into a kind of Whitmanesque prose, a paradox of immense bulk and grace that fits the subject exactly. The tempo is right, the sense of space. The arrogance and the humility.

The best poems are delicate conjectures of the self caught in the thicket of its own awarenesses.

Olson has a Whiteheadian sweep to his imagination that connects one shimmer of brightness with the first spark, the first spring, "the shoot, the thrust of what you are." Process is all, is the message of many of his investigations. His ability to link one detail with another is startling and often gives the feeling your eye has erred until then. (p. 6)

Olson is the most articulate theorist of the move toward "composition by field": the idea that the poem becomes the configuration ("the glyph") of its own instant of creation. That, together with his work in getting language back on its feet, make him one of the most interesting figures in recent American poetry. Though he may not be its most lucid practitioner there is this peculiar beauty to his work which balances the strength of his cerebral reach with the grace of his imagination to convey a genuine dance. When the lesson of his person has faded, this no doubt will suffice. (p. 25)

Matthew Corrigan, in The New York Times Book Review (© *1971 by The New York Times Company; reprinted by permission), July 18, 1971.*

It is difficult—awkward—to make this kind of evaluation, but Charles Olson, I think, has to be considered one of the strongest influences, one of the most decisive forces, on an entire area of modern American poetry. No one seems to quite measure up his size, despite the brilliance and the uniqueness of much of the writing around him. It's a sense of size and in some ways even more important a sense of place, a sense of being placed. American poetry comes out of a society that is uncertain and uneasy and the poetry has always had some of this uneasiness—not even developing traditions or any strong sense of direction. It always seems to be beginning, and every poet seems to be the beginning of a new American poetry. Olson, with his sense of having found a place, has the range and the strength to be a force —in his own way to be this kind of beginning, this kind of new American poet.

I think the feeling of place has to go beyond a personal focus. The first place a poet has to find is the ground he stands on—then he has to go out and find the distances to the places where other poets have decided to stand—to the place where they stand in the culture, and the place they stand in the society. Many contemporary poets have gotten to the first step. It's the larger vision of a place in the culture and the society that's beyond them. Olson got this far very early—partly by borrowing much of his early poetic stance and technique from Ezra Pound. There are early poems, important early writing, that could almost be unnumbered Cantos—"The Kingfishers" or "The Praises." . . . Olson found in Pound a feeling for the sweep of a culture and an angry alienation from some of the worst aspects of the American experience, and for him it was a beginning. Olson began writing late—in his middle thirties—so Pound was of considerable use to him. There is still, in almost all of Olson's poetry, a suggestion of Pound's technical devices and his artistic concerns. Pound opened him out and set him going and the feeling for Pound and his grasp of the poem will always be with Olson.

But with this strong connection there are still strong feelings of difference between the two men, especially as Olson's work has matured. There is no strong sense of place in Pound's work. . . . He has an intellectual sense of identity with his materials, but there is often no sense of a significant emotional involvement. With Olson his identity with the place, with Gloucester, gives his major work, *The Maximus Letters*, a deep emotional center. . . . Olson, in one of the Letters' most persistent themes, uses Gloucester as a poetic expression of the realities of history. Sometimes he has used materials similar to Thoreau's, and drawn some of the same inferences from similar documents, but in Thoreau there was always a sharp moral concern with the implications of his materials and he used them in the book to give an immediate clarity to his ideas. Olson, working in a larger concept that includes a whole new structure of the poem and of literature, is more ambiguous, but in some of the suggestions of his materials still as powerful. By not clearly forcing them into a place in the poem he has left them with their own interior force as document and history, instead of with the smaller place as example or illustration of some point. The structure and even some of the language

of *The Maximus Letters* has been strongly influenced by William Carlos Williams' *Paterson*, but Williams' poem is an extended allegory involving the man and the city. In some of the early Letters there is an extending of the figure of Maximus into an allegorical framework, but it's left as an ambiguous suggestion, and in the rest of the poem Maximus —Olson—stays at a distance from this kind of self-identification with Gloucester.

The sense of place in the Letters is—in a final sense—so compelling because what Olson is trying to hold on to is the sense of place in time, as well as the sense of the immediate place of Gloucester. In geometric terms he is developing place in vertical as well as horizontal planes. This gives the Letters a complex pattern of movement, as well as giving them some of their importance to contemporary poetry. It also gives them some of their difficulty. Sometimes the poetry has the clarity and the vividness—the loose, unconcerned line of the kind of American discourse that he so strongly defends and insists on. . . . The Letters become less of the poet's expression and more the historian's as they go on, even though the history is handled as poetic material. In any of the single Letters the history is almost without meaning—odd facts, lists of provisions, inserted paragraphs on the fishing industry—but with the growth of the poem as a whole it is clear that something else is involved. The same facts return again and again. He goes back again and again to look at Gloucester from every view point that the town's history gives him. The impetus—he would call it "thrust"—is moral—a New England transcendental morality concerned with the destruction of the early American ideal by commercial growth. (pp. 21-5)

Sometimes I find myself thinking of Olson as an artisan, a worker with his hands, a carpenter, a New England journeyman. The woodworkers who did the carvings, flutings, ceilings; ship carpenters who did the bowsprit figures, as well as the trim, railings, hatch covers, and hand gear. The sense of the work being finished, of being placed. It is difficult to be both a historian and a poet, but by using some of his materials as an artisan would he is usually able to keep the two together within the poem. His history, like the carpenter's plank, still has its own grain and smell when he gets through with it. And he uses more than history. There is a strong set of personal responses that also have become part of the Letters. In the earlier Letters there is a more open, more direct feel of language and image—even the simple, beautiful set of "The Songs Of Maximus." In the earlier sections it it much more Olson as artist that I feel— more poet than historian—the matter of the poetry coming out of someplace inside his own Gloucester experience. And the whole of the poem does seem to open out from the centering of himself in Gloucester, and from the feeling of himself within this place. In the earlier poems most of the themes that dominate the later have already been outlined, even if they have only been loosely threaded on the line of his own memories of the town's fishing fleet and the men of the boats. (p. 26)

I've never decided whether or not Olson considers his poems difficult to follow—or if he cares, but he is difficult, one of the most difficult of the modern poets to follow. Sometimes, as in the inner references of Letter 7, it's because he doesn't give enough away—at other times, as in the overall structure of the Letters, because he includes a maze of only distantly related material. Probably, since he knows the inference of everything he's saying he doesn't see the difficulty at all. (p. 27)

Olson's poetry has never been difficult in its imaginative image, only in its elisions and references. So difficult in these, that he could have been—often—uncomfortably trying to conceal the ordinariness of his materials by making the form of their presentation unnecessarily obscure. There is another implication, in the rejection of the imagination, that he makes more clearly in . . . Letter [7]. It is the vague feeling that there is a weakness, a softness, in the loose drift of the imagination. . . . His uneasiness with the imaginative vision has some of the gruffness of the New England countryman. As a poet he is also still the Charles Olson who was a fisherman, a carpenter, and postman. In this aspect of Olson is some of the poetry's brilliance, difficulty, insistence, and uniqueness. (pp. 32-3)

> *Samuel Charters, "Charles Olson," in his* Some Poems/Poets: Studies in American Underground Poetry Since 1945 *(copyright © 1971 by Samuel Charters), Oyez, 1971, pp. 21-35.*

*   *   *

OSBORNE, John   1929-

Osborne is a major British dramatist and writer for television. With his first play, "Look Back in Anger," Osborne gave both name and impetus to the writers known as Angry Young Men, the young "lower class" intellectuals who, like the Beats in America, were writing in protest of Establishment rules and values. (See also *Contemporary Authors*, Vols. 33-36.)

Jimmy Porter . . . is the angry one [of *Look Back in Anger*]. What is he angry about? It is a little difficult at first for an American to understand. The English understand, not because it is ever explicitly stated, but because the jitters which rack Jimmy, though out of proportion to the facts within the play, are in the very air the Englishman breathes. Jimmy, "risen" from the working class, is now provided with an intellect which only shows him that everything that might have justified pride in the old England—its opportunity, adventure, material well-being—has disappeared without being replaced by anything but a lackluster security. He fumes, rages, nags at a world which promised much but which has led to a dreary plain where there is no fiber or substance—only fear of scientific destruction and the minor comforts of "American" mechanics. His wife comments to the effect that "my father is sad because everything has changed; Jimmy is sad because nothing has." In the meantime Jimmy seeks solace and blows defiance through the symbolic jazz of his trumpet; while his working-class pal, though he adores Jimmy and his wife, wisely leaves the emotionally messy premises.

Immanent reality plus a gift for stinging and witty rhetoric are what give the play its importance. It is not realism of the Odets or Williams kind, nor yet poetry, although it has some kinship to both. It adds up to a theatrical stylization of ideas about reality in which a perceptive journalism is made to flash on the stage by a talent for histrionic gesture and vivid elocution. While the end product possesses a certain nervous force and genuineness of feeling it is also sentimental, for it still lacks the quality of an experience digested, controlled or wholly understood. (p. 56)

Jimmy Porter . . . is a sign, not a character. We accept him because in the final count he is more amusing than real. We can look beyond him and the flimsy structure of the fable in which he is involved and surmise some of the living sources in the civilization from which he issues.

That John Osborne is attached and attuned to those sources is the virtue and hope of his talent. (p. 57)

> *Harold Clurman, "John Osborne" (1957), in his* The Divine Pastime: Theatre Essays *(reprinted with permission of Macmillan Publishing Co., Inc.; copyright © 1946, 1948, 1949, 1950, 1951, 1952, 1953, 1954, 1955, 1956, 1957, 1958, 1959, 1960, 1961, 1962, 1963, 1964, 1965, 1967, 1969, 1970, 1971, 1974 by Harold Clurman), Macmillan, 1974, pp. 55-7.*

Jimmy Porter is often a detestable character from any point of view, including—at moments—the author's. With all its monotony of structure, its false starts into domestic melodrama or screwball comedy, *Look Back in Anger* has the courage of [Osborne's] talent for relentless portraiture. There's nothing wrong with Jimmy Porter that a good revolution wouldn't cure, if a good revolution were conceivable by him or anyone else connected with the play. But it isn't. And so a potentially political play becomes—again, I suppose, intentionally—a private lives play of the most suffocating kind. (p. 125)

> *F. W. Dupee, in* Partisan Review *(copyright © 1958 by Partisan Review, Inc.), Winter, 1958.*

A play like *Look Back in Anger* creates a world which, in essence, is familiar to us (reality, rather than an imaginative *dislocation* of reality), and it becomes easier for the mind to sidetrack onto an element which may be more pleasing to it than the main theme of the play. Constant reference is made, even by people who liked the play, to Jimmy Porter's *self-pity*, his *neurotic* behaviour, his *cruelty* to his wife. This makes nonsense of the play; Jimmy Porter is devoid of any neurosis or self-pity, and the play is summed up in his cry against a negative world, "Oh heavens, how I long for a little ordinary human enthusiasm. Just enthusiasm—that's all. I want to hear a warm, thrilling voice cry out Hallelujah! Hallelujah! I'm alive." . . . Would *Look Back in Anger* have been the success it was if people had been forced to listen to this damning indictment of themselves as dead souls, instead of being allowed to stray into less dangerous channels (guying of English Sundays, excitingly turbulent sex-life, downtrodden and maltreated wife, etc.)? (pp. 45-6)

> *Tom Milne, "The Hidden Face of Violence" (originally published in* Encore, *Vol. VII, No. 1, 1960; copyright © by Encore), in* Modern British Dramatists: A Collection of Critical Essays, *edited by John Russell Brown, Prentice-Hall, 1968, pp. 38-46.*

Whatever the merits of the writing, and they are considerable, *Look Back in Anger* is limited by the nihilism of its author and the crackle and sputter of fireworks in a mist. For a play characterized by admirably sustained dialogue and taut, fragmentary conflicts *Look Back in Anger* was curiously unsatisfying. . . .

The realism of seedy settings, vibrant acting, forthright staging, the sordid story, and the pungent dialogue was altogether appropriate here. But in the context of the play the realistic refinements are only arid achievements. There was a time, not so very long ago, when it was possible to associate realistic art with a positive attitude rather than with the negations of a *Look Back in Anger*. (p. 174)

> *John Gassner, "John Osborne's 'Look Back in Anger'," in his* Theatre at the Crossroads: Plays and Playwrights of the Mid-Century American Stage *(copyright © 1960 by Mollie Gassner; reprinted by permission of Holt, Rinehart and Winston, Publishers), Holt, 1960, pp. 173-75.*

If one looks closely at the crotchety, constipated, hypercritical figure of Martin Luther in John Osborne's [*Luther*], one is forcibly reminded of that fuming British malcontent, Jimmy Porter [protagonist of *Look Back in Anger*]; a protestant who bitched against the Welfare State as vehemently as the theologian wrangled with the Pope. The similarities do not end there.

Despite the jump in time, the clerical context and the change of venue, the play is not (as has been charged . . .) a *departure* for Osborne. There is a clear link-up between Luther's sixteenth-century Germany and our time. In both, the sense of cosmic imminence is very strong. "The Last Judgement isn't to come. It's here and now," says Luther, and the doomsday-mountain-squatters and the nuclear-psychotics echo his words. The church-sale of indulgences is put forward as if it were a commercial advertisement, and the suggestion here is that the Catholic Church at its lowest moral ebb is an appropriate symbol for modern ad-mass culture. And who is the cleric Tetzel but a kind of bloated Arthur Godfrey pushing piety with the same unctuousness used to boost Lipton's Tea?

The Osborne of *Look Back in Anger* and *The Entertainer* gave us the *temperature* of social protest. And it was blisteringly hot. In *The World of Paul Slickey*, no longer content with the charged implication and the social inference, Osborne issued indictments. One of these was made out for the church. There was something compulsive in the way that Osborne humiliated his churchmen in *Slickey*. I have a stark image of an obscenely capering clergyman shedding all the moral restraints one usually associates with the cloth. Osborne seemed to be taking it out on the church because of some fundamental failing, and it was tinged with a personal bitterness—as if Osborne himself had been let down.

The religious disturbance is implicit in all the earlier plays. In his first play, *Epitaph for George Dillon*, there is an arbitrary scene whose only purpose is to deflate the condescending, sold-on-God visitor to the Elliot home. And if we ask ourselves (as so many have) what was bugging Jimmy Porter and George Dillon, the answer would seem to be: loss of faith. (pp. 117-18)

It is almost as if Osborne, tracing skepticism down to its roots, had to move from George Dillon to Jimmy Porter to Archie Rice to Martin Luther—almost is if they were all part of the same family. (p. 118)

Structurally, [*Luther*] is a series of taut interviews interspersed with sermons and smeared thick with cathedral atmosphere. Formalistically, Osborne (like practically every other modern playwright) appears to be under the sway of Bertolt Brecht. Like Brecht, he has strung together a series of short, stark tableaux. Like Brecht, he has backed them with evocative hangings (flags, banners, tapestries, crucifixes). Like Brecht, he employs a narrator to fill in background and make comment. Like Brecht, he has balanced the man and the social structure so that every moment of one produces a gesture from the other. But unlike Brecht, he has not endowed his play with that added intellectual dimension around which the drama may cohere. He has not, in this tart dramatization of history, furnished an underlying concept with which to interpret events.

Spectacle and rhetoric propel the play's first two acts, but by Act Three it comes to a dead stop because language which has already posited the argument, no longer has a job to perform. The only promising dramatic situation in the play concerns Luther's encouragement and subsequent betrayal of the peasants in their revolt against the lords. This is merely reported after the event in a beautifully written narrative speech which doesn't make up for the lack of action. This is the Brechtian influence at its most destructive. The dramatic climaxes are siphoned dry; characters are involved with the intellectual implications of their behavior rather than with the blood and bone of their situations. A narrative, imagistic language is giving us the "point" of the Luther story in a series of historical passages annotated with theological footnotes. The strongest character in the second half is a Knight who helped put down the peasants' rebellion, and what gives him such presence is the fact that he has just waged war and arrives at least with the residue of an involvement. The real battle has been in Luther's conscience and we have felt only its mildest repercussions. No one has come foward to oppose our protagonist. His anti-clerical father has raged only against losing a son to the monastery. The Pope has threatened but backed down. The beaten peasants have shied off with their tails between their legs. From scene to scene we find ourselves being cheated by authenticity.

The play's final moments emphasize the dearth of development. . . . In place of the last-act solidification of ideas (not a desirable way to write a play, but obviously the kind of play Osborne *was* writing), we get the scene of pregnant ambiguity which invites us to moor the play in whichever dock we like, as the writer wasn't going anywhere in particular anyway. (pp. 118-20)

If the play proves nothing about Luther it proves a great deal about John Osborne. It proves that he has the ability to grasp dramatic ideas and the language to convey them on a hard, bright poetical level. Also, he can don period costumes and still hold a twentieth century stance, and in a theatre where an historical milieu automatically produces turgid posturing, this is a real asset. His structural and intellectual shortcomings do not diminish these gifts.

Osborne, I would guess, is fishing round for a new theme— or rather a new objective correlative in which to express his old theme: personal idealism in collision with institutional dogmas. He has gravitated from anger to contemplation, and that is a healthy progress. (p. 120)

At the start of what promises to be the swinging sixties [that is, at the time of this essay], Osborne remains the most ornery dramatist in England. He still smarts, seethes and occasionally rages. He refuses to conform to other people's idea of his nonconformity. He rejects the cosy club chair and the gutless protest that crackles in the lounge and smolders on the street. He still winces at the stench in his country and refuses to pretend it is only someone burning leaves in the back yard.

He is the closest thing England has to a Norman Mailer. . . . He produces in me a warm sense of security, for I always feel that he is one of the few (small "c") committed playwrights who really writes out of a conviction— that it is a social and humanist conviction and not an allegiance to maintain the fashion of the irate, verbose radical —and that unlike the (capital "C") Committed writers, he is not partial to anything except his art. (pp. 120-21)

> *Charles Marowitz, "The Ascension of John Osborne" (first published in* The Drama Review, *Vol. VII, No. 2, 1962;* © *1962 by The Drama Review; reprinted by permission; all rights reserved), in* Modern British Dramatists: A Collection of Critical Essays, *edited by John Russell Brown, Prentice-Hall, 1968, pp. 117-21.*

Osborne is unquestionably a born dramatist, and his vocabulary of invective is simply stunning, but I think he has yet to write a work that will endure. Too much of his writing remains unformulated, and too much remains unfinished: his plays have the quality of electrical particles without a nucleus to hold them in orbit. Osborne's dramatic discipline since *Epitaph for George Dillon* has grown increasingly loose, and more and more he has begun to indulge a weakness for dramatic ventriloquism: *Inadmissible Evidence*, for example, after a brilliant first act, collapses completely into structural chaos, as the author introduces rhetorical essays on subjects only remotely related to his theme. The typical Osborne scene consists of one person orating and another listening—the monologues are inspired but they do not admit of true argument. And he is capable, I think, of writing only one character fully: the cruel, blistering protagonist who evokes the spectator's pity when he reveals himself to be collapsing under the burden of his own unpleasantness. This suggests that under the hard veneer of Osborne's style there lurks considerable sentimentality, and makes it understandable why he has been successful on Broadway. . . . Until Osborne can put his wonderful eloquence at the service of consistently worked-out themes, he will remain a playwright of the second rank. (p. 129)

> *Robert Brustein, "The English Stage" (1965), in his* The Third Theatre *(copyright* © *1969 by Robert Brustein; reprinted by permission of Alfred A. Knopf, Inc.), Knopf, 1969, pp. 123-30.*

Osborne's first plays were structurally conventional: *Look Back in Anger* and *Epitaph for George Dillon* are three-act plays set within realistic walls like most of their immediate predecessors. Exposition, development, and conclusion, clear character presentation and progressive building of conflict and tension are all duly there. What was new was the kind of life these plays mirrored in detail: Osborne's own world—young, uneasily married and loving—and its thwarted idealistic pretensions. All the conventional discretion, polish, and good manners of the English drama had

gone; and there was no condescension—indeed there was a great show of sympathy—towards what his predecessors would have called "low" characters. Also, the central character in each was a misplaced artist, reduced to anger, double-talk and, temporarily, compliance. From this center, Osborne's later plays were to develop: the best of them are largely monologues, while the others use plot and situation to present an occasion for understanding and revaluation. (p. 9)

[In *Inadmissible Evidence*] Osborne is no longer angry and defiant; he is asking for compassion and understanding and, more surprisingly to judge from his early work, has found a way of recreating in physically realizable language, the inner, half-conscious pressures within his hero. The nightmare of a defeated idealist is not easily admissible in the theatre; even more rarely is it presented in palpable and challenging form, rather than in soliloquy. (This is the technique of *Lear* over against that of *Hamlet*, or a means of fusing the comic and serious plots of *The Changeling* or *'Tis Pity She's a Whore*.)

In other plays—*A Patriot For Me*, *Plays For England*, and *A Bond Honoured*—Osborne creates groups around his central characters that display their situation in society and, with the last play (developed from one by Lope de Vega), in the tradition of Christian thought and feeling. From his first play onwards Osborne has been moving with difficulty and energy towards a wider and truer relationship with the world around him. The plays have been fantastic and accurately realistic; large and small; historical and contemporary; monologue and babel. This variety is bred of responsibility and growing knowledge, not of ease or mere success. (p. 10)

> *John Russell Brown, "Introduction" to* Modern British Dramatists: A Collection of Critical Essays, *edited by John Russell Brown (*© *1968 by Prentice-Hall, Inc.; reprinted by permission of Prentice-Hall, Inc., Englewood Cliffs, New Jersey), Prentice-Hall, 1968, pp. 1-14.*

Like his apocalyptic sputtering about English society, Osborne wants language to "go down with dignity". But he is as much a rapist of the mother tongue as the institutions he criticizes. He cannot separate sound from sense, feeling from fury. Signalling the mind's retreat from the culture, his language loses the sinew that comes with struggle. It is a pose, not a probe.

Osborne's linguistic bind is also a theatrical stalemate. A large part of theatregoing pleasure is bearing witness to *something*, but nothing happens on Osborne's stage.

> *"Theatre without Adventure," in* The Times Literary Supplement *(*© *Times Newspapers Ltd., 1972; reproduced by permission), December 29, 1972, p. 1569.*

[In *Inadmissible Evidence* John Osborne] has created one of the towering roles of the theatre in our times. The most remarkable thing about this character [the protagonist, Bill Maitland,] is the fact that while it is impossible to like him, he nonetheless always commands our attention. It is a strange sensation: to be mesmerized by mediocrity. Bill Maitland is an inelegant lecher, an addicted personality who alternates between too much whiskey and too many pills, an insensitive and unprincipled lawyer who just barely survives on the petty wretchedness of others, and finally is a failure in every human relationship in which he has participated. (pp. 308-09)

Except to the most morbidly curious, such a character should be monstrously dull. But he isn't, and one of the chief reasons we find him so compelling is Osborne's incendiary brilliance of language. There is no one writing in the theatre today who has a surer mastery of stage rhetoric than he, and I believe the secret of his success lies in his ability to deal with disturbing themes without resorting to cheap or eccentric tricks of language. (p. 309)

Many people have seen *Inadmissible Evidence* as a play in which the young and angry Jimmy Porter of *Look Back in Anger*, having just reached middle age, discovers his own spiritual bankruptcy and turns his seemingly limitless capacity for bitter disgust away from the world and now directs it towards himself. Certainly, this is true.... But such a reading of the play doesn't explain why Maitland judges himself as he does. It seems to me that only when we recognize that from the beginning Osborne has been writing dramas of disengagement will the full import of this play become clear.

Jimmy Porter is angry because he has come to believe that everything about society is mean and hypocritical. In his disgust for the world he has consciously chosen to step outside it, no matter how this decision may affect his wife and friends. But Jimmy's whole angry existence is totally dependent upon the continued existence of that society which he rails at so bitterly. The judgment which Osborne makes on the life of Jimmy-Bill now that he has reached forty is not directed at his anger but at his act of disengagement. (pp. 309-10)

Bill Maitland (né Jimmy Porter) chose to detach himself from every claim which society can make on the individual. At the end of *Inadmissible Evidence*, as we see him broken and alone on the stage, we know he has at last succeeded in making the final cut. It has been a meaningless achievement, and John Osborne who fathered the "angry" generation in the British theatre has demonstrated most convincingly that when anger over the failures of society becomes so extreme that it leads to disengagement from that society, the anger will eventually turn into a caustic self-disgust which can produce only isolation and impotence. (p. 311)

> *Robert W. Corrigan, "Anger and After: A Decade of the British Theatre" (abridged versions originally published in anthologies edited by Robert W. Corrigan, 1962, 1965, 1968), in his* The Theatre in Search of a Fix *(copyright © 1973 by Robert W. Corrigan; used with permission of Delacorte Press), Delacorte Press, 1973, pp. 301-15.*

'Seems very long at beginning,' reads one of my programme jottings for *The Entertainer*; and, had not the production quite sapped my juices, I could have added 'very long in middle' and 'very long at end'. A new Unity of Length, in fact. Not that the writing isn't sometimes crisp and eloquent: it is, especially when anger or distress percolates into the lackadaisical Rice household. Not that the play's impressionistic view of 1956 has no aptness in

1974.... As dramatist, [John Osborne] has rarely flinched from the painful task of boring us to tears. (p. 872)

> *Benedict Nightingale, in* New Statesman *(© 1974 The Statesman & Nation Publishing Co. Ltd.), December 13, 1974.*

John Osborne ... ended a period of the British theatre, in *Look Back in Anger*, with a full stop. Since then he has carried on writing, but with increasing dependence for theatrical punctuation on the exclamation mark, wielding it indeed like a rubber truncheon in a Punch and Judy show, to belabour, or rather perhaps be-Tory, a succession of puppets, many of them wearing the masks of former friends and colleagues.....

Personally, I prefer *George Dillon* to *Look Back*, a work which came first in conception though late in delivery, because it provides us with the most satisfying, and workable, objective correlative for the question I believe obsesses its author. Crudely stated, this is: have I the right to behave like a shit even if it turns out that I am not after all a genius? *Luther* generated a kind of operatic eloquence, a spirituous distillation which caught fire in the throat, from the same theme, though some of it was an exercise in rewriting rather than writing, with hogsheads of Erik Erikson decanted and poured out neat in the dialogue. *Inadmissible Evidence* was the last play I thought nearly 100 per cent proof based on this formula, largely because it appeared to proclaim that the protagonist already knew in his guts the *eau de vie* was being diluted, that increased doses of sex, selfishness and booze provided diminishing returns. It was a case history of the narcissist as a closet alcoholic.

Since then, Osborne has been mining an exhausted seam, every rift loaded with either-or. *Time Present* and *Hotel in Amsterdam* were vamping till ready, raising the curtain on pseudo-dramas which went nowhere, lasted no time, yet seemed to go on forever. They were developers' signs announcing that someday, perhaps, if the talent is available, a play may be erected on this spot. *The End of Me Old Cigar* is just such another advertisement for Himself, a paper pattern for which no material can be found in the wardrobe. No matter that the holders of warrants as suppliers of invisible garments to His Majesty provide quotes in the Sundays to fig-leaf the naked Emperor, I cannot believe any free-floating playgoer, including even John Osborne, can regard this ham-fisted, word-clogged, blood-drained charade as suitable for anything but a party-game for beleaguered guests, trapped in the *huis clos* of whatever is the contemporary equivalent of Lady Ottoline Morrell's....

John Osborne, once an observer and participator on the street-level with us, now gives the impression of looking down with binoculars through the double-glazed windows of some *Playboy* eyrie. His slang is already out-of-date. His targets are now half-forgotten in the mists of nostalgia. He has boned up on his underground magazines, but he never seems to have met the people who write them, let alone read them.

> *Alan Brien, "Exhausted Stuntman," in* New Statesman *(© 1975 The Statesman & Nation Publishing Co. Ltd.), January 24, 1975, p. 118.*

Notices of new Osborne plays tend to fall into two camps.

One seems to be at pains to prove he's not the man he once was. The other argues with equal conviction that not only is he every bit as good as in his early hey-day, but time, experience and wisdom have tempered his anger investing his work with maturity. . . . Such is the fate—or privilege—of institutions and domesticated rebels. The privilege is that turn out a masterpiece or a failure there'll still be a theatre for your next play.

The End of Me Old Cigar sets out as one thing and ends as another. It begins very much as a Restoration satire. A confederacy of women plot to end male domination at a stroke. Their object is to catch a sufficiently large, representative, and influential sample of them with their trousers down and reveal to the world a two-way mirror's eye-view of their corruptibility, decadence and unfitness to rule. (p. 28)

But Osborne ducks out of the problem he has set himself. He ditches the satirical frame work he's built up, axes characters who've only just stuck their noses in and replaces it all with a little bedchamber-verité love scene. . . . Osborne then finishes the play with a haste that suggests either loss of interest or a need to take his type-writer in for servicing. . . .

But never let the ability of Osborne to thrill an audience be underestimated. He can always produce moments when a character soars into voice with a speed, fluency and mounted gusto that fair catches the breath. . . .

The piece has a contemporaneity about it, a sense that much of its detail will be outmoded within a 12-month and that the jokes are once-offs. It's an extended revue, as Osborne himself almost suggests in a programme note. He says that it was written while he was working on another, one supposes, more portentous play. (p. 29)

> *Ivan Howlett, in* Plays and Players *(© copyright Ivan Howlett 1975), March, 1975.*

* * *

OZ, Amos   1939-

Oz is an Israeli novelist. (See also *Contemporary Authors*, Vols. 53-56.)

Amos Oz has emerged in recent years as the best known of the younger Israeli novelists and a leading spokesman for the generation of *sabras* who grew up along with the State of Israel. In a country where "sensational" novels, and certainly those with any pretense to seriousness, are a relative rarity, Oz's works have gained considerable popularity, even notoriety, for both the controversiality of their themes and the boldness of their presentation. This was especially true of *My Michael*, the novel which served to introduce Oz to American readers, and which Oz wrote when he was scarcely twenty-eight years old. A study of the personal disintegration of a young Israeli housewife, *My Michael* succeeded in transforming a political "fact"— the Arab-Israeli dilemma—into a genuine metaphor of the imagination. The violence of its heroine's erotic fantasies of abduction and rape by Arab twins with whom she had grown up before the War of Independence in 1948 suggested another violence even more disturbing to the Israeli psyche than the political one. Jerusalem, the setting of the novel and a still-divided city, was depicted as a dense, opaque landscape mirroring the heroine's inner conflict, an

illusion of abstractions set upon a wilderness of suppressed violence, ever on the verge of upheaval by demiurgic powers.

Both in *My Michael* and in his later work, Oz has demonstrated a special talent for creating fiction out of the exigencies of Israel's political and historical legacy. It is a talent that is again evident, although to a considerably lesser degree, in *Elsewhere, Perhaps*, Oz's second novel—second, that is, to appear in English; actually, it is a reworked and truncated version of the author's first novel, published in Israel in 1966. Like *My Michael*, [this] work also purports to offer a critical glance at an aspect of Israeli society: the most sacrosanct of Israel's social institutions, the kibbutz. . . . The kibbutz, in short, [turns] into just another small town, an Israeli Peyton Place: one-third boredom, and two-thirds gossip. . . . Like all morality plays, this one deals in predictable dualities and opposites. (pp. 100-01)

Unfortunately, Oz's determination to force an allegory out of the implausible Zion-Diaspora conflict works at cross-purposes to and eventually defeats the novel's more interesting intention: the naturalistic exposé of the "other side" of kibbutz life. The members of Metzudat Ram [Oz's fictional settlement] never seem more than a bland force of personalized Goodness, while the Arabs and the Diaspora Jews are forever being straitjacketed into Oz's embodiment of the power of Evil. In a scheme as rigid and predetermined as this, little opportunity remains for specificity or nuance. There is, in fact, no essential difference between the "new" and "old" Jews *in* their Jewishness—neither are recognizably Jewish—except, perhaps, for the novel's "evil fairy," Siegfried Berger, who is embellished by Oz with all the grotesque flourishes that once marked the typical anti-Semitic caricature of the Jew.

Israeli literature, if it is ever to mature, will undoubtedly have to confront the critical issue of the relation of Diaspora Jewry to Israel, and the relation of Israel to Diaspora Jewry, in all its troubled complexity. That this issue has a special poignancy for the Israeli writer, whose own identity is forged in an ongoing dialectic between the secular values of Western culture and the religious-historical values of Judaism, should go without saying, But an allegory of the kind presented in *Elsewhere, Perhaps* is little more than a refusal to acknowledge the existence of the problem. The novel fails precisely where the imagination might have offered insight into the nexus of Zion and Diaspora. (p. 101)

> *David Stern, "Morality Tale" (reprinted from* Commentary *by permission; copyright © 1974 by the American Jewish Committee), in* Commentary, *July, 1974, pp. 100-01.*

[*Touch the Water, Touch the Wind* is a] lyrical, faintly allegorical novel [which] manages to sketch the life of a modest Jewish schoolteacher named Pomeranz, beginning with his persecution in Poland in 1939 and continuing to his sudden fame as a mathematician in Israel before the Six-Day War. If Pomeranz is an example of the wandering, wonder-struck Jew, his wife, who becomes separated from him and somehow rises to be the head of Soviet secret agencies, represents the conforming Jew who is comfortable with the established culture. . . . The book reverberates with motifs of recent Jewish history: the escape from terror, the commitment to a land, the persistent threat of a nemesis. It takes considerable risks with the fantastic and the supernatural. Though it never quite slows down enough to become very profound, its youthfulness and energy are exhilarating. (pp. 233-34)

The New Yorker (© *1974 by The New Yorker Magazine, Inc.), November 18, 1974.*

Among those younger Israeli authors who have in recent years been published in the U.S.—Aharon Megged, Yoram Kaniuk, Yehuda Amichai, and A. B. Yehoshua—Amos Oz has won particularly extravagant praise: For two novels, *Elsewhere, Perhaps* and *My Michael*, and the novella *Crusade*, which appeared in *Commentary* three years ago, he has been proclaimed "a writer of international importance." . . . *Elsewhere, Perhaps* was a kaleidoscopic account of life on a kibbutz hazardously close to the frontier, endangered continually by Arab guns from without and the petty, exhausting human frictions of collective life from within. In common with other sabra novelists of his generation, Oz regards the older world of Zionist idealists—the patriarchal heroes of the Palmach and the Haganah—with ironic amusement, the characteristically rebellious disdain of children toward the ideology of parents. Yet what he principally offered in *Elsewhere, Perhaps* was a cross-section of the kibbutz world: young love, middle-aged adultery, brush fires of gossip, the not always successful efforts of well-meaning teachers and poets and farmers and intellectuals to live in productive harmony for the good of their beleaguered country. A gathering of separate conflicts and personalities bound loosely together by the institutional setting, the novel was rather like *Grand Hotel* set on a communal farm. It was well-written but conventional, and Oz's satiric detachment was too often short-circuited by sentimentality.

Of *My Michael* one American reviewer declared: "It's quite the last kind of book one expects from a young writer living in the midst of a melodramatic political situation . . . a modern Israeli *Madame Bovary* . . . that is also a critique of a superficial 'masculine' society." When in doubt, call on Flaubert and feminism. But neither of these wild reaches into left field was relevant to the work, remarkable only for the flawless plausibility of the feminine-first-person voice that Oz assumed. *My Michael* was the story of a discontented marriage, told by the very neurotic Hannah Gonen. . . . Unfortunately, Oz never persuaded us of the singular qualities he obviously believed her to have. Hannah was a tiresome and very familiar sort of narcissistic nudnik, and *My Michael*, far from offering what still another critic hailed as "a fresh insight into the makeup of modern Israel," was too naggingly limited to the narrow, uninteresting boundaries of its heroine's self-absorbed world to cast any light at all on the society she inhabits. (The novella *Crusade*, set in the 11th century, is far more effective than the novels because the historical framework kept both the prose and the ideas in requisite focus.)

Nothing in the earlier fiction of Amos Oz in any way adumbrates his dense and puzzling new book, *Touch the Water, Touch the Wind*. . . . It is at first glance a juggler's act of symbols and magic, less a novel than a series of vaguely dovetailed meditations on Poland and Israel, on philosophy and mysticism, on the Jews as a people in constant flight from a hostile world. Oz seems to be saying that only through the nontemporal, intellectual magic of the mind— through mathematics, philosophy and music—can the Jew elude his inimical reality and live beyond the threat of death. "Can any Jew worthy of the name," he writes, "lay claim to a genuine passport?" (pp. 15-16)

After several readings, I am still maddeningly bewildered by *Touch the Water, Touch the Wind*. Oz appears to have abandoned the conventions of realism not out of a deeply felt literary necessity but for the purpose of a technical stunt. There is an air of meretricious contrivance about the book's jagged discontinuities, its random incidents and inexplicable declarations, as though its author were trying to prove that he, too, can handle the fashionable obscurities of disorientation. To justify the strain on one's credulity and powers of poetic connection, such fiction must have a consonant richness of thought and suggestion. Yet Oz's metaphor of the Jew in perpetual flight is not profound, and his stuggle to impose an innovatory "experimental" texture on this image seems more capricious than genuinely committed. Some novels of strangeness, marvels and unreality, like Dan Jacobson's *The Wonder Worker*, in time disclose astonishing vistas of imaginative clarity; to read them is an act of discovery. But *Touch the Water, Touch the Wind* seems more a maze without an exit, a willful act of confusion. (p. 16)

Pearl K. Bell, "Lost in the Land of Oz," in The New Leader (© *1975 by the American Labor Conference on International Affairs, Inc.), January 6, 1975, pp. 15-16.*

Touch the Water, Touch the Wind . . . is an attempt to present in fiction a representation of the European background and present situation of the Israelis. . . .

Unfortunately, as it seems to me, Oz has chosen to write in that portentous baby talk of the profound but simple soul, one of the more off-putting literary conventions.

> He was left to himself day and night. He thought about many different things. . . .

He has some other stylistic devices: a mixed whimsy and fantasy, presumably to remind us of fables and folk tales; a gaudy overwriting. . . . Persistently Oz uses the rhetoric of the big statement followed by a cute little homely detail. . . .

Amos Oz has elected to tell his story in the vein of fantasy. . . . Thus each crucial event of the story is fobbed off into what appear to me most inept bits of foolish and obscure legerdemain—to me this seems oddly and frivolously cruel, considering what was available to real people in similar circumstances. Many of these bits of fantasy, or "symbolism" if you will, are unbelievably tasteless, as is the irrelevant sadism, sexual at times, and also the attempts at humor, no better than tags. The presence or thought of Germans evokes always pork fried in pork fat, and so on. . . .

Surely the subjects that the Master Race has given us in our century are so difficult and painful that they may well be, as many have said, impossible for art. We might almost concede this, were it not for Tadeusz Borowski, Elie Wiesel, and a few others. Many have failed and especially in fantasy and fable. There can be no doubt that Amos Oz's heart is in the right place, but in this book everything else seems miserably wrong. (p. 40)

John Thompson, in The New York Review of Books *(reprinted with permission from* The New York Review of Books; *copyright © 1975 NYREV, Inc.), January 23, 1975.*

P

PERELMAN, S(idney) J(oseph)   1904-

A contributor to *The New Yorker* since 1930, Perelman is one of America's best-loved humorists. In addition to his satirical occasional pieces on almost every aspect of contemporary society, he has written plays and scripts.

One marvels that a man whose summits of wit appear to be "our son which he is home from Yale" (Eastern division) and "at the intersection of La Paloma and Alte Yenta Boulevards" (Western division) should have become a so-called major humorist, and, more amazing yet, one whose humor is said to be based on linguistic prowess. (p. 123)

> *John Simon, in* New York Magazine (© *1974 by NYM Corp.; reprinted by permission of* New York Magazine *and John Simon), November 18, 1974.*

There exist persons in the world to whom the very sight of Perelman's byline is enough to make them ready to guffaw and smirk at things that would draw sullen sighs were they perpetrated by any other writer. That this reviewer is such a person must be admitted at once. . . . In short, it is difficult to write about good Perelman and bad Perelman, when it is not the content of what Perelman writes that matters, or the jokes, but something so slippery as the tone: the arrogant sneer, the social bite, the mock-heroic posture that is likely to turn at any moment to sniveling, the elegant language likely to be brought down to earth any instant by an attack of Yiddish. . . .

For Perelman readers, the new collection *Vinegar Puss* will be an occasion for joy; for others, it is an opportunity to take up an addiction more beneficial than most that one could name. (p. 26)

> *Dorothy Rabinowitz, in* Saturday Review *(copyright © 1975 by Saturday Review/ World, Inc.; reprinted with permission), March 22, 1975.*

"Vinegar Puss" is Perelman's 19th book; he is now 71. If you want to familiarize yourself with his work, you probably shouldn't try to read all 19 books at once; one's vocabulary can take just so much enriching, or diminishing, as the case may be, by words you'll never use, "mommixed," "buttinsky," "goodge," "arble-bargle"; exclamations

you'll never exclaim, "let a snarl be your umbrella," "she's the bee's knees," "everything is leeches and cream," "no man ever buckled a better swash"; and ripostes you'll never riposte, "hie yourself to an asylum, my old," "don't be a sherbet, Herbert," "don't you know there's a peace on," "*numquam iterum, Carolus* (never again, Charlie)." . . .

The book consists of 22 pieces; I won't call it a gallimaufry, but it's pretty varied. I liked some of the shorter pieces and by-the-way bits and *mise en scènes* best. A famous Indian film star flees the country, leaving 17 partially completed films in the lurch, "I've been a naughty girl," pursued by various "handkerchief heads . . . hugging cans of films." She knows they'll catch up with her, "You don't know Indian vengeance like I know Indian vengeance." A gentleman dining alone, buttonholed by a stranger, finally just faints dead away from boredom . . . that sort of thing. . . .

Some of the pieces seem pretty slight, and the book offers fewer surprises, embellishments, somersaults, all the rest, than are generally found in some of those amazing earlier books of Perelman's. Yet actually I think "Vinegar Puss" yields more laughs and unexpected turns than did the last book ["Baby, It's Cold Inside"], which was rather heavy with social criticism. Perelman still takes a dim view of just about everything, . . . but overall he's less high dudgeoned this time around. . . .

It may be true that fine words butter no parsnips, but one still reads him very slowly, sentence by sentence, from start—"of a wild and windy night this winter, any noctambule pausing to light his cheroot (or extinguish it; it comes to the same thing) outside a public house off Shaftesbury Avenue called the Haunch of Pastrami might have observed two individuals of no special distinction descending from an equipage before the premises"—to finish. (pp. 6-7)

> *Robert M. Strozier, in* The New York Times Book Review (© *1975 by The New York Times Company; reprinted by permission), March 23, 1975.*

Ever since *Dawn Ginsbergh's Revenge* broke on an unsuspecting public in 1929, S. J. Perelman devotees have been lapping up his lapidary prose, scurrying to net his wild allusions, guarding against whiplash injuries from his abrupt twists of logic, and following his riotously disoriented express through Bucks County, Hollywood, Africa, Asia and paranomasia. As a long time member of the Perelman legion, I am more inclined to celebrate than criticize [*Vinegar Puss*] his first new book in five years. . . .

[For] the past 10 or 15 years, Perelman has been treated with the the sort of extreme unction usually lavished on humorists only after death. He has been enshrined alongside such golden '20s fellow-alchemists as Benchley, Lardner, Thurber and Kaufman, ranked with Balzac, James (both Henry and Joyce), Conrad, Roethke and Juvenal, and lofted from the category of humorist to the empyrean of nihilist, dadaist and surrealist. All of which has left him blushing and digging his toes into the hot sand, muttering that he writes to satisfy the grocer sitting on his shoulder and to amuse himself.

Perelman seems to have recognized his last from the first and stuck to it. Despite the pundits who feel that humor could only be legitimated by a larding of redeeming social value, he has retained his '20s/'20s vision and resolutely lived off the fatuities of the land. His inspirations have been drawn from advertisements, health journals, women's magazines, old novels and movies, and a preposterous series of personal pratfalls, all done to a turn and served in such small pieces that his oeuvres might best be described as hors d'oeuvres. Yet given a platter of his Bucks County antipastorales, only a cad could ask for meat and potatoes. His targets, from the start, have been the pompous, the absurd and the phony; he has attacked them with a bounding erudition, an unabridged vocabulary, a superb mastery of style, and a wild sardonic wit that shredded pretension into a lunatic fringe and dismembered linear thinking a generation before McLuhan.

Vinegar Puss . . . runs true to form. The Perelman face, so often drawn by Hirschfeld and quartered by his own pen ("bespectacled and snaffle-toothed, nervously scratching a chin you could hang a lantern on"), still shines from the pages with a king-sized leer; the familiar Perelman persona still capers along the newly cast lines ("Quixotic? Headlong? Possibly. But then such is my nature") with all the old braggadocio of Le Sid.

The material in his new book is cut from the same bolt as its predecessors and tailored, perhaps a trifle more soberly than in the past, to the classic Perelman patterns: parody, capsule drama, disastrous hegira, ludicrous adventure, improbable reminiscence. And the needlework is still so deft that nothing ever comes apart at the seams but the reader. . . .

His work continues to defy every sort of analysis including the psycho-, but Perelman is perdurable. Long may his *feuilletons* be collected. And recollected.

> Felicia Lamport, "The Perils of Perelman," in The New Republic (*reprinted by permission of* The New Republic; © *1975 by The New Republic, Inc.*), *March 29, 1975, p. 23.*

Perelman is in immediate danger of becoming solemnized, a process that begins as a stiffening in the joints where criticism is written, and is likely to end with an untenured English instructor laboring on "Laundry and Dry Cleaning as Objective Correlatives in the Humor of S. J. Perelman."

The humorist himself quite possibly anticipated this situation 25 years ago when he titled one of his essays *Don't Bring Me Oscars (When It's Shoesies That I Need).* (p. 76)

Perelman is one of the great nibblers of the mother tongue. In his impeccably cut parodies, words like wattles and dottle, boffin and horripilating are used in ways that have caused two generations of grown men with attaché cases to break up in solitary laughter on public transport. (pp. 78, K8)

With a few sparkling exceptions, the pieces collected in *Vinergar Puss* (written mostly during the past five years) show Perelman at his second best. But this is usually the case in humor collections: the author is always made to look as if he is playing *Can You Top This?* with himself. Pieces that look good in the casual format of a weekly magazine are rudely upstaged by the handful that are very good.

Around the Bend in 80 Days is only good. . . . Few writers can get away with first-degree malice as well as Perelman: "I drew a deep breath, brushed a small, many-legged Arab off my sleeves and went down to unpack." Most of the other lines, though, could have been written for Groucho Marx and perhaps were: "I was tempted to fling him a lakh of rupees with a princely gesture. Not knowing how many rupees there were to a lakh, though, I had to content myself with the princely gesture." . . .

Anatomists of the Perelman corpus may detect a slight twice-breathed air here, as well as in "Nostasia in Asia," the five-part piece that concludes the collection. Some of the ground and most of the mock dudgeon are reminiscent of *Westward Ha!* (1948). That magnificent Middle Eastern curse, "May you live a thousand years and a trolley car grow in your stomach annually!" appeared at least once before in *The Rising Gorge* (1961).

But *I Have Nothing to Declare but My Genius* is full of fizz and vinegar. It is a magnificently spiteful spoof about a rich, prolific hack written by a man who frequently describes himself as a bleeder and a firm believer "that easy writing makes hard reading." The hack is the kind of man who dashes off a few mysteries before breakfast and boasts of popularizing Shakespeare so that he will be "comprehensible to the veriest moron . . . to even a rock fan." He is also a painter with a worldwide reputation. "One has long enough been acquainted with your eminence in the belletristic sphere," André Malraux writes him in English. "Now we are overturned to uncover you as a painterly ace . . ." This is Perelman at his best, inspired by the pompous, the fake and tawdry, and hell-bent for leatherette. (p. K8)

> R. Z. Sheppard, "Idiom Savant," in Time (*reprinted by permission from* Time, The Weekly Newsmagazine; *copyright Time Inc.*), *April 7, 1975, pp. 76, K8.*

* * *

PLATH, Sylvia   1932-1963

Ms Plath was an American poet, novelist, and short story writer who lived in England. Her elegant and controlled style belied her images of anger, violence, and pain. Her finest work is the poetic realization of ultimate love and ultimate death. (See also *Contemporary Authors*, Vols. 19-20.)

The first review I ever wrote of a book of poems was of *her* first book of poems, that breviary of estrangement (the rhymes are all slant, the end-stop avoided like a reproach), *The Colossus.* . . . The conflict, or at least the confrontation between what I should designate the lithic impulse—the desire, the need to reduce the demands of life to the unquestioning acceptance of a stone, "taciturn and separate . . . in a quarry of silences"—and the impulse to live on, accommodating the rewards as well as the wrecks of existence so that "the vase, reconstructed, houses / the elusive rose": such was the dilemma I glimpsed as a departure at the end of *The Colossus.* (pp. 413-15)

Yet now that we have the whole thing together, the two books of poems and the novel . . .—now that we can see Sylvia Plath's life, as she kept meaning us to, from the vantage of her death, we must not make too great a disjunction between the "conceptual" and the "immanent," the bridged and the engulfed in her utterance. It was all one effort—as Hughes says perfectly: "she faced a task in herself, and her poetry is the record of her progress in the task. . . . The poems are chapters in a mythology"—and it was all one quest, as Sylvia Plath says imperfectly (that is, with the abiding awareness of imperfection), in an uncollected poem:

> . . . *With luck I shall*
> *Patch together a content*
> *Of sorts. Miracles occur,*
> *If you care to call these spasmodic*
> *Tricks of radiance miracles.*

Her entire body of work can be understood best as a transaction—out of silence, into the dark—with otherness: call it death, or The Stone, or as she came to call it, "stasis in darkness" ("Ariel"), "great Stasis" ("Years"), in the first book such negotiations taking the form of a dialogue ("your voices lay siege . . . promising sure harborage"), which is to say *taking a form*; while in the later poems she is speaking from a point of identification with stasis which is complete, resolved, irreversible ("the cold dead center / where spilt lives congeal and stiffen to history")—she is on the other side, within the Deathly Paradise, so that it is the triumph of her final style to make expression and extinction indivisible ("I like black statements"). Which is why A. L. Alvarez says that her poems read as if they were written posthumously, for the very source of Sylvia Plath's creative energy was her self-destructiveness. (pp. 415-16)

We shall best realize the goal and the gain of Sylvia Plath's poetry if we reckon with Joy as Nietzsche accounts for it:

> . . . All that suffers wants to live, longing for what is farther, higher, brighter. "I want heirs"—thus speaks all that suffers; "I want children, I do not want *myself*."
> Joy it is that wants *itself*—the ring's will strives in it . . .
> Joy, however, does not want heirs, or children—joy wants itself, wants eternity, wants everything eternally the same.

And we shall best recognize the vestal responsibilities of the woman occupied by such joy if we invoke the demonstrated responsibilities of other women—such heroic initiates as Pauline Réage and Doris Lessing; it is in the cause of a sacramental joy that *Histoire d'O* and *To Room Nineteen* survey the entire sweep of a spiritual evolution, an ascesis whose inevitable conclusion—after everything else has been endured—is the body's destruction. (pp. 417-18)

Sylvia Plath enters upon her apprenticeship to otherness, to ecstasy; more ceremonious than Lessing, more ingenuous than Réage, but like them prepared to obey a tragic ontogeny ("I am ready for enormity"), she sloughs off—we see her divest herself of—mere personality like the cloud . . . in order to achieve the ecstatic identity conferred by Joy. . . . Though she submits herself to the ordeal, the process refuses to *take*, and the would-be victim is left with only the impenetrable surface of existence. . . . [No]—joy cannot be willed, it can only be surrendered to, gained when it has been given over. . . . That is why the poems in this first book . . . are all confessions of failure, records of estrangement, even boasts of betrayal. . . . The exhaustion before its term of the lithic impulse, as I have called it, the impoverishment of the effort to escape effort ("the stars are no nearer . . . and all things sink / into a soft caul of forgetfulness . . . This is not death, it is something safer") is the worry of *The Colossus.* . . . (pp. 418-19)

> *Richard Howard, "Sylvia Plath," in his* Alone With America: Essays on the Art of Poetry in the United States Since 1950 *(copyright © 1965, 1966, 1967, 1968, 1969 by Richard Howard; reprinted by permission of Atheneum Publishers, New York), Atheneum, 1969, pp. 413-22.*

The poems in Sylvia Plath's *The Colossus* are largely flawed by a rhythmical and lexical vulgarity. However, many of them are very good poems, there is a powerful sense of them having come from a single, eccentric imagination, and they are full of strange and startling expressions. They are also identifiably by the author of *Ariel*. For example, there are forecasts of *Ariel*'s subject-matter, that evolution of psychological background, domestic oppression and public and private pain, into a private and ultimate specialisation. In order to achieve that unique and powerful poetry it was necessary to abandon the earlier clotted style. . . . [There is] a quite obvious liberation of tone and freedom of movement in her later verse which is unlike anything in *The Colossus*. It will be reasonable to suggest that the compulsion to dramatise what she had come to see as her identity was so strong, and so artistically felt, that it was necessary to devise a way of writing that would be a literary version of the identity she was obsessed with fulfilling—in other words she had to find her "own voice", that unriddable cliché. (p. 68)

Crossing the Water is much freer in style than the first book. There is still something formulaic and precious about her phrase-making: ". . . a valedictory, pale hand"; or "Black, admonitory cliffs." However, there is more of that zany, accurate and unexpected imagery that is so central to the style of *Ariel*, and also the first book. Alert, nervous, and often domestic, it is one of her peculiar strengths. (p. 69)

What struck me most after reading *Crossing the Water* was not just that it was so good, or that none of the poems there had been thought good enough for *Ariel*, but that *Ariel* itself represents such a unified stretch of work, such a strong and tragically magnificent working out of a single complicated theme. . . .

Crossing the Water is an indispensable book, and Sylvia Plath one of that handful of modern poets whom intelligent readers will feel, more and more, that they have no option but to try and understand. (p. 70)

Douglas Dunn, in Encounter (© 1971 by
Encounter Ltd.), August, 1971, pp. 68-70.

It is difficult to describe the peculiar quality of Sylvia
Plath's last poems. Their originality is not simply an originality of mood. Nor does it lie in the brilliance and precision of her language, although in a certain sense Sylvia
Plath's descriptive talent was greater than any other she
had. Perhaps what is most surprising is the complete avoidance of hysteria. For Sylvia Plath's poetry is never reflective; it contains no sympathy for attitudes that were not her
own. Her intelligence sought expression not in judgement
but in the lightning clarity of revelation. The poems present
a sudden glimpse of things, and, caught in that glimpse, a
moment of intense emotion. Her great achievement was to
evolve a style that would fit this precarious mode of lyrical
expression: the multiple metaphors, the quick rhythms, the
mastery of colloquial speech, the extraordinary language,
and the direct, unhesitant manner.

In the later poetry we find no attempt to *say* anything. Images enter these later poems as particulars only, without
symbolic significance, and however much the poet may
borrow the emotional charge from distant and surprising
sources (from the imaginary life in ocean depths, from the
real and imaginary calamities of modern history) it is never
with any hint of an intellectual aim. It is tempting to restore
to these poems some vestiges of generality, by interpreting
them as Freudian parables, or as complex symbols. But
although the poems of *Ariel* and *Winter Trees* invite such
an interpretation, they also show how valueless it is. It is
not through their coincidence with unconscious wishes that
these poems affect us, nor do they have any symbolic force
comparable to their overwhelming immediacy of impact.
Everything in them is objective, concrete, conscious; we
can feel moved by Sylvia Plath's obsessions without feeling
any need to share in them.

*Roger Scruton, ''Sylvia Plath and the
Savage God,'' in* The Spectator (© 1971 by
The Spectator; *reprinted by permission of*
The Spectator), *December 18, 1971, p. 890.*

Tragedy is not a woman, however gifted, dragging her
shadow around in a circle or analyzing with dazzling scrupulosity the stale, boring inertia of the circle; tragedy is cultural, mysteriously enlarging the individual so that what he
has experienced is both what we have experienced and
what we need not experience—because of his, or her, private agony. It is proper to say that Sylvia Plath represents
for us a tragic figure involved in a tragic action, and that her
tragedy is offered to us as a near-perfect work of art in her
books. . . . [The] cult of Sylvia Plath insists that she is a
saintly martyr, but of course she is something less dramatic
than that, though more valuable. The ''I'' of the poems is
an artful construction, a tragic figure whose tragedy is classical, the result of a limited vision that believed itself the
mirror held up to nature—as in the poem ''Mirror,'' the eye
of a little god that imagines itself without preconceptions,
''unmisted by love or dislike.'' This is the audacious hubris
of tragedy, the inevitable reality-challenging statement of
the participant in a dramatic action which he does not know
is ''tragic.'' He dies, and only we can see the purpose of his
death—to illustrate the error of a personality that believed
itself godlike. (pp. 501-02)

[The] creatures of ''Heavy Women'' . . . smile to themselves above their ''weighty stomachs'' and meditate ''devoutly as the Dutch bulb,'' absolutely mute, ''among the
archetypes.'' Between the archetypes of jealous, ruthless
power represented by the Father/Son of religious and social
tradition, and the archetype of moronic fleshly beauty represented by these smug mothers, there is a very small space
for the creative intellect, for the employment and expansion
of a consciousness that tries to transcend such limits. Before we reject Sylvia Plath's definition of the artistic self as
unreasonably passive, even as infantile, we should inquire
why so intelligent a woman should assume these limitations, why she should not declare war against the holders of
power and of the ''mysteries'' of the flesh—why her poetry
approaches but never crosses over the threshold of an active, healthy attack upon obvious evils and injustices. The
solitary ego in its prison cell is there by its own desire, its
own admission of guilt in the face of even the most crazily
ignorant of accusors. (p. 504)

Sylvia Plath did not like other people; like many who are
persecuted, she identified in a perverse way with her own
persecutors and not with those who, along with her, were
victims. But she did not ''like'' other people because she
did not essentially believe that they existed; she knew intellectually that they existed, of course, since they had the
power to injure her, but she did not *believe* they existed in
the way she did, as pulsating, breathing, suffering individuals. Even her own children were objects of her perception,
there for the restless scrutiny of her image-making mind
and not there as human beings with a potentiality that
would someday take them beyond their immediate dependency upon her, which she sometimes enjoyed and sometimes dreaded.

The moral assumptions behind Sylvia Plath's poetry condemned her to death, just as she, in creating this body of
poems, condemned it to death. But her moral predicament
is not so pathological as one might think, if conformity to
an essentially sick society is taken to be—as many traditional moralists and psychologists take it—a sign of normality. Miss Plath speaks very clearly a language we can
understand. She is saying what men have been saying for
many centuries, though they have not been so frank as she
and, being less sensitive as well, they have not sickened
upon their own hatred for humanity—they have thrived
upon it, in fact, ''sublimating'' it into wondrous achievements of material and mechanical splendor. Let us assume
that Sylvia Plath acted out in her poetry and in her private
life the deathliness of an old consciousness, the old corrupting hell of the Renaissance ideal and its ''I''-ness separate and distinct from all other fields of consciousness,
which exist only to be conquered or to inflict pain upon the
''I.'' Where at one point in civilization this very masculine,
combative ideal of an ''I'' set against all other ''I's''—and
against nature as well—was necessary in order to wrench
man from the hermetic contemplation of a God-centered
universe and get him into action, it is no longer necessary;
its health has become a pathology and whoever clings to its
outmoded concepts will die. If Romanticism and its gradually accelerating hysteria is taken as the ultimate end of a
once-vital Renaissance ideal of subject/object antagonism,
then Miss Plath must be diagnosed as one of the last Romantics; and already her poetry seems to us a poetry of the
past, swiftly receding into history.

The "I" that is declared an enemy of all others cannot identify with anyone or anything, since even nature—or especially nature—is antagonistic to it. Man is spirit/body, but as in the poem "Last Things," Sylvia Plath states her distrust of the spirit which "escapes like steam/In dreams, through the mouth-hole or eye-hole. I can't stop it." Spirit is also intellect, but the "intellect" exists uneasily inside a prison-house of the flesh, a small, desperate calculating process (like the Ego in Freud's psychology) that achieves only spasmodic powers of identity in the constant struggle between the Id and the Superego or between the bestial world of fleshly female "archetypes" and hypocritical, deathly male authorities. This intellect does not belong naturally in the universe and feels guilt and apprehension at all times. It does not belong in nature; nature is "outside" man, superior in brute power to man though admittedly inferior in the possibilities of imagination. When this intellect attempts its own kind of creation, it cannot be judged as transcendent to the biological processes of change and decay but as somehow conditioned by these processes and, of course, found inferior. Why else would Miss Plath call a poem about her own poetry "Stillborn" and lament the deadness of her poems, forcing them to compete with low but living creatures?—"They are not pigs, they are not even fish. . . ." It is one of the truly pathological habits of this old consciousness that it puts all things into immediate *competition*: erecting Aristotelian categories of X and non-X, assuming that the distinction between two totally unconnected phases of life demands a kind of war, a superior/inferior grading. (pp. 504-06)

The poems of hatred seem to us very contemporary, in their jagged rhythms and surreal yoking together of images, and in their defiant expression of a rejection of love, of motherhood, of men, of the "Good, the True, the Beautiful. . . ." If life really is a struggle for survival, even in a relatively advanced civilization, then very few individuals will win; most will lose (and nearly all women are fated to lose); something is rotten in the very fabric of the universe. All this appears to be contemporary, but Sylvia Plath's poems are in fact the clearest, most precise (because most private) expression of an old moral predicament that has become unbearable now in the mid-twentieth century. (p. 509)

The passive, paralyzed, continually surfacing and fading consciousness of Sylvia Plath in her poems is disturbing to us because it seems to summon forth, to articulate with deadly accuracy, the regressive fantasies we have rejected —and want to forget. The experience of reading her poems deeply is a frightening one: it is like waking to discover one's adult self, grown to full height, crouched in some long-forgotten childhood hiding place, one's heart pounding senselessly, all the old, rejected transparent beasts and monsters crawling out of the wallpaper. So much for Plato! So much for adulthood! Yet I cannot emphasize strongly enough how valuable the experience of reading Miss Plath can be, for it is a kind of elegant "dreaming-back," a cathartic experience that not only cleanses us of our personal and cultural desires for regression, but explains by way of its deadly accuracy what was wrong with such desires.

The same can be said for the reading of much of contemporary poetry and fiction, fixated as it is upon the childhood fears of annihilation and persecution, the helplessness we have all experienced when we are, for one reason or an-

other, denied an intellectual awareness of what is happening. For instance, the novels of Robbe-Grillet and his imitators emphasize the hypnotized passivity of the "I" in a world of dense and apparently autonomous things; one must never ask "Who manufactured these things? who brought them home? who arranged them?"—for such questions destroy the novels. Similarly, the highly praised works of Pynchon, Barthelme, Barth (the Barth of the minimal stories, not the earlier Barth), and countless others, are verbalized screams and shudders to express the confusion of the ego that believes—perhaps because it has been told so often—itself somehow out of place in the universe, a mechanized creature if foolish enough to venture into Nature; a too-natural creature for the mechanical urban paradise he has inherited but has had no part in designing. The "I" generated by these writers is typically a transparent, near-nameless personality; in the nightmarish works of William Burroughs, the central consciousness does not explore a world so much as submit pathetically to the exploration of himself by a comically hostile world, all cartoons and surprising metamorphoses. Sylvia Plath's tentative identity in such poems as "Winter Trees," "Tulips," and even the robustly defiant "Daddy" is a child's consciousness, essentially, seizing upon a symbolic particularity (tulips, for instance) and then shrinking from its primary noon, so that the poems—like the fiction we read so often today—demonstrate a dissolution of personality. (pp. 509-11)

There is never any integrating of the self and its experience, the self and its field of perception. Human consciousness, to Sylvia Plath, is always an intruder in the natural universe.

This distrust of the intellect in certain poets can result in lyric-meditative poetry of an almost ecstatic beauty, when the poet acknowledges his separateness from nature but seems not to despise or fear it. . . . It is a paradox that the poet believes he will honor the objects of his perception— whether swallows, trees, sheep, bees, or infants—only by withdrawing from them. Why does it never occur to Romantic poets that they exist as much by right in the universe as any other creature, and that their function as poets is a natural function—that the human imagination is, to put it bluntly, superior to the imagination of birds and infants?

In art this can lead to silence; in life, to suicide. (pp. 513-14)

Perhaps it is not just Sylvia Plath's position at the end of a once-energetic tradition, and the circumstances of her own unhappy life, that doomed her and her poetry to premature dissolution, but something in the very nature of lyric poetry itself. What of this curious art form which, when not liberated by music, tends to turn inward upon the singer, folding and folding again upon the poet? If he is immature to begin with, of what can he sing except his own self's immaturity, and to what task can his imagination put itself except the selection of ingenious images to illustrate this immaturity? . . . The risk of lyric poetry is its availability to the precocious imagination, its immediate rewards in terms of technical skill, which then hypnotize the poet into believing that he has achieved all there is to achieve in life as well as in his art. . . . Most lyric poets explore themselves endlessly, like patients involved in a permanent psychoanalysis, reporting back for each session determined to discover, to drag out of hiding, the essential problem of their personalities—when perhaps there is no problem *in* their personalities at all, except this insane preoccupation with the self and its moods and doubts, while much of the human universe struggles simply for survival. . . . The small, enclosed form of the typical lyric poem seems to preclude an active sanctifying of other people. . . . [The] lyric poet, if he is stuck in a limited emotional cul-de-sac, will circle endlessly inside the bell jar of his own world and only by tremendous strength can he break free. (pp. 514-16)

Again, lyric poetry is a risk because it rarely seems to open into a future: the time of lyric poetry is usually the present or the past. "This is a disease I carry home, this is a death," Miss Plath says in "Three Women," and, indeed, this characterizes most of her lines. All is brute process, without a future; the past is recalled only with bitterness, a stimulus for present dismay.

When the epic promise of "One's-self I sing" is mistaken as the singing of a separate self, and not the universal self, the results can only be tragic. (p. 518)

Sylvia Plath's essential innocence, her victimization by the pressures of an old, dying, ungenerous conception of man and his relationship to nature, must be made clear; this essay is not an attack upon her. She understood well the hellish fate of being Swift's true counterpart, the woman who agrees that the physical side of life is a horror, an ungainly synthesis of flesh and spirit—the disappointment of all the Romantic love poems and the nightmare of the monkish soul. (pp. 518-19)

In most of the poems, and very noticeably in *The Bell Jar*, Sylvia Plath exhibits a recurring tendency to dehumanize people, to flatten everyone into "cut-paper people," most of all herself. She performs a kind of reversed magic, a desacralizing ritual for which psychologists have terms—reification, rubricization. Absolute, dramatic boundaries are set up between the "I" and all others, and there is a peculiar refusal to distinguish among those who mean well, those who mean ill, and those who are neutral. Thus, one is shocked to discover in *The Bell Jar* that Esther, the intelligent young narrator, is as callous toward her mother as the psychiatrist is to her, and that she sets about an awkward seduction with the chilling precision of a machine—hardly aware of the man involved, telling us very little about him as an existing human being. He does not really *exist*, he has no personality worth mentioning. Only Esther exists.

"Lady Lazarus," risen once again from the dead, does not expect a sympathetic response from the mob of spectators that crowd in to view her, a mock-phoenix rising from another failed suicide attempt: to Sylvia Plath there cannot be any connection between people, between the "I" that performs and the crowd that stares. All deaths are separate, and do not evoke human responses. To be really safe, one must be like the young man of "Gigolo," who has eluded the "bright fish hooks, the smiles of women," and who will never age because—like Miss Plath's ideal self—he is a perfect narcissus, self-gratified. He has successfully dehumanized himself.

The Cosmos is indeed lost to Sylvia Plath and her era, and even a tentative exploration of a possible "God" is viewed in the old terms, in the old images of dread and terror. "Mystic" is an interesting poem, on a subject rare indeed in Miss Plath, and seems to indicate that her uneasiness with the "mill of hooks" of the air—"questions without answer"—had led her briefly to thoughts of God. Yet whoever or whatever this "God" is, no comfort is possible

because the ego cannot experience any interest or desire without being engulfed. . . . Sylvia Plath has made beautiful poetry out of the paranoia sometimes expressed by a certain kind of emotionally disturbed person, who imagines that any relationship with anyone will overwhelm him, engulf and destroy his soul. (For a brilliant poem about the savagery of erotic love between lovers who cannot quite achieve adult autonomy or the generosity of granting humanity to each other, see Ted Hughes's "Lovesong," in *Crow*, not inappropriate in this context.)

The dread of being possessed by the Other results in the individual's failure to distinguish between real and illusory enemies. . . . Sylvia Plath's inability to grade the possibilities of danger is reflected generally in our society, and helps to account for peculiar admissions of helplessness and confusion in adults who should be informing their children: if everything unusual or foreign is an evil, if everything *new* is an evil, then the individual is lost. The political equivalent of childlike paranoia is too obvious to need restating, but we have a cultural equivalent as well which seems to pass unnoticed. Surely the sinister immorality of films like *A Clockwork Orange* (though not the original, English version of the Burgess novel) lies in their excited focus upon small, isolated, glamorized acts of violence by non-representative individuals, so that the unfathomable violence of governments is totally ignored or misapprehended. (pp. 519-21)

What may come to seem obvious to people in the future—that unique personality does not necessitate isolation, that the "I" of the poet belongs as naturally in the universe as any other aspect of its fluid totality, above all that this "I" exists in a field of living spirit of which it is one aspect—was tragically unknown to Miss Plath, as it has been unknown or denied by most men. Hopefully, a world of totality awaits us, not a played-out world of fragments; but Sylvia Plath acted out a tragically isolated existence, synthesizing for her survivors so many of the sorrows of that dying age—Romanticism in its death throes, the self's ship, *Ariel*, prematurely drowned. (p. 522)

> *Joyce Carol Oates, "The Death Throes of Romanticism: The Poems of Sylvia Plath," in* The Southern Review *(copyright © 1973 by Joyce Carol Oates; reprinted by permission of the author and her agent, Blanche C. Gregory, Inc.), Vol. IX, No. 3, Summer, 1973, pp. 501-22.*

Sylvia Plath, martyr and archetype in the imagination of many, dangerously courted some portion of the blame for these irrelevant labels in more than one aspect of her poetry. Admiring critics in the decade since she committed suicide at the age of thirty have tried assiduously to dissociate her from the death-happy exultation of her cult. Yet this very ghoulishness has marked, often enough, their own accounts of her talent. It was A. Alvarez who, shortly after Sylvia Plath's own solemnizing gesture, established the orthodox tone of her praise [see excerpts in *CLC*-2]: "The achievement of her final style is to make poetry and death inseparable. . . ."

Poetry of this order is a murderous art.

Murderous, that is, rather than suicidal: Sylvia Plath is a martyr in this view to the demands of her art. It follows that to appreciate her poetry we must recognize the rightness, even the value, of her self-destruction.

The aesthetic that underlies this claim is not only confused but disastrous; though Alvarez's sympathy for the poet is incontrovertible, what he urges is ultimately unfeeling and inhumane. And though not all subsequent appreciation of Plath has struck his peculiar and abyss-dwelling note, it has been decisive for the conventional understanding of her poetry until now. . . . Alvarez has done much—very nearly everything—to influence our way of receiving the poems, and some of it has been useful. . . . But his disservice may be more enduring still.

What is most suspicious and disconcerting, however, about this intense and apparently irresponsible collation of her suicide and her poetry is the ease with which the case may be supported by citation from the poems themselves:

> The blood jet is poetry,
> There is no stopping it.

Equally troubling are those moments, for example in "Lady Lazarus," when Plath envisions suicide attempts, quite as the cult of Plath does, as fundamentally performances, pieces of art, like poetry itself:

> The peanut-crunching crowd
> Shoves in to see
>
> Them unwrap me hand and foot—
> The big strip tease.
> Gentlemen, ladies,
>
> These are my hands,
> My knees.

The notion of theatrical suicide is satirized, of course, but it is also relished, even sexually relished: "The big strip tease." (It may be said that the analogy between suicide and strip tease is not obscene only in the complicated sense in which Fellini is not obscene.) The poem records a series of three unsuccessful suicide attempts, each of which the lady is proud of having performed, proud of having survived:

> I have done it again.
> One year in every ten
> I manage it—
>
> A sort of walking miracle . . .

The tone is weirdly masochistic and show-offy. ("I guess you could say I had a call") and remarkably free of dread. But it's not the private and discreet suicide that appeals to her, nor, indeed, the successful one. Rather,

> It's the theatrical
>
> Comeback in broad day
> To the same place, the same face,
>   the same brute
> Amused shout:
>
> "A miracle!"
> That knocks me out.

I do not mean to say of such a poem that, having written it, Sylvia Plath had invited the "peanut-crunching crowd" to a celebration of her own, real suicide, though come they did. Nor does she imply that a performance of this kind could be painlessly observed: "There is a charge/ For the eyeing of my scars." But even in this detail, self-importance mixes with self-loathing: a decidedly public self-immolation.

The most suitable defense against the charge I have just made is that the "I" of Sylvia Plath's poetry is an artificial construct, and not Sylvia herself—in spite of the avowed "confessional" models, such as Robert Lowell and Anne Sexton, in spite of the unmistakable and direct autobiographical inspirations, in spite of the fact that more than a few of her poems, and among them the most important, are partially or wholly unintelligible without autobiographical gloss. It is not Sylvia Plath, but the *persona* of "Lady Lazarus," who is self-aggrandizing, the *persona* of "Daddy" who is vindictive, etc. I am not convinced by this defense, though it has New Critical good sense behind it, because in the case of Plath it leaves too much excepted, too much in awkward doubt. I suspect that when it is rigorously prosecuted, and it rarely is, it would end in a preference for the earliest Plath, the poems of *Colossus* (1960), a technically sure but derivative and generally bland first book. Plath's achievement, whatever its merits, rests on the posthumous collections, *Ariel* (1966), *Crossing the Water* (1971), and *Winter Trees* (1971), where indisputable originality of voice and subject matter abounds. One has the feeling, in turning from *Colossus* to these, that a mask has been dropped, and any understanding of her poetry which depends upon the assumption of a mask must stop where these begin. (pp. 47-8)

[Where] the poet chooses a method especially "confessional" and direct, as in Plath's poetry, or as in Robert Lowell's *Life Studies*, . . . a lack of self-knowledge can have dire aesthetic consequences. By self-knowledge I mean not some tidy, amateur delineation of psychic cause and psychic effect, but a sensitive, probative apprehension of root contradiction, root ambivalence in the self, without which the poetry, however "felt" or strident, must be shallow, unsponsored from within. The poem "Lady Lazarus" is, in the end, not autobiographical enough: it tells us something about how much she suffers, and less about how, and nothing about why. And that is true of Sylvia Plath's presentation of the other themes of her poetry: death, and bearing children, and hating one's father, and going without love. (p. 48)

I don't well see how anyone who has read James Dickey's *Deliverance* could call Plath's *The Bell Jar* (1963) a "poet's novel," though that is the rather evasive description it is usually given. . . . It is true that there is a tendency in the prose to dilate upon analogies and images until they achieve an autonomous significance rare in conventional novels. . . . All of this novel's successes are of this sort; as a narrative it is pedestrian. The chapter in which Esther Greenwood learns to ski, for example, could hardly be duller. But when we find her poised, alone, at the top of the slope, the novel becomes, for a paragraph, a "poet's" again. . . .

Of course, the genre to which *The Bell Jar* genuinely belongs is unmistakable. It would have been hard indeed to write a novel about adolescent *Weltschmerz* in the early 50's without feeling the influence of J. D. Salinger, even if one hadn't been an undergraduate of modish literary pretensions at the time. The confrontation between innocence and the big city, the embarrassed and embarrassing pretense at knowing its ways; the sexually advanced roommate, the first sexual encounter and its horrors, the inevitable boozy nausea; the return to a distant and uncomprehending parent, the withdrawal and mounting fascination with death, the ultimate breakdown.... [The] question upon which any judgment of *The Bell Jar* must turn [is] to what extent does the world beyond the parameters of Esther's psychosis seem real? Sylvia Plath is reported to have said of the novel that she tried to "show how isolated a person feels when he is suffering a breakdown.... I've tried to picture my world and the people in it as seen through the distorting lens of a bell jar.... My second book will show that same world as seen through the eyes of health." It is certainly unfair to adduce the genius of Proust, which was to write both these novels at once; but no novel could be unvaryingly one or the other without a damning thinness, and in respect of this it may be that [*Catcher in the Rye*] comes nearer the mark. Salinger succeeds in conveying to us that it is in his narrator's unwillingness to tell us "all that David Copperfield kind of crap" —the complex personal history, the why of suffering—that his trouble is fixed. The world beyond the parameters of the psychosis includes, then, not only the material world and its threatening "otherness," but the psychotic's own submerged past, the repressed realms of the self. It is here that *The Bell Jar* fails: we never see around the edges of the distorting lens, either outward into the world, or inward, into the self. But experiences whose effects the distortion of the lens will intensify—suicide, attempted rape, electroshock therapy—are here in abundant and vivid detail. They stack up like atrocities on the evening news. (p. 49)

A ... pertinent strain in Plath's work is her concern with a woman's experience of her own body. One essay in the volume *Radical Feminism* describes Plath as the poet of woman's body as "biological prison." It is a fact that, early and late, the poet was preoccupied with the imagery of female genitals, menstruation and menopause, child-bearing and miscarriage. But, as in a line like "The womb/ Rattles its pods," the tone of such preoccupation is sour, the presumed distance between the self and the body is great. The recurring desire for cleanliness and purity—

> I am too pure for you or anyone.
> Your body
> Hurts me as the world hurts God.

—is really the desire not to have a body at all, and manifests itself in disgust with all bodily functions, and especially sex:

> Obscene bikinis hide in the dunes,
>
> Breasts and hips a confectioner's sugar
> Of little crystals, titillating the light,
>
> While a green pool opens its eye,
> Sick with what it has swallowed—...

There is some question about the value of the lessons women can learn about themselves from a text of such self-hatred. (p. 50)

[It] is maudlin and depraved to speak of her death as if it were inevitable, or of her suicide as if it were murder. This, finally, is what Alvarez does, suggesting that the poet was (and is) a victim not in the sense in which we all are, but in some elect and especially stricken way. Plath herself goes further, and identifies suicide not only with murder but even with genocide....

Her comparison of her suffering to the suffering of the six million [Jews killed in the Holocaust] has been, of course, one of the most controversial features of her poems, as it is one of their most striking....

But what relevance do her poems establish? In "Lady Lazarus," the Belsen allusions tell us that she is oppressed, now by the "brute amused" crowd, now by "Herr Doktor" and "Herr God, Herr Lucifer." We know that she takes over from her oppressors the act of her own persecution, perhaps to win their approval, or to give to herself the sense of identity and self-command. We know also that such reversals were common in the concentration camps. The allusion has intensified her suffering in our imagination, and lent to it an air of cultural and historical importance. But where is there even a pretense of its legitimacy, a shred of support for such claims? There is none.... Moreover, what can Plath's claims for the "relevance" of her personal suffering mean? Despite the account of suffering it contains, and the larger amount that it invokes, "Lady Lazarus" conspicuously fails to tell us anything about the nature of suffering itself.

Plath's commitment to death was obscure—obscure to herself, we can only assume, because obscure in her art—and in her failure of insight, she left herself only the choice between a cold, still death and a "bed of fire." The sardonic triumph of the former is recorded in "Edge":

> The woman is perfected.
> Her dead
>
> Body wears the smile of accomplishment,
> The illusion of a Greek necessity . . .
>
> Each dead child, coiled, a white serpent,
> One at each little
>
> Pitcher of milk, now empty. . . .

[The] implication is that all accomplishment, all the earnest endeavor of our lives, tends toward this final perfection. It is a perfection that is achieved, moreover, with "the illusion of a Greek necessity," that is, as if our state were naturally and necessarily so perfect, which it is not. Instead, we must accomplish death: we die by art. Her poem itself is the penultimate gesture, the cutting "Edge." The ... serpent is an infant child. (p. 51)

[It] remains for me to say how mean a poem it is, how fundamentally cold-hearted and unkind. One may take as an example its very simplest unkindness: the image of the dead children "coiled" at the woman's breast. Their own deaths are, of course, irrelevant to the poem; they exist only as props. As such, they are examples of what the poet has called "flat," "cardboard" people, meaning "the other": ultimately, anyone but herself. The failure to imagine the other as having what George Eliot called an "equivalent center of self" is, of course, a moral lapse, but it is also an aesthetic one. Where Sylvia Plath's failure as an artist is not rooted in a failure to apprehend herself, it is rooted in a failure to apprehend the self in others.

Such judgments are possible—I would say, necessary— when we have wiped from our minds, "like chalk from a blackboard," the myth of Sylvia Plath's martyrdom. Her death, they say, begs all questions of sincerity in her poems. It may be so. It is impossible to read her poetry without being convinced of the pain in which it had its origin. It is impossible not to be moved. But in the end we must make judgments based upon our allegiance to life. (pp. 51-2)

John Romano, "Sylvia Plath Reconsidered" (reprinted from Commentary by permission; copyright © 1974 by the American Jewish Committee), in Commentary, April, 1974, pp. 47-52.

Alternately heroine or victim or martyr, [Sylvia Plath] has been symbolized so hauntingly in the cultural consciousness that it is difficult not to read her life—with its gestures of defiance, courage, compulsion and despair—rather than her work in which those gestures are reflected or re-imagined. The reasons can be sifted. Certainly in the last fifteen years the taste has been created by which she is so appreciated—with critics madly urging the Extremist visions of madness, and the new energies released by the increasing acceptance by poets and readers of the confessional mode. The way we live now, as well, must be counted: the context of a decade stalked by public violence and private nightmare, the lip-service paid to women as a class, and our desperate national psychoses that are run like films out of sequence. There is this and more, and none of it enough.

Some of the more obvious damage caused by this aghast, retrospective piety has been done to Plath's first, and now overpraised, collection, *The Colossus*. There is about this volume the self-consciousness of beginnings. It is poetry of chosen words, of careful schemes and accumulated effects; its voice is unsteady, made-up. It leans heavily on its models and sources; there are broad hints of help from Roethke and Stevens, and even Eliot is echoed without parody: "In their jars the snail-nosed babies moon and glow." Ted Hughes seems also to have been a strong influence, but one need only compare her "Sow" to his "View of a Pig" (or to any of his other early animals) to sense the more natural ease with which he urges and controls his language and the power it draws from strangeness. The awkward refinement which separates her from Hughes is evident as well in the literary cast of many poems which borrow Oedipus or Gulliver, Byron or Medea, Gabriel or Lucina for their authority, and in the stiff, stale diction which rattles around in them: cuirass, wraith, descant, bole, ambrosial, bruit, casque, ichor, pellicle. Too often the poems show their seams, and carry with them the musty smell of the underlined Thesaurus which Hughes remembers always on her knee at this time. . . . The reductive eye dominates the book and its slow figures, blocked landscapes and primary colors. There are times, though, when another vision intrudes, when the "moony eye" is "needled dark" and transformed to the "Red cinder around which I myself,/ Horses, planets and spires revolve" ("The Eye-Mote"). It is then that she sees most clearly, and at the same time allows us access to her deepest concerns. For the book's value seems finally to lie not in the promise or accomplishment of its verse, but in its introduction of themes that would recur more forcefully in later work. (pp. 155-56)

Crossing The Water and *Winter Trees* gather most of Plath's uncollected "transitional" poems, and while a few of them predict *Ariel*, most are more or less uncertain efforts to secure a new voice. At one extreme, Yeats lurks behind her "Magi", and at the other, there is a wholly un-

successful attempt at swagger ["Stopped Dead"]. . . . But generally, the lines are fuller and less studied than those in *The Colossus*, and her cadences are less tense, more closely adjusted to the speaking voice. . . . Perhaps this is due to the delayed influence of Robert Lowell—to whom she also admits a debt for his confessional "breakthrough." . . . Her own voice, the shrill, sharp sound that soars in *Ariel*, can be heard in such poems as "Whitsun", "Zoo Keeper's Wife", or in "Surgeon at 2 A.M." where the body is described as "a Roman thing". . . . The poems in *Winter Trees*—poems like "Purdah", "Childless Woman", "By Candlelight" and "Thalidomide"—are closer still to the hard exactness of tone in *Ariel*; they read like the negatives from which the later poems were printed. The images used to enclose personal relationships are more carefully worked, and poems like "The Babysitters", "Leaving Early" and "Candles" demonstrate her increasing ability to accommodate facts into poetry, to discover her experiences rather than merely to display her feelings about them. (pp. 159-61)

Ted Hughes has described the style of *Ariel* as one of "crackling verbal energy." But the exuberance is of a special sort. One hesitates to term it "American," except that Plath herself does, in her 1962 interview: "I think that as far as language goes I'm an American, I'm afraid, my accent is American, my way of talk is an American way of talk." The dynamics, the sharp, quick tonal contrasts, the hard exactness of word and image, the jaunty slang, the cinematic cutting—these are what she is pointing to. Even in poems—like "Tulips"—with quieter long lines, she sustains a new tension of menace and energy. . . . [In the] book's best poems, the lines are pared down, at times to a stark, private code, but always with purity and precision. Paradoxically, this taut, new control often creates effects of singular primitivism. She may have sought these; Hughes recalls her reading African folktales "with great excitement." They may also owe something to her marked identification of the imagination with the unconscious. Poems like "Getting There", "Medusa", and "Little Fugue" splay psychic scraps across dream landscapes with the mastery of Ingmar Bergman. The Gothic, or merely grotesque, aspects in the late poems which critics have commented on seem to be the weaker signs of this tendency, and the several mystical plunges she takes—for example, in "The Night Dances", "The Moon and the Yew Tree", and "Poppies in July"—are also attempts to approach, through the unconscious, higher states of being and art. Plath confesses the influence of Blake on these later poems, and like Blake she often seems to compel her vision through the poem.

That vision, again, is one of "perfection"—a term as central to Plath as "circumference" is to Emily Dickinson. Though "Ariel" and "Yeats" offer terrified, exultant arguments against "great Stasis," and "The Munich Mannequins" presents an ambiguous image of those bloodless idols to the self, the relentless hunt for a still completion, a condition beyond "the aguey tendon" of mortality, beyond the Shelleyan veils of life, continues. (pp. 163-64)

The familiar dilemma and longing in *Ariel* . . . take on an urgency and poignance that the earlier volumes lack. Part of it lies in a despair with the very language the poet now finally controls:

> Years later I
> Encounter them on the road—

Words dry and riderless,
The indefatigable hoof-taps.
While
From the bottom of the pool, fixed stars
Govern a life.

Perhaps this is her frequent distrust of voice, but the poem ["Words"], which closes *Ariel* except for the last blank page, implies that the vision forever escapes the language that alone can restore it. The silence that "perfection" demands, like the trusting, completed silence of her infants, becomes then a source of confusion for the poet, as though to contemplate an action were already to have accomplished its consequences. What she substitutes for the contradictory silence is "purity," the process towards perfection: "Pure? What does it mean?" Again, her technique is shaped into her theme, and purity, the spoken silence of great suffering and of the mystics, becomes a central concern among some of the book's strongest poems. (p. 165)

Sylvia Plath's suicide, which some critics read as her last, inevitable poem, has led most critics to assume a greater degree of fulfillment and completion in her work than it can justly claim. Her consistency, instead, lies in her experimentations with voice, and in her reworkings of the dilemma of the divided mind. That she was able, in *Ariel*, to include so much more of her experience and of her most persistent theme, in a voice equal to their demands and significance, does not mean that she might not have continued to seek a style that would have allowed her to write from beyond the limits of her longing. Her last poems are just arriving. (p. 166)

> *J. D. McClatchy, "Staring from her Hood of Bone: Adjusting to Sylvia Plath" (copyright © 1974 by J. D. McClatchy), in* American Poetry Since 1960: Some Critical Perspectives, *edited by Robert B. Shaw, Dufour, 1974, pp. 155-66.*

*   *   *

PORTER, Peter   1929-

Porter is an Australian poet now living in London. He has been praised for his ability to present traditional concerns in highly original forms and textures.

[Porter's] work is striking, not simply for its honesty, but for its balance: he is honest in tone as well as in content. . . . This honesty alone would have been a considerable achievement: but onto the integrity he has grafted a quality of daring, so that his range of achievement has grown successively with each book. Realism has become an adventure of thought, a trading with surprise as well as a harrying of truth. (p. 50)

As Edward Lucie-Smith points out, if we consider Porter a satirist, we must place him alongside the Elizabethan "biting satirists", in the tradition of Juvenal: accurate as it is in particulars and scathing as contemporary comment, his satire is essentially timeless, its subjects the omnipresence of death . . ., the limitations of human possibility. (p. 51)

Porter's originality as a satirist, and his particular relevance to this century, is that he concentrates, not on the kaleidoscope of folly, but on the monotony of human aspirations, the mean perspectives that, increasingly, we have in common. Every satirist has stressed that we all come to the same fate in the end: Porter's point is that we never get away from it in the first place. (p. 52)

From the beginning, Porter's imagery has been concrete in a particularly acute sense, the material defining the spiritual, not just representing it; but at the same time these concrete images have had a slightly surreal edge to them. . . . As the style has moved out of description into allusion, from orderly sequences into sudden epigrams, this edge has sharpened, but the imagery has shifted towards the allegorical. . . . It hasn't shifted far, though: Porter uses allegory as a bestiary rather than a shadowland of symbols . . . and it relates strongly back to . . . corporeal definition which is still Porter's basic habitat. . . . Two contrasting tendencies have both become stronger as his work has progressed: the first is towards an earthy, debunking common sense . . .; the second is towards a classic finality of statement. . . . It is a blend of these two, a sardonic classicism, which has become the distinctive voice of Porter's recent work. (pp. 54-5)

Porter's two latest books [*A Porter Folio* and *The Last of England*] are serious and uncompromising to the point of obsession—"death" and "pain" are probably the two most frequent words in his opus, "love" appears most often in the context of defeat—but the writing is filled with this sense of adventure, and the final tone is not heavy, but elusive, startling. (p. 55)

Porter's recent style is an act of courage. The keystone of his early work was honesty, though the expression had all the bite of rage. But the widening range of his material challenged his style. The combination of an increasing perspective, both forwards and backwards into history, with a more nervous apprehension of a fragmented moral world, made it necessary to break out of the confines of a four-square treatment. The present style is chancy—one would call it "transitional" if there wasn't a suspicion that part of the transition is to exclude the aim of coming to rest again. Porter has always had an instinct for good lines, and there have been plenty of them lately: but they tend to come singly, driven like plugs into layers of uneven material. . . . Peter Porter has been consistently careful not to let his gifts become predictable, and his development has been both adventurous and logical. Too often in the 'sixties, experiment was another name for whimsy, and integrity meant a conservative writing by rote: it is refreshing to find a poet whose courage is a function of his honesty. (pp. 56-7)

> *Roger Garfitt, "Peter Porter" (copyright © by Roger Garfitt), in* British Poetry Since 1960: A Critical Survey, *edited by Michael Schmidt and Grevel Lindop, Carcanet, 1972, pp. 49-57.*

Mr. Porter's books receive good reviews . . . but no one, to my knowledge, or to my satisfaction, stresses his importance. He is a major poet. In a sense, of course, it doesn't matter whether anyone knows it but me, not even Mr. Porter. (p. 83)

What is a major poet—is such a classification valuable description or literary purring—and is Mr. Porter one anyway? T. S. Eliot, for instance, is a major poet—that is, whatever you think of his politics, his religion, his aesthetic, his poems, he has made an indelible mark on our culture. All major artists make such marks, eventually. We measure by them—though they are not always self-evidently important to their immediate contemporaries. Mr. Eliot wasn't, Mr. Porter isn't. The latter needs a Dr. Leavis—not me.

But why? Not because Mr. Porter is writing poetry the only way it can be written—prescriptions are always surprisingly fashionable, always persuasive and, in the end, always stultifying. No, Mr. Porter's significance is that his conception, which is both traditional and original, of the world, is expressed in most eclectic terms. He draws metaphors and subjects from the spread of European culture—spread in time and distance. His conception is traditional in essence—the universals of love, insubstantiality, death—and original in appearance—violent, absurd, grotesque, anachronistic particulars. He presupposes the value of knowledge, of wanting to know, the virtue and unlikelihood of reason, the inevitability of death—he expresses the immortality of art (as in the act of writing) and thus of the self. Art presupposes the importance of self, yet survives the self which created it. Mr. Porter elegizes wittily the contradiction. . . . The converted to whom he is preaching are both the dead and the reader—the latter in the act of contemplating the greatness of art and his own frailty. The reader, by this definition, accepts the author's notions implicitly—notions whose relevance, almost everywhere, is increasingly denied or ignored.

There is a richness of texture in all of Mr. Porter's work, a richness of metrical forms, content, metaphor. . . . The poems abound in touchstones—from 'Story Which Should Have Happened', 'there should have been fictions to be real in' and from 'Fossil Gathering', '. . . every feeling thing ascends from slime/To selfhood and in dying finds a face'. The [latter] epitomises much of Mr. Porter's conception of the world—the accidental triumph of the self (a sea creature converted fortuitously into sculpture), the marbled dead conveying permanence.

A number of critics have pointed to the parallels between Martial's life and Mr. Porter's—poets, ex-colonials, writing in the capitals of dying, dead empires. Such parallels are intended, I think, as compliments to Peter Porter. They are patronising. Certainly, Martial's interest (except for sycophancy) coincide with Mr. Porter's—but the latter's are much more extensive. His senses of history and pathos are key instances of his superiority. He is much more important to us than Martial was to his contemporaries. Perhaps I ought to have written 'should be more important'. I know that *After Martial* will be more widely read than *Preaching to the Converted*, but, generally good though the former is, it does poorly, in comparison, as a measure of us. (pp. 83-5)

> *David Selzer, "Porter Major," in* Phoenix *(8 Cavendish Road, Heaton Mersey, Stockport, Cheshire, England), July, 1973, pp. 83-5.*

As a satirist Mr Porter is almost too brilliant for his own good. The sharp fragments and gobbets of fire fly from his anvil in every direction. His tone [in *Jonah*] never loses definition but the intensity is almost too great and the jokes, excellent ones, are almost too many, calling for a close reading that loses speed. . . . At times the poetry comes close to surrealism. . . . Some of the prose passages are surreal, but they go on too long, they are less substantial. The verse is best. . . .

"De Profundis," in The Times Literary Supplement *(© Times Newspapers Ltd., 1973; reproduced by permission), November 2, 1973, p. 1348.*

Peter Porter's subject in *Preaching to the Converted* is . . . death and the dying, whether it be people, towns, or civilizations. . . . Porter sees death as conferring significance on life itself: 'Man is ridiculous; if/ it weren't for his death,/ he'd have no value whatever' ('Timor Mortis'); and as unquestionably the greatest patron of the arts. The 'converted' are the dead themselves, accessible only through time . . . and the great dead are the artists who make this communication possible. Writers remain 'On the Isle of Ink, postmarked *Totenreich*' where 'The final purity is to have nothing to say', while composers' 'sounding notes/ go past like cart-loads of the glittering dead'. The dead attend the poet at his own work. . . . Under this overshadowing of death (like Wordsworth's crag) other themes are developed. Not least among these is the process of poetic creation itself, which Porter studies in the fine but difficult poem 'In the Giving Vein'. What should be more generally digestible are two of Porter's most recognizable ideas, an intense and complicated nostalgia for a vanished way of life on the one hand, and on the other a simultaneous mockery and weary acceptance of what modern life has to offer in exchange. These often overlap, and they combine in what seems to me to be the best poem in the book. This is 'Seaside Resort', a marvellous recreation of a decaying south coast town where 'the small black rained-on queen/ stares with disciplined eyes at the sea', where there is 'Nothing but the calm/ of history dying, the beautiful/ vulgarization of decay'. 'The polemic here is death' also; and the poet can introduce himself at the end in a mood of sober self-pity which is neither avoided nor indulged but fully expressed as a dramatic element in the poem's whole context. (pp. 83-4)

But what will prevent many readers from getting on terms with this book is the inordinate and unnecessary difficulty of many of the poems. I really don't see why Peter Porter's very public themes—death, love and sex, art—require him to take refuge behind the obsessive embedded allusion, clotted syntax, and other defensive gestures that make his poems appear so inhospitable to the reader. In 'The School for Love', a poem which is positively constipated with literary references (and which is presumably intended as an ironic comment on his own technique) he actually exclaims 'I have not heard of any natural style'. What is particularly frustrating about this is that Porter *does* have a natural style, if only he would trust to it; a natural lyrical impulse which is always trying to evade his intellectual guard. And this impulse frequently succeeds in carrying off the poem at the end. . . . I would say it is the poems that get off the ground in this way that are in the end the most successful. But despite the difficulties, intrinsic or overlaid, Porter is a poet worth persevering with; the fertility of his ideas, the power of his images, and the generally high level of craftsmanship in this volume are ample compensation for the frustrations it also contains. (pp. 85-6)

> *Damian Grant, in* Critical Quarterly, *Spring, 1974.*

* * *

POUND, Ezra   1885-1972

Pound, an American who lived most of his life abroad, was a

poet of immense stature whose major work, the *Cantos*, has done more than "express an individuality," as Hugh Kenner wrote. The *Cantos* "helped make twentieth-century experience intelligible." Pound's influence on other great writers of our time is immeasurable; in fact, it has been said that he is possibly the most representative figure of the cultural and literary climate of the early years of this century. (See also *Contemporary Authors*, Vols. 5-8, rev. ed.; obituary, Vols. 37-40.)

It startled us in our youth and always existed in the back of our minds—the fact that the madman of Pisa was writing the poem of poems. We turned to the prose and found him shouting at us. We read the books he recommended and found them dull, his friends and found them exciting. Much of the cachet of Pound comes from his having such exciting friends. He sought them out and bullied them into writing well. And he was—writing. Walter Kaufman shows us Hegel at thirty, the man of promise crazy to write something great so as not to disappoint his friends, who vomits up a great book. He too, in Marianne Moore's phrase, made us "accustomed to the recurring phosphorescence of antiquity." *The Cantos* is our White Whale, and four generations of minor poets learned that to ignore it was a kind of suicide. Major poets like Frost could do quite well without it.

The American poet's problem is propaganda. When Poe decided that preaching and teaching were taboo, he cut out from under us the only strategy which had made us accepted. The ground note of all his criticism is that art is something an adult can do, valuable to be busy about. He also abetted the century's reduction of poetry to lyric, a result of the decline of rhetoric—though his poems cut beautiful figures of grammar. Pound, drunk on elegiac cadences (dactyly, dactyly, dactyly, *thump* thump) and the idea of writing a long poem, can't make it cohere. Any page of Fletcher's *Divine Comedy* pleases more ways than a random Canto. Yet I suspect (and have never seen it suggested by a critic) that Pound thought he *was* writing like Dante. Through the thirties the ablest critic of other people's verse—in the sense of recognizing good new stuff—he seems to have genuinely mistaken his own. What I miss in him is the Elder Statesman, a wise combination of Saintsbury and Tennyson, writing unexpected letters to Roethke commending his ingenuity. But Pound aged more like Whitman, who was fully as embarrassing old as young. His philosophical cousins (if that makes any sense at all) are the German philosophers who got drunk on Will; the necessity of *The Cantos* is psychological. It says two things to a reader: I am important, and I am unintelligible. Critics like Noel Stock convince us that the unintelligibility is not profundity. What he withholds from us (when he says something rather than does something) is the contingent inane. But even when you *know* that, *The Cantos* is impressive, like Barnum, a triumph of imagination over common sense. Unlike Dante or Milton, his sideshow characters are merely what the barker says they are. International finance is the substitute for the medieval philosophy he hadn't the energy to understand. If we hunt through *The Cantos* looking for beauties, we treat Pound the way he probably treated Dante. Without logic and rhetoric (in the sense of the possibility of a large-scale *argument*, and the little squabbles and lectures that mean so much from Homer to Milton) to hold him up, he's got nothing except some dippy ideas on history *and verse* to see him through.

Wrong, we say, from the start. There is nothing in them of the sweep of humanity in the epics we read lots. Zukofsky's "*A*" poems have more life, more good sense, and more music. We will accept no cheap saves here, as that individual lines are all right, or that he spent a life writing them so we should at least read them. The history in *The Cantos* is oddly enough an outside history. I can't look at them—or even know they're on my shelf—without remembering their mythic existence in the back of the mind, of the minds of what seems a century of working poets—the idea of a Faustian old man in thick country clothes, writing a poem to save the world and put us all to shame. In this sense, even on the shelf, even looked at, his *Cantos* are the apotheosis of the Work in Progress, and for us what Burton's *Anatomy of Melancholy* would have been if it had announced itself as an epic. (pp. 210-11)

> *Gerald Burns, in* Southwest Review (© *1971 by Southern Methodist University Press), Spring, 1971.*

It appears that Pound the Orientalist scarcely existed. His celebrated translations have only a sketchy connection with the originals. This would be fine, hardly worth mentioning, except for the fact that in the later Cantos he goes one step further and instead of giving us his visual semantic intuitions, he gives us the Chinese characters themselves. He has stopped translating so we can all—what fun!—become sinologues or imagists or both.

At least part of this impulse, we may be sure, is to change the look of the poem. But a poet moving toward illustration —even as recondite as picture-writing—has either worn out his verbal resources or has started playing erudite games because he is bored. If poetry is rooted in the living tongue, as Pound has said, must we all learn the sound system of Chinese? Or do we regard the strokes as illuminations in the manuscript? The use of ideograms as a concrete element is really the culmination of a process begun long before, an insistence on naming things of personal significance to the writer. And so we must conclude that this visual delicatessen will yield up its full flavor only to one man and he is dead. (p. 36)

Pound says of Confucius, "He liked good music, he collected 'The Odes' to keep his followers from abstract discussion. That is, 'The Odes' give particular instances. They do not lead to exaggerations of dogma."

This is not only the voice of an elderly imagist who likes particular instances himself. It is the voice of a man obsessed with what could be hefted or shaped or seen or named. As if beyond the concrete lay the void of absolute terror, filled with creatures of no name. One wonders if this same obsession didn't underlie his love for the America of 1760-1830, an Edenic time of small farmers and craftsmen who worked with their hands and kept their savings under the cellar floor. It explains, perhaps, his equation of goodness with craftsmanship, his notion that from fit activity come fit thoughts. It is not unrelated to the fact that Mussolini, on first gaining power, cried out for a return to an artisan society—a cry that must have echoed Pound's creed joyously. And from here it is only a short step to his hatred of credit and capital—invisible money, the greatest abstraction of all, based on future demand instead of present satisfaction, the very opposite of what can be stored under the cellar floor. His downward progress from there has been chronicled—through his hatred of banking and usury to his hatred of Jews. It is ironic that the intention he ascribes to Confucius—the need to avoid exaggerations of dogma—was what proved his own undoing. He really had no head for anything but language, least of all for the illusionary constructs of finance.

Yes, language was what he knew. He was a tinkerer, a Ford or Edison out in the toolshed of English poetry, making it harder and tougher, giving it shape and speed and illumination. He was not interested in what your poems were about but in how hard-edge your lines were. If Pound goes unread now and in the future, except among academics, it will be because of this, because readers will sense that behind the brilliance he was only a technician, a better fabricator and no more. The social issues of his day didn't interest him. He cared about reforming the word only, and the time was never far off when this aestheticism would betray him into stupidity or worse. And his compassionless core locates him in the 19th century after all—the decade of Swinburne and Rossetti, of velvet jackets and flowing ties, all of which he hated so much.

His tragedy, then, is not merely a personal one—12 years in a place for the criminally insane. It is the tragedy of failed art (I almost wrote heart), art that only incidentally reached beyond craft or technology and into the ageless issues of poetry—love and freedom and justice and redemption. It is simply not enough to re-scrutinize the English sentence. The age demanded more.

But time passes and fairness requires that we acknowledge a last attempt at atonement, a belated apology by the poet. The Cookson anthology [*Selected Prose, 1909-1965*, edited by William Cookson] contains a brief Foreword written especially by Pound and dated July 4, 1972. He was 86 years old then and in failing health. Here are the last four lines:

> *In sentences referring to groups or races*
> *"they" should be used with great care.*
> *re USURY:*
> *I was out of focus, taking a symptom for*
> *a cause.*
> *The cause is AVARICE.*

Not enough really, but all we are likely to get.

R. I. P., Ezra. (pp. 36, 44)

> Richard W. Hall, "'Let the gods forgive . . .'," in The Village Voice (copyright © The Village Voice, Inc., 1974), May 23, 1974, pp. 35-6, 44.

There . . . seems to be no end to the making of books about Ezra Pound. Most of them see him not only as a great poet, but as a catalyst making other (modern) poetry possible. His influence on Eliot is noted and elaborated upon while his prose (which makes up nine-tenths of his work) is usually ignored. And his epic poem, *The Cantos*, is more often than not woefully misrepresented. . . .

[There is, in *The Cantos*,] false history (ancient, modern and medieval) combined with contempt for the many and compassion for the few—in fact, for one man only, Benito Mussolini.

In . . . Canto (Number 74, the first of the notorious "Pisan

Cantos," written *after* the Holocaust) we read: "the yidd is a stimulant, and the goyim are cattle [who] go to saleable slaughter with a maximum of docility." In Canto 80 we are informed that "Petain defended Verdun while Blum defended a bidet." And from Canto 91 we get this lesson in democracy—and in italics:

> *democracies electing their sewage*
> *till there is no thought of holiness*
> *a dung flow from 1913*
> *and in this their kikery functioned. . . .*

A full elucidation of all the crude Jew-baiting, race-hating, defamations to be found in Pound's "epic" would consume ten times the space a relatively short essay can encompass. (p. 21)

There is much in the writing about Pound that, as they say, boggles the mind. How, you may ask, can language so clearly stated, as Pound stated it, lead to such other-wordly conclusions? The answer probably lies in the need to elevate the poet—the writer—above the common run of humanity. Can a man, hailed as one of America's greatest poets, be an anti-Semite? It is, of course, possible in the sense that everything is possible. Whether Pound is paradigm here is arguable. There are those—Edmund Wilson, Robert Graves, Edward Dahlberg, among a host of others—who are not too much enamored with Pound as thinker *or* poet. Dahlberg thought his "epic" a hoax, Wilson saw bankruptcy in *The Cantos*, while Robert Graves once wrote: "It is an extraordinary paradox that Pound's sprawling, ignorant, indecent, and unmelodious Cantos . . . are now compulsory reading in many ancient centers of learning." . . .

When Pound says "Wellington was a jew's pimp" (Canto 50), he means just that. When he writes that the "yidd is a stimulant" whose lust for usury sends the poor "goyim" off to "saleable slaughter" (Canto 74) he means that, too. And when he tells us in Canto 87 of the "total dirt that was Roosevelt," he means "total dirt," even if [some critics are] convinced that these late Cantos (written in St. Elizabeth's Hospital where Pound was confined after he copped a plea of insanity to avoid standing trial for treason) "present a paradise of tenderness, delicacy and clarity absent from the literature since Dante."

Tenderness? Delicacy? Thus is language debauched and reason defiled to make a banquet for a "parasite," as Wyndham Lewis called Pound at the same time he said of him that he was "a person without a trace of originality of any sort." I don't agree. There was some originality in the man. Who else could have broadcast this (as Pound did) over the Rome radio warning America that it was nonsense to believe that it couldn't "happen" there. "What happen? Kikery, bolshevism happen right in your rationed nation, right where abundance has been bashed on the head by the high kikery. You have taken several things into yr. Lebensraum, Lebensraum. TOTEN's raum. Ezra Pound speaking." (Reproduced as recorded by Pound's mistress, Olga Rudge.)

[According to Michael Reck, writing in *Ezra Pound: A Closeup*,] Robert Graves said Pound should have been hanged. I tend to doubt this. I am more in accord with the gentler severities of Robert Frost. The New England poet pressed for Pound's release from confinement on the grounds that he did not want to help make "a martyr out of a traitor." (p. 22)

Max Geltman, "The Ezra Pound Apologists," in Congress Bi-Weekly, *May 24, 1974, pp. 21-2.*

* * *

PRIESTLEY, J(ohn) B(oynton) 1894-

An English novelist, playwright, short story writer, essayist, and man of letters, Priestley has been a versatile and prolific writer since 1922. His best-known novel is *The Good Companions***, but critics consider** *Angel Pavement* **and** *Bright Day* **his greatest artistic achievements. (See also** *Contemporary Authors***, Vols. 9-12, rev. ed.)**

[Priestley's] plays are seriously flawed, in my view, because, whilst they are always confoundedly careful, they lack care—that is, compassion, involvement—which, in one definition, is what separates art from entertainment. You feel that the author always calls the tune, that his characters scurry hither and thither at his bidding, always knowing far less than he does, never in any sort of ambiguous relationship with their creator. It's not something you feel of Chekhov, into whose waters Priestley sometimes sails. For Priestley is most definitely not a *subtle* ironist and his creatures are pushed down and dusted off without ceremony. We, the audience, are perforce as detached as he is. (p. 52)

W. Stephen Gilbert, in Plays and Players (© *copyright W. Stephen Gilbert 1973), October, 1973.*

J. B. Priestley is, to employ a sporting term he would surely appreciate, a good all-rounder; he is a novelist, playwright, essayist, literary critic, and—I intend no disrespect—something of a professional Englishman. In recent years he has added to a long inning of varied achievements as a man of letters his social histories of the Regency, the early years of Victoria's reign, and the Edwardian era. These characterizations in brisk prose, lavishly complemented by pictures, lead us to expect of his latest experiment in this mixed medium [*The English*] an original and appealing contribution to our understanding of the race to which the author so proudly belongs. (p. 29)

What Priestley has attempted is a personality profile based on his private analysis of the English. . . .

It is in the nature of guest lists to provoke astonishment and mirth; Priestley's is no exception. For instance, "Tudor, Stuart, and Hanoverian monarchs, Irish playwrights, Welsh poets, and Scottish painters and engineers" have been excluded on grounds of race and national origin; this exclusive little affair is for "true-born Englishmen-and-women" only. Well, who are the few to be favored with Priestley's hospitality? We should not look here to find Oscar Wilde (Irish), William Ewart Gladstone (Scotch), George Bernard Shaw (Irish), David Lloyd George (Welsh), Dean Swift (Irish), Thomas Stearns Eliot (American), Inigo Jones (Welsh), Richard Brinsley Sheridan (Irish), Anthony Vandyke (Flemish), William Butler Yeats (Irish), Richard Wilson (Welsh), or Benjamin Disraeli ("Jewish-dandy-novelist" and "impassive Oriental illusionist"!).

Priestley's own appointed laws, aside from being unjust, are also quite unenforceable. This is no mere procedural point; Priestley's narrow-minded definition of Englishness, based as it is almost exclusively on arbitrary considerations

of birth and blood, lies at the very heart of his enterprise. It is a species of cultural imperialism to exclude the donations made to the sum of English identity by, among others, the figures I have listed above. No survey, however sweeping, can truly comprehend the English "soul" if it seeks to divorce it from the cosmopolitan body which that soul inhabits; its "alien" distillations are of the English essence. And this is something the author overtly and covertly acknowledges time and again: Although Disraeli "has no place here," it is fully sixty-nine words before he is dismissed, whereas, to name only a few of the "true-born," Christopher Wren, Alexander Pope, Thomas Hobbes, Charlotte Brontë, Jeremy Bentham, Wilfred Owen, Edith Sitwell, and George Orwell don't get a look-in. . . . We can only conclude that the author is engaging in that traditional English pastime known universally as having your cake and eating it, too. . . .

The topography of the English spirit, as undertaken by Priestley, is crisscrossed by scenic routes; the tireless tourist will be rewarded with an eyeful of the picturesque and many idiosyncratic views. When Priestley writes well, and as often as not he does, his writing is a study in sturdy morality, shrewd wit, genial humor, and robust affection. He is on the side of life, and it is the English side of life. . . .

At the outset he sets down the slim hypothesis that what makes the English different is their freedom from the tyranny of reason; before he is through, this poor nag has been flogged to death. It is ironic that Priestley should thus unbalance his own equation of Englishness with the free operation of intuition by determining in advance of his findings what his measure of Englishness is to be. . . . Priestley is muddleheaded—that's one English characteristic we are agreed upon—in his analysis of the socioeconomic realities of the modern scene. He sounds at times as if he is whistling in the dark to keep his courage up. In their insular complacency the English are, after all, most English. (p. 30)

Michael George, "Priestley's English," in Saturday Review/World *(copyright © 1973 by Saturday Review/World, Inc.; reprinted with permission), December 18, 1973, pp. 29-30.*

Eden End [a play written in 1934, set in 1912, and reviewed to honor Priestley's 80th birthday] is in part a history lesson, taking us among the heavy curtains and mahogany chairs of the Yorkshire middle class and invoking an assortment of household names for our enlightenment: Wells, Asquith, Christabel Pankhurst, Gertie Millar, Scott of the Antarctic. It's also a sermon of sorts, using a somewhat heavy and deliberate irony to warn us against glib optimism. Priestley's Edwardians may be sceptical about the present: they are pretty smug about the future. . . . As far as the characters are concerned, Eden isn't ending: it's about to begin. But we know, my children, how very wrong they were.

Frankly, I don't see why the National chose this play as the cake for Priestley's 80th birthday. *An Inspector Calls* attacks nastier and more topical vices. . . . *Time and the Conways* has more energy and tension, perhaps because we actually see the bleak future into which the characters are hopefully peering. *Eden End* seems pretty limp beside them. Priestley has said himself that it 'owes much to the influence of Chekhov'; but his creditor is, I fear, the emasculated, elegiac Chekhov of British theatrical tradition, not the full-bloodied fellow they know in Russia. Chekhov himself would have made far more of the story of the prodigal daughter who returns home after years of failure as an actress, to rumple the rural tranquillity. In fact, he *did* make more of rather similar situations, notably in *The Seagull* and *Uncle Vanya*. The real, bouncing Chekhov would have given us at least some characters with minds as well as feelings, ideas as well as impressions. They'd probably have spoken of work and responsibility and heaven knows what, instead of presenting themselves, like Priestley's people, as the helpless spectators of social change. At any rate, they'd have provoked *some* solid discussion. They would also have been less flat as characters.

That, finally, is the trouble. What depresses me about *Eden End* is not its intellectual thinness, though it's surprising that as fine a mind as Priestley's should send us out of the theatre murmuring nothing more complicated than 'how sad that these people were so mistaken about the future'. It's the total failure of the characters to veer from their allotted tracks, their unerring inability to surprise us. When the old Yorkshire housekeeper calls the phone a 'daft machine', or tells a grown-up woman not to forget her mac, or confiscates the gramophone on the sabbath, it's exactly what one has expected since her first entrance. One smiles indulgently. . . . Such actions are so in character that one wonders, paradoxically, whether he's a character at all. And [one does the same] with the more important people. . . . (pp. 525-26)

> *Benedict Nightingale, in* New Statesman (© *1974 The Statesman & Nation Publishing Co. Ltd.), April 12, 1974.*

Priestley wrote *Eden End* in Coleridge's old rooms at 3 The Grove, Highgate Village when he was 40 odd and had already established himself in the theatre with *Dangerous Corner*. Some playwrights at 40 are still young at heart and iconoclastic, Shaw for instance; but Priestley had begun to regret the passing of the golden time and indulged in his favourite clever game of historical hindsight. He turned away from the concerns of 1934 to resuscitate those of 1912. . . .

[Once] the Priestley game's afoot we are quite prepared to join in and to observe the social historian and the novelist prompting the playwright. Confronted by *Eden End* critics nowadays reach for their *Cherry Orchard*, aided and abetted by Priestley himself: 'I owe,' he declared afterwards, 'much to the influence of Chekhov. . . . In this kind of play one's primary object is to conjure up the dramatic colour and shape, in all its absurdity and pathos, hope and heartbreak of life itself . . .'. This is an admirably fair declaration of intent, and quite true as far as it goes, but there is heartbreak and heartbreak; there are tears that are jerked out of you by playing upon the sense that life will never be the same as it was when our ambitions were untested, and the heartbreak that lies too deep for tears when we observe people of great richness of character and eccentricity become the victims of a historical process. The latter belongs to Chekhov and the former to Priestley.

What Priestley is really doing in this play is re-writing the world of his masters in the theatre, the world of St John Hankin, of Hubert Henry Davies, of Granville-Barker, of Barrie. Anything they could do, he is saying, I can do better, with more humanity and with greater irony; in fact he shares many of their attitudes; he regards the family as a sacred institution with a paramount claim over individual identity and maturity. (p. 34)

As the apologist for the family as being with reservations an essentially benevolent institution he was pre-eminently the practitioner of the ensemble play, of works in which the whole is greater than the parts. (p. 35)

> *Anthony Curtis, in* Plays and Players (© *copyright Anthony Curtis 1974), May, 1974.*

Several of [J. B. Priestley's] later novels as well as nonfiction works are commentaries on the changing world, often charged with indignation at unnecessary injustices and stupidities or poking fun at some of the absurdities—the conspiratorial airs and self-importance—of big corporate business. Since he isn't a moralist, however, even the novels of social criticism are first and foremost superbly told stories, and many incorporate a life-long concern with time and with magic, the magic inherent in the mystery in which we live. Here, I believe, one comes closest to the man himself, particularly in "Bright Day" (his own favorite) and the more recent "Lost Empires," the tale of a young man touring England in 1913-1914 in the variety show circuit as assistant to a master illusionist. This is a novel layered with meanings, those lost empires being the actual theaters with their "warm deep magic," the illusions of the theater (indeed illusion itself) and, on a deeper level still, the lost sense of enchantment which the narrator recalls as a "bright lost world that had taken [his] own youth with it." Perhaps most of all it is longing for the world that *might be*, a theme which haunts Priestley's work. One critic, praising the author's own skill as an illusionist was so diverted by the story he missed this point entirely.

For Priestley is a master illusionist, and out of sometimes outrageous tales float glimpses of something beautiful and important at the edge of consciousness—like the doves magicians produce out of all their paraphernalia which go winging away before we're quite sure we've seen them. And there, I think, is the paradox of his fiction: he writes in the older tradition, while his thinking and speculating are ahead of his time, and his sense of life's magic is outside either. What I believe concerns him as much as time is the mysterious intimations we are given of another world, "unmapped and outside solar space and time," from which we feel exiled. [One character tells us:] "There are some queer moments that seem to come out of a deeper reality, as if they were trying to tell us something we can never really know." Repeatedly Priestley celebrates such moments, and we are the richer for them. (p. 35)

> *Evelyn Ames, in* The New York Times Book Review (© *1975 by The New York Times Company; reprinted by permission), June 15, 1975.*

*   *   *

PRITCHETT, V(ictor) S(awden)   1900-

Pritchett is a British novelist, short story writer, literary critic, travel writer, autobiographer, and man of letters. In his beautifully written, very "English" prose, Pritchett exhibits a Dickensian eye for detail and a fine sense of humor.

Walter Allen, noting Pritchett's "unerring instinct for idiosyncrasy that reveals character," calls him "the complete master" of the short story form.

A Cab at the Door [is] the best 250-odd pages of autobiographical writing that I know of by a living author. What makes it so good is that Pritchett is, first of all, a master of the natural, direct style. As with Thoreau or Shaw, open any page and you are immediately in touch with the man. Or, as Pritchett has said of E. M. Forster, when he begins to speak the machine stops.

A Cab at the Door is written with plenty of candor, but it is also written with something even better, which is artistic tact. Reversing the customary procedure in contemporary autobiography, Pritchett places at the center of his memoir a solid and deliciously detailed commentary on lower-middle-class English life in the first two decades of the century, based on his family, educational, and early business experience; meanwhile he modestly lays around the rim the account of his own troubled development as a person and of his inchoate intentions as an artist.

The effect is a beautifully sustained priority of interests in which the depiction of concrete social conditions and forces, of manners and mores, stands by itself as a portrait of an age and a class, while serving as the ground that outlines the formation of his character. This not only places the emphasis where most readers would wish to see it—on the way things were rather than how they felt, on the individual life seen less through its accidents than as common experience—but also enables Pritchett, both as writer and as subject, to exist naturally and unselfconsciously among his interests and feelings. The result is a splendid montage of persons and places fixed in their individual being, casting their representative light, and suggesting the evolving personality of the author through his relations to them. By this kind of artistic strategy, mediating deftly between figure and ground, an autobiography turns into a life. (p. 285)

> *Theodore Solotaroff, "Autobiography as Art" (1968), in his* The Red Hot Vacuum and Other Pieces on Writing in the Sixties *(copyright © 1968, 1970 by Theodore Solotaroff; reprinted by permission of Atheneum Publishers, New York), Atheneum, 1970, pp. 284-90.*

A writer, V. S. Pritchett once explained, "is at the very least two persons. He is the prosing man at his desk and a sort of valet who dogs him and does the living." Few literary lives so genially and thriftily illustrate this peculiar symbiotic relationship as that of Victor Sawdon Pritchett. Two volumes of peerless memoirs (*A Cab at the Door* [and] *Midnight Oil*) chronicle his evolution from a shy, working-class English youth (born 1900) to eminence as an international man of letters: renowned lecturer, editor and critic. Pritchett's stories, meanwhile, regularly throb with the same grotesque scenes and sensuous memories as his life, recollected with a comic clarity and shrewd indulgence.

[*The Camberwell Beauty*] is mainly [a collection of] love stories, and in it life and letters support each other like an accomplished husband and wife team telling a family anecdote. . . .

Pritchett admits he is mainly interested in the spectacle of

people "floundering amid their own words, and performing strange strokes as they swim about with no visible shore in their own lives." Yet he is a romantic, a *coup de foudre* man for whom love strikes like a thunderbolt in the most preposterous ways. Still, it can produce instant chills and fever, practically as long as body draws breath or soul shudders at engulfing loneliness. (pp. E8-108)

Love stories! In the age of Alex Comfort and physical passion catered to almost as a culinary art? Yes, indeed. How does Pritchett do it? With a sharp eye, a fond heart and a lifetime's evidence that whatever silky Venus may insinuate, *The Joy of Sex* is not what Cupid had in mind at all. (p. 108)

> *Timothy Foote, "Venus Observed," in* Time *(reprinted by permission from* Time, The Weekly Newsmagazine; *copyright Time Inc.), September 16, 1974, pp. E8-108.*

Mr Pritchett fashions his stories with the same care as other men collect ferns or the rarer kinds of mollusc, warming them and drying them with his sighs. There is a capacious lugubriousness about *The Camberwell Beauty*. . . . Public secrets and private lies can find their ecological niche without discomfort in Pritchett's easy and assured style, a style that is so central to our tradition that it seems transparent, letting tiny objects and tiny people wink and gleam through. (p. 470)

Mr Pritchett creates his fictions in the form we most easily recognise and with the tone we most appreciate—neither high nor low, neither complex nor simple, neither too long nor too short. Recognisable human figures imitate words and actions in a recognisable landscape, and generally represent those sexual and personal bonds which are supposed to bring certain people together and keep others, alas, apart. The heights of the nineteenth century novel have been flattened until they leave only the barest traces, and we are regaled instead with comfortable entertainments which take us beyond ourselves—and into the warm, well lit, if somewhat cramped, purlieus of the suburban soul. (pp. 470-71)

> *Peter Ackroyd, in* The Spectator *(© 1974 by The Spectator; reprinted by permission of The Spectator), October 12, 1974.*

The pleasure [Pritchett] takes in writing translates itself into the pleasure one takes in reading him—the opportunity to acquaint oneself with a temperament that is humane, an intelligence that is acute and a technique that is masterly.

He has a supernal responsiveness to the eccentricity of ordinary life. Never conceiving of the story as a form of disguised autobiography or confession, he is never present as himself. . . .

Pritchett has a preternaturally sharp eye and ear, alert to the nuances of speech and behavior out of which the stories effortlessly, persuasively, naturally seem to arise. . . .

Clever he prodigiously is, but that is the least of it, measured against the empathy and unnerving understanding that reveals itself in every story, whether in the third or first person. (p. 22)

> *William Abrahams, in* The New Republic *(reprinted by permission of* The New Re-

public; © *1974 by The New Republic, Inc.),*
October 19, 1974.

V. S. Pritchett has turned a deft hand to the novel, to criticism, and even to travel writing, but he always outdoes himself in the short story. Few have mastered the form; even fewer can display the irony and balance evident in [*The Camberwell Beauty, and Other Stories*].

Pritchett's forte is creating eccentric characters and peculiar situations. . . .

Each of these nine stories is about the feelings and forces, exquisitely mixed, that bind men and women: exasperation, contempt, intrigue, lust. There is a hint of the old codger in Pritchett's tone, and his vision of women is not an altogether happy one: they are wistful virgins or bossy mothers, bores, deadly enchantresses, nitpickers. They encounter, rather than interact with, men. When they are young, they become infatuated ("The Lady From Guatemala"); when they are old, as in "The Spree," men are for them just ships that pass in the night. In Pritchett's stories, nothing is ever quite resolved; indeed, having come full circle, his situations seem to dissolve at the very place where they began. Yet, finally, there is a sense that you have come face to face with what is abrupt and unexpected in life, a pleasure that lingers long after you have put the book down. (pp. 28-9)

> *Susan Heath, in* Saturday Review/World
> *(copyright © 1974 by Saturday Review/*
> *World, Inc.; reprinted with permission),*
> *October 19, 1974.*

Pritchett is a romantic writer in the simplest sense—he writes about love in its happiest aspects, and especially well about the process of falling in love. No one could fail to find his stories [in *The Camberwell Beauty and Other Stories*] poetic and touching, but I confess that I am not deeply stirred by them. His world is too uncomplicated; in the end almost everyone gets off the hook . . .; every problem seems to vanish. His women are charming objects, but they are nearly all too fey, and the stories come near to a description. This is the best account I have read of the secret obsessions of antique dealers, obsessions in this case so powerful that they transform everything, including human beings, into antique objects of virtu: thus the dealer's pale and childlike wife, the Camberwell beauty herself, is metamorphosed into a strange mechanical doll blowing a bugle. Perhaps this is analogous to what Pritchett is doing in his fiction: he turns his characters and their surroundings into charming artifacts, the kind of antiques that I admire through a window, but do not want to make part of my life. (p. 32)

> *Matthew Hodgart, in* The New York Review of Books *(reprinted with permission from* The New York Review of Books; *copyright © 1975 NYREV, Inc.), March 20, 1975.*

Not many authors can have documented their own progress from small boy to Elder New Statesman of literature more completely and delightfully than Pritchett. Almost everything he writes stems from and refers to his family and childhood—his endearingly dotty father, man of strong principles and weak judgments, his scatty, 'put upon'

mother, and himself, the young Vic, inheriting his father's skills and energy but transforming them into a craftsmanship that called for the raw material of words, not wood, cloth, leather or ledgers. Wary of his father's cloudy romanticism and absurd aspirations, and therefore in his own work distrustful of dogma, he is always down to earth even when he indulges in fancy. He never divorces sense from sensibility. (p. 5)

New surroundings [he moved to France in 1920] and, above all, a new language intensified Pritchett's almost physical passion for words. It is not an aesthete's infatuation. He is the least precious of writers. He searches not for the rare, the exotic, word, but for the *mot juste*. . . . As he walked through the streets of Paris, relishing the new words spoken and displayed around him, he repeated the names of shops: *quincaillerie, boulangerie, bouquiniste*. 'Language and the sound of words had been my obsession from childhood; the pursed or the open subtlety of French vowels, the nasal endings, the tongue slipping along over silk and metal, the juiciness of the subjunctive, made my own lips restless.' I defy anyone to read that passage without wanting to be transported immediately to a French café and hear those sounds coming at him from every side. Words to Pritchett are tangible, like fabrics. Better still, you can taste them, savour them, like fruit. He is describing accurately, not just with enthusiasm and hyperbole; all those sibilant subjunctives, *fusse, eusse, puisse*, really do sound juicy, as if they were ripe figs from which double s after double s dribble down the speaker's chin. That was the inspiration (though I am sure Pritchett himself would consider it too grand a word) behind the first pieces he succeeded in getting published—evocative essays in local colour, describing his room in Paris, the bugle at the Champ de Mars and a neighbour's groans. (p. 7)

The best of Pritchett's reviews and criticisms are as enthralling as his short stories. Nothing is either a priori or ex cathedra. He applies no apparatus of preconceived theory. He is to literary criticism what Locke, Hume and Butler were to British philosophy. He observes and describes, simplifies and sympathizes, and finally illuminates by a combination of common sense and brilliant insight. He is excellent—of course—on the French, especially Balzac, Flaubert and Maupassant, from whom he himself had learned 'a sense of the importance of the *way* things are done, a thrift of the mind'. He has a deep understanding, too, of the Russians, although I can detect no close link between their writings and his. Above all, he has the knack of helping the common reader (e.g. me, from the time when I began reading his articles in the *New Statesman* nearly forty years ago) to clarify apparent obscurities and discrepancies in an author's work. (p. 10)

Pritchett's own novels are not in the same class as his stories and essays. His stories stay live and demand to be reread. The novels, on the other hand, although they hold you as you read them, relax their grip afterwards and do not ask to be given a second reading. They are genre paintings, flat canvases, static and fixed in their frames, however good the brushwork, however bright the colours. (pp. 10-11)

One's disappointment that the novels have never lived up to Pritchett's other achievements is mitigated by *A Cab at the Door* (1968) and *Midnight Oil* (1971). What could he have done in a novel that he hasn't succeeded in doing in these most memorable memoirs? Here are place, plot and people to satisfy the greediest novel-reader. The people, originals of so many of the characters in the stories and novels, are as colourful a gallery of eccentrics as any in fiction. . . . (p. 12)

John Mellors, "V. S. Pritchett: Man on the Other Side of a Frontier," in London Magazine (© *London Magazine, 1975), April/ May, 1975, pp. 5-13.*

Asked a few years back to comment on his work, V. S. Pritchett, equally distinguished as a writer of fiction, criticism, essays, biography and travel, confessed to valuing his short stories most. It is not surprising. His marriage to the genre—for it he abandoned even the novel—has been going on for nearly fifty years, and *The Camberwell Beauty and Other Stories*, the ninth collection to date, shows not only how valuable but how happy and durable the marriage has been.

Like the scores of other stories in his previous collections, those in *The Camberwell Beauty*—even the few that run a trifle thin—bear the unmistakable mark of Pritchett, a man with a gift for ironic comedy, humane, and endowed with an economical, colloquial style. Pritchett's rhetoric is as good as his sources. Should he happen to waver in invention, he can fall back on his native canniness . . ., should mother-wit fail, he can buoy up the story with the handy flotsam of detail . . .; and should all miscarry—as seldom happens—Pritchett saves all with scalpel-sharp incisions into character. . . .

Even when a Pritchett story does not altogether work either as a tidy fictional bundle or as a slice of life, it is generally amusing and instructive. But when all the elements of Pritchett's alchemy are working, he turns the mundane and the eccentric, the normal and the bizarre into something magical. To my way of thinking this happens twice in *The Camberwell Beauty*: once in the title story (perhaps because it is the longest), and again in "The Lady from Guatemala." (p. 570)

Robert K. Morris, "He Thinks People Are Human," in The Nation (*copyright 1975 by the Nation Associates, Inc.), May 10, 1975, pp. 570-72.*

*   *   *

PUIG, Manuel 1932-

Puig is an Argentinian novelist. (See also *Contemporary Authors*, Vols. 45-48.)

["Betrayed By Rita Hayworth"] sounds like a one-joke book. Manuel Puig . . . describes a provincial growing up in which movies were as vital as bread. As a bedtime story, the young hero, Toto, asks to be told the plot of "Intermezzo," which a fever prevented his attending after he had clipped out all the magazine photos of Ingrid Bergman in anticipation of its arrival. In turn, when he gets a little older, he is able to be a comfort to his mother when childbirth causes her to miss "Hold Back the Dawn" during its brief local run. Toto's mother failed to marry a suitor who became a movie actor ("We never really thought Carlos Palau would make it," one of the family wistfully recalls), but she has the consolation that her irascible husband looks "exactly" like that missed chance. The climax of young

Toto's school career is an essay competition on "The Movie I Liked Best," which he wins handily with his fervent entry on "The Great Waltz."

The novel's charm is in the tender gravity with which Puig records the chatter of Toto's family and neighbors. Kitchen conversations, awkwardly written letters and flowery schoolgirl diary entries . . . combine to evoke lives of humblest possibility and uncomplaining disappointment. Manuel Puig presents this quietly; the effect is moving. (pp. 120, 123)

Walter Clemons, in Newsweek (*copyright 1971 by Newsweek, Inc.; all right reserved; reprinted by permission), October 25, 1971.*

With *La traición de Rita Hayworth* and *Boquitas pintadas*, Manuel Puig established himself as a novelist able to combine cleverness, compassion and humour. He appropriated moreover in those novels a territory that was relatively new in Latin American fiction—the comic yet pathetic cultural aspirations of . . . lower middle-class families in the provinces. He showed these aspirations to be derived longingly from such people's principal or often sole entertainment, the cinema, whose models they try hard to imitate.

The Buenos Aires Affair is perhaps Sr Puig's most serious book to date. It is not devoid of the lucid and witty observation of absurd behaviour that characterized *Boquitas pintadas*, but it is altogether more anguished. . . .

Every chapter of the book is headed by excerpts from such films as *Grand Hotel* or *Shanghai Express*, which express the cinematic ethos that love is a vocation to which all else must be abandoned. Yet the chapters themselves demonstrate how far short of the cinematic models the characters fall, being in fact victims of the cinema's insistence that sex is the principal key to happiness. Sex is ultimately presented as man's worst enemy in *The Buenos Aires Affair*, a kind of curse that destroys concentration, dissipates compassion and love and in general places man at the mercy of "imperious erections" over which he has no control, and for which, unlike in the cinema, he can only rarely find shared satisfaction.

In spite of the harrowing story it tells, there is no self-pity in *The Buenos Aires Affair* because Sr Puig is an accomplished craftsman who keeps just the right distance from his material. *The Buenos Aires Affair* is technically even more accomplished than the previous novels, and Sr Puig is able to handle a wide variety of narrative devices in it without ever making them seem gratuitous.

"Common Complaint," in The Times Literary Supplement (© *Times Newspapers Ltd., 1973; reproduced by permission), August 31, 1973, p. 1007.*

Both *Betrayed by Rita Hayworth* and *Heartbreak Tango* by Manuel Puig present characters who suck the thumb of popular culture to avoid chewing the gristle of reality. . . . And both novels open with autonomous statements, theoretically independent of a narrator. In *Rita*, it is a script-like presentation, free of all theatrical indication, while in *Tango* it is a death notice from a newspaper. Before you reach that notice in *Tango*, however, you encounter an epigraph quoted from an actual tango. . . .

What Puig lends to *Tango*—what he so stringently withheld from his earlier novel—is exactly what the epigraph indicates: "his voice." Not Puig's own voice, of course, but a narrative voice announcing what follows the introductory music and also fills us in on actions Puig cannot put into his characters' mouths. In other words, Puig has supplied an indispensable announcer to his novelistic soap opera. It is a device we all remember from the radio soaps and Puig is trying to make us recall those soaps and their literary equivalent, the *folletín* or magazine serial. (p. 49)

As always in Puig, the core of [*Tango*] is both erotic and violent, while the form, as the subtitle of . . . *The Buenos Aires Affair* explicitly indicates, is that of a detective story. Here then, in *Tango*, is a newspaper-headline or soap-operatic drama; but again, as always in Puig, you are guided to see even this unheroic drama in collision with day-to-day reality, the collision of bourgeois romantic dream with poignantly objective fact.

The characters themselves are unaware of the romanticism in the class melodrama they inhabit and this lack of awareness is essential to Puig for the manufacture of that poignancy I spoke of. We readers must be aware of the sources of the characters' fantasies and thus see comic figures with absurd dreams epitomized in captions from popular movies . . . and in verses from tangos themselves. But, we must also be alert to the characters' pitiful victimization by what they do not recognize—the insidious power of unanalyzed popular culture. So all these epigraphs signal to you from a different typographical space from that inhabited by the characters, and they instruct your awareness with a different calculation of rhetoric. (p. 50)

But before you jump to the conclusion that *Tango* is just another rhetorical lash on the back of an already defeated romanticism, recognize that for Puig, for the vision of his novel, so-called objective fact is no less moving than subjective fantasizing. Characters like Nélida dream of imported tulle gowns and fashionably decorated apartments but inhabit a domestic barreness, it's true; and it would be easy to see this contradiction as the diagnostic analysis of Puig's novel. But if, once again, you turn to the prose—to the style or fashion of a novel so concerned with both style and fashion—you can see that the true voice of that purportedly objective narrative is one of the most elevatedly lyrical in all literature, lyric to the sublimity of elegance. (pp. 52-3)

[Whatever] the technique, [we are moved] to humor and pathos, tears and laughter. . . . [The] emotions are not *evoked* by means of an allusive complicity between author and reader in a plot that implicates not only literature and society but economics and politics as well. Rather, the emotions are *supplied* by the reader himself as he scans what at first seems to be the merely informational. (p. 53)

[The] technique of moving the reader by refining emotion out of the text's content and syntax recalls Joyce's great "mathematical catechism" chapter in *Ulysses* (Chapter Seventeen, "Ithaca") which Joyce himself called both "impersonal" and his favorite. . . . Less scientific or "mathematical" than Joyce—less *rigorous*, in a word—Puig nevertheless is straightfaced, if not truly pokerfaced, in causing us to feel a wide range of emotion as he confronts banal mentalities with banal facts without intimating the slightest disrespect for either.

Between modes of garrulous sentimentality and laconic factualness Puig has focused a vision of life like the vision of *Don Quixote*, and of *Madame Bovary*, that is inherently, accurately, *bi-focal*. He has not—and so you must not—conclude that to perceive ludicrous self-deception is to be free from it; or, for that matter, that to traffic in newspaper clippings, death certificates, medical reports and slightly breathless newscaster prose reminiscent of "You Are There" is to sterilize feelings. Such extremes are themselves delusions—vogues in intellectual or literary attitudes, no less preposterous or pathetically human than the outdated clothes Nélida and her companions desire. Clothes that are now coming back into style and seem to proclaim Puig a camp novelist while *Heartbreak Tango*, in addition to doing everything that *Rita Hayworth* did (and doing it better, too) actually proclaims Puig not only a major writer but a major stylist whose medium brings you both the heartbreak *and* the tango, but also reminds you, in several senses, that

> *As long as you can smile, success can be*
> *yours. . . .*   (p. 54)

> *Ronald Christ, "Fact and Fiction," in* Review 73 *(copyright © 1972 by the Center for Inter-American Relations, Inc.), Fall, 1973, pp. 49-54.*

Manuel Puig's *Heartbreak Tango* bombards us with "realism," arranging a terrifying welter of short, spasmodic fragments into a seedy "tragedy" that is coherent, poignant, and painfully funny. The setting is Buenos Aires in the 1940's-1960's; the characters are ambitious romantic daydreamers who all imagine—and act—out of an *idea* of the world which they derive from movies and radio serials. . . .

Sometimes Puig concentrates, minute-by-minute, on the detailed itinerary of a character's "day." He moves in and out of the novel surefootedly, sometimes commenting directly on his characters, or blandly offering lists and outlines to explain their motivations.

Though the novel is obviously *arranged* (into "Episodes," with quoted tango lyrics as epigraphs), a reader experiences it as a rich loose array of directly rendered personalities. Somehow, Puig does it by very consciously *varying* the kinds of attention that he brings to bear on his characters. We sense the keen compassionate intensity with which the Self (this time, the narrator-organizer's) views the World. (p. 128)

> *Bruce Allen, in* The Hudson Review *(copyright © 1974 by The Hudson Review, Inc.; reprinted by permission), Vol. XXVII, No. 1, Spring, 1974.*

Spanish American literature has been criticizing itself, folding back upon itself in poems, novels, and short stories for the last thirty years. The texts better known to the English reader—by Borges, Octavio Paz, Donoso, Carlos Fuentes, Lezama Lima—are only a few examples of a kind of writing that attempts to be everything and nothing at the same time, a literature that attempts to create a fiction and uncover the conventions that make this fiction possible. It is everything and nothing because in the interplay between building the individual work and pointing out its theoretical support, the illusions, the projections that non-self-critical texts produce in the reader are lost. . . . Most of these works tend to speak *about* literature in a thematized way. We find characters or privileged narrators operating in situations where the subject is clearly literature. . . . This situation has begun to change in more or less explicit ways with works like *One Hundred Years of Solitude* by García Márquez. But still, there is the gesture of integrating the meditation about literature into a discourse that tries to take simultaneously the place of fiction, philosophy, and linguistics by denying the existence of clear lines of demarcation between these languages. As a result of this denial of lines of demarcation, we have texts that convey the notion that there is no privileged language for truth, that the traits distinguishing levels of objectivity are tenuous and naive. The functions of discourses such as fiction, metaphysics, linguistics, etc., are denied specificity and locality; the notion of genre gives way to a text that attempts to lose itself in all the possibilities opened to it by the fact that it is made of language, that it is *only* language.

But all of the works we have mentioned still preserve one illusion about language and privileged discourses. Although they attempt to efface themselves as constituted by one particular language, they belong to a wider kind: they are *literature*. They are made out of what is considered to be acceptable written language. Their thrust towards orality is a literary gesture that locates itself in a tradition of attempts to achieve a "natural" prose. . . . If there is one untouched privilege it is the one of "good literature" over "bad literature," of beauty and intelligence over trash. In this sense the kind of break that they make with their tradition may be wide but not radical, since it preserves the notion of a good and a bad literature.

The three novels that Manuel Puig has produced up to now —*Betrayed by Rita Hayworth*, *Heartbreak Tango*, and *The Buenos Aires Affair*—come out of this tradition of breaking with the conventions of the naive realism of previous Spanish American literature but do not accept the notion of a privileged language for literature. They make this gesture of non-acceptance by taking an oblique position in relation to certain genres traditionally seen as trash, as ephemeral objects of mass consumption: *fotonovelas* and dime-store novels. (pp. 95-7)

This literature is read all over Latin America, France, and Italy. It has a long tradition, and its readership consists mainly of domestic servants, housewives, and shop attendants. It is a literature that clearly separates itself from the "good" one. Nobody would refer to it as anything but trash, thereby isolating its language and its conventions from the accepted reading material. Its mark is bad taste; its definition is the cliché. (p. 97)

Manuel Puig's writing is different. Puig supports his texts by constant references to these trashy works without ever presenting the line of demarcation that would help distinguish his novels from that trash. He has studied, accepted, and redefined the conventions of *fotonovelas* without separating the good from the bad, without trying to produce what traditionally was seen as beautiful and/or true. Trash appears in his novels as the effect of a complex system of artifices, as the result of a conventional network. Everyday

language, the repetitive nature of clichés, and the obsession with imitating models have been thoroughly integrated into a discourse that separates itself from the "literary" tradition by taking as its point of departure bad taste. But since there is no counterpart, there is no possibility of contrast. We know that this is bad taste because our exercise as readers of "good" literature tells us that, but nothing in the novels themselves speaks to us explicitly about the system of privileged discourses that exists outside it. In this way, Puig creates a surprisingly homogeneous novelistic discourse, with a texture that integrates trash and uses it as its only support.

Each of Puig's novels has to be read as part of a dialogue between the three novels that he has written. . . . The questions that we address to Puig's texts, the determinants that we find in this triple dialogue, concern the elaboration of a system of artifices through the absence of a voice that organizes levels of importance in the discourse of the novel. . . . The ghostly nature of the speakers, the lack of an organizing subject, the impossibility of seizing a referent, the gestures toward signification that are constantly frustrated constitute the interstice in which Puig's writing exists. The condition for the creation of the artifices, of convention, is the effect of a negative eroticism; his texts are the cipher for the loss of power over language as a bridge. The figure of castration lies behind the chain of allusions that we find in Puig and behind his notion of art as the "artificial," as that which is substituted for a natural object that has been lost. (pp. 97-8)

In displaying . . . the interstices that separate literature from its referents, Puig exposes his novels as samples of the thing for which all literature strives: the appropriation of an external object and its transformation into something else that appears to be the same, but only because of the radical difference which literature preserves with its referent. The loss of a structuring voice, the loss of a referent, is the attainment of Puig's writing. To enumerate these instances is to expose the precarious being of writing. Puig's writing posits castration as the necessary condition for the works' unfolding. The interstice, the absence, the loss of an eye/I, makes possible the existence of the novels' imaginative space. Convention, the work of art, is the product of a radical absence that masks itself. An interstice opens up the possibility of excess, of frivolity, of artifice.

Puig is a frivolous writer. His language is the archeological reconstruction of the language of others, its conventional nature is always present. His nostalgia for other songs, for other eras, for other movies, is part of going back in order to install himself at privileged moments in which language fails in its desire to create meaning. His writing produces artifacts, static museum pieces, enormous idiomatic paintings. The possibility of painting instances of the same interstice, time and again, is the luxury of the loss of a referent. (pp. 113-14)

Alicia Borinsky, "Castration: Artifices, Notes on the Writing of Manuel Puig," in The Georgia Review *(copyright, 1975, by the University of Georgia), Spring, 1975, pp. 95-114.*

Q

QUENEAU, Raymond   1903-

Queneau, a French surrealist writer, is the author of many novels, one play, screenplays, poetry, and essays. For Queneau, life is so absurd that only laughter makes it tolerable. He has been called a "virtuoso of style" and master of "bawdy language growing in a field of glorious rhetoric." In addition to his creative work, Queneau planned and edited the immense *Encyclopédie de la Pléiade*.

Queneau is not the first writer to contend with literature. Ever since "literature" has existed (that is, judging from the word's date, since quite recently), we can say that the writer's function is to oppose it. What distinguishes Queneau is that his opposition is a hand-to-hand combat: his entire *oeuvre* cleaves to the myth of literature, his contestation is alienated, it feeds on its object, always leaving substance enough for new meals: the noble edifice of written form still stands, but worm-eaten, scaling, dilapidated. In this controlled destruction, something new, something ambiguous is elaborated, a kind of suspension of formal values: rather like the beauty of ruins. Nothing vengeful in this impulse—Queneau's activity is not, strictly speaking, sarcastic, it does not emanate from a good conscience, but rather from a complicity.

This surprising contiguity (this identity?) of literature and its enemy is very apparent in *Zazie*. From the point of view of literary architecture, *Zazie* is a *well-made* novel. It embodies all the "virtues" criticism likes to inventory and praise: "classical" construction . . .; "epic" duration . . .; objectivity . . .; a full cast of characters . . .; a unified social milieu and setting . . .; variety and equilibrium of fictional methods (narrative and dialogue). In other words, the entire technique of the French novel, from Stendhal to Zola. Whence the work's familiarity, which is perhaps not foreign to its success, for we cannot be certain that all its readers have consumed this good novel in an altogether *distant* fashion: there is, in *Zazie*, a pleasure of cursive reading, and not only of contour.

Yet once the novel's entire positivity is established, Queneau, without directly destroying it, couples it with an insidious void. As soon as each element of the traditional universe solidifies, Queneau dissolves it, undermines the novel's security: literature's solidity curdles; everything is given a double aspect, made unreal, whitened by that lunar light which is an essential theme of deceit and a theme characteristic of Queneau. The event is never denied, i.e., first posited then negated; it is always *divided* . . ., mythically endowed with two antagonistic figures.

The moments of deceit are precisely those which once constituted the glory of traditional rhetoric. First of all, the *figures of thought*: here the forms of duplicity are countless: antiphrasis (the title itself [*Zazie dans le métro*], since Zazie never takes the metro); uncertainty (is it the Panthéon or the Gare de Lyon, Sainte-Chapelle or the Chamber of Commerce?); the confusion of contrary roles (Pedro-Surplus is both a satyr and a cop), of ages (Zazie "ages"), of sexes, this last doubled by an additional enigma, since Gabriel's inversion is uncertain; the error which turns out to be right (Marceline finally becomes Marcel); negative definition (the tobacco shop which is not the one at the corner); tautology (the cop arrested by other cops); mockery (the child who brutalizes the adult, the lady who intervenes), etc.

All these figures are inscribed within the texture of the narrative; they are not conspicuous. The *figures of words*, of course, effect a much more spectacular destruction, one familiar to Queneau's readers. These are first of all *figures of construction*, which attack literary dignity by a running fire of parodies. Every kind of writing is attacked: epic, Homeric, Latin, medieval, psychological, anecdotal, even the grammatical tenses, favorite vehicles of the myth of fiction, the historical present, and the Flaubertian *passé simple*. Such examples indicate that Queneau's parody has a very special structure: it does not parade a knowledge of the model being mocked; there is no trace of that Ecole-Normale complicity with high culture which characterizes Giraudoux's parodies, for instance, and which is merely a deceptively off-hand way of showing a profound respect for classical-national values; here the parodic expression is frivolous, it dislocates *en passant*—a scab picked off the old literary skin. Queneau's is a parody sapped from within, its very structure masking a scandalous incongruity; it is not imitation (however subtle) but malformation, a dangerous equilibrium between verisimilitude and aberration, verbal theme of a culture whose forms are brought to a state of perpetual deceit.

As for the *figures of speech*, they obviously go much farther than a simple naturalization of our orthography. . . . Queneau's reductions . . . produce, in place of the word pompously draped in its orthographic gown, a new word, indiscreet, natural, i.e., barbarous: here it is the *francité* of the writing which is undermined, the noble Gallic tongue, the *doux parler de France* abruptly dislocated into a series of stateless vocables, so that our Great Literature, after the detonation, might well be no more than a collection of vaguely Russian or Kwakiutl fragments (and if not, only because of Queneau's pure kindness). Which is not to say that Quenalian phoneticism is purely destructive (is there ever, in literature, a univocal destruction?): all of Queneau's labor on our language is inspired by an obsessional impulse, that of *découpage*, of cutting-up: this is a technique in which riddling is a first step, but whose function is to explore structures, for to code and to decode are the two aspects of one and the same act of penetration, as was indicated, long before Queneau, by the entire Rabelaisian philosophy, for example. (pp. 117-20)

[Conforming] to the most learned definitions of symbolic logic, Zazie clearly distinguishes the language object from metalanguage. The language object is that language which dissolves into action itself, which makes things *act*—it is the primary, transitive language, the one about which we can speak but which itself transforms more than it speaks. It is exactly within this language object that Zazie lives, she never distances or destroys this language. . . .

And it is from this language object that Zazie occasionally emerges in order to paralyze, with her murderous clausule, the metalanguage of the grown-ups. This metalanguage speaks not things but *apropos of* things (or *apropos of* the primary language). It is a parasitical, motionless, sententious language which doubles the act in the same way as the fly accompanies the coach; instead of the language object's imperative and optative, its principal mode is the indicative, a kind of zero degree of the act intended to *represent* reality, not to change it. This metalanguage secretes, around the letter of utterance, a complementary meaning—ethical, plaintive, sentimental, magisterial, etc.; in short, it is a song, an aria: in it we recognize the very being of literature. (p. 120)

For Queneau, literature is a category of speech, hence of existence, which concerns all of humanity. . . . It is not "the people," in Queneau's eyes, who possess the utopian literality of language; it is Zazie (whence, probably, the profound meaning of the role), i.e., an unreal, magical, Faustian being, since Zazie is the superhuman contraction of childhood and maturity, the superposition of "I am outside the world of adults" and of "How much I have lived." Zazie's innocence is not a bloom, a fragile virginity, values which could belong only to the romantic or edifying metalanguage: it is rejection of the aria, and a science of the transitive; Zazie circulates in her novel like a household god, her function is hygienic, counter-mythic: she calls to order. (pp. 120-21)

Zazie dans le métro is really an exemplary work: by vocation, it dismisses both . . . the serious and the comic. Which accounts for the confusion of our critics: some have taken it seriously as a serious work of art, suited to exegetical decipherment; others, judging the first group grotesque, have called the novel absolutely frivolous ("there is nothing to be said about it"); still others, seeing neither comedy nor seriousness in the work, have declared they did not understand. But this was precisely the work's intention—to wreck any dialogue about it, representing by the absurd the

elusive nature of language. There is, between Queneau and the serious and mockery of the serious, that very movement of control and escape which governs the familiar game, model of all spoken dialectic, in which paper covers stone, stone smashes scissors, scissors cut paper: one always has the advantage over the other—provided both are mobile terms, forms. The antilanguage is never absolute. . . .

[Zazie's] role is unreal, of an uncertain positivity, it is the expression of a reference more than the voice of a wisdom. This means that for Queneau, the contestation of language is always ambiguous, never conclusive, and that he himself is not a judge but a participant. (p. 122)

Queneau is on the side of modernity: his literature is not a literature of possession and fulfillment; he knows that one cannot "demystify" from the outside, in the name of an ownership, but that one must steep oneself in the void one is revealing: yet he also knows that this compromising of himself would lose all its virtue if it were spoken, recuperated by a direct language: literature is the very mode of the impossible, since it alone can speak its void, and by saying it, again establish a plenitude. In his way, Queneau takes a position at the heart of this contradiction, which perhaps defines our literature today: he assumes the literary mask but at the same time points his finger at it. This is a very difficult and enviable operation; it is perhaps because it is a successful one that there is, in *Zazie*, this last and precious paradox: a dazzling comedy yet one purified of all aggression. As if Queneau psychoanalyzes himself at the same time that he psychoanalyzes literature: Queneau's entire *oeuvre* implies a quite terrible imago of literature. (p. 123)

> *Roland Barthes, "Zazie and Literature" (1959), in his* Critical Essays, *translated by Richard Howard (copyright © 1972 by Northwestern University Press, Evanston, Ill.), Northwestern University Press, 1972, pp. 117-23.*

[*Zazie dans le métro* was] the first genuine success scored by . . . Raymond Queneau, who had, up to then, been greatly admired only by a small élite of connoisseurs. There was a contrived and highly self-conscious humor in some of his earlier volumes, *Loin de Rueil* (1944, translated as *The Skin of Dreams*), *Le Dimache de la vie* (1951), too wry and too geometrically calculated to arouse generous laughter. The author is immensely learned and the organizer and editor of several encyclopedias. . . . Not unlike Joyce, he has for years centered his meditations on language, and, not unlike Wordsworth in his famous preface, he has attempted to bring the French language 'near to the language of men.' Respect for their polished, perspicuous, often stylized language, laden with nuances which reveal the class stratification of the country, is the only cult which had survived the shattering downfall of most idols for the French people during the propaganda era of World War II. Queneau's words are artfully printed as they may be spoken by the unrefined and supposedly naïve common people of Paris. The effect is entertaining for a while, then soon palls upon the reader as it becomes monotonously mechanical. The characters are all wooden puppets and the teenager, Zazie, is a vulgar and would-be innocent little girl, about as tedious as the Lolita of the New World. (pp. 353-54)

Queneau . . . is perhaps not a great novelist but he is a

great writer and an incomparable virtuoso of style. His chief concern seems to be re-creating language through effective use of colloquial speech, of slang and of many of the devices of rhetoric, entertainingly used. But he owes as much to Charlie Chaplin as he does to James Joyce. His *Pierrot mon ami . . .*, which relates the hero's vicissitudes in an amusement park, in a truck in which he rides with apes, and his frustrated love affairs, is a masterpiece of hilarious comedy, as was his first and perhaps best novel, *Le Chiendent. . . . Le Dimanche de la vie . . .* has excellent parts on naïve and winning fools at odds with wily women and escaping scot-free, like Chaplin or even like Dostoevski's idiot, from the ordeals of modern life. The stumbling blocks for Queneau are probably his immense store of knowledge, rivaling that of Joyce and occasionally intruding into the tale as pedantry, his total disregard of the structure of his novels, hence some monotony in the 'flat' comic characters, and an ending usually unequal to a brilliant beginning. *Zazie dans le métro . . .* is in our opinion a strained and artificial *tour de force*; like many of the comic attempts by the author, it seems to have been synthetically contrived by a geometrician versed in philology. (p. 435)

> *Henri Peyre, in his* French Novelists of Today *(copyright © 1955, 1967 by Oxford University Press, Inc.; reprinted by permission of Oxford University Press, Inc.), Oxford University Press-Galaxy, 1967.*

American readers who have come to know the inimitable comic universe of Raymond Queneau through the charming but inconsequential *Zazie* or through the stylistic pyrotechnics of *Exercises in Style* [in which Queneau recounts the same anecdote in ninety-nine ways], can finally savor his first novel—and one of his best—*The Bark Tree (Le Chiendent)*, published in France in 1933 [and translated into English in 1971]. Then, as now, Queneau was preoccupied with problems of language. French, as it was written, he felt, no longer related to the way people spoke; he wanted the written idiom to reproduce the slang and colloquialism of ordinary street conversation.

Queneau set out to do a modern slang translation of Descartes' *Discourse on Method*; fortunately, he was carried further than he had expected and produced this strange, hilarious novel, which is a masterpiece of black humor and at the same time a meaningful, philosophic meditation. . . .

It would be almost as difficult—and as pointless—to "tell" the plot of *The Bark Tree* as to give a synopsis of a Marx Brothers film. Suffice it to say that everyone becomes hopelessly entangled in a search for a huge amount of money supposedly hidden behind a door by an old recluse junk dealer. After countless improbable happenings, it turns out that there is no treasure; behind the door there is nothing, only a wall: the old man had hung the door on the wall as one hangs a mirror, and all the competing devious plans to rob him of his purported wealth are foiled. The gratuitous, madcap quality of Queneau's novel is somewhat reminiscent of Gide's *Lafcadio's Adventures*, probably the only one of his meticulously styled works that the younger writer could stomach. . . .

The many colloquial philosophic monologues and dialogues are at once substantive and parodic. Queneau clearly views life as absurd (already!) and dwells insistently (though playfully) on the shadowy line that divides the actual from the

imagined. *The Bark Tree* is also a caricature before the fact of Sartre's meditations in *Nausea* on existence, nothingness, contingency.

This fascinating novel is prophetic in other ways too: not only does it presage the anti-novel so much in vogue in France since 1950 (concerned not with outward events but with the impossibility of narrating a story, *The Bark Tree* was hailed by Robbe-Grillet as a "new novel" twenty years' premature); it is also a pioneer work in stressing the very contemporary concern with communication and the crisis of language.

In Queneau's hands, language—vocabulary, spelling, syntax—is manipulated, squeezed, and pulled until it fairly explodes and becomes a "neolanguage" of slang and colloquialisms. These innovations, inspired by Joyce and Céline most of all, make translating Queneau a nightmarish task. . . .

But the English version retains more than enough fun to delight the reader.

At the end of the novel Queneau escalates the level of comedy, of satire and parody. Suddenly he launches into a mock-heroic conflict between France and the Etruscans, which enables him to draw a devastating caricature of war and of human greed and stupidity. Again there are echoes of Céline's ferocity though without his bitterness. Queneau is cynical but not pessimistic. No one who writes as funny a book as this could really be a pessimist. (p. 25)

> *Tom Bishop, in* Saturday Review *(copyright © 1971 by Saturday Review, Inc.; reprinted with permission), August 7, 1971.*

"The Bark Tree" is full . . . of nonsense and . . . naked contrivance. . . . A palpable Paris takes shape through a multiplicity of fine strokes . . . [and] Queneau's wonderful gift for simile tempts one to compile a list. . . . And above [the] odd events, [the] overanimated souls and artifacts, a real humanity presides; Queneau not only permits each character the dignity of eloquence but rises himself to a fury of sarcasm when he contemplates the chauvinistic farce of the "Etruscan" war: "even the strategists . . . said they'd never seen a simpler, easier, more amusing war."

Queneau's sympathy peculiarly falls upon the banal—upon the empty routines, that is, whereby human ordinariness propels itself along the quotidian. He says of certain conventional greetings that "their apparent complexity concealed a profound simplicity." Pierre, overhearing some clichés about the weather, "notes with some bitterness that these banalities correspond perfectly to reality." Perhaps, since Flaubert, banality is *the* challenge to serious novelists: the gales of romance have died, and the novelist is a sailor on a close reach, trying to use the constant wind of ordinary living to make some kind of headway against it. The melodrama by Queneau's plot is manufactured by the characters, as a vacation from boredom; his own vacation comes in the intervals of metaphysical speculation, and these—though he would not have written the book without them—seem rather mannered and pat. When Pierre talks to the reader about his boredom and his masks, or when Étienne drops the aphorism that "there isn't any gospel, there are only works of fiction," we are aware of an author pressing his claims upon our intelligence; when Ernestine, dying, formulates death as the disappearance of "the little voice that talks in your head when you're by yourself,'' we are in the presence of human experience and shared terror. Gertrude Stein said it: literature isn't remarks. What we want from fiction, and what fiction is increasingly loath to give us, is vicarious experience. Exiled from the great naïveté that nurtured the nineteenth-century masterworks of the novel, Queneau yet is old enough—humane enough—to spin, amid a metaphysics of relativity and uncertainty, affectionate images of human life in its curiosity, rapacity, and fragility. Compared to Queneau, [some younger] authors seem tired; a distance that cannot be exactly measured in generations or wars separates them from an instinctive belief that men are significant and that art must embody enduring principles. (pp. 138-39)

> *John Updike, in* The New Yorker *(© 1971 by The New Yorker Magazine, Inc.), September 25, 1971.*

Undoubtedly, Queneau was born before his time. His early novels were both more experimental and more ambitious than his later, better-known ones. Perhaps, consciously or unconsciously, Queneau became discouraged by the poor reception accorded his early experiments and allowed his energy to be diverted into other channels, notably his poetry and the immense enterprise of the *Encyclopédie de la Pléiade*, the planning and editing of which required all his vast knowledge as a modern polymath. Poetry and encyclopedic learning coalesce in his extraordinary work, *Petite cosmogonie portative* (''A Little Portable Cosmogony''), which takes for its province the history of the solar system, the evolution of life on earth, and the progress of human knowledge and invention down to the computer. (Published in 1950, it appeared too soon to include the exploration of outer space.) Its division into six *chants* challenges direct comparison with Lucretius' *De Rerum Natura*. While relatively shorter . . . than the great works of antiquity, *Petite cosmogonie portative*, by virtue of its tremendous range, entitles Queneau to be considered a modern Lucretius or Hesiod—endowed, however, with a sense of humor that his great predecessors might have considered a handicap. (pp. 44-5)

[There is] the possibility that Queneau may win his most lasting reputation as a poet rather than a novelist. . . .

Crucial influences were Joyce's *Ulysses* and Faulkner's *Sanctuary*. . . . Conrad's *Lord Jim* also influenced *Le Chiendent*. Later Queneau discovered *Tom Jones*. . . . Other important later discoveries were the notebooks of Henry James, *The Making of Americans* and other works by Gertrude Stein, and Edmund Wilson's *Axel's Castle*. This of course does not exhaust Queneau's knowledge of English literature, which can be traced in the excellent index to his volume of selected criticism, *Bâtons, chiffres, et lettres* (1950). . . . [He] acknowledges a general debt ''to the English and American novelists who taught me that a technique of the novel existed, and above all to Joyce.''

A carefully planned—and carefully concealed—structure, so important in the novels of Robbe-Grillet, Butor, and (sometimes) Simon, almost became a fetish with Queneau during the years of his discipleship to Joyce. . . . (pp. 45-6)

Queneau could hardly have known in 1933 of the variations upon a four-part organization that *Finnegans Wake* (then known as *Work in Progress*) would display when finally

published in 1939. But, besides being as fascinated by numerical symbolism as Joyce was, he had an almost professional knowledge of mathematics entirely outside the scope of the Irish writer. As Queneau reveals in *Technique du roman*, two of his first three novels [*Le Chiendent* and *Les Derniers jours*] had elaborate arithmetical structures. (p. 46)

Guele de pierre (1934) is less complex, mathematically at least. . . . However, each of [its] three parts also corresponds to one of the domains of nature—animal, vegetable, and mineral—and the third contains all twelve signs of the zodiac. . . .

[In *Bâtons, chiffres et lettres*, Queneau commented:] ''. . . I wrote . . . with this idea of rhythm, this intention of making a sort of poem out of the novel. It is possible to make situations or characters rhyme together just as one makes words rhyme; it is even possible to content oneself with mere alliteration. . . . I always compelled myself to follow certain rules which had no justification other than their satisfying my taste for figures or some purely personal whims. . . .'' (p. 47)

Implicit in this quotation is an attitude toward the reader which Queneau shares in greater or lesser degree with all the New Novelists. He is an author of the ''age of suspicion,'' to employ Nathalie Sarraute's term, and the reader must be constantly on the alert to make sure the author is not outwitting him in some way. Even so popular a book as Queneau's *Pierrot mon ami* conceals something basic from the unwary reader, namely an important complication of the plot; this in addition to whatever philosophical concepts, learned allusions, or symbolism there may be lurking for the more sophisticated reader to ferret out. . . .

Queneau has from the beginning taken full advantage of his awareness that he is writing in an age of suspicion. By the end of *Le Chiendent* it is impossible for any reader, however naïve, to believe that the characters are real people, but an explicit warning is given much earlier. Pierre le Grand, the intelligent observer through whose eyes we watch much of the early action, tells Narcense, ''I am observing a man.'' ''You don't say! Are you a novelist?'' ''No. A character.'' In other words, the person we readers have hitherto been most ready to identify with tells Narcense and us explicitly that he is nothing more than a character in a novel. . . .

Occasionally, in Queneau's later books, one finds a character one can believe in, but by so believing, one probably thwarts the conscious intent of the author. (p. 48)

One apparent link between Queneau and certain of the New Novelists—Robbe-Grillet, Cluade Mauriac—is his devotion to the film. . . .

Queneau, like most of the New Novelists, has drawn on the experiments in sentence structure, punctuation, verbal ''montage,'' and point of view engaged in by Joyce, Faulkner, and others, especially the Dadaist and Surrealist poets, between the world wars. Curiously, however, he has made almost no use of their very free handling of time. . . . Generally speaking, his narratives follow the accepted chronological order, and the only freedom he regularly allows himself is that of discontinuity: he will break off his narrative abruptly and resume it hours, days, or years later without any explicit indication of the passage of time, though of course implicit indications soon appear. There is one major exception (seemingly) to the above generalizations about Queneau's use of time—namely, the circular form of *Le Chiendent*. . . . To give Queneau full credit for his originality, we should take note that the circular structure of *Finnegans Wake*—which "ends" in the middle of a sentence, the continuation of which "begins" the book again—was not fully revealed until its publication in 1939.

Queneau differs most sharply from the New Novelists in the scope of his experiments with language. Like Joyce, though not to the same extreme point, he cannot remain content to experiment with word order, punctuation, and sentence structure; the individual word must also be liberated from convention. Most important among Queneau's linguistic preoccupations is his awareness of the gulf between most written and most spoken French. In both his novels and his poetry he constantly strives to write the spoken language. (pp. 49-51)

Queneau's copious use of argot, the French equivalent of slang, partly explains why so few of his novels have been translated into English. (p. 51)

Much of Queneau's attempt to capture the spoken language is, paradoxically, directed to the eye rather than the ear, through the use of phonetic spelling. (p. 52)

As a disciple of Joyce, Queneau does not balk at neologisms and portmanteau words, although he uses them sparingly. In *Bâtons, chiffres et lettres . . .*, he presents a translation into Joycean of the opening passage of *Gueule de pierre*. It shows a great many characteristics of the style of *Finnegans Wake*, though the basic language is French instead of English. (p. 53)

Another product . . . of his discipleship to Joyce is the extraordinary *Exercises de style* (1947), in which a brief prose anecdote is recounted in ninety-nine different styles. Among the weirdest variations are those called "Permutations": one written in groups of from two to five letters; one in groups of from five to eight; one in groups of from nine to twelve. Here we see again the mind of a mathematician rather than of a literary artist at work. The only similar permutations I can think of—and they are far from identical —are found in Beckett's second novel in English, *Watt* (completed in 1945, though not published until 1953). . . .

The literary critic who must analyze *Le Chiendent* cannot help wishing that Queneau shared still another trait of the New Novelists, their tendency to eliminate plot. In this work, as in almost all his novels, Queneau provides a most elaborate one, full of complications, coincidences, concealments, and discoveries. The reader, alternately baffled and surprised, wonders why Queneau felt it necessary to work so hard. To understand why, we must bear in mind Queneau's analogy between the novel and poetry—a very traditional kind of poetry, furthermore. In discussing *Le Chiendent* he has said:

> I set up for myself rules as strict as those of
> the sonnet. The characters do not appear
> and disappear by chance, nor do the scenes,
> nor the different modes of expression. . . .

Paradoxically, in *Le Chiendent* and *Pierrot mon ami* at least, this extreme artifice has at times the effect of naturalism; the arbitrariness of the plot resembles the arbitrariness of life, so that a single impulsive deviation from ev-

eryday routine can set off a chain of unforeseeable consequences prolonged virtually to infinity. (p. 54)

Of all the novels in which characters "talk philosophy" . . . *Le Chiendent* is probably the earliest which shares the preoccupations of mid-twentieth-century philosophers. This is hardly an accident; Georges Bataille wrote in 1948 that this novel marked "a beginning of existential philosophy in France." (p. 61)

Concern with plot and with philosophic content has led us to slight an important aspect of *Le Chiendent*: its experiments in the technique of narration and dialogue. It is true that these are not as radical as Queneau's experiments in philosophic exposition; probably no narrative device used by him is more than a variation on something already to be found in Joyce, the Surrealists, Rabelais, or Sterne. Indeed, one has to admit that certain passages in *Tristram Shandy*, which expound or exemplify—or simply plagiarize —the theory of association of ideas as treated in John Locke's *Essay Concerning Human Understanding*, anticipate Queneau's attempts to present philosophic ideas in colloquial language. (p. 64)

[The] ninety-one sections of *Le Chiendent* display a technical virtuosity akin to that of Joyce's *Ulysses*. Joyce employed a different technique in each of his eighteen episodes; Queneau does not claim to have employed ninety-one different techniques, but he has gone a good distance in that direction: no section is exactly like those which immediately precede and follow it. (pp. 64-5)

[Yet] *Le Chiendent*, . . . in spite of its careful structure, does not succeed in conveying the idea of a fundamental unity underlying its almost infinite variety. Perhaps the point implicit in its return to the *status quo ante* at the end is that no final resolution is possible for all the contradictions presented by life. The strange title of the novel may help us here. . . . Ultimately, each reader must give his own meaning to the title of *Le Chiendent*. (p. 66)

Saint Glinglin might be described as the perfect foil to *Le Chiendent* in both form and content. To the complex plotting of the earlier book it opposes the broad, free movement of myth. In place of the rigorous intellectual discipline of logic, existential philosophy, and mathematics, it offers the less stringent methods of the social sciences. . . . Though *Saint Glinglin* contains two lengthy philosophical meditations, the intellectual life is on the whole subordinated to the instinctual. (p. 67)

Despite a certain amount of willfully self-indulgent whimsicality on Queneau's part, *Saint Glinglin* is a remarkable work of fiction. While not as ambitious as *The Magic Mountain* or *Ulysses*, it can be mentioned without incongruity in the company of those tragicomic masterpieces. In its own way, it has something of their encyclopedic quality: instead of discussing some of the great ideas of the nineteenth and twentieth centuries, it exemplifies them in rather lighthearted parables. Existentialist philosophy in its German manifestation, Freudian psychology (at least in regard to father-son relationships), and some of the discoveries of cultural anthropology are implicit in the structure of *Saint Glinglin*. . . . *Saint Glinglin* is by turns strange, beautiful, ludicrous, and intellectually stimulating. Nothing in Queneau's later work except *Petite cosmogonie portative* reaches the same level. (pp. 76-7)

Un rude hiver (A Hard Winter) . . . like *Odile*, is a short exercise in the traditional novel. Unlike *Odile*, however, this little work is a masterpiece, written with the precision and economy of a craftsman who has learned most of what there is to know about narration. Queneau, in fact, has never had much difficulty in telling a fascinating story; his self-imposed difficulties have arisen from his desire to make the novel do so much more than this: to become a poem, a myth, a philosophic discourse. (p. 87)

In *Le Dimanche de la vie* Queneau has succeeded in creating a world virtually without dualism, without conflict. Even World War II, as presented here, becomes part of "the Sunday of life," and its real horrors are ignored. . . . If this be a Hegelian novel, it represents a period of synthesis in which the conflict of thesis and antithesis has been resolved. Here at last Queneau has escaped from the pessimism of his earlier work, and it is significant that Valentin is characterized not as a Gnostic but as a "benign atheist." His atheism, far from being a revolt against a God who permits evil, allows him a vision of the world that lies beyond good and evil. In spite of its characteristic touches of originality, this book is in no sense a New Novel. Perhaps its optimism would be sufficient to disqualify it, but in any case it is a carefully disguised didactic novel, more closely related to the *romans philosophiques* of Voltaire than to any later school of novel-writing. (pp. 97-8)

Queneau gave *Zazie dans le métro* an epigraph in Greek from Aristotle: *"Ho plasas ephanisen."* It means, roughly, "He who created it razed it to the ground". . . . This epigraph could also have been prefixed to *Le Chiendent*, to *Pierrot mon ami*, and to several other novels by Queneau. They remind us of those notoriously elaborate pieces of contemporary "sculpture" in the Dadaist tradition that, when set in motion, more or less efficiently destroy themselves. . . . [Many] other New Novels . . . are circular and/or self-destructive, from Robbe-Grillet's *The Erasers* to Simon's *The Flanders Road* and Pinget's *The Inquisitory*. All such works embody an anxious search for reality and a profound skepticism about the existence of the object of their search. But the priority in time belongs indisputably to Queneau. . . . (pp. 102-03)

> *Vivian Mercier, "Raymond Queneau: The Creator as Destroyer," in his* The New Novel: From Queneau to Pinget *(reprinted with the permission of Farrar, Straus & Giroux; copyright © 1966, 1967, 1968, 1971 by Vivian Mercier), Farrar, Straus, 1971, pp. 43-103.*

It is hard to imagine a novel lighter than ["The Flight of Icarus"] that would seriously engage the mind. Yet . . ., though it is continuously absurd, [the novel] never strikes us as silly. The style is chaste and swift, ornamented with inventions translated as "obnubilating," "spondulics," "ostreophagists," "petroliphagious," "cantharodrome." The many threads of the cat's-cradle plot are complicated and regathered with an impressive efficiency. (pp. 122-23)

Objecting to the plot's basic fantasy, the reader might say that one does not meet fictional characters on the street; the answer would be that one is not on the street but reading a book, where one meets fictional characters all the time. The reader's demand, that is, for reality is turned back upon itself. The characters are uniformly real, "characters" or not. And the milieu is perfectly convincing. (p. 123)

> *John Updike, "Mortal Games," in* The New Yorker *(© 1974 by The New Yorker Magazine, Inc.), February 25, 1974, pp. 122-23.*

R

RANSOM, John Crowe   1888-1974

A Southern American poet, critic, and man of letters, Ransom influenced the literary world as a major proponent of New Criticism and as a member of the "Fugitive Group" of poets (along with Robert Penn Warren and Allen Tate) writing in Nashville from 1915 to 1928. His gently ironic poems often contain domestic subjects and explore the dilemma of the romantic and the intellectual. (See also *Contemporary Authors*, Vols. 5-8, rev. ed.; obituary, Vols. 49-52.)

Structure is how you get there and texture is what you do with it or how you stay there. . . . [Ransom examined the structure-texture relationship in many papers.]

Epistemology and ontology are the media through which Ransom experiences the problem of the relation between thought and feeling. Here once again is the solipsist trying to find out how he knows the only thing he can trust in the world he creates—the formal aspects in which it appears; but trying also to find some formal means, through the relation of texture to structure, of discussing the actual burden of knowledge as also a set of formal relations. Ontology is being: being, one supposes, is not a relation at all, nor a form; and what Ransom is really after is what inhabits form and what suffers relations.

If Tate enjoys the power of received philosophy, Ransom enjoys the fascinated power of that mind which is concerned with manufacturing the mode of a philosophy that has not been received. He creates the scaffold of system after system for Tate to see through and beyond. This is why Tate instigates insight and why Ransom instigates practice, instigations which multiply each other's value. (pp. 623-24)

> *R. P. Blackmur, in* Sewanee Review *(reprinted by permission of the editor; © 1959 by the University of the South), Autumn, 1959.*

Ransom's angle of vision is essentially comic. Rueful, wry, ironic, he "endures," and, even more, accepts. The land which he loves has been so long in disorder that the right hierarchy can hardly be hoped for; it must be celebrated by the remnant in little "pockets of culture." . . . Good manners, courtesy, rituals are all important because man is cut off from the garden and must make his way in a world of desperate difficulties. But there is sentiment and devotion, and the world's body is inexhaustibly interesting. (p. 17-18)

One of Ransom's strongest aesthetic presuppositions . . . [is] that poetry is born of experience, not of innocence; it is "post-scientific," rather than "pre-scientific," as he later expresses it—not the work of a child or of "that eternal youth that is in some women," . . . but of a sensible and masculine adult. For, though poetry honors the feminine—the realm of feeling and value—it is not the expression of the feminine or of the childish. It is not written by sentimentalists or innocents or holy fools, but by those who have struggled with the world. . . . [It] is this attitude that has governed his own work all along, his poetry as well as his prose.

A second principle controlling his total vision has caused him to be called a "dualist": this is the tenet that in a poem the prose meaning, a logical "structure," . . . is made to submit to an apparently unrelated and independent body of sense particulars of both sound and imagery, the "texture" of the poem, in what he sometimes calls a "miracle" of equilibrium. All his other generative ideas—those concerning myth, form, "metaphysical poetry," and the anonymity of the poet—are related to this structure-texture reconciliation, a theme to which he has returned again and again throughout his entire career. His position on this question, however, does not in reality constitute a dualism so much as a dynamism; he is concerned with a total pattern of poetic action, the imaginative process. But however one wishes to categorize his position, what must be seen as underlying all Ransom's critical thought is the conviction that a complete act of knowledge consists, first, of the formation, by abstraction, of some general notion of how things ought to be and then, later, the discovery, in an encounter with the actual world, that things are not after all quite so simple. It is this submission to the reality outside the mind without any relinquishment of the governing idea within the mind that, according to Ransom, has created myth, culture, tradition, manners, and poems. (pp. 19-20)

God Without Thunder (1930) . . . is a work central to the understanding of Agrarianism, as well as the whole body of Fugitive-Agrarian criticism. It is surprising that the remarkable originality of this book has been so little noted; ideas throughout its pages anticipate Carl Jung, Mircea Eliade, Eric Voegelin, Susanne Langer, Philip Wheelwright, and other critics treating the topics of myth, symbol, and culture. But though Ransom's understanding of these matters is quite modern, his total vision is based very firmly on early Protestant Orthodoxy (the religious terminology provides the book with its richly wry and ironic tone). *God Without Thunder* is not about religion, however, despite its open references to it; it is about myth and culture and the way in which human beings transform abstract notions through their love of sensible objects. It is also about a tendency of society to destroy itself through what Ransom chooses to call "science"—actually a death drive that has the appearance of a life force. The fall of man came about, he maintains, from the hybris of attempting to control nature through scientific knowledge, as the myths both of the Garden of Eden and of Prometheus testify. (pp. 23-4)

Ransom was later to turn his attention away from the cultural and religious concerns of *God Without Thunder* but he was never to desert the principles which they caused him to formulate. Indeed, most of his critical writing during the thirties stemmed directly from his Agrarian commitment. In *The World's Body* (1938), one of the most important landmarks in modern criticism, Ransom brought together fifteen essays on poetry and the specifically poetic mode of knowledge; but far from being purely exegetical in their concerns, these essays imply an entire universe delineated by his social and cultural thought. At least two of the pieces in *The World's Body* are classics; both convey so intimate and engaging a sense of the pleasures of poetry that they teach as much by personal witness as by the formulation of principles.

In one of them, "Forms and Citizens," . . . Ransom [uses] analogy to justify formal versification in poetry. The poetic imagination is a model of indirection par excellence, he points out; formally restraining itself from immediate possession, its aim is to enhance the value of the object through close and reverent attention.

This enunciation of an epistemology of poetic knowledge is followed by an essay on the nature of poetry: "Poetry: A Note in Ontology" is the *locus classicus* for Ransom's elaboration upon the dualistic tension inside the poetic act. In this essay he differentiates between Physical poetry, which is about things, and Platonic poetry, which is about ideas. (pp. 26-7)

[For] Ransom, it must be the *order* which is the differentiating principle of a poem, not the kind of content or the strictly logical sequence of thought. The "worlds" given us by our scientific discourses are "reduced, emasculated, and docile versions" of the world in which we live . . . (p. 29)

What Ransom has discerned in the world—and found reflected in poetry—is a peculiar harmony, a "miraculous" blending of disparates into an ordered whole. He has declared in one of his most recent essays that he has never departed from the religion learned from his father at the turn of the century. And it is true that, for all his philosophical preoccupations, his view of the world is essentially religious and theistic; he has experienced it in the mode of the Biblical faith. His intellect was formed by the classics and matured by the moderns; Kant, Hegel, Schopenhauer, and Bergson, among others, have vied with Plato and Aristotle in his thinking. Like these nineteenth-century philosophers, he is fundamentally anti-rationalistic, with a mistrust of scientific abstraction deriving not so much from their influence

as from an inherently poetic mode of thought. Still, for all his anti-abstractionism, Ransom has never been able to relinquish in his poetic theory the emphasis on logical meaning. Poetic knowledge is, for him, not unrelated to life in general. He rebukes Cleanth Brooks for objecting to the paraphrase of a poem and quarrels with Richard Blackmur for treating the ideas in a poetic structure as having no importance in the real world, even though they may be ideas upon which, at the very moment, out in the world of action, crucially important issues of life and death depend. "No faith, no passion of any kind," he tells us [in *Poems and Essays*], "is originated in a poem; it is brought into the poem by the 'imitating' of life (to use Aristotle's term); it is the fact which is the heart of the fiction." (pp. 32-3)

The poetic universe, then, to Ransom is a small, complex model which sets in motion and reconciles three modes of experience which have become, to civilized man, quite disparate and unrelated: first, rational experience; second, the experience of feeling and desire; third, the grand universals that cannot be stated, but only sounded—in a measured rhythm that calls all the language of the poem to an observance of its punctuation. The poem gives men knowledge that is applicable to the world of affairs; it reminds them of their myths; it teaches them restraint and piety. (pp. 33-4)

> *Louise Cowan, in her* The Southern Critics *(copyright 1972 The University of Dallas Press), University of Dallas Press, 1972.*

John Crowe Ransom died . . . fifty-four years after the first issue of the *Fugitive* appeared. Donald Davidson died in 1968. Robert Penn Warren and I are left of the men who became poet-critics and whose lives were powerfully influenced by J. C. R. I would say, with Yeats, that I am accustomed to his lack of breath, but it will be harder to believe that he no longer occupies space, silent and unknowing as he was in the last few years. Now we may ignore, as we see fit, the destructive revisions which this great elegiac poet inflicted upon many of his finest poems. (p. 545)

Logic was the mode of his thought and sensibility. It limited his criticism to a kind of neoclassicism, but it contained, as "structure," his poetry; and thus the defect of the one became the virtue of the other. I have for years wondered how such an acute intelligence could seriously consider any formula for poetry, and I am still amazed that John Ransom, of all people, could come up with "structure" and "texture" as a critical metaphor. After the elaborate essays in Kantian philosophical aesthetics, the simple structure-texture formula is a sad anticlimax—as sad as the late Yvor Winters's formula. Winters said, over some thirty years, that "the concept motivates the emotion." . . . May we say that Winters's concept is Ransom's structure, and his emotion, Ransom's texture? All these correspondences are only proximate, but they witness a remarkably similar critical impulse in men of different ages and backgrounds. I have no explanation of the astonishing fact that three Americans but no Europeans in the modern age tried to encapsulate poetry. (pp. 546-47)

John Ransom was not an innovator in the sense that both Pound and Eliot were. He was a shy, subtle innovator in ways that could not be imitated and could not found a school. He wrote in conventional stanzas and meters, but his sensibility owed nothing to any poet, past or present. (Some critics have seen in him Hardy, others Donne. But this means little. Every poet resembles some other poet somewhere; if he didn't he would be an idiot.) Most of the great poems—"The Equilibrists," "Bells for John Whiteside's Daughter," "Vaunting Oak," "Spectral Lovers," "Winter Remembered," "Necrological," "Captain Carpenter"—all these in *Chills and Fever*—were written between 1922 and 1924. After 1924 his work lay in another direction: critical and philosophical prose. But he wrote, in the thirties, two of his finest—in my opinion his greatest—poems: "Painted Head" and "Prelude to an Evening." The latter he ruined by rewriting it so that it would have a "happy ending." Nevertheless the original version cannot be destroyed. I infer that "Painted Head" pleased him in his old age: until his literary executor finds a revised version among his papers, we may believe the poem is safe.

In the past ten years I have thought of John's mania (I don't know what else to call it) as the last infirmity of a truly noble mind. Yet one must see his compulsive revisions as a quite consistent activity—as an extension of his reliance on *logic* as the ultimate standard of judgment. (pp. 549-50)

Among his great essays, possibly written with his logical guard down—or perhaps the subjects bypassed it, are "Poets without Laurels" and "Wanted: An Ontological Critic." The ontological critic would investigate the grades of reality that a poem embodied. What other critic, almost an exact contemporary of John's, had arrived at the same doctrine though in very different terms? What other critic had also studied philosophy with the intention of teaching it or of becoming in some other capacity a professional philosopher? The one guess as to the answer is: T. S. Eliot. (Neither liked the other's criticism. Eliot liked Ransom's poetry better than Ransom liked his. Eliot's opinions I got by word of mouth; Ransom's, by word of mouth and from published essays and reviews.) The doctrine they shared is an ancient one that every age must rediscover. Eliot: whether a work is poetry must be decided by literary criteria; whether it is *great* poetry, by other than literary criteria. Ransom: the grade of being, or the ontological value, of a poem must be discerned philosophically by critics of sufficient wisdom; whether the work is poetry will depend on its degree of rightness in the structure-texture relation, neither obscuring the other. What both Eliot and Ransom arrive at in the end is that only persons of ripe experience both of literature and of the world can be proper critics of poetry.

Another great essay, "Poets without Laurels," I consider the *locus classicus* for insight into the relation of the modern poet to industrial-technological society. The poet is no longer a public figure; he is no longer "laureled." He is a private person who writes poems for other poets to read. He writes either pure poetry (Stevens) or obscure poetry (Tate!). All this is commonplace? The simple truth is never commonplace unless it is spoken by a commonplace mind. I risk the guess that Eliot's essays will be read, by that mythical character posterity, for their opinions; Ransom's, for their style, regardless of what they say. For John Ransom wrote the most perspicuous, the most engaging, and the most elegant prose of all the poet-critics of our time.

A few days after his death I came across (for at least the hundredth time) an essay entitled "In Amicitia." He wrote it for my sixtieth birthday. This essay isolates me; for

surely I am the only pupil who has ever had such affectionate approbation from his master. For John Crowe Ransom was Virgil to me, his apprentice. It is proper to recall the words of another apprentice: I salute thee, Montovano. . . . (pp. 550-51)

> *Allen Tate, "Reflections on the Death of John Crowe Ransom" (1974), in* Sewanee Review *(reprinted by permission of the editor;* © *1974 by The University of the South), Fall, 1974, pp. 545-51.*

In Ransom's writings there is always discernible a certain unease amid the heady currents of thought and attitude of the modern world, and a sense of his use of modernism as being a kind of strategy for coping with what he cannot avoid. (p. 591)

John Crowe Ransom's poetry and the philosophy that underlies it are built upon a dualism. The poetry illustrates and embodies the conflicting claims of the ideal and the real, the spirit and the flesh. The poems are based on divisions, usually that of heart versus head. What worried Ransom was the intellectual effort to falsify the perilous balance that he considered life to involve, by a too-strenuous assertion of the ideal, in the form of one variety or another of Platonic abstraction. (pp. 598-99)

He seemed to formulate his opinions and his ideas as the result of a rigorous reasoning process, and to use such a process to discipline and subjugate his emotions, so that he held not merely views but systematized intellectual positions, from which he could move by logic to cover his entire experience, and could order that experience with a consistency that was very important to him. (p. 606)

Ransom's philosophical stance was no merely catch-as-catch-can affair, but a highly sophisticated and logically developed position which, depending upon the form it took, might be extended into poetry, politics, society, philosophy, theology, or whatever and still reflect a consistent attitude. The dualistic base upon which Ransom erected his hypotheses and out of which he created his poetry is predicated upon the rival claims of the intellect and the feelings, the reason and the emotions, the idea and the fact. His definition of poetry is of a logical structure and a seeming textural "irrelevance" of language, which work against and upon each other to produce the unique artifact which is the poem, and which thereby, in the transaction between the idea and the image, produce a kind of suspended "miraculous" knowledge of the nature of reality, which is there not for use but for contemplation. Discussing "The Future of Poetry" in the *Fugitive* for February 1924, he declared that "no art and no religion is possible until we make allowances, until we manage to keep quiet the *enfant terrible* of logic that plays havoc with the other faculties." This approach involves a kind of Armageddon of its own: the contending forces of structure and texture, head and heart, meet and grapple with each other, and out of the combat comes a report from the battlefield, which is the poem, and which constitutes the peace settlement. It was usually Ransom's habit to portray the forces of the head, which he was apt to term Platonizing, scientific, structural, abstract, predatory, as the aggressor in such a battle. In his brilliant essay of the 1930s "Poetry: A Note in Ontology" he presented the matter this way: "The aesthetic moment appears as a curious moment of suspension; between the Platonism in us, which is militant, always sciencing and devouring, and a starved inhibited aspiration towards innocence which, if it could only be free, would like to respect and know the object as it might of its own accord reveal itself."

Without attempting any kind of psychological inquiry, one is nonetheless impelled to point out that the author of that brilliant definition was a reasoner of the first magnitude, a rigorous conceptual thinker who moved toward his conclusions with relentless logic. With Ransom it was never the flash of intuition, the sudden deduction that produces results, but the patient dialectical development. (pp. 607-08)

The dialectic method Ransom used was not open-ended in its possibilities; he started out from strongly-held moral, social, and ethical premises, and what he always moved toward, with masterful skill and subtlety of discrimination, was the restatement and reaffirmation of those premises in terms of the chosen context of the argument. (p. 609)

Ransom's poetics aims to recapture the claim to knowledge of the world from the scientists and the abstract philosophers by claiming for poetry a more complete, more comprehensive reality, based not merely upon its logical structure but upon the recalcitrant and unique particularities of its texture. The poem, through the imaginative and creative clash of these opposing tendencies, provides the world's body—the "body and solid substance of the world" in which we live, the "fulness of poetry, which is counterpart to the world's fulness." It is no accident that the product of this process is "miraculous"—an entity that cannot be apprehended through its idea structure or its physical imagic texture alone. "Specifically, the miraculism arises," he declared, "when the poet discovers by analogy an identity between objects which is partial, though it should be considerable, and proceeds to an identification which is complete." (pp. 609-10)

Throughout his career the identification of the artist and the moralist, of poetry and religion, was never dropped. It should be no surprise, therefore, to find him proclaiming in the uniqueness of the poem the affirmation of the world's body, the miraculism that actualizes the knowledge of God, and the creation of poetry as a religious act. What he has done, within the much broader and more sophisticated context of his literary and philosophical studies, is to reaffirm the rightness of the religious faith in which he was reared. He has, in effect, reasoned his reliance upon religious belief through poetic theory, in order to "quiet the *enfant terrible*" of a destructive logic. Not being a young man of the orthodox Methodism of the late nineteenth-century South, but a twentieth-century southerner educated at Vanderbilt and Oxford and unable to accept the kind of literal revealed Protestant theology he chides in his *Poems About God*, he has had to employ the logic of ontology and aesthetics to arrive at a justification for the religious impulse through poetry. (pp. 610-11)

He is not considered an "autobiographical" poet, and his poetics would appear to leave little room for first-person lyric self-justification. All the same it might be noted how often his poetry describes just such a cycle of early identification, then alienation, then ultimate reaffirmation as we have recognized in his career. (p. 615)

He had a compulsion to make logical sense of himself and his experience. He was powerfully drawn toward logic and reason, and he was also mightily attached to everyday middle-class society and the old religious community.

Unless we understand that Ransom's penchant for logical argumentation, his relentless dialectic, was in part at least a way of organizing and systematizing an intense emotional life, a method of discipline for his strenuous imagination, we will miss an essential truth about this very passionate man and poet. For Ransom, as those of his fellow Fugitives who have written about him all attest, was by no means the friendly avuncular man of reason that his genial manner and his courtly demeanor seemed to indicate; far from it. He did indeed have a formidable analytical mind; he took ideas very seriously, and his thinking was methodical and rigorous. . . . But there was more to the man than the thought; the same mind that worked out the poetics and the theory wrote the poems. He insisted on poetry as a way of knowing the world, superior in its fulness of apprehension to the partial truths of science and philosophy; and there can be no doubt that he believed that because he perceived it thus for himself. Out of this amiable and unpretentious but ultimately very private and strong-willed man came some of the best poetry of the twentieth century, and also some provocative and creative thinking about poetry and society; and these were the product of passion disciplined by logic and made formally felicitous by strategy. Ransom was no sweet reasoner; that was only his tactical method. He held strong convictions, felt emotions powerfully, and when he took his stand, he meant it. (pp. 617-18)

> *Louis D. Rubin, Jr., "The Wary Fugitive John Crowe Ransom," in* Sewanee Review *(reprinted by permission of the editor; © 1974 by The University of the South), Fall, 1974, pp. 583-618.*

For the past two decades or more John Crowe Ransom was the dean of American letters. This was as it should be, and the man's continuing fame was among the few pleasant aspects of the postwar literary scene. . . . Now that Ransom is lodged among the illustrious dead (his work had long since passed into literary history), his reputation as a man of letters will inevitably suffer; but the essential stature is certain and will endure. In the generations to come Ransom the elegiac poet will be read as long as poetry is valued; and he should always be remembered, though not rated so highly, as a teacher, editor, and critic. It will be hard to overestimate this man's contribution to modern letters. The same is true of Yeats, Eliot, and Auden in varying ways but in gaudier, more obvious fashion; in the course of time Ransom will probably occupy the same pantheon: his contribution to literature will ultimately be judged as great as Auden's and within reach of Yeats and Eliot.

It is Ransom the critic who has eluded definition—not Ransom the poet. The failure does not result from his having been neglected as critic: quite the contrary is the case. Criticism by friend and foe alike (especially Yvor Winters) has frequently been levelled at the writer for the inconsistencies and defects in his theory of structure and texture . . .; but when all is said and done, one must ask what modern critic has presented more comprehensive investigations into poetry. Since Coleridge, who in Great Britain or the United States has written a more searching and convincing formulation of poetry? (pp. 619-20)

Ransom wished to broaden and deepen the philosophical base of criticism so that it would possess an ontology which could fully contend with human behavior as one sees it re-fracted through the medium of art or instanced in "the con-tagion of art." With such a strategy any obstacle could be overcome: one could not only properly interpret the most demanding fiction but withstand the assault of unphilosoph-ical critics.

Ransom unquestionably located the Achilles heel of the New Criticism. The philosophical deficiency is of much greater importance than the alleged antihistorical or unhis-torical attitude which the new critics are said to evince. (They instead have inveighed against the useless impedi-menta of historical scholarship—not against history itself and the relation it bears to the proper study of literature, an entirely different matter.)

This is all to say that John Crowe Ransom was the most philosophical of the new critics, and yet we must remember that he regularly denounced the abstraction that is often associated with philosophical thinking and always de-manded concreteness and specificity in poetry. Therefore for him the true richness of a poem was to be found in its local texture of language and metaphor—not in the intended fable and theme, the logical structure or argument (whether the intention exists before or after the fact of the poem). (pp. 621-22)

Ransom argues for the primacy of the concrete element—the image, not the idea; the metaphor (and conceit), not the concept; the myth, not the dogma. But there must be a con-junction of the physical object and the Platonic idea; other-wise one gets the pure poetry of things—imagism—or the abstract poetry of ideas—allegory. In bringing together the natural object and the unattached idea the poet uses the greatest weapon in his arsenal—analogy—and if he brings it to bear properly, he forges metaphysical poetry, thus bal-ancing idea against fact.

In "Poetry: A Note in Ontology" Ransom defines modes; in "The Concrete Universal" he considers the largest phil-osophical bases upon which the metaphysical mode of po-etry may be grounded. Hence he can conclude: "The play between the understanding with its moral Universal on the one hand, and on the other hand Imagination presenting the purposive Concrete of nature, is unpredictable and inex-haustible." This summary statement provides the capstone for Ransom's house of poetry. He built a structure capable of sustaining infinite variety which can support many man-sions, and the foundation had been quarried out of Kant, Hegel, and Coleridge. (p. 623)

Ransom is less interested in the poet's choice of material—his imaginative projection so far as a particular kind of ex-perience is concerned—than he is in the writer's actual per-formance. This critic sees the subconscious mind and the conscious as far less significant than the work itself. For Ransom the poet's intention counts for little: what we need to examine is the document which results from his labors. Therefore Ransom characteristically examined the means of the poem's order: the ways in which the author has con-trolled the energy of his language which provides the ve-hicle by which he can at once enclose and reveal experi-ence. The language has got to be submitted to the restraining element of meter and the life-giving dimension of metaphor, and through the mechanical discipline of the one and the miraculous play of the other the poet can per-form his craft and make his poems. (pp. 624-25)

Ideally the poem embodies the essence of human behavior, a microcosm which contains "nearly everything we can possibly desire. It is the best of all possible worlds." Or, put differently, "poetry furnishes the perfect form of exper-ience; and reminds us that it is a dramatic rather than a real experience." (p. 627)

Logic (experience under the aspect of a governing idea or theme), metaphoric language, and meter are therefore the constituent parts of a poem as Ransom saw it. (The interac-tion of the three elements is much more complicated, sub-tle, and complex than the apparently simple relation of tex-ture to structure, the equation that was originally proposed and which has been ascribed to Ransom since.) (pp. 627-28)

The most serious possible deficiency in Ransom's theoret-ical formulations about poetry would seem to involve his neglect of the emotive dimension of the poem. . . . He seemed to be so chary of a poetry of the feelings which simply expresses the personality of the poet—a poetry that "taints us with subjectivism, sentimentality, and self-indulgence"—that he altogether discounted the importance of emotion and stressed cognition. Hence, for him, the best poetry is metaphysical—a poetry of knowledge; and one remembers that he on several occasions approvingly al-luded to Schopenhauer's phrase "knowledge without de-sire" as being indicative of an attitude appropriate for po-etry. (pp. 629-30)

John Ransom was a poet-critic who could write with equal authority about Shakespeare, Milton, Wordsworth, Hardy, Yeats, and Eliot. (p. 636)

[He] was never comfortable with the world he inhabited after 1914, and he took considerable pains to keep it at a suitable distance and in the right perspective. His literary criticism represents part of that taxing effort of the will and the imagination. The poetry is another aspect of the same effort. The criticism undergirds the poetry; the poetry spec-ifies the criticism; but neither art (and the criticism is an art) simply exists to complement the other.

As Robert Penn Warren has said, the criticism for all its concern with philosophical grounding is urbane and witty, charged by passion and delight. "The air is . . . of a collab-orative quest." He continues: "For Ransom, criticism, like poetry itself, is one of the ways of trying to live life with intelligence, logical scrupulosity, and moral rigor, but, withal, with gaiety, feeling, and respect for the human other." It is easy to neglect this dimension of Ransom's prose . . . in examining his characteristic formulations, his recurring concerns; it is more reprehensible to neglect the style and tone.

John Ransom was, as Allen Tate has observed, a gen-tleman in a dustcoat whose "civility of demeanor" was both gentle and severe (like Hardy before him). This sever-ity, the toughness of mind behind the smiling face and the apparently diffident manner, has often been misinterpreted. His was a classical severity (Hellenistic, as Arnold would have put it), an unrelenting stance which was ceremonious and courtly but still deeply felt and real—and no less impor-tant in the criticism than in the poetry. (p. 637)

John Crowe Ransom came graciously to terms with himself and his world—so must we, his readers, follow the configu-ration of the career in order to understand the complex man behind the prose and the poetry which are the principal record of that life. This, I am aware, violates a cardinal rule of the New Criticism as it is generally understood (or misunderstood). But how else can one understand the southern new critics? And how else can one realize the fullness of Ransom's call for an ontological criticism? It is this example—his performance as ontological critic—which not only powerfully influenced the southern literary renascence but deeply affected the whole course of contemporary criticism. (p. 638)

> *George Core, "Mr. Ransom and the House of Poetry,"in* Sewanee Review *(reprinted by permission of the editor;* © *1974 by The University of the South), Fall, 1974, pp. 619-38.*

*   *   *

REED, Ishmael   1938-

A distinguished Black American novelist, poet, and critic, Reed informs his fiction with black magic and satire. (See also *Contemporary Authors*, Vols. 23-24.)

Reed speaks bluntly and uses dialect, blues rhythms, and slang, not in conformity with some theoretical program but because he can make them work. He is at his best with the jaunty seriousness of "Loup Garoup Means Change Into" and "Railroad Bill, a Conjure Man," and at his worst, in "Kali's Galaxy," when he abandons the direct rhythms of speech and gets pinnacled dim in the intense inane. (p. 106)

It is surprising how utterly free from melancholy and the sweet languor of despair ["Chattanooga"] is. The seductiveness of death and the fascination of suffering hold no charms for Reed. He doesn't like victims, doesn't really believe in them. . . . Reed is at home in the world, content to talk about Chattanooga in the vernacular and not to grab the first gilded bus to Jerusalem Celeste. There is a lot to be said for a man who is bored by death, defeat, and martyrdom, who has the good taste to accost that prototype of righteous losers, the frequently insufferable Antigone, in no uncertain terms. (pp. 107-08)

> *Thomas Stumpf, in* Carolina Quarterly *(© copyright 1974 by* Carolina Quarterly*), Winter, 1974.*

In his first novel, *The Free-Lance Pallbearers* (1967), Ishmael Reed emphatically declares what he will *not* do as a Black writer. Bukka Doopeyduk's narrative retells the tale told by countless Black heroes in Afro-American literature of their journey into the heart of whiteness only to deride its formulary disclosures and protests. Yet in parodying this confessional mode (the denouement of Doopeyduk's tale is his own crucifixion), Reed also attacks those Black writers who adopt fashionable approaches to experimental writing, who strive to be "Now-here" in "Nowhere." To turn from the stiffening form of the traditional novel James Baldwin shares with John Updike only to fall into the linguistic despair of William Burroughs or the elaborate glosses of metafiction is an artistic fate Reed has taken great pains to avoid. And therein lies the problem that has informed his subsequent fiction, *Yellow Back Radio Broke-Down* (1969) and *Mumbo Jumbo* (1972). How does one comprehend the significance of Burroughs' narrative form, write in the parodic manner of Thomas Pynchon and Donald Barthelme, and at the same time hold an opposed view of history, an

optative, almost Emersonian sense of the dawning day? In his collection of poetry, *Conjure* (1972), Reed unequivocally asserts that Neo-HooDoo, this new direction in Afro-American literature, constitutes "Our Turn," a radical severance of his destiny as a writer from the fate of his White contemporaries. Appropriately the final poem, "introducing a new loa," transforms Burroughs' emblematic nova, the dying light of Western civilization, into a "swinging HooDoo cloud," the birth of a new Africanized universe of discourse. "I call it the invisible train," he writes, "for which this Work has been but a modest schedule."

The course of Reed's experimentation with narrative has thus increasingly involved his conception of Neo-HooDoo as a literary mode. My purpose in this essay is simply to take him at his word—the considerable claim that he has found a way of writing fiction unlike those decreative and self-reflexive fictive modes in which his White contemporaries seem imprisoned. Reed is careful, of course, not to establish Neo-HooDoo as a school. It is rather a characteristic stance, a mythological provenance, a behavior, a complex of attitudes, the retrieval of an idiom, but however broadly defined, Neo-HooDoo does manifest one constant and unifying refrain: Reed's fiercely professed alienation from Anglo-American literature. Ultimately, then, Neo-HooDoo is political art, as responsible as Richard Wright's *Native Son*, but without Wright's grim realism or the polemical separatism that characterizes Imamu Baraka's work. For Reed the problem is to get outside the "Euro-Am meaning world" (Baraka's term) without getting caught as an artist in a contraposed system. . . . In Reed's fiction, particularly the novels after *Pallbearers*, this rigorous denial of the "dominant culture" and its critical values has led to paradoxes and ambiguities that are exceptionally "good" in the terms of "that traditional critique." One can invent myths, invoke legends, change his name and dress, but he cannot will himself into another language. And it is specifically literary language with its seductive devices, its forms and rhetoric, that pulls the self-styled exile back into the consciousness he professes to despise. More than any other contemporary Black writer, Reed seems aware of this dilemma, the difficulty of fashioning an art form that will liberate him from the double consciousness signified by the hyphen between Afro and American. Yet this liberation is the objective of *Pallbearers*, the meaning of its negations, and the challenge of his later fiction.

As the narrator of *Pallbearers*, Doopeyduk speaks literally from the grave. The scat-singing voice that introduces the novel does not belong to the Doopeyduk who speaks within the narrative duration of *Pallbearers*. In killing off that latter Doopeyduk, Reed murders a style, the Black writer's appropriation of what D. H. Lawrence (in a different context) called "art-speech." Doopeyduk's attempt to fashion his discourse in formal English only reveals his stupidity, an ignorance not of correct grammar or proper diction, but of his world. For the language in which he invests his feelings and perceptions is a dead language. He speaks to his wife, the combustible Fannie Mae, as though he were translating a text, and her response is appropriately ribald. It is not, however, just the White man's "art-speech" in the Black man's voice that Reed burlesques. He attacks as well the conventions of Afro-American literature, its traditional modes of rendering and interpreting Black experience. . . . The structure on which Reed relies in this narrative, which he inflates and explodes, is the structure of Richard Wright's *Black Boy*, Ralph Ellison's *Invisible Man*, and the many subsequent books like them: *"read growing up in Soulsville first of three installments/or what it means to be a backstage darky."* Reed delivers the obligatory scenes of such confessional fiction with studied vulgarity.... The rites of passage established by Wright, Ellison, and Baldwin in their fiction are stripped of their dramatic force and reduced to the pratfalls of a burlesque routine. (pp. 126-28)

At his best, ... Reed achieves the surrealistic brilliance of Burroughs' skits in *Naked Lunch*. But between these extremes the prose often stalls in orthographical and grammatical posturing—misspelling for the hell of it. Finally, then, the problem with Doopeyduk's posthumous voice is that it is too obviously worked, too strained in its license. Burroughs' ability to transform street language, the idiom of the junk world, into powerfully stated and precise metaphors, a figurative language as dense and complex as any other in literature, remains the modern epitome of an accomplished colloquial style, an excellence Reed fails to attain in *Pallbearers*. What he does achieve, however, is the elliptical flow and quick displacements of Burroughs' narrative, the cutting edge of Burroughs' cold understanding of modern reality. The Hobbesian question—"Wouldn't you?"—posed in *Naked Lunch* as the resolution to the Algebra of Need is rephrased throughout *Pallbearers*.... Yet if Reed manages to erase the whiteness in his writing (the well-wrought form and rhetoric that won Baldwin so much critical praise) and breaks conclusively with the traditional novel, he does not emerge with a contrary Black style. The language of *Pallbearers* is an orchestration of idiolects, conflicting types of speech that caricature their speakers, but no single voice rules this contrived discordance....

Yellow Back Radio constitutes Reed's attempt to reconstruct a coherent perspective and viable form from the necessary wreckage of *Pallbearers*. Armed with supernatural "connaissance," the magic of poetry, the Loop Garoo Kid replaces Doopeyduk, the hapless victim, at the center of Reed's fiction. "One has to return," Reed writes in the introduction to *19 Necromancers*, "to what some writers would call 'dark heathenism' to find original tall tales, and yarns with the kind of originality that some modern writers use as found poetry—the enigmatic street rhymes of some of Ellison's minor characters, or the dozens. I call this neo-hoodooism; a spur to originality...." Neo-HooDoo as an experimental mode [is] the concept that informs *Yellow Back Radio*.... In its syncretistic composition, its diversity of gods and forms of worship, its avoidance of dogmatic structures, voodoo is Reed's reality-model, the known world forever hidden from the gaze of Westerners. Within it Loop is invulnerable; sheltered by ritual, aided by the endless resources of Nature, and empowered by the full possession of his body. (pp. 130-32)

The problem in *Yellow Back Radio* is to translate voodoo in a singular way of writing, to dislodge it from its status as a cultural myth and make it instead a state of consciousness. As we shall see, Reed does not write mythically—he writes about writing mythically.

If only in theory, then, Neo-HooDoo represents a new direction (so Reed argues) for the Black writer, an escape from the decadence of Anglo-American literature that re-

verses the path historically taken by Black writers and intellectuals in the United States. (p. 132)

But where are the "original folk tales" and native idioms in Reed's fiction? How far indeed does Neo-HooDoo (both as myth and mode) take him from established literary canons? His discourse in *Yellow Back Radio* and *Mumbo Jumbo* curves in and around colloquial Black English, which serves him as a stylistic device, not as a language. It is withal a learned and allusive discourse as mixed in its diction as Mark Twain's. His forms are not narrative legends taken from an oral tradition, but rather the popular forms of the Western and the Gangster Novel.... *Yellow Back Radio* is a Black version of the Western Burroughs has been writing in fragments and promising in full since the fifties. Not only is the content of the fiction eclectic in its composition, but Loop's performance as a *houngan* in it has a good deal of Burroughs' "Honest Bill." For the core of his narrative, Reed borrows almost intact the sociological drama Norman Mailer describes in *The White Negro*—that migration of White middle-class youth in revolt against the values of their own culture toward the counter-culture of Black America—and then weaves into this phenomenon a barely disguised account of the student uprisings at Berkeley and other campuses. The shooting at Kent State comes after the publication of *Yellow Back Radio*, but it is accurately prefigured in the book. (pp. 132-33)

Into this revised Western, ... Reed pours all the bitterness of present history. Certain Blacks betray Loop for the same dubious rewards that prompted Apache scouts to lead the cavalry to Geronimo. Official Washington is as blind and uncaring about the student massacre in the hinterland as it was during the Indian Wars of the 1880s. And like the Sioux after their crushing defeat at Wounded Knee, the victims of Gibson's peace (the students and Black militants of the sixties) dream apocalyptic dreams, create a drug culture (peyote/LSD), and retreat into themselves. So the narrative unfolds and draws to its necessary end. The only hold-out, the last authentic outlaw, is the artist, the worker of spells, Loop as necromancer. Yet in expanding the scope of the narrative in the final section to give Loop his mythopoeic due, Reed loses the bite of his allusive framework. The ending (Loop on a scaffold about to be hanged) presents a dazzling array of black-outs, bizarre Warholian bits, one-liners. But the laughter at the center of all this hilarity is so cold in its nihilism that it chills the book's critical perspectives.... [The] history that gives Reed his narrative line in *Yellow Back Radio* runs out on him.

When the Pope arrives near the end of the narrative ..., the book dissolves into lectures.... In effect, the Pope's arrival restores the hyphenated consciousness Reed seeks to annul in his fiction. It is the Pope who fills us in, who makes the connections that enable us to see how and why Loop works as a character. *Yellow Back Radio* thus turns into a book *about* Neo-HooDooism. And every explanation, every concealed footnote, betrays the artifice of the myth. Reed's mythopoeic lore is as arcane as the cryptic references strewn about in Burroughs' fiction. And his art, it would seem, bears as much relation to James Brown doing the "Popcorn" or Jimi Hendrix stroking his guitar as does T. S. Eliot's, whom Reed consigns in his manifesto to the graveyard of Christian culture....

In [*Mumbo Jumbo*] Reed concentrates on the Harlem Renaissance of the twenties (Langston Hughes, Countee Cullen, et al). . . . *Mumbo Jumbo*, then, is primarily an historical narrative, a tragicomical review of what went wrong in the twenties. . . . As such, the book is also an ingenious dissertation on the nature of Afro-American art, a dissertation with a program for the revival of that art.

By fracturing his narrative into a series of sub-texts (there is even a romance, Earline's love for Berbelang), Reed solves some of the problems that arise in *Yellow Back Radio*, notably the problem of introducing a great amount of mythological information. . . . Each story generates its own point of view . . . and gives Reed the ability to range widely over the dramatic possibilities within his myth. Similarly the diversity of these interpretations reflects the subtlety and complex nature of the Harlem Renaissance. (pp. 134-36)

Readers unfamiliar with the leading figures and notable disputes of the Harlem Renaissance will have a difficult time with *Mumbo Jumbo*. . . . Unlike *Yellow Back Radio*, where Reed's focus often seems simplistic and his energies diffused, *Mumbo Jumbo* swirls with the taut intricacy of a Jacobean revenge play. (p. 137)

[Though] Reed mercilessly attacks Eliot and Ezra Pound in *Conjure* as "Jeho-vah Revisionists," the archpriests of "atonist" literature, *Mumbo Jumbo* is as brocaded with mythic, literary, and historical allusions as either [*The Waste Land*] or the *Cantos*. . . . His fiction has become increasingly complex, learned, and witty (*Mumbo Jumbo* has a bibliography that extends for five pages). . . . In a sense, the problem with *Mumbo Jumbo* is that it is not mumbo jumbo at all. (p. 138)

Reed's Neo-HooDooist moves finally along the same metafictive angle that Pynchon and Barthelme take in their fiction, probing folklore and myth with the same seriocomic intent, to wrench from them their own truths. What distinguishes Reed's Neo-HooDooist is his adamant optimism, his belief that "print and words are not dead at all" . . ., the ringing note on which Reed ends his preface. (p. 139)

> *Neil Schmitz, "Neo-HooDoo: The Experimental Fiction of Ishmael Reed," in* Twentieth Century Literature *(copyright 1974, Hofstra University Press), April, 1974, pp. 126-40.*

In such original comic novels as *The Free-Lance Pallbearers*, *Yellow Back Radio Broke-Down* and *Mumbo Jumbo*, Ishmael Reed displayed powers of camouflage, mimicry and verbal play that drew praise from his peers—though very little cash from his publishers. As a black writer with a ticklish touch, Reed had to sit in the back of the literary omnibus until the white audience tired of having their heads whipped by the Cleavers and Joneses.

Yet Reed can hardly be accused of eye rolling and cakewalking for his supper. His angers and resentments are sheathed in intelligence, learning, scatological wit and showmanship. One thinks of Redd Foxx before he was Sanfordized, or Philip Roth confronting his middle-class American Jewish background in ways that have been judged, perhaps too hastily, as self-hateful and tasteless. Likewise, many blacks may find themselves both amused and offended by *The Last Days of Louisiana Red*, a combination circus freak show, detective story, Negro Dead Sea Scroll and improvised black-studies program. . . .

Reed spares precious few of his brothers and sisters. (He even offers a veiled suggestion that Angela Davis is the modern equivalent of the stern black mama figure trying to shape up her offspring in the absence of a father.) A minister named the Rev. Rookie is replaced by a Moog synthesizer; Maxwell Kasavubu, a button-down black literary critic, hallucinates that he is Richard Wright's illiterate murderer Bigger Thomas. Reed even brings back those veteran moochers from *Amos 'n' Andy*, the Kingfish and Andrew H. Brown, now trying to cash in on the street-corner Hindu racket. "Andy," says the Kingfish, "I think it's about time we went into the Karmel bizness."

Reed himself admits that he has more in common with Calvin Coolidge than with Dionysus. Bacchanalian plots and extended riffs of funky prose scarcely disguise the conservative folksiness within.

> *R. Z. Sheppard, "Gumbo Diplomacy," in* Time *(reprinted by permission from* Time, The Weekly Newsmagazine; *copyright Time Inc.), October 21, 1974, p. 119.*

It's not always easy to understand what is going on in . . . ["The Last Days of Louisiana Red"], and even when you do gain a slippery foothold, it is not necessarily for long. The pyrotechnics are all here, but the mixture of savage jokes, scathing social commentary, folklore, and black history that coalesced so well in his last novel, "Mumbo Jumbo," is a lot less funny and a lot more self-conscious and stagey. "Louisiana Red" is the author's euphemism for all the venal, cruel, competitive, self-deceiving, and self-defeating instincts in black men and women, which divide them and keep them enslaved. In the story, a huge, evil corporate entity called the Louisiana Red Corporation is pitted against an equally huge, but good, highly secretive company called the Solid Gumbo Works. Spies, double agents, liars, and hypocrites abound, and the antagonists drop like flies. Sometimes the social commentary is impressive and the satire quite funny, but the book hits out in so many directions at once that it eventually self-destructs. (pp. 208, 210)

> The New Yorker (© *1974 by the New Yorker Magazine, Inc.), November 4, 1974.*

Whoever called him Ishmael picked the right name. His hand is against every man's—and every woman's, too. Or so it seems. He is a black Juvenal, a man to whom satire comes as naturally as breathing. And, like Juvenal, he might well ask who could consider the last decade and not be a satirist. Especially if he concentrated on the San Francisco Bay area. So Ishmael Reed is a black satirist, which is not exactly the same thing as a black humorist. Oh no. Though his prose wickedly parodies everything from street talk to academic rhetoric, he is not to be confused with those who use their own cleverness as a shield against the ugly world. Ishmael Reed is a committed man, a satirist with a specific point of view. Beneath that funky facade beats the heart of a preacher.

Since his first novel, "The Free-Lance Pallbearers," appeared in 1967 he has been recognized as a writer of extraordinary facility. His prose has been compared to such masters of other media as Hieronymus Bosch and John Coltrane. With each new novel—"Yellow Back Radio Broke-Down" in 1969 and "Mumbo Jumbo" in 1972—his reputation has increased. In fact, people have been laughing at him so hard and praising him so indiscriminately that little attention has been paid to what he is saying. In his fourth novel ["The Last Days of Louisiana Red"] he is as funny as ever, but the message is coming through clearly, and not all those who understand it are going to find it palatable. For Reed is offering his own fiction as an antidote to certain elements of black mythology dear to the heart of liberal sociologists.

The world of "The Last Days of Louisiana Red" is a cartoonist's version of the last decade in Berkeley, Calif. . . .

Ishmael Reed has a shrewd eye, a mean ear, a nasty tongue. . . . [He] attacks self-serving hypocrisy wherever he finds it. . . .

[The hero] LaBas . . . exposes the false history of blacks in America, a history concocted and supported by white men and black women—who have always gotten along together very well. This false history fosters the myth that black women have been the only force holding families together over the years. LaBas [says] . . . that this belief is an insult to "the millions of negro men who've supported their families, freemen who bought their families freedom, negro men working as parking-lot attendants, busboys, slop emptiers, performing every despicable deed to make ends meet against tremendous odds." And through LaBas's words we hear the voice of Ishmael Reed, preaching up a storm. (p. 2)

> *Robert Scholes, in* The New York Times Book Review *(© 1974 by The New York Times Company; reprinted by permission), November 10, 1974.*

*   *   *

RICHLER, Mordecai   1931-

A Canadian novelist and journalist, Richler often draws on his urban Jewish background for his fiction.

[One] runs head-on into a curious discrepancy between what Mordecai Richler says he is writing about, what his heroes think they are railing against, and his novels' actual content. Granted that he employs the idiom and a few of the ideas ventilated by his American and English contemporaries, in terms of social viewpoint, feeling, and literary style Mordecai Richler unmistakably harks back to an earlier period. The best evidence for this is his preoccupation with the Marxist mirage and the Jewish middle-class family unit, the latter as it evolved in the East European *shtetl* and later in North America.

Neither is an issue of current validity. The subject of friction between first- and second-generation Jews and their American-born children is a noticeably exhausted one with such prominent American Jewish writers as Saul Bellow, Harvey Swados, Herbert Gold, Arthur Miller, Bernard Malamud, and Norman Mailer. Theirs is no cowardly neglect, no parvenu passion to disclaim their skullcap and prayer-shawl antecedents. In point of fact, this particular narrative vein began to peter out after the First World War with the cessation of the mass migrations from Russia and Poland. It dried up altogether by the time of the second world bloodbath. (p. 47)

Not that there is any scarcity of conflicts confronting the Jew as an individual or as a member of a group that would make the legitimate stuff of fiction. The point is that Mordecai Richler's concept excludes the middle-class Jew (the *lower* upper-middle-class Jew, to be precise) as he really is. *Son of a Smaller Hero* negotiates an obsolescent theme; moreover, the process is carried on in dated fashion. (p. 48)

The Richler vision embraces left-wing politics only, and the only type of left-wing politics and thinking that his novels appraise with any seriousness has a strong Marxist impulse. At that, it is a Marxism emotionally approached. There are few Communist characters in the books, and they are endowed with a blatantly bookish vocabulary. The impression grows that the author's contact with the ideology and its practitioners is based mostly on hearsay and casual encounters. Fundamentally his point is that the message of the Communist Manifesto formed our last chance to have something to believe in, something that gave the right answers to all questions. Now it has failed, and nothing remains. First went God, then gold, then Marx.

Now certainly Mordecai Richler has every right to concentrate on these matters. Only the writer can decide what material he should deal with. The people he feels are worth studying, the strains he cares to analyse and force and interpret, the dark corners of the human condition he chooses to light up—all are fitting grist for his mill. But he always takes the risk that his findings will be old and far from freshly seen, that they lack the broader, more universal meaning his limited experience suggests to him.

The salient fact about Mordecai Richler's blasting instruments (heavy irony, political attitudinizing, a pious taking for granted of one's superiority and greater wisdom) and his targets for attack is that of themselves they refute his belief that he is coping, squarely and frankly, with the relevant dilemmas of our time. (pp. 50-1)

Most of the men and women who pass through his pages are, by design, empty, trivial, disgusting, happy to vegetate in the safe cage of traditional principles, alarmed beyond belief by the perilous freedom of truth-seeking. They are so small, so worthless, so obviously (according to him) undeserving of compassion, that they are not worth caring about.

That Mordecai Richler is unable to see, and project, people as individuals is most demonstrable in the repetition of characters from novel to novel. Charlie Lawson, of *A Choice of Enemies*, appeared before in *Son of a Smaller Hero* as the culture-conscious professor and cuckold Theo Hall. Larkin, the foul-mouthed and foul-minded tourist visiting Spain with a gentile wife in *The Acrobats* is indistinguishable from Noah's uncle, Max, in *Son of a Smaller Hero*, a manufacturer with a gentile mistress. Sonny Winkelmann, the expatriates' leader in *A Choice of Enemies*, is simply an up-to-date version of the grandfather in *Son of a Smaller Hero*.

Then there are his women. Interestingly Mordecai Richler's novels deal with a man-dominated society; his treatment of the opposite sex suggests at the very least a deep distrust and contempt. Two kinds of female occupy his attention: the woman who takes for granted that an unpleasant time in bed is the contractual consideration for material security (Larkin's wife in *The Acrobats*, Margaret in *Son of a Smaller Hero*), and the woman who believes that happiness is only attainable through sexual gratification. The latter constitutes his heroine. Whether named

Toni or Miriam or Sally, she happily defies society's wrath to achieve her purpose. (pp. 53-4)

Essentially Mr. Richler's heroines are temporary pillows for his protagonists to lean on. Weak-minded creatures, they are stepping-stones leading his truth-seekers toward their freedom bridge. (p. 54)

The Richler heroes . . . never question the values they condemn. They just *know* they are bad. But how and why they fail, and by what means the light dawned on the hero and enabled him to grasp their falsity, we are never actually told.

As an example of the insufficiency of his heroes' value judgements, take the appraisal of the Canadian scene in Mordecai Richler's books. Canada in them consists of the Jewish ghetto in Montreal and a few adjacent neighbourhoods, a third-rate university and the attached teaching community, and a CBC television studio in Toronto. This minute landscape is enough, nevertheless, to make . . . [his protagonists take] for granted that the small subsection of it he has inherited is a microcosm, not just of the city but of the country. (pp. 55-6)

The dislike of Canada expressed in his novels does not issue from any genuinely-felt injury or effort to discover what this country is like, what elements hold it together, however shakily, or the nature of its identity such as that is. The unhappy truth is that Mordecai Richler is proffering what is scarcely more than the hit-and-miss, insubstantial chitchat of a pseudo-intellectual tea party as definitive, basic reasoning.

Here is the cruellest irony: the charges the heroes of the Richler view make against their antagonists apply, with equal validity, to themselves. They are selfish, oblivious to human dignity, cold, insensitive, conscienceless, wantonly destructive of personal relations. They have no nobility of spirit. Indeed, they are worse than the people around them since they presume to know better and insist on their superiority. Neither Nemesis nor Galahad, they run an erratic, footless course from anarchy to futility. Mordecai Richler is correct when he declares that few of his people are worth caring about, although there is more to most of them than he realizes. But he is wrong to suppose that his heroes are admirable exceptions. Alas, they are worth caring about the least of all. This is the weakness that causes the scaffolding of each of his novels to totter and give way. (pp. 56-7)

> *Nathan Cohen, "Heroes of the Richler View" (originally published in* Tamarack Review, *No. 6, 1957), in* Mordecai Richler, *edited by G. David Sheps (copyright ©️ McGraw-Hill Co. of Canada Ltd., 1971), McGraw-Hill/Ryerson, 1971, pp. 43-57.*

It is not seeing life steadily or whole to suggest [as Nathan Cohen, above, has] that Richler's novels express a dislike of Canada, any more than of Paris, Barcelona or the Finchley Road. . . . What is definitive and basic in *A Choice of Enemies* does not refer to Canada at all. It concerns the conflict for freedom and survival between a German . . ., a stunted gamma-product of defunct ideology, and a Canadian . . ., who, with all the weaknesses of being undetermined, has the strength of being not-quite-wholly defined. (p. 59)

In *The Acrobats*, Richler tended to write from within his characters, all of them; in *A Choice of Enemies* he tends to describe them as they appear and behave. This is a move towards maturity as a writer, even though, as is always the case with maturity, something must be lost. (p. 60)

In *Son of a Smaller Hero* one had the suspicion that Richler might develop more fully as a portraitist of a group than of an individual. His background seemed to come alive at a glance, while his intuitions of his hero were sometimes incoherent, sometimes unconvincing, sometimes embarrassingly personal. In *A Choice of Enemies*, however, the process of objectification has been almost completed. All of the characters are characters in themselves; no single one of them can be identified as the simply projection of Richler's *propria persona*. (p. 61)

[In] contrast to the facility with which his minor characters fall into view, Richler struggles to create his protagonists with a difficulty which is at once ungainly and arresting. They are, some would say, too important, his motives for creating them too serious, for the down-to-earth medium and style in which he works. Certainly it is true that at times there is a tendency for them to move, not according to their pattern, but to the simpler destiny of Richler's own. At the worst they are manipulated, do not behave but are made to behave, to reach more surely a previously conceived-of conclusion or inconclusion. . . . This tendency is one which Richler seems to have inherited obliquely from Sartre, his most obvious master: if indulged too far, it could reduce Richler's valid subject to a puppet or peep-show for the idiot-minded. In Sartre the problem is linked to the synthetic nature of existentialist psychology; it is both germane and irremediable. In the case of Richler, whose "philosophy" is eclectic, undisciplined, and tolerant, it is at odds with his deeper gift for accurate vision of diverse people in diverse situations. I would not suggest that the novel is a democracy, and that the author has not the right to order and dismiss his legions at will; but in the exercise of such arbitrary power Richler is still less subtle and skilled than Sartre, more like Arthur Miller, and yet more completely ambitious than Arthur Miller. (pp. 61-2)

There are [in *A Choice of Enemies*] other more disturbing features of manipulation and contrivance. What is ostensibly the plot, the contest between one man and another who has (unknown to either) murdered the former's half-brother, has an improbability which fits the Jacobean drama; but in the context of the novel's present conflict it is a thing of no meaning. . . . They are faults of a new and serious order. Richler was always an uneven writer, but his earlier blemishes were those of immaturity; these are blemishes of achievement and volition. (p. 63)

Throughout the postwar period we have seen fatigue with ideology and preoccupation with survival. Richler is one of the many authors to have caught this mood: his heroes, those endowed with the most consciousness, want above all to live, . . . not as flattened projections of history or of society, but as individuals grown free of their exhausted roots. To achieve this they must conquer their own hatreds and denials; to do this they must deny their own obsession with themselves. This is the moment of freedom which occurs in all three books, and which allows us to consider them as, if only in Thomas Mann's sense, comedies. (p. 64)

A Choice of Enemies closes with an ambiguity not of

words, but of situation: in this ambiguity lies Richler's true achievement. Perhaps he is no more sure than in *The Acrobats* of what, on this level, he is trying to say—or even that he is really trying to say anything, for it is so difficult for art to survive when statement begins. I certainly would not wish to impute to him the motives of Tom Thumb fighting to salvage the Western sensibility from individualism. But I do think we can trace in the shape of his writing hitherto the beginning of a powerful and complex insight.

To believe in this insight, one must take Richler's work, as one takes all works of art, partly on its merits, and partly on a kind of faith. . . . If we ask more for Richler on faith than on demonstration, that is because his novels are less articulate, and to that extent less conscious, than are the novels of any established European. But so are the lives of the Canadians he describes, especially against a European background: his very theme is this conflict of conscious and unconscious. (p. 68)

> *Peter Dale Scott, "A Choice of Certainties"* (originally published in Tamarack Review, *No. 8, 1958), in* Mordecai Richler, *edited by G. David Sheps (copyright © McGraw-Hill Co. of Canada Ltd., 1971), McGraw-Hill/Ryerson, 1971, pp. 58-68.*

The Acrobats brought to light one of the richest promises in the young tradition of Canadian literature. *The Acrobats* is in itself a mediocre novel, but, though it has all the pretentiousness and all the imperfections of a beginner's work, it reveals qualities which could equally well be those of a clever craftsman or those of a true writer.

Richler uses every means to avoid speaking directly of Canada and particularly of Canadian Jews. He sets his stage as far as possible from St. Urbain Street—in Valencia, in Spain. The complex intrigues, fruits of a fevered imagination, hide imperfectly the real anxieties of the young novelist. Since timidity and bashfulness prevent him from speaking in the first person, Richler disguises his characters to the best of his ability, clothing them in borrowed garments which barely hide the conventional faces of the wicked who succeed and the good who are defeated. (pp. 93-4)

In his second novel, *Son of a Smaller Hero*, the masks fall away. Richler does not speak in the first person, but the autobiographical tone of the book is not entirely deceptive. It is the world of his own childhood that he reveals in fictional form. The adolescent hero deprived of childhood takes his revenge. He sits in judgement on a family which has cut him off too early from an affection he desperately demanded. (p. 94)

The adolescent cannot cross the frontiers of the ghetto without doing violence to himself. He is too much affected by the traditions which nourished his childhood for him to be able to reject them except by force. It would be treating this rage of youth too seriously if we were to elevate Richler into the censor and critic of a whole community.

It is to his family that the hero owes a grudge; it is his family he accuses of not bearing the same love and feeling as he does toward a doctrine which he would like to maintain in its pristine purity, that is to say, without modification by the demanding laws of existence.

This is clearly the mental process of the adolescent. And this is what gives the novel movement, if not power. The ambitious youth who has made his reckoning with a narrow society is propelled by an irrepressible impulse. He wishes to deal as a man with adult problems. After all, has he not set himself free? Has he not said what he thinks of those who do not see beyond the wall of the ghetto? Now he must face them with the proofs of his initiation into manhood. (p. 95)

In [*A Choice of Enemies*] Richler places himself in the centre of great world problems. He brings before us the ex-Communist who fled from East Germany, the Ex-Nazi, and a whole assortment of North American fugitives who keep meeting in that vast city as if they were living in a little village where everyone knows everyone else, knows his petty habits and his grand manias. It is a novel in which skill is more in evidence than true passion.

In *The Apprenticeship of Duddy Kravitz* Richler returns to his childhood. He has not yet said all there is to be said. To the bitterness, the surly anger of *Son of a Smaller Hero* is added the dream of a world in which frankness, straightforwardness and love reign together. Great is the disenchantment of the unfortunate child who has put all his hopes in the mystery of non-Jewish society and has found there the same recurring faults as elsewhere. (p. 96)

In this novel, which is without doubt its author's most accomplished work, one can measure his talent against his limitations. Stirred by a demanding passion, he is led to destroy his characters through caricature. Facing a society which he wishes to conquer, he has no time to look at it, to understand it, to perceive its complete ambiguity. His characters are linear, for complexity would deprive them of the artificial consistency which is fabricated by a novelist whose wish to do battle is stronger than his desire to comprehend. This world without love or tenderness is at once sentimental and false—false because sentimental.

Richler manipulates situations and characters to fill a void which no degree of inventiveness can conceal. He does not succeed in breaking the yoke in which his sensibility imprisons him, for he takes no account of the sensibilities of others, and especially of his characters. These are his banner-bearers, the extensions of his own tastes and whims.

It is evident that Richler, who burns with the desire to plunge into the great ocean which he sees beyond the walls of the ghetto, can never quit St. Urbain Street. Whether he walks in England, France or Spain, he carries everywhere his little world, his secret fatherland, for he never succeeds in completing and going beyond his adolescence, which is its product.

In . . . [*The Incomparable Atuk*, he] is the master of artifice and appearance, and he intends to demonstrate the fact. In fabricating his caricatures he goes to the limit of his powers. He no longer pretends to create living personages or complex situations.

The Incomparable Atuk is a great piece of farce in which the child of the ghetto, once again disguised behind the mask of a fake Eskimo poet, makes his conquest of a world of imposters and hollow men. Richler turns his vengeful anger against all those personalities of swollen reputation and unmerited celebrity who people the intellectual world of Toronto. All of them are provincials puffed up with their false importance, blinded by their degree of influence, corrupted by the ambient complacency. The adolescent who reproached his parents and society in general for responding meagrely to his longing for purity, now directs a burst of mocking laughter against a world which was to blame for the mutilation of his dreams. (pp. 97-8)

> *Naim Kattan, "Mordecai Richler: Craftsman or Artist" (translated from the French by George Woodcock and originally published in* Canadian Literature, *Summer, 1964), in* Mordecai Richler, *edited by G. David Sheps (copyright © McGraw-Hill Co. of Canada Ltd., 1971), McGraw-Hill/Ryerson, 1971, pp. 92-8.*

Like Thoreau, who decided that Harvard taught all the branches of knowledge but none of the roots, Richler wants to get at the prime meaning of experience—to drive life into a corner and see whether it is a good thing or bad. But Richler does not live at Walden; his reality lies somewhere beneath the encrusted hypocrisies and orthodoxies of urban culture; and though in burrowing towards this reality he is often naïve, cranky, and even short-sighted, he is determined (in the words of his best critic, Peter Scott) "to keep to the experience at hand and to the truth which is available." Far from the reflective or analytical mood that has been characteristic of Canadian fiction, Richler's spirit resembles that of the "angry" young Englishman and the "beat" writers of "the great American night"; but though, like them, he strips away the world's pretences, he does not end as an outsider, in alienated or intoxicated freedom. Richler belongs (as Brian Moore does) in society, and he has enough nerve to refuse alienation. If orthodox frauds reject him, he will simply bypass them and create his own order—a crude one, perhaps, but bracing in its directness, and electric with energy. (pp. 712-13)

The Acrobats (1954) and *Son of a Smaller Hero* (1955) might both be described as "first novels"; both deal with a hero obsessed by self and in reckless opposition to a world which is stifling, corrupt, and Protean in its deceit. (p. 713)

The forced symbolism of [its] ending is only one of *The Acrobats'* shortcomings: the festival of San José glitters like the fireworks which conclude it, but falls short of the structural significance which similar rites achieve in Hemingway or Mann; the narrative method flickers uncertainly because the narrator is not sufficiently distinct from his hero; and the echoes of Hemingway, Sartre, and others are more often reflexes than conscious devices. But though the book is not, as one critic claims, "a guide to intelligent, contemporary pastiche," it has a nervous, exploratory power.

Son of a Smaller Hero (1955) is in effect an earlier chapter in fictional autobiography. But if Richler is on firmer ground in the Jewish community of Montreal than he was in Spain, he is still uncomfortably close to his hero's anger and confusion; the family and community described come magnificently to life, but the hero, Noah Adler, is such an unreliable guide to his own experience that the closing ambiguity of the novel appears inadvertent rather than deliberate. The step from this to *A Choice of Enemies* (1957) and *The Apprenticeship of Duddy Kravitz* (1959) is the enormous stride from denial to assertion, from rejection to deliberate choice. As in battle, the technical units lag be-

hind the attack forces in both of these works, but the objectives are taken and held. (pp. 713-14)

In *A Choice of Enemies*, Richler the film-writer occasionally interferes with Richler the novelist; suspense is introduced whether meaning requires it or not, and dialogue is often geared to the film editor's cut. In *The Apprenticeship of Duddy Kravitz* the novelist is again in control, but a new problem, the relation between realism and comedy or farce, presents itself. Duddy's apprenticeship—his chequered progress from a Montreal slum to a shaky status as landowner—is a story by turns comic, pathetic, bawdy, and farcical; and though the exuberant reality of Duddy himself is never in doubt, the modulation of other characters from pathos to farce makes the reader's suspension of disbelief something less than willing. But these flaws are principally evidence of the rapidity of Richler's artistic development. The theme of *Duddy Kravitz* extends the quest for values of the earlier books. (p. 714)

Mordecai Richler has asked piercing questions on issues which involve the self, the nation, and mankind, and he has dismissed the stock replies that religion, politics, and the polite social sciences and humanities customarily offer. His exuberant style and intellectual toughness make him the most exciting and promising of Canada's younger novelists. . . . (p. 715)

> *Hugo McPherson, "Fiction 1940-1960," in* Literary History of Canada: Canadian Literature in English, *edited by Carl F. Klinck and others (© University of Toronto Press, 1965), University of Toronto Press, 1965, pp. 694-722.*

Richler sometimes seems to sacrifice his art to a love-hate attitude to Hemingway's works, especially to *For Whom the Bell Tolls*. In the beginning of *The Acrobats* there is a noticeable Hemingway influence, in the artificial dialogue, in the sentence order and length. (p. 2)

All the directionless bar scenes of *The Acrobats* are like expatriate *The Sun Also Rises* scenes, but without even the desperate gaiety of the Jake Barnes crowd—rather with a soft and aimless self-hate. (p. 3)

This is the post-Hemingway world, the post-*For Whom The Bell Tolls* world, where the sermon from Donne takes on a grim cast. The language of Richler and his characters is also post-Hemingway, with all rapture gone, all romanticism sifted out. The (anti)hero's girl is not brave Maria in a sleeping bag, but the pregnant prostitute Toni, not the rebellious Pilar of the mountains but the city-slum girl tired of revolution and war. (p. 4)

Almost all the people in the novel are tired and disappointed. (p. 5)

Pretty obviously Richler intends in this first novel to show his own disillusionment in a postwar world he never made nor even had a hand in destroying. (p. 6)

Some critics have pointed out (and correctly, to a certain extent) that the people we meet in *The Acrobats* are stock characters. André is the young athlete, lost and in exile, searching for meaning in a confused world. Toni is the innocent prostitute, the traditional wry comment on a whole society that has sold its innocence for quick, mortal and illusory rewards. Chaim is the perennial wise old wandering

Jew and father figure to those who have lost all their own fathers. Barney is the rich boorish American abroad, hiding secret fears of his own sexual inability behind an aggressive social manner. And so on.

Probably more to the point is that in this first novel, Richler has not yet, as he has in his later books, submerged the techniques of writing below the surface of the story as we are allowed a look at it. (p. 12)

I believe that the young Richler scored a coup in this novel, in arousing compassion for characters who would superficially seem to be the enemy—Barney and Kraus the best examples. In this way, Richler speaks not to the smug liberal intelligence, but to the compassionate human being who may be lurking behind that mask. No author who speaks that way can hope to write an "accomplished" novel. But the book reaches at least determinedly beyond accomplishment toward the place where a man is forced to ask himself where he is, and how he feels. And there the sun also rises again. (p. 14)

> *George Bowering, "And the Sun Goes Down: Richler's First Novel" (originally published in* Canadian Literature, *No. 29, Summer, 1966), in* Mordecai Richler, *edited by G. David Sheps (copyright © McGraw-Hill Co. of Canada Ltd., 1971), McGraw-Hill/Ryerson, 1971, pp. 1-14.*

In every way, but particularly in their control of the sensationalism that at its best gives vitality to his writing and at worst makes it banal, the Montreal novels [*Son of a Smaller Hero* and *The Apprenticeship of Duddy Kravitz*] are the best; with a small number of short stories dealing with people in the same environment, they form the body of work that made Richler, before he reached the age of thirty, the most important of the younger generation of Canadian fiction writers.

It might be a metaphorical exaggeration to describe Canada as a land of invisible ghettos, but certainly it is, both historically and geographically, a country of minorities that have never achieved assimilation.

It is this fact that makes Montreal a great frontier city, where various traditions intermingle and react upon each other. It is a natural laboratory for examining the fears and fascinations that flow between the various communities, and Richler, working outward from the Jewish environment of his own childhood, has presented us with such an examination in *Son of a Smaller Hero*. Yet *Son of a Smaller Hero* is not a sociologically slanted novel about the "problem" of Jewish-Gentile relationships. . . . He does not, of course, ignore the social problems, yet at the same time he does not seek to abstract them from their context. They are part of the world he is trying to present in a fictionally viable form, part of the particular world of a divided city that he is using to illuminate a universal theme: the predicament of the man who sets out honestly to find and to be himself in a world where most men fear their own natures and try to live by comfortable falsehoods.

The inhabitants of the ghetto are depicted with a Dickensian eye for the foibles and tics of behaviour and speech; this makes them memorable, but too often we remember the habitual behaviour rather than the person, and Richler, in *Son of a Smaller Hero* at least, is inclined to present his minor figures as humours rather than characters. His sense of satire leads him perilously near the edge of caricature.

Son of a Smaller Hero is often amusing, but rarely pleasant, and never comforting; Richler would not have wanted us to find it so. His revelation of the ruthlessness of the man who seeks the truth is as deliberate as his exposure of the brutal world where men accept big lies and live by small evasions. Like most good satirists, he has his moments of compassion, but his most convincing tendernesses are those which emerge with the sharp rigours of candour. Richler's best line is taut, twanging, and a little discordant. (p. 21)

> *George Woodcock, "Introduction" (reprinted by permission of The Canadian Publishers, McClelland and Stewart Limited, Toronto) to* Son of a Smaller Hero, *by Mordecai Richler, New Canadian Library No. 45, McClelland and Stewart, 1966.*

Mordecai Richler is a satirist, and therefore a comparatively rare bird in our time. A great many writers toy with satire—insert satirical passages into a non-satirical work, or try to give an edge to farce by offering a satirical interpretation of their buffoonery. But Mr. Richler declares himself a conscious and deliberate satirist from the first page of [*Cocksure*]—I have read, alas, none of his earlier [novels] —and he keeps up the satirical pace from start to finish. (p. 106)

[A] general weakness of this funny and memorable book is that it is quite impossible to detect the moral platform on which Mr. Richler is standing and from which his darts are launched. Nobody wants a satirist to make a solemn declaration of faith, but that declaration is implied by the best satirists in everything they write. Here is a striking example of Mr. Richler's failure: an elderly and a highly reputable Canadian governess decides to take a job in the monstrous school, with the intention of counteracting its malignant influence. At first we are led to understand that she is having a great success just because she is introducing discipline, rewards, privacy, etc.—all the things which the school rejects but children need. Not a bit of it. It turns out that she is getting her splendid results simply by rewarding the children with her own techniques of mutual masturbation. Seeing ahead of it the fence of a positive moral judgment, Mr. Richler's horse has shied away from it. . . .

The weakness is a serious one, and before Mr. Richler writes a really good satire he will have to learn not only what he hates but where he hates it from. Meanwhile *Cocksure* is a highly entertaining book, and often a properly uncomfortable one. (pp. 108-09)

> *Philip Toynbee, "'Cocksure'" (originally published in* London Magazine, *May, 1968), in* Mordecai Richler, *edited by G. David Sheps (copyright © McGraw-Hill Co. of Canada Ltd. 1971), McGraw-Hill/Ryerson, 1971, pp. 106-09.*

The Apprenticeship of Duddy Kravitz . . . seemed to me when I first encountered it, hopelessly retrospective for all the talent that went into its making—the sort of fictional study of making it out of the ghetto appropriate for Americans only to the Thirties. *Having* made it was our new subject—and Richler's too, though he did not seem to know it at the start. Still, there was apparent in him a lust for surreal exaggeration and the grotesque, and an affinity for the atrocious—the dirty joke turned somehow horrific, the scene of terror altered somehow into absurdity—which made him, before he himself knew it, a member of the group later to be labelled Black Humorists.

Satire was his special affinity—not, to be sure, polished and urbane satire, but shrill and joyously vulgar travesty—directed, all the same, against pop culture, on the one hand, and advanced or experimental art on the other: middlebrow satire, in fact, however deliciously gross, an anti-genteel defence of the genteel tradition. It is this which makes Richler so difficult a writer for *me* to come to terms with, and—by the same token—so easy a one for the guardians of official morality to accept. . . . Richler himself belongs to the world of mass culture (in which he has laboured long, continues to support himself), so that he seems ultimately— *seems*, I think, rather than is—as harmless as *The Black and White Minstrel Show*.

It is quite another aspect of his work which makes Richler more dangerous than he seems perhaps even to himself: his concern with exile, his compulsion to define all predicaments in terms of that hopelessly Jewish concept, and his implicit suggestion that, after all, we are—everyone of us— Jews. . . .

The Incomparable Atuk, is not quite a successful book . . .; but in it Richler seems to have discovered at last where the demands of his real gifts were taking him—toward ultimate, absolute burlesque, i.e., burlesque that includes finally the book itself and its author, the sort of nihilism implicit unawares in all pop art, and consciously exploited in "Pop Art" of which *Cocksure* is an example. But ultimate burlesque requires a sense of the ultimate outsider, the real victim, the true Jew, who—in the realm of Anglo-Saxondom at least—turns out to be the Anglo-Saxon. . . . It is a book which seems always on the verge of becoming truly obscene, but stops short, alas, at the merely funny. Yet it is so close, so close—the sort of near miss that leaves permanent damage behind.

Perhaps it is close enough, then. Certainly Richler has come as near to saying how it is with us now when the ultimate exile has proved to be success, as anyone can out of the generation which dreamed that success, at a point when being poor and excluded seemed the only real indignity. (pp. 102-05)

> Leslie Fiedler, *"Some Notes on the Jewish Novel in English: or Looking Backward from Exile" (originally published in* The Running Man, *Vol. 1, No. 2, July-August, 1968), in* Mordecai Richler, *edited by G. David Sheps (copyright © McGraw-Hill Co. of Canada Ltd., 1971), McGraw-Hill/Ryerson, 1971, pp. 99-105.*

To be Canadian in any meaningful sense today one must come to grips with what [Mordecai Richler] has to say. To [some] he may be a "professional Jew," to many Jews he is a "jewish anti-Semite", to me he is one of the country's best writers and surely one of its most penetrating wits.

Considering the shallowness and hysteria of the attacks frequently levelled at him I sometimes wonder why Richler continues to bother with us at all. (p. 112)

Perhaps the best clue as to the difficulties Richler faces with his fellow Canadians is given by Richler himself. "To be a Jew and a Canadian," he says, "is to emerge from the ghetto twice, for self-conscious Canadians, like some touchy Jews, tend to contemplate the world through a wrong-ended telescope."

It is through this kind of telescope that Canadians most frequently view the giant phenomenon to the south of us. While it is true that many members of the Canadian élite differ sharply as to the merits of political and economic continentalism there is one type of continentalism the Canadian illuminati, en masse, are most fanatically opposed to. I refer, of course, (borrowing Richler's own phrase) to "the Jewish cultural take-over" in the United States.

That most distinctive and most influential segment of American culture is not part of the cultural continentalism the Canadian intelligentsia is prepared to buy. In the United States Phillip Roth, Saul Bellow, Norman Mailer, Bernard Malamud, Leslie Fiedler are *American* writers. In Canada Mordecai Richler is "a professional Jew."

In Canada the *good* Jew is a WASP. *Good* Canadian Jews never talk about Jews or being Jewish, don't think Jewish, don't look Jewish. Their noses are bobbed, and their minds are circumcised.

To people like this Mordecai Richler is a menace. They are not amused. (pp. 112-13)

What is really sad is what those Canadians who shout "professional Jew" and "Jewish anti-Semite" at a man of Richler's obvious talents, reveal about themselves and this country. What seems to link both these groups together is paranoia, a sense of inferiority, a feeling of alienation. The Canadian WASP élite is essentially cut off from the superior cultures of their American and British counterparts. Years ago it was a direct and vital part of the British Empire. It was getting part of the action. Being British was enough. The demise of the British Empire and non-membership in the new American one has left our WASP élite homeless, ghettoized, so to speak, in the northern half of the American continent. (pp. 113-14)

It's surely a typical Canadian irony that one-half of the tiny Jewish community in this country should live in Montreal and be English-speaking, making it in a French city a kind of ghetto minority squared.

It is doubly ironic that the Montreal Jewish Community should look to that city's WASP élite for inspiration and leadership. It is one beleaguered minority leading another in a basically hopeless situation. It is not surprising that the paranoia gauge of Canada's Jewish community, with its Montreal base and leadership, is high. (p. 114)

Richler . . . is a bad Jew and a worse Canadian but he tells it as it is. In *Hunting Tigers Under Glass*, a collection of his essays and reports, Richler writes about bad Jews and worse Canadians, superbly.

Take for example his hilarious account of that peculiar Canadian psycho-drama, the annual gathering of the Canadian Authors' Association. Listed by Richler as being in attendance, were such literary lights as Bluebell Phillips, Phoebe Erskine Kyde, and Una Wardelworth. Overlooked, much to my annoyance, were authors Carpathia Radish, Hathaway Yoyo, Paisley Goornisht, and Gay Abandon (she of Memoirs Of A Venetian Streetwalker fame).

Mentioned by Richler, as if in passing, was the Canadian literary hit of EXPO year, *Ripe And Ready*. Sad to say, this was not a Canadian *Fanny Hill* but rather a history of the Canadian apple. Unforgivably ignored by Richler were such Canadian literary hits of yesteryear as *Awake And Sing*, a history of the Canadian Opera Company; *Hail and Farewell*, a history of Canadian crop failures; and *From See To See*, a history of Canadian Catholic voyeurs.

Equally unforgivable in Richler is his tendency, at times, to view us provincial Canadians with the lofty disdain of the profligate, world-weary sophisticate. Air Canada does, after all, fly across the pond; the *Paris* and *Partisan Reviews* do find their way into the occasional household; the ladies from Dubuque and Coronation Street utter the same banalities as Anne of Green Gables.

Less irritating but a bit unnerving is Richler's tendency to drop the names of good friends and potential employers in some of his reports and essays. More disturbing is Richler's barely suppressed desire to be Canada's Edmund Wilson. His serious comments on writers and writing, filmmaking and politics are insightful and often valuable, but for the most part, are prissy and professorial in tone, often indistinguishable from the many academic prigs that already clutter up the field in these areas.

God forbid I should be labelled a professional Jew, but I like Richler best when he is idiosyncratic and autobiographical, first-person and Jewish. . . .

The final words on *Hunting Tigers Under Glass* should go to Richler. Says he: "If I'm able to communicate just some of my enjoyment of Israel, the Catskills, comicbooks, Jews in sport and the Canadian comedy, to readers, then I will count this collection a success."

Well start counting, Mordecai. It's a success, it's a success!! Me, I can hardly wait for the movie! (pp. 114-16)

> Larry Zolf, "Why, Why Should Mordecai Bother with Us At All?" (originally published in the Toronto Telegram, November 16, 1968), in Mordecai Richler, edited by G. David Sheps (copyright © McGraw-Hill Co. of Canada Ltd., 1971), McGraw-Hill/Ryerson, 1971, pp. 112-16.

At first glance, [*The Apprenticeship of Duddy Kravitz*] seems to fit into the tradition of Joyce's *Portrait of the Artist* and Lawrence's *Sons and Lovers*, each of which deals with the growing up of a young man to the point where he is on his own, alone and lonely, ready to strike out in life freed from the ties of his youth. . . . In both of these earlier novels the protagonist has made a choice of direction, aware of the chain of events that had made such a choice possible and necessary. Each has made a decision, based on thought and self-awareness, and each has chosen a way of life that is an affirmation of man's greatness or potential greatness.

Richler's novel, however, in spite of its superficial affinity with the two novels mentioned above, ends with no such affirmation. His protagonist, who has never weighted the consequences of his actions in any but material terms, is less alone in the physical sense than the earlier young men, but he is also much less of a man. His decisions have been made on the wrong terms, have been based on nothing at all. He has destroyed himself and others for a piece of land that means nothing to those who have loved him. He has devoted his energy to acquiring property; he has done nothing to develop himself. Whereas the other two, Stephen Dedalus and Paul Morel, have matured, and have decided the course of their lives for themselves, Poor Duddy has simply gone along without realizing where he was headed. He is a modern "anti-hero" (something like the protagonist in Anthony Burgess's *A Clockwork Orange*) who lives in a largely deterministic world, a world where decisions are not decisions and where choice is not really choice.

The novel ends . . . as a devastating attack on the world of Duddy Kravitz, which is the world of Jewish Montreal. It is interesting to note that Duddy's Montreal is a bicultural city, Jewish and non-Jewish. All non-Jews, French and English, are seen as pretty much the same; the two-culture theme of [Hugh MacLennon's] *Two Solitudes* takes on a new look in Richler's novel. He is obviously very aware of the flaws in his own society, and on one plane the novel is a bitter revelation of the vulgarity and raw materialism of middle-class Canadian life, for Richler well exemplified by the world he still probably knows best. There are a few admirable Jews presented very briefly and used to reveal even more clearly by contrast the glittering false standards of the many; but for the most part Richler emphasizes all too strongly the aspects of Jewish society that the anti-Semites do. The few warm and unselfish characters we meet remain largely undeveloped and lifeless. . . . But it is not only the sympathetic characters who fail to come to life; we also get to know very little about any character other than Duddy himself. Other characters are seen only in terms of their relationship with Duddy. . . .

Canadian novelists seem to me to be a very conventional lot, at least as far as experiments with form go . . ., and certainly in this novel Richler is a traditionalist. . . . In the narrative and descriptive sections of the novel Richler writes good, sound, correct English, perhaps a bit too much like a good term essay. It seems to me that Richler handles dialogue exceptionally well, giving us conversations of great range and convincing authenticity. . . . The book comes to life through its dialogue, and the vitality of dialogue is usually a reliable test of the success of a novel. . . . [This] novel with its satiric-tragic-comic attitude to man in the modern world is much more than a "mere" Canadian work. Richler's novel, it seems to me, can stand on its own by any standard.

> A. R. Bevan, "Introduction" (reprinted by permission of The Canadian Publishers, McClelland and Stewart Limited, Toronto) to The Apprenticeship of Duddy Kravitz, by Mordecai Richler, New Canadian Library No. 66, McClelland and Stewart, 1969.

As adults we thrive on constant change, but our childhood goes on forever, like a movie about a certain time and a certain place that keeps on running, with continuous showings in our heads. [Knelman is reviewing the film version of *The Apprenticeship of Duddy Kravitz*.] Our time and our place was different from Mordecai Richler's, but he puts us in touch with our own roots when he tells us the truth about growing up on St. Urbain Street in the 1940s. Richler's grandfather came to Montreal instead of Chicago because he traded tickets with somebody on the boat from Russia, and his work is about people who are Canadians more by a fluke than by historical design. His is the one voice in Canadian literature, as Brian Moore puts it, that is neither French Canadian nor English Canadian. He gives us the missing chapter of Canadian history whose absence made us sense that the official version we got in school, about destiny forged on the Plains of Abraham and the heritage of the United Empire Loyalists, had less to do with our lives than Judy Garland and Danny Kaye did. Richler gave us the story of our parents and our grandparents, and he took St. Urbain Street to London the way his grandfather had brought a Russian village to Canada. He speaks for those of us who in the third generation still feel like exiles because we've left even the transplanted ghettos of the new world. We're gypsies of the jet age, still scrambling and waiting for the next plane to somewhere, never quite going home again and never quite breaking away, either. And still trying to show somebody: "You see, Daddy, you see?" This isn't just a St. Urbain story or just a Jewish story. It's the theme that links the lives of Mordecai Richler and Ted Kotcheff and John Kemeny and Richard Dreyfuss and many of us in the audience who have never had a movie that came this close to us. That's why the making of *The Apprenticeship of Duddy Kravitz* matters emotionally even to people who are a bit afraid of it. We don't want it to be just another movie; we want them to get it right. (p. 24)

> *Martin Knelman, "How Duddy's Movie Brings Us All Back Home," in* Saturday Night *(copyright 1974), March, 1974, pp. 17-24.*

"What, who, why, when is a Canadian writer?"

An outraged and apparently depletable Canadian Authors' Association posed the question, then editorialized:

> *If a writer wants to make big money he will probably stop writing about Canada and almost certainly leave Canada. If a writer wants "instant fame" he will very likely have to prostitute his talent by such things as writing sex-dripping prose or taking a deliberately shocking stand on a touchy subject.*

Mordecai Richler qualifies as a living answer to the association's livid question. He left Canada and went to England and wrote for the movies for money. He has written novels like *Cocksure*, and *St. Urbain's Horseman*, full of sex-drippery, and he has taken radical stands on such touchy subjects as Jews in sport. The whole story is revealed in his newest collection of pieces [*Notes On an Endangered Species and Others*], and a scurvy tale it is. Richler may not have left Canada spiritually, literarily or reportorially, as these articles (and his novels) shamelessly prove, but he is nonetheless a cunning Canadian type. He will not run for mayor of Montreal. He will not streak at the National Book Awards affair to protest mountie brutality. He, sly fox, betrays his true nature instead by writing well. (p. 28)

Compared to *St. Urbain's Horseman* this collection of work is minor; but at that it has the capacity for outlasting far flashier, far more controversial journalism and criticism of the day, for it comes from a man who has, probably out of some appallingly splendid character defect, not yielded

to the pull of what was flimsy in his generational urges, but chose to steady it on, on through nine rewrites last time out, and who has produced book after book of quality fiction. And whatever the judgment of that body of work may eventually be, he certainly got one thing right: that without such work, the public man is only a clown of the time.

Richler fans will like this collection. Newcomers are advised to step first to the fiction counter for *St. Urbain's Horseman*, and come back to the *Endangered Species* as the hors d'oeuvres of another day. (p. 29)

> *William Kennedy, "Unsentimental Chronicler," in* The New Republic *(reprinted by permission of* The New Republic; © *1974 by* The New Republic, Inc.*), May 18, 1974, pp. 28-9.*

As black satirist, fearless lambaster of Jew and WASP, dirty comic writer, Mordecai Richler has consistently displayed a resolute sneer. But in his first children's book, *Jacob Two-Two Meets The Hooded Fang*, Richler stands revealed. Beneath the hardened accretions of cynicism, there's an incorrigible softy. Richler knows and loves children. (p. 65)

> *John Ayre, "Mordecai Richler's Subversive Accomplishment," in* Saturday Night *(copyright 1975), July/August, 1975, pp. 65-6.*

*   *   *

ROBBINS, Harold   1912-

Robbins is a best-selling American novelist who specializes in sex-and-violence and exposé of modern industry. His books include *The Carpetbaggers* and *The Betsy*.

The Inheritors, set in New York and Hollywood, is a glossy, beautifully-wrapped package deal in which everything is king-size and ostentatious. The men are hard-drinking, ruthless and dedicated to the fast buck. Sharper even than C P Snow's careerists, they never miss a trick. The girls are California-tanned, exquisitely clothed and still more exquisite unclothed. The men live for success, the girls for the men who have made it big. Copulation thrives but business always comes first. Nice guys finish last. . . .

Nobody can accuse Harold Robbins of not telling a story. He knows how to handle narrative and keep the novel on the move. As for style, it's crisp and throwaway. You won't need a dictionary to help you read this book. He drops in the occasional Hippie word ('uptight'), a few Yiddish ones ('schmuck') and comes up with a good deal of Americanese ('He sold like crazy').

There are hardly any births, an incredible number of fast copulations and only one death. . . . (p. 42)

This . . . is the story of the growth of American TV and the late flowering of the Dream City. It goes a long way to explain the revolt of the American young against the gods worshipped by their parents. (p. 43)

> *Robert Greacen, in Books and Bookmen (© copyright Robert Greacen 1971), April, 1971.*

It is difficult for me to say how disgusting I find [*The Betsy*]. Not because of the sex which afflicts almost everyone in it to an alarming degree, but because of its tone. *The Betsy* is the name of a brand new motor car—the car everyone will buy and which will sweep the market. It is the dream of 91-year-old Loren Hardeman, Number One of Bethlehem Motors, the family firm he started. . . . As the complications, board-room chicanery and industrial espionage get underway, we are given a full-length history of Loren in flashback form. This book is described hopefully as 'a devastating look at modern business', but is about as realistic and pungent as Batman. When in doubt unzip your flies seems to be the motto of everyone involved, and when cornered take off your belt and lay about you.

The superficiality of the characters is beyond belief; the mechanical setting-up of the sexual bouts is crude and the fact that everyone in the saga seems either vicious or bats or both doesn't help at all. (p. 67)

> *Roger Baker, in* Books and Bookmen (© *copyright Roger Baker 1971), April, 1971.*

Yes, junk fans, it's a *mano a mano* for novelists who are all thumbs. Two of the greatest schlockmeisters in the history of solid waste have just published novels about the auto industry. Arthur Hailey's *Wheels* appeared at the beginning of the fall season. . . . Now comes Harold Robbins to gun down Hailey with—*The Carburetors*? No, with *The Betsy*. . . .

Despite the literary failings of Hailey's and Robbins' competing car novels, the awards committee will announce its selections:

Worst title: basically a standoff with a slight edge for Robbins.

Number of pages: Robbins, 502 to Hailey's 374.

Most sensitive writing: Robbins' "giant shaft of white-hot steel" and "searing sheet of flame" far outclass Hailey's modest "her heart beat faster." . . .

Neatest reach for historical verisimilitude: Robbins, who in a flashback has Hardeman telephone Walter Reuther in 1937 to warn him that the Battle of the Overpass (in which auto company goons beat up unsuspecting union organizers) is about to occur.

> *John Skow, "Internal Combustion," in* Time *(reprinted by permission from* Time, The Weekly Newsmagazine; *copyright Time Inc.), December 13, 1971, p. E7.*

A Stone for Danny Fisher, published during the year that Dwight D. Eisenhower won office as President of the United States on the campaign formula K1 C2 (Korea, Communism, and Corruption), captured the agony of urban dwellers hungering to transmit their hopes, fears, dreams, and nightmares to their offspring. To some readers the book provided an escape from their problems; to others it was a nostalgic yet realistic journey into the recent past; finally, for many ethnic workers it was a mirror of their self-identity.

Harold Robbins, the bestselling American novelist, has been spurned and overlooked by literary critics because of the alleged mediocrity of his work. Nevertheless, he has won public affection by portraying identifiable life-situations in a realistic and titillating manner. His characters

resemble the common man even as their bizarre exploits, fascinating sex lives and heroic struggles exude an air of Walter Mitty. *A Stone for Danny Fisher* (1952), one of Robbins's earliest and most ambitious works . . . became one of the most popular and revealing urban handbooks of its era. Set in New York during the depression and war years, the novel dealt with the generational and environmental conflicts of a proud but sensitive Jewish youth. The protagonist was in a sense an urban Everyman as he encountered prejudice, poverty, corruption, and mobsters in treacherous settings. (pp. 295-96)

A Stone for Danny Fisher contained elements common to the most dominant and contrasting strains of urban literature: the sentimental, anti-urban, success-oriented Horatio Alger genre of the nineteenth century and the realistic, pessimistic works of social protest that reached their apotheosis with the proletarian novels of the 1930s. Robbins's characters shared the optimistic hope that with luck and hard work the world could be theirs, even as they suffered through tribulations that shattered their dreams. In its candor and raw mood *A Stone for Danny Fisher* resembled Nelson Algren's portrait of a tragic Skid Row gambler, *The Man With the Golden Arm* (1950). It would be too much to call Danny Fisher an existential man. Rather he was the prototype second- or third-generation American who dreamed the myth of opportunity and, like Algren's anti-hero, finally jettisoned his illusions one after another. Lacking the sustained force of Algren, Robbins was a master of the vignette, and some of the individual scenes in the book are quite compelling. . . . The book as a whole, however, resembled a carefully constructed mannequin, pleasant and enticing but bereft of a soul. . . .

In some respects *A Stone for Danny Fisher* was the male counterpart to the most famous urban novel of the previous decade, Betty Smith's *A Tree Grows in Brooklyn* (1943). (p. 296)

Smith appealed to the upwardly mobile, whereas Robbins had a special attraction for the ethnic urbanite still looking for his passport to success. (p. 297)

In a somewhat melodramatic fashion, *A Stone for Danny Fisher* recorded the epic battle of ethnic groups against inconsequentialness, and the disintegration of their rigid moral, ethical, and cultural standards under the stress and strain of survival. (p. 298)

Reviewers treated *A Stone for Danny Fisher* seriously and had words of praise for its author. Although they pointed out flaws in its structure and held reservations about its ample dosages of sex and violence, they recognized that it was the forerunner of a bright new genre of realistic urban novels. (p. 301)

Never again did Robbins win the respect of critics. He sold his considerable talents to the gods of wealth and fame, said some, even to the devil, said a few. . . . Robbins summed up his writing [to Thomas Thompson in a *Life* magazine interview] in this manner: "All my stories have this moral choice: the protagonist reaches the point where he has to choose his morality and live with it." Thompson, on the other hand, found the source of his appeal contained in his readable, anti-intellectual, sex-filled style. "His characters seldom think; they act." he wrote. (pp. 301-02)

> *James B. Lane, in* Journal of Popular Cul-

ture *(copyright © 1973 by Ray B. Browne), Fall, 1974.*

As Harold Robbins likes to point out, there is often more in a Harold Robbins novel than mere venery and violence. He shrewdly blends in topical interest to create a sort of non-fiction fiction. *The Carpetbaggers* (1961) offered thinly disguised views of Howard Hughes in his prime. *The Adventurers* (1966) traced jet-set life with the likes of the late Aly Khan. [*The Pirate,* a] timely extravaganza, is a picaresque about a financial wizard who might just be modeled on Abdlatif Al Hamad, the oil sheikdom of Kuwait's money manager.

But with a twist. Robbins' hero, Baydr Al Fay, is really a Jew—a changeling, by Allah! At 40, he is one of the world's richest men, traveling constantly between banking centers to invest Arab oil revenues. Like other Robbins figments, Baydr is also an international satyr whose feats are topped only by those of his insatiable California-born wife. (Yes, Hollywood is at work on the movie.)

There are some insights into the oil cartel's doings; the author leaves no doubt at all that the Arabs are going to buy up the world if they can. Robbins' fans may find that prospect less galvanizing than the usual steamy prose. . . . (p. E5)

Time *(reprinted by permission from* Time, The Weekly Newsmagazine; *copyright Time Inc.), November 11, 1974.*

S

SAMARAKIS, Antonis   1919-

A Greek poet, novelist, and short story writer, Samarakis writes as a member of the Resistance, voicing the need for freedom and human rights in his taut and incisive fiction. (See also *Contemporary Authors*, Vols. 25-28.)

From the start [Samarakis] was a renovator of contemporary Greek literature and a major world writer: a voice from Greece speaking to all humanity in acutely relevant and modern terms—about absurdity and disquietude, against depersonalization and dehumanization, war, violence, poverty, loss of freedom, and just plain hunger. His stories were beautifully written, stark but not grim, racing swiftly to the point. In other hands the author's affection and concern for Man and his fate might have led into the trap of sentimental homilies, or their converse, cynicism. But Samarakis does not preach—he shows. He shows his characters in situation, in action. We respond to *their* response, their speech, their inner dialogue. The author's deep mistrust of artistic gymnastics, of gratuitous formalism, of what he and his heroes scornfully call "literature," results in utter simplicity of style, classical in its density, its painstaking craft, its immediate impact. Samarakis does away with precious ornamentation, with nineteenth-century verbiage, or with the crowded rhetoric of today's "new" novel. He pares things down to the basic issues, gets to the heart of the matter and the nitty-gritty. He is also uncannily cinematic. No other body of high-quality fiction reads like so many scenarios ready for Take One. (pp. 531-32)

In the early stories ["Wanted: Hope," 1954], the typically lonely protagonists suffer from the impossibility of finding any human companionship; at least, while waiting for Godot, Beckett's Vladimir and Estragon have one another, *nolens volens*. In Samarakis, helplessness is total, be it a question of metaphysical or of social anguish. . . .

Many of the original themes are amplified in "Danger Signal" (1959). The economy of means and the filmic surprises are now augmented by irony and humor. (p. 532)

A former Resistance fighter during the occupation of Greece, Samarakis has remained . . . a totally committed man who fights for ideals "in a world full of ideologies and stripped of ideals," with a unique mixture of realistic and fantastic writing. Ethically and artistically his works are remarkably consistent. The stories in "I Refuse" (1961) and in "The Jungle" (1966), longer than the early "microstories" but still amazingly compact, develop some of the most poignant situations in contemporary literature. As in classical tragedy, they arouse fear and pity in the reader, but contrary to Aristotelian rules, they can also excite indignation. Not that the heroes are completely good—we do not really know, for Samarakis does not produce traditional portraits with as many facts filled out as the short-story format tolerates; instead, his "camera eye" selects those points of reference which will submit that, as an individual and as Everyman, his protagonist's misfortune is undeserved.

The world of Samarakis has a rather definite substructure as well as the kind of identity that true talent confers. A central figure, usually an anonymous and solitary man, moves about a sparse, Chirico-like urban landscape, tormented by the anguish of our time which he embodies. He is exceptionally sensitive, one might say pathologically so, were he not simultaneously rooted in tangible social indignity and in symbolic inhumane distress. (pp. 532-33)

It is impossible to summarize Samarakis' already terse parables, especially the episodic ones: "The Jungle," "The Window," "The Knife." Nor can one do justice to his style, now clinical, now a litany, now breathless, always distinctive—without examples. Language as a tool for the affirmation of a relative hope attains its high point in "The Flaw" (1965), a novel which ranks with the great works of Kafka, Orwell, or Koestler. It is a thriller, a political detective story which absorbs completely; it is also a metaphysical thriller, like *Oedipus Rex* and *Crime and Punishment*. It is the struggle for man's soul, the struggle between self-respect and the powers of darkness. (p. 533)

Edwin Jahiel, "Antonis Samarakis: Fiction as Scenario," in Books Abroad *(copyright 1968 by the University of Oklahoma Press), Vol. 42, No. 4, Autumn, 1968, pp. 531-34.*

The voice of Samarakis is heard again, years after *The Flaw* (1965; English [translation], 1969), one of the major humanistic thrillers of our time, and the splendid collection, "The Jungle" (1966). *To Diavatírio* (["The Passport"], . . . 1973) contains nine stories, six reprinted from "The Jungle" (now out of print) and three written in 1971-73 and previously published in Greek newspapers and periodicals.

That the junta allowed Samarakis's works to be reprinted (and all of them are, regularly) and that it permitted the publication of new stories in which the criticism of autocracy is hardly veiled, is something of a puzzle—but we do have some clues in the title story.

"The Passport" is an ironical and autobiographical title, for Samarakis himself was forced to remain in Greece for several years because the government confiscated his passport. In the story, a middle-aged bachelor and typical Samarakis loner has decided to go abroad for the first time in his life. His preparations, his mounting excitement, are described in a colorful crescendo of short, feverish phrases and with affectionate irony. But the trip, this departure which in the best Samarakis tradition is both fact and allegory, aborts: the hero, an entirely apolitical employee, is refused his passport. His file is marked "dangerous." Finally he goes through the labyrinth of hostile officialdom and discovers that some youthful poetry of his, sentimental innocuous trivia, is now considered dangerous. The carrot of a passport is dangled before him, however, in exchange for his composing a poem lauding "the System" (the State) and then reading it on the air in a special broadcast. At the station, after some ingenious twists, our hero makes a last-second change which now will really earn him the label "dangerous." At one point, he asks timidly if he can write his assigned poem in free verse. The answer is: "Of course you are free to use free verse. What do you take us for? . . . What do you think this is? . . . We don't do things here the way they do in totalitarian regimes!" Which probably explains why, although the Greek government may have thought that Samarakis was too dangerous for a passport, it chose, on balance, to suffer his writings without much fuss, by pretending that "those things don't apply to us." (pp. 58-9)

These stories point to the relatively new directions taken by Samarakis, but we will not be able to judge fully until we see what else he has (probably) written but has not been able to publish since 1966. Even so, it is significant that the three new stories could be collectively subtitled "Arrests." They are longer than usual, taking up as much text as the six from "The Jungle." Samarakis seems to take more time here in establishing characters and situations. Yet this new development does not result in cautious circumlocution; instead, it gives even more richness to the writer's prose. Previously, Samarakis dealt constantly with the themes of resistance, solidarity and charity; but until *The Flaw* the heroes' protests were politically ineffectual. Now Samarakis has his protagonists plunge squarely into political action. In earlier writings, too, Samarakis made it clear that there is no such thing as neutrality. All of life is seen as struggle or *agon*, and the author's favorite words are "human," "war," "battle," "resistance," "conquest," "surrender," "duel," "agony." In this turmoil there is hardly room for love-making, but ample room for love. Typically, any mention of sex or of couples is made in terms of battles, duels and the like, whether it concerns the professor and his mistress, or the idealistic lover in the reprinted, earlier story symbolically entitled "The Conquest." Now, not just neutrality is out of the question, but privacy and private concerns too.

There is, however, no sudden rupture with previous writings. There is an evolution which is consistent with earlier fiction by Samarakis: the tone has become more grotesque,

as befits the grotesqueness of government by little Caesars; and the changes in behavior have taken their next logical step. There is now active and overt resistance; but, as in previous works, the revolt is catalyzed by human, humane and personal factors—love for and loyalty to this man's soccer team, that girl's doll, that fellow's students—just as the captor in *The Flaw* betrayed his police-state masters, not for ideological reasons, but by succumbing to the sheer humanity of his prisoner. And this cautious but perceptible step toward optimism has already been glimpsed in Samarakis's work, namely in stories such as "The Window" and "The Apocalypse of John," reprinted in this volume.

In his newest stories, Samarakis's extraordinarily cinematographic writing is more pronounced than ever, in structures and in visuals. On a simple level, he uses tricks that Hitchcock calls Macguffins; but in a subtler fashion he reveals truth gradually, like Antonioni in *Blow-up* and Coppola in *The Conversation*. But, whereas Coppola's tricks become excessive, protracted and sly (not to mention his anti-human content), Samarakis's are revealed rapidly and honestly. There are many more cinematic equivalents in Samarakis. Repetitions of certain striking visual details, such as the spiders in the third story, could be annoying if seen strictly as text; but when interpreted as visuals, they become signposts that flash before our inner eye. (p. 60)

> *Edwin Jahiel, "Antonis Samarakis's 'To Diavatírio',"* in Books Abroad *(copyright 1975 by the University of Oklahoma Press), Vol. 49, No. 1, Winter, 1975, pp. 58-61.*

*   *   *

SANCHEZ, Sonia   1934-

Ms Sanchez is a Black American poet and playwright. (See also *Contemporary Authors*, Vols. 33-36.)

Sonia Sanchez . . . is concerned with black identity. Within this framework, however, she manages to achieve an amazingly wide variety of treatments. [She] feels that the return to black identity is a "home-coming" (the title, by the way, of her first published volume of verse) after a sojourn in a white-oriented society geared to UN-black the Black man —to mold him to a white standard of values. (p. 31)

As a protest poet, . . . Sonia Sanchez chooses themes from a wide range of the so-called "black experience." Her poems, however, are . . . personalized. She uses the first person "i" . . . frequently, and equates the black experience within the realm of her own identity as a black woman. Nevertheless, she is never maudlin. "A poet must never succumb to self-pity," she says. Self-pity spells the death of poetry. Her poems are strong, direct, and forcefully articulate in the free verse idiom of contemporary verse. (pp. 33-4)

> *R. Roderick Palmer, "The Poetry of Three Revolutionists: Don L. Lee, Sonia Sanchez, and Nikki Giovanni,"* in C. L. A. Journal *(copyright, 1971 by the College Language Association), September, 1971, pp. 25-36.*

[Sonia Sanchez] is an upfront woman, witty, bright, black, and utterly devoted to those revolutionary ideals she sees as the best hope for Black people. Her poems are raps, good ones, aimed like guns at whatever obstacles she detects standing in the way of Black progress. (p. 45)

Her praises are as generous as her criticisms are severe, both coming from loyalties that are fierce, invulnerable, and knowing. Whether she's addressing her praises to Gwendolyn Brooks or to the late Malcolm X, to her husband or to a stranger's child, always they emerge from and feed back into the shared experience of being Black. (p. 46)

> *William Pitt Root, in* Poetry (© *1973 by The Modern Poetry Association; reprinted by permission of the Editor of* Poetry), *October, 1973.*

* * *

SCHUYLER, James   1923-

Schuyler is an American poet and novelist.

James Schuyler's new book [*The Crystal Lithium*] contains the best poems he has ever written. In a time when many poets have designs on the immediate and provisional, when verse has the air of first-person notation, journals and improvisation, his is naturally a valued presence. His work has the coveted directness, the openness to experience of his plainest declarations: "All things are real/no one a symbol." He is often offhand, but never merely so. . . .

[His] is, as anyone can see, a poetry of nouns and adjectives, of apparent leaps, rags to nobility. If there is any point in mentioning the "New York School" of poets, where Schuyler began with the late Frank O'Hara and John Ashbery, it is only to remark how, in his very best poems, Schuyler transforms their original joy in random surfaces to something more inward, more mysterious. This is one of the hardest kinds of poetry to write, depending on perfect pitch to keep it from sounding like lists for sightseers and shoppers. When you uncouple the sentence, when you exchange a syntax of memory and judgment for a syntax of simultaneity, when you stop saying, "When to the sessions of sweet silent thought, I summon up . . .," the electric spark must jump from noun to seemingly unrelated noun, from event to seemingly disparate event.

Schuyler's effects aren't easily explained; he is somehow tuned to the way the awakened mind moves, to its guarded flirtations and powers. To be composed is, for him, to be at the same moment alive to things that threaten his poise. . . . (p. 6)

> *David Kalstone, in* The New York Times Book Review (© *1972 by The New York Times Company; reprinted by permission), November 5, 1972.*

James Schuyler appears to set up within the poem a kind of one-to-one correspondence between the imagery and language and the reality going on, as it were, behind it. It is as though the poem were a sensitized plate held up to a real landscape, transforming the objects actually there into poetry and creating form which is dictated by the rhythms of the sights and sounds actually present. . . . (p. 8)

Schuyler writes what I have called cloth-of-life poetry. Life goes on in front of one's eyes and has a very complex and rich texture. The senses receive it and transform it into poetry. . . .

One is right there, watching all this, and in its way it is extremely pleasurable. This poetry is close to a certain school of New York realist painting. Mr. Schuyler has lines which

are like those paintings in seeming entirely representational and yet with a clear black-and-white beautiful purity like Chinese brush drawings. . . . (p. 13)

> *Stephen Spender, "Can Poetry Be Reviewed?" in* The New York Review of Books (*reprinted with permission from* The New York Review of Books; *copyright* © *1973 NYREV, Inc.), September 20, 1973, pp. 8-14.*

Schuyler looks a little to one side at the minor motions of external nature, of the people around him, and of his own fluctuating attention, curiosity, and compassion.

While so many other poets are shouting at the top of their voices, Schuyler speaks softly and carries no *shtick* at all. The moments of relaxed awareness, of a serenity achieved in spite of suffering ("I've known un-happiness enough"), moments that many other poets would ignore or fail to see as poetic occasions—these moments Schuyler preserves and explores. He is the observer of quietly unfolding processes, and nowhere does he chart the growth of feelings and of an awakening springtime world more beautifully than in the long title poem of [*Hymn to Life*]. . . . (p. 25)

If Schuyler is a philosophical poet, his "abstractions and generalities" are never allowed to soar off into the heaven of supreme fiction. He is not a heroic forger of myths in the tradition of Whitman or Wallace Stevens. Unlike Whitman, he does not cannibalize everyone else's experience; Schuyler, the tranquil observer, does not have cosmic ambitions. Unlike Stevens, he has not adopted the grand tone and syntax of metaphysical discourse; Schuyler remains chatty and his connectives are loose associations, often puns: "To live! so natural and so hard / Hard as it seems it must be for green spears to pierce the all but / Frozen mold. . . ." But then why do I call Schuyler a philosophical poet at all? Could it be he is simply an autobiographical poet with an eye for nature?

I think not. He has not scrupulously effaced from his work all concern for the Big Questions. They haunt his verse like the smell of flowers that have just been removed from the room. He is always testing and trying on for size general ideas and then discarding them as poor fits. He considers religion as a refuge, then dismisses it ("But without the conviction of a truth, best leave / It alone. Life, it seems, explains nothing about itself"). He comes to doubt whether traditional ideas mean anything at all, or at least mean what they originally meant ("An idea may mutate like a plant, and what was once held basic truth / Become an idle thought . . .").

And yet, and yet Schuyler senses that time and nature are always *about* to surrender their meanings, if we could only decode them, the "untranslatable glyphs" of raindrops caught on a window screen or the gray April light that "spells out bare spots" on the lawn. We are surrounded by the stuff of meaning but we don't know how to fashion it into explanations. What we are left with are dark and bright scraps, with sumptuous, ordinary moments. . . . Schuyler may have written a hymn to life, but it is often in a minor key. No matter. He has found the only happiness that I, at least, can believe in. (pp. 25-6)

> *Edmund White, in* The Village Voice (*reprinted by permission of* The Village Voice;

*   *   *

SEFERIS, George (pseudonym of Georgios Stylianou Seferiadis)   1900-1971

A Nobel Prize-winning Greek poet, Seferis wrote with striking imagery and lyricism about the Hellenic world of culture, past and present. (See also *Contemporary Authors,* Vols. 5-8, rev. ed.)

What interests me about Seferis is his tone of voice in his poems. It is something to do with the building up of context inside a poem, and now that we have a broad mass of his poems to live with, one can see this power of context building up in whole collections and sequences of poems and from year to year, so that one can speak of something having a resonance in the whole context of the poetry of George Seferis. (p. 172)

Seferis' tone of voice (I am going to speak of him as if he existed only in poetry) is at once riveting to the attention. There is something very serious and very complicated about it. It obeys the important rule that poetry now has to be at least as serious, and speak of realities at least as complicated, as prose is capable of doing. (p. 173)

You cannot separate Seferis' tone of voice from the forms and the examples available to him. If you ask how a certain seriousness, a richness of tone that breaks through weaknesses, becomes available to a poet, there will always be an answer in terms of the progress of the poet's own work. . . . But where do the possibilities of verse come from? They belong to a particular moment in the language and a particular moment in the art of poetry. There is no poet who belongs more to his own language than Seferis; it is true of him—in a way it would not be true of Yeats—that he has created the Greek in which he speaks. But the possibilities of writing in such a tone and such a form as he has done belong to the modern movement and its masters all over Europe. No poetry could be more completely Greek than the best poetry of Seferis, and it is quite certain he has exploited veins of possibility in the Greek poetry of earlier generations that only an equally learned poet could ever rediscover, but he is a European poet in the same sense as Eliot or Quasimodo, which Yeats is not; he is a poet who became possible only because of the central traditions of European poetry in the late nineteenth century. (pp. 174-75)

There is no point in comparing stray lines of Seferis' poems with the work of individual European poets who are close to him. What is interesting is how he has reached such a point of easy compression, the kind of language he was already using with ease in *Mythistorema.* . . . Seferis in his early poems . . . is surely one of those who have had to write bad poetry in order to write good; who have had first to express a fineness of reaction, a hungry sharpness of the intellectual senses, in a full, unblushing way that, under the pressure of birth, was bound to appear to the world mannered and frail. A young poet must recapitulate in himself those stages of the history of earlier poetry that have done most to make his future work possible. But the technique is modern; it is Seferis from the beginning. The imagism and the half-rhymes, and above all the governing rhythm of the voice, as early as *The Cistern* in 1932, and (except for the half-rhymes) even in his first book, *Turning Point,* in 1931, are absolutely modern and his own. (p. 176)

[In] a certain sense in the poetry of George Seferis, you can see all the stages [of European poetry] in one man: first the mannerism, the dandy technique, and the confused fullness of feelings; then the liberated art, the freedom of language that could not have been built on any other beginnings.

This is not a question of particular conscious influences, or of a shared subject matter. If that is what you are looking for, it is impossible to see backward through the poems of George Seferis. Poems like his could not exist if they were not opaque. The writings of a poet are not simply original achievements of an individual genius; indeed, the more the poet seems to us a genius, the more certain it is that his work began in the lives and societies and lifework of earlier poets, even if he does not know their names, even if he cannot read their languages. . . . There are certain foreign writings that influenced [his] tone fundamentally, whether by direct or indirect knowledge. Of these the most important is Rimbaud and the most obvious is Eliot, although my personal impression, which I suggest very diffidently, is that Eliot was himself too perfect and too peculiar a poet to have been a fruitful influence on the poetry of other writers in his own time. The same might have been true of Rimbaud in his own time.

The world of Seferis' poems is clearly stated in *Mythistorema.* In that sequence, his first masterpiece, he wrote for the first time with a brush that made clear, economic marks on the page and left no traces on the air, as Basho puts it. The world of each poem is self-contained, but the poems belong together. In this they are very like the prose poems of Rimbaud. . . .

But one can say that Seferis' tone is more serious and more arresting than that of Rimbaud in these poems. He is more closely involved in his poem, and one has the impression it involved him from long before the point where you begin to overhear it. More important, you are involved also, nor can you ever be sure that the world is not yours: it is not quite a dream world but the real, ordinary world seen in the mirrors of a dream. . . . This is the secret of Seferis' tone of voice: everything in his mind that is not the poem is presupposed. We are always in the center of myths that we never understand because the whole story has never been told, the implications cannot be unraveled; probably, in fact certainly, if the lines of implication in *Mythistorema* were pursued to infinity they would contradict each other. . . . This poetry is more profound than the language of existentialism because there is no question that it matters; the self of the poet has a solidity and innocence—if that is the word—of a small boy. But at the same time the self is completely adult: only that he finds himself . . . in the center of [the] poem and has the godlike power of speaking about it. The myths extend outward in every direction into the bones of the language. They are not really stories at all; they are part of our consciousness of the language. In this they are like the central situations of Graham Greene or Conan Doyle that those writers have chosen to elaborate and rationalize into novels: journeys on great trains, the hunted criminal, the hound on the moors, the fog and the violin. It is the language, I believe, that contains the thoughts we inherit. (pp. 179-81)

The grief and the condemnation that Seferis has on very few occasions expressed in his poems have the force of powerful art: his poetry is an organ, not a flute. The rage and the despair of certain poems are Miltonic, but it is never like the anger of Brecht, a unified sensibility. Seferis is in the language like an alchemist among potions; however black his theme and his pronouncement, there are always other elements in the darkness, the solution is never resolved. That is because his myth is equivalent to the Greek language itself, and the force of his despair, whether it is public or personal, has the inevitability of something that belongs to the language itself: it is ourselves, we cannot alter it. I hope I am not speaking mystically about this: unless I am mistaken, as a foreigner may be, it is an objective matter. It is simply that Seferis is so true to the language he uses, his tone is so true to it, that the moral and aesthetic values that truly belong to the language are present to the reader in his use of it, in the same inevitable way as certain values are present in the *Iliad* almost in spite of the epic form of the poem. This is a mark of absolutely genuine language; it is often found in popular art, but I believe seldom in European poetry. Eliot imposes values of his own, even in the *Four Quartets*. The aesthetic and social values of Yeats' poetry are often flatly contrary to the sense of the English language. Seferis' tone of voice has a complicated purity about it that depends on his language always being quite genuine; everything in the poem, and the increasing weight of context that bears on each fresh line as you hear it, rings completely true. . . . There is a level at which the language of Seferis is simple, but with the apparent simplicity of ballads and chronicles, which is not simple at all. (pp. 185-86)

The general sense of Seferis' poetry is tragic, but it no more excludes his own people than the work of Shakespeare. A poet identifies with a wide range of humanity and reality by his identification with the breadth of his native language. In English the modern example is James Joyce. The economy and the intense power of Seferis' style as it has developed have limited his range. He is not a writer of Shakespearean comedies or of works like *Ulysses*, nor would that have been possible for a Greek writer of his generation; but the substance of breadth is there, and his writing has not ceased to develop, even at this time. There is a generosity of spirit in his poems that, if I may say so, is very Greek, even when his voice is one of black lamentation. . . . (p. 187)

> *Peter Levi, S. J., "Seferis' Tone of Voice," in* Modern Greek Writers, *edited by Edmund Keeley and Peter Bien (copyright © 1972 by Princeton University Press; reprinted by permission of Princeton University Press), Princeton University Press, 1972, pp. 171-89.*

The fascination of [Seferis's] poetic journal is in its density and depth of feeling. [*A Poet's Journal: Days of 1945-1951*] is not a record of events (though it covers a specific period) but a series of notes, apparently desultory, about the impact of man, nature and historic time upon a profoundly sensitive and educated writer, the greatest modern Greek poet. It would not be unfair to compare this work in its delicacy, passion and astuteness with that of the Valéry we meet with in the "Notebooks." Both the Frenchman and the Greek were determined to write poetry of deep but controlled feeling and metaphysical subtlety. . . .

[With George Seferis] Greek literature crossed the great divide into Europe and laid its firm claim upon the European consciousness, becoming a part of it. This is not to decry the great Greek poets of the last 50 years—far from it. But their sensibility remains Greek in the Balkan sense, and their work while brilliant is metropolitan Greek in spirit. They were not, as Seferis was, essentially cosmopolitan souls (Cavafy is the one exception), and one wonders whether Seferis's Smyrniot connections did not give him the same angle of vision as Alexandria's did for Cavafy. That, and the roving life of a diplomat. He always grew ironic over himself as a wanderer, and the persona or double he choose for himself (just as his admired friend Eliot chose "Prufrock," just as Pound chose "Mauberley") was "Stratis Thalassinos," an ironic seaman-traveler. He looked upon the impermanence and folly of life with the detached eye of a man who knows that he is leaving it, that his ship will be sailing in a few hours. He did not worry much about death—it was a voyage like any other; he was living in the midst of it. But he felt how provisional life was, and how absurd.

His temperamental relationship with T. S. Eliot will not elude anyone who knew them both, for they had much in common. They were both great critics, and they both worked coolly and quietly like great surgeons ("hastening slowly"). Both were mystics and savants. When Eliot speaks of "getting every ounce of tradition behind each word" one thinks of Seferis, so deeply steeped in the ancient Greek tragedies, and yet so modern in his approach. (p. 6)

> *Lawrence Durrell, in* The New York Times Book Review *(© 1974 by The New York Times Company; reprinted by permission), July 7, 1974.*

Few countries have had as painful a time in the 20th century as Greece; no poet has expressed Greece's pain better than George Seferis. With a visceral understanding of the plight of his native land (like an "umbilical cord that connects mother and child"), Seferis' poetry never loses sight of Greece ("Wherever I travel Greece wounds me"). Bold in style, utilizing a minimum of words ("I want no more than to speak simply"), his poetry draws from a reservoir of history and mythology. Seferis is the only Greek Nobel laureate in literature (1963), so honored for his "deep feeling for the Hellenic world of culture."

But Seferis was not parochial in perspective. While rooted in the Greek soil, Seferis' vision was not limited to the Hellenic world. He was influenced by T. S. Eliot and translated a number of Eliot's works into Greek. . . . Seferis' sense of the tragic pervades his poetry, tempered in intensity only by allegory: "And if I talk to you in fables and parables/it's because it's more gentle for you that way; and horror/really can't be talked about because it's alive."

It is difficult to know Seferis the man through his poetry. . . .

A Poet's Journal offers fresh insight into the life of Seferis. How, I wondered, could he reconcile his life as a poet with that of a diplomat serving a government whose hands were stained with Greek blood? The *Journal* shows the poet in the raw during a time that is the rawest, and in terms of human loss and suffering, the most tragic in modern Greek history. Seferis writes about the same postwar Greece—torn by civil war—that Kazantzakis so vividly portrays in

The Fratricides, so that we understand the most frigid of Cold War history on the poet's level, see his reaction to the chaos and death that engulf him. . . .

Damning the present, Seferis has no illusions about finding a paradise lost. His poem "The King of Asine" (1940) tells of the "permanent despair" experienced in searching for "ancient monuments" to overcome "contemporary sorrow." His despair leads neither to nihilism nor paralyzing frustration: "no problem can be solved by marking time; you must forge ahead or break." (p. 19)

Throughout Seferis' poetry, one finds a tension between a feeling of rootedness in Greek traditions and a sense of exile from the contemporary human condition. "Seferis" is a pen name—a contracted form of his family name, Seferiades—and the etymology of "sefer" connotes journey or wanderer. The wandering Odysseus searching for his identity is an important motif in Seferis' poetry. (pp. 19-20)

There seems little doubt that Seferis was a political conservative. But such a label inadequately describes the psyche of the poet. Despite his Dr. Jekyll/Mr. Hyde life of poet-diplomat, Seferis reacted to the political by an esthetic articulation of the tragic. Furthermore Seferis' respect for the individual transcends simply analysis; it is a respect deeply imbued with classical Greek tradition ("The free man, the just man, the man who is the 'measure' of life; if there is one basic idea in Hellenism, it is this one"). Moreover Seferis' popularization among Greek resistance writers today can hardly be attributed to his politics. (Seferis' persona takes on its most paradoxical guise when one considers that his poetry has become a major influence on the music of rebel composer Mikis Theodorakis.) Seferis' genius rested in his ability to capture in simple but moving images a suffering Greece. Most important, Seferis did so in a style peculiarly Greek, . . . steeped in classical imagery, fostered by the experiences of the Greek people.

Seferis is difficult for historians to evaluate because he expresses intense emotion without a sophisticated understanding of events. Only in passing—usually slighting references—does Seferis' journal mention the politicians and politics of the day. . . . For Seferis, his sense of the tragic is harnessed to the hope that his poetry will somehow awaken his people to a "Greekness" shattered by present politics. (p. 20)

James Goodman, "Poet Diplomat," in The New Republic *(reprinted by permission of* The New Republic; © *1974 by The New Republic, Inc.), September 7, 1974, pp. 19-20.*

*   *   *

SHAFFER, Peter   1926-

Shaffer is a British playwright noted for technical skill, versatility, and sophistication. His early successes were *Five Finger Exercise* **and** *The Royal Hunt of the Sun*. **(See also** *Contemporary Authors*, **Vols. 25-28.)**

[Without] spectacular theatricality, [*The Royal Hunt of the Sun*] amounts to very little; it may be total theatre but it is strictly fractional drama; and being exposed to Peter Shaffer's meditations on religion, love, life, and death for three solid hours is rather like being trapped in a particularly active wind tunnel with no hope of egress. (p. 114)

[The] conquest of Peru by the Spanish invaders is a natural subject for the theatre; it is the kind of dark myth that fascinated Antonin Artaud as an alternative to the decaying subject matter of the Occidental stage. The idea for the play, as a matter of fact, was probably suggested to Mr. Shaffer by Artaud's first scenario for his projected Theatre of Cruelty, a tableau sequence called *The Conquest of Mexico*. In this unproduced spectacle, Artaud hoped to "contrast Christianity with much older religions" and correct "the false conceptions the Occident has somehow formed concerning paganism and certain natural religions," while dramatizing, in burning images, the destruction of Montezuma and his Aztecs by the armies of Cortez. . . . Mr. Shaffer treats the annihilation of the Incas in a similar manner, and (having done his history homework carefully) occasionally engages in some speculative comparative anthropology. But at the same time that he is fashioning cruel Artaudian myths, he is mentalizing, psychologizing, and sentimentalizing these myths. Underneath the tumult and the swirl lie a very conventional set of liberal notions about the noble savage, the ignoble Catholic, and the way brotherly love can bridge the gulf that separates cultures. By the end of the play, in fact, the whole brutal struggle has degenerated into a fraternal romance between a lissome young redskin and an aging lonely paleface—a relationship which is illuminated less by Artaud than by Leslie Fiedler in his essay "Come Back to the Raft Again, Huck Honey." (pp. 114-15)

Robert Brustein, "Peru in New York" (1965) in his The Third Theatre *(copyright © 1969 by Robert Brustein; reprinted by permission of Alfred A. Knopf, Inc.), Knopf, 1969, pp. 114-16.*

On its most readily accessible level, Peter Shaffer's "Equus" . . . is a mystery story. . . . The plot of "Equus" is all simply and artfully, in a series of questions and answers, the working out of the mystery: How did an innocent boy come to reach the point where he felt obliged to blind the horses he loved?

Mr. Shaffer is an ingenious playwright, as we have had reason to observe in his "Five Finger Exercise," "The Royal Hunt of the Sun," and "Black Comedy." He is also a superb writer of dialogue, and in "Equus," which he might once have been content to turn into an exercise (this time for ten fingers, and perhaps for ten toes as well), he has taken far greater chances than before. His psychiatrist poses questions that go beyond the sufficiently puzzling matter of the boy's conduct to the infinitely puzzling matter of why, in a world charged with insanity, we should seek to "cure" anyone in the name of sanity. The doctor faces in his personal life a misgiving likely to paralyze him in his practice; he discovers that the boy, sick as he seemingly is, has had the joy of passion greater than any that the doctor himself has ever felt. If he cures the boy, it will be at the expense of that passion, which the doctor envies and would like to share.

Mr. Shaffer offers his big, bowwow speculations about the nature of contemporary life in the midst of a melodrama continuously thrilling on its own terms. . . . Mr. Shaffer convinces us that there is a pagan "horseness" separate from the life and death of individual horses and well worth our reverence; we violate it at our peril, as we violate our humanity at our peril. The word "equus" stands for more than a single horse, as the word "man" stands for more than a single man. It appears to be Mr. Shaffer's conviction that if only we could be who we are without having to bear the crushing weight of an identity, we would have no need for violence. (p. 123)

> Brendan Gill, "Unhorsed," in The New Yorker (© 1974 by The New Yorker Magazine, Inc.), November 4, 1974, pp. 123-24.

It took Shaffer 2½ years to write *Equus*, the dazzling psychological thriller ... about a boy who blinds six horses ... that is now Broadway's rarest ticket. [Shaffer] had heard in 1972 about the incident on which the play is based. A stableboy had been brought before the magistrates in a rural part of England, accused of blinding with a poker the 26 horses he cared for. The story haunted Shaffer. He never tried to find out the actual details because "I'm not a journalist or a photographer." He is, however, a consummate technician. He delved into the history of horses as sexual and religious symbols and read extensively in animal and child psychology. Then he worked out the boy's motivations to his own satisfaction. In the play they are revealed in long, troubled dialogues between the boy ... who actually worships horses, and a psychiatrist. ...

Shaffer ... resembles Noël Coward and Terence Rattigan, both of whom managed to write hits about such then queasy subjects as drug addiction (*The Vortex*) and homosexuality (*Ross*). Like them, Shaffer possesses an apparently flawless intuition about how much he can shock the audience without turning it off. Coming from a nation that reveres horses, he shrewdly placed a completely nude love scene—which might otherwise have caused a fuss—just before the boy's outrage on the horses. He also has an ear tuned to his audience's particular anxieties. He speaks of the modern struggle to live with ambiguities: the knowledge that any good course can be immediately opposed by another equally possible one. It is this constant weighing of trade-offs that forms Shaffer's conflicts. In *Equus*, the psychiatrist can cure the boy; he can exorcise his gods-demons, but he knows that in exchange he can offer only the dubious promise of "normality" and "adjustment." ...

Shaffer has fashioned a spectacle dominated by horses: actors who bear on their heads equine masks and on their feet wear 6-in.-high hoofs that thud with the menace of a jungle drum. Shaffer has been fascinated by mask drama ever since he wrote *The Royal Hunt of the Sun*, about the conquistador Pizarro in Peru. At his suggestion, Inca funeral masks were worn by the Indians in the last act. "Nobody could think how they should look during Pizarro's speech over the corpse of Atahuallpa," explained Shaffer. "I thought of the masks."

The results were rewarding. People asked Shaffer how he got the masks to change their expressions. "They hadn't, of course," said Shaffer. "But the audience invested so much emotion in the play that it looked as if they had." Many of the audience at *Equus* react similarly: they claim they see the horses' eyes roll. That to Shaffer is the fulfillment of his job. "The playwright must exercise the audience's muscle, its imagination." (p. 117)

> Richard Schickel, "Showman Shaffer," in Time (reprinted by permission from Time,

The Weekly Newsmagazine; *copyright Time Inc.*), November 11, 1974, pp. 117, 119.

Peter Shaffer is a dramatist of talent and intelligence who has always delighted me with his smaller and zanier plays, like *The Private Ear* and *Black Comedy*, but left me hungry and disappointed with his mightier efforts, like *The Royal Hunt of the Sun* and *The Battle of Shrivings*. ... [To me, *Equus*] is a bundle of anathemas.

First, *Equus* falls into that category of worn-out whimsy wherein we are told that insanity is more desirable, admirable, or just saner than sanity. At its lowest, this yields a film like *King of Hearts*; at its campiest, a farce like *Bad Habits*. Though much more sophisticated than these, *Equus* still asks us to believe that the crazed passion of a stableboy for horses, which, on the one hand, makes him create and fanatically worship a horse-god, Equus, and, on the other, drives him viciously to blind half a dozen harmless equines that witnessed his abortive love-making with a girl, is a fine and highflown thing, a love that must be quashed because it is too grand, wild, and beautiful for the humdrum world of plodding humanity. To me, this is nonsense, and I don't for a moment believe the play's psychiatrist who is made to verbalize this bull (or horse). ...

Next, and relatedly, the play asks us to believe that the psychiatrist who cures and "saves" this horse worshiper and blinder diminishes him: makes him plain, unpoetic, and common. Psychiatry, as its representative is made to confess, is a shriveler of souls. Now I hold no particular brief for psychiatry, having seen it not help about as many people as it has helped. But, fallible as it is—like all medicine, like all human endeavor—scoring facile points off it has always struck me as cheap and wrong-headed. I sympathize when a genius like Rilke or Ingmar Bergman refuses psychotherapy on the grounds that his greatness may somehow be lessened, that the achingly oversensitive artistic introspection may end up blunted. But what has this common stableboy to lose if, instead of naked nocturnal horseback-riding, and whipping himself, figuratively and literally, into a frenzy before a cloven-footed image, he makes love to a nice little girl, becomes a solid citizen, and occasionally wins or drops a few shillings at the races?

I particularly resent the further loading of the dice by making the psychiatrist, the spokesman for normality, an unhappily married man, his sex life with a dull and frigid wife completely atrophied, and his kicks coming from the perusal of illustrated tomes on Greek art. Not the goddesses of Phidias and Praxiteles, we are led to surmise, but the softly boyish *kouroi*, the charioteers and athletes of, say, Lysippus—after all, note the almost reverential ardor with which the psychiatrist treats and gazes at his ephebic patient's mind and body. ...

The play, furthermore, espouses the form of the case history, which, with the exception of the courtroom drama, is the most overworked and by now least imaginative form of theatrical offering. It is the difference between a great painting and its exploitation as a jigsaw puzzle: the art is no longer in the magnificent image, but in the fitting together of oddly shaped bits of wood. And then there is that obligatory (here not so obligatory) nude scene ... in which the girl is, of course, the aggressor, causing a breach in the boy's equine fidelity. Then comes the grand nude blinding scene, showing off the boy's organ to best advantage, and all that, combined with the far-fetchedness of this whole notion of hippophilia, makes me agree with [the] view that what is really meant here is pederasty. In a season when every second new play seems to be frankly concerned with homosexuality, the love-that-dare-not-speak-its-name strategy of *Equus* strikes me as particularly jejune.

Lastly, we get that fashionably bittersweet semihappy ending: even if being cured is a cosmic cop-out, the boy, at least, will be cured—as if psychotherapy were such a simple matter: a little hypnosis here, a bit of abreaction there, and our hideously disturbed protagonist's mind is safely on the way to total recovery. But the final blow is the ordinariness of the play's language. . . . What we need is more Lapithae, the mythic race who defeated the Centaurs and invented the bit and the bridle—only for horses, so far, but pretentious playwrights may be next. . . .

[No] amount of external embellishment can overcome the hollowness within.

> John Simon, *"The Blindness is Within,"* in New York Magazine (© *1974 by NYM Corp.; reprinted by permission of* New York Magazine *and John Simon), November 11, 1974, p. 118.*

When the good and ever-so-earnest doctor [in *Equus*] cries out in anger and agony at the fact that he, who in his therapeutic task on Alan [the co-protagonist] may be eliminating what is actually creative in the boy, is at the same time freezing his own best impulses, a good part of the audience applauds. The inference is that, once cured, that is, rid of his "divine" suffering, Alan will become a dullard like most normal people. Such applause is an echo of the new cant: that the schizophrenic is closer to the truth of life than the ordinary citizen. But positing such an alternative is false. One need not be "crazy" to live untrammeled by conventional proscriptions. Most of the insane (I have seen them in hospitals) are in every way far more wretched and pitiful than the average man in his quiet despair or humdrum gloom.

As dramatized, I find the play's "philosophy" bogus. Dysart [the psychiatrist] himself needs to be cured of his faulty reasoning. The playwright needs a more fitting "objective correlative" or story analogy for his defense of the irregular or anomalous person. (pp. 506-07)

> Harold Clurman, *in* The Nation (*copyright 1974 by the Nation Associates, Inc.), November 16, 1974.*

I was never able wholly to accept the psychiatric case-history that Shaffer invented [for *Equus*] to explain the strange and terrible aberration of the adolescent stable-lad who blinds the horses he supposedly dotes upon, but it's a beautifully organised, arrestingly written play. . . . (p. 714)

> Kenneth Hurren, *in* The Spectator (© *1974 by* The Spectator; *reprinted by permission of* The Spectator*), November 30, 1974.*

Peter Shaffer . . . who began, with *Five Finger Exercise* (1958), very much in the pre-1956 style and later borrowed rather superficially from Brecht for *The Royal Hunt of the Sun* (1964), has suddenly come into his own with *Equus* (1973). The play is still naturalistic but it moves with im-

pressive suppleness from past to present, reality to dream, narration to dialogue and at moments even into choric frenzy, with actors wearing the stylised masks of horses. It is clear that Shaffer's earlier rather unremarkable versions of psychological drama (though including the clever firework *Black Comedy* [1965]) were stages in a slow movement towards his real area of interest, a modern use of myth. *The Battle of Shrivings*, which seemed such an artistic disaster when it was performed in 1970 and which scarcely seems to be much improved in its rewritten version *Shrivings*, can now perhaps be seen as Shaffer's *adieu* to unmodified naturalism. *Equus* teaches us to call no playwright predictable until he is dead. (p. 65)

> John Spurling, *in* Encounter (© *1974-75 by Encounter Ltd.), January, 1975.*

Some American critics have found in [the] situation [of Martin, the psychiatrist in *Equus*,] a disguised statement of the plight of the timid homosexual, who lacks the courage to pursue the dangerous consummation of his desires. However, Shaffer has strongly denied any such intention, and the play works quite well if Martin is taken to represent the apparently ingrained tendency of many modern Britons to accept, without passion or anger, a well-ordered but watered-down existence. Yet the play's statement is less impressive than is Shaffer's skillful theatrical fabrication, which deftly finds layers of comic relief as he inexorably drills deeper into the hard rock of tragedy. Indeed, *Equus* emerges as a surprisingly painless modern tragedy, which accounts for both its popularity and the reservations some serious critics have expressed about its significance. . . .

All in all, one suspects *Equus* is at its truest when it is reflecting its author's anger at his own civilization.

> Henry Hewes, *"The Crime of Dispassion,"* in Saturday Review (*copyright* © *1975 by Saturday Review/World, Inc.; reprinted with permission), January 25, 1975, p. 54.*

Equus . . . surgically probes man's continuing fascination with violent forms of belief, those passionately fanatical, sometimes sacrificial manifestations of religious ecstasy. . . .

Shaffer's dramatic theme isn't new: obsession with the more primitive emotional drives inherent in extremely devout belief repeatedly has been treated in the drama and literature of our Freudian-shaped century, from D. H. Lawrence to Tennessee Williams and Carson McCullers. Shaffer's own previous work, the colorful and ritualistic *Royal Hunt of the Sun*, explored the self-sacrificial potentialities brought on by a confrontation of the Aztec and Spanish cultures.

Equus presents a psychiatric search for the reason for a specific violent act. A psychiatrist in a provincial British hospital . . . is given the case of the stableboy, Alan Strang. . . . In the argumentative relationship that develops between boy and doctor, Shaffer explores the boy's mental process—the usual ploy of psychiatric thrillers—but he additionally attempts, quite successfully, to set up and comprehend the elemental struggles in Everyman's concept of his individual world. . . .

Central to the playwright's dramatic concept is the idea of the horse as totemic animal, a creature-symbol of male power, an emblem of transcending mastery. Young Strang has come to understand intuitively, with his viewing and appreciation of television cowboys, that the coupling of man and animal can produce a type of grandeur, an intensification of religious experience, unknown in an era of commercial jingles and electrical appliances. In this sense, the boy is not unlike the repressed Army private in Carson McCullers' *Reflections in a Golden Eye* who rode naked through the Fort Benning forests.

Earlier, Strang had been attracted, his mother tells his doctor, to more "normal" religious images; he liked, for example, a picture of Christ ascending Calvary "loaded with chains" while the centurions "were really laying on the stripes." His father's objection to such "kinky" pictures causes the boy to change his worship to more Dionysian forms.

Of course, that traditional civil war of the psyche, the Apollonian and Dionysian struggle—the stress created between our simultaneous desires for, on the one hand, order, restraint, and rationality, and, on the other, passion, power, and violence—is evoked. Thomas Mann utilized the same confrontation in his *Death in Venice*, where the disciplined, craftsmanlike novelist Aschenbach fatally collided with his passionate vision, the boy-god Tadzio.

What is most gratifying about *Equus*, however, is the play's rich complexities. . . . Its principals, doctor and boy, are filled with ambiguity. If the boy is to return to "normal," he must lose the very meaningful religious sense he has developed; similarly, the analyst has come to have doubts about his psychiatric "religion" and about his role in it as priest or savior. Dysart, the psychiatrist, recognizes also that the boy he is treating has experienced "a passion more ferocious than I have felt in any second of my life." (p. 114)

With *Equus*, [Shaffer] has provided himself not only with a Lawrentian search into the dark night of the soul; he has also deeply explored the mythmaking necessity of man. (p. 115)

> *Jere Real, "A Rocking Horse Winner," in* National Review (© *National Review, Inc., 1975; 150 East 35th St., New York, N.Y. 10016), January 31, 1975, pp. 114-15.*

Shaffer is a playwright of very modest talents that, when put to a use commensurate with their scope, can produce a thin but pleasant amusement like *Black Comedy* or a competent family melodrama like *Five Finger Exercise*. However, when he attempted a heavier task in *The Royal Hunt of the Sun*, he turned the conquest of Peru into a public-school history pageant and made a conflict of cultures an exercise in English badinage. In *Equus* he has scaled down his scene of action but not his ambitions, for although the play is about a young man's undergoing the agony of mental therapy, much more is at stake in this drama than the rehabilitation of an individual psyche. The whole question of cultural vitality, of the Apollonian and Dionysian tension in civilization, is Shaffer's theme. (p. 77)

[This play] seems to me to be a perfect case-study in the mediocrity of insight necessary nowadays for a play to enjoy a popular reputation for profundity. From the schematic psychology to the simpleminded cultural criticisms, there is nothing in this play that either informs us what life is or what it ought to be. It is all contrivance, all middle-class whines and whimpers that generally belong to the fantasies of afternoon television. One sits through *Equus* and wonders how it could be possible that so much effort was spent trying to make this poor example of a young boy's derangement into a symbol of human vitality. The dark, irrational exhilarations of human life are made by Shaffer to seem so neat and precise a part of our psychology that *Equus* ends by making pure reason appear the real human adventure; and if one should embark on it during one of the play's many *longueurs* it comes to mind that the good doctor, and all those critics who agree with him, would not see Alan as such a romantic figure if he'd found his notion of deity in titmice or in a piece of very rare roast beef. The thesis that madness, if not outrightly divine, is at best preferable to the 20th century's ruthless and uninspired sanity, is in this play, as it is in so much fashionable philosophizing, totally dependent on a pleasant, aesthetically rational form of derangement for the credibility of its argument. Great foam-covered stallions in the moonlight are fine, but for titmice cults and roast-beef sects there is no public. (p. 78)

> *Jack Richardson, in* Commentary (*reprinted from* Commentary *by permission; copyright* © *1975 by the American Jewish Committee), February, 1975.*

After its success at Britain's National Theatre, Peter Shaffer's *Equus* took New York's critics and audiences by storm. It is well on its way to becoming the first dramatic hit on Broadway in heaven knows how many seasons. Serious plays have been failing year after year on the Broadway stage, where for some years now only comedies or musicals have paid off. . . .

What is there about *Equus* that may make it the exception to an ironbound rule?

First of all, *Equus* is pretentious, which the public falls for. (p. 97)

If "normality" is the patsy in this play, psychiatry, clearly, is the villain. (p. 103)

The play pullulates with dishonesty. Dishonesty toward its avowed purpose, the explication of "a dreadful event," by making that dreadfulness seem fascinating and even admirable. Dishonesty to the audiences, by trying to smuggle subliminal but virulent homosexual propaganda into them. Dishonesty toward the present state of the theatre, in which homosexuality can and has been discussed openly and maturely. Dishonesty to psychiatry, which is depicted as a castrator of bodies and souls. Dishonesty toward normality (whatever that is), by making its representatives and defenders, for the most part, pathetic or unappetizing. Dishonesty to art, which does not abide such facile equivocations as "You will be cured," "You won't be cured," "You will be cured, and less healthy for it," to say nothing of the fudging over of that horse-blinding by doing it as a nude scene, and to horses that are mere metallic masks. Greek tragedy showed no acts of violence either, but found a poetry that could richly convey them. It would not have settled for a Dysart [the psychiatrist] who says feebly—as he assumes, for no good reason given, the boy's sick identity—"I stand in the dark with a pick in my hand, striking at heads," followed by the no less feeble lines about *his* now having a permanent, painful chain in his mouth. Has Dysart become both Alan Strang and Equus?

In any case, the final dishonesty here is toward the very thing meant to be championed: homosexuality. Not only is it obliged to masquerade as zooerastia (also known as bestiality), it is also accorded a false and misleading image. What is the equivalent in basic homophile terms for the key incident of *Equus*, the blinding of the horses? I can find no valid analogies, yet the fundamental obligation of a metaphor or symbol is to create a thorough, functioning correspondence. *Equus* fails all the causes it seems to espouse, except for the dubious cause of spectacular theatricality. (p. 106)

> *John Simon, "Hippodrama at the Psychodrome," in* The Hudson Review *(copyright © 1975 by The Hudson Review, Inc.; reprinted by permission), Vol. XXVIII, No. 1, Spring, 1975, pp. 97-106.*

Equus clearly touches a nerve in the New York audience, as it did earlier in London, which means that it is something more serious (*i.e.*, more timely) than the effectively theatrical play it so obviously is. Not that I am completely taken with it as a play. Its main dramatic action lies in the psychiatrist's longing for an experience, however dangerous, as direct (as "primitive," he would say, tongue slightly in cheek) as that of the young man he is attempting to help (cure? turn to plastic?). . . .

No well-brought up audience can resist the combination of sexuality, religion and violence, and Shaffer attempts to weaken any possible resistance by organizing the play as a series of scenes in which the patient's acting-out becomes theatrical presentation. There is something a bit too concocted about the mechanism for my taste, the transformation of therapy into detective story, answering *why* rather than *who*. (p. 78)

We file out into the New York streets and—if I read that applause correctly—go back to our own narrow lives. *Equus*, it seems, is more than a high-class melodrama. It is a cry for the power of irrationality. Or an echo. (p. 79)

> *Gerald Weales, in* Commonweal *(copyright © 1975 Commonweal Publishing Co., Inc.; reprinted by permission of Commonweal Publishing Co., Inc.), April 25, 1975.*

*   *   *

SHAW, Robert   1928-

A British novelist, playwright, and actor, Shaw is best known for *The Man in the Glass Booth*, a courtroom drama of Nazi persecution of the Jews. (See also *Contemporary Authors*, Vols. 1-4, rev. ed.)

[*The Man in the Glass Booth*,] Robert Shaw's drama about a Jewish businessman who is exposed as a former SS colonel, a member of Eichmann's *Einsatzgruppen*, and then exposed again as a real Jewish businessman posing as a Nazi is, at bottom (and the way down isn't very far) at the very least insulting to the reality of Jewish suffering at the hands of Hitler. And this isn't because Shaw, a very good actor and a mediocre novelist whose first play this is, says anything openly calumniatory about the Jews but because he trivializes terrible actuality, plays with it and turns it into "entertainment."

But nobody seems to have noticed or cared, with the ex-

ception of Jack Kroll, whose . . . review touches with fine perceptiveness on all the play's strange perversions and ambitions. Shaw's chief ambition is to construct a hip moral drama, one informed by our contemporary awareness of how the oppressor and the victim may be united, how the sufferer may be a secret, powerless Nazi, dreaming of his torturer's jackboots. But crowding that ambition and muddying up the play is another motif: the Jew poses as a Nazi in order to say in the dock "what no German has said," that is, the world will now hear the voice of Hitlerism, strident, unashamed and brutally clear.

Well, as Kroll remarks, it would take a Dostoevsky to do justice to the first notion (although a . . . story by Irvin Faust, *Jake Bluffstein and Adolf Hitler*, isn't a bad try at it; but Faust is controlled, clear-headed and unpretentious, as Shaw is not), while the second strikes me as at best supererogatory and at worst dramaturgically thin. At any rate, those are the play's premises, and Shaw proceeds to build on them a confused melodrama whose air of significance comes more from the raw subject matter than from any internal accomplishment. (pp. 225-26)

> *Richard Gilman, "Murky Soup and Trivialized Actuality" (1968), in his* Common and Uncommon Masks: Writings on Theatre 1961-1970 *(copyright © 1971 by Richard Gilman; reprinted by permission of Random House, Inc.), Random House, 1971, pp. 223-27.*

Though *The Man in the Glass Booth* is clearly more of a major work than either of Shaw's other two plays, it does share with them a dramatic interest in extreme situations. Its style is, so to say, one of abstracted realism, in that the dialogue is realistic even if time and place are telescoped in a series of rapid transitions. As for the subject-matter, it shares with *Off the Mainland* and *The Pets* a preoccupation with that borderland between reality and fantasy, sanity and insanity in which the latest generation of British dramatists seem to feel most at home. *The Man in the Glass Booth* especially is a work of considerable, if enigmatic, power—enough so to make one hope Shaw will turn his attention to the theatre as a writer more frequently in future. (p. 202)

> *John Russell Taylor, in his* The Second Wave: British Drama for the Seventies *(reprinted with the permission of Farrar, Straus & Giroux, Inc.; copyright © 1971 by John Russell Taylor), Hill & Wang, 1971.*

Robert Shaw's *Cato Street* . . . illustrate[s] the difference between using history as inspiration and using it as a pretext. Like many dramatists before him, Mr. Shaw seems to have been confronted with the fact that historical events are often stubbornly undramatic, being either too simple or dull in themselves or too long to make a play.

The Cato Street Conspiracy falls into the first category: a hare-brained attempt by apparently simple-minded men to blow up the entire British cabinet. Revolutions are not made of such ideas or by such people. The conspiracy was foiled, and no effort by Mr. Shaw could breathe life into its story. (p. 40)

> *Randall Craig, in* Drama, *Spring, 1972.*

Robert Shaw's play [*The Man in the Glass Booth*], like his own novel on which it is based, is a compendium of deliberate—at times far too deliberate—attempts at obfuscation. (p. 147)

Goldman [the protagonist, in referring to the Nazi era, comments] . . .: "We're all Germans, Charlie. All Germans and all J . . . E . . . Ws."

The idea is familiar. Weiss insists on it in *The Investigation*, Hochhuth to a lesser extent in *The Deputy*. In similar circumstances men will behave in similar ways. The innocent will become the guilty, the victims the victimizers. It is all a question of opportunity, a matter of occasion. All men are at least partially guilty, at least potential aggressors, exploiters, killers.

Shaw wants to say this, of course, but also something more. It is how he combines the two that lends the play its early if distinctly flawed fascination. That and its not too subtly worn aura of intellectual mystery story. The game is called "Who is Arthur Goldman?" (p. 148)

Shaw obviously thinks . . . that a guilt that may be—very likely is—distributable should be distributed; that the manufacturer of yesterday, often the manufacturer of today, the priest who looked the other way, or the politician who managed to emerge with his hands relatively—apparently—clean, also was culpable. Is it possible that all men are Nazis? (p. 152)

One does not ask for "answers" to why [the Holocaust] happened—answers are perhaps impossible. What one does look for is some shaft of at least momentary illumination, some suggestion of new insight. It is here that Shaw fails. *The Man in the Glass Booth* is most of all "clever." In a serious kind of way. It takes a theme that has been used time and again in the past three decades and uses it yet once more, but without adding anything; at least without saying anything. Inevitably, one begins to resent its very cleverness, all those symbols and metaphors wandering about in search of an informing intelligence—or perhaps a sensibility—to transform them.

There is, however, a moment, a brilliant moment, late in the play, when Goldman-Dorff delivers a long monologue to the court [during his trial for war crimes]. It is a paean to Hitler, to what he meant to the German people at a moment in history and why he was able to so completely capture their loyalty—why, Shaw suggests, another Hitler might capture ours today. . . . And perhaps this is where the play has led. It is almost certainly where it should have ended. What follows—the picking up of pieces, the tying together of loose ends—says no more.

An old woman emerges from the audience to announce that "this man is not Dorff" and that she cannot let him continue. He is "enjoying himself too much." He, in fact, *is* Arthur Goldman and he is German-Jewish, a survivor of the camps. (pp. 152-53)

So it is all a "mistake." Goldman, with his millions, has contrived it all: bribed Israeli agents; planted the X-rays, the photographs, the handwriting samples; arranged for the forged records; made the anonymous phone calls that led to his being tracked down; burned the flesh under his arm so that they would think the scar concealed an SS insignia.

But *why* did he do it? Did he merely wish a forum from which to proclaim the collective guilt of mankind or of the German nation? Did he simply wish to have on trial—finally to have on trial—someone who would acknowledge responsibility and provide a true picture of the mentality that prevailed in those days, rather than an automaton only "taking orders?" Was he involved in an act of atonement—and for what? Did he view himself as some sort of Christ-surrogate?

All these, of course, and that is the play's major weakness. Encompassing everything, it embodies nothing fully, becomes a muddled rehashing of clichés, so diffuse in its effect that it almost might be said not to have one. . . .

But who is [Goldman] . . .? Does he see himself as God, a god, explaining, expiating? (In the novel, he does in fact cry into the microphone, "I am Christ, the chosen of God; offer me vinegar. I am the King of the Jews.") When, finally, he locks himself in his glass booth, innocent by their standards, is he even more guilty by his own? In the novel, he insists, "This is not a rabbinical school. There is no 'why' here." But today, in this context, *why* is the only question. To deny and diffuse it, as Shaw has, into an intellectual party game, meets neither historical nor theatrical imperatives. (p. 154)

> *Catharine Hughes, "'The Man in the Glass Booth'," in her* Plays, Politics, and Polemics *(copyright © 1973 by Catharine Hughes), Drama Book Specialists, 1973, pp. 145-54.*

*   *   *

SLAVITT, David   1935-
(Henry Sutton)

Slavitt is an American novelist, poet, and translator. His novels include *Anagrams* and *ABCD*. (See also *Contemporary Authors*, Vols. 21-22.)

Books by David Slavitt aren't actually reviewed. Critics seize upon them as opportunities to snipe at him for his histrionic disdain of them. Muggers, sex maniacs and murderers may find forgiveness, but there's no sympathy for Slavitt, who committed literary sacrilege by making fun of what he calls the Quality Lit Biz—and, worse yet, making money by making fun. An accomplished poet, he frequently mocks the profession. An astute commentator on current literature and cinema, he has stated that most criticism is slightly refined gossip. A talented comic novelist, he tossed off (under the pseudonym of Henry Sutton) a trio of best-selling potboilers that filled his enemies with outrage and envy, and his coffers with coin of the realm.

All this is worth recalling, since Slavitt's . . . novel ["Anagrams"] offers a satirical insight into the Quality Lit Biz as conducted on American campuses. A group of lesser-known writers converge upon a Midwestern college for one of those absurd exercises called Literary Festivals. Because critical esteem, or financial solvency, or both have escaped them, the poets and novelists grow verbally aggressive—what else?—and play punishing tricks on each other, their obtuse host, and the equally obtuse audience. Predictably, the event is neither festive nor literary—with one major exception. Jerome Carpenter, the protagonist (and a professional plagiarist for a dissertation service), manages to finish an important poem.

On this foundation Slavitt has fashioned dozens of grotesquely funny scenes. But as a novel, "Anagrams" doesn't quite work. The story is slender and at times creaky and unconvincing; an anagrams game and the composition of Carpenter's poem are forced to carry far too much dramatic freight. Then, too, other than Carpenter and his friend, John Royle, the characters remain curiously flat.

Yet as a display of verbal pyrotechnics, the book is unbeatable. Each page pulses with provocative opinions, puns, jokes and the sort of throwaway lines most authors parcel out for maximum mileage. Though some scenes are overly long, the reader never questions the timbre of the prose, or that he is in the presence of authentically poetic minds. Wild about words, delirious at the infinite possibilities of diction, these writers almost shape a world for themselves before reality intrudes.

Slavitt seems to suggest they suffer the kind of isolation usually associated with drug addiction. Shuffling words the way an anagrams player shuffles letters, they are estranged from mates, mistresses and one another, since the sensitivity of their creative perceptions has little effect on their personal relationships. Prisoners of an expensive vice, they pursue single-mindedly the satisfaction of their craving, and scramble madly for rip-offs. Rather than snatch purses, they pick up fees for lecturing, teaching and, yes, doing reviews.

Carpenter, however, feels superior to his colleagues. He never pretends to live by anything less than outright deceit. In providing fraudulent dissertations for aspiring academics, he exposes the absurdity of a system that rewards spurious scholarship yet fears creativity. He has no illusions this will change things. Experience has taught him that most students and faculty members are no more interested in serious contemporary literature than the average traveling salesman. (pp. 6-7)

Ultimately, "Anagrams" is not so much a novel as the record of a groping, sometimes lyrical, mind working its way through the problem of how to live as a poet. As a set of bitchy, subjective, cynical literary opinions, the book can be both irritating and entertaining. In the end, the idea that emerges most clearly is that good literature stands on its own, regardless of the story of its composition or the personality of its author. Judged by this standard, "Anagrams" stands forth as a funny, incisive, and sad examination of what it means to have a 50-dollar-a-day habit for poetry. (p. 7)

> Michael Mewshaw, in The New York Times Book Review (© 1971 by The New York Times Company; reprinted by permission), September 5, 1971.

The best of [the] poems [in *Child's Play*] are essay-like diversions that probe, expand, mock, and juggle human certitude and fate. Slavitt's thoughtfulness finds new points of view, and the thought masks the music and the varied pacing that carries it. . . . Although a number of the poems are simply things that occurred to him, not experiences deeply felt or considered, their laughter at man and praise of the survivor gives a gentle reminder of the variety of ways of hanging in. (p. lxii)

> Virginia Quarterly Review (copyright, 1973, by the Virginia Quarterly Review, The University of Virginia), Vol. 49, No. 2 (Spring, 1973).

For its epigraph, [*ABCD*] carries a quotation from Bach's *Art of the Fugue*. Musical readers, unless possessed of a supernatural wisdom, had better not spend too long in working out what it means. The key, D minor, often associated with tragedy and lamentation, is of little assistance here, and the sequence of notes would not offer a clue even to those with a mania for finding cruciform shapes in the Saint Matthew Passion or for detecting a code system in the songs of Schumann.

Music has in fact dictated the book's form as well as determining its title. Not that the author has resorted to the sonata principle or divided the narrative into four movements with Italian tempo markings, or had the thing printed on barred staves with clefs attached. Perhaps it might have been jollier if this were the case. No, these are, believe it or not, the Fugue Murders, in which, after appropriately staggered entries, D kills C kills B kills A. Apart, however, from this singular structural quirk, and a primitive urge to know how D finishes up, there is little to hold the reader's attention to the end.

As this is neither a whodunnit nor a psychological thriller, Mr Slavitt forces us to concentrate, with what often turns out to be an embarrassing directness, on his skills as a word spinner.

Story and characters wilt in an overheated greenhouse of artificiality. . . . Allusions to Leibniz, a disquisition on cigars (whose brand-names the author misspells), and an obligatory reference to the movies do not guarantee sophistication; neither does a barrage of self-conscious, neo-Jamesian rhetoric adequately suggest that dexterity of style to which it clearly pretends. A concerto, a symphonic poem, a set of variations, might better suit Mr Slavitt's talents. His fugue is but a mildly entertaining time-waster.

> *"Initial Impacts," in* The Times Literary Supplement (© *Times Newspapers Ltd., 1974; reproduced by permission*), *May 3, 1974, p. 465.*

ABCD is . . . thoroughly modern. It is a treatise on the art of self-indulgence. . . .

[The protagonists'] actions are mercifully unpredictable, and Mr Slavitt has a quirky, elliptical imagination which casts a long shadow over whatever his raised eyebrow brushes against. His is an ordinary, human story of incest, murder and intrigue but it is one that refuses to take any of them particularly seriously. I liked it. (p. 548)

> Peter Ackroyd, in The Spectator (© 1974 by The Spectator; reprinted by permission of The Spectator), May 4, 1974.

* * *

SNYDER, Gary 1930-

Snyder, a Pulitzer Prize-winning American poet associated with the San Francisco Renaissance, spent nearly ten years as a novice and student of Zen in a Japanese monastery. That experience, like his work as a logger, forester, carpenter, and seaman, is close to the heart of his accomplished poetry of innocence and primal ritual. (See also *Contemporary Authors*, Vols. 17-18.)

Once he has announced his occupational skills as logging, forestry, carpentry and seamanship, it is not surprising that Gary Snyder, who says that as a poet he holds "the most archaic values on earth," should have left this country where the forests have been stripped or burned off, where "the crews have departed," for the interior exile of Japanese monasteries and the rapturous life of a cosmic bum. . . . It is a departure from a world of fragments. . . . (p. 487)

It is perhaps his very aspiration to an illuminated existence *within* what other men call reality that makes Snyder so poignantly aware of the waste, the devouring slough of human life, and in his later work there ceases to be anything so neat as a division between a poem of detritus and a poem of ecstasy, for merely the litany of constatation provides the poet with his ascent. . . . (p. 493)

We are reminded that Snyder is the true heir of that Thoreau who retired to Walden in order to discover the meaning of the word "property" and found it meant only what was proper or essential to unbound human life. This self-exiled poet, like the one who withdrew from Concord, ballasts with what his senses tell him. . . . (p. 495)

No wonder the phenomenology of Snyder's landscape is so difficult to pin down! He is forever exchanging the trough of the wave for the crest, the mountain-top for the abyss, the world of cars and haircuts for the rocky desolation in which we are accustomed to find, reading the scroll inch by inch, a tiny, radiant sage under some tremendous crag—and that will be this odd American poet, our post-Hiroshima Lafcadio Hearn, who ends his latest excerpt from the endless poem-scroll of his life with this classic bit of spiritual geography, a human universal from Dante to Hiroshige:

> . . . *We were at the bottom of the gorge. We
> started drifting up the canyon. "This is the
> way to the back country."*   (p. 496)

> *Richard Howard, "Gary Snyder" (origi-
> nally published in* Perspective), *in his* Alone
> With America: Essays on the Art of Poetry
> in the United States Since 1950 *(copyright* ©
> *1965, 1966, 1967, 1968, 1969 by Richard
> Howard; reprinted by permission of Athe-
> neum Publishers, New York), Atheneum,
> 1969, pp. 485-98.*

The Back Country is a better introduction to [Gary Snyder's] work, but *Regarding Wave* is fine in a new way. One could say it's more confessional, though Snyder can always write about himself when he feels like it. He still writes Ginsberg chant sometimes, never as nice as his quieter, more genuinely tribal domestic ones, notes from the tipi and kiva. The poem "Meeting the Mountains" about his son Kai should have been written years ago by somebody. It's perfect Snyder and a perfect poem, ample repayment for all those deadly numbers the bad ones write about their preternaturally uninteresting offspring. It is a splendid, readable dawn book. I know young men whom Snyder has spoiled for anybody else; all they want is *The Back Country, Earth House Hold*, and a pack sack. Surely nobody is writing such excellent verse for that rockclimbing kind of person. Snyder is that ideal thing—the author you see scruffy copies of lying around. Adolescents are still unpleasantly fond of Rod McKuen. I've questioned them and

it's true—what comes back is the *mood* of a McKuen poem, not the words—all you do is tell them so and shunt them Snyder, and I swear they grow up before your eyes. William Stafford, Gary Snyder, and Robert Creeley work for you that way; Lowell and Berryman don't. . . . (pp. 209-10)

> *Gerald Burns, in* Southwest Review *(©
> 1971 by Southern Methodist University
> Press), Spring, 1971.*

I am uncertain about Snyder. Not uncertain about his effectiveness as a poet—Snyder is brilliant and unmistakeable—but I am uncertain of the innocence that could write a poem of the simplicity of "How To Make Stew In The Pinacate Desert." It is an innocence that somehow has the feeling of a stance, an attitude—which would make it not innocent—but his poem, like Snyder, has the feeling of completeness, that the poem, and he, is what it says it is. Within the poem are larger implications, but it is—simply—a recipe for cooking stew in the desert, written for some friends. (p. 57)

The simplicity is only an immediate face of the poem, an attitude that Snyder is using to direct the poem's movement. And it is a poem, even if it reads like a recipe. . . .

It is—also—more than a poem. In its simplicities and immediacies Snyder is describing a ceremony. The definiteness of the directions, the care of the details, for the vegetables, the meat, the times, places, spaces, all the movements of a ceremony. A simple ceremony, but by the act of ceremony itself the levels of meaning have become multiple, the steps of the ceremony followed with the image of their implied meanings. A ceremony for what, to yield what? Ceremonies have a circumference beyond their immediate event that gives even their confusions a larger importance. Even Gary Snyder's ceremony for making beef stew in the desert outside of Tucson, Arizona. (p. 58)

Snyder's ceremony is like much of his poetry, an attempt to reenact the experience of the natural environment. *Walden* written in a small hand. An American ceremony, affirmed over and over by American writers who, like Snyder, have felt the necessity of continuing this experience. They've thought of it either as a step toward a "true" environment—a positive stance—or as a step away from the "false" environment of the American city—a negative stance. For Snyder the ceremony is a step toward, a positive movement and direction, its affirmation so self-evident that he doesn't even feel the necessity of justifying it. His poetry has had this same clarity of affirmation from his earliest books. *Rip Rap* has as little artifice as his recipe for stew. The poems—it was his first book—almost completely outlined the spaces that his poetry has filled since. The opening poem, "Mid-August at Sourdough Mountain Lookout," ends,

> I cannot remember things I once read
> A few friends, but they are in cities.
> Drinking cold snow-water from a tin cup
> Looking down for miles
> Through high still air.

Even in a book as early as *Rip Rap* the innocence was directly and clearly present.

His poetry has this openness, this simplicity, but it also has a fullness, a sense of completeness. Everything in the poems comes out of his involvement with the earth in its deepest sense. In *Rip Rap* there is the shamanism of "Praise for Sick Women," poems from his loose wandering as a merchant seaman, poems from his life in the mountains of the Pacific Northwest, from his life in Japan—the "great stone garden in the sea"—the themes that have continued through his poetry. In all of it is the same innocence—the same guarded distance from the concept of a city and a crowd. Snyder would have liked to live his life as part of a tribe, without a tribe he has had to develop his own rituals toward the earth and its creatures. The years he has spent in Zen studies in Japan could have emphasized the ceremonial in a poem about a desert stew—since so much of the life in a monastery is ceremonial—but it could as well come out of his feeling of the necessity of the tribe and its ritual.

But the poetry still has a confusing element, its certainty is sometimes disquieting. The simplicity, the innocence sometimes has an overtone of obviousness, of insistence. Does Snyder mean it? Is his innocence genuine, despite the obvious complexity of his attitude toward it? Within its small frame even a poem like the stew recipe is insisting on the uniqueness of the wilderness experience, its attitudes—through his own involved feeling of tribe and earth—rooted in the Rousseauist vision of the romantic primitive, and to its manifestation through the American philosophic ideal of an essential innocence in the wild and the untouched. . . . Thoreau, ranging the same ground, would have stepped further, would have related the ceremony of cooking a desert stew to his own, and intensely personal, philosophy; but Thoreau, without being conscious of it, was less innocent than Snyder. (pp. 58-60)

Snyder's individuality has a complexity of depth and mood. He has come to it from a new conception, the concept of an innocence that builds itself through an awareness of what it has to avoid. A self-chosen innocence. Snyder has sensed that his response to much of what the American environment is forcing in on him has to be an act of rejection. His rejection is so complete that nothing of this response is even present in the poem. Nothing in his description of his stew making ceremony suggests that he is self-conscious—even self-aware that the simplicity of the poem, in itself, has to be an expression of his own complexity. The poem, for him, is as complete within itself as a piece of stone. . . .

The care for detail, the insistence on detail, has the same kind of concentration as a paragraph on fire building in a Boy Scout manual . . . and it is as isolated in its implications. (p. 61)

The moral implication is tangled and obscure, a denial of knowledge as a form of innocence, but he would probably refuse even to consider the implication. It could be that at this place in the American journey it is the only innocence left to us. (p. 62)

Samuel Charters, "Gary Snyder," in his Some Poems/Poets: Studies in American Underground Poetry Since 1945 *(copyright © 1971 by Samuel Charters), Oyez, 1971, pp. 57-63.*

Gary Snyder's "Trail Crew Camp at Bear Valley, 9000 Feet. Northern Sierra—White Bone and Threads of Snowmelt Water" is . . . deeply alien to traditional Western thought. (p. 59)

It may have occurred to the reader that the pattern of Snyder's poem very strikingly resembles that of a religious experience. Trails are like Ways, hence Snyder's occupation strongly suggests a process of meditation or spiritual exercise, clearing the path from temporal life to the moment of Enlightenment—the sudden dropping-away of the phenomenal world in the contemplation of the infinite and eternal, All and Nothingness. The ending of the poem reflects equally age-old processes: the return to the world, the greater awareness of reality paradoxically following on the awareness of its opposite, the insight that the Way Up is the Way Down. Yet we should beware of saying, in the usual sloppy way of critics, that the events in the poem (or the poem itself) *symbolize* such an experience; they contain the experience, as a Zen koan does, even if the content is to be unlocked only by arduous subsequent meditation. Thus, from a Zen point of view, skilful and concentrated work, work which tends to fuse the categories of subject and object, being and doing, is a kind of spiritual exercise likely to lead to Enlightenment; and this Enlightenment would be no less itself for arriving through a sudden vista of mountains. (Symbolism in our usual sense presupposes a hierarchic arrangement of kinds of experience and categories of consciousness, and it is this presupposition that I think Snyder, in keeping with many non-Western traditions, would wish to exclude.)

Poems like these have been referred to, derogatorily, as "Imagist." . . . But this seems to me a misapplied term; for I feel . . . no consciousness of restraint, no sense that hardness and indirection are aesthetic goods *per se*, and certainly no taboo against emotional or abstract language. The [poet does] choose subjects that are seemingly small and cool: rhythms of day and night, and the seasons; work, pleasure, and rest; the mind in unfixed contemplation. But [he does] so, clearly, because these areas of life seem stranger, more important, even more religious, to [him] than to earlier poets, poets committed to the ego or to one of its passionate or demonic antitheses. And meaning for [Snyder] . . . would inhere in an experience and not a paraphrase, and would therefore be betrayed by a less bodily, a more explanatory, language. (I do not mean to imply, however, that all poems written in this style deal with Enlightenment; many lead into darkness or into complexity, but they have the same method, the same sense of how important spiritual events happen.) Many of the surest achievements of this generation, the poems I am most convinced would hold up by the standards of any time and any aesthetic, are in this very short, very pure genre. (pp. 60-1)

Gary Snyder . . . [has] become, in America, a kind of patron saint of ecology. This has led to a certain amount of denigration of his thought, apparently on the theory that anything popular with the young has to be facile. Actually, Snyder, in rejecting Western culture, has prepared his peace with as eclectic and painstaking an apprenticeship as one could imagine: graduate study in Japanese and Chinese studies at Berkeley; review articles on Pacific Northwest Indian folklore at a time when the field was virtually unexplored; work in the "back country" as logger, forest ranger, and fire lookout; the greater part of six years as a Zen novice at the monastery in Kyoto. Snyder is a remarkable polemical essayist, pungent in aphorism ("A hand pushing a button may wield great power, but that hand will never learn what a hand can do"), but equally at home with the common sense, clarity, humor of a middle style. His short poems in *The Back Country* seem to me subtler in design, more intellectually suggestive than those of any of his contemporaries; I suspect this is partly due to his grounding in Zen, but I lack the knowledge to substantiate this guess further.... In its total structure, *The Back Country* seems to move outward from short poems toward more ambitious poems of religious and political criticism, poems remarkable alike for their historical insight and for the canny humor and daring that spring from Snyder's essential mystic's disbelief in history.... In sound, too, Snyder is perhaps the subtlest craftsman of his generation. He derives mainly from the Pound/Williams/Projectivist line, and hence writes the most "open", the least heavily accented free verse; but his most important inheritance from Pound (and from Robert Duncan) is perhaps his use of rhyme, and of syncopated versions of traditional meters, within a free form poem to bring it nearer incantation and song. This tendency (appropriate enough to Snyder's interest in the origins of poetry) becomes increasingly dominant in his more recent books; the early *Myths & Texts* still shows some of the crabbed and pedantic side of Pound's elliptical style, while the ... "Songs" from *Regarding Wave* have an intentional wave-pattern of intersecting consonances that becomes, at moments, almost Hopkinsian. (pp. 61-3)

> *Alan Williamson, "Language against Itself: The Middle Generation of Contemporary Poets" (copyright © 1974 by Alan Williamson), in* American Poetry Since 1960: Some Critical Perspectives, *edited by Robert B. Shaw, Dufour, 1974, pp. 55-67.*

Snyder's poems fall roughly into three categories: lyrical precepts (prayers, spells, charms) designed to instill an "ecological conscience" so that we will respect the otherness of nature, frequently personified as the tender, generative mother, and use her wisely. (Linked with these poems are a group that register his disgust at the heedless wasters, interlopers and marauders, the suburban developers for whom if you treat nature right, "it will make a billion board feet a year.") Several poems celebrate domesticity and the family, the poet as doting father and husband bestowing benedictions on his wife and sons. By far the largest segment of his work records quiet moments when he observes the "whoosh of birds," cloud movements, a volcanic crater, the coyote's wail, the Douglas fir or a red leaf. These imagistic poems employ a spare notation.

Snyder's subjects are often appealing: walks, mountains, children, the skinning of a deer, love-making, communion with friends on a camping trip—all the ceremonies of innocence. But the poems themselves are thin, scattered, forgettable, their rhythmical pulse sluggish, as in "Pine Tree Tops," a standard Snyder poem.... The reader feels he is watching home movies, leafing through snapshots of an exotic trip. What stays afterwards are silhouettes of experience....

Despite a few lovely poems—"The Egg," "Straight-Creek—Great Burn," and "The Hudsonian Curlew"—"Turtle Island" is flat, humorless and uneventful. (Snyder's prose is vigorous and persuasive.) The poems are also oddly egotistical. Any random scrap jotted into a journal, the miscellaneous thoughts and images that are the seeds of shaped poems and that most poets discard, are transferred into the poems without the imagination's critical intervention.

"Turtle Island" is a textbook example of the limits of Imagism.

I am reluctant to mention these doubts since as the bulldozers stand poised to despoil the wilderness by strip-mining the West for the sake of more dreck and civilized trumpery, Snyder's sane housekeeping principles desperately need to become Government and corporate policy. He is on the side of the gods. But as Snyder remarks, "Poetry is the vehicle of the mystery of voice," and the voice of "Turtle Island," for all its sincerity and moral urgency, lacks that mystery and "inspired use of language" we call style. (p. 2)

> *Herbert Leibowitz, in* The New York Times Book Review *(© 1975 by The New York Times Company; reprinted by permission), March 23, 1975.*

"Turtle Island" is our "Walden"—a sustained poetic testimony that we can, perhaps must, learn to live in psychic health with less organized human context, and more wild context, than civilization offers. Snyder describes nature better than any other living poet; moreover, like Wordsworth, he makes us feel the centering power, beyond the visible, that nature has for his mind. He is also a fine poet of nature-in-man, as in "The Bath"—a joyful and dignified corrective to bodily shame, and the over-extended incest taboos that induce it. Snyder is weak only in homily and satire, where his designs tend to be too obvious. (p. lvii)

> Virginia Quarterly Review *(copyright, 1975, by the* Virginia Quarterly Review, *The University of Virginia), Vol. 51, No. 2 (Spring, 1975).*

*   *   *

SOUSTER, (Holmes) Raymond   1921-

Souster is a Canadian poet. (See also *Contemporary Authors*, Vols. 13-16, rev. ed.)

Raymond Souster's *So Far, So Good*, selected from thirty years' work, shows well his tightness and opacity of line. Some of the early poems sound "holier-than-thou", but most of the work stands or falls on Williams's "direct treatment of the thing ...". The maturing Souster rids himself of pre-established solemnities. His persistent limitation has been a clash between his sense of the world (wonder, or disgust when wonder fails) and his view of technique, a preference for understatement. Wonder understated! He has, to a great extent, overcome the obvious handicaps by a double means—increasing precision of language and displacement of moralizing by tolerance and humour, as in *Battered* or *Yea Tigers*, in *Made in Canada*.

> *Mike Doyle, "Made in Canada?," in* Poetry *(© 1972 by The Modern Poetry Association; reprinted by permission of the Editor of* Poetry*), March, 1972, p. 358.*

Souster is one of those rare poets who, like a good wine, improves with age. I'm not sure whose age, Souster's or mine. My first encounter with Souster's work was in 1966 in Frank Watt's poetry seminar, somewhere in the catacombs of University College in Toronto....

Here was a Toronto poet-banker, not quite a Wallace Stevens, but a figure of some reputation, who read the American poets, who had correspondence with W. C. Williams and, most amazing of all, listened to jazz, wrote about it in poems, and identified in some mysterious way with the forces of resistance and anarchy that thrive (or throve then) in the subsoil of American culture. . . . And yet some of us still felt uneasy; we felt, first, that imagist poems at best were well-laid paving-stones on a dead-end street, that they gave little and asked little of a reader. All that one could say of them was, so what? Secondly, we suspected poets with ideas, especially those who expressed their ideas directly rather than indirectly through sound and image. Souster, after all, was a bit too raw, too common; perhaps, in retrospect, we thought he was just a bit too Canadian. His muse was flat-footed from pounding a beat in downtown Toronto. . . .

I discovered two years ago while making selections for *15 Canadian Poets* that Souster's didactic verses, his slices of seedy city life with embarrassing moral and philosophical tags, constitute only a small part of his work. . . . Souster's new selection, *The Years*, . . . makes it possible to see the range and scope of his abilities as a lyric poet and, also, to understand the relation between his lyricism and his didacticism. . . .

What emerges from almost all of Souster's social commentary is the question of personal responsibility. Souster is no Marxist or Socialist with a political or philosophical programme against which to measure the events of his time. His position is that of beleaguered humorist, troubled . . . with the matter of empathy, or sharing. . . . Souster's sense of his own guilt does not make good poetry when it expresses itself in the form of complacent moralizing or righteous indignation. The posture of complacency is mostly absent from *The Years*, but the indignation is not. . . .

Souster's lyrics also contain his best social criticism. This criticism seems most convincing when it comes indirectly, when, in the course of talking about what he knows intimately, Souster reveals his awareness of the texture and quality of life around him. (p. 27)

There is much to say about Souster's verse, about his concern for craft, especially his untiring preoccupation with the *line* as something more than an arbitrary way of breaking up prose poems. (p. 35)

Souster's range is not large but his concern for technique is, as Pound would say, a test of his sincerity. In *The Years*, he describes one of his Jazz favourites, Ed Hall, as "a man at one with his art, not fighting it, / not trying to prove a damn thing." The less Souster tries to prove, the more at ease he seems with his craft. (p. 36)

> Gary Geddes, *"A Cursed and Singular Blessing,"* in Canadian Literature, *Autumn, 1972, pp. 27-36.*

Singing small seems to be Raymond Souster's way of being a poet in the world (something he shares with . . . [his mentor] William Carlos Williams . . .). Souster is at his best when dealing with local, immediate, concrete experience. . . .

Noticing such things [as these] is Souster's chief strength: the face of the ragged postcard seller on Yonge Street, the movements of cats (another preoccupation shared with Wil-

liams), of small birds, the shapes and colours of old buildings, the small immediate actions of people. Yet, in the strict sense, Souster's are not the imagist poems they are often said to be, but rather (in Gary Geddes's phrase) "miniparables". They are "mini" in more than the obvious formal sense. As parables they tend to be judgments and when the judgments are small and local, involving the minutiae of daily life, they often contain a "shock of recognition", either painful or exhilarating, but in any case very real. (p. 123)

Souster presents himself (justly) as a man whose eye is determinedly on the object, as one who will not say more than is *there*. When in practice his aesthetic is most fully realized he often *says* a good deal less than is there. . . .

When he truly has his eye on the object Souster is good at recording nuances of behaviour, particularly in relationships between people or in capturing moments in which someone is revealing a particular sense of himself ("Dominion Square", "The Ugliest Woman", "Central Park South", "Decision on King Street"). What makes these poems is the recognition of a moment's uniqueness. Seeing clearly at the precise moment is the good thing, but simply seeing clearly in itself is not enough to make a poem, as the shrug which may attend upon a reading of Souster's flatter poems will attest.

The particular technique depends on a catch of the soul, or epiphany, and when it fails results only in (the very thing Souster would set himself against) explanation (see, for example, "Shoe Store"). (p. 124)

Souster's other strength is in his sense of humour, well exemplified in "The Spider Outside Our Window", wherein the spider has to cope with the problem of what to do with a rose petal which has fallen into his web:

> Then one day, inspiration! He painted up a
> sign in bug's blood, hung it out proudly:
>
> HAPPY CHARLIE'S ROSE GARDENS
> WHERE YOU'LL ALWAYS MEET A
> FRIEND.

Because of its characteristic brevity and opacity (in Pound's sense) Souster's work does not lend itself to (or require) analysis. (pp. 124-25)

> *Mike Doyle, "Singing Small," in* Canadian Literature, *Winter, 1974, pp. 123-25.*

*   *   *

SOYINKA, Wole   1934-

A Nigerian playwright, novelist, translator, and poet, Soyinka brings to his work a balance of both African and European influences. (See also *Contemporary Authors,* **Vols. 13-16, rev. ed.)**

What marks Soyinka and Armah so strongly is their unwillingness to fall back on the past as a solution for present-day social and political problems, and their interest, instead, in the current-day scene, the immediate. When Soyinka's drama, *A Dance of the Forests*, was presented at the Nigerian Independence celebrations in 1960, it, indeed, denigrated the glorious African past and warned Nigerians and all Africans that their energies henceforth should be spent trying to avoid repeating the mistakes that have already been made. *Kongi's Harvest* (Soyinka's last play prior to the Nigerian Civil War) was a scathing condemnation of the recklessness of post-independent African political leaders, and Soyinka's two years in prison during the Nigerian Civil War typify the renewed political concern of the African writer as critic of his own independent society. (pp. 244-45)

In the novels by Wole Soyinka and Ayi Kwei Armah there is one further marked distinction: the isolated individual is often the would-be artist, and the works by these two novelists are concerned with the pressing problem of the place of the artist in the independent African nation, the status and future of the intellectual who wants to be an artist only and not an appendage to the government and a part-time creator. (pp. 245-46)

The Interpreters, Wole Soyinka's only novel, . . . is one of the most impressive pieces of African fiction published in the last few years, and at the same time one of the most obscure African novels. The obscurity, however, is not due to culturally restricted materials. At the time of its publication, there was no precedent in African writing for this kind of work at all, and the critics were confronted with something totally different from what they had seen before. *The Interpreters* has no plot in a conventional sense; there is no real beginning or ending to Soyinka's story. The movement of the narrative instead of being temporal is figural, through space, and the pattern within the novel itself is based on a montage-like repetition of images, piled up on top of one another, overlapping upon one another, suggesting the works of Robbe-Grillet but only in the most generalized way. There is no conflict in the traditional sense of the well-made story; little, if anything, has been resolved by the end of the novel, and one has the impression that the arrangement of the scenes within the book itself could have been considerably different than it is without noticeably altering the impact or the meaning of the work itself. The fact that Soyinka is a playwright and a poet is apparent throughout much of the novel. Instead of basing his narrative on the orderly progression of events leading toward a suggested goal, Soyinka has given his narrative form and pattern by the repetition of certain scenes and images which are used as leitmotifs and short playlets incorporated into the texture of the novel. Soyinka's dialogue is especially effective and shows the influence of his years of work as a playwright. Many of the scenes read as if they were originally conceived as short plays and later incorporated into the novel.

Satire and social commentary are present in almost every incident of *The Interpreters*, and it is these aspects which especially relate Soyinka's only novel with Armah's two works, though Soyinka is not yet as bitter as Armah, nor as he himself is later, in his play *Madmen and Specialists*, written after the Nigerian Civil War. (pp. 246-47)

Technically, the structure is something altogether different from that of any previous African novels, with much more experimentation (in a Western sense) than in Camara Laye's *Le regard du roi* or even James Ngugi's *A Grain of Wheat*. At times, this obscurity is more harmful than beneficial to the novel itself, and it becomes extremely difficult to grasp Soyinka's meaning. Time is obscured almost completely except for occasional references to specific blocks of time, usually between chapters. The flashbacks are often spatial instead of temporal, and the imagery has a tendency to cluster around one given character but overlap upon others. (p. 254)

[The] theme of Soyinka's novel . . . is religion, ritual, the quest for the finer sensitivity which is missing from contemporary African society and above all the artistic side of it. Until these sensitivities are restored, until people have regained their faith in religion and art—bribery, corruption, religious quackery and pretense will reign. And the African intellectual will remain an interpreter instead of a creator.

What characteristics brand Wole Soyinka's *The Interpreters* as a distinctly African novel? No doubt this is a question which is asked by Africans more frequently than by non-Africans. The Western reader is already familiar with the kind of experimentation found in *The Interpreters* —in the Western novel of the twentieth century it is hard to miss this kind of thing. In answering the question, then, one is inclined to conclude that it is content only which will ultimately identify the African novel from any other novel— the inside point of view of an African culture as seen by an African himself, for it is slowly becoming obvious that it is in this direction that African fiction is moving as the second generation of writers becomes further and further removed from traditional African society, and as African oral literary materials are slowly forgotten. (pp. 257-58)

> *Charles R. Larson, in his* The Emergence of African Fiction, *revised edition (copyright © 1972 by Charles R. Larson), Indiana University Press, 1972.*

Soyinka at his best can write very well indeed, but his weakness is still a tendency to the grandiloquent—a tendency that proves fatal to his attempt to convey the inner reality of his experience [as a political prisoner]. Mostly these parts of his book [*The Man Died*] come out in just a whirl of words, most of them too large and fancy to be of much service for his purpose. There are, however, moments when he seems to strike a precise reality: not just what it feels like to be a prisoner but what it felt like for *him* to be a prisoner. Thus I shall never forget what he calls his moment of "self-definition," at the moment when fetters were placed on his legs for the first time: "I define myself as a being for whom chains are *not*, as, finally, a human being." . . .

Wole Soyinka as a person has every right to his indignation; as a writer he would have done well to control it. Thus he refers to the Nigerian police and other political controllers as the "Gestapo." If they had been, he would not have been alive to write what he has written. It is clear from his own narrative that his warders, however badly some of them may have treated other prisoners, were as decent as they were allowed to be to him personally. But in the eyes of the "being for whom chains are not," this was by no means decent enough: The warders and also the relatively decent prison governor remain "beings for whom chains *are*," that is to say below humanity. And below literature. (p. 46)

[He] is potentially a notable writer, but only potentially; and those who have praised him as already a mature writer, because it sounds nice to praise African writers, have done him no service by this particular version of racism. He has lived an extraordinary, interesting life at the center of events in a crucially important period in African and world history. If he would write about this straight and plain, with no prose poetry and with his indignation there but firmly under control, he would be giving us a testimony of world importance. We read Swift not just because his heart was lacerated by fierce indignation (to a much lesser extent I suspect than Soyinka's) but because he was able to control his expression of that emotion. Mr. Soyinka's indignation may in fact be so blazing as to be uncontrollable. If so, that would be a very great pity indeed. We need to hear—and really hear—the testimony of the man who did not after all die. (p. 48)

> *Rex Collings, "Literature and Indignation," in* World *(copyright © 1973 by Saturday Review, Inc.; reprinted with permission), February 13, 1973, pp. 46, 48.*

Mr Soyinka writes with great fluency and subtley, and *Season of Anomy* is an elaborate, careful book. I have one cavil and that is with an occasional over-lyricism, when he aspires towards being a black Mallarmé and the writing becomes too grandiose for its theme. I don't use 'theme' advisedly here, since the narrative diverges into romance, intrigue, high comedy, political statement and bloody description. The landscape of the novel is, apparently, an historical mess and Soyinka has smudged or erased the conventional boundaries of fiction. In each other's arms, his protagonists learn the politics of it all and in this particular revolution no aspect of life is left untouched. (p. 787)

> *Peter Ackroyd, in* The Spectator *(© 1973 by The Spectator; reprinted by permission of The Spectator), December 15, 1973.*

Wole Soyinka appears to have written much of *Season of Anomy* in a blazing fury, angry beyond complete control of words at the abuses of power and the outbreaks of both considered and spontaneous violence at a time when winds of change are blowing at gale force through societies, governments and individuals. The plot charges along, dragging the reader (not because he doesn't want to go, but because he finds it hard to keep up) through forest, mortuary and prison camp in nightmare visions of tyranny, torture, slaughter and putrefaction. The book reeks of pain. Ofeyi, the protagonist, struggles to find reasons and remedies for so much acute and seemingly needless suffering. Despite too many luridly purple passages of description and argument, and Ofeyi's irritating habit of making up ballads as trivial as the TV jingles a copywriter composes in the bus, the book compels attention, admiration and respect. Soyinka hammers at the point that the liberal has to deal with violence in the world however much he would wish he could ignore it; the scenes of murder and mutilation, while sickeningly explicit, are justified by Ofeyi's and the author's anger and compassion and insistence that bad will not become better by our refusal to examine it. Exuberance saves *Season of Anomy* from being solemn or pretentious, and it is good to see that Soyinka, despite his time in prison, has preserved intact his powers of observation and sense of the incongruously comic. . . .

Soyinka's style is at its worst in the dialogue in *Season of Anomy*, which is surprising when you look at *The Jero Plays*, two short plays. . . . They are lightweight, and not, I would guess, as amusing to read as to see acted, but the dialogue is as competent as in the novel it is clumsy and untrue to life, at least to any sort of life that I can imagine. (p. 136)

> *John Mellors, in* London Magazine *(© London Magazine, 1974), April/May, 1974.*

SPARK, Muriel   1918-

Muriel Spark, a Scottish-born Catholic convert, lived in England, Central Africa, and the United States before taking up her current residence in Rome. She is a novelist and short story writer, a poet, playwright, writer for children, critic, and biographer. A master of dialogue and mimicry, Ms Spark writes glittering, controlled, and formal novels distinguished as well by what has been called her "metaphysical wit." (See also *Contemporary Authors*, Vols. 5-8, rev. ed.)

The Abbess [title character of Muriel Spark's novel *The Abbess of Crewe*] is so insistent upon her plot that she neglects the energetic "strategies" of reality. She is betrayed by bumbling associates who break into her opponent's room and stupidly leave their tracks. She has to lie more completely than before; she has to change her scenarios. Oddly the Abbess is so enclosed in her own deceptions—a favorite sin of Spark's characters!—that she does not even *mind*. She loves her "art-forms" which, she claims, need "not be plausible, only hypnotic, like all good art." . . .

Spark does not tell us at any point that she borrows her plot from Watergate, but she offers so many of its elements that she need not belabor the fact.. . . .

She is a Catholic writer; she recognizes, therefore, that pride directs our desire to control the destiny of others. She demands that we condemn *sins*, that we see mythologies as crude attempts at deification. She suggests that we accept limits, boundaries and reality principles—there are, after all, differences between excommunication and sublimity, narcissism and true faith! (p. 29)

Spark has taken the Watergate mythology and transformed it into art. She possesses those very qualities of irony and lucidity lacked by the Abbess (and other great leaders), and as a consequence she enables us to observe the *shape of fleeting history*. (p. 30)

> *Irving Malin, in* The New Republic *(reprinted by permission of* The New Republic; *© 1974 by The New Republic, Inc.), October 12, 1974.*

Although the parallels between the fictive world created in [*The Abbess of Crewe*] and the very real happenings in Richard Nixon's Washington, D.C., are underlined, they are not belabored. Actually, though the book's plot most closely involves the political maneuverings of its main character and her top aides, the most interesting questions raised in *The Abbess of Crewe* are not merely political, but complex and moral ones. The abbess's motives are not self-serving in any crude or obvious way; her corruption is of a piece with the morally ambiguous climate in which she operates. If there is a "villain" in this "modern morality tale" it is defined as a historical process that has obscured the nature of good and evil and, hence, undermined the possibilities for ethical action of any description. *The Abbess of Crewe* has the closely woven texture and the structural coherence of good poetry; it is executed with a subtlety and intelligence that safeguard against the tones of complacent moralizing that might very easily have spoiled the articulation of the book's themes. (pp. 24, 28)

> *Jane Larkin Crain, in* Saturday Review/ World *(copyright © 1974 by Saturday Review/World, Inc.; reprinted with permission), October 19, 1974.*

If in summary the joke [that is the plot of "The Abbess of Crewe"] sounds intolerable, it is in fact delicious. Muriel Spark has spun a gossamer fable with tart wit, teasing malice, a springy gracefulness of prose. She neither belabors her parallel nor takes her story seriously. From the dirt of actuality sprouts the flower of fantasy; while studying the dirt, let us be grateful for such a pleasant blossom. (p. 110)

There is a precision and a poise to Muriel Spark's prose which suggest that we are in good hands. "The poplars," we read on the first page of *The Abbess of Crewe*, "cast their shadows in the autumn afternoon's end, and the shadows lie in regular still file across the pathway like a congregation of prostrate nuns of the Old Order." . . . This is a quiet, straight-faced world in which wry, comic slips and falls are about to take place. . . .

[There are heavy touches] and several jokes about dog and cat food being served up in the refectory of the abbey seem both coarse and weary, but such moments could be seen as the temporary wobbles of an otherwise brilliant balance. They could, that is, if the whole book were not conceived with a degree of coarseness and weariness which makes the poise and precision of the writing seem some kind of anomaly, an aristocratic style slumming in a parvenu's plot. For the story of *The Abbess of Crewe* concerns an election, . . ., a break-in, a cover-up, a bugged abbey, and a lot of tapes. For the slower-witted among us who may not quite catch the allusion, Miss Spark adds this cute little dab of irony: "Such a scandal could never arise in the United States of America. They have a sense of proportion and they understand Human Nature over there; it's the secret of their success."

The subtitle of the book is "a modern morality tale" and Miss Spark, I assume, is trying both to use the Watergate fiasco and to comment on it in some way. In fact, all the borrowed story does for her is prolong and reiterate her simple, central joke. When the abbess says, "I don't see that scenario," a stately representative of the past leaps into the seedy jargon of the present, and the effect is the kind of laugh that used to be elicited by the sight (or the thought) of a nun on a motorbike. The ancient and the modern, the sacred and the technical, the rule of St. Benedict and the principles of electronics—these are what meet up at the abbey of Crewe, and the morality tale never really moves, morally, much beyond its second page, where we learn that the poplars casting such elegant and pious shadows on the first page have been bugged. The nun on the motorbike has become the nun with the tapes, and the thin gag staggers on as best it can, propped up by its side effects rather than by anything we can make it mean.

Of course thin gags are better than no gags at all. What writers are supposed to do is write, and one can't come up with *War and Peace* (or even *Memento Mori*) every time. Still, there is a telling discrepancy between Miss Spark's topical plot and her real subject, which has been topical for the last few hundred years. The subject is class. The election of the new abbess is a contest between aristocratic Alexandra ("She is forty-two in her own age with fourteen generations of pale and ruling ancestors of England, and ten

before them of France") and middle-class Felicity ("The late Hildegarde tolerated Felicity only because she considered her to be a common little thing, and it befitted a Christian to tolerate"), and Alexandra swings the election, after the break-in, by an appeal to the snobbery of her flock-to-be. . . .

None of this is very powerful or very funny, but in the desire of the nuns to be ladies there is an emblem of all kinds of tangled and helpless and genuine English desires. In the Watergate-impelled plot there is only a distant, poorly understood American shadow, and a shadow which has nothing to do with the business of being ladies at that. Miss Spark has looked for reality in the newspapers and has found it, or a few scattered pieces of it at least, somewhere else; wherever novelists find such things.

But she looked in the newspapers first, which suggests a familiar contemporary diffidence, fiction feeling sheepish in the face of history. (p. 29)

[Comic] novelist Muriel Spark is one of the most serious practioners at work in English at the moment. Nothing truly serious can escape comedy and it has been Mrs Spark's method to use comedy for her kind of seriousness. Which is not Miss Iris Murdoch's or Miss Brigid Brophy's or anybody else's for that matter, but a thing she has made her own.

More recently it has also been her method to use incidents in real life as the basis of her parables, even if she rightly maintains that what the novelist relates, or she as a novelist relates, is 'a pack of lies'. A pack of lies, that is, which seeks the truth. In her latest novel, *The Abbess of Crewe*, briefer it seems, than ever: many of its sparse pages are taken up by most effective quotations from litanies and English poetry—she has taken the Watergate Affair and set it in a nunnery. At Crewe, a junction in all our lives. (pp. 28-9)

[To] help her reduce her own words to the minimum, she has called in the aid of poets, among them Marvell and Henry Vaughn, Pope, the anonymous Scots troubadour who sang of *Fair Helen of Kirconnell*; of the plainchant, the canticles, the bible, and—what more appropriate in this parable?—the *Discourses* of Machiavelli, who also placed expediency before political morality. The whole, however, has become a poem by Muriel Spark, and being a poem by Muriel Spark, even at its most serious moments it is ever conscious of the Absurd. (p. 29)

The book is, of course, utterly heartless. Yet it *has* a heart. That heart consists in words, the loving, proper, powerful use of language. The poetry quoted, its choice and timing, but, above all, the poetic control of Mrs Spark's own prose, not only raise the novel far above the level of a contemporary, Sparkian, at times almost vulgar joke, but form a potent, sad and even tight-lipped (if even that paradox is possible) comment on the whole Watergate Affair, the entire shoddy, ludicrously misguided ethics of a society and a type of human being, which makes Watergate Affairs possible all over the world.

Yet, moral though this tale is, as parables must be, to this reader at least it is words here, splendidly at work, which matter first and last. The writing is, as the Abbess of Crewe declares a cooked-up scenario 'based on fact' should be: 'hypnotic, like all good art.' (p. 30)

> *James Brockway, "Taking the Holy Water," in* Books and Bookmen *(© copyright James Brockway 1975), January, 1975, pp. 28-30.*

Since the ambitious "Mandelbaum Gate," Muriel Spark's novels have been short, brusque, bleak, harsh, and queer. They linger in the mind as brilliant shards, decisive as a smashed glass is decisive, evidences of unmistakable power rather casually applied. Beginning with her very first novel, "The Comforters"— utterly accomplished, perfectly her own—this author has exemplified the suitable virtue of *authority*. Under orders from first sentence to last, her books march unflinchingly to their dooms and always, to paraphrase Humpty Dumpty, mean what they choose to mean. Exactly what that is, however, has become something of a mystery, as is the event or idea that, during the years Mrs. Spark has been residing in Rome, has given an extra, tyranical twist to her command over words and characters. Three of her four recent novels have as their basic situation an odd encompassment, or annexation, of death by life: in "The Public Image" (1968), Annabel Christopher's husband commits suicide in order to embarrass her publicly; in "The Driver's Seat" (1970), Lise with cool madness courts her own murder; in "Not to Disturb" (1972), a household of servants plan how to capitalize on the scandal while upstairs the master, mistress, and their lover inexorably go through the fated motions of double murder and suicide. In "The Hothouse by the East River" (1973), most weirdly, an uncomfortable group of modern Manhattanites turn out to be ghosts, killed in London by a buzz bomb in 1944. Now, these books all had their scintillations of wit and slashes of dread, but, like letters from a daredevil friend abroad, they also had an unsettling air of concealing more than they told, and of having been posted in haste. Their most reassuring aspect was the photograph, like an enclosed snapshot, of the well-coiffed writer on the jacket. She was still alive. (p. 76)

"The Abbess of Crewe" is dragged to anticlimax by the pull of topical actualities; if the novel could have been freed to follow its original impudent inspiration, to be less an aping of Watergate than a transfiguration of it, we would have one of the purest, if the lightest, of this gaudy moralist's mock-worlds. As is, it is good to see Mrs. Spark, amused by our curious national occasion of self-betrayal and inscrutable justice, so near the top of her form. (p. 78)

> *John Updike, in* The New Yorker *(© 1975 by The New Yorker Magazine, Inc.), January 6, 1975.*

There was once a novelist called Muriel. She wrote several short books. Apart from the occasional comma and the necessary question-mark, she had little time for punctuation. She believed in a rather nasty God who did rather nasty things to His people. Early in her career she created a real character called Jean Brodie. Jean Brodie was real because you felt she could get the better of Muriel. Muriel was a very knowing writer. She enjoyed putting her charac-

ters down. The moment they threatened to come to life she killed them with a beautiful sentence. Muriel always wrote beautifully. Nothing was allowed to disturb the surface of her writing.

Early in her career (for Muriel was a mistress of repetition) she wrote a story. It was called 'You Should Have Seen The Mess'. After that you hardly ever saw it. There was no mess in her later works. Once she tried, very bravely, to write a really deep book. It was called 'The Mandelbaum Gate' and had its faults. It had virtues, too. Muriel ignored them and settled for a specious pithiness. She started to go in for poetry. One sniggering tombstone elegy on our fallen state followed another. She was always praised for them.

The praise for 'The Abbess of Crewe' was not as generous as it once had been. In this book certain seams were showing. Muriel had one idea in this novel. She had great trouble embroidering on it. You could see her having trouble as you read it. . . .

Earlier in her career Muriel wrote a book called 'Not to Disturb'. The people who didn't care for her books found that a beautiful description of them. Because they didn't like her nasty old God and the mean view of human aspirations He inspired Muriel to share with Him, they thought it rather apt. Muriel's calm was rarely disturbed. By love. By generosity. By kindness. Such things were always worth a snigger. (p. 117)

> *Paul Bailey, in* London Magazine *(© London Magazine, 1975), April/May, 1975.*

Muriel Spark—like Iris Murdoch so prolific that her very productivity becomes an image of depression transcended —attempts [in *The Abbess of Crewe*] a satiric transformation of the raw material of malaise. Although her wit has the power to make one forget the melancholy implications of her subject, she investigates, at a fastidious distance, some determinants of our national mood. . . . Like Swift's conversion of court affairs into the antics of beings six inches tall, Spark's story comments on politics by miniaturizing political concerns. (pp. 588-89)

Spark's dry tone, her spare rhetoric, her firmly shaped ironies are almost self-justifying: reading her narrative, one feels spellbound by that lucid, splendidly remote voice. Yet the novel—hardly a novel, really: a parodic imitation of one —finally seems distinctly less than satisfactory; the grounds for public depression cannot be so readily mastered. (p. 589)

The Abbess of Crewe aspires to the condition of myth, scenario, art object, and partakes of the nature of all three, abstracting and dramatizing the universal pattern underlying particularities, outlining the events of hypnotic high drama, using its characters as means to the reader's pleasure. Yet its preoccupation with formal manipulation involves neglect of human realities. Turning history into pseudo-mythology, it abandons rather than illumines the real; this separation itself has an aspect of despair. To imagine men six inches high who take themselves very seriously immediately clarifies an aspect of the society it mocks. To imagine Nixon transformed into a canny nun clarifies nothing: it is only a joke. Once you've thought of big men and little men, as Dr. Johnson pointed out, the rest is easy; Gulliver's story plays itself out with profound inevitability. Not so the abbess's, which flounders badly toward the end, trailing away in a chaos of irrelevant literary allusions, vain attempts to dignify. Watergate cannot be simply a joke, nor, on the other hand, are its mythic aspects yet truly perceivable. Muriel Spark, expert manipulator of style though she is, proves unable to confront the substance of her tale; she thus implies the possibility that substance is meaningless, only style provides power. Her story of victimization and self-assertion underlines the sense of helplessness that contributes now to everyone's misery. (p. 590)

> *Patricia Meyer Spacks, in* The Yale Review *(© 1975 by Yale University; reprinted by permission of the editors), Summer, 1975.*

*   *   *

SPENDER, Stephen   1909-

A major British poet, playwright, novelist, critic, and former editor of *Encounter*, Spender, along with Auden, MacNeice, and C. Day Lewis, formed the important Oxford group of the Thirties, influencing poetry and politics. (See also *Contemporary Authors*, Vols. 9-12, rev. ed.)

"Redeeming the world by introspection": Louis MacNeice's phrase (from his autobiographical sketch, *The Strings Are False*) about Stephen Spender in the late 1920s could serve as an epigraph to the whole body of Spender's poetic work as well. Indeed, it makes much better sense to look at the poems in this way, as attempts at redemptive and quasi-religious self-searching, than it ever did to see them as coming primarily from social or political concerns. Express trains, pylons, the unemployed at street corners, the burning of the Reichstag or the Spanish Civil War—all were merely grit for Spender's insatiably self-regarding oyster. But for some years the question has been about the quality of the pearls produced. . . .

Admiration for the force and achievement of the perfected will, and for the hero figure who personifies that will, is tempered by equally romantic notions of the inevitability of failure, death, darkness: "And all those other 'I's' who long for 'We dying'." The first-person of [the] early poems —and they are very much poems of the first-person—seems to be an amalgam of the majestic arch-creator Beethoven ("What else is iron but he?") and the slobbering scapegoat. Van Der Lubbe ("I laugh because my laughter/Is like justice, twisted by a howitzer"). The frequent images of the imprisoned self, painfully trying to communicate through vulnerable senses its need to love and be loved, suggests something almost autistic, certainly solipsist. They seem the last gasp of the stricken deer, the wounded romantic artist. . . .

The poems Spender wrote as a result of his experiences during the Spanish Civil War are almost the last in which he managed, perhaps almost unknowingly, to fuse his own "passive sufferings" successfully with those of others: his own emotional involvement at a thoroughly personal level (gone into with naked frankness in *World Within World*), together with his recoil from the waste of the only war he had seen at first-hand, combined to give the impetus to many of the poems in *The Still Centre* (1939). . . . In all these poems the objective correlative was utterly unsatisfactory from any partisan political point of view—they must, indeed, have been an embarrassment to any loyal Communist—yet they create their own authentic world, verify it, and add to the sum of experience rather than simply notating or qualifying it. . . .

Apart from the handful of new work towards the end of the *Collected Poems*, Spender's most recent book of verse until the other day was *The Edge of Being* (1949). *The Generous Days* therefore draws, potentially, on the products of more than twenty years. But it is a slim offering for such a time span.

Some of the poems look like reworkings of old ones, perhaps products of a wartime notebook; others are marginal notes, either variations on someone else's themes (such as the "Four Sketches for Herbert Read") or—like "Bagatelles"—half-hearted epigrams or memorabilia; and there is the persistent feeling of poems being grubbed up from "occasions", such as "Central Heating System", which, with an uneasy mixture of imagism and expressionism, attempts to memorialize what was evidently a long night of the soul spent in Storrs, Connecticut. The most direct is a hasty character-sketch called "Art Student", clumsily and rawly done, but the clumsiness and rawness might be justified by arguing that, after all, they embody what the poem is about. For the rest, there are some wan and rather abstract love poems, and a title-poem which speaks with a formal rhetoric unfamiliar in Spender. . . . (p. 1629)

> *"A Self-Revealing Poet," in* The Times Literary Supplement *(© Times Newspapers Ltd., 1971; reproduced by permission), December 31, 1971, pp. 1629-30.*

Though Spender has constructed [*Love-Hate Relations*] historically, he has not written it neutrally, or even objectively. I don't say this as a criticism—neutrality is a pale virtue in issues that matter to a man—but simply descriptively. He is a poet, a man of letters, and perhaps most of all he is a European, and he has a stake in the future of his language, and the tradition that he values. For him, the words England and Europe are heavy with accreted meaning: they stand for a present in touch with the past. America represents the opposite of this, a society without a past, eclectic, restless, energetic, commercial, living in the present and endlessly exporting itself. In this opposition, Spender's commitment is clear: "The past is—or ought to be—the door opening onto freedom from today which is a time-prison." And to be American, "to see the whole of human life on this planet from the standpoint of the contemporary 'continuous present' is to abdicate ninety-nine hundredths of consciousness *as a whole experience of living in the world . . .*". . . .

Love-Hate Relations is not, strictly speaking, a work of literary criticism, though it contains many acute critical passages. It is rather a meditation on literature and nationality, by an English writer who knows and understands America, but writes always as an Englishman. Like most meditations, it is deeply personal, turning and returning upon certain preoccupations. To English readers it will no doubt be a book about the survival of Englishness, but for us, it is a book about how to be an American, but not *those* Americans—how to find the moral resources outside the present bankrupt moment, how to open the door of the time-prison and recreate a moral culture. Spender is pessimistic about the chances of our doing that, and so am I. But perhaps the chances are a bit better for the existence of this fine, personal testament to the importance of the task.

> *Samuel Hynes, "The Yankee Peril," in*

Book World—The Washington Post (© The Washington Post), *June 16, 1974, p. 1.*

In ["Love-Hate Relations"] taste is doing the work of thought, snobbery stands in for understanding. . . . The claim is always to be speaking on behalf of literary culture, but the voice behind the claim is usually one speaking on behalf of class culture. It is precisely such views that make it possible to be elegantly left wing and simultaneously contemptuous of all that is working class or prole in style.

"Love-Hate Relations" closes on a threnody of sorts for English literary life, with Spender still holding out a thread of hope. He hopes, specifically, that the literary situation in England at present and in the years ahead might be roughly analogous to that of Ireland in relation to England at the turn of the century. He hopes that perhaps the English can avoid the extremes of American experience and "maintain distance and sanity." . . .

"Love-Hate Relations" prompts the question of why it is that a man such as Stephen Spender, soaked in literary culture, seems all wet on everything outside literature. His book, while insisting on the importance of literature, simultaneously casts doubt on literary study as a method of social analysis. It makes one ache for Orwell, bearer of a literary culture firmly anchored in social realities. Of Orwell, Spender notes that he "had a moral grudge against the literary who held views which, in the abstract, were variations of his own." Yet it was not in the abstract but in the concrete that Orwell found the truth about culture and where Spender loses it. If the literary man as a type is to go under, Spender's book points up the fact that a certain class of literary man will not be entirely blameless. (p. 30)

> *Joseph Epstein, in* The New York Times Book Review *(© 1974 by The New York Times Company; reprinted by permission), June 23, 1974.*

Love-Hate Relations: English and American Sensibilities is a curious potpourri of criticism, literary speculation, cultural history, autobiography, testament of faith. Yet Spender's ostensible purpose is more fastidious: to explore the constantly altering area of Anglo-American literary relationships that has obsessed, infuriated and confounded writers on both sides of the Atlantic for almost two centuries. . . .

The trouble with *Love-Hate Relations* is not a matter of attitude and opinion, but of structure and organization, a bungling of priorities. The discussion is unfocused and monotonously rambling; the pace is shuffling and indecisive, marred by a strangely viscous indolence. Both Spender's exposition and his argument are too casually discursive, digressive, ragged. He hops erratically from one writer to another, one era to another; for 50 pages at a throw he loses sight entirely of the subject stated in his title. *Love-Hate Relations* reads like a tape-recording of some rather maundering lectures that was rushed, unedited, into print. (And the book itself is riddled with typographical howlers.) In sum, what might have been a major critical investigation is an eccentric grab-bag filled with unequal parts of treasure and junk. (p. 15)

At the age of 65, with the trendy battles of radicalism and modernity firmly consigned to memory, Spender has come to feel unexpectedly at home in the conservative, nostalgic world of the Georgian poets (Housman, Bridges, Hardy, Edward Thomas) and the prewar British novelists of "poetic sensibility" (Forster, Woolf, Lawrence, Joyce) who despised the thumping social realism of Bennett, Wells and Galsworthy. In his romantic tribute to the Georgian poets, Spender shrewdly remarks that although Pound and Eliot, the expatriate American firecrackers, "woke the English poets out of their complacent dream," the British were unable to assent to Eliot's extreme view that all of Western civilization was in ruins. Instead, Spender notes admiringly, they "returned to their tradition, but had become able to question the way in which they were making use of it."

To one's immense surprise, Spender concludes with an elegiac lament for the vanished Britain preserved by Forster in *Howards End* and by Virginia Woolf in *Between the Acts.* And only in this last section of the book—"English Threnody and American Tragedy"—does Spender come strongly to grips with his real theme, one that has little to do with the love-hate relations of England and America, except as a means of emphasis. Against the objectivity imposed by modern society, which captivated the "novelists of saturation" like Bennett and Wells, Spender invokes the rich subjectivity of the poetic novelists, with their intensely self-conscious devotion to English tradition, their lyrical feeling for the English countryside, their fertile involvement in the English past, their incorruptible commitment to privacy and individual values, their concern for the survival not of modern society but of "the smaller civility of personal relations."

In his very English way, Spender now affirms the indispensability of the civilized past in the life of the present, and thus rejects the apocalyptic obsessions of the "orgasmic culture," with its antinomian contempt for the solacing continuity of tradition and its mind-blowing absorption in the intensities of nowness. Spender identifies this nowness as peculiarly American, yet here he is being somewhat unjust. The national label seems in any case less important and relevant than his humanistic creed: Moral energy must be measured not by its ability to explode (and destroy) but by its capacity to sustain, preserve, endure.

Had Spender concentrated on his beautiful and moving defense of civility and tradition, what a fine book this might have been! Unfortunately, he consistently undercuts the strength of his mature judgment with a messy web of ill-fitting rhetoric, specious Anglo-American generalization, and the obligatory glib sniping at America's "bubble-gum" culture. Lacking a crucial lucidity of structure, *Love-Hate Relations* is an anomaly—an elegiac tribute to continuity and order that is itself a model of their opposite. (p. 16)

> *Pearl K. Bell, "Anglophiles and America-phobes," in* The New Leader *(© 1974 by the American Labor Conference on International Affairs, Inc.), July 8, 1974, pp. 15-16.*

* * *

STEAD, Christina 1902-

Miss Stead is an Australian novelist and short story writer now living in England. Her particular talent, according to one critic, is her ability to create "memorably menacing characters," and to fuse "the commonplace and the bizarre

into a single, compelling poetic vision.'' Christina Stead is best known for *The Man Who Loved Children*, a novelistic masterpiece. (See also *Contemporary Authors*, Vols. 9-12, rev. ed.)

House of All Nations (first published in 1938 and deservedly re-issued now) . . . deals with men at their money-making, men for whom lust for food and women offers little more than a diversion of excess energies. The book centres on the *Banque Mercure*, a private merchant-bank in Paris in the early Thirties, directed by the elegant Jules Bertillon, whose financial manipulations and gigantic currency speculations give the book its main narrative thrust. . . . Essentially, it is a house of illusions, sustained against the onset of gun-fire; what Bertillon provides is the illusion of stability, grandeur, and his own infinite capacity for making money. . . . Miss Stead gives a shrewd account of a collapsing world, where the soundest financial advice is Bertillon's 'Bet on disaster'; an Australian herself, she worked in Paris for some years in a bank that ultimately sank; and we always have the sense of overhearing and watching from the inside. It has to be said, however, that this is not altogether a virtue in the book. Miss Stead understands the financial repercussions of England going off the gold standard rather better than the political implications of a sinking Europe; and even more sadly, she has fallen victim to her characters' own sense of invulnerability. . . .

[This is] a series of extraordinary set pieces which are, in their own way, magnificent in a range of experience no English-born writer I can think of could, or would, attempt. And it must be added that the entire novel is written with such a pressure of event and diverse personality that even at its huge length it is never less than compulsively readable.

The Little Hotel is an altogether meaner book. The people who inhabit the small Swiss hotel in the late Forties, and indeed the proprietors themselves, are much less sharply delineated. . . . It may be that the proprietress hears a good deal; but we are given little insight into what she feels, or rather we are led into her curious lack of feeling (not necessarily Miss Stead's) by a bewildering blankness of tone. . . . This particular difficulty is intensified through her use of a first person narrative structure; though indeed this is not severely maintained. We do not only see through the narrator's eyes, or overhear what she hears. We are even allowed to enter the minds of other characters. This makes the blankness of the central mind all the more disquieting; especially set against a few memorable conversations, ringing true as a tape-recorder, reminding us of the casual cruelties of the age we live in.

Miss Stead has declared in an interview that she finds the English 'tepid'. It may be. In contrast, and in her seventies, Miss Stead seems to have become cold to the point of bleakness. Her reputation will surely rest on the work written 30 years ago (*The Man Who Loved Children* . . .); and *The House of All Nations* for all its flaws, marks out an extraordinary terrain of avarice with as much passion as other novelists have given to the violence of sexual love.

> Elaine Feinstein, *''Bleak Houses,''* in New Statesman (© *1974 The Statesman & Nation Publishing Co. Ltd.), June 14, 1974, p. 856.*

In her native Australia, Christina Stead's writing has long been valued as part of the national literary treasure. American readers today know her, if they do at all, as a one-book author. *The Man Who Loved Children* was the only Stead novel in print here until her reputation began growing with the aid of the women's movement, whose support, ironically, she would rather not have. Nevertheless, *The Man Who Loved Children* is appearing on reading lists for women's studies classes. *House of All Nations* has just come out in paper. And when *The Little Hotel* was announced this year, it seemed a good time to look once more at Christina Stead's work in print and to signal what is missing. . . .

Although there are no great themes, no significant events and no literary experiments in *The Little Hotel*, the guests' own chatter reveals their characters—and their situation as the castaways of European history—with the same merciless accuracy that makes the conversations of Stead's more ambitious novels so riveting. *The Little Hotel* is an engaging though minor Stead novel.

Stead knew a wealth of people, and she took care to understand their social connections, their politics, their professions and their speech before using them in her fiction. She was as familiar with the Australian milieu of Socialist journalists and working-class women depicted in her first novel, *Seven Poor Men of Sydney*, as she was with their London counterparts in *Dark Places of the Heart*. She knew as much about the political import of the great banks in *House of All Nations* as she did the details of lace making and the lace trade necessary for writing *The Beauties and Furies*. When she took apart a marriage in *The Man Who Loved Children*, every detail of family life contributed to the conjugal war of attrition. In short, Christina Stead had and used an exceptionally wide canvas for her fiction. . . .

In most Stead novels, women who do not work waste their lives. Superfluous women cling to a humiliating dependency upon a man when they have no training that will allow them to leave and take a job. In her novels you can see Stead's women struggling, successfully or not, to free themselves from the biological and social roles imposed upon them. (p. 501)

Stead has a very select, piercing set of values. She refuses to take sides in her fiction or in private opinion on the basis of sex. As a political orientation, and a natural choice, she always opts for the exploited over the exploiters, for the poor over the rich, but not because the working people or the women are saintly and unselfish. In her novels, you feel that individual workers, and sometimes women, simply have more spunk, daring and social conscience than those individuals with wealth and power. The hideaway rich, whether bankers in *House of All Nations* or misers in *The Little Hotel*, are simply thrown aside by historical circumstances.

Nor does Stead seem to believe that a woman's condition or possibility for success is basically different from a man's. Men without a strong identification through their work are as powerless as women. (p. 502)

> Barbara L. Baer, *''Castaways of History,''* in The Nation (*copyright 1975 by the Nation Associates, Inc.), April 26, 1975, pp. 501-03.*

''The Little Hotel'' is a small, daringly perfect novel from which all excess has been elided—a method not usually associated either with its author or our century. Christina Stead is best known here for "The Man Who Loved Children," a book which rocks on the torrential conversation of its hero. Her huge tale of a Paris banking-house, the recently reprinted "House of All Nations," accumulates in telegraphic sentences, like one enormous financial communique. In her other books the style is clear 19th-century England, as a gifted Australian might still hear it sounding across the waters to a broader continent—rambling but precise, baroque with ideas but never obscure in the expression of them, and never mincing into the wrong poetry. Yet in all her work there are two alternative voices, the one a cataract carrying everything before it—or, as some think, a massive garrulity—the other witty, tender or caustic in the small way, shyly interpolated, even exquisite. This latest novel, brief as it is, raises the same questions as the big ones. And the same answers. Why is Stead's originality so hard to define? Because there's so much of it. Does her strange blend of outmoded interest in character and avant-garde sensibility have anything to say to the doctrinaire American novel?

Yes. A lot.

"The Little Hotel" takes almost sly advantage of an age-old convention—various characters reported in the daily events of a milieu where they are almost accidentally confined. The Grand Hotel tradition, is it? The story's narrator takes pains to tell us that the Swiss-Touring, the hotel she runs with her husband, is fourth-rate, the lowest grade in which her patrons can stay without loss of reputation. . . .

Stead has always loved the mixed company of the spa, the restaurant, the party-meeting and the party anywhere—all the high-class lowlife of those who live vivaciously above their income, or greedily below. All these people are recognizably the pension-haunters of a certain kind of literature. When Stead is finished with them, they seem to us the staples of a certain kind of life.

What we get are the echoes of their excess, the hints of their compromise. All comes to us muted, as if we ourselves are in the hotel. . . . [Scenes] less than a page in length are vivid with presence and flow seamlessly. Stead's narration can remind one of those jugglers who fling an object over the shoulder with the right hand and present it with the left, all the while facing us. The narrator herself all but disappears; only a technician would notice when.

Nor has Stead's notably political conscience become anything but more deft. These *rentiers* whose income is dubiously expropriated either from the Nazis or from each other, who are forever discussing where to put their money now that America is no longer safe and England tax-rotten—are political without knowing it. . . .

Behind them all in this marvelously stenographic novel is that chaos we all know so well, though sometimes more from books and movies than from our actual lives. Here, our planetary madness is present only by the lightest implication. Stead is a genius at locale (see her Maryland Eastern Shore, her 1930's New York in "Letty Fox, Her Luck," a novel once banned in her homeland)—and chaos localized is less often cliché. Moreover, she has been writing about it for years now, and is above replicating chaos on the page in order to portray it in the world.

No wonder her work has reminded many of Tolstoy, Ibsen,

Joyce—any tag to signify that the reader is offered breadth of vision and honest depth of enjoyment, with neither sacrificed to the other. Now in her seventies, she has witnessed much, and used it. Her works bridge the gap between that humanistic preoccupation with character which the novel is said to have lost to the past, and that modern spirit which any novel worthy of its time must have. What her books teach us is that wisdom is the novelist's ultimate requirement. "The Little Hotel" carries that bouquet. (p. 6)

Hortense Calisher, in The New York Times Book Review (© *1975 by The New York Times Company; reprinted by permission), May 11, 1975.*

Written by the great author of *The Man Who Loved Children*—among the most strange and powerful achievements of literary realism in our time—*The Little Hotel* deals in acidulous miniature with the very large subject of Europe's social transformations following World War II. The residents of Monsieur and Madame Bonnard's impecunious little Swiss residential hotel are baffled, touching, contemptible relics of European colonial administration and the homeless, compromised leisure class it once sustained. Filled with a quaintness based more on absurdity than on charm, they are not attractive people. Besotted with their political paranoia and genteel racism, they numbly live through their heartbreaking, insufferable rituals, clinging to dwindling bank accounts, which, instead of providing them with freedom, lock them all the more tightly into small and hopeless lives. The book describes these lives with a focus that is almost disorienting in its precision.

To say that Christina Stead writes well verges on the impertinent; what is basically the plain style of English expository fiction has rarely been rendered with such originality, given such a continuously absorbing texture. In the age of realism's exhaustion, Stead has sustained herself as a great realist by bringing to bear on the banal an intelligence so closely tuned and penetrating that it renders everything as compelling, eccentric, and bizarre. And though she is the least sentimental of writers, this focus provides her with an almost (she would hate the word) theological comprehension of human pathos and vanity. In passing, one might mention that the feminists' indifference to Stead is slightly baffling. She is, for example, a much more profound—and far more politically aware—writer than the justly rehabilitated, but now vastly overpraised, Jean Rhys. Quite apart from *The Man Who Loved Children*, one thinks of Stead's overwhelming novella, *The Puzzleheaded Girl*, standing in a class by itself as a treatment of a young woman in America. In *The Little Hotel*, as in all her work, Stead's eye is cold indeed, and the trivia she sees terrible indeed. But here, as elsewhere, her intelligence, toughness, and charm also give a strange voice to the even rarer quality that one must call wisdom. (p. 28)

Stephen Koch, in Saturday Review (*copyright* © *1975 by Saturday Review/World, Inc.; reprinted with permission), May 31, 1975.*

Christina Stead . . . probably will be most honored for her horrifying *The Man Who Loved Children.* But when that was first published in 1940 it received little attention. Her immediate triumph was *House of All Nations*, 1938; it won both critical acclaim and, considering how formidable it is, a surprising popular success. It concerned the spectacular Banque Mercure and relentlessly detailed in nearly 800 pages all its intricate financial speculations. The cast of hundreds was made up of the rapacious *richissime* of several continents and the assorted profiteers who leeched on their vices.

While the House of All Nations was a fashionable though corrupt Paris bank, the Little Hotel is a modest but proper Swiss *pension*; instead of the decadent international set, the clientele is mainly postwar English of meager means. But the most significant difference is in style and tone. The flamboyant flood of incident and compulsive torrent of language, which even admirer Randall Jarrell criticized for excess and lack of discrimination, has narrowed to a quiet stream of simplicity and restraint. The rage and revulsion, as intense as that of Nathanael West, has simmered down to an almost gentle satire. And even that is peripheral to the portrayal of a major character unthinkable in Stead's earlier novels, a frail, naive, loving woman. (p. 1)

The House of All Nations ended with the fall of the Banque Mercure and the loss of huge fortunes. Attempted murder and suicide conclude *The Man Who Loved Children*. But neither of these dramas are as sad as [the] death of a long love affair [in *The Little Hotel*]. One has to regret the loss of the coruscating vitality of Christina Stead's former mordant misanthropy. Yet it is some achievement to have acquired such perfect control of style and material. And it must have taken courage to present to readers avid for wit and vitriol so artless and gentle a heroine, and to record without a flicker of mockery her ingenuous faith: "People suffer and we call them names; but all the time they are suffering. I know I am not clever: it is partly because I cannot believe that life is meant to be ugly." (p. 2)

> *Audrey C. Foote, "Pensioned Off," in* Book World—The Washington Post (© The Washington Post), *June 1, 1975, pp. 1-2.*

*   *   *

STEINBECK, John   1902-1968

An American novelist and short story writer, Steinbeck won both the Pulitzer Prize and the Nobel Prize for Literature. His realistic accounts of rural poverty in the United States, most notably *The Grapes of Wrath* and *Of Mice and Men*, are American classics. (See also *Contemporary Authors*, Vols. 1-4, rev. ed.; obituary, Vols. 25-28.)

Travels with Charley in Search of America, a series of travel articles from *Holiday* that became a leading bestseller . . ., is a hodge-podge of superficial social criticism, ripe sentimentality, one endless joke about the urination of Steinbeck's dog, bad prose, encounters that surely must have been invented, and factual inaccuracies. There are streaks of honesty and insight in the book, and one chilling and effective look at New Orleans racism. *Travels with Charley* and *The Winter of Our Discontent* are clearly the work of a writer who, if he was not always a lightweight, is a lightweight now.

> *Stanley Edgar Hyman, "John Steinbeck and the Nobel Prize," in his* Standards: A Chronicle of Books for Our Time (© 1966; *reprinted by permission of the publisher, Horizon Press, New York), Horizon, 1966, pp. 113-17.*

The reason so many of Steinbeck's former admirers no longer enjoy his work is that the weaknesses of the earlier writings, excusable enough in a young novelist, have prevailed: the woodenness and the sentimentalism. Over the years he has become the idol of book clubs and movie audiences, and of a vast uninstructed reading public. Literary experts of high standing have either ignored Steinbeck or, in critical books and journals of limited circulation, have exposed his defects. Edmund Wilson, Alfred Kazin, and Maxwell Geismar are three important critics, for example, who have detailed Steinbeck's imperfections. . . .

At a time when people were hungry and dispossessed and wandering, Steinbeck was one of their literate spokesmen. But too many readers mistook his sentimentalism for compassion; sentimentalism, that is, in the sense of tearfully expecting too much from life. We can perform a service to our culture, to the preservation of its truest values, by not overrating the work of this man of goodwill who was sometimes a competent novelist, though never "great."

> *Harry T. Moore, "Epilogue" (© 1968 by Harry T. Moore), to his* The Novels of John Steinbeck, *2nd edition, Kennikat Press, 1968.*

Steinbeck was never a utopian because he was always a man with a place. He was a Californian, and his writings never succeeded very well when he tried to walk alien soil. Yet his California was a very special one, a narrow strip embracing Monterey, San Benito, Santa Cruz and San Luis Obispo counties, sleepy California that time passed by. He ignored the great cities except in glimpses and if he wrote of other places, it was likely to be the New England village of *Winter of Our Discontent* or the Northwest orchards of *In Dubious Battle*. In a literal sense, he was a conservative, a man who valued and even clung to the old America; the real power of *Grapes of Wrath* is the savage anger at the impersonal process that uproots men from the land and rapes it, substituting rattletraps and highways for place and kindred.

In that sense, he was romantic, sure that past times were far from perfect and yet possessed of virtues and qualities now lost, human even in their cruelties and stupidities as the industrial age is not. . . .

Conservative and romantic, Steinbeck stuck to the sturdy rationalism that insists that the old questions will not be wished away, that the old virtues cannot be dispensed with, that the rule of first things first still applies. The direct route is the best, because the best cannot be captured unaware or bought cheap.

That did not make him lapse into quietism, or leave him indifferent to social reform. Far from it: compassion and concern lie on the direct route too. So, for that matter, does violence, and Steinbeck knew that there is a love which must take up the knife to slay another, because it is the same love which leads to a knowing willingness to sacrifice the self. (p. 230)

> *Wilson C. McWilliams and Nancy R. Mc-Williams, "John Steinbeck, Writer," in* Commonweal (reprinted by permission of Commonweal Publishing Co., Inc.), May 9, 1969, pp. 229-30.

405

Steinbeck is entirely representative of an American type of great influence during the first two decades following World War II, the Stevenson Democrat. Steinbeck was indeed preeminent among the men of letters to whom this label could be applied; he was one of the many who, having lived through the frustrations of the Depression and the horrors of the war, hoped that the direction of the country might at last be entrusted to a quiet, introspective, cautiously idealistic man with roots in a characteristically American agrarian community.

The trouble with the Stevensonians during an age of affluence like the 1960's is that they were rarely able to convert their nebulous vision of a better society into meaningful specifics. They were driven into trying to see in the pacification of the Mekong Delta the restoration of Candide's garden. (p. 297)

Steinbeck's political views became increasingly irrelevant, because—like many others of his liberal persuasion—he insisted on seeing the present in terms of the past. Steinbeck had frozen into a political position that in the 1930's enabled him to avoid fashionable error and made him the champion of common sense, but that in the 1960's isolated him from the problems of affluence. (This judgment is grounded in the idea that in the 1930's the nation's problems were primarily those of underproduction and physical survival, but that in the 1960's—although there are still a sizable number of "disadvantaged" persons in the society—the problems were principally those of overproduction and spiritual disenchantment.)

What is most significant is how closely the thinking of the man who, regardless of critical demurrers, was one of the most distinguished twentieth-century American writers mirrored that of Lyndon Johnson, whose once awe-inspiring reputation as a political operator crumbled because of his inability to communicate with most people under forty. Johnson, like Steinbeck, insisted on responding to the problems of the 1960's as if they were those of the 1930's. (p. 299)

Steinbeck was able to see the Vietnamese conflict not in ideological terms but as a necessary stimulant to American morale. He embraced—again like many of his countrymen—the puritanical notion that a nation can flourish only when it is fighting against physical odds—"westering." . . .

In effect, Steinbeck was arguing, we were using Vietnam simply to establish the continuing virility of our local brand of morality. In an interview after belatedly receiving the Nobel Prize, Steinbeck observed that it was more difficult in the 1960's than in the 1930's to determine who was an underdog, more difficult—to borrow the title of one of his most famous essays—to tell good guys from bad. The admission shows that Steinbeck's thinking had not become sophisticated enough to deal with the subtle problems of an age of affluence. Part of the trouble is that when values are principally physical—as in problems of survival—it is not difficult to perceive the differences between contenders; but when values are principally intellectual or spiritual—as in problems of adjustment—it may be very difficult to perceive differences. (pp. 303-04)

In his great novels of the 1930's Steinbeck intentionally alerted the nation to the dangers that persistence in the stereotyped thinking fostered by the chimerical speculative abundance that a virgin continent once promised presented

to a land that had failed to solve the problems of fairly distributing its resources. In the 1960's his novels unintentionally alert us to the dangers that persistence in the stereotyped thinking derived from the privations endured during the Depression and World War II present in coping with the problems of an age of affluence in which economic momentum can be maintained only by a program of controlled waste that is not destructive of human resources.

Steinbeck had trouble during the last two decades—as *The Winter of Our Discontent* especially suggests—because he still saw human problems in the currently irrelevant terms of clashes between exploiter and victim, the ignoble and the noble. He failed to grasp that in an age when a potential threat of atomic destruction hangs over the whole world—when man could annihilate himself—the question of who "wins" this or that particular physical engagement can hardly be a burning issue. Nobility is no longer even a possibility. The failure of Steinbeck's private politics was to reflect a general failure of American politics. There are many luxuries we can no longer afford. The political fastidiousness of the polite liberal—epitomized by Steinbeck—is surely one of them. (pp. 304-05)

Warren French, "John Steinbeck (1902-1968)," *in* The Politics of Twentieth-Century Novelists, *edited by George Panichas (reprinted by permission of Hawthorn Books, Inc.; copyright © 1971 by The University of Maryland; all rights reserved), Hawthorn, 1971, pp. 296-306.*

Talismanic symbols take many and various forms in Steinbeck's novels. In *To A God Unknown* the rock in the forest glade is a talisman to Joseph Wayne, and the rock is described much like the pink piece of stone in *The Winter of Our Discontent*. In these two cases the talisman is true to the dictionary definition of a stone, but in other novels the idea is expanded to include anything that men believe in or go to for some kind of nonrational fulfillment, anything that sparks a man to identify with it and project the mystery of his being upon it. On a larger scale, the idea is manifest in the land in *Of Mice and Men* and *The Grapes of Wrath*; on a smaller scale, the talisman is the image of the virgin that Juan Chicoy communes with but does not accept as a Christian symbol in *The Wayward Bus*, Kino's pearl, Danny's house in *Tortilla Flat*, and a wide variety of other objects throughout Steinbeck's fiction.

One prevalent form of the talismanic pattern is the relationship between men and particular "places." In *The Winter of Our Discontent* Ethan has a hidden cave along the side of the sea, a sanctuary of sorts where he can retreat from worldly traumas and, through a sense of harmony and oneness with his environment, gather together the fragments of his being and find wholeness and unity within himself. Virtually all of Steinbeck's characters have a talismanic place such as Ethan's. (pp. 263-64) Steinbeck is reluctant to offer any simple explanation for the need men have of such places, but throughout his writing there is the implicit suggestion that some sort of fundamental relationship exists between the places and the deeper parts of the human psyche. (p. 264)

Identification results when man transfers part of his own being to his symbols, when an object becomes suffused with human spirit so that a complete interpenetration exists.

On a simple level Steinbeck is merely describing the common psychological quirk of a man identifying with his tools or with the object of his work, infusing his spirit into his physical environment. At bottom, however, the identification has wider implications and is grounded in Steinbeck's basic monism, his belief that one thing is all things and all things are one thing—that whole which "Is"—and thus share a fundamental relatedness. (pp. 265-66)

With many of Steinbeck's characters the attempt to express this tacit sense of relatedness is channeled into talismanic identification. The talisman becomes a vehicle to help man feel his oneness with the whole and express that feeling, and the pattern of talismanic identification becomes a ritual —such as the Viking burial ceremony, and generally with religious overtones—for overcoming the cosmic alienation of a separate being and for reaffirming the oneness of creation. Such a ritual contributes greatly to Steinbeck's second novel, *To A God Unknown*, in the person of an old man who lives alone on a cliff overlooking the sea. Every night he watches the sun go down and makes some small sacrifice to it. He waits for the perfect time to offer the ultimate sacrifice of himself, just as the main character, Joseph Wayne, will sacrifice himself to the land for rain at the end of the book. (pp. 266-67)

By far the strongest and most enduring of the talismanic identifications in Steinbeck's fiction is that of men with the land. As a talismanic symbol, land fuses the three main elements of the pattern of identification that I have mentioned: man attaching spiritual value to an object as a means of satisfying some deep and unidentifiable need; man infusing his spirit into his possessions or the objects of his work; and man using the talisman as a vehicle for perceiving and affirming his relatedness to a larger whole. The desire for land is, of course, physical, but it is also talismanic, charged as Ethan Hawley's stone and place are, with more than material or rational significance. (p. 267)

The pattern of talismanic identification is most successful to the characters in Steinbeck's later novels when the sense of relatedness and continuity that it helps them achieve and express becomes organic and is translated, as it is in *The Pearl*, into a principle of right action in the world. The talisman itself remains necessary primarily as a vehicle and as a sort of emotional prop, something, such as Ethan Hawley's Place, that a man can use to periodically recharge his courage and moral energy. (p. 271)

The transcendence of the talisman that is manifest in *The Pearl* and *Sweet Thursday* is prefigured in *The Grapes of Wrath* in somewhat different terms. Here the talismanic pattern is handled in a far more naturalistic manner and is subsumed within the larger narrative design. One of the major structural devices of *The Grapes of Wrath* is the movement from a lone individual (Tom) to a group of individuals (Tom, Casey, and Muley) to a family (Tom's reunion with the Joads) to a union of families (Joads and Wilsons) to a community (Weedpatch) to the family of mankind. The center of this movement is the Joad family, and while the family is not a talisman, it nevertheless performs a talismanic function. Like Danny's house in *Tortilla Flat* it is the vital force that gives form, meaning, and sustenance to the life of the Joads. Unlike *Tortilla Flat*, however, when the Joad family diffuses, creation does not collapse into chaos. Instead, as in *The Pearl*, the talismanic pattern leads beyond itself to an awareness of the whole.

The Joad family becomes the family of man. Tom verbalizes this awareness in his parting speech to Ma, and Rosasharon puts his words into action at the end of the novel, as the most intimate and private of family functions becomes an act of relinquishment, of love and compassion for mankind as a whole.

In Steinbeck's other "big" novel, *East of Eden*, the talismanic pattern is centered in the Cain and Abel story. Here, as in *Tortilla Flat*, Steinbeck uses an archetypal narrative as the key to his novel. But there is a significant difference: the Arthurian legend simply furnished him with a possible model of the talismanic pattern; in *East of Eden* Steinbeck conceives of the story itself as having talismanic power. (p. 272)

To many followers of Steinbeck . . . it has long been evident that beneath their surface diversity his novels contain a unified body of thought. This blend of consistency and versatility also characterizes the talismanic patterns of his novels. In each book the pattern is distinctive; it changes from novel to novel throughout his career, often merging with the larger structural designs of specific books. But as I have suggested, the principle itself has deep roots in Steinbeck's imagination and forms an underlying structural pattern in much of his major fiction. It is not difficult to speculate on the motive behind its extensive use. At the heart of Steinbeck's work is a conviction that the writing most worth doing is that which can penetrate to the sources of human thought and behavior and present in the form of some objective correlative the archetypal and mythopoeic knowledge that lies deep in the mystery of human experience. The talismanic pattern in its various guises is one of these correlatives. (pp. 274-75)

> *Todd M. Lieber, "Talismanic Patterns in the Novels of John Steinbeck," in* American Literature *(reprinted by permission of the Publisher; copyright 1972 by Duke University Press, Durham, North Carolina), May, 1972, pp. 262-75.*

From as far back as *Cup of Gold* (1929) to his most recent work, John Steinbeck has shown a proclivity for dealing with people who are searching for a golden land of happiness, the fulfillment of a dream, quests that of course entail an escape both into and away from the past. Indeed, the past in the novels of Steinbeck constantly forms the design not only of rare exotic moments but of those more mundane periods in the daily lives of his people, who are tied to those earlier times that produced them and that gave birth to what has come to be called the American Dream.

Like that first modern American novel of escape, *Adventures of Huckleberry Finn*, *The Grapes of Wrath* (1939) is not only a book of travel but a novel of escape—as in Tom Joad's instance, from the consequences of his acts; as in the instance of the Joad family, from the conditions and economics of the land; as in the instance of Preacher Casy, from an untenable past with its irreconcilable split between what the preacher is (or becomes) and the tenets he has long preached but now no longer believes in. If Tom Joad is the hero of this novel of escape, he is a hero who shares the characteristics of countless picaresque heroes who so often seem to be fleeing from something that threatens their well-being. But if he shares something of the tradition of the picaresque hero, he shares that tradition with the comic overtones omitted. (p. 95)

Sam Bluefarb, "The Joads: Flight Into the Social Soul," in his The Escape Motif in the American Novel *(copyright © 1972 by the Ohio State University Press; all rights reserved), Ohio State University Press, 1972, pp. 94-112.*

[Although] Steinbeck had written "Of Mice and Men" as a novel—it was published earlier the same year—he had had the intention from the first of turning it into both a play and a movie. [George S.] Kaufman took over the manuscript of the play while Steinbeck was busy gathering material for the novel that was eventually to become "The Grapes of Wrath." Kaufman was a brilliant director and the ablest play doctor of his time; in that capacity, he set great store by a well-turned, strongly motivated plot. In the present instance, the dialogue is obviously Steinbeck's and the tidy laying out of the scenes owes much to Kaufman.

Styles in playwriting change, and by an irony it may be that to contemporary audiences Kaufman's careful workmanship will seem a mere patness; we tend to like plays to be looser and more open-ended and therefore more ambiguous than they were in the thirties. What allows "Of Mice and Men" to triumph over the neat joins of its manufacture is the extraordinary amount of emotion that continues to reverberate in its lines; after thirty-seven years, their semiliterate simplicities of hope and despair are as touching as ever. Big, simpleminded, affectionate, and inadvertently murderous Lennie and his banty companion and protector, George, are true friends. They are bound together by a love that has scarcely a trace of the sexual in it, save to the extent that everything Lennie loves he must move close to and caress. . . .

Lennie is George's doom, which he accepts in part because he knows that Lennie cannot live without him and in part because love—even poor Lennie's defective love—is precious to him. Year after year, they go on cherishing the dream of someday settling down on a little farm together, where Lennie will raise rabbits. This never-to-be-realized dream is a startlingly precise equivalent of Beckett's never-arriving Godot: in each case, the painful absurd is made bearable by the presumption of an alternative that, though it can be described, doesn't exist. Beckett's icy existential fastidiousness causes him to draw back from the melodrama of any action that would signal "The End," since for him "The End" amounts to an unacceptable artifice. Being at heart a sentimentalist, Steinbeck believes in endings, whether happy or sad. The ending of "Of Mice and Men" is a shocker, and it is no less shocking because we have been anticipating it all evening long.

Brendan Gill, "Recalled to Life," in The New Yorker *(© 1974 by The New York Magazine, Inc.), December 30, 1974, p. 52.*

When this play [*Of Mice and Men*] was first produced in the '30s, the Natural Man enjoyed something of a vogue. Eugene O'Neill's *Hairy Ape*, Hemingway's grunting heroes and Steinbeck's wretched Okies were the common components of tragedy. But even milestones can erode with the years and weather. Depression America is not Recession America; economic determinism is no longer in literary style. The ranch hands who surround George and Lennie are types rather than characters, and the stagecraft contains

all the ungainly devices of yesteryear: the breathless entrances, the lamplit confessionals, the contrived pathos that redeems criminal actions.

Stefan Kanfer, "Brute Strength," in Time *(reprinted by permission from* Time, The Weekly Newsmagazine; *copyright Time Inc.), December 30, 1974, p. 53.*

Of Mice and Men . . . strikes me in retrospect as one of the best pieces of dramatic writing since our country's coming-of-age in the 1920s.

It is something more than a rugged tale of itinerant agricultural workers during the Great Depression. It is a sort of American "legend." There is a mythic simplicity about it. What emerges is not only a sense of the loneliness of American existence, the separation between persons, the lack of brotherhood, our incapacity to fructify our vast continent with the warm blood of fellow feeling, but an inference to the effect that until brawn and brain become one in our land we shall suffer the dumb ache of isolation, a perpetual state of partial being.

It may well be that Steinbeck did not think of his story in these terms, but that is nonetheless what he created. Its moral point lies in the telling. There is no artifice or "aesthetic" design in it; it is rather stark. The mood and meaning spring naturally from the authentic Americanism of the language, the spareness of the character delineation. Even those who do not get the play's "message" as conscious content must be touched by direct contact with the naked material. The play is modest in form and large in emotional implication. (p. 27)

Harold Clurman, in The Nation *(copyright 1975 by the Nation Associates, Inc.), January 11, 1975.*

In the prewar heyday of sentimental socialism, *Of Mice and Men* may have seemed lean and forceful; now its mentality appears antiquated, and it depends solely on whatever craft it can muster. But, alas, it is very much of a storyteller's play, proceeding linearly by piling up brief episode on episode, usually by the introduction of a new character and his or her story, or by the mere intensification of plot elements. It does not operate in breadth and depth, as drama must; it does not develop characters by deepening our understanding of their backgrounds, needs, and interplay, but simply pushes them into further and stickier plot situations or recitatives. It is still a much better play than, for example, [such a current success as] *All Over Town*, but it can no longer ride the crest of a historical wave. (p. 56)

John Simon, "Off Base, Off Color, Off and Running," in New York Magazine *(© 1975 by NYM Corp.; reprinted by permission of* New York Magazine *and John Simon), January 20, 1975, pp. 56-7.*

Steinbeck's play [*Of Mice and Men*] is one of the American best. . . . I can't imagine a list of, say, Twenty Best that could omit it. The tragic inevitability at which Steinbeck aimed is dimmed by the creakiness of the arrangements. We know with somewhat pleasant ironical foreknowledge in the first scene, when the two friends discuss their plans to have a place of their own, that they will never get it; but

Steinbeck ensures the grim ending with the nervous young husband at the ranch and his arbitrarily restless wife. Besides, Lennie's feeblemindedness mitigates the tragedy. He is a "case" on the loose, not a man susceptible to trouble. If he were only slow-witted, instead of defective, there would be some hint of what his life might have been. With the idiot Lennie there are no alternatives.

Still Steinbeck touched some deep American themes, the great myths of the road and of the two male companions. (Snickers in today's audience at the lines about two men traveling together; the ceremony of innocence is drowned.) And there is a strong residue of 19th-century feeling about the land—working on the land is the basic good, owning some of it is salvation. I can't think of another successful American play since 1937 with that feeling, or even one centered on rural work. Because of what has happened since it was written, *Of Mice and Men,* with its faults unchanged, has become a play about the end of something in America and in American drama. (p. 18)

> *Stanley Kauffmann, in* The New Republic *(reprinted by permission of* The New Republic; © *1975 by The New Republic, Inc.),* January 25, 1975.

*   *   *

STONE, Robert   1937?-

Stone, an American novelist and short story writer associated with the San Francisco counterculture of the Sixties, wrote the prize-winning novel *Dog Soldiers*.

During the waning days of U.S. involvement in Viet Nam, a journalist named John Converse takes up with a bored American expatriate woman in Saigon. She invites him to buy an interest in three kilograms of pure heroin. Once this deadly package is safely Stateside and distributed to her friends, Converse will earn $40,000. He agrees, persuades an acquaintance, Ray Hicks, to smuggle the heroin to California. There, Converse's wife Marge will take possession and pay Hicks off.

The stark evil in this plan quickly flowers into nightmare. . . .

Dog Soldiers is more than a white-knuckled plot; it is a harrowing allegory. The novice smugglers evade a sense of their own villainy through sophistry or indifference. Converse rationalizes that in a world capable of producing the horrors of war, "people are just naturally going to want to get high." Hicks concentrates on the exploit's challenge and itches to hurl his own aggressiveness into the void he imagines around him. Marge, already hooked on pills, accepts the heroin's arrival as fated for her.

Such equivocations blind them to the truth of their situation, which is also the novel's truth. The heroin is as shackling a possession as the bag of gold in Chaucer's *Pardoner's Tale*. Indeed, it is worse. Chaucer's three thieves at least thought that the gold was benign. Their catastrophe stemmed from disregarding Christian doctrine: *radix malorum est cupiditas* (greed is the root of all evil). Without a moral compass, Stone's characters cannot even plead ignorance. The irony that the heroin's value is rooted in its destructiveness does not escape them, but they cannot drop it. Its force has irradiated their world. They know of no good that will shelter them. . . .

This elemental tale is played out against a backdrop of the here and now. Heroin brings the Viet Nam War home to a sunny California filled with burnt-out cases from the '60s: deracinated hippies, faded gurus, old people driven mad by the gap between promise and truth. This Western strip of civilization has become a collection of competing manias, and its traces—rooming houses, motels, highways—are perched on the edge of primitive wilderness. Driving out of Los Angeles, Hicks comments on the quick change of scenery: "Go out for a Sunday spin, you're a short hair from the dawn of creation."

Novelist Stone's language is spare, constantly earning maximum effects with all but invisible efforts. A military career is summed up as years "of shining shoes and saluting automobiles." Much of the novel is dialogue, simultaneously as laconic and menacing as a scene by Harold Pinter.

Brooklyn-born Robert Stone . . . spent time in New Orleans and San Francisco during the early '60s as an "active participant" in the counterculture. Some of these experiences spilled out in *A Hall of Mirrors* (1967), a surrealistic vision of a New Orleans rife with political paranoia. This second novel confirms the talent betrayed in *A Hall of Mirrors* and reveals added discipline. The book has its flaws, of course. It occasionally luxuriates in baroque bleakness for its own sake. For example, Converse's addled mother is gratuitously trotted on like a lab specimen. The characters' motives, seen through moments of fragmentary introspection, are not always adequate. Still, most of *Dog Soldiers* is as precise as the cross hairs on a rifle sight. With fearful accuracy it describes a journey to hell and pronounces an epitaph on a time that has not ended.

> *Paul Gray, "Flowers of Evil," in* Time *(reprinted by permission from* Time, The Weekly Newsmagazine; *copyright* Time Inc.), *November 11, 1974, p. 111.*

Part melodrama, part morality play, "Dog Soldiers" offers a vision of a predatory, insensate society from which all moral authority has fled. It is a world in which innocence or vestigial remnants of decent behavior prove fatal to their owners: Hicks, whom the author sees as a kind of latter-day samurai, is nearly violent enough to survive, but he is done in by his loyalty to Marge. All of this corruption and vulnerability, this savagery and stoned withdrawal, this combination of passion and cynicism works convincingly, for Stone is a very good storyteller indeed. (pp. 111-12)

> *Peter S. Prescott, in* Newsweek *(copyright 1974 by Newsweek, Inc.; all rights reserved; reprinted by permission), November 11, 1974.*

If one were forced to choose the most important novel of the year, [*Dog Soldiers*] would be it: on the surface a gripping chase across Southern California involving three kilograms of heroin; deeper than that a stunning immorality tale about war and dope and violence. Don't expect to be elevated; this is not a cheering book and there are no very good guys in it. As one of the characters observes, "The desires of the heart are as crooked as a corkscrew." Robert Stone writes like a Graham Greene whose God is utterly dead, and he favors the same sort of setting, the same juxtaposition of the exotic and the banal. (p. 1)

Book World—The Washington Post (© The Washington Post), *December 8, 1974.*

Robert Stone's first novel, *A Hall of Mirrors*, was a baggy, zany affair, filled with goodies like "a California of the mind." *Dog Soldiers* is anything but zany; it is tight and, although exciting, grim. Whereas the texture of *A Hall of Mirrors* was hallucinogenic like its characters' grass, *Dog Soldiers* owes its insistent rhythm to heroin addiction and a kind of accelerated greed which are the book's subjects....

Dog Soldiers raises several old-fashioned questions about the nature of fiction.... All the characters' lives are sordid, violent and grim, relieved only (if at all) by unpleasant cynicism.... None of them is interesting except as a new subspecies, the counterculture turned ratty and sour. They deserve their own misery; they are addicted to it.

Perhaps Stone wants to make some sweeping indictment of America. Perhaps he is a moralist of the Vietnam war.... The implication is, of course, that . . . the American addiction [is] to violence, the embrace of weaponry, produced the Vietnam war, dope addiction, smuggling, and police brutality and corruption. It's an easy message—even if it may be true.

The trouble is, the characters in the novel all deserve what they get. The children blown out of sleep to death are merely a formal gesture, a nod toward what we all viewed for years on TV with dinner. None of the victims is made real.... Unlike the Vietnamese children these people could choose better lives. If there are moral objections to the war or to American life the book fails to make them. Where everyone deals, no one suffers. It's hard to care very much.... Greed and fear do not make a man.

But they do make a plot. Despite my profound moral disgust at this novel, my utter inability to sympathize with the characters, and my suspicion that my good liberal notion that the Vietnam war is as American as apple pie is cheaply manipulated, I have to admit I read the book straight through, addictively flipping the pages. Like James Dickey's *Deliverance*, to which similar objections might be made, this novel relies brilliantly on suspense: Will they make it? Who will kill whom? For the moment, at least *while you read*, these questions are paramount; they take precedence over What does it mean? and Is it art? Here, then, is the second issue *Dog Soldiers* raises. How important is plot, that excited concatenation of events, in the final assessment of a novel? What does it mean to be contemptuous of the characters and skeptical of a book's morality and yet to enjoy the *reading*.

Because these questions are unanswerable, *Dog Soldiers* compels a grudging admiration. It may even be that the reader's addiction to the plot is a counterpart as real as sympathy to the character's violence, greed, and fear. Suspense is the reader's scag. (pp. 29-30)

> *Joan Joffe Hall, in* The New Republic *(reprinted by permission of* The New Republic; © 1975 by The New Republic, Inc.), Jan-uary 4 & 11, 1975.*

Robert Stone's second novel [*Dog Soldiers*] is . . . really good, reminded me frequently of Hemingway (the epigraph from *Heart of Darkness* extends the line further back) and

has thus far met with universal praise. Good as the book is, it may be that its subject matter—Vietnam and drugs, the Great Confusion and various momentary stays against confusion—is partly responsible for the acclaim....

[The] story is as elaborately twisty, as challenging to try and follow along without leaving something out, as a Raymond Chandler thriller, say *The Big Sleep*; the dialogue is ever-present, arresting and often very funny indeed—Lenny Bruce funny, that is.... No friendly author-narrator, winking at the reader, stands behind these assorted losers, these junkies, creeps and U.S. riff-raff circa 1970. (p. 159)

Stone sees all his characters as funny little fuckers—dog soldiers who soldier on but just may be inclined, things being what they are, to speed up the trip towards death. As with the earlier *Hall of Mirrors*, it is a claustrophobic world; barely a moment of impulse allowed in the direction of a better life; no figure from his ill-assorted gallery likely to take time out to read, oh, say Wordsworth or Dickens, or make up a large corned beef sandwich on rye and watch the late show. Everybody is tainted, even the old people round the television in a cheap hotel . . . have "reptile faces." If it weren't for the razor's edge of comic brilliance, the rich lore about other modes of behavior (I speak as an East Coast Straight), the flick and spring of exchange—hardly conversation—this would be a dreary and deathly book. But no, the novel is the book of life said the dying Lawrence as through gritted teeth he saluted Hemingway and Huxley and would have *The Day of the Locust*. Reading Robert Stone's book you know more about how life was never worse than in 1974 and how art is still art, doing ruthlessly and strangely what it does. (p. 160)

> *William H. Pritchard, in* The Hudson Review *(copyright © 1975 by The Hudson Review, Inc.; reprinted by permission), Vol. XXVIII, No. 1, Spring, 1975.*

Dog Soldiers is a truly grim book, relentless in a way that makes other books claiming to look at the dark side of American life seem at least slightly deflecting or palliative in their final effect. Robert Stone's publishers say he offers a "vision of our predicament," but if that were true one could turn aside, call it just a vision and Stone a grouse, and that's not the way it works. *Dog Soldiers* does not expose, or show, or put on a performance for readers. It is an absorbed realistic novel, telling a story, always working to get it told right, much closer to Theodore Weesner's *The Car Thief* in this respect than to *Something Happened* or *Gravity's Rainbow*, which are "visions" of life that a reader can finally take or leave. As a result, one presumes, these books can be popular in a way that *Dog Soldiers*, homely and serious as wood, beautiful only in its integrity, will probably never be....

Stone seems to have realized, here more than in his first novel *A Hall of Mirrors*, that he wanted to see the lives of his main characters as having shapes for all that they seem to have none, and to use plot as his major means of articulating those shapes....

It's not daily life in the usual sense we are considering, because these lives have no habits or direction; still, it is only the moment-to-moment experience in which Stone is interested. Even people who have no characters have lives.

Stone cannot love his characters, or urge us in any way to admire them, because they are not lovable or admirable. But they count, he keeps insisting, which is why the book is so grim. How much easier it would be to think they don't matter. . . .

Stone, as I see it, is a nineteenth-century moralist, as eager as Carlyle or George Eliot to make the precise assessments required to judge the choices made by an individual or a society. John Converse has scurried about creation with casual arrogance, and there is no better judgment to be made. Yet if aimlessness, destruction, and institutional wantonness do not preclude choice and so do not preclude judgment, they make Stone's task far different from that of any writer of a century ago. What if one did see the bombs fall on the Cambodians? How easy then to make judgments, and of anything but oneself. Converse, at that moment, only cries. But . . . as he remembers the scene, after having chosen to put the world once again murderously at his throat, he neither shrinks nor sentimentally implicates himself in the bombing. He . . . can only soldier on, a dog, but alive. . . .

Dog Soldiers could have been one of the best American books of his generation. The first half does something with all the myths and clichés about current living that no other novel I know has done: it takes on the grimness of our worst fears about ourselves and gives meaning to the lives it thereby embodies. Such unappetizing characters these are, such figures for satire and horror stories—yet that is not the sense we have of them at all. (p. 9)

The more seriously Stone takes his characters, the more carefully he brings their aimlessness to a decision, the more he eventually either jettisons the aimlessness or falsifies the decisiveness and its importance. I'm not sure how he could better have pondered his materials and his wonderful first half, but the remainder is good writing that seems divorced from a wider purpose than its own existence, and so seems just like writing.

The problem here is an old problem, one that has haunted the realistic novel as it has persisted in these latter days when, though the novel itself is alive and well, the conventions with which the realistic novel began certainly seem dead. The myth had it that the atomization of society destroyed the importance the novel as a form had sought to impart to individual lives. To support the myth, one could point to the way many of the best novels of the past generation have invested importance only in the imagination of the performing novelist; language is set free, the result is comic, visionary, and grotesque by turns. But the realistic novel has persisted, and at its recent best, as in *Dog Soldiers*, it does so not as a literary vestige but as a way of still seeing and knowing the life that goes on. Converse, Marge, and Hicks are not complex figures, but they are not symbolic figures or mouthpieces either. The first half of *Dog Soldiers* takes them as they are, and seriously, without once overrating their importance; the second half falls victim to a plot, as so many older realistic novels do, that does not so much realize these characters' lives as finish off an action in which novelist and characters have become enmeshed.

Yet even in its most headlong and least effective pages, *Dog Soldiers* shows Stone's clear eye for detail and clear-eyed determination to see these lives through to some end

without sentimentalizing them. Throughout, thus, his integrity gives us a sense of learning at first hand what most of us have known only as hearsay or freakout. He brings the news, as novelists are supposed to do; he makes one think we have only begun to understand our immediate past. (p. 10)

> *Roger Sale, "Bringing the News," in* The New York Review of Books *(reprinted with permission from* The New York Review of Books; *copyright © 1975 NYREV, Inc.), April 3, 1975, pp. 9-10.*

In *Dog Soldiers*, the action moves—along with plenty of heroin—from Saigon to America, bringing the war home. Robert Stone is a very sure writer, and his characters—the journalist (sort of); his wife; and the carrier, a savvy dumbhead—slide into destruction along with their sense of decency. It's not entirely their fault or Robert Stone's. On the other hand the author doesn't openly take on the challenge of why they are destroyed, though perhaps if he did the book would not be in print. Moments of really fine writing peak through the book's early leisure. And when it is tough it is very tough. He does not risk his readership with self-confrontation, but plays with murder and flashes of unpleasant insight into depravity. It should appeal to people who want to mind-mess both with drugs and with those who lose hardest. Stone shows his own kind of heroism here by taking on the exploration of a world that most people don't deal with by choice. (p. 3)

> *John Bart Gerald, in* Bookletter *(copyright 1975 by* Harper's Magazine; *reprinted from the April 28, 1975 issue by special permission), April 28, 1975.*

*   *   *

STOPPARD, Tom   1937-

Stoppard, a Czech-born British playwright for stage, radio, television, and screen, and the author of one novel, has won both the Tony and New York Drama Critics' Circle Awards. The premise for much of his work is the Beckettian notion that man is a minor character in a drama he cannot understand. C.W.E. Bigsby has written that the central concern of *Rosencrantz and Guildenstern Are Dead* and several other plays is that wrenching object from setting and event from context "results not merely in a revealing absurdity but in a perception of the contingent nature of truth."

I misconceived the meaning of [Tom Stoppard's *Jumpers*] when I reported on it here last summer. . . .

Stoppard, or at any rate, the play's protagonist George Moore, a professor of moral philosophy, wishes to prove that a belief in the existence of God is reasonable. There is a certain absurdity in this, for, as the professor himself declares, "The fact that I cut a ludicrous figure in the academic world is largely due to my aptitude for traducing a complex and logical thesis to a mysticism of staggering banality."

Apart from the fact that Stoppard has made his professor laughably absentminded, unkempt and generally disorganized in his workaday behavior . . . there is little else in the play besides its intellectual argument.

Clearly the play, in its humor and in its brilliant writing, in addition to its basic subject, is an exceptional and superior entertainment. But Stoppard impresses me chiefly as a gifted university wit. I cannot take him seriously as an important dramatist. Even his *Rosencrantz and Guildenstern Are Dead* struck me as a deft variation on a Beckett-like theme, and *The Real Inspector Hound* as a nimble jape. He is, to use Samuel Goldwyn's phrase, "a very clever genius." (p. 604)

Harold Clurman, in The Nation *(copyright 1974 by the Nation Associates, Inc.), May 11, 1974.*

'Man—good, bad, or indifferent?' the philosopher-hero of Tom Stoppard's *Jumpers* was apt to ask himself; and practically everyone in his *Travesties* seems to be discussing a similar, if smaller question. Art—good, bad, or indifferent? The play is set in Zurich, and capitalises on the coincidence that Lenin, Joyce and the Dadaist Tristan Tzara were all to be found in its libraries and cafés at about the time of Passchendaele. . . . Stoppard's great gift is to treat solemn subjects with a gaiety that enlightens without trivialising. So it was with *Jumpers*, which was about the discomfort of inhabiting a world left bereft of all moral certainties; and so, to a lesser extent, it is here. Perhaps I expected too much. Perhaps we've grown accustomed to his amusement-arcade style. Whatever the reason, I couldn't respond as wholeheartedly as I'd wished to the puns and Wildean *mots*, the long, sparkling monologues, the limericks and songs, the disguises and misunderstandings, all packing the action like pinball machines in a debating chamber. Stoppard's wit isn't in question, nor his intelligence, nor his audacity . . . What troubles me is his propensity to get carried away in his own mental helter-skelter. Joyce, when first mentioned, is mistaken for a woman, then called Doris, then Janice, then Phyllis, then Deirdre—get Stoppard stuck into a joke, and you have to prise him out with a crowbar. Indeed Johnson's notorious words about Shakespeare apply more aptly to him: a quibble is 'the gilded apple for which he will always turn aside from his career, or stoop from his elevation'. There's so much chasing of ideas that we never get around to evaluating them, so much fun with characters that we cannot finally tell what, why, how or even who they are.

But Stoppard has his own reply to such criticism: in a pluralistic world, who can make an adequate judgment on any matter or person? . . . So we're to savour the intellectual questions as they bounce by, murmuring 'who knows?' into our whiskers—'who knows?', but not, let me emphasise, 'who cares?'. For all his unbelief, Stoppard is no nihilist; for all his manic frivolity, he's still, somehow, a serious writer. . . . (p. 859)

Benedict Nightingale, in New Statesman *(© 1974 The Statesman & Nation Publishing Co. Ltd.), June 14, 1974.*

Travesties . . . is another Stoppard study in human irrelevance. Like Rosencrantz and Guildenstern, like George, the professor in *Jumpers*, Carr [in *Travesties*] is a poohstick in the River of Fate, swirled to and fro by currents, not recognising the bridges under which he slowly drifts. After three or four plays, this harping on irrelevance seems irrelevant in itself. Is Stoppard suggesting that men are always adrift, in which case he could have selected a more startling pooh-stick, such as Lenin? Or is he simply pointing out that, from different angles, history changes colour and shape, a familiar point but one which, in a world full of dogmas, is worth stressing?

My view is that Stoppard merely uses this theme of irrelevance as a pad from which to launch a variety of literary pastiches, the chief being that of Wilde's play [*The Importance of Being Earnest*], but with a cluster of secondary ones, such as Joycean limericks and Dadaistic poems which prove accidentally to have more sense than their originals. The extracts from Lenin's writing and the brief adulatory passages from his biography sit awkwardly in this company, occupying too much room in the second act. The chief delight of *Travesties*, an entertaining play, is similar to that of reading *New Statesman* competitions, of tracking down literary sources, of groaning at awful puns ('My art belongs to Dada') and of admiring the stylistic cleverness without bothering about the content. For this reason a genteel boredom creeps in, a yawn of pleasure, which we try politely to cover. . . . (p. 801)

John Elsom, "Pooh-sticks," in The Listener *(© British Broadcasting Corp. 1974; reprinted by permission of John Elsom), June 20, 1974, pp. 801-02.*

Based on a true incident in the Geneva of 1918—a minor British consular employee's suing James Joyce over the unreimbursed cost of a pair of trousers for an amateur production of *The Importance of Being Earnest* Joyce had coproduced—[*Travesties*] proceeds to weave together outrageous fictions about the lives of Joyce, Henry Carr (the employee), the dadaist poet Tristan Tzara, and Lenin, all of whom lived in Geneva at that time and might have known one another but didn't. What Stoppard has fabricated, using Wilde's play as a maze into which his own keeps wandering and briefly losing itself, is one of the most ingenious, uproarious, preposterous, and genuinely sophisticated comedies ever—in its first act. But in the second, where Lenin preponderates, things get serious, in fact, downright ponderous. . . . Did Stoppard consider Lenin's humorless zeal, transposed to the stage, a funny enough *objet trouvé* as is? Or is he too much of a Marxist to dare poke fun at Lenin? Or are some of his best friends, whom he wants to keep, Marxists? Whatever the reason, the second act goes to pot; even *The Importance* obtrudes too insistently, and though there are still some genuine laughs, they are few and far between. . . .

But there remains for me a crucial problem here, and one that has been dogging Tom Stoppard—unless he has been dogging it. It is the problem of a profound nugacity, an inveterate trifling—the fact that this play is ultimately about nothing at all. True, some pretty good farces have been written about very little—though the best ones are redolent with genuine human foibles—but Stoppard's characters, although they sometimes impinge on humanity, are only sight gags and word plays romping around a stage. And not without a certain pretentiousness, either. *C'est magnifique, mais ce n'est pas l'art*. When you invoke names like Joyce, Lenin, and Tzara, something more is expected of you. (p. 67)

John Simon, in New York Magazine *(© 1974 by NYM Corp.; reprinted by permission of* New York Magazine *and John Simon), August 26, 1974.*

Mr. Stoppard has the rare gift of intellectual high spirits and he writes with the freshness that characterised the *Beyond the Fringe* quartet in their early days. It was a brilliant idea to think of James Joyce, Tristan Tzara and Lenin as being all together in the public library in Trieste during the First World War, so as to juxtapose serious avant-garde art, Dadaist non-art and political activism which looks upon art as a distraction from the serious business of refashioning life. It was equally brilliant to show them through the eyes of the unknown consular official, Henry Carr, who fell foul of Joyce in connection with an amateur performance of *The Importance of Being Earnest*. Carr is the central monologuist [in *Travesties*], like the philosopher in *Jumpers* and the Rosencrantz-Guildenstern couple in the earlier play; he is remembering the whole thing in seedy retirement and, by his ramblings, uncertainties and sudden bursts of bad temper, illustrates the unreliability of history, which can present any of these famous men as a fascinating person or a repellent one.

This is the oft-repeated Existentialist point: we live only in the present, and the past is a perpetual recreation. The past, in fact, is always art, myth or retrospective extrapolation, and so our hold on "real life" is always much more precarious than most of us care to think. Mr. Stoppard conveys this idea beautifully in Carr's monologues....

By the way in which he juggles with Lenin, Joyce and Tzara, Mr Stoppard shows that he has a point of view. He is in favour of genuine art, represented by Joyce, against aleatory art, minimal art or non-art—all those activities which blur the distinction between art and life—represented by Tzara. He is also against Lenin, who chose to disregard art as a disturbing luxury, being too obtuse to understand that art, in the last resort, is the most profoundly serious human occupation above the subsistence level. As somebody remarks at one point: "If you can't be an artist, you may as well be a politician!" It is perhaps because Mr Stoppard is in love with art and not quite sure that he himself is a true artist that he loads every rift with other men's ore, and dazzles with quotations and imitations. (p. 59)

John Weightman, in Encounter (© *1974 by Encounter Ltd.), September, 1974.*

I could fill whole issue of *Drama* by simply tracing the intellectual cat's-cradle, the verbal dexterities of this dramatic *salmagundi* [*Travesties*]. I enjoyed my evening in the theatre, to be sure; but I was undeniably disappointed, and at the last unsatisfied. Here, if you like, is some sort of burlesque of the higher reaches of Western civilization, encapsulated in Zurich during the first world war. There, as it happened, two artistic would-be revolutionaries—Tristan Tzara, the Romanian preacher of Dada, the art of the meaningless, and James Joyce, the Irish singer of solipsistic bliss—and one very real political revolutionary, later known as Lenin, were all to be found while the guns crashed and the corpses rotted in the mud on the Western Front and the great disgruntled masses of Russia came to the boil. The first two Mr. Stoppard mixes into a parody of bits of *The Importance of Being Earnest*, which we are probably meant to take as the purest, most abstract comedy yet written. It is not abstract at all, in fact; like all English comedy, it is about manners and money in a certain class at a certain time. And Tzara was no real revolutionary, for Dada has remained a symptomatic sport in the history of

art in our time; and Joyce was no real revolutionary either, for neither *Ulysses* nor *Finnegans Wake* has had any effect upon the significant fiction of our century. At one time or another, in between the burlesque acts, the limerick-swapping, the puns and the song-and-dance acts and the comic costumes (Joyce, for example in a white suit patterned with shamrocks) there is quite a bit of potentially interesting talk about the nature and purpose of art in one form or another; but it goes nowhere in particular, and Mr. Stoppard does not seem to be using his puppets to say anything in particular.... But what, you are asking, of the real revolutionary, Lenin? Him Mr. Stoppard has totally failed to blend with his masquerade. Initially all three revolutionaries are seen together in the public library; but Lenin and his wife are mere background figures until, totally detached from all the rest, they give us passages from Lenin's speeches ..., which not only disrupted the fragile party fun-and-games of the rest of the piece, but made me feel that I would quite happily, though no Communist, have gone on listening to them for the rest of the evening. No such luck; we were soon back to the sixth-form high jinks. (pp. 38-40)

Also in Zurich was a man called Henry Carr ... [and] out of him Mr. Stoppard has made a fine character. He frames the play as an old man living in dim retirement, remembering the days when he rubbed shoulders with the great (not always recognizing them as such, and now not always able to get their names right); he bounds through the play as a young embodiment of God's Englishman, ... a philistine —though a remarkably intelligent one when necessary for purposes of the dialogue—a boyish adventurer and a preening prig. His old self and his young self alternate with bewildering rapidity, and both are enormously enjoyable. (p. 40)

Mr. Stoppard is doubtless, like David Storey in *Life Class*, using that by now familiar evasive tactic of putting opinions in which he believes (art must not be destroyed either by travesties or by politics) into unlikely mouths, so that he cannot be accused of being what used to be called square.... If only the rest of *Travesties* had approached the tattered stoicism of Henry Carr, we should have had a play indeed; as it is, ... we are left with an ingenious plaything. (p. 41)

J. W. Lambert, in Drama, *Autumn, 1974.*

[An] early play by Tom Stoppard called "Enter a Free Man" ... would perhaps be a less interesting play for us to watch if we were unaware of the Stoppard of "Jumpers" and "Travesties," because it is written in a realistic vein, and the nature of its plot prevents the sort of gorgeous high fooling with language that now distinguishes Stoppard from almost all his contemporaries. The characters in "Enter a Free Man" are lower-middle-class and therefore tonguetied. Such eloquence as they possess is that which springs not from speaking well but from speaking badly; they struggle to find words commensurate with their feelings, and they always fail....

The author of "Enter a Free Man" betrays his youth by the trouble he has taken to work out at length a plot of no very great originality and to give it an ending too neat for its own good. Along the way, we catch glimpses of the Stoppard to come, especially when ... his characters, with every sign of perfect satisfaction, chatter away at cross-purposes. (p. 50)

Brendan Gill, in The New Yorker (© *1975 by The New Yorker Magazine, Inc.), January 6, 1975.*

[*Enter a Free Man*] is Stoppard's first, and although it doesn't have the complexity and texture of his later work, like "Rosencrantz and Guildenstern Are Dead" and "Jumpers," it's a fascinating harbinger of those plays.

Troubled England's young playwrights seem to be shaping up into two rough camps—the political and the philosophical. Stoppard is perhaps the most philosophical of the latter, and in his very first work he looks behind social tensions to human tensions and aberrations of spirit. His chief aberration is George Riley, who is British Everyman gone bonkers. George thinks he's a great inventor; he's spent his adult life being supported by his wife and daughter while he creates such breakthroughs as an envelope with gum on both sides of the flap and a system to water plants by piping in the rain. George is a multiple human parody—of a husband, of a father, and finally no doubt of the aspirations of contemporary Britain itself. . . .

It was angry young men who brought in the British theater revolution, but Stoppard has something with more staying power than anger—an empathy into the pathos, inevitably funny, of people who screw up their little lives by reaching for big truths. Even George's wife and daughter have their own illusions. The mother believes in a domesticity now sadly decayed, and the daughter, despite her shrewdness, falls into the old romantic traps.

Stoppard's special trick is finding the sweet, sad craziness hidden in real behavior. . . .

Jack Kroll, "Everyman Bonkers," in Newsweek *(copyright 1975 by Newsweek, Inc.; all rights reserved; reprinted by permission), January 8, 1975, p. 64.*

* * *

STOREY, David   1933-

Storey is an award-winning English playwright and novelist. In both his fiction and drama, Storey uses ordinary people and commonplace situations to work out powerful emotional conflicts and complicated ideas about family and social class relationships.

A Temporary Life is an odd book, occasionally brilliant, always intelligent and absorbing. Mr Storey's command both of pathos and of comedy is increasingly sure: he switches here from the harrowing to the farcical with unnerving speed, and complete conviction. But the sum total is both cryptic and frustrating. For some reason, Mr Storey has chosen to channel his impressive understanding of modern society, the nature of change within it, and the effect of that change on the individual, into a sort of mannered parable. A host of characters who at first actually live, vigorously, through the abundant psychological realism, the quirks and eccentricities, which the author gives them, slip one by one into allegorical roles, and peter out in fantasy. The finely economical, staccato prose is clipped and pared down to a portentously meaningful minimalist style. Everything works with clockwork efficiency and intricacy—clues and symbolic pointers are dropped in every sequence and ingeniously explained, or taken up, at some later stage. But the final impression is of a writer putting his intense and disquieting perceptions of the way life is going through a nightmarish squaredance which muffles rather than clarifies the effect of what he wants to say. Few novelists now writing see so vividly, think so intelligently, command so much sheer understanding of people and society. It is sad to watch these abilities turned to an exercise in stylish evasion.

"Latest Developments," in The Times Literary Supplement (© *Times Newspapers Ltd., 1973; reproduced by permission), September 21, 1973, p. 1073.*

[The] essential quality of [David Storey's] work comes, above all, from the characteristic balance he achieves between the literary and the visual. Structure is particularly important in his plays: their overall shape is almost sculptured. *The Contractor* takes its form from the erection and dismantling of the tent. After starting with an empty stage, we see the tent being put up and then being prepared for the wedding breakfast. This takes place in the interval between Act II and Act III, and the lights next go up on the chaos of empty bottles, dirty glasses and plates, damaged decorations and overturned furniture that the wedding guests have left. This is cleared up, the tent is taken down and we end, as we began, with an empty stage. *In Celebration* also centres on a celebration meal, which again takes place in the interval. The play is about a family reunion occasioned by the fortieth wedding anniversary of a coalminer and his wife. As the play begins, one of their three sons is arriving in the heavily-furnished living-room of their home. The other two arrive, the conversation between sons, parents and neighbours produces a series of insights into the lives they are all leading, and we see that those of the parents and neighbours have changed very little since the sons, now all in their thirties, were children. They stay overnight but leave in the morning. The excitement over, the parents resume their lives. (p. 12)

[In] *The Changing Room* the focus is wider, taking in all thirteen members of a professional rugby team, the cleaner of the changing room, the trainers, the referee and the club manager and chairman. Again, though the play is about the people, its shape—like that of Wesker's *The Kitchen*—is determined by the place, and though the place (unlike the tent in *The Contractor*) has a continuing existence both before and after the action, it comes to life only at the time of the game, and what we see is constructed around two busy climaxes, with the players changing first into their rugby clothes and, later, out of them. Again the main climax of action—the game itself—is excluded from the play, and again we begin and end very quietly, this time with the old cleaner, who never watches the game but whose life centres on the changing room. The wooden benches, the clothes-pegs, the towels, the rugby boots, socks, singlets and shorts, and the physical actions, including massage and the referee's inspection, contribute to the life of the play on almost exactly the same level as the words. (pp. 12-13)

Ronald Hayman, "David Storey," in his Playback *(copyright © 1973 by Ronald Hayman; reprinted by permission of A. D. Peters & Co. Ltd.), Davis-Poynter, 1973, pp. 7-20.*

Storey's [*The Contractor*] is minimal theatre, like his *Home* and *The Changing Room*, but with slightly more discernible shreds of plot adhering to the documentary structure. And structure it truly is; Ewbank, a Yorkshire contractor, has his men erect a marquee for his daughter's wedding (which, significantly, is not shown) in his suburban garden; later the structure is taken down again. The foreman and workers tease one another, bicker, and come to blows; the Ewbank family—gently pathetic elders, befuddled middle generation, and more or less alienated young—display their puzzlement, quiet cynicism, dislocation, or despair; somewhere in the invisible foreground, the city sprouts an ever more threatening Birnam Wood of TV antennas, encroaching on the view from the Ewbanks' hillside stronghold.

There is envy and dissension among the working-class contingent; uneasy comfort in the middle-class family. . . .

Out of these elements, without ever allowing them to congeal into a real plot, Storey creates an atmosphere of general unfulfilment, unstable compromise, and poignancy, as slippery objects of desire elude hands drenched with the sweat of existential anxiety. And over it all looms the tent, whose erection, decoration, and dismantling constitute, respectively, the play's three acts. It becomes thus the embodiment of work, which is what finally keeps men from going totally purposeless, restless, mad; and also the emblem of the rise, culmination, and decline of all human endeavor, including life itself. The play talks around rather than into its theme: everything is indirection and implication, and very often only silence. There is a good deal of humor, more often raucous than gentle, and a rare bit of strangulated pathos, made more touching by its self-effacing brevity. In some ways this suggests a kinship with Pinter, but this is, happily, only superficial. Storey's pauses, non sequiturs, sudden changes of mood grow out of his conception of character: they represent genuine human weaknesses, hesitancies, derailments; in Pinter, these devices are calculated for effect, and represent undue cleverness on the part of the characters, and flashy prestidigitation on the part of the author. Pinter's weirdness is imposed from without, meant to stun the audience with the depth of its inscrutability; Storey's fumblings are those of people protesting against or subsiding into perplexity. Pinter tries to impress us; Storey impresses things on us. Pinter invents a teasing, distorted unreality; Storey allows the strangeness of ordinary reality to dawn on us, as when, let's say, we first see a hair under a microscope.

One more good thing about *The Contractor*: Storey, a man who has held many odd jobs, understands the intricacy and fascination of labor, which makes something come to be where, formerly, nothing was. He gets us painstakingly involved with the minutiae of tent-building, and we are exhilarated to see the thing go up and proudly assert its existence. We are further thrilled to see how furnishings and decorations make a veritable, even if gaudy, environment out of the edifice. At last, when it is dismantled, we experience a keen sense of loss, transience, mortality. (pp. 82-3)

John Simon, in The Hudson Review *(copyright © 1974 by The Hudson Review, Inc.; reprinted by permission), Vol. XXVII, No. 1, Spring, 1974.*

The young men at the centre of David Storey's plays are a pretty sorry lot. His composite juvenile lead, lifted mainly from *In Celebration, The Contractor* and *The Farm*, seems usually to be visiting his old folks' place near Barnsley, a squat, stony womb that fills him with love and loathing in roughly equal parts. He's university-educated, despises his white-collar job, writes poetry and paints desultory abstracts, is planning to leave his wife and children if he can summon up the courage, and will soon have a nervous breakdown. His ever-admiring mother hovers with a teapot, while his father takes off his hobnail boots and grumbles into the fire. 'Sithee, lad,' says the old man helpfully, 'thou hast never done aught worth aught, hast thou?'; and the boy, thinking enviously of the career as a coal-miner or hill-farmer he's missed, will probably agree. He is, it seems, doomed to spend his rag-bag life on the outside, looking back in: a voyeur and, though not always regarded by the world as a failure, invariably a failure to himself. . . .

Life Class may not have one of Storey's authentic fathers to show us, but it does have a father-figure of sorts, and here he is, living up to the part both by his rejection of Allott [the protagonist] in the last reel and by the aggressive and dogmatic conservatism of his views. Sometimes one wonders if his dramatic function might be to provoke a debate about the place, if any, of art and the artist in the modern world. But, if so, it doesn't amount to much: he and Allott provide, not a debate, but a blunt collision of extremes of opinion. What useful conclusion can the listener reach when one side seems to expect a second Renaissance to rise over Wakefield Cathedral, and the other hopes for nothing better than a random series of more or less sensational happenings?

None, of course, except that the world is a pretty confused and confusing place: precisely David Storey's view of it. Indeed, don't think he's as interested in assessing his characters' attitudes as in showing us how diverse and irreconcilable those attitudes are. His plays are all about disintegration, fragmentation: of society, of belief, of the family, of the individual psyche. From *The Restoration of Arnold Middleton* to *Home* to *The Changing Room*, they tell us how difficult it is for man to cooperate with man, or even to achieve much coherence and unity within himself. In artistic endeavour, if anywhere, the mind, emotions and hands should function as one: they patently don't do so in *Life Class*. (p. 558)

As often with Storey's plays, much is asked of the audience: it's up to you and me to speculate about character and ideas on the basis of far less direct evidence than modern playwrights customarily offer. But the evidence exists, and the rewards are there to be grabbed. Those who are prepared to do a little homework in the stalls, instead of slumping back and passively absorbing, will leave the theatre feeling that a good deal more has occurred than they can remember having actually seen and heard on the stage. (p. 559)

Benedict Nightingale, "Everyman on His Uppers," in New Statesman *(© 1974 The Statesman & Nation Publishing Co. Ltd.), April 19, 1974, pp. 558-59.*

The boredom that Storey inflicts upon an audience is, or so it seems to me, wilful rather than inadvertent, and I'm bound to say that indignation at his impertinence is tempered a little by admiration for his nerve. It used to be said of Ibsen that his plays (or some of them) began at the point where, in other hands, they would have ended. Storey is getting away with a rather simpler operation: he ends his plays (or some of them) at the point where they might more stimulatingly begin. His characters are drawn with an almost obsessive attention to detail that extends into all manner of irrelevance (the sort of thing that most dramatists probably jot down as notes on their characters, so that they know where they've been before getting down to the business of where they're going), and then, having familiarised himself with them, he calls it a day. Reviewers who praise this sort of thing are somewhat in the position of motoring correspondents who might rhapsodise over the bodywork of a car from which the engine has been left out.

It is an indolent approach to the dramatist's craft if there ever was one, and in the case of *Life Class* it seems to have required even less effort than meets the eye, since all the adult characters—including the central figure, an art teacher at some dubious college of art somewhere in the drearier northern provinces—are lifted from the novel, *A Temporary Life*, which Storey had published last year. Giving them different names seems to have been the limit of his further inspiration about them. (pp. 489-90)

Life Class, despite this character overlap, is in no sense an adaptation of *A Temporary Life*. The book was not exactly overdone with incident, but its quaint little threads of narrative were a frenzy of plotting compared with the fatiguing uneventfulness of the proceedings on the stage, which have an aimlessness extravagant even for Storey. . . . The scene throughout is the 'life class' presided over by the disenchanted Allott character, who moves among his unappetising students dispensing philosophical reflections on art that I took at first to indicate some wickedly satirical motive on Storey's part, but it gradually becomes miserably clear that this scourge of the captive audience is more or less the author's spokesman and that his half-baked aphorisms are intended to be taken seriously. (p. 490)

> *Kenneth Hurren, "Still Life," in* The Spectator *(© 1974 by The Spectator; reprinted by permission of* The Spectator*), April 20, 1974, pp. 489-90.*

Life Class, . . . unless I'm very much mistaken (which is conceivable) . . . is in the nature of a valediction. The stuff of the play is a dialectic on life and art, enduring and creating, proceeding and observing. Storey takes a naked figure and sets about it a group of student artists, a posse of teachers and a commentator. (p. 26)

Storey is not, I suspect, a writer to condone speculation. As he once said on TV, 'the bird sings, and that is all'. Allott, his teacher in *Life Class*, puts it less succinctly—'a bird sings in its tree but doesn't contemplate its song . . . we are life's musicians, life's singers and what we sing has no meaning'. All very fine. But I can't help pricking up my ears when Allott also issues the dark threat: 'My next effort may be something altogether less commendable' and, looking round the life class studio and the Royal Court theatre beyond, considers he's done some of his best work there. The valediction I'm busily detecting is to the life class, to the careful portrayal of 'that incredible miasma we call life', which has made Storey's name and about which he has surely said all he's got to say. Is there a promise here of a new direction, a farewell not so much to the

theatre itself as to the safety of the Royal Court theatre of life-as-she-is-lived? God, I hope so. Because without this tantalising suggestion which, for me, lit up the last 40-odd minutes of the play and in retrospect the whole of it, I should be reporting on a very heavy evening.

It's as well, though, to consider the play as the singing bird, without such overtones. The tune is the polished artifice of the new establishment theatre. . . . All wrapped up in the good old slice-of-life show.

The students—or at least the lads—are broad types, easily despatched with a pair of adjectives. Saunders is prissy and conscientious (we know that on sight because he wears specs), Mathews is boyish and horny, Warren is jokey and aggressive, and so on. But considering the reflections on sexism, it's interesting to note that the girls are unable to establish sharp characters, having no arresting or idiosyncratic things to say and never holding, rarely passing through, centre-stage. Even their names—Catherine Smith, for instance—are anonymous. Moreover, the continuous ribaldry about the model is hard to take. A lot of the lines might have been written for 10-year-olds. . . .

The ruminations on art are not, of themselves, very resonant (though totally fascinating if they relate to a farewell to farms, tents, rugby players and teachers). Thoughts like 'no work of art is complete without a personal statement' fall exhausted to the ground half-way up the stalls. . . . I've never thought Storey's laugh-lines came easy. . . . The mock-rape scene is quite preposterous, unbelievable on any level, save as a metaphor for what Storey allows his invented characters to do to real life, whilst Allott/Storey considers the event with a detached, slightly alarmed dignity.

No, it was definitely that note of *congé* that caught my fancy. Storey is in real danger of going round in diminishing circles at the Court. Now would be an excellent time to branch out, perhaps to avail his undoubted skills to an experimental group. I have no way of knowing how he sees his future, but I urge him to pursue the radical departure that I believe *Cromwell* was a false start towards and that *Life Class* presages. (p. 27)

> *W. Stephen Gilbert, in* Plays and Players *(© copyright W. Stephen Gilbert 1974), May, 1974.*

Admittedly, [*Life Class*] appears, at first sight, to deal with the same kind of situation [as *The Contractor* and *The Changing Room*]. A group of people are engaged on a practical pursuit and the truth about them is meant to emerge incidentally as they carry through the *project*. In *Life Class*, instead of a gang of workmen setting up a tent or a rugby team before, during and after the match, we have a class of art-students in some provincial academy assembled on a cold winter's day to draw from the nude, under the direction of their disillusioned and sarcastic teacher. The pattern is similar to that of the other two plays: preparation for the action, the action under way, and the dismantling of the action for a return to zero; coming together in the morning, the class in operation leading to a dramatic climax, and then disruption and dispersal in the evening. The teacher allows, and perhaps encourages, something to happen which causes his dismissal, so that the life class is a symbolic crisis in his life. Instead of the students succeeding in drawing the nude model, one of them leaps on to her and simulates an orgasm so convincingly that the rest of the class is momentarily taken in and shocked, and a sexually-repressed student reports the matter to the principal. Real life nudity has produced a gross physical response instead of a work of art. Since, as the teacher keeps implying in his ironical speeches, we don't really know what art is, life has, in this instance, interrupted the life class and destroyed the supposed purity and sublimity of art, by showing that a nude is a system of sex-signals to be acted on immediately, with no nonsense about transposition to a different plane.

My central disappointment with the play arises from this implied message, which is a surprisingly crude simplification of the truth about life and art. It is a fact that artists have traditionally fornicated with their models, and good luck to them, but anybody can fornicate, whereas only an artist qua artist can produce the Rokeby Venus or any other collocation of forms celebrating the poetry of sex. I wonder if Mr Storey has not been misled by the new permissiveness into putting a nude on the stage and then making too facile a use of her, charming though she is. (p. 57)

[There] is never any indication that they are specifically art students, *i.e.* people who, in addition to their randiness and bowel-movements, are genuinely interested in the problems of art. They are all perfectly philistine, and the only art-object they produce is a hat that one of the girls has made at home.... The kind of art school he presents would only be appropriate in a farce, but *Life Class* is clearly meant as a serious statement.

The seriousness, alas, is little more than sentimentality. Allott, the sophisticated teacher, is a failed artist, who says he has ruined his marriage to devote himself to art, and then has found that his talent, or art itself, is non-existent. He consoles himself with the assertion that real life is his material and pads around the room creating an atmosphere with snooty-clever remarks, like any soured schoolmaster or university teacher. This is meant to be life as continuous happening. But the happening is quite lacking in salt, and ... the play does not attempt to convey why there has been tension between his private life and his art, or between art and himself. He is no more than a rather dim *fruit sec*, who is presented in an aura of unjustified approval, a sort of minor Jimmy Porter who has strayed into an arts school to continue his grumbling there. (pp. 57-8)

> *John Weightman, in* Encounter (© *1974 by Encounter Ltd.), September, 1974.*

Life Class is a garrulous and pretentious play, astonishing from a dramatist as spare and understated as Storey has been in the past. Lately Storey has turned out plays too quickly, I believe, and if worthiness has become wordiness, the reason may simply be that concentrated leanness takes longer than prodigal prolixity....

In past plays, Storey was able to make some human activity—erecting a tent, playing Rugby, hanging on in an old folks' home—become absorbing on, or just off, stage, and unassumingly take on symbolic implications. But art school does not even provide a dramatic enough initial activity: charcoal sketches never seen by the audience are less than involving, and the petty animosities among immature students and untutored teachers refuse to grow into an overarching image of human endeavor and strife. And whereas Storey's characters formerly spoke tersely, bumblingly, or with a self-revealing evasiveness, allowing meanings to emerge against their will and all the more poignantly, here there is mostly verbose pontification or persiflage about life and art whose sardonic deflations by Allott sound not a whit less attitudinizing than the rest....

Unlike so many of our playwrights, Storey has had an eventful and varied life, which provides him with potent, strongly felt dramatic metaphors. Conceivably even a life class could have functioned in this way, had he again espoused inwardness and implication rather than portentous noise.

> *John Simon, "London Diary, VII ... And Out," in* New York Magazine (© *1974 by NYM Corp.; reprinted by permission of* New York Magazine *and John Simon), September 23, 1974, p. 67.*

David Storey's plays have invited comparison with Harold Pinter—and some scenes of implicit menace and unspoken dread in Storey's ... novel ["A Temporary Life"] justify that comparison....

Like Pinter, Storey develops his narrative with a minimum of action yet manages to create a super-charged atmosphere. Enigmatic and episodic, "A Temporary Life" is far bigger than the sum of its parts—and far better than any Storey novel since "This Sporting Life." (p. 119)

> *Arthur Cooper, in* Newsweek (*copyright 1974 by Newsweek, Inc.; all rights reserved; reprinted by permission), November 11, 1974.*

David Storey's *Home* extends this dramatist's dim view of "things as they are." In this play, however, the picture is more abstract and more "poetic" than in *The Contractor.* The atmosphere—well caught in the bare setting—is gentler and more muted. (p. 240)

[The] "home" of the title, though we do not know it at first, is an institution for the mentally disturbed, people given to some more or less harmless but probably incurable aberration. At the same time this "home" may be construed as England or, quite baldly, the world today.

At the center of the play stand two elderly gentlemen, who seem to be meeting casually at a glum seaside resort. They exchange banalities, desolate and ludicrous; they hardly ever complete a thought and when they do, how lamentable, self-contradictory and laughable it is. They yearn for communication but each dwells in a realm of which only the periphery touches that of the other.... Their lives are shadowy dreams, shattered memories. From time to time, without apparent cause, they quietly weep.

Pitifully, one laughs at them and ruminates, "Yes, this is typical of much that we too have seen, apart from the certifiably lunatic sphere." The horizon here is even less fleshed than are those with which Pinter has acquainted us. How pathetically bleak is the picture. But, I must confess, I do not fully believe in it: even the dullest beings have more substance, greater density of experience.

Near-farcical traits are drawn in the presentation of two women inmates of the asylum. They are less "symbolic."

They may be likened to colorful cartoons of cockney characters. In these there are sudden intimations of violence and suicidal bitterness. Contemporary youth is limned in the image of a boy maimed by an operation which has removed part of his brain. He is nothing but brute muscle. His only address, to man and woman alike, is: "Do you want to fight?" spoken with no real hostility.

All this might become depressing, not to say monotonous, if it were not lightened by humor—saturnine, but still funny—and softened by an ambience of regret and restrained compassion. (pp. 240-41)

> *Harold Clurman, in his* The Divine Pastime: Theatre Essays *(reprinted with permission of Macmillan Publishing Co., Inc.; copyright © 1946, 1948, 1949, 1950, 1951, 1952, 1953, 1954, 1955, 1956, 1957, 1958, 1959, 1960, 1961, 1962, 1963, 1964, 1965, 1967, 1969, 1970, 1971, 1974 by Harold Clurman), Macmillan, 1974.*

*   *   *

STYRON, William   1925-

A Southern American novelist, Styron won the Pulitzer Prize for his controversial "meditation on history," *The Confessions of Nat Turner*. Ihab Hassan has written that, in his novels, Styron reveals "a brooding imagination, sometimes obsessive, and a dark gift of poetry." *Lie Down in Darkness* was considered one of the finest first novels of its generation. (See also *Contemporary Authors*, Vols. 5-8, rev. ed.)

It is now several years since the appearance of William Styron's novel *The Confessions of Nat Turner*. But that novel, like Styron's earlier works, continues to generate critical interest primarily because Styron is absorbed in the central psychological subject of twentieth-century fiction, identity, and growth. For similar reasons much critical effort has been expended on his earlier novel *Set This House on Fire*, a novel which has a number of situations and themes parallel not only to *The Confessions* but to Styron's previous novels as well. (p. 1007)

[*Set This House on Fire*] basically remains a contest between two related attitudes. The first attitude is caricatured in the artist, Cass Kinsolving, who is the sum of all the flaws of men living in a romantic-puritan society (self-indulgence, self-pity, guilt-obsession) but who is marked as a rebel by his urgent discontent. Hyperbole in deed and word is his medium.

The second caricature is Mason Flagg, a monstrous extension of the hero and a personification of all the defects of an anti-human society. The contest takes place within a gothic nightmare of brutal violence and the result is a combination of satire and the tale of horror.

Set This House on Fire is in many respects an enlargement, thematically and structurally, of Styron's earlier work. As in *Lie Down in Darkness*, *The Long March*, and *The Confessions of Nat Turner*, Styron's third novel focuses on a violent episode which affects the lives of the major characters. Flashbacks, the confessional tone, the slow revelations of all the details which return the reader to the moral consequences of the central action give *Set This House on Fire* some of the mystery of Conrad. But where in *Lie Down in Darkness* the overwhelming sense of futility in the

Loftises' lives dominates the book, in *The Long March* and *Set This House on Fire* the note of survival and acceptance of the possibilities and limitations of existence is preeminent. Even the titles of the latter two suggest a movement of physical and spiritual struggle rather than passivity. For Styron demonstrates in these novels as he does later in *The Confessions of Nat Turner* that acceptance and passivity are not synonymous for him. Acceptance, which means involvement in humanity to Styron, is arrived at paradoxically through the exorcism of rebellion. (p. 1008)

Set This House on Fire, which appeared in the same year as Leslie Fiedler's *Love and Death in the American Novel*, fulfills Fiedler's prescription for the sort of gothic fiction which can best express an American nightmare: the super-real grotesque characters, even the exotic and gothic setting, the incidents of sexual and fatal violence joined with the moral struggle of Cass Kinsolving to free himself from his masochistic guilt. Fiedler reminds us that Melville, Hawthorne, Twain, and Faulkner each satisfied "the dimly perceived need of many Americans to have their national existence projected in terms of a pact with the devil. . . . There is scarcely a heroic ideal of our native life which is not, in one or another of these writers' gothic books, illuminated by a weird and lurid light. Such ideals are not . . . merely travestied and debunked . . . [but are] raised to a tragic power." My contention is that unlike those earlier writers Styron is not so much concerned with the tragic consequences of such a pact in *Set This House on Fire* as he is involved in Cass Kinsolving's struggle to exorcise those defects of the society in himself. In the process the values of contemporary society are satirized and vilified equally with the romantic puritanism which binds Cass. (pp. 1009-10)

In Styron's gothic world, like Nathanael West's, forms and shapes are grotesquely presented; and the sense of proportion and scale and order necessary to a classic Sophoclean tragic view are clearly lacking. In this respect *Set This House on Fire* is too hallucinatory and surreal in its violence and too ambiguous in its resolution to be tragic. (p. 1011)

Styron is using the trappings of tragedy, but his purpose is more satiric than tragic. (p. 1014)

One should not expect some profound philosophical truth in *Set This House on Fire* for Styron is much more of a psychological than a philosophical novelist. Basically, in *Set This House on Fire*, Styron presents us with psychological truths about American guilt and responsibility in a fiction which goes beyond the limits of the realistic novel because he is telling something about a false world from which one can be freed by a transforming miracle.

Styron's whole approach to the situation is that of a satirist who employs the gothic and grotesque to attack his subject, and the novel is as concerned with what is false in American life as it is with its central character. In fact, the two themes of social satire and personal tragicomedy are inextricably tied, and more successfully, I believe, than in *Lie Down in Darkness*, where family tragedy dominates the novel. (pp. 1018-19)

Like William Faulkner, John Hawkes, and Nathanael West, Styron gives us a comic-grotesque vision of the horror of the American Nightmare, and symbolically offers the means to the freedom of self-purgation. (p. 1020)

Marc L. Ratner, "Rebellion of Wrath and Laughter: Styron's 'Set This House on Fire'," in The Southern Review *(copyright, 1971, by the Louisiana State University), Vol. VII, No. 4, Autumn, 1971, pp. 1007-20.*

William Styron's *The Confessions of Nat Turner* has called forth a greater variety of approaches and evaluations than any other American novel of the past decade. Historians and sociologists continue to debate, often bitterly, whether the book is an accurate recreation of history, a plausible mythic interpretation of it, or a white liberal's attempt to emasculate black radicals. Religious commentators discuss Nat as a mystic, a messiah *manqué*, or a Christian pilgrim, and they disagree as to whether Styron has created a convincing or a contrived story of revelation and conversion. Psychologists are either interested in or amused by the pop-Freudian relations of sexual repression, violence and religious fanaticism. And more purely literary critics consider the prose style either masterful and fully orchestrated or bombastic, self-indulgent, and too literary. But there has been no full-scale attempt to comprehend the basic form of this omnibus work, to describe a literary structure that can accommodate so many approaches and cause so much controversy. (p. 19)

Seeing the *Confessions* as a melodramatic romance eliminates many of the objections to its stock characters, historical simplifications, and obtrusively rhetorical style; these techniques are staples of melodrama and to object to them entirely is to demand a thoroughgoing realism that Styron does not, and need not, attempt. Despite some convincing social sketches in his earlier work, Styron has never been primarily a realistic novelist, and this historical melodrama gives him an adequate form for the virtuosity that disrupted his other novels. But recognizing the proper genre does not solve all the problems of the book.... Although melodrama is an overly maligned genre that has been important in American fiction from Hawthorne to Mailer, it usually does seem too facile when it is not qualified by complementary techniques. And Styron does qualify it with an ironic structure that makes melodrama a major subject as well as the major genre of the book.

The irony works mainly through his use of the first-person narrative. Unfortunately, this confessional form has led to an endless, futile debate as to whether or not this Nat Turner thinks like, speaks like, feels like, and fantasizes like an honest-to-blackness revolutionary slave. These attempts to judge the stylized romance as an historical documentary have obscured an important function of the first-person narrative: to show how the character makes consoling melodramatic fictions out of his intolerable understanding of his condition. The prevailing melodramatic form of the book reflects Nat's perceptions, and Styron implicitly and ironically uses it to explore his character's point of view. This does not mean that the book is a study of a unique, neurotic aberration any more than it is a realistic documentary about slaves. Nat's condition is a heightened symbol of all men's condition, and he creates his melodramas from the stereotypes, popular myths, and obsessive images that our culture has used to avoid painful understanding. Styron's Nat Turner is an Everyman; Styron's melodrama is truly an American melodrama; and his "meditation on history," as he calls it, is an attempt to understand human causes of the racial myths he has wrongly been accused of perpetuating.

In brief, throughout the book Nat is haunted by what we often think of as a modern, or post-Romantic, tragic vision of life. With its lenses ground by Kierkegaard, Dostoevsky, and Nietzsche and polished by twentieth century existentialists, this vision ... sees man as questioner, naked, unaccommodated, alone, facing mysterious, demonic forces in his own nature and outside, and the irreducible facts of suffering and death.... Nat repeatedly tries to replace that vision with neatly ordered and culturally conditioned stereotypes, to repress the terror of the irrational with the melodramatic assurances of the known and simplified. But because these defenses are so contrived, they are often destroyed by a complex, minutely particularized reality they can no longer contain. Then Nat reorders his perceptions, recasts his characters, and creates a new set of fictional defenses. Finally, in the last section of the book, he makes a leap of faith that transcends, rather than represses, terror, and that takes him beyond both tragedy and melodrama. (pp. 19-21)

Nat Turner is not only the physically and socially bound slave; he is also man, living under sentence of death in an arbitrary universe that destroys his freedom and dignity. Styron, in effect, suggested this when he explained that the narrative structure of his book came from his first reading of Camus' *The Stranger* in 1962. Like Meursault, Nat is condemned man whose awareness of his mortality is intensified by his imprisonment and impending execution, both of which press his submerged fears into consciousness. (p. 21)

One out of many instances should demonstrate Styron's technique of juxtaposing description and symbolism. As the lawyer Gray reads the confession of murder, Nat looks out of his prison window and sees black children gathering firewood on the other side of the river.... For the moment Nat does not see these unknowing black children as mindless flies living on offal. They seem to him like lively birds, quick and bright as they call out to each other things he cannot understand. But since he is also aware of their rags and their burdens, they soon become for him more examples of the doomed and hopeless. (p. 22)

Styron is not giving us sentimentalized pickaninnies, natural and happy in their slavery and much better off than a fanatical revolutionary would make them. The black children are clearly exploited and degraded, as the novel frequently shows in its descriptions of slave life, and Nat would lack all heroic proportions if he were not aware of that. His dilemma, however, grows out of that awareness: tormented by his horror at such bondage (both social and metaphysical), he obsessively reduces life to a symbolic drama, thereby losing touch with the very nature of life out of which his visions grew. His acute consciousness of man's frustrations has separated him from God, other men, and much of his own self, as his experiences of isolation and spiritual dryness show. This tragic irony is more worthy of Dostoevsky than of U. B. Phillips, the apologist for slavery with whom Styron has been linked by some of his black critics. (p. 23)

Styron's black critics have been most hostile about his portrayal of this military leader as losing control of his men, vomiting at the sight of the slaughter, and failing in his own attempts to kill. Where, they ask, is the virile and courageous figure of history? ... Instead of the melodramatic hero whom Styron once describes as an "amalgamated black Paul Bunyan and Daniel Boone," Styron has created a tragic hero who struggles through error toward a psychological and spiritual salvation that he glimpses only in his defeat. Like most tragic heroes, his greatness is inseparable from the causes of his errors and destruction: acute consciousness, a religious and symbolic imagination, and a passionate sense of social and metaphysical absurdities.

Also, like many modern heroes, Nat is a complex and ambiguous character who cannot easily quiet his conflicting feelings or ignore experiences that do not fit his dominant scheme of things. On the day of the insurrection he is nearly overcome by fear and despair, showing much more anxiety than any of his followers and wondering whether Biblical leaders felt so when they thought of the slaughter to come. Styron dwells on Nat's terror but not to emasculate the black commander or simply to give his character realistic emotions on the eve of battle. As the action nears its climax he is intensifying and sharpening the central clash between Nat's symbolic, messianic view of life and the literal nature of both his emotions and the people involved in his apocalyptic drama. (pp. 28-9)

In creating the hero of this religious parable Styron has deliberately worked against the legend of the black Napoleon, but his refusal to add to black militant propaganda does not mean that he is therefore reinforcing racist stereotypes or writing art-for-art's-sake arabesques. Instead, he is exploring the universal fears of death, powerlessness, and uncertainty that cause, and eventually bring to life, those melodramatic stereotypes of infinitely desirable white women, omniscient patriarchs, animalistic Negroes, and avenging black angels. Far from advocating such stereotypes, Styron shows that their creation, and the obscuring of the real humanity they mask, is a destructive attempt to hide from a surmountable tragic vision of life. And by taking his character through this compulsive symbol-making to some acceptance of man as he is and some intimation of man as he ought to be, Styron goes beyond the topical issues of the 1830s and 1960s to reach problems that underlie them all. (p. 32)

> *David Eggenschwiler, "Tragedy and Melodrama in 'The Confessions of Nat Turner'," in* Twentieth Century Literature *(copyright 1974, Hofstra University Press), January, 1974, pp. 19-33.*

William Styron's *The Confessions of Nat Turner* (1967) aims to be the recreation of a man and an era as well as "a meditation on history." Quite apart from garbling some matters of fact about the slave revolt of 1831, the novel projects far too much of the bi-sexuality of a twentieth-century James Baldwin into its image of an early nineteenth-century messianic black preacher. This anachronistic attitude aborts the story's contribution to our historical understanding of the protagonist. (p. 19)

> *Cushing Strout, in* Diacritics *(copyright © Diacritics, Inc., 1975), Spring, 1975.*

*   *   *

SWADOS, Harvey   1920-1972

Swados was an American novelist, short story writer, and essayist. (See also *Contemporary Authors*, Vols. 5-8, rev. ed.; obituary, Vols. 37-40.)

Swados is especially adept at short, incisive descriptions of people, a talent which is best exploited in *On The Line*. What is even a rarer talent is his ability at catching the spirit of a particular place in a particular time. Thus the Felton family is seen as rooted in contemporary, urban America, and, as the novel progresses, we begin to understand how their haunted lives, in many ways, tells us about ours. While *Out Went The Candle* is a powerful work, it suffers, at times, from ever shifting points of view, for often the transitions are rough. Unfortunately Swados has also seen fit to lace his tale with a number of super-obvious coincidences. And, most troublesome of all, the Lear equals Felton equation becomes too much of a literary cryptogram, a gimmick rather than an artistic device. . . .

Swados, in a number of important articles, has shown his understanding for the problems of the industrial laborer; and in *On The Line* he extends this compassion. Not since Upton Sinclair's *The Jungle* have we had such a direct, steady look at the worker's world, one of hard dullness, continual pressures, and very little satisfaction. (pp. 188-89)

References to *The Brothers Karamazov* abound [in *The Will*], enough to offer hours of pleasure to the *PMLA* boys, but the horror of the suffering is more akin to, say, Saltykov-Schedrin's *The Golovlovs*. While the Swados book is a noble and often successful experiment, none of the characters [is] as well realized as Herman Felton, and not one is as successful as several of the figures who featured in Swados' shorter fictional pieces. What is splendid in *The Will* is the intelligence behind the narration and the quality of the structure. (pp. 190-91)

A good deal of Swados' most effective work appears in his stories, a genre in which he takes chances and more often than not succeeds in making art out of his severe social criticism. While he failed, in *False Coin*, to effectively depict the artist as he is spoiled by American life, this important theme does succeed in "The Man in the Toolhouse" and "The Dancer" (*Nights in the Gardens of Brooklyn*) . . . , two stories which are strikingly different in concept. (p. 191)

Keenly aware of the social realities of today, Swados, as a splendid and imaginative creative artist is well equipped to transform these realities into fiction, a fiction that will give the lie to all who so patronizingly announce that the novel of social criticism is dying. (p. 192)

> *Charles Shapiro, "Harvey Swados: Private Stories and Public Fiction," in* Contemporary American Novelists, *edited by Harry T. Moore (copyright © 1964, Southern Illinois University Press; reprinted by permission of Southern Illinois University Press), Southern Illinois University Press, 1964, pp. 182-92.*

"Celebration" is Mr. Samuel Lumen's planet, an 89-year-old man's journal entries, resembling the "short views" of Saul Bellow's Mr. Sammler. "Inhumanly deified" for his long history of commitments to radical political causes and child welfare, Lumen lives in carefully managed repose. When memories and an insistent present disturb his packaged peace, Lumen begins a journal to explain to himself—perhaps to others—why the private man makes the public statue scream in the night. That journal, with almost daily entries, extends from April to September of 1975, from doubt to desperation and finally to a celebration as moving as Sammler's "we know, we know, we know." . . .

[Eventually, Lumen addresses] those questions Swados so often measured in his essays: How can radical ideas best be adapted to present circumstances? What is the proper use of personal and cultural authority? Where do the unique individual and the group action, private history and public work, best meet?

Swados's achievement is to gather these into one question: Does one celebrate American life in ritual or liberation? . . .

Sam Lumen wants to know if his past will allow him to celebrate at all. Ultimately, none of the alternatives is as important as the celebration of truth that is the journal itself. Realizing, like Eliot's "Gerontion," that "Unnatural vices/Are fathered by our heroism. Virtues/Are forced upon us by our impudent crimes," Lumen resists both the temptations of phony marble immortality and of phony youthful gesture. With a Whitmanian embracing of contradictions, Lumen celebrates himself, soiled but free. In the end, near his end, Sam Lumen begins: "No more explanations. It no longer matters to me what kind of figure I will cut for posterity. Posterity is here. Hello, from this old boy! Take it away!"

Swados avoids sentimentality by making Lumen earn his celebration; his test is understanding the ironies of living long. Sam has been a public man concerned with the future of others but he learns that the past is most real and, from Jung, that "only what is interior has proved to have substance." . . .

Although fable-like in its outlines, "Celebration" is longer than it needs to be. The journal form gives Swados an intellectually interesting voice, but it also introduces too much trivia, leads to artificial delays of information, and lets Sam include too many dreams. There is nothing drearier in fiction than a dream—unless it's the dreamer's interpretation. The question of how Sam Lumen will be used is also overdeveloped, perhaps because of the slow progress of the journal, perhaps for an unneeded suspense. However, despite the undue complications and quotidian fullness, the reader's after-image is not of a set of details but of a man thinking, both devouring and creating himself. While Sam Lumen purifies his life, the reader does so too by setting aside the verisimilitude necessary for life but not for fiction.

Readers who know all of Swados's novels may find "Celebration" his best, his most artful. While his essays were appreciated for their lucidity, passion and understanding of mass culture, his novels elicited artistic objections: old-fashioned, diffuse, linguistically impoverished. The language of "Celebration" remains analytical, rather than presentational, and the journal form leads to technical weaknesses, but the novel has qualities that suggest Swados may have been moving toward a different kind of fiction. His concentration of social themes into metaphor, his attention to subtleties of character rather than ideology, and his creation of an ironic complexity are signs of an intensive fiction more like his best stories than "Standing Fast." These qualities do not make "Celebration" a great novel, but they do combine with the perfect Swados persona—an educator and man of conscience—to demonstrate his considerable humane skills.

Josef Pieper has said that to celebrate means "to live out, for some special occasion and in an uncommon manner, the universal assent to the world as a whole." Sam Lumen achieves this assent at the end of his journal. It's something Harvey Swados knew all along. (p. 4)

> *Thomas LeClair, in* The New York Times Book Review (© *1975 by The New York Times Company; reprinted by permission), March 9, 1975.*

Harvey Swados uses lines from Neruda as an epigraph to his last novel: "I have lived so much that someday/they will have to forget me forcibly,/rubbing me off the blackboard. My heart was inexhaustible." . . .

Celebration is a wonderfully serene novel. It accepts the conflict of generations as an inevitable fact of life; it acknowledges the need for liberation of fathers *and* sons. It refuses to flee from political, sexual and educational strife. It is an appropriate testament—not only to Lumen [the protagonist] but to Swados himself. . . .

> *Irving Malin, "Posterity Now," in* The New Republic *(reprinted by permission of* The New Republic; © *1975 by The New Republic, Inc.), March 22, 1975, p. 27.*

Celebration [is] complex. . . . Most of the complexity makes for richness of concept, luxury of emotion: Generation conflict. Self-analysis in the classic Freudian context of pleasure and ego gratification. The difference between intelligence and wisdom. The passage of the myth as reality. The confusion of sex and love. Some of the complexity, however, cannot support its weight, for the characters and events of *Celebration* often miss the necessary conviction that this is how it had to be, there could be no other way. Despite an uncomfortable vagueness about his educational contributions, Sam Lumen [the protagonist] does live. He has space and time. The other characters of *Celebration* behave like ideas about characters. Perhaps the problem lies in their presentation through a diary. Or maybe in their conception as representatives of social attitudes—Sarah Lawrence liberalism, the inevitable conservatism of the power elite, naive youth in pointless revolt. And the seemingly endless comings and goings of Lumen's diary . . . do not take us deeper into the characters, but further from them. . . .

Heir to the social novelists of the 1930s, cultural historian to radicalisms and upheaval, [Swados] seems to have been trying to put everything he knew into his last novel. What he knew most about—or tells us most about in this didactic fiction—was the terrible price a man must pay in human relationships to leave even a modest imprint on the world. And then, having made the imprint, to realize in time that he is alone and must seek self-preservation. . . .

Swados seeks the bitterness of aging, the crookedness of achievement and the mysteries of personal and social change in *Celebrations*. He reaches enough to engage us. But the themes are great ones calling for, I suppose, the gift of genius. Swados did not have that. He had compassion and skill. Sometimes *Celebration* is an inspired novel. Usually it's a good one. We will remember him for it.

> *Webster Schott, "The Shrunken Vision," in* Book World—The Washington Post (© The Washington Post), *March 23, 1975, p. 3.*

Celebration . . . has the virtues one cherished in Swados' fiction: decency, compassion and a gentle wit. Yet the book suffers from what was always Swados' noble flaw as a novelist: a talent never quite up to the demands he put upon it.

Celebration combines all the elements that should produce readability and substance in fiction. Sam Lumen's secret diary is told in the form of mixed memories, snatches of dreams and unsentimental musing about old age. But the clash of ideas, between old and new radicals, for instance, never reaches higher than Lumen's easy parries of nihilistic rhetoric. Above all, Sam Lumen's eminence is never convincing.

The diary form of the novel sees to this. Lumen is more intent on confessing his frailties than on contemplating the ideas and works that made him famous or the changes and conditions that are about to immortalize an old radical in federal concrete. The evolution of American radicalism was apparently much on Swados' mind when he wrote *Celebration*. He was a serious man whose leftist politics and social conscience developed during the Depression '30s. Sympathetic members of his own generation and background are likely to fill in the gaps. (p. K11)

> R. Z. Sheppard, "September Song," in Time (*reprinted by permission from* Time, The Weekly Newsmagazine; *copyright Time Inc.*), March 24, 1975, pp. K9, K11.

It is no accident that there are so few serious novels about old people. We resist thinking about the very old; indeed, as Simone de Beauvoir has observed, we seem incapable of imagining ourselves old: it is someone else that we imagine in our place. Our novelists, who tend to write from experience, are themselves neither very old nor familiar with the very old, who in our society are usually hustled out of sight.

Furthermore, to write about old people with insight and compassion—as Saul Bellow did in "Mr. Sammler's Planet" and Harvey Swados did in "Celebration"—presents the author with a nasty array of technical problems. His hero will almost surely be in retreat from life, whether through loss of zest or an assortment of incapacities. His memory will fail him. He is likely to be paranoiac, garrulous, obsessed with trivia. He may fall asleep or have to be hurried from the scene just as the action grows heated. Poets and dramatists have an easier job; it is hard to write fiction about old age that is both realistic and interesting.

Swados (who died before this book was published) did not overcome these obstacles, but I salute him for trying. His protagonist, Sam Lumen, is an antique radical, a former pioneer in education, child care and lechery. As his 90th birthday approaches, he begins a diary in which he confides his guilt about his past and his fears that those who love him are trying to use him for their own sordid purposes. . . .

Haunted by his past idealism and weakness, he is unable now to dismiss the puerile demands of the radicals laying siege to him, unable to see that his son is arrogant and cruel. An irritable, unlikable old buzzard, he is redeemed partly by his struggle against fossilization as a living monument and partly by his awareness of his own senility.

And so we have an ambitious, realistic novel, one in which Swados labored mightily to create a convincing old man

who constantly observes his own deteriorating physical and mental performance. Denying himself the lengthy flashbacks that John Marquand applied in similar stories, Swados gives us only glimpses of Lumen's past—and no sense at all of his former greatness. We are left, then, with a very long portrait of a tedious man; the portrait, for all its virtues, cannot escape a certain tedium of its own.

> Peter S. Prescott, "Antique Radical," in Newsweek (*copyright 1975 by Newsweek, Inc.; all rights reserved; reprinted by permission*), March 31, 1975, p. 76.

The title of Harvey Swados' posthumous novel, *Celebration* . . ., could not have been more fitting. Swados was a man who lived not orgiastically, or even indulgently, but he had the capacity for infusing almost any encounter with a spirit of celebration, and his joy was happily communicable.

He was also the author of serious essays on literature for such periodicals as *Partisan Review* and *New World Writing*; contributed political articles, as a self-proclaimed socialist, to *Anvil*, *Monthly Review*, and *The Nation*; was a tough-minded intellectual and hard-muscled man who had served as a merchant seaman and an automobile assembly-line worker and who was deeply committed to both life and letters. (p. 91)

I have to admit that Swados' first three novels, *Out Went the Candle*, *False Coin*, and *The Will*, seemed to me, for all their virtues, to be strained, as if the characters were bowed down beneath the weight of the ideas and themes they were designed to carry. I felt, up to that time, that his most successful fiction was his short story collections, *Nights in the Gardens of Brooklyn* and *A Story for Teddy —and Others*. The writing in these seemed at once sharper and more relaxed, as if the author, under no constraint to create a masterpiece, was able to be at ease, almost playful, and his prose took on mellow flavor and charm that was missing in the first three novels.

[Despite] the praise for his non-fiction, and sometimes his stories, at the expense of his novels, he still thought of himself first and foremost as a novelist, insisted on being a novelist, gloried in being a novelist—and the world be damned.

And so, in spite of everything, he sat down in the mid-sixties and started writing his Big Novel. It was a panoramic political novel with many interwoven threads of plot and character, stretching from the Great Depression of the thirties to the freedom rides of the civil rights movement in the early sixties. It was big in scope and achievement; it was stubbornly "old-fashioned" in its Dos Passos realism; and it carried in it the craft and passion of a lifetime. It was called *Standing Fast*. But by 1970, the year the book was published, its subject matter seemed as dated as the Children's Crusade.

The timing of Swados' novel was rather like that of Fitzgerald's story of the hedonistic Americans on the Riviera published at the height of the Depression, and James Agee's great book about the sharecroppers of Alabama which appeared at the opening of World War II. Those books were eventually appreciated for their intrinsic merits, but the hope of future appreciation is cold comfort to an author. (pp. 92-3)

As originally conceived, [*Celebration*] was to be the diary of an old man who had been a successful musician. . . . But somewhere between that early concept of the novel and its completion, the aged musician was transformed into an aged man of politics—not in the sense of elective, establishment politics, but as a social innovator, a journalistic muckraker, a pacifist who chose jail over combat in World War I, an educator who founded a famous progressive school, who fought for child labor reform and child welfare laws, and even in his later years was a champion of the causes of youth, both social and political.

It was artistically inevitable that Swados would make this hero a political figure, for it gave him the opportunity to grapple once more—and with his most subtle and successful results—with the complexities of politics in the most personal sense, with the ironies of self-aggrandizement through good causes. (p. 93)

When he wrote this novel in the vibrant first years of his fifties, Harvey Swados was able to make that leap of imagination to the feelings and perceptions of advanced age. That was the kind of dangerous fictional feat he had often ventured, but he never so successfully achieved it as he did in this, his final *Celebration*. (p. 94)

> *Dan Wakefield, "Celebration Man," in* The Atlantic Monthly *(copyright © 1975 by The Atlantic Monthly Company, Boston, Mass.; reprinted by permission), April, 1975, pp. 91-4.*

I have never wanted to like a novel more, but *Celebration* is not, I must admit, among the books I will remember Harvey Swados for. Because it is about a man on the verge of death, it will inevitably be read as Swados' literary last will and testament, perhaps even a premonition of his fate. . . .

Exactly why Swados found the subject of *Celebration* appealing is puzzling. One cannot be certain of what he wanted to do. It is about the relationship between ideology and death, ideology and reputation, ideology and the need for a measured optimism in times such as our own. And it is recorded by a man who has experienced the necessity and joy of surviving not as a victim but as one who triumphs within his lifetime. . . .

The journal technique is peculiar in that it works against Sam Lumen's credibility. There is a strange lack of intimacy about the narrative, as if Sam's consciousness had been born public. . . .

At times, [Sam's] self-consciousness gives way and he sheds his pomposity, his sense of himself as a monumental force. At such moments, we see a man wounded by mortality and waiting to die but insisting on the prerogatives of individuality. But such moments are infrequent. One can care passionately about the people in the last novel Swados published during his lifetime, *Standing Fast*; their radicalism is the stuff of their lives. But Sam and his young photographer wife and the Children of Liberty—there is little we can care about here. Long before the novel's conclusion, Sam Lumen has been defeated, even if his integrity remains intact.

And yet, there is much here that is characteristic of Harvey Swados. His literary signature is upon all his work. And to read him today is to be made uncomfortable by one's adopted sophistication. For one thing, Swados wrote out of a compassion that was the basis of his honesty: it is noteworthy that Swados, whose politics was socialism and whose deepest sympathies were with the working-class victims of industrial society, should have written so sympathetically of that *bête noire* of the contemporary American writer, the much-berated middle class. In this, he resembles George Gissing and Arnold Bennett more than he does his American contemporaries. . . . But it was as a journalist and creator of short stories that Swados was particularly of our time. He refused to accept the myths of the 1950s. *On the Line* was not the only indication of that. At a time when other writers found the working class boring, Swados wrote a brilliant series of essays which showed exactly how the American worker had been victimized by the limited success of the trade union movement. (p. 565)

His commitment to socialism was matched by his commitment to the truth. In our world, the two do not necessarily go together. Like Orwell, Swados examined the working class, warts and all, while he retained his faith in its capacity to behave in a human way.

And yet, Swados wanted to be thought of as a writer of fiction. . . . In rereading his work, I have asked myself why he never attempted to achieve the kind of synthesis of novelist and journalist that one finds in Clancy Sigal's *Weekend in Dinlock*. No writer appears better equipped, both by temperament and talent, to have achieved such a synthesis. His fiction, whatever its stylistic limitations, makes sense to any reader who believes that the writer is the historian of his time, and his work must echo the discord of life.

Swados' imagination was so firmly rooted in the problems of our age that even his best fiction tends toward polemic. (p. 566)

He was a writer for whom words were instrumental to the deed, not the deed itself. And if his books emerged out of the man, as books inevitably do, they are not really autobiographical. He does not seem to have been particularly interested in himself. (pp. 566-67)

> *Leonard Kriegel, "A Distinctive Literary Voice," in* The Nation *(copyright 1975 by the Nation Associates, Inc.), May 10, 1975, pp. 565-67.*

T

TAYLOR, Eleanor Ross   1920-

Eleanor Taylor is a Southern American poet.

Maybe the spirit of the times is catching up to Eleanor Ross Taylor, and "Welcome Eumenides," her second book, will find readers waiting for it. Her first, "Wilderness of Ladies," published in 1960, recognized by a handful of people including the late Randall Jarrell, has remained an underground book, fierce, rich and difficult, though it seems less difficult with every passing year, just as Emily Dickinson does. In that book are two poems I've carried about with me for a decade as a kind of secret knowledge and reinforcement: "Woman as Artist" and "Sister." They, like many of Eleanor Taylor's poems, speak of the underground life of women, the Southern white Protestant woman in particular, the woman-writer, the woman in the family, coping, hoarding, preserving, observing, keeping up appearances, seeing through the myths and hypocrisies, nursing the sick, conspiring with sister-women, possessed of a will to survive and to see others survive. (The Southern black woman and the Southern white woman share a history and a knowledge that we are barely on the edge of exploring.)

"Welcome Eumenides" reaches out from this scene yet has its roots there. The South is the only part of the United States to have lost a war and suffered the physical and psychic trauma of military defeat; this is another kind of knowledge that Eleanor Taylor, as a Southern woman, possesses. . . .

[The] truly remarkable poem in the book, one for which it should be read even if it did not contain other strong poems, is the title poem, "Welcome Eumenides." Out of the world and the wars that men have made she conjures the voice of Florence Nightingale, reliving her days and nights at Scutari, the death-ward of the Crimean War, with glimpses back into the family-centered, trivializing life of 19th-century English women of the leisure class. (Many lines and phrases of the poem are directly quoted from actual notes Florence Nightingale left behind her.) In this heroic, oral poem, densely woven and refrained, Eleanor Taylor has brought together the waste of women in society and the waste of men in wars and twisted them inseparably. . . .

What I find compelling in the poems of Eleanor Taylor, besides the authority and originality of her language, is the underlying sense of how the conflicts of imaginative and intelligent women have driven them on, lashed them into genius or madness, how the home-nursing, the household administration, the patience and skill in relationships acquired at such expense in a family-centered life, became an essential part of the strength of a woman like Nightingale, but at tremendous price. "Welcome Eumenides" is a writing-large, in terms of a celebrated and powerful woman, of unanswered questions that hover throughout Eleanor Taylor's poems, and throughout the history and psychology of all women. (p. 3)

> Adrienne Rich, in The New York Times Book Review (© 1972 by The New York Times Company; reprinted by permission), July 2, 1972, p. 3.

Mrs. Taylor's world is anything but bright. Her poetry [in Welcome Eumenides] has warmth yet lingers on one as a freezing snowfall clings to branches. There is an intense reality in her images, a firmness and strength to her style. She maintains all the qualities necessary to welcome Eumenides. (p. cxxiv)

> Virginia Quarterly Review (copyright, 1972 by the Virginia Quarterly Review, The University of Virginia), Vol. 48, No. 4 (Autumn, 1972).

Taylor's poems [in Welcome Eumenides] draw blood; they have knowingness which distinguishes a real maker of poetry from someone with talent who aspires to the role of poet. The first hints of this always come with sudden stabs of language. Eleanor Ross Taylor brings off lines that sound like no one else's. You recognize a real poet by certain cadences before you even grasp the "meaning" or the "subject-matter". . . . [Her poems] reveal an ear for rhythmic free verse, an eye for piercing description, and that remarkable gift for condensation which makes a good poem like a little container of pure energy which explodes when the reader's eye focuses upon it. (p. 79-80)

[Her] subjects are always bigger than the immediate excuses for her poems. None of her poems is occasional.

Her great theme is loss; loss of comfort, loss of blood, loss of children. In her poems about women, she often seems to be concerned with the stripping away of outward roles that hide a woman's true identity even from herself. The role of mother, the role of wife, all the evasions a woman's life provides. Florence Nightingale is the perfect speaker of a dramatic monologue about the condition of a woman's soul because she has consciously renounced all these evasions ("To hide in love!") and crying *"No More love/No more marriage!"* she has sought a larger and less personal sort of love, and with it, the discovery of her own soul. The poem recalls some of Shakespeare's soliloquys. Its fragmented style—somewhat reminiscent of Browning, somewhat reminiscent of Eliot yet totally Ross Taylor—seems haphazard at first, but later emerges as a fugue of all the poet's obsessive themes. (pp. 81-1)

> *Erica Jong, "Three Sisters," in* Parnassus *(copyright © by* Parnassus: Poetry in Review*), Fall/Winter, 1974, pp. 77-88.*

Eleanor Ross Taylor lives in the South, not the South of Governor Wallace crowning a black homecoming queen, or the South of missile centers and crazy police, that "one big armed camp down there" as radicals like to say, but a South that still seems miraculously "rocked in homespun," where the floors of the houses still smell "seasonround of guano." It's a land where an unhappy moment in a garden at evening can appropriately be called "starfall on savagery," where a "Flagg Bros. store / With new glass front" or "Falcons and Mustangs" can be dismissed as "bourgeois rot," where whenever the things of the earth or the heart are ripe you have to pick them, give them—where, too, Whitman could say, as he did say obstreperously up North, "I wear my hat as I please, indoors and out," and be cherished, not for being a nut, but for the spontaneity of his observation, the spunk of his conviction. During most of my hitch in the army I was stationed in Georgia and Mrs. Taylor's South was not the South I found. But if it's not there in fact, it's there on the page.

Her poems, however, do not affect to "laugh at disillusion" as Whitman the irreverent bachelor did: managing alone is impossible in Mrs. Taylor's world. Her characters may be separate or inconstant, a mother may moan the loss of her son, a wife may giddily shout, "A husband, more or less! A family, more or less!"—still these people and their lives are always at the farthest remove from isolation. Kinships, legacies, ghostly estates, "a changing and pacing in the rooms of next year" or the year after, a perennial opening and closing of accounts, the injury rates in human affairs—these are the rhythms that shape her world. A throb of pathos, a current of universality seem to run through the poems where we catch all the moments that lie behind us or all the moments that await us, as in a wedding or a funeral, where Mrs. Taylor's men and women weep for all the brides that have ever been, for all the dead who were once alive.

Far from being sentimental, though, her work, both in spirit and interest, is strict and classical, fastidious even in its verve. It comes out of and sustains, as Randall Jarrell once observed in a marvelous essay on her work, the traditions of the Puritan South, a world as "dualistic as that of Freud." Yet it is full too of the folkloric or prosaic habits and rites, or the gratuitous, contingent aspects of one's humanity—one's *compromised* humanity especially. If some of the poems seem governed by a gossipy generalized texture, the small, lyric, slightly querulous, at times some-

what histrionic voice of the poet can always be felt. For Mrs. Taylor is a little like a Southern belle who has uncharacteristically read all the big books, thought all the gray thoughts, who is a bit fearful perhaps of expressing grief or depth or the cruel chemical wit of which she is capable, yet who, against "cyclonic gust and chilly rain," expresses them forthrightly anyway.

She seems to me better at dramatic monologues, which make up most of her earlier book, *Wilderness of Ladies*, than she is at dramatic reveries, which make up most of . . . *Welcome Eumenides*. Either way, though, her poems depend on a sense of character, a coherence of manner and motive, as much as they depend on anything. If they are not readily quotable, demand the full strength of the full context to be faithfully represented, still her virtues can be enumerated easily enough. In "Victory," one of the best of the new poems, she has a novelist's eye, Faulkner's in miniature. In "Buck Duke and Mama," one of the best of the older ones, she can incorporate bits of stray humor, idiomatic quirkiness, the sort of catchy effect you get in Welty or O'Connor or in Peter Taylor, her husband, but it's always rare in poetry. . . . She can use words we all know—words like posterity, constellation, kinless, beseech—but rarely use because they might sound too awkward or too grand, but in her poems they almost always hit the proper note. Or she can employ a more exotic grammar—dominie, rheum, disfestooned—yet these do not misbecome her, as she might say, but have a natural sparkle, seem just. Her language always has something going on beneath its lines. . . . The meter has its own pace and duration, suggests, as an odd analogy, Schopenhauer's description of rhythm as melody deprived of pitch; her adjectives and verbs, especially those in her still lifes, project a strange delicacy and weight. . . . (pp. 21-2)

Many of the poems . . . seem to be wise in the way that the old proverbs are wise, poems that know it is better to be invited to herbs with love than to a fatted calf with hatred, poems that may regret life, indeed can and do make judgments against life, against people, but there's no *hostility* in them. And that's rare—considering life, considering people. The characters quarrel with God, are restless among themselves, but the flux has an unusual balance, like water, whose underlying characteristic is patience, so that the wearing away of the spirit occurs slowly, diffidently, the sea wearing away the rocks on a strand. The domestic details are often as exact as in Vermeer, the settings as shapely as in Manet—nothing grandiloquent, nothing askew (though much of the subject matter can appear almost willfully odd). And the figurative presences that shine in her portraits are often there in the manner of Manet saying that the real figure in the painting is the light—the light in Mrs. Taylor's case being the dignity and sympathy of her response, the clarity of her memory.

Of course her work *is* peculiar—sometimes too tense, too skittery. *Welcome Eumenides* is not as conclusive in its impact as is *Wilderness of Ladies*. A few of the newer lines tend to leap in the air without having first touched ground. Others are so wispy or so austere as to be almost obscure. Her poems in general, I guess, take a while to reveal themselves just as it takes the reader a while to surrender to them. But they are distinctly her own, unlike that of any other American writing. They set their own standard for honesty and wit, for rueful downrightness, for sparkle and restraint few other poets reach. (p. 22)

Robert Mazzocco, in The New York Review of Books *(reprinted with permission from* The New York Review of Books; *copyright © 1975 NYREV, Inc.), April 3, 1975.*

*   *   *

THEROUX, Paul   1941-

Theroux, an American novelist, short story writer, critic, and poet, has travelled and lived abroad—primarily in England and equatorial lands—for the last decade. (See also *Contemporary Authors*, Vols. 33-36.)

"Sinning With Annie and Other Stories" is a finely written [short story] collection about the come-uppance of the mildly ruthless, those nasties who abuse people to get what they want only to find no joy in their prize. . . . For their nastiness always breeds guilt, and the fight for their great goody always leaves them sickish. Their success is muted by remorse; their remorse is dampened by the impulse to do it again. Theroux's talent is for this middle grayness, for the mellowest anxiety and the thinnest vibrations of evil. . . .

Theroux is a master of trimmers, those neither-here-nor-there sorts who cannot feel happy, but who are not too miserable either. He writes with elegance of the wry, the rueful, the nagging complaints of middle grayness and middle confusion. And he is so successful that his stories have only a middling force. (p. 4)

> *Josephine Hendin, in* The New York Times Book Review *(© 1972 by The New York Times Company; reprinted by permission), November 5, 1972.*

In a picaresque novel [*Saint Jack*] laid in Singapore and having an irresistible rogue as hero, Mr. Theroux maintains the dizzying pace he has set for himself as a new novelist, displaying here an elaborate knowledge of Oriental palaces of sin operating in the very heart of the mysterious if not entirely inscrutable East. As an author he shows much ingenuity in writing about sex as a divertissement quite unrelated to love, unemotionally, as a virtual vocation for beachcombers otherwise gifted with a quick-witted ability to survive in an alien world. (p. viii)

> Virginia Quarterly Review *(copyright, 1974, by the* Virginia Quarterly Review, *The University of Virginia), Vol. 50, No. 1 (Winter, 1974).*

It is a tribute to Paul Theroux's energy and industry that at the age of 33 he has produced seven books of fiction. Moreover, it is a tribute to his integrity and ambition that he is not content to keep repeating himself. But unfortunately his new novel, "The Black House," an abrupt departure from the comic vision of his earlier work, does a serious disservice to his talent and will likely disappoint those who enjoyed "Jungle Lovers" and "Saint Jack."

The book might best be described as a hybrid composed of unequal parts of social satire, commentary on colonialism, anthropological insights, some randy sex and an inconclusive gothic tale. In the author's mind there must have been a theme or thread that linked these disparate elements, but if so, Mr. Theroux has deleted the unifying substance from the final version, which is held together by nothing except the thinnest integument of prose. (p. 18)

After each event the reader thinks things will implode and form a pattern that permits deeper, or at least broader, understanding. But nothing is hot or bright enough to burn away the haze that hides Mr. Theroux's intentions, nothing is powerful enough to overcome the inertia of the narrative. And the story stands still, the style grows attentuated, mainly because Munday [the protagonist] has a tendency to analyze the least significant actions and to repeat and italicize his ideas. Since he is a scholar this may be believable, but it doesn't make for interesting reading since his mind is neither remarkable nor particularly appealing—he's petty, pedantic, squeamish and often appallingly cold and unkind. . . .

Granting credit where it's due, it appears that Paul Theroux is searching for new material and perhaps a method of pushing beyond the conventional—even if successful—limits of his previous work. He hasn't found it here, yet he can't be faulted for trying. Much as one might wish he hadn't published "The Black House," he has earned the right to make such mistakes without losing the respect and patience of readers who care about fiction. (p. 20)

> *Michael Mewshaw, in* The New York Times Book Review *(© 1974 by The New York Times Company; reprinted by permission), September 8, 1974.*

Paul Theroux is a young novelist who writes with uncommon assurance and grace. His last effort, *Saint Jack*, told of an American drifter in Singapore, a pimp wallowing among the local flora, who brought his own story to its mildly upbeat conclusion by forfeiting a lot of money to help a fellow lost soul. Highly praised in this country, it seemed to me an energetic but not very satisfactory picaresque jab. Yet the prose, quick, lucid and continually gazing over the brink of events, appeared ready for anything. *The Black House* is perhaps a recasting of old virtues: Theroux's execution is lively once again, whereas his conception is just a little dim. All the same he has a smart thriller-like plot to dally with, and the result to my mind is a marked invigoration of his talent. . . .

The Black House seems to have been influenced a good deal by Iris Murdoch's fiction, especially *The Bell*. Yet the influence, if I may say so, creates a happy effect precisely because it has been absorbed quite thoroughly. (p. 2)

> *David Bromwich, in* Book World—The Washington Post *(© The Washington Post), September 15, 1974.*

It takes courage for a writer to abandon a tone of voice which he has mastered and attempt something completely different; but it is the sort of courage a serious writer needs. Paul Theroux started publishing novels in 1967 and has produced a series of brilliant and much-praised books each of which, though more than funny, was without doubt very funny indeed. *The Black House* marks a departure from this series: any jokes lurking in the narrative are of a depressed and bitter kind, jokes involving disappointment, betrayal of friends, disgust with the way things are. This may be partly because the hero is neither a young man nor even—as Theroux's last hero, 'Saint Jack' was—a middle-aged man able to comfort himself with fantasy. Sickness, sourness and despair afflict Alfred Munday, an anthropologist forced into early retirement away from a sunny African location and 'his' people, the Bwamba, into the damp Dorset village his wife Emma has hankered after.

In part, then, it is a novel about the expatriate condition, a condition Theroux is in a good position to explicate; he has lived and set novels in Africa and Singapore since leaving his native America, and is now himself settled in England. He has to an unusual degree the qualities a travelling writer needs if he is to be more than a travel writer: he can soak up atmosphere as quickly and thoroughly as a sponge, and he does not intrude his own personality. His English village, its flora and fauna, topography and moods, indoor and out, are here as sharply outlined as any of his earlier exotic settings. Anyone who has been an interloper in an English village—and it's the commonest way of experiencing country life today—will recognise the accuracy of the descriptions. Pleasure has to be found in cold, rain and early darkness ('it never gets this dark in London', as one baffled visitor points out); there is a good deal of slyness, social unease, bonhomie that cracks quickly. Munday's views on Africa, delivered at the village hall, do not help him along any more than his bad temper when he is baited at the pub by the villagers or condescended to by the squire over sherry. . . .

'I sometimes feel I could have discovered all I needed to know about isolation and perhaps even tribalism right here . . . and witchcraft of a sort,' says Munday at one point; the parallel between the African village community and the English one is never far from his mind. And in fact he is caught up in some English witchcraft, a haunting providing the other strand to the plot. Sinister and erotic, this is the most technically adventurous part of the narrative, and it put me in mind of a Henry James ghost story; only there the sexual element is never allowed to surface, whereas here it is not only explicit but insistent.

There is perhaps a tremor of uncertainty at the end of the book. Munday reaches some resolution whose value is not quite made clear; and he himself grows shadowy at times, more possessed by his ghost (one feels) than in possession of himself. But then the book is about a man panicked by doubts about just where he and other creatures do belong. The degree of skill with which Theroux handles these various themes, and the level mastery of his writing, have produced a novel of unusual scope and promise still more for the future.

> *Claire Tomalin, "Out of Africa," in* New Statesman *(© 1974 The Statesman & Nation Publishing Co. Ltd.), October 4, 1974, p. 475.*

Mr Theroux . . . is an intelligent writer who manages to use his intelligence without jokiness or self-aggrandisement. [In "The Black House,"] Alfred and Emma Munday have returned from that romantic haven, 'darkest' Africa, to an English countryside which is no less dark and considerably more hostile. Their new home, the "Black House" of the title, gleams like wet coal and will not let them alone. . . . A series of small but ominous events gather their own momentum and the narrative reaches a point of almost visible darkness. It is all very [neatly] done, and the novel ar-

ranges itself into patterns almost as deliberate as those of Theroux's ideal landscape: the language is ordered, the theme is settled. "But it was frozen, the green looked infertile, threatening to die and discolor for the winter."

Some obvious analogy might be made here with Africa's rather more fertile chaos, but it is the book itself which must bear the strain of comparison. For it, too, is threatening to fade away precisely when Mr Theroux lavishes the most care and intelligence upon it. The initial gathering of moods and moments, so cleverly suggesting menace, is dissolved by what appears to be a wilful spending of Theroux's powers; his sure line in characterisation, his wit and his ear for dialogue become the substance rather than the shadow of the novel, and the scene is clouded by lightweights and *leit-motifs*. The power is undoubtedly there, if only Mr Theroux would keep a firmer hold upon it. (p. 471)

> *Peter Ackroyd, in* The Spectator *(© 1974 by* The Spectator; *reprinted by permission of* The Spectator*), October 12, 1974.*

Connoisseurs of ghost stories know that the very best are often least encumbered by supernatural paraphernalia; the ghost's existence may even be problematical, perhaps no more than the neurotic projection of the story's protagonist. So it is here [in *The Black House*]. . . .

Theroux emphasizes the realistic details of English country life and keeps us interested in the fate of the thoroughly unpleasant [protagonist]. And (as if he had not assumed enough technical problems) he has abandoned the wit that graced his earlier novels, replacing it with a tone of anxiety and anticipation. (p. 116)

> *Peter S. Prescott, in* Newsweek *(copyright 1974 by Newsweek, Inc.; all rights reserved; reprinted by permission), November 11, 1974.*

[While] I think *The Black House* is mostly a mistake, I also found it very impressive, the work of a real novelist writing with real authority, someone who from the first page is intent on the serious business of other people's lives. The story is . . . a reverse "Heart of Darkness": an English anthropologist, after ten years of studying an isolated African tribe, returns home and discovers in an English village in Dorset the same village as the one he left, an isolated tribal world of suspicion, acrimony, and suppressed violence. Theroux creates the English countryside slowly and very well indeed. . . . Furthermore, there is a chapter describing a day the Mundays have in London, mostly seeing sad and corrupted old African acquaintances, that is a little masterpiece as well as a full warning to the Mundays that the heart of England is indeed dark.

But the wages of homelessness are mutedness, suspicion, and ineffectuality, so the Mundays themselves are unpleasant folk to have around, and Theroux feels he has to have at least a ghost story to expose Munday to himself. Parts of the ensuing psychodrama are very exciting, but the story seems only partly to understand itself, and at the same time it leads Theroux away from his original desire to establish the Dorset village alongside the remembered African one. There is less need here to say precisely what it is that doesn't work than to say that the total effect is indeed murky and unsatisfactory—but there is less need to insist on that than to repeat that Paul Theroux, whatever the tangles he has gotten himself into here, is a real writer, full of achievement even in this unachieved novel, full of promise. (pp. 630-31)

Roger Sale, in The Hudson Review *(copyright © 1974 by the Hudson Review, Inc.; reprinted by permission), Vol. XXVII, No. 4, Winter, 1974-75.*

*   *   *

THURBER, James   1894-1961

Thurber was an American humorist, short story writer, cartoonist, and essayist. With Harold Ross, Thurber contributed much to the style and tone of *The New Yorker* during its formative years. Thurber's great appeal was his ability to see universal human weaknesses in terms of a precarious balance of tragedy and comedy, bitterness and fantasy.

I am not sure what poetic sensitivity is, but I am practically certain Thurber has got it. Though artists work in different forms there is a contemporary tissue which connects them, and the things they have in common spiritually are greater than the differences among them technically. Thurber has more in common with modern poets than, for instance, he has with any other present-day humorist you might mention.

I do not know whether the critical landlords of Axel's Castle—our customary symbol for Symbolism—list him among the occupants or not, or whether they are aware he is on the premises. It is that house (to call a partial roll) through whose silences can be heard the interminable scratching of the pen of Proust, and the sad sound of his cough. Here Prufrock, lost in the fumes of introspection, lay damned in the late afternoon. From its window Yeats saw the centaur stamp in the black wood, and Joyce labored mightily in its towers. If fancy and the imagination and "subjective" as opposed to "objective" reality is the emphasis we are talking about, then Thurber can certainly be included. The filaments of individual sensibility are seldom more sharply wrought, or more constantly manifest, than in his work. The psychological nuance is rarely more intricately drawn, even in those tidy sketches in which he is reducing it to absurdity. His inner states and private convolutions are, if not as profound, as skillfully projected as any. He may be least of the family—indeed perhaps just a quizzical lodger cutting up in some remote corner of the premises—but this is the address all right.

It is hard to think of anyone who more closely resembles the Prufrock of Eliot than the middle-aged man on the flying trapeze. This preoccupied figure is Prufrock's comic counterpart, not in intensity of course, but in detail. There is, for instance, the same dominating sense of Predicament. The same painful and fastidious self-inventory, the same detailed anxiety; the same immersion in weary minutiae, the same self-disparagement, the same wariness of the evening's company. And the same fear, in summary, that someone—in Thurber's case a brash halfback or maybe even a woman—will "drop a question on his plate." (pp. 37-8)

Poetry is where you find it, and I find it in *The Black Magic of Barney Haller*, one of the best of those exquisite little sketches which see more drafts than many poems. You will remember it as the account of the caretaker whom storms follow home, whom Thurber suspects of trafficking with the devil and exorcises by incantations of Frost and Lewis Carroll. (p. 39)

The woman satirized in *The Portrait of a Lady* was trite, but she was alive and certainly operating conversationally, and the women lampooned in Thurber are alive and operating too, at their worst when they are a little too much like the preoccupied men (like the woman who came up and announced to the man shrinking in the chair: "I have a neurosis"), at their best possessing a certain virility lacking in the male. They perch confidently on the arms of sofas, drag their men to bridge parties, drive cars well, are in the embalming game. The male is on the wane, corroded with introspection, deflated by all his own inefficient efficiency, without "strength to force the moment to its crisis," his love lyric in desuetude. There is a sketch in which Thurber does not want to go some place—out some place, perhaps a bridge party or something like that—and he says he would rather stay home. "That's the place for a man to be anyhow—home." It is not a long step from there to: "A man's place is in the home," a generalization the feminists of the hour might like to adopt as a battle cry. (pp. 39-40)

"The poet of *The Waste Land*," writes Edmund Wilson, "is living half the time in the real world of contemporary London and half the time in the haunted wilderness of medieval legend." Thurber too is half the time God knows where. "One's head may be stored with literature but the heroic prelude of the Elizabethans has ironic echoes in modern London streets and modern London drawing rooms." Reality in Thurber undergoes filterings and transmutations as curious and as abrupt. . . . Confronted by details, moments, of that dull environment with which he is long weary of coping, he contrives his own little substitutions, and his transformer is always at work altering, to suit his fancy, the currents of experience. . . . "The kingdom of the partly blind," he assures us, jesting of his affliction, "is a little like Oz, a little like Wonderland, a little like Poictesme." He never drives alone at night "out of fear that I might turn up at the portals of some mystical monastery and never return." He has but to do that, and the parallel with Eliot is complete. (pp. 41-2)

I referred, with rather loose whimsicality I suppose, to Thurber as jester in Axel's Castle, and his work may be a rivulet running "individual sensiblity" off into a kind of *reductio ad absurdum*—not that some of the serious exponents of Symbolism haven't already done so. But whatever the excesses of Symbolism may have been, it has not only made a notable contribution to modern literature but by its emphasis on subjective experience has helped us to a richer idea of what "reality" is. Just as poetry and profit are where you find them, reality is what you make it. The angle of refraction according to the perceiving psyche is *always* there, and the individual's extracting from the world around him constitutes an experience that is itself a reality; a point which modern artists have been trying to make for over a generation. (p. 42)

Peter De Vries, "James Thurber: The Comic Prufrock" (originally published in Without a Stitch in Time, *by Peter De Vries; copyright 1943 by Peter De Vries), in* Thurber: A Collection of Critical Essays, *edited by Charles S. Holmes, Prentice-Hall, 1974, pp. 37-43.*

[Thurber's] effort through most of a long career has been to write lucid, correct, and expensively simple English.

I would hesitate to say that his prose is the best now being written in this country. Other things being equal, the best prose would be that which was most effective in presenting the boldest subjects. Except in his fables, where he can touch them lightly, Thurber has always avoided bold subjects like war and revolution, love and death; he prefers to write about the domestic confusions of people whose sedentary lives are not too different from his own. It isn't a very complicated society that he presents, or one with a rich fabric of inherited values, or one in which men and women are destroyed by their splendid passions. His most ambitious hero is Walter Mitty, who has his visions of glory while buying puppy biscuits. His tragic lover (in "The Evening's at Seven") goes back to a *table d'hôte* dinner at his hotel and, in token of a shattered life, orders consommé instead of clam chowder.

Comedy is his chosen field, and his range of effects is deliberately limited, but within that range there is nobody who writes better than Thurber, that is, more clearly and flexibly, with a deeper feeling for the genius of the language and the value of words.

He tries never to intone or be solemn. (p.140)

His loss of vision has had an effect on his style that will be noted by almost every reader of his new fables [*Further Fables for Our Time*]. All the sound effects have been intensified, as if one sense had developed at the cost of another, and the language is full of onomatopoeia and alliteration. "The caves of ocean bear no gems," one studious lemming reflects as all the others plunge into the water, "but only soggy glub and great gobs of mucky gump." Man tells the dinosaur, in one of the best fables, "You are one of God's moderately amusing early experiments . . . an excellent example of Jehovah's jejune juvenilia." There are puns too, like "Monstrosity is the behemother of extinction," and there are rhymes not only in the morals but scattered through the text, so that whole passages could be printed as verse.

But this preoccupation with words, with their sound, sense, and arrangement into patterns, has affected more than the style of the fables. It is also transforming the imagination of the author, who seems to be presenting us with a completely verbalized universe. The only conceivable end for the inhabitants of such a universe would be mass suicide resulting from complete verbal confusion; and that is exactly how Thurber pictures them as ending, in the fable about lemmings which also ends the collection.

It seems that a single excited lemming started the exodus by crying "Fire!" when he saw the rising sun. Hundreds followed him toward the ocean, then thousands, each shouting a different message of fear or exultation. "It's a pleasure jaunt!" squeaked an elderly female lemming. "A treasure hunt!" echoed a male who had been up all night; "Full many a gem of purest ray serene the dark unfathomed caves of ocean bear." His daughter heard only the last word and shouted, "It's a bear! Go it!" Others among the fleeing thousands shouted "Goats!" and "Ghosts!" until there were almost as many different alarms as there were fugitives. Then they all plunged into the seas, and that was the end of the lemmings.

Symbolically it was also the end of mankind as only Thurber could have imagined it: not with a bang, not with a whimper, but in a universal confusion of voices and meanings. (pp. 142-43)

> Malcolm Cowley, "Lions and Lemmings, Toads and Tigers" (originally published in The Reporter, *XV, December 13, 1956; copyright © 1956 by Malcolm Cowley), in* Thurber: A Collection of Critical Essays, *edited by Charles S. Holmes, Prentice-Hall, 1974, pp. 138-43.*

James Thurber's fifteen-year journey from *Fables for Our Time* (1940) to *Further Fables for Our Time* has taken him, as it has taken all of us, through a world war, immediate postwar period of hope for peace that has begun to go a little sour in our mouths, the years of the McCarthy ascendancy when fear and distrust were served up with our breakfast coffee, into the present moment [note, though, that this essay was written in 1957] when social conformity has become such a force that even the anti-conformists appear to be conforming. Thurber's own steps through these times have been further darkened by the gradual loss of his sight. The new fables are quite plainly marked with the national and personal uneasiness that these years represent. They are harsher and more bitter than the early fables without succumbing to a facile or fashionable despair; they are richer, wiser, more serious, and, by comparison, the early fables now seem flip and a little smart-alecky. (p. 144)

The somber streaks that run with the laughter in the new fables are not completely new to Thurber, not a sudden reversal or discovery, not the unveiling of a new man. Thurber said in an interview . . ., "It's very hard to divorce humor from other things in life. Humor is the other side of tragedy. Humor is a serious thing." Humor has always been serious for Thurber. Back in 1929, E. B. White wrote a mock serious explanation of Thurber's drawing, which appeared at the end of their *Is Sex Necessary?* Although White's note kids the pretentiousness of critical over-elaboration, just as the book kids the terrible solemnity of all sex books, his remarks cannot escape being touched with truth. "When one studies the drawings," White writes, "it soon becomes apparent that a strong undercurrent of grief runs through them." (pp. 145-46)

Thurber's relationship to politics has never been an overt one, yet a political climate informs all his later work, either directly or by implication. (p. 146)

Until [*Further Fables*] appeared, however, Thurber's war and post-war work had been admittedly a kind of escape from a world that was becoming increasingly difficult to face. The escape took two paths, one into the fantasy of children's books, the other into memory. The escapes were as profitable to readers as they were to Thurber, who has come back strangely strong, for without them we would not have had *The Thirteen Clocks* and *The Thurber Album.* Thurber turned first to children's books in 1943 with *Many Moons* and then passed through *The Great Quillow* and *The White Deer* to *The Thirteen Clocks*, which is, by any standard, one of the best books that he has ever written. Still, it is significant that Thurber should feel the need to say in the Foreword to that book that it is the result of "escapism and self-indulgence" and to add, "Unless modern Man wanders down these byways occasionally, I do not see how he can hope to preserve his sanity." *The Thurber Album*, the collection of profiles of relatives and friends from an earlier and seemingly solider Ohio, was also a "kind of an escape," as he said. (p. 147)

[The] strength of *Further Fables* lies in more than a balance of word music against a harsh and sometimes angry view of the world, seen through darkness darkly. It lies in a kind of faith that pervades the whole work, even at its saddest. The opening fable, "The Sea and the Shore," finds some amorphous water creatures crawling toward the undergrowth on land, life in its beginnings; the last fable, "The Shore and the Sea," finds the lemmings, panicked by misunderstanding, in a headlong race to destruction. These two fables would seem to round out not only Thurber's book, but the story of man, to hint at hopelessness. The moral, "All men should strive to learn before they die what they are running from, and to, and why," however, contains the possibility of finding out, or at least the desirability of finding out. The scholarly lemming in the fable, the one who does not run, "shook his head sorrowfully, tore up what he had written through the years about his species, and started his studies all over again." But he did start again. The moral of "The Turtle Who Conquered Time" asks sadly, "Oh, why should the shattermyth have to be a crumplehope and a dampenglee?" There is some quality in these fables, and Thurber knows it because he put it there, that insists that the shattermyth can be something quite different from a crumplehope. (p. 149)

> Gerald Weales, "Thurber's Fifteen-Year Journey" (originally published under a different title in The Commonweal, IV, January 18, 1957; copyright © 1957 by The Commonweal), in Thurber: A Collection of Critical Essays, edited by Charles S. Holmes, Prentice-Hall, 1974, pp. 144-49.

For more than a generation James Thurber has been writing stories, an impressive number of them as well shaped as the most finely wrought pieces of Henry James, James Joyce and Ernest Hemingway, as sensitively worded as the most discriminatingly written prose of H. L. Mencken, Westbrook Pegler and J. D. Salinger, and as penetrating—especially during what we can call his "major phase"—as the most pointed insights of those two large poets of our century, E. A. Robinson and Robert Frost. (p. 87)

[Amongst] our living writers [this essay was written in 1958] he is virtually our only creator of serious comedy and one of the few humanists who can make an affirmation without either a chip or a Christ symbol on his shoulder. Indeed, in Thurber's prose the individual is best off when freed of all the paraphernalia of systems, whether mechanical, social, literary or just plain transcendental. . . .

Thurber's protagonists, usually but not always men, . . . are engaged in self-preservation—struggling to keep inviolate the realms of chance, individuality, reflection and purpose, which give the will substance to work with and freedom occasion for exercise. The self, as Thurber shows, is in danger of extinction when persons are driven inward until society becomes impossible, or forced outward until there is no residue to socialize. The most interesting aspect of Thurber's artistic development is in terms of his search for a place where the individual can finally reside—or preside.

Since almost the beginning of his career as a story writer Thurber has insisted that the menace to the individual lurks in the world of man-made systems, whether mechanical or mental, and that the promise waits in the uncircumscribed realms of instinct and the imagination. (p. 88)

If anyone doubts the character of Thurber's affirmation, *My Life and Hard Times* (1933) should dissipate the doubt at once. Although Thurber writes mainly about the decade preceding the First World War, one is scarcely aware that the past may have been sought by the writer as escape. The positive value of being at odds with the facts of a commonplace world is what dominates the book. (p. 90)

[An] older generation's oddities, however delightful, cannot adequately enable a responsible person to come to terms with himself in the present. (p. 91)

The older generation had a vigorous humanity that encompassed their oddities, but the Bidwells and Winships [in "The Private Life of Mr. Bidwell" and "The Breaking Up of the Winships," respectively], and others who might be listed, unhappily illustrate all that the phrase "the modern temper" has come to signify. Here is dehumanization in action. Persons have no resources beyond their rituals and their nerves, or their reflexes. Society becomes the graveyard of individuality, and it is the man with ordinary feeling and simple compassion who would appear eccentric in his ability to forsake detachment in the face of another's pain. The old centers do not hold. Men and women are being flung apart, atomized. The very thing that would hold them together—conformity—is the one thing that takes no account of them as persons. In short, what makes old-fashioned eccentricity alone no answer is that in Thurber's time its corollary may well be loneliness: it may be loneliness when society itself is a mere form rather than a place for persons to exhibit what distinguishes one from another. If in *My Life and Hard Times* misunderstandings are funny, in the later stories they border on the tragic. And the worst aspect of it is that men and women, scarcely unconventional, fail to examine their habits and complacently spin along the disturbed orbit to disaster. The automatic response has superseded the purposeful commitment. Abstraction takes the place of experience, and class names obliterate the self. Persons have become indistinguishable from the little quanta that spot film plates. Appropriately, Thurber declares their isolation a sad rather than glad plight. Indeed, even if they were reflective people they would be defeated, for they would retire from a tawdry world into a hotel room, or seek a box to hide in.

Thurber, though, is clearly no misanthrope. One always feels that something worth recovering has been defeated; hence that recovery of this something is still a good. Man is not necessarily *all* destruction, but he is so *unless*—. This *unless*—is what distinguishes Thurber's preoccupation from 1939 onward. (pp. 93-4)

[Human] needs clearly require a sense of what Thoreau called "the infinite state of our relations." The human being is lost when he loses his sense of his limitation, his mortality; when he equates the private with the absolute. Emerson could preach self-reliance because he had the oversoul in the offing; but Thurber's society has ignored the relationship and thereby denied both the self and the context for its being. Our only morality is embodied in our clichés. Heed their purveyors and be saved. *The Last*

Flower, a Parable in Pictures (1939) and *Fables for Our Time and Famous Poems Illustrated* (1940) remind us how suicidal unself-critical man can be. The acceptance of empty forms is not only frustrating; it is utterly catastrophic. *The Last Flower* exhibits the disastrous course of human habits, the way men and women forget that their source and inspiration lie in what we may term nature—and the way that this forgetting allows mankind to become pretentious, arrogant and, finally, fatally warlike. The last, the best, the only hope is of earth itself: it is lodged in the natural cycle, the regenerative power of nature whose lone flower will seek invincibly to bloom again. The *Fables* makes this point in another way. (pp. 94-5)

The sense of relation that humanity needs is, thus, a sense of a saving connection with a primary spirit, something elemental that civilization disclaims at its peril. To disclaim this something is ultimately to deny the whole self. It is nothing less than this truth that Thurber and Elliott Nugent show Professor Tommy Turner in *The Male Animal* (1940). . . . But the lesson is not simply to affirm the nakedly primitive. (Compare William Inge's *Picnic* and some of Tennessee Williams' plays.) Turner is, after all, always the embodiment of thought and imagination, the man capable of asserting the freedom to think as one will; the memorable drinking scene even underscores this, for were he to come to his illumination in a moment of sober reflection the words of the lesson would be left with only their face value, but instead, the hilarity of the occasion is part of the argument. . . . It is analysis without feeling, without passionate commitment, that is condemned. . . . What the play finally argues, then, is that the good life lies in recovering a certain principle of action, in establishing a source for responses that can make those responses trustworthy. Over-refinement and intellectualism can reduce persons to a level on which their problems are capable of solution by tranquilizers. The fact is, Thurber states elsewhere, "that the bare foot of Man has been too long away from the living earth, that . . . [Man] has been too busy with the construction of engines, which are, of all the things on earth, the farthest removed from the shape and intention of nature." (pp. 95-6)

By subtly and wittily introducing a modern point of view, Thurber makes clear that the fairy tale is itself something of an act of faith in the innocence and purity that fairy tales usually celebrate. At the same time, the fact of that intrusion also declares that it is a large awareness rather than an immature belief that is at work. . . . [That] awareness is the property of a mature and humble mind that encompasses the ability to believe quite as much as it does the ability to act. (pp. 96-7)

"The Secret Life of Walter Mitty" may be said to usher in the major period. As ever, Thurber is trying to find a realm where the individual can maintain his self; and as ever, too, there seems to be no answer without qualifications—an appropriate enough way of assaulting rigid forms. Yet there is ultimately what has already been suggested, a humanistic affirmation. Of course, at no time does Thurber forsake one kind of writing and immerse himself exclusively in another. Although there may be no *My Life and Hard Times*, there are still instances of great humor, more fairy tales and fables. But most of them are marked by the increasing complexity and depth that are best embodied in such important and challenging masterpieces as "The Secret Life of Walter

Mitty" (1939), "The Whip-Poor-Will" (1941), "The Catbird Seat" (1942), "The Cane in the Corridor" (1943), "A Friend of the Earth" (1949), "Teacher's Pet" (1949) and *The Thirteen Clocks* (1950). (p. 97)

[The] very use of language is related to the argument in behalf of individuality and the sense of relation. Insofar as perceptions are verbalized, words must be precise, sharp, telling. Whether employing an arresting metaphor or playfully juxtaposing the trite and the fresh, or simply inveighing against jargon, "polysyllabic monstrosititis," Thurber is warring for meaning—and for the only mind for whom that objective can make sense. It is fitting that . . . *The Wonderful O*, should argue the value not only of love and hope and valor, but also of freedom; and it is equally fitting that he identifies the threat to freedom with an assault on language, on communication. (p. 99)

The concluding fable [of *Further Fables for Our Time*] tells of a scholarly lemming who refuses to join his fellow lemmings in their excited exodus to the sea. . . . [His] studies long ago have told him that there is no devil in the forest or gems in the sea. He simply shakes his head sorrowfully, tears up all he has written about the species, and starts his studies all over again. "All men," the moral reads, "should strive to learn before they die what they are running from, and to, and why." To attribute to man the ability both so to learn and then to act in consequence is almost to pay him the tribute that painters represent with the halo—almost but not quite—and yet better—because ordinary men are more complex than the saints. (pp. 99-100)

> *Robert H. Elias, "James Thurber: The Primitive, the Innocent, and the Individual" (originally published in* The American Scholar, *Vol. 27, No. 3, Summer, 1958; copyright © 1958 by the United Chapters of Phi Beta Kappa; reprinted by permission of the publishers), in* Thurber: A Collection of Critical Essays, *edited by Charles S. Holmes, Prentice-Hall, 1974, pp. 87-100.*

[Thurber] was both a practitioner of humor and a defender of it. The day he died, I came on a letter from him, dictated to a secretary and signed in pencil with his sightless and enormous "Jim." "Every time is a time for humor," he wrote. "I write humor the way a surgeon operates, because it is a livelihood, because I have a great urge to do it, because many interesting challenges are set up, and because I have the hope it may do some good." Once, I remember, he heard someone say that humor is a shield, not a sword, and it made him mad. He wasn't going to have anyone beating his sword into a shield. That "surgeon," incidentally, is pure Mitty. During his happiest years, Thurber did not write the way a mouse waltzes.

Although he is best known for "Walter Mitty" and "The Male Animal," the book of his I like best is "The Last Flower." In it you will find his faith in the renewal of life, his feeling for the beauty and fragility of life on earth. Like all good writers, he fashioned his own best obituary notice. Nobody else can add to the record, much as he might like to. And of all the flowers, real and figurative, that will find their way to Thurber's last resting place, the one that will remain fresh and wiltproof is the little flower he himself drew, on the last page of that lovely book. (pp. 171-72)

> *E. B. White, "James Thurber" (originally published in* The New Yorker, *XXXVII, November 11, 1961; copyright © 1961 The New Yorker Magazine, Inc.), in* Thurber: A Collection of Critical Essays, *edited by Charles S. Holmes, Prentice-Hall, 1974, pp. 171-72.*

[Toward] the end Thurber's humor was overwhelmed by puns and dismay.

The puns are understandable. Blindness, in severing language from the seen world of designated things, gives words a tyrannical independence. Milton and Joyce wrung from verbal obsession a special magnificence, and Thurber's late pieces, at their best—for example, "The Tyranny of Trivia," collected in "Lanterns and Lances"—do lead the reader deep into the wonderland of the alphabet and the dictionary. But in such weak rambles as, in this collection, "The Lady from the Land" and "Carpe Noctem, If You Can," logomachic tricks are asked to pass for wit and implausible pun-swapping for human conversation. (p. 150)

Television, psychoanalysis, the Bomb, the deterioration of grammar, the morbidity of contemporary literature—these were just a few of Thurber's terminal pet peeves. The writer who had produced "Fables for Our Time" and "The Last Flower" out of the thirties had become, by the end of the fifties, one more indignant senior citizen penning complaints about the universal decay of virtue. (pp. 150-51)

Of the humorists of this century, he and Don Marquis were the most complex, the most pessimistic and the most ambitious. Thurber, in comparison to Marquis and Benchley, was not especially sensitive to the surface currents of American life, and as a journalist, uncomfortable, and, as a writer of straight fiction, unconvincing.

His great subject, springing from his physical disability, was what might be called the enchantment of misapprehension. His masterpieces, I think, are "My Life and Hard Times" and "The White Deer"—two dissimilar books alike in their beautiful evocation of a fluid chaos where communication is limited to wild, flitting gestures and where humans revolve and collide like glowing planets, lit solely from within, against a cosmic backdrop of gathering dark. Thurber's genius was to make of our despair a humorous fable. It is not surprising that such a gallant feat of equilibrium was not maintained to the end of his life. (pp. 151-152)

> *John Updike, "Indignations of a Senior Citizen" (originally published in* The New York Times Book Review, *November 25, 1962; copyright © 1962 by* The New York Times), *in* Thurber: A Collection of Critical Essays, *edited by Charles S. Holmes, Prentice-Hall, 1974, pp. 150-52.*

In a basic Thurber situation the man and the dog, clutching each other lovingly, are dancing to the radiogram. The savage wife-figure, glaring at them with her arms crossed, says: "Will you be good enough to dance outside?" The assumption is that men are smaller, more helpless and touching, than their galumphing mates; but they also have more wisdom. They alone can see the frightful black beast swooping down on them from the air. In the end they may

turn and strangle their womenfolk at restaurant tables (and earn the gentle rebuke from the head waiter: "There's a place for that, sir''); or receive the symbolic baseball-bat of surrender from the Women's General.

The Thurber little man, short-sighted, put-upon creature, bruised and frightened by life, is appealing. The trouble is that he goes not at all with cocktails at the Algonquin; and perhaps the unease with which I early greeted Thurber's work stems from a suspicion that the "little man" may not have seemed entirely true to the author. . . . Not only was the put-upon little man quite different from the tough, happy and sophisticated artist . . ., but his sufferings were a standing joke kept up for the readers of the *New Yorker*—just as the fiction of the unpleasantness of mothers-in-law is preserved for the audiences at holiday camps in Shoeburyness. So the Battle of the Sexes comes to appear part of the Great American dream, something longed for, in those glossy *New Yorker* pages, but no more substantial than that watch from Cartier's or the nest egg in the Chase National Bank. Perhaps that is why, read in this great bulk [that is, in the collection *Vintage Thurber*], the humour of Thurber comes to wear so thin. The creators of "Little Men" are ever in a spot. From the heights of Switzerland and his genius Chaplin now speaks of the "Little Fellow" he once was with wistful alienation. In the same way the small, bumbling Thurber innocent came less and less to represent anything his author felt, and resort was had to the whimsy of the fairy-tales, the animals and the Last Flower. And that's why the best pieces are still about Thurber's youth. Better far the nights spent in hilarious insomnia with his parents and his cousin Briggs Beall than those latter-day carouses in the distinguished company of Robert Benchley, Heywood Broun, Scott Fitzgerald, Thomas Wolfe and Sinclair Lewis. (pp. 154-55)

> *John Mortimer, "Insomniac's Companion" (originally published in* The New Statesman, *LXVII, January 10, 1964; copyright © 1964 by* The New Statesman), *in* Thurber: A Collection of Critical Essays, *edited by Charles S. Holmes, Prentice-Hall, 1974, pp. 153-55.*

In his nonfictional essays Thurber sometimes wears the mask of the same figure who cowers in his fiction, with the minor difference that the Little Man of the essays often writes for a living. As a writer, he may easily be portrayed as a wise fool and sad clown. . . . Saddened by his own ineptitude and by his encounters with women, psychiatrists, business, bureaucracy, gadgets, and automobiles this *persona* was further depressed by the disasters of the nineteen-thirties at home and abroad. (p. 287)

[An] orthodox Freudian would see Thurber's Little Man as tormented by the conflict between the unconscious "beast" of sex and the repression of it by the superego, which is shaped and dominated by this man's "civilized" environment. The repressed animal finds its outlet in anxieties, fixations, and obsessions. Basically, society is at fault for repressing rather than channeling the primary urge. (p. 288)

[Some] of Thurber's ideas about sex and personality are not necessarily in conflict with those of Freud. Thurber feels that the male animal is unduly repressed by his environment, an environment which includes another animal, his wife, who both abets and conceals her ruthlessness by means of more resolution, solicitude for her mate, and competence in the small matters of everyday living than he shows. Part of his environment is also a society going mad through a misapplication of technology; so-called neurosis is often merely "a natural caution in a world made up of gadgets that whir and whine and whiz and shriek and sometimes explode." Thurber differs from Freud in ignoring the Oedipus complex, whereas Freud regarded this as the major component of sex. He also differs in feeling that it is futile for man to expect to throw off his repressions or even to sublimate them satisfactorily. The civilized (or repressing and repressed) elements in the Little Man's character and environment often have the same cosmic finality as the natural traits. Thurber's people rarely succeed in changing any aspect of either their surroundings or themselves, and such "adjustment" as the male achieves usually comes only through complete withdrawal, as in the cases of Mitty, and of Grandfather in *My Life and Hard Times*. . . .

Several of the fables carry a message also found in *Is Sex Necessary?* and *Let Your Mind Alone*: namely, the naturalistic theme that man, in trying to act as if he were above his place in nature's order, has muddled himself into disaster. . . . But since the animal kingdom can match the human race in showing an irrational urge to destroy itself—witness the lemmings—there is little consolation or wisdom to be found in the nonhuman world, except for the courage and tranquillity of certain dogs. (pp. 288-91)

A pessimistic naturalism has thus permeated Thurber's depiction of the Little Man, but in the late nineteen-thirties, as the economic depression persisted and war began to threaten, he began to say things about public affairs that call for classifying his literary double also with the heirs of the Progressive "New Citizen," that is, with the liberals of the thirties and forties and with the active opponents of McCarthyism in the frightened fifties. In the anger of *The Last Flower* itself one senses—. . . in Auden's words—"an affirming flame" of zeal and hope which is scarcely consistent with despair, and for over a quarter of a century Thurber was outspoken in his attacks on authoritarianism of both left and right. (pp. 291-92)

Thurber's humor in his last decade shows the same inconsistent mixture of despair and of militancy with its concomitant of hope. In *Further Fables for Our Time* (1956), one finds some of the older, skeptical pessimism about the human race—see "The Human Being and the Dinosaur"—but one also finds that at least ten out of the forty-seven fables in this book are disguised tracts in defense of free expression. In "The Peacelike Mongoose," an animal of that species is persecuted for his use of "reason and intelligence" by those who cry "Reason is six-sevenths of treason." Two more fables are likewise thrusts at McCarthyism: "The Trial of the Old Watchdog" and "Ivory, Apes, and People," but at least two of these *Further Fables* are satires of Soviet communism, which Thurber hated as much as he disliked professional Americanism. (pp. 294-95)

Thurber's liberalism resembles that of Day and Benchley in being sharply limited by his middle-class angle of vision. Most of his neurotic males and females are suburbanites with hired "help" and summer cottages; people who earn their living with their hands are among the threats to this white-collar cocktail crowd. Mr. Monroe shrinks before the furniture movers; Walter Mitty is buffaloed by the parking-

lot attendant; Mr. Pendly by garage mechanics, and several of Thurber's protagonists by waiters, maids, or butlers. . . . Oftener than any humorist of note since Bangs, Thurber makes comedy out of "difficult" servants. The maid in *The Male Animal* is a nineteenth-century stereotype. If their employers are neurotic, Emma Inch, Barney Haller, and several Negro maids are "odd," cross-grained, stupid, or downright psychotic. The servants of the Thurber family in *My Life and Hard Times* usually seem even more unbalanced than their employers, and in a revealing piece called "A Friend of the Earth," Thurber's *alter ego* psychologically grapples with Zeph Leggins, a village roustabout, philosopher, and joker who can also be taken as a symbol of the author's rejection of crackerbarrel humor.

Only occasionally are the manual workers shown as mentally healthy, in contrast to the neurotic persons with more money and book-learning. . . .

The point is not that Thurber makes a principle of relating neurosis to social class, but that nearly all manual workers in his writings are seen only from the viewpoint of their employers, and the author does not seem interested in any other viewpoint. When not butts of satire, they are mere foils for his educated, middle-class neurotics. (pp. 295-96)

[A] contradiction remains between the view of man as a helpless bit of animated earth and the view that he can and ought to achieve his freedom and improve his lot. This contradiction is reduced but not resolved by the fact that Thurber's pessimistic determinism appears chiefly in his writings about personal and domestic matters, whereas his belief in free will and freedom crops out mainly in his pieces dealing with social and political topics. Rarely, as in *The Male Animal*, does he try to fuse the two realms of subject matter and the two philosophies, and when he does try, the result is not convincing either as ideology or as art.

In the work of Benchley one sees a family man and citizen who is seldom victorious and often defeated but who rarely gives up his theoretical hold on certain hard and fast values. In Thurber's writing, this figure is more often driven over the brink to psychosis and separated from any sense of values. The *persona* who fights the liberal fight for a freedom he refuses to consider dead in theory or in practice is separate and distinct from the beaten-down Little Man. Faced with the dilemma of naturalism—the belief that man is an animal whose character and fate are predetermined by his heredity and his environment—and the contradictory need for some form of belief in free will and morality if one is to live harmoniously among one's fellows or to write humor, Thurber solved the problem no better than did Mencken. Mencken blithely ignored the dilemma; Thurber divided his conception of man and embodied each conception in a separate image inconsistent with the other. (pp. 297-98)

Norris Yates, "James Thurber's Little Man and Liberal Citizen," in his The American Humorist: Conscience of the Twentieth Century *(© 1964 by the Iowa State University Press, Ames, Iowa; reprinted by permission), Iowa State University Press, 1964, pp. 275-98.*

What distinguished . . . [*Fables for Our Time* from *Further Fables for Our Time*] was a greater playfulness and the joy of variation he had been patient enough to practice. In the later work, his repetitions and overextensions are technical counterparts of a moral decline and bitterness.

In his extremism he pushes the antiproverbialist and antirhetorical qualities he always had to absolute limits. There is no communication at all possible in the comic misapprehensions of language that he dramatizes. And that leads him to the defeatism figured in the connivance and stupidity of "The Daws" and to the nihilism of his concluding fable, "The Shore and the Sea."

There are still comic attempts at literalism, comic metaphor, and confusionism, to be sure, along with the now obsessive punning. But his disabusement, barely and cannily saved from diatribe by these last comic gestures, is comprehensive and deep—and, at the last, not very funny. (p. 287)

Thurber's last stage represents a retreat from humor. And his irritabilities, his explicitness, his animus, his borderline perversities and grotesqueries, his final hopelessness, and his ingrownness are indices to the whole contemporary epoch, not only to his own career. (p. 288)

Thurber . . . moved from his attack on certain women, on American women, to an onslaught on women in general and into a war on reality. And in his tightened equation of fantasy with honorific male idiosyncrasy and confusionism, he capitulated not only to a final grandiose oversimplification but to frank neurosis. Comic social criticism is possible on grounds that are more sophisticated and less extreme than that.

But Thurber increasingly withdraws from outer subjects anyway and seeks his comedy in anagrammatical humor and word play. . . . Almost a generation before, in "Ladies' and Gentlemen's Guide to Modern English Usage" (*The Owl in the Attic*, 1931), he had sustained exquisite comedy in the grammatical confusions of "who," "which," the correct use of "the subjunctive," etc. But in every case his demonstrations were actually rescued by his supplying the right and unaffected style to employ and a common-sensical tact. That implicit hopefulness disappears and, with it, his capacity for situational and sustained humor along with the verbal confusion. He is led to strained punning, insistent alliteration, or general intellectual gamesmanship in his last stage. "We battle for the word where the very Oedipus of reason crumbles beneath us." He becomes our comic Joyce, likewise degenerating into a fascination with ingrown verbal resources. It is his final refuge. (pp. 288-89)

The strains and grotesqueries of the later Thurber are also apparent in other contemporary authors, in a host of fellow cartoonists, especially those who treat the outré in full abandon, in the efflorescence of sick humor in this period, our own latter-day Baudelaireism, in comic enfeeblements and excesses on the air and on the screen, and in the uncertain position of Jewish humor in this period. If there are exceptions and resurgences, as there clearly are, they appear as yet insufficient to counter the evidence for the decline and even fall of American humor. Such judgment is impersonal and pragmatic. In the material before us corroborations are alternately subtle and notoriously flagrant. (p. 290)

> *Jesse Bier, in his* The Rise and Fall of American Humor *(copyright © 1968 by Jesse Bier; reprinted by permission of Holt, Rinehart and Winston, Publishers), Holt, 1968.*

[Thurber's] work should be called a pleasure dome of the American imagination. . . . It seems strange that a nation which is eager to praise its own genius has not praised Thurber more, but possibly our ignoring his work merely follows the familiar habit of slighting our genuine man of talent, like Poe [or] Melville, until a foreigner discovers him. I do not think we should wait for a foreigner to find Thurber for us. (pp. 7-8)

His work, to make discussion easier, falls into three natural periods. In a creative period that runs from 1929 to 1961 his work falls into three clusters, one for each decade. The first group, starting with his collaboration *Is Sex Necessary?* and ending around 1937, develops the comedy of the little man menaced by civilization. In addition to *Is Sex Necessary?* Thurber published his comic autobiography *My Life and Hard Times* and three other collections. These essays and sketches, originally written for the *New Yorker*, are witty excursions into the impossibility of life or heroism because of large women, automobiles, and the flummery of a complicated civilization. Peter De Vries says that in these books Thurber puts into action a comic Prufrock, an epithet which is both appropriate and accurate. The characters never quite dare, and when they do, they are squelched by dogs, psychologists, women, shower faucets and overcoats. These books contain the vintage Thurber; he springs to life full-grown in them without faltering juvenilia. (p. 8)

The Last Flower (1939), a cartoon sequence with a minimum of prose commentary, and *Fables for Our Time* (1940) inaugurate a second phase of his writing. He refurbishes old themes, probes more deeply into human experience, and tries new methods: in this period he collaborates on a play, discovers the fable form, and writes his children's books. In January, 1940, his play *The Male Animal* (written with Elliott Nugent) opened for a successful run in New York; for the first time the tart, astringent Thurber dialogue gets a larger framework. His three collections of essays may appear to continue the old habits, but the laughter in them is muted and the stories advance toward a terror that the earlier stories suggested but did not explore. But the most important work in this decade, I am convinced, is to be found in the fairy tales. These stories appear without warning—except as the fables themselves have announced a different direction—but in them he advances his insight and his art. His five tales are the only books that were written to appear without prior magazine publication. Thurber makes no particular claim for these five books (he mentions them only once and then slightly when he talks about his work), but they seem to me to contain the quintessence of his vision. Although the stories seem to be written for children, they are more rich for an adult mind that catches and enjoys the outrageous tricks played in them upon experience and time. Like *Alice in Wonderland*, each book is larger than its words seem to indicate. The books of the 1930's show him as an amusing and effective critic of manners and behavior, but these tales show him an interested and acute critic with subjects echoing up and down our own and the general American experience. He works his way through the comic despair of the 1930's to an imaginative reconstruction of experience that explains and comments on that experience. To know

Thurber is to know these books, and it is a measure of the unsatisfactory and slight criticism that he has received that no one (with the exception of Edmund Wilson in a review of *The White Deer*) has had the courage to explore their meaning.

Thurber never abandons his old methods, but he is always developing new ones. Thus he continues to write sketches, fables, and children's stories in the 1950's, but he also discovers a new way to communicate the vision he has learned in the books for children. In *The Thurber Album* (1952) he returns to the same autobiographical subjects he exploits in his third book, *My Life and Hard Times*, but he returns to them with the benefit of the insight dramatized in the children's stories. He considers once more the remembered time of late nineteenth- and early twentieth-century America. He pits his remembrance of the past against the fact of mid-century and, in the contrast, the reader intuits, senses, a third possibility that neither accepts all of the past nor rejects all of the present. Thus we discover a golden vision beyond the remembered past and the sad present. *The Years with Ross* (1959) is similar; it looks back to a heroic time to contrast that past with a disturbing present and to envision a New Found Land. He now writes a comedy of fulfillment; his heroes and heroines are menaced by civilization, as are the heroes of the tales, but they find a way to surmount its obstinate mindlessness, carelessness, and disrespect for intelligence. They live against all odds. The characters act against a debilitated landscape; when they touch a thing, however, "the ugliness, God knows how, goes out of it." And he is convincing.

The writing of the 1930's creates a kind of *Inferno*, the writing of the 1940's a *Purgatorio*, and the writing of the 1950's a *Paradiso*. Of course, the inferno is frenetically gay; the purgatory contains a vision; and the paradise is tinged with so much regret that only the astute reader catches its vision. Further, it is audacious to suggest that a twentieth-century writer has Vision; to describe him that way is a nasty way of condemning him. Visions of paradise are not common, and when tried, they seldom satisfy. The fact remains that these last books do satisfy, and I am astonished that no one yet has shown why. Thurber continued to write his sketches, fables, and stories, and in the most effective of these pieces his anger and his vision (both always potential) are rigidly and thoroughly dressed in what has become a perfect artistic form. He waits now for readers able to see the value in these last examples of his art. (pp. 9-11)

Despite all [his] acid comments about critics and criticism, Thurber's comedy shows a strong underlying awareness of the desperate need for felt understanding. It is not that he is opposed to the intellect's search for understanding. The trouble, as he sees it, is that feeling and understanding may get separated. (p. 12)

Thurber's comedy, like any successful comedy, displays variations on the design—variations that surprise and delight the reader. Surprise and delight are the qualities that give comedy its life and interest; it is impossible to conceive of comedy without them. Comic writers create expectations and then, to our great delight, belie these expectations. In the endings of his stories, Thurber's characters surprise us by celebrating tiny, unnoticed private victories instead of the public marriage and triumphs of older comedy. This variation is significant, for it helps to distinguish the particular pleasure to be discovered in Thurber.

In addition to the basic element of surprise, comedy does five other things. (1) Comedy celebrates the victory of witty man over the obstacles of chance and fortune; it celebrates a vital surge of felt life. Hence our pleasure in the happy ending. Our word *comedy* comes from the Greek word *comos*, standing for the marriage hymn that accompanied the bawdy dance at the end of the Greek rite of spring. Thurber's handling of this conventional expectation is not only his most brilliant accomplishment, but also the key to the changing pattern in his comedy. (2) Comedy deliberately encourages us to think about aspects of life that we try to ignore or that society wants us to ignore. It loves to puncture sacred cows. We feel a tension or excitement when a comedian audaciously insults public officials or when he teases us by forays into sex or funerals. If, as Freud suggests, laughter is a release from the tension of society, then the comic writer will deliberately choose subjects to create this tension or excitement. Again Thurber's subjects not only vary from our expectation (in addition to sex, he chooses scientism and efficiency), but also reveal much about his developing power as an artist. (3) Comedy also arises when any law, habit, custom, or quirk is continued beyond what is ordinarily considered as normal or appropriate. We laugh at the repeated "pocketa-pocketa" of Mitty's automobile that is transformed into the "pocketa-pocketa" of an airplane motor because Mitty is stuck in a "humor," rigidly bound to a quirk of his own nature which makes him daydream instead of function according to normal suburban expectations. (4) Comedy occurs when we recognize that an apparent behavior or an apparent truth is not what it seems to be. Disguise is funny the moment we recognize the incongruity between the real man and the appearance of the mask. (5) Comedy praises admirable qualities in society by laughing *with* them and condemns violations of what is socially appropriate by laughing *at* them. Thus our laughter at an actor in a strange costume tells him and us to conform to the notions of appropriate dress. When we laugh at a man speaking a dialect, we force him and other dialect speakers to conform to our notion of appropriate language. By giving its successful characters the dress and language considered admirable, comedy enforces admirable social qualities. Thus comedy shapes and modifies its audience, though to what degree it succeeds is difficult to assess. Comic writers frequently speak of their desire to "correct" man's knowledge or behavior. Thurber, for example, says much about improving taste and intelligence. Finally, since the essence of comedy is unpredictability and surprise, each of these actions of comedy that I list must astound us if it is to be genuinely comic. Comedy must do all of these things and yet not seem to do them; it is a difficult and sophisticated art form. (pp. 15-16)

I have two convictions about James Thurber. The first is that his comic form provides him with a perspective to view the confusion of the twentieth century and make it meaningful. The second follows directly: that therefore his form needs serious study. (p. 21)

[*Is Sex Necessary?* and *The Owl in the Attic*] are astonishing performances for the beginning of a career. When they succeed, they illustrate the point that comedy at its best grapples with the human condition just as thoroughly as tragedy, satire, or romance. . . . Later books modulate and develop the ideas—freedom, imprisonment by gadgets and systems, female vitality, illusive meaning—beyond all expectations of our fathers, but it is in the early books that he finds the themes and discovers their validity for the comic view of experience. (pp. 40-1)

Every comedy, when stripped down to its basic essentials, involves only two characters: on one side a young hero (a New King) representing life and freedom and on the other an old man (the Old King) who threatens the hero. The old man represents authority, order, repression, and since he is frequently a liar or a pretender, he is known by the technical name of *imposter*. When he is overthrown, the hero is awarded a prize, a young lady, and the marriage that ends the comedy signifies the birth of a new society that the young hero has given us a glimpse of. Lesser characters in the drama exist only to heighten the distinction between the hero and the impostor or to bring the struggle to a successful victory for the young man. . . .

Ancient man enacted the ritual of the Old King, associated with the sins and errors of his community during the winter, and a New King, representing the new hopes for life, fertility, and the community's desires for the coming summer. The most ancient comedies are clearly fertility rites, celebrating the god of fertility; they were performed in the spring of the year and they represent mankind's constant hope for rebirth and eternal life. (p. 61)

This pattern of the death of winter and the birth of summer helps us to see what is happening in Thurber's comedy, a comedy written for a civilization that thinks of spring as a season of daffodils and winter as a season when the theater is active and the streets are full of slush. Thurber's comedy is both very much like the ancient ritual and very different. Even his essays, which do not seem dramatic in the ordinary sense of the term, resemble the ancient form. Because his comedies repeat the ancient ritual, they truly impinge on our humanity and enable us to re-enact the basic struggles of civilization. Civilization is the game that we play to act out perennial and serious questions in a distant and removed world of art forms so that we can understand, see, and even appreciate the experience that most of us are too busy to taste and savor. I must compare Thurber's comedy —and . . . the play [*The Male Animal*] is the clearest example for comparison—with this primary human drama of rebirth in order to demonstrate the great seriousness of his comedy. *The Male Animal* concerns primitive and primary qualities of our character. The play is not just a story about an English professor who insists on reading a letter to undergraduates at a large midwestern university; the play says it concerns the need and right of expression against repressive, stupid, powerful forces which will, if they can, kill American society. By comparing the play to the ancient ritual, I am showing how complicated and interesting this well-constructed play is. By comparing the essays to this play, I am showing how much more Thurber accomplishes in the little room of his essays. (pp. 61-2)

The play that Thurber and Nugent wrote is a complicated examination of issues that man has been concerned with as far back as our records go. . . . Thurber wrote to show how life triumphs over forces which make it a mere formula. He makes what might be old and familiar seem bright and new. (pp. 62-3)

Comic endings range from one extreme in which the comic victory is full and triumphant to an opposite in which the victory is so slight that it may be barely noticeable. The most ironic or bitter comedy is that in which the hero is nearly smothered by his opposition; in the romantic comedy, the victory is so complete that the hero seems to be founding a newly born society with the new life and value that he represents. Comedy ranges from one extreme in which the comic hero's very presence is a kind of lament against society for not allowing this man to live more triumphantly to the other extreme where it is almost a religious vision (recall the *Divine Comedy*), in which the comic hero redeems the society. The victory may range from a token victory, the mere fact of survival, to the victory that changes and completely reanimates the world in which it takes place. Thurber comes closest to the triumphant comedy in *The Male Animal* and, much later, in his five fairy tales.

Thurber prefers the bitter. Granting his impostors, I suspect that only small victories are possible. Is there any comic victor in *My Life and Hard Times?* The mother seems to qualify sometimes; the narrator rarely qualifies since he is nearly inundated in most contests he engages in; Grandfather's saving common sense sometimes qualifies him to near triumphs. *Let Your Mind Alone* has endings ranging from the very bitter to a point that is still considerably less that the limited victory of *The Male Animal*. (p. 75)

While Thurber's basic struggle is the same as that in Greek comedy, his contestants wear different clothes and his endings celebrate a life in the mind. I have used the model [of ancient comedy], then, as a heuristic device. Thurber can stand without it, but with it *we* can see how the artist has played a new song. We still celebrate witty man's struggle with his universe, but we require a new victory. We do not arrange ceremonies to insure that crops will grow, rivers flow, and women bear children; we fertilize our crops, dam our rivers, and seek out gynecologists to study our reproductive organs. Our danger, a more terrifying danger, lies not so much in imponderable forces of weather or reproduction, but in those imponderable forces of our own nature that restrain us from the life that our soul needs. In Thurber the struggle has moved from the universe of natural forces into the universe of the mind. (pp. 79-80)

Thurber laughs, according to [Francis Hackett, in *On Judging Books* (1947), pp. 29-40], to cover the wound made when society threatens to ridicule Thurberean feeling. Thus, to understand Thurber's comedy we need to know the particular aspects of his personality that make him vulnerable to this potential ridicule. The argument is persuasive, since Thurber does create sensitive men like George Bidwell, Charlie Deshler, Mr. Pendly and Mr. Bruhl and invites us to laugh when these men are under attack. Thurber's friends report that anger and rage were basic to his character, and Mark Van Doren attests to that rage in his poem for Thurber, "Anger Is, Anger Was." To argue, however, that Thurber's comedy is merely the result of his Ohio sensitivity is to demean both Thurber and his comedy. The Sad Clown Theory of comedy reduces comedy to a social accident, a product of erring society's persecution of the poor clown. It is a theory which . . . falls short of accounting for the purpose and achievement of the comic *artist*. . . .

We should care less about Thurber's own sensitivities than about his ability to make laughter possible for us by deliberately choosing subjects that will create nervous, unsettling and unbearable tensions. This is not to deny that Thurber's own sensitivity is great and is a very powerful ingredient in his comedy. (p. 82)

Thurber's comedy, especially that of the 1940's, consummately exploits fears, uncertainties, and inhibitions about the relationship between the mind and the world. (p. 83)

The Last Flower, a fable with drawings about the twelfth and thirteenth world wars, inaugurates the "high middle period" of Thurber's writing. The period deserves the name *high* because of his increased sense of the mind as a threat and because of his increased ability to dramatize that threat. . . .

The tension or the drama comes from three sources. First it comes from within the mind of the individual who deludes himself. This placement is familiar in Thurber. In "The Black Magic of Barney Haller" and "The Remarkable Case of Mr. Bruhl" (both in *The Middle-Aged Man*), fears and ideas with their own nature drive the characters to distraction (and death). The idea is brilliantly exploited in *My World and Welcome to It*. A second category of threat comes from the public mind, the intellectual clichés and political habits never wholly lost to view and never clearly seen but surely keeping us from the spoor of bigger game. A third category is the threat from our efforts to discover meaning in our familiar truths, the little ways and habits of our own behavior. In this last category, Thurber gets very close to enunciating a code for the artist that his own work justifies. (p. 84)

Giving [Thurber's] graceful fables any ponderous meaning takes away from their ease, but they create a new awareness of transitory life and suggest values. In the dimension of the fables, almost anything seems possible, for they balance the impulse to statement with their detachment to allow a reader's perception of meaning beyond what paraphrase or summary can suggest. The fable form permits Thurber to speak about such basic ideas of his civilization as the use of intelligence and the concept of imagination. . . . He dares to use his style to make us understand ideas. (p. 116)

The fable form is the lever by which Thurber and his readers move the world. On the fulcrum of the comic plot, Thurber employs the artificial means which are his human powers: his sense of metaphor, symbol, and language. We sense the power that he applies and in the fable itself we see that power increased to its fullest potential. We "see through it" in that we know why the power has increased. Further, since the power is exerted on matters of significance—human vanity, behavior of massman, attempts to violate and even pervert human abilities, complexity, and beauty—the act attracts us. We "see through it" also, when we recognize that the man using the power is repeating a mode of behavior, that he is behaving inelastically when he tells fables, and we laugh with pleasure as we see him repeat his foolish habit. But at the same time that we realize his foolishness, we also appreciate his result: the foolishness isolates what is basic and essential to the human condition and gives it the harmony or repose of artistic form. (pp. 117-18)

The Romance provides Thurber with another form (like the fable) by means of which he can fulfill the writer's ancient duty of advising man on his true condition. Behind the guise of a fairy tale he can speak of a world of ideals and delight his reader in the process. He puts real toads, as Marianne Moore advises the writer to do, in an imaginary garden. (p. 122)

In the five books which I call Romances [*Many Moons, The Great Quillow, The White Deer, The Thirteen Clocks*, and *The Wonderful O*] Thurber sustained his most creative flight. Except in these books (and possibly in *The Male Animal*) Thurber always follows the injunction to the comic writer that he be short and swift. Even the shortest of these stories, *Many Moons*, is several times the length of his usual sketch, and *The White Deer* and *The Wonderful O* come near to the length of a short novel. I am not going to argue in favor of these books because of their length, but I can notice that his art has a deeper meaning here because we sense an interplay between a larger patter of surface perception—the quest-motif of romance—and the pressures of depth-perception which makes us see that he writes about a power that exists in our civilization, the power that gives us ivory, apes, and peacocks but cannot give us the moon or free us from plundering giants, idiot rulers, and robbers. In the larger space of these books, he has room to define those qualities of the Jester which can bring life back into our wasted land suffering its surfeit of ivory and peacocks. (pp. 135-36)

Thurber, then, has not just chosen an available form, but he has chosen the one form that communicates the reality of our experience. He writes about a world in which the dream of pleasure is the commonplace. He writes about a real world where time is stopped. Now more than ever before the imaginative intelligence is needed to give value and significance to our real gardens. What begins by arousing our laughter—the comic incongruity between an imagined world and fact—turns out to be more than a comic device. It is a means of commenting on and understanding our strange and bizarre experience. (p. 137)

Thurber's final comedy succeeds because his sense of form persists in his shift from a stereotyped comedy to a comedy of human action. The unsound and fuzzy impostors threatening in Thurber's final books are not constructions but facts of human experience just as the impostors in primitive comedy represent natural forces in the world which threaten to destroy humanity. His heroes are not artfully created men but rather existential heroes, men who have the power to form the chaotic world of experience into meaning. The comedy of Ross and the men and women like Jacob Fisher and Aunt Margery Albright is a comedy of seeing things as they really are, a comedy of finding in experience itself the ritual action of challenge, defeat, despair, and final victory. While the action often ends in death, the spirit of his heroes survives. His comedy therefore is a human comedy (rather than a divine comedy), and it gives his readers a very human revelation of a very human and transitory *Paradiso*. (p. 162)

I admire particularly Thurber's . . . artistic and humanistic growth in his fairy tales. In these stories the implicit comic idea—that Man must triumph over sterile and unprofitable men who reduce life to a stereotype—is given explicit dramatic statement. These stories move from a wasteland of strange, enticing, and unusual appearance to a reality. The reality is the order made by the creative mind of the poet who reanimates the world. The world is our world, torn and dying but capable of rebirth. The American imagination has typically used the strange and distant world to project its fears, frustrations, and hopes, and thus Thurber mines a vein familiar to Hawthorne, Twain, Faulkner and Fitzgerald. Truth, beauty, and meaning exist, these stories say, not in the world nor in its social institutions, but in the mind of the Jester who discovers that the moon is just as large as the little girl who wants it imagines it to be. In truth, the moon is a golden disk caught in the branches of a tree. (pp. 184-85)

> *Richard C. Tobias, in his* The Art of James Thurber *(copyright © 1969 by Richard C. Tobias), Ohio University Press, 1969.*

Though Thurber's satire would seem to resemble the eastern school of the mannerist absurd—the continuity of Stephen Leacock, Robert Benchley, and S. J. Perelman—there is a wild, Dionysian spirit hiding beneath the mask of Apollo, which like those clocks of Columbus is associated with Thurber's dreams of home. From his college days on, Thurber admired Henry James's mastery of style, but in his heart's core he was much closer to Mark Twain. (p. 16)

In his old age, racked by disease and incapacitated by blindness, Thurber became a sort of resident western curmudgeon, snarling at a changing world he could not comprehend. But during the thirties and forties, his essentially western voice spoke through parables of exquisite texture, giving form to the spirit of wildness which redeems his early mistakes and his later failures. (p. 18)

> *John Seelye, "From Columbus to New York" (originally published under a different title in* Book World—The Washington Post, *October 22, 1972; copyright © 1972 by* The Washington Post), *in* Thurber: A Collection of Critical Essays, *edited by Charles S. Holmes, Prentice-Hall, 1974, pp. 15-18.*

The major themes of [Thurber's] earlier work cluster around the conflict between the individual (free, spontaneous, eccentric) and the system (ordered, repressive, conventional). His view of life is romantic, liberal, optimistic. His basic form is the narrative anecdote, revealing oddities of character and behavior. After his blindness, he begins to create his comedy out of extravagant word-play rather than out of action and character. The change is gradual, but it is clearly evident in *The Beast in Me.* Accompanying this change in artistic method is a growing pessimism and misanthropy, as personal frustrations and a despairing concern over the state of the world upset his precarious psychic balance.

The peak achievement of Thurber's early career is *My Life and Hard Times.* For many readers it is his one unquestioned masterpiece. . . . The book is the definitive image of Thurber's special comic world. Here the eccentric characters, chaotic situations, and the strange blend of the realistic and the fantastic which are the hallmarks of his work are present in their purest and most concentrated form. It mines one of his richest veins of subject matter—the days of his youth in Columbus—and out of these autobiographical materials he creates a mad comic world in which the normal order of things is constantly exploding into chaos and confusion. (p. 148)

Disorder and confusion are anathema to the world at large, but for Thurber they are sources of possible liberation.

They are at the heart of a set of closely related values which, until his very last years, he habitually champions in opposition to the dominant ideals of contemporary society. In a world committed to logic, organization, conformity, and efficiency, Thurber stands for fantasy, spontaneity, idiosyncrasy, and confusion. Hence Thurber's fondness for situations involving eccentric behavior, elaborate practical jokes, breakdowns of communication, and the disruption of bureaucratic machinery. . . . The whole of *My Life and Hard Times* is a celebration of what might be called the Principle of Confusion, or the Fantasy Principle. Nearly every episode shows the disruption of the orderly pattern of everyday life by the idiosyncratic, the bizarre, the irrational. (p. 149)

Throughout *My Life and Hard Times* eccentricity of character is seen as a life-enhancing value. The mild insanities and picturesque obsessions of the people Thurber remembers from the days of his youth are not only diverting examples of the human comedy, they are also something important—they represent freedom, independence, the irrepressible stuff of life which refuses to be caught in formulas and conventions. (p. 154)

In *My Life and Hard Times* Thurber has arrived at full artistic maturity and nowhere is this more evident than in the style. Working on *The New Yorker* and emulating the easy informality of E. B. White, he developed a style that was natural, easy, and unself-conscious. It was colloquial without being slangy (although it could be that, too), and disciplined without being stiff. It was plain to the point of invisibility—a style which pretended not to be a style at all. It had no idiosyncrasies: sentence structure and word order were unobtrusively normal, and the language seldom called attention to itself. . . . Thurber's prose is a transparent medium, reporting action and character in the simplest possible way.

All this he had by 1929, when *Is Sex Necessary?* first identified him as a writer of consequence. The difference is that in *My Life and Hard Times* his style has become not only a versatile comic instrument but a highly personal mode of expression as well. In *My Life and Hard Times* Thurber has developed a vocabulary and a pattern of phrasing which reflect his own unique temperament and cast of mind. (p. 158)

> *Charles S. Holmes, "Columbus Remembered: 'My Life and Hard Times',"* in his The Clocks of Columbus: The Literary Career of James Thurber *(copyright © 1972 by Charles S. Holmes; reprinted by permission of Atheneum Publishers, New York), Atheneum, 1972, pp. 145-60.*

The landscape of Thurber's mind was not quiet and orderly like Trollope's; it was a clutter of domestic objects bouncing and banging down hill towards chaos. It terrified Thurber. As E. B. White put it, "His mind [is] unbelievably restless and [makes] him uncomfortable at all hours. (p. 32)

[He refused to deliver his message] with mechanical, rational clarity, deliberately leaving it to hover in its truest form just beneath the verbal surface.

Thurber's best drawings work the same way. The famous lady on the bookcase, for example, began as an attempt to draw a woman crouching at the head of the stairs, the obvious beginning of a perfectly reasonable joke. But Thurber fudged the perspective and suddenly had a woman on all fours on a bookcase. Without hesitation he filled in the rest of the drawing—a man blandly introducing his wife to a visitor who peers up at the fiercely glowering lady on the bookcase—and wrote the caption, "That's my first wife up there, and this is the *present* Mrs. Harris." (p. 34)

> *Arthur Mizener, in* The New York Times Book Review (© *1973 by The New York Times Company; reprinted by permission), March 25, 1973.*

One tends to think of Thurber—a man who, after all, made his living writing for the very style-conscious *New Yorker*—as an adroit and inventive prose stylist, one who, through his verbal pyrotechnics, wrought humor out of the commonplace. Yet, in fact, Thurber's basic style is remarkably neutral, exhibiting a marked avoidance of verbal acrobatics. Thurber always regarded himself as a journalist, and much of his prose is written in the clear, flat, economical style of the reporter; it is a style which does its best not to call attention to itself through any deviations from the norm. Thurber was intensely concerned with the purity of the language, and he wrote many pieces decrying its abuse. Language, to Thurber, as Charles S. Holmes, in ["James Thurber and the Art of Fantasy"] states, is "a necessary principle of order, and an instrument of precision and beauty," a besieged force for clarity in an increasingly confusing world. (p. 75)

Yet Thurber, and here we see the other side of his professional and hence stylistic coin, was an inveterate dabbler with language, "fascinated," as Holmes says, "by its capacity to create an Alice-in-Wonderland world where ordinary rational communication is transcended." He was a connoisseur of chaos. To the journalist, then, Thurber improbably grafted the fantasist; and out of the collision of the two (out of the collision of two styles and, finally, of two world views) issued his humor. (pp. 75-6)

In his later work, . . . reflecting a more bitter attitude toward a growingly chaotic world, Thurber's prose is packed with puns, scrambled literary allusions, anagrams and other forms of wordplay, and sequences of words linked phonemically in a hectic conjunction in which meaning, ordered meaning, is lost; and characters, tricked by what was once an "instrument of precision," fall into the confusion of fantasy. Further, Thurber was a great parodist; to analyze the style of, say, "The Secret Life of Walter Mitty," "The White Rabbit Caper," or *The Thirteen Clocks* would be to track down, not Thurber, but Thurber as writer of the adventure tale, the murder mystery, and the fairy tale. . . . *My Life and Hard Times,* . . . I believe, best represents the quintessential Thurber, the mimic speaking in his own voice, the journalist whose taste for fantasy is under tight rational control. (p. 76)

[It] is in his diction that Thurber's humor lies. The base style, which I have called "journalistic," involves the rather colorless features—or rather *lack* of features, lack of morphemic, phonemic, syntactic, or grammatical experimentation—. . . and a rather stilted, archaic vocabulary, heavy in Latinisms, which reflects Thurber's nostalgia for past, more ordered, patterns of life and forms of expression. . . . He will often use phrases, to introduce or further

his narrative, drawn from the repertoire of the nineteenth-century storyteller, and reminiscent of, say, Henry James, who was Thurber's favorite author. (p. 78)

In contrast, but in conjunction with this ordered, formal, impersonal, slightly archaic diction, is a vast amount of idiom, often expressive of violent action and chaotic and idiosyncratic states of mind, but almost invariably, also, nostalgic, in that these usages belong mainly to the rural, familial past of Thurber's childhood. . . .

In contrast both with the base style and with the events described (which, I should mention, are usually of the most ordinary, simple nature), Thurber uses a whole range of words and phrases found normally in contexts of danger and intrigue; this is the diction of the mystery novel or the romance. (p. 79)

All the apparatus of an impersonal, crisp journalistic style, fraught with diction expressive of events and people of significance, is brought to bear upon simple, ordinary men and the events of daily existence. The effect is that of the mock-heroic: inflated diction is satirized, the people and events described are satirized, and, finally, in spite of the satire involved, those people and events take on a kind of heroic, if nostalgic, dignity commensurate with the language in which they are treated. (p. 80)

> *Michael Burnett, "James Thurber's Style"* (© *1973 by Michael Burnett), in* Thurber: A Collection of Critical Essays, *edited by Charles S. Holmes, Prentice-Hall, 1974, pp. 75-82.*

James Thurber has long been recognized as one of America's leading modern humorists. His stories, sketches, and cartoons are engaging, often leading to chuckles of wry reminiscence. But when he created "The Secret Life of Walter Mitty," Thurber wrought better than he knew, for he had touched upon one of the major themes in American literature—the conflict between individual and society. Mitty's forerunners are readily observable in native folklore and fiction. On one side Mitty is a descendant of Rip Van Winkle and Tom Sawyer. On the other side he dream-wishes qualities customarily exhibited by the legendary frontier hero. Yet, while Thurber's story derives from American culture tradition, it presents the quest for identity in an unmistakably modern context. In what may be the final scene in an unfolding tapestry of heroic situations, Mitty struggles to achieve a measure of self-respect, but finds himself restricted to the pathways of retreat and wish-fulfillment.

Mitty's closest literary forerunner is Rip Van Winkle, the "good-bad boy" of American fiction. Like Rip, Mitty has a wife who embodies the authority of a society in which the husband cannot function. Mitty's world is routine, trivial, and fraught with pigeon-holes; it persecutes the individual, strips his life of romance, and dictates what his actions (if not his thoughts) should be. The husband is often reduced to the status of a naughty child (as demonstrated by a pre-pubertal mentality); and he attempts to escape rather than confront a world symbolized by a wife who, more often than not, seems to be a mother-figure rather than a partner. Because of the threat which the wife-mother poses to the American male psyche, Rip must go hunting, Deerslayer cannot marry and dwell in the town, and Huck seeks the river rather than be *sivilized*. (p. 283)

Because his imagination depends upon what he has read rather than what he has done, Mitty lives a vicarious existence. And, conversely, Mitty's misuse of words and concocted over-dramatizations betoken his unwillingness to dwell in a dimension which cannot feed his imaginative faculties. Given his routine external life, how could it be otherwise? . . . A dual purpose is evident here, for while Thurber deliberately places these wrong-way signposts to reveal Mitty's ignorance of the heroic experience Mitty remains oblivious of his blunders as he succeeds in fashioning his own reality. Simultaneously it is a sad and amusing show.

Mitty's visions, however, are more than mere adolescent fantasies with their theatricality and simplistic crises; they are surprisingly true to what Lawrence in *Studies in Classic American Literature* defined as the fundamental American male psyche: "The essential American soul is hard, isolate, stoic, and a killer." . . . It must be noted that nearly all of Mitty's visions deal with violence, and even the one exception dramatizes a matter of life and death. This kind of situation allows the ultimate in symbolic action in which the questions of self can be answered and personal values defined. One can speculate whether Mitty's visions of crises and correspondingly heroic responses are so familiar because they are inherent in the national unconscious or because they recur with such frequency in the national literature. The speculative game is one of chicken and egg; the undeniable fact suggests serious and alarming possibilities concerning the American male mentality in a time when football and military force provide over-simplified moral and physical confrontations.

This quality of self-reliance, so directly traceable to the American past, is manifested by Mitty's dream-self to a considerable degree. In both the frontier literature and that of the New England Romantic tradition, the hero always defined himself through actions which dramatically delineated his inner self and established his identity. . . . A youthful culture naturally produced heroes with youthful qualities, most notably an unshaken self-confidence which framed their belief that they could always adapt to the world, no matter what the world might prove to be. This kind of unqualified optimism in one's ability (one side of the Romantic coin) reveals itself most clearly in Cooper's Natty Bumppo, Emerson's "Self-Reliance" and Thoreau's exploits in *Walden*. It is this swaggering self-assertion and a conviction regarding the control of one's destiny which characterize at once the American hero and Mitty's alter ego. (One need only recall how Mitty substitutes the fountain pen for the faulty piston in the failing anaesthetizer, how he strikes the villainous District Attorney from a sitting position with his one good arm in the chivalrous defense of a Byronic heroine, and how he prepares to fly, alone and weary, on a vital mission against the "Archies.") Like Davy Crockett, Mike Fink, and Natty Bumppo, the dream-Mitty can out-shoot, out-fight, and out-do any and all opposition. But the man who can surmount catastrophes, man-made or natural, exists today only in the mind of a bewildered and hen-pecked protagonist. Whether the potential for heroic action was greater in the past, or whether there were indeed giants in those days, Mitty, like Miniver Cheevy, can only *think* about it. "The greatest pistol shot in the world" is reduced to ordering puppy-biscuit, to fetching and carrying for his wife, and he has difficulty even recalling the name of the product. (pp. 284-86)

The current world of industrialism and specialization severely restricts any potential for heroic action. With the frontier gone, and physical and psychological space limited, the typical male is reduced to fantasy-visions as outlets for that action which is now denied him. If it is depressing that Mitty cannot rise to traditionally heroic statue in today's world, it is also realistic. Today, Thurber seems to say, the combat is so unequal that the path to heroic action lies through the inner mind. The would-be hero must resort to the world of dream in order to inflate himself to that state where he can psychologically compete and win. Lacking the resources of the natural hero, the modern man acquires them by wish-fulfillment. Unfortunately, the victory, if and when it is attained, must occur in that same world of make-believe. (p. 286)

[Mitty's comment, "Things close in," circumscribes] much of the contemporary American male's feelings toward adult responsibilities. Small wonder that he returns to boyhood methods of dealing with a world which confuses him—and small wonder that he conceives his wife as threat and stifler of his inner self. . . . In so many ways the American male resembles a child who has not yet awakened, or who prefers to pull the blanket over his drowsy head rather than confront and cope. Babbitt's coventional escapes—his lukewarm affair and fishing trip—are less disturbing than Paul Riesling's solution of shooting the wife. And just as serious is Harry "Rabbit" Angstrom's method of running away physically from adult relationships after he has committed himself to fatherhood. Mitty's internal flights are harmless by comparison, but the motivating factors are identical. (pp. 287-88)

The heroic mold has generally been cast by a juvenile imagination in America. Certainly the folk heroes were inflated to larger-than-life proportions. And the Romantic imagination would naturally have seized upon the frontier as a natural landscape whereon heroic deeds of a corresponding size and nature could be performed. But in Thurber's modern man only a dim memory of a heroic past remains, nurtured on puerile fantasies propagated by films and pulp fiction. With the frontier gone, and space and privacy at a premium, there is only one place where Mitty can hope to fulfill himself—in a world of self-projection. And even here he cannot totally escape, for the real world apprizes him of its presence by shattering each delusion before it can be climaxed.

As a result of being perpetually interrupted at crucial moments in these fantasies, it seems only proper that Mitty's final role should be that of the condemned man about to be executed by a faceless firing squad for reasons not explicitly given. This vision is a marvelously telling projection of Mitty's place in the world as he feels it. How fitting it is that the story ends, as it began, with a day-dream and that, to the external world (his wife, among others), Walter Mitty wears that "faint, fleeting smile" and remains "inscrutable to the last." (pp. 288-89)

> *Carl M. Lindner, "Thurber's Walter Mitty —The Underground American Hero," in* The Georgia Review *(copyright, 1974, by the University of Georgia), Summer, 1974, pp. 283-89.*

Generally speaking, British readers find something authentically American in Thurber's voice as well as in his subject matter. They like the vein of fantasy in his work, and they are more responsive than American readers to the dark side of his imagination, to the pessimism and the sense of disaster which give Thurber's world its special atmosphere. At the same time, they admire his "civilized" qualities—the craftsmanship and the classic economy of style. (p. 5)

The first American recognition of Thurber's importance as an interpreter of modern life was Peter De Vries's 1943 essay . . ., "James Thurber: The Comic Prufrock." De Vries's argues that Thurber's true affinity is with the Symbolist poets rather than with the humorists. Like them, he celebrates the subjective vision, and in his work there are the same quick shifts from outer to inner experience, the same transformations of reality into dream and fantasy that we find in T. S. Eliot. . . . For him, as for the Symbolists, the life of fantasy is superior to the life of reality. In De Vries's fine phrase, Thurber is the "jester in Axel's Castle," giving us a comic version of the areas of experience explored by the poets of the Symbolist tradition. His timid, neurotic protagonists are the direct descendants of Eliot's J. Alfred Prufrock—and, as Edward Stone suggests, of Henry James's "poor sensitive gentlemen."

Thurber's great subject is the predicament of man in a baffling and alien world. Cut off from the simpler, stabler order of the past, which Thurber's nostalgic pieces constantly evoke, modern man leads a precarious existence. Trapped in a world of machines and gadgets which challenge his competence and threaten his sanity, a world of large organizations and mass-mindedness which threatens his individuality, and—most painfully—a world of aggressive women who threaten his masculine identity, he is forced to go underground, so to speak, and to fight back in small, secret ways. Unlike Prufrock, Thurber's protagonists do resist, finding in daydream and fantasy the means to reshape outer defeat into inner victory, as Walter Mitty does. Occasionally, the victory is unequivocal, like that of the husband in "The Unicorn in the Garden" and of Mr. Martin in "The Catbird Seat," but open triumph is not the usual destiny of the Thurber male. (pp. 5-6)

Thurber's Little Man has a good deal in common with the antiheroes of twentieth-century fiction. Thurber did not invent this character for American humor—Benchley did that, following the model of Stephen Leacock—but he enlarged it, gave it a new psychological dimension, and made it into a highly effective dramatic persona. (p. 6)

The Little Man is the most famous of Thurber's personae, but . . . it is not the only one. Throughout his career he wrote as a reporter, social historian, memoirist, and biographer, in addition to his work as a humorist; and, in these roles, he customarily speaks in the voice of the educated and enlightened observer of the human scene. As he became more and more concerned over what was happening to American life in the 1940s and 1950s, the identity of the Little Man no longer served his needs, and he adopted instead the traditional role of the social critic and satirist, speaking out as rational man and public-spirited citizen against the fanaticisms and vulgarities of the day. These two personae—one, the helpless Little Man, the other the aggressive reformer and man of liberal principles—embody two conflicting views of life; and . . . Thurber never harmonized or reconciled them. When he tried, in the character of Tommy Turner, in *The Male Animal*, the result was unconvincing. (p. 7)

[One] can identify two ways of looking at Thurber: one, the "dark," psychological view, emphasizing the neurotic and unsettling elements in his work; the other the "light," rational view, emphasizing its aesthetic and humanistic qualities. The humanistic view sees Thurber as the defender of the individual in an age of mass culture, the champion of imagination over the logic-and-formula-ridden mind, the enemy of political fanaticism, whether of the Right or Left. This is the Thurber of *My Life and Hard Times, Let Your Mind Alone, The Male Animal, Fables for Our Time, The Last Flower* (if read optimistically, as E. B. White does), *The White Deer*, and perhaps *The Thurber Album*. (p. 10)

The darker view focuses on Thurber as a man writing to exorcise a deep inner uncertainty, to come to terms with fears and resentments which threatened his psychic balance. Images of these neurotic forces are everywhere in his work—in the Preface to *My Life and Hard Times*, in the discords of *The Middle-Aged Man on the Flying Trapeze*, in the strange drawings, in Walter Mitty's escapism, in stories such as "The Whippoorwill," in *Further Fables for Our Time*, and in the compulsive wordplay of the late pieces. (pp. 10-11)

The effect of blindness on Thurber's style and subject matter was profound. First of all, it drove him inward and backward to the world of childhood fantasy. The fairy tales —*Many Moons* (1943), *The Great Quillow* (1944), *The White Deer* (1945), *The Thirteen Clocks* (1950)—are not only escapes from a painful present reality into a world of romance and make-believe; they are also affirmations of certain values which had come to have a special importance for him. All of them . . . tell the story of a blighted land, of the failure of the king's advisers—scientists and men of power—to remedy the situation, and of the lifting of the spell by the lowly regarded court jester, toymaker, poet, or minstrel, in short, by the man of creative imagination.

Blindness also intensified Thurber's lifelong preoccupation with language. Cut off from the visible world, he became obsessed with words as things in themselves. The grounds of his comedy shift from the play of character and situation to that of verbal encounter, repartee, and word gamesmanship. Beginning with *The White Deer*, he develops a style very different from the understated economy of his earlier prose. This new style is elaborate and decorative, full of puns, garbles, coinages, and literary allusions. (pp. 11-12)

The theme of all of Thurber's late work is decline—of form, style, good sense, "human stature, hope, humor." The spirit of the late pieces is satiric rather than humorous: "anger," he observed . . . has become "one of the necessary virtues." The center of his concern became the state of the language, which for him, as for Ezra Pound and George Orwell, was the index to the state of a culture. . . . Earlier in his life, Thurber celebrated disorder, illogic, and confusion, feeling that these were desirable counterbalances in a society overcommitted to science and efficiency. Later, as history changed the world he grew up in, and his own view of life changed, he looked for stability and continuity, and championed those qualities which hold a society together. (p. 13)

The world Thurber created is both intensely American and enduringly universal. Although he wrote no single masterpiece like *Huckleberry Finn* or *Don Quixote*, his prose and his drawings, taken together, give us an image of life so original and so outrageously true that his place among the great comic writers seems already to be assured. (p. 14)

> *Charles S. Holmes, "Introduction" to* Thurber: A Collection of Critical Essays, *edited by Charles S. Holmes (copyright © 1974 by Prentice-Hall, Inc.; reprinted by permission of Prentice-Hall, Inc., Englewood Cliffs, New Jersey), Prentice-Hall, 1974, pp. 1-14.*

Thurber has often been compared to Mark Twain, whom he indignantly denied having read. This is unbelievable, but the springs of his manner were too delicate and his mind too inturned for the long masterpiece. One can see this in his brief parodies, in his love of impromptu, in his vision of Walter Mitty, and, above all, in those long letters that were written to start useful hares. He was profitably uninventive in the large sense and trapped by autobiography; although he boasted of his powers of total recall, his best things are the result of weeding this deadly faculty. (p. 106)

> *V. S. Pritchett, "Thurber," in* The New Yorker *(copyright 1975 by V. S. Pritchett; reprinted by permission of Harold Matson Co., Inc.), June 23, 1975, pp. 104-07.*

*   *   *

TUTUOLA, Amos   1920-

Tutuola is a Nigerian novelist of international reputation. (See also *Contemporary Authors*, Vols. 9-12, rev. ed.)

That conflict between tribal beliefs and modern technology, between intuitive faith in the past and rational optimism engendered by prospects for the future, is found in all of the four books written by Amos Tutuola, the first Nigerian novelist to be celebrated abroad. It is one of the ironies of literature that Tutuola is probably the best-known West African fiction writer in Europe and the United States (with the possible exception today of Chinua Achebe), yet Nigerians think little of him. His work has sold well on both continents, and his original and translated works have been the literary sensation of Paris. The reason for his French success may be laid to his style: it is an amalgam of African rhythms and structure with pidgin-English locutions. But just as Nigerians generally frown on the Négritude movement, so do they look on Tutuola's work as an artificial product and a dead end.

Tutuola is more a mythologist than a novelist. All his work is cast in the guise of fiction, but his heroes and heroines are more dream-figures than people of flesh and blood. (p. 69)

The journey motif, or the end to innocence, seems at the core of all Tutuola's work. What seems especially important is the change of his heroes' attitude to their journey. In *My Life in the Bush of Ghosts* and *The Palm-Wine Drinkard* the heroes return to earth, but they yearn for the mysterious forces of Deads Town and the world of spirits. In anticipation of their return to these worlds they revel in the eternal fears of the forest. In *Simbi* and *The Brave African Huntress* the heroines are content to have returned home from their journey. Home is dull, it lacks the throbbing passion of the forest, but it is secure. Indeed, the theme of Tutuola's third book [*The Brave African Huntress*] is Simbi's foolish desire to venture into "Poverty" and "Punish-

ment." The brave African huntress is driven at least as much by a positive social goal—destruction of the ugly Pygmies—as by a psychological one. Tutuola seems to have progressed from a need to explore evil and darkness, a need compounded by fear of punishment for possessing that compulsion, to a more rational social approach to the conquest and elimination of evil. Even the styles of the books reflect the change of attitude. The bouncing, tossing sentences of *The Palm-Wine Drinkard* almost disappear from *The Brave African Huntress*, which has a stately, more conventional sentence structure.

Tutuola has had little influence on Nigerian writers principally because he has relied on a personal mythology and because many Nigerians feel he has been playing the court jester to the European literary kingmakers. (pp. 71-2)

Nigerians regard him as a primitive showing no desire to move from his "primitive habitat." Yet it is likely that in time he will be seen as a real talent, not merely as a phenomenon that introduced the exotic barbarities of an African jungle to a living-room world. Even today he is not without influence abroad: as has already been affirmed, his easeful, vital rhythmic style brought the first wave of European and American attention to West African writers. His preference for English over his native language of Yoruba has in itself been significant, and his books, in spite of their mythical primacy, reflect the ambivalence of an African rooted in the tribal past yet caught up in a modern power struggle. (p. 72)

> *Martin Tucker, in his* Africa in Modern Literature: A Survey of Contemporary Writing in English *(copyright © 1967 by Frederick Ungar Publishing Co., Inc.), Ungar, 1967.*

The romances of Amos Tutuola of Abeokuta in western Nigeria have put criticism on its mettle. These strange works, strange alike in their merits and their shortcomings, have taken criticism aback both in the West and in Nigeria, producing a kind of misinformed, surprised delight in the West and (usually) shocked anger and bewilderment in Nigeria. (p. viii)

Most reviewers of Tutuola's books have taken for granted that they are meant to be novels, and this misconception has made for a good deal of critical clumsiness in judgment and some unfairness. If we suppose that the novel proper is a piece of prose fiction that has realistic characters, that deals with man in social relations, usually in a more or less contemporary setting, then surely the Tutuola works are something else again and are not fairly judged as novels.

Gerald Moore notices this mistake in placing Tutuola's fiction and reorients us by saying [in *Seven African Writers* (1962)] that Tutuola's "affinities are with Bunyan, Dante and Blake rather than with the Western novel." He calls Tutuola a "visionary" and his books "prose epics rather than novels." But though the names of Bunyan, Dante, and Blake usefully highlight the mythopoeic, non-realistic quality of Tutuola's works, only Bunyan is a fiction writer, and Moore does not pursue the very significant parallels between Bunyan and Tutuola beyond saying that neither had much formal education and both "seize upon the images of popular imagination and use them for their own purposes." The term "visionary" is somewhat vague for literary analysis, and "prose epic" is easily confused with Fielding's "comic epic in prose."

A really accurate genre-name for Tutuola's works would be "naive romances"; "naive" to distinguish them from the more sophisticated romances of William Morris or perhaps Hawthorne. The romance genre has been brilliantly distinguished and analyzed by Northrop Frye in his *Anatomy of Criticism*. Frye's placing of the "romance mode of fiction" by the degree of the "hero's power of action" seems exactly pertinent to Tutuola's ghost novels. (pp. 43-4)

[To] be really impressed with the pristine Africanness of Tutuola's novels one must hear something of his folklore marvels: the magical juju powers, especially the transformations. No more than the traditional Yoruba tale teller is Tutuola cribbed and confined in his literary imagination by such considerations as the dicta of logic, the literary canons of plausibility, or the scientific truths of vertebrate anatomy and physics. We can readily imagine that Tutuola's magical marvels are so many affronts to the positivistic and progressive creed of educated West Africans. (p. 71)

[The] first thing about [Tutuola's] work to strike the reader —and it strikes hard—is his language. It is probably altogether unique in the history of our literature. Vigorous and magnificently assured, it is wildly "incorrect," a kind of grand literary defiance of all the English-teaching schoolmarms of the world. (p. 96)

One quality not mentioned by the critics but noticeable to any reader who immerses himself in Tutuola's work and certainly worth mentioning is the stability, the self-consistency, the inevitableness of the language. The quality is not easy to describe, but we might say that when we have read a number of Tutuola's works, we catch ourselves reading conventional English as though it were Tutuolese, very much as when we return from abroad we read English signs as though they were in the foreign language we have recently been living with. Perhaps this is just a way of saying that Tutuola's English is not, like the clumsy freshman themes, merely ineptitude, but a real language with power.... [It] is not nearly as important to place Tutuola's English in the proper social and usage level as it is to recognize its power and grace. Gerald Moore quite correctly calls Tutuola "one of the two supreme stylists among living African prose writers" (the other is the French-speaking novelist Camara Laye). (pp. 98-9)

Tutuola's innocent manhandling of our language gives results that are extremely interesting for language study; [it suggests] the malleability of the language, the possibilities in the language for creative expansion and development, for freshness, and for the assimilation of alien ideas. (p. 103)

In Tutuola's fiction the imaginatively conceived monsters, the fanciful transformations, and other marvels of oral literature are somehow intellectually refreshing, like brainstorming sessions, utopian thinking, and the wild absurdities of *risqué* jokes. It would seem that our minds are in danger of getting petty and stuffy if we feed too regularly on commonplace reality. (p. 117)

The appeal of [Tutuola's] monsters and marvels is not escapist—that is, psychologically harmful. Tutuola's dream world is every bit as difficult for human intelligence and courage as our real world. The difficulties are often different in kind from those in the real world and so are many

of the means of opposing the difficulties, but the human qualities are much the same. And, in a sense, modern science and technology—and their own ingenuity—will one day provide the Nigerians with marvels almost as incredible as those in Tutuola's novels. (p. 118)

Although Tutuola is devoted to the mythical mode of thought, his works are full of graphic touches, clear and lively descriptions showing striking imaginative power, that should make the most inveterate partisans of realism lend momentary belief to his magical world. (p. 119)

Tutuola is a master in the evocation of the simple, uncomplicated emotion of fear. If in some romances terror is transmuted to delicious thrill, in Tutuola's romances it is terror pure—of course, a vicarious literary version of it— much like the intense fear of nightmares. It is the fear of trapped, helpless humanity in the presence of, or in the grip of, bestiality and malignancy. (p. 121)

Tutuola's humor is one of his most ingratiating qualities, both the humor he draws from his traditional sources and that due to his own creativity.... [Humor] is one of Tutuola's fortes and one likely to help him gain popularity.... Sometimes it is wild fancy that charms (a traditional Yoruba quality).... Much of Tutuola's humor is, of course, humor of hyperbole, which is also a traditional quality.... But perhaps Tutuola's best humor is humor of situation. (pp. 123-25)

But Tutuola's most important literary virtue is what we must call, for lack of a better term, his humanity—his compassionate view of human beings and his dramatizing and offering for his readers' admiration some of the saving traits of humanity: courage, resolution, persistence, ingenuity, resourcefulness, tolerance, kindness, and forbearance. His main characters, untrammeled by the usual human modes of moral bondage, are free from such idolatries as the devotion to slogans and fanatical ideals, to a domineering god or gods, to social standards, to war, to tribal traditions, to class mores, to sexual demands. They exhibit, after their own fashion, not a few of the cardinal virtues ascribed to the heroes and heroines of *Pilgrim's Progress* or *The Faerie Queene*—works in which, it might be added, monstrous elements exist in great abundance. (pp. 126-27)

It might be objected that [the] simple, uncomplicated virtues of Tutuola's characters are more admirable and pertinent in Tutuola's mythical world of physical and magical conflict with demons and ghosts than they are in our real world with its painfully complex moral conditions and its conflicts on so many different planes and in so many different relations. But surely simple virtues may have complicated applications, and just as surely in our day we are continually in danger of sophisticating our virtues into outright vices.

It might also be objected that a paralyzing fear in Tutuola's characters makes the moral atmosphere of Tutuola's mythical world unwholesome. It is true that fear is almost constantly in the minds of Tutuola's heroes and heroines and that this fear inspires in them some very rough combat tactics. On the other hand, this fear does not debase or brutalize the characters, or make them mean, suspicious, and cruel. Toward human beings, Tutuolan heroes and heroines are almost always generous, open, and kindly. Toward demons and hostile ghosts, they are at least open and aboveboard in their hostility.

One of the most striking peculiarities of Tutuola's protagonists is that they are wonderfully free from rancor and the desire for revenge.... In spite of the superficial paganism of Tutuola's romances, there are clear reflections of his Christian beliefs and his personal gentleness.

What then is the significance of Tutuola's work? He has made available to the world the human values of the Yoruba folk tales, in the way the folk tale collectors could never do. He is in the true Yoruba tradition of the professional storytellers, the *akpalo kpatita*, but he performs in every place in the world where there are readers. This fairly catholic reader believes Tutuola's work will endure for the vigor and interest of his language (never mind the errors and hardly ever mend them!), the force and economy and dramatic effect of his storytelling, his fertile imagination, his graphic descriptions, his wild humor, the compelling power of his nightmare flights, tortures, horrors, ogres, and transformations, and the great humanity of his gentle Christian soul, unembarrassed by the African past, Western technology, or indeed anything else. Surely one day Amos Tutuola will be recognized as West Africa's first classic in world literature. (pp. 127-28)

> *Harold R. Collins, in his* Amos Tutuola *(copyright 1969 by Twayne Publishers, Inc.; reprinted with the permission of Twayne Publishers, A Division of G. K. Hall & Co., Boston), Twayne, 1969.*

Tutuola's *The Palm-Wine Drinkard* stands out in its exuberant fantasy as *sui generis,* a light that never was on sea or land. This romance presents itself as a piece of spontaneous and primitive surrealism, the product of a dream-like imagination nourished by the marvels of traditional folklore and quite naively at ease before the supernatural. Tutuola's attitude is undisciplined by a European sense of reality, yet he seems at times ironically conscious of things European and of the contrast between Europe and Africa. The European may wonder whether these tales have been perhaps conceived in a more or less deliberate effort to escape the drab realities of an uncongenial colonialism or its subsequent dictatorships. In ... Tutuola's dream world ..., the *Drinkard* is fantastic and carefree. (pp. ix-xi)

> *Newton P. Stallknecht, "Foreword" to* The Emergence of African Fiction, *by Charles R. Larson, revised edition (copyright © 1972 by Charles R. Larson), Indiana University Press, 1972, pp. ix-xi.*

Amos Tutuola became the first "novelist" from tropical Africa to gain extensive exposure among Western literary audiences. Tutuola was not, however, the first novelist from Africa to be published by a European house. (p. 3)

These ... early African novelists [Thomas Mofolo, E. Casely-Hayford, and R. E. Obeng] shared one common bond: a certain reverence and awe for Christianity, which had led them along the pathway to Western education in the first place. Mofolo's novels were published by the church mission from which he had received his education. Tutuola, however, was strikingly different from these earlier novelists in that he broke away from Christianity.

Moreover, his use of the English language was notably original. Purists were shocked by Tutuola's irreverent use of

the English language, and ... the novel as a genre took on a slightly different shape because of Tutuola's imaginative use of Yoruba folk materials. (p. 4)

It was undoubtedly the language itself which first struck the non-African reader of Tutuola's work. In a certain sense, Tutuola has been fighting a battle ever since then with his fellow Africans, who have been embarrassed by what they have regarded as Tutuola's "irregular" use of English. And the *Drinkard* misled a number of Western literary critics into believing that Tutuola's language would be the language future Anglophone African writers would employ in their writing. Dylan Thomas, in a now famous review of *The Palm-Wine Drinkard*, referred to Tutuola's language as "young English by a West African ...". He was not alone. Anthony West, reviewing the American edition of the *Drinkard*, commented to much the same effect: "One catches a glimpse of the very beginning of literature, that moment when writing at last seizes and pins down the myths and legends of an analphabetic culture." West further added, *The Palm-Wine Drinkard* must be valued for its own freakish sake, and as an unrepeatable happy hit."

Yet, Tutuola has repeated his "hit" [several] times since the publication of the *Drinkard*, publishing ... novels and ... short stories in essentially the same Tutuolan style. And the critics—who if they are a little less awed now than they were in the early 1950's—have continued to contradict one another in their attempts to make his works fit into some pigeonhole of Western literature.... Lee Rogow referred to the work as a "fantastic primitive ... written in English, but ... an English with inflections and phrasings which make it seem like a new-born language...." Rogow, who appears to be amazed that Africans can write, adds, "The interest lies in the primitive play of language," a statement which in retrospect appears to be completely erroneous. For, if anything, the interest in Tutuola should be in his original use of mythology and folklore, that is, in what he has carried over from the oral tradition into a non-African literary genre known as the novel. (pp. 5-6)

More recently, Tutuola has begun to gain the recognition he deserves including a respect among his fellow Africans, who no longer seem to be quite as embarrassed about his presence as they were in the early 1950's. He is still, however, at the center of a continuous debate about his true stature in African literature, a debate which has still not decided exactly what it is that Tutuola has been writing for twenty years, to what genre his works belong. Tutuola is only an archetype in this instance, only one of a number of pioneer African writers who have frequently been misunderstood by non-African critics in their passion for place and order. Again and again, reading Western criticism of African writers one has the impression that the critic has noticed that something is different in African literature; yet this "differentness" is something the critic all too frequently has failed to put his finger on....

In a generally fine study called *Amos Tutuola*, Harold R. Collins struggles with the problem of categorization, yet never quite comes to the crux of the issue: the African writer's penchant for "bending" the novel form. (p. 7)

[Any] number of contemporary Western novelists would not fit in Collins' definition [of "the novel proper"] at all (Kafka, Nathanael West, Robbe-Grillet, among others.)... Collins is attempting to categorize Tutuola as an eighteenth or nineteenth century novelist, is trying to force him into a literary tradition dead both in the West and in Africa. (pp. 7-8)

The problem with Tutuola, as [Gerald] Moore notes [in *Seven African Writers*], is indeed the problem of the African writer in general today. The latter has long been caught in the curious dilemma of on the one hand being praised for the wrong reasons, and on the other hand tormented and attacked—again, usually for the wrong reasons. Moore also, it seems to me, has said the last word on the future of Tutuola's "curious form." No, Tutuola's novels are not the typical form of African fiction, (nor has his language been imitated by later writers) and as twenty years have shown, the African novel has not fallen into the Tutuolan pattern. Moore concludes: "Tutuola's books are far more like a fascinating cul-de-sac than the beginning of anything directly useful to other writers. The cul-de-sac is full of wonders, but is nevertheless a dead end." (pp. 8-9)

Amos Tutuola's universe is almost totally different from that of the Onitsha pamphleteers [African writers specializing in brief, topical, racy, pulp fiction]. While theirs is a world of urbanization and neo-realism, Tutuola's is one of jungle and bush—fantasy, supernaturalism, and surrealism. Whereas the Onitsha writers as a group regularly break almost every grammatical rule in the English language, Tutuola's private idiom is almost uniquely his own—sometimes heard in West African English but rarely duplicated by any other African writers. . . . It is easy to conclude that Tutuola's novels would be impossible to translate into other languages, yet Tutuola's works have been successfully translated into French, Italian, German, and many other languages. . . . Tutuola in the eyes of many students of African writing remains a "pure" example of contemporary African writing—the African writer par excellence—the only original African talent, almost totally uninfluenced by the West. No doubt these admirers of his work have come to this conclusion because of his clear relation to the oral tradition, myth, and archetype.

The oral tradition is an integral part of every work by Amos Tutuola, and it is exactly this reliance on the traditional tale which is anathema to many of Tutuola's readers, for he is not the kind of writer one is likely to have mixed opinions about. One either likes him or one does not. . . . Tutuola is first and foremost a story-teller—the major similarity he shares with his Onitsha contemporaries, for both are a link between traditional and modern African literature. In Tutuola's case, however, the story is not formula fiction but a highly skilled weaving of material from Yoruba culture—filtered through Tutuola's never-flagging imagination and reshaped in a narrative form often more closely related to the medieval quest or voyage narrative, *Gulliver's Travels, Pilgrim's Progress*, or, more recently, Nathanael West's *The Dream World of Balso Snell*, Céline's *Journey to the End of the Night*, or Kafka's *The Castle*. As with these later works, it is the psychological implications of Tutuola's world that many readers find so enthralling, his personal groping toward an understanding of man's relationship to the external world and the spirit world—the ontological gap. (pp. 93-4)

In Tutuola, West African "experimentation" in prose fiction reaches its zenith, for the oral tradition which he uses is more specifically a private mythology where daring tricks and innovations in time, space, and description—no doubt

at times unintentionally—attain a level which makes them almost pure examples of surrealism. This surrealism is indigenous or even spontaneous—not based on Tutuola's knowledge of the French surrealist movement. However, Tutuola's remarks about the brief amount of time he spends writing a novel suggest something akin to André Breton's theory of automatic writing: ". . . an attempt . . . to express, either verbally, in writing or in any other manner, the true functioning of thought. The dictation of thought, in the absence of all control by the reason, excluding any aesthetic or moral preoccupation." Except for the last comment about the "moral preoccupation," this definition characterizes Tutuola's writing quite patly.

Outwardly, like parts of Achebe's *Things Fall Apart*, Tutuola's *Palm-Wine Drinkard* is fragmented and shaped by many short and often apparently unrelated tales and incidents. Like Ekwensi's *Jagua Nana*, Tutuola takes his main character through a series of picaresque-like incidents and events. Thematically, there is the outer quest of the Drinkard in search of his lost palm-wine Tapster; inwardly this is paralleled by the voyage toward an understanding of the ontological gap—the relationship of man to his surrounding, his environment, the universe in which he lives. It is this essence of the voyage or inner journey of the Drinkard which makes it tempting to relate Tutuola's narrative to the symbolist and surrealistic writing of the early part of this century, and a case could be made for Tutuola's writing as an almost ideal marriage of the symbolist archetype of the dream, the subconscious, the super-ego. It must be acknowledged, too, that the non-African reader is often at a disadvantage in understanding many of the subtle nuances, private referents, and ethnic myths in Tutuola's writing. But also the reactions of his fellow Nigerians—including Yorubas—indicate that even being a Yoruba might not automatically lead to a full understanding of Tutuola's private world, in spite of the fact that a Yoruba student once told me that he had heard many of the tales and separate events in *The Palm-Wine Drinkard* as a child. Like all good storytellers, Tutuola makes up many of the incidents or substories in his novels, especially when he cannot find something suitable from his reserve of Yoruba folklore. (pp. 95-6)

It is in his use of time that Tutuola differs so widely from the Western writers with whom he has often been compared and even from some of his African contemporaries. In *The Palm-Wine Drinkard*, the reader is always conscious of time, because Tutuola constantly makes references to hours, days, weeks and months, even years; still there is the impression that many of the events that the Drinkard encounters are beyond the control of the normal dictates of time. (p. 102)

It may be easier to understand Tutuola's presentation of time by considering his references to temporal factors and their relationship to a more traditional value system. Such an interpretation gives us "evil time" and "good time" and in both categories time may be speeded up or slowed down. (p. 103)

It is easy to argue that in many literary works which are outside the bounds of realism—that in all tales and stories, and especially in folklore and mythology—time operates in no logical manner. Tutuola's world is not that simple, however, as his occasional references to time in his own life clearly indicate. In the five-page autobiographical account appended to *The Palm-Wine Drinkard*, Tutuola describes a youthful experience, by informing the reader:

I was trekking this distance of 23¾ miles. . . . If I left home at 6 o'clock in the morning, I would reach the village at about 8 o'clock in the same morning or when my people were just preparing to go to farm, and this was a great surprise to them, because they did not believe that I trekked the distance but joined a lorry. (p. 128)

Twenty-three and three-fourths miles in two hours through African bush would indeed make Tutuola one of the fastest runners in the world! When asked during an interview . . . how long it took him to write *The Palm-Wine Drinkard*, Tutuola replied "three days," later stating that most of his works take no more than two or three weeks. If this is true, one wonders why Tutuola has published only six works during his eighteen-year literary career.

The implication is certainly that Tutuola views time in some other way than we do in the West, as related to some definite system involving good (accomplishment) and evil (hindrance or stagnation); and, by extension, that time in an African sense has little to do with actual blocks of time as measured in a Western sense but rather with human values and human achievements. Certainly this is true of a number of other African novels far removed from the folkloristic domain. (pp. 105-06)

As a corollary, space and its treatment in *The Palm-Wine Drinkard* is also something frequently quite removed from the Western concept as shown in much Western fiction. Tutuola makes constant references to vast distances (to miles and miles and miles) that his hero and other characters are capable of covering in very limited periods of time in spite of the fact that in many cases there are no roads or pathways. . . . The Drinkard's advance [in one incident] is much like K's attempt to reach the castle in Kafka's novel, *The Castle*; time and space frequently repel one another. (pp. 106-07)

Also like Kafka, Tutuola's merging of time and space frequently leads to surrealistic passages, as the physical as-pects of the environment divide, alter, and coalesce into new forms. (p. 107)

It should also be noted that the Tutuolan world is replete with humor—often in the form of puns and curious anachronisms. There is a tendency, also, toward the didactic at the end of many of the incidents in the narrative and at many of the transitions from story to story. This didactic tendency, as we have . . . noted with other African writers, is in part a carry-over from traditional literary materials—in Tutuola's case the Yoruba oral tradition.

Storytelling is clearly at the heart of Tutuola's art, and Tutuola himself has said that even as a child he was admired by his playmates as a teller of tales. If this storytelling borders on the dreamlike, the surreal, the fantastic and the archetypal, we have only to note that Tutuola's tales are rooted in an oral tradition which is still very much alive in Yoruba society today—and the African reader often responds to these tales in a manner different from the non-African. In spite of the reshaping he often gives to his tales, Tutuola is for the African reader clearly a man whose work is grounded in the real world in which the African lives. When reading his work I am constantly reminded of the many essays I corrected when teaching English in Nigeria. Time and again, students related what to me appeared fantastic accounts of spirits and wild animals they had supposedly encountered in the bush. Tutuola's writing does just about the same thing. If Tutuola's imagination is frequently a bridge between the internal and the external world (the ontological gap), between the real and the surreal, between the realistic and the supernatural, we must at least point out in conclusion that passages of Tutuola's novels are rooted in a reality comparable to that of the more realistic works of his African contemporaries. . . . Yet how can we be certain that [any apparently realistic] passage may not be fantasy, and . . . may not represent reality to a mind that could create the writings of an Amos Tutuola? (pp. 111-12)

Charles R. Larson, in his The Emergence of African Fiction, *revised edition (copyright © 1972 by Charles R. Larson), Indiana University Press, 1972.*

U

UPDIKE, John   1932-

Updike is an American novelist and poet. A traditional novelist, he writes with ironic and literate complexity on contemporary themes. The "Rabbit" novels and the sensational *Couples* are particularly well known. (See also *Contemporary Authors*, Vols. 1-4, rev. ed.)

Although the ordered structures of the physical universe are endlessly fascinating to him and receive his admiring attention, the ambiguities of flesh are what bring out the best in John Updike. His work constantly takes up the theme of man as the Adam who awakens to a knowledge of his fallen state and to a realization of the immensity of the issues of good and evil. (p. 14)

Updike expects his readers to be literate. He assumes that references to world literature—to the Bible, to Boethius, to Beatrix Potter—will be recognized without being laboriously spelled out. In the greater part of Updike's work, indeed, there is a dialogue between the story he tells and other stories on the same theme that have established themselves within our cultural heritage and have helped to shape the Western imagination. Sometimes this dialogue is explicit; more often it is not. In "You'll Never Know, Dear" the theme of the world as a fair inevitably harks back to the classic presentation of Vanity Fair in Bunyan's *The Pilgrim's Progress*. Yet a more intimate link seems to exist between Updike's story and James Joyce's "Araby," from *Dubliners*, which itself contains clear reminiscences of Bunyan. (pp. 19-20)

The interplay of dualities and the experience of life as a series of paradoxes bulk large in Updike's fiction. This is the result of his viewing the world in the perspective of Christian faith. Taking such a stance, he does not simply use Christian motifs (as Joyce does) in order to point to the universality of the fall from the ideal to the actual, from the sacred to the profane. He sees existence as that which simultaneously hides and reveals the truth about itself, since truth ultimately lies beyond the bounds of space and time and yet must be grasped by creatures who are temporally and spatially limited. Thus he regards the passage from innocence to experience as neither a triumph nor a disaster, as neither a casting off of foolish illusion nor a fall from eternity into time. Insofar as innocence means an intuition of the eternal and the sacred, men should never travel so far away from it that they cannot return to the vision it

gives; and, insofar as experience means encounter with the actual world in all its ambiguity and complexity, men should never turn away from it under the impression that they can somehow escape the risks inherent in the human condition. (pp. 22-3)

One Updike story links with others, because Updike presents at all times a consistent universe where men reap what they sow and are rewarded by the god at whose shrine they serve, according to the nature of that god. (p. 24)

Even if the surface of his stories gives only the lesser part of his intention, this does not mean that the surface is irrelevant, or that any melody at all would serve as the sufficient foil to the countermelody. The two levels of his fiction, the literal and the symbolic, are mutually dependent. . . .

He has a high estimate of human intelligence, and a belief that every individual can use it to discover the kind of world he is living in. The givenness of an intelligible (though mystery-laden) universe, and the questioning mind of the individual who can respond to the given—these are the poles between which Updike slings his creative vision. In sharp contrast to despairing or defiant dogmatists who proclaim this terrestrial stage to be a cosmic Theater of the Absurd, he finds the world of nature and of man to be a place of intricate and marvelous patterns of meaning. (p. 28)

Updike's theme remains constant: earth seen in relation to heaven. Only the focus changes. And Updike's technique remains consistent also. Like Kierkegaard, he is adept at indirect communication. Kierkegaard explains that if a writer wishes to talk about religion to those who are immersed in the aesthetic sphere, then the necessary approach is to say: "Let us talk about aesthetics." Updike, in effect, says: "You think the Sexual Revolution to be highly topical and a particularly American theme? Well, let's talk about it." This—directly—he proceeds to do through the four hundred and fifty-eight pages of *Couples*, and the critics make comments about the author's self-indulgence and his lack of serious purpose or sense of responsibility. Meanwhile, the book sells, having been labeled "the thinking man's *Peyton Place*." Kierkegaard, in his day, complained that the public took in its right hand what he held out with his left. (pp. 215-16)

Couples is not in the least a sex-novel. Its purpose is neither to celebrate nor to denigrate sexuality, though it is true that many of the features of the analysis of Eros which have occupied such a prominent place in Updike's later short stories are to be seen here. The whole book finds its focus in precisely that aspect of life which the critics generally have accused Updike of failing to be concerned about: the social consequences of individual beliefs and choices. As in *The Poorhouse Fair*, so here Updike asks the question: "How fares America now?" And, even more pointedly than in his first novel, he gives the answer in terms of accounts left unsettled, talents buried in the ground of this world, and lines of division ignored until it is too late to escape judgment. (p. 216)

Technically regarded, *Couples* is the most ambitious of Updike's novels. . . . [Behind] the complex exterior action, Updike places an equally complex structure of biblical parallelism. . . . It is an ironical comment upon the quality of our educated consciousness that so many critics of *Couples* should think that Updike has written a superficial sex-novel and then dressed it up with a few "pretentious" allegorical motifs. The irony of the situation is the more complete in that Updike has built into his story indications that those who most pride themselves upon being the heirs and interpreters of Western culture are the very people least able to understand the living voice of that culture. These are prodigal sons who chew the dried husks of the wisdom inherited from the past and remain with empty bellies. (p. 217)

Updike's refusal to be heavily pretentious is the sign of his genuine seriousness. Because he sees the smallness of all earthly things set under heaven's jurisdiction, he also knows that nothing is too small to reflect the radiance of eternity. No event can be trivial in a universe ordered by truth and justice. (p. 243)

Updike's fiction is fully parabolic both in intention and in execution. . . . Updike's parables remind us that the quantitative and the qualitative are forever distinct. (p. 248)

Updike directs us to those aspects of earth which can speak to us of heaven and show us how to relate ourselves qualitatively to it. He gives us scenes from childhood, adolescence, young manhood, maturity, and old age—specific scenes set in one particular place at one particular time. He turns us from generalizations about a New Age to the concrete situations confronting us from day to day. And he lets us see that, behind the shifting surface of the experiences life brings us, there is one constant question which each of us must answer for himself: Does the universe, blindly ruled by chance, run downward into death; or does it follow the commands of a Living God whose Will for it is life?

Updike's answer to that question is unambiguous and given in Christian terms. Whether we agree with him or not is our own concern, for no man can answer for another or choose for him. But the elements of Updike's world are displayed before us so that we can enter imaginatively into his vision of the reality of things, a vision of earth set under heaven. (pp. 248-49)

Alice and Kenneth Hamilton, in their The Elements of John Updike *(copyright © 1970 by Wm. B. Eerdmans Publishing Co.; used by permission), Eerdmans, 1970.*

Updike [has] puzzled and disconcerted his audience, hanging them upon the horns of a critical dilemma. His work refuses to fit into the critics' neat formulations—which is all right since no novelist worth his salt will snuggle comfortably into anybody's prefabricated boxes; but it refuses *not* to fit into them as well—and that, too, is all right since it permits his work to be examined in context with and in juxtaposition to that of his contemporaries. But in insisting on having it both ways, Updike confuses his issues and opens himself to the charge of inconsistency. (p. 14)

I suggest that [Updike's intention] is to reveal the thing itself—scene, situation, character, even argument—as perceived, with no revelation beyond the perception. Because he honestly has no revelation to make. . . . Hence the ambivalence and inconclusiveness of the novels; hence the aimlessness of Rabbit's running and the promiscuity of Piet's coupling. They are logical results of Updike's intention. This does not mean that Updike is simply a mindless recorder or camera, unconcerned with ideas or themes, unaware of the truism and all its ramifications. Quite the contrary: ideas dominate his work, and the truism structures it. . . .

Updike does send his protagonists, after *Poorhouse Fair* at least, off on quests, presumably for identity, for a means to square themselves with the enigmatic universe. He confronts them with all the temptations both of flesh and spirit which the questing hero must face, with all the problems and the myriad solutions to them. But he is only nominally concerned with bringing his protagonists through successfully—or even unsuccessfully. His real concern is a critical examination of the temptations, the problems, the questions, and the answers as they conflict both inside and outside the protagonist, alternately promising and denying solutions to the quest. It is a question of emphasis: perception and examination rather than revelation are in fact his theme; the quest functions primarily as a structural motif. (p. 16)

Without identifying them specifically, Updike delineates the two philosophical forces in conflict carefully and unmistakably in all the novels as the two idealisms, pragmatic and transcendental, which have dominated American thought since colonial days. And in the process, he consistently introduces a subordinate third force, the Christian church, which he portrays most often as a compromising, frequently stupid, always inadequate keeper of the values which precipitate the conflict.

The primary thrust of Updike's conception of the conflict is anti-pragmatic. He decries the bastardization of the Jamesian ideal which results in the "vulgar" pragmatic Babbitry in the opening scenes of *Rabbit, Run*, in Mr. Springer's occupation, and in Reverend Pedrick's sermon at the outset of *Couples*. But, as his scorn for modern organized Christianity and his withering portrayals of do-gooders like Conner and Eccles illustrate, he also rejects the utilitarian reform aspects of applied pragmatic idealism. It should be noted, however, that Updike seldom sacrifices his objectivity to his contempt for pragmatic social reform. He is intent upon examining the phenomenon, perhaps critically, even negatively; but he retains his ironic detachment. He betrays little desire to effect a change, to reform the reformer as it were. As a matter of fact, if the pragmatist retains his individualism and his idealism, as does George Caldwell in *The Centaur*, he may earn Updike's grudging admiration.

But, though Updike implicitly favors the transcendental side in the conflict, he has little faith or confidence in it as an alternative to pragmatism. At the same time that it is the positive and desirable force, it lacks specificity and strength of the negative. It is nebulous, indefinable, and weak to the point of impotence. (p. 17)

Understandably, given his implied preferences, the irony in Updike's treatment of the transcendentalist position is hardly as cutting as that which he reserves for the pragmatic, though it serves the same purpose of establishing his detachment. Neither of the alternatives offers a satisfactory direction for the quest—the one because it is too shallow and earth-centered, the other because it is so unearthly as to be incapable of articulation or even of attainment. The conflict, in whatever terms it be cast, remains irresolvable.

As long as Updike maintains the objectivity which this method is meant to insure, his intention merely to portray the conflict without resolving it is clearly communicated. The intention is unmistakable in the intellectual and artistic, as well as physical, impotence of the Harry Angstrom of *Rabbit Redux*, in the open cynicism of the end of *Couples*, and even in *Of the Farm*, where Updike toys with existentialism as a possible alternative resolution. But when he allows himself to become intimately involved with his story and his people, as I believe he does in *Rabbit, Run*, he loses his detachment and the intention as a consequence becomes muddied and unclear.

Thus, those ironic fillips and twists which serve Updike to keep his people at arm's length don't work anymore, or else they double back upon themselves and become, ironically, unironic. And his abortive striving at the end of the novel to reaffirm his intention by portraying his Rabbit as mechanical and winding him up to run compulsively is, unlike Hook's unanswerable question and Peter's straining to say the unsayable and the "cured" Rabbit's broken lance, finally unsuccessful.

Curiously then, those things which contribute to the strengths of the other novels are the weaknesses of this one; and those things which would be the weaknesses of the others—involvement, commitment, the suggestion that Rabbit's quest might succeed—are the strengths of [*Rabbit, Run*]. For with the loss of detachment, Rabbit, Ruth, and Eccles become the most believable and sympathetic characters in Updike's canon, and the conflict which rests at the heart of all his work (indeed, the pragmatic-transcendental battlelines are more clearly drawn here than in any other) takes on an importance for the first and only time outside itself. It attaches to someone, to Rabbit, in a way that it doesn't in any of the other novels, and so it seems far more relevant, far less academic, though no less resolvable, here than elsewhere. For these reasons, *Rabbit, Run* is at once Updike's most imperfect and aggravating novel, and his most stimulating and important. Perhaps paradoxically, I believe that it is also his best. . . . (pp. 18-19)

> *Joseph Waldmeir, "It's the Going That's Important, Not the Getting There: Rabbit's Questing Non-Quest," in* Modern Fiction Studies (© 1974, by Purdue Research Foundation, West Lafayette, Indiana), Spring, 1974, pp.13-27.

Updike finds both his greatest challenge and his ultimate satisfaction as a fiction writer in the problems of narrative, in the recounting of patterned action in a voice enthralling to the listener. Because of this passion for telling stories, he is driven to seek the essence of the story, its original form, in which it satisfied some profound need of the human psyche for that pleasure which is found in the relief of anxiety through immersion in past event. But in following this movement backward into origins and essence, Updike encounters—as the examples of *Beowulf*, the *Mabinogian*, and Greek tales indicate—myth. In doing so, he finds, however, not a bloodless abstraction, an eternal thematic pattern of wisdom, but what the audience of Homer and Herodotus had found before him, namely, a traditional story about the past of the human, a story originally identified by the interchangeable terms "mythos" and "logos." In such stories the mythic and historical elements are not antagonistic forces vying for supremacy and ultimate authenticity but coordinate aspects of a narrative that unflinchingly encompasses the spectrum of conceivability. Thus, in *The Centaur* the quotidian details of a Trumanesque, cold-war America and the limpid vision of an immemorial Chiron and his pupils interact in a cooperative effort to render in a viable form the story of the nature of narrative in the twentieth century.

The novel's story in its most inclusive form is not so much a narrative about George Caldwell, his putative artist son Peter, Chiron, Prometheus, Zeus, or Ceres as it is a tale about the modern writer's drive, efforts, and need "to keep an organized mass of images moving forward." . . . *The Centaur* does not overtly introduce the writer as character or as voice into the narrative. The novel does, however, utilize several narrative styles and points of view whose effect is to increase our consciousness of the fictiveness of the narrative, of the presence behind the narrative masks of a shaping, manipulative voice speaking in several idioms. The end result of this technique is to create through the action and narrative of the novel the shadowy, spectral, but dominant figure of the story-teller himself (not . . . to be identified with John Updike the man) bringing something into the world that did not exist before without destroying something else. . . . The story of man's story-telling propensity is one in which, as *The Centaur* subtly and luminously demonstrates, myth and history, the archetypal and the quotidian are inextricably intertwined.

Perhaps the central quality of the story-teller is suggested by the novel's epigraph from Karl Barth: "Heaven is the creation inconceivable to man, earth the creation conceivable to him. He himself is the creature on the boundary between heaven and earth." Since Updike has avowed himself predisposed theologically to Barth, critics have related the epigraph to the prevailing religious dilemma of twentieth-century man as emblematically rendered by the twy-form of Chiron. Without in the least denying this dimension of the novel, I would like to suggest that the epigraph has additional, even more significant connections with myth and the story-teller. The crucially operative terms for *The Centaur* are not the religiously flavored one of "heaven" and "hell" but the imaginatively oriented ones of "conceivable" and "inconceivable." The inconceivability of heaven is an index of creative, imaginative limitation, whereas the conceivability of earth circumscribes the ordinary scope of the human imagination. But since a variety of religious narratives have rendered something of the nature of heaven, there is clearly a sense in which the inconceivable is expressible. Man's ultimate and basic position on the boundary between the conceivable and the inconceivable is identical with his power to narrate what Aristotle called probable impossibilities, to tell stories that breach the constrictions of what mankind conceives to be the case. And the individual who regularly encompasses the ordinary and the extraordinary, the conceivable and the inconceivable, is the maker of fictions, the teller of stories, whom today we call the writer.

While Barth and Updike as Christians stress the creatureliness and finiteness of man, *The Centaur* reveals a secular variant of the later Barth's stress upon the sacred narrative and God's entrance into man's world through the Word. As the central figure described in the novel, Chiron's centauric nature represents Barth's boundary creature struggling to reconcile the conceivable and the inconceivable but destined to find them forever antinomies, however variable and shifting their content. On the other hand, the narrative developed through nine chapters and an epilogue and cast in a variety of styles and points of view is a made thing that includes not only inconceivable mythic monsters, gods, goddesses, and events but also all too conceivable ordinary fathers, sons, mothers, sweethearts, and actions. Its maker is the teller of the story, and it is he who through the narrative word provides the means by which the more-than-human impinges directly on ordinary mankind, who in this case is identified with the reader of the novel.

Seen from this perspective, *The Centaur* appears less a piece of tricksy ingenuity, stylistic bravura, and leg-pulling pastiche than a daring, tautly economical exploration of the meaning and scope of narrative and the potentialities of the story-teller as a figure at the very heart of human achievement. At the core of the story-teller's art, as we have seen, is myth, "what is said." . . . Updike himself specifies five distinct ways the Chiron myth functions in *The Centaur*. Given this, it is not perhaps too much to suggest that he is not only utilizing many of the major modalities of myth but also striving to structure them into a single narrative form. (pp. 32-5)

> *John B. Vickery, "'The Centaur': Myth, History, and Narrative," in* Modern Fiction Studies (© 1974, by Purdue Research Foundation, West Lafayette, Indiana), Spring, 1974, pp. 29-43.

The problem with *Couples*, of course, is all that sex. All that sex, however, can be understood as a complex metaphor for man's relation to and examination of death. Just as the characters seem to be continually alert for the sexual main chance or gauging someone else's sexual liaisons, so they carry an ever growing shadow of knowledge of their own mortality. Freddy Thorne says that the two comical things in this world are "the Christian church and naked women. . . . Everything else tells us we're dead." "Comical" here involves the classic Aristotelian understanding of the word "comedy" as opposed to tragedy. It suggests that Updike divides the world into two kinds of experiences, tragic and comic. Death and its relatives, "everything else," characterize the tragic (Lear, Orestes), and relief from that, hope and faith, comes in the Christian church and sex which turn a person away from himself. On the most obvious level, "naked women" draw male attention away from themselves, outward. In Freddy's comment, the

sexual encounter is a way the participants face death and are released from its bonds. Just as people are "lost" when they give themselves up entirely to the sexual experience, so the Christian Church preaches that a man should "lose himself" in God. (pp. 45-6)

Except for Piet and Foxy, the couples have abandoned the Puritan virtues of duty and work, the mores setting institutional church, and the Horatio Alger dream. "Virtue, that which defines manhood, strength, and meaning was no longer sought in temple or marketplace but in the home—one's own home, and then the homes of one's friend". . . . The center of the community's social life and standards has become their circle of friends. As the church has been adorned by craftsmen, a blending of the world's art and status objects (pew cushions, air conditioning), so have the homes been. As the behavior and values of the marketplace had been rationalized and justified, so the couples' have been. As the church and American dream stood between man and *timor mortis*, so the couples' social life. Rituals of helping one another, examination of soul, corporate worship, and communion exist. *The New Yorker* and *The Nation* replace hymnals, Freddy Thorne's perverted humanism the sermon. (p. 46)

Piet is a non-believer, a throw-back to the pre-Pill accountable world, a man unwilling to play games. . . . The novel's movement is Piet's search for the vote for happiness and his progression from one false God to another. His success is marked in part by his ability to regard Thorne benignly at the end. He can joke "my mentor and savior" . . . and acknowledge the truth in that as well as in Freddy's good intentions. But he is not Freddy's or anyone elses' disciple at last. (p. 47)

Updike is a realist, however. Undergirding Piet's revelation is the affirmation that nothing very much is changed. (p. 52)

> *Paula and Nick Backscheider, "Updike's Couples: Squeak in the Night," in* Modern Fiction Studies (© 1974, by Purdue Research Foundation, West Lafayette, Indiana), Spring, 1974, pp. 45-52.

The results of [Updike's] painstaking care are apparent on every page of [*Couples*], but perhaps never as impressively as in the two extensive parlor games he makes his characters play. These are formal activities in the process whereby these "heirs of the Puritans" are observed "growing old and awful in each other's homes." The less formal activities in this process, drinking, quarrelling, love-making, and so forth, call forth Updike's many other skills, but these two games, "Impressions" in part II and "Wonderful" in part III, reveal how meticulously he had worked out the construction and relationship of character, theme, and detail in the book. One is reminded (in spite of the differences in reticence and irony) of the parlor games in Jane Austen's *Emma*, where formal exchange under intentionally ambiguous circumstances is also skillfully exploited to reinforce the implications of other passages in the novel. (p. 53)

If a study of these two games leads to a realization of the careful construction and precise detail throughout the novel, then the . . . analogy with Jane Austen will not seem so far-fetched. This may serve to place the emphasis on *Couples* where it belongs, and where its author put it, on the craftsmanship, and not on the sex. (p. 58)

Alan T. McKenzie, "'A Craftsman's Intimate Satisfactions': The Parlor Games in 'Couples'," in Modern Fiction Studies (© 1974, by Purdue Research Foundation, West Lafayette, Indiana), Spring, 1974, pp. 53-8.

Updike . . . carefully details minutia, not of "American reality," whatever that is, but of our ordinary experience. Updike has too much to say and, worse, he says it much too late. *Rabbit Redux*, for instance, chronicles the history of the sixties, and it tells us what we have already known about youth, drugs, the Vietnam war, black protest, the loss of the American dream. . . . *Rabbit, Run* . . . told us what we knew, not what we should know. . . . And even though Updike uses the present tense in the Rabbit books, the form in general is that of the traditional sociological novel, with an especially high degree of symbolic and metaphorical artistry.

The shortcoming of the Hamiltons [Alice and Kenneth, in their study, *The Elements of John Updike*, excerpted above] is that their interpretation of Updike places all the emphasis upon the individual's relationship with God, specifically a Christian encounter. Updike admittedly seems Christian in his interests and in one aspect of his cosmic vision, but in *The Centaur*, for instance, the richness of the book derives from strata of time—geologic, mythic, and Biblical, and not from a Christian interpretation. The obvious irony is that the Christian values Rabbit was inculcated with as a child are a handicap to his human well-being, which may be fine for Christians in an afterlife, but which seem inimical to secular life which surely might include harmony between the earthly and the heavenly—in human values of love, brotherhood, and kindness. Can either Updike or the Hamiltons seriously believe that Christianity is the solution to urban blight, pollution, drug addiction, adultery, unemployment, and war? Or do they naively believe after nearly 2,000 years of Christianity, it will suddenly solve men's secular problems, not only for Christians, but also for skeptics, Jews, Moslems, and atheists? Such an interpretation of Updike's works stems from his concern with the kind of corrupt humanism that the contemporary world has been battered with, but is there a significant difference between corrupt Christianity and corrupt humanism? Updike values human life, sacrifice, and kindness, and these values need no foundation in Christianity in order to be valid. (pp. 59-60)

Updike calls attention to white American Protestant bigotry as much as he condemns a Protestantism that increasingly dismisses concepts of sin and God in favor of a social do-goodism which requires no necessary religious justification. He mourns, in *Rabbit Redux*, the loss of values which are Christian but only incidentally so. The Hamiltons are correct in asserting that Updike is an allegorist, but his allegories deal with broadly American values and not with a puritanical conception of God and Satan at war for men's souls. . . .

He has allowed self-knowledge on the part of Rabbit in *Redux*, a quality few of his characters have previously had. It is as if the author himself has been holding in abeyance the inevitable truth that knowledge brings sadness, and, consequently, *Redux* can rightfully be called Updike's most mature work, because finally the vision presented in his fic-

tion is tough enough to withstand the truth. In his previous works, the "truth" exists, but it is just beyond reach. (p. 61)

Rabbit Redux is a curiously old-fashioned novel, dealing with America's heightened consciousness of wrong-doing, at home in its oppressive treatment of black Americans, and abroad in its waging so futilely so brutal a war. Just over the horizon is America's bicentennial, and it is as if Updike is writing a spiritual and sociological history of the nation as it approaches its third century. Updike perhaps appropriately deals with the loss of the American dream though for students of American culture it seems bizarrely late to risk so threadbare a theme. (p. 62)

Alice and Kenneth Hamilton have argued aggressively and convincingly that Updike has constantly dealt with the abundance of God's saving grace for those who will freely accept it. Their explication of Updike rather diminishes the complexity of his characters, makes Christianity sound like the only plausible theoretical understanding of human existence, and loses sight of the large capacity for compassion in Updike. It has to be acknowledged that the meaning of God has always been a concern of Updike and that Biblical allusion is common, but the Hamiltons' interpretation of these seems, at times, arbitrary and almost too pat, too simple, as if religious belief is as easy as buying a new household appliance. Religious belief in Updike's works is far more difficult to achieve than that, and rather than seeing Updike as somewhat indignantly and impatiently developing his main characters as examples of obtuse disbelievers, it is surely more accurate to see sympathy for those who suffer while wanting to believe. . . . Christianity as it is presented in *Rabbit, Run* hardly seems to be an answer to the problems of contemporary Christian Americans. The final symbol for it is the darkened church window which Rabbit glances at in order to find that physical presence in which to glimpse, through its colored fragments of glass, some bright spiritual reality. But the church (Christianity) has turned off its light, and the Hamiltons don't seem to perceive that. (pp. 64-5)

For the Hamiltons to argue that Updike finds the turning from God responsible for America's problems reduces Updike to a simple-minded WASP. That Updike denounced Conner's scientific humanism in *The Poorhouse Fair* does not mean that Updike hates humanism. Rather, Updike's fiction is calling for a humanism that has little justification in theology. Its elements are rather simple: joy, love, warm family ties, beauty in our lives, social justice. To achieve these in modern America is difficult in part because our technology, not our loss of faith in God, is inimical to these values. . . . This does not indicate that Updike is skeptical about humanism, but rather that he is skeptical that technology is going to produce a humanism that is not totally corrupt. It is evident that the value of Updike's analysis lies in his sensitivity to the complexity of the problem. Neither technology nor religion offers hope, so where then should we turn? (pp. 65-6)

The contradictions in Updike are symptomatic of the society he fictionalizes. Where he differs from his contemporaries is in his lack of despair, perhaps the most fashionable mode of the present time. Pop Angstrom and Rabbit are both pleased with the essential goodness and fairness of their fellow beings, and this kind of American faith underlies Updike's fiction. His is a sober concern for human life, one too few critics have been willing to perceive because of a presumed aridity of thought and sterility of style. It is surprising perhaps to find so talented a writer apparently dealing with the tiredest of clichés, yet American fiction, for all its brashness of subject matter and lavishness of experimental forms, has hardly yet gone beyond anything other than the dominant theme of the fall from innocence, the failure of the American dream (which may never have had conscious existence), and the most dominant theme of all, of attempting to find the connections which should link the individual to a society and to a cosmic scheme in oneness and harmony. Whitman tried hardest, and even he breaks down in the consideration of death by proclaiming its beauty and rightness or advising his reader-disciples not to bother their brains about it or about God. John Updike has been on this large quest throughout his novels, and with the reconciliation of Rabbit to time as the element human life lives in, there is some promise in genuine détente with dissolution. In many ways *Rabbit Redux* reaffirms that American fiction cannot portray maturely either love or death, but that, unlike some other national literatures, the insolvability of love and death is our national literary riddle. (pp. 70-1)

One of the striking oddities of Updike's fiction is the predominance of nearly pornographic depiction of sexual acts, presented with puritanical disgust, but relish, to symbolize the denial of life urges, an assertion of loneliness, or as exploitation. One might imagine that if love is an achievable value, we might be shown it. Instead, Updike generates even less emotional feeling about sexually expressed love than Hemingway. Few characters in Updike's fiction are capable of love on any level. Although they engage compulsively in free sexuality, they find no pleasure, no relief or release. (p. 71)

In his urgency to exploit the open interest in sexuality while simultaneously being critical of it, Updike loses sight of the significance of both love and sex. As symbols for degradation of a human being or a nation, the sexuality of *Rabbit Redux* functions well: but there is always in Updike's work a contradiction between the ideal of sexual love and genuine depiction of it. (p. 72)

As a *vade mecum* to survival in the seventies, *Rabbit Redux* will not attract a large following. There is little "style" to be emulated; the doctrine is not fashionable, nor does it promise entertainment. . . . If we live in a secular world, partitioned from God, at least temporarily, how are we to conduct ourselves? Nelson would answer with pop culture existentialism that we must assume responsibility for our lives and actions; Rabbit would answer skeptically that, given theoretically unlimited possibilities for happiness, beauty, and good, but an actuality in which nothing is any more what it once seemed to be or is, in fact, not what it pretends to be, we have recourse only to unattractive compromise, to time among other things, to enduring sorrow, to trying to cope with the mess we have made, without cynicism and without much hope except in a faith that human beings are essentially kind, though frequently ignorant, selfish, and shortsighted. (p. 75)

> *Wayne Falke, "'Rabbit Redux': Time/Order/God," in* Modern Fiction Studies (© 1974, by Purdue Research Foundation, West Lafayette, Indiana), Spring, 1974, pp. 59-75.

For those who condemn Updike (and to a lesser extent, Durrell) for the deliberately self-conscious and mannered virtuosity of his language and who deride him for failing to explain the mystery and wonder that pervade his stories and for those who condemn him for neatly closing his stories in the gnomic, didactic, and perfectly circular manner of an Aesopian Fable, all I can say in earnest rebuttal is this: being committed to the eye, and to things near and known within its periphery and being fully—if not tragically —aware of the Kantian artifice and gratuity of the mind's fictional constructions, and being reverentially devoted to mandala imagery as the psychic manifestation of God's graceful intervention, Updike is, therefore, not so much in pursuit of perfection, as he is of "completion"; or, rather, say that perfection IS completion and that Updike's completed circular stories are themselves a kind of superimposed "pattern of order" which, like the repetitive appearance of Jung's compensatory mandalas, make oblations of order and harmony to a human psyche distraught with chaos and confusion. (pp. 95-6)

> *Robert Alton Regan, "Updike's Symbol of the Center," in* Modern Fiction Studies (© 1974, by Purdue Research Foundation, West Lafayette, Indiana), Spring, 1974, pp. 77-96.

Updike feels that his meticulous stylistic ornamentation deserves more careful evaluation than it generally receives [according to his comment in "Henry Bech Redux"]: "All the little congruencies and arabesques prepared with such delicate anticipatory pleasure are gobbled up [by insensate critics] as if by pigs at a pastry cart." But if Updike's critics befoul his stylistic lacework, often-times they feel that they have to dig too deeply for his contentual truffles, the "larger issues." The question of whether Updike's characterizations elicit our compassion and sympathy is pertinent here. Much of his fiction does, in fact, seem to be emotionally vapid; one senses successful pathos or poignancy in characterization only infrequently. . . . The fact is . . . that Updike does have a great deal to say. His fiction is indeed surcharged with hidden meaning and so "highbrow" as to be intimidating. To a greater degree than most of his contemporaries, Updike treats the larger issues in the subsurface architechtonics of his fiction. (pp. 98-100)

Updike is concerned with human needs vs. society's demands. There is an inherent tension in man, much of which derives from the pressures of civilized society, the codes of conduct that would legislate the human condition. Updike feels that "to be a person is to be in a situation of tension, is to be in a dialectical situation. A truly adjusted person is not a person at all—just an animal with clothes on or a statistic". . . . For Updike, "unfallen Adam is an ape." Man is a *naked* ape who attempts "to lead on this terrestrial ball,/With grasping hand and saucy wife,/The upright life," but who inevitably vacillates between individual wants and social dictates. Unlike all other animals, he is a "thinking animal" with a "grasping hand," which is both responsible for a highly technological society and symbolic of his acquisitive nature. His "saucy wife" signals the less attractive aspects of monogamy; the "upright life" of a faithful marriage and righteousness *per se* are threatened by instinctual desires. (p. 101)

Other than his concern with religious elements and the

treatment of nostalgia, Updike's treatment of "sex and death as riddles for the thinking animal" remains the most important focal point for examining his fiction. Indeed, especially in his later fiction, a good case can be made for the sex-and-death themes being his chief concerns. With such a focus in mind one cannot fail to discern the meaningfulness and richness of texture in Updike's fiction. What is often mistaken as a pretentious style is merely Updike's . . . objective amplification of surface detail and his particular and express refusal to preach to the reader. Updike . . . is very much concerned with "the problems of the human heart in conflict with itself." But he deals not so much with individual psychologies as with an aggregate portrayal of the human condition. If his characters are often on the psychological level emotionally jejune, as focal points for the human paradox they are ample. Not only the "little congruencies and arabesques" of his prose but his social commentary, too, places him squarely within the first rank of contemporary writers. A hasty perusal of his fiction will invariably result in disparagement and esthetic "indigestion." (p. 105)

> *Robert S. Gingher, "Has John Updike Anything to Say?," in* Modern Fiction Studies *(© 1974, by Purdue Research Foundation, West Lafayette, Indiana), Spring, 1974, pp. 97-105.*

Because of their brevity, Updike's short stories often provide more accessible examples of structural subtlety than his novels where the architectonics are more cumbersome and, consequently, more difficult to comprehend as a whole. "Should Wizard Hit Mommy?", one of the finest stories from the 1962 collection *Pigeon Feathers*, provides an excellent illustration of the way structure can, with the greatest economy, invest a superficially simple story with deep layers of meaning.

"Should Wizard Hit Mommy?" employs a structural technique much used in other genres, but not much used in short stories (with the notable exception of those in the local color tradition)—namely, the "form within a form" technique, here the story within a story. In the frame story, a young father, Jack, is telling his four-year-old daughter, Jo, a ritualistic nap-time tale. In this instance, however, Jack varies the formula of the familiar narrative in such a way as to create discomfort and dismay in the child who is his supple audience. Finishing his story-telling, Jack goes dutifully downstairs to assist his pregnant wife, who is beginning the task of painting the living-room woodwork. Updike's frame story then ends with a haunting word-picture of Jack's weary feeling of being in a cage with his wife and of not wishing "to speak with her, work with her, touch her, anything."

Although the frame story is rendered with those superb touches of everyday realism for which Updike is so famous, there are few details with which the reader can avail himself for the construing of Jack's character or for the intellectual understanding of the resentment which seethes in Jack at the story's close. The reader may be hard-pressed to say what major truths are revealed in the story, but he is, nevertheless, unlikely to feel totally disappointed in the work: he will sense that the denouement is somehow right and that Jack's depression at the end is justified somehow by the story itself. What the reader instinctively but unconsciously responds to is the delicately contrived interrelationship of the frame story and the story within the story. (pp. 111-12)

"Should Wizard Hit Mommy?" the title of the story asks. Because of the interplay of the structural parallels Updike has created, it also asks, "Should Jack strike out at Clare?" And what is this but the concrete expression of the artist's universal dilemma: should the artist defend himself against the prosaic responsibilities that circumscribe his creative imagination? (p. 115)

> *Albert J. Griffith, "Updike's Artistic Dilemma: 'Should Wizard Hit Mommy?'," in* Modern Fiction Studies *(© 1974, by Purdue Research Foundation, West Lafayette, Indiana), Spring, 1974, pp. 111-15.*

Two-thirds closet drama and one-third lumpy essay, the whole once intended to coalesce into a novel—no wonder John Updike presents [*Buchanan Dying*] to us much as a father would introduce an ill-formed child: affectionately, and with a parent's commitment, but a little nervous, too, about how it looks to us. And the sorry truth is, it doesn't look very good. I'll summon a few kind words in a moment, but from any realistic perspective, Updike's first attempt at a play must be considered the runt of his otherwise impressive litter.

First, the form. It is a play meant to be read, which is another way of saying it is not a good *play*. (pp. 82, 85)

Updike attempts to re-create the diction of Buchanan's times. Virtually every writer of historical fictions from Shakespeare to Anthony Burgess has made contemporaries of his characters; for the sake of vitality it is only sensible to have Caesar speak as an Elizabethan or a sardonic American statesman. But Updike has gone to speeches and letters for his phrases and the result lies thick in the ear: "Then cast off this prothonotarial tether," cries one of Buchanan's drinking buddies. Buchanan's own speech frequently presses against the rhythms of blank verse. (pp. 85-6)

Updike's portrait of the man is sympathetic, intelligent, concerned. There are scenes in the play, and sections in the long concluding essay, that are felicitous and interesting—but not enough to redeem this wordy, ungainly and ultimately ill-advised attempt at theater. (p. 86)

> *Peter S. Prescott, "Immobile President," in* Newsweek *(copyright 1974 by Newsweek, Inc.; all rights reserved; reprinted by permission), June 24, 1974, pp. 82-6.*

Updike has chosen to build his play [*Buchanan Dying*] around . . . the education of Buchanan's heart. The focus of Act I is young Buchanan's engagement to marry Anne Coleman. Unwilling to face the abyss of unreason that passionate love would open, he subtly rejects the girl, who then kills herself. The focus of Act II is the constitutional impasse of Buchanan's last months as president. Here the unreasoned passions of the South meet the same cautious, legalistic response as did Miss Coleman's libido. The last act shows Buchanan finally confronting the horror of human life in a world purged of divine reason. He recoils, turns back to conventional faith, and dies.

If Updike's play held one's attention, its unhistorical features would matter less. But the story must bewilder any reader unacquainted with the details of Buchanan's life. The scene is the dying man's bedroom. As his now disorderly mind produces events or illusions, they are acted out. Real people come to see him, interrupt the reveries, and are absorbed into them. The sequence of episodes is not chronological but dreamlike.

For this poetic blending of internal idea and external reality there are precedents in Updike's novels, where he often dwells on the ghostliness of his people. The structure of the novels is rarely a line of probable actions, each producing the next. The arrangement of the incidents is more often arbitrary, associative, poetic. The motives and affections of the characters change unpredictably. Even scenes of high drama, like the burning of the church in *Couples*, are undercut by Updike's taste for parody and ventriloquism. The expanding use of recent public events in *Couples, Bech*, and *Rabbit Redux* might have prepared us for the poetic use of history in *Buchanan Dying*. The displays of mimicry in the novels also foreshadow Updike's pleasure in catching the voices of the forty-odd speakers in his play.

The dreamlike pattern of the play rests on the repetition of themes and gestures, images and situations. The bells that punctuate various sections take us back to the bell Mrs. Buchanan is said to have hung about her son's neck when he was tiny, so he would not be lost while exploring the woods. So their sound suggests the lure and danger of the irrational, the mystery of human wickedness, the fragility of institutions meant to keep us in the ways of righteousness. The women keep dissolving into Anne Coleman. Buchanan's failure to respond to her is the crucial event that echoes through other memories and hallucinations; and her loss deepens the guilt he suffered (according to the playwright) over his elder sister Mary, who died the year he was born. Letters, messages, decisions tend to revive scenes from the early love affair. One infers that all the crises of a man's life are re-enactments of those that first shaped his character—an insight (if it is one) neither fresh nor exciting enough to compensate readers who persist to the end of the play.

For all the scholarly apparatus of the book, Updike's account remains dubious history. Information about Buchanan's connection with Miss Coleman is exceedingly thin, and his later treatment of women does not suggest that her death scared him away from them. The tale of the girl's suicide is a remote piece of unreliable gossip. Updike represents her as an anti-establishment intellectual, rich and neurotic, pulsing with eros—a spiritual ancestor of Jill in *Rabbit Redux*. But history gives us no reason to believe that Miss Coleman was a devotee of new thought or of sexual experiment.

Neither does it trouble Buchanan with the eccentric theology that Updike ascribes to him. Here we possess reliable information, and it contradicts Updike's representation of a man unable to digest the element of evil in humanity. Even a softened Calvinism would acquaint any systematic thinker with the depravity of mankind. As Dr. Johnson said, only the desert or the cell can exclude it from notice; and Buchanan was neither a hermit nor a nun. The fear of the irrational that drives the character in the play does link Buchanan's frigidity to his legalistic politics. But Updike does not try to make the rest of the person cohere. Instead,

he has Buchanan confess that his own deepest problem is the split between self and action.

The feature of the play that should transcend its confusion is the vividness of the separate dialogues and their revelation of personality. In *Rabbit Redux* the first meeting of Harry, Babe, and Skeeter, at Jimbo's, shows with how much brilliance and conviction Updike can reproduce voices not his own. In the play this talent is whittled away. If one knows the background well, the language will often sound anachronistic or false. A woman capable of writing Mrs. Buchanan's letters would hardly talk to her son in the primitive idiom the play allots to her. But even if one has no history, the speeches too often sound flat and mechanical, perhaps because many of them are quick paraphrases of historians' accounts. (pp. 6, 8)

One does not get the impression that Updike has worked overtime to elaborate the design and smooth the seams of the play. The line of action will puzzle most readers, with its arbitrary leaps in time, its mixture of living, dead, and illusory figures, its quick succession of half-identified persons and little speeches. The treatment of the characters changes inexplicably from sympathetic to ironical, and Updike stands on surprisingly neutral ground in the judgment of Buchanan's virtues and faults.

Some illumination is provided by the long afterword, in which Updike validates his scholarship while chatting about the sources of his information and the way he came to write the play. Here he spreads out some of the materials he could not fit into the text, and here he offers what is the most careful and valuable literary accomplishment in the book, an excellent ballad imitation dealing with an episode in Buchanan's early career. (p. 8)

> *Irvin Ehrenpreis, "Buchanan Redux," in* The New York Review of Books *(reprinted with permission from* The New York Review of Books; *copyright © 1974 NYREV, Inc.), August 8, 1974, pp. 6, 8.*

John Updike is a slummer. In his fiction. Extradited from the real world to imaginary Brewer or Tarbox, I doubt if he could sustain ten minutes' conversation with Rabbit Angstrom, with any of the many singles in *Couples*. Updike's characters don't deserve a form letter obituary, let alone a novel. They are pathetic folk; even the pathos is undistinguished. Great issues aren't at issue in Updike's fiction. When ignorant armies clash by night, his people are somewhere else on the beach, skinny dipping perhaps.

Updike is our genteel Gentile: the sweet, lonesome singer of Protestant mediocrity. For his first historical venture [*Buchanan Dying*] Updike has chosen America's rabbit, run President: James the Worst. In another novelist it would seem affectation. In Updike it's merely shyness, modesty, and—despite all the bestsellers—under-confidence. . . .

Eccentric, sure: Updike belongs in a Cheever novel. And, like most eccentrics, he is not a funny man. You may laugh at the aptness of his characterizations or, for joy, at the nifty metaphors, but there is no slapstick in his heart. Updike people don't astonish you; they don't do preposterous things. That, after all, would be another gross abuse. Updike, the gentleman, never asks you to suspend disbelief. He takes Rabbit and Pennsylvania and, yes, James Buchanan dead seriously. This is a nice trick. The title itself appears crammed with bathos, *Buchanan Dying*. Might as well be *The Dialogues of Calvin Coolidge* or *Archie Bunker Agonistes*. But Updike has been fair to Buchanan. This fairness is certainly a strength: his first ground rule. It's also a severe limitation. Updike takes none of those liberties which are the novelist's only pleasure. He's a middle class realist. By all standards Updike should be unread. He is read a lot. It's the best tribute yet to frankness and deft style. . . .

Yet, one or two stage directions aside, that style is absent with leave in *Buchanan Dying, A Play*. Updike, of course, has perfect pitch: his mimic ear fixes the several accents of nineteenth century America. But these are mostly public accents. . . . The play is trite in form: a pastiche of letters, speeches, reported confrontations. Blackouts over the death bed provide bridges. Updike handles it well enough; still this dramatic mechanism is hackneyed as the flashback montage in film.

Buchanan is Updike's kind of people. The well-intentioned, middling man, hung up in a rundown between North and South, abolitionist and slave-holder. Despite presidential prerogatives, he's hardly more decisive than Rabbit Angstrom, vegetating between moonwalkers and militant blacks. Buchanan is also Updike's kind of Christian: that's to say, he'd made agnosticism look zealous. (pp. 987-88)

Updike is fair to just about everyone; he must be a superb father and husband. There are neither villains nor saints in his fiction. He plumps for no ideology: that would be an abuse of the artist's position. In fact, John Updike, out of kindness or acedia, has very little to say. And no one writing in America says it better. (p. 988)

> *D. Keith Mano, "Doughy Middleness," in* National Review (© *National Review, Inc., 1974; 150 East 35th St., New York, N.Y. 10016), August 30, 1974, pp. 987-88.*

About *Buchanan Dying*, John Updike's long play dealing with the last days of America's fifteenth president, the reader will probably also ask the one truly fatal question: who cares? I'll admit to caring deeply about Updike, but the book is almost heroically boring, a tribute to the author's beloved Pennsylvania which should have been put away in a drawer and forgotten. What's happened to Updike over the past decade would be interesting to discuss. But all I can say here is that his gifts for lyric social observation don't function in historical drama, and when things aren't fully meshed for him, Updike leans too hard on his pen. (p. 50)

> *Peter Straub, in* New Statesman (© *1975 The Statesman & Nation Publishing Co. Ltd.), January 10, 1975.*

John Updike may be America's finest novelist; he is, with Saul Bellow, the most intelligent, and surely he is one of the most interesting—a self-mocking, sex-obsessed Christian of the strict construction, and chronicler, in the waning days of our century, of the small-town Babylons, the post-Pill paradises, as he once described them, that dot the map of our Northeast. His seventh and newest novel, *A Month of Sundays*, is quintessential Updike, a veritable Rosetta Stone to his hieroglyphs and likely to be scrutinized a gen-

eration or two or three from now as runic clues to the times we live in.

"Forgive me my denomination and my town; I am a Christian minister, and an American," he begins, writing in the person of his protagonist Tom Marshfield, who is spending a month in a desert sanitarium, a sort of half-way house for slipped clerics. Some will find it necessary to forgive Updike more than his narrator's vocation and milieu. There are, for instance, the florid metaphors and alliterative excesses to contend with, the self-consciously convoluted, Nabokovian prose, the parodies of himself (no one mocks Updike as well as he mocks himself, and with more exquisite irony). Then there are his women—strong, placid, enduring receptacles; occasions of sin, little more. But no matter. One forgives him—or ought to—as one forgives one's friends their minor quirks and even major faults, for friend and flaw are indistinguishable. The secret is to relax and enjoy them. . . .

Few of our writers have been vouchsafed—to use a word dear to the hearts of Sunday sermonizers—a vision at once so robustly voluptous and so stringent; so keenly, deliciously aware of the mingling of pleasure (sex, "this human contact, this blank-browed thing we do for one another") and pain (the sense of sin, the anticipation of death) in the possibility of salvation. Nathaniel Hawthorne is the American writer who comes most readily to mind—and is quite consciously in Updike's. . . . Indeed, Updike is an earthier, wittier, 20th-century version of the 19th-century master. They share the same eschatological concerns, and a vision as remorselessly terrifying: of a stern and utterly mysterious God ("There's something out there that wants me to find it," Updike writes in *Rabbit, Run*), of man as a very fallen angel, and of the social forces that work as gravity in the universe to keep men revolving in their proper orbits.

> *William McPherson, "Sacramental Relations," in* Book World—The Washington Post (© *The Washington Post), February 16, 1975, p. 1.*

As [*A Month of Sundays*] reveals, Marshfield is a stock character from Updike's central casting. He snorts at liberal Protestantism and pumps for devotion inspired by awe and terror ("Mop up spilt religion! Let us have it in its original stony jars or not at all!"). At the same time he pushes graphic, adulterous sex as suburbia's best anodyne; coupling is sweetest with the ashen taste of sin. He sees women chiefly as attractive hurdles in the heavenly sweepstakes, where all the runners are male.

To perk up this familiar rehash, Updike gives his clergyman a bag of Nabokovian wordplays and tries to pass him off as Humbert Humbert (in *Lolita*, Humbert observed, "You can always count on a murderer for a fancy prose style"). Marshfield rattles off alliterations as if he were on death row. He describes a local nursery "which piously kept its Puerto Rican peony-pluckers in a state of purposeful peonage." With nary a blush he writes of returning home to the "fusty forgiveness of my fanlighted foyer." His frequent dissections of sex and theology revolve around a central question: How many matrons can dance on the head of a pun? "More power to the peephole!" the Rev. Marshfield exults after describing a session of spying on his curate and his mistress of the moment.

Before long, Marshfield's worst problem seems to be a case of terminal cuteness. Unlike Humbert, he is not facing a murder trial. He is passing through a clerical dude ranch, free to resume his pallid philandering as soon as he leaves.

Updike is too talented to write undistinguished fiction, and *A Month of Sundays* contains more than its share of finely wrought *aperçus*: "In the end, fashion overcomes personality: all the mistresses of Louis XV look alike." Marshfield's sermons (he writes one each Sunday of his stay) are sly pastiches of biblical scholarship and sophistry. Few writers can be as entertainingly cerebral as Updike. Yet after nearly two decades of distinguished service as the thinking man's John O'Hara, Updike seems to have reported everything he knows about the sexually tormented middle class. The ground covered in *A Month of Sundays* is fast becoming scorched earth.

Paul Gray, "Ring around the Collar," in Time *(reprinted by permission from* Time, The Weekly Newsmagazine; *copyright Time Inc.), February 17, 1975, p. 82.*

John Updike emerges in his new novel [*A Month of Sundays*] as a writer of sermons. And a splendidly witty sermonizer he is. Perhaps one can see his work tending that way: the minister in *Rabbit, Run*, the father in *The Centaur*, Rabbit himself *Redux* as a social commentator.

The sermons in *A Month of Sundays* are written by a *bona fide* preacher, the Rev. Thomas Marshfield, shipped off by his wife and his assistant to a desert retreat. Tom has been easing the distress of his female parishioners by applying himself. (p. 29)

For all its cleverness—maybe because of its cleverness— the novel as a whole is shallow in a way that its sermons are not. The male characters are sketchy and the female characters are by and large only the locations for sexual congress (pubic hair, breasts, mouths). Is this view of women part of Tom's early sexual hysteria and not part of the author's vision? (*Couples*, Updike's novel about a man who liked sex, pretended to be a novel about a man who liked women; the present novel at least does not confuse the issue.) . . .

The prose *is* clever, of course—*A Month of Sundays* must have been fun to write—but only as a writer of sermons is Tom worthy. The distinction between man and priest may hold for him, but it cannot hold for us; in both roles he's still a character, and like other characters he's a bore. Clever language and witty design are not cure-alls, nor is confession; both can be tedious. One may be saved by faith and works but not by speech, by the Word, but not by words. (p. 30)

Joan Joffe Hall, in The New Republic *(reprinted by permission of* The New Republic; © *1975 by* The New Republic, Inc.), *February 22, 1975.*

[A] way with words, a cross between the styles of Bellow's Herzog and Nabokov's Humbert (Tom [the protagonist] also likes word golf and makes telling slips in the style of Nabokov's Kinbote), is one of the things worthy of praise in [*A Month of Sundays*]. Another is its elegance of form. Others are a number of setpieces, such as an interview between Tom and his senile father, and a cracked but inge-

nious sermon on adultery ("We *are* an adulterous generation; let us rejoice"). Still others are the quick, deft sketches of minor characters, such as Tom's children and his equally, although differently, distracted clergymen golfing partners. But what from my incurably secular point of view above all deserves praise is the novel's decency, humanity, charity; its sense of "the spaghetti of motives and emotions heaped in our hearts"; its vivid insistence that "there is something gritty, practical, mortised, functional in our lives, something olefactory and mute, which eludes our minds' binomial formulations." The quality of "lived life's muddle" is the novel's primary concern— rather than, say, religious belief or the Object of it, which in any case are interesting only to the extent that they reveal the believer.

Much as there is to praise about this novel, good as it is, it is not good enough, not as good as its own possibilities demand. Like Tom, it does not always rise to its own occasions. At a few crucial points it is only adroit. Consider . . . this sentence: "That I continued to wish, and continue to wish, to please my wife, I append as a sorry frill upon, as an ulcerated blemish beneath the belt of, these confessions." The sentence is shapely, witty and apt, but if it had been written by Nabokov, the images of frill, blemish and belt would be more than *ad hoc* embellishment, mere decor; they would be strands of interwoven patterns of imagery working through the whole novel to form the ground of its substance and meaning; they would make up the novel's argument by design. (p. 4)

George Stade, in The New York Times Book Review (© *1975 by The New York Times Company; reprinted by permission), February 23, 1975.*

No stock character in all of Christian storytelling is more venerable than the lecherous clergyman, which is perhaps why John Updike has propped him up again to serve as narrator of [*A Month of Sundays*], his most overtly Christian novel. . . .

Updike has long been an accomplished amateur in theology, knows more about it, surely, than any other contemporary American novelist. . . . There is much byplay between love of spirit and love of flesh, between faith and potency, between waiting for Christ and waiting for a woman, and some of this works well, while some seems only ambitious. The parallels between sex and religion have not gone unnoticed in our century's literature, and Updike offers no new insights, only new wit instead.

For this is also Updike's most playful, most cerebral, most self-regarding novel. He is usually most reliable when writing in a light vein and this is always a clever, witty story. . . . There is also much of Updike's best writing here —a high incidence of the right image or metaphor for any given scene—and, in a sermon justifying adultery and divorce, a set piece that is perhaps the best that Updike has ever done. A special novel, then, for the happy few: "so those of us who live by the irrational may moderate our shame."

Peter S. Prescott, "The Passionate Cleric," in Newsweek *(copyright 1975 by Newsweek, Inc.; all rights reserved; reprinted by permission), March 3, 1975, p. 72.*

Novels by John Updike are luxury products, as a thousand reviewers have noted: The exterior trim is burnished, the inside hides are matched, the doors thunk gorgeously behind one, and few travelers feel the road. Unremittingly observant, the creator catches even tiny differences between toilets—flushing action at home and away. His eye for the "speaking" incongruity—chewing-gum wrappers crumpled on the floor of the choir—is acute. As for his way with a metaphor: It resembles that of a compactor with kitchen rubbish. In a trice the miscellaneous welter and muck of social existence is packaged in impeccably symmetrical phrases. (p. 20)

But there is a problem [with "A Month of Sundays"], namely, that this author, who knows everything about the age and its tenants, lacks a principle on which to build resistance. He nowhere glorifies corruption or weakness, but nowhere, either, does he discover resources of pride or clarities of discrimination of the kind that unhorse urbanity and shrugging compliance. Church and theology are open doors to his gift, but religion is closed: his "word" charms but does not instruct. It is true, of course, that "resistance" in a novelist, if unaccompanied by an instinct for true values, can be simply a show-biz number (morally, Mailer and Updike weigh roughly the same). But time and again in Updike's stories, you feel an aptitude for something better than stylized No! in thunder, a capacity for a more active and earnest address to experience, an interest in playing in other than the sad-song keys, even a trace of moral authority. (pp. 20-1)

A writer publishing his seventeenth highly readable book deserves to be spared absurd talk about Possibility, Growth, Hope, and the rest. . . . When you recall, in addition, that the author in question is barely out of his 30s, it's extremely hard not to look ahead: not to wonder whether, sooner than later, he won't be bound to look the thing straight in the eye without winking. I, for one, can't wait. (p. 21)

> *Benjamin DeMott, "Mod Masses, Empty Pews," in* Saturday Review *(copyright © 1975 by Saturday Review/World, Inc.; reprinted with permission), March 8, 1975, pp. 20-1.*

John Updike has been an enviable problem. Gifted at once with a supremely alert ear and eye for the pulse and sinew of contemporary American speech and with a passion for the rare word, for the jewelled and baroque precisions still vital beneath and around the current of common idiom, he has been able to write about literally *anything*. Whether it be the stubble in a Pennsylvania field, the swerve of a basketball under gymnasium lights, the rasp of a tire on gravel, the tightening at a man's temples under pressure of sexual fantasy, Mr. Updike has made these planes of experience brilliantly his own yet true to the evidence, penetrative into the fabric of American discourse and gesture to a degree that future historians and sociologists will exult in. He has written of rich and poor, of urban and rural, of science and political intrigue, of gregariousness and cold solitude with an unforgiving yet strangely solicitous, almost tender intelligence. The critic and the poet in him (a minor but sparkling poet of occasion and humor of a kind infrequent now) are at no odds with the novelist; the same sharpness of apprehension bears on the object in each of Updike's modes. But it

is precisely this ubiquity, the sheer range of whatever elicits his luminous dispassions, that has made it difficult for him to find a mastering theme.

Not only in "The Centaur" but, indeed, in all of his novels Updike has tested elements of fable and allegory, ancient formal devices with which to knit into comely and probing shape the dazzling singularity, the vital ordinariness of his perceptions. "The Poorhouse Fair," still one of his finest achievements, aims at control, at a sharp and exemplary meaning, through compression. "Couples" is a panoramic mapping rescued from indiscrimination by recourse to deliberately symbolic, terminal devices (the raging fire at the close). "Bech" is a book held in place, mirrored within a book—again a fine solution to the problem of focus, of finding a structure both firm and supple enough to contain such wealth and scruple of style. Sexuality has over and over provided the key. . . . Eroticism is, in a serious artist, an ascetic pursuit.

To invoke the pathos, the enigmatic humanity of lust is, of course, to borrow the language of St. Augustine and of Kierkegaard. Where eros and sadness meet, theology begins. This realization has long been a part of Mr. Updike's work. Looking back, one comes to realize how deeply his sense of American experience is religious, and religious in a vein related particularly to the history of New England Calvinism on the one hand and to the thought of Barth and Tillich on the other. It is a commonplace that recent American fiction and criticism have to a drastic extent been the product of a Jewish tone and explosion of talent. Updike is the counterpoise: his sensibility is, among practicing American novelists, the most distinctly Christian and Protestant. The eroticism of his fiction has been a long prelude to a radically theological view of American existence. In "A Month of Sundays" . . ., the sexual and the clerical, the scatological and the eschatological are intimately, almost violently meshed. (p. 116)

"A Month of Sundays" is a meditation on, a contradictory echo of that first classic of the American Protestant erotic imagination, Hawthorne's "The Scarlet Letter." Adultery was to Hawthorne the crucial, emblematic motif of the American condition, posing the full paradox of the inherited weakness of the flesh and of social institutions in a new Eden, in a world predestined to innocence and the renovation of man. Updike turns the tables on Hawthorne and on the legacy of Calvinist prohibition: "But who that has eyes to see cannot so lust? Was not the First Divine Commandment received by human ears, 'Be fruitful, and multiply'? Adultery is not a choice to be avoided; it is a circumstance to be embraced. Thus I construe these texts." (p. 117)

Working so near the innermost of his concerns, that congruence—at once farcical and tragic—of sexuality and religious feeling in post-Puritan America, Updike trusts himself almost blindly to his verbal skills. His use of puns, Freudian malapropisms, and portmanteau words . . . runs riot. Too often the level is that of a Hasty Pudding script in an off year. . . .

Whether "A Month of Sundays" is substantial, controlled enough to make [Updike's] vision emotionally plausible is less [than] certain. It is an impatient text enforced by rather than enforcing its pyrotechnics. One would guess that it is a transitional novel in Updike's work, a rapid staking-out of territory that the next fictions will map at leisure. (p. 118)

George Steiner, "Scarlet Letters," in The New Yorker *(© 1975 by The New Yorker Magazine, Inc.), March 10, 1975, pp. 116-18.*

[It] wasn't until the publication of *Rabbit Redux* in 1971 that Updike achieved in his own work the self-restraint and craftsmanship he had admired in others. Before then, he had flailed about somewhat unsteadily, tending toward verbal cuteness and gimmickry. Novels like *The Centaur* and *Bech: A Book* were deft but diversionary, more finger exercises than compositions.

Happily, these are now well behind him. *A Month of Sundays* is Updike's newest novel: its competence is prodigious. It is a composed and careful book whose success lies largely in its scarcity of faults. It is less coy, less evasive, less precious than is Updike's wont—a more substantial claim than might at first be apparent. (p. 11)

In the past, Updike's linguistic virtuosity often intruded into the narrative, and there was an inevitable disparity between the intellectual fastidiousness of the author and the mediocrity of his heroes. But the verbal gymnastics here seem very much to the point. More than Rabbit Angstrom or Peter Caldwell or Henry Bech, Marshfield is the Updike protagonist *par excellence*: guilt-ridden, word-conscious, querulous, and wry.

Though the novel has nothing of the scope or complication of *Rabbit Redux*, it may yet be the best formulation of a problem that has preoccupied Updike for years: the modern spirit-sapping retreat from dogma into passionless compromise. The figure of Marshfield, anxious but orthodox, corresponds nicely to Updike's sense of his own role as purveyor of unfashionable conservative truths to a liberal age ("androgynous, homogenizing liberals," Marshfield complains at one point).

There are large themes lurking in the background—the silence of God, the weakness of humankind—but Updike is able to approach them discreetly and without fanfare. The particular accomplishment of *A Month of Sundays* is to intimate the larger questions without sinking into ponderousness. Updike is no philosopher, and he keeps the range of inquiry manageable. He is writing within the reach of his talents, not trying to push beyond them. That may make for limitation, but it makes equally for control. The issues Updike is concerned to argue are at bottom simple ones, and he argues them without fuss. (pp. 11-12)

Michael Levenson, "Cataloging a Life," in Bookletter *(copyright 1975 by* Harper's Magazine; *reprinted from the March 31, 1975 issue by special permission), March 31, 1975, pp. 11-12.*

I suppose that Updike was drawn to the idea of a clerical hero for a number of reasons. Ministers aren't bad surrogates for novelists—they too, at least by repute, are literate, thoughtful, sensitive to human pain, good with words, devoted to more than immediate and transient values, accustomed to the presence of attentive audiences. And Updike's Thomas Marshfield [In *A Month of Sundays*], though stronger in some of these qualities than in others, can indeed sum up his experience as a passable outline for a novel. . . . [But there] are problems . . . in Marshfield's way of turning the outline into images of life.

For one thing, this account, with its insinuation of a "romance" quest-motif toward the end, seems rather self-protective, right down to the little typo which immediately generates a footnote making nervous comedy out of the "impotent-omnipotent" confusion and its implications for a reader of Meister Eckhart and Aquinas. And the character's defensiveness, his offer of charm and whimsicality to ward off the simple disapproval his behavior might otherwise seem to call for, reflects a difficulty for which the novelist must be held responsible.

The writing in the book often is almost aggressively overwrought, even for Updike, never one to pretend that his prose hasn't been *written*. (p. 18)

What exactly is the matter with Tom Marshfield? Married to the daughter of an old-fashioned theology professor named Chillingworth and entrusted to the rehabilitative care of the large and most un-nubile Ms. Prynne, whom he worshipfully beds before leaving the desert, he evidently is meant to be a weird updating of Hawthorne's Arthur Dimmesdale; but plain, dull, Puritan guilt isn't part of his penitential repertory. . . . (pp. 18-19)

[The question is] whether Marshfield makes sense as a human self-portrait. For me he doesn't. Just as I'm not sure that he's supposed to be quite the monster he usually seems, I'm not sure how far to trust the conclusion, in which he appears to regain (with the help of Confucius, Pascal, and Bergson) a perilous faith that may be the only one possible for intelligent modern people. . . .

A Month of Sundays doesn't hang together well enough to prove that Updike's interest in sex and his interest in religion have come together to say something that is impressive or interesting about love. Perhaps to my shame, I can't see the novel as being a great deal more than disappointing self-indulgence by a very gifted writer. (p. 19)

Thomas R. Edwards, "Busy Minister," in The New York Review of Books *(reprinted with permission from* The New York Review of Books; *copyright © 1975 NYREV, Inc.), April 3, 1975, pp. 18-19.*

[*A Month of Sundays*] is, at least in formal terms, a change of pace for the author. It is his freest, most loosely structured work to date. In fact, this is perhaps its most conspicuous and interesting feature. The narrative of Reverend Tom Marshfield is digressive, disjointed, and repetitious, an extended monologue, an ornate, overwrought confession. The author seems to be making a very conscious effort to loosen up, break free from the restraints of traditional narration. Though a number of Updike's other novels, notably *The Poorhouse Fair* and *The Centaur*, sometimes seemed more like prose poems than novels, they did possess a concreteness of character and detail. Here character is often eclipsed by Marshfield's voice, his overripe language, his frequent sermons. There is a wealth of physical detail, but it tends to give us bits and pieces of a world rather than a full, distinct environment. While it is encouraging to see an established author trying something a little different, taking chances with his work, one wishes that the results were more successful. . . .

In this novel Updike's prodigious verbal energy is as much a curse as it is a blessing. There are, to be sure, a number of fine set pieces. . . . But for all the elegant, striking prose there seems to be an equal, if not even greater amount of irritatingly classy, bloated language. (p. 679)

[The protagonist's] frequent flights of language and his lengthy sermons prevent us from getting any clear picture of the human beings who share his story. We do get, among other things, lovely details of rooms, streets, bodies, references to the philosophy of Barth and Tillich, and great chunks of rhetoric. These elements, however, distance us from the matter at hand instead of illuminating it and bringing it closer to us. Since the people hold little reality for us, the passion and urgency of Tom's voice seem rather contrived and uncalled for. We don't quite believe it. It is too overwhelming. The author doesn't help matters by filling his narrative with puns, parenthetical asides, and footnotes. We strongly detect here the influence of Nabokov, whom Updike has so often praised. . . . It is unfortunate that he has chosen to employ the old master's most annoying devices.

Still, we are often taken by Updike's style and intelligence, and we are almost willing to forgive him his excesses. Parts of *A Month of Sundays* work very well, but the book as a whole does not, jumping as it does from bits of personal history to generalities to minor details. It is a thoroughly professional though diffuse performance by one of our most gifted writers, who has given us and, no doubt, will give us more satisfying and memorable books than this. (pp. 679-80)

Ronald De Feo, "Sex, Sermons, and Style," in National Review *(© National Review, Inc., 1975; 150 East 35th St., New York, N.Y. 10016), June 20, 1975, pp. 679-80.*

V

Van der POST, Laurens   1906-

A South African writer of novels, travel journals, and other nonfiction, and formerly an explorer, a farmer, and a career officer in the British Army, van der Post now spends most of his time in England. Most of his work deals with life and its problems in South Africa. (See also *Contemporary Authors*, Vols. 5-8, rev. ed.)

[Laurens van der Post's] three novels show the influence of Christian socialism, Jungianism, and a personal mysticism. Van der Post is an heir to the literary tradition bequeathed by E. M. Forster, but he also reflects the influence of William Plomer and Joseph Conrad. His first novel, *In a Province* (. . . 1934), dealt with two men, of different cultures and races, trying and failing to understand each other. (p. 212)

This theme of personal and spiritual isolation is found throughout van der Post's writing. All his heroes are unmade men searching for the vital relationship which will connect them to a sense of sharing in the ocean of experience. Van der Post ties this theme of isolation to the color issue in South Africa so that the psychological journey within the individual is completed through identification with one's black brother. In *In a Province* the hero comes to maturity through accepting his commitment to the native boy; in *The Face Beside the Fire* (. . . 1953) the hero accepts his role in life after a dream in which he identifies with the white-stubbled negroid face of an old man; in *Flamingo Feather* (. . . 1955) the hero continues his fight for racial harmony after identifying himself in guilt with African rioters. (pp. 212-13)

Van der Post's emphasis on the necessity and joy of love of white men for black men is the symbolic counterpart of miscegenation. Sexual love rarely occurs in his novels; the passion of friendship, of deep platonic affection, takes its place. He substitutes symbolic and emotional identity for sexual union. (p. 213)

Although van der Post has treated Communist agitation in his novels, he is more interested in the psychological lessons of the African scene than in its political and social complexes. In this sense he is a representative of the Conradian tradition, seeing Africa in terms of the deep center of a man's soul. Thus, Africa, more than a state of people, becomes a condition of man. Or as van der Post put it in *The Dark Eye in Africa*, a book in which he related his personal mythology to *Mata Kelap*, a Malayan phrase referring to a gentle person who erupts suddenly into violence, "Nevertheless, the interest of the world is compelled by events in Africa because, unconsciously, the world apprehends that Africa may hold the secret of its own lost and hidden being." . . . [If] van der Post fears violence, he also sees it as an unavoidable condition. In his novels riot and violence are the beginning, not the end, of racial harmony. The violence is the necessary catharsis, the expulsion of the festering wound. (p. 214)

In van der Post's novels friendship between men is never achieved till they have accepted their black or white brothers; no man is free of the chains of his immaturity till he has crushed and despoiled himself of all reserves of racial prejudice. The problem of color, as in all South African literature, dominates these novels; other issues remain secondary. (p. 217)

> *Martin Tucker, in his* Africa in Modern Literature: A Survey of Contemporary Writing in English *(copyright © 1967 by Frederick Ungar Publishing Co., Inc.), Ungar, 1967.*

The philosophic travelogue is a distinguished enough genre, and it might be useful trying to approach Laurens van der Post's . . . novel, *A Far-Off Place*, in the light of it. Certainly, the action is mechanical to the point of absurdity, and serves mainly as a vehicle for disquisitions on the evils of modern civilisation, the life-enhancing wonders of primitive (especially Bushman) culture, and for ecstatically detailed sunsets, sunrises, lions, elephants, bees, and extraordinary facts about the wilderness of (it seems) South-West Africa. There is nothing cold about Mr van der Post, and nothing that is flippant or relaxed. Every bush, and every bird in it, burns with meaning and with moral intensity. When a boy makes himself creep slowly at night he does so 'despite the temptation to hasten that the sense of imminent danger brings to the human spirit'—and it is this portentous 'human spirit', and other spirits, that are the true protagonists of a book bent on restoring us to the world of natural magic from which Descartes expelled us (as the Romantic myth has been claiming for 200 years).

Much of this, considered contemplatively, is admirable, and the scheme of values—liberal-individualist yet quasi-mystical—has a traditional appeal to the English imagination. But even a meditative travelogue needs shape, variation, basic sensitivity of language, and some intellectual acuity—at least a recognition that truth is complex, and most values ambiguous. And no amount of well-observed natural history, African folklore or decent Christian kindliness will bear up moral banality, repetitiousness and an apparatus of coyly awkward or grandiloquent metaphors. The concluding Moralitas, spoken by a figure representing Haile Selassie, 'the only authentic royal voice of Africa', is that we must all (but especially African terrorists and Communist mercenaries) learn to love and to forgive.

No, as a meditation and vision of life, *A Far-Off Place* will not do, though its heart is in the right place—with the Noble Savage still. So that one is forced back on its merits as a novel, which is clearly how we are asked to take it. It comes as a sequel to *A Story Like the Wind*, and though it claims to stand by itself, it in fact begins very much where the other left off, and would make no sense without the . . . synopsis of the first volume which the author thoughtfully and laboriously provides. (p. 381)

Impossible episodes, ungainly prose, fossilised character-types, and wooden dialogue are straight out of the old world of Biggles and Bulldog Drummond. The terrorists (and anti-Nature forces) are led by a Chinese 'Chairman' who says 'velly funny'; a bad Scot with a worried conscience who says (like all Scots) 'Ach, dinna fash yourself, mon' (the World Council of Churches, or Kirks, is behind the invasion); and a cynical Frenchman who says '*mon cher*' and gives Gallic shrugs.

It is all very preposterous and more than a little pretentious. A boy-scout's yarn has been inflated into a gauche, if well-meant, fable for our times, and into a would-be 'epic of Africa'; but the only true and fresh things in it are the springbok, the honey-badger, the bitter melon, and the wild fig-tree. (p. 382)

Kenneth Graham, "Back to Biggles," in The Listener (© British Broadcasting Corp. 1974; reprinted by permission of Kenneth Graham), September 19, 1974, pp. 381-82.

A Far Off Place, the concluding sequel to *A Story Like the Wind*, is itself the tale of a journey, physical and allegorical, but it reaches no very convincing destination. On one level, as its author hints in his prologue, it tries to do for Africa what *Kim* did for India. It is a yarn, no other word for it, about a young European couple who find themselves orphaned and made homeless by a Communist-led nationalist rebellion somewhere in southwest Africa. Accompanied only by a Bushman couple and a dog, they make their way with appalling difficulty to the coast, where they are able to break the news of the conflict to a NATO fleet which is conveniently exercising its marines at the very point of their emergence, and are subsequently presented to the Emperor of Ethiopia, who talks to them in French and offers the apologies of Africa for their discomforts.

In many ways it is preposterous. Colonel van der Post's characterisation is embarrassingly *jejune*. . . .

It is an old man's book. Exercising warships are no longer, alas, painted a tropical white. Naval officers no longer introduce themselves as "Michael Featherstone, Commander, Her Majesty's Royal Navy sir". Cockney sea-

men, if there are any, certainly do not observe "Cor strike me pink". I cannot believe that mercenary officers of revolutionary armies habitually address each other, even in irony, as "My guid gentleman of France" or "Mon cher Ecossais", and I have severe doubts about the high-born Portuguese lady who, tied to the Makoba Tree of Life, is obliged to sing a *fado* every night to satisfy an Old Prophecy of liberation.

Never mind, in this book the message is the medium. The story does not matter, the characters are mere instruments, and the true fascination of the work is the spectacle of Colonel van der Post trying to come to terms with a world apparently determined to block his every path of enlightenment. He is such a good man, so kind, so *right*, that the failure of this attempt, which is really a life-long dedication, provides a sombre conclusion to an exciting adventure—even perhaps, if it is not impertinent or premature to say so, to a noble life. . . .

Colonel van der Post is constantly up against ideas which confuse his own convictions. He loves the innocent African, but he knows that given a machine-gun or a battery egg farm, the African becomes as awful as the rest of us. He feels a true brotherhood with wild creatures, yet he accepts the need to kill and eat them. He responds to the ancient unity of Africa, yet cannot stomach the methods of the African insurgents. He hates industrialisation, but warms to the splendour of a ship or the elegance of a good rifle. He loathes war but is a soldier born, distrusts power yet responds to it, searches always for an absolute which does not exist, except in the ideal.

He is a mystic, disguised as a novelist and man of action, and he is here in the world to ponder its incalculables, and allow us to share his conjectures. Yet he seems dissatisfied with the role, and wishes always to translate his long ecstasy into something more positive, some plan of action, some practical purpose. It is as though a sense of guilt, inherited perhaps from the Calvinist conscience, drives this inspired dreamer into a closer involvement with the world's reality: as though the dream, and the vision, is not reality enough.

It takes a very special kind of yarn to invoke these speculations in a reader. *Kim* itself, the yarn of yarns, hardly does as much. If I have laughed at *A Far Off Place*, and probed insolently into Colonel van der Post's privacies, I have done so only with respect and gratitude. I think I see some of the quandaries that lie behind his contradictory epic, and I certainly recognise the grandeur of its conception, and the love that lies between its every line. Laurens van der Post's absurdities are other men's achievements, and one of his doubts is worth a dozen of our poor certainties.

Jan Morris, "Mystic Gleam," in The Spectator (© 1974 by The Spectator; reprinted by permission of The Spectator), September 21, 1974, p. 369.

*　　*　　*

VONNEGUT, Kurt, Jr.   1922-

Vonnegut is an enormously popular American novelist, short story writer, and playwright. His deceptively simple fantasies and science fiction are incisive commentaries on contemporary life; his slapstick comedy is black. (See also *Contemporary Authors*, Vols. 1-4, rev. ed.)

Kurt Vonnegut's *Breakfast of Champions* is more provocative as a straw in the wind than a work of literature. It has almost no narrative interest, almost no "solidity of specification," almost no moral complication, and almost none of the inside-dopesterism characteristic of books that sell very well; yet it has sold not merely well but best. What it does have is play, wit, structural unpredictability, some ingenious mimicry of American speech, and an absurdist vision continuous with Vonnegut's previous work, though here with a different tonal range. It seems to me possible that our literary sociology is changing in some ways that are not yet clear and that Vonnegut's rather unpretentious book, so astonishingly different from any previous bestseller, may mark the beginning of a different and wider public for new, unconventional fiction.

Vonnegut's principal strategy is to contrive the voice of a naïf, which in his case is the voice of a fifty-year-old naïf. "Everybody in America," the narrator tells us, "was supposed to grab whatever he could and hold onto it. Some Americans were very good at grabbing and holding, were fabulously well-to-do. Others couldn't get their hands on doodley-squat." Elsewhere the mention of a Colonel Sanders franchise evokes the following explanation. "A chicken was a flightless bird which looked like this: [Vonnegut here inserts his own drawing of a chicken, apparently done with a felt-tip pen, in the style of a child's coloring book]. The idea was to kill it and pull out its feathers, and cut off its head and feet and scoop out its internal organs—and then chop it into pieces and fry the pieces, and put the pieces in a waxed paper bucket with a lid on it, so it looked like this: [here a drawing of a bucket of fried chicken]." The two obvious risks of such a voice are that it will pall and weary the reader with its limitations of tone and, secondly, that the naive observations will finally seem to represent the mind of the author, which is to say that the book is apt to make Vonnegut himself appear simpleminded. On the other hand, the possibilities of the naive voice are considerable, and Vonnegut exploits them all: being naive, the narrator has no sense of structure or priority and thus can include anything, as indeed he does, moving in a few pages through matters of eschatology and teleology, cornball manners of the Midwest, irrelevant statistics, perverse sexuality, washroom graffiti, and automobile sales techniques. The satiric possibilities of the naive voice, moreover, are classic, and Vonnegut directs his innocent voice at American guile and idiocy with considerable effect. He explains, for example, with the same dull ingenuousness that he uses to explain the bucket of fried chicken, the function of the body bag in gathering together the fragments of a soldier killed in action. Ordinarily, however, the audience for naive narration is explicit and contained: Candide explains naively to Pangloss who explains naively to Cunegonde who explains naively to Candide while we readers overhear; Gulliver explains naively to the King of Brobdingnag while we, knowing more than either of them, listen, with some humiliation and much ironic amusement. Vonnegut's narrator, on the other hand, is explaining to nobody in particular, to the generalized reader, or perhaps to himself. And thus the naïveté seems especially bald and uncontrolled, without a plausible setting. (p. 302, 304)

[The] life of the book does not reside in the continuity of its central figures. The life of the book resides in its "bits," its gags, its lines, its long succession of comic-apocalyptic events, even its drawings. So it is that it seems pointless to criticize the book for being self-indulgent and messy; of course it is. It does not, however, seem pointless to criticize the book for its triviality. For, touching again and again on the curious and desperate backwaters of American culture, the book nevertheless dissipates much of its force with schoolboy bathroom jokes, penis measurements, and a good portion of foolishness that seems neither buoyant enough nor clever enough to justify its existence. (p. 304)

> *Philip Stevick, in* Partisan Review *(copyright © 1974 by Partisan Review, Inc.), Vol. XLI, No. 2, 1974.*

Vonnegut's success can be attributed largely to the skill with which he blends humorous fiction and a popular moralistic vision.

On the surface, it would appear that Vonnegut's rhetoric is nihilistic and that his humor merely punctuates the "history of human stupidity" which must inevitably end in The Grand Ah-whoom. The bombing of Dresden informs his authorial memory which in turn matches the paranoia of his audience. His perfectly timed grim humor is an artistic gesture of defiance but cannot by itself transcend the apocalyptic vision which underlies all his subjects. How, then, can Vonnegut be called a moralist?

Critical reading reveals that he does not always use grim humor nihilistically. . . . Vonnegut, like Twain, often deploys that humor as a weapon. In addition, like Dickens, he makes sentimental appeals to his audience. Jerome Klinkowitz, who has taken the trouble to dig out from *Collier's* and *Galaxy Science Fiction* Vonnegut's earliest short stories, shows [in *The Vonnegut Statement*; see excerpts in *CLC*-4] that he has spoken continuously for a return to a plain, middle-class, "fundamental American decency." What does America need and want? Vonnegut himself says that Americans are homesick for Mommy and Daddy. He aims his stories at the generals and senators who run things but is sure that they do not read them. He recognizes instead an audience which includes those who will someday be the generals and senators, and he works deliberately to "poison their minds with humanity." The humane values his fiction declares are common and simple: pacifism, family responsibility, love of the land, freedom from "the unbridled intellect," and being kind to one's neighbors. It should be no surprise that Vonnegut is middle-aged, has raised children, tries to pay his bills on time. The cult-hero of "the radical young" is none other than good old Dad from Indiana! . . .

[He is] a true rarity among modern American novelists—a moralist deploying traditional satire, iconoclastic grim humor, and a lucid view of what is wrong with man. (p. 243)

> *Richard Boyd Hauck, in* American Literature *(reprinted by permission of the Publisher; copyright 1974 by Duke University Press, Durham, North Carolina), May, 1974.*

Vonnegut's undercutting of pleasant and humorous space fantasy [in *Slaughterhouse-Five*] by horrible earth-reality is typical of black comedy's operant tensions. The book's repeated dictum, "Concentrate on the good times," is its only offer of solace. *Slaughterhouse-Five* is slightly different from many black comic novels in that Vonnegut presents his hero as dominated by the reality of his existence, analogous, perhaps, to an absurdist character's status. When one remembers that in the opening chapter, the narrative "I" (should one say Vonnegut?) promises that his novel will contain no roles for John Wayne, a reason for Billy Pilgrim's nature is more easily discerned. Value in *Slaughterhouse-Five* is developed subjectively, "Concentrate on the good times." Men perpetrate evils on other men. One may not be able to change the state of things, but one need not add to it. (pp. 204-05)

> *John Boni, "Analogous Form: Black Comedy and Some Jacobean Plays," in* Western Humanities Review *(copyright, 1974, University of Utah), Summer, 1974, pp. 201-15.*

Wampeters, Foma & Granfalloons is . . . a collection of essays, reviews, speeches, etc. Only a writer with Vonnegut's power base could get a book of occasional writings published today, let alone get away with giving it such a title. Simply the sound of the apparently nonsensical words is enough to kindle recognition in those who have been initiated into Vonnegut's universe, and by the most cautious estimate the number of reader-initiates must be in the hundreds of thousands. The very definite *meaning* of these not-so-secret words is stored in the memories of probably almost as many people, and is fairly often retrievable and can be recited in paraphrase—the novel (*Cat's Cradle*) in which Vonnegut invented the words and originally set forth their meanings in 1963 has gone through thirty-two printings in the last four years. But *Cat's Cradle* is not the only book in which Vonnegut has made up words; in this practice, as in other ways, his work is of a piece, and once the reason is understood why any of his writing should have become immensely popular, it is understandable why all of his books—almost impossible to find in bookstores when first published—are now continuously in print. The prevalence of Vonnegut cannot be overstated. Another of his novels (*Slaughterhouse-Five*) has been translated into fifteen languages, and another (*Breakfast of Champions*) recently spent a year on the best-seller list, at the top of it much of that time. (p. 40)

Vonnegut is the champion—actually in a class by himself. The sale of his books and the love accorded them and their creator are such as are ordinarily reserved for the reading matter that caters best to a larger public's appetite for violence, inside dope, and sentimentality, and those who produce it (examples are unnecessary). (pp. 40-1)

Considering the ability of his books to hold the attention of large numbers of people in a society supplied with many distractions more vivid than books, it is not surprising that Vonnegut's standing with literary critics should be unsettled. Some seem to think he is suspect because his work enjoys a success that is anomalous for "serious" writing; others, having skimmed or read his books, say more or less that they are not worth a critic's time. Vonnegut is a "sententious old salt in ontological drag," the late Charles Thomas Samuels wrote [see *CLC*-2], and his is "a bogus talent. . . . [He] can tell us nothing worth knowing except what his rise itself indicates: ours is an age in which adolescent ridicule can become a mode of upward mobility." . . . But as Benjamin DeMott sees it, "the kids' lighting on

Kurt Vonnegut is an undeservedly good break for the age" [see *CLC*-2], and, in Leslie Fiedler's opinion, the Vonnegut novels do belong "to what we know again to be the mainstream of fiction," by which Fiedler does not mean what he calls "High Art," but rather "American Pop . . . the quest of the absolute wilderness." Graham Greene is less sly, more explicit: Vonnegut is "one of the best living American writers."

Vonnegut's novels are full of stories—no plotless novels in the hyper-modern manner could have become so popular. They are also full of characters, surprises, episodes, suicides, apocalypses, science-fiction fantasies, morals drawn and underlined. And certain persistent motifs run through all of them. The Vonnegut hero is typically an American who has either been born or worked his way into what society considers a privileged position. But he is more than dissatisfied—he is ashamed, and tries to redeem himself by dropping out and associating with those believed less privileged, by helping the unwashed, the insulted, or merely exploited, the little people worn down by industrial and scientific consequences. Sometimes this saintly program is an obsession, an end in itself (*God Bless You, Mr. Rosewater*), sometimes a nagging temptation along the way of a quest or odyssey (*Player Piano; The Sirens of Titan; Cat's Cradle*). One way or another, it continually seems that it might be the right thing if the main character devoted what energy and ingenuity he had to it, in spite of the fact that he realizes such a program cannot change anything for the better, that the unfortunate are no more lovable or deserving than the intelligent, the high, and the mighty, and that in any event fate has an absurd and painful end in store for all.

To note this recurring theme is misleading, if it suggests that Vonnegut creates failed saints to study and dissect them, like a psychologist. With several exceptions, the characters, even the presumptive heroes, who appear and reappear in his novels are not deep enough and they do not stay in one place long enough to be studied as in a psychological novel. Mostly, Vonnegut's figures are mechanical contrivances bathed in a stroboscopic glare—fleshless robots galvanized by his will, moving jerkily toward the next joke, moral, or plot-advancing surprise.

Another thread: In all his novels, and even when he uses the whole universe for scenery, Vonnegut has originated this repertory of characters in upstate New York, Rhode Island-Cape Cod, and Indiana. In *The Vonnegut Statement*, a *Festschrift* compiled by some of his academic admirers in the Middle West, these locales are compared to Faulkner's Yoknapatawpha County. As Vonnegut sketches them, the places are meant to seem sadly comic, haunted by American ghosts: of the coastal Indians and whalers, the Iroquois tribes and Erie canalmen, the pioneers. Technology and salesmanship have stripped and raped the land and divested the people of pride, leaving them ridiculous—mechanical men and women whom it is a duty to love. In his speeches, Vonnegut has explicitly blamed all this degeneration and suffering on American scientists and technologists, the inspired tinkerers, the sons of Edison in the employ of the Rockefellers and Rosewaters and the government. . . . [Only] late, in *Breakfast of Champions*, is a good word said for any product of modern technology and it turns out to be tranquilizers, which the narrator swallows to restore his chemical balance.

It is risking nothing to take a quick guess that some of these ideas about America—let them be called political instead of philosophical, though they are connected to no party or program—eventually helped Vonnegut's books win an appreciative audience among college-age readers and, later, their elders: it was a matter of waiting for the *Zeitgeist* to catch up. His politics—implied, inferred—are a factor in his appeal, and need to be examined. But while they may have become agreeable to an even larger audience, it is probably the style that they, and the story line, are presented in which first pleased, delighted, seduced. Vonnegut's is a brief, repetitious style, rhetorically mock-naive, relying for effect on the regular delivery of a quantity of some kind of satisfaction every page or so. It arrives in the shape of a surprise, a moral, a giggle, a laugh. After what now looks like a false start in *Player Piano*, Vonnegut fastened on the form that works best with such a style: a series of self-contained, sometimes arbitrarily divided, "chapters" of no more than five hundred words, often as few as fifty. "My books are essentially mosaics made up of a whole bunch of tiny little chips," he says . . ., "and each chip is a joke." Whether he is speaking here in all honesty, or out of false modesty (he evidently thinks of himself as more than a comedian, and harbors exalted ideas of the role of writers), as a description of his method it is not bad.

Vonnegut's novels are constructed in a way that can also be likened to the structure of an old-fashioned cartoon booklet with figures painted in primary colors which is flipped with the thumb. *Cat's Cradle,* for example, has 121 "chapters", headed with ironical inscriptions like title-cards, contained in a grand total of 191 pages. The divisions between each "chapter" function like the frames between cartoons, so that read over quickly (as Vonnegut's novels are meant to be read on first encountering them, before going back to search out, talmudically, allegories, symbols, and designs), they blur into a semblance of motion. The effect is cinematic, as if a basic pattern, and resource, of the movies had been appropriated to a book without pictures. (pp. 41-2)

[*Player Piano*] is a recognizable literary project in the approved manner, down to the basic device of casting a misfit in the anti-utopia. "I cheerfully ripped off the plot of *Brave New World*," Vonnegut [has said]. Although the perfectly bad society that irks the hero is not coercive or totalitarian, but rather a benevolent welfare state where corporations look out for what they consider the public interest and bright young men in crewcuts do not get too drunk, *Player Piano* is another cautionary fantasy extrapolating from what is actual, in the tradition of Zamyatin, Huxley, and Orwell. Sometimes it also reads like *Babbitt*. It partakes in a gently pessimistic way of anger at what the boosters of mass production and the assembly line are doing to bodies and souls, and fear of what they may do still worse. . . .

[His] stories, which Vonnegut says he wrote to buy time, and which have been collected in *Welcome to the Monkey House*, adhere to formula while mildly worrying the strain of disaffection evident in *Player Piano*. Their heroes are eccentric villagers, precocious dropouts, average U.S. citizens taking advantage of a windfall to improve their model train sets or HAM radio apparatus. In the meantime, *Player Piano* was issued in paperback, renamed *Utopia 14*. It took Vonnegut seven years to write the first of a couple of books (*The Sirens of Titan* and *Cat's Cradle*) that, with the help of the bosomy covers their publishers wrapped them in,

assured his consignment to the demeaning science-fiction drawer. These novels made Vonnegut's underground reputation; in them he found his form and oracular voice.

The Sirens of Titan (1959) and *Cat's Cradle* (1963), unlike *Player Piano*, are fairly original in conception, quite consistent in tone. They are also highly contrived and as didactic as sermons. (p. 42)

This was one of Vonnegut's achievements, that he could make a certain audience read what are essentially books of ideas, using multiple plots, self-consciously intricate designs, and flashy characters, and intruding himself continually, without breaking the spell. A load of moralistic message is what puts *Sirens* and *Cat's Cradle* into the category of science fiction—more precisely, into that subcategory of science fiction, fantasy, that depends, for credibility, not on detailed descriptions of possible machines or experiments with nature, but on a seamless web of dreaming about a universe that can never be, populated by impossible beings, humanoids embodying urges and ideas.

It is more the stuff of teleology than ontology; paperback readers who do not know the meanings of these words can appreciate that the dreamlike quests of Vonnegut's heroes in fantastic worlds and universes are about finding purpose here, in this world. And purpose there is, finally. The mocking voice, seemingly parodying itself, denying any aim in life, demands not to be believed, yet always taken seriously—this is the unspoken understanding between writer and reader in Vonnegut's books.

Preachy as it is, the voice never talks down, nor does it depress. It is breezy, charming, confidential, fully clued in to the popularity of sticking gun turrets on model aircraft carriers with Duco cement and other pre-pubescent American joys; it shares rather than imparts dark-sounding truths, funny jokes. An American "kid" who had bought *Sirens* or *Cat's Cradle* in a bus station (both novels were published in paperback, went unreviewed) could wish when done reading that the author was a terrific friend of his, whom he could call up on the phone whenever he felt like it. In fact, during the years when rare copies of *Sirens* were being being sold for up to fifty dollars, many of Vonnegut's young enthusiastic readers did that. . . .

An anti-scientific bias is also less unusual, more popular now than fifteen years ago. "You scientists *think* too much," a Miss Pefko says in *Cat's Cradle*, which ends with the end of the world. A marked animus against scientists, and thinking, and a propensity to toy with apocalypse, characterize all of Vonnegut's books. He has another preoccupation. Except in two books, it is never more than continually alluded to. The Martian soldiers in *The Sirens of Titan* "wore knee spikes, and glossy black uniforms. . . . Their insignia was a skull and crossbones." Von Koenigswald, saintly jungle doctor of *Cat's Cradle*, has "the terrible deficit of Auschwitz in his kindliness account."

World War II, the Nazis, the war's long-lasting effect on individual Americans and America, are themes that loom large for Vonnegut for autobiographical and other reasons. He gets around to facing them directly in *Mother Night* (1961) and *Slaughterhouse-Five* (1969).

At first, it seems that *Mother Night* is intended as the study of an insane man, in the form of that well-known fictional conceit, the self-portrait or confession. "I've always been able to live with what I did," writes Howard W. Campbell, an American double agent awaiting trial in Israel as a Nazi war criminal. "How? Through that simple and widespread boon to modern mankind—schizophrenia." To try and create a character who will bear scrutiny would seem to be a departure for Vonnegut.... This is a very ambitious project—locating a publicly harmful madman within modern history, undercutting revulsion for him by showing his all-too-human, even sympathetic sides, never losing sight of his diseased soul under the welter of well-known documentary facts that needn't be mentioned but are, and always, "in his own words."

The prime prerequisite in a confessional novel has always been that the novelist get inside his creature, becoming invisible. Nabokov did this with Humbert Humbert, also a disturbed man in jail, Salinger with Holden Caulfield, Roth (almost) with Alexander Portnoy. However, Howard Campbell's words are not all his own; many of them, and his ideas and sentiments as well, are Vonnegut's. Instead of strategically subsuming his intentions in Campbell's craziness, Vonnegut mainly uses him as a mouthpiece, so that *Mother Night* quickly turns into an exercise in ventriloquism. Often the voice does not even trouble to disguise itself, and sounds just like . . . Vonnegut's. (p. 43)

If *Mother Night* were intended as a psychological novel, the flat characterization of Campbell could be blamed for the book's failure to move beyond the level of a slapstick, melodramatic spy story. But the main intention is, again, moralistic, and the book is a vehicle for messages, attached this time to events and personalities in the unimagined world, in a contemporary history that is already legendary for younger readers. The message is to the effect that reality and men are such masses of contradiction, that, among other things, it is useless saying who is finally villainous or heroic, though villainy and evil are obvious. As for what looks like unmitigated villainy, the best one can do, looking back, is provoke laughter at it. . . .

Günter Grass wrote raucously in *The Tin Drum* without in the least depriving Nazism of an aura of important, brutal force, or getting smeared by nearness with sentimentality. Vonnegut makes the Nazis, and by implication, evil itself, seem absurd, ridiculous, and inevitable. To counter it, he enlists laughter, but not only that. . . .

While *Mother Night* is grotesque, like mummery on a stage, *Slaughterhouse-Five*, Vonnegut's first hardback best-seller, has a maudlin feel about it. Both books present the spectacle of a writer facing the world, trying to write saving myths about it using documentary material.

That this is what Vonnegut was about in *Slaughterhouse-Five* can easily be inferred. The story—told by a narrator who is a writer established on Cape Cod—concerns a harmless optometrist, Billy Pilgrim who, as a prisoner of the Germans in World War II, lived through the American bombing of Dresden and is obsessed to the point of madness with the memory. Coming "unstuck," Billy lives simultaneously on earth and on the planet Tralfamadore where he learns a new religion of stoicism. The kinship of Billy Pilgrim with his namesake in Bunyan, not to mention Christ and Everyman, is obvious. The style, "in the telegraphic schizophrenic manner of the planet Tralfamadore," attempts to get at something by accretion of extremely unconnected bits in time and space, and the bombing of

Dresden actually disappears in the shadows thrown by placard-like announcements from the narrator: "I have told my sons that they are not under any circumstances to take part in massacres, and that the news of massacres of enemies is not to fill them with satisfaction or glee." . . .

Breakfast of Champions, as seemingly miscellaneous as *Slaughterhouse-Five*, is the summation of the discoveries Vonnegut has made in writing, the whole held together by the crude drawings he supplies to illustrate it. It is like a children's encyclopedic picture album with detours and definitions, naming the animals, presuming to treat as if for the first time of pornography, suicide, racism, and madness in Middle America, without neglecting the plot, or despairing of methods of salvation proposed in earlier novels. The drawings are the logical goal of Vonnegut's writing over the years. They supplement the words, and begin substituting for them. They are meant, in their crude friskiness, to increase the horror by playing against it, as a comedian in silent films might deadpan against a hilarious or hazardous situation. The effect is not necessarily the one intended. They also mean to charm, to draw forth love and mercy, and there can be no doubt that for some reader-viewers they succeed. (p. 44)

[It] is not enough to say that Hoenikker, the atomic scientist in *Cat's Cradle*, was a cliché ten years ago. It is necessary to add that this cliché speaks with increasing force to a generation of students, and their parents who take after them, because of what they read in the papers and breathe in the air. "I was in Dresden," Vonnegut says, "when America dropped scientific truth on it." . . . Although the pacifism Vonnegut preaches is couched in absolute terms, and his imaginary ideal American hero is a man who absolutely refuses to kill or be a party to killing, Vonnegut does not fail to say in speeches now that during his war the enemy deserved to be crushed by any means—so long as innocent, defenseless people (for example, the Dresdeners) were not incinerated. Vonnegut is not unaware of the tortured relation of guilt and innocence, and of the practical difficulty, probably the impossibility once the logic of total war is rolling, of sparing civilians. Indeed, he is ever ready to indicate moral dilemmas and paradoxes, in the best manner of innocence lost, while never really altering or complicating the thrust of his simple, absolute preachment.

The preacher is a sinner, too, of course; he does not deny it. In denying his own virtue Vonnegut can go to such extremes of language and hypothetical example that one can either be disarmed by his honesty, or begin suspecting that this writer not only has the power to do harm, but actually does it—by the crude, unreal, and actually soothing pictures of human behavior that he draws. "If I'd been born in Germany," he says in the preface to *Mother Night*, "I suppose I would have been a Nazi, bopping Jews and Gypsies and Poles around, leaving boots sticking out of snowbanks, warming myself with my secretly virtuous insides. So it goes." (p. 45)

Villains and heroes do not exist in such accounts, needless to say, but neither do any humans, if humans think, decide, act, regret. Yet Vonnegut's fictions, with their flat characters who are put through their paces to make the author's humanistic point ("only humans are sacred"), most probably do not leave Vonnegut's devotees feeling empty or sad.

Vonnegut is not an apologist for evil, nor does he mean to sound neutral; he is sure it exists, and that he knows what it is—he could not be so popular if he did not. Of World War II he says in *Wampeters, Foma & Granfallons*, "We had fought something which was totally obscene." That is only the beginning, however, for "this was very bad for us." The war against Hitler gave Americans a long-lasting sense of righteousness and of a global mission finally expressing itself, he says, in what Lieutenant Calley did at Mylai. If the after-effects of Vonnegut's generation's war were bad for America, they were and continue to be worse for people in the rest of the world, because of the power America acquired to harm with its good intentions. In Vonnegut's books, greed and narrowmindedness go with self-righteousness and power. The world is on the road of war, pollution, and starvation, of final extinction around the corner, and so far as humans can be, his generation of Americans is responsible for this.

During the last decade or so such ideas have become common currency in this country, and surely would have been if Vonnegut had not contributed his share. Obviously it takes more to attract the young man than to blame the world's troubles on their parents. In fact, it would be bizarre if reading or listening to Vonnegut set a young person against his elders, or reinforced a previous hatred or contempt. Vonnegut's anger at his generation is mild, as his pessimism concerning the human prospect is gentle, and presumably all-inclusive: though he sympathizes with the young founders of backwoods communes, who try to adapt Bokononism (the religion of fatalism practiced in Tralfamadore) to their separate realities, he has little or no hope of their success. It is either too late for that, or it is written somewhere, in the book of Fate, that these experiments, too, are doomed. (pp. 45-6)

Vonnegut says in his new book that one of the reasons he no longer gives so many speeches is that "a recent refugee from Middle Europe" interrupted him once with the question, "You are a leader of American young people—What right do you have to teach them to be so cynical and pessimistic?"

But one can only understand the anger of Vonnegut's Czech or Polish questioner if one is convinced of many things—that the Vonnegut phenomenon is a cultural-political test case, that books really are bisected into "High Art" and "Pop," that taste is debased, that books are important. Most of all, one would have to believe, as Vonnegut says he does, that good or bad ideas in books have the power to do good or to harm. (p. 46)

> Edward Grossman, "Vonnegut & His Audience" (reprinted from Commentary by permission; copyright © 1974 by the American Jewish Committee), in Commentary, July, 1974, pp. 40-6.

I would like to examine . . . the relationship between Vonnegut's fiction, which essentially defies problem solving, and the reader's conventional expectation of finding meaning, if not solutions, in the texts of Vonnegut's fiction. My suggestion is that the conclusions to Vonnegut's novels develop out of, and preserve, a complex awareness of the interplay between imagination and death; which is to say that Vonnegut, unlike any contemporary American author I am aware of, has it *both* ways for perfectly legitimate rea-

sons. A favorite question, variations of which appear explicitly in every one of Vonnegut's novels, is "What are people for?" Each one of the conclusions I have cited [*Player Piano, Sirens of Titan, Mother Night, Cat's Cradle, God Bless You, Mr. Rosewater, Slaughterhouse-Fire*, and *Breakfast of Champions*] captures or arrests this question within the paradoxical framework of an imaginative assertion poised against the presence of death. Such a device preserves our sense that individuals are free to "do their own thing"—that people can have at least the illusion of growth imaginatively and sometimes practically—but at the same time their "own thing" is continually set against a resistant pattern which we call human history. There exists a continual contest in Vonnegut's work between the inner space of imagination and the outer space of history. To put it another way: people, including Kurt Vonnegut, Jr., are free to self-actualize but they must never expect such self-actualization to alter, fundamentally, the course of human history. As a consequence, what we see in Vonnegut's fiction is a continuum of imagined alternatives—a spectrum of people self-actualizing—which at the same time preserves our sense, to use Vonnegut's phrase, that "the fix is on" ["In a Manner That Must Shame God Himself," *Harper's Magazine*, November, 1972]. (pp. 165-66)

What we see repeatedly in Vonnegut's fiction is individual action reduced to sham theatricality—to gestures without ultimate significance but desperately laden with personal meaning. The actions are imagined attempts at meaning, but they will in no way alter the forces of human history. Individuals try to evolve toward significance and value, but history continually intrudes, denudes, and reduces human aspiration to nothing more than static posturing. (p. 168)

Vonnegut's humor, which is doubtless deserving of an essay in itself, strikes me as being only part of, and not an antidote to, the all-encompassing problem of human imagination pitted against the forces of historical extinction. Vonnegut's humor represents a perceptual slant that makes destruction a bit more tolerable; it is a mode of consciousness which permits the reader to accept his apparent condition with some detachment, if not with good cheer. But Vonnegut's humor in no way alters (indeed, it highlights) the apparent meaning of his fiction, which is that, individually, we try to imagine a meaning for ourselves in an inner space that, historically, is continually violated. (p. 170)

From *Player Piano* to *Slaughterhouse-Five*, Vonnegut's fiction depends, in a variety of ways, on an interplay between death and the imagination. The confrontation between these two forces is rarely weighted exclusively toward one pole or the other, the idea being that the exercise of imagination in the face of death constituted what social scientists call the "human condition." In *Breakfast of Champions*, however, it appears that this dialectic has been replaced by an obsessive split between Vonnegut's nostalgic lament for a lost past and his bitter denunciation of a coercive present. Where Vonnegut formerly expressed a fear that men were being displaced by machines, now he is fearful that men have become machines. (p. 171)

[The] chief "character" of [*Breakfast of Champions*] is clearly Kurt Vonnegut, Jr. He is the master of ceremonies, or better yet, the master mortician. Vonnegut is out to kill his former fiction—to clear his head, he says, "of all the junk in there." It is significant that the book is written in primer prose, for *Breakfast of Champions* is a kind of children's book (complete with drawings) in which Vonnegut tries to sort out innocence and experience. He himself must appear front and center, for the book, finally, is about Vonnegut's sense of awareness. Thus we watch Vonnegut almost ritually stalk his own biographical past while he also pursues his former characters down the seamy streets of Midland City; all this is done to establish that what he once created he now wishes to destroy. Destruction, of course, is often a prelude to regeneration, but before Vonnegut will be able to regenerate his fiction, to his own satisfaction, it appears that he will have to sort out his own past. In a sense, then, this book does not simply frustrate the reader's customary pursuit of meaning: it records Vonnegut's own frustrated pursuit of meaning in his own fiction. The reader of *Breakfast of Champions* is thus being asked to participate in, or at least observe, Vonnegut's own self-analysis. (p. 172)

[The] question Vonnegut continually asks of himself in this book is whether he can create art out of his American experience or whether America has replaced art—his art—with advertising. (p. 173)

If my reading of *Breakfast of Champions* is at all plausible, it then follows that the reader's expectation of meaning takes an especially curious turn in Vonnegut's latest book. There is a sense in which the reader's frustrated pursuit of meaning now converges with Vonnegut's—not simply his characters'—sense of frustration. For reader and author alike *Breakfast of Champions* is at once a dead-end and a possible prelude to liberation. . . . It is [the] very willingness to confront tragedy—the tragedy of America together with Vonnegut's sensitivity to tragedy—that makes *Breakfast of Champions* such a moving, tortured, and honest book. What *Breakfast of Champions* does, even as Vonnegut abandons his prior characters, is to reconfirm, in a highly personal way, the basis of his fiction: namely, that imagination and death are inextricably bound together, and that only as they are fully contemplated in terms of one another can Vonnegut's art and his reader's response remain humane. (pp. 173-74)

> *Robert W. Uphaus, "Expected Meaning in Vonnegut's Dead-End Fiction," in* Novel: A Forum on Fiction *(copyright © Novel Corp., 1975), Winter, 1975, pp. 164-74.*

I enjoyed [*Venus on the Half-Shell*, allegedly written by Kilgore Trout, a Vonnegut character]. The story rolls right along from one escapade to another, and the philosophy is so thin and silly it never gets in the way. At one point, having received something less than a satisfactory answer to his query from a cannibalistic wise man, Wagstaff explodes: "You have the same philosophy as a college sophomore's!" Trout knows his audience, anyway.

As I read the book, a great many words beginning with "r" sprang into my mind. These were the words: ribald, risque, revolutionary, revolting, raunchy, rowdy, raucous, randy, Rabelaisian. . .

If it had started with an "r" I might also have thought "Voltairean," for there is a certain *Candide* quality to the work. The ineffectual, not especially intelligent hero wanders from one allegorical, satirical situation into another. But Trout is no Voltaire, and there is nothing so profound it provokes serious thought; nothing you can sink your teeth into. It's more like cotton *Candide*.

After all it is the originality of a satirist's vision, rather than the object of his satire that makes his work endure; his powers of invention rather than his philosophical perspective that makes him memorable. We remember Candide and Pangloss, not the ideas of Leibniz they were meant to parody. Lilliput, Brobdingnag, and the Yahoos have become part of the language, though their relationship to 18th-century politics may be utterly lost on us.

Trout recognizes this. His philosophy is only a flimsy pretext for adventure; the Space Wanderer's question-and-answer only a device to keep him moving around from planet to planet. Vonnegut, on the other hand, seems to take himself seriously. He is best when he is like Trout, inventive and right on the edge of silliness, when his fantasy takes over and he writes of Tralfamadore and the chronosynclastic infundibulum. When he writes of war and death and Dresden he is occasionally profound, but more often embarrassing.

Vonnegut once claimed that "Kilgore Trout's unpopularity was deserved. His prose was frightful. Only his ideas were good." And in the synopses he gave, he seemed to back up that statement. But *Venus on the Half-Shell* does not. Trout's prose is at least as good as Vonnegut's. It is strange ("clouds as black as rotten spots on a banana . . . the horizon had been as unbroken as a fake genealogy"), but it is lively and inventive and goes by faster than a holiday weekend. Some of the incidents—obsessed as they are with sex and excrement—are a little hard to stomach, but the next reissue of Trout, perhaps *Oh Say Can You Smell?* or *2BR02B* is something I'm definitely looking forward to.

Thanks, Kurt. (p. 4)

> *Chris Dickey, "Fishing for Trout," in* Book World—The Washington Post *(© The Washington Post), March 2, 1975, pp. 1, 4.*

There is a certain kind of American writing that resembles the cement industry in Sri Lanka. On the hungry island that was once known as Serendip coral reefs are blasted off the coast and the coral is burned in kilns to make lime. But then the reefless places let in the heavy surf and this causes erosion. Lime is an essential ingredient in cement, so the reefs are replaced with a by-product of the coral—concrete. It is a joke industry, self-perpetuating and finally self-consuming. 'So it goes,' as Kurt Vonnegut says, and well he might. After all, *Slaughterhouse-Five* was partly a novel about a man writing a novel called *Slaughterhouse-Five* ("'Listen," I said, "I'm writing this book about Dresden. . . .'"). You can't get any more self-perpetuating than that, and as Mr Vonnegut's experience has shown, this kind of candour goes down well with the college crowd. Art looks like an intimidating gimmick to the fairly ignorant. . . . It is an enterprise in repetition, another joke industry. At the high point of his fame the celebrated American writer, who has nothing to say, says, 'I have nothing to say' and makes a fortune on the lecture circuit repeating it.

It is also the making of modesty into a conceit so unique it borders on arrogance. Mr Vonnegut's modesty is breathtaking. (p. 452)

The impression one is left with [after reading *Wampeters, Foma & Granfalloons*] is of a writer who wishes to appear in a state of undress in order to be thought innocent, who sees a kind of eloquence in being inarticulate. The subtitle of his collection is 'Opinions', and yet even he must see that he is the opposite of opinionated: a wide-eyed boy of 51, astonished and a little embarrassed by his success. (p. 453)

> *Paul Theroux, "Joke Industry," in* New Statesman *(© 1975 The Statesman & Nation Publishing Co. Ltd.), April 4, 1975, pp. 452-53.*

W

WAGONER, David   1926-

Wagoner is an American poet, editor, and novelist endowed with a "lyrical ear and an alert but disciplined imagination." Themes of innocence and corruption, of the individual trapped in a violent society, recur in his tragicomic novels. (See also *Contemporary Authors*, Vols. 1-4, rev. ed.)

Though his eight books, as I mean to show, have nourished and renewed one another, the poems gaining precisely the humanity and texture of reality we look for in the novel, and the novels acquiring that "abandon, wild calculation and seriousness" which James Dickey locates in Wagoner's poetry; though the four volumes of poetry alternating with four novels since 1953 have garnered a lot of cross-pollinating praise, it is surely because they insist so securely on being poems and novels that most of us have still to discover this writer's contribution to our literature. That is just it: Wagoner will not come out from behind his literature, and thereby protects himself from becoming another casualty of Success. . . .

The first of Wagoner's books of poetry, *Dry Sun, Dry Wind*, was published in 1953 and dedicated to Roethke, who remains a pervasive force in all this poet's work—even the novels. What Wagoner gets from Roethke is a preoccupation with the movement from external to created reality, the sense that we awaken in a world possessed and informed by something in our dream, so characteristic of the older poet. (p. 534)

The slant rhymes and assorted rhythms [of the first book] keep us from collecting the material presented into a charm, an incantation. There is no self here to "breathe what I am"—just as, in the poems about selves, there is so little breakthrough to vision ("the eye turns feebler, year by year"); the partitioning of the beautiful lyrics from the bruised lives brings Wagoner to a strange alienation, a sense that Being itself, even while he watches, is being withheld from him, or rather, not from him, but that he is not yet himself entirely *there*, in the sense of selfhood that Keats intended when he wrote, "that which is creative must create itself"—for by the end of *Dry Sun, Dry Wind*, Wagoner has not yet created himself, but only the estranged world of "familiars" in which he will henceforth operate by an alienation-effect whose apparent suspension of energy, of process, turns every known thing Other. (p. 537)

The year after *Dry Sun, Dry Wind* . . ., Wagoner published his first novel, *The Man in the Middle* and in 1955 his second, *Money Money Money*; and it was not until 1958, five years after *Dry Sun, Dry Wind*, that he had sufficiently released himself from the indenture to plausible surfaces, to accident and "the ravelled edge of everything" which we think of as the impulse of fiction, or at least its expedient, to produce his second collection of poems, *A Place to Stand*. The intuition of futility in most biography, the awareness that we are impotent in the clutch of what *happens* to us, finds, in Wagoner's first three novels, a more appropriate rehearsal than in his early poems, which are committed—it is, of course, the lyric responsiblity—to an order of knowledge and a hierarchy of Being. *The Man in the Middle* takes for its exergue a sentence from Donne which may stand over all of Wagoner's prose enterprises: "This minute I was well, and am ill, this minute. I am surprised with a sodaine change, and alteration to worse, and can impute it to no cause, nor call it by any name." Wagoner's hero in each instance is a creature from outside the community life—invalid, obsessed, even idiotic—who knows what he takes for his own mind and wants to be left alone with that knowledge, not to enjoy it perhaps ("it was harder to invent life by yourself") but to nurse it along, to "favor" it, in the sense of something felt to be vulnerable; but chance puts him in the world's way, and the ensuing adventures must lead to disaster along with a surrender of the separateness cherished by "the man in the middle," crushed by the social and erotic forces he is called upon to mediate even as he unleashes them. (p. 538)

[In] the overflowing poems of [*The Nesting Ground*, the] third book, Wagoner has found a modulation, a cadence grateful to the range of his own voice. He has also learned to exploit the determinations already encysted in our speech (as when he refers to "drivers driven by themselves. . . . The far-afield, the breakers of new ground/who cartwheel out of sight, end over end": here the condensation which makes death an exploration as well as an impasse in "breakers of new ground" and the doom of "end over end" have a rightness beyond mere invention, a finality due to something discovered in the idiom itself). Further, he shows a flickering grace with slant rhymes, as if to remind the discourse—so relaxed at times as to be beneath the tension of the lyre—that he is still touching the strings. . . . [It] is only justice to say that Wagoner's music *has* consumed its instruments. His mastery of his own means liberates him for a kind of observation, an acknowledgment of the given world, . . . which he had previously been obliged, as by some lack in himself, some failure of nerve, to siphon off into the novels. (p. 544)

The very thing one felt to be absent in Wagoner's early poems, or to be partitioned off without much mercy for the terrain thus distributed, has now—by a curious apprehension of opposites or at least oppositions, in his own and in an outer nature—been resolved into a *presence*, and what is more, a presence within a *scene*. (p. 545)

In 1966, . . . Wagoner published *Staying Alive*, his fourth book of poems and, in the nature of things—a phrase, by the way, which bears a particular application to this preeminently Big Woods series, a *preserve* where the poet "sets loose, like birds / in a landscape, the old words"—his finest achievement to date. . . . The quest for some retrieved wholeness which will venture into that country of "love's divisions" is the burden of this book, and its motley wisdom can be summed up—though Wagoner resists the summary process; he likes the separate effort, the unparaphrasable enterprise: "springing again, as the birds will, to climb through wilder country before falling"—in the wry phrase "Staying Alive By Going to Pieces," with its suggestion of Osiris beneath the colloquial profanity. The very history of his art becomes something to oppose, and by opposing to extend, as in Wagoner's beautiful epithalamion, "Water Music for the Progress of Love in a Life-Raft Down the Sammamish Slough," the true Northwest Passage this explorer has been looking for so long. (pp. 548-49)

[There] is, finally, an acceptance in David Wagoner's poetry, an assenting invocation to the very fractured and fragmented existence he had once most feared as a kind of death; indeed, there is a sense in which death itself is reckoned the "missing all," as Emily Dickinson called it, in the totality of experience which this poet, at the end of his book, puts together in a kind of mad song, a Christopher Smart rhapsody called "Come Before His Countenance with a Joyful Leaping". . . . (p. 550)

> *Richard Howard, "David Wagoner," in his* Alone With America: Essays on the Art of Poetry in the United States Since 1950 *(copyright © 1965, 1966, 1967, 1968, 1969 by Richard Howard; reprinted by permission of Atheneum Publishers, New York), Atheneum, 1969, pp. 533-51.*

[*The Road to Many a Wonder* is] American Escapiana in which virtue and industry triumph while the mean and greedy get their just retribution against a genuine historical background. . . . [Mr. Wagoner] . . . does it all pretty well, but never well enough so we're not always aware that he's "doing it." This is very far indeed from the contemporary champion in its vein—Charles Portis's admirable, neversmug "True Grit." (p. 36)

> *Sara Blackburn, in* The New York Times Book Review *(© 1974 by The New York Times Company; reprinted by permission), April 21, 1974.*

[With *The Road to Many a Wonder*] Mr. Wagoner has not attempted an especially large or weighty work . . .; still [this] is a consistently charming book, saved from banality or sentimentality by something ultimately uncompromising, intelligent, and hardheaded in the makeup of its heroes. Also, a number of secondary characters, most of them marked by laziness, cupidity, and a dangerous hunger for unearned rewards, are drawn with enough texture to give some depth and tension to the plot. Mr. Wagoner has drawn unabashedly on some of the more heartening impulses in American myth-making, and the book itself partakes of the same spirit of generosity and confidence that imparts energy and substance to the experience portrayed in it. (p. 19)

> *Jane Larkin Crain, in* Saturday Review/World *(copyright © 1974 by Saturday Review/World, Inc.; reprinted with permission), June 29, 1974.*

David Wagoner is a personable, gentle and soft-spoken artist whose reputation as a novelist is slowly beginning to equalize his formidable and well-deserved reputation as a poet. . . .

Wagoner's new novel ["The Road to Many a Wonder"] is a total delight: a fresh, charming insight into Western America of the late 1850's that, in spite of its captivating hero and heroine, is a realistic, clear-eyed view of the rags to riches complex that dominated American character during and after the Pike's Peak Gold Rush of 1859. . . .

To read this novel is to understand once again the hope and optimism that characterized so much of the American frontier; an optimism that over a century later, Wagoner has come to firmly believe in, although civilization has made deep scars on the landscape of the American Dream.

"The Road to Many A Wonder" pursues the themes that have fascinated Wagoner since his first excellent novel, "The Man in the Middle," was published in 1953. Simply put, Wagoner's basic theme involves an innocent person who becomes involved in a corrupt situation, finds himself trapped and eventually is either destroyed or badly wounded by the experience.

However, since "The Escape Artist" (1965), the last part of this formulae has begun to change, and the road to despair has branched off into a road of many wonders indeed. Further, in his last three novels, Wagoner has allowed his considerable poetic talents to gently introduce themselves into his always strong, flowing narrative prose. The result is not only first-rate story-telling, but story-telling enhanced with the holding power of poetic myth.

> *Jack Leahy, "David Wagoner: An Artist in Search of Wonders," in* The Seattle Post–Intelligencer, *July 7, 1974.*

David Wagoner, in my opinion, is a novelist to read, a high opinion that I have held ever since reading *The Man in the Middle*. . . . He has a particular genius for portraying men in hysterical motion, and women too, as [*The Road to Many a Wonder*] shows. And here, as in his . . . *Where Is My Wandering Boy Tonight?*, the hysteria erupts in continuous laughter. This is a very funny book, further proof of Leslie Fiedler's adage that the best way to regard the mythic Great West is as a big joke. It is a book that you may place with assurance in the hands of children, though you may have to pry it loose in order to get in back. In such parlous times, such a book is a treasure, but *Road to Many a Wonder* is not merely entertainment; it is that kind of literature we call American.

In patent imitation in style and subject matter of *The Adventures of Huckleberry Finn*, Wagoner has taken another step and stuffed Huck's skin with Horatio Algerish *Excelsior!* resulting in Ike (Isaac) Bender, whose motto is "Bound to Rise." That his bread may do likewise, Ike sets out for the Pike's Peak goldfields with salterus in his pocket, but the yeast in Ike's particular dough is Millicent Slaughter. . . .

[As] Ike has a Huckish ring to his metaphors and an Algerish hike to his trousers, so Millicent's is a familiar voice in American literature, with a schoolmarmish edge to her voice, apparently taken from a fabled "Miss Wilkerson" back home. But it recalls something of the quality of Katharine Hepburn in company with Humphrey Bogart as they chug down the Congo in the *African Queen*. Hepburn is the undisputed salvation of Bogart, and so Millicent with Ike, and though their journey is overland it follows the course of the Platte—a good enough Congo for their purposes. (p. 28)

This book, quite frankly, is a fairy tale of marvelous encounters filling golden roads leading out of Kansas to wonder, and the dialogue crackles with the rude wit that is the stuff of that indigenous American fairy tale, the folk tale, for like Huck himself Ike and Millicent Bender have traveled a long, long road indeed—like Sweet Betsy from Pike who crossed those big mountains with her lover. Always the master of a dialogue that matches his fast-paced plots, Wagoner here elevates exchange into the kind of transcendent patter a more sophisticated version of which made a Raymond Chandler famous, redolent of the drawl that makes Davy Crockett and Sam Spade brothers under the hard-boiled shell. That this drops like manna before the moving picture camera should go without saying, but I mention it so that when this happens you will have read it here first, and be sure to read the book first also, because it may not be better than the movie but I'm betting that it is, and don't forget you read that here first as well. (p. 29)

John Seelye, in The New Republic *(reprinted by permission of* The New Republic; © *1974 by the New Republic, Inc.), July 20, 1974.*

[Wagoner's] best achievements are among his poems, but a number of his earlier novels had flaws that were the result of serious effort. . . . [Now he] writes only successes. Here is the opening of *The Road to Many a Wonder*:

> I'd probably have went Pikes-Peak-or-Busting without any extra help or discouragement, but what made it certain sure was my old man cussing our farm. We'd been scratching to hang on to it for five years, but I could tell there wasn't going to be no sixth when he stood there . . . and commenced laying his extra-special Sunday-miss-the-meeting curse on it.

Since that language is about as native to Wagoner as Bantu, it must have been hard to write, but as in all literary writing, when the effort goes into the language devoid from

everything else, the mountains keep bringing forth mice as they labor. . . . There can't be many motives, and none of them good, for writing this way, words tossed around like cracked ping-pong balls, as though the only task were to *sound like* Huck, or Jamie McPheeters. It is no occupation for a grown person, and I'm sorry Wagoner chose to write it. (pp. 625-26)

Roger Sale, in The Hudson Review *(copyright* © *1974 by The Hudson Review, Inc.; reprinted by permission), Vol. XXVII, No. 4, Winter, 1974-75.*

David Wagoner has been the poet to look to for the "narrative poem." *Sleeping in the Woods*, his eighth volume of poetry, is not quite another collection in a continuing saga, although he remains one of the most *readable* poets around. Immediately, upon entering his poems, we are taken into his world. Intrigued, we drink the liquor of his story's weave, instantly interested. Although he is the author of numerous novels, his poetry has that one (out of many?) aspect that distinguishes poetry from prose: a sense of line. There is tension of syntax and diction in his work. In this book he leaves behind much of his narrative acumen, moving on to something new for him, something more contemplative, more difficult—an uneasiness that makes this book, if not my favorite Wagoner, perhaps his most important. In this deeper realm, he is once again novice, a word I use cautiously. Wagoner is a master technician. He knows how to write well, a novelty in much contemporary verse. It is as a departure that I recommend his new collection. (p. 26)

Daniel Halpern, in The New Republic *(reprinted by permission of* The New Republic; © *1975 by The New Republic, Inc.), March 29, 1975.*

Though David Wagoner's new volume, *Sleeping in the Woods*, is not entirely successful, his honesty and his craftsmanship are splendidly apparent, and his (occasionally annoying) affectations are genuinely consistent with his interests. In many of these poems, the poet rather uncertainly compels our sympathy with his particular commitment, while leaving to luck our own commitment to that compulsion. Often, he carries it off with a flourish, for he has a pleasant skill. . . . But in some cases, even when the poem is quite well ordered, it is disappointingly inadequate to compel a sense of the significance to which it is committed. (pp. 123-24)

The significance that Wagoner sees in all things is a very demanding one, and these demands become the reader's expectations through the instrument of the poet's transparency. The scheme is fairly simple: nature exists to provide a lesson in organic form and its processes, in whose imitation and recreation poetry excels, surpassing painting and music with a delicate burst of inimitable complexity. Such poetry is compounded of the major aesthetic traditions, the classical and the romantic; and its arrogance in insisting that its sister arts are relatively toothless when it comes to defending oneself against the barbarian has not been recognized. For the advantage of poetry which Wagoner takes is that it can say something in its saying. (p. 124)

The best poems in this volume are of two kinds. Most numerous are those in which the truth of the moment appears (at the least) to give validity to the style, though the precise distinctions, and the points at which the validity impresses itself upon us, are never quite clear. . . . And then there are those in which, very clearly, the style compels our belief in the truth which the poet presents to us . . . in which our belief is the root, our believing the stem and the leaves, and the thing believed is the flower. The psalms are perhaps our noblest example of this process; and Wagoner's "Seven Songs for an Old Voice" belong in their general company. . . . (pp. 124-25)

J. E. Chamberlin, in The Hudson Review *(copyright © 1975 by The Hudson Review, Inc.; reprinted by permission), Vol. XXVIII, No. 1, Spring, 1975.*

* * *

WALKER, Alice   1944-

Ms Walker is a Black American novelist, short story writer, and poet, born in Georgia and now living and teaching in Massachusetts. (See also *Contemporary Authors,* **Vols. 37-40.)**

Alice Walker has delivered a magnificent first novel in *The Third Life of Grange Copeland*. It is about three generations of black sharecroppers in Georgia. Suffering deprivations foisted upon them by white bosses, they are still significantly the victims of cruelties inflicted upon each other —cruelties that emanate from a profound lack of self-respect, fostered by whites and blacks alike, and a powerfully destructive despair. The tremendous difficulty of emerging from these depths is what Miss Walker sets out to dramatize. She begins with Grange Copeland's early failure as a sharecropper, father, husband, and man—a life he abruptly and unilaterally abandons for a new one in the North, which almost predictably turns out to be no less degrading. Meanwhile, his abandoned son, Brownfield, repeats in his life the worst errors in his father's: he marries a good and lovely woman whose higher education he sees as a threat and therefore does not rest until he brings her down to a misery so abject that it all but crushes her. . . . Grange brings up the youngest of his grandchildren, Ruth, whom he tries not only to protect but to provide with a sense of self-esteem that his son has totally lacked and that, up until his own return south, he himself has missed. It is too easy, he has found, to blame everything on the white man. Somewhere along the way a man, even a black man, must assume responsibility for what happens to himself, if he is ever to become truly a man. (pp. 464-65)

Grange dies believing that there is no future for black men in this country, that it is too late for blacks to forget or forgive the harm that has been done them, regardless of changes that may bring equality for all men. But he also knows that "Survival was not everything. *He* had survived. But to survive *whole* was what he wanted for Ruth". . . . The self-respect, tenderness, and love that Grange has taught Ruth in their years together can support something bigger, including as it does even the bitter memories of her girlhood. She will not repeat the mistakes of her mother or grandmother, nor let the bitterness triumph. . . .

[The] honest treatment of both past and present, the worst aspects of which Miss Walker does not flinch at, help make *The Third Life* a convincing and stirring novel. So do its firm, tight control and its eloquence: it is no surprise to learn that the author is also a poet. (p. 465)

Jay L. Halio, in The Southern Review *(copyright, 1973, by the Louisiana State University), Vol. IX, No. 1, Spring, 1973.*

There is little doubt that, [with *In Love & Trouble*, a collection of stories,] Alice Walker has touched us all. Whether a JuJu woman convincing an ole evil white woman to die or a black lady being ejected from worship because it's the wrong church. In "Strong Horse Tea" the question posed—When will this one learn to depend on those who will come?—awaits our answer. Alice has begun peeling an essence. They are not pretty—these short stories—nor happy—as one traditionally thinks of stories about black women and their men, black mothers and their children, old black ladies and their gods. I applaud *In Love & Trouble*. I welcome the examination without polemics. I certainly welcome the love Alice so painfully shares.

Nikki Giovanni, "So Black and Blue," in Book World—The Washington Post *(© The Washington Post), November 18, 1973, p. 1.*

Alice Walker has focused her fictional eye on the black woman, her loves and, as the blues idiom puts it, her 'bukes and scorns . . .'. And, like the lyrics of good blues, [the stories in "In Love and Trouble"] are terse, ironic and humorous. Alice Walker writes efficiently and economically, and the shorter pieces here, even when thin as fiction, are often prose poems.

While not as ambitious as her novel, "The Third Life of Grange Copeland"—which traced a poor, rural black family through three generations and established its author as a skillful recorder of the Southern character—these stories are perceptive miniatures, snapshots, that capture their subjects at crucial and revealing moments. In this collection, Miss Walker is moving without being maudlin, ironic without being [gimmicky]. (p. 41)

Mel Watkins, in The New York Times Book Review *(© 1974 by The New York Times Company; reprinted by permission), March 17, 1974.*

Reading Alice Walker is like hearing John Coltrane's *Alabama*. Each bites into strange Southern fruit and finds a sweetness almost as unbearable as the bitterness of violence, humiliation and oppression. As Walker's character Grange Copeland says after his granddaughter's birth: "'Out of all kinds of shit comes something clean, soft and sweet smellin','" Pain and joy, tenderness and power, helplessness and cruelty flow through her writing and are beautiful because of the wholeness of her talent.

In Walker's hands wholeness is an all-inclusive, open-ended theme. Pointing beyond human guilt, it suggests that an oppressed people's first step away from helplessness is to take responsibility for their actions toward each other. . . .

In Walker's poems black women mostly survive and, even when one doesn't—like Sammy Lou who, after killing the cracker who murdered her husband, is carried off to the electric chair—her death is heroic. . . .

In Walker's fiction there is often nothing but pain, violence and death for black women. I shouldn't say *nothing* because the two women who die violently in *The Third Life of Grange Copeland* are lovely, strong and in love as they marry and begin working shares on the white man's plantation. (p. 21)

In Love and Trouble is full of . . . challenging and movingly realized stories. . . .

Alice Walker's power as a writer is exactly that power she [once noted] in Jean Toomer. "He is both feminine and masculine in his perceptions." Alice Walker is Ruth, and she is Grange Copeland. She is old Mr. Sweet and the girl who revives him. As I've heard Michael Harper say as he reads his poems and those of the neglected Sterling Brown: "I been down so long that down don't bother me." (p. 22)

> *John F. Callahan, "Reconsideration: The Higher Ground of Alice Walker," in* The New Republic *(reprinted by permission of* The New Republic; © *1974 by The New Republic, Inc.), September 14, 1974, pp. 21-2.*

*   *   *

WALLANT, Edward Lewis   1926-1962

Wallant, an American novelist, was the author of *The Pawnbroker*. His protagonists are Jewish-Americans immersed in anguish; his settings, harshly urban; his message, optimistic. (See also *Contemporary Authors*, Vols. 1-4, rev. ed.)

Edward Lewis Wallant . . . can be considered "minor" only in terms of what he might have done had he lived beyond the age of thirty-six. I shall not be surprised if future critics award him a high place in our literature on the basis of the four novels he did complete; but in the meantime his inclusion in a volume devoted to minor figures is justified by the fact that he is almost unknown to the public. (p. 118)

It is . . . the sudden hunger to know what lies in the hearts of others . . . that is at the center of Wallant's fiction; or rather, as the theme characteristically appears in a framework of exhortation, the absolute obligation of all men to acknowledge this hunger, and to satisfy it by communion with their fellows.

This is the battle cry of the romantics; it does not require much reflection to locate it in central position in such important contemporary works as *Franny and Zooey, A New Life, Henderson the Rain King,* and *One Flew over the Cuckoo's Nest.* (p. 122)

Wallant was [deeply involved] in the affairs of the new romanticism, which combines the moral concern and savage sincerity of a Nathanael West, a Dos Passos, or Hemingway with a new, sometimes mystical acceptance of life, and most of all, an imperative call to action. (pp. 122-23)

Wallant says it this way: "We all have to hold hands in all this dark." The words are given to that *daemon ex machina,* Sammy, the orderly of *The Children at the Gate.* To take the hand of one's neighbor may be an unsavoury task, and in any case will prove a difficult one, because all of the wisdom of the world is ranged against it. Yet Wallant like other romantics insists that the effort be made; and the clash of that effort against that wisdom—sensibility against sense, if you will—resounds through his fiction.

Wallant sets up these confrontations with great skill. No contemporary novelist was more gifted in the sheer grace of constructing a novel. . . . In each [of his novels] there is a careful positioning of the central figure from the beginning in a fixed state symbolic of his life—in each case, an unsatisfactory life. The characters then initiate or take part in certain symbolic acts which eventually result in freeing them for the kind of deep human relationship which their author demands for all men.

The key word is *separation.* In each novel the hero is set apart, sometimes bound; more often fixed in unproductive orbit around a world of chained sufferers. (pp. 123-24)

> *Charles Alva Hoyt, "The Sudden Hunger: An Essay on the Novels of Edward Lewis Wallant," in* Minor American Novelist, *edited by Charles Alva Hoyt (copyright © 1970, Southern Illinois University Press; reprinted by permission of Southern Illinois University Press), Southern Illinois University Press, 1970, pp. 118-37.*

[The] New York where Holden Caulfield has his nervous breakdown is an almost benign place when compared with the urban landscapes, created only a few years later, of Edward Lewis Wallant. He lived to write only four novels, but that was long enough to plummet the city to the absolute nadir of the human line. Whether the city is of middling size, like the New Haven of his first novel, *The Human Season* (1960), or the vast New York sprawl of the last three, it bears the accumulated stigmata of the century: it is squalid, noisy, oppressive to the senses, numbing to the mind, antithetical to the spirit, hostile to hope, ambition, and the free flow of human energy. No matter at what end of the physical or spiritual scale one takes it, Wallant's city is horrendously, wonderfully ugly—ugly *à l'outrance.* A necessary stage in his art as an urban landscapist is that he carry the idea of the anti-Periclean city to its logical end, to paint it as a *reductio ad absurdum* of horror and frustration. The Athens that was friend to man is now the modern megalopolis that is his foe.

But it is not Wallant's intention simply to state, even in its ultimate form, the verdict of the century. It is indeed his peculiar distinction that he embraces that verdict imaginatively only to reverse it. The city is a nightmare but contains at some inscrutable source within itself the seeds of its own resurrection. Resurrection is a theological term. There are others. Rehabilitation is the sociological synonym, restoration the architectural, reawakening the emotional, revival the secularly human. Wallant embraces this whole verbal and modal range. He believes uncannily in the regenerative powers of the city, and his novels bear intimate witness to the rebirth of his wounded characters inside the urban framework. This is made both possible and credible only because they and the cities they inhabit have, in a kind of spectacular symbiosis, reached bottom, the very bottom, at the same time. Because Wallant catches this descent with mordant accuracy, the movement, or the first stirrings of the movement, upward are rendered psychologically convincing. It is part of his difficult creed that sentimentality be avoided at all cost, that he stay deliberately clear of *la nostalgie de la boue,* that he be as hard-eyed on the way up as on the way down. It is my sustained impression that he succeeds. And in succeeding, he performs a miracle that is at once astonishing and unexpected: he revives and dramatizes in contemporary form nothing less than the Periclean ideal.

Wallant's first novel [*The Human Season*] sets the stage for all the others. Its protagonist is a fifty-nine-year-old plumber named Joe Berman who has just suffered a devastating injury, the death of his wife to whom he was profoundly attached. He feels as though his nerves have been severed, as though his connections with the world have suddenly disappeared.

The city in which he lives and works supplies his misery with an appropriate background. It is high summer, Wallant's favorite urban season, and utterly merciless. Joe and his partner are pounding along in their truck: "He tried to rest his arm on the door but the metal was burning hot. Even the wind of their passage was a warm breath of heated tar and pavement. The trolley tracks were fiery ribbons leading them to the shimmering distance. The people they passed moved slowly, resigned to the harsh dream of summer". . . . (pp. 253-55)

Toward the end of the book, on a particularly hot afternoon, [Berman] leaves the city and goes off to the beach, only to sit on the sand fully clothed—a bizarre and alien figure among the semi-nude bathers. Wallant's characters do not know what to do with themselves away from the city. On ritual occasions they may find themselves in the country, where they act like displaced persons and return to their native habitat with a sense of obscure relief. (p. 256)

In *The Pawnbroker* (1961), Wallant's second novel, the city is just as overwhelmingly there. Again it is high summer: "The air was thick and hot. . . . The sky stared down at all the stone and brick, a pale-blue monstrous eye". . . . "The heat seemed to soften the very stone and brick of the buildings. . . . Metal burned to the touch, and there was a constant density to the air that made him feel he moved through an infinite number of transparent woolen curtains". . . . Nor have the odors changed: "The hallway, with its tile floors and broken windows, smelled of garbage and soot; Tessie's apartment gave forth the more personal odors of bad cooking and dust". . . . Nor has the city's surrealist quality: "The evening sun made the street shimmer in a golden bath through which the passers-by moved like dark swimmers in no hurry to get anywhere". . . .

All these urban effects have been deliberately intensified to suggest the pawnbroker's total despair. A concentration camp survivor, with a tattoo number on his arm, his wife molested and killed by the Nazis, the very bones in his body rearranged in medical experiments, he is physically alive and emotionally dead. He simulates all the life acts—earns a living operating a Harlem pawnshop as a front for a powerful gangster, lives with his sister and supports her unappetizing family, makes love to another survivor of the Holocaust—but goes through these activities mechanically, without feeling anything.

Perversely, his disengagement from life makes him a power figure in the eyes of others. . . . Even his customers, trailing their miseries into the shop, look upon his cold, remorseless detachment with awe. Berman had been badly injured, but not like this. With the pawnbroker, we descend to the absolute last rung of Wallant's Inferno. Only there could the following horrifying curse on man be issued: "Ah, our youth, the progenitor of our future. Maybe the earth will be lucky, maybe they will all be sterile". . . . Only there can the pawnbroker boast somberly that he is

free of racial prejudice: "'I am nonsectarian, nondiscriminatory. Black, white, yellow are all equally abominations' . . .". (pp. 256-57)

Having written two books which dealt with men severely injured in middle age, Wallant wrote two more—his final two—about young men waiting to be born. The younger, Angelo, appears in *The Children at the Gate* (1964), a book that was composed third among the four novels, though published last. At nineteen, Angelo's mind—tough, clear, scientifically rational—exercises such a tyranny over his feelings that they can be said not to exist. (pp. 257-58)

In the end the whole thickened carapace of Angelo's disillusioned rationalism shatters, allowing his smothered emotional sensibilities to breathe at last. . . .

In Wallant's final novel, the comic masterpiece *The Tenants of Moonbloom* (1963), the city and its inhabitants become one, fusing in a joyous renaissance last heralded in the words of Pericles. Norman Moonbloom, at thirty-three, is still waiting to be born. It is the year not of death and resurrection but of birth and resurrection. (p. 259)

No brief account of the novel can do justice to its brilliant images, its apt handling of semi-hallucinatory states, its poignant gallery of human types, its sense of bottom-level urban immediacy—rotting pipes, cockroaches, and the smell of urine are Wallant's attar of roses. He is a poetic naturalist, touched by the influence of Joyce, Dos Passos, and Nathanael West. And his virtuosity is uncommon. He is as deft with offstage presences . . . as he is with figures onstage. (p. 260)

But dominating the field of his art is his vision of the great city, at once sickeningly ugly and disintegrative, yet in its swarming vitality holding forth the promise of some soul-stirring, spellbinding rejuvenation. Not to allow reality to enslave possibility, to keep both yoked in energetic fusion, suggests Wallant as our ultimate urban novelist. He carries the landscape we inhabit as far as it can go in both directions—into the dark abyss of *The Secret Agent* and into the invigorating light of Pericles' sublime oration. (p. 261)

> Leo Gurko, "Edward Lewis Wallant as Urban Novelist," in Twentieth Century Literature *(copyright 1974, Hofstra University Press), October, 1974, pp. 252-61.*

* * *

WELTY, Eudora 1909-

A Southern American short story writer and novelist, Eudora Welty is one of this country's most notable regionalists. Her stories of family life in small towns in the Deep South are built around what Paul Marx has called "the complex network of judgments, misjudgments, and rejudgments," sometimes taking on the elusive quality of dreams. Ms Welty is a quintessential storyteller. (See also *Contemporary Authors*, Vols. 9-12, rev. ed.)

Eudora Welty's long-awaited novel—her first since *The Ponder Heart* (1954)—might well be cited as evidence that most writers of authoritative fiction are often severely limited in the stories they choose—or are forced—to tell. . . . In any case, *Losing Battles* is in many ways the Welty "mixture as before": the family, the community—the blood ties of heart and home, and the teasing paradoxes they pose for those who can see the least bit around or outside them. Here is again what Robert Penn Warren years ago called the love and the separateness in Miss Welty's work: the individualism, the identity which must be cherished—even fought for—in the face of the pre-emptive and often devouring claims of the group, with all its traditional sanctions. And the tension between these two "pulls"—these twin allegiances which may be likened to the two faces of love itself—has constituted one of Miss Welty's principal thematic concerns. (p. 766)

It will be said that this novel has an extremely dense texture, that its many characters and thematic motifs—in all their permutations and combinations—weave in and out in a seamless philosophical and social garment. And so they do, almost to the point of constituting an embarrassment of riches—to say nothing of disproportionate thematic development. One feels somehow disappointed here—perhaps most so during the birthday reunion scenes, where there is a good deal more self-conscious, mannered sentiment (and consequent stylization, even affectation, in the prose) than the narrative can assume and support. There are just too many "blessed sweethearts" and too much family pet-naming and verbal cuddling. And it's so sad to see (or rather to hear) Miss Welty's ear succumbing to what often sounds factitious and even—God forbid—quaint and folksy. She's at her best when she remembers her characters'—and perhaps her own—real grounding in the lusty, robust Faulknerian humor of the old southwest, when she lets them all go to it without further ado. "Arty" tendencies have manifested themselves in her earlier fiction —in certain stories in *The Bride of the Innisfallen* (1955) and *The Golden Apples* (1949); and one always hoped that she would suppress them in light of her great gift for the real, the elemental thing. They were held well in check in *Delta Wedding*, where the characters and their social position would admit of more ambitious things. But they are, I believe, out of place here: one sighs for the real authority of voice found in *The Ponder Heart* and some of the earlier stories.

Nevertheless, though I cannot place *Losing Battles* in the front rank of Miss Welty's fiction, I admire the wonder, the reverence, the joy she has once again brought to her great, her inevitable theme. Her style, her art may occasionally have played her false here; but she has never really been false to the truth of the compelling story she has told again and again. She remains one of the most distinguished of 20th century American writers of fiction. (pp. 766-67)

Robert Drake, *"Miss Welty's Wide World,"* in The Christian Century (copyright 1970 *Christian Century Foundation; reprinted by permission from the June 17, 1970 issue of* The Christian Century), *June 17, 1970, pp. 766-67.*

Miss Welty's sense of inevitable loneliness and the mysteries of the human heart purge her fiction of sentimentality. Her humor—ranging from slapstick, farce and W. C. Fields-like satire to subtle irony and down-home understatement—purges it of romanticism. The tension she creates between concealment and revelation, surprise and fate, mystery and actuality, love and rage, the delicate balance she commands between these poles while showing their discord, stamps her talent as major. But then, *Losing*

Battles is the deceptively simple work of a great technician. The string of tall tales resembles a six-act grand old oprey about the Mississippi hills, yet the novel is intricately, deviously plotted. Characters emerge almost exclusively through dialogue, with the author invisible and her compassionate view of people and events tacit. Through their interaction with environment, characters transmit setting—the crude farmhouse, the maze of treacherous backroads, rickety wooden bridges, the nearby Bywy River, Banner Top. Time rushes forward in a lyric progression from the rooster's first crow that morning to the full moon that night, from the clarity of daylight when loquacity compensates for loneliness to the opacity of night when the heart beats to the tune of imponderables. (p. 466)

Linda Kuehl, in Commonweal (copyright © 1970 Commonweal Publishing Co., Inc.; reprinted by permission of Commonweal Publishing Co., Inc.), September 18, 1970.

It is bad luck how established, but not showy, writers are taken for granted. If [*The Optimist's Daughter*] were an early [novel] from a new writer, it would be hailed as a masterpiece.

It is about grieving: something commoner in life than in current fiction. Verse, from pop lyric to elegy, can express the concentrated scream of grief; the novel has the harder job of somehow suggesting grieving as *activity*, negative, monotonous and passive as it is, and at the mercy of the griever's relationship with time. Eudora Welty's skill in this book lies in the way she incorporates, without obtrusive use of flashback, a long span of passed and passing time within the framework of a few days. . . .

A very subtle book; not solemn or pretentious; and it even has that old trick of making you want to know how it will turn out.

"In Mourning," in The Times Literary Supplement (© *Times Newspapers Ltd., 1973; reproduced by permission), March 30, 1973, p. 341.*

Like Hawthorne and [Katherine Anne] Porter, Eudora Welty is concerned . . . with depicting characters who are so spiritually maimed that they have lost the basic human qualities. . . . *Petrified Man* clearly illustrates the problem of arousing in the reader a strong emotional response without using a conventional theological or moral set of values.

Eudora Welty imposes a further restriction upon herself by omitting any positive standard of the good or beautiful by which her sordid characters may be compared. There is nothing in the story that fulfils the same purpose as does Hawthorne's majestic landscape . . . or the beauty of Katherine Anne Porter's writing and composition. . . . Eudora Welty shows unadulterated sordidness or, to use . . . Porter's phrase, "vulgarity absolute, chemically pure, exposed mercilessly to its final subhuman depths." (p. 35)

Eudora Welty chooses to convey the sterility of these lives in aesthetic terms, to show spiritual poverty by means of bad taste. She sets the scene in a beauty shop and the stroke is a clever one since the women are clearly physically repulsive (even a convicted rapist is unmoved by the sight of Mrs. Pike at his bedside). She works every ironic possibility in this paradoxical situation, observing with her sharp photographic eye the most telling details of ugly decor and vulgar posture. She records the vulgar language and gross sentiments of the women and presents a devastating picture of blunted sensibilities. The picture, however, in spite of its potential for horror, does not so far arouse shock. The main reason is that the kind of ugliness she describes is so widespread that it no longer astonishes. The scene strikes the reader as familiar and amusing.

But the writer is not satisfied with arousing merely an amused wince, she wishes to provoke a stronger reaction and in order to do so she moves into the grotesque world of the freak show. The freaks are described in loving detail by the "beauty operator," Leota, and the equation between them, Leota, Mrs. Fletcher and Mrs. Pike is inescapable. Like these women the freaks are stunted from birth, grotesquely joined together and the most interesting one of all is reportedly turning into stone. The point of this detail is to suggest that the physical transformation into stone which the "petrified man" simulates is taking place actually and spiritually in the women. Eudora Welty's indebtedness to Hawthorne for this central image has been noted. She probably is indebted also to the legend of the Gorgons, whose horrendous aspect turned men to stone. The reference is one of many in the story to the women of legend and mythology. The Trojan women, the Sabine women and the Gorgons are all evoked with the purpose of showing that the women of the story are totally disqualified from either heroic virtues or heroic vices. Their last act is to swoop down, like the Thracian women, and wreak a pointless vengeance for their miscellaneous grievances upon the only available male object, Billy Boy.

This final act is the dramatic climax of the story and like the account of Mrs. Pike's "treachery" it seems strained and superfluous. Apparently it proved difficult to resolve satisfactorily an account of characters whom the writer has endowed with no sympathetic traits and no capacity for introspection. In her conclusion she resorts once again to exaggerated and forced effects. Hence Mrs. Pike's unlikely discovery of the man's improbable disguise and Leota's unaccountable outrage. (pp. 35-6)

Eudora Welty . . . [does not] analyze her characters' spiritual states. Instead she shows at once that they are rotten and proceeds to externalize their flaws by piling one crudity upon another. Her exertions are successful in that the impact is truly startling. But her assault on the reader is similar to that of the neon sign and no more moving, in spite of its being directed against a serious human failure. Her success, in this story at least, is of a very minor kind. (p. 37)

> *Joan Givner, "Katherine Anne Porter, Eudora Welty and 'Ethan Brand'," in* The International Fiction Review, *January, 1974, pp. 32-7.*

[A] detail which not only characterizes all those persons in [*The Golden Apples*] who embody its life and action but also constitutes the link between it and much of the rest of Miss Welty's fiction, early and late . . . , can best be described as a special way of seeing, or perceiving, which conditions in some degree the total vision of most of the principal characters and which, if they persist in it, may drive them to go on strange quests or otherwise wander from the patterns of normal behavior. Perception of this

special kind is not unknown in other fiction, but all too often commentators and even authors sentimentalize it as a visionary dream of some sort, the possessor of which is expected to seek and find appropriate fulfillment—in love, adventure, self-realization or some other accomplishment. The characters of *The Golden Apples* do not reach goals or attain prizes or even seem to know what such things are. For them, or so the book would have us believe, seeing is its own fulfillment, a reward that carries with it a rare kind of vitality which more than compensates for the restlessness and anguish it sometimes causes. "June Recital" [the second chapter of *The Golden Apples*] helps us to understand that unusual gift by presenting several examples of it in action. (pp. 300-01)

Again and again we find in Eudora Welty's world, as in the world of Lewis Carroll's Alice—that all things are double, at least double—and that the fortunate person among us is the one who habitually, occasionally, or even once in his lifetime has the necessary fire in his head to see the golden possibility of that doubleness in some fragment or detail of the world about him. (p. 303)

In this late twentieth-century post-Christian and technological age we reach as readily as in any other for the transcendent; but all too often in our eagerness we grasp at the occult, cast horoscopes, attempt to raise spirits, or glorify seagulls. It is reassuring to have among us one writer who begins with life as it appears in all its richness and undeniable immediacy and . . . finds in the tangible stuff of our day-to-day existence the ground for a kind of miracle that can redeem life from the dullness that rationalism and common sense have often reduced it to. For that reassurance *The Golden Apples* with its collection of gifted wanderers is of central importance. Even without *The Golden Apples*, however, Miss Welty's work would give us our miracles; for the miraculous lurks just beneath the surface of all that she has written, establishing thereby that her relationship with the wanderers she has created is one of kissing kin and not mere acquaintance. If some readers prefer to call her craft fantasy or magic, we should allow their terms and remember that even Shakespeare's skeptical Leontes refused to quibble over such trivialities when what appeared to be his wife's statue suddenly came to life. "If this be magic," he exclaimed, "let it be an art lawful as eating." Apply Leontes's exclamation to the art of Eudora Welty—which like the statue in *The Winter's Tale* derives its special life from being first and finally a part of this credible world—and we can only say amen. (p. 315)

> *J. A. Bryant, Jr., "Seeing Double in 'The Golden Apples'," in* Sewanee Review *(reprinted by permission of the editor; © 1974 by The University of the South), Spring, 1974, pp. 300-15.*

*   *   *

WESKER, Arnold 1932-

Wesker, a British Jew of Russo-Hungarian descent, is one of the foremost of the New Wave dramatists of the working class. *The Kitchen* and *Roots* are considered theatrical masterpieces. In addition to his plays for stage, television, and screen, Wesker has written criticism, essays, and, most recently, a collection of short stories. (See also *Contemporary Authors*, Vols. 1-4, rev. ed.)

Future historians of mid-twentieth century drama will have to do a lot of homework on the political background, and I don't envy them the job. Stock responses along one or another political groove were the main obstacle to critical assessment of the new English playwrights who came to the front from 1956 onwards. The artistic vitality of this new wave came from an upsurge of attitudes, diction, and characters formerly unknown to our stage; but it seems that the release of energy among the supposedly inhibited English could only take place in the absence of genteel restraint. At all events, most of the new writers had an education well short of university standards. The result is a freshness of imaginative response side by side with conceptual poverty, as if they were artistically mature and intellectually virgin.

In many critical opponents of the New Wave this condition seemed to have been reversed. They . . . shirked the issue and fell back on the snobbish formula 'kitchen sink'. Although they had the advantage over the dramatists in education and experience, they greeted the dramatic equivalent of a social revolution with vague gestures of distaste and never brought their minds to bear on it. (pp. 71-2)

Having failed to define the New Wave's admittedly meagre stock of ideas, its opponents went on to reveal an astonishing ignorance of dramatic form. They repeatedly invoked the Edwardian concept of a 'well made play' without, apparently, having broken down even that limited vehicle to its elements, which are in fact two or three star actors in scenes contrived for the display of personality and technique. Such parochialism, leaving out as it did most of the world drama's expressive range, including Shakespeare's method in the histories, was especially unsuited to coping with the new English work. The new playwrights were actively opposed to boulevard drama, and in Wesker's case any objection to it in principle was reinforced by total ignorance of it. Working as a kitchen porter in Paris, he never went to the theatre at all. (p. 72)

Wesker's most notable qualities are emotional maturity and his command of action in depth. The first means that he never condescends to his characters, the second that what happens on stage is always more interesting in performance than we would be likely to guess from quotation. . . . Under the surface of dialogue which, like O'Neill's, is often limp and colourless on the page, there comes into focus a network of relationships more significant than the interplay in the foreground, which can be written off as a quarrel between cooks or the gushing quotation of a half-educated young man's ideas, accurate but uninspiring. The inner framework, on the contrary, contains social and political issues, held together dramatically by the playwright's urgent concern for them and by his conviction that they affect the homely characters in front. Thus, behind Ronnie Kahn lies the Hungarian revolution of 1956 and behind both is the fact of the author's Russo-Hungarian descent; behind Peter the cook lies German idealism and violence; and behind Beatie Bryant is a generation faced with a new kind of choice. In each case there are three sources of pressure: current affairs, the author's attitude, and the characters in the play.

At the end of *Roots* there is a good example of the way this three-fold pressure is applied. The elementary theatrical situation is that of a heroine ditched by her fiancé and alone with a family she has outgrown. From the current sociological angle, Beatie Bryant is a working-class girl, newly awakened to the joys of abstract painting, classical music, and extra-marital love. From Wesker's angle she is all that, and also a creature with a choice between self-realisation and absorption by the greedy mass of spenders corrupted by advertising; from her own, she is a woman in love who has done her best to reconcile her boy-friend's view of life with that of her mother. By the end of the play she has been let down by everybody, yet she chooses that moment to assert herself with all the zest of a woman who at last knows her own mind. It works, because the commonplace events on stage register a series of pressures beyond those undergone by the characters. (pp. 73-4)

Is there really anything more in [*The Kitchen*] than close observation of a sleazy environment, arbitrarily whipped into a crude approximation to drama from time to time? Many think not; but what worries me about their attitude is a suspicion that they might think the same of *The Iceman Cometh* and *The Lower Depths*. (pp. 75-6)

When it comes to [the characters in *The Kitchen*], we will be disappointed if we look for any great insight or complexity; there are too many of them and there is too little time. Moreover, not one of them develops, as Beatie Bryant does, or learns anything new from start to finish. These might appear to be crippling defects, were it not for the fact that the characters do take on independent life, mainly because they speak in varied accents and dialects. We get the flavour of distinct personalities from the brief incidents which detach them from the crowd. This has been taken too much for granted, and seems to me remarkably skilful. An obvious parallel is O'Neill's definition of his crowd in *The Iceman Cometh*, but he takes four times as long to do it. Wesker's people are less characters than personalities, indeed it is part of the statement that they are not characters, but as usual with him they refer to a social context far bigger than themselves, to boring work, misused leisure, incentives, retirement, and other subjects of mid-century anxiety or debate. (p. 76)

A kitchen on stage can be accepted as a Capitalist microcosm with the proprietor standing in for God. The relationships and conflicts resemble those in other industries enough to prevent the documentary aspect from obscuring the point. First we are introduced to the people and, rare in the theatre, their work. Then they are shown under stress. In the subsequent lull a few of them go as far as they can towards reflecting on their situation. Finally, there is the feverish progress to an overwhelming question. The contours of significant action rise to the break period, structurally a climax though subdued in tone. I am plotting the inner action; the usual critical method would mark the lunch-hour rush as a climax and the break period as a relaxation, merely because one is noisy and the other quiet. In fact the reverse is true. The core of the play is a conversation in which Peter asks five of the others what they want from life. One wants tools and gadgets, the second sleep, the third money, the fourth women, the fifth human understanding. When the same question is put to Peter himself, he doesn't answer, or rather he answers in character by forgetting that the question has been asked. He has just caught sight of Monique, the waitress he is in love with. This wonderful scene, with the ovens at half-power, a guitar playing, and men of limited intellect fumbling with the issues which convulse the mid-century world, is a masterpiece by any standard. In the formal scheme it comments on what has gone before and enriches the seemingly trivial conflicts before and after. It recalls in various ways O'Neill, Gorki, and Chekhov. (pp. 77-8)

Peter's place in the scheme remains a debating point, because the scheme itself is so good. Two lines of defence, neither of them wholly convincing, can be followed. One is to take him as an essay in expressionist violence, an instrument registering the extremes of conflict elsewhere stated through people whose interest is limited by apathy or brutish prejudice. If working-class drama is to be more than reporting, at least one character must be given insight enough to lend events a shape. It would be cheating in this environment to introduce the necessary factor on an intellectual plane, so it is done emotionally instead, by the presence of a sensibility unstable but superior. The other artistic defence of Peter would be to adapt Kedrov's dictum that *Uncle Vanya* is an orchestra of which Vanya is the 'cello, to call Peter the solo instrument in a concerto. Either way, Peter is an impressive creation with the special appeal of characters who seem to break out of a play's design and take on independent life. As a part he might become a challenge to distinguished actors.

Wesker's claim to serious critical attention can very well rest on *The Kitchen* and *Roots*. (pp. 78-9)

Chicken Soup with Barley is remarkably mature. There are three acts, in 1936, 1946, and 1956. The action is that of time, politics, and social change on a Jewish East End family, the Kahns; and one way to appreciate it is to imagine what a mess this or that other 'committed' playwright would be likely to make of the same subject. The route is littered with invitations to get lost, as, say, Osborne does, in a piquant stage relationship or lay down the law at political slogan level. Instead of that, the political issues are almost inseparable from Wesker's characters and seem as much a part of the household as a cup of tea. (p. 79)

Although he arrives there with greatly inferior intellectual equipment and totally different techniques, Wesker reaches commanding heights from which he is able to ask questions as urgent as those asked by Shaw. He has the advantage over Shaw in emotional maturity and at times in the layers of meaning piled up behind external action. . . . Art as well organised as [his] will not yield its full flavour to criticism fettered by political opinion, Right or Left, still less to oversimplified notions of dramatic form. (p. 80)

> *Laurence Kitchin, "Drama with a Message: Arnold Wesker" (originally published in* Experimental Drama, *edited by W. A. Armstrong, G. Bell and Sons Ltd., 1963; copyright © 1963 by G. Bell and Sons Ltd.), in* Modern British Dramatists: A Collection of Critical Essays, *edited by John Russell Brown, Prentice-Hall, 1968, pp. 71-82.*

Let us pass over [Wesker's] irrepressible impulse to indoctrinate the working classes with Higher Forms of Art, though this may some day constitute one of the most embarrassing episodes in recent English cultural history. His plays are a good deal more complicated about such missions than his behaviour warrants, and when he deals—in the *Chicken Soup* trilogy and in *Chips With Everything*—with the intellectual's poignant failure to merge with the masses, he uncorks a theme which is both convincing and

deeply felt. His writing, on the other hand, though full of sincerity, is almost completely wanting in art, being crude, zealous, garrulous and naive; his sense of style has not developed much beyond the grey, exacting realism of Galsworthy; and his relentless missionary temperament and perennial innocence frequently turn his characters into caricatures from agit-prop. (pp. 168-69)

> *Robert Brustein, "The English Stage" (originally published in* New Statesman, *August 6, 1965; copyright © 1965 by The Statesman and Nation Publishing Co., Ltd.), in* Modern British Dramatists: A Collection of Critical Essays, *edited by John Russell Brown, Prentice-Hall, 1968, pp. 164-70.*

Arnold Wesker's first two plays, *Chicken Soup with Barley* and *The Kitchen*, broke all the rules. They are written like films. The setting for *The Kitchen* involves several large gas ovens, a butcher's table, storage units, sinks, swingdoors—the whole apparatus of a large kitchen serving a busy restaurant. It is inhabited by thirty people: cooks, waitresses, and menials. The action is dispersed in a series of brief interludes embedded and almost immersed in the routine complexity of kitchen work. Each individual episode is severely curtailed in time and leaves little mark on its successors. There is only one major climax that must serve both phases of the play—Wesker does not call them "acts"—and this occurs when Peter, the most verbally articulate character, grabs a chopper, cuts through a gas main, and stops what for him is an intolerable routine. Then he rushes out and leaves the manager and others to sustain and rapidly contain the consequences of his action.

The play was of course criticized for its lack of dramatic construction; and its first professional production in London had to wait for the success of later plays by Wesker. But the playwright defended his innovations: "for Shakespeare the world may have been a stage," but for him "it was a kitchen," where men and women were imprisoned and dwarfed by a grueling routine, and where specifically human actions could not have development and climax and consequence. He had found a form for what he had seen and felt.

Wesker must then have read a book on "how to write a play," for his next two plays are more conformist, each with three acts and far fewer *dramatis personae*; the passage of time is more usual, the settings are easily realizable in the three walls of a box set. In *Roots*, the most eloquent of all these early plays, a heroine dominates the action.

But with *Chips With Everything* Wesker returned to a broader theme and presented two more of his "worlds." One shows conscripts in the R.A.F. on the parade-ground, developing from ill-coordinated individuals into a "fine body of men," efficient and faceless at the passing-out ceremony. The other shows, in interspersed scenes, the same conscripts in their barracks, but now bringing their individual needs and affections to various, disconnected, and imperfect life; in these scenes Wesker shows another development towards a group-life, but far less certain or effective than that of the parade ground. When the recruits voluntarily follow a leader, the group reaction is efficient, and when they combine to protect and aid the unfortunate Smiler—the rejected and suffering fool—their corporate life becomes considerate. But at the end, these actions have no consequence; the random collection of individuals disperses as the airmen are posted to different stations.

With *Chips* and *The Kitchen*, Wesker was recognized as a social dramatist whose plays need large casts and are made effective by choreographic direction. But then his next play to be performed was *The Four Seasons*, which has only two characters and tells the story of a love affair. His director and the critics seemed quite unprepared for this: it was a new and unexpected development. But the love affair was private, intimate, and finally inconclusive: Wesker was magnifying one of the individualistic incidents of *The Kitchen* or *Chips*, artificially sustaining a confrontation (that in any of his ways of life is naturally tentative and impermanent) for as long as a symbolistic framework of Winter-Spring-Summer-Autumn would permit. His dialogue attempted to hold on to moments by the use of song or formal address, and so it suggests the antipathies, submissions, and cruelties at the heart of short moments of apparent concord.

With *Their Very Own and Golden City*, . . . Wesker once more used the wide scene, only less restricted in time, place, and type of character. Here is the whole life of a working-class boy becoming a famous Town Planner, knighted for his services. Like *The Four Seasons* it did not please the critics: flashbacks in the last scenes from middle-age to youth (involving two actors for a single character); a setting that has to change during the action (especially in the last eleven scenes, where Wesker wants to have the progression of a film rather than of a play); the obvious propagandist and autobiographical elements combined with the compression of characters to types that was necessary in order to contain such wide-ranging subject matter within bounds of a three-hour performance—all this gave offense. If Wesker had been content with his own earlier dramatic forms he would have been in less danger of being judged a failure. But a more demanding form is what he seeks—in order to present the themes he has always considered significant. He is using the theater to explore, to demonstrate in more comprehensive and more subtle ways: that is why he is a dramatist before he is a propagandist. (pp. 12-14)

> *John Russell Brown, "Introduction" to* Modern British Dramatists: A Collection of Critical Essays, *edited by John Russell Brown (© 1968 by Prentice-Hall, Inc.; reprinted by permission of Prentice-Hall, Inc., Englewood Cliffs, New Jersey), Prentice-Hall, 1968, pp. 1-14.*

Love Letters On Blue Paper [a collection of short stories] dwells, despite its title, on death, decay and socialism but not necessarily in that order—socialism is torment reserved for the living. The three stories included in this collection are somewhat ambiguous, though, since they deal with these unpleasantly sentimental themes with a prose which is dry to the point of artificiality. Sheridan Brewster is 'The Man Who Became Afraid,' a humourless and pedantic creature whose timorous death promises to be as uninteresting as his life, and I suppose that we must put it down to Wesker's unerring dramatic sympathy that the prose should be as heavy as the hero. . . .

The second story, 'A Time of Dying', is in fact "autobiographical," which simply means that quotidian experience

has been ruthlessly subjected to nineteenth-century laws of chronology, causation, aesthetic unity and rhetorical effect. It is a memorial to the death of some close relations, and as such it can be interesting only to those who were naturally involved. The last of the stories is the titular head of the collection, 'Love Letters On Blue Paper', and it returns again to Wesker's favourite study of those who discover that they have lived to no purpose. It is here, of course, that Wesker's dry prose comes into its own as he articulates the even dryer processes of fear and failure. . . .

The story is carefully written, apparently without irony and certainly without humour, and although the mawkishness is reserved for Wesker's protagonists it is this mawkishness which, finally, suffuses the whole book. (p. 246)

> *Peter Ackroyd, in* The Spectator *(© 1974 by* The Spectator; *reprinted by permission of* The Spectator), *August 24, 1974.*

Predictably low on middles, short stories grab inevitably for endings. In short, you might say, short stories are obsessed by finality. What apter, then, than that Arnold Wesker should pursue his own obsession with human finality by means of short stories. Even the least successful of Wesker's three stories [in *Love Letters on Blue Paper*]—the first one, about a man whose way of boasting he's afraid of nothing is to profess that he's 'afraid of everything' and who is visited by the nemesis his words invoke—has the satisfying moral panache of great fable. Wesker, of course, doesn't merely seek the rounded and plausible satisfactions of parable: the man who becomes afraid is also a Labour Party supporter whose decline involves his realisation that he no longer believes in equal opportunity. On this occasion the political theme and the fabliau shape don't quite manage to mesh, but 'A Time of Dying' and 'Love Letters on Blue Paper' do contrive confidently to animate their political as well as their more general concerns. . . . In both, memory, particularly family memory, is shown focused and strengthened by dying, and, involved in a variety of traditions and continuities, the death of the individual becomes a kind of triumph. Wesker's writing is, especially in these two tales, finely sensitive, strongly humane, and quite convincing. It proves that the kind of realism he's often sought is much more attainable through the generous particularities of prose fiction than in the stylised artificialities of the stage. (p. 293)

> *Valentine Cunningham, in* New Statesman *(© 1974 The Statesman & Nation Publishing Co. Ltd.), August 30, 1974.*

Arnold Wesker has moved from plays to short stories [*Love Letters on Blue Paper*] with happy results. Doubtless, one of the reasons for his success is the fact that he has an inherent respect for his characters, when he is not outright in love with them. He commits himself wholeheartedly to their vision of things, refusing them nothing, permitting them to believe in themselves and their lives, to scream at death, to yearn for victories of whatever sort—even when the victory belongs to an elderly woman whose dreams of selfhood center on winning money in the football pools. Few writers of fiction nowadays are so fearlessly generous as Wesker is with his characters (the most successful of whom are old East End types), and the result is a collection of stories of stunning dramatic power. (p. 36)

Dorothy Rabinowitz, in Saturday Review *(copyright © 1975 by Saturday Review/ World, Inc.; reprinted with permission), May 17, 1975.*

Of all the playwrights of England's "Angry" renaissance of the late '50s, Arnold Wesker is perhaps the least known here in America. He happens also to be about the best of a good lot. John Osborne, Wesker, Shelagh Delaney, Brendan Behan—it's easy to think of them all (and not just poor Behan) in the past tense. Nothing fails with such finality as a revolution that succeeds.

But Arnold Wesker is a special case. It is puzzling, really, that his plays have not traveled well to this side. He is Jewish and of working class origins—and his writing (in particular his early work) seems to have quite a lot in common with that of American Jewish playwrights, such as Clifford Odets and Arthur Miller. But that, perhaps, is just the trouble: it may be that Wesker seems *too* familiar, that his work may be too much in a mode we think of as more or less American. Perhaps theater audiences here look for something more exotic in their imported plays—something distinctly "English."

If that is the case, I wonder how this collection of stories, *Love Letters on Blue Paper*, will fare here. It cannot possibly get the audience it deserves, for if it did that, it would shoot to the top of the best-seller list. . . . [Three] of the five stories in it ["Six Sundays in January," "The Man Who Became Afraid," and the title story] are remarkably good; and one of them, the title story, is as fine as any I've read for a very long time. The trouble is, these, just as some of his plays did, seem somehow "American": some in their Jewishness and others in their technique—the way they go beyond basic storytelling and into a kind of existential mode, communicating a quality of life, making them novels in summary. I suppose that you would, in fact, call the three very good stories "short novels," for they are well over what is usually considered story length. . . .

[The] beautiful "Love Letters on Blue Paper": it is a story of death, of dying, but as the title has it, this one is also, and most importantly, a love story. . . . [It] is beautifully faceted, suggesting an *entire* marriage, man and woman, as death comes to part them.

As all this may suggest, Arnold Wesker's great themes are death and the family. Even the two shorter stories in the book, "Pools" and "A Time of Dying," conform perfectly, treating both. His attitude is best summed up in the curtain line of his first play, *Chicken Soup With Barley*, spoken by a tough matriarch to her son, the would-be-poet: "If you don't care you'll die." Wesker cares. And the extent and depth of the concern he shows in these stories may yet win him at least the beginning of an audience here in America. Then, perhaps, the plays.

Bruce Cook, "Return to Sender," in Book World—The Washington Post *(© The Washington Post), June 1, 1975, p. 2.*

Mr. Wesker, a Londoner, has been known here mainly as a playwright, and three of the five stories in ["Love Letters on Blue Paper"] might well be improved if they could somehow be staged. Like many modern dramas, they tell of unexceptional people struggling with vague and confused feelings, and the forms in which they express these feelings —the inner monologues of a thirty-five-year-old Hampstead mother overtaken by ennui and self-doubt, the jottings and musings of a Jewish widow living on dreams of winning the football pool, and the sudden, surprising love letters of a wife to her dying husband—are histrionic in a way that doesn't stand up on paper but that might be effective in the speech of a resourceful actress. Of the two remaining stories, one is a gentle, factual account of a period of deadly coincidences in the author's family, and the other is a formal tale—almost a fable—about a British businessman whose spiritual malaise curiously resembles that of his fictional suburban-American counterparts. On the whole, this book isn't quite funny enough or touching enough to be enthusiastically recommended, but it has its rewards of sentiment and insight. (p. 126)

The New Yorker *(© 1975 by The New Yorker Magazine, Inc.), June 9, 1975.*

* * *

WHITE, Patrick 1912-

White, an English-born Australian novelist, playwright, and short story writer, won the Nobel Prize for Literature in 1973. His novels, vast in scope, are "multilayered and exquisite."

Throughout this long book [*The Eye of the Storm*], Mr White curbs what his detractors have considered to be his excesses and, possibly in the curbing, dilutes some of his prodigious gifts. Gone are the baroque satirical setpieces such as the magnificent party for the artist in *The Vivisector*; instead a small dinner party or two which deflate the idle burghers of Sydney, but the targets seem hardly worth it. We are no longer treated to those superb passages of elliptical, truncated and barbarous Strine; just the odd phrase from Mrs Cush, the cleaning woman; but why give her such a crude joke name? Why call the most stupid, self-satisfied nurse Sister Badgery? Mr White is too great a writer to trifle with such vulgarity in a book so finely wrought as this. Why, also, does he bring in some of his favourite themes, invite comparison with earlier versions, and produce definite regressions? After the wonderfully moving and piteous Greek heiress who so loved the vivisector, why introduce briefly, and inevitably palely, the Greek mother of Sister de Santis? The noble, loving and eternally baffled nurse is a superb creation compared with which her mother seems dross.

The German-Jewish housekeeper with her incompetent theatrical past is an interesting near-victim of the holocaust, but when she recalls her escape from the gas, she also recalls that other escaper from Nazi Germany, Professor Himmelfarb in *Riders in the Chariot* and the comparison seems sacrilegious. These are harsh criticisms but they are aimed at weaknesses in the work of a writer who has long overtaken the need to toy with characters and situations which are less than perfect, and they are faults in a book which, by its own ambition, should not contain them.

These faults, irritating as they are, do not, however, detract from the marvellous precision of the writing. They are perhaps best described as errors of taste in a work whose complex structure is architecturally perfect and whose style is much freer, more devastatingly precise than even its most august predecessors. In earlier books there was a tendency towards the densely clotted, inexorable slow march of Faulkner. In *The Eye of the Storm* Mr White has attained, without the orotundity, some of the deadly irony and the epigrammatic skill of Henry James. James himself could hardly have bettered the mutually embarrassed encounter of Princess Dorothy and Sister Manhood. . . .

As one surveys this book and its substantial number of characters, it is almost impossible . . . to find a single human being who engages the reader's sympathy, let alone, and much more importantly, the author's. Mr White's formidable satirical gifts have previously seemed apposite and just, linked from *Voss* onwards with huge compassion and the creation of men and women with true nineteenth-century fictional grandeur. In *The Eye of the Storm* no stone of human character is left unturned without the revelation of some evil or distasteful worm beneath. . . .

If one takes as basic a theme as sibling rivalry, sibling love and sibling sex, and considers that cold climax between Dorothy and Basil Hunter at Kudjeri and compares it with the Dostoevskian intensity and compassion of the two brothers in *The Solid Mandala*, one sees the disastrous gap between this chillingly brilliant new book and the sheer moral grandeur of its great predecessors. . . .

The weight of hatred, disgust and dislike is overpowering, and, one suspects, finally excessive and hence fatally detrimental to what should have been a great novel. In comparison with most of today's fiction, *The Eye of the Storm* is truly remarkable, with its relentless narrative thrust, the lucidity of its style, the all-seeing comprehension of the characters. But, in the final analysis, it does not survive comparison with the heights of White's genius, *Voss, Riders in the Chariot, The Solid Mandala*, and *The Vivisector*.

> *"High Wind in Australia," in* The Times Literary Supplement *(© Times Newspapers Ltd., 1973; reproduced by permission), September 21, 1973, p. 1072.*

The Eye of the Storm . . . is a good novel to read to get a sense of White's power.

In a way, White reminds me of a contemporary Jane Austen. As a modern, though, he has learned to use stream of consciousness, to intersperse playlets into his novel, to multiply points of view into comment on his subject, and to distrust the consolations of society. But like Austen at her best, he makes tempests in teapots feel like violent storms. . . .

Ideas as such don't exist within this novel; White seems as innocent of Great Ideas and Great Events as Austen.

I mention all this only to pay tribute to White's unique achievement, for *The Eye of the Storm* is a rather long novel (over 600 pages) written within extremely severe limits. It succeeds, I think, because White knows his cliché characters so well that he makes us know them fully. Somehow, they never depart from the stereotype, yet they consistently surprise. Whether it be the usually dowdy Sister deSantis ashamed of the garish hat she has bought, or Mrs. Hunter remembering the tenderness of caring for her dying husband, from whom she had been estranged for years, the effect is akin to our first realization that Falstaff can suffer. The type remains, but we understand, feelingly, what it

must mean to be a human being of that type. I know of no other novelist capable of writing a novel in which each character is both static and complexly moving. (p. 269)

> *Lee T. Lemon, "Static and Moving," in* Prairie Schooner *(© 1974 by University of Nebraska Press; reprinted by permission from* Prairie Schooner*), Fall, 1974, pp. 268-69.*

Was it O'Faolain who looked for both punch and poetry in short stories? [In *The Cockatoos*] Patrick White has both, in abundance. His events would all rate at least a paragraph in the most sensation-seeking newspaper. They are transformed to the status of works of art by the author's poetic imagination and the power of his prose. He is the most eminent of his own cockatoos, 'real dazzlers of birds . . . heartless from the way they slash at one another, kind, too, when they want to be'. (pp. 61-2)

> *John Mellors, in* The Listener *(© British Broadcasting Corp. 1975; reprinted by permission of John Mellors), January 9, 1975.*

["The Cockatoos"] are six stories (a few are short novels) to do with lives often driven or hopeless, but what they are ultimately about is what might have been. They bring together the possibilities and the impossibilities of human relationships. They happen in Australia, Egypt, Sicily, Greece, where they go off like cannons fired over some popular, scenic river—depth charges to bring up the drowned bodies. Accidentally set free by some catastrophe, general or personal—war, starvation, or nothing more than a husband's toothache—Patrick White's characters come to a point of discovery. It might be, for instance, that in overcoming repugnancies they are actually yielding to some far deeper attraction; the possibilities of a life have been those very things once felt as its dangers. Or they may learn, in confronting moral weakness in others, some flaw in themselves they've never suspected, still more terrifying.

The common barriers of sex, age, class, nationality *can* in uncommon hands operate as gates, which open (for White's characters) to experience beyond anything yet traveled, hope of which may have beckoned from earliest years and gone ignored, only haunting dreams and spoiling the day at hand. Passing us through these barriers is what Mr. White is doing in his writing. (p. 4)

> *Eudora Welty, in* The New York Times Book Review *(© 1975 by The New York Times Company; reprinted by permission), January 19, 1975.*

When Australian novelist Patrick White was awarded the Nobel Prize for Literature in 1973, the good judgment and sanity of the Swedish Academy came once again under suspicious international scrutiny. (p. 34)

Patrick White is known to American readers, but reviewers here have tended to see in him a kind of bush D. H. Lawrence, a pretentious primitivist who assembles characters burning with thematic *purpose*—intense, dreaming Prometheuses—within vast, creaking narrative structures that offer individual experiences as universal myths. The looming continent embraced and traversed by White's uprooted Europeans is an abstract and primeval test of their ability to "break through" to self-understanding. "Down under" (especially when it maps the route of a protagonist's soul-journey) is hell, nor are they out of it.

Each of White's novels is a search for ultimate meanings. Oddly, each is also an ambitiously comprehensive sweep over a large and confusing terrain, nevertheless focusing on an individual character or several characters—and on such individuals' ways of perceiving the life that clamors around them. Thus, a plain, awkward woman's willed retreat from her ugly life becomes a rich romantic escape into idealized selfhood (*The Aunt's Story*). A laborious trek across the Australian continent is elevated, by the imaginations that fuel it, into a Christ-like epic of aspiration and sacrifice (*Voss*). The painfully entwined lives of two brothers—one priggish and hateful, the other gentle but retarded—writhe in an operatic struggle that aims to oppose the creative and destructive halves of the human soul (*The Solid Mandala*).

It is the apparent distortion of focus, I believe, that makes White's books confusing. Our attention is pulled toward individual characters; emphatic images and phrases direct us to infer grand meanings from their conflicts. But their actions, and the announced significances therefrom, are frequently credible *only* as symbol and are unconvincing as drama. We wonder, a bit resentfully, how cataclysmic universals can be latent, behind a "realism" that has been so patently fabricated. White's fourth novel, *Riders in the Chariot* (1961), drearily exemplifies his weakness for contrivance. It is a complicated interweaving of the life-altering "visions" that possess four starkly imagined, tormented characters: a gnarled, pathetic madwoman; a patiently long-suffering farm wife; a Blakean aborigine painter; and a despised Jew (whom White will not resist crucifying, in an insanely feverish climax). The novel is about the irresistible permeability of evil in all of us; when the novel concentrates on its people, there is superbly convincing drama. But White is interested in the intersection of their fates, and the metaphoric momentum rips every realistic detail away from its location, as the riders lumber toward their prepared apocalypse. It's an unusually strong novel, owing to its *potential*. There are four striking, separate centers of interest, but the direction the novel takes is toward the interlocking and relating of its separable meanings. We lose our sense of the characters' powerful individuality, because we're encouraged to perceive the blueprints that explain them and schematize their relationships.

White's style poses additional problems. The prose is densely packed, jangling with implied resonances. The rhythms place heavy emphasis on single words and phrases. We're forced to read slowly and look for the critical object or image. But the syntax frequently deceives, because White's language doesn't concentrate in a way that is related to meaning; it stretches for vivid devices to express even subsidiary meanings. Essentials, and incidentals as well, are worked over with bone-crushing emphasis. (pp. 34-5)

It's obvious that White's avidity for gargantuan effects makes him a clumsy writer, in the noticeable element of sentences and paragraphs. And yet this stylistic crudeness has never seemed to bother White's British critics, who almost unanimously assert his importance as a Homeric celebrator of heroic psyches. (*The Eye of the Storm*, labeled elephantine and unintelligible by most American reviewers, was respectfully praised throughout the United

Kingdom.) One can argue that the tradition of the serial novel, with its jerry-built crisis points and unabashed inset summaries, has inured British critics to verbosity and overwriting. But it's also true that they tend to view single books as parts of a writer's total output, and it may be this practice, too often ignored by American criticism, that contributes to the world's high opinion of Patrick White.

I think that if one reads all of White's novels and short stories (not necessarily in their order of publication), one can sense a central strength inhering in White's view of the relationship of individuals to universals. Abstractions and eternalities are the quarry of the journeys and quests and symbolic confrontations that occupy the forefront of his novels. But it is *individuals* who dominate his spacious canvases: We see the huge and menacing intimations of eternity as they are seen by White's seekers after enlightenment and transcendence. (p. 35)

The short stories seldom match the flawed but genuinely imaginative grandeur of the novels. What they gain is *focus*, for White employs the story form for creating characters uneasily involved in exterior relationships, who recoil into deep self-absorption or recapturable (thus, comforting) pasts. An early collection, *The Burnt Ones* (1964), contains several remarkable examples of White's technique of slow, patient revelation. In stories such as "A Glass of Tea" and "A Cheery Soul," challenging outward conflicts force people backward and inward, toward discovery of the forces that have made them what they are and that continue to rule their lives.

The stories collected in *The Cockatoos* are reputedly recent work, but at least two display flaws that suggest they may be early stories, later rewritten. . . .

[The] stories are credible in direct proportion to the use White makes of their characters' inner lives. . . .

Only in "A Woman's Hand" do we see White's peculiar strengths and weaknesses in exhilarating combination. Evelyn and Harold Fazackerley, in retirement from a life of cautiously borne disappointments, meet, and awkwardly destroy, a friend from Harold's childhood. . . . Telling the story, White stays near the psyche of the coarse, selfish Evelyn; but when a devastating impression of waste and folly echoes out from the carnage, it is Harold who briefly assumes understanding—as if to remind us that pockets of sanity are only slender islands amid the upheaval, often glimpsed too late and too distant. It is the opening story in this collection, and a good one, I think, with which to begin one's reading of Patrick White. Its style sometimes verges on obscurity, its organization succumbs to illogic. But the confusions are the kind that are suffered by people who venture deeply into their own—and others'—souls. At the story's outset, it is the quirky strangeness of the Fazackerleys that impresses. As the story ends, we've come to know that they are the same kind of people we are—and the shock of recognition is genuinely appalling. (p. 37)

Bruce Allen, "In Lawrence's Shadow," in Saturday Review (*copyright © 1975 by Saturday Review/World, Inc.; reprinted with permission*), January 25, 1975, pp. 34-7.

White is a master of the novel. At his best he draws us in, but only so far: the vise that grips the reader is carefully distanced, and that distance can provide an oracular power.

But the short story is a form that demands immediate rapport between artist and audience; and White, the most austere of modern novelists, isn't an intimate writer. The stories in his early collection *The Burnt Ones* are either whimsical, with O. Henry twists and lovable Greeks talking in English except for occasional italicized Greek words, or portentous without delivering. *The Cockatoos*, a new collection of novellas and stories, shows White trying to shape the short form to his own special gifts rather than degrading those gifts by trying to be cozy. The title story and two others, "Sicilian Vespers" and "Five-Twenty," are too attenuated to hold much interest; but the rest, although one doesn't necessarily *like* them, command attention. (p. 23)

"The Full Belly," about a family of starving Greek aristocrats during the German occupation, isn't quite bearable. Although White's prose has never been more razor-sharp, he uses it to slice his characters to bits. . . . I think that White intended us to sense our own atavistic potentiality in the family's dehumanization, but what we sense is that the author loathes his characters. White has compressed his grimmest personal vision into 20 pages—a feat of storytelling, but the compulsive read seems an eternity.

The opening novella, "A Woman's Hand," is less accessible and, perhaps for that reason, not nearly so repellent. I shuddered at the central figure, a frigid busybody wife who brings about a marriage that leads to insanity and death. She appears throughout White's work in one form or another, and he clearly despises her. Although I'm not sure what "A Woman's Hand" is supposed to be about and don't understand the motivations, and although I suspect that White shares my uncertainties, the novella is riveting. White has gone further with one of his stylistic specialties: prose rhythms that provide equivalents for the characters' hang-ups and eruptions into madness, eruptions that the reader can only partially intuit. The madness in "A Woman's Hand" is never clarified; it's suggested by the insane friends perception of ocean sunsets as blazing peacocks, emblems of a voluptuous redemption that is unattainable. White has taken the most lucid passages of madness from *The Aunt's Story* into pure impressionism. He almost succeeds, because his subliminally erotic imagery, tinged with religious elements, pulls one in although the imagery has nothing coherent behind it.

It's a measure of White's artistry that *The Cockatoos*, flawed and disturbing as it is, makes one eager to see what he will do next. But the short form is not, and probably never will be, the best showcase for his genius. Since White is now a Nobel winner, many readers are eager to encounter his work for the first time and may imagine that a new story collection is a good introduction. *The Cockatoos*, although it should be read, isn't the ideal starting point. It will tantalize some; others need to respond to the breadth of vision in the major novels before they approach these strange but impressive minor works.

Patrick White's procession of novels is majestic; no other living novelist in English is so consistently audacious or writes on such a large scale. In America only pulp novelists like Michener are interested in full-dress productions. White, a serious artist, has given us *Voss*, a historical epic of Tolstoyan proportions; and his work ranges from the spacious epic to the fiercely introverted writhings of his new book, *The Cockatoos*. We are drawn to White's heroic

writing even when he puts us off. His satiric dialogue can be overly vicious, as in *Riders in the Chariot*; and his schematized conceptions cripple a poor novel like *The Living and the Dead* and mar one of his best, *The Solid Mandala*. His hatred of his characters reaches a culmination in *The Cockatoos*. But White is full of surprises. He follows his worst novel, *The Vivisector*, which loads an overheated Passion Play tone onto a standard tortured-artist story of the Irving Stone variety, with *The Eye of the Storm*, a serenely visionary work in which his prose reaches new heights.

In the seven-year hiatus between his false starts (*Happy Valley* and *The Living and the Dead*) and the appearance of *The Aunt's Story*, White began developing his prose, a mixture of the tangy, lazy rhythms of Australian diction and glittering bursts of imagery that sometimes emerge from the text with a beautiful naturalness, sometimes with a shock that is like a slap in the reader's face—a prose style both precise and flexible. Speaking voices overlap into description; and points of view can be separated by slight modulations in one brief scene, even in one paragraph. Pitch is heightened by minor chord changes from sentence to sentence, from phrase to phrase. The prose daringly calls attention to itself in such passages as the German housekeeper's cabaret act before her painted death-doll mistress in *The Eye of the Storm*, or the aged Waldo's preening in his dead mother's ball gown in *The Solid Mandala*. These scenes are incomparable pieces of stage direction, but White provides everything—actors and props aren't needed. (Oddly, his plays are hopelessly "literary" and derivative, while his fiction is miraculously scenic.)

In *The Aunt's Story* White rearranges the pieces of an Australian spinster's mind as though they were chips in a mosaic. Although he doesn't entirely control his effects, parts of the novel even today read like a breakthrough. Unfortunately the middle section is a stiffly self-conscious nightmare-reverie, possibly modeled after "Nighttown" in *Ulysses*, in which Theodora is supposed to be crossing over into madness. White records the tiny alterations in Theodora's perceptions of reality without resorting to conventional explanations and metaphors for insanity.

The Tree of Man, unlike *The Aunt's Story*, has no obvious experimentation. It's an Australian farm saga told, for White, as simply as possible. A basic fallacy creeps in: because of the Parkers' poverty, White grants them a wholeness he denies his more affluent characters. But this epic of the soil avoids most Pearl Buck overtones by the power of the images; the fire and flood are White's first great descriptive scenes. Another important factor in White's growth as an imaginative artist first appears: the view of Australia as a primordially unshaped, almost mythic continent. The transportation of the first convicts is like Lucifer cast into hell; and the natural disasters in *The Tree of Man* are plagues, manifestations of divine wrath at those who would try to shape the wilderness. (pp. 23-4)

Voss is one of those rare novels that pulls the reader up successive peaks of intensity until he emerges, purged, at the top. The book is completely achieved, despite a typical last White touch: a trivializing epilogue that neatly wraps up all the narrative threads that might better have been left free.

Voss is the last of White's straight narratives. The later novels, except for *The Vivisector*, form a trilogy of symbolic works. Instead of archetypal characters, like Voss and the Parkers, White gives us characters who are extensions of another kind of archetype—a risky attempt for a novelist, but White has never been one to avoid risks. Each novel's title is the governing metaphor. *Riders in the Chariot*, the least successful, presents four characters, various examples of the earth's wretched, who will finally ride in triumph in the apocalyptic chariot of fire. The riders are joined by tenuous plot linkages, and White uses them questionably.... Does White really like his miserable creatures, or does he only think he should? *Riders in the Chariot* is split down the middle; but it has powerful scenes, such as the Jew's recollection of the death camps (with White's characteristic connections between violent death and sex, connections that increase the horror), and curious exchanges, that suggest Jane Bowles, between bizarrely matched couples drawn together by mutual freakishness.

White, whose fiction is rarely far from the feel of flesh, can't get his winged chariot to soar. He does much better with earthbound symbols: the storm's eye, and the mandala, which is an ordering of chaos, not a transcendence of it. *The Solid Mandala* is a glass marble, a child's toy, with twin strands of color that in different lights twist and untwist in colors that blind and illuminate....

The Solid Mandala probes further beneath the surface of human frailty than any other White novel. *The Eye of the Storm*—about a dying woman, once a great beauty and sexual monster, and those who wait for her to die—is a panoramic view, suggesting what is underneath by resonant language and juxtaposition of shifting time and place. The themes are highly charged: the helplessness with which we anticipate death, the shame of old age and the body's ugly tyranny (the imagery, as George Steiner notes, is largely fecal), the ways that recollections of sex and sexual failure and continuing desires push us into collision with others; who are pursued by their own demons. This is the most highly plotted of White's works, and some of the subplots are embarrassments; but the plotting advances the action only slightly. The plots principally serve as supporting metaphors to the central scene: the dying woman's memory of being trapped in the eye of a hurricane. The savage beauty of destruction as seen from that small area of calm brings back her entire life, the past recaptured in that one instant of revelation. The novel is structured around the storm scene, like ripples spreading in a pool. White seems to be writing from the storm's eye, from that lucidity that is reached only after tortuous mazes have been traveled. (p. 24)

> *John Alfred Avant, "The Oeuvre of Patrick White," in* The New Republic *(reprinted by permission of* The New Republic; © *1975 by* The New Republic, Inc.*), March 22, 1975, pp. 23-4.*

*   *   *

WHITEHEAD, E. A.   1933-

Whitehead is a British dramatist.

I can appreciate the brilliance of Mr Whitehead's writing at individual moments, though it does also disturb me slightly that his style veers from terse and violent naturalism to

overweight phrase-making (Frank announces, for instance, that he is merely 'lurching from one derelict sunset to another') without warning and with little justification in terms of character. But the cumulative effect of [*Alpha Beta*] suffers from too much unvaried harping on one note, too many short-lived explosions and empty threats that lead nowhere very much. It is impossible to doubt the strength of feeling behind the play, but it does seem possible that the author is too close to his material to abstract it sufficiently to make it stand on its own as an independent dramatic entity. (pp. 42, 44)

> *John Russell Taylor, in* Plays and Players, *(© copyright John Russell Taylor 1972), March, 1972.*

The Sea Anchor is a calculated attack on the myths accompanying pleasure.... [With] mathematical puritanism, Whitehead proves that all is vanity. *The Sea Anchor* is already being compared to Eugene O'Neill's early plays, and indeed they have much in common: a telling sense of atmosphere, an impending doom, a careful realism in the dialogue and a determination not to be fooled by life.

> *John Elsom, "Empty Embraces," in* The Listener *(© British Broadcasting Corp. 1974; reprinted by permission of John Elsom), July 18, 1974, p. 89.*

If there's one thing that seems to disgust and sadden E. A. Whitehead more than women, it is men. He has given stage-room to male misogyny in *The Foursome*, whose climax was a frenzied ode to lipstick, eye-shadow, Tampax and other female clutter, and in *Alpha Beta*.... [In *Sea Anchor*] he concentrates on male inadequacies, hauling onstage characters that might be the Liverpudlian tearaways of *The Foursome*, one marriage, several children, umpteen affairs and some 15 years later. They are in Dublin, waiting for the arrival of a friend, Nick, who is asserting his declining virility by sailing over from England in a dinghy....

It's a well-written, tense, depressing piece. Tense, because we're never allowed to forget that one major character may be drowning out there in the Irish Sea; depressing, because all the others seem resigned to anomie and sexual misery. The women are painfully dependent on the men; the men see their wives as burdens to be endured, and all other women as anonymous alcohol to which they're addicted. True, one purports to find joy in his children, but that's only because 'it makes me feel young again'. The other takes grim satisfaction in loving nothing and no one. For both, the end of life is 'freedom', which may be roughly defined as slavish subservience to the bodily processes.... The language positively oozes with distaste, both for self and others....

Indeed, we're left to wonder if Nick hasn't deliberately opted out of the degradation of it all, by jumping a ship or drowning himself; an ambiguous ending to a piece that grabs the ear and stomach whether it's considered as a quasi-sociological study of perverted puritanism, or a personal yowl of distress, or (probably) both. No one but Whitehead could have written it; but then none but Whitehead would have *wanted* to write it. He is to sex what Edward Bond is to violence and cruelty, a highpriest of misanthropy.... (p. 91)

Benedict Nightingale, in New Statesman (©
*1974 The Statesman & Nation Publishing
Co. Ltd.), July 19, 1974.*

Superficially [Whitehead's] plays seem to be about getting
drunk and making love inside and outside marriage. Deeper
down he is more interested in illusions of liberty. He
writes, as he has said himself, about characters who are
trapped—by limited opportunities and by moral and emotional pressures. The husband in *Alpha Beta* is trapped not
so much by marriage and the family situation as by his own
idea of liberty, which he equates with the right to sleep with
as many women as he can. Nick, the offstage character in
The Sea Anchor, also thinks he's achieved something every
time he beds a new girl, but the ironies of the play work
against his attitude. He treats his wife as badly as his
steady girlfriend treats her husband, and she is not more
generous to Nick than his wife is in allowing him the liberty
he takes anyway to sleep around. (p. 70)

We are in Dublin Bay, sharing the edgy anxiety of the four
characters as they scan the horizon with binoculars, worried about Nick's non-appearance. They are asserting their
freedom by having a dirty weekend in Ireland, while Nick
has been more desperately asserting his by sailing over
from Liverpool alone on a dinghy. In this Whitehead play,
therefore, it is not just the pursuit of pleasure that turns out
to be painful, it is the growing certainty that his bravado
has been suicidal. Death, the final trap, has been his only
possible escape from the traps that his misguided quest for
liberty has caught him in. (pp. 70-1)

Randall Craig, in Drama, *Autumn, 1974.*

*   *   *

WIDEMAN, J(ohn) E(dgar)   1941-

Wideman is a Black American intellectual novelist.

John Edgar Wideman's *Hurry Home* is a story of blackness
told in a very private, poetic, sensitive way. A sequence of
lifelike events, a pattern of relationships among identifiable
people, can be seen in the glinting, running river of prose.
But so can nightmares, Moorish warrior kings, the visions
of Hieronymus Bosch, water and night and stillborn children more symbolic than real, and a young, modern American Negro who remembers being locked in a slave ship 300
years ago. . . .

Hurry Home is primarily an experience, not a plot: an experience of words, dense, private, exploratory, and nonpro-
gressive. The clusters of words are sometimes clever
(sometimes too clever); sometimes "literary," in an over-
conscious way; sometimes as elusive as cigarette smoke.
But they are sometimes also eloquent, vivid, and direct.
They represent the voice of a highly cultured man (but cultured for what between Oxford and the Washington slums,
between the slave ships and the Prado?), a painfully sensitive black American who is trying to find a shape, a pattern
of words that will allow him to ask certain deep, personal,
existential questions. (p. 40)

David Littlejohn, in Saturday Review (copyright © 1970 by Saturday Review, Inc.; reprinted with permission), May 2, 1970.*

[*The Lynchers*] is an "important" black novel. . . . Large
analogies . . . come to mind when reading this novel. The
inclusion of a "Matters Prefatory" section containing historical documents on slave revolts and lynching suggests
Melville's use of quotation in preface to *Moby-Dick*. Also,
the analogy to Melville goes deeper in the pervasive vein of
irony that juxtaposes the romantic expectations of the characters with the intransigence of experience's refusal to take
beautiful and natural form. Analogies to Melville may be as
invidious as analogies to *War and Peace*, but they do place
the novel more closely in its national framework where its
importance lies. (p. 99)

[The] "crisis of the Negro Intellectual" [is an issue] faced
directly in the novel in the conflict between Littleman, the
crippled genius whose idea it is to lynch a white policeman
as a way to save the spirit of the black community and who
is willing to sacrifice a few insignificant black lives to that
higher purpose, and Orin Wilkerson, the school-teacher
who finally destroys the bizarre plot for its inhuman implications. The issue is also faced implicitly in the relation
between *The Lynchers* and the other major works in the
tradition of black novels, particularly Wright's *Native Son*,
the novel that led black writers away from the minstrel-
novels of the Harlem Renaissance into serious naturalistic
fiction that spoke of and to the condition of the black
masses. Being a crime and punishment novel, *Native Son*
provides an opportunity to judge social institutions for their
inability to make a true judgment. The inadequacy of the
jury's judgment of Bigger Thomas in condemning him to
death for the murder of Mary Dalton is counterpointed by
Bigger's own process of self-definition, his complexly related feelings of pride and compassion through which he
can come to his own judgment of himself and society. Justice is the main theme of *The Lynchers* as well, but in substituting execution (or punishment) for trial (or judgment) as
the central metaphors, Wideman leads us to a deeper, more
primitive awareness of the fantasies of violence and frustration than Wright does. (p. 100)

[Wideman's] characters represent aspects of the black
mind; they are figures for the sense of impotence, the frustrations, aggression and selfishness that have been at the
center of the recent black experience. Through this range of
characterization that suggests the allegorical without being
restricted by its technical demands, Wideman has confronted not merely the crisis of the Negro intellectual, but
has placed that crisis in the context of the more general
crisis of all black Americans. In *Invisible Man* Ellison provided as a figure for the black social condition in white society the battle royal, whether it be a mob of blindfolded
black youths knocking each other down for the entertainment of a Southern town's white fathers or a ghetto riot in
Harlem. Wideman brilliantly develops this image by juxtaposing the family and social quarrels that finally undercut
all the relationships and many of the characters of the novel
against the images of beauty, order and control in the basketball games in the city playground. His terms exemplify a
critical awareness of the narrowness of abstraction in Ellison's terms and provide a richer and more varied image of
life. (p. 102)

Philip Keith, "Philadelphia Story," in Shenandoah (copyright by Shenandoah; reprinted
from Shenandoah: The Washington and Lee
University Review with the permission of the
Editor), Winter, 1974, pp. 99-102.*

Much of the force of Wideman's novel [*The Lynchers*] resides in its presentation of the ways in which the myth takes over the conspirators' mind. While there is violence, talk of revolution, salty dialogue, and much naturalistic detail in *The Lynchers,* it is not a novel of the angry black, nor is it a novel where story or suspense dominates. Rather Wideman tells his story in a complex way, reducing the impact of suspense and the dramatic. Time is jumbled; Wideman relies heavily on interior monologue. Joycean also is the dash at the beginning of the speech to indicate dialogue. For Littleman, the originator of the conspiracy, especially, history is a nightmare from which he is trying to escape. A novel about revolution, *The Lynchers* is not a novel for revolutionists. Rather it suggests in its psychological approach how myth can overwhelm a mind. The revolutionist is a special kind of magician. (p. 104)

> *Joseph M. Flora, in* The Michigan Quarterly Review *(copyright © The University of Michigan, 1975), Winter, 1975.*

*   *   *

WIESEL, Elie(zer)   1928-

Born in Transylvania, "somewhere in the Carpathian mountains," Wiesel is now an American citizen writing "Jewish-inspired" novels in French. He and his family were sent to Auschwitz when Wiesel was fifteen; he emerged alone from Buchenwald when he was not quite seventeen, and he has spent his life trying to reconcile—in novels, stories, prose poems, and essays—the evil of Auschwitz and the apparent indifference of God. Whether Wiesel is an artist or simply a witness is of little importance; his fiction is probably the most powerful and passionate of all Holocaust writing. (See also *Contemporary Authors*, Vols. 5-8, rev. ed.)

Elie Wiesel's fourth book, *The Town Beyond the Wall*, marks a continuation of the anguished bitterness, born of the Nazi destruction of European Jewry, that characterized his earlier works. . . .

The mood of the story is reminiscent of Kafka at his most depressed, of Samuel Beckett's "end of the world" dialogues, of that incredible Mexican novel of despair and brooding death, Juan Rulfo's *Pedro Paramo*. The central figure, the agonist, is Michael, a Jewish refugee from the Nazi holocaust. . . .

[Much] of the story has been foreshadowed by the Kafkas and the Becketts of this century, men who are not in the least writing about anything like a Nazi or a Communist reign of terror. This passage about Michael's bleak life in Paris, for example, seems to pop right out of Kafka's wish-fulfillment nightmare, *Amerika*: "One day the uncle in New York cut off his monthly money. He was angry, the uncle: his burst of charity was over."

And as for Michael's Hungarian imprisonment under the most mind-destroying circumstances, Wiesel appears to be translating Beckett's *Malone Dies, Endgame*, and *Krapp's Last Tape* into contemporary European geopolitical terms. Literary influences aside, however, *The Town Beyond the Wall* is moving and utterly absorbing. . . .

> *Samuel I. Bellman, "The Agony Relived,"* in Congress Bi-Weekly, *February 1, 1965, p. 14.*

Part One of [*The Oath*] is entitled "The Old Man and the Child." Wiesel [here] underlines the "marriage" of two opposing forces, old age and childhood. We wait to see whether this relationship will lead to tears.

The first word of the section is "No." The old man does not want to speak of yesterdays; he prefers to remain silent forever. Of course, we are made to wonder about the secrets he holds, but we are even more puzzled by his strong denial of progress, of any tomorrows. He says: "There is no more tomorrow." He is at the end of the line; he is haunted by imminent (or past?) doom.

Before we can discover more about the old man—the entire novel is a series of unanswered questions—we are offered an italicized passage. The very presence of italics startles us—there is a hint of discontinuity between the certainty of the old man's denial and the wavy lines of speculation. Another person is obviously thinking, but his thoughts are more disturbing than the denial we have previously heard. . . .

When the old man, who is named Azriel, speaks, he refuses to enlighten the stranger (and us) about Kolvillág. He wants to talk about *everything else*; and his unspoken words merely reinforce our desire to hear the forbidden secret. Wiesel shrewdly conveys the conflict between words and silence (one of his favorite themes). (p. 79)

Azriel has observed "scenes of apocalypse, nightmares begotten by sleeping corpses," but he is "sworn to silence." He cannot tell his story of survival, although he warns us darkly that "I am Kolvillág and I am going mad." It is ironic that he obsessively drops hints; he is a teasing storyteller or, better yet, a teasing story. He is *being told— by some other storyteller*. There is a sense of stories within stories, of words within words, worlds within worlds. Azriel understands the circularity of narration: "That is why you will not succeed in making me talk. I will circle around the story, I will not plunge into it. I'll beat around the bush. I'll say everything but the essential. For you see, I am not free. My voice is a prisoner." He recognizes that he is a "character" in some more complex story.

And as he listens to Azriel's unspoken words, the young man receives some message. He recognizes underlying truths. But he does not tell *us* what he learns. We are always in the middle of things, not able to strike through the masks of both men. (pp. 79-80)

Part two, entitled "The Child and the Madman," takes up more space than the earlier one; yet it concentrates upon a series of closely following events. Time narrows; "space" broadens. The effect is to create a dramatic focus, a concentrated description of destruction.

Wiesel changes his style. In place of jagged, unanswerable hints and incomplete omens, he sketches vividly the progress of apocalypse. A Gentile boy is missing; the friends and relatives turn to the "simple" explanation: the Jews have killed him! It is an old story—almost a cliché—but this quality enables Wiesel to dispense with lengthy, modernist interpretations of behavior and concentrate upon broad details. We may object to the stock characters, but we should realize that he wants us to see the "eternal return" of events. (p. 80)

Part three, "The Madman and the Book," may seem an anti-climax, but it partially resolves the tensions posed by all of the "separations" described earlier. It continues, at first, with the "ancient images of pogroms"—"smashed doors, shattered windows, broken dishes"—but it does not end with complete destruction. There is one survivor, Azriel, who miraculously escapes with the Book and, more significantly, with his remembered vision of the events. It is this remembered vision which contains the seeds of new life. There is a symbolic rebirth—although Moshe preached a new vision, he merely transmitted it to his disciple who, in effect, sees more—the end and . . . the beginning.

Wiesel does not stop here. The stories continue; the worlds increase. We read an italicized passage describing the present. Old Azriel and the young man stare at each other at dawn break. The young man, having just heard the story of Kolvillág, is transformed. He no longer wants to die; he also regards himself as some kind of survivor. He reawakens. (p. 81)

And yet there is another turn. After the two men depart on their separate journeys, there is another voice which proclaims in the italicized last words of the novel: "Azriel had returned to die in my stead, in Kolvillág." We are shocked. How can Azriel die in Kolvillág? How can death occur in a dead town? And how can Wiesel know the event will occur? The real and the unreal, life and the Book, author and character—those dualities we tend to separate clearly are suddenly clouded. We sense darkly that existence is, despite Moshe's glorious truths, a mingled story. Only a writer like Wiesel, unsure of his "life," can proclaim that he must try to define it day by day, line by line. Salvation is earned by irony, laughter, and symbol—by the ability to note dualities and to embrace none (or both) at the same time. Now we understand the repetition of "and" in the titles of the three sections. Wiesel wants us to be aware of continuities, parallels, inconclusions, perpetual beginnings. *The Oath* does not really end because its last words force us to reread it, to start once more, to recreate another pattern. (p. 82)

> *Irving Malin, "Worlds within Worlds," in* Midstream *(copyright © by The Theodor Herzl Foundation, Inc.), February, 1974, pp. 79-82.*

The documentary nature of *Night*, with its overwhelming content of hideous facts, pre-empts one's response to all three stories [*Night, Dawn,* and *The Accident*]. If one were to assume that the other two were fiction and judge them only by what is written on the page, they might appear somewhat crudely handled; the central notion of a Lazarus unable to respond to life might seem too simplified and too superficially expressed; yet taken as the later writings of a child who actually endured the experience of *Night*, they become evidence rather than art and their over-emotional style (which in any case probably sounds better in French) reads as the true voice of a witness rather than as the material of a fiction. (p. 159)

> *John Spurling, in* New Statesman *(© 1974 The Statesman & Nation Publishing Co. Ltd.), February 1, 1974.*

Elie Wiesel, journalist and novelist of the Holocaust, claims to owe his writing career to three years of imprisonment in Nazi concentration camps, starting at the age of fourteen. He relates in his quasi-autobiographical works that in the Hungarian *shtetl* of his early years he had been completely immersed in Talmudic studies (in the time-honored manner of intelligent Jewish boys), presumably preparing for life as a Talmudic scholar. His world was that of orthodox Judaism, governed in every detail by Jewish law, outside the mainstream of European culture.

To the young Wiesel the notion of an "absurd" universe would have been a completely alien one. Indeed, the world of orthodox Judaism would appear to allow no place in it for notions of the absurd in the contemporary, existential sense. For the traditional Jewish view holds that life's structure and meaning are fully explained and indeed derive from the divinely granted Torah. Yet, this view of Judaism, while accurate on the most basic level, is simplistic, ignoring, as it does, the well-established Jewish tradition of challenging God by questioning His ways. While Job is the most obvious (and perhaps the best) example to cite in this connection, it should not be forgotten that other prominent figures of the Old Testament, including Abraham, Moses, and Jeremiah, rebel against God and hold Him responsible for the injustice of the world.

As witness to the Holocaust, Elie Wiesel, remaining firmly within this Judaic tradition of protest, cries out against the destruction of European Jewry, against God's failure to intercede on behalf of His creatures. Wiesel's first five novels, in fact, can be meaningfully read as a sustained, developing revolt against God from within a Jewish context. Jewish tradition provides not only adequate precedents for such revolt, but the legal and moral sanction as well, in the unique covenant with God into which the Jewish people entered. . . .

In effect, the covenant brings God and man into a moral partnership, with each of the two parties having a clearly defined responsibility to the other.

Against this background the reality of Auschwitz confronts the Jew with a dilemma, an "absurdity" which cannot be dismissed easily and which stubbornly refuses to dissipate of its own accord. [As Emil Fackenheim noted in *God's Presence in History*,] "In faithfulness to Judaism . . . [the] Jew must refuse to disconnect God from the holocaust." Since the Jewish God is "a God who is Lord of actual history, its external events included," it is an inescapable conclusion that "Auschwitz is not an accident . . . because of the fact that God is part of it." . . . The only possible response that remains within the framework of Judaism is denunciation of God and a demand that He fulfill His contractual obligation.

This is the religious and moral context within which Wiesel attempts to apprehend and assimilate the events of the Holocaust. It would appear to be an underlying purpose of Wiesel's creative efforts to reconcile Auschwitz with Judaism, to confront and perhaps wring meaning from the absurd, which emerges as the true antagonist in his fiction. In this respect Wiesel is on common ground with other Jewish writers of the Holocaust, notably André Schwarz-Bart and Nelly Sachs. (pp. 212-14)

In sharp distinction to Wiesel, for whom the absurd is the breakdown of the accustomed order in God's world, the dissolution of a long established relationship between man and God, for Camus no such order and relationship ever existed, since Camus is, quite simply, an atheist. Indeed, in the thinking of Camus the absence of a Higher Authority in the world seems to be connected with the roots of man's absurd condition, for Camus describes the absurd as arising from man's realization that he can have no direct knowledge of the world, that he can make no contact with absolute truths and values. . . . Camus concludes that "there is but one truly serious philosophical problem, and that is suicide. Judging whether life is or is not worth living amounts to answering the fundamental question of philosophy."

Wiesel too has seriously considered this problem in his novel, *The Accident*, whose protagonist-narrator is almost killed in an "accident" that is an apparent attempt at suicide. With this act Wiesel's rebellion against the God of Judaism, begun passionately in the setting of Nazi concentration camps in the autobiographical *Night* and continued on a more detached, philosophical plane in his second novel, *Dawn*, reaches a climax. For the sacredness of life, as God's gift to mankind, is basic to Judaism and in fact arguably the most basic tenet of the Jewish faith. In the Jewish view it is not for man to judge "whether life is or is not worth living"; only the God of Israel, as Creator and Giver of Life, is to determine when life is to end. In Wiesel's peculiarly Jewish context, therefore, the suicide attempt takes on added significance as a kind of ultimate defiance of God, explainable only on the basis of a recognition, in reaction to Auschwitz, that God encompasses evil as well as good, that in violating His covenant with man, God has not only withdrawn His protection but has left man free of the restraints of His laws and commandments.

Wiesel's hero has thus come to share the attitude which characterizes Camus' protagonist, Meursault, at the beginning of *The Stranger*—a sense of the absurdity of the world and the pointlessness of human existence. In contrast to Meursault, however, Wiesel's character is obsessed by the relationship of man and God. . . . Wiesel's survivor questions incessantly, though expecting no answers, aware that the existence of answers is itself in question. (pp. 214-16)

Like Meursault, the protagonist of *The Accident* refuses to deny the absurd; he avoids what Camus had termed "philosophical suicide," that is, the attitude of existential philosophies which *a priori* reject the idea that life has some transcendental meaning and then, by a sudden "leap of faith," find such meaning, abandon revolt, become reconciled. . . . The message of *The Accident* . . . is essentially the same as that conveyed by Meursault—that man, like Sisyphus, can find fulfillment (if not meaning) in confronting his fate with lucidity rather than denial, in not hesitating "to draw the inevitable conclusions from a fundamental absurdity," in struggle itself. Yet, in *The Accident* (as in *The Stranger*), lucidity is unaccompanied by meaningful action that might lead to such fulfillment for the protagonist. (pp. 216-17)

The passivity of the narrator of *The Accident* gives way to the positive action of Michael, protagonist of Wiesel's succeeding novel, *The Town Beyond the Wall*. Michael is also a survivor of the Nazi death camps and he too is obsessed by the memory of those who died. Yet his longing to return to the town in Hungary in which he was born and raised is the opposite of indifference; it is, in fact, a passion for clarity, a desire to confront and understand, within the limits of human possibility, the catastrophe which befell him, his family, the Jewish community. (p. 217)

Michael confronts the absurdity of the Holocaust by focusing upon the spectator, . . . [who] makes a telling point:

"A few policemen—not more that ten—led you all to the slaughterhouse: why didn't you seize their arms?" (pp. 217-18)

We may conjecture that those unresisting Jews were awaiting until the end the intervention of God, who would save them as He had saved their ancestors fleeing from the Pharaoh, that they would rather face death than acknowledge the breakdown of the covenant, the indifference of the universe. This steadfast trust in God, in the face of impending disaster, places these victims of the Nazi extermination close in spirit to Father Paneloux of *The Plague*, who refuses to accept medical attention when he contracts the disease. The priest's death is thus as suicidal as are the deaths of Wiesel's Jewish victims. The underlying cause is the same in both cases—the inability or unwillingness to surrender faith, the inability to cope with an irreducible absurdity, the refusal to acknowledge the possibility of evil within God.

In contrast, Michael is able to make this acknowledgment and, in so doing, is freed to take positive action. (p. 218)

Moral madness reappears as an important force in Wiesel's succeeding novel, *The Gates of the Forest*. At the beginning of the work it is not Gregor, the young protagonist, but Gavriel, his philosopher-teacher, who displays moral madness in reacting to the horrors of the war: "I'm listening to the war and I'm laughing" . . . [and who] bursts suddenly into overwhelming laughter at the moment he is taken prisoner by the German soldiers. . . . [The] Hasidic Rebbe . . . advocates song, dance, prayer, and joy in the face of the Holocaust: "The man who goes singing to his death is the brother of the man who goes to death fighting". . . . (p. 218-19)

The moral madman is closely linked in spirit to the "absurd man" in the sense of Camus; both are able to face the world's absurdity unflinchingly, with aversion, perhaps, but without denial. . . . The end result is the same in either case —that genuine confrontation with the absurd advocated in *The Myth of Sisyphus*. Camus' thoughts on the necessity of such confrontation is reflected in Pedro's message: "Remaining human—in spite of all temptations and humiliations —is the only way to hold your own against the Other". . . . Michael stands in direct opposition to that divinely inspired passivity in the face of death displayed by the Jewish victims of the Holocaust and by Father Paneloux, who feels that in fighting the plague he may well be thwarting the will of God.

In the same way that Father Paneloux's confrontation with the plague is overlaid with difficulties stemming from faith, Wiesel's confrontation with the absurd is complicated (as compared with that of Camus) by his adherence to Judaism. However, Paneloux's resolution of the problem through suicide is not the answer for Wiesel, who finds his solution instead in protest, not merely against absurdity, but against God Himself. . . . For him the object of protest against God is not nihilism, not denial of God, but the very opposite—the re-establishment of God's order in a world which has witnessed the destruction of order. Indeed, through Michael, Wiesel confesses his inability to repudiate God: "I want to blaspheme, and I can't quite manage it. I go up against Him, I shake my fist, I froth with rage, but it's still a way of telling Him that He's there, that He exists . . . that denial itself is an offering to His grandeur". (pp. 219-20)

Though Wiesel clings to God in the face of injustice, his position cannot be termed philosophical suicide, in the sense in which Camus understands that phrase. On the contrary, Wiesel is a perfect example of Camus' "absurd man," striving for clarity whatever the consequences, recognizing the complicity of God in the evil perpetrated by man, in spite of the shattering effect of such recognition. . . . Ivan Karamazov believes that without God all things are possible; Wiesel shares with us his discovery that all things are possible even with God and therein lies his unique contribution to our understanding of the human condition. (p. 220)

> *Josephine Knopp, "Wiesel and the Absurd," in* Contemporary Literature *(© 1974 by the Board of Regents of the University of Wisconsin System), Vol. 15, No. 2, Spring, 1974, pp. 212-20.*

"The Madness of God" belongs to the Joan of Arc genre. This is where an individual troubled by integrity and filled with immortal longings risks his or her life ("The Crucible")—or at least respectable position in the community ("An Enemy of the People")—in order to speak The Truth, angering the temporal establishment but pleasing the gods who sit in both heaven and the balcony. The particular galvanizing power of Wiesel's play is that the problem is real and contemporary: the political persecution of Jews in Russia. . . .

"The Madness of God" is always interesting and occasionally quite moving. But too often the action and dialogue are predictable, probably because Wiesel has chosen to create spokesmen for political points of view rather than character. A legitimate choice only if the argument takes off and transcends. . . .

"The Madness of God" is Jewish propaganda on behalf of our brethren in Russia. But in a curious and probably unintended way, I found the play speaking directly to American Jews about their own delinquent worship and belief. In both Russia and America we are witnessing the disintegration of an ethnic-religious tradition. But the greater pathos is on these shores. For it is here in America that we have willingly turned wine into grape juice. . . .

"The Madness of God" may be propaganda, but it is mythic too. Because Jews are mythic. Because history has made them so.

Auschwitz and Israel. Death and resurrection.

Elie Wiesel's play asks if it will be death again.

> *Dan Isaac, "Turning Wine into Grape Juice," in* The Village Voice *(reprinted by permission of* The Village Voice; *copyright © The Village Voice, Inc., 1974), June 13, 1974, p. 87.*

Wiesel, out of the horror of his own experience at Auschwitz and that of his entire generation, has wrestled with the Messianic problem in an autobiographical chronicle, half a dozen novels, and three books of essays. With infinite variety, the Messianic theme is raised, the question is asked, responses are sought. The strands of hope seem slender and often virtually invisible, but there always remains a willingness to persist in asking the questions. For if man

often seems to be "hope turned to dust," he is also, amazingly, "dust turned to hope." On occasion, most notably perhaps at the conclusion of *The Gates of the Forest*, a hope is expressed that the Messiah is not one man, but can and must be present in all men, whose very presence in the world, singing, praying, crying and obdurately questioning, is somehow a sign that forsakenness is not the only world.

Ani Maamin is Wiesel's latest and most poignant pressing of the Messianic question. It is the libretto of a cantata, set to music by Darius Milhaud, and appears in the text in both French and English. The writing is in blank verse, spare and taut, and its very economy of line, apparent in both languages, contributes to the enormous anguish built up as the questions addressed to God assume an almost unbearable poignancy. *Ani maamin beviat ha-Mashiah* is one of Maimonides' thirteen articles of faith: "I believe in the coming of the Messiah." Wiesel sang the song as a young Hasidic Jew in Transylvania, and believed it. He heard it sung in the death camps and wondered how it could continue to be sung. How could one "believe in the coming of the Messiah" during and after the holocaust? So the song was "lost." Could it possibly be "found" again? The Book is Wiesel's exploration of that possibility. (pp. 384-85)

> *Robert McAfee Brown, "Eli[e] Wiesel's Song: Lost & Found Again," in* Commonweal *(copyright © 1974 Commonweal Publishing Co., Inc.; reprinted by permission of Commonweal Publishing Co., Inc.), July 12, 1974, pp. 384-86.*

Elie Wiesel's first attempt at drama, *Zalmen, or The Madness of God*, is an energetic fusion of mystical longings and worldly, political insights. (p. 20)

The triumphs that . . . exist in the play are tenuous triumphs of existential choice and self-decision. The play is a call for self-assertion and struggle against passive defeat. But it is, at the same time, a realistic assessment of the Jewish situation in the Soviet Union. For, although Zalmen, in both a prologue and epilogue, informs us that this story is unreal, it nevertheless is a story of concrete potential.

Wiesel's ironies and paradoxes are multiple. Heroism may fail, prudence can become imprudent. Bureaucrats may act intelligently and thus become even more formidable. In the end, there is no choice but to pursue madness, if madness means a rejection of silence and acquiescence. It is in the eyes of the young that our madness is reflected in all its clarified saneness.

Wiesel's drama is poignant and resonant. It is at once a demand and insistent call on Jews and a powerful exploration of spiritual depths and the human condition. (p. 21)

> *Lawrence J. Epstein, "Wiesel's Drama of Survival," in* Congress Monthly, *April, 1975, pp. 20-1.*

*   *   *

WILDER, Thornton   1897-

Wilder, a Pulitzer Prize-winning American playwright and novelist, writes elegant and inventive "dramatic hymns to human endurance" about ordinary human beings "living in an inscrutable but benevolent universe." His great plays, *Our*

Town and *Skin of Our Teeth,* are distinguished as experiments in theatrical technique and by what is considered particularly American charm and humor. (See also *Contemporary Authors,* Vols. 13-16, rev. ed.)

Thornton Wilder . . . is thought of, together with O'Neill, Miller, and Williams, as one of our "Big Four," and yet his reputation is based on only three full-length plays and was made on one. . . . For some he is the great American satirist; for others he is a soft-hearted sentimentalist; and for still others he is our only "religious" dramatist. Furthermore. . . . Brecht, Ionesco, Duerrenmatt, and Frisch have all acknowledged their debt to this "great and fanatical experimenter." (p. 239)

Wilder has dealt boldly and affirmatively with the themes of Life, Love, and Earth. Each of his plays is a hymn in dramatic form affirming life. But the important question is: What is the nature of this affirmation? It is not, as some would have it, Christian. To begin with, Wilder has no belief—at least as expressed in his plays—in a religion that is revealed or historical. These are basic premises of Christianity. To be sure Wilder is deistic, but as almost all of his critics have pointed out, he is essentially a religious Platonist; and this position must ultimately reject the historic dimension as meaningful. (pp. 239-40)

Wilder is a humanist, an affirming humanist, a "yeasayer to life" as Bernard Hewitt calls him. When we examine the nature of Wilder's humanistic affirmation, what do we discover? His plays celebrate human love, the worth and dignity of man, the values of the ordinary, and the eternity of human values. From the little boy in Wilder's first play who says: "I am not afraid of life. I will astonish it!" to Dolly Levi and her cohorts in adventure in *The Matchmaker,* Wilder has always been on the side of life and life is seen to be most directly affirmed through love. Love, then, is his most persistent theme and it has been for him an inexhaustible subject. Of its worth he is convinced, but it is interesting to note that Wilder has never been able to make any commitments as to the reasons for its worth. Wilder can deal with life and love directly and concretely; but when he moves to the edges of life, the focus becomes less sharp. Certainly, Wilder deals with death—he is not afraid of it, but death in his plays is terminal. When Mrs. Soames says in Act Three of *Our Town:* "My, wasn't life awful—and wonderful," Wilder is reminding us that beauty is recognizable because of change and life is meaningful because of death. But as both John Mason Brown and Winfield Townley Scott have pointed out, Wilder never deals adequately with Death's own meaning. And as for what's beyond death?. . . Life is reality and eternity is the perfected essence of that reality to which we are too often blind and of which we can't stand too much.

It is this tendency, a tendency consistent with his Platonism, to reduce the dimension of eternity so that it can be encompassed by life itself, that has led me to believe, although he has written no tragedies, that Wilder has essentially a tragic rather than a Christian or even religious view of life. To be sure, Wilder has not created any Ahabs or Lears, but this is not because he lacks a tragic vision. He happens to believe, as did Maeterlinck, that there are times in each of our lives when we are conscious of moving into the boundary situations of the tragic realm, and that furthermore, life's tragedies can best be seen in the drama of the everyday, in life's smallest events. For this reason he

does not dramatize great conflicts in order to capture the quintessence of tragedy. I think it is important to see the validity of this, although we must point out that while this approach is tragic it is not always dramatic. And this, I think, accounts for the fact Wilder's plays are usually referred to as "hymns", "odes," "songs," and so on, and most critics feel that there isn't much conflict in their plots. (pp. 240-42)

Over and over again in Wilder's work, the belief is stated directly and indirectly that "life is what you make of it." The fullest discussion of the idea is in his novel *The Ides of March,* where Caesar says: "Life has no meaning save that which we confer upon it.". . . [This] is really an existential position and . . . Wilder is very close to Sartre's "Man is condemned to be free."

In fact, upon reflection, we discover that in starting from "Life is what we make of it," Wilder is really in the mainstream of the modern drama beginning with Ibsen and Strindberg. And this is a dangerous position and usually in the drama has led to despair. The image of man in this drama is an image of collapse. . . . I think [Wilder] averts despair—and also tragedy, even though his view of life is essentially tragic—with a kind of Santayana-like belief in life. In fact, Wilder's Platonism can make sense only if it is seen as coming through Santayana. Wilder is, as probably most of us are, saved from despair and its paralyzing effects by what Santayana has called "animal faith.". . . [Our] animal faith, which bids us believe in the external world, is much stronger than all the logical arguments which tend to make life seem absurd. (pp. 242-43)

But although Wilder can assert meaning to life, the meaning is almost in the assertion itself and this is not a very comfortable position to be in. One gets the feeling that Wilder has to keep saying it to make sure that it is true. The danger of this position is that it lacks the necessary polarity and tension for full meaning. This in itself keeps Wilder from being a religious dramatist. In all great religious drama—the works of Sophocles, Calderón, *Everyman,* and in more recent times the later plays of Hofmannsthal, Eliot, and even Fry—there is the backdrop of religious belief which gives meaning to and informs the hero's "life is what you make of it." There is the greater stage. . . [and] the idea of man as a player on the world's stage becomes the very principle of the *mise-en-scène.* For God, the master, speaking from the top of the scaffold, actually orders the world to produce a play under his eyes, featuring man who is to act out his part on earth.

More important than the absence of a religious dimension to Wilder's work, however, are the many experiments he has made in theatrical technique to compensate for this lack of an ultimate perspective. (pp. 243-44)

Wilder has not been interested in psychology and [unlike most modern dramatists, according to this critic,] has never used psychological techniques to solve the "modernists'" problems in the theatre. This accounts, I think, for his great influence on the Continental avant-garde dramatists who are rebelling against our psychologically oriented theatre. Wilder sought to achieve the sense of an ultimate perspective by immaterializing the sense of dramatic place on stage. The bare stage of *Our Town* with its chairs, tables, and ladders, together with the Stage Manager's bald exposition, are all that he uses to create the town. The same is true of *The Skin of Our Teeth*; you never really know where the Antrobuses live, nor when. This is his second dominant technique; by destroying the illusion of time, Wilder achieves the effect of any time, all time, each time. But this is risky business, for without the backdrop of an ultimate perspective to inform a play's action, it can very easily become sentimental or satirical, or even pretentious. Wilder at his best keeps this from happening, but his only weapons are wit and irony. And a production which does not succeed in capturing these qualities (as, alas, most college and school productions do not) is bound to turn out pathetic and sentimental; when technique is used as a compensation for the ultimate perspective, the resultant work of art always lies precariously under a Damoclean sword.

It is important that we see the dangers in Wilder's methods, but that a tragic sense of life informs his plays is best illustrated by his sense of destiny. (p. 245)

What Wilder [says] is that human beings cannot stand to have a sense of destiny—the awareness that there is a continuity in all our acts, the awareness that every present moment comes from a past and is directed to a future. Only at moments, usually of emotional crisis, do we have this sense of destiny, this sense of awareness of the future. It is this sense of destiny that is the great human reality and the tragedy of life lies in our fragmentary and imperfect awareness of it. Wilder is aware, like Eliot, that "human kind cannot bear very much reality," but his plays fall short of tragedy because he takes the Platonic escape, he moves into a world that denies the reality and the nemesis of destiny. Nor does he have the solution of an Eliot. For in denying, finally, the reality of destiny he shuts out the possibility of ever providing the means to perfect our fragmentary and imperfect vision. He fails, to use Karl Jaspers' phrase, to go "Beyond Tragedy." That Wilder lacks this dimension is not to discredit him, however, for no other American dramatist more fully affirms that miracle of life which so much modern drama would deny. (p. 246)

> *Robert W. Corrigan, "Thornton Wilder and the Tragic Sense of Life" (originally published in* Educational Theatre Journal, *Vol. XIII, No. 3, 1961), in his* The Theatre in Search of a Fix *(copyright © 1973 by Robert W. Corrigan; used with permission of Delacorte Press), Delacorte Press, 1973, pp. 239-46.*

Thornton Wilder announced himself at once as an experimenter. The audience that entered the theatre at the first performance of *Our Town* . . . found itself facing a curtainless, sceneryless stage. The beginning of the play was marked by the entrance of the Stage Manager, who lighted his pipe, cocked his hat over his eyes, and sat down to chat informally with the spectators about the play they were going to see. If the audience was at first startled by the novelty, they were soon able to adjust to it, and, through the necessarily sharpened focus on the actors, found themselves engrossed by a story so simple and commonplace that in other hands and under other conditions of production they might never have noticed it at all. The play is without the conflicts and tensions that are normally considered dramatic or theatrical: a young girl grows up, marries and dies in a New England village so isolated from the burning issues of the greater world that they are never

hinted at. And yet this very isolation, emphasized by the bareness of the stage, brought to vivid life the problems, the conditions, the situation of everyman, so that this little play, seemingly so American in its frame of reference and its attitudes, has found an instant and continuing response in the hearts and minds of world audiences.

The Skin of Our Teeth . . . is in many ways Wilder's most creative use of the theatre. His theme is the survival of the human race in the face of ignorance, catastrophe, and folly, and he moves backward and forward in time with a rapidity that reminds some critics of the *Finnegans Wake* of James Joyce. . . . For sheer variety and mingling of emotions, *The Skin of Our Teeth* approaches most closely a musical comedy, but its theme is a celebration rather than a mere exhibition of humanity. Wilder's use of familiar materials and conventions in a fresh way comes very close to that creative, poetic theatre toward which O'Neill urged his fellow workers to aspire. (pp. 52-3)

> *Alan S. Downer, "The Revolt from Broadway," in* A Time of Harvest, *edited by Robert E. Spiller (reprinted with the permission of Farrar, Straus & Giroux, Inc.; copyright © 1962 by Robert E. Spiller), Hill & Wang, 1962, pp. 42-53.*

[It] is within the frame of Wilder's total endeavor as playwright and novelist that [his] short pieces stand out most meaningfully. And, conversely, [the] little masterworks [in *The Long Christmas Dinner*] help to define their author, concerning whom opinions have been frequently divided and rarely cogent despite the attention paid to his writings and the regard in whch he is held on two continents. In this collection of early plays we find (not unexpectedly in the case of so disciplined and self-aware an artist) the configurations of a talent that combines sensitivity with a strong awareness of form and embraces both the commonplaces of life and the life of the imagination, which fluctuates between fantasy and philosophy, skepticism and mysticism, playfulness and sobriety. We see him poised between "life" and "theatre," and this not merely as a beguiling technician but as an observer of reality who does not hesitate to throw off the shackles of realistic play construction in order to come closer to reality. (pp. viii-ix)

The Woman of Andros may not be a substantial novel; it is nonetheless an enchanting and affecting book, and it is more satisfying in my opinion than many an acclaimed contemporary novel. But the historical situation was plainly unfavorable to the reflective and tastefully distanced artistry which is one of the two worlds of art Wilder has inhabited in the course of his distinguished literary career. He would have to move into the other world of common reality which he had fastidiously avoided but with which he soon made a successful compromise that accounts for much of his originality and his special genius—the compromise of combining intensive observation of the common world with uncommon transcendence or sublimation of that world. Wilder himself was apparently aware of a limitation in his art when he declared some years later (in 1938) that he had shrunk from describing the modern world and was "alarmed at finding a way of casting into generalization the world of doorbells and telephones." He was ready, he believed, "to accept the twentieth century, not only as a fascinating age to live in, but as assimilable stuff to think with."(pp. x-xi)

Henceforth he was to inhabit two worlds, the real and the imaginary, or to blend the two in the same work. This was apparent in his later fiction—in *Heaven's My Destination*, an amusing yet rueful novel about a moralistic innocent adrift in American society, published in 1935, and in *The Ides of March* (1948), in which he combined a novel of manners in Julius Caesar's times with a penetrating portrait of Caesar and exquisitely reflective prose often intensified with emotion and lightened with humor. . . . But it is especially in the plays published after *The Angel That Troubled the Waters* that Wilder effected the reconciliation of reality and imagination which proved so rewarding in *Our Town* in 1938 and *The Skin of Our Teeth* in 1942. (pp. xiii-xiv)

He is at once a radical and a traditionalist in employing a form of the drama instead of sedulously sustaining the so-called illusion of reality required by the conventions of modern realism. The artificial nature of the theatre was the established convention of classic, Oriental, Renaissance, Elizabethan, neoclassic, and romantic theatre; realistic convention, which became firmly established only in the second half of the nineteenth century, is a very late development. In returning to "theatricalism" or "theatre for theatre's sake" (rather than "theatre for the sake of illusion"), Wilder associated himself with tradition in dramatic art. But returning to tradition in the twentieth century was an innovation, and Wilder's manner of returning to it was personal and unique. It came about not without some dangers, the greatest of these being in his case some frolicsome bookishness and self-conscious skittishness, but it amounted to a minor revolution in the American theatre. (pp. xvii-xviii)

> *John Gassner, "The Two Worlds of Thornton Wilder" (introduction copyright © 1963 by Harper & Row, Publishers, Inc.; reprinted by permission of the publishers), the introduction to* The Long Christmas Dinner, and Other Plays in One Act, *by Thornton Wilder (copyright 1931 by Yale University Press and Coward-McCann, Inc.), Harper & Row, 1964, pp. vii-xx.*

*   *   *

WILLIAMS, John A(lfred)   1925-

Williams, a Black American novelist, poet, and journalist, has produced increasingly complex fictions which transcend the personal, or protest, novel.

In his latest novel Williams . . . turns to black history, and while it is evident that the author has done his homework, his failure here is as a novelist. *Captain Blackman* is an ambitious attempt at a fictional chronicle covering about two centuries of black military history. Its hero is named, appropriately enough, Abraham Blackman; his archenemy of many years, now his battalion commander, bears the equally symbolic name of Ishmael Whittman. . . .

The novel is a stinging polemic demonstrating how blacks have been used by a racist military establishment that encouraged them to fight and die for a freedom ultimately denied them. . . . *Captain Blackman* has the merit of bringing a buried past to our consciousness and our conscience; the work, however, suffers from a doggedly mechanical structure.

> *Leonard Fleischer, in* Saturday Review *(copyright 1972 by Saturday Review, Inc.; reprinted with permission), May 13, 1972.*

John A. Williams' *The Man Who Cried I Am* (1967) has attracted considerable attention among the general public not so much for its literary excellence but because in the last pages of the novel its protagonist, Max Reddick, discovers a monstrous plot—code named "King Alfred"—to eradicate the black population of the United States. The plot, similar in many ways to Nazi Germany's "final solution," employs enough facts from everyday life to give the reader an uneasy feeling that perhaps this section of the book is not pure fiction: only slightly disguised, James Meredith, Malcolm X, Martin Luther King, Richard Wright, and James Baldwin all appear in the novel; so do numerous black organizations ranging from the Urban League to the Black Muslims (the Black Panther Party had not come to prominence at the time Williams was writing the book). Add to these facts the recent furor over detention camps still in existence and the growing suspicion of the CIA and the FBI, and it is not surprising that a black critic such as David Henderson should approach the book as a social document, a part of the protest school of black writing, which points out and documents real examples of racial prejudice and persecution.

This feature of the novel is not to be ignored. By suggesting the logical extension of America's past and present treatment of black people, the novel, hopefully, may jolt the conscience of the nation and influence its future policies. However, Williams deserves credit for the art of the novel as well as its message. The King Alfred extermination plan is only one item in a series of nightmarish elements which Williams uses to dramatize not only the psychological problems of the main character but also the frightening social conditions which foster them. Like most nightmares, these particular elements of the novel evoke emotions of fear and repugnance and often a frantic refusal to accept what is detestable or unbelievable. As in a nightmare, the seemingly impossible happens, and evil or death is manifested in peculiarly horrifying ways; perversion, savagery, and hatred may threaten one's humanity, reason, or life itself. Employing these gothic elements with considerable artistic success, Williams frees himself from the naturalistic protest format which for a time seemed the sole métier of the black novelist. (pp. 186-87)

What purpose does the King Alfred portion of the novel serve? White readers are likely to dismiss King Alfred as something like science fiction, while black readers are likely to accept it as showing real insight into contemporary attitudes and conditions. Viewed from a literary perspective, however, . . . King Alfred serves a valid artistic purpose. In one sense, black people have been systematically killed off in the United States since their first introduction to its shores. Malnutrition, disease, poverty, psychological conditioning, and spiritual starvation have been the tools, rather than military operations and gas chambers, but the result has often been the same. King Alfred is not only a prophetic warning of what might happen here but a fictional metaphor for what has been happening and is happening still.

What has Williams accomplished by his use of bizarre and horrible metaphors for racial conflict and the plight of the black American? Perhaps his most important achievement is his escape from the protest novel tradition that has threatened to confine black writers within one narrow school. Since the publication of *Native Son* (1940), black novelists have either written naturalistic protest novels only to be compared unfavorably with Wright or have attempted to find a new form which would bring a freshness to their work but would still express their powerful moral indignation. (pp. 195-96)

Williams has demonstrated his ability to work with a type of horror tale which transcends mere documentation of ghetto conditions yet still carries the message he feels he must convey to his readers. The nightmarish scenes which emerge from his otherwise realistic novel startle the reader into attention and leave him with memories that he will not forget as soon as he may wish. Williams' success with this shock technique suggests one of the new directions that may be taken by the black novelist. (p. 196)

> *Robert E. Fleming, "The Nightmare Level of 'The Man Who Cried I Am'," in* Contemporary Literature (© *1973 by the Regents of the University of Wisconsin), Vol. 14, No. 2, Spring, 1973, pp. 186-96.*

The human spirit transcends the accidents of history and is not bound by the brutal processes of nature. . . . The theme of [*The Man Who Cried I Am*] seems to be that by resisting the oppressive forces of cancer and politics Max Reddick insists on the value and dignity of his life as a man and as a Black and, by extension, affirms the value of all individual life.

The novel also illustrates a basic pattern in Williams' fiction: in each of his novels the black protagonist, much like the wounded Hemingway hero, suffers from some physical or emotional affliction, at bottom a symbol of interracial relations in the world. (p. 13)

Of all [his] characters, . . . Max Reddick of *The Man Who Cried I Am* best illustrates Williams' concern with oppression and the will to resist it. Reddick is the most knowledgeable—he has traveled widely in three continents; he has worked as a journalist, writer, and presidential adviser; he has developed a sense of history. The novel, too, ranges further in time, space, and ideas than any of the others, thus providing a panoramic background that lends depth to the figure of Max Reddick. The most significant of Williams' protagonists, he has a greater awareness of the diverse forces that afflict him; and because his death from cancer is imminent, his resistance becomes even more meaningful. Indeed, Max Reddick dramatizes in a grand manner what the other protagonists have been concerned with implicitly: the need to affirm one's worth by resisting the racism that would deny it. (p. 14)

> *William M. Burke, "The Resistance of John A. Williams: 'The Man Who Cried I Am'," in* Critique: Studies in Modern Fiction (*copyright* © *by* Critique, *1974), Vol. XV, No. 3, 1974, pp. 5-14.*

John A. Williams may not be an incarnation of the "black writer" of the 1960's, but he stands pretty much at the center of the black fiction of that decade. Not only a writer, he has become a monitor of black writing in general,

working hard for its propagation and improvement. He is not the overt activist that Amiri Baraka has become, nor a militant pusher of "black aesthetic." He is concerned with a revolution, and just as the beginning of his writing career coincides with the early activist phase of the Civil Rights Movement (his first novel, *The Angry Ones*, was published in 1960), so all of his work has a distinctly political focus.

His subject is race, and his themes reflect the most advertised concerns of the revolution: the economic and psychological emasculation of the black man by the white, the struggle of the black man to preserve his manhood, the black will to survive and the enduring strength that brings victory. He is not the kind of political novelist Irving Howe speaks of, whose main challenge is "to make ideas or ideologies come to life, to endow them with the capacity for stirring characters into passionate gestures and sacrifices." Instead, he seeks to convince the reader that his picture of society, with its black ideological tilt, is accurate, bringing home to white Americans the extent of their crime and demonstrating to blacks the means by which they might triumph over white discrimination. He has picked up the baton from Richard Wright and set out to use his art to help his people, to embody the sociopolitical concerns of black Americans in fictional form. (pp. 81-2)

Williams's novels are consistent in reflecting his ideological bias, but artistically they are quite uneven. *The Angry Ones*, dealing with discrimination against blacks who try to get specialized employment, and *Night Song* (1961), an excursion into the world of black jazz, indicate that from the beginning Williams knew how to put a novel together, but that he had not developed the emotional restraint or insight to put a *good* novel together. *Sissie* (1963), about the changing black family and the emergence of a new generation, is a great improvement. Williams, having learned much about himself and his subject, found a way to capture the complexities of both. *The Man Who Cried I Am* (1967) rises to art, as if the three earlier novels were exercises of preparation. Its story of two black novelists makes one of the best novels of the 1960's. But *Sons of Darkness, Sons of Light* (1969) and *Captain Blackman* (1972) show a sharp falling off. The former, about the use of Mafia techniques in a "possible" future, and the latter, about the role of the black soldier in America's military history, are both thin and theme-ridden.

That he has not been more frequently successful is largely explained by the fact that he has expended his talents more on politics than on art. Perhaps more important, the course upon which his political and racial loyalties have guided him is not completely the course of his natural bent. The arena in which he is most comfortable is the world of the black intellectual. His prototypical character is the man of thought whose creativity is sapped by racism. The strength of the character and his interest for the reader lie in his powers of self-analysis and understanding. (p. 82)

He can write first-rate fiction; the irony is that his first-rate fiction, which is less loaded with doctrinal intentions than his second-rate, seems more effectively to do the job he sets out to do. Honest politics—good politics—is much better served by good art that is not overtly or designedly political than by bad art that is. In fact, the politics that calls on its artists to falsify their vision and slant the findings of their personal observation cannot be good politics and cannot produce good art. (pp. 85-6)

The Man Who Cried I Am is Williams's adaptation of the rhetoric of black power to his own needs as a novelist. It is a gloss on a sentence in *This Is My Country Too:* "Today the strength of the contemporary Negro is in being ready to die." But the novel also expresses a feeling about the implications of prototypical black militancy no other novel has. It does not end with a flourish of trumpets and a martyred death of a black victim who triumphs even in defeat; it ends on a note of sadness and uncertainty, of lament for the necessary metamorphosis of the new black into a revolutionary ready to die. Melancholy pervades the novel, not heroic anger or righteous wrath. The violent ending cannot erase the sorrow that dominates every scene, sorrow over the tarnishing of America's bright dream. After the political implications in the failure of the American Creed comes yet another discovery that makes the politics of the novel so complex and effective: men, black and white, can be petty and self-serving; women can be grasping and self-centered. Every relationship carries with it warm human promise, and every promise gradually dissipates in the air of human frailty and the deficiency of conditions. No motive is pure, no act is untinged with bias. Blacks as well as whites display greed, jealousy, duplicity, opportunism. (pp. 98-9)

The Man Who Cried I Am is in a sense Williams's *Huckleberry Finn*. It reflects his deep skepticism over the capacity of America to live up to its professed ideals, and a development of deep pessimism about whites in particular and man in general. The intensity of its melancholy demonstrates the strength of Williams's emotional attachment to America. The gloom that the novel conveys is the result of seeing that one's most optimistic convictions are laid in sand, and that the building of the pure ideal was doomed from the start. (p. 99)

In *The Man Who Cried I Am*, Williams fuses the pessimism and the optimism that divide his own mind and feelings and makes good fiction and good politics. By recognizing men's moral, mental, and physical limitations, he delivers to politics a vision that is both more realistic and more human than the conventional political rhetoric gives us. He frees politics of its exaggerations and posturing and helps the reader avoid the danger of believing in the oversimplified version of the struggle that reduces all contention to the conflict between hero and villain. Though Williams resolves the paradox of "fortunate oppression" in *The Man Who Cried I Am*, he has perhaps gone too far on the road to polemics to turn back. He has chosen, more often than not, to use his art for the narrow rather than the larger political purpose, and it has led him into implausible exaggeration and offensive sentimentality. Unless a change in the times frees him of his deep sense of obligation to the narrower purpose, he will probably never write another novel as good as *Sissie* or *The Man Who Cried I Am*. (p. 100)

> Jerry H. Bryant, "John A. Williams: The Political Use of the Novel," in Critique: Studies in Modern Fiction *(copyright © James Dean Young 1975), Vol. XVI, No. 3, 1975, pp. 81-100.*

*   *   *

WILLIAMS, Tennessee   1911-

Williams is a Southern American playwright, screenwriter, short story writer, and novelist. *The Glass Menagerie* **is rec-** ognized as the prototype of the American theatrical trend to explore the vanished hopes of the dispossessed. Most of Williams' work is derived from his understanding of the impossibility of communication and what Signi Falk has called his "awareness of the appalling emptiness and cruelty in the hearts of many well-fed Americans." Williams, one of the world's most popular playwrights, is probably America's greatest living dramatist. (See also *Contemporary Authors,* Vol. 5-8, rev. ed.)

The plays that first thrust Tennessee Williams into the front rank have much in common besides their clear focus and economical construction. Both *The Glass Menagerie* and *A Streetcar Named Desire* transmute the base metal of reality into theatrical and, frequently, verbal poetry. Both supplement the action with symbolic elements of mood and music. A major theme is Southern womanhood helpless in the grip of the new world, while its old world of social position and financial security is a Paradise Lost. (p. 84)

The Glass Menagerie is a memory play in which crucial episodes from family history are evoked in the comments of a narrator, the poet Tom, who is now in the merchant marine. . . . Tom's memory takes him back to his straitened home life and the need to revolt that finally sent him to sea. In episodes softened by the patina of time he recalls the painful shyness of his lovable crippled sister, Laura, and the tragicomic efforts of his mother, Amanda, to marry her off, as well as his own desperation as an underpaid shoe company clerk who dreams of escaping from his drab life. The climax comes when, nagged by the desperate mother, Tom brings Laura a gentleman caller, who turns out to be engaged to another girl. (pp. 84-5)

In *A Streetcar Named Desire* health and disease are again at war, but more openly and more sensationally. The lines of conflict are sharply drawn in this naturalistic drama whose story, unlike that of *The Glass Menagerie*, is not revealed impressionistically through a mist of memory. Nothing is circuitous in *Streetcar*, and the dramatic action drives directly to its fateful conclusion as the plebeian Stan Kowalski and patrician Blanche Du Bois confront each other. Like Williams' other Southern heroines, who invariably suggest Picasso's dehydrated "Demoiselles d'Avignon," Blanche Du Bois is not only a recognizable human being but also an expressive abstraction. She is decadence, pretension, hysteria, charm faded, sensibility misapplied, sensitivity rudely jolted by the world, hope deferred, life wasted. It is her final tragedy that the life she encounters in her married sister's home becomes a hell of humiliation precisely when she is most desperately in need of sympathy. (pp. 85-6)

Concerning the plays that followed *Summer and Smoke* in the Fifties, it is worth observing how differently their author worked in each case. *The Rose Tattoo*, which reached Broadway early in 1951, was written as a *comedy*. This alone is a departure. . . . But in addition, Williams makes his central heroine a full-blooded woman quite unlike the more or less wilted Southern ladies he had hitherto favored. (p. 88)

It is to Williams' credit that he showed himself in possession of a will to health along with his fascination with the underworld of the id. In *Camino Real* historical characters have escaped from the infernal world of his imagining. Byron escapes when he goes out to die for Greek liberty, as does Don Quixote when he recklessly follows the call of his delusionary idealism. But these escapes are not worked out dramatically; they are an ill-fitting, if deeply intended, coda. It is not so much that the author's matter or idea is obscure as that his manner is choppy and his story diffuse. If anything, his ideas suffer as mere ideas or symbols and literary allusions. The play is at once too badly abstruse and too strenuously theatrical.

Despite the criticism I have just summarized, it is evident that only a man of exceptional dramatic talent could have written *Camino Real*. No one else would have dared to write it; no one else could have written it in so snarled a manner, attempting to say so much about human life and the state of the world. Though *Camino Real* looks like a deliberate literary exercise (chiefly because of its literary allusiveness), it was wrung out of its author's consciousness. (p. 89)

During the Fifties Tennessee Williams moved in various directions with different degrees of range and intensity in *Camino Real, Orpheus Descending*, and *Suddenly Last Summer*. These plays represent the most intensive use of the dramatic imagination in a single decade by any American playwright since O'Neill. At the same time Williams continued to make profitable use of his flair for naturalistic drama in two great box-office successes: *Cat on a Hot Tin Roof* and *Sweet Bird of Youth*. . . .

It is fair to say that Williams is the mid-century theatre's most impressive, though not necessarily most gratifying, American playwright. Whether he fails with fantasy or succeeds with reality, he makes indifference to the theatre virtually impossible. (p. 90)

Like all effective *play*wrights, Tennessee Williams has been virtually from the start of his career a vivid and exciting *scene*wright. But in composing a balance sheet of credits and debits we must take one final matter into consideration: Williams' consuming theatricality. This theatricality is partly the poet's and partly the showman's. It is truly difficult to know, as it is not in the case of the indisputably great dramatists before him, to what degree theatricality in his work has sensationalized life instead of illuminating it. (p. 91)

> John Gassner, *"Tennessee Williams 1940-1960," in his* Theatre at the Crossroads: Plays and Playwrights of the Mid-Century American Stage *(copyright © 1960 by Mollie Gassner; reprinted by permission of Holt, Rinehart and Winston, Publishers), Holt, 1960, pp. 77-91.*

By now it should be clear that Tennessee Williams' real subject is the painfulness (not the tragedy) of existence, and the fate of human dignity (not of the soul) in the face of suffering. It should also be clear that however neurotic Williams himself may be and however widely neurosis enters into and affects his work, there is little point in looking for the roots of his art, and less in searching out the meaning of any particular play, on one or another categorical Freudian plot of ground; because to Williams *everything* is painful—sexuality, touch, communication, time, the bruteness of fact, the necessity to lie, the loss of innocence. And finally it should be clear that toward his material Williams has alternately been elegist, soothsayer, mythmaker, immolator,

exorcist or consoler—none of the incarnations final and no one incarnation carried through to finality.

> Richard Gilman, *"Williams as Phoenix" (1962), in his* Common and Uncommon Masks: Writings on Theatre 1961-1970 *(copyright © 1971 by Richard Gilman; reprinted by permission of Random House, Inc.), Random House, 1971, pp. 140-43.*

The Milk Train Doesn't Stop Here Anymore is not diseased in the way that certain detractors of Williams find the bulk of his work to be. If anything, it is in subject the "healthiest" play he has written, which establishes once again how unimportant subject in art really is. For this thrust into allegory, which speaks of renunciation and transcendence and a way of the spirit, represents so nearly complete a collapse of Williams' imaginative powers, such a massive failure of rhetoric and structure, impulse and control, that next to it a "black" play like *Suddenly Last Summer* or *Orpheus Descending* seems robust and encouraging simply because of the relative victory of the shaping imagination; it is form, in other words, that most directly answers questions of health in art. (pp. 144-45)

Iguana got by, narrowly against its tendencies to self-debasement, because its symbolism was sparser and more controlled, because its central proposition—that there is a need for courage and for the acceptance of mortal frailty in ourselves and others—was sustained by an adequate structure and a frequently distinguished rhetoric, and because its characters had the dramatic existence proper to their intellectual and imaginative intentions. But *Milk Train* has almost no structure (originally a one-acter, it is agonizingly overextended), no decisive language beyond the most pretentious ("We all live in houses on fire" is a fair example) and no characters with a greater degree of existence than long residence in Williams' hothouse can confer on them. (pp. 146-47)

> Richard Gilman, *"Mistuh Williams, He Dead" (1963), in his* Common and Uncommon Masks: Writings on Theatre 1961-1970 *(copyright © 1971 by Richard Gilman; reprinted by permission of Random House, Inc.), Random House, 1971, pp. 144-47.*

[*The Glass Menagerie,*] one of [Williams'] earliest [plays], holds up wonderfully well. A drama of "memory," which transforms autobiography into lucid, objective art, it is small, domestic, deeply felt, its lyricism reined in by perception, sentimentality tightened by insight, experiment anchored in sure classical techniques. All Williams' later concerns have their seeds here: neurosis as a form of stamina, the vulnerability of the spirit, the interaction of myth and reality, the body as both hope and betrayal—all displayed in guarded, oblique shapes.

This domestic, seemingly ingratiating surface is what inspires the excessive nostalgia for this play on the part of reviewers who have always been disturbed by Williams' sensuality and periodic efforts to use the stage for dangerous encounters. Of all his works it is the one which most readily satisfies that craving for the "haunting" and the "magical" which to the Broadway intellect substitutes for dramatic experience. But the play is deceptive. The tale of a Southern family's erosion by its loss of the past and incapacity for the present conceals a stern awareness: that there are no solutions or exits from necessity, that men endure despite having natures opposed to the nature of things. (p. 148)

> *Richard Gilman, "The Play's the Thing" (1966), in his* Common and Uncommon Masks: Writings on Theatre 1961-1970 *(copyright © 1971 by Richard Gilman; reprinted by permission of Random House, Inc.), Random House, 1971, pp. 148-51.*

Tennessee Williams is [a] nonabsurdist nay-sayer. His nihilism is personal rather than abstruse and formal, as is Beckett's or Ionesco's. Williams has not flaunted an unbreakable negativistic commitment, being ready to break any compact he seems to have made with morbid negation whenever he feels an urge to oppose despair with strongly romantic affirmations. His Don Quixote character in *Camino Real* surmounts the wall that imprisons the rest of faltering humanity. Williams is much taken with his vivid Sicilian heroine Serafina, in *The Rose Tattoo*, in whom the vital need to love overcomes her humiliation on discovering that her deceased husband had been unfaithful. Williams also fancies Maggie, the plucky heroine of his *Cat on a Hot Tin Roof*, who drives so hard toward life while her hopeless husband Brick plunges headlong into the destructive element. Nevertheless, Williams has an obvious affinity for the school that finds no solace or resting point in the universe. (p. 703)

> *John Gassner, in his* Dramatic Soundings: Evaluations and Retractions Culled From 30 Years of Dramatic Criticism, *introduction, and posthumous editing by Glenn Loney (© 1968 by Mollie Gassner; used by permission of Crown Publishers, Inc.), Crown, 1968.*

Williams is a dramatist of lost souls. His work describes a long laceration. No American playwright is altogether a pessimist. The conclusion of *Camino Real*, "the violets in the mountains have broken through the rocks," simply means that idealism will ultimately smash the battlements of villainy in which we are immured. But this thought only marks a pause along the road. Williams' path leads to no final statement. He has no doctrine, unless it be the need for compassion. He traces a chart of the fevers that he has experienced in looking at the world outside and within himself. (pp. 227-28)

With only a few exceptions, Williams' characters are lost souls because they are torn between the god-seeking impulse and the pull of desire. In the shambles of our civilization, desire has been debased into raw carnality. Sex without the blessedness of love is death-dealing corruption. In this corrupt atmosphere—always captivatingly colorful in Williams, even to the very names of the vicinities in which his dramas take place—his men and women are destroyed by the poisons which emanate from it. The lacerations they suffer are the result of their bodies and souls being at odds. The sharpness of this division is a characteristic of Puritan consciousness. Unity of spirit is achieved only by the chaste Hannah in *Iguana* and the impassioned and therefore utterly loyal Rosa in *The Rose Tattoo*, in which sex becomes glorified through its pure flame. But Rosa is a Sicilian—a foreigner to our way of life.

When we speak of the world and of society, we imply a realm beyond the strictly personal. Sex, it is commonly held, is Williams' major theme. This, I believe, is only partly true; when this preoccupation with sex in Williams is insisted upon as the determining ingredient, such insistence leads to a falsification. Williams is also very much a social playwright. Sex being a central factor in existence, it becomes the area in Williams' plays where the social battles as well as the battle of angels rage.

It is in a fatal incapacity to integrate the conflict of body and soul, or, to put it more concretely, the struggle between power and love, egotistical acquisitiveness and social generosity, that we find the thematic core of Williams' work. The tension in these forces creates a split in the social order as well as in the individual personality. It causes his people to grope, trembling and bewildered, between that light and shadow to which he repeatedly refers. It also gives rise to personal self-deception and public hypocrisy. (pp. 229-30)

The doppelgänger or second-self ascribed to Alma in *Summer and Smoke* is his own. The accusatory ferocity in regard to our society, which becomes a debilitating fixation in his later plays, alternates with a certain calm or balance in *The Night of the Iguana* or even takes the form of good-natured comedy in his *Period of Adjustment*.

There is a salutary humor in all his work. It is quizzical and given to grassroots laughter. His violence too is softened by the colorfulness and musicality which bathe his plays in glamour. "A kind of lyricism," a stage direction in *Streetcar* reads, "gracefully attenuates the atmosphere of decay." There is magic in Williams' realism.

In the illusionist sense of theatricality, he has no match in American dramatic writing. The rhythms of his colloquial speech are seductive. His dialogue excels in euphony and ease. It has a fragrance like that of a tropical flower planted in a northern soil. The diction is at once limpid and elusive, achieving both mystery and suspense.

Williams writes rich roles for actors. They are gratifying because they represent people who mirror some of his own ambivalence, assertive and tremulously vulnerable, staunch and retreating. His particular nature has enabled him to fashion several of the most perceptive and touching portraits of women our drama has produced. He is one of the few dramatists among us who writes genuine love scenes.

He is no intellectual. Some of his views and sentiments—as in *Camino Real*—are couched in terms which betray an almost adolescent sentimentality. His weaknesses, however, should not dim for us his mastery of stage poetics, his immense gift for theatrical effect and, above all, his vital contribution to the understanding of formerly undisclosed phases of American life.

Through his fascination with sin and his affinity with sinners, Williams, even more than O'Neill, has opened our eyes and hearts to the victims of our savagely mechanized society, the company of the "somehow unfit," the fragile, the frightened, the different, the odd and the lonely, whose presence in our world we have so long sought to avoid thinking about and recognizing as our kin. (pp. 230-31)

> *Harold Clurman, "Tennessee Williams: Poet and Puritan" (1970), in his* The Divine Pastime: Theatre Essays *(reprinted with permission of Macmillan Publishing Co.,*

Inc.; copyright © 1946, 1948, 1949, 1950, 1951, 1952, 1953, 1954, 1955, 1956, 1957, 1958, 1959, 1960, 1961, 1962, 1963, 1964, 1965, 1967, 1969, 1970, 1971, 1974 by Harold Clurman), Macmillan, 1974, pp. 227-31.

Tennessee Williams has probably sold more plays to the movies than any other dramatist of the twentieth century. . . . *The Glass Menagerie* did not translate well to the screen. Actually *A Streetcar Named Desire* is not very cinematic at all. Most critics probably would agree that the two plays mentioned above, together with *Cat on a Hot Tin Roof,* represent Williams's finest work for the stage (with *Suddenly Last Summer* and *The Night of the Iguana* not far behind Williams's most notable achievements). Plays such as *The Glass Menagerie,* in which Williams employs cinematic devices rather extensively, do not film successfully because at the same time they are extremely *theatrical* (which is why *Suddenly Last Summer* fails as a movie). The more "realistic" plays, such as *A Streetcar Named Desire* and *Cat on a Hot Tin Roof*—wherein the cinematic imagination is much less in evidence—are actually better on the screen (which is why *The Night of the Iguana* pleases where *Suddenly Last Summer* disappoints). Generally speaking, plays—especially distinguished plays—do not provide satisfactory motion picture material. In rare cases, however, some of the greatness of the original work survives the transition from stage to celluloid. Such works may not represent the best use of the film medium, they may not possess their most authentic existence on the screen, but nevertheless—due to outstanding character portrayal—they manage to hold a motion picture audience. Of course, it also helps if a gifted screenwriter and a brilliant director are given charge of the adaptation.

A Streetcar Named Desire—which opened on Broadway in December 1947 and was a tremendous hit—represents a major turning point in motion picture history. Many people in Hollywood were afraid to handle the play due to its themes involving insanity, compulsive promiscuity, homosexuality, and rape. . . . The censors wanted to eliminate the rape scene; but since, as Williams rightly pointed out, Stanley Kowalski's violation of Blanche DuBois represents the structural and thematic climax of the piece it could not very well be omitted. (pp. 56-7)

In some ways *Cat on a Hot Tin Roof* . . . is the most interesting example of a Williams play adapted to the screen. It is no secret that *Cat on a Hot Tin Roof* succeeds as a play in spite of its structural defects. There are actually two published versions of the last act, neither of which is wholly satisfactory. Analysis reveals that both versions have an Ibsenian structure. . . . [In both versions], though, Brick avoids squarely facing the question of his latent homosexuality. Most critics speak of "evasion" here on the part of Williams. However that may be, *Cat on a Hot Tin Roof* remains one of the most powerful—though flawed—plays in the modern theater.

Homosexuality was a strong theme for the American screen in the fifties. (p. 59)

One of the two best later Williams efforts for the stage is *Suddenly Last Summer* (1958). In spite of some cinematic touches in this short play—such as the hot spot of light on Catherine which resembles a close-up, the bird cries behind Mrs. Venable's description of the beach of the Encantadas

which function like background film music, and the "dissolve" within Scene Four—it basically remains one of the playwright's most theatrical (in the good sense of course) presentations. *Suddenly Last Summer* is a morality play; the names of the characters alone suggest the symbolical nature of the piece: Mrs. Venable, Dr. Cukrowicz (Dr. Sugar), Mrs. Foxhill, Sister Felicity, and the like. Scene One is very largely a monologue by Mrs. Venable, and throughout the play the language used is rich in poetic imagery. (pp. 63-4)

Actually the movie is less than candid on the score of "sexual deviation," with the result that the theme is left hazy for those unfamiliar with the play.

The Night of the Iguana, which opened on Broadway in 1961, is Williams's most impressive drama since *Cat on a Hot Tin Roof.* Like most of the author's plays, *The Night of the Iguana* depends heavily on characterization through protracted confrontations involving two actors—much of the time through recourse to lengthy monologues—in which theme is developed by analogy, image, and symbol. There is the use of another "hot light" in this play, similar to the cinematic effect achieved in *Suddenly Last Summer,* and still another filmic transition between scenes within Act Two; but the soul of the work is verbal and theatrical. (pp. 65-6)

Edward Murray, "Tennessee Williams— after 'The Celluloid Brassiere'," in his The Cinematic Imagination: Writers and the Motion Pictures *(copyright © 1972 by Frederick Ungar Publishing Co., Inc.), Ungar, 1972, pp. 46-67.*

Tennessee Williams continued his public decomposition with an item called *Out Cry,* the very spelling of the title emblematic of Williams's desperate striving for originality, even if it amounts to no more than an extra empty space. The play, already produced in at least two . . . cities under a different title, is like all of its author's more recent works a combination of bloodless blather and unintentionally parodistic self-imitation. It concerns a brother and sister abandoned as mad by their theatrical troupe in an unnamed country, in what may or may not be a theatre and before what may or may not be an audience. They are broke and desperate and possibly insane, but proceed gallantly to enact their "Two-Character Play" about an orphaned brother and sister (their father killed their mother and himself), destitute and scarcely daring to leave the house in quest of food. There is very little difference between the play and the play-within-the-play, and none in quality. It is all windy pastiche, with an awkward and belated bow to absurdism, as when the performing siblings find themselves mysteriously locked into that putative theatre. The thing that may or may not be dialogue is mostly on the level of, "Only the dead can get away with doing nothing, Clare." "Yes, they do get away with it very nicely." Or: "Your hair has grown so long, you look hermaphroditic." "Good. Thank you." On a deeper level, we get, "There are punctuation marks in life and they include periods, one of which is final," or this last exchange that sums up everything: "Magic is habit." "Magic is the habit of our existence."

Williams was, apparently, dramatizing the two components of his psyche: the more fearful, self-deluding side as a sister; the more persistent and pugnacious side, as a brother. But this rather barren metaphor cannot sustain an inert two-character play for a whole evening, even if the writing were appreciably better than the piteous but representative examples I have quoted. (pp. 343-44)

John Simon, in The Hudson Review *(copyright © 1973 by The Hudson Review, Inc.; reprinted by permission), Vol. XXVI, No. 2, Summer, 1973.*

Powerful and wrenching, this latest of Tennessee Williams's plays [*Out Cry*] explores the relationship between two actors, brother and sister, on the stage of a "state theatre in an unknown state." The rest of the company has abandoned them and they are alone with the audience waiting for their performance. Crying out in loneliness, fear, despair, they perform "The Two Character Play," moving in and out of the real world as the play-within-the-play and the drama itself drive to their simultaneous and devastating conclusion. "Out Cry" contains some of Williams's most brilliant writing—lyrical, sensitive, compelling. It is a difficult play, but one that demands attention. (p. xvi)

Virginia Quarterly Review *(copyright, 1974, by the* Virginia Quarterly Review, *The University of Virginia), Vol. 50, No. 1 (Winter, 1974).*

By an early age most artists have stored up enough "life" to draw upon forever. Even the greatest have a finite number of themes, which they vary throughout their careers. The variation is refinement, re-experienced experience, echo. Art manipulates echo by refashioning (or personalizing) works by another, or by oneself at another time. Still, there is a golden echo and a leaden echo, as one poet sang years ago and as Tennessee Williams demonstrates today.

His style has always been personal despite the proximity of excellent friends—"southern" and otherwise. Yes, he does show a dash of the meanness, whimsy, blasé anger, and pussycat anxiety of McCullers, Capote, Vidal, and Jane and Paul Bowles. He, too, blends sexuality with horror. But he seems to have more fun than the others, and certainly more ease with words.

His content, too, is his own—or, to situate through analogy, a mix of Jean Genet with Isaac Singer. Though Williams is as goyish as Singer is Yiddish, both share an affection for (indeed, extract their identity from) what lies directly underhand, even when that is neither a bagel nor a bourbon but a dybbuk's sigh or a Martian spacecraft. They render the fantastic usual and the usual fantastic. Though Williams is as American as Genet is French, both are drawn to the glamour of injustice, and both call forth a similar *dramatis personae*: tough guys, mad queens, policemen, angels.

By 1965, Tennessee Williams's major themes had been nourishing each other for 20 years. Big and little tales and plays ricocheted off each other, igniting always apparently novel combinations of energy, as a kaleidoscope confects endless patterns from a limited number of colors. It comes as no surprise, then, that the six tales in Williams's [*Eight Mortal Ladies Possessed*] should prove to be reconsiderations of their writer's younger triumphs. But the ricochet

has boomeranged, self-nourishment is now self-cannibalism, the echo lacks resonance and falls like lead. The eight mortal ladies possessed are caricatures, all more or less unpleasant, of Tennessee's gold stars. (p. 24)

Clearly the author does believe in these stories both as art and as message, and possibly as a "breakthrough" in style. His belief is his privilege—nor dare one find fault with new language. But this is not new language, or even new grammar—merely new accents that inelegantly blur the line between grandiloquence and satire. (p. 25)

Ned Rorem, "Tennessee Now and Then," in Saturday Review/World *(copyright © 1974 by Saturday Review/World, Inc.; reprinted with permission), September 21, 1974, pp. 24-6.*

Tennessee Williams's success and achievement as a playwright have tended to obscure his very real significance as a writer of short fiction. Such stories as "The Field of Blue Children," "Three Players of a Summer Game," "Portrait of a Girl in Glass," "The Resemblance between a Violin Case and a Coffin," and half a dozen others are of their kind as good as anything produced during recent years. *Eight Mortal Ladies Possessed*, his collection of six stories —his fourth—will not add to his reputation.

"Happy August the Tenth" is good Williams: the portrayal of two upper-class ladies, a New Yorker and a Virginian ("middle age was not approaching on stealthy little cat feet . . . but was bursting upon them"), belongs with the author's best work. A similar case might be made for "Oriflamme," a moving characterization reminiscent of several of the bewildered, helpless women of the plays, and "Completed" is redeemed from triviality by a hasty but effective characterization of a black servant.

About the others the less said the better. The author's characterizations of sex-ridden females are emetic rather than cathartic: a century-old principessa who dreams of her fifth husband's prowess in bed ("The Inventory of Fontana Bella"); an ugly and aging American poetess addicted, among other unpleasant personal habits, to lallacropia and an Italian lover ("Sabbatha and Solitude"); and a nymphomaniac liberated by the death of an aged grandmother ("Miss Coynte"—do you yokels get the point?—"of Greene"). Gone is the compassion that gave meaning to the twisted lives of so many of Williams's earlier misfits, grotesques, and freaks; in its place is a continuing kind of ugliness, almost glee in the depiction of debasement.

It's sad to see this sort of thing from the pen of one of the great talents of our time. (p. 725)

William Peden, in Sewanee Review *(reprinted by permission of the editor; © 1974 by The University of the South), Fall, 1974.*

Tennessee Williams is the George Balanchine of American playwrights. Like New York City Ballet's great choreographer, he persists in tinkering with his works long after they have opened. *Orpheus Descending* (1957) is a rewrite of the 1940 failure *Battle of Angels*; *Small Craft Warnings* (1972) an expansion and reworking of *Confessional* (1970); other versions of *Out Cry* (1973) had been produced in Chicago in 1971 and, under the title *The Two-Character Play* . . . in 1967 and *The Gnädiges Fräulein* (1966) was presented off-

Off Broadway in a new version last spring. *The Milk Train Doesn't Stop Here Anymore* and *Kingdom of Earth (The Seven Descents of Myrtle)* also have experienced more than one incarnation. Williams clearly means it when he says, 'A play is never an old one until you quit working on it'.

As with Balanchine, the work sometimes turns out for the better, sometimes for the worse, and on occasion the differences are hardly as significant as Williams himself seems to believe. With the new *Cat on a Hot Tin Roof*, . . . things definitely work for the better. . . . Because *Cat* is 'major' Williams, though not on a level with *The Glass Menagerie* and *A Streetcar Named Desire*, the nature of the changes and restorations is of more than passing interest.

Cat is one of Williams's most highly theatrical plays. Its major characters have vitality and, with the exception of the underwritten Brick—ex-footballer hero and sports commentator, latent homosexual and active alcoholic—sufficient inherent or suggested interest to hold the attention throughout, despite the play's unnecessary repetitiousness. . . .

Williams attempts to keep too many balls in the air at one time for the play to be completely successful. On the one hand, there is Big Daddy, who tragically and too late has discovered that he has disliked his wife for years and now wants both a final fling, which he is destined not to have, and an heir from Brick. On another, the guilt-ridden Brick, asserting the purity of his friendship with the dead Skipper, refusing to acknowledge it for what it was—for at least one of them; because of it refusing also to go to bed with his wife. And what of Maggie? Are her intensity and passion prompted more by a craving for wealth or a craving for Brick, even at the moment at the end of the play when she denies him his liquor, telling the hobbling, crutch-bound man she will return it only after he impregnates her, after which they'll 'get drunk together'?

Holding it all together should be two factors: the theme of 'mendacity', the curse that tells his father is responsible for his alcoholism, and Brick himself. The mendacity theme works considerably better in this version, presumably thanks to restorations from the original text. It is seen to pervade virtually all the relationships, virtually all the major moments of confrontation, whether they have to do with Brick's relationship with Skipper, the impending death of Big Daddy or the vying for those 28,000 acres. For Brick has denied not only his guilt concerning Skipper, but Skipper himself; doing so, he has become an attractive nonentity, a fading shadow of the golden boy's promise (and, let us face it, by now something of a cliché). Big Daddy must be kept from the truth—and not only out of kindness—save in an explosive confrontation with Brick. . . .

But through it all we are asked to take on faith whatever it is that Maggie, Big Daddy and Big Mama find so attractive, so worthy of love, even of admiration, in Brick. . . . It is not sufficient to have Maggie remind us Brick is one of those 'weak, beautiful people who give up with such grace' —especially when the grace is not on view—and to witness instead only his ironically polite indifference. Brick is far too pivotal to everyone else's motivation for that. . . .

Williams has dropped the Kazan-inspired Broadway third act, leaving something both closer to his original and more ambiguous. (p. 45)

[The] homosexual element and the language are more explicit and various lines have been clarified, updated or restored, almost to positive effect. After nearly two decades, . . . the play does hold up remarkably well, confirming . . . that Williams has every right to be considered America's foremost living playwright. (pp. 45, 47)

> *Catharine Hughes, in* Plays and Players *(© copyright Catharine Hughes 1974), October, 1974.*

As a writer of fiction, Tennessee Williams has two things going for him: he is never dull; and he knows how to ingratiate himself. If, in [the] collection ["Eight Mortal Ladies Possessed"] Williams is so captivating as a narrator, it is because he had invented a tone of voice that is both racy and genteel, that slyly alternates between juicy vulgarity and the mellifluous circumlocutions of a gentleman of the old school. . . .

The important quality in Williams's style (as befits a playwright) is that it is *spoken*; you can imagine someone (an eloquent and mannered someone, of course) drawing you aside and telling you these sweet somethings. And because a conversational voice is recounting an incident of interest (usually of bizarre interest), Williams appears to write effortlessly. He never seems to fuss over exposition or scene-painting, no more than you would fuss if you were telling one of your best after-dinner stories.

Some of the pieces in this collection, however, might sound a good deal better if told over brandy and cigars. In fact, one, "Miss Coynte of Greene," is repellent in the cold light of the printed page. . . . [It appeared to me to be] sexist and racist tripe, the product of a shallow if agitated imagination. The cliché characters (domineering mother, sex-crazed spinster, well-endowed bucks) could have been conceived by a Freudian analyst c. 1950—which is my way of saying that if the story weren't so silly it would be degrading to all concerned, author, reader and characters alike.

Fortunately the book is redeemed by one perfect tale, "Happy August the Tenth.". . . The story is sad and funny, terse but not so terse that it excludes the meandering feel of those spiteful, frightening, inconclusive events, those simultaneous monologues, called lovers' quarrels. The book should be read for this one tale alone; the last story, "Oriflamme," also merits attention. . . .

Happy August the Tenth," alas, has no sex interest to offer. Just beauty. (p. 14)

> *Edmund White, in* The New York Times Book Review *(© 1974 by The New York Times Company; reprinted by permission), October 6, 1974.*

[What] a rousing melodrama [the revised version of "Cat on a Hot Tin Roof"] is and . . . [what] luscious roles! Williams is a playwright in the nineteenth-century tradition, and one observes in him the qualities that our ancestors admired in Dion Boucicault; nothing is here for tears and scarcely anything is here even for credulity, but the evening roars past in a glory of gorgeous Southern fustian, and one leaves the theatre like a happy sleepwalker, reluctant to be waked. One has had such a good time that to question the means by which the prestidigitator-playwright has achieved his effects would seem a dour Yankee incivility. Let the Technicolored dream go on and on, let the bright birds flutter up out of the black cape perpetually. (p. 73)

Brendan Gill, "Family Troubles," in The New Yorker *(© 1974 by The New Yorker Magazine, Inc.), October 7, 1974, pp. 73-4.*

Cat on a Hot Tin Roof [in its revised version] possesses a number of striking assets. It has much of Williams' stage canniness and power, euphonious writing of American tang and humor, three well-drawn characters made arresting by the author's concern with them. . . .

Williams seemed intent on tearing the mask of moral fraud and lying (mendacity, he calls it) from the face of middle-class "respectability." Many things worth saying are voiced in the course of the play, though most of them are stated in passing or for purposes of character delineation. They assert the imperative of clinging to life—the impulse to survival, the need for love, the nullity of existence without genuine connection among fellow human beings, the dangers involved in the refusal to stand up to the fact of mortality.

But . . . the play remains centrally ambiguous. The evidence for greater thematic clarity is present but never clinched. For all his determination to be courageously frank, Williams beclouds the issue—which is not simply sex but homosexuality. (p. 349)

Williams' original third act—in which Big Daddy does not appear—lets the play hang in the air except for the tying up of some loose ends. There still remains an overlong scene demonstrating family greed: Brick's older brother and sister-in-law trying to take charge of the rich estate after Big Daddy's imminent death. The ending now, pretty much as it was in 1955, suggests that Maggie's lie about being pregnant by Brick makes Big Daddy happy and wins Brick's admiration so that he may consent to turn her lie into a truth. But this compounds the play's confusion. Still, it hardly matters. The play is virtually complete after the second act. (pp. 349-50)

Williams writes about women with a sympathy and an understanding unusual among our playwrights. Most of his women, however, are victims. Maggie fights being one. (p. 350)

Harold Clurman, in The Nation *(copyright 1974 by the Nation Associates, Inc.), October 12, 1974.*

Tennessee Williams is one of the two American dramatists of enduring substance and [*Cat on a Hot Tin Roof*] is not one of his best plays. The other man, obviously, is O'Neill, and his later plays are well above Williams; still *A Streetcar Named Desire* is truly an American tragedy and *The Glass Menagerie* stands, even if a bit unsteadily, as one of the few successful poems in our theater. *Cat* is significantly less than either.

It came after the two best plays in Williams' very prolific career, and it's among the first in a series that, though laced with fire, nevertheless declines toward a mere rehash like *Small Craft Warnings* and a feeble protest against its author's sterility like *Out Cry*. To say that Williams' career describes an arc is too neat. For one thing it isn't over; for

another such plays as *Period of Adjustment* and *The Gnädiges Fräulein* show a largely untapped spring of humor in him. But nothing since *Streetcar* (1947) has so beautifully fused the elements of the Williams "mainstream" in so beautiful a form.

Cat deals with that mainstream. This means, on the surface or near it, such matters as loneliness, buried and released violence, sex and "difference"—the last often signified by physical difference, like lame Laura in *The Glass Menagerie* and injured Brick here. More deeply, Williams has been concerned with American change, with the extension of the Civil War by other means, with the course of our history as we have moved from a 19th-century society of adventure and idealism circumscribed by puritanism to a 20th-century society that is increasingly liberated and increasingly devoid of appetite for adventure or ideal. Fundamentally *Streetcar* is about the end of a romantic America that had rot under the romance, and the onslaught of a brass-and-beer America that has mere bareness where the rot used to be. *Cat*, taking another tack on the same theme, deals with questions of continuity, with death and birth. The play asks: isn't death, as much as sex, a prerequisite of birth? (p. 16)

But his articulation of these themes is clumsy. Much of the first act is laborious exposition, cramming us with facts while pretending not to know that we are there. And it's particularly tortuous because Brick is mostly restricted to cynical taciturnity and bourbon-pouring; thus a huge burden falls on Margaret. Brick's little nephews and nieces, the "no-neck monsters," are cartoons; their parents, Gooper and Mae, are barely two-dimensional; Big Mama is not much more; the preacher is out of a revue sketch. . . . The best scene in the play is the long one in Act Two between Big Daddy and Brick, but that scene is all revelation and exploration. The dynamics of the play depends on Margaret, who is offstage for most of Act Two. (pp. 16, 33)

The dialogue is garlanded with litanies of repetiion, apt enough for characters who enjoy speaking, but sometimes Williams intrudes into their rhetoric. For instance Brick says that he and his football friend used to toss long high passes "that couldn't be intercepted except by time." (p. 33)

[The] play itself, second-rate Williams though it is, reminds us that he was (is?) a writer who saw (sees?) life through a dramatist's eyes, as distinct from people who go around looking for material for plays. (p. 34)

Stanley Kauffmann, in The New Republic *(reprinted by permission of* The New Republic; *© 1974 by The New Republic, Inc.), October, 1974.*

Blanche DuBois [in *A Streetcar Named Desire*] . . . is classic—a nearly perfect combination of tyrannical aspiration, idealism, failure, and dignity, all engendered by her region's history and romantic ambience. However, these heroic qualities are not always recognized by the academic critics of the play. Popular critics did perceive them.

Though produced in 1947, midcentury indeed, the frank portrayal of thc power of sex in *A Streetcar Named Desire* burst shockingly enough nearly to overwhelm the tragic themes that Tennessee Williams put into his play. For two decades, learned critics treated *Streetcar* as if it were an

Ibsenian drama about a forbidden subject. Beclouded by the sad nymphomania of Blanche DuBois, the vigorous, imperial virility of Stanley Kowalski, the comfortable, satiated sensuality of Stella DuBois Kowalski, and the striking rape scene that climaxes the next to last scene of the play, Herbert Muller [in *The Spirit of Tragedy*] saw sexuality as Williams' "tragic theme," and "restoration of sexual order [as] the key to salvation and peace. . . . [There is] no wider or deeper tragic import." John Von Szeliski [in "Tennessee Williams and the Tragedy of Sensitivity"] agreed: "The only communication and comprehension is in sex and the survivors are the sexually, albeit bestially, adjusted ones." And Robert Heilman reiterates [in "Tennessee Williams: Approaches to Tragedy"]: "The sexual commonground points up a world of imperfect choices" in which Stanley represents "a coarse new order, vigorous but rude and boorish. . . . Hope lies in Stanley and Stella."

Undeniably, the air crackles with the subject. Nevertheless, sex is not beautiful in *A Streetcar Named Desire*; it is but animalistically satisfying. It certainly is not the paradisial state for Blanche; sex destroys her. It is what Stella merely settles for. Sexuality does not make Stanley into a god by any means. If he represents a well adjusted new order, then we can only conclude that either Williams has thrown up his hands in despair or is declaring that Stanley represents mere survival, and there must be more to life than such a new order.

The point is that Williams uses sexuality tragically. It looms alongside history and time as an external power, with a like capriciousness, uncontrollability, and relentless inevitability. Like Ibsen, in *Ghosts*, Williams did not interpose sex into his play for its own sake as a theme of shock or liberation from staid, artificial gentility, but as a symbol of a relentless, nemesic past, in which the sins of the father are visited upon the children in proper Old Testament fashion. Williams uses sex in *A Streetcar Named Desire* as the catalyst in the tragedy of a personality broken by death, history, and her own destined psyche. We ought not to delimit his concept to the mere portrayal of maladjusted and tawdry individuals, who need mental help and don't know it. No amount of therapy can save Blanche DuBois from confronting these powerful, uncontrollable modern surrogates of the supernal beings of old. "Williams has a long reach," his fellow tragedian Arthur Miller once wrote [in "The Shadow of the Gods: A Critical View of American Theatre"], "and a genuinely dramatic imagination. . . . His greatest value, his aesthetic valor, so to speak, lies in his very evident determination to unveil and engage the widest range of causation conceivable to him."

To justify this range of causation and confrontation, Williams needed an equivalent protagonist because character, not plot, is the concern of modern tragedy. Williams' choice of a Blanche DuBois to undergo the tragic enactment and the point *in medias res* with which he begins his plot present problems, but also indicate the angle of his tragic vision. . . . She is beyond the capability of even attempting to control and manipulate the world about her. Nonetheless, her recollections of her former world do limn in our minds a personality that once had strength to manipulate. There still rests a deal of heroism in her. (pp. 83-5)

Sordid though she be, she has come to represent the social destruction that still lingers after a century as the inescapable punishment for slavery and the Civil War; the dissolu- tion of a tinseled gentility founded upon inhumanity; the inexplicable victimization of a class of womanhood by a society that forced them to marry inadequately in order to fulfill a dream forever shattered. (p. 86)

Blanche . . . knows truth and reality, knows them so well that she builds bulwarks against them—pitiful ramparts of paper shades around glaring light bulbs, of cheesy old-fashioned dresses and hats, of threadbare rituals of outmoded, inappropriate gentility, of shabby subterfuges that dissolve upon the most superficial investigation.

But until the very last scene Blanche does not lose touch with reality. She is, indeed, in a constant state of self-awareness, of recognition of who she is and what she is and what her world is like and what her immediate situation treacherously holds out to her. (p. 87)

Obviously she recognizes truth, and the truth is that her life is compounded of fate and individual error and fear. Brooks Atkinson complimented the actress who created the role in New York, Jessica Tandy, by saying [in "'Streetcar' Tragedy"] that she captured the essence and the nuances that Williams wrote into the role: "the terror, the bogus refinement, the intellectual alertness and the madness." It's the intellectual alertness . . . that becomes the madness of vital truth which Herman Melville had seen in the dark characters of Shakespeare.

Not the least among the terrors that Blanche perceives looms the inevitability that Stanley Kowalski will be the instrument of her final catastrophe. (p. 88)

Blanche is right. Stanley does become her executioner. He applies the *coup de grâce* to her psyche. If sex represents the old-time power of the Greek gods, then Stanley represents a perverse *deus ex machina*, the final piece of machinery that produces, rather than resolves, the catastrophe. All that is left here is the preservation of dignity, amidst the shards of the hero's life and self, an ironic dignity devised from the anagnorisis of the self's limitations and the power of the Other. (pp. 88-9)

> Dan Vogel, "The Mask of Oedipus Tyrannos," in his The Three Masks of American Tragedy *(copyright © 1974 by Louisiana State University Press), Louisiana State University Press, 1974, pp. 13-102.*

Though it is billed as a novel, Tennessee Williams' new book [*Moise and the World of Reason*] reads more like a series of notebook entries in which the author muses at random on art and sex. Williams is the most intensely personal of writers; his compulsively voluble narrator clearly speaks to us in Williams' own palpitating voice. *Moise and the World of Reason* is a portrait of the author as a sensual young man, "a distinguished failed writer" at 30. Obsessed with his past, his sexual desires and his rejection slips, the narrator uses his diary jottings as a defense against emptiness. His desk is the center of his world; his writing imposes order and dignity on the experiences of a sometimes shabby life. Art heals, and the book records the process of the writer's salvation through the patterned arrangement of words on a page.

Since it has no real story or tangible dramatic conflict, the novel is designed to show off its narrator's sensibility—Williams attempts to hold us with the fractured, fevered ruminations of a character who nakedly enacts his own fears of failure and isolation. . . . Characters, anecdotes, images from the author's past compete for our attention. Williams, of course, is an exuberant, though inconsistent master of ceremonies, and the quality of the remembered moments varies. Some are tantalizing, while others seem like pale carbon copies of past routines. (pp. 24-5)

As always, Williams is a poet of sexual longing; and the most lyrical of the memories involve the writer and his first lover Lance, a black ice-skater with an ideal physique and a generous, yielding spirit. . . .

Typically Williams' attitude to sex is dense and contradictory as he sees it as both holy and infected, transcendent and tainted. Lance is a Williams stud like Chance Wayne and Stanley Kowalski who offers ecstatic release. Yet throughout these reminiscences sex is also sinister, as in the bizarre passage in which the young writer meets and feels threatened by a once-famous playwright who tries to entice him to go on a long journey. The crumbling playwright, so patently an embittered self-portrait, uses sex as magic but also as punishment. Williams therefore remains a reluctant Dionysian, a guilt-ridden reveler; and for this Southern puritan, sex still promises catastrophe.

The novel is Williams' true confession. He has never before written so unguardedly about himself. The narrator is openly, at times even joyously, homosexual; sexual desire isn't disguised here as it was in many of the plays. But Williams is one of those writers for whom telling all may have a therapeutic effect on his spirit but a dampening result on his art. Written before gay liberation, his major plays required distance from and transformation of his actual experience. Williams benefited from the pressures of social convention. On one level *A Streetcar Named Desire* is a homosexual fantasy with Blanche as an effeminate male masked as a magnificently neurotic Southern belle; but American drama can be glad that Williams didn't write Blanche as a man! In terms of sexual candor, *Moise and the World of Reason* is Williams' most liberated statement, and yet it has little of the surging erotic comedy of the great plays.

Williams has always been a self-conscious writer. Here he shares with us his design for his own book and he lets us know that he's aware of his eccentricities—his fondness for ending sentences in mid-air, his pleasure in repeating words, phrases and images, his almost impish delight in inverting normal word order. . . .

For all its ornery formlessness, its stylistic self-indulgence, its avoidance of high drama, the book has genuine rewards, descriptive passages that remind us of Williams' special lyrical gifts and his distinctive personality, evocation of downtown New York at night conveying the macabre isolation of an Edward Hopper painting. Even when the narrative voice is whining or out of control, even when it is lazy and repetitive, it is still, manifestly, the voice of America's greatest playwright. There is bristling wit here, and charm, and temperament. (p. 25)

> *Foster Hirsch, in* The New Republic *(reprinted by permission of* The New Republic; © *1975 by The New Republic, Inc.), May 24, 1975.*

The purpose of [*Moise and the World of Reason*], I'm sure, is to flex Williams's fantasy. And to unburden him on the subject of homosexuality. He's for it, and *Moise* will tell you more about its procedures than you may want to know. Sex is Williams's antidote to the world of reason—and the world of unreason as well.

What holds the bits, pieces, and roles of *Moise* together is Williams's lovely writing, not his cockeyed people or erotic celebrations. Some of his descriptive passages, especially with elderly figures, unfold like dark flowers. He plucks aphorisms as if they grew on bushes. . . .

Opinions will differ as to whether *Moise* was written or drafted. Often it's a silly and transparent fraud. Williams's 30-year-old author has the wisdom and experience of a worldly 50-year-old shrunk by a team of Viennese analysts. His mock seriousness—about loving, growing old, dying—turns to lead. Yet there's charm, grace, beauty here. *Moise* has the sound and feel of art. Instinctively, Williams makes something like literature.

> *Webster Schott, "Catamite on a Hot Tin Roof," in* Book World—The Washington Post (© *The Washington Post),* June 15, 1975, p. 1.

* * *

WILLIAMS, William Carlos   1883-1963

One of America's most influential poets, Williams also wrote novels, plays, essays, and a fascinating autobiography. He maintained his practice of medicine throughout his career. Williams' work toward the poetic depiction of urban America ultimately produced *Paterson***, his finest long poem, which has served as a model for innumerable younger writers. Although Williams was a friend of both Pound and Amy Lowell and although he never abandoned their poetic dictum concerning treatment of "the thing itself," he remained free of the mainstream of Imagism. Williams was awarded posthumously the Pulitzer Prize in Poetry in 1963.**

Williams' entire literary career has been dedicated to the struggle to preserve spontaneity and immediacy of experience. His explanations of these aims are certainly not as impressive as Eliot's and in fact lead to such confusing theories as Objectivism. In defense of Williams one can say that his theorizing is innocent, while in the case of the Pounds and Eliots it is calculated and tricky. Williams does not stand or fall on theory; he is willing to void it at a moment's notice. But it is unfortunate for him that he must engage in theory at all. At bottom Williams is not an intellectual, and he is too human, too sympathetic, too natural to become a symbol of the anti-intellectual. Besides, as he says in his published letters, he is illogical. He would never be able to impress the quarterly reviews or the highbrows who consider him a kind of intellectual slob. (p. 144)

Williams is a guinea pig of modern poetry. He lends himself to the literature of the laboratory and a thousand trials and errors of criticism. He even writes a "mythic epic" like Pound and Eliot which all the culture critics seize on as proof that Williams is not a literary imbecile but one you can practically write books about. *Paterson* is a typical culture poem, the only full-dressed one Williams ever wrote but, according to the critics, the real thing, a kind of New Jersey *The Waste Land*. Williams is so innocent that he would even do that. In writing his large bad poem Williams was perhaps trying to test the validity of works like the *Cantos* and *The Waste Land*, even to compete with them. (pp. 144-45)

Williams is the American poet who tries to fight off Europeanism. He fights it off, singlehanded, but he cannot impress the European with his cause. Neither can he impress the American. Lacking the arrogance of an Eliot or a Pound, lacking philosophy or religion or logic, he is battered back and forth by the literati, who are always armed to the teeth with Positions and who can make anything out of him they want, except a bad poet. (pp. 145-46)

[In] between *Kora* and *Paterson* we have close to a thousand pages of some of the best or most interesting American poetry in our history. Almost all of this poetry is in a style which is immediately recognizable as Williams' own; further, it is a workable style, one which permits him to write a poem almost at random. At its best, which is a good bit of the time, it is not "experimental" poetry or crank technique. Naïve it certainly is, even what some writers call primitive; it is precisely Williams' innocence of forms that frees him to respond to daily experience as a poet. Williams went on writing, day after day, year after year, losing manuscripts, not finishing them, giving them away, but never letting up. Poetry to him was a daily function of life, a means of seeing. In a sense, he is our first American poet since Whitman. It hardly matters that his counselors poisoned his mind against Whitman; Whitman is his mentor after all. (p. 154)

It can never be said of Williams that he writes a well-rounded poem like "Ode on a Grecian Urn" or "The Love Song of J. Alfred Prufrock" or even "my father moved through dooms of love." He loathes the *fait accompli* in poetry or in painting. On the other hand, he does not worship the "fragment" for the fragment's sake. He tries to find the center of his experience in relation to the art of poetry; and he finds it over and over again. (p. 157)

All the appurtenances of the closed poem, especially the stanza, become anathema to Williams from the beginning. Rhyme itself seems to him meretricious; when he uses it (and he uses it as well as anybody), it is with a slur. The poem must not be governed by meters—any meters—nor by periods and paragraphs (stanzas), nor by the figures of speech. What is left? Nothing. The raw material of the poem is all. It is the same process that Whitman went through: a rebirth. (pp. 161-62)

Had Williams been as good a theoretician as he was a poet he would probably be the most famous American poet today. But Williams cannot explain, fortunately for him, or he explains badly when he does. It is the poem he is after. His kind of poem may be the chief development of the American poem since *Leaves of Grass*. When it is successful, as it is an amazing number of times, it abolishes the dualism of form-content, expression-artistry, and all those other dualisms which get in the way of art. Williams' almost mystical repetitions about "the line" (and somewhat wildly in *Paterson* about the *Language*) are a decree against critical speculation about forms. He knows that forms are not predetermined, not inherited, not traditional. He knows, too, that forms do not matter for the honest artist, whether he uses them or not. It is when form becomes a fetish that he draws back and howls. (pp. 164-65)

Williams knows too much about poetry to set up a critical shop or lay out a curriculum like Pound. He is the godfather, all the same, of nearly all the existent *avant-garde* poetry, all the free poetry that exists in the English world today. This is recognized by the young poets who long ago branched away from the cultural highway and took to the backstreets and bohemias of the land. Williams is no bohemian; he is a serious man of letters (as the stuffy expression goes) but he is closer to the life of the poet than any of his contemporaries. (p. 165)

I do not mean that Williams' works are perfection or even that he has written a score or two of poems which will set him beside Milton or Catullus or Marlowe. It is hard to judge such work comparatively; it is too new, too unlike anything else. But there is one sure sign of its value; it has already penetrated the poetry of a whole generation of American poets, not the ones we read month after month in the apple-pie-order journals of letters or the fat anthologies, but in the less-known, less-official magazines and pamphlets strewn over the countryside, which Williams has always lent his hand to. With D. H. Lawrence, Williams is the leader of what authentic American poetry is being written today. Little enough of it is up to his mark, yet the tendency is the right one. The example is there in Williams' poems, not in his criticism. And it is being followed. When I read his poems I feel I am reading a foreign language, my language. After all, there is practically no American poetry to speak of, and nearly all of it has come in the twentieth century, and a good portion of that has been written by William Carlos Williams. (pp. 168-69)

> *Karl Shapiro, "William Carlos Williams: The True Contemporary," in his* In Defense of Ignorance *(copyright © 1960 by Karl Shapiro; reprinted by permission of Random House, Inc.),* Random House, 1960, pp. 143-69.

There is no simple way to speak of [Williams' *Pictures from Breughel and Other Poems*]. It is so singularly the work of a man, one man, that it moves thereby to involve all men, no matter what they assume to be their own preoccupations. . . .

The insistence in our lives has become a plethora of plans, of solutions, of, finally, a web of abstract commitments—which leave us only with confusions. Against these Dr. Williams has put the fact of his own life, and all that finds substance in it. He had earlier insisted, "No ideas but in things," meaning that all which moves to an *elsewhere* of abstractions, of specious 'reliefs,' must be seen as false. We live as and where we are. (p. 117)

What device, means, rhythm, or form the poem can gain for its coherence are a precise issue of its occasion. The mind and ear are, in this sense, stripped to hear and organize what is given to them, and the *dance* or *music* Williams has used as a metaphor for this recognition and its use is that which sustains us, poets or men. (p. 118)

Coming then to the later poems, what can be said now is that there is all such truth, such life, in them. I cannot make that judgment which would argue among the poems that this or that one shows the greater mastery. I think there must come a time, granted that one has worked as Williams to define the nature of this art, when it all coheres, and each poem, or instance, takes its place in that life which it works to value, to measure, to be the fact of. (p. 120)

> *Robert Creeley, "The Fact" (1962), in his* A Quick Graph: Collected Notes & Essays,

edited by Donald Allen (copyright © 1970 by Robert Creeley), Four Seasons, 1970, pp. 117-20.

In providing pieces of art that would go beyond him into the lives of the young, William Carlos Williams takes up in his final books a problem which he thought to solve in 1928 by his Objectivist theory. The theory asserts that past objects like the sonnet, having about them past necessities which have conditioned them and from which, as a form itself, they cannot be freed, must give way to objects consonant with the present; no art will long endure the attacks on its vitality which time makes. (p. 278)

For Williams as for Ezra Pound, art, science, and literature became permanent products of the state and along with the state's "social justice," the bases on which states would be judged. Their permanence—again not always distinguishable from form—lay in the very way they colored the present—often in terms of the state's "being a second body for the human mind"—and Williams' preoccupation with literature, science, and art as indications of Paterson's development as city and as man reflects the centrality which he assigns their suasive powers. Moreover, as the history of culture became for Pound the history of ideas in action, so, too, did it for Williams, except that for Williams ideas passed through an intermediary stage of "things." No ideas, Williams insisted, but in things, but things of action, and, in "A Reading of *Paterson III*" (1970), Charles Doyle indicates that much of the revision to that book was to make static scenes active. Nonetheless, "things" do have form and, if Williams' Objectivist theory was correct, these forms must in time be subject to decay. (p. 280)

[What] is indicated by Williams' last two books [*Paterson V* and *Pictures from Brueghel*] is not quite a reopening of the problem of the immortality of the art so much as a new probing of the immortality of the artist by virtue of his art. The emphasis is to be put on the intelligence shaping the poems rather than on the poems, and, as if to point this stress, Williams chooses subjects for them that make incontrovertible his indebtedness. Both books use established art works to explore those instants when experience crystalizes into artistic inspiration, and, like the set pieces of art school, mastery lies not in the choice of subject but in the artist's skill at execution. (p. 281)

Jerome Mazzaro, "The Descent Once More: 'Paterson V' and 'Pictures from Brueghel'," in Modern Poetry Studies *(copyright 1970, by Jerome Mazzaro), Vol. I, No. 6, 1970, pp. 278, 280-1.*

Williams sought from the beginning a poetic Americanism. (p. 33)

[When] he appropriated a poetic form invented by French poetry, Williams changed it and transformed it into a method of exploration of language and of the subterranean strata of the collective soul. *Kora in Hell* is a book that could have been written only by an American poet and it should be read in the perspective of a later book which is the centre of Williams' Americanism, his *Ars Poetica: In the American Grain* (1925). . . . [His] novels, short stories, and theatrical works . . . are extensions, irradiations of his poetry. The frontier between prose and verse, always hard to trace, becomes very tenuous in this poet: his free verse borders on prose, not written prose but spoken prose, with everyday language; and his prose is always rhythmic, like a coast bathed in poetic waves—not verse but the verbal surge and resurge that is the creator of verse.

Since he first began to write, Williams revealed his distrust of ideas. It was a reaction against the symbolist aesthetic shared by most poets of that time and in which, in his case, were combined American pragmatism and his profession as a doctor. In a famous poem he defined his search: 'To compose: no ideas but in things.' Except that the things are always beyond, on the other side: the 'thing itself' is intangible. Thus Williams does not depart from things but from sensation. But in turn, sensation is shapeless and instantaneous; one cannot construct or create anything with pure sensation; the result would be chaos. Sensation . . . itself must be transformed into things. Language is the agent of change: sensations become verbal objects. A poem is a verbal object, a fusion of two contradictory properties: the liveliness of the sensation and the objectivity of the things.

Sensations become verbal things through the operation of a force that to Williams is not essentially different from electricity, steam or gas: the imagination. In some reflections of 1923 (included among the poems of the first edition of *Spring and All* as 'displaced prose'), Williams says that imagination is 'a creative force that makes objects'. . . . Williams twists the neck of traditional aesthetics: art does not imitate nature, it imitates its creative procedures. It does not copy its products but its mode of production. 'Art is not a mirror reflecting nature, rather, the imagination rivals the compositions of nature. The poet becomes nature and works like nature.' Of course, we are dealing with ideas that appear in many poets and artists of the period. (pp. 34, 36)

Williams conceives the poetic imagination as an activity that complements science and rivals it. Nothing is farther from magic than Williams. . . . To Williams artists—it is significant that he depends upon and draws inspiration from the example of Juan Gris—*separate* the things of the imagination from the things of reality: cubist reality is not the table, the cup, the pipe, and the newspaper of reality; it is *another* reality, no less real. This *other* reality does not deny the reality of real things: it is *another* thing which is simultaneously the *same* thing. 'The mountain and the sea of a picture of Juan Gris,' says Williams, 'are not mountain and sea but a picture of mountain and sea.' The poem-thing is not the thing: it is another thing that exchanges signs of intelligence with the thing.

[This is the] non-imitative realism of Williams. (pp. 36-7)

In his search for the American language, Williams finds (hears) the basic measure, a metre of variable foot but with a triadic accentual base. 'We know nothing', he says, 'save the dance: the measure is all we know.' The poem-thing is a verbal, rhythmic object. Its rhythm is the transmutation of the language of a people. Through language Williams leaps from things and sensations into the world of history.

Paterson is the result of these preoccupations. . . . *Paterson* belongs to that poetic genre invented by modern North American poetry and which oscillates between the *Aeneid* and the *Treatise of Political Economy*, the *Divine Comedy* and journalism. (p. 39)

Williams' poem is complex and uneven. Beside magic or

realistic fragments of great intensity there are long disconnected selections. Written in the face of and at times in opposition to *The Waste Land* and the *Cantos*, he reveals the effect of his polemic with these two works. In this lies his principal limitation; a reading of him depends on other readings, so that the judgment of the reader unavoidably becomes a comparison. The vision that Pound and Eliot had of the modern world was rather sombre. Their pessimism was steeped in feudal nostalgia and in pre-capitalist concepts; therefore their just condemnation of money and modernity became transformed immediately into conservative attitudes and, in the case of Pound, into fascist attitudes. Although Williams' vision is not optimistic either—how could it be?—it does not have reminiscences of other ages. This, which could be an advantage, is really a disadvantage: Williams does not have a philosophical or religious system, a coherent sum-total of ideas and beliefs. The one that was offered him by the immediate tradition (Whitman) was unusable. There is a kind of vacuum at the centre of the concept of Williams (not in his short poems) which is the very vacuum of contemporary American culture. (p. 40)

Paterson does not have the unity of *The Waste Land* or its religious authenticity—although Eliot's religiousness is negative. The *Cantos*, moreover, are a poetry incomparably vaster and richer than that of Williams, one of the few contemporary texts at the height of our terrible epoch. What of it? The greatness of a poet is not measured by the scale but by the intensity and the perfection of his works. Also by his vivacity. Williams is the author of the most *vivid* poems in modern North American poetry. . . . [Is] Williams really the most American of the poets of his epoch? I don't know and I don't care about knowing. On the other hand, I do know that he is the freshest and most limpid. As fresh as a stream of brook water, as limpid as that same water in a glass pitcher on a rough wood table in a whitewashed room in Nantucket. Wallace Stevens once called him 'a kind of Diogenes of contemporary poetry'. His lantern, lit in the brightness of day, is the only little sun that it has. (p. 41)

> Octavio Paz, *"Saxifrage: Some Notes on William Carlos Williams," in* London Magazine (© London Magazine, *1974*), June/July, *1974, pp. 33-43.*

William Carlos Williams's "Prologue" to *Kora in Hell* (in *Imaginations*, . . . 1970) is one of the most important documents in the history of the avant-garde because of its defensiveness. Williams has been attacked. Pound has called *Kora* "incoherent" and "un-American," in fact claims that Williams is opaque and that "opacity is not an American quality." Hilda Doolittle wants to rid the poem of all its "flippancies," what she seems to consider self-mockery, un-seriousness. Wallace Stevens refers to Williams's "tantrums." The pseudo-avant-garde, derivative, conventional, *déjà vu*, confronts the genuine avant-garde—the hitherto *undone*—and is confused. They aren't up to it. Anything off their beaten paths and they are genuinely lost. Anything hitherto *undone* is tantrums, flippancy, opacity . . . they don't see (as Williams does) that they are confronting a new language and they have to learn how to decipher it before they can savor it.

Williams's answer to the rarefied obscurantism of much of the avant-garde dismisses Eliotesque and Poundian postur-

ing, sees the *real* function of the imagination as breaking through the alienation of the near at hand and reviving its wonder: ". . . the thing that stands eternally in the way of really good writing is always one: the virtual impossibility of lifting to the imagination those things which lie under the direct scrutiny of the senses, close to the nose."

Kora in Hell—the poem itself—is an extension and illustration of Williams's own theory of the imagination: "Having once taken the plunge, the situation that preceded it becomes obsolete which a moment before was alive with malignant rigidities." (p. 285)

In the introduction to *Spring and All*, Williams further clarifies exactly what he sees as the function of the imagination, not a world in itself, separated a la Coleridge from "reality," but a kind of reality-augmenting and intensifying faculty that enables the artist to break through to reality: "To refine, to clarify, to intensify that eternal moment in which we alone live there is but a single force—the imagination." . . .

Spring and All is a kind of Credo of Williams's later work and explains Williams's "realism" as "*not* 'realism' but reality itself." He doesn't attempt to create a scholastic definable Realism as movement or attack or approach, but realism as "separate existence," not "representation." In other words, the function of the imagination is to create a Reality *more* "real" than reality itself. (p. 286)

In *The Great American Novel* (. . . 1923), Williams both experiments with current 1920s avant-garde novel styles (notably Joyce and Stein) and also confronts the dynamic and structural problems limiting *all* writing—the problems inherent in words. (p. 287)

Williams plays Word-Magician/Reality-Creator to show in a sense how the WORD is a kind of platform in the void, a thing that takes shape in the midst of shapelessness. Again back to the artist as God/Creator. The whole *Great American Novel* is Williams's play-creation, his experimental universe. . . .

[Williams captures] the shorthand of reality with an appropriate jagged, overturned literary shorthand—the methodology of the antimethodological, the same antipattern pattern that he ends his career with in *Paterson*, what in someone else's hands would be mere pyrotechnical "avant-gardism," here being turned by W. C. Williams, the Yankee empiricist, into a means of not *avoiding*, but *capturing* reality. The American doesn't have the European luxury of anti-reality art, but is constantly tugged back *to* reality so that all methodologies and techniques no matter *how* avant-garde become reality-grabbers and recorders. (p. 288)

Interestingly enough, W. C. W. in his poetry—true to avant-garde patterns—moves from a simple, derivative statement to a complex originality. In his prose the shift is from the complex to the simple. It's as if Joyce wrote *Dubliners* after *Ulysses* and *Finnegans Wake*. And then one *would* have to suspect the seeming simplicity of the "simple surface."

The great pitfall of Williams's objectivity, though, is surfaceness. He theorizes that *the surface is all*: things themselves, people, conversation, actions. Very Lockean, physiological, the person as a sensory apparatus. Only, at least in *White Mule*, by avoiding the Kafkaesque expressionist approach, emptying the Total Person with all his layers on the page, and sticking with an *almost* naturalistic surface (*impressionist*) presentation, a definite flatness occurs, which fits the nature of the characters, but also—at times—drags. *Or is even the "drag" planned?*

At the same time, too, when you are brought so solidly into the life of *things*, are suddenly *there*, then the mind-life, the extras, nuances, psychic extensions and growths fill themselves in. In a sense this thing-centrism forces the reader to complete the reality with a part of himself. (p. 292)

The avant-gardist is not really a member of the proletariat, the bourgeoisie, or the aristocracy, and since he is the outsider his experimentation is "outsiderese." Williams as doctor is an insider, consequently the William Dean Howells Insider in him here surfaces—at least in the prose. In the poetry he remains "difficult"—part of him never really *can* slip inside U.S. society.

Why should avant-garde Williams choose an immigrant family "making it" as *the* theme of three novels? Shades of Silas Lapham. Except perhaps as a symbolic incorporation of himself into the rituals of acceptance and conformity. By putting these ego-projections through the initiation rites of capitalism, Williams sidesteps these rites (and their consequences) himself, *remains* an Outsider. The "making it" trilogy is a kind of continuing anticapitalism *exorcism.* (pp. 292-93)

White Mule is the first volume of a trilogy. *The Build-Up* is the third. It suffers not from "actualism" but from "realism"—at times Williams loses the magic of surface imagery, which is the real strength of *White Mule*, and becomes very "realistic," alienating himself from the essential life of things/actions, and gets trapped in trivia. (p. 293)

Except in the very early *Imaginations*, Williams is never consciously avant-garde. His experimentalism, instead of being consciously and purposefully added on, in a sense is forced on him by the necessities of his basically realistic (objectivist) purposes. The jagged, juxtaposed collage effects in *Paterson* are one way to try to break through words to reality. In the *White Mule* trilogy his method is as straightforward and simple a presentation as possible. Which is also the case in the short stories, the plays, and much of the other poetry. The important thing, though, always is how to be effectively a spokesman for the autonomous kingdom of the imagination. As Williams wrote in a review "A 1 Pound Stein" in 1934 (reprinted in the *Selected Essays, . . .* 1954): "It's the words, the words we need to get back to, words washed clean."

This cleansing can be mistaken for either radical experimentalism (*Paterson*) or cloddish realism (the *White Mule* trilogy and the short stories), but ultimately they are *both* experiments at reaching objective reality employing subjectively overused communication symbols (words) within the historical context of just as shabby social conventions. Williams never succeeds, nor does he pretend to succeed. Among the papers found on his death was the statement: "Words are the burden of poems, poems are made of words." (pp. 298-99)

> Hugh Fox, "The Genuine Avant-Garde: William Carlos Williams Credo," in Southwest Review (© 1974 by Southern Methodist University Press), Summer, 1974, pp. 285-99.

In contrast to Stevens, [Williams'] whole effort was to demystify poetry, to overcome the conceptual quality of words with their *thinginess.* "No ideas, but in things," is a famous Williams aphorism.

Instead of saying something about the universe, poetry, Williams believed, was analogous to facts in their quiddity. He may not have been terribly clear about all this—Pound spoke of him as "*the* most bloody inarticulate animal that ever gargled"—but [one] is less concerned with elucidating Williams' muddled theoretical statements than with [noting] the poet's intense groping toward a particular view of the autonomy and *reality* of language: Innocent and unillusioned, unburdened by history or poetic tradition, the imagination for Williams meant the new world, albeit not in Whitman's sense of hopeful anticipation. Reborn things "enter the new world,/cold, uncertain of all save that they enter." (p. 21)

> Eugene Goodheart, in The New Leader (© 1975 by the American Labor Conference on International Affairs, Inc.), June 9, 1975.

*   *   *

WILLINGHAM, Calder   1922-

Willingham is a Southern American novelist and screenwriter. (See also *Contemporary Authors*, Vols. 5-8, rev. ed.)

Reach to the Stars, which concerns Dick Davenport, the youthful would-be writer working as a bellboy in a hotel near Hollywood, has no actual plot; instead the book consists of a series of fragmented scenes, jumbled as to chronological development, in which are depicted a variety of eccentric hotel guests and employees; and interwoven are some mock versions of Science Fiction stories, plus a number of letters written to and by Davenport. *Reach to the Stars* is apparently nothing more, except that the contents are extremely funny. Nothing profound, seemingly, has been "said" about the spiritual dilemmas of Twentieth Century Man. Curiously enough, however, this seeming triviality of artistic intention—the presenting of a series of comic events that do not appear to have any particular point—is really the measure of Willingham's tremendous achievement.

The significance of his writing becomes more evident if one sees it in relation to the general pattern of American fiction. For instance, Willingham's early novels center on a quest theme, and the quest motif essentially characterizes the traditional American novel. The quest is customarily a search for some kind of self-transformation: either through experience with the natural elements (the Mississippi in *Huckleberry Finn*, of powerful sea creatures in *Moby-Dick* and *The Old Man and the Sea*) or various social orders (Europe with the expatriates of James and Hemingway, or America itself for Thomas Wolfe's wandering protagonists and Fitzgerald's Gatsby). Distinctive about this quest format in Willingham's novels is the lack of a sense of ultimate purpose. (pp. 58-9)

[Willingham's first five novels] are masterful comic achievements, distinguished as well by having brought new life to American fiction by altering its basic themes and manner of presentation—anticipating the later "Black Humorists." Willingham seemed to sense the kind of world coming into being, what David Reisman described in the 1950's as the other-directed society, and what Marshall

McLuhan now calls a global village. Willingham worked out from his awareness a suitable way of dealing with that world in fiction. Since the traditional novel involving some heroic individual (Reisman's inner-directed man, or McLuhan's linear-Renaissance type of man) engaged in a quest for near-magical self-transformation was evidently finished (no realistic basis for it existing in reality), Willingham offered instead a kind of mock quest series of situations: quests leading nowhere, except possibly toward marriage—which is what George, to his dismay, finds in *Natural Child*. Otherwise, everything—man's experience and his inner life, which could be affected only by Hollywood movies and "bug eyed monster" Science Fiction stories—was simply ridiculous. (pp. 60-1)

[In] the 1950's the serious novel in America virtually collapsed. Not only Willingham seemed to have nothing further to say; his contemporaries also experienced a prolonged state of muteness. Realization seemed to be that the traditional novel form, centered on the myth of the solitary individual seeking out some wondrous personal destiny, could no longer continue. Of course, Willingham had already managed to achieve considerable success through such a realization, but apparently his own special fictional milieu was unable to sustain him any further.

Some new conception of fiction had to emerge if the novel was to continue as a significant literary form. (Fiction would have to change, since society obviously was not going to. In fact, the other-directed trends noted by Reisman were becoming more and more pronounced. McLuhan, in preference to his earlier term "global village," now describes the world as a global theatre, where what matters are social performance and the communal arts: an excellent situation for movies, folk singing, and mixed media happenings, but a very grim one for the individually addressed written word.) What did emerge was Black Humor, accompanied by varying shades of Gray: a great wave of novels and stories by such writers as Joseph Heller, John Barth, Terry Southern, Bruce Jay Friedman, Donald Barthelme, and Thomas Pynchon, closely modelled on early Willingham in their dealing with an absurd lack of pattern in life, but usually fiercer in tone. Then came Willingham's own contribution to this genre, *Eternal Fire*, a diabolically explosive fantasy set in the South of the 1930's—a work of such startling dramatic impact that, by comparison, his previous writings seem almost as gently soothing as the White Humor of P. G. Wodehouse or Thorne Smith. (pp. 61-2)

Eternal Fire is not simply an S. J. Perelman-like parody [of the Southern novel], but rather an ironic depiction of material that is customarily tragic. The black shadows of Gothic despair and decay have been exposed to the brilliant sunlight of Willingham's imagination and thus vanish from view. The usual guilt-ridden Southern novel, represented by, say, William Faulkner, Carson McCullers, and Truman Capote, has therefore been replaced by a new sort of Southern novel: one in which there are no absolutes of good and evil, but instead one in which there is an intermediate moral milieu filled with sardonic laughter. . . . Unlike his early novels, this novel has a definite story line, worthy of being compared to that of any other American novel for spellbinding appeal. As to why Willingham altered his fictional methods, the most obvious reason would be that he wishes to strengthen the nature of his artistic vision: instead

of dealing with a fragmented society, he is concerned now with exploring a more fully realized fictional world, one of logical sequence, which is what is implied by a chronological plot development. At the same time, *Eternal Fire* resembles the earlier novels in its constantly unfolding series of ironies. Aside from narrative structure, another major difference is that Willingham has abandoned a real-life frame of reference (largely autobiographical, one might assume) in favor of an obviously make-believe tableau, more than likely to give free rein to his imaginative speculations about whatever reality lies beyond the ostensible real world. In other words, he is moving away from a social framework of McLuhanesque surface events to develop his own comic-demonic version of human experience.

Eternal Fire would thus appear to be a logical conclusion to the problem posed by all his earlier novels. Essentially what these novels concerned was the dilemma of the modern artist: how to find a meaning to life in a society that presented no discernible unifying pattern. Willingham's various young heroes were usually from the South, and were usually writers—or they wanted to write but could find nothing in their travels that would give them the necessary insight or sense of artistic purpose. With *Eternal Fire*, however, set as it is in the South and with a solidly established social framework, the suggestion is that the quest of Willingham's wandering artists has been fulfilled: they have returned to the land from which the wanderers had originally come, a spoiled Eden which is nonetheless a setting far richer in spiritual possibilities than anything encountered by Dick Davenport and all the others.

Willingham's [more] recent novel, *Providence Island*, lacks his usual impact, perhaps because the basic conception (a Madison Avenue television executive stranded on a desert island with two young women) is all wrong for him. The usual Willingham approach is along the lines of an ironic anti-myth: in the early novels he dealt with an anti-quest myth, and then in *Eternal Fire* he reversed the traditional myth of Southern novels. But leaving aside the debatable merits of *Providence Island*, one notices only one disturbing drawback to Calder Willingham's splendid list of achievements—a series of delightful models of how modern American fiction should be conceived and carried out; and that drawback is that they have not received the respect due them. Such disregard of literary distinction may perhaps represent one more irony of our times, a grim joke Willingham could certainly understand if not fully appreciate. (pp. 63-5)

> J. L. Parr, "Calder Willingham: The Forgotten Novelist," in Critique: Studies in Modern Fiction *(copyright © by* Critique, *1969), Vol. XI, No. 3, 1969, pp. 57-65.*

Calder Willingham's more knowing admirers may find the notion difficult to believe, but it would seem that he had rather serious things in mind when he began [*Rambling Rose*], his eighth and in many ways his best novel. It is a fictional memoir of his small-town boyhood in the deep South during the Depression, written "with love and continuing affection and bitter-sweet nostalgia for days long ago," but it is no exercise in sentimentality. . . .

Rambling Rose is, as Willingham says in a funny "Necessary Note to the Reader," "unlike others I have written." That is because it is distinctly autobiographical and strongly motivated by nostalgia, qualities that give it a depth of feeling not always evident in his fiction. But the old antic spirit is there as well, the "pure sheer mischief" that has made Willingham one of our most irreverent and perceptive satirists. Each new Willingham novel is cause for laughter and celebration, so as we laugh let us celebrate *Rambling Rose*.

> Jonathan Yardley, "Cause for Laughter and Celebration," in Book World—The Washington Post (© The Washington Post), October 29, 1972, p. 6.

Funny, inventive, boisterously dirty, cunningly crafted as it sometimes is, the dark nightside of ["The Big Nickel"] is essentially superior vaudeville—fine, clever clowning of an improvisional order, one good turn creating the terms and conditions of the next, a set-piece preparing the way for its successor, each tall tale providing possibilities for taller ones. While the joke lasts, it is cracking good.

It lasts a surprisingly long while, but not long enough. Willingham himself appears to tire of it before it is over. . . .

And suddenly we are pitched onto another plane—no gradations, no steady descent, a violent catapult from comic pornographic fantasy (I say this with respect and admiration: Willingham is one of a handful of American virtuosi of pornography, and if anyone supposes that is a mean art let him count fingers against those reeking multitudes of pretenders). . . .

To say "The Big Nickel" is about art and life, success and failure, experience and imagination would be stretching the point past breaking: and to conclude as Davenport [the protagonist] does, and Willingham may, in a vertiginous lapse into homely sentimentality, that "one smile from a living and breathing human being was worth more than all the works of civilization" and that it is "in the service of that smile that those whose works existed" is entirely beside the point—beyond the life and energy of the novel, though it is one way out of it, the easy, ingratiating, popular way, which is no more available to serious novelists than to Presidents of all the people. One doesn't want to be unfair: Willingham's gifts are various, rich, prodigal; the novel is eminently "worth" reading for the simple pleasures it gives, never mind the "human condition", but it is a "brilliant," "promising," fitful, unresolved . . . novel. . . . (p. 12)

> Saul Maloff, in The New York Times Book Review (© 1975 by The New York Times Company; reprinted by permission), March 23, 1975.

Willingham . . . is not an especially "serious" novelist, despite occasional lapses into Deep Meaning; his plots, to use a favorite Willingham verb, tend to ramble; his penchant for self-indulgence is considerable. He is, however, one of the most skilled, observant and purely funny satirists of the postwar generation. He took on, in *Eternal Fire*, every creaking convention of Southern gothic and destroyed the genre in a storm of laughter. In *Providence Island*, he took on both the "sex novel" and middle-class sex obsession, with similar results. In his screenplay for *The Graduate*, he had equal success demolishing the affluent society and its array of pretensions.

Even at his least successful, Willingham is fun to read—

which is about all that can be said on behalf of *The Big Nickel*. There are a lot of entertaining passages in it, and one or two that Willingham nuts doubtless will want to read aloud when the impious spirit moves them, but a collection of occasional good moments does not a good novel make. *The Big Nickel* is barely coherent structurally, its characters sustain only marginal interest, and its conclusion is oddly sentimental.

Perhaps the problem is that Willingham is too consciously preoccupied here with theme—in this case, the theme of early success and the burdens it imposes on American writers. It is a solid, important theme . . . [but] Willingham doesn't seem to know quite what to do with it. . . .

But if *The Big Nickel* fails as a work of fiction, it still contains enough of those marvelous Willingham moments to keep admirers happy. (p. 24)

> Jonathan Yardley, in The New Republic (reprinted by permission of The New Republic; © 1975 by The New Republic, Inc.), April 5, 1975.

*   *   *

WILSON, Angus   1913-

Wilson is an English novelist, short story writer, essayist, and critic. Although some critics have discussed his agnostic humanism and have grouped him with the "angry young men" of the 1950s, most note that his are traditional sensibilities and skills, and emphasize his precise sense of social fact. (See also *Contemporary Authors*, Vols. 5-8, rev. ed.)

Angus Wilson is one of the most devoted exponents of traditionalism in fiction on the contemporary English scene. (p. 64)

The English novelists to whom Wilson is most often compared are Dickens, George Eliot, Henry James, Jane Austen, and Arnold Bennett; and these are the novelists whom Wilson praises most often in his criticism. (p. 67)

There is also a strain in Wilson's writing which goes back to George Eliot, though the Dickensian element may at times eclipse it. (p. 71)

Wilson's analysis of his own writing, *The Wild Garden*, is written using the same biographical technique employed in [his] study of Zola. Wilson feels, moreover, that his own writing has a similar blending of imaginative and naturalistic elements.

Wilson also learned about handling controversial sexual themes from Zola. Zola helped to show that sexual themes could be used for artistic, and not prurient reasons. (p. 74)

Zola, Wilson feels, gave him ideas about the basic form of fiction, but he also learned from Proust: "Zola has certainly influenced me a great deal in the form and shape of my novels. From Proust I get the feeling about paradox and the truth of improbability—especially the latter" [*Paris Review*, No. 17, 1957]. By "improbability" Wilson means that strange events do occur in real life, and the inclusion of such events in fiction may actually lend verisimilitude to the plot. The principal sort of improbability which Wilson refers to is the juxtaposition of people who seem to have very little in common and the revelation that, contrary to expectation, strong links can be forged between them. (p. 75)

Wilson's novels usually have an important moral issue at their centers, with lesser moral problems occurring in the subplots. (p. 80)

Wilson does not use only round characters. A number of his minor characters, most notably Mrs. Curry in *Hemlock and After*, are entirely evil and at the same time quite Dickensian. . . . On the other hand, Wilson's other characters are almost never entirely good or moral; his heroes all have flaws.

Wilson explains that there are two types of evil characters in his novels; the first kind are the flat characters of Mrs. Curry's type, people who are committed to evil; the second kind are people who are not aware of the moral implications of their actions. . . . The heroes in Wilson's novels are always morally self-aware; if they do evil, they know it while they are doing it or soon thereafter.

This presentation of evil on three moral planes—intrinsic evil, unconscious evil, and conscious, reluctant evil—is quite effective: the serpent, Eve, and Adam are presented in similar terms. Instead of using morality within a theological framework, however, Wilson has used liberalism and humanism as a basis for the moral code of his heroes.

Wilson is far too intelligent a writer to present the liberal humanism of his major characters in simple or dogmatic terms; indeed, this would be a capitulation to his sin of doing evil through lack of moral self-awareness. His characters prefer the opposite end of the spectrum: a self-awareness so analytical and introspective that it ends in paralysis of the will and inaction. Attempting to live decently and morally, intellectually unable to accept religious ethics, Wilson's heroes govern their lives with a set of impeccable humanistic precepts. The inevitable conflicts occur. The most carefully considered moral actions give pain to others, and Wilson's protagonists withdraw to a world of moral inactivity. (pp. 83-4)

The bitterest hell is the one with a memory of paradise; the most tragic fall is from high estate where the chance for salvation is narrowly missed. Wilson's hell is depressing more than anything else; the absence of salvation or the possibility of salvation produces resignation and not tragedy. (p. 85)

Wilson's interest in psychoanalysis, the self-analytic nature of his fictional methods, and the knowledge of Freud which he acquired in the thirties might lead one to expect a Freudian bias in his fiction. Actually, this is only partially true. A good deal of Wilson's writing is concerned with understanding the psychological makeup of his characters. (p. 92)

[Characters] Wilson himself seems to dislike are insufficiently analyzed. . . . Characters who are conservative or fascistic in Wilson's fiction rarely have an unconscious; their nastiness is taken for granted and seldom is analyzed. (pp. 94-5)

Another fault which is connected with Wilson's traditionalism is his weakness in using symbolism. Wilson's only sustained attempt at using symbols occurs in his fourth novel, *The Old Men at the Zoo*; the novel he wrote after this one, *Late Call*, is a reversion to his usual less symbolic style. (p. 95)

Rubin Rabinovitz, "Angus Wilson," in his

The Reaction against Experiment in the English Novel, 1950-1960 *(copyright © 1967 Columbia University Press; reprinted by permission of the publisher), Columbia University Press, 1967, pp. 64-96.*

Knowledge of literature as counterfeit is a recurrent theme in modern writing; in Wilson's case, the understanding cuts deep into the speech and words of his characters, giving them something of that self-mimicking quality which is a typical attribute of tenure in his universe. But it also reaches back into the writer and implicates him. It promotes the admirable pastiche qualities of *No Laughing Matter*, but also those strange positional insecurities that keep on arising as the relationship between Wilson's narrative posture and his characters keeps proving oblique and surprising. Those who have seen his work as a realistic fiction of social range and moral maturity have always this side of his work to come to terms with; it is the biggest problem his writing poses. Of course he is that sort of writer: he offers himself as a moral power; there *is* in his work a singular moral maturity and perceptiveness. But to overlook the elements of self-doubt and self-mockery would be to miss something quite as essential, and quite as creatively significant, having to do with an uncertainty towards, or a qualification of, that fiction of adult social seriousness he so much admires. (pp. 212-13)

Wilson is unmistakable in his tough-minded interest in moral responsibility, and the milieu of extreme strain and tension in which moral acts are conducted; at times he is unsparing in his capacity for satirical exposure. Even as he relishes his world for its style, its social flamboyance, he measures and judges according to a comic and ironic mode. And one of the functions of irony and comedy in his work is to be directed, as it is in Forster's novels, towards a centre, showing up moral and emotional atrophy, self-deceit and unrecognized failure in the realm of the personal. (pp. 215-16)

Wilson's politics are ostensibly liberal and progressive, and he seems to condemn false social institutions and values; there are hints of political exposé, and of higher historical promises, of better worlds that might be, greater equality, increased tolerance. His bourgeoisie is insecure and in some ways sunk in an illusion which the novelist exposes. But history, though an active force in all his writing, hardly looks, on closer inspection, regenerative. The world of the welfare state, of which he has offered many apt portraits—including the brilliant one of the new town in *Late Call*—does not transcend evil, but simply provides a new frame for its continuance; the revolutionary promise is never made real, but is another falsification or illusion. The point is that Wilson acts as if historical redemption might come; he writes the liberal-humanistic, or the radical, novel but qualifies it, taking its world often for his essential world but then touching in many insecurities. (p. 218)

["God's eye view"] is in fact a commonplace form of the times, and we find it in much modern realism, satire, and comedy. But the point about Wilson's way with it is that he uses it very freely and unpuristically, as a story-teller above all interested in his story might, moving in and out of his characters as the need arises, presenting his material through many eyes, committing himself to extended episodes of exposition, allowing himself to make acerbic moral points and judgements. This use is imprecise, which is to say that Wilson performs many transactions which writers for whom such things are prime ends, basic organizational instruments for eliciting the form of art, would eschew. His material has to grow of itself, by being freely mimed and acted, in a mock-theatre in which the author creates fixed terms within which the play may occur. What Wilson needs indeed is a mode of writing which allows him a high degree of social mimicry and involvement and then a means for the assertive control of it; this duplicates the narrative activity, and potently divides it. This, I think, he has seen and worried over, which is one reason why the mode has become itself a matter for study in some of his more recent books. (pp. 218-19)

The bourgeois generational novel, the dynastic novel as we have it in *Buddenbrooks* or *Der Stechlin* or *The Forsyte Saga*, is a well-established realistic form, a very substantial and material species of fiction, able to give the sense of social substance, of historical motion, of familial rise and fall, of the interlocking of a family and a culture; but the telling point in *No Laughing Matter* is the subversion of this—the family is not a communion or a coherence, its financial roots are weak, and the substantive relationship between individual and culture is itself unreal. (p. 221)

No Laughing Matter is very much a laughing matter, or history as a certain kind of farce. It is shrill farce; the farce is itself conditioned, for one feels that the comedy and absurdity, the entire theatre, is a theatre derived from society. But theatre it is; the metaphor is very exact, and it is very total. The idea exists in all of Wilson's novels; in the earlier books we have the text presented as a kind of play, in which well-defined characters exist and well-defined scenes occur, the author then participating as actor and mime and standing back as dramatist to produce his distinctive scenario. But in this novel the metaphor is very obsessive and extensive.

It is, at one level, a figure for illusion, the social illusion, the false-seeming which allows the bourgeois family to feel that, whatever the facts of society and history, they stand at the centre of the stage. But to do that they cast off character and assume roles, roles with artificial social meanings; they are players in the sense of being people who take on other identities. The distinctive thing about the Matthews family, especially in the early pages of the novel, is that they are self-knowing actors, mocking as well as mocked people. They speak in an elaborate, self-parodying discourse drawn from stage, literature, music-hall, newspapers and general cliché ('His Nibs'); they play their part in life, so that they seem at once curiously over-full and over-empty, people with great self-awareness but no substance, people through whom society or cliché speaks. This is all part of a prevalent self-awareness, the knowledge each has of the self-deceptions practised by others; it has much to do with the insecure foundations in family, and money, and society, on which their lives are built. But the theatrical metaphor is also obviously a figure not alone for false illusions in society, the disjunctive images of a declining class, but for life.

Malcolm Bradbury, "The Fiction of Pastiche: The Comic Mode of Angus Wilson," in his Possibilities: Essays on the State of the Novel *(copyright © 1973 by Malcolm Bradbury; reprinted by permission of Oxford University Press, Inc.), Oxford University Press, 1973, pp. 211-31.*

While [Wilson] has been a most impressive short story writer, he has yet to write a completely satisfying novel. Either his plots creak badly (*Hemlock and After, Anglo-Saxon Attitudes*) or drag on interminably (*The Old Men at the Zoo*) or else his central characters are not involving enough to sustain full-length works (Meg Eliot of *The Middle-Age of Mrs. Eliot*, Sylvia Calvert of *Late Call* and pretty much the entire Matthews clan of *No Laughing Matter*). Still, each Wilson book contains several saving graces—crisp dialogue (Wilson is an accomplished mimic), a number of lively secondary characters, and some perceptive descriptive passages. I remember fondly, for example, the evil Mrs. Curry of *Hemlock and After*, the eccentric Rose Lorimer of *Anglo-Saxon Attitudes*, the nightmarish passages in *The Old Men at the Zoo* and the glimpse of New Town life in *Late Call*. With that truncated tribute out of the way, I must report, sadly, that . . . [*As If by Magic*] is absolutely dreadful and that it will only support his detractors charges that he is an author who writes and writes but has next to nothing to communicate. . . .

Throughout the novel Wilson changes tone so often that we never know when to take him seriously, when to laugh with him or at him. Add to this a short-story-length epilogue in which the author desperately tries to tie his big, sloppy bundle together, and you have, as if by perverse magic, Wilson's worst novel thus far, one that will only embarrass the sensible Wilson devotee. (pp. 780-81)

Ronald De Feo, in The Hudson Review *(copyright © 1973 by The Hudson Review, Inc.; reprinted by permission), Vol. XXVI, No. 4, Winter, 1973-74.*

[In *As If by Magic*] Wilson has been so copiously and freely inventive, so frank in his construction of a great machine-like plot, that his novel tends to transform its documentation into symbol. Wilson has worked out an elaborate series of episodes, of satiric and comic turns, that carry the actual, one hopes, a stage or two beyond its verifiable limits. And yet, one suspects, if he has outrun the actual, it will surely have overtaken him before we can impeach his extravagances. He has a fine ear for the litanies of the young. . . . He can catch more in a sentence than most observers see in a day. (p. 563)

Wilson's novel has been called Dickensian, and the term has its point. This novel does not have the movement between levels of a single society, the gradual uncovering of a buried secret, and the remarkable interweaving of characters and incidents that make *Anglo-Saxon Attitudes* the most Dickensian of Wilson's novels. But it does have a central theme that is pursued in various guises, richly imagined scenes if not characters, and a play of coincidence that is at once shocking and ironic. If the plot comes together with stunning calculation, what it yields is, after all, somewhat dry and anticlimactic; there are no festivities that involve redeemed prodigals, heavenly brides, and beautiful infants. What celebration we find at the close is somewhat like Bernard Shaw's, the freedom from illusion, with all the loneliness that its independence may cost.

Wilson has always been, to a considerable degree, a moralist. . . . [He] does not delight in irony for its own sake.

He is skeptical enough, but not radically skeptical; he is, in fact, profoundly concerned with truth. (pp. 563-64)

Wilson makes frequent allusions to traditional English novels—as he did in *The Middle Age of Mrs. Eliot*—to Jane Austen, Dickens, Lawrence, E. M. Forster. Yet one is not so much struck by the game of self-conscious artifice as by the moral insight. (p. 565)

Wilson's characters gradually win sympathy in spite of the fatuities that are recorded with such lucid precision. They shade into states of madness that are hard to distinguish from self-indulgence, but they come through them and learn from the process. Such states are always more pathetic or comic, more terrible or ludicrous, than the comparative sobriety and wisdom which may succeed them, but they finally interest us most as transitional states, movements of disintegration or repair. Where they remain fixed and endlessly repetitive, as in horror comics or comic turns, they may become symbolic dimensions of a fuller self that is capable of change, that is potentially the stuff of more than fiction. So it is with the conventions that are so disarmingly parodied or so frankly employed; they provide games we are accustomed to play, and they remind us, too, of the freedom of games (where we can be as greedy and ruthless in Monopoly as we try not to be in life). Yet the novelist's games would not interest us as much as they do if they were not in some way making an assertion or a discovery we value in all our experience. Fiction, like magic, can solve our problems, but only to the extent that we are willing to become the stuff of fiction ourselves; one value of magic is to remind us of the stubbornness of things, of fiction to recall the responsibilities of selves. (pp. 565-66)

> *Martin Price, in* The Yale Review *(© 1974 by Yale University; reprinted by permission of the editors), Summer, 1974.*

As If by Magic is a genuine novel, and a good one. It is, despite the dust jacket's calling it Mr. Wilson's "most Dickensian novel to date," decidedly twentieth century, both in technique and in its unremittingly bleak view of human nature. Almost without exception, the characters are hateful or pathetic or both. The plot concerns the round-the-world voyages of Hamo Langmuir, an aging homosexual scientist, and of his neurotic goddaughter, Alexandra Grant. Hamo's story gradually shifts from black comedy to tragedy, in the superbly written center section of the book. Alexandra is less satisfactory. The narrator says with no detectable irony that she has finally understood that there is no Magic—either religious or literary or scientific or political—to solve all our problems for us. But I don't believe it. Whatever the narrator says, Alexandra's own words and actions in the last scene tell me that she is not much changed from the muddleheaded, paranoid young woman we met 400 pages ago. Her perception is perfectly valid (although her specific social prescriptions are simplistic), but she has seemed to reach it so often, falling back from it each time, that I see no reason why this time should be different. By having Alexandra disparage E. M. Forster and Jane Austen, Mr. Wilson sets up a standard of comparison that emphasizes his own unsureness of tone and reminds the reader of the difference between a good novel and a great one. (p. 1055)

> *Linda Rogers, in* National Review *(© National Review, Inc., 1974; 150 East 35th St.,*

New York, N.Y. 10016), September 13, 1974.

* * *

WODEHOUSE, P(elham) G(renville)   1881-1975

Wodehouse was an English-born American novelist, short story writer, playwright, and essayist. One of this century's most beloved writers, Wodehouse, with his unchanging world of upper-class characters—Bertie Wooster, Jeeves, Psmith— came to be taken as much for granted as the Royal Family. His elaborate plots, filled with the comic absurdities of farce and set in an England that almost, but never really, existed, are worked out with affectionate satire in "feather-light" prose that is casual, sophisticated, mock-pompous, and completely inimitable. (See also *Contemporary Authors*, Vols. 45-48; obituary, Vols. 57-60.)

Useless to describe the plot of a P. G. Wodehouse novel: [in "Jeeves and the Tie that Binds"] they are all made to stand on their heads as often as a Slinky toy coming down the staircase. . . .

Except for the discovery that Jeeves's first name is Reggie —"It had never occurred to me before that he had a first name," says Bertie—nothing has changed in this novel which marks Wodehouse's 90th birthday. As always, it is a mistake to send Bertie out to deal with a woman whose "eye could have been used for splitting logs in the teak forests of Borneo" or a man described as "a twenty-minute egg." "Where one goes wrong when looking for the ideal girl," says Bertie's pal, "is in making one's selection before walking the full length of the counter." Wit? The world's wisdom writ in little space. One of the master's better novels, I would say if I could, but I can't because, in the warder of the brain (as Jeeves would say of memory), they are all equally good. Buy it against the certain agues of winter. (p. 116)

> *Peter S. Prescott, in* Newsweek *(copyright 1971 by Newsweek, Inc.; all rights reserved; reprinted by permission), October 25, 1971.*

[Two of Wodehouse's old] novels, one of 1913 (*The Little Nugget*) and the other (*Sam the Sudden*) of 1925 [are] characteristic examples of his use of the New World to unbalance the Old, and both of them [are] first rate stories. . . . We are reminded of this anyway every time he brings back the old characters. . . . [Alas], they are not the men they were, more like manoeuvrable puppets.

You need only open *Sam the Sudden*, which is understandably one of Mr Wodehouse's own favourites, to see how much richer the human material once was. Here [the main characters] make a thick, meaty background to the story of Sam himself and Kay Derrick, who may suffer from some of the usual difficulties of heroes and heroines (such as undue good looks) but are not nearly so two-dimensional as those who came since. The same goes for the earlier *The Little Nugget*, with its schoolmasters and American crooks and its slightly more unconventional heroine; the two hardbitten Drassilis women seem particularly well-observed, as well as that transatlantic Bunter, the Nugget himself. In those days there was a romantic thread in Mr Wodehouse's work, linking it to the stories of such writers as Dennis Mackail, which doubtless aggravated the highbrows but now proves to have been a source of variety, and even of strength. It kept his range much wider than it subsequently became.

"Saga Habits," in The Times Literary Supplement (© *Times Newspapers Ltd., 1973; reproduced by permission), January 26, 1973, p. 84.*

The novels of P. G. Wodehouse's eighties (writes A Fan, nostalgically), were on the whole remarkable for two things. There was the odd unexpected innovation—a new category of character or a sudden intrusion from the modern world—coupled with a certain weakening in the structure: loose threads or unsatisfactory endings. Together they kept the reader on his toes; one had to watch out. This is not the case, however, with . . . *Bachelors Anonymous*, which is slight but efficiently organized along well-worn lines. Dialogue and comment are as well phrased as ever, but the characters, though their names are mainly new, are all from stock and the situations hardly original. That is no reason for not recommending the book to new readers, who will surely start laughing as their fathers and grandfathers did before them. But there is not much here to intrigue the habitué, aside from a brief return to one of Mr Wodehouse's most cherished settings, the south-east London suburb of Valley Fields. (p. 1338)

The Times Literary Supplement (© *Times Newspapers Ltd., 1973; reproduced by permission), November 2, 1973.*

[The stories in *The Golf Omnibus*] are not merely golf stories, but are examples of sprightly fiction about the unbelievable addictions suffered by followers of the Ancient and Royal Game. Collected together like old treasured scorecards, these stories are unbeatable in their wit and elegance. Wodehouse, who has written over 75 books and gave butlering immortality through his creation of Jeeves, is writing for golfers primarily; but those who may laugh the most at his stories are ones who, like The Oldest Member, sit on the high veranda and watch the rest of us torture ourselves in the valley below. Sometimes, we shoot a 110 and there is *no* shot worth remembering. If that happens, there is nothing to do but follow the sound advice of Sam Snead, another ageless miracle like Wodehouse: lay off golf for three weeks, and then quit altogether.

Colman McCarthy, "Welcome to the Club," in Book World—The Washington Post (© *The Washington Post), March 31, 1974, p. 2.*

A new novel by Wodehouse always stirs the kind of awe in me that would be evoked by the discovery that Hepplewhite was still making chairs. Wonder of wonders. This wonder ["Bachelors Anonymous"] conforms to the classic Wodehouse mythology: nice but dim young men; nice, clever young women; crusty, rich senior citizens rattling around in impossible adventures terminating in matrimony. In Wodehouse, characters are broke but not poor, marriages are closed and the impossible invariably happens. Why not? What could be more unlikely than the author himself, a 93-year-old writer turning out novels as though he were 20?

"Bachelors Anonymous" features a young playwright and

pugilist named Joe Pickering, hired temporarily by movie potentate Ivor Llewellyn to protect him from getting married for the fifth time. Llewellyn's lawyer, a member of Bachelors Anonymous, lends a helping and nearly disastrous hand. For Wodehouse readers, no further explication should be necessary. (p. 27)

Martin Levin, in The New York Times Book Review (© *1974 by The New York Times Company; reprinted by permission), August 4, 1974.*

Those who have no enthusiasm for [Wodehouse's] work are often irritated by the exuberant hyperbole and even aggressiveness of [his] fans, who sometimes show all the least attractive characteristics of religious zealotry. I confess I find myself slightly shocked when anybody admits to not liking Wodehouse, although I can see that this is an unreasonable reaction. But I think I can be dogmatic on a few points from my own observation: that Wodehouse has been more read than any other English novelist by his fellow novelists; that nobody with any genuine feeling for the English language has failed to recognise at least an element of truth in Belloc's judgment of 1934, that Wodehouse was 'the best writer of English now alive, the head of my profession'; that the failure of academic literary criticism to take any account of Wodehouse's supreme mastery of the English language or the profound influence he has had on every worth-while English novelist in the past 50 years demonstrates in better and conciser form than anything else how the Eng. Lit. industry is divorced from the subject it claims to study; finally, that the university departments of English Literature are manned to a large extent by people with no particular love for or understanding of the English language and no appreciation of English literature beyond a few rubbishy opinions about Lawrence, Joyce and Wyndham Lewis which they push backwards and forwards at each other. . . .

To dismiss him with a sneer as a purveyor of light entertainment . . . is to betray a blinding ignorance of the structure, form, language and philosophy of the English novel. What Wodehouse has done is to distil for all time a form of pure comedy in more or less abstract guise: without any social application, let alone political commitment; with no bitterness, cruelty, sex, rancour or any other impure purpose which comedy may serve. Whatever uses other writers may put it to, the essence remains what Wodehouse has distilled. . . .

There are many people who object to the Wodehouse *mise-en-scène* on grounds of its sociological partiality and political cretinism. The fact that he concerns himself more or less exclusively with the imaginary rich may indeed be an obstacle to enjoyment among those who disapprove of the rich. It is a question of taste. . . . Those who complain that there is no account of the sources of Wooster's income, no glance at the exploited urban industrial masses who sustain life at Blandings, are registering a political objection, not a literary one. He never set himself the task of writing a realistic novel and can scarcely be blamed for having failed. Nobody ever said that Wodehouse was the greatest living novelist, only the greatest living writer, to which I would add that as a writer he has had more influence on the English novel than any other writer in history, and about twenty times as much as Lawrence, Joyce and Kafka combined, even on such consciously experimental novels as B. S. Johnson's *Christie Malry's Own Double Entry*.

Auberon Waugh, "The Best Writer," in New Statesman (© 1975 The Statesman & Nation Publishing Co. Ltd.), February 21, 1975, p. 240.

Wodehouse seemed uniquely to exist outside time: the latest Jeeves and Bertie Wooster tale, *The Cat-Nappers*, is as sprightly as the first one was in 1916. Wodehouse was both the delight of gerontologists and insurance actuaries and the despair of writers a third his age struggling in the toils of second-novel constipation. His plots in his 90s were as maniacally intricate as ever—Sir Pelham was the fastest man with a peripeteia since Euripides—the dialogue as crackling, the literary allusions as hilariously apt. Perhaps only by hindsight does there seem just the faintest tinge of autumnal wisdom in this last Jeeves story. At one point Bertie reflects about a bully described by his own daughter as "a cross between Attila the Hun and a snapping turtle" that: "I didn't like his tone, but then one often doesn't like people's tones."

Certainly not in the modern world, which I think Wodehouse made the mistake of occasionally trying to render here. There are wildly anachronistic references to peace marches, muggings, and girls who "radiant-beautywise" are "in the top ten." Since the overwhelming ambiance of the novel is that vaguely Edwardian Arcadia we particularly associate with Wodehouse, this is a mistake.

Another is that Jeeves doesn't occupy as large a role in extricating Bertie from his self-induced disasters as was once his wont. . . . [He] shows an uncharacteristic and unfortunate tendency to melt into the middle distance.

Bachelors Anonymous . . . is set entirely in the modern world, although it is a world with strong deja-vu sensations of 1930s movies. . . .

The World of Mr. Mulliner contains 42 stories, some going back to the 1920s, about the garrulous Mr. Mulliner who regales his fellow barflies at the Angler's Rest with whoppers about his various relatives, all of whom are talented at getting into Woosterian scrapes. They prove that tall tales about people are more interesting than fables about fish, but Wodehouse was correct in recommending a medium adult dosage of "not more than two or three stories, taken at breakfast or before retiring."

Richard Freedman, "Pelham Grenville Wodehouse is not a name that translates easily into Chinese," in Book World—The Washington Post (© The Washington Post), March 30, 1975, p. 1.

Filling winter's bare, ruined choirs with joyful cuckoos, P. G. Wodehouse's *Aunts Aren't Gentlemen* is vintage fluff. (p. lvii)

In P. G. Wodehouse's novels, the best-laid plans, even those of good aunts, go wildly astray. According to John Locke extravagant behavior was best explained by the association of ideas. Ideas "not at all of kin," Locke wrote, come by chance or custom or education "to be so united in men's minds" that it becomes hard to separate them. They always keep company, and one no sooner appears in the

understanding but its associate wanders after it, "and if there are more than two which are thus united, the whole gang, always inseparable, show themselves together." Quite right—thus Bertie Wooster is not the only wise man from Gotham living in a cottage and breathing the peppermint air of Maiden Eggesford. The whole gang is there livening up the rural grave. (p. lviii)

Even with the help of a score of Ariadnes, and Daedalus pitched in for good measure, Theseus himself could not lay bare the delightful windings of Mr. Wodehouse's labyrinthine plot. Suffice it to say that a minotaur does not lurk in the center, for Mr. Wodehouse knows the importance of no tragic relief. Life is too important to be taken seriously. In his *Defence of Politics* Bernard Crick argues that boredom with established truths is the great enemy of free men. Would that Mr. Crick had gone further, for boredom is the enemy of life itself. When the world is too much with us and we suffer from deadly apple-disease of seriousness, there is no better tonic than one of P. G. Wodehouse's eighty-four novels. His laughter falls brightly from the air; boredom vanishes like the ghost of Christmas past, and established truths become warmly alluring. In this literary-critical world which often seems ponderous enough to bore the behind off an elephant, we ought to thank whatever powers that be for P. G. Wodehouse and his sights that make us less forlorn. (p. lix)

Sam Pickering, Jr., "The Wisdom of Foolishness," in Sewanee Review (reprinted by permission of the editor; © 1975 by The University of the South), Spring, 1975, pp. lvii-lix.

"The Cat-nappers" is Wodehouse's 97th novel. Released first in England some months ago, it is the last to appear during his lifetime. (Other books, drawn from his papers, are expected in the future.) Appropriately enough "The Cap-nappers" features those favorites of the Wodehouse stock company, Jeeves the butler ("Would pusillanimous be the word for which you are groping, sir?") and Bertie Wooster ("Quite possibly. I know it begins with pu.") The ingredients are quite familiar: a theft, a sundered heart, an aunt, "a hearty good morning to you, aged relative," and numerous concatenations. People cross paths and call each other things like "wee sleekit timorous cowering beastie" and "elderly little gawd-help-us," but, as always, everything rights itself in the end, with no real harm done to anyone.

Wodehouse has, of course, rotated the same crops hundreds of times: the setting—Edwardian England—rarely varies ("I hardly think it would be an improvement if I were to write a novel laid in Yugoslavia or the Crimea"); the chief characters are typically the young idle rich, who wear morning coats and spatterdashes (spats), who, if they're not at the Drones Club, are spending long week-ends with various formidable aunts and loopy uncles at posh country estates such as Totleigh Towers or Matcham Scratchings, trying to disentangle themselves from, or entangle themselves with, assorted young women named Honoria Glossop or Corky Pirbright. Almost everybody is slightly ridiculous but never contemptible, as Orwell once pointed out, and the real world—whatever that is—rarely intrudes.

Many writers avoid the numerous stock devices of plot and

language; Wodehouse embraces them with relish. His bag of tricks is considerable. Clichés, slang and off-center classical allusions come together in various self-defeating combinations. . . .

His books abound in inflated euphemisms . . ., slightly batty orotund phrases . . ., and genial insults. . . .

Perhaps more than anything else Wodehouse is a master of a kind of nonsense prose, non-sequiturish phrases and absurd concords and wonderfully silly repetitions. . . . Finally, probably no one has written so well about pigs. (p. 23)

[The] books consist mostly of dialogue and are carefully plotted around inconsequential doings—truly the novel as musical comedy. (p. 24)

> *Robert M. Strozier, in* The New York Times Book Review *(© 1975 by The New York Times Company; reprinted by permission), April 27, 1975.*

* * *

WRIGHT, James 1927-

An American poet and recipient of the Pulitzer Prize and other awards, Wright is considered by many critics among the best poets of his generation. (See also *Contemporary Authors*, Vols. 49-52.)

Not margins but centers, not edges but spaces, not contiguities but distances: the thematic insistence of this poet—who by forty had written four volumes of poetry, two in verse and two (it is tempting to say) inversely—is plain, indeed is plane: from Martins Ferry, Ohio to Stateline, Nevada, with significant stopovers in Minneapolis and in Fargo, North Dakota, it is a landlocked, borderless life whose terms are *spread out*, articulated by James Wright in a dialect of dispossession and deprival, "a vowel of longing" unique among his contemporaries for its final bleakness, singular in its ultimate solitude. (p. 575)

The point is to reach a point, literally, of no return, a true event which would be one that cannot recur—as Wallace Stevens calls it, "an escape from repetition, a happening in space and the self that touched them both at once and alike." For this escape, for this event the instruments of a *convention* are felt to be thereby not instruments but obstacles. Traditional versification, rhyme, the discourse which submits itself to an asymptotic norm sensed to govern *the line* however great the departures from it—these are, for James Wright's ultimate art, no means at all. Yet it is an *art*, not merely a compliance, not merely a rapture, which we are entitled to see as Wright's achievement. An art constituting itself out of what it gives away, and out of the very process of giving itself away. (p. 576)

It is not until Wright has made himself over, from *The Branch Will Not Break* (1963) onward, converted himself from an elegiast into an apocalypst, discovering the whole of nature not as a rhythmical series of sad events but as the singular content of a ceaseless human soma . . . that he can mount to the ecstasy so marvellously his own, momentarily given and not repeated but possibly followed by yet another, which is the achievement of his later poems.

Few poets, one may say, enable us to take the expression *ground form* so literally as James Wright enforces, implants

the acceptation: the easy sorrows, the more difficult splendors of earth engender his utterance; the wrecked landscapes of the Ohio strip-mines and the ruined lives scattered upon them compel a recognition, once the enemy is discovered within rather than projected upon the surrounding sordor, that mortality is its own recompense. (pp. 578-79)

The recognition that one must be a naturalized inhabitant of the self in order to converse with love is crucial to Wright's persistence as a poet—"the main thing is not to get on in the world but to get home," Wright says of Theodore Storm, and of himself in that somatic landscape of his own discovery:

> *Close by a big river, I am alive in my own country*
> *I am home again. . .*

When what you have always thought was outside yourself and therefore against you is found to be within and therefore with you, you can deal with its mortal as with its ecstatic consequences. For the creating mind, Wright has remarked of [René] Char, there is no such thing as irrelevancy—the corporeal and the chthonic are collected into "a single human word for love of air." (p. 579)

He wants his poetry to be a *finding*, an *invention* in the literal sense of the word, not a loss comforted by rite but a discovery, however brutal, made bearable by art. (p. 582)

In the third and fourth books, *The Branch Will Not Break* and *Shall We Gather at the River*, James Wright reaches occasionally—but it is the occasions which justify the effort, which ransom the expense—beyond even such rectitude of desolation which is the self's first calisthenic in the achievement of recognition, or identity made ecstatic. And the guide to this final or at least fulfilling mode of his poetry is an elusive Virgil indeed, the "silence-haunted" Georg Trakl, whose poems Wright calls—and the relevance to his own enterprise is patent—"attempts to enter and to recognize one's very self." With Robert Bly, James Wright has translated twenty of Trakl's poems "from which all shrillness and clutter have been banished." and the still raptures of these interior landscapes, with their abrupt drops and ascents into the "merely personal" and beyond it, certainly qualify and prepare all that Wright creates in his own broken but incandescent later poems, generated from moments of beatitude like the one recorded in "Today I Was So Happy I Made This Poem" and concluding—it is the *summum bonum* of Wright's whole undertaking—with these lines:

> *Each moment of time is a mountain.*
> *An eagle rejoices in the oak trees of heaven,*
> *Crying*
> *That is what I wanted.*

The aphoristic resonance of this ("aphorisms, representing a knowledge broken," Bacon says), the elliptical *sentences* of some seraphic wanderer, suggest what Wright found in Trakl's mysterious verses, his statements of stillness. (pp. 583-84)

In "Milkweed," for example, the apocalypse is not only invoked, it is *experienced*, reminding us of Éluard's great discovery: "there is another world, but it is this one." Wright's ecstasy is earned by a tremendous renunciation, the abjuring of ritual—and in consequence his poems are not lovely, are not conveyed in a language of polished facets; rather they are splinters, jagged cleavages on which the sun, momentarily, explodes. . . . (p. 584)

Richard Howard, "James Wright," in his Alone With America: Essays on the Art of Poetry in the United States Since 1950 *(copyright © 1965, 1966, 1967, 1968, 1969 by Richard Howard; reprinted by permission of Atheneum Publishers, New York), Atheneum, 1969, pp. 575-86.*

James Wright [has] renounced . . . the opalescent visual style, with its incantatory grammatical clearness, which at the moment has won Wright more mediocre imitators even than Lowell. As Wright's use of imagery has become sparer, his grammar has become more complex, with unexpected tenses, shifting antecedents, and a general tendency to suggest multiple contexts. . . . *Two Citizens* is a book of direct statements, with ambiguous contexts, but with a very American downrightness, too. The emotional exclamatoriness that some have called sentimental in Wright is more prominent than ever; but I for one, have been led to a new insight about it. It is a part of the American speech that Wright . . . wants to speak: a vocal violence needed to break the *macho* barrier against uttering feeling at all in our culture. It has, for Wright, the beauty of the men who must always live roughly, yet can remain fundamentally gentle.

The criticism of myth, both patriotic and personal, is a large concern in *Two Citizens*. Jenny, the prostitute-saint and martyr of *Shall We Gather At The River*, here thins (if that is the word for so airy a translation) to a tree, a season, a half-self. The paradoxical St. Judas, the holy outcast, also goes, through a Blakean repudiation of the "good" and "evil" that made him necessary. . . . Having denounced America, Wright falls late and hard for the American love of a Europe which, lacking our myths of opportunity, also lacks our need for rootless and violent self-assertion. But Europe is finally less important than the discovery of an unsolipsistic loneliness, persisting even in love, which enables one to bear rootlessness and outward ugliness without myth. This discovery is set forth early, in the beautiful "Afternoon and Evening at Ohrid," and in the end it leads Wright back to America. . . . *Two Citizens* is a deeply moving book, and it establishes Wright's quest for integrity of statement, "the pure clear word," on an even firmer basis than his splendid earlier volumes did. (pp. 88-9)

Alan Williamson, in Shenandoah *(copyright by* Shenandoah; *reprinted from* Shenandoah: The Washington and Lee University Review *with the permission of the Editor), Winter, 1974.*

As is evident in ["At the Executed Murderer's Grave" and "American Twilights, 1957"], and in poems such as "My Grandmother's Ghost" and "A Poem about George Doty in the Death House" from *The Green Wall*, Wright envisions his creative role in dualistic terms of outcast and savior from the very beginning, familiar stances not too far removed from Pound's concept of the artist as hero in the *Cantos*. This enables him to wander freely beyond society's pale in search of themes and characters, evoking compassion for the inarticulate victims of our inequitable, antihuman institutions, while indulging a personal passion for the confessional voice, and the thematic freedom it entails.

Like Diane Wakowski, a much better poet, he strives always to yoke private memory to surrealistic techniques.

Verging on the sentimental throughout, Wright usually manages to avoid complete capitulation in his next and best volume, *The Branch Will Not Break* (1963), only through a fierce neoclassical restraint, a restraint of style, not substance or feeling. It is this willingness to confront the unsaid, to appreciate and utilize selective silences and great white spaces, which lets him maintain the required distance between self and subject matter. More important, perhaps, it helps him introduce another notion of romantic oases into contemporary poetry's bleak terrain, a mission he seemingly deems fundamental.

For Wright, redemption is found in the old-fashioned verities of our pastoral past and its poets' Wordsworthian traditions, in crickets, owls, horses and wheat stalks, which are almost inevitably appealed to in climatic stanzas as significant means of flight from the depressing emotional inscape already established by previous stanzas. . . . Furthermore, their delightful gestures of being imply a cosmological harmony (with nature and themselves) which appears to guarantee human survival. The risk of sentimentality, unthinking sentimentality, remains, of course. (pp. 258-59)

The majority of poems in *The Branch Will Not Break* accomplish their moving (if modest) ends, and, in style and final poetic success, "Two Hangovers" can be viewed as a sort of prototype for the rest. The surface is confessional in its apparently personal, unheroic experience, or in its "deep subjective images," and in its valid attempt to seek an analogue for that experience. (p. 259)

The pattern so prevalent in previous poems has again reasserted itself: despair and celebration, ritual damnation and ritual salvation, the agony of human existence miraculously made bearable by nature's endless eloquence. Although seemingly open to manifestations of the universe's mysterious design, Wright's poems are closed structures, circular staircases winding forever down towards a sensual basement paradise in which Darwinian rats are either ignored or explicitly refuted. Reminiscent, at times, of Emily Dickinson, he cannot or will not take his nature straight. It must always be transmuted into epistemological tableaus through the child's golden eye, with the observer's art becoming a primitive form of animism in the process, not in itself dangerous, but fraught with seductive potential for over-statements, as well as over-simplifications. . . .

And yet, the poem does succeed, particularly in the second section, where Wright is operating inside the sparse anecdotal format he prefers. Its major flaws are all located in the first section, which is predicated upon favorite motifs of haunted recollections and blatant social protests, but Yeats's "cold eye" is notable by its absence. (p. 260)

Taken as a whole, the poem attains a high degree of lyric grace and manages to overcome Wright's almost innate sentimentality. A state of grace is what the poet is seeking, and his characters remain innocent in their miseries, as do nature's tokens of seasonal endurance. Religious or not, Wright has thus refused an irrational universe. The logical path chosen, from physical discomfit through terrible dreams and memories to the closing affirmation, presents an integrated world of balanced alternatives in which the state of grace, or innocent purgation, can forgive everyone everything. For all its coy simplicity, the artist's redemption does not strike false, though his descent into childish death images nearly upsets the coal cart. His art in "Two Hangovers" is a positive, healing act of will thrust upon a harsh reality.

Unhappily, with the publication of *Shall We Gather at the River* (1968), Wright's penchant for the sentimental finally overwhelmed his very real, if limited, talent. The book's title, a question without a question mark taken from the declarative line of a revival hymn, significantly indicates a preordained affirmation. It is this imposed affirmation, a religious one, which drags him and his frail aesthetic to earth. Without the probing doubt evident in his earlier volumes—despair remains and, indeed, appears to increase, but it is more hysterical than true—his poetry loses its necessary tension. The ultimate benevolence of God's entire creation has become a secret conviction that allows his sentimental inclinations to loom unchecked. On the surface, he often gives the impression of operating within the same lyric confines present in previous work, within a relaxed, conversational style, but the patterns of neo-classical restraint are now mere trappings as sentimental distortions slop over their sides like pea soup. Always a strong point, his metaphors suffer the most, frequently disappearing altogether. He is too often content with unquickened, untransfigured pathos, the pathos of a stark situation, as in "I Am a Sioux Brave, he said in Minneapolis" and "In Terror of Hospital Bills," which revolve around the plight of an American Indian trapped in a hostile culture. Even the collection's best piece, "A Christmas Greeting," which again utilizes Charlie, Wright's favorite representative for the down-trodden, stumbles, at the end, into inadequate soap opera. (pp. 263-64)

As is clear from references in "The Minneapolis Poem" and "Inscription for the Tank," Wright has come to regard himself as another Walt Whitman, singer of the common man. Alas, he possesses neither Whitman's eloquence nor his gigantic soul, and his particular perception of America is as narrow as his limited characters'. (p. 265)

The decline into mawkishness continues into *The Collected Poems*, which won the 1972 Pulitzer Prize, reasserting that award's continued dedication to preserving mediocrity. Of the thirty-three new poems included, only two of them could be described as unqualified successes, and they, "To the August Fallen" and "Small Frogs Killed on the Highway," are substantially returns to the subjective-imagistic techniques of *The Branch Will Not Break*. Their modest rosaries of metaphors never preach or whine, are content to let their imaginative potentialities carry the burden of the poems to its logical summation. For instance, at the end of "Small Frogs Killed on the Highway," the image of tadpoles dancing "on the quarter thumbnail/ Of the moon" precisely reflects the speaker's earlier desire to leap "Into the light." Similarly, in "To the August Fallen," Wright's lament for generations of dead strangers finds a beautiful echo in the fall of insects into a pond, which, in turn, leads to memories of Chinese Tartars (historical) and a cyclical climax that returns the speaker to his perch (literary) above death.

In spite of exceptional whole stanzas and individual lines, the rest of the new poems are almost embarrassing in their lack of sensitivity and basic poetic skill. Horror and despair are treated with such elementary sentimentality that they soon become grotesque. . . . Wright has obviously read Pablo Neruda, but he has been unable to penetrate or dupli-

cate his surrealistic ethic, except at the most superficial level. (pp. 265-66)

And the few war protest poems included, such as "A Mad Fight Song for William S. Carpenter" and "Echo for the Promise of Georg Trakl's Life," further convince me that the Vietnam folly, besides destroying countless innocent lives and compromising America's honor, has ruined a large number of our contemporary poets. Being a deliberate craftsman, and a sincere one, Wright occasionally pauses to defend his new aesthetic, claiming his task as the restoration of "the pure clear word" to poetry. But instead of bold metaphors and diamond hardness, which this kind of vision should provide, he can only offer cute tricks, such as a blank page entitled "In Memory of the Horse David, Who Ate One of My Poems," or simplistic Hemingwayese, "The giant killer is/ A dirty little bastard," which will reach an absurd zenith in a poem called "Northern Pike."

Whatever the grave faults (pun intended) of the new poems in the collected edition, and a whine is unappealing in any form, none of them can approach the disasters of Wright's most recent volume, *Two Citizens* (1973). . . . From the standpoint of artistic achievement, *Two Citizens* is an almost total failure. (pp. 266-67)

Without the despair and horror that pulsed in his earlier poems, Wright has nothing left to restrain his inordinate taste for sentimental resolutions of difficult problems. He has betrayed us and betrayed himself by refusing to accept the implications of his own gift, by insisting upon filtering all experience through the wringer of drunken emotions, regardless of their irrational narrowness. (p. 267)

> *Edward Butscher, "The Rise and Fall of James Wright," in* The Georgia Review *(copyright, 1974, by The University of Georgia), Summer, 1974, pp. 257-68.*

James Wright started out in the fifties with a great bolt of visionary silk, which he cut, in the fashion of the day, to symmetrical patterns. His poems won prizes, but were so hard to believe, so safely and slickly "art," that they seemed only a vast closet of ceremonial robes to be taken out, worn as one bowed before the formal dignity of poetry, and returned, spotless.

It was toward the end of "Saint Judas," his second volume, that, with a slam, Wright walked out on high art. His voice suddenly sharpened:

> *I waste no pity on the dead that stink,*
> *And no love's lost between me and the crying*
> *Drunks of Belaire, Ohio, where police*
> *Kick at their kidneys till they die of drink.*

Of course, it was just because he did "waste" pity—on all the "cursed"—that Wright gave way to anger. In "The Branch Will Not Break" (1963), his best volume, and "Shall We Gather at the River" (1968), his poems became so wincingly resentful and chagrined that their wires seemed disengaged. Wright lost the heart for wholeness.

More, he nursed his subjects, spoiled them with pity. And this too unhitched the lines from discipline. For instance, from the terse Oriental delicacy of

> *The black caterpillar*
> *Crawls out, what with one thing*
> *And another, across*
> *The wet road.*

he could pass at once—shockingly—to "How lonely the dead must be." He had only a pennyworth of trust in the implicit. His adverbs and adjectives were crying towels. Even his happiness was too permissive:

> *Suddenly I realize*
> *That if I stepped out of my body I would break*
> *Into blossom.*

This conclusion to the well-known poem "A Blessing" belies the love for *finite* realities that, despite soft writing, gives the poem force. Besides, it is bumbling: circumlocutious and a mishmash of the corporeal and incorporeal. Only a writer who neglected, as it were, to read his own poems would have retained it.

But it is just out there, in the *reader's* place—that detached perspective, that point at which the poem becomes a limited "whole"—that Wright fears to be; for there, so it seems, lurk the causes of pain: the unpitying mind, business America, the police, "men," death. The truth of *feeling* is in the individual lines—stuffed there by the poet himself, a hoard. The result—more aggravated than ever in "Two Citizens"—is a defiant, protective incoherency. Wright refuses both the rigors and the pacifications of wholeness. He twists about in his poetry as if in a cocoon, but he doesn't want to break out, doesn't want "distance"—distance is cold, the truth hot.

Reading the new Wright is, in consequence, an uncomfortable wriggle. You must go with the poem, and the poem doesn't know where it is going. Mostly it is shifting about for a place to feel satisfied with being James Wright. It forgets its own beginnings, indeed forgets where it is. . . .

The pain is frank in the first poems, on the poet's childhood; covered over, yelling through, in the later poems of love. At first Wright licks and licks at the old thorn in his paw, to show what, as a lover of America, he had to overcome. But how he seems to relish the renewed tingle:

> *Hell, I ain't got nothing.*
> *Ah, you bastards,*
> *How I hate you.*

In truth, as always, he is *too* defeated to compel interest as a critic of American life. Instead of ruthlessly amassed evidence, or canny objectives, only pouts, whimpers, growls. Wright seems lodged in pugilistic, grudge-bearing adolescence. . . .

Wright's unusual tenderness for animal and beaten human life, his suffering over the inability to wing upward, to embrace creation ("what are you going to do?"), makes his a moving, enlarging sensibility, but his relation to the poetic medium has always been misjudged. If his early poems carried a formal will like a knife between the teeth, the recent work is either too bitter or too painfully happy for its own self-possession: all wound. (p. 6)

> Calvin Bedient, in The New York Times Book Review (© 1974 by The New York Times Company; reprinted by permission), August 11, 1974.

James Wright is . . . lyrical and . . . purely imaginative; he is also . . . bent on vulnerability, on getting immediately to the essentially poetic material. He has turned to Georg Trakl, and to modern Spanish and Latin American poets, for models of such openness. He has sometimes been criticized for the foreign sound of his idioms; but (except in his earliest experiments) they seem to me as suited to his voice —and, consequently, enriching to the possibilities of English poetry—as comparable assimilations in Eliot and Auden.

Wright's themes have remained remarkably constant, from his earliest formalist work. There is the "profound poetry of the poor and of the dead"—to quote Stevens—and of the outcast (a category so comprehensively important as to include executed murderers, Swift's poetry, and Warren G. Harding). There is what I can only call a strength of misery in love; and an equally strong desire to transcend the bodily self into conditions of delicacy intuited from animals, stones, dreams. Like Goethe, Wright is drawn towards a double transcendence, pure creature and pure spirit; but oddly, his commitment to a style centered on bodily states makes his account of this tension one of the most precise and interesting in existence.

But Wright is also, unlike his contemporaries, a part of the American tradition of mythopoeic regionalism, a "sole owner and proprietor" of names and places. He names the important names in his private history with a confident insouciance that springs partly from the bardic role itself. . . . And perhaps the key is, finally, the knowledge of place: of the northern Great Plains, which remind Wright of "the sea, that once solved the whole loneliness / Of the Midwest"; but especially of his native southeastern Ohio, where the fate and exhaustion of Eastern Europe repeats itself in towns named for the super-corporations, beside the river that is at once Indian sacred place and "Tar and chemical strangled tomb." Like Winesburg or Yoknapatawpha, Wright's places seem less the accidents of one life than scenes the American experience itself has chosen for its agons. This quality sometimes seems to me to give a necessary larger importance to Wright's poetry of emotional daring; but I am not sure one can separate the two. (pp. 64-5)

> Alan Williamson, "Language against Itself: The Middle Generation of Contemporary Poets" (copyright © 1974 by Alan Williamson), in American Poetry Since 1960: Some Critical Perspectives, edited by Robert B. Shaw, Dufour, 1974, pp. 55-67.

[In] *Two Citizens* . . . [Wright] displays amazing mastery of a colloquial style he has been developing since before the widely discussed appearance in 1963 of *The Branch Will Not Break. Two Citizens* is alive with an honest energy which colloquial free verse can have only if it is strictly and knowledgeably controlled. . . .

The power . . . does not spring from particularly fresh language; "I loved her only in my dreams," for example, seems to have appeared in countless song lyrics. But it is precisely by abandoning rhetoric at the right moments that Wright gains the authenticity of his tone, which comes not only from our previous knowledge of his strong traditional craftsmanship; abandoning rhetoric and writing bad poems is as easy for a good poet as it is for a bad one. What Wright retains of his earlier virtuosity is his clear view of how a whole poem must move in order to gain credibility. (pp. 93-4)

> Henry Taylor, in The Michigan Quarterly Review (copyright © The University of Michigan, 1975), Winter, 1975.

Y

YOUNG, Andrew   1885-1971

Young, a Scottish-born British clergyman and an authority on wild flowers, received the Queen's Gold Medal for Poetry in 1952. A Scottish nature poet and an English metaphysician, he was untouched by fashion. He also wrote plays and literary criticism; and his nonfiction works, such as *A Prospect of Flowers* and *A Retrospect of Flowers*, have found a wider public than his poetry. (See also *Contemporary Authors*, Vols. 5-8, rev. ed.)

Born while Tennyson, Arnold and Hopkins were alive, and still at work (on a prose book) a year after the publication of Ted Hughes's *Crow*, Andrew Young neither influenced nor—remarkably—was influenced by any of the passing trends in English poetry. His work takes little account of current events or the changeable climates of this century's thought. His concerns are with the eternal themes, his imagery drawn almost exclusively from what is permanent and immutable in nature; his poems only seem dated on those rare occasions when he introduces an *aeroplane*, a *gramophone*, a *flying-boat*. For all this quality of timelessness, Andrew Young's poetry belongs unchallengeably to the modern movement, admired and respected by nearly every one of his fellow-practitioners. But owing to its special elusiveness, the poetry is still often under-estimated. To dismiss or patronise a poet of Andrew Young's great gifts as a mere, minor nature poet is to misconstrue what his poems are essentially *about*.

His powerfully individual brand of modernity springs not from his subject-matter but from his attitudes and the clarity of style he adopts to express these attitudes. Fiercely intellectual and objective in approach, unrhetorical and terse in his use of language, he achieves a simplicity of expression both in the miraculously-wrought lyrics and in the long poems which, with their casual and everday speech-patterns, recreate the standard pentameter by a tightly-controlled process of demolishing and rebuilding it. Andrew Young is a master-craftsman—a poet's poet—but he's impossible to parody or to steal from.

He wears his scholarship lightly, and his vast knowledge of theology, natural history, topography, literature and philology is a vital ingredient of his vision, but seldom intrudes on the page. What it does do, in conjunction with his religious and mystical demeanour, is to create a metaphysical poetry full of wit and intellectual conceits; a poetry very far removed from the nature-notes of his Georgian contemporaries. Natural objects are used, with love, sometimes for their own sake; but usually they are no more than the starting-points from which the poet presents a world, a life, a way of seeing, which we might never have perceived for ourselves. His image-making, a blend of exact observation and fanciful allusion, makes us see both the similarities and the significant dissimilarities existing between incongruous objects or ideas. We enter a new dimension of awareness, astonished to re-examine the clichés of common experience; we recognise that rivers can be *drowned* in flood or frozen brooks be *their own bridges*, that an albino blackbird can be *white as sin*, that idleness can be shirked, that a spider's web really is like a Greek theatre. Vivifying as these images are, the best surprises are those which startle or terrify.

> Ted Walker, "Ancient but Modern," in New Statesman (© 1974 The Statesman & Nation Publishing Co. Ltd.), February 22, 1974, p. 266.

Is it at all significant for poets to be parsons (rather than doctors, teachers or university librarians)? It's certainly easy to feel that in theological terms, and even in pastoral terms, they are likely to be mavericks. For Andrew Young,

> churches were my love and study,
> Not theology.

In this passage of 'Into Hades' he goes on to describe his favourite ecclesiastical buildings in a way that shows that, although he is claiming that they convert strange pagan lore into shining Christian truth, they nonetheless survive by being pagan or pantheistic, betraying the rich anthropomorphism of nature. And his short poems bear this out: nature is an arena in which life and death perform their quaint or disturbing parables as a substitute for religious doctrine. . . .

Young . . . offers a discursive lyricism and fondness for conceits characteristic of the late-flowering Edwardian taste often labelled Georgian. . . .

The cuckoo's double note, the lark small as a flint arrow, the kestrel pinned to air, the mole buried within the blue vault of the air: Young's anthology pieces find their level among hundreds of poems just as observant or as bizarrely logical. There is something of Marvell's loaded symbolism here and there, in the mole's life and death—

> For you to raise a mound
> Was as for us to make a hold—

or in cows plagued by a 'god of flies'—

> Strange that we both were held divine,
> In Egypt these, man once in Palestine.

To the nature-poet, who can do nothing about their itch, the cows are divine anyway, and presumably the parson in him believes in Christ. The strangeness lies only in the confrontation: one god unable to assist another because everything is a god. Many of Young's poems seem a little inconclusive, as though their conceits have nothing much to do with what they are trying to say about reality. (p. 311)

> *John Fuller, in* The Listener *(© British Broadcasting Corp. 1974; reprinted by permission of John Fuller), March 7, 1974.*

What do entrepreneurs of intellectual or critical fashion do when faced with the peculiarities of Andrew Young . . . ? It is an exclamatory question. The evident answer is they do nothing; or rather they do not allow themselves to be faced by a poet whose structures and substance—or apparent substance, quickly looked at and passed over—are not of the most intricate, and do not fit usefully into their scheme of relationships and their critical formulae. They leave him alone, outside argument, no doubt to be enjoyed along with Herrick on Tistietosties or Dorothy Wordsworth on foxgloves, or Kilvert on blue hills and dog roses, or Dufy painting a regatta, by the unserious. And others take him up, and he is reduced to a simplistic property, to a "nature poet", owned, managed, proclaimed and interpreted or characterized in their own image by simpletons.

This won't do. But let us see how it has happened (not without some help from Andrew Young himself, it has to be confessed). Here was a clerical poet, from Scotland, on terms with nature. He liked flowers (a questing field-botanist or treasure-botanist of persistence and ability). So he was evidently rather Georgian and not disgustingly modern. He liked as well seeds, mushrooms, birds, quadrupeds, insects, slow-worms, crabs, snails, stars, feathers, leaves, seasons, snow, wind, mist, barrows, roads, signposts, quarries, hills, mountains, rocks, rivers. His poems had been full of them, delineated or indicated at once surprisingly, convincingly and evocatively, ever since they began to appear more than half a century ago, in pamphlets of the smallest circulation. Then in 1957, when Andrew Young was an old man of seventy-two and when he had nearly written himself out, a number of admirers united in a small book of tributes, entitled *Andrew Young, Prospect of a Poet.*

Setting the tone, the editor . . . told readers of this strong oddity of a poet that "it was as if the childlike, elfin hand of Blake had guided him on his explorations". . . .

One contributor, John Betjeman, did nothing but quote in Young's face, so to say, minor clerical poets, "gentle parsons"—as if tough and tortured Young was one of them. . . .

Other contributors used Young to mock or knock what they considered modernism to be. . . .

Only one of the fourteen tributaries, the poet Norman Nicholson, realized that their man was a writer of the twentieth century, in the curt activity and firm plasticity of his language and his conveyance of the subjective in objectivity. Only Norman Nicholson knew how much Young was admired by several poets in the wake of Eliot and Auden; and why. They realized that on the whole he rejected an easy, effete stylization. He rejected coy elves behind rose-cottages, they liked his use of concrete language both for the concrete and the elusive. . . .

Words were fitted by him to words, and made into poems of mosaic or of tile, the effectiveness of which outweighed brusqueness or awkwardness.

Every now and then it is of course possible to catch a whiff of origins, or rather of slight influences which helped Young to his ultimate strictness of authenticity and freedom —a whiff of Hardy, Housman, Crabbe, Bishop King, George Herbert, Lovelace, Spenser, Drayton.

Best poems certainly came, in ones and twos, out of all periods of Young's reading and writing life, back to the earliest booklets; but the most assured collection of his brief poems was the last, *The Green Man* of 1947 . . . [and] the most disturbing.

Disturbance is his mark. It is everywhere. It can be detected in very early poems, in the *Boaz and Ruth* of 1920, for instance, where it already indicated a man with questions to ask, who was unlikely to be satisfied by answers. Some day biography may join the poems in supporting the likeliest account of this man's slow turmoil. . . .

Was he both god-given and god-suspicious? The sensualist never quite reconciled with the discipline he imposed on the senses? . . .

Poem after poem (his "oldest fear" . . . was to be buried alive) has to do with death or the churchyard, or with meeting his own dead self—in *The Green Man* especially— until the disturbance culminates in those two long final poems, "Into Hades" and "A Traveller in Time", which bring Andrew Young, or in which he brings himself, in sharper earnest, from what he had called in one poem "playing at death", to the final affront of being dead, and being buried in his own churchyard in Sussex, from which he moves away as a ghost. (p. 393)

Why had he called that last book of his short poems *The Green Man*, unless he had been thinking of the spring sacrificial victim, the nature victim, carved in churches, frowning, agonized, and wreathed in the leaves of the oak or the may which grows out of his mouth? (He knew about such things, and one can imagine he would have read Lady Raglan's article on 'The Green Man in Church Architecture", which had appeared in *Folklore* in 1939.)

He was the victim. Eventually he wrote, or had to write, this lover of nature and the "amorous earth", this older edition of "that young lover, Who pitched his tent in heaven and read Plato", this poet who like Cowper, when he saw the leaves falling off the willows, wanted to live for ever and ever here and nowhere else. . . . Does he or doesn't he take the side of living, here and not elsewhere? Yes and no, as this searching man searches and does not find.

We must—even if we cannot as yet explain it entirely—

acknowledge the pull, now stronger one way, now stronger the other, out of which Young's poems were made; while also realizing that what an Edinburgh Calvinist—or a Claude!—might call a great villainy of the sensual, can have a greater, unvillainous issue in the arts. Young wasn't a Victor Hugo, though he was haunted; he wasn't a Pasternak, a conscious guest of livingness more freely able to be glad and to urge his readers to an unrestricted ecstatic thankfulness. He was a little short or uncertain . . . in the rhetoric and sound of verse; but from an outer province of our time he was a genuine, rewarding poet all right. (p. 394)

"The Disturbances of Andrew Young," in The Times Literary Supplement (© *Times Newspapers Ltd., 1974; reproduced by permission), April 12, 1974, pp. 393-94.*

Andrew Young's work, almost from the first, is brief, spare, hard as flint. . . .

He has been too easily called a nature poet. This is accurate enough as far as it goes, since he writes with grace and economy of the countryside and the plants and animals living there. But he uses nature for a more important purpose than merely to observe it even with his clear eye and the knowledge of a fine naturalist. He was a metaphysical poet, exploring the layers of meaning that exist within a single word, now playfully, now transforming a small lyric into an important and profound statement by a single stroke of the imagination. Words fascinated him, to an extent unusual even among poets. He read widely in his dictionaries, for the sheer delight of wandering among words. His clear, exact vocabulary, simple enough to allow his poems to be read and loved by young children, was chosen from a wealth of language. (p. 133)

Young's observation of the natural world owes nothing to anyone else. He sees the world as if it were being looked at for the first time. . . . The combination of exact observation and a language which is hard, sinewy and precise within changing contexts is what allows him to say that 'mist that gathered from nowhere/With a bright darkness filled the air', or to see the shot magpie fall 'with feathers heavier than lead'.

His lyrics occupy a world in which the poet is usually alone and aware of great stretches of time. Many of his poems celebrate his kinship with the men who are buried in the long barrows, 'the silent men of bones'. He mourns, too, the small creatures whose lives are short, the mole 'buried within the blue vault of the air', the bird so still 'I almost say/"You are not a dead *bird*"'; the rat, the dead crab, a host of others. He sees the nearness of life and death clearly. (pp. 133-34)

Young's verse-forms are unmistakeable. Apparently orthodox and traditional, he has a trick of unexpectedly shortening a line by a syllable or two without ever losing his firm rhythm, or he'll gently insist on an accent in an unlooked for place. The result is always highly personal. . . .

The long poem, 'Into Hades', is where Young used his considerable learning and examined his beliefs. I think this work still under-rated. It has great strength, is eloquent and visionary, and reveals aspects of Young's poetry one would not suspect from reading the lyrics. After completing it he virtually gave up the writing of poetry. (p. 134)

Leslie Norris, "A Complex Clarity," in London Magazine (© *London Magazine, 1974), June/July, 1974, pp. 132-35.*

Reading Andrew Young's poems the impression that they are little more than residual excellences from an earlier, pastoral England is complicated by real admiration for the fact that they work and have effect. What literary upheavals there were in his time—and, born in 1885, he was the same age as Pound, three years older than Eliot, and seven years older than "Hugh MacDiarmid"—fall away as beside the point.

Whether it is right for a reader to submit to the luxurious abdication of his historical consciousness in this way is a different matter. The question is central to contemporary poetry in English. . . .

Young's poems . . . are latched on to as proof of a secret English world, an incorruptible country in which an endearing countryside and its appropriate arts are like old soldiers and never die. No matter what happens in dark, satanic cities, or on foreign fields—the accepted phrases quickly remove them from the secret country—the fields, wild-flowers and landscapes are the same, and continue to elicit spiritual and personal dramas from the observer. It is both reassuring and appalling.

And yet hardly as English as all that. His poems are a version of *England Their England*, written by a man who thought it was his as well. Young was a Scotsman. But it is worth noting that when he writes about Scottish scenery, it occasionally releases his distaste for it, or a less placid melancholy. In the Cuillins, he says he is in Hell. I've never been there; but other poems by Scotsmen about these particular mountains led me to think they were in heaven. Young appears to have cultivated an English sensibility by preference, being suited to a miniature art of observation which Scottish temperaments seldom come to with ease.

As a clergyman, Young naturally paid attention to spiritual predicaments and celebrations. Far from being the strongest impulse in his work, Young's religious feeling is more effectively conveyed through his love of nature and his overall benevolence. The voice in his poems is generally one of personal loneliness, inevitably aroused or calmed by Nature. His perception of what Nature is and does was not one to admit of change. The secret country is permanent. Significantly, it is in a poem with a Scottish setting where Young says he fixes his concentration on the cries of seagulls, blotting the sounds of traffic from a nearby road out of his mind. His England seldom, if ever, allows so modern an intrusion. His visitors are ghosts from the past. The poet becomes like a ghost himself. . . .

[Any] reader of poems must constantly be surprised by the loyalty of a temperament to itself, risking the insults that may come from appearing to be wilfully out of date. Even if the vision of his poetry may have a nostalgic appeal for some, to read it in that way is to accept that there was once a purity of nature and society, which Young's poetry somehow embodies, when in fact his vision is as much imaginative as a matter of recall. (p. 82)

Douglas Dunn, in Encounter (© *1974 by Encounter Ltd.), September, 1974.*

One of the crucial distinctions between 'major' and 'minor'

Nature poetry surely lies in the degree of complex interplay allowed between the natural object and its observer. Andrew Young . . . is clearly indebted to Thomas Hardy and Edward Thomas, but his work lacks the dialectical force and torsion of their work, the sense of a ceaselessly problematical relation between man and Nature enacting itself in the structural ironies, syntactical shiftings and ruffled rhythms of the poetry itself. *Collected Poems* . . . seems to me remarkable for a Georgian conventionality of feeling stiffened by an unGeorgian austerity of technique . . . Young was almost wholly by-passed by 'modernism' (he disliked the work of both Yeats and Eliot); and it's difficult to see how that bypassing was anything but a loss, even while one perversely admires the unmitigated consistency with which Young kept it up. (pp. 71-2)

Young lacks both the original imagery and idiosyncratic eye of Hardy and Thomas, and that lack reflects a failure of imaginative penetration which betrays itself in the over-finished quality of his work, in contrast with the ambiguous, ironic openendedness of the older poets. It also means that the relations between natural object and human subject in his work are considerably over-simplified: a typical poem either delineates a scene and then turns away in its final stanza to point a human analogy or response— . . . or, alternatively, sets up a natural landscape which is too palpably directed by the demands of subjective mood. Young has a problem about how to situate himself in terms of what he sees; and the upshot of this is that what personal meaning he derives from a landscape is either too often conventional closing gesture, or conversely what's actually observed is limited to what can be the bearer of a personal impulse. . . .

[A] combination of not-too-specific natural detail and not-over-precise feeling seems to me to characterise much of his work. Impressively crafted and constructed as much of that work is, it can't avoid an emotional and thematic thinness which springs ultimately from its isolation from a wider, nourishing history. . . .

Young hoards and clips his language in the interests of artistic austerity. . . . (p. 72)

Terry Eagleton, in Stand *(copyright © by* Stand), *Vol. 15, No. 4, 1974.*

Cumulative Index to Critics

Cumulative Index to Authors